MARTIN
LUTHER'S
BASIC THEOLOGICAL WRITINGS

MARTIN
LUTHER'S
BASIC THEOLOGICAL WRITINGS

edited by
Timothy F. Lull

Foreword by
Jaroslav Pelikan

Fortress Press   Minneapolis

This anthology of Luther's writings is dedicated to:

Brevard S. Childs

in thanks for encouraging me to read Luther
and in appreciation for his teaching and his writing
which have been a constant witness to all the churches
to the power of the Word of God.

MARTIN LUTHER'S
BASIC THEOLOGICAL WRITINGS

Cover art: Lucas Cranach, Portrait of Martin Luther from the holdings of the art collections at Weimar.

Cover and text design: Carol Evans-Smith.

Library of Congress Cataloging-in-Publication Data

Luther, Martin, 1483–1546.
   [Selections. English. 1989]
   Martin Luther's basic theological writings / edited by Timothy F. Lull.
     p.   cm.
   Translated from German and Latin.
   ISBN 0-8006-2327-4
   1. Theology—Early works to 1800. I. Lull, Timothy F. II. Title.
BR331.E5   1989a
230'.41—dc20   89-34201
                             CIP

Printed in the United States of America   AF 1-2327

98   97   96   7   8   9   10

CONTENTS

CHRONOLOGICAL LIST OF LUTHER'S WRITINGS IN THIS VOLUME

All references are to *Luther's Works:* American Edition, volumes 31–54, and to *Book of Concord* (ed. Tappert) published by Fortress Press.

Foreword

The preparation of collections of "basic" writings of Martin Luther has been going on since Luther's own time. Inevitably any such collection requires of the editor a series of decisions about what to include, and on what basis. Indeed, even so extensive a collection as the American Edition of *Luther's Works* involved a constant process of selecting and deciding: Which of several successive editions (the first or the last) would be the most faithful? Should we use lecture notes, either Luther's own or those of his students, or printed versions, some of them evidently doctored by editors? Where there is both a German text and a Latin text (e.g., for *The Freedom of a Christian* of 1520, and for that matter the Augsburg Confession of 1530), which should be taken as normative? The history of such theological compilations—like the history of anthologies, *florilegia*, and *Sentences* in Byzantium and in the medieval West, and behind them in Greek and Roman antiquity—has of course been shaped by the presuppositions and interests of the theologians and scholars who have prepared them. This has been true in special measure of the history of Luther editions and of Luther study as a whole; for as a group of us sought to show in a volume of essays published by Fortress Press in 1968 under the title *Interpreters of Luther*, the variety and complexity of Luther's thought and personality could, and did, give rise to an astonishing variety of *Lutherbilder*, each of them possessing at least some legitimate claim to accuracy and authenticity but each of them also showing unmistakable marks of when, by whom, and for what purpose it was drawn.

Timothy F. Lull's Luther reader also reflects the orientation of its editor and of his time, and that in several respects. It is, for one thing, unabashedly *theological* in its intent. (Somewhat to my regret, although I do appreciate the reasons for it, that has required him to slight the massive corpus of Luther's exegetical works; Luther was, after all, *Doctor in Biblia* and did not teach systematic or doctrinal theology at Wittenberg, but biblical interpretation.) But the theological concentration of the book also protects it from capitulating, as so much of contemporary theological literature does, to the trendy and the excessively topical. Much of the debate over the thought of Luther since the years of the church struggle under the Nazis has, for understandable reasons, concentrated on his political ideas, and has done so, moreover, even when it was debating his theological ideas. The issue of the relation betrween Law and Gospel is, as Professor Lull notes in his introductions, basic to Luther's thought about the Bible, about the nature of God, and about the economy of God's dealing with the human race. But it is also an important element—and, in the judgment of so profound an interpreter as Karl Barth, a fatal one—in Luther's interpretation of the authority of temporal government and in his views about the validity and the limits of the Christian witness of the Word of God in relation to government. Several of the selections in Part VI have been chosen with this debate in mind, but they come where they do because the editor believes, and rightly, that the fundamental theses about the Word of God that are the business of Part II and about grace and justification that appear in Part III must be clear if the reader is to make sense of the social and political ethics of Part VI. There is no apology here for taking Christian doctrine seriously as an object of study in its own right, not merely as a preface to politics.

Much of what Luther said and wrote about politics pertained chiefly to his own time and place, but the Luther who speaks in this volume is primarily an *international* figure. As Heinrich Heine observed in his brilliant essay on the Reformation, there was something quintessentially Germanic about Luther's character as well as about his writings. I have reason to know that no translation can hope to capture the riches of his language, especially in the German works. Sometimes he saw himself in almost exclusively German terms, as "the prophet of the Germans" and as the defender of Germanic values against Roman ones. But more often he strove to articulate his teachings in a larger, more international context. Like Moscow after the Revolution, the Wittenberg of Luther's day became a crossroads for students from many countries—it should be recalled that Hamlet, prince of Denmark, is described as having studied there—who returned to bring the Reformation to their own peoples and churches. For much of its history, Luther study has likewise been almost exclusively a German preserve, and none of us could get anywhere in the field without the pioneering work that has been done for all these years by German scholars and editors. But in the twentieth century, and especially since the Second World War, that has changed substantially, as Luther scholars in many lands have gone on from the tutelage of their German mentors to create a truly international community, reflected for example in the attendance at the International Congresses for Luther Research since 1956, in which researchers from Europe, America, and Asia have all participated.

Those researchers also come from all the branches of Protestantism and from Roman Catholicism. Like the Congress for Luther Research, therefore, this compendium is also explicitly *ecumenical* in its orientation and intent. In the history of theological controversy Luther occupies a special place, both because he had a remarkable intuition for recognizing the key issue in a doctrinal debate (what he himself called, in the conflict with Erasmus, an instinct for the jugular, although he was referring to Erasmus rather than to himself) and because his powers as a veritable sorcerer of language enabled him to express that recognition with a pungency and force that was always memorable and that often verged on polemical overkill. With a few exceptions, such as the Wittenberg Concord of 1536 and his negotiations with the Hussites during those same years, Luther was usually suspicious of the "ecumenical" efforts of his own time, and he even found the Augsburg Confession, as authored by Philip Melanchthon, to be a bit too gentle. That Luther, the archpolemicist and descendant of Epiphanius and Jerome (and of Saint Paul), is represented here, for example in substantial selections from *The Bondage of the Will* in 1525 and from the defenses of Baptism and the Real Presence in 1526 and 1528. But these are outweighed, quantitatively and especially qualitatively, by those writings in which Luther is expressing, with characteristic force and eloquence, the great consensus of most Christian teachers and of their churches. That is, it seems to me, as it should be, for in a variety of ways the Luther study of our time has been locating him within the spectrum of that consensus.

Closely related to the ecumenism of this compend is its *churchly* orientation. Luther has often been seen as the prototypical modern individualist: "you must do your own believing," he said, "as you must do your own dying." But if twentieth-century Luther research has made any point that is sure to remain central in future study, it is that, according to Luther, this believing and this dying must go on in the company of the church as it listens to the Word of God and as it prays. A Reformation treatise like Luther's *Babylonian Captivity of the Church* of 1520 is not an attack on the church, but a defense of the church by its faithful servant, against all its enemies foreign and domestic. His *Small Catechism* of 1529 stands alongside his translations of the Bible as a contribution to the total life of the Church. And *On the Councils and the Church* of 1539 is documentation for the thesis that even twenty years after the Leipzig Disputation Luther was still probing the meaning of the doctrine of the church both in its theological dimensions and in its practical implications. Luther on the reading of the Old Testament and the New, Luther on the sacramental life, Luther on the liturgy, Luther on daily life—this is the theologian who speaks in these pages.

For it is ultimately with the practical implications—that is, with the implications for Christian *praxis*—that Martin Luther was concerned, and that Timothy Lull is concerned. If my reading of the state of the church—and the state of all the churches— is accurate, the crisis both of their *praxis* and of their doctrine has reached the point where it will require the witness of the communion of saints "of every time and every place" to summon them to discipleship. In that communion of saints, Luther occupies a special place, and in this volume his witness comes through, loud and clear.

Jaroslav Pelikan
Sterling Professor of History
Yale University

Preface

Martin Luther has been much discussed in recent years, especially during the 500th anniversary of his birth in 1983. Many splendid new books about Luther have recently been published. But there is still need for a new one-volume anthology of Luther's basic theological writings.

Luther did not write a single compend of theology comparable to Thomas Aquinas' *Summa Theologiae*, Calvin's *Institutes of the Christian Religion*, or Schleiermacher's *The Christian Faith*. Because of this his important proposals concerning issues in current theological discussion are sometimes hard to find. This volume is intended to help readers correlate Luther's various writings with some major topics in theology, so Luther can be seen as a formidable and perhaps even systematic theologian, without losing the contextual nature of his writings.

His most important treatises are readily available in English thanks to the 55-volume American edition of *Luther's Works* published by Concordia Publishing House and Fortress Press. This splendid scholarly tool, edited by Jaroslav Pelikan and Helmut T. Lehmann, provided the texts for this collection. But the documents that are included here are scattered in fifteen of those volumes (and in *The Book of Concord.*) Serious readers of Luther will want to buy several of the volumes of the American edition, but even those who already have all those volumes in their library may need help in focusing their reading.

There is an even more pressing reason for a new anthology. In a changed ecumenical situation many now are willing to admit that Luther is not so much a Lutheran or Protestant figure as an important theologian of the church catholic—*doctor ecclesiae* (doctor of the church). This volume has been prepared with the hope of introducing Luther to a wider range of readers, and to speak to those questions that have emerged in the last twenty years of ecumenical dialog and study.

One curious person asked the editor whether this meant "cleaning Luther up." This is both impossible (as the reader who confronts Luther's bold style for the first time will see) and quite unnecessary. But it has been one of my goals to include selections that may have bearing on the current debates among the churches.

For example, a much wider range of Luther's sacramental writings is needed than was included in some earlier collections in order to do justice to the complexity of his thought in this area. Many older interpretations tended to concentrate on his writings through 1520; for all the importance of the early Luther, this approach failed to show how Luther's thought continued to develop (including its more catholic side) when he was no longer simply fighting the Roman authorities but also other versions of reform.

This anthology has been assembled with the hope of including both the most important of Luther's shorter writings and showing the range of his theological interests. Wherever possible (in 25 of the 31 documents contained in this anthology) entire treatises have been presented. In the case of the six partial documents, all but one of these are self-contained sections.

The material has been arranged in six parts, as one suggestion of how these texts might be studied. But any number of ways might be proposed to approach these writings. Luther's own method leads him to range widely while discussing any subject, and one who wanted to read these selections chronologically instead could easily do so by consulting the chronological list included after the table of contents.

Because of the wide range and great length of Luther's writings, a decision had to be made to limit the kinds of material included. The most basic decision was to include only those documents from the so-called Reformation writings *Luther's Works*, American Edition, volumes 31-54 (Fortress Press). It would take another anthology of at least this length to give a fair sampling of Luther as biblical interpreter.

A second difficult decision had to do with three important treatises of 1520: "Appeal to the German Nobility," "The Babylonian Captivity of the Church," and "The Freedom of a Christian." These documents are readily available in an inexpensive paperback edition, and two of them are rather long. But they do have a major claim on the reader of Luther.

The decision was to include in its entirety "The Freedom of a Christian" and Part I of "The Babylonian Captivity," with the hope that this new volume might be seen as a companion piece to the *Three Treatises* (Philadelphia: Fortress Press, 1970), rather than as a substitute for it. This strategy allowed many shorter works to be included that do show something of Luther's range over a longer period of time and that have been less widely known. (Actually, a fourth key writing from 1520, "On Good Works" [Luther's *Works* 44] also had to be omitted because of its length.)

Next were the questions of what to do about Luther's three writings that have been included in the official collection of confessions of the Lutheran church, *The Book of Concord* (Philadelphia: Fortress Press, 1959). The "Large Catechism" is simply too long to reproduce in a volume of this size, despite the importance of Luther's treatment of the First Commandment in it. But we have provided the other two items because of their importance for Luther's theology.

The "Small Catechism" has surely been the most widely known writing of Luther, and it is here along with his "Smalcald Articles" of 1537. The catechism shows Luther's pastoral energy engaged to give an irenic summary of the basics of the faith. The articles, written at a time rather late in his career when Luther was full of fear about the coming general council, show his personal and fully developed views about what matters could not be compromised.

Finally, one should be aware that Luther's controversial writings could not be given much space in this anthology. Some of these are crucial for understanding Luther in his times, and certainly his limitations—especially those concerning the papacy, the Jews, and the peasants' war. But Luther's sharp tongue and polemical judgments are not completely absent from this volume.

Limitations of space have made it impossible to include an introduction to Luther's life or thought. Among the books now available, readers of this volume will be especially helped by consulting two excellent recent works: Bernard Lohse's *Martin Luther: An Introduction to His Life and Work* (Philadelphia: Fortress Press, 1986), and Eric Gritsch's *Martin—God's Court*

Jester (Philadelphia: Fortress Press, 1983). Gritsch provides an excellent eighty-page summary of the career of Luther in the first part of his book; both volumes, in somewhat different formats, discuss the intellectual background, major controversies, and Luther's own writings.

But for all that has not been included, much is here—especially for those who are just beginning to know Luther and those who want an essential and ecumenical Luther anthology. My chief concern has been to let Luther speak—to all the churches and to the theological task today throughout the world. This means, above all, letting the reader encounter Luther directly without too much interference.

For this volume's appearing, many deserve thanks. Colleagues at the Lutheran Theological Seminary at Philadelphia, especially Lyman T. Lundeen and Christopher R. Seitz (now of Yale Divinity School), offered suggestions and encouragement while this work was being planned. Pastors Joseph A. Burgess and Richard E. Koenig helped me think about what such a book might include and about its potential audience.

Other theologians offered detailed reactions to an anonymous proposal for such an anthology that was circulated to them. They will see that we have been able to include many (although not all) of their good suggestions. But we were not able, within the scope of this project, to do anything about the very real need for new translations of several of these documents.

Pastor Ross Goodman offered a great deal of technical assistance while he was a graduate student at the Lutheran Theological Seminary at Philadelphia. That seminary's library staff was consistently helpful throughout the editing of this book. The seminary also provided funds for research expenses, and our faculty secretary Laurie E. Pellman took charge of manuscript corrections. St. Edmund's College, Cambridge, England, provided computer facilities in the summer of 1987.

The editors at Fortress Press, especially Thelma Megill Cobbler, Harold W. Rast, and John A. Hollar, and at a later stage Stefanie Ormsby Cox, deserve special thanks for their support for this project throughout its long development.

Anyone who has ever written, edited, or even read a book will understand that I also wish to thank my family, especially my wife, Mary Carlton Lull, and our sons Christopher and Peter, for their very concrete help, encouragement, and support in this project. Many thousands of books have been written with such thanks at the end of the preface, but this will be a worse world when that custom stops. Here is one "human tradition" that Luther himself would have applauded.

This anthology is dedicated to Professor Brevard S. Childs of Yale Divinity School. Over twenty years ago he was one of the strong voices at that school urging me to read more Luther (and, to be sure, also Calvin). The whole church has benefited from the way in which he has pointed to the richness and continuing relevance of reformation theology in his teaching and writing. But of course his deeper importance is that, like the reformers themselves, he has always pointed to the Word of God as that living voice through which the Spirit still instructs the church.

> Timothy F. Lull
> *Cambridge, England*
> *and Philadelphia*

LUTHER'S CHALLENGE TO THEOLOGY TODAY

This anthology has been prepared with the special hope that it might be useful in making the writings of Martin Luther available as a resource for contemporary work in theology, both in academic settings and in current struggles about theology in the life of the churches. Is this hope realistic? There are several obstacles.

First of all, there is no question that Luther is interesting nowadays—historically, psychologically, and ecumenically. There is also no question that Luther—in contrast to some other theologians—is a man whose life and work are closely connected, so that his own particular voice and struggles come through clearly in his writings. But can the theologians and the churches actually hear Luther today? What is initially interesting can come to seem merely personal.

Second, Luther is an occasional theologian, not a systematic theologian! He wrote no single summary of his own teaching that can stand next to the greatest compends of Christian doctrine. The person who wants to listen to Luther has to follow him through the concrete struggles for the gospel in the context of the sixteenth century church and society. This serves as valuable protection against bringing Luther into current discussions in too facile or immediate a way, but it also makes him seem somewhat dated, time-bound, and even old-fashioned.

Third, Luther has extremely strong views about theology and is hard on opponents (and on himself, to be fair about the matter). He is extreme in language and is passionate about any issue that seems to have bearing on how the gospel is heard in the church. This makes Luther a lively person to read and study. But the impression persists that he is unfair, unbalanced, and not a steady guide to the subtle distinctions of which much of theology consists.

Finally, the deepest obstacle to hearing Luther in today's theological discussions is that his theology is so rich, complex, and dialectical that he seems unreliable both as an opponent and as an ally. There is always with Luther the element of surprise. That s...ne "on the other hand . . ." which seems to give depth to Thomas Aquinas leads many people to distrust this element in Luther as a sign of muddled thinking or evasive paradox.

That impression is correct in one sense. Luther concentrates on the question of the gospel and the right way of speaking of God so intently that he can rarely offer a simple yes or no to a question. A survey of his concerns in this anthology will show that he is at odds with many of the favorite causes and slogans in contemporary theology.

But a closer look might show that Luther is not simply one who would say no (or *Nein!*) to the hopes and legitimate concerns of theology today. He is a valuable resource and a classic source for theology partly because he is able to generate dialog. A careful reading of these writings of Luther will *both* challenge *and* affirm many of the characteristic features of current theology.

Three examples can help to show how Luther can offer us a very stimulating yes and no:

1. *The Question of Theological Method* (See Part I of this anthology). Luther's authorship, as contained in these selections, begins with the "Disputation Against Scholastic Theology" from 1517. Here he makes a powerful case that the reigning scholastic method, with its dependence on certain forms of philosophy, has played a major role in obscuring the gospel. That word of grace from God in Jesus Christ is not something that emerges within human wisdom or moral achievement but is a word of judgment and mercy set *over against* even the best that humans could achieve. The heavy dependence of theology on philosophy, he

argues, has led to a situation in which the distinctiveness of the gospel was so blunted that it could not be understood.

Luther's judgments against reason sound harsh when applied to recent theology with its high level of interest in dialog with philosophy, with the social sciences, with culture and with the world religions. It also seems narrow and triumphantly Christian. But contemporary theologians who favor apologetics and try to fit the gospel into the needs and world-view of modern humanity need to consider to what extent Luther's critique is a fair judgment on their work. Or is the situation now so different from that of late scholasticism that Luther's warnings are irrelevant to contemporary projects?

Yet other starting points may be more promising. In his "theology of the cross" set forth in the "Heidelberg Disputation" of 1518 (see again Part I), Luther develops a theme that could open an interesting and more positive dialog with current theology. His insistence that God is not to be found in the great successes of humanity, whether intellectual or moral, but instead in the cross of Jesus, has an affinity with some strands of liberation theology. Of course Luther was no proto-Marxist, no friend of political revolution in any form. But this sense that God has been hidden from the powerful and the wise and revealed to the lowly and the humble could be the starting point for a fruitful and perhaps surprising dialog.

2. *The Bondage of the Will* (See Part III of this anthology). Luther considered his finest theological work to be his defense of the bondage of the human will against the views of Desiderius Erasmus. Those who read this anthology will find this theme was already central to his theology as early as 1517. Yet the bondage of the will is a particularly distasteful theme for theology today!

Most contemporary theologians wish to set a different course, developing a basically positive or affirming view of human capacity. They often claim that Scripture has been misread in a negative way by the Christian tradition. Or they insist that humanity be held more accountable than a grace-centered theology would seem to do. Others argue that concepts like sin and guilt have been too prominent in past theologies.

Over against this, Luther's insistence on the bondage of the will deserves exploration. Two things emerge quickly: First, of course, Luther speaks of the bondage of the will not in terms of human capacity for ordinary or even extraordinary action, but in reference to that salvation question—the God relationship— which is always the center of his thinking.

Second, Luther insists that the bondage of the will has less to do with pessimism about humanity (although some of that is surely there) than with the grace of God that has been revealed in Jesus Christ. The bondage of the will is an implication of his Christology, rather than an item of free-floating pessimism about human nature.

Modern theology would benefit from a close dialog with Luther on these issues. Does optimism about human will in its theoretical form really lead to humanity's being more accountable and more responsible? Or do many other factors come into play? And what does modern theology say about the connection between its typically optimistic view of human prospects and its own Christology? It may be that the contemporary sense of discontinuity with classical Christology is to be found not only because the categories seem alien, but more basically because there is little for Jesus to do or to be, beyond serving as moral exemplar or a sage for the ages.

3. *The Shape of Christian Ethics* (See Part VI of this anthology). Contemporary ethics seems to be deeply divided about the general form that Christian action ought to take. Many Christian theologians, fearing the current moral laxity and permissive society of the West, are eager to find new ways to ground a binding moral code of human behavior to stand against the relativism of the age. Other Christian theologians, and many nonreligious persons, see in this new stress on virtue and character the old Christian tyranny of standing against human freedom, particularly in such an area as sexual behavior.

Luther, often dismissed as an antinomian or a dispenser of "cheap grace," actually has something vital to offer to this debate. His own proposal about the shape of the Christian life, as set out in "The Freedom of a Christian" from 1520, places freedom and service together as the indivisible marks of what life in Christ must include.

Against those who really do resent human autonomy, who are convinced that the church always knows what is best for people, Luther is a vigorous advocate of Christian liberty. But against any reduction of this freedom to an opportunity for license, self-preoccupation, or indifference to the needs of others, Luther makes the service of others the hallmark and goal of how Christian liberty is to be used.

Other examples of how Luther might address contemporary theology could be developed from the other sections of this anthology:

- □ Luther's hermeneutic of law and gospel (See Part II) can be misused, and often has been, as when the law/gospel distinction is seen as setting the New Testament against the Old. But Luther offers a clear and preachable approach in striking contrast to many of the current proposals that appear too complex ever to influence the life of the church.

- □ Luther's view of the sacraments (See Part IV) insists on critique in light of the gospel, to ensure that the sacraments are the means of grace rather than human tasks, however gloriously performed. But the mystery of God in Christ present in water, bread, and wine is vigorously preserved against all attempts of interpretation to give a rationalizing account.

- □ Luther's approach to reform in the church (See Part V) is striking in its caution and deliberation. But his insistence on education and on concern for popular understanding of what the church is doing could be a crucial missing factor in many of the current church campaigns which seem to falter when the dreams of the leaders are set over against the wishes and opinions of the people.

The best connections that the reader can make may well be the ones that she or he is personally able to discover. The way to read this book as a text in theology is with both generosity toward Luther's own context, so that he is not dismissed by the critical standards of the twentieth century, and with imagination about those academic and pastoral problems with which the reader is currently engaged.

For in many instances Luther has been there before us, in this task of faithful reforming, and he is always at least a helpful case-study, whether his own proposals are embraced, altered, or rejected. Luther deserves more from the church today than to be ignored or consigned to being an interesting exhibit in the museum of church history. Luther deserves to be read rather than read about. This anthology seeks to bring his voice more fully into both the study of theology and our current debates.

PART I

THE TASK OF THEOLOGY

In this first part the reader will find five documents that reveal Luther's basic stance toward theology and show his own major convictions, from early and from much later in his career. Though the first three selections are difficult reading (because of their compressed format as theses for debate), all of them reveal Luther's distinctive sharp language and passionate way of speaking of God and salvation.

By Luther's time Christians had developed a rich and diverse set of answers to the question of how theology should be pursued. Luther looked at all of these answers critically in light of the Word of God in Scripture, and he felt especially uncomfortable with the dominant scholastic theology of his own day.

1   Disputation Against Scholastic Theology

In this crucial document from the early fall of 1517, Luther offers a number of theses for debate that are sharply critical of the currently reigning method of scholastic theology, with its high confidence in human reason and free will. The philosophical dependence of theology on Aristotle, going back two hundred and fifty years to St. Thomas Aquinas, may initially have been a creative and worthwhile experiment. But now as Luther views the scholastic theology of his own time, this approach has blunted the distinctiveness of the gospel.

The reader may well find the thesis-form forbidding and find some of the issues that Luther is addressing difficult to understand. These theses were written for a student to defend in an academic exercise at the University of Wittenberg and therefore were designed only to provide initial clues about these positions. Their very pointed, exaggerated nature is part of the intellectual challenge of the disputation for those who must develop and defend them.

But the reader who perseveres will find in them many of the major themes of Luther's own theology as they had been emerging in his biblical lectures of the preceding years. One can at least see that Luther already had strong convictions on a number of issues, especially the relations between sin, grace, free will, and good works, even before the debate about indulgences began.

Luther's language is sharp, but his official posture is still deferential. He concludes the attack on scholastic theology with the claim that "we believe we have said nothing that is not in agreement with the Catholic church and the teachers of the church." But within weeks Luther had launched a debate about the selling of indulgences that brought him and his theology to the attention of the highest church authorities.

2   The Ninety-Five Theses

This document, which is officially a "Disputation on the Power and Efficacy of Indulgences," is one of Luther's best-known writings. It shows that from the beginning his concern about the right formulation of the gospel was not simply one regarding church teaching or theology but intended to provide a critique of church practice as well.

The selling of indulgences developed slowly throughout the Middle Ages. Originally its conception was limited to removing the temporal or earthly punishment that the church had the right to inflict as part of the sacrament of penance. But it was clear to Luther that many simple persons were not understanding indulgences in this way. Those who arranged for their sale had their own stake in keeping the precise theology of indulgences obscure.

Luther wrote the "Ninety-Five Theses" as a call for debate, similar to that called for regarding the nature of theology in the preceding document. He seems to have offered these theses for discussion on October 31, 1517. (This date has often been considered the beginning of the Lutheran Reformation. Where and even whether Luther posted these theses is a major subject of debate among contemporary historians.)

While the initial reaction to the call for debate was disappointing, subsequent translation into German and publication of the document set off a storm of comment. It was clear that Luther had touched a vital nerve, both from the support that he generated and the hostility with which some church authorities began to view his work. The reader will want to explore the many points at which these first two documents are connected, especially in the centrality of Luther's concern for a right understanding of sin and forgiveness in the church. (Luther's ideas on purgatory, papal authority, and the sacraments were soon to undergo considerable development.)

3   Heidelberg Disputation

The next spring, in April of 1518, the Augustinian order of Germany held its General Chapter at Heidelberg. Luther was by this time under a great cloud of controversy, and so he was asked to present and defend his theological thinking to his fellow Augustinians. He did this in the form of a third set of theses named for the town where that meeting took place.

This is perhaps the most important of the five documents in Part I for understanding Luther's developed theology. Here he not only expanded his theology of sin, grace, and free will, but also offered his own positive theological agenda centered in the "theology of the cross" (*theologia crucis*). In this formulation of theological method we begin to hear Luther's distinctive contribution.

Luther had come to think that the trouble with the whole tradition that had developed from Thomas Aquinas was that it tended to be dominated by its opening theological moves. Since the existence of God could be shown rationally or philosophically, a style of theology developed that moved too smoothly *from* what could be known and comprehended clearly in creation *to* the grace of God in Jesus Christ. Though Thomas himself was clear that the saving mysteries could not be known by reason, much of the energy of subsequent theology went into these foundational questions.

This could obscure what St. Paul had taught so forcefully: the cross of Christ is not a concept compatible with human wisdom and philosophy, but only with deep folly and offense. The cross is not inspiring but a scandal. Therefore the true theologian is not the one who argues from visible and evident things (following Aristotle), but rather the one who has learned from the cross that the ways of God are hidden (*deus abscondItus*), even in the revelation of Jesus Christ.

This document is more developed than the first two selections. Why? Here Luther provides not only theological and philosophical theses, but also elaborations of each one, showing the connection of many of the issues which he is discussing with the views of Scripture and various theologians.

What emerges in this document is Luther's radically grace-centered theology that sets the righteousness of God not only against the claims of philosophy for wisdom, but also against all the best moral achievement of humanity. It is an appeal to re-discover the sharp voice of Augustine (especially in his contro-versy with Pelagius), which apparently had become muted even in the Augustinian order.

4 Confession Concerning Christ's Supper—Part III

The fourth document in Part I comes from almost a decade later. This period (late 1527/early 1528) was a difficult time for Luther. He was experiencing illness himself and in his family, plague in Wittenberg, and deepening sacramental controversy with the Swiss and the Strassburgers over the Lord's Supper.

At that point in the controversy Luther wrote a major re-futation of Zwingli's views in a lengthy treatise. This key work will be discussed more fully in the introduction to Part IV of this anthology. But here we have included the final part of that con-fession, which is a summary by Luther of his developed theology.

The reader will find here Luther's mature views, organized in relation to the doctrine of the Trinity. Luther strongly affirms the historic trinitarian and christological dogmas of the church catholic. He continues to protest against the concept of free will or human merit playing any role in salvation. He offers his re-flections on the sacraments and the church and explains his reasons for distrusting monasticism. He provides a foundation for Christian ethics in the concept of orders and institutions linked with the "common order of Christian love."

This important summary of Luther's thought, prepared be-cause both friends and enemies were thought to be misrepre-senting him, influenced the Schwabach Articles and the structure of the "Augsburg Confession" itself. But it is not Luther's last word on the task and content of theology.

5   Preface to the Wittenberg Edition

The final document in Part I is a personal preface that Luther wrote to an edition of his German writings that was being prepared in 1539. Luther had not been enthusiastic about this project of some friends in Strassbourg because it seemed to mark a moment of turning him into a monument, rather than a living voice pointing toward Christ as known in the Word. But even as Luther complains about the danger of other books (including his own books) obscuring the Book, the Bible, he offers some reflections looking back on most of his writings concerning the three marks of a theologian.

The first mark of a good theologian (despairing of your own reason) reaches back to the first documents in this anthology. The second (the need to meditate on the Word day and night) points forward to Part II. The third (the inevitability of suffering), is not only a true reflection of the uncertainty and danger that Luther experienced throughout his career, but also a clear implication of what it means to do theology as "theology of the cross."

And yet the last word is not somber but joyful. Luther was himself sustained by the grace of God, but also by his own sense of humor. The end of this preface is a famous moment of irony about self and accomplishment that has often been cited (noted even by the young theologian Karl Barth as a reminder not to take himself too seriously). It is good warning from Luther not to be unduly dazzled by any of the five selections in Part I or by anything in the subsequent parts of this book.

1.

DISPUTATION AGAINST SCHOLASTIC THEOLOGY

1. To say that Augustine exaggerates in speaking against heretics is to say that Augustine tells lies almost everywhere. This is contrary to common knowledge.

2. This is the same as permitting Pelagians[1] and all heretics to triumph, indeed, the same as conceding victory to them.

3. It is the same as making sport of the authority of all doctors of theology.

4. It is therefore true that man, being a bad tree, can only will and do evil [Cf. Matt. 7: 17-18].

5. It is false to state that man's inclination is free to choose between either of two opposites. Indeed, the inclination is not free, but captive. This is said in opposition to common opinion.

6. It is false to state that the will can by nature conform to correct precept. This is said in opposition to Scotus[2] and Gabriel.[3]

7. As a matter of fact, without the grace of God the will produces an act that is perverse and evil.

8. It does not, however, follow that the will is by nature evil, that is, essentially evil, as the Manichaeans[4] maintain.

---

[1] Pelagius (360?-420?), a native of Britain, denied original sin. He held that justifying grace is given according to merit and regarded sinless perfection possible after baptism. His teachings were vigorously attacked by St. Augustine (354-430), bishop of Hippo.

[2] John Duns Scotus (d. 1308) was the leader of the Scotist school which taught freedom of the will and the superiority of the will over the intellect. He denied the real distinction between the soul and its faculties.

[3] Gabriel Biel (1425?-1495) was "the last of the scholastics" and the first professor of theology in the newly founded University of Tübingen. He was the author of *The Canon of the Mass* which Luther studied diligently as a young man.

[4] Manichaeism is a form of religious dualism consisting of Zoroastrian dualism, Babylonian folklore, and Buddhist ethics superficially combined with Christian elements. It was founded in the latter half of the third century by the Persian prophet Mani (215?-276?). According to Mani, everything material and sensual is created evil and must be overcome.

9. It is nevertheless innately and inevitably evil and corrupt.

10. One must concede that the will is not free to strive toward whatever is declared good. This in opposition to Scotus and Gabriel.

11. Nor is it able to will or not to will whatever is prescribed.

12. Nor does one contradict St. Augustine when one says that nothing is so much in the power of the will as the will itself.

13. It is absurd to conclude that erring man can love the creature above all things, therefore also God. This in opposition to Scotus and Gabriel.

14. Nor is it surprising that the will can conform to erroneous and not to correct precept.

15. Indeed, it is peculiar to it that it can only conform to erroneous and not to correct precept.

16. One ought rather to conclude: since erring man is able to love the creature it is impossible for him to love God.

17. Man is by nature unable to want God to be God. Indeed, he himself wants to be God, and does not want God to be God.

18. To love God above all things by nature is a fictitious term, a chimera, as it were. This is contrary to common teaching.

19. Nor can we apply the reasoning of Scotus concerning the brave citizen who loves his country more than himself.

20. An act of friendship is done, not according to nature, but according to prevenient grace. This in opposition to Gabriel.

21. No act is done according to nature that is not an act of concupiscence against God.

22. Every act of concupiscence against God is evil and a fornication of the spirit.

23. Nor is it true that an act of concupiscence can be set aright by the virtue of hope. This in opposition to Gabriel.

24. For hope is not contrary to charity, which seeks and desires only that which is of God.

25. Hope does not grow out of merits, but out of suffering which destroys merits. This in opposition to the opinion of many.

26. An act of friendship is not the most perfect means for accomplishing that which is in one.[5] Nor is it the most perfect means

---

[5] "To do what is in one" is a scholastic phrase which implies that a Christian can do meritorious works agreeable to God.

for obtaining the grace of God or turning toward and approaching God.

27. But it is an act of conversion already perfected, following grace both in time and by nature.

28. If it is said of the Scripture passages, "Return to me, . . . and I will return to you" [Zech. 1:3.], "Draw near to God and he will draw near to you" [Jas. 4:8], "Seek and you will find" [Matt. 7:7], "You will seek me and find me" [Jer. 29:13], and the like, that one is by nature, the other by grace, this is no different from asserting what the Pelagians have said.

29. The best and infallible preparation for grace and the sole disposition toward grace is the eternal election and predestination of God.

30. On the part of man, however, nothing precedes grace except indisposition and even rebellion against grace.

31. It is said with the idlest demonstrations that the predestined can be damned individually but not collectively. This in opposition to the scholastics.

32. Moreover, nothing is achieved by the following saying: Predestination is necessary by virtue of the consequence of God's willing, but not of what actually followed, namely, that God had to elect a certain person.

33. And this is false, that doing all that one is able to do can remove the obstacles to grace. This in opposition to several authorities.

34. In brief, man by nature has neither correct precept nor good will.

35. It is not true that an invincible ignorance excuses one completely(all scholastics notwithstanding);

36. For ignorance of God and oneself and good work is always invincible to nature.

37. Nature, moreover, inwardly and necessarily glories and takes pride in every work which is apparently and outwardly good.

38. There is no moral virtue without either pride or sorrow, that is, without sin.

39. We are not masters of our actions, from beginning to end, but servants. This in opposition to the philosophers.

40. We do not become righteous by doing righteous deeds but, having been made righteous, we do righteous deeds. This in opposition to the philosophers.

41. Virtually the entire *Ethics* of Aristotle is the worst enemy of grace. This in opposition to the scholastics.

42. It is an error to maintain that Aristotle's statement concerning happiness does not contradict Catholic doctrine. This in opposition to the doctrine on morals.

43. It is an error to say that no man can become a theologian without Aristotle. This in opposition to common opinion.

44. Indeed, no one can become a theologian unless he becomes one without Aristotle.

45. To state that a theologian who is not a logician is a monstrous heretic—this is a monstrous and heretical statement. This in opposition to common opinion.

46. In vain does one fashion a logic of faith, a substitution brought about without regard for limit and measure. This in opposition to the new dialecticians.

47. No syllogistic form is valid when applied to divine terms. This in opposition to the Cardinal.[6]

48. Nevertheless it does not for that reason follow that the truth of the doctrine of the Trinity contradicts syllogistic forms. This in opposition to the same new dialecticians and to the Cardinal.

49. If a syllogistic form of reasoning holds in divine matters, then the doctrine of the Trinity is demonstrable and not the object of faith.

50. Briefly, the whole Aristotle[7] is to theology as darkness is to light. This in opposition to the scholastics.

51. It is very doubtful whether the Latins comprehended the correct meaning of Aristotle.

---

[6] Luther refers to the Cardinal of Cambrai, Pierre d'Ailly (1350-1420), a French theologian, a commentator on the *Sentences* of Peter Lombard and guiding spirit of the conciliar movement which led to the calling of the Council of Constance (1414-1418).

[7] The logical and metaphysical writings of Aristotle were well known in the Middle Ages and were incorporated in scholasticism. His scientific writings became known to Europeans in the late Middle Ages and caused much concern because they contained statements contrary to Christian doctrine. It is to these writings that Luther refers in his phrase "the whole Aristotle."

52. It would have been better for the church if Porphyry[8] with his universals had not been born for the use of theologians.

53. Even the more useful definitions of Aristotle seem to beg the question.

54. For an act to be meritorious, either the presence of grace is sufficient, or its presence means nothing. This in opposition to Gabriel.

55. The grace of God is never present in such a way that it is inactive, but it is a living, active, and operative spirit; nor can it happen that through the absolute power of God an act of friendship may be present without the presence of the grace of God. This in opposition to Gabriel.

56. It is not true that God can accept man without his justifying grace. This in opposition to Ockham.[9]

57. It is dangerous to say that the law commands that an act of obeying the commandment be done in the grace of God. This in opposition to the Cardinal and Gabriel.

58. From this it would follow that "to have the grace of God" is actually a new demand going beyond the law.

59. It would also follow that fulfilling the law can take place without the grace of God.

60. Likewise it follows that the grace of God would be more hateful than the law itself.

61. It does not follow that the law should be complied with and fulfilled in the grace of God. This in opposition to Gabriel.

62. And that therefore he who is outside the grace of God sins incessantly, even when he does not kill, commit adultery, or become angry.

63. But it follows that he sins because he does not spiritually fulfil the law.

64. Spiritually that person does not kill, does not do evil, does not become enraged when he neither becomes angry nor lusts.

---

[8] Porphyry (233-303) was a Neoplatonic follower of Plotinus and a bitter opponent of Christianity.
[9] William of Ockham (*ca.* 1280-1349) was a Franciscan schoolman, a nominalist who stated that reason could not be applied to theology. He published commentaries on Aristotle and Porphyry.

65. Outside the grace of God it is indeed impossible not to become angry or lust, so that not even in grace is it possible to fulfil the law perfectly.

66. It is the righteousness of the hypocrite actually and outwardly not to kill, do evil, etc.

67. It is by the grace of God that one does not lust or become enraged.

68. Therefore it is impossible to fulfil the law in any way without the grace of God.

69. As a matter of fact, it is more accurate to say that the law is destroyed by nature without the grace of God.

70. A good law will of necessity be bad for the natural will.

71. Law and will are two implacable foes without the grace of God.

72. What the law wants, the will never wants, unless it pretends to want it out of fear or love.

73. The law, as taskmaster of the will, will not be overcome except by the "child, who has been born to us" [Isa. 9:6].

74. The law makes sin abound because it irritates and repels the will [Rom. 7:13].

75. The grace of God, however, makes justice abound through Jesus Christ because it causes one to be pleased with the law.

76. Every deed of the law without the grace of God appears good outwardly, but inwardly it is sin. This in opposition to the scholastics.

77. The will is always averse to, and the hands inclined toward, the law of the Lord without the grace of God.

78. The will which is inclined toward the law without the grace of God is so inclined by reason of its own advantage.

79. Condemned are all those who do the works of the law.

80. Blessed are all those who do the works of the grace of God.

81. Chapter Falsas concerning penance, dist. 5,[10] confirms the fact that works outside the realm of grace are not good, if this is not understood falsely.

---

[10] *Decretum Magistri Gratiani, Decreta Secunda Pars*, causa XXXIII, ques. III, dist. V, cap. 6. *Corpus Iuris Canonici*, ed. Aemilius Friedberg (Graz, 1955), I, col. 1241. Cf. Migne 187, 1636.

82. Not only are the religious ceremonials not the good law and the precepts in which one does not live (in opposition to many teachers);

83. But even the Decalogue itself and all that can be taught and prescribed inwardly and outwardly is not good law either.

84. The good law and that in which one lives is the love of God, spread abroad in our hearts by the Holy Spirit.

85. Anyone's will would prefer, if it were possible, that there would be no law and to be entirely free.

86. Anyone's will hates it that the law should be imposed upon it; if, however, the will desires imposition of the law it does so out of love of self.

87. Since the law is good, the will, which is hostile to it, cannot be good.

88. And from this it is clear that everyone's natural will is iniquitous and bad.

89. Grace as a mediator is necessary to reconcile the law with the will.

90. The grace of God is given for the purpose of directing the will, lest it err even in loving God. In opposition to Gabriel.

91. It is not given so that good deeds might be induced more frequently and readily, but because without it no act of love is performed. In opposition to Gabriel.

92. It cannot be denied that love is superfluous if man is by nature able to do an act of friendship. In opposition to Gabriel.

93. There is a kind of subtle evil in the argument that an act is at the same time the fruit and the use of the fruit. In opposition to Ockham, the Cardinal, Gabriel.

94. This holds true also of the saying that the love of God may continue alongside an intense love of the creature.

95. To love God is at the same time to hate oneself and to know nothing but God.

96. We must make our will conform in every respect to the will of God (in opposition to the Cardinal);

97. So that we not only will what God wills, but also ought to will whatever God wills.

1. The Task of Theology

In these statements we wanted to say and believe we have said nothing that is not in agreement with the Catholic church and the teachers of the church.

1517

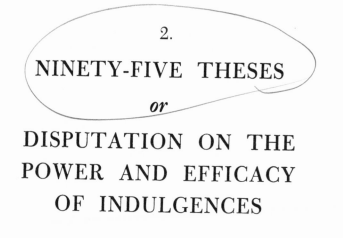

2.

NINETY-FIVE THESES

or

DISPUTATION ON THE POWER AND EFFICACY OF INDULGENCES

Out of love and zeal for truth and the desire to bring it to light, the following theses will be publicly discussed at Wittenberg under the chairmanship of the reverend father Martin Lutther,[1] Master of Arts and Sacred Theology and regularly appointed Lecturer on these subjects at that place. He requests that those who cannot be present to debate orally with us will do so by letter.[2]

In the Name of Our Lord Jesus Christ. Amen.

1. When our Lord and Master Jesus Christ said, "Repent" [Matt. 4:17],[3] he willed the entire life of believers to be one of repentance.

2. This word cannot be understood as referring to the sacrament of penance, that is, confession and satisfaction, as administered by the clergy.

3. Yet it does not mean solely inner repentance; such inner repentance is worthless unless it produces various outward mortifications of the flesh.

---

[1] Luther spelled his name Lutther in this preamble.

[2] There was actually no debate, for no one responded to the invitation. The contents of the ninety-five theses were soon widely disseminated by word of mouth and by the printers, and in effect a vigorous debate took place that lasted for a number of years.

[3] The Latin form, *poenitentiam agite,* and the German, *tut Busse,* may be rendered in two ways, "repent," and "do penance."

4. The penalty of sin[4] remains as long as the hatred of self, that is, true inner repentance, until our entrance into the kingdom of heaven.

5. The pope neither desires nor is able to remit any penalties except those imposed by his own authority or that of the canons.[5]

6. The pope cannot remit any guilt, except by declaring and showing that it has been remitted by God; or, to be sure, by remitting guilt in cases reserved to his judgment. If his right to grant remission in these cases were disregarded, the guilt would certainly remain unforgiven.

7. God remits guilt to no one unless at the same time he humbles him in all things and makes him submissive to his vicar, the priest.

8. The penitential canons are imposed only on the living, and, according to the canons themselves, nothing should be imposed on the dying.

9. Therefore the Holy Spirit through the pope is kind to us insofar as the pope in his decrees always makes exception of the article of death and of necessity.[6]

10. Those priests act ignorantly and wickedly who, in the case of the dying, reserve canonical penalties for purgatory.

11. Those tares of changing the canonical penalty to the penalty of purgatory were evidently sown while the bishops slept [Matt. 13:25].

12. In former times canonical penalties were imposed, not after, but before absolution, as tests of true contrition.

13. The dying are freed by death from all penalties, are already dead as far as the canon laws are concerned, and have a right to be released from them.

14. Imperfect piety or love on the part of the dying person necessarily brings with it great fear; and the smaller the love, the greater the fear.

---

[4] Catholic theology distinguishes between the "guilt" and the "penalty" of sin.

[5] The canons, or decrees of the church, have the force of law. Those referred to here and in Theses 8 and 85 are the so-called penitential canons.

[6] Commenting on this thesis in the *Explanations of the Ninety-five Theses* (p. 114), Luther distinguishes between temporal and eternal necessity. "Necessity knows no law." "Death is the necessity of necessities." Cf. *WA* 1, 549.

15. This fear or horror is sufficient in itself, to say nothing of other things, to constitute the penalty of purgatory, since it is very near the horror of despair.

16. Hell, purgatory, and heaven seem to differ the same as despair, fear, and assurance of salvation.

17. It seems as though for the souls in purgatory fear should necessarily decrease and love increase.

18. Furthermore, it does not seem proved, either by reason or Scripture, that souls in purgatory are outside the state of merit, that is, unable to grow in love.

19. Nor does it seem proved that souls in purgatory, at least not all of them, are certain and assured of their own salvation, even if we ourselves may be entirely certain of it.

20. Therefore the pope, when he uses the words "plenary remission of all penalties," does not actually mean "all penalties," but only those imposed by himself.

21. Thus those indulgence preachers are in error who say that a man is absolved from every penalty and saved by papal indulgences.

22. As a matter of fact, the pope remits to souls in purgatory no penalty which, according to canon law, they should have paid in this life.

23. If remission of all penalties whatsoever could be granted to anyone at all, certainly it would be granted only to the most perfect, that is, to very few.

24. For this reason most people are necessarily deceived by that indiscriminate and high-sounding promise of release from penalty.

25. That power which the pope has in general over purgatory corresponds to the power which any bishop or curate has in a particular way in his own diocese or parish.

26. The pope does very well when he grants remission to souls in purgatory, not by the power of the keys, which he does not have,[7] but by way of intercession for them.

27. They preach only human doctrines who say that as soon

---

[7] This is not a denial of the power of the keys, that is, the power to forgive and to retain sin, but merely an assertion that the power of the keys does not extend to purgatory.

as the money clinks into the money chest, the soul flies out of purgatory.

28. It is certain that when money clinks in the money chest, greed and avarice can be increased; but when the church intercedes, the result is in the hands of God alone.

29. Who knows whether all souls in purgatory wish to be redeemed, since we have exceptions in St. Severinus and St. Paschal,[8] as related in a legend.

30. No one is sure of the integrity of his own contrition, much less of having received plenary remission.

31. The man who actually buys indulgences is as rare as he who is really penitent; indeed, he is exceedingly rare.

32. Those who believe that they can be certain of their salvation because they have indulgence letters will be eternally damned, together with their teachers.

33. Men must especially be on their guard against those who say that the pope's pardons are that inestimable gift of God by which man is reconciled to him.

34. For the graces of indulgences are concerned only with the penalties of sacramental satisfaction[9] established by man.

35. They who teach that contrition is not necessary on the part of those who intend to buy souls out of purgatory or to buy confessional privileges[10] preach unchristian doctrine.

36. Any truly repentant Christian has a right to full remission of penalty and guilt,[11] even without indulgence letters.

---

[8] Luther refers to this legend again in the *Explanations of the Ninety-five Theses* below, p. 178. The legend is to the effect that these saints, Pope Severinus (638-640) and Pope Paschal I (817-824), preferred to remain longer in purgatory that they might have greater glory in heaven.

[9] Satisfaction is that act on the part of the penitent, in connection with the sacrament of penance, by means of which he pays the temporal penalty for his sins. If at death he is in arrears in paying his temporal penalty for venial sins, he pays this penalty in purgatory. Indulgences are concerned with this satisfaction of the sacrament of penance—they permit a partial or complete (plenary) remission of temporal punishment. According to Roman Catholic theology, the buyer of an indulgence still has to confess his sins, be absolved from them, and be truly penitent.

[10] These are privileges entitling the holder of indulgence letters to choose his own confessor and relieving him, the holder, of certain satisfactions.

[11] To justify the placing of absolution before satisfaction, contrary to the practice of the early church, theologians distinguished between the guilt and the penalty of sins.

37. Any true Christian, whether living or dead, participates in all the blessings of Christ and the church; and this is granted him by God, even without indulgence letters.

38. Nevertheless, papal remission and blessing are by no means to be disregarded, for they are, as I have said [Thesis 6], the proclamation of the divine remission.

39. It is very difficult, even for the most learned theologians, at one and the same time to commend to the people the bounty of indulgences and the need of true contrition.

40. A Christian who is truly contrite seeks and loves to pay penalties for his sins; the bounty of indulgences, however, relaxes penalties and causes men to hate them—at least it furnishes occasion for hating them.

41. Papal indulgences must be preached with caution, lest people erroneously think that they are preferable to other good works of love.

42. Christians are to be taught that the pope does not intend that the buying of indulgences should in any way be compared with works of mercy.

43. Christians are to be taught that he who gives to the poor or lends to the needy does a better deed than he who buys indulgences.

44. Because love grows by works of love, man thereby becomes better. Man does not, however, become better by means of indulgences but is merely freed from penalties.

45. Christians are to be taught that he who sees a needy man and passes him by, yet gives his money for indulgences, does not buy papal indulgences but God's wrath.

46. Christians are to be taught that, unless they have more than they need, they must reserve enough for their family needs and by no means squander it on indulgences.

47. Christians are to be taught that the buying of indulgences is a matter of free choice, not commanded.

48. Christians are to be taught that the pope, in granting indulgences, needs and thus desires their devout prayer more than their money.

49. Christians are to be taught that papal indulgences are use-

ful only if they do not put their trust in them, but very harmful if they lose their fear of God because of them.

50. Christians are to be taught that if the pope knew the exactions of the indulgence preachers, he would rather that the basilica of St. Peter were burned to ashes than built up with the skin, flesh, and bones of his sheep.

51. Christians are to be taught that the pope would and should wish to give of his own money, even though he had to sell the basilica of St. Peter, to many of those from whom certain hawkers of indulgences cajole money.

52. It is vain to trust in salvation by indulgence letters, even though the indulgence commissary, or even the pope, were to offer his soul as security.

53. They are enemies of Christ and the pope who forbid altogether the preaching of the Word of God in some churches in order that indulgences may be preached in others.

54. Injury is done the Word of God when, in the same sermon, an equal or larger amount of time is devoted to indulgences than to the Word.

55. It is certainly the pope's sentiment that if indulgences, which are a very insignificant thing, are celebrated with one bell, one procession, and one ceremony, then the gospel, which is the very greatest thing, should be preached with a hundred bells, a hundred processions, a hundred ceremonies.

56. The treasures of the church,[12] out of which the pope distributes indulgences, are not sufficiently discussed or known among the people of Christ.

57. That indulgences are not temporal treasures is certainly clear, for many [indulgence] preachers do not distribute them freely but only gather them.

58. Nor are they the merits of Christ and the saints, for, even without the pope, the latter always work grace for the inner man, and the cross, death, and hell for the outer man.

59. St. Laurence said that the poor of the church were the

---

[12] The treasury of merits is a reserve fund of good works accumulated by Christ and the saints upon which the pope could draw when he remitted satisfaction in indulgences.

Keys are Gospel not indulgences

treasures of the church, but he spoke according to the usage of the word in his own time.

60. Without want of consideration we say that the keys of the church,[13] given by the merits of Christ, are that treasure;

61. For it is clear that the pope's power is of itself sufficient for the remission of penalties and cases reserved by himself.

62. The true treasure of the church is the most holy gospel of the glory and grace of God.

63. But this treasure is naturally most odious, for it makes the first to be last [Matt. 20:16].

64. On the other hand, the treasure of indulgences is naturally most acceptable, for it makes the last to be first.

65. Therefore the treasures of the gospel are nets with which one formerly fished for men of wealth.

66. The treasures of indulgences are nets with which one now fishes for the wealth of men.

67. The indulgences which the demagogues acclaim as the greatest graces are actually understood to be such only insofar as they promote gain.

68. They are nevertheless in truth the most insignificant graces when compared with the grace of God and the piety of the cross.

69. Bishops and curates are bound to admit the commissaries of papal indulgences with all reverence.

70. But they are much more bound to strain their eyes and ears lest these men preach their own dreams instead of what the pope has commissioned.

71. Let him who speaks against the truth concerning papal indulgences be anathema and accursed;

72. But let him who guards against the lust and license of the indulgence preachers be blessed;

73. Just as the pope justly thunders against those who by any means whatsoever contrive harm to the sale of indulgences.

74. But much more does he intend to thunder against those

---

[13] The office of the keys: the preaching of the gospel, the celebrating of the sacraments, the remitting of sins to the penitent, and the excommunicating of impenitent sinners.

who use indulgences as a pretext to contrive harm to holy love and truth.

75. To consider papal indulgences so great that they could absolve a man even if he had done the impossible and had violated the mother of God is madness.

76. We say on the contrary that papal indulgences cannot remove the very least of venial sins as far as guilt is concerned.

77. To say that even St. Peter, if he were now pope, could not grant greater graces is blasphemy against St. Peter and the pope.

78. We say on the contrary that even the present pope, or any pope whatsoever, has greater graces at his disposal, that is, the gospel, spiritual powers, gifts of healing, etc., as it is written in I Cor. 12 [:28].

79. To say that the cross emblazoned with the papal coat of arms, and set up by the indulgence preachers, is equal in worth to the cross of Christ is blasphemy.

80. The bishops, curates, and theologians who permit such talk to be spread among the people will have to answer for this.

81. This unbridled preaching of indulgences makes it difficult even for learned men to rescue the reverence which is due the pope from slander or from the shrewd questions of the laity,

82. Such as: "Why does not the pope empty purgatory for the sake of holy love and the dire need of the souls that are there if he redeems an infinite number of souls for the sake of miserable money with which to build a church? The former reasons would be most just; the latter is most trivial."

83. Again, "Why are funeral and anniversary masses for the dead continued and why does he not return or permit the withdrawal of the endowments founded for them, since it is wrong to pray for the redeemed?"

84. Again, "What is this new piety of God and the pope that for a consideration of money they permit a man who is impious and their enemy to buy out of purgatory the pious soul of a friend of God and do not rather, because of the need of that pious and beloved soul, free it for pure love's sake?"

85. Again, "Why are the penitential canons, long since abrogated and dead in actual fact and through disuse, now satisfied by

the granting of indulgences as though they were still alive and in force?"

86. Again, "Why does not the pope, whose wealth is today greater than the wealth of the richest Crassus,[14] build this one basilica of St. Peter with his own money rather than with the money of poor believers?"

87. Again, "What does the pope remit or grant to those who by perfect contrition already have a right to full remission and blessings?"[15]

88. Again, "What greater blessing could come to the church than if the pope were to bestow these remissions and blessings on every believer a hundred times a day, as he now does but once?"[16]

89. "Since the pope seeks the salvation of souls rather than money by his indulgences, why does he suspend the indulgences and pardons previously granted when they have equal efficacy?"[17]

90. To repress these very sharp arguments of the laity by force alone, and not to resolve them by giving reasons, is to expose the church and the pope to the ridicule of their enemies and to make Christians unhappy.

91. If, therefore, indulgences were preached according to the spirit and intention of the pope, all these doubts would be readily resolved. Indeed, they would not exist.

92. Away then with all those prophets who say to the people of Christ, "Peace, peace," and there is no peace! [Jer. 6:14].

93. Blessed be all those prophets who say to the people of Christ, "Cross, cross," and there is no cross!

94. Christians should be exhorted to be diligent in following Christ, their head, through penalties, death, and hell;

95. And thus be confident of entering into heaven through many tribulations rather than through the false security of peace [Acts 14:22].

1517

---

[14] Marcus Licinius Crassus (115-53 B.C.), also called Dives ("the Rich"), was noted for his wealth and luxury by the classical Romans. Crassus means "the Fat."

[15] See Theses 36 and 37.

[16] The indulgence letter entitled its possessor to receive absolution once during his lifetime and once at the approach of death.

[17] During the time when the jubilee indulgences were preached, other indulgences were suspended.

3.

HEIDELBERG DISPUTATION

Brother Martin Luther, Master of Sacred Theology, will preside, and Brother Leonhard Beier, Master of Arts and Philosophy, will defend the following theses before the Augustinians of this renowned city of Heidelberg in the customary place. In the month of May, 1518.[1]

THEOLOGICAL THESES

Distrusting completely our own wisdom, according to that counsel of the Holy Spirit, "Do not rely on your own insight" [Prov. 3:5], we humbly present to the judgment of all those who wish to be here these theological paradoxes, so that it may become clear whether they have been deduced well or poorly from St. Paul, the especially chosen vessel and instrument of Christ, and also from St. Augustine, his most trustworthy interpreter.

1. The law of God, the most salutary doctrine of life, cannot advance man on his way to righteousness, but rather hinders him.

2. Much less can human works, which are done over and over again with the aid of natural precepts, so to speak, lead to that end.

3. Although the works of man always seem attractive and good, they are nevertheless likely to be mortal sins.

4. Although the works of God always seem unattractive and appear evil, they are nevertheless really eternal merits.

5. The works of men are thus not mortal sins (we speak of works which are apparently good), as though they were crimes.

6. The works of God (we speak of those which he does through man) are thus not merits, as though they were sinless.

---

[1] This is an approximate date. The disputation actually took place April 26, 1518.

7. The works of the righteous would be mortal sins if they would not be feared as mortal sins by the righteous themselves out of pious fear of God.

8. By so much more are the works of man mortal sins when they are done without fear and in unadulterated, evil self-security.

9. To say that works without Christ are dead, but not mortal, appears to constitute a perilous surrender of the fear of God.

10. Indeed, it is very difficult to see how a work can be dead and at the same time not a harmful and mortal sin.

11. Arrogance cannot be avoided or true hope be present unless the judgment of condemnation is feared in every work.

12. In the sight of God sins are then truly venial when they are feared by men to be mortal.

13. Free will, after the fall, exists in name only, and as long as it does what it is able to do, it commits a mortal sin.

14. Free will, after the fall, has power to do good only in a passive capacity, but it can always do evil in an active capacity.

15. Nor could free will endure in a state of innocence, much less do good, in an active capacity, but only in its passive capacity.

16. The person who believes that he can obtain grace by doing what is in him[2] adds sin to sin so that he becomes doubly guilty.

17. Nor does speaking in this manner give cause for despair, but for arousing the desire to humble oneself and seek the grace of Christ.

18. It is certain that man must utterly despair of his own ability before he is prepared to receive the grace of Christ.

19. That person does not deserve to be called a theologian who looks upon the invisible things of God as though they were clearly perceptible in those things which have actually happened [Rom. 1:20].

20. He deserves to be called a theologian, however, who comprehends the visible and manifest things of God seen through suffering and the cross.

21. A theologian of glory calls evil good and good evil. A theologian of the cross calls the thing what it actually is.

22. That wisdom which sees the invisible things of God in

---

[2] Cf. p. 14, n. 5.

works as perceived by man is completely puffed up, blinded, and hardened.

23. The law brings the wrath of God, kills, reviles, accuses, judges, and condemns everything that is not in Christ [Rom. 4:15].

24. Yet that wisdom is not of itself evil, nor is the law to be evaded; but without the theology of the cross man misuses the best in the worst manner.

25. He is not righteous who does much, but he who, without work, believes much in Christ.

26. The law says, "do this," and it is never done. Grace says, "believe in this," and everything is already done.

27. Actually one should call the work of Christ an acting work and our work an accomplished work, and thus an accomplished work pleasing to God by the grace of the acting work.

28. The love of God does not find, but creates, that which is pleasing to it. The love of man comes into being through that which is pleasing to it.

PHILOSOPHICAL THESES

29. He who wishes to philosophize by using Aristotle without danger to his soul must first become thoroughly foolish in Christ.

30. Just as a person does not use the evil of passion well unless he is a married man, so no person philosophizes well unless he is a fool, that is, a Christian.

31. It was easy for Aristotle to believe that the world was eternal since he believed that the human soul was mortal.

32. After the proposition that there are as many material forms as there are created things had been accepted, it was necessary to accept that they all are material.

33. Nothing in the world becomes something of necessity; nevertheless, that which comes forth from matter, again by necessity, comes into being according to nature.

34. If Aristotle would have recognized the absolute power of God, he would accordingly have maintained that it was impossible for matter to exist of itself alone.

35. According to Aristotle, nothing is infinite with respect to ac-

tion, yet with respect to power and matter, as ma
been created are infinite.

36. Aristotle wrongly finds fault with and der
Plato, which actually are better than his own.

37. The mathematical order of material thing ~~~1y
maintained by Pythagoras, but more ingenious is the interaction of
ideas maintained by Plato.

38. The disputation of Aristotle lashes out at Parmenides' idea
of oneness[3] (if a Christian will pardon this) in a battle of air.

39. If Anaxagoras posited infinity as to form, as it seems he did,
he was the best of the philosophers, even if Aristotle was unwilling
to acknowledge this.

40. To Aristotle, privation, matter, form, movable, immovable,
impulse, power, etc. seem to be the same.

PROOFS OF THE THESIS DEBATED IN THE CHAPTER
AT HEIDELBERG, MAY, 1518, A.D.

1

*The law of God, the most salutary doctrine of life, can-
not advance man on his way to righteousness, but rather
hinders him.*

This is made clear by the Apostle in his letter to the Romans (3
[: 21]): "But now the righteousness of God has been manifested
apart from the law." St. Augustine interprets this in his book, *The
Spirit and the Letter (De Spiritu et Littera):* "Without the law,
that is, without its support."[4] In Rom. 5 [:20] the Apostle states,
"Law intervened, to increase the trespass," and in Rom. 7 [:9]
he adds, "But when the commandment came, sin revived." For
this reason he calls the law a law of death and a law of sin in Rom.
8 [:2]. Indeed, in II Cor. 3 [:6] he says, "the written code kills,"

---

[3] Parmenides was a well-known Greek philosopher who, with Zeno, headed
the Eleatic school and taught a monistic cosmology.

[4] In *Basic Writings of St. Augustine*, trans. P. Holmes, ed. Whitney J. Oates
(2 vols.; New York, 1948) I, 461-518. Cf. Migne 44, 199-246.

which St. Augustine throughout his book, *The Spirit and the Letter*, understands as applying to every law, even the holiest law of God.

2

Much less can human works which are done over and over again with the aid of natural precepts, so to speak, lead to that end.

Since the law of God, which is holy and unstained, true, just, etc., is given man by God as an aid beyond his natural powers to enlighten him and move him to do the good, and nevertheless the opposite takes place, namely, that he becomes more wicked, how can he, left to his own power and without such aid, be induced to do good? If a person does not do good with help from without, he will do even less by his own strength. Therefore the Apostle, in Rom. 3 [:10-12], calls all persons corrupt and impotent who neither understand nor seek God, for all, he says, have gone astray.

3

Although the works of man always seem attractive and good, they are nevertheless likely to be mortal sins.

Human works appear attractive outwardly, but within they are filthy, as Christ says concerning the Pharisees in Matt. 23 [:27]. For they appear to the doer and others good and beautiful, yet God does not judge according to appearances but searches "the minds and hearts" [Ps. 7:9]. For without grace and faith it is impossible to have a pure heart. Acts 15 [:9]: "He cleansed their hearts by faith."

The thesis is proven in the following way: If the works of righteous men are sins, as Thesis 7 of this disputation states, this is much more the case concerning the works of those who are not righteous. But the just speak in behalf of their works in the following way: "Do not enter into judgment with thy servant, Lord, for no man living is righteous before thee" [Ps. 143:2]. The Apostle speaks likewise in Gal. 3 [:10], "All who rely on the works of the law are under the curse." But the works of men are the works of the law, and the curse will not be placed upon venial sins. Therefore they are mortal sins.

In the third place, Rom. 2. [:21] states, "You who teach others not to steal, do you steal?" St. Augustine interprets this to mean that men are thieves according to their guilty consciences even if they publicly judge or reprimand other thieves.

4

Although the works of God always seem unattractive and appear evil, they are nevertheless really eternal merits.

That the works of God are unattractive is clear from what is said in Isa. 53 [:2], "He had no form of comeliness," and in I Sam. 2 [:6], "The Lord kills and brings to life; he brings down to Sheol and raises up." This is understood to mean that the Lord humbles and frightens us by means of the law and the sight of our sins so that we seem in the eyes of men, as in our own, as nothing, foolish, and wicked, for we are in truth that. Insofar as we acknowledge and confess this, these is no form or beauty in us, but our life is hidden in God (i.e. in the bare confidence in his mercy), finding in ourselves nothing but sin, foolishness, death, and hell, according to that verse of the Apostle in II Cor. 6 [:9-10], "As sorrowful, yet always rejoicing; as dying, and behold we live." And that it is which Isa. 28 [:21] calls the alien work of God that he may do his work (that is, he humbles us thoroughly, making us despair, so that he may exalt us in his mercy, giving us hope), just as Hab. 3 [:2] states, "In wrath remember mercy." Such a man therefore is displeased with all his works; he sees no beauty, but only his ugliness. Indeed, he also does those things which appear foolish and disgusting to others.

This ugliness, however, comes into being in us either when God punishes us or when we accuse ourselves, as I Cor. 11 [:31] says, "If we judged ourselves truly, we should not be judged" by the Lord. Deut. 32 [:36] also states, "The Lord will vindicate his people and have compassion on his servants." In this way, consequently, the unattractive works which God does in us, that is, those which are humble and devout, are really eternal, for humility and fear of God are our entire merit.

5

The works of men are thus not mortal sins (we speak of works which are apparently good), as though they were crimes.

For crimes are such acts which can also be condemned before men, such as adultery, theft, homicide, slander, etc. Mortal sins, on the other hand, are those which seem good yet are essentially fruits of a bad root and a bad tree. Augustine states this in the fourth book of *Against Julian (Contra Julianum)*.[5]

6

The works of God (we speak of those which he does through man) are thus not merits, as though they were sinless.

In Eccles. 7 [:20], we read, "Surely there is not a righteous man on earth who does good and never sins." In this connection, however, some people[6] say that the righteous man indeed sins, but not when he does good. They may be refuted in the following manner: "If that is what this verse wants to say, why waste so many words?" or does the Holy Spirit like to indulge in loquacious and foolish babble? For this meaning would then be adequately expressed by the following: "There is not a righteous man on earth who does not sin." Why does he add "who does good," as if another person were righteous who did evil? For no one except a righteous man does good. Where, however, he speaks of sins outside the realm of good works he speaks thus [Prov. 24:16], "The righteous man falls seven times a day." Here he does not say, "A righteous man falls seven times a day when he does good." This is a comparison. If someone cuts with a rusty and rough hatchet, even though the worker is a good craftsman, the hatchet leaves bad, jagged, and ugly gashes. So it is when God works through us.

7

The works of the righteous would be mortal sins if they

---

[5] Migne 44, 641-880.
[6] By "some people" Luther means St. Jerome above all.

would not be feared as mortal sins by the righteous them-selves out of pious fear of God.

This is clear from Thesis 4. To trust in works, which one ought to do in fear, is equivalent to giving oneself the honor and taking it from God, to whom fear is due in connection with every work. But this is completely wrong, namely to please oneself, to enjoy oneself in one's works, and to adore oneself as an idol. He who is self-confident and without fear of God, however, acts entirely in this manner. For if he had fear he would not be self-confident, and for this reason he would not be pleased with himself, but he would be pleased with God.

In the second place, it is clear from the words of the Psalmist [Ps. 143:2], "Enter not into judgment with thy servant," and Ps. 32 [:5], "I said, 'I will confess my transgressions to the Lord,'" etc. But that these are not venial sins is clear because these passages state that confession and repentance are not necessary for venial sins. If, therefore, they are mortal sins and all the saints intercede for them, as it is stated in the same place, then the works of the saints are mortal sins. But the works of the saints are good works, wherefore they are meritorious for them only through the fear of their humble confession.

In the third place, it is clear from the Lord's Prayer, "Forgive us our trespasses" [Matt. 6:12]. This is a prayer of the saints, therefore those trespasses are good works for which they pray. But that these are mortal sins is clear from the following verse, "If you do not forgive men their trespasses, neither will your father forgive your trespasses" [Matt. 6:15]. Note that these trespasses are such that, if unforgiven, they would condemn them, unless they pray this prayer sincerely and forgive others.

In the fourth place, it is clear from Rev. 21 [:27], "Nothing unclean shall enter into it" [the kingdom of heaven]. But everything that hinders entrance into the kingdom of heaven is mortal sin (or it would be necessary to interpret the concept of mortal sin in another way). Venial sin, however, hinders because it makes the soul unclean and has no place in the kingdom of heaven. Consequently, etc.

8

By so much more are the works of man mortal sins when they are done without fear and in unadulterated, evil self-security.

The inevitable deduction from the preceding thesis is clear. For where there is no fear there is no humility. Where there is no humility there is pride, and where there is pride there are the wrath and judgment of God, for God opposes the haughty. Indeed, if pride would cease there would be no sin anywhere.

9

To say that works without Christ are dead, but not mortal, appears to constitute a perilous surrender of the fear of God.

For in this way men become certain and therefore haughty, which is perilous. For in such a way God is constantly deprived of the glory which is due him and which is transferred to other things, since one should strive with all diligence to give him the glory—the sooner the better. For this reason the Bible advises us, "Do not delay being converted to the Lord."[7] For if that person offends him who withdraws glory from him, how much more does that person offend him who continues to withdraw glory from him and does this boldly! But whoever is not in Christ or who withdraws from him withdraws glory from him, as is well known.

10

Indeed, it is very difficult to see how a work can be dead and at the same time not a harmful and mortal sin.

This I prove in the following way: Scripture does not speak of dead things in such a manner, stating that something is not mortal which is nevertheless dead. Indeed, neither does grammar, which says that "dead" is a stronger term than "mortal." For the gram-

---

[7] This quotation is from Sirach 5:8. The Vulgate Bible contained the apocryphal books.

marians call a mortal work one which kills, a dead work not one that has been killed, but one that is not alive. But God despises what is not alive, as is written in Prov. 15 [:8], "The sacrifice of the wicked is an abomination to the Lord."

Second, the will must do something with respect to such a dead work, namely, either love or hate it. The will cannot hate a dead work since the will is evil. Consequently the will loves a dead work, and therefore it loves something dead. In that act itself it thus induces an evil work of the will against God whom it should love and honor in this and in every deed.

11

Arrogance cannot be avoided or true hope be present unless the judgment of condemnation is feared in every work.

This is clear from Thesis 4. For it is impossible to hope in God unless one has despaired in all creatures and knows that nothing can profit one without God. Since there is no person who has this pure hope, as we said above, and since we still place some confidence in the creature, it is clear that we must, because of impurity in all things, fear the judgment of God. Thus arrogance must be avoided, not only in the work, but in the inclination also, that is, it must displease us still to have confidence in the creature.

12

In the sight of God sins are then truly venial when they are feared by men to be mortal.

This becomes sufficiently clear from what has been said. For as much as we accuse ourselves, so much God pardons us, according to the verse, "Confess your misdeed so that you will be justified" [Cf. Isa. 43:26], and according to another [Ps. 141:4], "Incline not my heart to any evil, to busy myself with wicked deeds."

13

Free will, after the fall, exists in name only, and as long as it does what it is able to do, it commits a mortal sin.

The first part is clear, for the will is captive and subject to sin.

Not that it is nothing, but that it is not free except to do evil. According to John 8 [:34, 36], "Every one who commits sin is a slave to sin. . . . So if the Son makes you free, you will be free indeed." Hence St. Augustine says in his book, *The Spirit and the Letter*, "Free will without grace has the power to do nothing but sin";[8] and in the second book of *Against Julian*, "You call the will free, but in fact it is an enslaved will,"[9] and in many other places.

The second part is clear from what has been said above and from the verse in Hos. 13 [:9], "Israel, you are bringing misfortune upon yourself, for your salvation is alone with me,"[10] and from similar passages.

14

Free will, after the fall, has power to do good only in a passive capacity,[11] but it can always do evil in an active capacity.

An illustration will make the meaning of this thesis clear. Just as a dead man can do something toward life only in a passive capacity, so can he do something toward death in an active manner while he lives. Free will, however, is dead, as demonstrated by the dead whom the Lord has raised up, as the holy teachers of the church say. St. Augustine, moreover, proves this same thesis in his various writings against the Pelagians.

15

Nor could free will endure in a state of innocence, much less do good, in an active capacity, but only in its passive capacity.

The Master of the *Sentences*,[12] quoting Augustine, states, "By these

---

[8] Chap. 3, par. 5, Migne 44, 203.
[9] Chap. 8, par. 23, Migne 44, 689.
[10] This is a free rendering of the passage, "I will destroy you, O Israel; who can help you?"
[11] This is Luther's way of stating that the free will could before the fall determine to do good. That it could do so after the fall would seem likely because of its name, but not in actual fact.
[12] Peter Lombard. Migne 192, 519-964. The chapter to which Luther refers is in col. 586.

testimonies it is obviously demonstrated that man received a righteous nature and a good will when he was created, and also the
help by means of which he could prevail. Otherwise it would
appear as though he had not fallen because of his own fault." He
speaks of the active capacity, which is obviously contrary to Augustine's opinion in his book, *Concerning Reprimand and Grace* (*De
Correptione et Gratia*), where the latter puts it in this way: "He received the ability to act, if he so willed, but he did not have the
will by means of which he could act."[13] By "ability to act" he
understands the passive capacity, and by "will by means of which he
could," the active capacity.

The second part, however, is sufficiently clarified by the Master
in the same distinction.

16

*The person who believes that he can obtain grace by doing
what is in him adds sin to sin so that he becomes doubly
guilty.*

On the basis of what has been said, the following is clear: While
a person is doing what is in him, he sins and seeks himself in everything. But if he should suppose that through sin he would become
worthy of or prepared for grace, he would add haughty arrogance
to his sin and not believe that sin is sin and evil is evil, which
is an exceedingly great sin. As Jer. 2 [:13] says, "For my people
have committed two evils: they have forsaken me, the fountain of
living waters, and hewed out cisterns for themselves, broken cisterns, that can hold no water," that is, through sin they are far
from me and yet they presume to do good by their own ability.

Now you ask, "What then shall we do? Shall we go our way
with indifference because we can do nothing but sin?" I would
reply, By no means. But, having heard this, fall down and pray for
grace and place your hope in Christ in whom is our salvation, life,
and resurrection. For this reason we are so instructed—for this
reason the law makes us aware of sin so that, having recognized our
sin, we may seek and receive grace. Thus God "gives grace to the

---

[13] Migne 44, 915-946.

humble" [I Pet. 5:5], and "whoever humbles himself will be exalted" [Matt. 23:12]. The law humbles, grace exalts. The law effects fear and wrath, grace effects hope and mercy. "Through the law comes knowledge of sin" [Rom. 3:20], through knowledge of sin, however, comes humility, and through humility grace is acquired. Thus an action which is alien to God's nature results in a deed belonging to his very nature: he makes a person a sinner so that he may make him righteous.

17

Nor does speaking in this manner give cause for despair, but for arousing the desire to humble oneself and seek the grace of Christ.

This is clear from what has been said, for, according to the gospel, the kingdom of heaven is given to children and the humble [Mark 10:14, 16], and Christ loves them. They cannot be humble who do not recognize that they are damnable whose sin smells to high heaven. Sin is recognized only through the law. It is apparent that not despair, but rather hope, is preached when we are told that we are sinners. Such preaching concerning sin is a preparation for grace, or it is rather the recognition of sin and faith in such preaching. Yearning for grace wells up when recognition of sin has arisen. A sick person seeks the physician when he recognizes the seriousness of his illness. Therefore one does not give cause for despair or death by telling a sick person about the danger of his illness, but, in effect, one urges him to seek a medical cure. To say that we are nothing and constantly sin when we do the best we can does not mean that we cause people to despair (unless they are fools); rather, we make them concerned about the grace of our Lord Jesus Christ.

18

It is certain that man must utterly despair of his own ability before he is prepared to receive the grace of Christ.

The law wills that man despair of his own ability, for it leads him into hell and makes him a poor man and shows him that he is a sinner in all his works, as the Apostle does in Rom. 2 and 3 [:9], where he says, "I have already charged that all men are under the power of sin." However, he who acts simply in accordance with his ability and believes that he is thereby doing something good does not seem worthless to himself, nor does he despair of his own strength. Indeed, he is so presumptuous that he strives for grace in reliance on his own strength.

19

That person does not deserve to be called a theologian who looks upon the invisible things of God as though they were clearly perceptible in those things which have actually happened [Rom. 1:20].

This is apparent in the example of those who were "theologians" and still were called fools by the Apostle in Rom. 1 [:22]. Furthermore, the invisible things of God are virtue, godliness, wisdom, justice, goodness, and so forth. The recognition of all these things does not make one worthy or wise.

20

He deserves to be called a theologian, however, who comprehends the visible and manifest things of God seen through suffering and the cross.

The "back" and visible things of God are placed in opposition to the invisible, namely, his human nature, weakness, foolishness. The Apostle in I Cor. 1 [:25] calls them the weakness and folly of God. Because men misused the knowledge of God through works, God wished again to be recognized in suffering, and to condemn wisdom concerning invisible things by means of wisdom concerning visible things, so that those who did not honor God as manifested in his works should honor him as he is hidden in his suffering. As the Apostle says in I Cor. 1 [:21], "For since, in the wisdom of God, the world did not know God through wisdom, it pleased God through the folly of what we preach to save those who believe." Now it is not sufficient for anyone, and it does him no good to recognize God in his glory and majesty, unless he recognizes him in the humility and shame of the cross. Thus God destroys the wisdom of the wise, as Isa. [45:15] says, "Truly, thou art a God who hidest thyself."

So, also, in John 14 [:8], where Philip spoke according to the theology of glory: "Show us the Father." Christ forthwith set aside his flighty thought about seeking God elsewhere and led him to himself, saying, "Philip, he who has seen me has seen the Father" [John 14:9]. For this reason true theology and recognition of God are in the crucified Christ, as it is also stated in John 10 [John 14:6]: "No one comes to the Father, but by me." "I am the door" [John 10:9], and so forth.

21

A theologian of glory calls evil good and good evil. A theologian of the cross calls the thing what it actually is.

This is clear: He who does not know Christ does not know God hidden in suffering. Therefore he prefers works to suffering, glory to the cross, strength to weakness, wisdom to folly, and, in general, good to evil. These are the people whom the apostle calls "enemies of the cross of Christ" [Phil. 3:18], for they hate the cross and suffering and love works and the glory of works. Thus they call the good of the cross evil and the evil of a deed good. God can be found only in suffering and the cross, as has already been said. Therefore the friends of the cross say that the cross is good and works are evil, for through the cross works are destroyed and the old Adam, who is especially edified by works, is crucified. It is impossible for a person not to be puffed up by his good works unless he has first been deflated and destroyed by suffering and evil until he knows that he is worthless and that his works are not his but God's.

22

That wisdom which sees the invisible things of God in works as perceived by man is completely puffed up, blinded, and hardened.

This has already been said. Because men do not know the cross and hate it, they necessarily love the opposite, namely, wisdom, glory, power, and so on. Therefore they become increasingly blinded and hardened by such love, for desire cannot be satisfied by the acquisition of those things which it desires. Just as the love of money grows in proportion to the increase of the money itself, so the dropsy of the soul becomes thirstier the more it drinks, as the poet says: "The more water they drink, the more they thirst for it." The same thought is expressed in Eccles. 1 [:8]: "The eye is not satisfied with seeing, nor the ear filled with hearing." This holds true of all desires.

Thus also the desire for knowledge is not satisfied by the acquisition of wisdom but is stimulated that much more. Likewise the desire for glory is not satisfied by the acquisition of glory, nor is the desire to rule satisfied by power and authority, nor is the desire for praise satisfied by praise, and so on, as Christ shows in John 4 [:13], where he says, "Every one who drinks of this water will thirst again."

The remedy for curing desire does not lie in satisfying it, but in extinguishing it. In other words, he who wishes to become wise does not seek wisdom by progressing toward it but becomes a fool by retrogressing into seeking folly. Likewise he who wishes to have much power, honor, pleasure, satisfaction in all things must flee rather than seek power, honor, pleasure, and satisfaction in all things. This is the wisdom which is folly to the world.

23

The law brings the wrath of God, kills, reviles, accuses, judges, and condemns everything that is not in Christ [Rom. 4:15].

Thus Gal. 3 [:13] states, "Christ redeemed us from the curse of the law"; and: "For all who rely on works of the law are under the curse" [Gal. 3:10]; and Rom. 4 [15]: "For the law brings wrath"; and Rom. 7 [:10]: "The very commandment which promised life proved to be the death of me"; Rom. 2 [:12]: "All who have sinned without the law will also perish without law." Therefore he who boasts that he is wise and learned in the law boasts in his confusion, his damnation, the wrath of God, in death. As Rom. 2 [:23] puts it: "You who boast in the law."[14]

24

Yet that wisdom is not of itself evil, nor is the law to be evaded; but without the theology of the cross man misuses the best in the worst manner.

Indeed the law is holy [Rom. 7:12], every gift of God good [I Tim. 4:4], and everything that is created exceedingly good, as in Gen. 1 [:31]. But, as stated above, he who has not been brought low, reduced to nothing through the cross and suffering, takes credit for works and wisdom and does not give credit to God. He thus misuses and defiles the gifts of God.

He, however, who has been emptied [Cf. Phil. 2:7] through suffering no longer does works but knows that God works and does all things in him. For this reason, whether man does works or not, it is all the same to him. He neither boasts if he does good works, nor is he disturbed if God does not do good works through him. He knows that it is sufficient if he suffers and is brought low by the cross in order to be annihilated all the more. It is this that Christ says in John 3 [:7], "You must be born anew." To be born anew, one must consequently first die and then be raised up with the Son of Man. To die, I say, means to feel death at hand.

25

He is not righteous who does much, but he who, without work, believes much in Christ.

For the righteousness of God is not acquired by means of acts frequently repeated, as Aristotle taught, but it is imparted by faith, for "He who through faith is righteous shall live" (Rom. 1 [:17]), and "Man believes with his heart and so is justified" (Rom. 10 [:10]). Therefore I wish to have the words "without work" understood in the following manner: Not that the righteous person

---

[14] The editor has followed the text in *CL* 5, 390 rather than *WA* 1, 363.

does nothing, but that his works do not make him righteous, rather that his righteousness creates works. For grace and faith are infused without our works. After they have been imparted the works follow. Thus Rom. 3 [:20] states, "No human being will be justified in His sight by works of the law," and, "For we hold that man is justified by faith apart from works of law" (Rom. 3 [:28]). In other words, works contribute nothing to justification. Therefore man knows that works which he does by such faith are not his but God's. For this reason he does not seek to become justified or glorified through them, but seeks God. His justification by faith in Christ is sufficient to him. Christ is his wisdom, righteousness, etc., as I Cor. 1 [:30] has it, that he himself may be Christ's action and instrument.

26

The law says, "do this," and it is never done. Grace says, "believe in this," and everything is already done.

The first part is clear from what has been stated by the Apostle and his interpreter, St. Augustine, in many places. And it has been stated often enough above that the law works wrath and keeps all men under the curse. The second part is clear from the same sources, for faith justifies. "And the law (says St. Augustine) commands what faith obtains." For through faith Christ is in us, indeed, one with us. Christ is just and has fulfilled all the commands of God, wherefore we also fulfil everything through him since he was made ours through faith.

27

Actually one should call the work of Christ an acting work and our work an accomplished work, and thus an accomplished work pleasing to God by the grace of the acting work.

Since Christ lives in us through faith so he arouses us to do good works through that living faith in his work, for the works which he does are the fulfilment of the commands of God given us through faith. If we look at them we are moved to imitate them. For this reason the Apostle says, "Therefore be imitators of God, as beloved children" [Eph. 5:1]. Thus deeds of mercy are aroused by the works through which he has saved us, as St. Gregory says: "Every act of Christ is instruction for us, indeed, a stimulant." If his action is in us it lives through faith, for it is exceedingly attractive according to the verse, "Draw me after you, let us make haste" [Song of Sol. 1:4] toward the fragrance "of your anointing oils" [Song of Sol. 1:3], that is, "your works."

28

The love of God does not find, but creates, that which is pleasing to it. The love of man comes into being through that which is pleasing to it.

The second part is clear and is accepted by all philosophers and theologians, for the object of love is its cause, assuming, according to Aristotle, that all power of the soul is passive and material and active only in receiving something. Thus it is also demonstrated that Aristotle's philosophy is contrary to theology since in all things it seeks those things which are its own and receives rather than gives something good. The first part is clear because the love of God which lives in man loves sinners, evil persons, fools, and weaklings in order to make them righteous, good, wise, and strong. Rather than seeking its own good, the love of God flows forth and bestows good. Therefore sinners are attractive because they are loved; they are not loved because they are attractive. For this reason the love of man avoids sinners and evil persons. Thus Christ says: "For I came not to call the righteous, but sinners" [Matt. 9:13]. This is the love of the cross, born of the cross, which turns in the direction where it does not find good which it may enjoy, but where it may confer good upon the bad and needy person. "It is more blessed to give than to receive" [Acts 20:35], says the Apostle. Hence Ps. 41 [:1] states, "Blessed is he who considers the poor," for the intellect cannot by nature comprehend an object which does not exist, that is the poor and needy person, but only a thing which does exist, that is the true and good. Therefore it judges according to appearances, is a respecter of persons, and judges according to that which can be seen, etc.

4.

CONFESSION CONCERNING CHRIST'S SUPPER

* * *

The Third Part

I see that schisms and errors are increasing proportionately with the passage of time, and that there is no end to the rage and fury of Satan. Hence lest any persons during my lifetime or after my death appeal to me or misuse my writings to confirm their error, as the sacramentarian and baptist fanatics are already beginning to do, I desire with this treatise to confess my faith before God and all the world, point by point. I am determined to abide by it until my death and (so help me God!) in this faith to depart from this world and to appear before the judgment seat of our Lord Jesus Christ. Hence if any one shall say after my death, "If Luther were living now, he would teach and hold this or that article differently, for he did not consider it sufficiently," etc., let me say once and for all that by the grace of God I have most diligently traced all these articles through the Scriptures, have examined them again and again in the light thereof, and have wanted to defend all of them as certainly as I have now defended the sacrament of the altar. I am not drunk or irresponsible. I know

---

270 Luther did not carry out his intention directly, though he did preach on John 6:26-28 in a series of sermons, 1530-1532, transcripts of which were published by Aurifaber in 1565. *LW* 23, 7 ff. Melanchthon's *Annotations on the Gospel of John* had been published in 1523, John Brenz's *Exposition of the Gospel of John* in 1527. *WA* 26, 498, n. 1.

what I am saying, and I well realize what this will mean for me before the Last Judgment at the coming of the Lord Jesus Christ. Let no one make this out to be a joke or idle talk; I am in dead earnest, since by the grace of God I have learned to know a great deal about Satan. If he can twist and pervert the Word of God and the Scriptures, what will he not be able to do with my or someone else's words? [271]

First, I believe with my whole heart the sublime article of the majesty of God, that the Father, Son, and Holy Spirit, three distinct persons, are by nature one true and genuine God, the Maker of heaven and earth; in complete opposition to the Arians, Macedonians, Sabellians,[272] and similar heretics, Genesis 1 [:1]. All this has been maintained up to this time both in the Roman Church and among Christian churches throughout the whole world.

Secondly, I believe and know that Scripture teaches us that the second person in the Godhead, viz. the Son, alone became true man, conceived by the Holy Spirit without the co-operation of man, and was born of the pure, holy Virgin Mary as of a real natural mother, all of which St. Luke clearly describes and the prophets foretold;[273] so that neither the Father nor the Holy Spirit became man, as certain heretics have taught.[274]

---

[271] This paragraph is quoted in the *Formula of Concord,* Solid Declaration, VII, 29 ff.
[272] Of the heresies listed here only Arianism is mentioned by name in the *Book of Concord,* e.g. *Augsburg Confession,* Art. I. Cf. p. 120, n. 198, above. Macedonianism, named after Macedonius, a fourth century archbishop of Constantinople, affirmed that the Holy Spirit is less than divine, not one of the divine persons; this view was condemned at a council at Alexandria in 362 and subsequently. Sabellianism, a third century form of Modal Monarchianism, treated the terms Father, Son, and Holy Spirit not as distinct divine persons but simply as different modes or even successive phases of the one God. It was Arius' accusation of Sabellianism against his bishop which opened the controversy leading to the Council of Nicaea, 325, where both Arianism and Sabellianism were excluded.
[273] Cf. Luke 1:26 ff. With the Middle Ages generally, Luther found the virgin birth foretold in other prophecies besides Isa. 7:14, e.g. Isa. 9:6 (cf. WA 40III, 680), but eventually he rejected most of those interpretations as farfetched.
[274] The second and third century Patripassians (Monarchians) Noetus and Praxeas, opposed by Tertullian, taught the absolute unity of God in such a way as to affirm that the Father in the person of Jesus suffered on the cross. Montanus, a second century prophet, claimed to be the incarnation of the Holy Spirit.

Also that God the Son assumed not a body without a soul, as certain heretics have taught,[275] but also the soul, i.e. full, complete humanity, and was born the promised true seed or child of Abraham and of David and the son of Mary by nature, in every way and form a true man, as I am myself and every other man, except that he came without sin, by the Holy Spirit of the Virgin Mary alone.

And that this man became true God, as one eternal, indivisible person, of God and man, so that Mary the holy Virgin is a real, true mother not only of the man Christ, as the Nestorians teach,[276] but also of the Son of God, as Luke says [1:35], "The child to be born of you will be called the Son of God," i.e. my Lord and the Lord of all, Jesus Christ, the only, true Son by nature of God and of Mary, true God and true man.

I believe also that this Son of God and of Mary, our Lord Jesus Christ, suffered for us poor sinners, was crucified, dead, and buried, in order that he might redeem us from sin, death, and the eternal wrath of God by his innocent blood; and that on the third day he arose from the dead, ascended into heaven, and sits at the right hand of God the Father almighty, Lord over all lords, King over all kings and over all creatures in heaven, on earth, and under the earth, over death and life, over sin and righteousness.

For I confess and am able to prove from Scripture that all men have descended from one man, Adam; and from this man, through their birth, they acquire and inherit the fall, guilt and sin, which the same Adam, through the wickedness of the devil, committed in paradise; and thus all men along with him are born, live, and die altogether in sin, and would necessarily be guilty of eternal death if Jesus Christ had not come to our aid and taken upon himself this guilt and sin as an innocent lamb, paid for us by his sufferings, and if he did not still intercede and plead for us as a faithful, merciful Mediator, Savior, and the only Priest and Bishop of our souls.

I herewith reject and condemn as sheer error all doctrines

---

275 Apollinaris in the fourth century taught that the Word assumed human flesh and biological life (*psuchē*) but not a human higher soul or mind. Apollinarianism was condemned in the 370's.
276 On Nestorianism see p. 212, n. 75, p. 292, n. 218.

which glorify our free will,[277] as diametrically contrary to the help and grace of our Savior Jesus Christ. Outside of Christ death and sin are our masters and the devil is our god and lord, and there is no power or ability, no cleverness or reason, with which we can prepare ourselves for righteousness and life or seek after it. On the contrary, we must remain the dupes and captives of sin and the property of the devil to do and to think what pleases them and what is contrary to God and his commandments.[278]

Thus I condemn also both the new and the old Pelagians[279] who will not admit original sin to be sin, but make it an infirmity or defect. But since death has passed to all men, original sin must be not merely an infirmity but enormous sin, as St. Paul says, "The wages of sin is death" [Rom. 6:23], and again, "Sin is the sting of death" [I Cor. 15:56]. So also David says in Psalm 51 [:5], "Behold, I was conceived in sin, and in sin did my mother bear me." He does not say, "My mother conceived me with sin," but, "I—I myself—I was conceived in sin, and in sin did my mother bear me," i.e. in my mother's womb I have grown from sinful seed, as the Hebrew text signifies.

Next, I reject and condemn also as sheer deceptions and errors of the devil all monastic orders, rules, cloisters, religious foundations, and all such things devised and instituted by men beyond and apart from Scripture, bound by vows and obligations,[280] although many great saints have lived in them, and as the elect of God are misled by them even at this time, yet finally by faith in Jesus Christ have been redeemed and have escaped. Because these monastic orders, foundations, and sects have been maintained and

---

[277] Luther is thinking particularly of Scotist and Occamist scholasticism, cf. *Disputation Against Scholastic Theology,* 1517. *LW* 31, 9 ff., and Erasmus' humanism, cf. *Bondage of the Will,* 1525. *LCC* 17, 101 ff. Erasmus in turn influenced many of the left-wing reformers.

[278] This paragraph is quoted in the *Formula of Concord.* Solid Declaration, II, 43.

[279] Pelagianism is condemned in the *Augsburg Confession,* Arts. II and XVIII. Pelagius, a fifth century heretic opposed especially by Augustine, taught that man's salvation was due to the faithful exercise of his free will. Though Pelagianism was condemned at councils in Ephesus, 431, and Orange, 529, subtle versions of this doctrine of self-salvation persistently reappeared. Luther objected to Zwingli's conception of original sin, cf. p. 16, n. 7, as well as that of the modernist scholastics and the humanists.

[280] Cf. *Address to the Nobility,* 1520. *LW* 44, 179 ff.; *On Monastic Vows,* 1521. *LW* 44, 251 ff.

perpetuated with the idea that by these ways and works men may seek and win salvation, and escape from sin and death, they are all a notorious, abominable blasphemy and denial of the unique aid and grace of our only Savior and Mediator, Jesus Christ. For "there is no other name given by which we must be saved" than this, which is Jesus Christ [Acts 4:12]. And it is impossible that there should be more saviors, ways, or means to be saved than through the one righteousness which our Savior Jesus Christ is and has bestowed upon us, and has offered to God for us as our one mercy seat, Romans 3 [:25].[281]

It would be a good thing if monasteries and religious foundations were kept for the purpose of teaching young people God's Word, the Scriptures, and Christian morals, so that we might train and prepare fine, capable men to become bishops, pastors, and other servants of the church, as well as competent, learned people for civil government, and fine, respectable, learned women capable of keeping house and rearing children in a Christian way. But as a way of seeking salvation, these institutions are all the devil's doctrine and creed, I Timothy 4 [:1 ff.], etc.

But the holy orders and true religious institutions established by God are these three: the office of priest, the estate of marriage, the civil government.[282] All who are engaged in the clerical office or ministry of the Word are in a holy, proper, good, and God-pleasing order and-estate, such as those who preach, administer sacraments, supervise the common chest, sextons and messengers or servants who serve such persons. These are engaged in works which are altogether holy in God's sight.

Again, all fathers and mothers who regulate their household wisely and bring up their children to the service of God are engaged in pure holiness, in a holy work and a holy order. Similarly, when children and servants show obedience to their elders and masters, here too is pure holiness, and whoever is thus engaged is a living saint on earth.

---

281 The term "mercy seat," *propitiatorium* (cf. Luther's gloss on Rom. 3:25 in *Commentary on Romans*, 1515-1516. WA 56, 37 f.) is more accurately referred to Heb. 9:5, cf. Exod. 25:17 ff.

282 Luther does not always name the "orders," i.e. the basic social units, in just this fashion. Cf. *Large Catechism*, Fourth Commandment, 158, and Melanchthon's *Augsburg Confession*, Art. XVI.

Moreover, princes and lords, judges, civil officers, state officials, notaries,[283] male and female servants and all who serve such persons, and further, all their obedient subjects—all are engaged in pure holiness and leading a holy life before God. For these three religious institutions or orders are found in God's Word and commandment; and whatever is contained in God's Word must be holy, for God's Word is holy and sanctifies everything connected with it and involved in it.

Above these three institutions and orders is the common order of Christian love, in which one serves not only the three orders, but also serves every needy person in general with all kinds of benevolent deeds, such as feeding the hungry, giving drink to the thirsty, forgiving enemies, praying for all men on earth, suffering all kinds of evil on earth, etc.[284] Behold, all of these are called good and holy works. However, none of these orders is a means of salvation. There remains only one way above them all, viz. faith in Jesus Christ.

For to be holy and to be saved are two entirely different things. We are saved through Christ alone; but we become holy both through this faith and through these divine foundations and orders. Even the godless may have much about them that is holy without being saved thereby. For God wishes us to perform such works to his praise and glory. And all who are saved in the faith of Christ surely do these works and maintain these orders.

What was said about the estate of marriage, however, should also be applied to widows and unmarried women, for they also belong to the domestic sphere. Now if these orders and divine institutions do not save, what can we say about the effects of the devil's institutions and monasteries, which have sprung up entirely without God's Word, and further, rage and contend against the one and only way of faith?

Thirdly, I believe in the Holy Spirit, who with the Father and the Son is one true God and proceeds eternally from the

---

[283] *Amptleute* are civil officers in general. The title *Cantzler* not only means "chancellors" at court but also includes many of their underlings in embassies, etc. *Schreiber* (scribes) include prothonotaries, notaries, and other state officials in small localities.

[284] The medieval church had commended the "seven acts of mercy," consisting of the six acts mentioned in Matt. 25:35 f., plus burying the dead.

Father and the Son, yet is a distinct person in the one divine essence and nature. By this Holy Spirit, as a living, eternal, divine gift and endowment, all believers are adorned with faith and other spiritual gifts, raised from the dead, freed from sin, and made joyful and confident, free and secure in their conscience. For this is our assurance if we feel this witness of the Spirit in our hearts, that God wishes to be our Father, forgive our sin, and bestow everlasting life on us.

These are the three persons and one God, who has given himself to us all wholly and completely, with all that he is and has. The Father gives himself to us, with heaven and earth and all the creatures, in order that they may serve us and benefit us. But this gift has become obscured and useless through Adam's fall. Therefore the Son himself subsequently gave himself and bestowed all his works, sufferings, wisdom, and righteousness, and reconciled us to the Father, in order that restored to life and righteousness, we might also know and have the Father and his gifts.

But because this grace would benefit no one if it remained so profoundly hidden and could not come to us, the Holy Spirit comes and gives himself to us also, wholly and completely. He teaches us to understand this deed of Christ which has been manifested to us, helps us receive and preserve it, use it to our advantage and impart it to others, increase and extend it. He does this both inwardly and outwardly—inwardly by means of faith and other spiritual gifts, outwardly through the gospel, baptism, and the sacrament of the altar, through which as through three means or methods he comes to us and inculcates the sufferings of Christ for the benefit of our salvation.

Therefore I maintain and know that just as there is no more than one gospel and one Christ, so also there is no more than one baptism. And that baptism in itself is a divine ordinance, as is his gospel also. And just as the gospel is not false or incorrect for the reason that some use it or teach it falsely, or disbelieve it, so also baptism is not false or incorrect even if some have received or administered it without faith, or otherwise misused it. Accordingly, I altogether reject and condemn the teaching of the Anabaptists and Donatists, and all who rebaptize.[285]

---

[285] Cf. *Babylonian Captivity of the Church*, 1520, LW 36, 57 ff., and *On*

In the same way I also say and confess that in the sacrament of the altar the true body and blood of Christ are orally eaten and drunk in the bread and wine, even if the priests who distribute them or those who receive them do not believe or otherwise misuse the sacrament. It does not rest on man's belief or unbelief but on the Word and ordinance of God—unless they first change God's Word and ordinance and misinterpret them, as the enemies of the sacrament do at the present time. They, indeed, have only bread and wine, for they do not also have the words and instituted ordinance of God but have perverted and changed it according to their own imagination.[286]

Next, I believe that there is one holy Christian Church on earth, i.e. the community or number or assembly of all Christians in all the world, the one bride of Christ, and his spiritual body of which he is the only head. The bishops or priests are not her heads or lords or bridegrooms, but servants, friends, and—as the word "bishop" implies—superintendents, guardians, or stewards.[287]

This Christian Church exists not only in the realm of the Roman Church or pope, but in all the world, as the prophets foretold that the gospel of Christ would spread throughout the world, Psalm 2 [:8], Psalm 19 [:4]. Thus this Christian Church is physically dispersed among pope, Turks, Persians, Tartars, but spiritually gathered in one gospel and faith, under one head, i.e. Jesus Christ. For the papacy is assuredly the true realm of Antichrist, the real anti-Christian tyrant, who sits in the temple of God and rules with human commandments, as Christ in Matthew 24 [:24] and Paul in II Thessalonians 2 [:3 f.] declare; although the Turk and

---

Rebaptism, 1528. LW 40, 229 ff., and Augsburg Confession, Art. IX. The Donatists were a rigorist sect in North Africa, originating in the fourth century, who insisted that the holiness of the church must be judged in terms of the moral purity of its members, and that the ministerial acts of an unholy priest were invalid. Baptism in the orthodox church therefore was invalid, and converts from that church had to submit to a true baptism. What the Christian Roman empire thus considered "rebaptism" was made punishable by death in the Code of Justinian, as subversive of Christian society itself, and on that basis the sixteenth century "Anabaptists" were persecuted.

[286] This paragraph is quoted in the Formula of Concord, Solid Declaration, VII, 32. Cf. also Augsburg Confession, Arts. X and VIII.

[287] Cf. Augsburg Confession, Art. VII. On the word "bishop," see Answer to Goat Emser, 1521. LW 39, 154 f.; Misuse of the Mass, 1522. LW 36, 155 ff.; and Augsburg Confession, Art. XXVIII.

all heresies, wherever they may be, are also included in this abomination which according to prophecy will stand in the holy place, but are not to be compared to the papacy.[288]

In this Christian Church, wherever it exists, is to be found the forgiveness of sins, i.e a kingdom of grace and of true pardon. For in it are found the gospel, baptism, and the sacrament of the altar, in which the forgiveness of sins is offered, obtained, and received. Moreover, Christ and his Spirit and God are there. Outside this Christian Church there is no salvation[289] or forgiveness of sins, but everlasting death and damnation; even though there may be a magnificent appearance of holiness and many good works, it is all in vain. But this forgiveness of sins is not to be expected only at one time, as in baptism, as the Novatians teach, but frequently, as often as one needs it, till death.[290]

For this reason I have a high regard for private confession, for here God's word and absolution are spoken privately and individually to each believer for the forgiveness of his sins, and as often as he desires it he may have recourse to it for this forgiveness, and also for comfort, counsel, and guidance. Thus it is a precious, useful thing for souls, as long as no one is driven to it with laws and commandments but sinners are left free to make use of it, each according to his own need, when and where he wishes; just as we are free to obtain counsel and comfort, guidance and instruction when and where our need or our inclination moves us. And as long as one is not forced to enumerate all sins but only those which oppress him most grievously, or those which a person will mention in any case, as I have discussed in my *Little Book on Prayer.*[291]

---

[288] From 1520 on (cf. *Address to the Nobility. LW* 44, 133) Luther's writings regularly identified the papacy with the Antichrist. On the Turk, see *War Against the Turk*, 1529. *LW* 46, 181, 196.

[289] On Luther's understanding of this famous dictum of Cyprian see *Large Catechism*, Creed, Art. III, 56, where Luther closely connects the church with the forgiveness of sins.

[290] Novatian, a third century rigorist, insisted that once baptized, a Christian could not be forgiven a grave sin. Some Left-Wing Protestants revived this teaching, cf. *The Keys*, 1530. *LW* 40, 374. The *Augsburg Confession*, Art. XII, condemns Novatianism.

[291] This paragraph was added by Luther when Part III of this treatise was issued separately. On private confession see *Babylonian Captivity of the Church. LW* 36, 86 ff.; *The Sacrament—Against the Fanatics*, 1526. *LW* 36,

But the pardons or indulgences which the papal church has and dispenses are a blasphemous deception, not only because it invents and devises a special forgiveness beyond the general forgiveness which in the whole Christian Church is bestowed through the gospel and the sacrament and thus desecrates and nullifies the general forgiveness, but also because it establishes and bases satisfaction for sins upon the works of men and the merits of saints, whereas only Christ can make and has made satisfaction for us.[292]

As for the dead, since Scripture gives us no information on the subject, I regard it as no sin to pray with free devotion in this or some similar fashion: "Dear God, if this soul is in a condition accessible to mercy, be thou gracious to it." And when this has been done once or twice, let it suffice. For vigils and requiem masses and yearly celebrations of requiems are useless, and are merely the devil's annual fair.[293]

Nor have we anything in Scripture concerning purgatory. It too was certainly fabricated by goblins. Therefore, I maintain it is not necessary to believe in it; although all things are possible to God, and he could very well allow souls to be tormented after their departure from the body. But he has caused nothing of this to be spoken or written, therefore he does not wish to have it believed, either. I know of a purgatory, however, in another way, but it would not be proper to teach anything about it in the church, nor on the other hand, to deal with it by means of endowments or vigils.[294]

---

354 ff.; the two *Catechisms*, and *Augsburg Confession*, Arts. XI and XXV.

[292] A full year before posting his *Ninety-five Theses*, Luther had publicly criticized the current indulgence doctrine. In the *Theses*, 1517, and the *Explanations of the Ninety-five Theses*, 1518 (*LW* 31, 25 ff., 83 ff.) Luther questioned the propriety of the practice and the clarity of the doctrine; by late 1520 he rejected indulgences in principle, cf. *Babylonian Captivity of the Church*. LW 36, 11; *Defense and Explanation of All the Articles*, 1521. LW 32, 33 f., 64 f.

[293] A requiem mass (*seelmesse*) is celebrated on the anniversary of decease; a vigil is a commemoration on the eve of the anniversary. Luther had questioned the celebration of masses for the dead in Thesis 83 of the *Ninety-five Theses*. LW 31, 32; he sharply criticized the practice in *Address to the Nobility*, 1520. LW 44, 180 f.

[294] On Luther's reinterpretation of purgatory see *Explanations of the Ninety-five Theses*. Thesis 15. LW 31, 125 ff., and *Defense and Explanation of All the Articles*, esp. Arts. 4 and 37. LW 32, 31 f., 95 ff.

Others before me have attacked the invocation of saints, and this pleases me. I believe, too, that Christ alone should be invoked as our Mediator, a truth which is scriptural and certain. Of the invocation of saints nothing is said in Scripture; therefore it is necessarily uncertain and not to be believed.[295]

If unction were practiced in accordance with the gospel, Mark 6 [:13] and James 5 [:14], I would let it pass. But to make a sacrament out of it is nonsense. Just as, in place of vigils and masses for the dead, one might well deliver a sermon on death and eternal life, and also pray during the obsequies and meditate upon our own end, as it seems was the practice of the ancients, so it would also be good to visit the sick, pray and admonish, and if anyone wished in addition to anoint him with oil, he should be free to do in the name of God.[296]

Neither is there any need to make sacraments out of marriage and the office of the priesthood. These orders are sufficiently holy in themselves.[297] So, too, penance is nothing else than the practice and the power of baptism.[298] Thus two sacraments remain, baptism and the Lord's Supper, along with the gospel, in which the Holy Spirit richly offers, bestows, and accomplishes the forgiveness of sins.

As the greatest of all abominations I regard the mass when it

---

[295] Precursors in criticizing the cult of saints included high ecclesiastics, e.g. Gerson, popular preachers, e.g. Berthold of Regensburg, would-be reformers, e.g. Huss, humanists, e.g. Erasmus. On Luther's critique see *Explanations of the Ninety-five Theses*, Thesis 58. *LW* 31, 212 ff., *Fourteen Consolations*, 1520. *LW* 42, 121 ff. Cf. *Augsburg Confession*, Art. XXI. Matters treated in these four paragraphs above are crisply criticized by Luther as a "vermin-brood and poison of idolatries" begotten by the "dragon's tail," the mass, in *Smalcald Articles*, 1537, II, Art. II, 11 ff.; cf. *Augsburg Confession*, Art. XXIV.
[296] Cf. *Babylonian Captivity of the Church*. *LW* 36, 118 ff.
[297] Cf. *Babylonian Captivity of the Church*. *LW* 36, 92 ff., 106 ff. Melanchthon would not have been averse to calling ordination, properly understood, a sacrament. *Apology*, Art. XIII, 11. He was less willing to call marriage a sacrament. *Ibid.*, 14 ff. Cf. Sasse, *This Is My Body*, p. 25, n. 10.
[298] The Wittenbergers wavered for a long time between acknowledging and not acknowledging absolution—part of the Roman Catholic sacrament of penance—as a third sacrament; see the ambiguity on the subject in *Babylonian Captivity of the Church*. *LW* 36, 18 and 124, and Melanchthon's explicit recognition of it in *Apology*, Art. XIII, 4. Luther preferred to subsume repentance under baptism, *Babylonian Captivity of the Church*. *LW* 36, 58 f., 61, 69, 81 ff.; *Large Catechism*, Baptism, 74 ff. Cf. *Augsburg Confession*, Art. XII.

is preached or sold as a sacrifice or good work, which is the basis on which all religious foundations and monasteries now stand,[299] but, God willing, they shall soon be overthrown. Although I have been a great, grievous, despicable sinner, and wasted my youth in a thoughtless and damnable manner, yet my greatest sins were that I was so holy a monk, and so horribly angered, tortured, and plagued my dear Lord with so many masses for more than fifteen years.[300] But praise and thanks be to his unspeakable grace in eternity, that he led me out of this abomination, and still continues to sustain and strengthen me daily in the true faith, despite my great ingratitude.

Accordingly, I have advised and still advise people to abandon religious foundations and monasteries and their vows and come forth into the true Christian orders, in order to escape these abominations of the mass and this blasphemous holiness, i.e. "chastity, poverty, and obedience," by which men imagine they are saved.[301] Excellent as it was in the early days of the Christian Church to maintain the state of virginity, so abominable is it now when it is used to deny the aid and grace of Christ. It is entirely possible to live in a state of virginity, widowhood, and chastity without these blasphemous abominations.

Images, bells, eucharistic vestments, church ornaments, altar lights, and the like I regard as things indifferent. Anyone who wishes may omit them. Images or pictures taken from the Scriptures and from good histories, however, I consider very useful yet indifferent and optional. I have no sympathy with the iconoclasts.[302]

---

[299] *Babylonian Captivity of the Church.* LW 36, 35 f.; *Treatise on the New Testament,* 1520. *LW* 35, 75 ff. Cf. *Augsburg Confession,* Art. XXIV.

[300] Luther's reminiscences about his life in Roman Catholicism are collected in Scheel, *Dokumente zu Luthers Entwicklung,* (2nd ed.; Tübingen, 1929); cf. also *WA* 58I, *Gesamtregister.* Interpretations in Bainton, *Here I Stand* (New York, 1950), esp. chaps. 1-3; Rupp, *Luther's Progress to the Diet of Worms* (Chicago, 1951); Fife, *Revolt of Martin Luther* (New York, 1957), esp. chaps. 6-8, 11.

[301] Luther here lists the traditional monastic vows; "chastity" here means celibacy. Cf. *Babylonian Captivity of the Church.* LW 36, 74 ff.; *On Monastic Vows,* 1521. *LW* 44, 251 ff. *Augsburg Confession,* Art. XXVII.

[302] Cf. Luther's *Eight Wittenberg Sermons,* 1522. *LW* 51, 70 ff., and his writings against Karlstadt and Münzer in 1524-1525, *LW* 40; and *Formula of the Mass,* 1523. *LW* 53, 30 ff.

Finally, I believe in the resurrection of all the dead at the Last Day, both the godly and the wicked, that each may receive in his body his reward according to his merits. Thus the godly will live eternally with Christ and the wicked will perish eternally with the devil and his angels. I do not agree with those who teach that the devils also will finally be restored to salvation.[303]

This is my faith, for so all true Christians believe and so the Holy Scriptures teach us. On subjects which I have treated too briefly here, my other writings will testify sufficiently, especially those which have been published during the last four or five years. I pray that all godly hearts will bear me witness of this, and pray for me that I may persevere firmly in this faith to the end of my life. For if in the assault of temptation or the pangs of death I should say something different—which God forbid—let it be disregarded; herewith I declare publicly that it would be incorrect, spoken under the devil's influence. In this may my Lord and Savior Jesus Christ assist me: blessed be he for ever, Amen.

---

[303] Origen in the third century taught that the devils would ultimately be converted. Though this view was condemned at Constantinople in 553, it was revived in the sixteenth century.

5.

PREFACE TO
THE WITTENBERG EDITION
OF LUTHER'S GERMAN WRITINGS

Dr. Martin Luther's Preface

I would have been quite content to see my books, one and all, remain in obscurity and go by the board. Among other reasons, I shudder to think of the example I am giving, for I am well aware how little the church has been profited since they have begun to collect many books and large libraries, in addition to and besides the Holy Scriptures, and especially since they have stored up, without discrimination, all sorts of writings by the church fathers, the councils, and teachers. Through this practice not only is precious time lost, which could be used for studying the Scriptures, but in the end the pure knowledge of the divine Word is also lost, so that the Bible lies forgotten in the dust under the bench (as happened to the book of Deuteronomy, in the time of the kings of Judah[1]).

Although it has been profitable and necessary that the writings of some church fathers and councils have remained, as witnesses and histories, nevertheless I think, *"Est modus in rebus,"*[2] and we need not regret that the books of many fathers and councils have, by God's grace, disappeared. If they had all remained in existence, no room would be left for anything but books; and yet all of them together would not have improved on what one finds in the Holy Scriptures.

It was also our intention and hope, when we ourselves began to translate the Bible into German,[3] that there should be less writing,

---

[1] Cf. II Kings 22:8. In Luther's German Bible, Deuteronomy is referred to as "the fifth book of Moses."

[2] "There is a reason for the way things happen." Horace *Satires* I, 1, 106.

[3] Luther began to translate the Bible into German during his confinement to the Wartburg. In a letter to Johann Lang, December 18, 1521, he announced his

and instead more studying and reading of the Scriptures. For all other writing is to lead the way into and point toward the Scriptures, as John the Baptist did toward Christ, saying, "He must increase, but I must decrease" [John 3:30], in order that each person may drink of the fresh spring himself, as all those fathers who wanted to accomplish something good had to do.

Neither councils, fathers, nor we, in spite of the greatest and best success possible, will do as well as the Holy Scriptures, that is, as well as God himself has done. (We must, of course, also have the Holy Spirit, faith, godly speech, and works, if we are to be saved.) Therefore it behooves us to let the prophets and apostles stand at the professor's lectern, while we, down below at their feet, listen to what they say. It is not they who must hear what we say.

I cannot, however, prevent them from wanting to collect and publish my works through the press (small honor to me), although it is not my will. I have no choice but to let them risk the labor and the expense of this project. My consolation is that, in time, my books will lie forgotten in the dust anyhow, especially if I (by God's grace) have written anything good. *Non ero melior Patribus meis.*[4] He who comes second should indeed be the first one forgotten. Inasmuch as they have been capable of leaving the Bible itself lying under the bench, and have also forgotten the fathers and the councils—the better ones all the faster—accordingly there is a good hope, once the overzealousness of this time has abated, that my books also will not last long. There is especially good hope of this, since it has begun to rain and snow books and teachers, many of which already lie there forgotten and moldering. Even their names are not remembered any more, despite their confident hope that they would eternally be on sale in the market and rule churches.

Very well, so let the undertaking proceed in the name of God, except that I make the friendly request of anyone who wishes to have my books at this time, not to let them on any account hinder him from studying the Scriptures themselves. Let him put them to use as I put the excrees and excretals[5] of the pope to use, and the

---

intention to translate the New Testament into German. *WA,* Br 2, 413. This letter contains the first reference to Luther's intention to translate the Bible.

[4] I Kings 19:4. "I am no better than my fathers."

[5] That is, "decrees and decretals." The translator has attempted to render Luther's pun *"Drecket und Drecketal"* in English.

Luther describes Studying the word of God is better than study man's books. Psalm 119 he suggest an Outline to accomplish this

Preface to the Wittenberg Edition

books of the sophists. That is, if I occasionally wish to see what they have done, or if I wish to ponder the historical facts of the time, I use them. But I do not study in them or act in perfect accord with what they deemed good. I do not treat the books of the fathers and the councils much differently.

Herein I follow the example of St. Augustine,[6] who was, among other things, the first and almost the only one who determined to be subject to the Holy Scriptures alone, and independent of the books of all the fathers and saints. On account of that he got into a fierce fight with St. Jerome, who reproached him by pointing to the books of his forefathers; but he did not turn to them. And if the example of St. Augustine had been followed, the pope would not have become Antichrist, and that countless mass of books, which is like a crawling swarm of vermin, would not have found its way into the church, and the Bible would have remained on the pulpit.

Moreover, I want to point out to you a correct way of studying theology, for I have had practice in that. If you keep to it, you will become so learned that you yourself could (if it were necessary) write books just as good as those of the fathers and councils, even as I (in God) dare to presume and boast, without arrogance and lying, that in the matter of writing books I do not stand much behind some of the fathers. Of my life I can by no means make the same boast. This is the way taught by holy King David (and doubtlessly used also by all the patriarchs and prophets) in the one hundred nineteenth Psalm. There you will find three rules, amply presented throughout the whole Psalm. They are *Oratio, Meditatio, Tentatio.*[7]

Firstly, you should know that the Holy Scriptures constitute a book which turns the wisdom of all other books into foolishness, because not one teaches about eternal life except this one alone. Therefore you should straightway despair of your reason and understanding. With them you will not attain eternal life, but, on the contrary, your presumptuousness will plunge you and others with you out of heaven (as happened to Lucifer) into the abyss of hell. But kneel down in your little room [Matt. 6:6] and pray to God with real humility and earnestness, that he through his dear Son may give

---

[6] *Epistola 82.* Migne 33, 277.
[7] Prayer, meditation, *Anfechtung.*

you his Holy Spirit, who will enlighten you, lead you, and give you understanding.

Thus you see how David keeps praying in the above-mentioned Psalm, "Teach me, Lord, instruct me, lead me, show me,"[8] and many more words like these. Although he well knew and daily heard and read the text of Moses and other books besides, still he wants to lay hold of the real teacher of the Scriptures himself, so that he may not seize upon them pell-mell with his reason and become his own teacher. For such practice gives rise to factious spirits who allow themselves to nurture the delusion that the Scriptures are subject to them and can be easily grasped with their reason, as if they were *Markolf*[9] or Aesop's Fables, for which no Holy Spirit and no prayers are needed.

Secondly, you should meditate, that is, not only in your heart, but also externally, by actually[10] repeating and comparing oral speech and literal words of the book, reading and rereading them with diligent attention and reflection, so that you may see what the Holy Spirit means by them. And take care that you do not grow weary or think that you have done enough when you have read, heard, and spoken them once or twice, and that you then have complete understanding. You will never be a particularly good theologian if you do that, for you will be like untimely fruit which falls to the ground before it is half ripe.

Thus you see in this same Psalm how David constantly boasts that he will talk, meditate, speak, sing, hear, read, by day and night and always, about nothing except God's Word and commandments. For God will not give you his Spirit without the external[11] Word; so take your cue from that. His command to write, preach, read, hear, sing, speak, etc., outwardly[12] was not given in vain.

Thirdly, there is *tentatio, Anfechtung*. This is the touchstone

---

[8] Ps. 119:26 *et al.*
[9] The very popular medieval legend of Solomon and Markolf was treated in a verse epic, chapbooks, dialogues, and farces. The figure of Markolf, a sly and unprincipled rogue, was known in Germany as early as the tenth century.
[10] *Eusserlich.*
[11] *Eusserlich.*
[12] *Eusserlich.* The correspondence Luther intends to show between actual (*eusserlich*) study of the Bible in its outward (*eusserlich*) form and the external (*eusserlich*) Word as a medium of God's address cannot be rendered in idiomatic English by translating *eusserlich* with one word.

which teaches you not only to know and understand, but also to experience how right, how true, how sweet, how lovely, how mighty, how comforting God's Word is, wisdom beyond all wisdom.

Thus you see how David, in the Psalm mentioned, complains so often about all kinds of enemies, arrogant princes or tyrants, false spirits and factions, whom he must tolerate because he meditates, that is, because he is occupied with God's Word (as has been said) in all manner of ways. For as soon as God's Word takes root and grows in you, the devil will harry you, and will make a real doctor of you, and by his assaults[13] will teach you to seek and love God's Word. I myself (if you will permit me, mere mouse-dirt, to be mingled with pepper) am deeply indebted to my papists that through the devil's raging they have beaten, oppressed, and distressed me so much. That is to say, they have made a fairly good theologian of me, which I would not have become otherwise. And I heartily grant them what they have won in return for making this of me, honor, victory, and triumph, for that's the way they wanted it.

There now, with that you have David's rules. If you study hard in accord with his example, then you will also sing and boast with him in the Psalm, "The law of thy mouth is better to me than thousands of gold and silver pieces" [Ps. 119:72]. Also, "Thy commandment makes me wiser than my enemies, for it is ever with me. I have more understanding than all my teachers, for thy testimonies are my meditation. I understand more than the aged, for I keep thy precepts," etc. [Ps. 119:98-100]. And it will be your experience that the books of the fathers will taste stale and putrid to you in comparison. You will not only despise the books written by adversaries, but the longer you write and teach the less you will be pleased with yourself. When you have reached this point, then do not be afraid to hope that you have begun to become a real theologian, who can teach not only the young and imperfect Christians, but also the maturing and perfect ones. For indeed, Christ's church has all kinds of Christians in it who are young, old, weak, sick, healthy, strong, energetic, lazy, simple, wise, etc.

If, however, you feel and are inclined to think you have made it, flattering yourself with your own little books, teaching, or writing,

---

[13] *Anfechtungen.*

because you have done it beautifully and preached excellently; if you are highly pleased when someone praises you in the presence of others; if you perhaps look for praise, and would sulk or quit what you are doing if you did not get it—if you are of that stripe, dear friend, then take yourself by the ears, and if you do this in the right way you will find a beautiful pair of big, long, shaggy donkey ears. Then do not spare any expense! Decorate them with golden bells, so that people will be able to hear you wherever you go, point their fingers at you, and say, "See, See! There goes that clever beast, who can write such exquisite books and preach so remarkably well." That very moment you will be blessed and blessed beyond measure in the kingdom of heaven. Yes, in that heaven where hellfire is ready for the devil and his angels. To sum up: Let us be proud and seek honor in the places where we can. But in this book the honor is God's alone, as it is said, "God opposes the proud, but gives grace to the humble" [I Pet. 5:5]; to whom be glory, world without end, Amen.[14]

---

[14] The last two sentences are in Latin in the original text.

See summary pg 65 Top.

PART II

THE POWER OF THE WORD OF GOD

Luther's passion for a grace-centered theology came neither simply from dissatisfaction with current options, nor from personal preference and need. He had the courage to speak of God in this way because of his work as a professor of Scripture, lecturing extensively in the years between 1513 and 1518 on the Psalms, Romans, Galatians, and Hebrews. The bulk of his theological writing did not involve the kinds of documents included in this anthology, but lectures on the various books of the Bible. In addition, he became a major translator of Scripture. See, for instance, his "Prefaces to the Books of the Bible" (*Luther's Works*, vol. 35, p.225).

Luther became convinced that the standard approach of interpreting the Bible in light of tradition, while not altogether useless, had greatly blunted the biblical teaching about the righteousness of God in Christ. He used Scripture, especially certain parts that seemed to him to present the gospel in an especially clear way, as a means to critique both theology and current church practice. This method was exciting, at times radical, and yet reasonably subtle because Luther was convinced that the message contained in the Bible was itself complex. A simple appeal to Scripture would not do.

6   "Concerning the Letter and the Spirit"

An early opponent, Hieronymous or Jerome Emser of Leipzig (1478-1527), engaged in a series of polemical exchanges with Luther, attacking him for his failure to heed papal authority and for what Emser saw as Luther's simplistic or literal approach. Emser took Luther to task using the Pauline distinction from 2 Cor. 3:6: "The letter kills, but the Spirit gives life." Emser seemed to be suggesting that Luther wanted to solve every complex problem in the church by a direct appeal to the Bible.

This gave Luther an excellent opportunity to show how his own Biblical theology was conceived. Selection 6 is a portion of Luther's sharp response, "Answer to the Hyperchristian, Hyperspiritual, and Hyperlearned Book by Goat Emser in Leipzig." Drawing on Augustine's famous treatise, "On the Spirit and the Letter," Luther demonstrated that one could not simply extol the spiritual interpretation of all passages (which Emser saw as equivalent to the traditional development of Catholic practice). At points the literal sense was best; at other points a spiritual interpretation was demanded by the text itself.

But Luther's real attack on Emser came in his charge that the Leipzig theologian had totally misunderstood the Pauline passage from which he took his text. There Paul was distinguishing the letter of the *law*, which can only bring judgment and death, from the life-giving and grace-bringing *Spirit*. And what Spirit brings, which was especially missing in the church of their day, is *freedom*. The Pope, says Luther, actually opposes the Spirit by structuring a church in which everything, even the basic message, is law. This treatise will challenge the reader, but there are many lively (even outrageous) passages along the way in the spirit of sixteenth century polemic.

7   A Brief Instruction on What to Look for and Expect in the Gospels

Luther's concept of the power of the Word and its proper interpretation is even more clearly spelled out in the four treatises (7-10) that follow. Selections 7 and 8 deal with how to read the Bible, especially the New Testament. In 1521, while in exile at Wartburg Castle, Luther had begun a series of model sermons for the Sundays of the church year. As an introduction, but also as a separate short consideration of the nature of the good news, Luther published in the spring of 1522 "A Brief Instruction on What to Look for and Expect in the Gospels."

Luther teaches that while many different books are to be found in the Bible, there is only one gospel: "a story about Christ, God's and David's Son, who dies and was raised and is established as Lord." The gospel is not a literary genre but a name for the message on which the church is founded and in which Christians put their hope. That gospel is to be found not only in the Gospels of Matthew, Mark, Luke, and John, but at any place in Scripture where human beings are taught to put their trust in this gracious God.

Luther believed that this message was missing in the church of his day. Instead, Christ had been made into a new Moses, a law-giver, or at best an example. Christ is an example, of course, but for Luther this was to fail to grasp the "higher level" of Christ as gift. Only preaching Christ as the Crucified One brings humanity to the true and central message of the gospel, "the overwhelming goodness of God," or ". . . the great fire of the love of God for us, whereby the heart and conscience become happy, secure and content."

8   Preface to the New Testament

These same themes are restated in selection 8, "Preface to the New Testament" (1522, revised last in 1546), written to introduce Luther's fresh translation of the New Testament. Here again Luther insists that the chief thing the gospel demands is not the good works that we expect God to want from us. "Rather the gospel demands faith in Christ."

This led Luther to see all of Scripture as valuable, since the law and the gospel are each parts of the story of God that we need to hear repeatedly. But it led him to value most highly those parts of Scripture in which the gospel as grace and promise is most clearly expressed. This means that for Luther the most valuable books are not the four Gospels themselves, but the Gospel of John and the gospel proclaimed in certain of Paul's epistles.

9   Preface to the Old Testament

This strongly gospel-centered theology has often led critics to charge Luther with being a Marcionite—one who presents the God of the Old Testament in overly sharp contrast to the God of the New. To explore the truth or falsity of this common charge against Luther, the reader has two good sources in selections 9 and 10 of this anthology (and even more extensive evidence in Luther's writings on the Old Testament in *Luther's Works*, vols. 1-20).

Luther goes right to the heart of this accusation in his "Preface to the Old Testament" (1523, revised 1545). He admits that some have little use for the Old Testament. But they are wrong, for in it, despite "the simplicity of language and stories frequently encountered there," are found "the very words, works, judgments, and deeds of the majesty, power, and wisdom of the most high God."

The popular contrast between Old and New Testament is partly correct. The chief work of the New Testament is "the proclamation of grace and peace through the forgiveness of sins in Christ" just as the chief message of the Old Testament is "the teaching of laws, the showing up of sin, and the demanding of good." But Luther knows full well that both law and gospel are found in both Old and New Testament. There follows an extensive discussion of the Torah, the five traditional books of Moses.

10   How Christians Should Regard Moses

This question of the authority of the Old Testament is taken up by Luther again two years later in "How Christians Should Regard Moses" (1525). This is a reworking of a sermon on the book of Exodus preached on August 27, 1525. It was directed especially against those enthusiastic opponents of Luther who found in the Old Testament, especially in the Law of Moses, a detailed model for society in Luther's time, and one that they thought could be actually realized.

Basically Luther counters these contemporaries by the strong insistence in the first part of this treatise that "the law of Moses binds only the Jews and not the Gentiles." Here he follows St. Paul, especially in Galatians, in celebrating the freedom of dependence on the law that the gospel brings to Christians.

But Luther's approach to the Old Testament is more subtle and complex than rejection. Moses is to be retained (and the whole Old Testament with him) for three reasons: (1) He gives laws that are wise and useful for the structuring of society (a different aspect or use of the law for Luther than that of driving us to God's grace in Christ). (2) In many passages in Moses and in the whole Old Testament are "promises and pledges of God about Christ." (3) Finally, the Old Testament is filled with helpful examples of "faith, love and the cross" for those who read them with right understanding.

Law and gospel together serve as Luther's hermeneutical key to unlock the knowledge of God in the Bible. But these are keys that he uses skillfully, and the reader (perhaps especially today's reader) would do well to notice Luther's warning against a too facile application of the biblical text to a current situation:

> One must deal cleanly with the Scriptures. From the very beginning the word has come to us in various ways. It is not enough simply to look and see whether this is God's word, whether God has spoken it; rather we must look and see to whom it has been spoken, whether it fits us. That makes all the difference between night and day (p. 144).

6.

ANSWER TO THE HYPERCHRISTIAN, HYPERSPIRITUAL, AND HYPER-LEARNED BOOK BY GOAT EMSER IN LEIPZIG—INCLUDING SOME THOUGHTS REGARDING HIS COMPANION, THE FOOL MURNER[1]

* * *

---

[1] *Murnarr*, a pun on the name Murner.

Concerning the Letter and the Spirit

St. Paul says, in II Corinthians 4 [3:6], "The letter kills, but the Spirit gives life." My Emser uses and interprets this to mean that Scripture has a twofold meaning, an external one and a hidden one, and he calls these two meanings "literal" and "spiritual." The literal meaning is supposed to kill, the spiritual one is supposed to give life. He builds here upon Origen,[63] Dionysius,[64] and a few others who taught the same thing. He thinks he has hit the mark and need not look at clear Scripture because he has human teaching. He would also like me to follow him, to let Scripture go and take up human teaching. This I refuse to do, even though I too have made the same error. I intend, in precisely this example, to give reasons and to show clearly that Origen, Jerome, Dionysius, and some others have erred and failed in this matter, that Emser builds upon sand, and that it is necessary to compare the fathers' books with Scripture and to judge them according to its light.

First, if their opinion were correct that the spiritual meaning gives life and the literal one kills, we would have to confess that all sinners are holy and all saints are sinners. Indeed, Christ himself, together with all the angels, would have to be simultaneously alive and dead. We intend to make this so clear that even Emser with all his lying powers cannot fight against it. We shall consider the passage from Paul in Galatians 4 [:22], "Abraham had two sons, Isaac and Ishmael, by two women, Sarah and Hagar." This is said according to the literal meaning and the letter. Now this is the meaning Christ has. God the Holy Spirit and all angels and saints hold fast to it and insist that it is as the literal meaning and the letter say, and this is truly the way it is. What now, Emser? Where is your Origen? If you are really the man who does not

---

[63] Origen of Alexandria (ca. 184-253), a Greek church father whose principles of allegorical exegesis were the source of many lengthy controversies. Cf. *The Babylonian Captivity of the Church*, 1520. LW 36, 30.

[64] Dionysius (ca. 500), the "Areopagite" (a pseudonym based on Acts 17:34), is associated with Christian neo-Platonism and mystical ideas about the church. Cf. LW 36, 109.

strike with the sheath and wounds only with the blade, you had better say now that the letter and literal meaning kill Christ and the Holy Spirit together with all the angels and saints. What can anyone say more blasphemously than that the truth in all of Scripture is deadly and harmful, as Emser rages here?

Again, (as you say) the spiritual meaning is that Abraham is Christ, the two women are the two testaments [Gal. 4:24], the two sons are the people of the two testaments, as St. Paul interprets. Now not only the saints but also the worst sinners, indeed, even the devils in hell, hold to this same meaning. So step onto the battlefield, my Emser, strike out merrily with the blade, and say that all the devils and knaves are alive and holy since the Holy Spirit gives life. Now admit it: is it not true that if you take this piece of Origen, Dionysius, Jerome, and many others, you have taken almost all their skill? Is not Scripture here clearer than all of them put together? With what do I test, judge, condemn, and defeat them all so that no one can deny it, other than with the same passage of St. Paul which they take as their basis, namely, "The letter kills, the Spirit gives life" [II Cor. 3:6]? What kind of glosses do I add? Is not the text itself so clearly against them that everyone is forced to say Yes?

This is the way one should deal with the whole Scripture, even with the ancient figures like the one prohibiting Jews from eating either pork or rabbit since pigs and rabbits do not ruminate [Lev. 11:6-7]. This was the literal meaning and letter. This is the way David, all the holy prophets, and Christ himself with his disciples have understood it and obeyed it. If they had not understood and obeyed it in this way they would have been in opposition to God. Then why did the letter not kill them? On the other hand, great deadly sinners and, above all, devils may understand that the pig means carnal teaching, or whatever one wants to interpret here spiritually; so why does the Spirit not give them life? Where are you now, man from Leipzig with the cutting sword? Better go and write even more about me, that I have praised ceremonies as being "holy, just, and good, given by a good God." You yourself must now see and confess that the result is as I said it would be. Did I not tell you that you do not know even one jot about what Spirit and letter are in Scripture? You should mind your own business and leave Scripture in peace. Do you see now what good it does to refer to many teachers and to rely on their writings?

St. Paul says further in Romans 7 [:14], "Divine law is spiritual but I am carnal," and he cites one of the Ten Commandments, "*Non concupisces*, you shall not covet!" [Rom. 7:7]. He argues here with rich words and wisdom that this same spiritual law kills. What do you intend to do here, Emser? Where are you, man with the spear, dagger, and cutting sword? St. Paul says here, "The spiritual law kills"; you say, "The spiritual meaning gives life." Start whistling; let us hear your skill: which is the literal and which is the spiritual meaning in this commandment, "You shall not covet"? You certainly cannot deny that no other meaning can be understood here but the one given by the letters themselves; and he speaks here of the evil lusts of the flesh. Yet St. Paul still calls the law spiritual and says it kills. And you say that it would be better to read a poetic fable than such a meaning of Scripture. St. Paul thinks that anyone who understands a meaning different from this literal meaning in regard to the evil lusts does not understand anything at all in this commandment. How nicely Emser harmonizes with St. Paul, just like the ass with the nightingale. This is the way one must deal with all of God's commandments, be they ceremonial or other commandments, small or great. Thus it is quite obvious that Emser fails miserably here and knows less about Scripture than a child.

Moreover, his erroneous and false understanding leads to the humiliation of all of Scripture as well as to his own great disgrace. For the diligence and efforts of all teachers are directed solely to discovering the literal meaning which alone is valid for them too. Thus Augustine also writes that "figures prove nothing."[65] This means that Emser's spiritual understanding counts for nothing; but the other one [the literal one] is the highest, best, strongest, in short, the whole substance, nature, and foundation of Holy Scripture. If one abandoned it, the whole Scripture would be nothing. But the spiritual one, which Emser inflates, counts in no dispute and does not stand the test; it would not matter at all even if no one knew it, as I have proven in my book on the papacy.[66] For it

---

[65] Cf. *On the Unity of the Church,* I, 5, 8. MPL 43, 396.
[66] Cf. *On the Papacy in Rome,* 1520. LW 39, 70.

would not matter if no one knew that Aaron is spiritually Christ, nor can it be proven. One must let Aaron be just Aaron in the simple sense, unless the Spirit himself interprets him in a new sense, which then would be a new literal sense—as when St. Paul makes Christ out of Aaron for the Hebrews [Hebrews 9–10].

Why are you so bold now, Emser, that you dare to say that this literal meaning is deadly? You babble on, not knowing yourself what you are saying, when you claim it is better to read one of Virgil's fables than such a meaning in Scripture. This means to condemn the whole Scripture and to prefer the devil's lies or fables to the holy word of God, especially since it [Scripture] has no other meaning that counts but the one you teach as deadly and to be avoided. This is called striking with the blade and a true Emserian spiritual interpretation! This is the way to strike the heretic Luther! Turn the leaf over, Emser, and you will find that the meaning you call spiritual and alive is precisely the one which, if one adheres to it alone and lets the literal meaning go, would better be replaced by the mere fables of poets. For it is dangerous, and Scripture can exist without it. But Scripture cannot exist without the other meaning. That is why Origen received his due reward a long time ago when his books were prohibited, for he relied too much on this same spiritual meaning, which was unnecessary, and he let the necessary literal meaning go. When that happens Scripture perishes and really good theologians are no longer produced. Only the true principal meaning which is provided by the letters can produce good theologians.

The Holy Spirit is the simplest writer and adviser in heaven and on earth. That is why his words could have no more than the one simplest meaning which we call the written one, or the literal meaning of the tongue. But [written] words and [spoken] language cease to have meaning when the things which have a simple meaning through interpretation by a simple word are given further meanings and thus become different things [through a different interpretation] so that one thing takes on the meaning of another. This is true for all other things not mentioned in Scripture because all God's creatures and works are sheer living signs and words of God, as Augustine and all the teachers say. But one should not therefore say that Scripture or God's word has more than one meaning.

The fact that a painted picture signifies a living man without any words or writing should not cause you to say that the little word "picture" has two meanings, a literal one, signifying the picture, and a spiritual one, signifying the living man. Likewise, even though the things described in Scripture mean something further, Scripture should not therefore have a twofold meaning. Instead, it should retain the one meaning to which the words refer. Beyond that we should give idle spirits permission to hunt and seek the manifold interpretations of the things indicated besides the words. But they should beware of losing themselves in the hunt or the climb, as happens to those who climb after chamois, and as also happened to Origen. It is much more certain and much safer to stay with the words and the simple meaning, for this is the true pasture and home of all the spirits.

Now see how well Emser rides along with his twofold Bible. The result [of his effort] is that nothing remains certain. When St. Peter says, "We are all priests" [I Pet. 2:9], he says this is said in the spiritual sense and not in the literal one. But when I ask why it is not the literal sense, he answers, because the literal sense kills. He does not understand a jot of what he says. He does not see that he himself now really disgraces his own priesthood by teaching clearly that it is not the living and spiritual, but rather the literal, deadly, and harmful priesthood, and that it would really be better to be a poet-priest than such a literal priest. If whatever is not Spirit does not live and cannot be understood according to the spiritual meaning, then it must certainly be understood according to the letter as dead, harmful, and worse than pagan, if the high and hyperspiritual theology of Emser is to endure. That is why it would be good if a smith remained a smith, a verse-maker a verse-maker, and let those who have power and marrow in their fists and arms wield the spiritual sword. Scripture does not tolerate the division of letter and Spirit, as Emser so outrageously [divides them]. It contains only a simple priesthood and a simple meaning.

Those who have called the letter a veiled and hidden word, as Augustine also did for a while, have committed a more reasonable error. For example, if I said, "Emser is a crude ass," and a simple man following the words understood Emser to be a real ass with long ears and four feet, he would be deceived by the letter, since through such veiled words I wanted to indicate that he had a crude and unreasonable mind. One teaches such flowery words to boys in school, calling them *schemata* in Greek and *figurae* in Latin, because one dresses up and ornaments speech with them just as one ornaments a body with a jewel. Scripture is full of such flowers, especially in the prophets. For example, John and Christ in Luke 3 [:7] call the Jews "a brood of vipers." And St. Paul calls them "dogs" in Colossians 2 [Phil. 3:2]. Psalm 110 [:3] says, "The dew of your children will come from the womb of the morning." Again, "The Lord will send forth from Zion the scepter of your power" [Ps. 110:2], that is, Christ's children will not be born from the womb of a physical woman or mother, but rather without the work of a man, like the dew from the sky, from the womb of the morning of the Christian church. Again, Christ, in Matthew 5 [:13-14] says, "You are the salt of the earth, and the light of the world." But St. Paul does not mean a letter like this; this belongs to grammar and to elementary school.

If you can humble yourself and not despise me completely, then listen to me: I shall do my Christian duty toward you as I am bound to do it to my enemy; and I shall not withhold from you God's gift to me. In this matter I shall teach you better (to speak without boasting) than you have ever been taught by any other teacher, with the exception of St. Augustine—if you have read his *On the Spirit and the Letter*.[67] None of the others will teach you this. You will not find a single letter in the whole Bible that agrees with what you, along with Origen and Jerome, call the "spiritual meaning." St. Paul calls it *mysteria*, that is, veiled and secret meaning. Therefore, the earliest fathers called it *anagogas*, that is, "the more withdrawn meanings, separate knowledge" (*remotiores sensus, separatas intelligentias*). At times they also called it "allegory," as St. Paul himself does, Galatians 4 [:24]; but this is not yet Spirit, although the Spirit grants this as well as the letter and all gifts. As we read in I Corinthians 14 [:2], "The Spirit utters the hidden meaning." Some people, out of ignorance, therefore,

[67] *De spiritu et litera, ad Marcellinum* (412). MPL 44, 199-246; PNF 5, 83-114.

attributed a fourfold meaning to Scripture: the literal, the allegorical, the anagogical, and the tropological. But there is no basis for it.

Thus "literal meaning" is not a good term, because Paul interprets the letter quite differently than they do. Those who call it "grammatical, historical meaning" do better. It would be appropriate to call it the "meaning of the tongue or of language" as St. Paul does in I Corinthians 14 [:2-19], because, according to the sound of the tongue or speech, it is understood in this way by everyone. For the language or tongue which hears that Abraham had two sons from two wives retains this same meaning and does not think beyond the meaning [given] by the tongue or language until the Spirit leads it on and discloses the hidden understanding about Christ, about two kinds of testaments and peoples. These are called *mysteria*, just as Paul, Ephesians 5 [:32], calls [the unity of] Christ and the church in one body *mysterium*, although Scripture and the letter speak of husband and wife—Genesis 2 [:24]. But here it is necessary that no one invent mysteries on his own, as some people have done and are still doing. The Spirit himself must do it—or else one must prove it with Scripture, as I have written in the book on the papacy.[68]

That is why Paul's saying, II Corinthians 4 [3:6], "The letter kills, but the Spirit gives life," harmonizes with these two meanings, the literal and the spiritual, as well as Emser's mind harmonizes with philosophy and theology. At the moment I shall ignore how and why Origen, Jerome, and some other fathers have stretched and misused this passage. Certainly they stretched more passages in the same way to fend off Jews and heretics, as everyone well knows or is able to know. They should be excused for this, but we should not follow them in this as these unclean animals are doing who have no judgment with regard to the work and teaching of the fathers; they gobble up everything they find until they obey the fathers only in those things in which the dear fathers slipped as men. And they drop them when they did well, as I could easily prove with regard to all the teachings and lives now held to be the very best.

---

[68]Cf. *LW* 39, 73.

II. The Power of the Word of God

Let us deal now with the passage concerning the Spirit and the letter. In this passage [II Cor. 3:6], St. Paul does not write one iota about these two meanings, only about two kinds of preaching or preaching offices. One is that of the Old Testament, the other is that of the New Testament. The Old Testament preaches the letter, the New [Testament] preaches the Spirit. And, to avoid the kind of dreaming goat Emser does, let us hear the Apostle's own clear words spoken about the servants or preachers of the New Testament. They are written in II Corinthians 4 [3:3-6]: "You are a letter from Christ made through our preaching and written not with ink but with the Spirit of the living God, not on stone tablets but on tablets of human hearts. That is why we need no other letter of recommendation. Such is the confidence we have through Christ in God. Not that we are sufficient in ourselves to claim anything as coming from us; our sufficiency is from God, who has qualified us to be servants and preachers of the New Testament, not of the letter but of the Spirit; for the letter kills, but the Spirit gives life," etc.

Are not these clear words about preaching? Here we see clearly that St. Paul names two tablets and two sermons. Moses' tablets were made of stone in which God's finger inscribed the law, Exodus 20 [:1-17; 24:12; 31:18]. Christ's tablets, or (as he says here) Christ's letters, are the hearts of Christians in which not letters, as in Moses' tablets, but the Spirit of God is inscribed through the preaching of the gospel and through the office of the apostles. What does all this mean? The letter is nothing but divine law or commandment which was given in the Old Testament through Moses and preached and taught through Aaron's priesthood. It is called "letter" because it is written in letters on stone tablets and in books. It remains letter, and does not yield more than that, because no man improves through the law; he only becomes worse. Thus the law does not help, nor does it grant grace; it only commands and orders something done which man is neither able nor willing to do. But the Spirit, the divine grace, grants strength and power to the heart; indeed, he creates a new man who takes pleasure [in obeying] God's commandments and who does everything he should do with joy.

This Spirit can never be contained in any letter. It cannot be written, like the law, with ink, on stone, or in books. Instead, it is inscribed only in the heart, and it is a living writing of the Holy Spirit, without [the aid of] any means. That is why St. Paul calls it Christ's letter and not Moses' tablets, for it is not written with ink but with God's Spirit. Through this Spirit or grace man does what the law demands. He pays what he owes the law, and thus becomes liberated from the letter which kills him, living now through the grace of the Spirit. For everything which does not have the grace of the living Spirit is dead, even though external obedience to the whole law glitters. That is why the Apostle says of the law that it kills, gives no one life, and holds one eternally in death if grace does not arrive to redeem and give life.

These then are the two ways of preaching: the priests, preachers, and sermons of the Old Testament deal with no more than the law of God. The Spirit and grace are not yet openly preached. But in the New Testament only Spirit and grace, given to us through Christ, are preached. For the New Testament preaching is but an offering and presentation of Christ, through the sheer mercy of God, to all men. This is done in such a way that all who believe in him will receive God's grace and the Holy Spirit, whereby all sins are forgiven, all laws fulfilled, and they become God's children and are eternally blessed. Thus St. Paul here calls the New Testament preaching the "ministry of the Spirit" [II Cor. 3:6], that is, the office of preaching whereby God's Spirit and grace are offered and put before all those who are burdened by the law, who are killed, and who are greedy for grace. He calls this law "a ministry of the letter," that is, the office of preaching whereby no more is given than the letter or law. No life flows from it, the law is not fulfilled by it, and man can never satisfy it. That is why it remains letter, and in the letter it can do no more than kill man, that is, show him what he should do and yet cannot do. Thus he recognizes that he is dead and without grace before God and that he does not fulfil the commandment, which, however, he should fulfil.

From this it is now clear that the words of the apostle, "The letter kills, but the Spirit gives life," could be said in other words: "The law kills, but the grace of God gives life." Or, "Grace grants help and does everything that the law demands and yet is unable to do by itself." St. Paul therefore calls the law of God a law of death and of sin, saying in Romans 8 [:2-4], "The law of the Spirit of life in Christ has set me free from the law of sin and death. For it was impossible for the law to help me; indeed, it only made things worse because of the malice of the old flesh. That is why God sent his Son in our likeness and let him put on our sinful flesh. Thus he destroyed our sin through the sin Christ took upon himself in his suffering, in order that the just requirement of the law might be fulfilled in us." Thus we see that in a masterful way St. Paul teaches us how to understand Christ, God's grace, and the New Testament correctly—namely, that it is nothing but [the story] of how Christ stepped into our sins, carried them on the cross in his flesh, and destroyed them, so that all who believe in him are set free from sin through him and receive the grace to enable them from now on to satisfy the law of God and the letter that kills, and to live in eternity. You see, this is "ministry of the Spirit and not of the letter," the preaching of the Spirit, the preaching of grace, the preaching of true indulgence, the preaching about Christ. This is the New Testament about which there would be much to say if the evil spirit had not blinded the world through the pope and had not led human teaching into the abyss of utter darkness.

Now we see that all commandments are deadly, since divine commandments are also deadly. For everything that is not Spirit or grace is death. Therefore, it is a crude misunderstanding to call allegories, tropologies, and the like "Spirit," since all of them are contained in letters and cannot give life. Grace has no other vessel than the heart. Now just as not all men accept the life of this Spirit—indeed, the majority let this Spirit's servants present and preach this rich grace in vain, and do not believe the gospel—so too, not everyone takes up the ministry of the letter or the preaching of the law. They do not want to let themselves be killed; that is, they do not understand God's law, and they go on without receiving either the letter or the Spirit. But let us set forth goat Emser's blind mind even more clearly: he thinks the letter should be avoided and the death of the letter should be escaped. This is what happens to those who read only the books of the fathers and leave Scripture aside. They juggle with their spears and daggers, making an obscure fog out of Scripture and a light out of the teaching of the fathers.

The Apostle does not want us to avoid the letter or to escape its death. Indeed, he complains in the same passage [II Cor. 3:7] that there was a veil hanging over the law for the Jews, just as over the face of Moses (Exodus 34 [:33-35]), so that they failed to see the letter, its death, or its brilliance. He wants us to preach and make the letter clear and to lift the veil from Moses' face. This is how it happens: he who understands the law of God correctly and looks it in the face—without the veil—will find that the works of all men are sin and that there is nothing good in them unless the grace of the Spirit enters into them. This then is the end of the law and its meaning, of which Paul speaks in II Corinthians 4 [3:13], "They did not see the end of Moses." For it [the law] wants to make everyone a sinner and all that is ours into sin; in this way it wants to show us our misery, our death, and our merit, and lead us into true knowledge of ourselves. As St. Paul says, Romans 7 [:7], "If it had not been for the law, I should not have known sin"; and Romans 3 [Gal. 3:22], "Scripture consigned all men to sin," so that the whole world's mouth might be stopped and it might know that no man can be upright before God without grace, even though he does works of the law.

Those who want to emphasize their good works and boast about free will do not allow all human works to be sin. They still find something good in nature, just as the Jews and our sophists, together with the pope, do. They are the ones who do not want to let Moses' face shine clearly. They put a veil over the law and do not really look it in the face. They refuse to let everything belonging to them be either sin or death before God; that is, they do not really want to know themselves or to be humble. They only strengthen their pride. They flee the letter and a true understanding of it, just as the Jews fled the face of Moses. That is why their mind remains blind and they never come to the life of the Spirit. Therefore, it is impossible for someone who does not first hear the law and let himself be killed by the letter, to hear the gospel and let the grace of the Spirit bring him to life. Grace is only given to those who long for it. Life is a help only to those who are dead, grace only to sin, the Spirit only to the letter. No one can have the one without the other. Therefore, what Emser calls the letter and death is, in reality, nothing but the veil, the harmful misunderstanding of the letter, and the damnable flight from this blessed death. In fact, it is not even this good an understanding. So far away is this poor and blind man from Scripture, and he pretends to hit the mark with the sword blade! I think he has only struck his own cheek!

My good advice to such unlearned minds would be to give up writing books. For while they madly cite the words of a few fathers, they thumb their noses at the poor people so that they fall for it and accept this error, perhaps for life. Thus such books are not without harm, and their insane author is guilty before God because of such corruption. Who will give Emser the grace to eradicate, as he ought to, the errors and lies resulting from his book? It would have been better for him, as Christ says, to have a millstone fastened around his neck and to be drowned in the depth of the sea [Matt. 18:6]. For not only does he write erroneous, harmful, and scandalous teaching, but he also blasphemes the very best teachings of Christ and completely poisons the poor people and drives them away. Woe to you, Emser! If you had waited until God called you and drove you, he would have worked with you too and given you his Spirit to write something useful. But now you do as Jeremiah says, "I did not send the prophets, yet they ran; I did not speak to them, yet they prophesied" [Jer. 23:21]. The hateful and deceitful spirit has driven you. That is why you do not write anything but lies and error. I can do no more than to warn everyone against your poison. And if I were not afraid for these poor people I would not have considered you worth answering, just as I did not before,[69] for in these matters you are ignorance itself!

But to return to our topic: it is certainly true that wherever the law alone is preached and only the letter is dealt with, as happened in the Old Testament, and where the Spirit is not preached afterward, there is death without life, sin without grace, misery without consolation. This creates miserable and imprisoned consciences who in the end despair and are forced to die in sin. They are thus condemned to eternity through such preaching. In our day the murderous sophists have done this kind of thing and are still doing it with their "systems" [*summae*] and "confessionals" [*confessionales*],[70] in which they drive and torture people

---

[69]Cf. *To the Goat in Leipzig*, 1521. LW 39. 105-115.
[70]Systems of theology and manuals of confession.

with commands to do penance, to confess, to repent, and to make satisfaction. After this they teach good works and preach good doctrine, as they say. But never once do they hold the Spirit and Christ up to the sorrowful consciences, so that Christ is now unknown in the whole world and the gospel is pushed under the rug.[71] The whole New Testament office is silenced and only the very best people explain Moses and the commandments, and even they are quite rare. The majority deals only with tomfoolery, teaching canon law, papal laws, human teaching, and their own statutes. To these things they cling, these they keep, these they teach daily; and they no longer have an opportunity to know the truth, as St. Paul says [II Tim. 3:7].

If God's commandment, preached and explained as well as possible, is harmful and damning, as St. Paul says here, why then do the sophists and the goat pretend to make people godly with human teachings, with their own laws and an increase in good works? Indeed, since the law kills and condemns everything which is not grace and Spirit, they do no more with their many laws and works than to give the law much to kill and to condemn. Thus all their labor and effort is in vain, and the more they do the worse they become; for it is impossible to satisfy the law with works and teachings. Only the Spirit can satisfy it. That is why Scripture calls their nature *aven* and *amal* [in Hebrew], that is, "trouble" and "effort" [Ps. 10:7]; and it calls this same lost crowd *Behaven*, that is, the "church or crowd of trouble" [Hos. 4:15]. Again, Amos 7 [:16] calls it *Beth-Ishac*, that is, the "church of deceit," because everyone under it is deceived by their false teaching, work, and life.

That is why I advised, and still advise, that one should not pretend to institute a reformation to better such human teaching and canon law as Emser foolishly suggests, for that is impossible. Rather, they [human teaching and canon law] should be burned, eliminated, destroyed, and reversed. Or else they should be reduced as much as possible and the two offices of the letter and the Spirit advanced once again, which can only be done if human teaching is left far behind. It is only fair that they give way to the letter and the Spirit of God, since they hinder it and are detrimental to it. We

---

[71]Cf. *Answer to the Hyperchristian Book,* 1521. *LW* 39, 167, n. 46.

have more than enough to preach on the letter and the Spirit, even if we preached from the beginning of the world until the end of it.

But even though we are already in the New Testament and should have only the preaching of the Spirit, since we are still living in flesh and blood, it is necessary to preach the letter as well, so that people are first killed by the law and all their arrogance is destroyed. Thus they may know themselves and become hungry for the Spirit and thirsty for grace. So [the letter] prepares the people for the preaching of the Spirit, as it is written about St. John [the Baptist], that he made the people ready for Christ through the preaching of repentance [Matt. 3:1-12]. This was the office of the letter. After that he led them to Christ, saying, "Behold, the Lamb of God, who takes away all the sins of the world" [John 1:29]. This was the office of the Spirit. These then are the two works of God, praised many times in Scripture: he kills and gives life, he wounds and heals, he destroys and helps, he condemns and saves, he humbles and elevates, he disgraces and honors, as is written in Deuteronomy 32 [:39], I Kings 2 [I Sam. 2:6-8], Psalm 112 [:7-8], and in many other places. He does these works through these two offices, the first through the letter, the second through the Spirit. The letter does not allow anyone to stand before his wrath. The Spirit does not allow anyone to perish before his grace. Oh, this is such an overwhelming affair that one could talk about it endlessly! But the pope and human law have hidden it from us and have put up an iron curtain in front of it. May God have mercy! Amen.

On the basis of this [discussion] everyone can easily understand what St. Paul means when he says, Romans 7 [:12], "The law is good, just, holy, and spiritual," and yet, it is still a killing letter. For it shows how man should be truly good, just, holy, spiritual, and in harmony with all things. But, as the law discloses, things are quite different with man; he is evil, unjust, sinful, carnal, and out of harmony with the law in every measure. This disharmony brings him eternal death, God's wrath, and disgrace before God, who wants his law fulfilled (as is only right) to the last letter and iota. Thus man recognizes himself in the mirror and in face of the letter or the law—how dead he is and in what disgrace he is with God. This knowledge makes him afraid and drives him to seek the

Spirit, who makes him good, godly, holy, spiritual, brings all things into accord with the law, and leads him to God's grace. The law then becomes dear to him, and the letter never kills him. Instead, he lives in the Spirit as the law demands; indeed, he no longer needs any law to teach him, for he knows it now by heart. Everything the law demands has become his nature and essence through the Spirit.

Thus we want to finish this [discussion] now with St. Augustine's fine comment regarding Psalm 17, in which he defines nicely and briefly what the letter is. He says, "The letter is nothing but LAW WITHOUT GRACE."[72] We, on the other hand, may say that the Spirit is nothing but GRACE WITHOUT LAW. Wherever the letter is, or the law without grace, there is no end to making laws, to teachings, and to works. And yet they are of no avail; no one becomes better through them, everything remains dead in the letter. On the other hand, wherever the Spirit of God exists, there is freedom, as St. Paul says [II Cor. 3:17]; there no teaching or law is needed; everything happens as it should happen. It is just like the man who has healthy, good vision; he does not need anyone to teach him how he should see. His vision is unhindered, and he has more than any teaching could help him get or give to him. But if his vision is not healthy, he is no longer free, and there is not enough teaching to help and protect him. He will have to worry about every single glance and have a rule about it in order to see. Thus it is St. Paul's opinion, I Timothy 1 [:9], that "the law is not laid down for the just," for the Spirit gives him everything that the law demands. Thus when he says, "God has made us preachers of the Spirit and not of the letter," he means that in the New Testament only grace and not law should be preached, so that men become truly godly through the Spirit.

Where are you now, Goliath Emser, with your spear and sword? You have buckled on this sword and let your own head be cut off with it. You could not have found a passage in the whole Bible which serves me as well against you as does this one on which you base your argument and comfort. You boast to strike with the blade, but you do not even get to the point of touching

---

[72] Luther's quote reflects the core of Augustine's commentary. Cf. *Expositions on the Book of Psalms*. MPL 36, 448-454; PNF 8, 49-50.

either sheath or hilt! Do you see now how you torture this saying spiritually, dragging it to the point that the letter means literal meaning and the Spirit means spiritual meaning? And you say that one should flee the letter and death. What a fine fencer you are! What a fine round you have fought with the famous fencer! Now then, since I have unbuckled your sword and have beheaded your arrogance, we shall come back again to your spear, your dagger, and your whole armor. I hope I shall uncover a dead Goliath, hold up his head, and show everyone your abomination, your threat, and your Goliath-like blasphemy. Let us see where your idol the pope will be with his laws, and where the entire army of these Philistines will be with their human teachings.

If the pope, with his bishops and priests, is a pious and loyal follower and heir to the apostolic see, I hope he is also obliged to execute their office and to preach the Spirit, in accord with these words of St. Paul. But if he is to preach the Spirit, he is not to preach any law but rather freedom from even the laws of God, as was said. Thus I ask: Where do this pope and priesthood come from? Not only do they never preach this Spirit, indeed, they do not even explain the letter correctly. Instead, they [preach] their own law, canon law, and nothing but human teaching—consecrated salt, water, vigils, masses, and whatever other tomfoolery like this you can name. They fill the world with them, obscure the law of God, and replace the veil of Moses which the apostles had lifted. Furthermore, they imprison the world in their law, destroy Christian freedom, ruin the Spirit, and drive away grace. [In return] for such abominable evil they steal, rob, and take all our money and property. St. Paul says that even the brilliance of Moses, that is, the law of God, is annulled through the preaching of the Spirit, so that only the brilliance of the Spirit shines in the church. But the pope does not only reintroduce Moses (which would still be a favor), but also replaces the veil before his eyes and, indeed, with his innumerable laws builds a stone wall before him so that now neither Spirit nor letter is recognized or preached, only fables about human teaching, of which Christ says in Matthew 15 [:8-9], "In vain do they serve me with human laws and teachings; they honor me with their lips, but their heart is far from me."

Where does such a pope come from with his priesthood?

Indeed, he is not the heir to the apostolic see, for he surely destroys the apostles' office and teaching with his teaching. St. Paul stands firm here, saying, "We are servants or preachers of the Spirit and not of the letter." But what does the pope say? "We are preachers neither of the Spirit nor of the letter, but only of our own dream which is written down nowhere." Where then does he come from? I shall tell you: Christ names him in Matthew 24 [:15, 23-26], "When you see the desolating sacrilege in the holy place" (that is, the pope with his own teaching in the church, sitting in the chair of the apostles) "let the reader understand. For false prophets, teachers, and Christs will arise, saying, 'Lo, here is the Christ!' or 'There he is!' and they will lead many people astray." That is, they will present human teachings with which one looks for Christ here and there, thinking one could find him through works and cere-monies. Instead, he [Christ] lets himself be found only in the heart, Spirit, and faith, everywhere, every time, and by everyone. St. Paul [says], II Thessalonians [2:3, 9], "The man of sin and perdition will be revealed through the activity of Satan"; and in Daniel 7 [8:23-25] [we read], "At the end of the Roman Empire, a king will arise. His strength will consist of externals and appearance" (that is, of human teachings which teach only external ways and habits, as, for example, the lives of bishops, priests, and monks with their vestments and external works and ways). "He will cause fearful destruction, his cunning will be swift and geared to mak-ing human laws and increasing them," etc. More another time.

Now listen to what else God says about your idol and human teachings: St. Paul, Colossians 2 [:8], "Take care that no one deceives you through philosophy and empty deceit, human teach-ings, commandments concerning temporal, external things, which are not according to Christ's teaching."[73] What kind of teachings these are follows later when he says, " If you died with Christ, why do you live as though you still lived with human laws and submit to regulations, 'Do not eat, Do not drink, Do not handle, Do not touch'? These are nothing but temporal things which perish as they are used, on which human commandments and laws center—and yet they [human laws] have the appearance of being well and

---

[73] Luther added to the text, "commandments concerning temporal, external things."

wisely ordered. Yet they are nothing but superstition and false, foolish humility, intent only on hurting the body and perverting it. They [human laws and teachings] satisfy their animal-like mind, but they are of no value."[74] Where is the blade of the goatish spirit here? Did not St. Paul in a masterful manner here expose the lives of pope, bishops, clerics, and monks? Such lives consist only of not eating this, or not drinking that, of not touching money or not wearing a certain vestment or color and so on. Their spirituality is geared to temporal things which perish as they are used and represent nothing but an illusion and a shadow of holiness. But they thus deceive everyone and subjugate the world to themselves with their foolish humility. This is the king whose strength consists only of externals and not of armor, word, or word of God, Daniel 8 [:23-25].

Again, Christ says in Matthew 7 [:15], "Beware of false teachers, who come to you in sheep's clothing but inwardly are ravenous wolves." What else is sheep's clothing but such external holiness in vestments, shoes, tonsures, eating, drinking, days, and places? These are temporal things, and inwardly, in faith, which grants eternal holiness and rests on eternal goods, they are nothing. Indeed, they are only destroyers of such faith and ravenous wolves, as St. Paul confesses too, I Timothy 2 [II Tim. 3:5, 7], saying, "They have a form of piety without substance. They always teach and learn and can never arrive at a knowledge of the truth." If all of this were removed and changed, as it should be, where then would the papacy be, since it rests upon only this? Christ himself has to remove it on the Last Day; otherwise, nothing will come of it. Here we see clearly that we should flee sheep's clothing, namely, human laws and works.

Again, St. Paul [writes], Galatians 1 [:8], "If anyone, even an angel from heaven, should teach you differently than you learned, let him be accursed." And Colossians 2 [:7-8], "Beware of that which is not taught according to Christ."[75] Indeed, St. Paul wants nothing taught here except Scripture. What do you say to that, Emser? Perhaps you will introduce SS. Augustine, Benedict,[76]

---

[74] Col. 2:20-23. Luther translated very freely here.

[75] Luther summarized these two verses in this manner.

[76] Benedict of Nursia (*ca.* 480-*ca.* 547), founder of the Benedictine Order.

Francis,[77] Dominic, and other fathers, all of whom taught and maintained holy but human teachings. I answer that this is not enough to satisfy Scripture. God's word is more than all the angels, saints, and creatures. Therefore, no one can say that these same saints never erred. Who will guarantee, then, that they did not err in this either, since Aaron and all the elect could err here, and since Scripture is clearly before me? I want to be and must be defeated with Scripture, not with the uncertain teachings and lives of men, no matter how holy they may be.

Moreover, these same saints kept their teachings free and open, without making commandments out of them. Thus he who wanted to live accordingly could do so, and, if he desired, could also give up doing so. And even if they had erred so much as to make a commandment and law out of them, which I do not believe, I would judge them according to the words of Ezekiel [14:9], "If the prophet be deceived, I, the Lord, have deceived that prophet." I would count them among those of whom Christ says, Matthew 24 [:24], that the rule of the Antichrist will be so brilliant, with such erroneous teachings, and will perform so many signs and wonders, that, if possible, even the elect will be led astray. Accordingly, these holy fathers with the Spirit they had in faith may have miraculously escaped from the dangers of human teaching, and yet, their successors may all be lost, for they hold only to their works and human teachings at the expense of their faith and Spirit. But your pope, who should allow these teachings to be as free as the saints had them, makes necessary eternal commandments and laws out of them with his confirming, just as he does with his own laws.

Furthermore, I think you know that in the Old Testament the people were as much obliged to listen to their priests as we are obliged to listen to ours. Nor did God permit them to teach their own teachings and he forbade their doing so. That is why Moses and all the prophets so often preferred the little word, "My voice." He commands in Deuteronomy 4 [:2], "You shall not add to the words I command you, nor take from them." And in Zechariah 2 [Mal. 2:7], "The people should seek God's commandments and

---

[77] Francis of Assisi (*ca.* 1182-1226), founder of the Franciscan Order.

teaching from the mouth of the priest for he is the messenger of God." And Christ says in Matthew 23 [:2-3] that one should listen to the scribes because they sit in the chair of Moses, that is, because they teach the law of Moses. On the other hand, Scripture calls all those who teach their own laws false prophets, false priests, deceivers, seducers, wolves, ravenous animals, of whom He says in Jeremiah 23 [:32], "They have led my people astray when I did not send them or charge them to teach such things." Indeed, all the priests were sent and, on the basis of their office, charged with teaching the law; but they were not charged with teaching their own law. Again, [He says in] Jeremiah 25 [23:21-22], "I did not send the prophets, yet they preached. I did not command anything to them, yet they taught. If they had remained in my teaching, then they would have proclaimed my words to the people, and I could have turned them from their evil lives."

How will you survive in the face of such passages, pope? Where are you, Emser, you who pretend that one must have more than God's word? You invent dagger and spear. God says here one should teach nothing but his word. Otherwise, he would not convert anyone. Thereby he teaches us this: if something more than God's word is presented to us, it is certainly erroneous, seductive, un-Christian, lying, and deceiving. It only hinders God's work and grace within us. For this reason St. Paul calls the Antichrist the "man of lawlessness and son of perdition" [II Thess. 2:3-4], because he will turn the whole world away from God through his own law and teaching and thus prevent its encounter with God. Thus he will be a master of all sin and of all perdition, and yet he will use the name and image of Christ, calling himself "most holy" [*Sanctissimum*], "vicar of God" [*Vicarium dei*], and "head of the church" [*caput Ecclesiae*]. He will persecute all those who do not obey him in this regard, as is more than evident and obvious in the example of the pope.

Is there any greater labor on the part of all prophets than that of fighting against human teaching and keeping only God's word in a people? All idolatry is nothing but human teaching—for example, the cows of Bethaven [Hos. 4:15-16], Aaron's calf, the idol Baal, and the like. Who can safeguard himself enough against such teachings? Aaron, the highest priest, worshiped the golden calf, and Christ himself says, Matthew 24 [:24], that such deceit and imagery could even lead the elect astray. If the pope did not have such a great following and so much deceit, he could never be the Antichrist. There has to be deceit and a following among all the bishops, priests, monks, universities, princes, and all authorities. There is but one item God does not permit him to cover up—here the ears of the ass still stick out—and that is his disregard for the word of God, which he does not preach either. He is content to preach his own teaching. His singing betrays the kind of bird he is.[78] Just as John envisaged in Revelation 13 [:11] an animal with two horns, looking like a lamb yet speaking like a dragon, so too the crowd of papists has to be viewed; they appear to be Christians yet preach like the devil. Daniel 11 [:37-38] said regarding this that the Antichrist will give no heed to the god of his fathers, will not propagate his teaching, and will not be married; instead he will honor his god *Maozim*[79]—that is, he prohibits marriage only for the sake of his appearance and that of his papists. In place of God and his gospel he erects the idol *Maozim,* his decretals and his teachings, and binds spirituality to external places, as Christ says, "They will say, 'Here is Christ!' and, 'There is Christ!'" [Matt. 24:23].

Again, Jeremiah 19 [:5] says regarding the great Baal worship that they even sacrificed and burned their children, thinking they thereby did a great service to God. But God said, "I have not commanded it, and it never entered my heart," etc. From this it also becomes clear that nothing should be preached or presented to the people that God has neither commanded nor desired. Now we are certain that the pope with his papists has no commandment from God to propagate his own teaching in Christendom. It is nothing but a trick of the devil to hinder God and his commandment and the salvation of all men. Therefore, my goat should first prove and

---

[78] From the German proverb, *den Vogel erkennt man an seinen Federn,* meaning, "the bird is recognized by his feathers."

[79] Hebrew for "god of fortresses." The Vulgate, which Luther quoted, made a proper noun of the Hebrew word. In a letter concerning secret masses in 1534, Luther related the word to "mass": "He [the Antichrist] calls the idol *Maozim,* using the very letters of the word mass. Obviously he would have preferred to call it mass if he had not been constrained to use words of concealment. But he portrays the idol in such a way that we can certainly see he has the abominable mass in mind." Cf. *EA* 31, 390, and 41, 302.

make clear that God approves of his spear and dagger. He thinks it is sufficient when the spear is long and the dagger is short. It should be sufficient to call the one usage and the other human teaching, and [he thinks] that I should drop Scripture and make my judgment according to his mind instead.

So that you may also see the extravagance of your cleverness, listen to me: I certainly know about human teaching and usage with which you fight against me. How could I not know them, since I fight against them? What are you doing, you great philosopher, by bringing up against me the very thing that I am attacking? You should instead protect it by other means. If I besieged a city with an army and shot against its walls and gates until they collapsed, and you, from inside, became very angry at me and determined to get up and fight me, and yet if you did no more than to point out with your hand precisely these same walls and gates which I had shot down, shouted menacingly that I should look at them, and then pretended you had defeated me in this manner— what should I think of you? I would summon a cooper to have him put one or two hoops around your head so that it would not burst from too much nonsense. But even though you have heard how I make use of Scripture and attack human teaching and usage and will not accept their validity unless they have Scripture on their side, you are so smart that you do not protect them with Scripture but only carry them around, showing them to me as if I had never seen them. You claim you have won and have broken open the cuirassier, but everyone can see how desperate you are.[80] St. Augustine, in *Against the Donatist Petilian,*[81] considered it a great joke that when Ticonius introduced the thunder of Scripture against him [i.e., Petilian], he could answer only with the human teachings of his ancestors. He [Augustine] thought it was the most foolish

---

[80] Proverbial German, *wie dich die hunds tage reytten,* literally, "how the dog days plague you."

[81] Cf. *MPL* 43, 246-383; *PNF* 4, 519-628. Actually, Augustine's argument on this particular issue of Donatism (a schismatic movement in North Africa emphasizing the morality of the person over against the office of the ministry) is found in his tract *Against the Epistle of Parmenian. MPL* 43, 34-107. Ticonius (*ca.* 380), founder of a reformatory Donatist group, opposed the strict Donatists led by Petilian and Parmenian on the basis of Scripture. Augustine praised him for this, but at the same time denounced him for maintaining membership in schismatic Donatism.

answer. And I, who also introduce only Scripture, should regard goat Emser's answer as dear and precious wisdom when it is but human fancy and imagination presented without scriptural foundation! Nevertheless, he immediately threatens with it, calling it dagger and usage. It would therefore be good to advise you to stay home with your spear and dagger and to fight with Scripture against me, just as I do against you. What has become of your philosophy now which teaches "not to beg the question" (*petere principium*)? I think it is idiotic and your Aristotle is an arch-fool.[82] The same fate awaits a verse-maker[83] who wants to be a philosopher and theologian as awaited the ass with the bagpipes.

If the Manichaean heresy were to arise today and men pretended that Scripture did not give us enough, but that the Holy Spirit had awakened them and one should follow them, how would you, with all your papists, fend them off? In this case would you also not do any more than point with your finger to your teaching? Or would you say, "Oh, you are too slow; we ourselves have already discovered that one should believe and obey more than Scripture offers"? How nicely you papists would stand if you strengthened your enemy with your own example and admitted teaching and living outside Scripture! Now, is it not foolish and shameful that we ourselves not only confess freely but also boast that our cause is not founded upon Scripture? We go so far as to follow the example of the cuckoo[84] and sing our own praises as good Christians, berating everyone else as heretics, even though they have all of Scripture on their side, as we well know. This should be so intolerable to us, if we were not completely mad, that if our enemy accused us of doing it, we would risk life and limb [to deny] it. Is there anyone who would not rightfully mock us, if we ourselves confess that our foe has Scripture but our cause does not? How could we sing about ourselves more disgracefully and about our

---

[82] *Ertzstultus,* a pun on Aristotle.

[83] *Versifex.* Luther repeatedly used this expression against Emser, who composed a Latin poem in his tract *Answer to the Raging Bull in Wittenberg.* Enders, *op. cit.,* II, 43-44. One of Emser's poems dealt with the disputation at Leipzig in 1519. Cf. the German translation in *St. L.* 18, 1488-1489.

[84] From the German proverb, *Der Kuckuc ruft sein eigen namen aus,* which literally says, "The cuckoo calls out his own name." Cf. Thiele, *Luthers Sprichwörtersammlung,* No. 210.

enemies more honestly? Nor should we present such crude folly to the whole world as wisdom. Indeed, it is time that we used the scabbards of these brave war heroes for latrines!

Moreover, what I wanted [to show] in all my books was precisely what Emser confesses here. Yet he complains about me with a great, earnest, and murderous noise! Did I not also say that the affairs of the pope and of all papists are nothing but human teaching and usage, without any Scripture—something Emser wants to extort from me at all cost? What else am I fighting about but precisely this? I do it so that everyone may understand the true difference between divine Scripture and human teaching or usage and so that a Christian heart does not buy the one for the other—straw for gold, hay for silver, and wood for jewels—as St. Paul teaches, I Corinthians 2 [3:12], and St. Augustine too in many places, as well as the holy carnal law, if the hyperlearned "licentiate of holy canon law" had looked at it soberly. Why does this goat accuse me so fiercely when we both are of one mind and agree on the matter? Perhaps it was my sin to have spoken impolitely when I did not call human teaching a short dagger and usage a long spear? The reason is that I am not a rhymester. Moreover, since he has no other reason to write books than to show off his masterly skill in inventing names, to call human teaching a short dagger and usage a long spear, it would not have helped me at all to call it that. He might still, just to teach us, have called human teaching "goat horn" and usage "goat beard" and thereby knocked me down and confused me. Such wise and intelligent masters do philosophy and the arch-fool Aristotle create through the sophists!

If, then, goat Emser makes a murderous noise about me throughout the whole book for the sake of his anti-Christian head in Rome and thus gains great honor, it is only proper for me to make a noise about him for the sake of my head in heaven, whom he slanders and blasphemes. He may pretend that the Holy Spirit and Christ did not teach us enough, that Scripture is not enough, and that God's word must have an addition; and that whoever has nothing more than God's word, Scripture, and teaching is poison, a heretic, an apostate, and the worst man on earth and that all those who live with such words of God and such teaching and do not keep human teaching are condemned, cursed, and to be burned.

Thus Christ and the Holy Spirit too must be guilty and responsible; indeed, they deserve such blasphemy, since they produced and daily preserve such blasphemous, accursed, and condemned people through their word and teaching.

Look here! Is he not the greatest blasphemer ever known? Who indeed has ever heard more blasphemous, poisonous, hellish, heretical, raging, and nonsensical words than those Emser here pours from his poisonous and hellish mouth and lets stink to heaven? This poor creature spits and sprays his spit at God his Creator so terribly and gruesomely that it is abominable to listen to or speak of. If he could at least show where the Holy Spirit teaches too little and where Scripture needs the additions of men, there would be some appearance of reason. But now he himself admits that Scripture is on our side and he is unable to criticize us on the basis of Scripture; he also freely admits that his human work is not in Scripture, yet he nevertheless pours out such blasphemy upon us—that is, upon Scripture, as he himself admits —that I would not have thought even a devil in hell would be permitted to do such things. I say this only so that you, dear goat, may see that if sheer murderous noise and raging amplification could strengthen your cause, I could strengthen my cause even more with them. My cause does not need them. It is well grounded in Scripture. Yours certainly does, because it is built upon human dreams and upon the chamber of his [the pope's] heart.[85]

I trust that from all this everyone may see what Emser's spear and dagger are and what kind of bout he has fought with the famous fencer. I shall improve things for him when he returns for another round. But I do not swear to it either by my priesthood or by my holiness.[86] I shall satisfy him in other ways. Here I shall conclude with the three main parts of his book, the sword, the spear, and the dagger. They are so overcome that the whole book built upon them is also overcome. But to explain my view again: since

---

[85] *Scrinium pectoris.* A reference to the habit of storing official documents in a "chest" *(scrinium)* during the days of the Holy Roman Empire. Pope Boniface VIII (1294-1303), who added his own collection to existing canon law, claimed authority over canon law by saying, "The Roman pontiff has all laws in the chamber [*scrinium*] of his heart." Cf. *LW* 44, 202, n. 215; and below p. 281, n. 34.

[86]Cf. *Concerning the Answer of the Goat in Leipzig*, 1521. *LW* 39, 131, n. 29.

Emser concedes that I have opposed neither the articles of faith nor Scripture—whereby he becomes my unwilling, unfavorable, but therefore all the more convincing witness to the fact that I am a truly devout Christian and have falsely been called a heretic by him for no reason—I shall wrest one more thing from him which he never expected and which he does not like to let go.

He should grant us freedom from human laws so that it is up to us whether or not we obey them. And if we are indeed to live under them, as I have taught and still teach, he should nevertheless grant us permission to state that they are neither necessary nor good for us and that we do not have to obey them; that moreover the pope is a tyrant, without any right to make these laws and that he thus commits an injustice; that we may obey them, not because it is our duty or the pope's due, but because it is our own free will to do so to serve him, just as Christ says in Matthew 6 [5:25] that we should make friends with the accuser; and that those who do not obey them [laws] should rightly not be called heretics. All this should be granted to us, and we shall prove it in the following manner.

When we have Scripture and Scripture has us, as Emser admits —which is undoubtedly satisfactory to God—we are more than sufficiently praised as devout Christians; those who slander us have to give the lie to themselves. What more do you people want from us? When you call us heretics, whom do you call heretics, since you yourselves admit that we are in agreement with Scripture? Can you condemn those whom God justifies? Does not truth punish you through your own Caiaphian and Baalian mouths? For you are only put in office to lead us to God and to God's word and to tend us with God's word, as Christ says in Matthew 4 [:4], "Man shall live by every word that proceeds from the mouth of God." Why do you pretend to lead us further and indeed pull us away from God toward yourselves and drive us from his word to your teaching and usage? Is this the office of shepherds or of wolves?[87]

---

[87] Cf. Emser's statement in *Against the Un-Christian Book of the Augustinian Martin Luther:* "Help me, you true and living Son of God, Holy Lord Jesus Christ, against the raging wolf, who aims to lead astray your sheep which you have bought and redeemed with your rose-colored blood." Enders, *op. cit.,* I, 15.

Therefore I say: Let us be free, Emser, and admit, as your conscience implores you, that the pope is a tyrant who has no right to make laws which are neither good nor necessary for us anyway. And, so that conscience does not vanish from the pope and you papists, admit that you are thieves, robbers, wolves, seducers, and betraying Judases with your laws. Then we shall gladly obey and endure them, just as Christ endured his rope and cross, to which Judas, the ancestor of the pope, had brought him. Then they do not harm us, and we endure them in the same way we endure someone's taking clothes, money, property, even life from us. We will even endure you too, when you burden our Christian freedom with your insane, foolish, and useless laws. But our conscience remains free from you and unburdened. But if you were to insist (as you do) that it is your right to do so and that we should take it as proper and right—just as though a murderer forced me to say that he has a claim on my life and property—then, Emser, we shall cry No as long as there is breath in us. For you wish to imprison our conscience so that we should stand in fear as before the law —even when it is an unjust law. Thus you want to catch us and strangle us with innumerable ropes, just as you do with your unlawful ban, forcing people to obey your roguery.

We shall endure injustice from you, but we shall never approve of it. Therefore, tell your idol the pope that he may make laws over me—as many as he pleases. I shall obey them all. But also tell him that he has no right to do so and that I do not owe obedience to him. However, I shall gladly endure his injustice, as Christ teaches [Matt. 5:39-42], and I shall no longer oppose the pope. Everything might as well be bad! What more do you want from me? Did I not teach this in [the commentary on] Galatians[88] and in all my books? But when the pope drives the whole world as though he had a right to do so, he confuses innumerable souls and seduces them into hell. That is why he is the "man of lawlessness and the son of perdition" [II Thess. 2:3], because he has imprisoned consciences and forced them to sanction his injustice, thus filling the world with sin and destruction. For anyone who believes the

---

[88] Cf. *Lectures on Galatians*, 1519. *LW* 27, 151-410.

pope has the right and power to make laws soon thinks he has to obey them as good and necessary and he does not endure them as tyranny and injustice. He obeys them unwillingly; he would like to get rid of the law but is not able to, and so he finally suffocates in sins. For whoever dislikes doing something he must do or thinks he must do, sins in his heart. Accordingly, all the pope's commandments (which are innumerable) are nothing but a rope strangling souls. With these he causes only sin and destruction in the whole world and thus destroys all of Christendom, as Daniel prophesied [Dan. 8:24-25; 9:27]. Christ therefore calls him an "abomination" [Matt. 24:15]. Few people, if any, escape him, except those who die in the cradle.

Do you understand me now, Emser? I do not desire to be free of human laws and teachings. I only desire to have the conscience free and to have all Christians make the sign of the cross against a faith which believes that the pope is right in his rule. For such a faith destroys faith in Christ and drowns the whole world in nothing but sin and destruction. The pope and you papists are the pious heirs of this sort of thing. You, who do no more than propagate such superstition, seduce the world, destroy Christian faith, and lead all souls to the devil when you should believe only in Christ and preach freedom from human laws so as to remain "ministers of the Spirit" and not "of the letter." Likewise, I do not desire to be free of Emser's slandering, hatred, and envy; but I do desire to be free in conscience so that I am allowed to believe Emser is tyrannizing me and doing me an injustice. For if I should sanction this as right, my conscience would already be imprisoned and could not be free until Emser ceased to hate, which might never happen. For if I had to sanction it, which I would not do willingly (since I cannot), I would be sinning endlessly against my conscience. Thus the whole world is now sinning endlessly and is perishing if it believes that the pope is right with his rule, domination, and governance. Yet no one is doing so willingly, since everyone hates the papacy—except those who want to enjoy it—so that it is justifiably called an abomination. The pope has therefore imprisoned the whole world with false conscience and superstition. People have to sin endlessly and unwillingly and [finally] perish. Woe to you, you terrible abomination! Come, Lord Jesus Christ, and save us from the Antichrist! Push his see into the abyss of hell, as he deserves, so that sin and destruction may cease. Amen.

7.

A BRIEF INSTRUCTION ON WHAT TO LOOK FOR AND EXPECT IN THE GOSPELS

It is a common practice to number the gospels and to name them by books and say that there are four gospels. From this practice stems the fact that no one knows what St. Paul and St. Peter are saying in their epistles, and their teaching is regarded as an addition to the teaching of the gospels, in a vein similar to that of Jerome's[1] introduction.[2] There is, besides, the still worse practice of regarding the gospels and epistles as law books in which is supposed to be taught what we are to do and in which the works of Christ are pictured to us as nothing but examples. Now where these two erroneous notions remain in the heart, there neither the gospels nor the epistles may be read in a profitable or Christian manner, and [people] remain as pagan as ever.

One should thus realize that there is only one gospel, but that it is described by many apostles. Every single epistle of Paul and of Peter, as well as the Acts of the Apostles by Luke, is a gospel, even though they do not record all the works and words of Christ, but one is shorter and includes less than another. There is not one of the four major gospels anyway that includes all the words and works of Christ; nor is this necessary. Gospel is and should be nothing else than a discourse or story about Christ, just as happens among men when one writes a book about a king or a prince, telling what he did, said, and suffered in his day. Such a story can be told in various ways; one spins it out, and the other is brief. Thus the gospel is and

---

[1] Jerome (ca. 342-420), Eusebius Hieronymus, was the foremost biblical scholar of the ancient church and a friend of St. Augustine. He translated the entire Bible from the original Hebrew and Greek into popular Latin (Vulgate).
[2] In the prologue to his commentary on the Gospel of Matthew, Jerome writes, "It has been clearly demonstrated [on the basis of Ezek. 1:5, 10, and Rev. 4:7-8] that only four gospels ought to be acknowledged." Migne 7, 20.

should be nothing else than a chronicle, a story, a narr
Christ, telling who he is, what he did, said, and suffered
which one describes briefly, another more fully, one this w
that way.

For at its briefest, the gospel is a discourse about Christ, that
he is the Son of God and became man for us, that he died and was
raised, that he has been established as a Lord over all things. This
much St. Paul takes in hand and spins out in his epistles. He bypasses
all the miracles and incidents[3] [in Christ's ministry] which are set
forth in the four gospels, yet he includes the whole gospel adequately and abundantly. This may be seen clearly and well in
his greeting to the Romans [1:1-4], where he says what the gospel
is, and declares, "Paul, a servant of Jesus Christ, called to be
an apostle, set apart for the gospel of God which he promised
beforehand through his prophets in the holy scriptures, the gospel
concerning his Son, who was descended from David according to
the flesh and designated Son of God in power according to the Spirit
of holiness by his resurrection from the dead, Jesus Christ our
Lord," etc.

There you have it. The gospel is a story about Christ, God's and
David's Son, who died and was raised and is established as Lord.
This is the gospel in a nutshell. Just as there is no more than one
Christ, so there is and may be no more than one gospel. Since Paul
and Peter too teach nothing but Christ, in the way we have just
described, so their epistles can be nothing but the gospel.

Yes even the teaching of the prophets, in those places where
they speak of Christ, is nothing but the true, pure, and proper
gospel—just as if Luke or Matthew had described it. For the prophets
have proclaimed the gospel and spoken of Christ, as St. Paul here
[Rom. 1:2] reports and as everyone indeed knows. Thus when
Isaiah in chapter fifty-three says how Christ should die for us and
bear our sins, he has written the pure gospel. And I assure you, if a
person fails to grasp this understanding[4] of the gospel, he will never

---

[3] *Wunder und wandel* may be the equivalent of *die Wunder und das Leben Jesu* according to WA 10^I, ^{1}, 729, nn. 9, 22.

[4] *Wahn* is the equivalent of *Meinung* and the Latin *opinio*. WA 10^I, ^{1}, 10, n. 1.

be able to be illuminated in the Scripture nor will he receive the right foundation.

Be sure, moreover, that you do not make Christ into a Moses, as if Christ did nothing more than teach and provide examples as the other saints do, as if the gospel were simply a textbook of teachings or laws. Therefore you should grasp Christ, his words, works, and sufferings, in a twofold manner. First as an example that is presented to you, which you should follow and imitate. As St. Peter says in I Peter 4,[5] "Christ suffered for us, thereby leaving us an example." Thus when you see how he prays, fasts, helps people, and shows them love, so also you should do, both for yourself and for your neighbor. However this is the smallest part of the gospel, on the basis of which it cannot yet even be called gospel. For on this level Christ is of no more help to you than some other saint. His life remains his own and does not as yet contribute anything to you. In short this mode [of understanding Christ as simply an example] does not make Christians but only hypocrites. You must grasp Christ at a much higher level. Even though this higher level has for a long time been the very best, the preaching of it has been something rare. The chief article and foundation of the gospel is that before you take Christ as an example, you accept and recognize him as a gift, as a present that God has given you and that is your own. This means that when you see or hear of Christ doing or suffering something, you do not doubt that Christ himself, with his deeds and suffering, belongs to you. On this you may depend as surely as if you had done it yourself; indeed as if you were Christ himself. See, this is what it means to have a proper grasp of the gospel, that is, of the overwhelming goodness of God, which neither prophet, nor apostle, nor angel was ever able fully to express, and which no heart could adequately fathom or marvel at. This is the great fire of the love of God for us, whereby the heart and conscience become happy, secure, and content. This is what preaching the Christian faith means. This is why such preaching is called gospel, which in German means a

---

[5] I Pet. 2:21; cf. 4:1.

joyful, good, and comforting "message"; and this is why the apostles are called the "twelve messengers."[6]

Concerning this Isaiah 9[:6] says, "To us a child is born, to us a son is given." If he is given to us, then he must be ours; and so we must also receive him as belonging to us. And Romans 8[:32], "How should [God] not give us all things with his Son?" See, when you lay hold of Christ as a gift which is given you for your very own and have no doubt about it, you are a Christian. Faith redeems you from sin, death, and hell and enables you to overcome all things. O no one can speak enough about this. It is a pity that this kind of preaching has been silenced in the world, and yet boast is made daily of the gospel.

Now when you have Christ as the foundation and chief blessing of your salvation, then the other part follows: that you take him as your example, giving yourself in service to your neighbor just as you see that Christ has given himself for you. See, there faith and love move forward, God's commandment is fulfilled, and a person is happy and fearless to do and to suffer all things. Therefore make note of this, that Christ as a gift nourishes your faith and makes you a Christian. But Christ as an example exercises your works. These do not make you a Christian. Actually they come forth from you because you have already been made a Christian. As widely as a gift differs from an example, so widely does faith differ from works, for faith possesses nothing of its own, only the deeds and life of Christ. Works have something of your own in them, yet they should not belong to you but to your neighbor.

So you see that the gospel is really not a book of laws and commandments which requires deeds of us, but a book of divine promises in which God promises, offers, and gives us all his possessions and benefits in Christ. The fact that Christ and the apostles provide much good teaching and explain the law is to be counted a benefit just like any other work of Christ. For to teach aright is not

---

[6] *Tzwellff botten.* In Middle High German the singular form of the composite word was used to designate a single apostle. Luther derives the term for "messenger" *(Bote)* from the term for "message" *(Botschaft).* Cf. Grimm, *Deutsches Wörterbuch,* XVI, 1437.

the least sort of benefit. We see too that unlike Moses in his book, and contrary to the nature of a commandment, Christ does not horribly force and drive us. Rather he teaches us in a loving and friendly way. He simply tells us what we are to do and what to avoid, what will happen to those who do evil and to those who do well. Christ drives and compels no one. Indeed he teaches so gently that he entices rather than commands. He begins by saying, "Blessed are the poor,[7] Blessed are the meek," and so on [Matt. 5:3, 5]. And the apostles commonly use the expression, "I admonish, I request, I beseech," and so on. But Moses says, "I command, I forbid," threatening and frightening everyone with horrible punishments and penalties. With this sort of instruction you can now read and hear the gospels profitably.

When you open the book containing the gospels and read or hear how Christ comes here or there, or how someone is brought to him, you should therein perceive the sermon or the gospel through which he is coming to you, or you are being brought to him. For the preaching of the gospel is nothing else than Christ coming to us, or we being brought to him. When you see how he works, however, and how he helps everyone to whom he comes or who is brought to him, then rest assured that faith is accomplishing this in you and that he is offering your soul exactly the same sort of help and favor through the gospel. If you pause here and let him do you good, that is, if you believe that he benefits and helps you, then you really have it. Then Christ is yours, presented to you as a gift.

After that it is necessary that you turn this into an example and deal with your neighbor in the very same way, be given also to him as a gift and an example. Isaiah 40[:1, 2] speaks of that, "Be comforted, be comforted my dear people, says your Lord God. Say to the heart of Jerusalem, and cry to her, that her sin is forgiven, that her iniquity is ended, that she has received from the hand of God a double kindness for all her sin," and so forth. This double kindness is the twofold aspect of Christ: gift and example. These two are also signified by the double portion of the inheritance which the law of

---

[7] Martin Bucer's Latin translation of 1525 adds, "in spirit." WA 10^I, 1, 13, n. 2.

Moses [Deut. 21:17] assigns to the eldest son and by many other figures.

What a sin and shame it is that we Christians have come to be so neglectful of the gospel that we not only fail to understand it, but even have to be shown by other books and commentaries what to look for and what to expect in it. Now the gospels and epistles of the apostles were written for this very purpose. They want themselves to be our guides, to direct us to the writings of the prophets and of Moses in the Old Testament so that we might there read and see for ourselves how Christ is wrapped in swaddling cloths and laid in the manger [Luke 2:7], that is, how he is comprehended [*Vorfassett*] in the writings of the prophets. It is there that people like us should read and study, drill ourselves, and see what Christ is, for what purpose he has been given, how he was promised, and how all Scripture tends toward him. For he himself says in John 5 [:46], "If you believed Moses, you would also believe me, for he wrote of me." Again [John 5:39], "Search and look up the Scriptures, for it is they that bear witness to me."

This is what St. Paul means in Romans 1[:1, 2], where in the beginning he says in his greeting, "The gospel was promised by God through the prophets in the Holy Scriptures." This is why the evangelists and apostles always direct us to the Scriptures and say, "Thus it is written," and again, "This has taken place in order that the writing of the prophets might be fulfilled," and so forth. In Acts 17 [:11], when the Thessalonians heard the gospel with all eagerness, Luke says that they studied and examined the Scriptures day and night in order to see if these things were so. Thus when St. Peter wrote his epistle, right at the beginning [I Pet. 1:10-12] he says, "The prophets who prophesied of the grace that was to be yours searched and inquired about this salvation; they inquired what person or time was indicated by the Spirit of Christ within them; and he bore witness through them to the sufferings that were to come upon Christ and the ensuing glory. It was revealed to them that they were serving not themselves but us, in the things which have now been preached among you through the Holy Spirit sent from heaven, things which also the angels long to behold." What else does St. Peter here desire than to lead us into the Scriptures? It is as if he should be saying, "We preach and open the Scriptures to you through the Holy Spirit, so that you yourselves may read and see what is in them and know of the time about which the prophets were writing." For he says as much in Acts 4[3:24], "All the prophets who ever prophesied, from Samuel on, have spoken concerning these days."

Therefore also Luke, in his last chapter [24:45], says that Christ opened the minds of the apostles to understand the Scriptures. And Christ, in John 10 [:9, 3], declares that he is the door by which one must enter, and whoever enters by him, to him the gatekeeper (the Holy Spirit) opens in order that he might find pasture and blessedness. Thus it is ultimately true that the gospel itself is our guide and instructor in the Scriptures, just as with this foreword I would gladly give instruction and point you to the gospel.

But what a fine lot of tender and pious children we are! In order that we might not have to study in the Scriptures and learn Christ there, we simply regard the entire Old Testament as of no account, as done for and no longer valid. Yet it alone bears the name of Holy Scripture. And the gospel should really not be something written, but a spoken word which brought forth the Scriptures, as Christ and the apostles have done. This is why Christ himself did not write anything but only spoke. He called his teaching not Scripture but gospel, meaning good news or a proclamation that is spread not by pen but by word of mouth. So we go on and make the gospel into a law book, a teaching of commandments, changing Christ into a Moses, the One who would help us into simply an instructor.

What punishment ought God to inflict upon such stupid and perverse people! Since we abandoned his Scriptures, it is not surprising that he has abandoned us to the teaching of the pope and to the lies of men. Instead of Holy Scripture we have had to learn the *Decretales*[8] of a deceitful fool and an evil rogue. O would to God

---

[8] Papal and conciliar decisions, decrees, and pronouncements had been assembled and supplemented through the centuries until they constituted a very sizeable "body of canon law." Luther had consigned the entire collection to the flames on December 10, 1520, along with the papal bull which called for the burning of his books. Cf. *LW* 31, 381-395; and E. G. Schwiebert, *Luther and His Times* (St. Louis: Concordia, 1950), pp. 19-20.

that among Christians the pure gospel were known and that most speedily there would be neither use nor need for this work of mine. Then there would surely be hope that the Holy Scriptures too would come forth again in their worthiness. Let this suffice as a very brief foreword and instruction. In the exposition[9] we will say more about this matter. Amen.

[9] The reference is to Luther's commentary on the various texts of the Wartburg Postil to which this *Brief Instruction* was intended as a foreword.

- There is only one Gospel
- There are several writers
- The Gospel is the main thing in OT & NT.
- Don't write off NT.
- Gospel should be spoken!

8.

PREFACES TO THE
NEW TESTAMENT
Preface to the New Testament[1]
1546 (1522)

[It would be right and proper for this book to go forth without any prefaces or extraneous names attached and simply have its own say under its own name. However many unfounded [*wilde*] interpretations and prefaces[2] have scattered the thought of Christians to a point where no one any longer knows what is gospel or law, New Testament or Old. Necessity demands, therefore, that there should be a notice or preface, by which the ordinary man can be rescued from his former delusions, set on the right track, and taught what he is to look for in this book, so that he may not seek laws and commandments where he ought to be seeking the gospel and promises of God.

Therefore it should be known, in the first place, that the notion must be given up that there are four gospels and only four evangelists.[3] The division of the New Testament books into legal, historical, prophetic, and wisdom books is also to be utterly rejected. Some make this division,[4] thinking thereby (I know not how) to compare

---

[1] Prior to the 1534 edition of the complete Bible this preface—intended perhaps as a preface to the entire New Testament or at least to the first part of the New Testament including the gospels and Acts (see WA, DB 7, xxxi)—carried as a title the single word, "Preface." We have based our translation on the version which appeared in the 1546 edition of the complete Bible, noting significant variations from earlier versions, particularly from the first version as it appeared in the September Testament of 1522. WA, DB 6, 2-11. See pp. 227-232 for the general introduction to all of Luther's biblical prefaces.
[2] On the ancient practice of providing prefaces, see the Introduction, p. 231. On the prefaces which appeared in early printed German Bibles, including the text of that to the book of Romans in the Mentel Bible—the first printed Bible in High German published by Johann Mentel in Strassburg about 1466—see Reu, *Luther's German Bible*, pp. 35 and 305, n. 71.
[3] Limiting the number of gospels to four was an ancient practice going back at least to Jerome, who based his position on the existence of but four living creatures in Ezekiel 1 and Revelation 4—the man, lion, ox, and eagle. Migne 30, 531-534. WA, DB 6, 536, n. 2, 12. Cf. p. 360, n. 9.
[4] This division had been made, e.g., in the 1509 Vulgate printed at Basel, which Luther had probably used. WA, DB 6, 537, n. 2, 14.

the New with the Old Testament. On the contrary it is to be held firmly that][5]

Just as the Old Testament is a book in which are written God's laws and commandments, together with the history of those who kept and of those who did not keep them,[6] so the New Testament is a book in which are written the gospel and the promises of God, together with the history of those who believe and of those who do not believe them.[7]

For "gospel" [*Euangelium*] is a Greek word and means in Greek a good message, good tidings, good news, a good report, which one sings and tells with gladness. For example, when David overcame the great Goliath, there came among the Jewish people the good report and encouraging news that their terrible enemy had been struck down and that they had been rescued and given joy and peace; and they sang and danced and were glad for it [I Sam. 18:6].

Thus this gospel of God or New Testament is a good story and report, sounded forth into all the world by the apostles, telling of a true David who strove with sin, death, and the devil, and overcame them, and thereby rescued all those who were captive in sin, afflicted with death, and overpowered by the devil. Without any merit of their own he made them righteous, gave them life, and saved them, so that they were given peace and brought back to God. For this they sing, and thank and praise God, and are glad forever, if only they believe firmly and remain steadfast in faith.

This report and encouraging tidings, or evangelical and divine news, is also called a New Testament. For it is a testament when a dying man bequeaths his property, after his death, to his legally

---

[5] The portions here set in brackets did not appear in any editions of the complete Bible, nor in editions of the New Testament after 1537. Divergences from the original 1522 text were due primarily to Luther's desire to accommodate the text of the New Testament prefaces to that of the Old Testament prefaces with which they were—in the 1534 complete Bible—to appear for the first time, rather than to criticism on the part of Emser or other opponents. That these divergences were not taken into account in the 1534-1537 separate editions of the New Testament was probably due to the carelessness of the printer, Luther having likely given no personal attention to these particular editions. *WA, DB* 6, 536.
[6] Cf. p. 119.
[7] The editions prior to the 1534 complete Bible here add, "Thus one may be sure that there is only one gospel, just as there is only one book—the New Testament—one faith, and one God who gives the promise" (Eph. 4:4-6).

defined heirs.[8] And Christ, before his death, commanded and ordained that his gospel be preached after his death in all the world [Luke 24:44-47]. Thereby he gave to all who believe, as their possession, everything that he had. This included: his life, in which he swallowed up death; his righteousness, by which he blotted out sin; and his salvation, with which he overcame everlasting damnation. A poor man, dead in sin and consigned to hell, can hear nothing more comforting than this precious and tender message about Christ; from the bottom of his heart he must laugh and be glad over it, if he believes it true.

Now to strengthen this faith, God has promised this gospel and testament in many ways, by the prophets in the Old Testament, as St. Paul says in Romans 1[:1], "I am set apart to preach the gospel of God which he promised beforehand through his prophets in the holy scriptures, concerning his Son, who was descended from David," etc.

To mention some of these places: God gave the first promise when he said to the serpent, in Genesis 3[:15], "I will put enmity between you and the woman, and between your seed and her seed; he shall bruise your head, and you shall bruise his heel." Christ is this woman's seed, who has bruised the devil's head, that is, sin, death, hell, and all his power. For without this seed, no man can escape sin, death, or hell.

Again, in Genesis 22[:18], God promised Abraham, "Through your descendant shall all the nations of the earth be blessed." Christ is that descendant of Abraham, says St. Paul in Galatians 3[:16]; he has blessed all the world, through the gospel [Gal. 3:8]. For where Christ is not, there is still the curse that fell upon Adam and his children when he had sinned, so that they all are necessarily guilty and subject to sin, death, and hell. Over against this curse, the gospel now blesses all the world by publicly announcing, "Whoever believes in this descendant of Abraham shall be blessed." That is, he shall be rid of sin, death, and hell, and shall remain righteous, alive, and saved forever, as Christ himself says in John 11[:26], "Whoever believes in me shall never die."

Again God made this promise to David in II Samuel 7[:12-14] when he said, "I will raise up your son after you, who shall build

---

[8]Cf. *A Treatise on the New Testament*, 1520. LW 35, 87-90.

a house for my name, and I will establish the throne of his kingdom forever. I will be his father, and he shall be my son," etc. This is the kingdom of Christ, of which the gospel speaks: an everlasting kingdom, a kingdom of life, salvation, and righteousness, where all those who believe enter in from out of the prison of sin and death.

There are many more such promises of the gospel in the other prophets as well, for example Micah 5[:2], "But you, O Bethlehem Ephrathah, who are little to be among the clans of Judah, from you shall come forth for me one who is to be ruler in Israel"; and again, Hosea 13[:14], "I shall ransom them from the power of hell and redeem them from death. O death, I will be your plague; O hell, I will be your destruction."

The gospel, then, is nothing but the preaching about Christ, Son of God and of David, true God and man, who by his death and resurrection has overcome for us the sin, death, and hell of all men who believe in him. Thus the gospel can be either a brief or a lengthy message; one person can write of it briefly, another at length. He writes of it at length, who writes about many words and works of Christ, as do the four evangelists. He writes of it briefly, however, who does not tell of Christ's works, but indicates briefly how by his death and resurrection he has overcome sin, death, and hell for those who believe in him, as do St. Peter and St. Paul.

See to it, therefore, that you do not make a Moses out of Christ, or a book of laws and doctrines out of the gospel, as has been done heretofore and as certain prefaces put it, even those of St. Jerome.[9] For the gospel does not expressly demand works of our own by which we become righteous and are saved; indeed it condemns such works. Rather the gospel demands faith in Christ: that he has overcome for us sin, death, and hell, and thus gives us righteousness, life, and salvation not through our works, but through his own works, death, and suffering, in order that we may avail ourselves of his death and victory as though we had done it ourselves.

To be sure, Christ in the gospel, and St. Peter and St. Paul besides, do give many commandments and doctrines, and expound the law. But these are to be counted like all Christ's other works and

---

[9] Each of the four gospels had its own preface in Jerome's Vulgate. Luther's concern for the "one gospel" kept him from ever writing four such separate prefaces. Indeed at the beginning it seems likely that he envisioned but one preface for the entire New Testament. WA, DB 6, 537, n. 8, 5; WA, DB 7, xxi.

good deeds. To know his works and the things that happened to him is not yet to know the true gospel, for you do not yet thereby know that he has overcome sin, death, and the devil. So, too, it is not yet knowledge of the gospel when you know these doctrines and commandments, but only when the voice comes that says, "Christ is your own, with his life, teaching, works, death, resurrection, and all that he is, has, does, and can do."

Thus we see also that he does not compel us but invites us kindly and says, "Blessed are the poor," etc. [Matt. 5:3]. And the apostles use the words, "I exhort," "I entreat," "I beg," so that one sees on every hand that the gospel is not a book of law, but really a preaching of the benefits of Christ, shown to us and given to us for our own possession, if we believe. But Moses, in his books, drives, compels, threatens, strikes, and rebukes terribly, for he is a law-giver and driver.

Hence it comes that to a believer no law is given by which he becomes righteous before God, as St. Paul says in I Timothy 1[:9], because he is alive and righteous and saved by faith, and he needs nothing further except to prove his faith by works. Truly, if faith is there, he cannot hold back; he proves himself, breaks out into good works, confesses and teaches this gospel before the people, and stakes his life on it. Everything that he lives and does is directed to his neighbor's profit, in order to help him—not only to the attainment of this grace, but also in body, property, and honor. Seeing that Christ has done this for him, he thus follows Christ's example.

That is what Christ meant when at the last he gave no other commandment than love, by which men were to know who were his disciples [John 13:34-35] and true believers. For where works and love do not break forth, there faith is not right, the gospel does not yet take hold, and Christ is not rightly known. See, then, that you so approach the books of the New Testament as to learn to read them in this way.

[Which are the true and noblest books of the New Testament][10]
[From all this you can now judge all the books and decide among them which are the best. John's Gospel and St. Paul's epis-

---

[10]See p. 113, n. 5.

tles, especially that to the Romans, and St. Peter's first epistle are the true kernel and marrow of all the books. They ought properly to be the foremost books, and it would be advisable for every Christian to read them first and most, and by daily reading to make them as much his own as his daily bread. For in them you do not find many works and miracles of Christ described, but you do find depicted in masterly fashion how faith in Christ overcomes sin, death, and hell, and gives life, righteousness, and salvation. This is the real nature of the gospel, as you have heard.

If I had to do without one or the other—either the works or the preaching of Christ—I would rather do without the works than without his preaching. For the works do not help me, but his words give life, as he himself says [John 6:63]. Now John writes very little about the works of Christ, but very much about his preaching, while the other evangelists write much about his works and little about his preaching. Therefore John's Gospel is the one, fine, true, and chief gospel, and is far, far to be preferred over the other three and placed high above them. So, too, the epistles of St. Paul and St. Peter far surpass the other three gospels, Matthew, Mark, and Luke.

In a word St. John's Gospel and his first epistle, St. Paul's epistles, especially Romans, Galatians, and Ephesians, and St. Peter's first epistle are the books that show you Christ and teach you all that is necessary and salvatory for you to know, even if you were never to see or hear any other book or doctrine. Therefore St. James' epistle is really an epistle of straw,[11] compared to these others, for it has nothing of the nature of the gospel about it. But more of this in the other prefaces.][12]

---

[11] On the term "straw" cf. Luther's reference on p. 395 to I Cor. 3:12. Luther's sharp expression may have been in part a reaction against Karlstadt's excessive praise of the book of James. Cf. *WA*, DB 6, 537, n. 10, 6-34, and the literature there listed.

[12] See especially the Preface to James in this volume, pp. 395-398. Cf. also Luther's negative estimate of the book of James already in his 1520 *Babylonian Captivity of the Church* in LW 36, 118, and in his *Resolutiones* of 1519 in WA 2, 425.

9.

PREFACES TO THE OLD TESTAMENT

Preface to the Old Testament[1]

1545 (1523)

There are some who have little regard for the Old Testament. They think of it as a book that was given to the Jewish people only and is now out of date, containing only stories of past times. They think they have enough in the New Testament and assert that only a spiritual sense[2] is to be sought in the Old Testament. Origen,[3] Jerome,[4] and many other distinguished people have held this view. But Christ says in John 5[:39], "Search the Scriptures, for it is they that bear witness to me." St. Paul bids Timothy attend to the reading of the Scriptures [I Tim. 4:13], and in Romans 1[:2] he declares that the gospel was promised by God in the Scriptures, while in I Corinthians 15[5] he says that in accordance with the Scriptures Christ came of the seed of David, died, and was raised from the dead. St. Peter, too, points us back, more than once, to the Scriptures.

They do this in order to teach us that the Scriptures of the Old

---

[1] Luther finished translating the five books of Moses by the middle of December, 1522. They were published as a group by Melchior Lotther in Wittenberg by early summer, 1523, and revised six times by 1528. In contradistinction to the New Testament, the Psalter, Jesus Sirach, and the Books of Solomon, the Pentateuch was never published in separate edition after its incorporation into the complete Bible of 1534 (WA, DB 8, xix-xxi). This preface, composed after completion of the translation of the Pentateuch and first published with the Pentateuch in 1523, was retained almost intact in the 1534 and later versions of the complete Bible. It has reference, of course, primarily to the first five books of the Old Testament (WA, DB 8, xli). Our translation is based on the 1545 text as given in WA, DB 8, 11-31. See pp. 227-232 for the general introduction to all of Luther's biblical prefaces.

[2] *Geistliche sinn.* The allegorical sense of Scripture was differentiated from its literal sense and its moral sense by the early exegetes.

[3] Origen (*ca.* 185-*ca.* 254) at Alexandria was the principal exponent of allegorical exegesis.

[4] Jerome (*ca.* 342-420) sought to combine the literal and the allegorical methods of interpretation, giving somewhat greater emphasis to the former than to the latter.

[5] I Cor. 15:3-4; cf. Rom. 1:3 and II Tim. 2:8.

Testament are not to be despised, but diligently read. For they themselves base the New Testament upon them mightily, proving it by the Old Testament and appealing to it, as St. Luke also writes in Acts 17[:11], saying that they at Thessalonica examined the Scriptures daily to see if these things were so that Paul was teaching. The ground and proof of the New Testament is surely not to be despised, and therefore the Old Testament is to be highly regarded. And what is the New Testament but a public preaching and proclamation of Christ, set forth through the sayings of the Old Testament and fulfilled through Christ?

In order that those who are not more familiar with it may have instruction and guidance for reading the Old Testament with profit, I have prepared this preface to the best of the ability God has given me. I beg and really caution every pious Christian not to be offended by the simplicity of the language and stories frequently encountered there, but fully realize that, however simple they may seem, these are the very words, works, judgments, and deeds of the majesty, power, and wisdom of the most high God. For these are the Scriptures which make fools of all the wise and understanding, and are open only to the small and simple, as Christ says in Matthew 11[:25]. Therefore dismiss your own opinions and feelings, and think of the Scriptures as the loftiest and noblest of holy things, as the richest of mines which can never be sufficiently explored, in order that you may find that divine wisdom which God here lays before you in such simple guise as to quench all pride. Here you will find the swaddling cloths and the manger in which Christ lies, and to which the angel points the shepherds [Luke 2:12]. Simple and lowly are these swaddling cloths, but dear is the treasure, Christ, who lies in them.

Know, then, that the Old Testament is a book of laws, which teaches what men are to do and not to do—and in addition gives examples and stories of how these laws are kept or broken—just as the New Testament is gospel or book of grace,[6] and teaches where one is to get the power to fulfil the law. Now in the New Testament there are also given, along with the teaching about grace, many other teachings that are laws and commandments for the control of the flesh—since in this life the Spirit is not perfected and grace alone

---

[6]Cf. p. 113.

cannot rule. Similarly in the Old Testament too there are, beside the laws, certain promises and words of grace, by which the holy fathers and prophets under the law were kept, like us, in the faith of Christ. Nevertheless just as the chief teaching of the New Testament is really the proclamation of grace and peace through the forgiveness of sins in Christ, so the chief teaching of the Old Testament is really the teaching of laws, the showing up of sin, and the demanding of good. You should expect this in the Old Testament.

We come first to the books of Moses. In his first book [Genesis] Moses teaches how all creatures were created, and (as the chief cause for his writing) whence sin and death came, namely by Adam's fall, through the devil's wickedness. But immediately thereafter, before the coming of the law of Moses, he teaches whence help is to come for the driving out of sin and death, namely, not by the law or men's own works (since there was no law as yet), but by "the seed of the woman," Christ, promised to Adam and Abraham, in order that throughout the Scriptures from the beginning faith may be praised above all works and laws and merits. Genesis,[7] therefore, is made up almost entirely of illustrations of faith and unbelief, and of the fruits that faith and unbelief bear. It is an exceedingly evangelical book.

Afterward, in the second book [Exodus], when the world was now full and sunk in blindness so that men scarcely knew any longer what sin was or where death came from, God brings Moses forward with the law and selects a special people, in order to enlighten the world again through them, and by the law to reveal sin anew. He therefore organizes this people with all kinds of laws and separates it from all other peoples. He has them build a tent, and begins a form of worship. He appoints princes and officials, and provides his people splendidly with both laws and men, to rule them both in the body before the world and in the spirit before God.

The special topic of the third book [Leviticus] is the appointment of the priesthood, with the statutes and laws according to which the priests are to act and to teach the people. There we see that a priestly office is instituted only because of sin, to disclose sin to the people and to make atonement before God, so that its entire

---

[7]Cf. p. 135, n. 1.

function is to deal with sin and sinners. For this reason too no temporal wealth is given to the priests, neither are they commanded or permitted to rule men's bodies. Rather the only work assigned to them is to care for the people who are in sin.

In the fourth book [Numbers], after the laws have been given, the princes and priests instituted, the tent and form of worship set up, and everything that pertains to the people of God made ready, then the whole thing begins to function; a test is made as to how well the arrangement operates and how satisfactory it is. This is why this very book says so much about the disobedience of the people and the plagues that came upon them. And some of the laws are explained and the number of the laws increased. Indeed this is the way it always goes; laws are quickly given, but when they are to go into effect and become operative, they meet with nothing but hindrance; nothing goes as the law demands. This book is a notable example of how vacuous it is to make people righteous with laws; rather, as St. Paul says, laws cause only sin and wrath.[8]

In the fifth book [Deuteronomy], after the people have been punished because of their disobedience, and God has enticed them a little with grace, in order that by his kindness in giving them the two kingdoms[9] they might be moved to keep his law gladly and willingly, then Moses repeats the whole law. He repeats the story of all that has happened to the people (except for that which concerns the priesthood) and explains anew everything that belongs either to the bodily or to the spiritual governing of a people. Thus Moses, as a perfect lawgiver, fulfilled all the duties of his office.[10] He not only gave the law, but was there when men were to fulfil it. When things went wrong, he explained the law and re-established it. Yet this explanation in the fifth book really contains nothing else than faith toward God and love toward one's neighbor, for all God's laws come

---

[8] Cf. Rom. 5:20; 7:7-9; 4:15.
[9] Cf. p. 138 and *A New Preface to the Prophet Ezekiel*, 1545. *LW* 35, 289-290.
[10] Throughout this preface with but two exceptions we have rendered the German word *Amt* by its closest English equivalent, "office." We have done so for the sake of preserving the continuity in Luther's discussion of the law, even though *Amt* in various contexts is really susceptible of numerous more felicitous English renderings which may or may not be implied in the term "office," such as work, ministry, function, and even dispensation (the RSV term in II Cor. 3:7, which we have retained on p. 242). Cf. the use of the same term on p. 348, l. 19, in connection with the gospel as well as the law.

to that. Therefore, down to the twentieth chapter, Moses, in his explanation of the law, guards against everything that might destroy faith in God; and from there to the end of the book he guards against everything that hinders love.

It is to be observed in the first place that Moses provides so exactly for the organization of the people under laws as to leave human reason no room to choose a single work of its own or to invent its own form of worship. For Moses not only teaches fear, love, and trust toward God, but he also provides so many ways of outward worship—sacrifices, thanksgivings, fasts, mortifications, and the like —that no one needs to choose anything else. Besides he gives instructions for planting and tilling, marrying and fighting, governing children, servants, and households, buying and selling, borrowing and repaying, and for everything that is to be done both outwardly and inwardly. He goes so far that some of the prescriptions are to be regarded as foolish and useless.

Why, my friend, does God do that? In the end, because he has taken this people to be his own and has willed to be their God. For this reason he would so rule them that all their doings may surely be right in his eyes. For if anyone does anything for which God's word has not first given warrant, it counts for nothing before God and is labor lost. For in Deuteronomy 4[:2] and 12[:32] he forbids any addition to his laws; and in 12[:8] he says that they shall not do merely whatever is right in their own eyes. The Psalter, too, and all the prophets lament that the people are simply doing good works that they themselves have chosen to do and that were not commanded by God. He cannot and will not permit those who are his to undertake anything that he has not commanded, no matter how good it may be. For obedience, which depends on God's word, is of all works the noblest and best.

Since this life, however, cannot be without external forms of worship, God put before them all these forms and included them in his commandment in order that if they must or would do God any outward service, they might take one of these and not one they themselves had invented. They could then be doubly sure that their work was being done in obedience to God and his word. So they are prevented on every hand from following their own reason and free will in doing good and living aright. Room, place, time, person, work, and form are all more than adequately determined and prescribed, so that the people cannot complain and need not follow simply the example of alien worship.

In the second place it should be noted that the laws are of three kinds. Some speak only of temporal things, as do our imperial laws. These are established by God chiefly because of the wicked, that they may not do worse things. Such laws are for prevention rather than for instruction,[11] as when Moses commands that a wife be dismissed with a bill of divorce [Deut. 24:1] or that a husband can get rid of his wife with a "cereal offering of jealousy" [Num. 5:11-31] and take other wives besides. All these are temporal laws. There are some, however, that teach about the external worship of God, as has already been mentioned.

Over and above these two are the laws about faith and love. All other laws must and ought to be measured by faith and love. That is to say, the other laws are to be kept where their observance does not conflict with faith and love; but where they conflict with faith and love, they should be done away entirely. For this reason we read that David did not kill the murderer Joab [I Kings 2:5-6], even though he had twice deserved death [II Sam. 3:27; 20:10]. And in II Samuel 14[:11][12] David promises the woman of Tekoa that her son shall not die for having slain his brother. Nor did David kill Absalom [II Sam. 14:21-24]. Moreover David himself ate of the holy bread of the priests, I Samuel 21[:6]. And Tamar thought the king might give her in marriage to her stepbrother, Amnon [II Sam. 13:13]. From these and similar incidents one sees plainly that the kings, priests, and heads of the people often transgressed the laws boldly, at the demand of faith and love. Therefore faith and love are always to be mistresses of the law and to have all laws in their power. For since all laws aim at faith and love, none of them can be valid, or be a law, if it conflicts with faith or love.

Even to the present day, the Jews are greatly in error when they hold so strictly and stubbornly to certain laws of Moses. They

---

[11] *Nur Wehrgesetz, mehr denn Leregesetz.*

[12] Where Luther cites correctly the Vulgate, in which the four books of I and II Samuel and I and II Kings were numbered as I, II, III, and IV Kings, we have given the corresponding RSV reference.

would rather let love and peace be destroyed than eat and drink with us, or do things of that kind. They do not properly regard the intention of the law; but to understand this is essential for all who live under laws, not for the Jews alone. Christ also says so in Matthew 12,[13] that one might break the sabbath if an ox had fallen into a pit, and might rescue it. Now that was only a temporal necessity and injury. How much more ought one boldly to break all kinds of laws when bodily necessity demands it, provided that nothing is done against faith and love. Christ says that David did this very thing when he ate the holy bread, Mark 3[2:25-26].

But why does Moses mix up his laws in such a disordered way? Why does he not put the temporal laws together in one group and the spiritual laws in another and the laws of faith and love in still another? Moreover he sometimes repeats a law so often and reiterates the same words so many times that it becomes tedious to read it or listen to it. The answer is that Moses writes as the situation demands, so that his book is a picture and illustration of governing and of living. For this is the way it happens in a dynamic situation: now this work has to be done and now that. No man can so arrange his life (if he is to act in a godly way) that on this day he uses only spiritual laws and on that day only temporal. Rather God governs all the laws mixed together—like the stars in the heavens and the flowers in the fields—in such a way that at every hour a man must be ready for anything, and do whatever the situation requires. In like manner the writing of Moses represents a heterogeneous mixture.

That Moses is so insistent and often repeats the same thing shows also the nature of his office. For one who is to rule a people-with-laws [*Gesetzuolck*] must constantly admonish, constantly drive, and knock himself out struggling with the people as [he would] with asses. For no work of law is done gladly and willingly; it is all forced and compelled. Now since Moses is a lawgiver, he has to show by his insistence that the work of the law is a forced work. He has to wear the people down, until this insistence makes them not only recognize their illness and their dislike for God's law, but also long for grace,[14] as we shall show.

---

[13] Matt. 12:11; cf. Luke 14:5.
[14] Cf. Luther's *Brief Explanation of the Ten Commandments, The Creed, and The Lord's Prayer. PE* 2, 354-355.

In the third place the true intention of Moses is through the law to reveal sin and put to shame all presumption as to human ability. For this reason St. Paul, in Galatians 2[:17], calls Moses "an agent of sin," and his office "a dispensation of death," II Corinthians 3[:7]. In Romans 3[:20] and 7[:7] he says, "Through the law comes nothing more than knowledge of sin"; and in Romans 3[:20], "By works of the law no one becomes righteous before God." For by the law Moses can do no more than tell what men ought to do and not do. However he does not provide the strength and ability for such doing and not doing, and thus lets us stick in sin. When we then stick in sin, death presses instantly upon us as vengeance and punishment for sin. For this reason St. Paul calls sin "the sting of death" [I Cor. 15:56], because it is by sin that death has all its right and power over us. But if there were no law, there would be no sin.[15] Therefore it is all the fault of Moses, who by the law precipitates and stirs up sin; and then upon sin death follows with a vengeance. Rightly, then, does St. Paul call the office of Moses a dispensation of sin and death [II Cor. 3:7], for by his lawgiving he brings upon us nothing but sin and death.

Nevertheless this office of sin and death is good and very necessary. For where there is no law of God, there all human reason is so blind that it cannot recognize sin. For human reason does not know that unbelief and despair of God is sin. Indeed it knows nothing about man's duty to believe and trust in God. Hardened in its blindness, it goes its way and never feels this sin at all. Meanwhile it does some works that would otherwise be good, and it leads an outwardly respectable life. Then it thinks it stands well and the matter has been satisfactorily handled; we see this in the heathen and the hypocrites, when their life is at its best. Besides reason does not know either that the evil inclination of the flesh, and hatred of enemies, is sin. Because it observes and feels that all men are so inclined, it holds rather that these things are natural and right, and thinks it is enough merely to guard against the outward acts. So it goes its way, regarding its illness as strength, its sin as virtue, its evil as good; and never getting anywhere.

See, then! Moses' office is essential for driving away this blindness and hardened presumption. Now he cannot drive them away

---

[15] Cf. Rom. 4:15.

unless he reveals them and makes them known. He does this by the law, when he teaches that men ought to fear, trust, believe, and love God; and that, besides, they ought to have or bear no evil desire or hatred for any man. When human nature, then, catches on to this, it must be frightened, for it certainly finds neither trust nor faith, neither fear nor love to God, and neither love nor purity toward one's neighbor. Human nature finds rather only unbelief, doubt, contempt, and hatred to God; and toward one's neighbor only evil will and evil desire. But when human nature finds these things, then death is instantly before its eyes, ready to devour such a sinner and to swallow him up in hell.

See, this is what it means for sin to bring death upon us and kill us. This is what it means for the law to stir up sin and set it before our eyes, driving all our presumption into despondency and trembling and despair, so that a man can do no more than cry with the prophets, "I am rejected by God," or, as we say in German, "The devil has me; I can never be saved." This is to be really cast into hell. This is what St. Paul means by those short words in I Corinthians 15[:56], "The sting of death is sin, and the power of sin is the law." It is as if he were saying, "Death stings and slays us because of the sin that is found in us, guilty of death; sin, however, is found in us and gives us so mightily to death because of the law which reveals sin to us and teaches us to recognize it, where before we did not know it and felt secure."

Notice with what power Moses conducts and performs this office of his. For in order to put human nature to the utmost shame, he not only gives laws like the Ten Commandments that speak of natural and true sins, but he also makes sins of things that are in their nature not sins. Moses thus forces and presses sins upon them in heaps. For unbelief and evil desire are in their nature sins, and worthy of death. But to eat leavened bread at the Passover [Exodus 12–13] and to eat an unclean animal [Leviticus 11, Deuteronomy 14] or make a mark on the body [Lev. 19:28, Deut. 14:1], and all those things that the Levitical priesthood deals with as sin—these are not in their nature sinful and evil. Rather they became sins only because they are forbidden by the law. This law can be done away. The Ten Commandments, however, cannot be done away, for here there really is sin, even if there were no commandments, or if they were not known—just as the unbelief of the heathen is sin, even though they do not know or think that it is sin.

Therefore we see that these many laws of Moses were given not only to prevent anyone from choosing ways of his own for doing good and living aright, as was said above,[16] but rather that sins might simply become numerous and be heaped up beyond measure. The purpose was to burden the conscience so that the hardened blindness would have to recognize itself, and feel its own inability and nothingness in the achieving of good. Such blindness must be thus compelled and forced by the law to seek something beyond the law and its own ability, namely, the grace of God promised in the Christ who was to come. Every law of God is good and right [Rom. 7:7-16], even if it only bids men to carry dung or to gather straw. Accordingly, whoever does not keep this good law—or keeps it unwillingly—cannot be righteous or good in his heart. But human nature cannot keep it otherwise than unwillingly. It must therefore, through this good law of God, recognize and feel its wickedness, and sigh and long for the aid of divine grace in Christ.

For this reason then, when Christ comes the law ceases, especially the Levitical law which, as has been said, makes sins of things that in their nature are not sins. The Ten Commandments also cease, not in the sense that they are no longer to be kept or fulfilled, but in the sense that the office of Moses in them ceases; it no longer increases sin [Rom. 5:20] by the Ten Commandments, and sin is no longer the sting of death [I Cor. 15:56]. For through Christ sin is forgiven, God is reconciled, and man's heart has begun to feel kindly toward the law.[17] The office of Moses can no longer rebuke the heart and make it to be sin for not having kept the commandments and for being guilty of death, as it did prior to grace, before Christ came.

St. Paul teaches this in II Corinthians 3[:7-14], where he says that the splendor in the face of Moses is taken away, because of the glory in the face of Jesus Christ. That is, the office of Moses, which makes us to be sin and shame with the glare of the knowledge of

---

[16]Cf. pp. 122-123.

[17] Separate editions of the Pentateuch prior to the 1534 complete Bible here read, "For through the grace of Christ the heart has now become good, loving the law and satisfying it." WA, DB 8, 24, n. 25/26.

our wickedness and nothingness, no longer causes us pain and no longer terrifies us with death. For we now have the glory in the face of Christ [II Cor. 4:6]. This is the office of grace, whereby we know Christ, by whose righteousness, life, and strength we fulfil the law and overcome death and hell. Thus it was that the three apostles who saw Moses and Elijah on Mount Tabor were not afraid of them, because of the tender glory in the face of Christ [Luke 9:32]. Yet in Exodus 34[:29-35], where Christ was not present, the children of Israel could not endure the splendor and brightness in the face of Moses, so that he had to put a veil over it.

For the law has three kinds of pupils. The first are those who hear the law and despise it, and who lead an impious life without fear. To these the law does not come. They are represented by the calf worshipers in the wilderness, on whose account Moses broke the tables of the law [Exod. 32:19]. To them he did not bring the law.

The second kind are those who attempt to fulfil the law by their own power, without grace. They are represented by the people who could not look at the face of Moses when he brought the tables of the law a second time [Exod. 34:34-35]. The law comes to them but they cannot endure it. They therefore put a veil over it and lead a life of hypocrisy, doing outward works of the law. Yet the law makes it all to be sin where the veil is taken off. For the law shows that our ability counts for nothing without Christ's grace.

The third kind of pupils are those who see Moses clearly, without a veil. These are they who understand the intention of the law and how it demands impossible things. There sin comes to power, there death is mighty, there Goliath's spear is like a weaver's beam and its point[18] weighs six hundred shekels of brass, so that all the children of Israel flee before him unless the one and only David—Christ our Lord—saves us from all this [I Sam. 17:7, 24, 32]. For if Christ's glory did not come alongside this splendor of Moses, no one could bear the brightness of the law, the terror of sin and death. These pupils fall away from all works and presumption and learn from the law nothing else except to recognize sin and to yearn for

---

[18] *Stachel*, meaning a sharp point such as the head of a spear, has additional overtones in this context, for it was also the word Luther had used in I Cor. 15:56 to speak of the "sting" of death (cf. p. 243). WA, DB 7, 134.

Christ. This is the true office of Moses and the very nature of the law.

So Moses himself has told us that his office and teaching should endure until Christ, and then cease, when he says in Deuteronomy 18[:15-19], "The Lord your God will raise up for you a prophet like me from among your brethren—him shall you heed," etc. This is the noblest saying in all of Moses, indeed the very heart of it all. The apostles appealed to it and made great use of it to strengthen the gospel and to abolish the law [Acts 3:22; 7:37]. All the prophets, as well, drew heavily upon it. For since God here promises another Moses whom they are to hear, it follows of necessity that this other one would teach something different from Moses; and Moses gives up his power and yields to him, so that men will listen to him. This [coming] prophet cannot, then, teach the law, for Moses has done that to perfection; for the law's sake there would be no need to raise up another prophet. Therefore this word was surely spoken concerning Christ and the teaching of grace.

For this reason also, St. Paul calls the law of Moses "the old testament" [II Cor. 3:14], and Christ does the same when he institutes "the new testament" [I Cor. 11:25].[19] It is a testament because in it God promised and bequeathed to the people of Israel the land of Canaan, if they would keep it. He gave it to them too, and it was confirmed by the death and blood of sheep and goats. But since this testament did not stand upon God's grace, but upon men's works, it had to become obsolete and cease, and the promised land had to be lost again—because the law cannot be fulfilled by works. And another testament had to come which would not become obsolete, which would not stand upon our deeds either, but upon God's words and works, so that it might endure for ever. Therefore it is confirmed by the death and blood of an eternal Person, and an eternal land is promised and given.[20]

Let this be enough about the books and office of Moses. What, then, are the other books, the prophets and the histories? I answer: They are nothing else than what Moses is. For they all propagate the office of Moses; they guard against the false prophets, that they

---

[19] Cf. Heb. 8:13: "In speaking of a new covenant he treats the first as obsolete." In Luther's Bible, as in the Vulgate, the adjective "new" appeared also in the synoptic accounts of the Last Supper, Matt. 26:28, Mark 14:24, and Luke 22:20.
[20] Cf. Heb. 9:11-12.

may not lead the people to works, but allow them to remain in the true office of Moses, the knowledge of the law. They hold fast to this purpose of keeping the people conscious of their own impotence through a right understanding of the law, and thus driving them to Christ, as Moses does. For this reason they also explicate further what Moses says of Christ, and furnish two kinds of examples, of those who have Moses right and of those who do not, and also of the punishments and rewards that come to both. Thus the prophets are nothing else than administrators[21] and witnesses of Moses and his office, bringing everyone to Christ through the law.

In conclusion I ought also to indicate the spiritual meaning[22] presented to us by the Levitical law and priesthood of Moses. But there is too much of this to write; it requires space and time and should be expounded with the living voice. For Moses is, indeed, a well of all wisdom and understanding, out of which has sprung all that the prophets knew and said. Moreover even the New Testament flows out of it and is grounded in it, as we have heard[23] It is my duty, however, to give at least some little clue[24] to those who have the grace and understanding to pursue the matter further.

If you would interpret well and confidently, set Christ before you, for he is the man to whom it all applies, every bit of it. Make the high priest Aaron, then, to be nobody but Christ alone, as does the Epistle to the Hebrews [5:4-5], which is sufficient, all by itself, to interpret all the figures of Moses. Likewise, as the same epistle announces [Hebrews 9–10], it is certain that Christ himself is the sacrifice—indeed even the altar [Heb. 13:10]—who sacrificed himself with his own blood. Now whereas the sacrifice performed by the Levitical high priest took away only the artificial sins,[25] which in their nature were not sins, so our high priest, Christ, by his own sacrifice and blood, has taken away the true sin, that which in its very nature is sin. He has gone in once for all through the curtain to God to make atonement for us [Heb. 9:12]. Thus you should

---

[21] *Handhaber* has the sense of uphold, support, or defend as well as of perform or execute. WA, DB 8, 29, n. 22; cf. Grimm, *Deutsches Wörterbuch*, IV, 393-396.

[22] *Geistliche Deutung;* cf. p. 235, n. 2.

[23] Cf. p. 118.

[24] *Grifflin* means a trick, device, or stratagem. Grimm, *Deutsches Wörterbuch*, IV, 312; cf. WA, DB 8, 29, n. 30.

[25] *Die gemachten sunde.* See 126-127.

apply to Christ personally, and to no one else, all that is written about the high priest.

The high priest's sons, however, who are engaged in the daily sacrifice, you should interpret to mean ourselves. Here on earth, in the body, we Christians live in the presence of our father Christ, who is sitting in heaven; we have not yet passed through to him except spiritually, by faith. Their office of slaughter and sacrifice signifies nothing else than the preaching of the gospel, by which the old man is slain and offered to God, burned and consumed by the fire of love, in the Holy Spirit. This sacrifice smells really good before God; that is, it produces a conscience that is good, pure, and secure before God. This is the interpretation that St. Paul makes in Romans 12[:1] when he teaches that we are to offer our bodies to God as a living, holy, and acceptable sacrifice. This is what we do (as has been said) by the constant exercise of the gospel both in preaching and in believing.

Let this suffice for the present as a brief suggestion for seeking Christ and the gospel in the Old Testament.[26]

Whoever reads this Bible should also know that I have been careful to write the name of God which the Jews call "Tetragrammaton"[27] in capital letters thus, LORD [*HERR*], and the other name which they call *Adonai*[28] only half in capital letters thus, LOrd [*HErr*].[29] For among all the names of God, these two alone are

---

[26] In editions of the complete Bible from 1534 on, the preface ended at this point. The paragraphs which follow were found only in the earlier editions.

[27] Tetragrammaton, literally "four letters," is the technical term for the four-consonant Hebrew word for the name God, which is now commonly thought to be represented in English by the word "Yahweh." When the Hebrews came to this name in speaking or reading they avoided uttering it because of its sacred character, pronouncing instead the word Adonai (Lord) unless (as at Gen. 15:2) it immediately followed the word "Adonai" in the text, in which case "Elohim" (God) was read. In written Hebrew texts the vowel-points of Adonai were given to the consonants of the Tetragrammaton with the resultant rendering in English, "Jehovah."

[28] Adonai literally means "my lord," but by usage it was in effect a proper name.

[29] While the Hebrew *YHWH* always had reference to God alone, *ADN* could mean either the divine Lord, or a lord or ruler who was not divine. Luther distinguished clearly between the two words by rendering *HERR* for *YHWH* and either *HErr* or *herr* for *ADN* (cf. *LW* 12, 99-101 and *LW* 13, 230). The distinction between the divine and human within *ADN*, however, was not consistently maintained in translation by the use of *HErr* and *herr* (cf. *WA*, DB 6, 538-539, note on Matt. 1:20). Cf. Luther's *HERR-HERR* in Jer. 23:5-6 with the RSV LORD-LORD, Luther's *HERR-herr* in Gen. 24:12 with the RSV LORD-master,

applied in the Scriptures to the real, true God; while the others are often ascribed to angels and saints. I have done this in order that readers can thereby draw the strong conclusion that Christ is true God. For Jeremiah 23[:6] calls him LORD, saying, "He will be called: 'The LORD, our righteousness.' " The same thing is to be found in other passages. Herewith I commend all my readers to Christ and ask that they help me get from God the power to carry this work through to a profitable end. For I freely admit that I have undertaken too much, especially in trying to put the Old Testament into German.[30] The Hebrew language, sad to say, has gone down so far that even the Jews know little enough about it, and their glosses and interpretations (which I have tested[31]) are not to be relied upon. I think that if the Bible is to come up again, we Christians are the ones who must do the work, for we have the understanding of Christ without which even the knowledge of the language is nothing. Because they were without it, the translators of old, even Jerome,[32] made mistakes in many passages. Though I cannot boast of having achieved perfection, nevertheless, I venture to say that this German Bible is clearer and more accurate at many points than the Latin. So it is true that if the printers do not, as usual, spoil it with their carelessness, the German language certainly has here a better Bible than the Latin language—and the readers will bear me out in this.

And now, of course, the mud will stick to the wheel,[33] and there will be no one so stupid that he will not try to be my master in this work, and criticize me here and there. Let them go to it. I figured from the very beginning that I would find ten thousand to criticize my work before I found one who would accomplish one-twentieth

---

and Luther's *HERR-HErr* in Ps. 110:1 (1545 version only, the earlier versions being both *HERR-HERR* and *HERR-herr*, *WA*, DB 10^I, 476-477) with the RSV Lord-lord. In Luther's Matt. 22:44 rendering of the first "Lord" of the Psalm quotation he went from *Gott* in 1522 through *Herr* and *HErr* to *HERR* in 1539 and later editions (*WA*, DB 6, 100, note). See Gen. 15:2, 8 where Luther translates *ADN YHWH* as *HErr HERR* (*WA*, DB 8, 73). Cf. also *WA*, DB 10^{II}, xxiii, n. 26.

[30] Cf. Luther's statement, "It was necessary for me to undertake the translation of the Bible, otherwise I would have died under the mistaken impression that I was a learned man." *WA* 10^{II}, 60, ll. 13-15; cf. also *WA*, Br 2, 423, ll. 48-50.

[31] Cf. Luther's *Defense of the Translation of the Psalms*, 1531. *LW* 35, 209-223.

[32] Cf. p. 104, n. 1.

[33] Cf. Wander (ed.), *Sprichwörter-Lexikon*, II, 1556, "Koth," Nos. 4 and 16.

of what I have done. I, too, would like to be very learned and give brilliant proof of what I know by criticizing St. Jerome's Latin Bible; but he in turn could also defy me to do what he has done. Now if anyone is so much more learned than I, let him undertake to translate the whole Bible into German, and then tell me what he can do.[34] If he does it better, why should he not be preferred to me? I thought I was well educated—and I know that by the grace of God I am more learned than all the sophists in the universities—but now I see that I cannot handle even my own native German tongue. Nor have I read, up to this time, a book or letter which contained the right kind of German. Besides no one pays any attention to speaking real German. This is especially true of the people in the chancelleries, as well as those patchwork preachers and wretched writers.[35] They think they have the right to change the German language and to invent new words for us every day, such as *behertzigen,*[36] *behendigen,*[37] *erprieslich,*[38] *erschieslich,*[39] and the like. Yes, my dear fellow, there are [and this is] also *bethoret* and *ernarret.*[40]

In a word, if all of us were to work together, we would have plenty to do in bringing the Bible to light, one working with the meaning, the other with the language. For I too have not worked at this alone,[41] but have used the services of anyone whom I could

---

[34]Cf. *On Translating: an Open Letter,* 1530. *LW* 35, 183-184 and 221-223.

[35] *Lumpen prediger und puppen schreyber.*

[36] Deriving largely from Swabian origin, the term had been used frequently by Emser. Friedrich Kluge, *Etymologisches Wörterbuch der deutschen Sprache* (17th ed.; Berlin: de Gruyter, 1957), p. 61.

[37] In a letter from Luther and Karlstadt to Duke Frederick of Saxony dated August 18, 1519, Luther—or perhaps his co-author—had himself used the term *Behendigkeit.* *WA* Br 1, 477, 1. 410. The use of *behendigen* is documented as early as 1484 in Wetterau. Moritz Heyne, *Deutsches Wörterbuch* (3 vols.; Leipzig: Hirzel, 1890-1895), I, 324.

[38] Meaning originally to spring forth or sprout, *erspriessen* early came to be used in New High German in the sense of "be useful, profitable, advantageous." The adjective too was given this derived meaning from about the beginning of the sixteenth century. Kluge, *op. cit.,* p. 173.

[39] Luther apparently was unaware that the intransitive verb *erschiessen* was used rather extensively in a sense synonymous with that of *erspriessen.* Grimm, *Deutsches Wörterbuch,* III, 962.

[40] *Bethören* means to make a fool of, in the sense of infatuate, seduce, or deceive. *Ernarren* means to play the fool, in the sense of be silly, astonish, or amaze. The construction of Luther's sentence conveys a double meaning: not only that these words too are recent innovations, but also that all such innovating is sheer folly.

[41]See the Introduction, *LW* 35, 229.

get. Therefore I ask everyone to desist from abuse and leave the poor people undisturbed, and help me, if he can. If he will not do that, let him take up the Bible himself and make a translation of his own. Those who do nothing but abuse and bite and claw are actually not honest and upright enough to really want a pure Bible, since they know that they cannot produce it. They would prefer to be Master Know-it-all[42] in a field not their own, though in their own field they have never even been pupils.

May God bring to completion his work that he began [Phil. 1:6]. Amen.

— Luther discusses the relevancy of the O.T.

— 1st He summarizes Gen → Deu. Pentateuch

— mostly he stresses the role of

— Law
— Moses
— Grace
— Christ

— 3rdly he in retrospect (unapologetically) defends his German translation.

10.

HOW CHRISTIANS SHOULD REGARD MOSES

Dear friends, you have often heard that there has never been a public sermon from heaven except twice. Apart from them God has spoken many times through and with men on earth, as in the case of the holy patriarchs Adam, Noah, Abraham, Isaac, Jacob, and others, down to Moses. But in none of these cases did he speak with such glorious splendor, visible reality, or public cry and exclamation as he did on those two occasions. Rather God illuminated their heart within and spoke through their mouth, as Luke indicates in the first chapter of his gospel where he says, "As he spoke by the mouth of his holy prophets from of old" [Luke 1:70].

Now the first sermon is in Exodus[1] 19 and 20; by it God caused himself to be heard from heaven with great splendor and might. For the people of Israel heard the trumpets and the voice of God himself.

In the second place God delivered a public sermon through the Holy Spirit on Pentecost [Acts 2:2-4]. On that occasion the Holy Spirit came with great splendor and visible impressiveness, such that there came from heaven the sudden rushing of a mighty wind, and it filled the entire house where the apostles were sitting. And there appeared to them tongues as of fire, distributed and resting on each of them. And they were all filled with the Holy Spirit and began to preach and speak in other tongues. This happened with great spendor and glorious might, so that thereafter the apostles preached so powerfully that the sermons which we hear in the world today are hardly a shadow compared to theirs, so far as the visible splendor and substance of their sermons is concerned. For the apostles spoke in all sorts of languages, performed great miracles, etc. Yet through our preachers today the Holy Spirit does not cause

---

[1] Where Luther refers to a specific book of the Pentateuch by number (e.g., "The Second Book of Moses") we have given the corresponding English title.

himself to be either heard or seen; nothing is coming down openly from heaven. This is why I have said that there are only two such special and public sermons which have been seen and heard from heaven. To be sure, God spoke also to Christ from heaven, when he was baptized in the Jordan [Matt. 3:17], and [at the Transfiguration] on Mount Tabor [Matt. 17:5]. However none of this took place in the presence of the general public.

God wanted to send that second sermon into the world, for it had earlier been announced by the mouth and in the books of the holy prophets. He will no longer speak that way publicly through sermons. Instead, in the third place, he will come in person with divine glory, so that all creatures will tremble and quake before him [Luke 21:25-27]; and then he will no longer preach to them, but they will see and handle him himself [Luke 24:39].

Now the first sermon, and doctrine, is the law of God. The second is the gospel. These two sermons are not the same. Therefore we must have a good grasp of the matter in order to know how to differentiate between them. We must know what the law is, and what the gospel is. The law commands and requires us to do certain things. The law is thus directed solely to our behavior and consists in making requirements. For God speaks through the law, saying, "Do this, avoid that, this is what I expect of you." The gospel, however, does not preach what we are to do or to avoid. It sets up no requirements but reverses the approach of the law, does the very opposite, and says, "This is what God has done for you; he has let his Son be made flesh for you, has let him be put to death for your sake." So, then, there are two kinds of doctrine and two kinds of works, those of God and those of men. Just as we and God are separated from one another, so also these two doctrines are widely separated from one another. For the gospel teaches exclusively what has been given us by God, and not—as in the case of the law—what we are to do and give to God.

We now want to see how this first sermon sounded forth and with what splendor God gave the law on Mount Sinai. He selected the place where he wanted to be seen and heard. Not that God actually spoke, for he has no mouth, tongue, teeth, or lips as we do. But he who created and formed the mouth of all men [Exod. 4:11] can also make speech and the voice. For no one would be able to speak a single word unless God first gave it, as the prophet says, "It would be impossible to speak except God first put it in our mouth."[2] Language, speech, and voice are thus gifts of God like any other gifts, such as the fruit on the trees. Now he who fashioned the mouth and put speech in it can also make and use speech even though there is no mouth present. Now the words which are here written were spoken through an angel. This is not to say that only one angel was there, for there was a great multitude there serving God and preaching to the people of Israel at Mount Sinai. The angel, however, who spoke here and did the talking, spoke just as if God himself were speaking and saying, "I am your God, who brought you out of the land of Egypt," etc. [Exod. 20:1], as if Peter or Paul were speaking in God's stead and saying, "I am your God," etc. In his letter to the Galatians [3:19], Paul says that the law was ordained by angels. That is, angels were assigned, in God's behalf, to give the law of God; and Moses, as an intermediary, received it from the angels. I say this so that you might know who gave the law. He did this to them, however, because he wanted thereby to compel, burden, and press the Jews.

What kind of a voice that was, you may well imagine. It was a voice like the voice of a man, such that it was actually heard. The syllables and letters thus made sounds which the physical ear was able to pick up. But it was a bold, glorious, and great voice. As told in Deuteronomy 4[:12], the people heard the voice, but saw no one. They heard a powerful voice, for he spoke in a powerful voice, as if in the dark we should hear a voice from a high tower or roof top, and could see no one but only hear the strong voice of a man. And this is why it is called the voice of God, because it was above a human voice.

Now you will hear how God used this voice in order to arouse his people and make them brave. For he intended to· institute the tangible [*eusserliche*] and spiritual government. It was previously stated how, on the advice of Jethro, his father-in-law, Moses had

---

[2] Cf. Num. 22:38.

established the temporal government and appointed rulers and judges [Exod. 18:13-26]. Beyond that there is yet a spiritual kingdom in which Christ rules in the hearts of men; this kingdom we cannot see, because it consists only in faith and will continue until the Last Day.

These are two kingdoms:[3] the temporal, which governs with the sword and is visible; and the spiritual, which governs solely with grace and with the forgiveness of sins. Between these two kingdoms still another has been placed in the middle, half spiritual and half temporal. It is constituted by the Jews, with commandments and outward ceremonies which prescribe their conduct toward God and men.

The law of Moses binds only the Jews and not the Gentiles

Here the law of Moses has its place. It is no longer binding on us because it was given only to the people of Israel. And Israel accepted this law for itself and its descendants, while the Gentiles were excluded. To be sure, the Gentiles have certain laws in common with the Jews, such as these: there is one God, no one is to do wrong to another, no one is to commit adultery or murder or steal, and others like them. This is written by nature into their hearts; they did not hear it straight from heaven as the Jews did. This is why this entire text does not pertain to the Gentiles. I say this on account of the enthusiasts. For you see and hear how they read Moses, extol him, and bring up the way he ruled the people with commandments. They try to be clever, and think they know something more than is presented in the gospel; so they minimize faith, contrive something new, and boastfully claim that it comes from the Old Testament. They desire to govern people according to the letter of the law of Moses, as if no one had ever read it before.

But we will not have this sort of thing. We would rather not preach again for the rest of our life than to let Moses return and to let Christ be torn out of our hearts. We will not have Moses as ruler or lawgiver any longer. Indeed God himself will not have it either. Moses was an intermediary solely for the Jewish people. It was to

---

[3]On the two kingdoms cf. *A New Preface to the Prophet Ezekiel*, 1545. LW 35, 289-290.

them that he gave the law. We must therefore silence the mouths of those factious spirits who say, "Thus says Moses," etc. Here you simply reply: Moses has nothing to do with us. If I were to accept Moses in one commandment, I would have to accept the entire Moses. Thus the consequence would be that if I accept Moses as master, then I must have myself circumcised,[4] wash my clothes in the Jewish way, eat and drink and dress thus and so, and observe all that stuff. So, then, we will neither observe nor accept Moses. Moses is dead. His rule ended when Christ came. He is of no further service.

That Moses does not bind the Gentiles can be proved[5] from Exodus 20[:1], where God himself speaks, "I am the Lord your God, who brought you out of the land of Egypt, out of the house of bondage." This text makes it clear that even the Ten Commandments do not pertain to us. For God never led us out of Egypt, but only the Jews. The sectarian spirits want to saddle us with Moses and all the commandments. We will just skip that. We will regard Moses as a teacher, but we will not regard him as our lawgiver—unless he agrees with both the New Testament and the natural law. Therefore it is clear enough that Moses is the lawgiver of the Jews and not of the Gentiles. He has given the Jews a sign whereby they should lay hold of God, when they call upon him as the God who brought them out of Egypt. The Christians have a different sign, whereby they conceive of God as the One who gave his Son, etc.

Again one can prove it from the third commandment that Moses does not pertain to Gentiles and Christians. For Paul [Col. 2:16] and the New Testament [Matt. 12:1-12; John 5:16; 7:22-23; 9:14-16] abolish the sabbath, to show us that the sabbath was given to the Jews alone, for whom it is a stern commandment. The prophets referred to it too, that the sabbath of the Jews would be abolished. For Isaiah says in the last chapter, "When the Savior comes, then such will be the time, one sabbath after the other, one month after

---

[4] In a letter to Chancellor Brück of Saxony dated January 13, 1524, Luther wrote that the people of Orlamünde, Karlstadt's parish, would probably circumcise themselves and be wholly Mosaic. *MA*³ 4, 402, n. 182.

[5] *Zwingen* probably means *zwingend beweisen* as *MA*³ 4, 402, n. 183, 4 suggests.

the other," etc.[6] This is as though he were trying to say, "It will be the sabbath every day, and the people will be such that they make no distinction between days. For in the New Testament the sabbath is annihilated as regards the crude external observance, for every day is a holy day," etc.

Now if anyone confronts you with Moses and his commandments, and wants to compel you to keep them, simply answer, "Go to the Jews with your Moses; I am no Jew. Do not entangle me with Moses. If I accept Moses in one respect (Paul tells the Galatians in chapter 5[:3]), then I am obligated to keep the entire law." For not one little period in Moses pertains to us.

Question:

Why then do you preach about Moses if he does not pertain to us?

Answer to the Question:

Three things are to be noted in Moses.

I want to keep Moses and not sweep him under the rug,[7] because I find three things in Moses.

In the first place I dismiss the commandments given to the people of Israel. They neither urge nor compel me. They are dead and gone, except insofar as I gladly and willingly accept something from Moses, as if I said, "This is how Moses ruled, and it seems fine to me, so I will follow him in this or that particular."

I would even be glad if [today's] lords ruled according to the example of Moses. If I were emperor, I would take from Moses a model for [my] statutes; not that Moses should be binding on me, but that I should be free to follow him in ruling as he ruled. For example, tithing is a very fine rule, because with the giving of the tenth all other taxes would be eliminated. For the ordinary man

---

[6] Our rendering of Isa. 66:23 is here based on the Douay version, as Luther's was on the Vulgate.

[7] *Unter den banck stecken* (literally, "put under the bench") is a proverbial expression meaning to put aside, hide, or forget some despicable thing. WA 51, 661 and 724, No. 468. Wander (ed.), *Sprichwörter-Lexikon* I, 229, *"Bank,"* No. 40. Cf. p. 253, n. 53.

it would also be easier to give a tenth than to pay rents and fees. Suppose I had ten cows; I would then give one. If I had only five, I would give nothing. If my fields were yielding only a little, I would give proportionately little; if much, I would give much. All of this would be in God's providence. But as things are now, I must pay the Gentile tax even if the hail should ruin my entire crop. If I owe a hundred gulden in taxes, I must pay it even though there may be nothing growing in the field. This is also the way the pope decrees and governs. But it would be better if things were so arranged that when I raise much, I give much; and when little, I give little.

Again in Moses it is also stipulated that no man should sell his field into a perpetual estate, but only up to the jubilee year.[8] When that year came, every man returned to the field or possessions which he had sold. In this way the possessions remained in the family relationship. There are also other extraordinarily fine rules in Moses which one should like to accept, use, and put into effect. Not that one should bind or be bound by them, but (as I said earlier) the emperor could here take an example for setting up a good government on the basis of Moses, just as the Romans conducted a good government, and just like the *Sachsenspiegel*[9] by which affairs are ordered in this land of ours. The Gentiles are not obligated to obey Moses. Moses is the *Sachsenspiegel* for the Jews. But if an example of good government were to be taken from Moses, one could adhere to it without obligation as long as one pleased, etc.

Again Moses says, "If a man dies without children, then his brother or closest relative should take the widow into his home and have her to wife, and thus raise up offspring for the deceased brother or relative. The first child thus born was credited to the deceased brother or relative" [Deut. 25:5-6]. So it came about that one man had many wives. Now this is also a very good rule.

When these factious spirits come, however, and say, "Moses has

---

[8] *Laut jar.* Cf. Lev. 25:8-55.
[9] This "Saxon code of law" was a thirteenth century compilation of the economic and social laws obtaining in and around Magdeburg and Halberstadt; it was influential in the codification of German law until the nineteenth century. The radical Reformers sometimes sought to replace it with the law of Moses or the Sermon on the Mount. Cf. *LW* 21, 90, n. 37 and *LW* 40, 98, n. 20.

commanded it," then simply drop Moses and reply, "I am not concerned about what Moses commands." "Yes," they say, "he has commanded that we should have one God, that we should trust and believe in him, that we should not swear by his name; that we should honor father and mother; not kill, steal, commit adultery; not bear false witness, and not covet [Exod. 20:3-17]; should we not keep these commandments?" You reply: Nature also has these laws. Nature provides that we should call upon God. The Gentiles attest to this fact. For there never was a Gentile who did not call upon his idols, even though these were not the true God. This also happened among the Jews, for they had their idols as did the Gentiles; only the Jews have received the law. The Gentiles have it written in their heart, and there is no distinction [Rom. 3:22]. As St. Paul also shows in Romans 2[:14-15], the Gentiles, who have no law, have the law written in their heart.

But just as the Jews fail, so also do the Gentiles. Therefore it is natural to honor God, not steal, not commit adultery, not bear false witness, not murder; and what Moses commands is nothing new. For what God has given the Jews from heaven, he has also written in the hearts of all men. Thus I keep the commandments which Moses has given, not because Moses gave commandment, but because they have been implanted in me by nature, and Moses agrees exactly with nature, etc.

But the other commandments of Moses, which are not [implanted in all men] by nature, the Gentiles do not hold. Nor do these pertain to the Gentiles, such as the tithe and others equally fine which I wish we had too. Now this is the first thing that I ought to see in Moses, namely, the commandments to which I am not bound except insofar as they are [implanted in everyone] by nature [and written in everyone's heart].[10]

The second thing to notice in Moses

In the second place I find something in Moses that I do not have from nature: the promises and pledges of God about Christ.

---

[10] The bracketed phrases in this paragraph are from the version given in the 1528 *Exposition of the Ten Commandments*. WA 16, 380, ll. 26, 31.

This is the best thing. It is something that is not written naturally into the heart, but comes from heaven. God has promised, for example, that his Son should be born in the flesh. This is what the gospel proclaims. It is not commandments. And it is the most important thing in Moses which pertains to us. The first thing, namely, the commandments, does not pertain to us. I read Moses because such excellent and comforting promises are there recorded, by which I can find strength for my weak faith. For things take place in the kingdom of Christ just as I read in Moses that they will; therein I find also my sure foundation.

In this manner, therefore, I should accept Moses, and not sweep him under the rug: first because he provides fine examples of laws, from which excerpts may be taken. Second, in Moses there are the promises of God which sustain faith. As it is written of Eve in Genesis 3[:15], "I will put enmity between you and the woman, and between your seed and her seed; he shall bruise your head," etc. Again Abraham was given this promise by God, speaking thus in Genesis [22:18], "In your descendants shall all the nations be blessed"; that is, through Christ the gospel is to arise.

Again in Deuteronomy 18[:15-16] Moses says, "The Lord your God will raise up for you a prophet like me from among you, from your brethren—him you shall heed; just as you desired of the Lord your God at Horeb on the day of the assembly," etc. Many are these texts in the Old Testament, which the holy apostles quoted and drew upon.

But our factious spirits go ahead and say of everything they find in Moses, "Here God is speaking, no one can deny it; therefore we must keep it." So then the rabble go to it. Whew! If God has said it, who then will say anything against it? Then they are really pressed hard like pigs at a trough. Our dear prophets have chattered thus into the minds of the people, "Dear people, God has ordered his people to beat Amalek to death" [Exod. 17:8-16; Deut. 25:17-19].[11] Misery and tribulation have come out of this sort of thing. The

---

[11] Thomas Münzer in a sermon of July, 1524, at Allstedt demanded that the princes wipe out all the godless, including godless rulers, priests, and monks. *MA*[8] 4, 402, n. 187, 9. Cf. *LW* 40, 47.

peasants have arisen,[12] not knowing the difference, and have been led into this error by those insane factious spirits.

Had there been educated preachers around, they could have stood up to the false prophets and stopped them, and said this to them, "Dear factious spirits, it is true that God commanded this of Moses and spoke thus to the people; but we are not this people. Land, God spoke also to Adam; but that does not make me Adam. God commanded Abraham to put his son to death [Gen. 22:2]; but that does not make me Abraham and obligate me to put my son to death. God spoke also with David. It is all God's word. But let God's word be what it may, I must pay attention and know to whom God's word is addressed. You are still a long way from being the people with whom God spoke." The false prophets say, "You are that people, God is speaking to you." You must prove that to me. With talk like that these factious spirits could have been refuted. But they wanted to be beaten, and so the rabble went to the devil.

One must deal cleanly with the Scriptures. From the very beginning the word has come to us in various ways. It is not enough simply to look and see whether this is God's word, whether God has said it; rather we must look and see to whom it has been spoken, whether it fits us. That makes all the difference between night and day.[13] God said to David, "Out of you shall come the king," etc. [II Sam. 7:13]. But this does not pertain to me, nor has it been spoken to me. He can indeed speak to me if he chooses to do so. You must keep your eye on the word that applies to you, that is spoken to you.

The word in Scripture is of two kinds: the first does not pertain or apply to me, the other kind does. And upon that word which does pertain to me I can boldly trust and rely, as upon a strong rock. But if it does not pertain to me, then I should stand still. The false prophets pitch in and say, "Dear people, this is the word of God." That is true; we cannot deny it. But we are not the people. God has not given us the directive. The factious spirits came in and wanted to stir up something new, saying, "We must keep the Old Testa-

---

[12]On the Peasants' War see the Introduction, *LW* 35, 157.

[13] *Da scheidet denn sich sommer und winter.*

ment also." So they led the peasants into a sweat and ruined them in wife and child. These insane people imagined that it had been withheld from them, that no one had told them they are supposed to murder. It serves them right. They would not follow or listen to anybody. I have seen and experienced it myself, how mad, raving, and senseless they were.[14]

Therefore tell this to Moses: Leave Moses and his people together; they have had their day and do not pertain to me. I listen to that word which applies to me. We have the gospel. Christ says, "Go and preach the gospel," not only to the Jews as Moses did, but to "all nations," to "all creatures" [Mark 16:15]. To me it is said, "He who believes and is baptized will be saved" [Mark 16:16]. Again, "Go and do to your neighbor as has been done to you."[15] These words strike me too, for I am one of the "all creatures." If Christ had not added, "preach to all creatures," then I would not listen, would not be baptized, just as I now will not listen to Moses because he is given not to me but only to the Jews. However because Christ says: not to one people, nor in this or in that place in the world, but to "all creatures," therefore no one is exempt. Rather all are thereby included; no one should doubt that to him too the gospel is to be preached. And so I believe that word; it does pertain also to me. I too belong under the gospel, in the new covenant. Therefore I put my trust in that word, even if it should cost a hundred thousand lives.

This distinction should be noticed, grasped, and taken to heart by those preachers who would teach others; indeed by all Christians, for everything depends entirely upon it. If the peasants had understood it this way, they would have salvaged much and would not have been so pitifully misled and ruined. And where we understand it differently, there we make sects and factions, slavering among the rabble and into the raving and uncomprehending people without any distinction, saying, "God's word, God's word." But my dear fellow, the question is whether it was said to you. God

---

[14] In April and May, 1525, Luther had preached personally against the insurrection, both in Mansfeld and in Thuringia. MA^3 4, 402, n. 188, 11.

[15] Cf. Matt. 7:12.

indeed speaks also to angels, wood, fish, birds, animals, and all creatures, but this does not make it pertain to me. I should pay attention to that which applies to me, that which is said to me, in which God admonishes, drives, and requires something of me.

Here is an illustration. Suppose a housefather had a wife, a daughter, a son, a maid, and a hired man. Now he speaks to the hired man and orders him to hitch up the horses and bring in a load of wood, or drive over to the field, or do some other job. And suppose he tells the maid to milk the cows, churn some butter, and so on. And suppose he tells his wife to take care of the kitchen and his daughter to do some spinning and make the beds. All this would be the words of one master, one housefather. Suppose now the maid decided she wanted to drive the horses and fetch the wood, the hired man sat down and began milking the cows, the daughter wanted to drive the wagon or plow the field, the wife took a notion to make the beds or spin and so forgot all about the kitchen; and then they all said, "The master has commanded this, these are the housefather's orders!" Then what? Then the housefather would grab a club and knock them all in a heap, and say, "Although it is my command, yet I have not commanded it of you; I gave each of you your instructions, you should have stuck to them."

It is like this with the word of God. Suppose I take up something that God ordered someone else to do, and then I declare, "But you said to do it." God would answer, "Let the devil thank you; I did not tell you to do it." One must distinguish well whether the word pertains to only one or to everybody. If, now, the housefather should say, "On Friday we are going to eat meat," this would be a word common to everybody in the house. Thus what God said to Moses by way of commandment is for the Jews only. But the gospel goes through the whole world in its entirety; it is offered to all creatures without exception. Therefore all the world should accept it, and accept it as if it had been offered to each person individually. The word, "We should love one another" [John 15:12], pertains to me, for it pertains to all who belong to the gospel. Thus we read Moses not because he applies to us, that we must obey him, but because he agrees with the natural law and is conceived better than the Gentiles would ever have been able to do. Thus the Ten Commandments are a mirror of our life, in which we can see wherein we are lacking, etc. The sectarian spirits have misunderstood also with respect to the images;[16] for that too pertains only to the Jews.

Summing up this second part, we read Moses for the sake of the promises about Christ, who belongs not only to the Jews but also to the Gentiles; for through Christ all the Gentiles should have the blessing, as was promised to Abraham [Gen. 12:3].

The third thing to be seen in Moses

In the third place we read Moses for the beautiful examples of faith, of love, and of the cross, as shown in the fathers, Adam, Abel, Noah, Abraham, Isaac, Jacob, Moses, and all the rest. From them we should learn to trust in God and love him. In turn there are also examples of the godless, how God does not pardon the unfaith of the unbelieving; how he can punish Cain, Ishmael, Esau, the whole world in the flood, Sodom and Gomorrah, etc. Examples like these are necessary. For although I am not Cain, yet if I should act like Cain, I will receive the same punishment as Cain. Nowhere else do we find such fine examples of both faith and unfaith. Therefore we should not sweep Moses under the rug. Moreover the Old Testament is thus properly understood when we retain from the prophets the beautiful texts about Christ, when we take note of and thoroughly grasp the fine examples, and when we use the laws as we please to our advantage.

Conclusion and Summary

I have stated that all Christians, and especially those who handle the word of God and attempt to teach others, should take heed and learn Moses aright. Thus where he gives commandment, we are not to follow him except so far as he agrees with the natural law. Moses is a teacher and doctor of the Jews. We have our own master, Christ, and he has set before us what we are to know,

---

[16]The iconoclasm of the radical leftists, who took Moses literally and destroyed images, windows, and other church art, aroused Luther's indignation. Cf. his fuller treatment of this subject, also during 1525, in *Against the Heavenly Prophets. LW* 40, 84-101.

observe, do, and leave undone. However it is true that Moses sets down, in addition to the laws, fine examples of faith and unfaith—punishment of the godless, elevation of the righteous and believing—and also the dear and comforting promises concerning Christ which we should accept. The same is true also in the gospel. For example in the account of the ten lepers, that Christ bids them go to the priest and make sacrifice [Luke 17:14] does not pertain to me. The example of their faith, however, does pertain to me; I should believe Christ, as did they.

Enough has now been said of this, and it is to be noted well for it is really crucial. Many great and outstanding people have missed it, while even today many great preachers still stumble over it. They do not know how to preach Moses, nor how properly to regard his books. They are absurd as they rage and fume, chattering to people, "God's word, God's word!" All the while they mislead the poor people and drive them to destruction. Many learned men have not known how far Moses ought to be taught. Origen,[17] Jerome,[18] and others like them, have not shown clearly how far Moses can really serve us. This is what I have attempted, to say in an introduction to Moses how we should regard him, and how he should be understood and received and not simply be swept under the rug. For in Moses there is comprehended such a fine order, that it is a joy, etc.

God be praised.

---

[17] Origen (*ca.* 185-254), Alexandrian theologian and ascetic, always sought in his exegesis the deeper, hidden spiritual meaning that lay back of the unspiritual grammatical-historical meaning of the text. See p. 403, n. 7.
[18] On Jerome see p. 104, n. 1.

PART III

THE RIGHTEOUSNESS OF GOD IN CHRIST

The first two parts of this anthology have shown Luther's passion for a grace-centered theology of the cross, and his confidence that this gospel is the deep message of Scripture when it is rightly interpreted. Next we want to see more precisely how that sense of the love of God is to be found in Jesus, and how this is related to sin (especially in the form of the bondage of the human will) and to justification by faith.

See how this approach fits Christian Motivation.

11   Two Kinds of Righteousness

The first document in this part is a sermon from late 1518 or early 1519. Since it is based on the traditional epistle text for Palm Sunday, it may come from that occasion in 1519. But in any case it is a relatively early and very clear statement of Luther's understanding of how the righteousness of God has been manifested in Christ Jesus.

The first type of righteousness is alien or external righteousness, that which can never be found in a sinful human individual intrinsically, but which has been freely given in Jesus. This righteousness, given to the baptized and in repentance, allows the poor human being to claim all that Christ has accomplished on the cross:

> Mine are Christ's living, doing, and speaking, his suffering and dying, mine as much as I have lived, done, spoken, suffered and died as he did (p. 155).

And this alien righteousness is the primary form; it, and it alone, is "the basis, the cause, the source of all our own actual righteousness" (p. 156).

This alien righteousness comes to us by grace alone, in preaching and in the sacraments. It comes both decisively and repeatedly, for "it is not instilled all at once, but it begins, makes progress, and is finally perfected at the end through death." The gospel is precisely the news that this surprising possibility exists for humanity, that God accepts sinners not through some exertion on their part, but freely, and for Christ's sake.

Alien righteousness must come first. But there is also a second kind or type of righteousness, that which flourishes in that woman or man who has found justification in Christ Jesus. Here Luther comes to ethics, to good works, to the love of neighbor and life in the world. But all of this is lived not according to one's own inherent possibility; the woman or man in Christ lives only in reflection of and response to that alien righteousness that has been received as a gift.

But what about the need to keep order and restrain sin in a fallen world? Luther offers some preliminary reflections, admitting that one may have to do such things, either because one holds a public office (and therefore is charged to maintain order) or because one (with great maturity) is in a position to rebuke another for the sake of his or her own good. But Luther warns that such looking at others and worrying about their behavior is a dangerous undertaking. It can so easily lead us away from that humility appropriate for faith and toward a pride in ourselves and superiority toward others.

[handwritten margin notes: "Council holds this danger"]

12   A Meditation on Christ's Passion

A second document ties the righteousness of God in Christ even more closely to the "theology of the cross" which Luther had proposed. This treatise, written by Luther in the spring of 1519, was a very popular work in his own lifetime. It was included in the *Church Postil* of 1525 as the sermon for Good Friday. Many of the early editions of this meditation were published illustrated with woodcuts of the crucifixion to underscore the human reality of Christ's suffering.

The first part of the treatise warns against inadequate ways to consider Christ's passion, including blaming the Jews. In contrast, true contemplation of the cross begins with seeing it as a judgment against oneself. Here Luther shows the cross as the revelation of the wrath of God not only against those who crucified Jesus, but against all humanity. And the individual person must be able to see "that you are the one who is torturing Christ thus, for your sins have surely wrought this" (p. 167).

If this were all, it would lead Christians only to despair. But the special glory of the cross is the realization that it is the revelation not only of the judgment of God, but also of God's great love. "You cast your sins from yourself and onto Christ when you firmly believe that his wounds and sufferings are your sins, to be borne and paid for by him" (p. 170). This is the external or alien righteousness discussed in the first document, and brought to bear not abstractly as a property of God, but concretely as the good news of the Crucified One for all who believe.

13   The Bondage of the Will

The longest selection in this part consists of three selections from Luther's most complex theological treatise, "The Bondage of the Will" (1525). This was written in the fall of 1525 as a reply to criticisms of Luther in Erasmus's treatise, "The Freedom of the Will," which had been published a year earlier.

Although Luther and Erasmus had some common points of criticism of the Roman Church and shared a passion for the renewal of learning, there was tension between them almost from the beginning of Luther's published works. Erasmus was a perceptive reader in seeing the theme of the bondage of the will as a key one for Luther's theology (the reader of this anthology has already encountered it in Part I, selections 1 and 2 from 1517). While Luther generally was trying to revive the Pauline/Augustinian doctrine of grace, there were moments, especially in a treatise of 1520, when he seemed to express himself so extremely on the subject that all dimensions of human freedom were denied.

Why was the bondage of the will so important to Luther? It is the negative implication of the theology of the cross. Luther feels that lurking behind Erasmus's concern for freedom, merit, and good works is human pride—a desire to have something to offer God that will blunt the enormity of our need for grace.

Luther feared that the wrong kind of concern for human responsibility would soon connect with the self-centeredness that is the result of original sin. Such pride of self is the enemy of the gospel, which calls all to receive what God offers in Christ humbly, and without conditions. The truth is that both human wickedness and human achievement stand judged by the cross, to the extent that either represents an attempt to live without God and by human strength alone.

Luther had developed a very different theology from the humanist Erasmus, who had been so concerned to uphold moral accountability. So Luther defends the radical Pauline gospel of Jesus Christ that is sharply set against human wisdom and human achievement—even, and especially, the best that humans have to offer:

> . . . show me any one of the whole race of mortals, even if he is the holiest and most righteous of them all, to whom it has ever occurred that the way to righteousness and salvation is the way of faith in One who is both God and man, who for the sins of men both died and rose again and is seated at the right hand of the Father; or show me any who has ever dreamed that of this wrath of God which Paul here says is revealed from heaven. Look at the greatest philosophers; what have been their thoughts about God, and what have they left in their writings of the wrath to come? (p. 181)

The serious student of Luther will want to follow the entire debate, either in *Luther's Works* vol. 33 or in *Luther and Erasmus: Free Will and Salvation*, eds., E. Gordon Rupp and Philip S. Watson (Philadelphia: Westminster, Library of Christian Classics, 1978), which includes both Erasmus's treatise and Luther's response.

The selections included here are the introduction, the final main section (Part VI), and Luther's brief conclusion. They give an especially rich sense of how Luther felt that he was basing his argument on the theology of St. Paul and St. John, writings that Luther believed stood at the heart of the canon of Scripture.

14   Sermon on the Afternoon of Christmas Day

Though Luther valued his achievement in "The Bondage of the Will" highly, it strikes a rather abstract or theoretical note, given Luther's own conviction was that he was here defending the gospel itself. So Part III ends with a "Sermon on the Afternoon of Christmas Day" from 1530. Luther loved Christmas and preached extensively on it, for it was another way in which the story of God's love for humanity could be brought home to the listener in its radically gracious form.

Luther held to the traditional christological confession of the church that the one who was born of Mary was true God and true human. But Luther points out in this sermon that such faith is not, in itself, that helpful. It can too easily become a kind of general religious proposition, true enough, but not relevant to my need as a sinner standing before God. Even Muslims (the Turk, in Luther's terminology) may well believe this about Jesus.

The more radical form of the gospel (which Luther even speaks of as "second faith") is not only to believe that the child born in Bethlehem is *the* Lord, but more decisively that he is *my* Lord. Such faith is overwhelming and deeply humbling:

> One who hears the message of the angel and believes it will be filled with fear, like the shepherds. True, it is too high for me to believe that I should come into this treasure without any merit on my part. And yet, so it must be (p. 233).

Thus there is a great continuity running through the four documents in Part III. The negative aspect of Luther's writings speak of human incapacity, of the need for alien righteousness, of humility and awe that such a gift could be given unconditionally. But the positive, personal name for all of this is Jesus Christ the Lord, born of Mary, obedient unto death on a cross, raised by the glory of God for the justification of all who have faith in him.

11.

TWO KINDS
OF RIGHTEOUSNESS

By

The Reverend Father

Martin Luther

Brethren, "have this mind among yourselves, which you have in Christ Jesus, who, though he was in the form of God, did not count equality with God a thing to be grasped" [Phil. 2:5-6].

There are two kinds of Christian righteousness, just as man's sin is of two kinds.

The first is alien righteousness, that is the righteousness of another, instilled from without. This is the righteousness of Christ by which he justifies through faith, as it is written in I Cor. 1 [:30]: "Whom God made our wisdom, our righteousness and sanctification and redemption." In John 11 [:25-26], Christ himself states: "I am the resurrection and the life; he who believes in me . . . shall never die." Later he adds in John 14 [:6], "I am the way, and the truth, and the life." This righteousness, then, is given to men in baptism and whenever they are truly repentant. Therefore a man can with confidence boast in Christ and say: "Mine are Christ's living, doing, and speaking, his suffering and dying, mine as much as if I had lived, done, spoken, suffered, and died as he did." Just as a bridegroom possesses all that is his bride's and she all that is his—for the two have all things in common because they are one flesh [Gen. 2:24]—so Christ and the church are one spirit [Eph. 5:29-32]. Thus the blessed God and Father of mercies has, according to Peter, granted to us very great and precious gifts in Christ [II Pet. 1:4]. Paul writes in II Cor. 1 [:3]: "Blessed be the God and Father of our Lord Jesus Christ, the Father of mercies and

God of all comfort, who has blessed us in Christ with every spiritual blessing in the heavenly places."[1]

This inexpressible grace and blessing was long ago promised to Abraham in Gen. 12 [:3]: "And in thy seed (that is, in Christ) shall all the nations of the earth be blessed." [2] Isaiah 9 [:6] says: "For to us a child is born, to us a son is given." "To us," it says, because he is entirely ours with all his benefits if we believe in him, as we read in Rom. 8 [:32]: "He who did not spare his own Son but gave him up for us all, will he not also give us all things with him?" Therefore everything which Christ has is ours, graciously bestowed on us unworthy men out of God's sheer mercy, although we have rather deserved wrath and condemnation, and hell also. Even Christ himself, therefore, who says he came to do the most sacred will of his Father [John 6:38], became obedient to him; and whatever he did, he did it for us and desired it to be ours, saying, "I am among you as one who serves" [Luke 22:27]. He also states, "This is my body, which is given for you" [Luke 22:19]. Isaiah 43 [:24] says, "You have burdened me with your sins, you have wearied me with your iniquities."

Through faith in Christ, therefore, Christ's righteousness becomes our righteousness and all that he has becomes ours; rather, he himself becomes ours. Therefore the Apostle calls it "the righteousness of God" in Rom. 1 [:17]: For in the gospel "the righteousness of God is revealed . . .; as it is written, 'The righteous shall live by his faith.'" Finally, in the same epistle, chapter 3 [:28], such a faith is called "the righteousness of God": "We hold that a man is justified by faith." This is an infinite righteousness, and one that swallows up all sins in a moment, for it is impossible that sin should exist in Christ. On the contrary, he who trusts in Christ exists in Christ; he is one with Christ, having the same righteousness as he. It is therefore impossible that sin should remain in him. This righteousness is primary; it is the basis, the cause, the source of all our own actual righteousness. For this is the righteousness given in

---

[1] The section "who has blessed, etc." is not from II Corinthians, as indicated by Luther, but from Eph. 1:3.

[2] Gen. 12:3 has "in thee" instead of "in thy seed." The quotation above is actually from Gen. 22:18 (A.V.). Cf. also Gal. 3:8.

place of the original righteousness lost in Adam. It accomplishes the same as that original righteousness would have accomplished; rather, it accomplishes more.

It is in this sense that we are to understand the prayer in Psalm 30 [Ps. 31:1]: "In thee, O Lord, do I seek refuge; let me never be put to shame; in thy righteousness deliver me!" It does not say "in my" but "in thy righteousness," that is, in the righteousness of Christ my God which becomes ours through faith and by the grace and mercy of God. In many passages of the Psalter, faith is called "the work of the Lord," "confession," "power of God," "mercy," "truth," "righteousness." All these are names for faith in Christ, rather, for the righteousness which is in Christ. The Apostle therefore dares to say in Gal. 2 [:20], "It is no longer I who live, but Christ who lives in me." He further states in Eph. 3 [14-17]: "I bow my knees before the Father . . . that . . . he may grant . . . that Christ may dwell in your hearts through faith."

Therefore this alien righteousness, instilled in us without our works by grace alone—while the Father, to be sure, inwardly draws us to Christ—is set opposite original sin, likewise alien, which we acquire without our works by birth alone. Christ daily drives out the old Adam more and more in accordance with the extent to which faith and knowledge of Christ grow. For alien righteousness is not instilled all at once, but it begins, makes progress, and is finally perfected at the end through death.

The second kind of righteousness is our proper righteousness, not because we alone work it, but because we work with that first and alien righteousness. This is that manner of life spent profitably in good works, in the first place, in slaying the flesh and crucifying the desires with respect to the self, of which we read in Gal. 5 [:24]: "And those who belong to Christ Jesus have crucified the flesh with its passions and desires." In the second place, this righteousness consists in love to one's neighbor, and in the third place, in meekness and fear toward God. The Apostle is full of references to these, as is all the rest of Scripture. He briefly summarizes everything, however, in Titus 2 [:12]: "In this world let us live soberly (pertaining to crucifying one's own flesh), justly (referring to one's neightbor), and devoutly (relating to God)."

This righteousness is the product of the righteousness of the first type, actually its fruit and consequence, for we read in Gal. 5 [:22]: "But the fruit of the spirit [i.e., of a spiritual man, whose very existence depends on faith in Christ] is love, joy, peace, patience, kindness, goodness, faithfulness, gentleness, self-control." For because the works mentioned are works of men, it is obvious that in this passage a spiritual man is called "spirit." In John 3 [:6] we read: "That which is born of the flesh is flesh, and that which is born of the Spirit is spirit." This righteousness goes on to complete the first for it ever strives to do away with the old Adam and to destroy the body of sin. Therefore it hates itself and loves its neighbor; it does not seek its own good, but that of another, and in this its whole way of living consists. For in that it hates itself and does not seek its own, it crucifies the flesh. Because it seeks the good of another, it works love. Thus in each sphere it does God's will, living soberly with self, justly with neighbor, devoutly toward God.

This righteousness follows the example of Christ in this respect [I Pet. 2:21] and is transformed into his likeness (II Cor. 3:18). It is precisely this that Christ requires. Just as he himself did all things for us, not seeking his own good but ours only—and in this he was most obedient to God the Father—so he desires that we also should set the same example for our neighbors.

We read in Rom. 6 [:19] that this righteousness is set opposite our own actual sin: "For just as you once yielded your members to impurity and to greater and greater iniquity, so now yield your members to righteousness for sanctification." Therefore through the first righteousness arises the voice of the bridegroom who says to the soul, "I am yours," but through the second comes the voice of the bride who answers, "I am yours." Then the marriage is consummated; it becomes strong and complete in accordance with the Song of Solomon [2:16]: "My beloved is mine and I am his." Then the soul no longer seeks to be righteous in and for itself, but it has Christ as its righteousness and therefore seeks only the welfare of others. Therefore the Lord of the Synagogue threatens through the Prophet, "And I will make to cease from the cities of Judah and from the streets of Jerusalem the voice of mirth and the voice of gladness, the voice of the bridegroom and the voice of the bride" [Jer. 7:34].

This is what the text we are now considering says: "Let this mind be in you, which was also in Christ Jesus" [Phil. 2:5]. This means you should be as inclined and disposed toward one another as you see Christ was disposed toward you. How? Thus, surely, that "though he was in the form of God, [he] did not count equality with God a thing to be grasped, but emptied himself, taking the form of a servant" [Phil. 2:6-7]. The term "form of God" here does not mean the "essence of God" because Christ never emptied himself of this. Neither can the phrase "form of a servant" be said to mean "human essence." But the "form of God" is wisdom, power, righteousness, goodness—and freedom too; for Christ was a free, powerful, wise man, subject to none of the vices or sins to which all other men are subject. He was pre-eminent in such attributes as are particularly proper to the form of God. Yet he was not haughty in that form; he did not please himself (Rom. 15:3); nor did he disdain and despise those who were enslaved and subjected to various evils.

He was not like the Pharisee who said, "God, I thank thee that I am not like other men" [Luke 18:11], for that man was delighted that others were wretched; at any rate he was unwilling that they should be like him. This is the type of robbery by which a man usurps things for himself—rather, he keeps what he has and does not clearly ascribe to God the things that are God's, nor does he serve others with them that he may become like other men. Men of this kind wish to be like God, sufficient in themselves, pleasing themselves, glorying in themselves, under obligation to no one, and so on. Not thus, however, did Christ think; not of this stamp was his wisdom. He relinquished that form to God the Father and emptied himself, unwilling to use his rank against us, unwilling to be different from us. Moreover, for our sakes he became as one of us and took the form of a servant, that is, he subjected himself to all evils. And although he was free, as the Apostle says of himself also [I Cor. 9:19], he made himself servant of all [Mark 9:35], living as if all the evils which were ours were actually his own.

Accordingly he took upon himself our sin and our punishment, and although it was for us that he was conquering those things, he acted as though he were conquering them for himself. Although as far as his relationship to us was concerned, he had the power to be our God and Lord, yet he did not will it so, but rather desired to become our servant, as it is written in Rom. 15 [:1, 3]: "We . . . ought . . . not to please ourselves . . . For Christ did not please himself; but, as it is written, 'The reproaches of those who reproached thee fell on me'" [Ps. 69:9]. The quotation from the Psalmist has the same meaning as the citation from Paul.

It follows that this passage, which many have understood affirmatively, ought to be understood negatively as follows: That Christ did not count himself equal to God means that he did not wish to be equal to him as those do who presumptuously grasp for equality and say to God, "If thou wilt not give me thy glory (as St. Bernard says), I shall seize it for myself." The passage is not to be understood affirmatively as follows: He did not think himself equal to God, that is, the fact that he is equal to God, this he did not consider robbery. For this interpretation is not based on a proper understanding since it speaks of Christ the man. The Apostle means that each individual Christian shall become the servant of another in accordance with the example of Christ. If one has wisdom, righteousness, or power with which one can excel others and boast in the "form of God," so to speak, one should not keep all this to himself, but surrender it to God and become altogether as if he did not possess it [II Cor. 6:10], as one of those who lack it.

Paul's meaning is that when each person has forgotten himself and emptied himself of God's gifts, he should conduct himself as if his neighbor's weakness, sin, and foolishness were his very own. He should not boast or get puffed up. Nor should he despise or triumph over his neighbor as if he were his god or equal to God. Since God's prerogatives ought to be left to God alone, it becomes robbery when a man in haughty foolhardiness ignores this fact. It is in this way, then, that one takes the form of a servant, and that command of the Apostle in Gal. 5 [:13] is fulfilled: "Through love be servants of one another." Through the figure of the members of the body Paul teaches in Rom. 12 [:4-5] and I Cor. 12 [:12-27] how the strong, honorable, healthy members do not glory over those that are weak, less honorable, and sick as if they were their masters and gods; but on the contrary they serve them the more, forgetting their own honor, health, and power. For thus no member of the body serves itself; nor does it seek its own welfare but that of the other. And the weaker, the sicker, the less honorable a member is, the more the other members serve it "that there may be no discord in the body, but that the members may have the same care for one another," to use Paul's words [I Cor. 12:25]. From this it is now evident how one must conduct himself with his neighbor in each situation.

And if we do not freely desire to put off that form of God and take on the form of a servant, let us be compelled to do so against our will. In this regard consider the story in Luke 7 [:36-50], where Simon the leper, pretending to be in the form of God and perching on his own righteousness, was arrogantly judging and despising Mary Magdalene, seeing in her the form of a servant. But see how Christ immediately stripped him of that form of righteousness and then clothed him with the form of sin by saying: "You gave me no kiss. . . . You did not anoint my head." How great were the sins that Simon did not see! Nor did he think himself disfigured by such a loathsome form as he had. His good works are not at all remembered.

Christ ignores the form of God in which Simon was superciliously pleasing himself; he does not recount that he was invited, dined, and honored by him. Simon the leper is now nothing but a sinner. He who seemed to himself so righteous sits divested of the glory of the form of God, humiliated in the form of a servant, willynilly. On the other hand, Christ honors Mary with the form of God and elevates her above Simon, saying: "She has anointed my feet and kissed them. She has wet my feet with her tears and wiped them with her hair." How great were the merits which neither she nor Simon saw. Her faults are remembered no more. Christ ignored the form of servitude in her whom he has exalted with the form of sovereignty. Mary is nothing but righteous, elevated into the glory of the form of God, etc.

In like manner he will treat all of us whenever we, on the ground of our righteousness, wisdom, or power, are haughty or angry with those who are unrighteous, foolish, or less powerful than we. For when we act thus—and this is the greatest perversion—righteousness works against righteousness, wisdom against wisdom, power against power. For you are powerful, not that you may make the weak weaker by oppression, but that you may make them powerful by raising them up and defending them. You are wise, not in order to laugh at the foolish and thereby make them more foolish, but that you may undertake to teach them as you yourself would wish to be taught. You are righteous that you may vindicate and pardon the unrighteous, not that you may only condemn, disparage, judge, and punish. For this is Christ's example for us, as he says: "For God sent the Son into the world, not to condemn the world, but that the world might be saved through him" (John 3:17). He further says in Luke 9 [:55-56]: "You do not know what manner of spirit you are of; for the Son of man came not to destroy men's lives but to save them."

But the carnal nature of man violently rebels, for it greatly delights in punishment, in boasting of its own righteousness, and in its neighbor's shame and embarrassment at his unrighteousness. Therefore it pleads its own case, and it rejoices that this is better than its neighbor's. But it opposes the case of its neighbor and wants it to appear mean. This perversity is wholly evil, contrary to love, which does not seek its own good, but that of another [I Cor. 13:5; Phil. 2:4]. It ought to be distressed that the condition of its neighbor is not better than its own. It ought to wish that its neighbor's condition were better than its own, and if its neighbor's condition is the better, it ought to rejoice no less than it rejoices when its own is the better. "For this is the law and the prophets" [Matt. 7:12].

But you say, "Is it not permissible to chasten evil man? Is it not proper to punish sin? Who is not obliged to defend righteousness? To do otherwise would give occasion for lawlessness."

I answer: A single solution to this problem cannot be given. Therefore one must distinguish among men. For men can be classified either as public or private individuals.

The things which have been said do not pertain at all to public individuals, that is, to those who have been placed in a responsible office by God. It is their necessary function to punish and judge evil men, to vindicate and defend the oppressed, because it is not they but God who does this. They are his servants in this very matter, as the Apostle shows at some length in Rom. 13 [:4]: "He does not bear the sword in vain, etc." But this must be understood as pertaining to the cases of other men, not to one's own. For no man acts in God's place for the sake of himself and his own things, but for the sake of others. If, however, a public official has a case of his own, let him ask for someone other than himself to be God's representative, for in that case he is not a judge, but one of the parties. But on these matters let others speak at other times, for it is too broad a subject to cover now.

Private individuals with their own cases are of three kinds. First, there are those who seek vengeance and judgment from the representatives of God, and of these there is now a very great number. Paul tolerates such people, but he does not approve of them when he says in I Cor. 6 [:12], "'All things are lawful for me,' but not all things are helpful." Rather he says in the same chapter, "To have lawsuits at all with one another is defeat for you" [I Cor. 6:7]. But yet to avoid a greater evil he tolerates this lesser one lest they should vindicate themselves and one should use force on the other, returning evil for evil, demanding their own advantages. Nevertheless such will not enter the kingdom of heaven unless they have changed for the better by forsaking things that are merely lawful and pursuing those that are helpful. For that passion for one's own advantage must be destroyed.

In the second class are those who do not desire vengeance. On the other hand, in accordance with the Gospel [Matt. 5:40], to those who would take their coats, they are prepared to give their cloaks as well, and they do not resist any evil. These are sons of God, brothers of Christ, heirs of future blessings. In Scripture therefore they are called "fatherless," "widows," "desolate"; because they do not avenge themselves, God wishes to be called their "Father" and "Judge" [Ps. 68:5]. Far from avenging themselves, if those in authority should wish to seek revenge in their behalf, they either do not desire it or seek it, or they only permit it. Or, if they are among the most advanced, they forbid and prevent it, prepared rather to lose their other possessions also.

Suppose you say: "Such people are very rare, and who would be able to remain in this world were he to do this?" I answer: This is not a discovery of today, that few are saved and that the gate is narrow that leads to life and those who find it are few [Matt. 7:14]. But if none were doing this, how would the Scripture stand which calls the poor, the orphans, and the widows "the people of Christ?" Therefore those in this second class grieve more over the sin of their offenders than over the loss or offense to themselves. And they do this that they may recall those offenders from their sin rather than avenge the wrongs they themselves have suffered. Therefore they put off the form of their own righteousness and put on the form of those others, praying for their persecutors, blessing those who curse, doing good to evil-doers, prepared to pay the penalty and make satisfaction for their very enemies that they may be saved [Matt. 5:44]. This is the gospel and the example of Christ [Luke 23:34].

In the third class are those who in persuasion are like the second type just mentioned, but are not like them in practice. They are the ones who demand back their own property or seek punishment to be meted out, not because they seek their own advantage, but through the punishment and restoration of their own things they seek the betterment of the one who has stolen or offended. They discern that the offender cannot be improved without punishment. These are called "zealots" and the Scriptures praise them. But no one ought to attempt this unless he is mature and highly experienced in the second class just mentioned, lest he mistake wrath for zeal and be convicted of doing from anger and impatience that which he believes he is doing from love of justice. For anger is like zeal, and impatience is like love of justice so that they cannot be sufficiently distinguished except by the most spiritual. Christ exhibited such zeal when he made a whip and cast out the sellers and buyers from the temple, as related in John 2 [:14-17]. Paul did likewise when he said, "Shall I come to you with a rod, or with love in a spirit of gentleness?" [I Cor. 4:21].   FINIS

12.

A MEDITATION ON
CHRIST'S PASSION

1. Some people meditate on Christ's passion by venting their anger on the Jews.[1] This singing and ranting about wretched Judas[2] satisfies them, for they are in the habit of complaining about other people, of condemning and reproaching their adversaries. That might well be a meditation on the wickedness of Judas and the Jews, but not on the sufferings of Christ.

2. Some point to the manifold benefits and fruits that grow from contemplating Christ's passion. There is a saying ascribed to Albertus[3] about this, that it is more beneficial to ponder Christ's passion just once than to fast a whole year or to pray a psalm daily, etc. These people follow this saying blindly and therefore do not reap the fruit of Christ's passion, for in so doing they are seeking their own advantage. They carry pictures and booklets, letters and crosses on their person. Some who travel afar do this in the belief that they thus protect themselves against water and sword, fire, and all sorts of perils.[4] Christ's suffering is thus used to effect in them a lack of suffering contrary to his being and nature.

3. Some feel pity for Christ, lamenting and bewailing his innocence. They are like the women who followed Christ from Jeru-

---

[1] Luther's attitude toward the Jews finds frequent expression in his works. At the beginning of his career his position was one of benevolent hope of converting them to Christianity. This is reflected in this treatise, as well as in his *That Christ Was Born a Jew*, 1523 (*LW* 45, 195-229). Over the years his position changed, due largely to the adamant refusal of the Jews to accept his invitation to acknowledge Christ. This is evidenced in his treatise of 1547, *On the Jews and Their Lies. WA* 53, (412) 417-552.

[2] Luther alludes to a medieval German hymn, *O du armer Judas, was hast du getan* ("Ah, Thou Wretched Judas, What Is It You Have Done?"). *MA*[3] 1, 520.

[3] Albert Magnus (1193-1280) was a scholastic theologian, often called *"Doctor universalis,"* and a teacher of Thomas Aquinas.

[4] Luther here directs his criticism at those who carry holy pictures, prayer books (cf. *LW* 43, 5-7), rosaries, etc., as amulets to ward off harm and danger, as well as those who undertake pilgrimages.

salem and were chided and told by Christ that it would be better to weep for themselves and their children [Luke 23:27-28]. They are the kind of people who go far afield in their meditation on the passion, making much of Christ's farewell from Bethany[5] and of the Virgin Mary's anguish,[6] but never progressing beyond that, which is why so many hours are devoted to the contemplation of Christ's passion. Only God knows whether that is invented for the purpose of sleeping or of waking.[7]

Also to this group belong those who have learned what rich fruits the holy mass offers. In their simplemindedness they think it enough simply to hear mass. In support of this several teachers are cited to us who hold that the mass is *opere operati, non opere operantis,*[8] that it is effective in itself without our merit and worthiness, and that this is all that is needed. Yet the mass was not instituted for its own worthiness, but to make us worthy and to remind us of the passion of Christ. Where that is not done, we make of the mass a physical and unfruitful act, though even this is of some good. Of what help is it to you that God is God, if he is not God to you?[9] Of what benefit is it to you that food and drink are good and wholesome in themselves if they are not healthful for you? And it is to be feared that many masses will not improve matters as long as we do not seek the right fruit in them.

4. They contemplate Christ's passion aright who view it with a terror-stricken heart and a despairing conscience. This terror must be felt as you witness the stern wrath and the unchanging earnestness with which God looks upon sin and sinners, so much so that he was unwilling to release sinners even for his only and dearest Son

---

[5] John 12:1-8. The veneration of Martha was widespread in medieval Germany. See Stephen Beissel, *Geschichte der Verehrung Marthas in Deutschland während des Mittelalters* (Freiburg, 1909).

[6] John 19:25-27.

[7] It was not unusual for such contemplations to last four or five hours. Often they were much longer, and the pious frequently fell asleep. On these devotional exercises, see Florenz Landmann, *Das Predigtwesen in Westfalen in der letzten Zeit des Mittelalters* (Münster, 1900), p. 75.

[8] I.e., the mechanical performance of the mass makes it valid and effective, not the inward intent or disposition of the one who celebrates the mass.

[9] Ever more pronounced from this point on is Luther's emphasis on the *pro me, pro nobis* ("for me, for us"), reflecting the personal aspect of faith which Luther himself experienced and now expressed in all his writings.

without his payment of the severest penalty for them. Thus he says in Isaiah 53 [:8], "I have chastised him for the transgressions of my people." If the dearest child is punished thus, what will be the fate of sinners?[10] It must be an inexpressible and unbearable earnestness that forces such a great and infinite person to suffer and die to appease it. And if you seriously consider that it is God's very own Son, the eternal wisdom of the Father, who suffers, you will be terrified indeed. The more you think about it, the more intensely will you be frightened.

5. You must get this thought through your head and not doubt that you are the one who is torturing Christ thus, for your sins have surely wrought this. In Acts 2 [:36-37] St. Peter frightened the Jews like a peal of thunder when he said to all of them, "You crucified him." Consequently three thousand alarmed and terrified Jews asked the apostles on that one day, "O dear brethren, what shall we do now?" Therefore, when you see the nails piercing Christ's hands, you can be certain that it is your work. When you behold his crown of thorns, you may rest assured that these are your evil thoughts, etc.

6. For every nail that pierces Christ, more than one hundred thousand should in justice pierce you, yes, they should prick you forever and ever more painfully! When Christ is tortured by nails penetrating his hands and feet, you should eternally suffer the pain they inflict and the pain of even more cruel nails, which will in truth be the lot of those who do not avail themselves of Christ's passion. This earnest mirror,[11] Christ, will not lie or trifle, and whatever it points out will come to pass in full measure.

7. St. Bernard[12] was so terrified by this that he declared, "I regarded myself secure; I was not aware of the eternal sentence that had been passed on me in heaven until I saw that God's only Son had compassion upon me and offered to bear this sentence for me. Alas, if the situation is that serious, I should not make light of it or feel secure." We read that Christ commanded the women not to weep for him but for themselves and their children [Luke 23:28].

---

[10] Cf. Luke 23:31.

[11] I.e., the one in and through whom we see our sin in its starkness.

[12] St. Bernard of Clairvaux (1090-1153), Cistercian monk, mystic, and founder of the abbey of Clairvaux, was held in high regard and frequently quoted by Luther.

And he adds the reason for this, saying, "For if they do this to the green wood, what will happen when it is dry?" [Luke 23:31] He says as it were: From my martyrdom you can learn what it is that you really deserve and what your fate should be. Here the saying applies that the small dog is whipped to frighten the big dog. Thus the prophet[13] said that all the generations on earth will bewail themselves over him; he does not say that they will bewail him, but that they will bewail themselves because of him. In like manner the people of whom we heard in Acts 2 [:36-37] were so frightened that they said to the apostles, "O brethren, what shall we do?" This is also the song of the church: "I will ponder this diligently and, as a result, my soul will languish within me." [14]

8. We must give ourselves wholly to this matter, for the main benefit of Christ's passion is that man sees into his own true self and that he be terrified and crushed by this. Unless we seek that knowledge, we do not derive much benefit from Christ's passion. The real and true work of Christ's passion is to make man conformable to Christ, so that man's conscience is tormented by his sins in like measure as Christ was pitiably tormented in body and soul by our sins. This does not call for many words but for profound reflection and a great awe of sins. Take this as an illustration: a criminal is sentenced to death for the murder of the child of a prince or a king. In the meantime you go your carefree way, singing and playing, until you are cruelly arrested and convicted of having inspired the murderer. Now the whole world closes in upon you, especially since your conscience also deserts you. You should be terrified even more by the meditation on Christ's passion. For the evildoers, the Jews, whom God has judged and driven out, were only the servants of your sin; you are actually the one who, as we said, by his sin killed and crucified God's Son.

9. He who is so hardhearted and callous as not to be terrified by Christ's passion and led to a knowledge of self, has reason to fear. For it is inevitable, whether in this life or in hell, that you will

---

13 Cf. Jer. 4:31.

14 This hymn cannot be named with certainty, though it may well have been Bernard of Clairvaux's *Salve Caput cruentatem,* later paraphrased freely by Paul Gerhard in his "O Sacred Head Now Wounded."

have to become conformable to Christ's image and suffering.[15] At the very least, you will sink into this terror in the hour of death and in purgatory[16] and will tremble and quake and feel all that Christ suffered on the cross. Since it is horrible to lie waiting on your deathbed, you should pray God to soften your heart and let you now ponder Christ's passion with profit to you. Unless God inspires our heart, it is impossible for us of ourselves to meditate thoroughly on Christ's passion. No meditation or any other doctrine is granted to you that you might be boldly inspired by your own will to accomplish this. You must first seek God's grace and ask that it be accomplished by his grace and not by your own power. That is why the people we referred to above fail to view Christ's passion aright. They do not seek God's help for this, but look to their own ability to devise their own means of accomplishing this. They deal with the matter in a completely human but also unfruitful way.

10. We say without hesitation that he who contemplates God's sufferings for a day, an hour, yes, only a quarter of an hour, does better than to fast a whole year, pray a psalm daily, yes, better than to hear a hundred masses. This meditation changes man's being and, almost like baptism, gives him a new birth. Here the passion of Christ performs its natural and noble work, strangling the old Adam and banishing all joy, delight, and confidence which man could derive from other creatures, even as Christ was forsaken by all, even by God.

11. Since this [strangling of the old Adam] does not rest with us, it happens that we occasionally pray for it, and yet do not attain it at once. Nevertheless we should neither despair nor desist. At times this happens because we do not pray for it as God conceives of it and wishes it, for it must be left free and unfettered. Then man becomes sad in his conscience and grumbles to himself about the evil in his life. It may well be that he does not know that Christ's passion, to which he gives no thought, is effecting this in him, even as the others who do think of Christ's passion still do not gain this knowledge of self through it. For these the passion of Christ is hidden and genuine, while for those it is only unreal and mislead-

---

[15] Cf. I Cor. 15:49.
[16] At this point in his career Luther did not question the doctrine of purgatory.

ing. In that way God often reverses matters, so that those who do not meditate on Christ's passion do meditate on it, and those who do not hear mass do hear it, and those who hear it do not hear it.

12. Until now we have sojourned in Passion Week and rightly celebrated Good Friday.[17] Now we come to the resurrection of Christ, to the day of Easter. After man has thus become aware of his sin and is terrified in his heart, he must watch that sin does not remain in his conscience, for this would lead to sheer despair. Just as [our knowledge of] sin flowed from Christ and was acknowledged by us, so we must pour this sin back on him and free our conscience of it. Therefore beware, lest you do as those perverse people who torture their hearts with their sins and strive to do the impossible, namely, get rid of their sins by running from one good work or penance to another, or by working their way out of this by means of indulgences. Unfortunately such false confidence in penance and pilgrimages is widespread.[18]

13. You cast your sins from yourself and onto Christ when you firmly believe that his wounds and sufferings are your sins, to be borne and paid for by him, as we read in Isaiah 53 [:6], "The Lord has laid on him the iniquity of us all." St. Peter says, "in his body has he borne our sins on the wood of the cross" [I Pet. 2:24]. St. Paul says, "God has made him a sinner for us, so that through him we would be made just" [II Cor. 5:21]. You must stake everything on these and similar verses. The more your conscience torments you, the more tenaciously must you cling to them. If you do not do that, but presume to still your conscience with your contrition and penance, you will never obtain peace of mind, but will have to despair in the end. If we allow sin to remain in our conscience and try to deal with it there, or if we look at sin in our heart, it will be much too strong for us and will live on forever. But if we behold it resting on Christ and [see it] overcome by his resurrection, and then boldly believe this, even it is dead and nullified. Sin cannot remain on Christ, since it is swallowed up by his resurrection. Now you see no wounds, no pain in him, and no sign of sin. Thus St. Paul de-

---

[17]See *LW* 35, xiv-xv.
[18]Luther was often critical of pilgrimages. See, for example, *LW* 35, 40 and *LW* 44, 86-87.

clares that "Christ died for our sin and rose for our justification" [Rom. 4:25]. That is to say, in his suffering Christ makes our sin known and thus destroys it, but through his resurrection he justifies us and delivers us from all sin, if we believe this.

14. If, as was said before, you cannot believe, you must entreat God for faith. This too rests entirely in the hands of God. What we said about suffering also applies here, namely, that sometimes faith is granted openly, sometimes in secret.

However, you can spur yourself on to believe. First of all, you must no longer contemplate the suffering of Christ (for this has already done its work and terrified you), but pass beyond that and see his friendly heart and how this heart beats with such love for you that it impels him to bear with pain your conscience and your sin. Then your heart will be filled with love for him, and the confidence of your faith will be strengthened. Now continue and rise beyond Christ's heart to God's heart and you will see that Christ would not have shown this love for you if God in his eternal love had not wanted this, for Christ's love for you is due to his obedience to God. Thus you will find the divine and kind paternal heart, and, as Christ says, you will be drawn to the Father through him. Then you will understand the words of Christ, "For God so loved the world that he gave his only Son, etc." [John 3:16]. We know God aright when we grasp him not in his might or wisdom (for then he proves terrifying), but in his kindness and love. Then faith and confidence are able to exist, and then man is truly born anew in God.

15. After your heart has thus become firm in Christ, and love, not fear of pain, has made you a foe of sin, then Christ's passion must from that day on become a pattern for your entire life. Henceforth you will have to see his passion differently. Until now we regarded it as a sacrament which is active in us while we are passive, but now we find that we too must be active, namely, in the following. If pain or sickness afflicts you, consider how paltry this is in comparison with the thorny crown and the nails of Christ. If you are obliged to do or to refrain from doing things against your wishes, ponder how Christ was bound and captured and led hither and yon. If you are beset by pride, see how your Lord was mocked

and ridiculed along with criminals. If unchastity and lust assail you, remember how ruthlessly Christ's tender flesh was scourged, pierced, and beaten. If hatred, envy, and vindictiveness beset you, recall that Christ, who indeed had more reason to avenge himself, interceded with tears and cries for you and for all his enemies. If sadness or any adversity, physical or spiritual, distresses you, strengthen your heart and say, "Well, why should I not be willing to bear a little grief, when agonies and fears caused my Lord to sweat blood in the Garden of Gethsemane? He who lies abed while his master struggles in the throes of death is indeed a slothful and disgraceful servant."

So then, this is how we can draw strength and encouragement from Christ against every vice and failing. That is a proper contemplation of Christ's passion, and such are its fruits. And he who exercises himself in that way does better than to listen to every story of Christ's passion or to read all the masses. This is not to say that masses are of no value, but they do not help us in such meditation and exercise.

Those who thus make Christ's life and name a part of their own lives are true Christians. St. Paul says, "Those who belong to Christ have crucified their flesh with all its desires" [Gal. 5:24]. Christ's passion must be met not with words or forms, but with life and truth. Thus St. Paul exhorts us, "Consider him who endured such hostility from evil people against himself, so that you may be strengthened and not be weary at heart" [Heb. 12:3]. And St. Peter, "Since therefore Christ suffered in the flesh, strengthen and arm yourselves by meditating on this" [I Pet. 4:1]. However, such meditation has become rare, although the letters of St. Paul and St. Peter abound with it. We have transformed the essence into semblance and painted our meditations on Christ's passion on walls and made them into letters.[19]

---

[19] Text T, printed at Wittenberg in 1520, adds a final line: *Soli deo gloria.* WA 2, 142.

13.

THE BONDAGE OF THE WILL

To the Venerable Master Erasmus of Rotterdam, Martin Luther
sends grace and peace in Christ.

[INTRODUCTION]

[Luther Explains His Delay in Replying and Admits Erasmus' Superior Talent][1]

That I have taken so long to reply to your *Diatribe Concerning Free Choice*,[2] venerable Erasmus, has been contrary to everyone's expectation and to my own custom; for hitherto I have seemed not only willing to accept, but eager to seek out, opportunities of this kind for writing. There will perhaps be some surprise at this new and unwonted forbearance—or fear!—in Luther, who has not been roused even by all the speeches and letters his adversaries have flung about, congratulating Erasmus on his victory and chanting in triumph, "Ho, ho! Has that Maccabee, that most obstinate Assertor,[3] at last met his match, and dares not open his mouth against him?" Yet not only do I not blame them, but of myself I yield you a palm such as I have never yielded to anyone before; for I confess not only that you are far superior to me in powers of eloquence and native genius (which we all must admit, all the more as I am an uncultivated fellow who has always moved in uncultivated circles),[4] but that you have quite

---

[1] WA 18, 600–602.
[2] Erasmus' *De libero arbitrio* was published in September, 1524, Luther's *De servo arbitrio* not until December, 1525. For the meaning of *Diatribe* and the translation of *arbitrium* see pp. xi f. and 8.
[3] The Maccabees were the intrepid leaders of the Jewish revolt against the tyranny of Antiochus Epiphanes (*ca.* 166 B.C.). "Assertor" refers to Luther's *Assertion of all the Articles Condemned by the Latest Bull of Leo X* (1521).
[4] Literally: "a barbarian who has always lived among barbarians." Possibly an ironic allusion to Erasmus' *Book Against the Barbarians (Anti-barorum liber)*, first published in 1520. For Erasmus the "barbarians" were those who opposed *bonae literae* or "good letters."

damped my spirit and eagerness, and left me exhausted before I could strike a blow.

There are two reasons for this: first, your cleverness in treating the subject with such remarkable and consistent moderation as to make it impossible for me to be angry with you; and secondly, the luck or chance or fate by which you say nothing on this important subject that has not been said before. Indeed, you say so much less, and attribute so much more to free choice than the Sophists[5] have hitherto done (a point on which I shall have more to say later) that it really seemed superfluous to answer the arguments you use. They have been refuted already so often by me,[6] and beaten down and completely pulverized in Philip Melanchthon's *Commonplaces*[7]—an unanswerable little book which in my judgment deserves not only to be immortalized but even canonized. Compared with it, your book struck me as so cheap and paltry that I felt profoundly sorry for you, defiling as you were your very elegant and ingenious style with such trash, and quite disgusted at the utterly unworthy matter that was being conveyed in such rich ornaments of eloquence, like refuse or ordure being carried in gold and silver vases.

You seem to have felt this yourself, from the reluctance with which you undertook this piece of writing. No doubt your conscience warned you that, no matter what powers of eloquence you brought to the task, you would be unable so to gloss it over as to prevent me from stripping away the seductive charm of your words and discovering the dregs beneath, since although I am unskilled in speech, I am not unskilled in knowledge, by the grace of God. For I venture thus with Paul [II Cor. 11:6] to claim knowledge for myself that I confidently deny to you, though I grant you eloquence

---

[5] A contemptuous term, used also by Erasmus, to denote the Scholastic theologians.

[6] E.g., in the *Lectures on Romans* (1516; WA 56, 155–528; LCC 15, 3–419), the *Quaestio de viribus et voluntate hominis* (1516; WA 1, 145 ff.), the *Disputation Against Scholastic Theology* (1517; WA 1, 224 ff.; LW 31, 9 ff.), the *Heidelberg Disputation*, esp. Theses 13–15 (1518; WA 1, 354; LW 31, 40), the *Lectures on the Psalms* (1519–1521; WA 5, 172 ff.; 622 ff.), the *Assertio* (1521; WA 7, 142 ff.), and *Defence and Explanation of All the Articles* (*Grund und Ursach*) (1521; WA 7, 446 ff.; LW 32, 3 ff.).

[7] The *Loci communes rerum theologicarum*, first edition 1521.

and native genius such as I willingly and very properly disclaim for myself.

What I thought, then, was this. If there are those who have imbibed so little of our teaching or taken so insecure a hold of it, strongly supported by Scripture though it is, that they can be moved by these trivial and worthless though highly decorative arguments of Erasmus, then they do not deserve that I should come to their rescue with an answer. Nothing could be said or written that would be sufficient for such people, even though it were by recourse to thousands of books a thousand times over, and you might just as well plow the seashore and sow seed in the sand or try to fill a cask full of holes with water. Those who have imbibed the Spirit who holds sway in our books have had a sufficient service from us already, and they can easily dispose of your performances; but as for those who read without the Spirit, it is no wonder if they are shaken like a reed by every wind.[8] Why, God himself could not say enough for such people, even if all his creatures were turned into tongues.[9] Hence I might well have decided to leave them alone, upset as they were by your book, along with those who are delighted with it and declare you the victor.

It was, then, neither pressure of work, nor the difficulty of the task, nor your great eloquence, nor any fear of you, but sheer disgust, anger, and contempt, or—to put it plainly—my considered judgment on your *Diatribe* that damped my eagerness to answer you. I need hardly mention here the good care you take, as you always do, to be everywhere evasive and equivocal; you fancy yourself steering more cautiously than Ulysses between Scylla and Charybdis as you seek to assert nothing while appearing to assert something. How, I ask you, is it possible to have any discussion or reach any understanding with such people, unless one is clever enough to catch Proteus?[10] What I can do in this matter, and what you have gained by it, I will show you later, with Christ's help.

There have, then, to be special reasons for my answering you

---

[8] Cf. Matt. 11:7.

[9] Cf. Luke 19:40.

[10] A figure of Greek mythology, supposed to have the power of changing himself into different shapes so as to avoid capture. Cf. Ovid *Metamorphoses* viii. 730 f.; Erasmus, *Adagia* XLIII.

at this point. Faithful brethren in Christ are urging me to do so, and point out that everyone expects it, since the authority of Erasmus is not to be despised, and the truth of Christian doctrine is being imperiled in the hearts of many. Moreover, it has at length come home to me that my silence has not been entirely honorable, and that I have been deluded by my mundane prudence[11]—or knavery—into insufficient awareness of my duty, whereby I am under obligation both to the wise and to the foolish [Rom. 1:14], especially when I am called to it by the entreaties of so many brethren. For although the subject before us demands more than an external teacher, and besides him who plants and him who waters outwardly [I Cor. 3:7], it requires also the Spirit of God to give the growth and to be a living teacher of living things inwardly (a thought that has been much in my mind), yet since the Spirit is free, and blows not where we will but where he wills [John 3:8], we ought to have observed that rule of Paul, "Be urgent in season and out of season" [II Tim. 4:2], for we do not know at what hour the Lord is coming [Matt. 24:42]. There may be, I grant, some who have not yet sensed the Spirit who informs my writings, and who have been bowled over by that *Diatribe* of yours; perhaps their hour has not yet come.

And who knows but that God may even deign to visit you, excellent Erasmus, through such a wretched and frail little vessel of his as myself, so that in a happy hour—and for this I earnestly beseech the Father of mercies through Christ our Lord—I may come to you by means of this book, and win[12] a very dear brother. For although you think and write wrongly about free choice, yet I owe you no small thanks, for you have made me far more sure of my own position by letting me see the case for free choice put forward with all the energy of so distinguished and powerful a mind, but with no other effect than to make things worse than before. That is plain evidence that free choice is a pure fiction; for, like the woman in the Gospel [Mark 5:25 f.], the more it is treated by the doctors, the worse it gets. I shall therefore abundantly pay my debt of thanks to you, if through me you become better informed, as I through you

---

[11] Literally: "the prudence or knavery of my flesh."
[12] "*Lucrifaciam*"; cf. Matt. 8:15; I Cor. 9:19 ff.

have been more strongly confirmed. But both of these things are gifts of the Spirit, not our own achievement. Therefore, we must pray to God that he may open my mouth and your heart, and the hearts of all men, and that he may himself be present in our midst as the master who informs both our speaking and hearing.

But from you, my dear Erasmus, let me obtain this request, that just as I bear with your ignorance in these matters, so you in turn will bear with my lack of eloquence. God does not give all his gifts to one man, and "we cannot all do all things";[13] or, as Paul says: "There are varieties of gifts, but the same Spirit" [I Cor. 12:4]. It remains, therefore, for us to render mutual service with our gifts, so that each with his own gift bears the burden and need of the other. Thus we shall fulfill the law of Christ [Gal. 6:2].

* * *

[PART VI. A DISPLAY OF THE FORCES ON LUTHER'S SIDE]

We have come to the last part of this book, in which, as we promised, we must produce our forces against free choice. But we shall not produce all of them; for who could do that in one small book,

---

13 "*Non omnia possumus omnes*," Virgil *Eclogue* viii. 63.

when the whole of Scripture, every jot and tittle of it, is on our side? Nor is it necessary; on the one hand, because free choice is already vanquished and prostrate by a twofold conquest—once where we prove that everything Diatribe thought to be in its favor is actually against it, and again where we show that the arguments she sought to refute still stand invincible. On the other hand, even if free choice were not already vanquished, no more than a couple of missiles would be required to lay it low, and·that would be enough. For what need is there, when an enemy has been killed by any one shot, to riddle his dead body with a lot more? Now, therefore, we shall be as brief as the subject will allow. And out of our numerous armies we will bring forward two high commanders with a few of their battalions, namely, Paul and John the Evangelist.

[*St. Paul: Universal Sinfulness Nullifies Free Choice*][1]

This is how Paul, writing to the Romans, enters into an argument against free choice and for the grace of God: "The wrath of God is revealed from heaven against all ungodliness and wickedness of men who in wickedness hold back the truth of God" [Rom. 1:18]. Do you hear in this the general verdict on all men, that they are under the wrath of God? What else does this mean but that they are deserving of wrath and punishment? He gives as the reason for the wrath, the fact that they do nothing but what deserves wrath and punishment, because they are all ungodly and wicked, and in wickedness hold back the truth. Where now is the power of free choice to attempt anything good? Paul represents it as deserving the wrath of God, and pronounces it ungodly and wicked. And that which deserves wrath and is ungodly, strives and prevails against grace, not for grace.

There will be smiles here at sleepy old Luther, who has not looked carefully enough at Paul; and someone will say that Paul is not there speaking about all men, nor about all their doings, but only about the ungodly and wicked and, as is expressly stated, those who in wickedness hold back the truth, so that it does not follow that all men are like that. To this I reply that for Paul it makes no

---

[1] WA 18, 757–763.

difference whether you say "against all ungodliness of men" or "against the ungodliness of all men"; for Paul almost everywhere uses Hebraisms, so that the meaning is: "All men are ungodly and wicked, and in their wickedness they suppress the truth, hence they are all deserving of wrath." Furthermore, in the Greek there is no relative, "of men who," but an article, like this: "The wrath of God is revealed against all ungodliness and wickedness of men the suppressors of the truth in wickedness"; so that the clause translated "who in wickedness hold back the truth" is, as it were, adjectival to "all men," just as the relative clause is adjectival in "our Father who art in heaven," for which an alternative rendering would be "our heavenly Father" or "our Father in heaven." The objection, on the other hand, is designed to separate out those who believe and are godly.[2]

But all this would be mere empty talk were it not so compellingly confirmed by the drift of Paul's argument itself. For shortly before, he has said: "The gospel is the power of God for salvation to everyone who has faith, to the Jew first and also to the Greek" [Rom. 1:16]. Here are no obscure or ambiguous words; "to Jews and Greeks" means that to all men the gospel of the power of God is necessary in order that they may have faith and be saved from the wrath that is revealed. I ask you, when he declares that the Jews, rich as they are in righteousness, the law of God, and the power of free choice, are without distinction destitute and in need of the power of God to save them from the wrath that is revealed, and when he makes this power necessary for them, does he not deem them to be under wrath? What men will you pick out, then, as not liable to the wrath of God when you are obliged to believe that the finest men in the world, the Jews and the Greeks, were in that condition? Again, what exceptions will you make among the Jews and Greeks themselves when Paul without any distinction puts

---

[2] Literally: "For it is said (*or*: It is said, to be sure), for the differentiation of . . ." Precisely what the "it" refers to here is obscure. The rendering in the text refers it to the statement of the smiling objector at the beginning of the paragraph, since this seems to make the best sense; but it could be referred to the adjectival clause in the preceding sentence. What is quite clear is Luther's conviction that all men without exception are ungodly by nature, and "those who believe and are godly" are so only by grace.

them all into one category and brings them all under the same judgment? Must we suppose that among these two most distinguished peoples there were not any who aspired to virtue? Did none of them strive with all the might of their free choice? But Paul pays no attention to this; he puts them all under wrath, declares them all ungodly and wicked. And must we not believe that in similar terms the rest of the apostles, each in his own sphere, consigned all the other nations also to this wrath?

This passage of Paul's, therefore, stands unyielding in its insistence that free choice, or the most excellent thing in men—even the most excellent men, who were possessed of the law, righteousness, wisdom, and all the virtues—is ungodly, wicked, and deserving of the wrath of God. Otherwise, Paul's whole argument is valueless; but if it is not, then the division he makes leaves no one on neutral ground, when he assigns salvation to those who believe the gospel, and wrath to all the rest, or takes believers as righteous and unbelievers as ungodly, wicked, and subject to wrath. For what he means is this: The righteousness of God is revealed in the gospel as being of faith, so it follows that all men are ungodly and wicked. For it would be foolish of God to reveal righteousness to men if they either knew it already or possessed the seeds of it. But seeing that God is not foolish, and yet he reveals to them the righteousness of salvation, it is evident that free choice, even in the highest type of men, neither possesses nor is capable of anything, and does not even know what is righteous in the sight of God—unless perhaps the righteousness of God is not revealed to the highest type, but only to the lowest, despite Paul's boasting that he is under obligation both to Jews and Greeks, wise and foolish, barbarians and Greeks [Rom. 1:14].

Therefore, Paul in this passage lumps all men together in a single mass, and concludes that, so far from being able to will or do anything good, they are all ungodly, wicked, and ignorant of righteousness and faith. And this conclusion indisputably follows from the fact that God reveals to them, as ignorant and sitting in darkness, the righteousness of salvation; for this means that in themselves they are ignorant, and being ignorant of the righteousness of salvation, they are certainly under wrath and damnation, from which in their ignorance they can neither extricate themselves nor even try to. For how can you try, if you do not know what there is to try about, or how, why, and wherefore to try?

With this conclusion, plain fact and experience agree. For show me any one of the whole race of mortals, even if he is the holiest and most righteous of them all, to whom it has ever occurred that the way to righteousness and salvation is the way of faith in One who is both God and man, who for the sins of men both died and rose again and is seated at the right hand of the Father; or show me any who has even dreamed of this wrath of God which Paul here says is revealed from heaven. Look at the greatest philosophers; what have been their thoughts about God, and what have they left in their writings about the wrath to come? Look at the Jews, constantly instructed by so many signs, so many prophets; what do they think of this way? Not only have they not accepted it, but they so hate it that no nation under heaven has more fiercely persecuted Christ, down to the present day. But who would venture to say that among so great a people there was not one who cultivated his free choice and endeavored all he could by its power? How is it, then, that they all endeavor in the opposite direction, and that the most excellent thing in the most excellent men has not only not followed this method of righteousness, and has not only been ignorant of it, but since it has been published and revealed, has actually rejected it with the greatest hatred and sought to destroy it? So much so that Paul in I Corinthians 1[:23] says that this way is a stumbling block to Jews and folly to Gentiles.

Now, whereas he names Jews and Gentiles without distinction, and it is certain that the Jews and the Gentiles were the principal peoples under heaven, it is at the same time certain that free choice is nothing else but the supreme enemy of righteousness and man's salvation, since there must have been at least a few among the Jews and Gentiles who toiled and strove to the utmost of the power of free choice, yet just by doing so they did nothing but wage war against grace. Now go and say that free choice inclines toward the good, when goodness and righteousness themselves are a stumbling block and foolishness to it! And you cannot say that it applies to some but not to all, for Paul speaks of all without distinction when

→ Uu SAVED
Cannot evoke because
Free choice they would never choose
God.

III. The Righteousness of God in Christ

he says "to Gentiles folly and to Jews a stumbling block" and excepts none but believers. "To us," he says, meaning those who are "called" and "saints" [I Cor. 1:2], it is "the power and wisdom of God" [I Cor. 1:18]. He does not say "to some Gentiles and some Jews," but simply "to Gentiles and Jews" who are not of "us"; and thus he separates believers from unbelievers by a clear line of division, leaving no one in between. But we are discussing the Gentiles as they act apart from grace, and it is these to whom Paul says the righteousness of God is a folly that they abhor. So much for the laudable endeavor of free choice toward the good!

Consider, moreover, whether Paul himself is not citing the most outstanding among the Greeks when he says it was the wiser among them who became fools and whose minds were darkened, or who became futile in their reasonings, that is, in their subtle disputations [Rom. 1:21 f.]. Tell me, does he not here touch the sublimest achievement of Greek humanity—their reasonings? For this means their best and loftiest ideas and opinions, which they regarded as solid wisdom. But this wisdom, which he elsewhere calls foolish [I Cor. 1:21], he here calls futile, as having succeeded by its many endeavors only in becoming worse, so that at length with darkened minds they worshiped idols and perpetrated the consequent enormities which he records. If, therefore, the noblest effort and achievement of the noblest of the Gentiles is evil and ungodly, what must we think of the rest, the common herd or the lower orders (so to say) of the Gentiles? For even here among the noblest he makes no distinction, but condemns their devotion to wisdom without any respect of persons. And when the achievement or the attempt at it is itself condemned, then all who devote themselves to it are condemned, even though they exercise the utmost power of free choice in doing so. Their very best endeavor itself, I say, is asserted to be vicious, so how much more those who engage in it?

In a similar way, he goes on to reject without any distinction the Jews who are literally but not spiritually Jews [Rom. 2:29]: "You," he says, "with the letter and circumcision dishonor God" [v. 27]. Also: "For he is not a Jew who is one outwardly, but he is a Jew who is one inwardly" [vv. 28 f.]. What could be plainer than this division? The outward Jew is a transgressor of the law! Yet how many Jews do you think there were, who though not having faith were most wise, religious, and virtuous men, and men who strove with might and main to attain to righteousness and truth? Why, he frequently bears them testimony, that they have a zeal for God [Rom. 10:2], that they pursue the righteousness of the law [Rom. 9:31], that they earnestly seek night and day to attain to salvation [Acts 26:7], that they live blamelessly [cf. Phil. 3:6]. Even so they are transgressors of the law, because they are not Jews spiritually, and they stubbornly resist the righteousness of faith. What then remains but that free choice is worst when it is best, and the more it endeavors the worse it becomes and behaves? The words are plain, the division is certain, there is nothing to contradict it.

But let us hear Paul himself as his own interpreter! In the third chapter, in a sort of peroration, he says: "What then? Are we better off than they? Not at all. For we have argued that Jews and Greeks are all under sin" [Rom. 3:9]. Where is free choice now? All, he says, all Jews and Greeks are under sin. Are there any "tropes" or "knots" here? What is the whole world's interpreting worth in face of this clear as possible statement? When he says "all" he excepts none, and when he declares that they are under sin, or in other words, are slaves of sin, he leaves nothing of good in them. But where has he stated this case, that Jews and Gentiles are all under sin? Nowhere but the place we have shown, where he says: "The wrath of God is revealed from heaven against all ungodliness and wickedness of men" [Rom. 1:18]. And he goes on to prove this from experience, pointing out that in God's displeasure they have been given up to so many vices, as though these fruits of their own ungodliness convict them of willing and doing nothing but evil.

Then he judges the Jews separately, when he says that the Jew according to the letter[3] is a transgressor, and proves this similarly by fruits and experience, saying: "You preach against stealing, yet you steal; you abhor idols, yet you commit sacrilege" [Rom. 2:21 f.]; and he excepts none at all but those who are Jews according to the Spirit [cf. Rom. 9:6 ff.; Gal. 4:22 ff.]. Nor can you get away from this by saying that although they are under sin, yet what is best in

---

[3] I.e., one who has the outward marks but not the inward spirit of his religion. Cf. Rom. 2:28 f.; II Cor. 3.

them, such as their reason and will, has a bias toward the good. For if a good tendency remains, it is false when he says that they are under sin. For when he names Jews and Gentiles, he includes everything there is in Gentiles and Jews, unless you are going to turn Paul upside down and insist that he wrote: "The flesh of all Jews and Gentiles, that is to say, their lower passions, are under sin." But the wrath that is revealed from heaven against them is going to damn their whole being, unless they are justified through the Spirit; and that would not be the case if they were not with their whole being under sin.

However, let us see how Paul proves his point from Holy Writ, and whether "the words have more polemic force in Paul than in their own context."[4] "As it is written," he says, " 'None is righteous, no, not one, no one understands, no one seeks for God. All have turned aside, together they have become worthless'; no one does good, not even one," and so forth [Rom. 3:10 ff.]. Here give me a "suitable interpretation" if you can! Invent tropes, allege that the words are obscure and ambiguous, and defend free choice against these damning sentences if you dare! Then I, too, will willingly yield and recant, and will myself be a confessor and assertor of free choice. It is certain that these things are said of all men, for the prophet represents God as looking down on all men and passing this judgment on them. For so it says in Psalm 13[14:2 f.]: "The Lord looks down from heaven upon the children of men, to see if there are any that understand or that seek after God; but they have all gone astray," etc. And lest the Jews should think that this did not apply to them, Paul forestalls them with the assertion that it applies above all to them: "We know," he says, "that whatever the law says, it speaks to those who are under the law" [Rom. 3:19]. He meant just the same where he said: "To the Jew first, and also to the Greek" [Rom. 2:9 f.]. You hear, therefore, that all the children of men, all who are under the law, Gentiles and Jews alike, come under this judgment in the sight of God, that not even one of them is righteous, understands, or seeks after God, but all have turned aside and become worthless. Now, I imagine that among the children of men

---

[4]See *The Bondage of the Will*, 1525. *LW* 33, 196, n. 46.

and those who are under the law there are included also the best and noblest of them, who by the power of free choice strive after virtue and the good, concerning whom Diatribe loudly proclaims that they have an awareness of the good and certain seeds of virtue implanted in them—unless perhaps she maintains that they are children of angels!

How, then, can they strive after the good, when they are totally ignorant of God and neither seek after God nor pay any regard to him? How can they have a power worth anything as a means to the good when they have all turned aside from the good and are altogether worthless? Are we ignorant of what it means to be ignorant of God, not to understand, not to seek after God, not to fear God, to turn aside and become worthless? Are not the words entirely clear, and do not they teach us just this, that all men are devoid of the knowledge of God and full of contempt for him, and they all turn aside to evil and are worthless as regards the good? For it is not a question here of ignorance about where to find food or of contempt for money, but of ignorance and contempt for religion and godliness. And such ignorance and contempt are beyond doubt not in the flesh and the lower and grosser passions but in the highest and most excellent powers of men, in which there ought to reign righteousness, godliness, the knowledge of God and reverence for God. In other words, they are in the reason and the will, and therefore in the power of free choice itself, or in the very seeds of virtue and the most excellent thing there is in man.

Where are you now, friend Diatribe, with the promise you gave earlier[5] that you would willingly agree that the most excellent thing in man is flesh, i.e., ungodly, if this were proved from the Scriptures? Agree now, then, when you hear that the most excellent thing in all men is not only ungodly, but ignorant of God, contemptuous of God, inclined to evil and worthless as regards the good. For what does it mean to be wicked but that the will—which is one of the most excellent things—is wicked? What does it mean to be without understanding of God and the good but that reason—which is another of the most excellent things—is ignorant of God and the good, or is

---

[5] *Diatribe, EAS* 4, 126.

blind to knowledge of godliness? What does it mean to turn aside and become worthless but that men have simply no ability in any part of themselves, and least of all in their most excellent parts, to turn to the good, but only to evil? What does it mean not to fear God, but that in all their parts, and especially the higher ones, men are despisers of God? But to be despisers of God is to be at the same time despisers of all the things of God—his words, works, laws, precepts, and will, for example. What now can reason dictate that is right when it is itself blind and ignorant? What can the will choose that is good when it is itself evil and worthless? Or rather, what choice has the will when reason dictates to it only the darkness of its own blind ignorance? With reason in error, then, and the will misdirected, what can man do or attempt that is good?

But someone will perhaps venture the sophistry that although the will goes astray and reason is ignorant in actual fact, yet it is inherently possible for the will to make some attempt at the good and for reason to know something of the right, since there are many things we can do which we do not do; and after all, we are discussing here what is possible, not what actually happens. I reply that the words of the prophet include both actuality and potentiality, and to say that a man does not seek for God is the same as saying that he cannot seek for God. You may gather this from the fact that if there were a power or ability in man to will good, then since no inaction or idleness is permitted by the motion of divine omnipotence, as we have shown above, it would be impossible for it to avoid being set in motion and, at least in one instance if not more, displayed in some employment. But this is not what happens, for God looks down from heaven and does not see even one who seeks or attempts to seek him; hence it follows that there is nowhere any power which might attempt or wish to seek him, but instead they all turn aside. Besides, if Paul were not understood as implying man's impotence, his argument would lose its point. For his whole concern here is to make grace necessary for all men. But if they were able to initiate anything of themselves, there would be no need of grace. As it is, however, they are not able and therefore they do need grace.

So you see that free choice is completely abolished by this passage, and nothing good or virtuous is left in man, since he is flatly stated to be unrighteous, ignorant of God, a despiser of God, turned aside from him, and worthless in the sight of God. The prophet's words are weighty enough, and not less in their own context than in Paul's quotation of them. It is no small matter to say that man is ignorant of God and despises God, for these are the sources of all crimes, the sink of all sins, nay, the hell of all evils. Could any evil not be there where there is ignorance and contempt of God? In short, the reign of Satan in men could not have been described in fewer or more expressive terms than by his saying that they are ignorant of God and despisers of God. That betokens unbelief, it betokens disobedience, sacrilege, and blasphemy toward God; it betokens cruelty and lack of mercy toward our neighbor; it betokens love of self in all the things of God and men. There you have a picture of the glory and power of free choice!

However, Paul goes on to state explicitly that he is speaking of all men, and especially of the best and noblest among them when he says: "So that every mouth may be stopped, and the whole world may be held accountable to God. For no human being will be justified in his sight by works of the law" [Rom. 3:19 f.]. Tell me, how can every mouth be stopped if there still remains a power by which we can do something? For we shall be able to say to God: "There is not absolutely nothing here; there is something you cannot condemn, a measure of ability you yourself have given; this at least will not be silenced, and will not be accountable to you." For if the power of free choice is sound and valid, it is not true that the whole world is accountable and guilty before God; for that power is no insignificant affair in an insignificant part of the world, but most conspicuous and most common throughout the whole world, and its mouth ought not to be stopped. Or else, if its mouth ought to be stopped, it must be accountable to God and guilty, together with the whole world. But by what right can it be said to be guilty unless it is unrighteous and ungodly, or in other words, deserving of punishment and retribution? Show me, please, by what interpretation this power of man can be absolved of the guilt with which the whole world is charged before God, or by what device it can be exempted from inclusion in the whole world.

These words of Paul: "All have turned aside, the whole world is guilty, there is none righteous," are mighty rolls of thunder and piercing lightning flashes, and in truth the very "hammer that breaks the rocks in pieces," as Jeremiah calls it [Jer. 23:29], by which everything that exists is shattered, not only in one man or some men or some part of them, but in the whole world and all men without a single exception, so that at these words the whole world ought to tremble, fear, and take to flight. What stronger or graver terms could have been used than that the whole world is guilty, all the children of men are turned aside and worthless, no one fears God, no one is not wicked, no one understands, no one seeks for God? Nevertheless, such was and is the hardness and insensate obstinacy of our hearts that we have neither heard nor felt these thunderings and lightnings, but have set up and extolled free choice and its powers in spite of them all, so that we have truly fulfilled the saying in Malachi 1[:4]: "They build, but I will tear down."

[Free Choice May Do the Works of the Law but Not Fulfill the Law][6]

In similarly grave terms, this also is said: "No human being will be justified in his sight by works of the law" [Rom. 3:20]. This is strong language—"by works of the law"—just as is also "the whole world" and "all the children of men." For it should be observed that Paul refrains from mentioning persons and speaks of pursuits, which means that he involves all persons and whatever is most excellent in them. For if he had said that the common people of the Jews, or the Pharisees, or certain ungodly people are not justified, it might have been thought that he had left out some who by the power of free choice and the help of the law were not altogether worthless. But when he condemns the works of the law themselves and makes them impious in the sight of God, it is clear that he is condemning all those whose strength lay in their zeal for the law and its works.

But it was only the best and noblest that were zealous for the law and its works, and that only with the best and noblest parts of themselves, namely, their reason and will. If, therefore, those who exerted themselves in respect of the law and works with the utmost

---

6 WA 18, 763–769.

zeal and endeavor both of reason and will—in other words, with the whole power of free choice, and were assisted besides by the law itself as with divine aid, finding in it instruction and stimulation—if these, I say, are condemned for ungodliness and, instead of being justified, are declared to be flesh in the sight of God, what is there now left in the whole race of men that is not flesh and not ungodly? For all are alike condemned who rely on works of the law.[7] For whether they have exercised themselves in the law with the utmost zeal or with only moderate zeal or with no zeal at all does not matter in the least. None of them could do anything but perform works of law, and works of law do not justify; and if they do not justify, they prove their doers ungodly and leave them in this condition; and the ungodly are guilty and deserving of the wrath of God. These things are so clear that no one can utter one syllable against them.

But they are in the habit of trying to get round Paul here, by making out that what he calls works of the law are the ceremonial works, which since the death of Christ are deadly. I reply that this is the ignorant error of Jerome, which in spite of Augustine's strenuous resistance[8]—God having withdrawn and let Satan prevail—has spread out into the world and persisted to the present day.[9] It has consequently become impossible to understand Paul, and the knowledge of Christ has been inevitably obscured. Even if there had never been any other error in the Church, this one alone was pestilent and potent enough to make havoc of the gospel, and unless a special sort of grace has intervened, Jerome has merited hell rather than heaven for it—so little would I dare to canonize him or call him a saint. It is, then, not true that Paul is speaking only about ceremonial laws; otherwise, how can the argument be sustained by which he concludes that all men are wicked and in need of grace? For someone could say: Granted we are not justified by ceremonial works, yet a person might be justified by the moral works of the Decalogue, so you have not proved by your syllogism that grace is necessary for these. Besides, what is the use of a grace that liberates us only from

---

[7] Cf. Gal. 3:10.

[8] *Letter 82, To Augustine*, 2, 18 (*MPL* 33.283).

[9] Luther had complained of this error in Erasmus as early as 1516, in a letter written to the latter by Spalatin at his request.

ceremonial works, which are the easiest of all, and which can at the lowest be extorted from us by fear or self-love? It is, of course, also untrue that ceremonial works are deadly and unlawful since the death of Christ; Paul never said that, but he says they do not justify and are of no advantage to a man in the sight of God as regards setting him free from ungodliness. Once this is accepted, anyone may do them without doing anything unlawful—just as eating and drinking are works that do not justify or commend us to God [I Cor. 8:8], yet a man does nothing unlawful when he eats and drinks.

They are also wrong in that the ceremonial works were as much commanded and required in the old law as was the Decalogue, so that the latter was neither more nor less important than the former. And as Paul is speaking primarily to Jews, as he says in Romans 1[:16], no one need doubt that by works of the law he means all the works of the entire law. For it would be meaningless to call them works of the law if the law were abrogated and deadly, since an abrogated law is no longer a law, as Paul very well knew. He is therefore not speaking of an abrogated law when he speaks of the works of the law, but of the law that is valid and authoritative. Otherwise, how easy it would have been for him to say: "The law itself is now abrogated!"—then we should have had a clear and unambiguous declaration.

But let us appeal to Paul himself as his own best interpreter, where he says in Galatians 3[:10]: "All who rely on works of the law are under a curse; for it is written, 'Cursed be everyone who does not abide by all things written in the Book of the Law, and do them.'" You see here, where Paul is making the same point in the same words as in the epistle to the Romans, that every time he mentions the works of the law he is speaking of all the laws written in the Book of the Law. And what is more remarkable, he actually quotes Moses, who curses those who do not abide by the law [Deut. 27:26], although he himself preaches that those are accursed who rely on the works of the law. He thus makes two contrary statements, the one being negative, the other affirmative. He can do this, however, because the fact is that in the sight of God those who are most devoted to the works of the law are farthest from fulfilling the law, because they lack the Spirit that is the true fulfiller of the law, and while they may attempt it by their own powers, they achieve nothing. So both statements are true and both types are accursed—those who do not abide by the law, as Moses puts it, and those who rely on works of the law, as Paul puts it; for they each lack the Spirit, without whom the works of the law, no matter how much they are done, do not justify, as Paul says [Rom. 3:20], and therefore they do not abide in all the things that are written, as Moses says [Deut. 27:26].

In short, Paul's division is confirmation enough of what we teach, for he divides men as doers of the law into two classes, putting those who work according to the Spirit in one, those who work according to the flesh in the other, and leaving none in between. For this is what he says: "No flesh will be justified by works of the law" [Rom. 3:20]; and what else does this mean but that those of whom he is speaking do the works of the law without the Spirit, because they are "flesh," or ungodly and ignorant of God, and that these works are of no help to them at all? He draws the same distinction in Galatians 3[:2], where he says: "Did you receive the Spirit by works of the law, or by hearing with faith?"; and again in Romans 3[:21]: "But now the righteousness of God has been manifested apart from law"; and again: "We hold that a man is justified by faith apart from works of law" [Rom. 3:28].

From all this it is unmistakably plain that for Paul the Spirit is opposed to works of law in just the same way as he is to all other unspiritual things and to the whole gamut of powers and pretensions of the flesh. It is thus clear that Paul takes the same view as Christ, who in John 3[:6] says that everything not of the Spirit is of the flesh, no matter how splendid, holy, and exalted it may be, even including the very finest works of God's law, no matter with what powers they are performed. For there is need of the Spirit of Christ, without whom all our works are nothing else than damnable. It can be taken as settled, then, that by works of the law Paul means not simply ceremonial works, but all the works of the law in its entirety. With this it will also be settled that everything connected with the works of the law is condemned if it is without the Spirit. And one of the things without the Spirit is that very power of free choice—for this is the matter at issue—which is held to be the most outstanding thing a man has. Now, nothing more excellent can be said of a man than that he is engaged in works of the law; and Paul is speaking not of those who are engaged in sins and impiety contrary to the law but of these very ones who are engaged in works of the law, that is to say, the best of men, who are devoted to the law, and who, besides the power of free choice, have the help of the law itself to instruct and inspire them. If, therefore, free choice, assisted by the law and occupying all its powers with the law, is of no avail and does not justify, but remains in the ungodliness of the flesh, what may we suppose it is able to do by itself, without the law?

"Through the law," he says, "comes knowledge of sin" [Rom. 3:20]. He shows here how much and how far the law helps. In other words, he shows that free choice by itself is so blind that it is not even aware of sin, but has need of the law to teach it. But what effort to get rid of sin will anyone make who is ignorant of sin? Obviously, he will regard what is sin as no sin, and what is no sin as sin. Experience shows this plainly enough by the way in which the world, in the persons of those whom it regards as the best and most devoted to righteousness and godliness, hates and persecutes the righteousness of God proclaimed by the gospel, calling it heresy, error, and other abusive names, while advertising its own works and ways, which in truth are sin and error, as righteousness and wisdom. With this text, therefore, Paul stops the mouth of free choice when he teaches that through the law sin is revealed to it as to someone ignorant of his sin. That is how far he is from conceding to it any power of striving after the good.

Here we have also the answer to that question which Diatribe so often repeats throughout her book: "If we cannot do anything, what is the point of so many laws, so many precepts, so many threatenings and promises?" Paul here replies: "Through the law comes knowledge of sin." He replies to this question very differently from the way man or free choice thinks. He denies that free choice is proved by the law and cooperates with it to produce righteousness; for what comes through the law is not righteousness but knowledge of sin. It is the task, function, and effect of the law to be a light to the ignorant and blind, but such a light as reveals sickness, sin, evil, death, hell, the wrath of God, though it affords no help and brings no deliverance from these, but is content to have revealed them. Then, when a man becomes aware of the disease of sin, he is troubled, distressed, even in despair. The law is no help, much less can he help himself. There is need of another light to reveal the remedy. This is the voice of the gospel, revealing Christ as the deliverer from all these things. It is not reason or free choice that reveals Christ; how should it when it is itself darkness and needs the light of the law to reveal its disease, which by its own light it does not see, but believes to be health?

So also in Galatians [3:19], dealing with the same question, he says: "Why then the law?" He does not, however, reply as Diatribe does, that it proves the existence of free choice, but he says: "It was added because of transgressions, till the offspring should come to whom the promise had been made." It was because of transgressions, Paul says; not meaning, however, that it was in order to put a stop to them, as Jerome dreams,[10] since Paul is arguing that a promise had been given to the future offspring that God would take away and put a stop to sins by the gift of righteousness; but it was in order to increase transgressions, as he says in Romans 5[:20]: "Law came in to increase sin." Not that sins were not committed or did not abound without the law, but that they were not known to be transgressions or sins of such grave consequence; on the contrary, most of them and the greatest of them were regarded as righteousness. Now, when sins are unrecognized, there is no room for a remedy and no hope of a cure, because men will not submit to the touch of a healer when they imagine themselves well and in no need of a physician. Therefore, the law is necessary to make sin known so that when its gravity and magnitude are recognized, man in his pride who imagines himself well may be humbled and may sigh and gasp for the grace that is offered in Christ.

Notice how simple the words are: "Through the law comes knowledge of sin"; yet they alone are powerful enough to confound and overthrow free choice. For if it is true that when left to itself it does not know what sin and evil are—as he says both here and in Romans 7[:7]: "I should not have known that covetousness is sin if

---

[10] *Commentary on the Epistle to the Galatians* (*Comment. in Ep. ad Gal.*), II, 3 (*MPL* 26.366).

The law makes us realize we can never be Righteous by your own efforts alone.

the law had not said, 'You shall not covet,' "—how can it ever know what righteousness and goodness are? And if it does not know what righteousness is, how can it strive toward it? If we are unaware of the sin in which we were born, in which we live, move, and have our being, or rather, which lives, moves, and reigns in us, how should we be aware of the righteousness that reigns outside of us in heaven? These statements make complete and utter nonsense of that wretched thing, free choice.

This being so, Paul speaks with full confidence and authority when he declares: "But now the righteousness of God is manifested apart from law, although the law and the prophets bear witness to it; the righteousness of God, I say, through faith in Jesus Christ for all and upon all who believe in him. For there is no distinction; since all have sinned and fallen short of the glory of God, they are justified by his grace as a gift, through the redemption which is in Christ Jesus, whom God put forward as an expiation by his blood," etc. [Rom. 3:21–25]. Paul's words here are absolute thunderbolts against free choice.

First: "The righteousness of God is manifested apart from law." This distinguishes the righteousness of God from the righteousness of the law; for the righteousness of faith comes from grace apart from law. The phrase "apart from law" cannot mean anything else but that Christian righteousness exists apart from the works of the law, in the sense that works of law are utterly useless and ineffective for obtaining it, as he says immediately below: "We hold that a man is justified by faith apart from works of law" [Rom. 3:28], and as he has said above: "No human being will be justified in his sight by works of the law" [Rom. 3:20]. From all of which it is very clearly evident that all the devoted endeavors of free choice are worth absolutely nothing. For if the righteousness of God exists apart from law and the works of law, must it not much more exist apart from free choice? Especially as the highest aspiration of free choice is to practice moral righteousness, or the works of the law, with the help afforded by the law to its own blindness and ignorance. This expression "apart from" excludes morally good works; it excludes moral righteousness; it excludes preparations for grace. In a word, imagine whatever you may as being within the power of free choice, Paul will still persist in saying that the righteousness of God avails "apart from" that kind of thing. And suppose I allow that free choice can by its own endeavor achieve something—good works, let us say, or the righteousness of the civil or moral law—yet it does not attain to the righteousness of God, nor does God regard its efforts as in any way qualifying it for his righteousness, since he says that his righteousness functions apart from the law. But if it does not attain to the righteousness of God, what will it gain if by its own works and endeavors (if this were possible) it achieves the very sanctity of angels? The words are not, I think, obscure or ambiguous here, nor is there room for any kind of tropes. For Paul clearly distinguishes the two righteousnesses, attributing one to the law and the other to grace, maintaining that the latter is given without the former and apart from its works, while the former without the latter does not justify or count for anything. I should like to see, therefore, how free choice can stand up and defend itself against these things.

A second thunderbolt is his saying that the righteousness of God is revealed and avails for all and upon all who believe in Christ, and that there is no distinction [Rom. 3:21 f.]. Once more in the plainest terms he divides the entire race of men into two, giving the righteousness of God to believers and denying it to unbelievers. Now, no one is crazy enough to doubt that the power or endeavor of free choice is something different from faith in Jesus Christ. But Paul denies that anything outside this faith is righteous in the sight of God; and if it is not righteous in the sight of God, it must necessarily be sin. For with God there is nothing intermediate between righteousness and sin, no neutral ground, so to speak, which is neither righteousness nor sin. Otherwise, Paul's whole argument would come to nothing, since it presupposes this division, namely, that whatever is done or devised among men is either righteousness or sin before God: righteousness if faith is present, sin if faith is absent. With men, of course, it is certainly a fact that there are middle and neutral cases, where men neither owe one another anything nor do anything for one another. But an ungodly man sins against God whether he eats or drinks or whatever he does, because he perpetually misuses God's creatures in his impiety and ingratitude, and never for a moment gives glory to God from his heart.

It is also no small thunderbolt when he says: "All have sinned and fall short of the glory of God" and "There is no distinction" [Rom. 3:23, 22]. I ask you, could he put it more plainly? Show me a worker of free choice and tell me whether in that enterprise of his he also sins. If he does not sin, why does not Paul make an exception of him? Why does he include him "without distinction"? It is certain that one who says "all," excepts no one in any place, at any time, in any work or endeavor. Hence if you except any man for any kind of effort or work, you make Paul a liar, because the subject of such work and endeavor of free choice is also included in "all," and Paul ought to have had enough respect for him not to place him so freely and without qualification among sinners.

Then there is the statement that they lack the glory of God. You can take "the glory of God" here in two senses, active and passive. This is an example of Paul's habit of using Hebraisms. Actively, the glory of God is that by which God glories in us; passively, it is that by which we glory in God. It seems to me, however, that it ought to be taken passively here—like "the faith of Christ," which suggests in Latin the faith that Christ has, but to the Hebrew mind means the faith we have in Christ. Similarly, "the righteousness of God" in Latin means the righteousness that God possesses, but a Hebrew would understand it as the righteousness that we have from God and in the sight of God. So we take "the glory of God" not in the Latin but in the Hebrew sense as that which we have in God and before God, and which might be called "glory in God." Now, a man glories in God when he is certain that God is favorable to him and deigns to look kindly upon him, so that the things he does are pleasing in God's sight, or if they are not, they are borne with and pardoned. If, then, the enterprise or endeavor of free choice is not sin, but good in God's sight, it can certainly glory and say with confidence as it glories: "This pleases God, God approves of this, God counts this worthy and accepts it, or at least bears with it and pardons it. For this is the glory of the faithful in God, and those who do not have it are rather put to shame before him." But Paul here denies this, saying that men are completely devoid of this glory. Experience proves that he is right; for ask all the exercisers of free choice to a man, and if you are able to show me one who can sincerely and honestly say with regard to any effort or endeavor of his own, "I know that this pleases God," then I will admit defeat and yield you the palm. But I know there is not one to be found.

Now, if this glory is lacking, so that the conscience dare not say for certain or with confidence that "this pleases God," then it is certain it does not please God. For as a man believes, so it is with him; and in this case he does not believe with certainty that he pleases God, although it is necessary to do so, because the offense of unbelief lies precisely in having doubts about the favor of God, who wishes us to believe with the utmost possible certainty that he is favorable. We thus convict them on the evidence of their own conscience that free choice, when it is devoid of the glory of God, is perpetually guilty of the sin of unbelief, together with all its powers, efforts, and enterprises.

[*"Congruous" and "Condign" Merit*][11]

However, what will the patrons of free choice say in the end to what follows: "justified by his grace as a gift"? What does "as a gift" mean? What does "by his grace" mean? How do endeavor and merit accord with a righteousness freely bestowed? Perhaps they will say here that they attribute to free choice as little as possible, and by no means condign merit.[12] But these are empty words. For

---

[11] WA 18, 769–771.

[12] Scholastic theology distinguished between two kinds of merit: *de congruo* and *de condigno*, or the merit of "fitness" and the merit of "worthiness." The former was due to man's well-intentioned efforts when he "did what in him lay" (*facere quod in se est*) to seek the good; for although nothing achieved by such efforts was strictly meritorious, it was "fitting" that God should reward them with his grace. The latter kind of merit arose from good works done with the aid of the grace thus received (*gratia gratum faciens*), which were meritorious in the strict sense of the term—and were rewarded with yet more grace and finally with salvation and glory. Just how much, if anything, it lay in a man to do without the stimulus of "special" grace (*gratia peculiaris, praeveniens, operans*), was much debated. Some held (like Aquinas) that man could make no effort whatsoever toward the good, and therefore could acquire no merit, apart from grace; and that any such effort inspired by grace carried both kinds of merit—"congruous" inasmuch as it was a work of man's free choice, "condign" inasmuch as it was a work of God's grace. The prevailing trend in later scholastic thought, however, was more optimistic as to what man could do "by his own natural powers" to acquire congruous merit, though it was universally agreed that for condign merit the assistance of grace was essential.

what is sought by means of free choice is to make room for merits. Diatribe has shown this all along by her insistent demand: "If there is no freedom of choice, what room is there for merits? If there is no room for merits, what room is there for rewards? To what are we to ascribe it if a man is justified without merits?" Paul here replies that there is no such thing as merit, but all who are justified are justified freely (*gratis*), and this is to be ascribed to nothing but the grace of God. With the gift of righteousness, moreover, there are given also the Kingdom and eternal life. What about your "endeavoring" now? What about your "earnest striving" and "works"? What about the merits of free choice? What use are they? You cannot complain of obscurity and ambiguity; the facts and the words are very clear and very simple.

For suppose they do attribute as little as possible to free choice, nevertheless they teach that by means of this minimum we can attain to righteousness and grace. Nor have they any other way of solving the problem of why God justifies one man and abandons another than by positing free choice, and inferring that one has endeavored while the other has not, and that God respects the one for his endeavor but despises the other, and he would be unjust if he did anything else. And although they protest both in speech and writing that they do not seek to obtain grace by condign merit, and in fact do not use the term, yet they are only playing a trick on us with the word, and holding on to the thing it signifies just the same. For what excuse is it that they do not call it condign merit, when they attribute to it everything that belongs to condign merit? When they say that the man who endeavors finds favor with God, while the one who does not endeavor does not find favor, is not this plainly a case of condign merit? Are they not making God a respecter of works, merits, and persons? They say that one man lacks grace by his own fault, because he has not striven after it, while the other, because he has striven, obtains grace, as he would not have done if he had not striven. If this is not condign merit, I should like to know what there is that deserves the name. You could play about with any word in this fashion, and say: It is not, of course, condign merit, but it has the same effect as condign merit; the thorn is not a bad tree, but only produces the fruit of a bad tree; the fig is not a good tree, but it produces what a good tree usually does.[13] Diatribe is not indeed ungodly, though she speaks and acts only as an ungodly person does.

For these advocates of free choice, it turns out as the proverb says: "In avoiding Charybdis he runs into Scylla."[14] For in their anxiety not to agree with the Pelagians, they start denying condign merit, and by their very denial they establish it more firmly than ever. They deny it in the words they speak and write, but affirm it in fact and in their hearts, and they are on two accounts worse than the Pelagians. First, because the Pelagians confess and assert condign merit, simply, candidly, and ingenuously, calling a spade a spade[15] and a fig a fig, and teaching what they really believe. These friends of ours, however, though they believe and teach the same, make dupes of us with deceptive words and a false pretense, as if they dissented from the Pelagians, though this is the last thing they do; so that if you go by their hypocrisy, they seem to be the bitterest foes of the Pelagians, while if you look at the facts and their real opinion, they themselves are Pelagians double-dyed. The second reason is that by this hypocrisy they both value and purchase the grace of God for far less than the Pelagians. For the latter do not assert that there is a tiny little something in us by which we can attain to grace, but that there are whole, full, perfect, great, and many efforts and works. But our friends say that it is a very little thing, and almost nothing, by which we merit grace.

If we must have error, then, there is more honesty and less pride in the error of those who say that the grace of God costs a great deal, and so hold it dear and precious, than of those who teach that it costs only a trifling amount, and so hold it cheap and contemptible.[16] But Paul kills both these birds with one stone when he says that all are justified freely, or again, are justified apart from law and works of law. For when he asserts that justification is freely bestowed on all who are justified, he leaves no one to work, or earn,

---

[13] Cf. Matt. 7:16 f.
[14] Gualtherus ab Insulis, *Alexandreis* i. 301.
[15] Literally: "a boat a boat."
[16] Grace is not cheap, but priceless—and free. It is free to us, but immensely costly to God; cf. p. 210.

or prepare himself, and he leaves no work that can be called congruous or condign; and thus by a single stroke of this thunderbolt he shatters both the Pelagians with their total merit, and the Sophists with their little scrap of merit. Free justification allows of no workers, because there is an obvious contradiction between "freely given" and "earned by some sort of work." Besides, justification by grace excludes consideration of anyone's personal worthiness, as he says below in chapter 11: "If it is by grace, it is no longer on the basis of works; otherwise grace would no longer be grace" [Rom. 11:6]. He says the same in chapter 4: "Now to one who works, his wages are not reckoned as a gift, but as his due" [Rom. 4:4]. Thus my Paul, unconquerable conqueror of free choice that he is, wipes out two armies with a single word. For if we are justified "apart from works," then all works are condemned, whether small or great, for he makes no exception but thunders equally against all.

You will notice here how unobservant all these friends of ours are, and what good it does to rely on the venerable old Fathers, who have been approved through such a long succession of ages. Were not they too all equally blind, or rather, did they not simply overlook the clearest and most explicit statements of Paul? Can anything, I ask you, be said clearly and explicitly in defense of grace against free choice if Paul's language here is not clear and explicit? He first extols grace by contrasting it with works, and then in the clearest and simplest terms he states that we are justified freely, and that grace would not be grace if it were earned by works, so that he quite unmistakably excludes all works in the matter of justification in order to establish grace alone and free justification. Yet with all this light we still search for darkness, and when we cannot claim large and all-inclusive things for ourselves, we try to claim little modest things, just to ensure that justification by the grace of God shall not be free and apart from works. As if he who denies us all the important things will not even more deny that the little modest things help us in any way toward justification, when he has laid it down that we are justified only by his grace apart from all works, and therefore apart from the law itself, in which all works, great and small, congruous and condign, are included. Now go and boast of your ancient authorities, and rely on what they say, when you see that they have one and all overlooked the clearest and plainest teaching of Paul as if they deliberately shunned this morning star, or rather this sun, because of the carnal notion they doubtless entertained that it would be absurd to have no place left for merits.

[*The Righteousness of Works and of Faith; and a Summary of St. Paul's Testimony Against Free Choice*][17]

Let us take a look here at what Paul says later about the example of Abraham [Rom. 4:1–3]. "If Abraham," he says, "was justified by works, he has something to boast about, but not before God. For what does the Scripture say? 'Abraham believed God, and it was reckoned to him as righteousness.'" Please notice here too the distinction Paul makes by referring to a twofold righteousness of Abraham.

First, there is the righteousness of works, or moral and civil righteousness; but he denies that Abraham is justified in God's sight by this, even if he is righteous in the sight of men because of it. With this righteousness, he has indeed something to boast about before men, but like the rest he falls short of the glory of God. Nor can anyone say here that it is the works of the law, or ceremonial works, that are being condemned, seeing that Abraham lived so many years before the law was given. Paul is speaking simply about the works Abraham did, and the best ones he did. For it would be absurd to argue as to whether anyone is justified by bad works. If, therefore, Abraham is not righteous because of any works, and if both he himself and all his works remain in a state of ungodliness unless he is clothed with another righteousness, namely, that of faith, then it is plain that no man is brought any nearer to righteousness by his works; and what is more, that no works and no aspirations or endeavors of free choice count for anything in the sight of God, but are all adjudged to be ungodly, unrighteous, and evil. For if the man himself is not righteous, neither are his works or endeavors righteous; and if they are not righteous, they are damnable and deserving of wrath.

The other kind of righteousness is the righteousness of faith,

---

[17] WA 18, 771–776.

which does not depend on any works, but on God's favorable regard and his "reckoning" on the basis of grace. Notice how Paul dwells on the word "reckoned," how he stresses, repeats, and insists on it. "To one who works," he says, "his wages are not reckoned as a gift but as his due. And to one who does not work but has faith in him who justifies the ungodly, his faith is reckoned as righteousness, according to the plan of God's grace" [Rom. 4:4 f.].[18] Then he quotes David as saying the same about the "reckoning" of grace: "Blessed is the man against whom the Lord will not reckon his sin," etc. [Rom. 4:6 ff.]. He repeats the word "reckon" nearly ten times in this chapter. In short, Paul sets the one who works and the one who does not work alongside each other, leaving no room for anyone between them; and he asserts that righteousness is not reckoned to the former, but that it is reckoned to the latter provided he has faith. There is no way of escape for free choice here, no chance for it to get away with its endeavoring and striving. It must be classed either with the one who works or with the one who does not work. If it is classed with the former, so you are told here, it does not have any righteousness reckoned to it, whereas if it is classed with the latter—the one who does not work but has faith in God—then it does have righteousness reckoned to it. But in that case it will no longer be a case of free choice at work, but of a being created anew through faith.

Now, if righteousness is not reckoned to the one who works, then clearly his works are nothing but sins, evils, and impieties in the sight of God. Nor can any impudent Sophist break in here with the objection that a man's work need not be evil, even if the man himself is evil. For Paul purposely speaks, not simply of the man as a man, but of the man as a worker, in order to make it unmistakably plain that the man's works and endeavors themselves are condemned, no matter what their nature, name, or sign may be. It is, however, with good works that he is concerned, since he is arguing about justification and merit. Hence although with the phrase "one who works" he refers quite generally to all workers and all their works, it is particularly of their good and virtuous works that he is

---

[18] The phrase "according to the plan of God's grace" is the reading of the Clementine Vulgate.

speaking. Otherwise, there would be no point in his distinction between the "one who works" and the "one who does not work."

I will not here elaborate the very strong arguments that can be drawn from the purpose of grace, the promise of God, the meaning of the law, original sin, or divine election, any one of which would be sufficient by itself to do away completely with free choice. For if grace comes from the purpose or predestination of God, it comes by necessity and not by our effort or endeavor, as we have shown above. Moreover, if God promised grace before the law was given, as Paul argues here and in Galatians, then grace does not come from works or through the law; otherwise the promise means nothing. So also faith will mean nothing—although Abraham was justified by it before the law was given—if works count for anything. Again, since the law is the power of sin [I Cor. 15:56] in that it serves only to reveal and not to remove sin, it makes the conscience guilty before God, and threatens it with wrath. That is what Paul means when he says: "The law brings wrath" [Rom. 4:15]. How, then, could there be any possibility of attaining righteousness through the law? And if we receive no help from the law, what help can we expect from the power of choice alone?

Furthermore, seeing that through the one transgression of the one man, Adam, we are all under sin and damnation, how can we attempt anything that is not sinful and damnable? For when he says "all," he makes no exception either of the power of free choice or of any worker, but every man, whether he works or not, endeavors or not, is necessarily included among the "all." Not that we should sin or be damned through that one transgression of Adam if it were not our own transgression. For who could be damned for another's transgression, especially before God? It does not, however, become ours by any imitative doing of it ourselves, for then it would not be the one transgression of Adam, since it would be we and not Adam who committed it; but it becomes ours the moment we are born—a subject we must deal with some other time. Original sin itself, therefore, leaves free choice with no capacity to do anything but sin and be damned.

These arguments, I say, I will not elaborate, both because they are so very obvious and so very substantial, and also because we have already said something about them earlier in the book. But if we wished to list all the points made by Paul alone by which free choice is overthrown, we could not do better than make a running commentary on the whole of Paul, showing how the much vaunted power of free choice is refuted in almost every word. I have already done this with the third and fourth chapters,[19] on which I have chiefly concentrated in order to expose the inattentiveness of all these friends of ours who have a way of reading Paul that enables them to find, even in his clearest passages, anything but these very strong arguments against free choice. I also wanted to show the foolishness of the confidence they repose in the authority and writings of the ancient doctors, and to leave them to consider what the effect of these most evident arguments must be if they are treated with due care and judgment.

For my own part, I confess to being greatly astonished. Paul again and again uses these universal terms, "all," "none," "not," "nowhere," "apart from"—for example: "All have turned aside"; "None is righteous"; "No one does good, not even one"; "All are sinners and damned through one man's transgression"; "We are justified by faith, apart from law, apart from works"—so that although one might wish to put it differently, he could not speak more clearly and plainly. Hence I am, as I say, astonished that in face of these universal words and sentences, contrary and even contradictory ideas have come to prevail, such as: "Some have not turned aside, are not unrighteous, not evil, not sinners, not damned," and "There is something in man that is good and strives after the good"—as if the man that strives after the good, whoever he may be, were not included in the words "all," "none," "not"!

I should not myself find it possible, even if I wished, to make any objection or reply to Paul, but should have to regard my power of free choice, endeavors and all, as included in those "alls" and "nones" of which Paul speaks, unless a new kind of grammar or a new use of language were introduced. It might have been possible to suspect a trope and give a twist to the words I have cited if Paul had used this kind of expression only once or in only one passage;

---

19 Of the Epistle to the Romans.

but in fact he uses it continually, both in the affirmative and the negative form, treating his theme through a polemical partition of categories which on both sides have universal application. In consequence, not only the natural sense of the words and the actual statement he makes, but both the immediate and wider context and the whole purpose and substance of his argument lead alike to the conclusion that what Paul means to say is that apart from faith in Christ there is nothing but sin and damnation—it was in this way that we promised we would refute free choice, so that all our opponents would be unable to resist; and I think I have done it, even though they will neither admit defeat and come over to our view, nor yet keep silence. That is not within our power; it is the gift of the Spirit of God.

However, before we hear John the Evangelist, let us add a crowning touch from Paul—and if that is not enough, we are prepared to bring out the whole of Paul against free choice, commenting on him verse by verse. In Romans 8[:5]: where he divides the human race into two types, namely, flesh and spirit (just as Christ does in John 3[:6]), he says: "Those who live according to the flesh set their minds on the things of the flesh, but those who live according to the Spirit set their minds on the things of the Spirit." That Paul here calls carnal all who are not spiritual is evident both from this very partition and opposition between spirit and flesh, and from his own subsequent statement: "You are not in the flesh but in the Spirit if the Spirit of God really dwells in you. Anyone who does not have the Spirit of Christ does not belong to him" [Rom. 8:9]. What else is the meaning of "You are not in the flesh if the Spirit of God is in you" but that those who do not have the Spirit are necessarily in the flesh? And if anyone does not belong to Christ, to whom else does he belong but Satan? Clearly, then, those who lack the Spirit are in the flesh and subject to Satan.

Now let us see what he thinks of the endeavor and power of free choice in those he calls carnal. "Those who are in the flesh cannot please God" [Rom. 8:8]. And again: "The mind of the flesh is death" [v. 6]. And again: "The mind of the flesh is enmity toward God" [v. 7]. Also: "It does not submit to God's law, indeed it cannot" [v. 7]. Here let the advocate of free choice tell me this: how something that is death, displeasing to God, hostility toward God, disobedient to God, and incapable of obedience can possibly strive toward the good? For Paul did not choose to say simply that the mind of the flesh is "dead" or "hostile to God," but that it is death itself, hostility itself, which cannot possibly submit to God's law or please God, just as he had said a little before: "For what was impossible to the law, in that it was weak because of the flesh, God has done," etc. [v. 3].

I, too, am familiar with Origen's fable about the threefold disposition of flesh, soul, and spirit, with soul standing in the middle and being capable of turning either way, toward the flesh or toward the spirit.[20] But these are dreams of his own; he states but does not prove them. Paul here calls everything flesh that is without the Spirit, as we have shown. Hence the loftiest virtues of the best of men are in the flesh, that is to say, they are dead, hostile to God, not submissive to the law of God and not capable of submitting to it, and not pleasing to God. For Paul says not only that they do not submit, but that they cannot. So also Christ says in Matthew 7[:18]: "A bad tree cannot bear good fruit," and in Matthew 12[:34]: "How can you speak good when you are evil?" You see here not only that we speak evil, but that we cannot speak good. And although he says elsewhere that we who are evil know how to give good gifts to our children [Matt. 7:11], yet he denies that we do good even when we give good gifts, because although what we give is a good creation of God, we ourselves are not good, nor do we give these good things in a good way; and he is speaking to all men, including his disciples. Thus the twin statements of Paul are confirmed, that the righteous live by faith [Rom. 1:17], and that whatsoever is not of faith is sin [Rom. 14:23]. The latter follows from the former, for if there is nothing by which we are justified but faith, it is evident that those who are without faith are not yet justified; and those who are not justified are sinners; and sinners are "bad trees" and cannot do anything but sin and "bear bad fruit." Hence, free choice is nothing but a slave of sin, death, and Satan, not doing and not capable of doing or attempting to do anything but evil.

---

[20] Cf. *Diatribe*, EAS 4, 126 (quoted p. 223, n. 19); cf. also Erasmus, *Enchiridion* 7.

Take also the example in chapter 10 [Rom. 10:20], quoted from Isaiah: "I have been found by those who did not seek me; I have shown myself to those who did not ask for me" [Isa. 65:1]. He says this with reference to the Gentiles, because it has been given to them to hear and to know Christ, though previously they could not even think of him, much less seek him or prepare themselves for him by the power of free choice. From this example it is clear enough that grace comes so freely that no thought of it, let alone any endeavor or striving after it, precedes its coming. It was the same also with Paul when he was Saul. What did he do with his wonderful power of free choice? He certainly gave his mind to very good and virtuous things from the point of view of reason. But observe by what endeavor he finds grace! Not only does he not seek it, but he receives it even while raging furiously against it. On the other hand, he says concerning the Jews in chapter 9 [Rom. 9:30]: "Gentiles who did not pursue righteousness have attained it, that is, righteousness through faith; but Israel who pursued the righteousness which is based on law did not succeed in fulfilling that law." What murmur can any defender of free choice raise against this? The Gentiles, just when they are full of ungodliness and every kind of vice, receive righteousness freely by the mercy of God, while the Jews, who devote themselves to righteousness with the utmost zeal and endeavor, are frustrated. Does not this simply mean that the endeavoring of free choice is in vain, even when it strives after the best, and that of itself it rather "speeds toward the worse, and backward borne glides from us?"[21] Nor can anyone say that they did not strive with the utmost power of free choice. Paul himself bears them witness in chapter 10, "that they have a zeal for God, but it is not enlightened" [Rom. 10:2]. Therefore, nothing is lacking in the Jews that is attributed to free choice, and yet nothing comes of it, or rather, the opposite comes of it. In the Gentiles there is nothing to be found of what is attributed to free choice, and yet the righteousness of God results. What is this but a confirmation by the unequivocal example of the two nations and the clearest possible testimony of Paul that grace is given freely to those without merits

---

[21] Virgil *Georgics* i. 200.

and the most undeserving, and is not obtained by any efforts, endeavors, or works, whether small or great, even of the best and most virtuous of men, though they seek and pursue righteousness with burning zeal?

[*St. John: Free Choice Is of "the World," "the Flesh"; Grace Is of Christ, by Faith. The Two Are Opposites*][22]

Let us now come to John, who is also an eloquent and powerful devastator of free choice. At the very outset, he represents free choice as so blind that it cannot even see the truth, let alone be able to strive toward it. For he says: "The light shines in the darkness, but the darkness does not comprehend it" [John 1:5]; and shortly afterward: "He was in the world, and the world knew him not. He came to his own, and his own received him not" [vv. 10 f.]. What do you think he means by "world"? Will you exempt any man from this description unless he has been recreated by the Holy Spirit? It is characteristic of this apostle to use this word "world" to mean precisely the whole race of men. Hence, whatever he says about the world applies also to free choice as the most excellent thing in man. Thus according to this apostle, the world does not know the light of truth [v. 10], the world hates Christ and those who are his [John 15:18 f.], the world neither knows nor sees the Holy Spirit [John 14:17], the whole world is in the power of the evil one [I John 5:19], all that is in the world is the lust of the flesh and the lust of the eyes and the pride of life [I John 2:16]. "You," he says, "are of the world" [John 8:23]. "The world cannot hate you, but it hates me because I testify of it that its works are evil" [John 7:7]. All these and many similar passages proclaim the glories of free choice, that principal part of the world and that which governs it under the overlordship of Satan.

For John too speaks of the world antithetically, so that "world" means everything that has not been taken out of the world into the Spirit, as Christ says to the apostles: "I took you out of the world and appointed you," etc. [John 15:16, 19]. If now there were any in the world who by the powers of free choice were endeavoring to-

---

22 WA 18, 776–783.

ward the good (which should be the case if free choice were able to do anything), John ought surely to have limited the word out of respect for these people, so as not to implicate them, by using a general term, in all the evils of which he accuses the world. As he does not do this, it is evident that he makes free choice guilty of all the charges brought against the world, since whatever the world does, it does by the power of free choice, or in other words, by means of reason and will, which are its most notable components.

He goes on: "To all who received him, who believed in his name, he gave power to become children of God; who were born, not of blood nor of the will of the flesh nor of the will of man, but of God" [John 1:12 f.]. By this absolute distinction he drives out of the Kingdom of Christ "blood," "the will of the flesh," "the will of man." I think "blood" means the Jews, that is, those who claimed to be sons of the Kingdom because they were sons of Abraham and the Patriarchs, and thus gloried in their blood. The "will of the flesh" I take to mean the zeal with which the people devoted themselves to the law and works. For "flesh" here means those who are carnal and without the Spirit, so that although they certainly have the ability to will and endeavor, they do so, in the absence of the Spirit, in a carnal way. The "will of man" I understand as the strivings of all men generally, whether under the law or without the law, Gentiles or whatever they may be, so that the meaning is: "They become sons of God neither by natural birth nor by zeal for the law nor by any other human doing, but only by a divine birth." If therefore they are not born of the flesh, nor trained by the law, nor prepared by any human discipline, but are born anew from God, it is plain that free choice counts for nothing here. For I think the word "man"[23] in this passage is to be taken in the Hebrew sense as meaning any and every man, just as "flesh" is understood in contrast with Spirit to mean the people without the Spirit; and the "will" I take to be the highest power in men, as the principal element in free choice.

But supposing we do not so understand the individual terms, the matter itself as a whole is quite clear. For by his division John rejects everything that is not born of God, inasmuch as he says we

---

23 "*Virum*," "male."

do not become sons of God except by being born of God; and this takes place, as he himself explains, by believing in the name of Christ. In this rejection, moreover, the will of man, or free choice, being neither a birth from God nor faith, is necessarily included. But if free choice were worth anything, the will of man ought not to be rejected by John, nor should men be drawn away from it and directed to faith and the new birth alone; otherwise, the word of Isaiah would apply to him: "Woe to you who call good evil" [Isa. 5:20]. As it is, since he rejects equally blood, the will of the flesh, and the will of man, it is certain that the will of man can no more do anything toward making men sons of God than can blood or carnal birth. But no one doubts that carnal birth does not make men sons of God. As Paul says in Romans 9[:8]: "It is not the children of the flesh who are the children of God," and he proves this by the example of Ishmael and Esau.

The same John introduces the Baptist speaking thus of Christ: "And of his fullness we have all received, grace for grace" [John 1:16]. He says that grace has been received by us from the fullness of Christ; but for what merit or effort? "For grace," he says, meaning Christ's grace; just as Paul also says in Romans 5[:15]: "The grace of God and the free gift in the grace of that one man Jesus Christ abounded for many." Where is now the endeavor of free choice by which grace is obtained? John says here, not only that grace is not received by any effort of ours, but that it is received through another's grace or another's merit, namely, that of the one man Jesus Christ. It is therefore either false that we receive our grace in return for another's grace, or else it is evident that free choice counts for nothing. For we cannot have it both ways; the grace of God cannot be both so cheap as to be obtainable anywhere and everywhere by any man's puny endeavor, and at the same time so dear as to be given us only in and through the grace of one Man and so great a Man. I wish the defenders of free choice would take warning at this point, and realize that when they assert free choice they are denying Christ. For if it is by my own effort that I obtain the grace of God, what need have I of the grace of Christ in order to receive it? Or what do I lack when I have the grace of God?

Now, Diatribe has said, and all the Sophists say, that we secure grace and prepare ourselves to receive it by our own endeavor, even if not "condignly," yet at least "congruously."[24] This is plainly a denial of Christ, when it is for his grace that we receive grace, as the Baptist testifies. For I have already exposed that fiction about "condign" and "congruous," showing that these are empty words, and that what they really have in mind is the merit of worthiness, and this to a more ungodly degree than the Pelagians themselves, as we said. The result is that the ungodly Sophists and Diatribe alike deny the Lord Christ who bought us, more than the Pelagians or any heretics ever denied him. So little can grace tolerate the power of free choice or even the slightest hint of it. The fact that the defenders of free choice deny Christ is proved, moreover, not only by this Scripture but also by their very way of life. For they have turned Christ from a kindly Mediator into a dreaded Judge for themselves, whom they strive to placate by the intercessions of his mother and the saints, and by a multitude of invented works, rites, religious orders, and vows, in all of which their aim is to placate Christ so that he may give them grace. They do not believe that Christ is their advocate with God, and obtains grace for them by his own blood, and as it says here, "grace for grace" [John 1:16]. And as they believe, so it is with them. Christ is truly and deservedly an inexorable Judge to them, inasmuch as they abandon him as a Mediator and most merciful Savior, and count his blood and his grace of less value than the efforts and endeavors of free choice.

Let us look also at an example of free choice. Nicodemus [John 3:1 ff.] surely is a man who leaves nothing to be desired as regards the capabilities of free choice; for what is there that he fails to do in the way of effort or endeavor? He confesses that Christ is true and has come from God; he praises his signs, he comes by night to hear him and converse with him. Does he not seem to have sought by the power of free choice the things that belong to godliness and salvation? Yet see how he comes to grief. When he hears the true way of salvation by means of a new birth as taught by Christ, does he recognize it or profess that it is what he himself has been seeking? On the contrary, he is so shocked and perturbed that he not

---

[24] Cf. *Diatribe*, EAS 4, 50.

only says he cannot understand it, but he rejects it as impossible. "How," he says, "can this be?" [John 3:9]. Nor indeed is it surprising, for whoever heard that a man must be born anew of water and the Spirit in order to be saved? [v. 5]. Whoever thought that the Son of Man would have to be lifted up, that whosoever believes in him should not perish but have eternal life? [vv. 14 ff.]. Did the greatest and most discerning philosophers ever make mention of this? Did the princes of this world ever possess this knowledge? Did any man's free choice ever strive toward this? Does not Paul confess it to be "wisdom hidden in a mystery" [I Cor. 2:7], which though foretold by the prophets and revealed by the gospel, has yet from eternity been kept secret and unknown to the world [Rom. 16:25]?

What can I say? Let us ask experience. The whole world, human reason itself, indeed free choice itself, is obliged to confess that it never knew Christ nor heard of him before the gospel came into the world. And if it did not know him, much less did it seek after him, or even could seek after him or make any endeavor to come to him. Yet Christ is the way, the truth, the life, and salvation [John 14:6]. It must therefore confess, willy-nilly, that by its own powers it has been unable either to know or to seek after the things that pertain to the way, the truth, and salvation. Nevertheless, despite this confession and our own experience, we insanely argue with empty words that there still remains in us a power capable of both knowing and applying itself to the things that pertain to salvation. That is as good as saying it can know Christ the Son of God lifted up for us, although no one has ever known or been able to think of such a thing. So ignorance here is no longer ignorance, but knowledge of Christ, that is, of the things that pertain to salvation. Do you still not see and feel that the assertors of free choice are clearly mad when they call a thing knowledge that they themselves admit to be ignorance? Is not this putting darkness for light, as Isaiah says [Isa. 5:20]? To think that God so mightily stops the mouth of free choice by its own confession and experience, yet not even so can it keep silence and give God the glory!

Furthermore, when Christ is called the way, the truth, and the life [John 14:6], and that antithetically, so that whatever is not Christ is not the way but error, not the truth but a lie, not the life but death, then it necessarily follows that free choice, since it is neither Christ nor in Christ, is included in the error, the lie, and the death. Where and whence, then, have we that intermediate and neutral thing, the power of free choice, which although it is not Christ or the way, the truth, and the life, must still not be error, or a lie, or death? For unless everything said about Christ and grace were said antithetically, so as to be set over against its opposite—for instance, that outside of Christ there is nothing but Satan, apart from grace nothing but wrath, apart from light only darkness, apart from the way only error, apart from the truth only a lie, apart from life only death—what, I ask you, would be the point of all the discourses of the apostles and of Scripture as a whole? They would all be in vain, because they would not insist on the absolute necessity of Christ, which in fact is their chief concern; and they would not do so because some intermediate thing would be found, which of itself would be neither evil nor good, neither Christ's nor Satan's, neither true nor false, neither alive nor dead, perhaps even neither something nor nothing, and that would be called "the most excellent and exalted thing in the whole race of men"!

Choose then which you please. If you grant that the Scriptures speak antithetically, you will be able to say nothing about free choice but what is contrary to Christ, namely that error, death, Satan, and all evils reign in it. If you do not grant that they speak antithetically, then you enervate the Scriptures, so that they lose their point and fail to prove that Christ is necessary. Hence, inasmuch as you maintain free choice, you cancel out Christ and ruin the entire Scripture. Moreover, although verbally you may make a show of confessing Christ, yet in reality and in your heart you deny him. Or if the power of free choice is not wholly in error or damnable, but sees and wills what is virtuous and good and what pertains to salvation, then it is in sound health and has no need of Christ the physician [Matt. 9:12], nor has Christ redeemed that part of man; for what need of light and life is there where there is light and life? And if that part has not been redeemed by Christ, the best thing in man has not been redeemed, but is in itself good and saved. But then God is unjust if he damns any man, because he damns what is best and soundly healthy in man, or in other words, he condemns the innocent. For there is no man who does not have the power of free choice; and although a bad man may misuse it, this power is not thereby destroyed, we are told, but still strives or can strive after the good. And if that is so, then it is undoubtedly good, holy, and righteous, and ought not to be damned but separated from the man who is to be damned. This, however, cannot be done; and if it could, a man no longer possessed of free choice would not be a man at all. He would have neither merits nor demerits, nor could he be saved, but would be simply a brute and no longer immortal. It therefore remains that God is unjust if he damns, along with the evil man, that good, righteous, and holy power which even in an evil man has no need of Christ.

But let us proceed with John. "He who believes in him," he says, "is not judged; he who does not believe is judged already, because he has not believed in the name of the only Son of God" [John 3:18]. Tell me, is free choice counted among those who believe, or is it not? If it is, then again it has no need of grace, since of itself it believes in Christ, though of itself it neither knows him nor gives him a thought. If it is not, then it is already judged; and what does that mean but that it is damned in the sight of God? But God damns none but the ungodly, so therefore it is ungodly. And what godliness can the ungodly aspire to? We cannot, I think, make an exception of the power of free choice here, since John is speaking of the *whole man*, who he says is damned. Besides, unbelief is not one of the grosser passions, but sits and holds sway at the summit—the citadel of the will and reason, just like its opposite, faith. Now, to be unbelieving is to deny God and make him a liar, as I John 1[:10] says: "If we do not believe God, we make him a liar" [cf. John 5:10]. And how can a power that is contrary to God and makes him a liar strive toward the good? If this power were not unbelieving and ungodly, John should not have said of the *whole man* that he is judged already, but rather that with regard to his grosser passions man is already judged, but with regard to what is best and most excellent in him he is not judged, because this strives after faith, or rather, already believes. Hence where Scripture says, as it so often does, that every man is a liar, we must say on the authority of free choice that, on the contrary, it is rather the Scripture that lies, because man is not a liar in the best part of him, his reason and will, but only in his flesh, blood, and bones, so that the whole of that which entitles man to be called man, namely reason and will, is soundly healthy and holy. Again, there are the words of the Baptist: "He who believes in the Son has eternal life; but he who does not believe in the Son shall not see life, but the wrath of God rests upon him" [John 3:36]. This will have to be understood as follows: "Upon him" means that whereas the wrath of God rests upon the grosser passions of man, upon his power of free choice, that is to say, his will and reason, there rests grace and eternal life. On this model, in order that free choice may be maintained, you can twist anything that is said in the Scriptures against ungodly men, to apply by synecdoche[25] to the brute part of man, so that the rational and truly human part may be left untouched. I shall then return thanks to the assertors of free choice, and shall sin with confidence, safe in the knowledge that reason and will, or free choice, cannot be damned, since it is never extinguished but remains forever sound, righteous, and holy. And with will and reason thus beatified, I shall rejoice that the filthy, brutish flesh is separated from them and damned; so far shall I be from wishing to have Christ as its Redeemer. Do you see what the dogma of free choice leads us to, how it denies all things divine and human, temporal and eternal, and with all these monstrous notions makes itself a laughingstock?

Again, the Baptist says: "No one can receive anything except what is given him from heaven" [John 3:27]. Diatribe may here stop that parading of her forces where she enumerates all the things we have from heaven.[26] We are not disputing about nature but about

---

[25] A figure of speech in which a part is used to express the whole, or vice versa.
[26] *Diatribe*, EAS 4, 136: "From this saying of John the Baptist it does not follow that there is no power or use of free choice. The fact that fire warms comes from heaven; the fact that we naturally seek what is useful and shun what is harmful, comes from heaven; the fact that after the Fall our will is impelled to better desires, comes from heaven; the fact that with tears, alms, and prayers we attain the grace that makes us acceptable to God, this too is from heaven. Nor does our will in the meantime do nothing, although it cannot attain what it seeks without the help of grace; but since what is done by us is so very little, the whole is ascribed to God, just as a sailor who has brought his ship safely into port out of a severe storm, does not say "I have saved the ship," but "God has saved it," although his own skill and toil were not useless. . . ."

grace, and we are not asking what we are on earth, but what we are in heaven before God. We know that man has been constituted lord over the lower creatures, and in relation to them he has authority and free choice, so that they obey him and do what he wills and thinks. What we are asking is whether he has free choice in relation to God, so that God obeys man and does what man wills, or rather, whether God has free choice in relation to man, so that man wills and does what God wills and is not able to do anything but what God wills and does. The Baptist says here that a man can receive nothing except what is given him from heaven; consequently, free choice must be nothing. Also, "He who is of the earth belongs to the earth, and of the earth he speaks; he who comes from heaven is above all" [John 3:31]. Here again he makes all men earthly who do not belong to Christ, and says they savor and speak of earthly things; and he leaves no room for any in between. Free choice, therefore, which is not in any event "he who comes from heaven," must necessarily be of the earth and must savor and speak of the earth.

But if ever at any time, in any place or work, there was any power in any man that did not savor of earthly things, the Baptist ought to have made allowance for this man and should not have said of all men generally that apart from Christ they are of the earth and speak of the earth. So also below, in chapter 8, Christ says: "You are of the world, I am not of the world; you are from below, I am from above" [John 8:23]. Now those to whom he was speaking possessed free choice, or reason and will, yet even so he says they are of the world. But what new thing would he be telling us, to say they were of the world as regards the flesh and the grosser passions? Did not the whole world know this already? Besides, what need is there to say that men are of the world as regards the brute part of them, when in this respect even beasts are of the world?

Now take the saying of Christ in John 6[:44]: "No one comes to me unless my Father draws him." What does this leave to free choice? For he says that everyone needs to hear and learn from the Father himself, and that all must be taught by God. He plainly teaches here, not only that the works and efforts of free choice are fruitless, but that even the message of the gospel itself (which is what this passage is about) is heard in vain unless the Father himself speaks, teaches, and draws inwardly. "No one can come," he says, "no one"; and thus that power by which a man is able to make some endeavor toward Christ, or in other words, toward the things that pertain to salvation, is asserted to be no power at all. Nor is free choice helped by Diatribe's attempt to depreciate this clear and most powerful passage by quoting from Augustine to the effect that God draws us in the same way as we draw a sheep, by holding out a green twig to it.[27] By this simile she claims it is proved that there is in us a power to follow the drawing of God. But this simile is valueless in connection with this passage. For God holds out not only one of his good things, but all of them, and even Christ his Son himself, yet not a man follows unless the Father inwardly does something else and draws in some other way; instead, the whole world persecutes the Son whom he holds out to it. The simile fits very well the case of the godly, who are already sheep and know God their Shepherd; for they, living in the Spirit and moved by him, follow wherever God wills and whatever he holds out to them. But the ungodly does not come even when he hears the Word, unless the Father draws and teaches him inwardly, which He does by pouring out the Spirit. There is then another "drawing" than the one that takes place outwardly; for then Christ is set forth by the light of the Spirit, so that a man is rapt away to Christ with the sweetest rapture, and rather yields passively to God's speaking, teaching, and drawing than seeks and runs himself.

Let us take one more passage from John, where he says: "The Spirit will convince the world of sin, because they have not believed in me" [John 16:8 f.]. Here you see that it is sin not to believe in Christ. And this sin is surely not seated in the skin or the hair, but precisely in the reason and the will. But when he makes the whole world guilty of this sin, of which experience shows that the world is as ignorant as it is of Christ until the convincing Spirit reveals it, then it is evident that in the sight of God free choice, with its will and its reason alike, is reckoned as a captive of this sin and as damned by it. Therefore, so long as it is ignorant of Christ and does

---

[27] Augustine, *On the Gospel of John* (*Tract. in Joan. Evang.*), XXVI, 5 (*MPL* 35, 1609).

not believe in him, it cannot will or strive after anything good but necessarily serves this sin without knowing it.

In a word, since Scripture everywhere preaches Christ by contrast and antithesis, as I have said, putting everything that is without the Spirit of Christ in subjection to Satan, ungodliness, error, darkness, sin, death, and the wrath of God, all the texts that speak of Christ must consequently stand opposed to free choice; and they are innumerable, indeed they are the entire Scripture. If, therefore, we submit the case to the judgment of Scripture, I shall win on all counts, and there will not be a jot or a tittle left that will not damn the dogma of free choice. Moreover, the fact that Scripture preaches Christ by contrast and antithesis, even if the great theologians and defenders of free choice are or pretend to be ignorant of it, is nevertheless known and commonly confessed by all Christians.

[*The Two Kingdoms, of Christ and of Satan. The Assurance of Faith*] [28]

For Christians know there are two kingdoms in the world, which are bitterly opposed to each other. In one of them Satan reigns, who is therefore called by Christ "the ruler of this world" [John 12:31] and by Paul "the god of this world" [II Cor. 4:4]. He holds captive to his will all who are not snatched away from him by the Spirit of Christ, as the same Paul testifies, nor does he allow them to be snatched away by any powers other than the Spirit of God, as Christ testifies in the parable of the strong man guarding his palace in peace [Luke 11:21]. In the other Kingdom, Christ reigns, and his Kingdom ceaselessly resists and makes war on the kingdom of Satan. Into this Kingdom we are transferred,[29] not by our own power but by the grace of God, by which we are set free from the present evil age[30] and delivered from the dominion of darkness.[31]

The knowledge and confession of these two kingdoms perpetually warring against each other with such might and main would

---

28 *WA* 18, 782–783.
29 Col. 1:13 f.
30 Gal. 1:4.
31 Col. 1:13.

alone be sufficient to confute the dogma of free choice, seeing that
we are bound to serve in the kingdom of Satan unless we are delivered by the power of God. These things, I say, the common people know, and they confess them abundantly in their proverbs and
prayers, their attitudes and their whole life.

I leave aside that truly Achillean text of mine,[32] which Diatribe
has bravely passed over and left intact. I mean, where Paul in
Romans 7[:14 ff.] and Galatians 5[:16 ff.] teaches that there is in
the saints and the godly a battle between the Spirit and the flesh, so
fierce that they cannot do what they would. From this I argued
thus: If human nature is so evil that in those born anew of the Spirit
it not only does not endeavor after the good but actually strives and
fights against it, how should it endeavor after the good in those who
are not yet born anew but are still "in the old man" and in bondage
to Satan? For even here Paul is not speaking only of the grosser
passions, in which Diatribe commonly takes refuge when she wants
to evade the Scriptures, but he lists among the works of the flesh
heresy, idolatry, dissension, strife, which undoubtedly have their
seat in those highest faculties, the reason and the will. If, therefore,
the flesh wages war against the Spirit with such passions as these in
the saints, it will fight against God all the more in the ungodly and
in free choice. That is why in Romans 8[:7] he calls it hostility to
God. I should like to see *this* argument pulled to pieces, and free
choice defended against it.

For my own part, I frankly confess that even if it were possible,
I should not wish to have free choice given to me, or to have anything left in my own hands by which I might strive toward salvation. For, on the one hand, I should be unable to stand firm and
keep hold of it amid so many adversities and perils and so many
assaults of demons, seeing that even one demon is mightier than all
men, and no man at all could be saved; and on the other hand, even
if there were no perils or adversities or demons, I should nevertheless have to labor under perpetual uncertainty and to fight as one
beating the air,[33] since even if I lived and worked to eternity, my

---

[32] Cf. *The Bondage of the Will*, 1525. LW 33, 145 n. 68 and 234, n. 36.
[33] I Cor. 9:26.

conscience would never be assured and certain how much it ought to do to satisfy God. For whatever work might be accomplished, there would always remain an anxious doubt whether it pleased God or whether he required something more, as the experience of all self-justifiers proves, and as I myself learned to my bitter cost through so many years. But now, since God has taken my salvation out of my hands into his, making it depend on his choice and not mine, and has promised to save me, not by my own work or exertion but by his grace and mercy, I am assured and certain both that he is faithful and will not lie to me, and also that he is too great and powerful for any demons or any adversities to be able to break him or to snatch me from him. "No one," he says, "shall snatch them out of my hand, because my Father who has given them to me is greater than all" [John 10:28 f.]. So it comes about that, if not all, some and indeed many are saved, whereas by the power of free choice none at all would be saved, but all would perish together. Moreover, we are also certain and sure that we please God, not by the merit of our own working, but by the favor of his mercy promised to us, and that if we do less than we should or do it badly, he does not hold this against us,[34] but in a fatherly way pardons and corrects us. Hence the glorying of all the saints in their God.

[*The Mercy and Justice of God in the Light of Nature, Grace, and Glory*][35]

Now, if you are disturbed by the thought that it is difficult to defend the mercy and justice of God when he damns the undeserving, that is to say, ungodly men who are what they are because they were born in ungodliness and can in no way help being and remaining ungodly and damnable, but are compelled by a necessity of nature to sin and to perish (as Paul says: "We were all children of wrath like the rest,"[36] since they are created so by God himself from seed corrupted by the sin of the one man Adam)—rather must God be honored and revered as supremely merciful toward those whom he

---

[34] Or: "does not impute this to us."
[35] *WA* 18, 784–785.
[36] Eph. 2:3.

justifies and saves, supremely unworthy as they are, and there must be at least some acknowledgement of his divine wisdom so that he may be believed to be righteous where he seems to us to be unjust. For if his righteousness were such that it could be judged to be righteous by human standards, it would clearly not be divine and would in no way differ from human righteousness. But since he is the one true God, and is wholly incomprehensible and inaccessible to human reason, it is proper and indeed necessary that his righteousness also should be incomprehensible, as Paul also says where he exclaims: "O the depth of the riches of the wisdom and the knowledge of God! How incomprehensible are his judgments and how unsearchable his ways!"[37] But they would not be incomprehensible if we were able in every instance to grasp how they are righteous. What is man, compared with God? How much is there within our power compared with his power? What is our strength in comparison with his resources? What is our knowledge compared with his wisdom? What is our substance over against his substance? In a word, what is our all compared with his?

If, therefore, we confess, as even nature teaches, that human power, strength, wisdom, substance, and everything we have, is simply nothing at all in comparison with divine power, strength, wisdom, knowledge, and substance, what is this perversity that makes us attack God's righteousness and judgment only, and make such claims for our own judgment as to wish to comprehend, judge, and evaluate the divine judgment? Why do we not take a similar line here too, and say, "Our judgment is nothing in comparison with the divine judgment"? Ask Reason herself whether she is not convinced and compelled to confess that she is foolish and rash in not allowing the judgment of God to be incomprehensible, when she admits that everything else divine is incomprehensible. In all other matters we grant God his divine majesty, and only in respect of his judgment are we prepared to deny it. We cannot for a while believe that he is righteous, even though he has promised us that when he reveals his glory we shall all both see and feel that he has been and is righteous.

---

[37] Rom. 11:33.

I will give an example to confirm this faith and console that evil eye which suspects God of injustice. As you can see, God so orders this corporal world in its external affairs that if you respect and follow the judgment of human reason, you are bound to say either that there is no God or that God is unjust. As the poet says: "Oft I am moved to think there are no gods!"[38] For look at the prosperity the wicked enjoy and the adversity the good endure, and note how both proverbs and that parent of proverbs, experience, testify that the bigger the scoundrel the greater his luck. "The tents of the ungodly are at peace," says Job [Job 12:6], and Psalm 72[73:12] complains that the sinners of the world increase in riches. Tell me, is it not in everyone's judgment most unjust that the wicked should prosper and the good suffer? But that is the way of the world. Here even the greatest minds have stumbled and fallen, denying the existence of God and imagining that all things are moved at random by blind Chance or Fortune. So, for example, did the Epicureans and Pliny; while Aristotle, in order to preserve that Supreme Being of his from unhappiness, never lets him look at anything but himself, because he thinks it would be most unpleasant for him to see so much suffering and so many injustices. The prophets, however, who did believe in God, had more temptation to regard him as unjust—Jeremiah, for instance, and Job, David, Asaph, and others. What do you suppose Demosthenes[39] and Cicero[40] thought, when after doing all they could they were rewarded with so tragic a death?

Yet all this, which looks so very like injustice in God, and which has been represented as such with arguments that no human reason or light of nature can resist, is very easily dealt with in the light of the gospel and the knowledge of grace, by which we are taught that although the ungodly flourish in their bodies, they lose their souls. In fact, this whole insoluble problem finds a quick solution in one short sentence, namely, that there is a life after this life, and whatever has not been punished and rewarded here will be punished and

---

[38] Ovid *Amores* iii. 8.36.

[39] Athenian orator and statesman (*ca.* 383–322 B.C.), opponent of Philip of Macedon; took poison after the failure of the Athenian revolt against the Macedonians.

[40] Roman orator, writer and statesman (106–43 B.C.); outlawed, pursued and murdered after a speech in the Senate against Mark Antony.

rewarded there, since this life is nothing but an anticipation, or rather, the beginning of the life to come.

If, therefore, the light of the gospel, shining only through the Word and faith, is so effective that this question which has been discussed in all ages and never solved is so easily settled and put aside, what do you think it will be like when the light of the Word and of faith comes to an end, and reality itself and the Divine Majesty are revealed in their own light? Do you not think that the light of glory will then with the greatest of ease be able to solve the problem that is insoluble in the light of the Word or of grace, seeing that the light of grace has so easily solved the problem that was insoluble in the light of nature?

Let us take it that there are three lights—the light of nature, the light of grace, and the light of glory, to use the common and valid distinction. By the light of nature it is an insoluble problem how it can be just that a good man should suffer and a bad man prosper; but this problem is solved by the light of grace. By the light of grace it is an insoluble problem how God can damn one who is unable by any power of his own to do anything but sin and be guilty. Here both the light of nature and the light of grace tell us that it is not the fault of the unhappy man, but of an unjust God; for they cannot judge otherwise of a God who crowns one ungodly man freely and apart from merits, yet damns another who may well be less, or at least not more, ungodly. But the light of glory tells us differently, and it will show us hereafter that the God whose judgment here is one of incomprehensible righteousness is a God of most perfect and manifest righteousness. In the meantime, we can only *believe* this, being admonished and confirmed by the example of the light of grace, which performs a similar miracle in relation to the light of nature.

[CONCLUSION]

[*That the Case Against Free Choice is Unanswerable Let Erasmus Be Willing to Admit*][1]

I will here bring this little book to an end, though I am prepared if need be to carry the debate farther. However, I think quite enough has been done here to satisfy the godly and anyone who is willing to admit the truth without being obstinate. For if we believe it to be true that God foreknows and predestines all things,[2] that he can neither be mistaken in his foreknowledge nor hindered in his predestination, and that nothing takes place but as he wills it (as reason itself is forced to admit), then on the testimony of reason itself there cannot be any free choice in man or angel or any creature.

Similarly, if we believe that Satan is the ruler of this world, who is forever plotting and fighting against the Kingdom of Christ with all his powers, and that he will not let men go who are his captives unless he is forced to do so by the divine power of the Spirit, then again it is evident that there can be no such thing as free choice.

Similarly, if we believe that original sin has so ruined us that even in those who are led by the Spirit it causes a great deal of trouble by struggling against the good, it is clear that in a man devoid of the Spirit there is nothing left that can turn toward the good, but only toward evil.

Again, if the Jews, who pursued righteousness to the utmost of their powers, rather ran headlong into unrighteousness, while the Gentiles, who pursued ungodliness, attained righteousness freely and unexpectedly, then it is also manifest from this very fact and experience that man without grace can will nothing but evil.

To sum up: If we believe that Christ has redeemed men by his blood, we are bound to confess that the whole man was lost; otherwise, we should make Christ either superfluous or the redeemer of only the lowest part of man, which would be blasphemy and sacrilege.

---

[1] WA 18, 786–787.
[2] Rom. 8:29.

My dear Erasmus, I beg you now for Christ's sake to do at last as you promised; for you promised you would willingly yield to anyone who taught you better.[3] Have done with respecting of persons! I recognize that you are a great man, richly endowed with the noblest gifts of God—with talent and learning, with eloquence bordering on the miraculous, to mention no others—while I have and am nothing, unless I may venture to boast that I am a Christian. Moreover, I praise and commend you highly for this also, that unlike all the rest you alone have attacked the real issue, the essence of the matter in dispute, and have not wearied me with irrelevancies about the papacy, purgatory, indulgences, and such like trifles (for trifles they are rather than basic issues), with which almost everyone hitherto has gone hunting for me without success. You and you alone have seen the question on which everything hinges, and have aimed at the vital spot; for which I sincerely thank you, since I am only too glad to give as much attention to this subject as time and leisure permit. If those who have attacked me hitherto had done the same, and if those who now boast of new spirits and new revelations would still do it, we should have less of sedition and sects and more of peace and concord. But God has in this way through Satan punished our ingratitude.

Unless, however, you can conduct this case differently from the way you have in this Diatribe, I could very much wish that you would be content with your own special gift, and would study, adorn, and promote languages and literature as you have hitherto done with great profit and distinction. I must confess that in this

---

[3] *Diatribe, EAS* 4, 92 f.: ". . . I do not knowingly resist the truth, and with all my heart I favor true evangelical liberty and detest whatever is opposed to the gospel. Nor do I here act the part of a judge, as I have said, but of a debater, and yet I can truly say that in the debate I have kept the oath that used to be demanded in capital cases from sworn judges. And although I am an old man now, I shall not be either ashamed or reluctant to learn from any young man who can teach me better things with evangelical courtesy. Here I know someone will say: 'Let Erasmus learn Christ and have done with human wisdom; no one understands these things unless he has the Spirit of God.' If I do not yet understand what Christ is, I have indeed been wandering far from the mark hitherto; though I should like to know what Spirit so many doctors and Christian people have possessed—the people being likely to have believed what their bishops taught—for the past thirteen hundred years without understanding this."

for Erasmus was not a theologian.

direction you have done no small service to me too, so that I am considerably indebted to you, and in this regard I certainly respect and admire you most sincerely. But God has not yet willed or granted that you should be equal to the matter at present at issue between us. I say this, as I beg you to believe, in no spirit of arrogance, but I pray that the Lord may very soon make you as much superior to me in this matter as you are in all others. There is no novelty in it, if God instructs Moses through Jethro[4] and teaches Paul through Ananias.[5] For as to your saying that you have wandered very far from the mark if you are ignorant of Christ, I think you yourself see what it implies. For it does not follow that everybody will go astray if you or I do. God is preached as being marvelous in his saints,[6] so that we may regard as saints those who are very far from sanctity. And it is not difficult to suppose that you, since you are human, may not have rightly understood or observed with due care the Scriptures or the sayings of the Fathers under whose guidance you think you are attaining your goal; and of this there is more than a hint in your statement that you are asserting nothing, but have only "discoursed."[7] No one writes like that who has a thorough insight into the subject and rightly understands it. I for my part in this book *have not discoursed, but have asserted and do assert,* and I am unwilling to submit the matter to anyone's judgment, but advise everyone to yield assent. But may the Lord, whose cause this is, enlighten you and make you a vessel for honor and glory.[8]

Amen.

---

[4] Exod. 18:13 ff.

[5] Acts 9:10 ff.

[6] Ps. 67:36 (Vulgate); English versions (Ps. 68:35) read: "terrible in his sanctuary."

[7] Erasmus ends his *Diatribe* by saying: "*CONTULI, penes alios esto judicium,*" "I have discoursed, let others pass judgment." *Contuli* can also mean "I have made comparisons," and it is this sense Luther has in mind here. He does not think it his business simply to discourse on the subject, comparing different views, but he must assert and proclaim the truth about it.

[8] Rom. 9:21.

14.

SERMON ON THE AFTERNOON
OF CHRISTMAS DAY
1530

Sermon on the Afternoon of Christmas Day,

Luke 2:1-14, December 25, 1530

You have heard today the story from the Gospel of St. Luke of how it came to pass that our Lord Christ was born and then also the message of the angel, who announced who the boy was who was born.[1] Now we shall go on and take up the message of the angel. So for today you have heard only that the child was born and that he is the Lord and Savior. Thus we spoke of the story, how it unfolded, and who the persons in it were. This article is so high that even today it is believed by only a few. Nevertheless, God has preserved

---

[1] Luther is referring to the sermon he preached that morning on Luke 2:1-10 (text in WA 32, 251-261; Buchwald, *Martin Luther Predigten, op. cit.,* II, 47-53).

it even through those who have not believed it. For at all times in the monasteries and universities there have been disputations and lectures which dealt with the fact that Christ the Lord, born of Mary, is true man and God. But it went no further than saying and hearing it.[2] But this belief is held by the devil too and the Turks and all the godless among the Christians, and is the kind of belief which everybody believes that it is true but would not die for it, as Eck[3] and many others show today. If they had as much from Christ and the teaching of the gospel as from the devil, they would also think as much of Christ. The Turk too admits that Christ was born of the Virgin Mary, that Mary was an immaculate virgin, and that Christ was more than a man; but the Word of God, as it is given in the gospel, he denies, and yet I fear that the Turk believes more of this article than does the pope. Therefore it is a high article to believe that this infant, born of Mary, is true God; for nobody's reason can ever accept the fact that he who created heaven and earth and is adored by the angels was born of a virgin. That is the article. Nobody believes it except he who also knows this faith, namely, that this child is the Lord and Savior.

But for whom was he born and whose Lord and Savior is he? The angels declare that he was born Lord and Savior. The Turks, the pope, and the scholars say the same thing, but only to the extent that it brings in money and honor. But that anyone could say, "to *you* is born," as the angel says, this is the faith which we must preach about. But we cannot preach about it as we would like to do. Indeed, who could ever grasp [the full meaning of] these words of the evangelist: "a Savior, who is the Lord," and, "to you"! I know well enough how to talk about it and what to believe about it, just as others do. So there are many who have this belief and do not doubt this first belief that Christ is the Lord, the Savior, and the virgin's Son. This I too have never doubted. But if these words are planted no higher than in my thoughts, then they have no firm roots. We are certain that this was proclaimed by the angel, but the firm faith does not follow. For the reason does not understand both sides of this faith, first that Christ is a man, but also the Savior and Lord

---

[2] This sentence supplied from Nürnberg Codex Solger.
[3] Johann Eck (1486-1543), one of Luther's earliest opponents. Cf. *The Leipzig Debate. LW* 31, 308-325.

or King. This needs to be revealed from heaven. One who really has the first faith also has the other.

Who, then, are those to whom this joyful news is to be proclaimed? Those who are faint-hearted and feel the burden of their sins, like the shepherds, to whom the angels proclaim the message, letting the great lords in Jerusalem, who do not accept it, go on sleeping. Beyond the first faith there must be the second faith, that Christ is not only the virgin's Son, but also the Lord of angels and the Savior of men. The words anyone can understand, antisacramentarians, fanatics, sectarians, and Turks; but they do not proceed from the heart, they come only from hearing and go no farther than hearing. This is not faith, however, but only a memory of what has been heard, that one knows that he has heard it. Nobody ventures upon it, so as to stake goods, life, and honor upon it. And yet we must preach it for the sake of those who are in the multitude to whom the angel preached.

This is our theology, which we preach in order that we may understand what the angel wants. Mary bore the child, took it to her breast and nursed it, and the Father in heaven has his Son, lying in the manger and the mother's lap. Why did God do all this? Why does Mary guard the child as a mother should? And reason answers: in order that we may make an idol of her, that honor may be paid to the mother. Mary becomes all this without her knowledge and consent, and all the songs and glory and honor are addressed to the mother. And yet the text does not sound forth the honor of the mother, for the angel says, "I bring to you good news of a great joy; for to you is born this day the Savior" [Luke 2:10-11]. I am to accept the child and his birth and forget the mother, as far as this is possible, although her part cannot be forgotten, for where there is a birth there must also be a mother. Nevertheless, we dare not put our faith in the mother but only in the fact that the child was born. And the angel desired that we should see nothing but the child which is born, just as the angels themselves, as though they were blind, saw nothing but the child born of the virgin, and desired that all created things should be as nothing compared with this child, that we should see nothing, be it harps, gold, goods, honor, power, and the like, which we would prefer before their message. For if I receive even the costliest and best in the world, it still does not have the name of Savior. And if the Turk were ten times stronger than he is, he could not for one moment save me from my infirmity, to say nothing of the peril of death, and even less from the smallest sin or from death itself. In my sin, my death, I must take leave of all created things. No, sun, moon, stars, all creatures, physicians, emperors, kings, wise men and potentates cannot help me. When I die I shall see nothing but black darkness, and yet that light, "To you is born this day the Savior" [Luke 2:11], remains in my eyes and fills all heaven and earth. The Savior will help me when all have forsaken me. And when the heavens and the stars and all creatures stare at me with horrible mien, I see nothing in heaven and earth but this child. So great should that light which declares that he is my Savior become in my eyes that I can say: Mary, you did not bear this child for yourself alone. The child is not yours; you did not bring him forth for yourself, but for me, even though you are his mother, even though you held him in your arms and wrapped him in swaddling clothes and picked him up and laid him down. But I have a greater honor than your honor as his mother. For your honor pertains to your motherhood of the body of the child, but my honor is this, that you have my treasure, so that I know none, neither men nor angels, who can help me except this child whom you, O Mary, hold in your arms. If a man could put out of his mind all that he is and has except this child, and if for him everything—money, goods, power, or honor—fades into darkness and he despises everything on earth compared with this child, so that heaven with its stars and earth with all its power and all its treasures becomes as nothing to him, that man would have the true gain and fruit of this message of the angel. And for us the time must come when suddenly all will be darkness and we shall know nothing but this message of the angel: "I bring to you good news of great joy; for to you is born this day the Savior" [Luke 2:10-11].

This, then, is the faith we preach, of which the Turks and the pope and all the sectarians know nothing. The fanatics do, it is true, snatch to themselves the words of the angels, but how earnest they are is plain to see. For they receive the Word only as a piece of paper, as the cup and corporal receive the body and blood of Christ. The paper does no more than contain something and pass it on to others, but yet it remains paper. Thus you copy something from one paper on another paper; from my tongue the Word sounds in your ear, but it does not go to the heart. So they receive this greatest of treasures to their great harm and still think they are Christians, just as though the paper were to say: I certainly have in me the written words, "to you is born this day the Savior"; therefore I shall be saved. But then the fire comes and burns up the paper.

Therefore this is the chief article, which separates us from all the heathen, that you, O man, may not only learn that Christ, born of the virgin, is the Lord and Savior, but also accept the fact that he is your Lord and Savior, that you may be able to boast in your heart: I hear the Word that sounds from heaven and says: This child who is born of the virgin is not only his mother's son. I have more than the mother's estate; he is more mine than Mary's, for he was born for me, for the angel said, "To you" is born the Savior. Then ought you to say, Amen, I thank thee, dear Lord.

But then reason says: Who knows? I believe that Christ, born of the virgin, is the Lord and Savior and he may perhaps help Peter and Paul, but for me, a sinner, he was not born. But even if you believed that much, it would still not be enough, unless there were added to it the faith that he was born for you. For he was not born merely in order that I should honor the mother, that she should be praised because he was born of the virgin mother. This honor belongs to none except her and it is not to be despised, for the angel said, "Blessed are you among women!" [Luke 1:28]. But it must not be too highly esteemed lest one deny what is written here: "To you is born this day the Savior." He was not merely concerned to be born of a virgin; it was infinitely more than that. It was this, as she herself sings in the Magnificat: "He has helped his servant Israel" [Luke 1:54]; not that he was born of me and my virginity, but born for you and for your benefit, not only for my honor.

Take yourself in hand, examine yourself and see whether you are a Christian! If you can sing: The Son, who is proclaimed to be a Lord and Savior, is my Savior; and if you can confirm the message of the angel and say yes to it and believe it in your heart, then your heart will be filled with assurance and joy and confidence, and you will not worry much about even the costliest and best that this world has to offer. For when I can speak to the virgin from the bottom of my heart and say: O Mary, noble, tender virgin, you have borne a child; this I want more than robes and guldens, yea, more than my body and life; then you are closer to the treasure than everything else in heaven and earth, as Ps. 73 [:25] says, "There is nothing upon earth that I desire besides thee." You see how a person rejoices when he receives a robe or ten guldens. But how many are there who shout and jump for joy when they hear the message of the angel: "To you is born this day the Savior?" Indeed, the majority look upon it as a sermon that must be preached, and when they have heard it, consider it a trifling thing, and go away just as they were before. This shows that we have neither the first nor the second faith. We do not believe that the virgin mother bore a son and that he is the Lord and Savior unless, added to this, I believe the second thing, namely, that he is my Savior and Lord. When I can say: This I accept as my own, because the angel meant it for me, then, if I believe it in my heart, I shall not fail to love the mother Mary, and even more the child, and especially the Father. For, if it is true that the child was born of the virgin and is mine, then I have no angry God and I must know and feel that there is nothing but laughter and joy in the heart of the Father and no sadness in my heart. For, if what the angel says is true, that he is our Lord and Savior, what can sin do against us? "If God is for us, who is against us?" [Rom. 8:31]. Greater words than these I cannot speak, nor all the angels and even the Holy Spirit, as is sufficiently testified by the beautiful and devout songs that have been made about it. I do not trust myself to express it. I most gladly hear you sing and speak of it, but as long as no joy is there, so long is faith still weak or even non-existent, and you still do not believe the angel.

You can see what our papists and Junkers, who have chosen innumerable saviors, have felt about this faith. Indeed, the papists still want to retain the mass, the invocation of saints, and their invented works by which we are to be saved. This is as much as to say, I do not believe in the Savior and Lord whom Mary bore; and yet they sing the words of the angel, hold their triple masses [at Christmas] and play their organs. They speak the words with their tongues but their heart has another savior. And the same is true in the monasteries: if you want to be saved, remember to keep the rule and regulations of Francis[4] and you will have a gracious God! And at the Diet of Augsburg they decided to stick to this. In the name of all the devils, let them stick there! It has been said sufficiently that this Savior lies in the manger. But if there is any other thing that saves me, then I rightly call it my savior. If the sun, moon, and stars save, I can call them saviors. If St. Bartholomew[5] or St. Anthony[6] or a pilgrimage to St. James[7] or good works save, then they surely are my savior. If St. Francis, then he is my savior. But then what is left of the honor of the child who was born this day, whom the angel calls Lord and Savior, and who wants to keep his name, which is Savior and Christ the Lord. If I set up any savior except this child, no matter who or what it is or is called, then he is not the Savior. But the text says that he is the Savior. And if this is true—and it is the truth—then let everything else go.

One who hears the message of the angel and believes it will be filled with fear, like the shepherds. True, it is too high for me to believe that I should come into this treasure without any merit on my part. And yet, so it must be. In the papacy this message was not preached in the pulpit, and I am afraid that it will disappear again. It was the other message that the devil initiated and has allowed to remain in the papacy. All their hymns are to this effect. Among the Turks the devil has completely wiped it out. Therefore, remember it, sing it, and learn it, while there is still time! I fear that the time will come when we shall not be allowed to hear, believe, and sing this message in public, and the time has already come when it is no longer understood; though Satan does allow it to be spoken with the mouth, as the papists do. But when it comes to declaring that he is born for you, and to singing:

> *In dulci jubilo*
> Now sing with hearts aglow!
> Our delight and pleasure

---

[4] Francis of Assisi (1182-1226), founder of the Franciscan Order, who was canonized two years after his death by Pope Gregory IX.

[5] According to Matt. 10:3, Mark 3:18, Luke 6:14, and Acts 1:13, Bartholomew is one of the twelve Apostles. His feast day is usually observed on August 24.

[6] St. Anthony (b. *ca.* 250 A.D.), a hermit who is considered the forerunner of the monastic movement.

[7] St. James of Compostella was the most frequented place of pilgrimage in Europe for many centuries.

> Lies *in praesepio*,
>   Like sunshine is our treasure
> *Matris in gremio*
> *Alpha est et O!*[8]

—this he is unwilling to allow.

What we have said, then, has been about that second faith, which is not only to believe in Mary's Son, but rather that he who lies in the virgin's lap is our Savior, that you accept this and give thanks to God, who so loved you that he gave you a Savior who is yours. And for a sign he sent the angel from heaven to proclaim him, in order that nothing else should be preached except that this child is the Savior and far better than heaven and earth. Him, therefore, we should acknowledge and accept; confess him as our Savior in every need, call upon him, and never doubt that he will save us from all misfortune. Amen.

---

[8] Fourteenth century macaronic German carol. *The Oxford Book of Carols* (Oxford University Press, 1928), No. 86.

PART IV

THE PROMISE OF THE SACRAMENTS

The first three parts of this anthology introduce aspects of Luther that are generally well known: that Luther took a strong stand for faith against the prevailing theological method of his time; that he was a translator and interpreter of Scripture; and that he was passionate for proclaiming the righteousness of God in Christ. This last made him opposed to all human claims for excellence that might obscure faith, even that freedom of human will might play any part in salvation.

But when it comes to the sacraments, the full range of Luther's theological contribution is not so well known. Many who have seen Luther only as the primordial Protestant will know his critique of the Mass, and of the Roman Catholic sacramental system generally. But they may not know that Luther is not only a critical theologian regarding the sacraments, but also a constructive one.

This is one area where it is safe to say that Luther's full views emerged slowly and in response to the debates of the age. Some of his early writings are quite traditional. Then follow treatises that are sharply polemical against claims for the sacraments that seem to set them alongside or apart from the gospel.

But as a range of other voices begin to emerge, including those more sharply critical of catholic sacramental theology, Luther soon found that he was in even deeper disagreement with these persons. The five long selections included here attempt to show something of this range of Luther's interests, and above all the positive contribution he made toward understanding the full meaning of the sacraments within the Christian faith.

Luther found in Baptism and in the Lord's Supper powerful and efficacious forms of the gospel itself. That Christ who must come to be known not only as *the* Lord but even more intimately as *my* Lord can be discerned in a number of ways, but certainly not exclusively through the preaching of the Word. Baptizing and sharing the Lord's Supper are also strong ways of proclaiming the gospel, which also provide a powerful, personal encounter for the individual believer.

15 The Blessed Sacrament of the Holy and True Body and Blood of Christ, and the Brotherhoods

The first document in this part was written in 1519. Luther's writing here shows many signs of continuity with traditional catholic teaching. He speaks of a change in the bread and wine that sounds compatible with the doctrine of transubstantiation. He emphasizes the need for frequent reception.

Even his proposal for laity to receive both bread and wine (which had been forbidden only as recently as the Council of Constance in 1414-18) is put forward with great caution. But here Luther already speaks of Baptism and the Lord's Supper as the two "principal sacraments in the church," rather than two among seven.

Two strongly evangelical themes are sounded here. One is the great stress on the relation between faith and the sacrament. Luther does not say that faith makes Christ present—this is never a position he would have maintained. But he does exhort his readers toward faith:

> Christ and all his saints are coming to you with all their virtues, sufferings, and mercies to live, work, suffer, and die with you, and . . . they desire to be wholly yours, having all things in common with you. If you will exercise and strengthen this faith, then you will experience what a rich, joyous, and bountiful wedding feast your God has prepared for you upon this altar (p. 254).

The other evangelical emphasis here concerns the nature of Christian community or fellowship as experienced in the Supper. Christians find true unity in Christ and with one another in the Lord's Supper. Luther contrasted this exchange of blessings and burdens with the practices of the brotherhoods. These were primarily lay groups that met ostensibly for devotional purposes, but whose meetings often had a largely social (sometimes even rowdy) character.

16   The Babylonian Captivity of the Church—Part I

Luther's critique of Roman Catholic sacramental practice is much more sharply focused in the second document, Part I of his great treatise from 1520. This entire writing is an attack on the system of seven sacraments (as the introduction makes clear), but this first part is especially important in its indictment of three aspects of the current Roman teaching concerning the Lord's Supper:

    □ The withholding of the cup from the laity summarizes the whole tyrannical, arbitrary, power-oriented side of the medieval church.

    □ The doctrine of transubstantiation (which the church lived well without for twelve hundred years) is an unnecessary, speculative philosophical imposition on simple faith that Christ is present in the bread and wine as he promised.

    □ Most serious of all, the doctrine of the sacrifice of the mass turns what ought to be a gracious gift of God into a human work or human action.

It is evident that much had happened in the one year since the previous treatise was written, and at the beginning of this section Luther reviews the events that have moved him beyond his earlier simple conviction that "it would be well if a general council were to decide that the sacrament should be administered to the laity in both kinds."

17   The Sacrament of the Body and Blood of Christ—Against the Fanatics

Luther was now perceived as a strong opponent of the sacraments. King Henry VIII of England even received the papal title of "defender of the Faith" for his refutation of Luther's "Babylonian Captivity." But this was hardly Luther's final word.

In the next few years, much more violent critics of sacramental theology and practice began to appear, claiming Luther's example in justification of their own views. In the debates that followed Luther seems to have discovered that he was far more "catholic" in regard to sacramental theology than he might earlier have imagined.

The third document comes from the year 1526. For all of its polemical title ("Against the Fanatics"), it is a clear, simple, pastoral text, based on a series of three sermons that Luther preached to the Wittenberg congregation in the season of Easter, 1526.

It does have as its background the controversies near home with radical reformers like Andreas Karlstadt and debates with voices at a greater distance, like that of the Swiss Reformer Ulrich Zwingli, whose influence was growing at this time. It shows us Luther expounding the sacrament in a simple way that the people can understand, but with the controversies of the day clearly in mind.

The first part is a passionate defense of the reality of the bodily presence of Christ in the bread and the wine. Luther's attack on transubstantiation in the "Babylonian Captivity" had never called into question this "real presence."

Luther shows that while his opponents on the radical edge of the Reformation claim that it is neither fitting nor necessary for Christ to be in the bread and in the wine, these same arguments can really be used against the incarnation itself. The bread and wine are as fitting vehicles for the presence of Christ as was his human body. The finite is capable of bearing the infinite.

The second part of the treatise is a discussion of the proper spirit in which to come to the sacrament and a celebration of the fruits or benefits that one receives. The third part is an evangelical presentation of a long-standing sacramental concern about confession and forgiveness. Here Luther's chief stress is on the way in which penance is presented. Private confession must not be demanded, but rather the people invited to come "with kind words and not with coercion."

18   Concerning Rebaptism

The next document in this part is another one that grew out of the controversies of the 1520's. Luther wrote this expansion of his earlier baptismal theology late in 1527 and early in 1528 as a response to the growing influence of the anabaptists.

He was stimulated by their attacks on infant baptism both to an affirmation of that traditional practice and even more deeply to a meditation on the meaning and gift of baptism itself. If baptism were to be repeated and grounded on certain faith, then "baptizing without end would result." One could never be sure of baptism if it were grounded in personal faith, rather than in the promise and action of God.

> Assume that the first baptism is without faith. Tell me which is the greater and the more important in the second baptism, the Word of God or faith? Is it not true that the Word of God is greater and more important than faith, since faith builds and is founded on the Word of God rather than God's Word on faith? Furthermore faith may waver and change, but God's Word remains forever (p. 372).

19   Confession Concerning Christ's Supper— from Part I

The final selection in this group is from a document that has already been introduced in selection 4, "Confession Concerning Christ's Supper" from 1528. Here we find Luther in the midst of the fully developed conflict with Zwingli about the mode of Christ's presence in the Eucharist. Zwingli, who had argued that since Christ is now at the right hand of the Father, he cannot be present in local celebrations of the sacrament, accused Luther of misunderstanding the Ascension.

But Luther exhorts Zwingli (and modern readers) to think more energetically about the promise of Christ, and therefore about ways in which the mode of presence might be understood.

Perhaps it is Zwingli's understanding of the Ascension that is too literal, locating Christ in glory in a far-off place.

In fact, Luther wonders by the end of this spirited and conceptually challenging excerpt whether Zwingli and his followers may have misunderstood the incarnation itself. And he challenges the reader to think more deeply about the nature of God:

> God . . . is a supernatural, inscrutable being who exists at the same time in every little seed, whole and entire, and yet also in all and above all and outside all created things. There is no need to enclose him here, as this spirit dreams, for a body is much, much too wide for the Godhead; it could contain many thousand Godheads. On the other hand, it is also far too narrow to contain one Godhead (p. 397).

Zwingli, for all his distrust of catholic tradition, has in the end put the same faith in reason that Luther had been attacking ten years earlier in his writings against scholastic theological method. Reason cannot accept a gracious God, let alone a God bound by a promise to be present in the flesh of Jesus Christ, in the water of baptism, and in the bread and wine of the sacrament.

But the Christian community knows by faith that God is graciously present in just this place. Thus the theologian writing about the sacraments must keep struggling until he or she can present a doctrinal account that is faithful to this full reality of the church's experience.

15.

THE BLESSED SACRAMENT OF THE HOLY AND TRUE BODY OF CHRIST, AND THE BROTHERHOODS

1. The holy sacrament of the altar, or of the holy and true body[1] of Christ, also has three parts[2] which it is necessary for us to know. The first is the sacrament, or sign. The second is the significance of this sacrament. The third is the faith required with each of the first two. These three parts must be found in every sacrament. The sacrament must be external and visible, having some material form or appearance. The significance must be internal and spiritual, within the spirit of the person. Faith must make both of them together operative and useful.

2. The sacrament, or external *sign*, consists in the form or appearance of bread and wine, just as baptism has water as its sign; only the bread and wine must be used in eating and drinking, just as the water of baptism is used by immersion or pouring. For the sacrament, or sign, must be received, or at least desired, if it is to work a blessing. Of course at present both kinds are not given to the people daily, as in former times.[3] But this is not necessary since the priesthood partakes of it daily in sight of the people. It is enough

---

[1]*Waren Leychnams* is the actual body which was given into death. MA³, Er 2, 540, n. 382, 2.

[2]Cf. *The Sacrament of Penance* (1519), *LW* 35, 11, and *The Holy and Blessed Sacrament of Baptism* (1519), *LW* 35, 29-30.

[3] The custom of giving only the bread but not the wine to the laity was enacted into canon law by the Council of Constance which burned an earlier advocate of both kinds, John Huss, as a heretic, even though the council itself admitted the custom's divergence from the institution of Jesus and the practice of the early church. Denzinger, *The Sources of Catholic Dogma*, No. 626.

that the people desire it daily and at present receive one kind, as the Christian Church ordains and provides.[4]

3. For my part, however, I would consider it a good thing if the church should again decree[5] in a general council that all persons be given both kinds, like the priests. Not because one kind is insufficient, since indeed the desire of faith is alone sufficient, as St. Augustine says, "Why do you prepare stomach and teeth? Only believe, and you have already partaken of the sacrament."[6] But it would be fitting and fine that the form, or sign, of the sacrament be given not in part only, but in its entirety, just as I said of baptism: it would be more fitting to immerse in the water than to pour with it, for the sake of the completeness and perfection of the sign.[7] For this sacrament [of the Body of Christ], as we shall see, signifies the complete union and the undivided fellowship of the saints; and this is poorly and unfittingly indicated by [distributing] only one part of the sacrament. Nor is there as great a danger in the use of the cup as is supposed,[8] since the people seldom go to this sacrament. Besides Christ was well aware of all future dangers, and yet he saw fit to institute both kinds for the use of all his Christians.

4. The *significance* or effect of this sacrament is fellowship of all the saints. From this it derives its common name *synaxis* [Greek] or *communio* [Latin], that is, fellowship. And the Latin *communicare* [commune or communicate], or as we say in German, *zum sacrament*

---

[4] Later Luther continued to allow for the voluntary use of one kind, but he soon expressed himself more forthrightly on the propriety of both kinds and the wickedness of forbidding both kinds. Cf. *A Treatise on the New Testament, that is, the Holy Mass*, in this volume, pp. 106-107. *LW* 36, 19-28.

[5] The Council of Basel had concluded the *Compactata* of Prague (November 30, 1433), which reversed the decision of Constance to the extent of allowing the followers of Huss to administer the sacrament in both kinds. Cf. *LW* 36, 27 and 13.

[6] *Sermo* 112, cap. 5. Migne 38, 645.

[7] Cf. *The Holy and Blessed Sacrament of Baptism*, 1519. *LW* 35, 29.

[8] The danger, readily conceded by pious laity who trembled at the thought of it, was that a drop of the consecrated wine might fall to the floor. Since the bread was regarded as the more important anyway–and could be placed in the mouth of the communicant without his even having to touch it–it seemed possible, by expending with reception of the wine, to avoid the danger of desecrating the sacrament. Cf. Albert Hauck (ed.), *Realencyklopädie für protestantische Theologie und Kirche* (3rd ed., 24 vols.; Leipzig: Hinrichs, 1896-1913), XII, 721.

gehen [go to the sacrament], means to take part in this fellowship. Hence it is that Christ and all saints are one spiritual body,[9] just as the inhabitants of a city are one community and body, each citizen being a member of the other and of the entire city. All the saints, therefore, are members of Christ and of the church, which is a spiritual and eternal city of God.[10] And whoever is taken into this city is said to be received into the community of saints and to be incorporated into Christ's spiritual body and made a member of him. On the other hand *excommunicare* [excommunicate] means to put out of the community and to sever a member from this body; and that is called in our language "putting one under the ban"—though a distinction [is to be made in this regard] as I shall show in the following treatise, concerning the ban.[11]

To receive this sacrament in bread and wine, then, is nothing else than to receive a sure sign of this fellowship and incorporation with Christ and all saints. It is as if a citizen were given a sign, a document, or some other token to assure him that he is a citizen of the city, a member of that particular community. St. Paul says this very thing in I Corinthians 10[:17], "We are all one bread and one body, for we all partake of one bread and of one cup."

5. This fellowship consists in this, that all the spiritual possessions of Christ and his saints[12] are shared with and become the common property of him who receives this sacrament. Again all sufferings and sins also become common property; and thus love engenders love in return and [mutual love] unites. To carry out our homely figure, it is like a city where every citizen shares with all the others the city's name, honor, freedom, trade, customs, usages, help,

---

[9] Cf. Rom. 12:5; I Cor. 12:5.

[10] Cf. Isa. 60:14; Heb. 12:22; Rev. 3:12.

[11] See *A Treatise Concerning the Ban* (1520) (*PE* 2, 35-54), where Luther distinguishes between the external ban (excommunication) which excludes from the church's sacramental fellowship and the internal ban (sin and unbelief) which excludes from the fellowship with Christ.

[12] As early as 1515-1516 in his lectures on Romans [12:13] Luther distinguished between the contemporary understanding of "saints" as those who "are blessed and participating in glory" and the biblical understanding of "saints" as "all those who believe in Christ." *WA* 56, 469; *MA³*, Er 2, 398. This second sense is implicit in his use of the term here and throughout this treatise.

support, protection, and the like, while at the same time he shares all the dangers of fire and flood, enemies and death, losses, taxes, and the like. For he who would share in the profits must also share in the costs,[13] and ever recompense love with love.[14] Here we see that whoever injures one citizen injures an entire city and all its citizens; whoever benefits one [citizen] deserves favor and thanks from all the others. So also in our natural body, as St. Paul says in I Corinthians 12[:25-26], where he gives this sacrament a spiritual explanation, "The members have [the same] care for one another; if one member suffers, all suffer together; if one member is honored, all rejoice together." This is obvious: if anyone's foot hurts him, yes, even the little toe, the eye at once looks at it, the fingers grasp it, the face puckers, the whole body bends over to it, and all are concerned with this small member; again, once it is cared for all the other members are benefited. This comparison must be noted well if one wishes to understand this sacrament, for Scripture uses it for the sake of the unlearned.

6. In this sacrament, therefore, man is given through the priest a sure sign from God himself that he is thus united with Christ and his saints and has all things in common [with them], that Christ's sufferings and life are his own, together with the lives and sufferings of all the saints. Therefore whoever does injury to [the believer], does injury to Christ and all the saints, as he says through the prophet [Zech. 2:8], "He who touches you touches the apple of my eye." On the other hand whoever does him a kindness does it to Christ and all his saints; as he says in Matthew 25[:40], "As you did it to one of the least of these my brethren, you did it to me." Again, man must be willing to share all the burdens and misfortunes of Christ and

---

[13] Cf. the English aphorism, "What's none of my profit shall be none of my peril" (Vincent Stuckey Lean, *Lean's Collectanea* [Bristol: Arrowsmith, 1904], IV, 178) with its German equivalents in Karl F. Wander (ed.), *Deutsches Sprichwörter-Lexikon* (5 vols.; Leipzig: Brockhaus, 1867-1880), I, 1557, "*Geniessen*," Nos. 3, 4, 10, 14.

[14] Cf. the English aphorism, "Love is love's reward" (*Lean's Collectanea*, IV, 39), with its German equivalents in Wander (ed.), *Sprichwörter-Lexikon*, III, 136ff., "*Liebe*," Nos. 146, 386, 388, 635, 661, and especially No. 410 which also cites the English, "Love can neither be bought nor sold, its only price is love."

his saints, the cost as well as the profit. Let us consider more fully these two [sides of the fellowship].

7. Now adversity assails us in more than one form. There is, in the first place, the sin that remains in our flesh after baptism: the inclination to anger, hatred, pride, unchastity, and so forth. This sin assails us as long as we live.[15] Here we not only need the help of the community [of saints] and of Christ, in order that they might with us fight this sin, but it is also necessary that Christ and his saints intercede for us before God, so that this sin may not be charged to our account by God's strict judgment. Therefore in order to strengthen and encourage us against this same sin, God gives us this sacrament, as much as to say, "Look, many kinds of sin are assailing you; take this sign by which I give you my pledge that this sin is assailing not only you but also my Son, Christ, and all his saints in heaven and on earth. Therefore take heart and be bold. You are not fighting alone. Great help and support are all around you." King David speaks thus of this bread, "The bread strengthens a man's heart" [Ps. 104:15]. And the Scriptures in numerous places ascribe to this sacrament the property of strengthening, as in Acts 9[:18-19] [where it is written] of St. Paul, "He was baptized, and when he had received the food, he was strengthened."

In the second place the evil spirit assails us unceasingly with many sins and afflictions. In the third place the world, full of wickedness, entices and persecutes us and is altogether bad. Finally our own guilty conscience assails us with our past sins; and there is the fear of death and the pains of hell. All of these afflictions make us weary and weak, unless we seek strength in this fellowship, where strength is to be found.

8. Whoever is in despair, distressed by a sin-stricken conscience or terrified by death or carrying some other burden upon his heart, if he would be rid of them all, let him go joyfully to the sacrament of the altar and lay down his woe in the midst of the community [of saints] and seek help from the entire company of the spiritual body—just as a citizen whose property has suffered damage or misfortune at the hands of his enemies makes complaint to his town council and

---

[15]Cf. Introduction, *The Blessed Sacrament of the Holy and True Body and Blood of Christ*, 1519. LW 35, 30-34.

fellow citizens and asks them for help. The immeasurable grace and
mercy of God are given us in this sacrament to the end that we might
put from us all misery and tribulation [*anfechtung*] and lay it upon
the community [of saints], and especially on Christ. Then we may
with joy find strength and comfort, and say, "Though I am a sinner
and have fallen, though this or that misfortune has befallen me,
nevertheless I will go to the sacrament to receive a sign from God
that I have on my side Christ's righteousness, life, and sufferings,
with all holy angels and the blessed in heaven and all pious men on
earth. If I die, I am not alone in death; if I suffer, they suffer with
me. [I know that] all my misfortune is shared with Christ and the
saints, because I have a sure sign of their love toward me." See, this
is the benefit to be derived from this sacrament; this is the use
we should make of it. Then the heart cannot but rejoice and be
strengthened.

9. When you have partaken of this sacrament, therefore, or
desire to partake of it, you must in turn share the misfortunes of the
fellowship, as has been said. But what are these? Christ in heaven
and the angels, together with the saints, have no misfortunes, except
when injury is done to the truth and to the Word of God. Indeed,
as we have said, every bane and blessing of all the saints on earth
affects them. Here your heart must go out in love and learn that
this is a sacrament of love. As love and support are given you, you
in turn must render love and support to Christ in his needy ones.
You must feel with sorrow all the dishonor done to Christ in his
holy Word, all the misery of Christendom, all the unjust suffering
of the innocent, with which the world is everywhere filled to overflowing. You must fight, work, pray, and—if you cannot do more—
have heartfelt sympathy. See, this is what it means to bear in your
turn the misfortune and adversity of Christ and his saints. Here the
saying of Paul is fulfilled, "Bear one another's burdens, and so fulfil
the law of Christ" [Gal. 6:2]. See, as you uphold all of them, so they
all in turn uphold you; and all things are in common, both good and
evil. Then all things become easy, and the evil spirit cannot stand
up against this fellowship.

When Christ instituted the sacrament, he said, "This is my body which is given for you, this is my blood which is poured out for you. As often as you do this, remember me."[16] It is as if he were saying, "I am the Head, I will be the first to give himself for you. I will make your suffering and misfortune my own and will bear it for you, so that you in your turn may do the same for me and for one another, allowing all things to be common property, in me, and with me. And I leave you this sacrament as a sure token of all this, in order that you may not forget me, but daily call to mind and admonish one another by means of what I did and am still doing for you, in order that you may be strengthened, and also bear one another in the same way."

10. This is also a reason, indeed the chief reason, why this sacrament is received many times, while baptism is received but once. Baptism is the taking up or entering upon a new life,[17] in the course of which boundless adversities assail us, with sins and sufferings, both our own and those of others. There is the devil, the world, and our own flesh and conscience, as I have said. They never cease to hound us and oppress us. Therefore we need the strength, support, and help of Christ and of his saints. These are pledged to us here, as in a sure sign, by which we are made one with them—incorporated into them—and all our woe is laid down in the midst of the community [of saints].

For this reason it even happens that this holy sacrament is of little or no benefit to those who have no misfortune or anxiety, or who do not sense their adversity. For it is given only to those who need strength and comfort, who have timid hearts and terrified consciences, and who are assailed by sin, or have even fallen into sin. How could it do anything for untroubled and secure spirits, who neither need nor desire it? For the Mother of God[18] says, "He fills only the hungry [Luke 1:53], and comforts them that are distressed."

11. In order that the disciples, therefore, might by all means be worthy and well prepared for this sacrament, Christ first made them

---

[16]Cf. *A Treatise on the New Testament*, 1520. *LW* 35, 82, n. 5.

[17]Cf. Introduction, *LW* 35, 30.

[18] Luther often called the Virgin Mary by this term of veneration which was common in Western Christendom. Cf. his discussion of the name in *The Magnificat* (1521). *LW* 21, 326-327.

sorrowful, held before them his departure and death, by which they became exceedingly troubled. And then he greatly terrified them when he said that one of them would betray him. When they were thus full of sorrow and anxiety, disturbed by sorrow and the sin of betrayal, then they were worthy, and he gave them his holy body[19] to strengthen them.[20] By which he teaches us that this sacrament is strength and comfort for those who are troubled and distressed by sin and evil. St. Augustine says the same thing, "This food demands only hungry souls, and is shunned by none so greatly as by a sated soul which does not need it."[21] Thus the Jews were required to eat the Passover with bitter herbs, standing and in haste [Exod. 12:8, 11]; this too signifies that this sacrament demands souls that are desirous, needy, and sorrowful. Now if one will make the afflictions of Christ and of all Christians his own, defend the truth, oppose unrighteousness, and help bear the needs of the innocent and the sufferings of all Christians, then he will find affliction and adversity enough, over and above that which his evil nature, the world, the devil, and sin daily inflict upon him. And it is even God's will and purpose to set so many hounds upon us and oppress us, and everywhere to prepare bitter herbs for us, so that we may long for this strength and take delight in the holy sacrament, and thus be worthy (that is, desirous) of it.

12. It is Christ's will, then, that we partake of it frequently, in order that we may remember him and exercise ourselves in this fellowship according to his example. For if his example were no longer kept before us, the fellowship also would soon be forgotten. So we at present see to our sorrow that many masses are held and yet the Christian fellowship which should be preached, practiced, and kept before us by Christ's example has virtually perished. So much so that we hardly know any more what purpose this sacrament serves or how it should be used. Indeed with our masses we frequently destroy this fellowship and pervert everything. This is the fault of the preachers who do not preach the gospel or the sacra-

---

[19] *Leychnam;* cf. p. 49, n. 1.
[20] Following Matt. 26:20-25 and Mark 14:17-21, Luther places the announcement of the betrayal prior to the institution of the Lord's Supper.
[21] Cf. Augustine's commentary on Ps. 22:26 (Vulgate 21:27) in Migne 36, 178.

ments, but their humanly devised fables about the many works [of satisfaction][22] to be done and the ways to live aright.

But in times past this sacrament was so properly used, and the people were taught to understand this fellowship so well, that they even gathered food and material goods in the church, and there—as St. Paul writes in I Corinthians 11[23]—distributed among those who were in need. We have a vestige of this [practice] in the little word "collect" in the mass,[24] which means a general collection, just as a common fund is gathered to be given to the poor. Those were the days too when so many became martyrs and saints. There were fewer masses, but much strength and blessing resulted from the masses; Christians cared for one another, supported one another, sympathized with one another, bore one another's burdens and affliction. This has all disappeared, and now there remain only the many masses and the many who receive this sacrament without in the least understanding or practicing what it signifies.

13. There are those, indeed, who would gladly share in the profits but not in the costs. That is, they like to hear that in this sacrament the help, fellowship, and support of all the saints are promised and given to them. But they are unwilling in their turn to belong also to this fellowship. They will not help the poor, put up with sinners, care for the sorrowing, suffer with the suffering, intercede for others, defend the truth, and at the risk of [their own] life, property, and honor seek the betterment of the church and of all Christians. They are unwilling because they fear the world. They do not want to have to suffer disfavor, harm, shame, or death, although it is God's will that they be thus driven—for the sake of the truth and of their neighbors—to desire the great grace and strength of this sacrament. They are self-seeking persons, whom this sacrament does not benefit. Just as we could not put up with a citizen who wanted to be helped, protected, and made free by the community, and yet in his turn would do nothing for it nor serve it. No, we on our part must make the evil of others our own, if we desire Christ and his

---

[22]Cf. *The Sacrament of Penance*, 1519. *LW* 35, 12-18.
[23]I Cor. 11:21, 33; cf. Acts 2:44-46.
[24]Cf. *The Holy and Blessed Sacrament of Baptism*, 1519. *LW* 35, 95.

saints to make our evil their own. Then will the fellowship be complete, and justice be done to the sacrament. For the sacrament has no blessing and significance unless love grows daily and so changes a person that he is made one with all others.

14. To signify this fellowship, God has appointed such signs of this sacrament as in every way serve this purpose and by their very form stimulate and motivate us to this fellowship. For just as the bread is made out of many grains ground and mixed together, and out of the bodies of many grains there comes the body of one bread,[25] in which each grain loses its form and body and takes upon itself the common body of the bread; and just as the drops of wine, in losing their own form, become the body of one common wine and drink—so it is and should be with us, if we use this sacrament properly. Christ with all saints, by his love, takes upon himself our form [Phil. 2:7], fights with us against sin, death, and all evil. This enkindles in us such love that we take on his form, rely upon his righteousness, life, and blessedness. And through the interchange of his blessings and our misfortunes, we become one loaf, one bread, one body, one drink, and have all things in common. O this is a great sacrament,[26] says St. Paul, that Christ and the church are one flesh and bone. Again through this same love, we are to be changed and to make the infirmities of all other Christians our own; we are to take upon ourselves their form and their necessity, and all the good that is within our power we are to make theirs, that they may profit from it. That is real fellowship, and that is the true significance of this sacrament. In this way we are changed into one another and are made into a community by love. Without love there can be no such change.

---

[25] The figure is very ancient, going back at least into the second century as attested by a document unknown to Luther, *The Didache* 9:4, "As this piece [of bread] was scattered over the hills [the reference is likely to the sowing of wheat on the hillsides of Judea] and then was brought together and made one, so let your church be brought together from the ends of the earth into your kingdom." Cyril C. Richardson (trans., ed.), *Early Christian Fathers* ("The Library of Christian Classics," Vol. I [Philadelphia: Westminster Press, 1953]), p. 175.

[26] In the Vulgate of St. Jerome, the Greek word *mysterion* (mystery) in Eph. 5:32 is translated *sacramentum*. Cf. Luther's later discussion of the term in *LW* 36, 93-95.

15. Christ appointed these two forms of bread and wine, rather than any other, as a further indication of the very union and fellowship which is in this sacrament. For there is no more intimate, deep, and indivisible union than the union of the food with him who is fed. For the food enters into and is assimilated by his very nature, and becomes one substance with the person who is fed. Other unions, achieved by such things as nails, glue, cords, and the like, do not make one indivisible substance of the objects joined together. Thus in the sacrament we too become united with Christ, and are made one body with all the saints, so that Christ cares for us and acts in our behalf. As if he were what we are, he makes whatever concerns us to concern him as well, and even more than it does us. In turn we so care for Christ, as if we were what he is, which indeed we shall finally be—we shall be conformed to his likeness. As St. John says, "We know that when he shall be revealed we shall be like him" [I John 3:2]. So deep and complete is the fellowship of Christ and all the saints with us. Thus our sins assail him, while his righteousness protects us. For the union makes all things common, until at last Christ completely destroys sin in us and makes us like himself, at the Last Day. Likewise by the same love we are to be united with our neighbors, we in them and they in us.

16. Besides all this, Christ did not institute these two forms solitary and alone, but he gave his true natural flesh in the bread, and his natural true blood in the wine, that he might give a really perfect sacrament or sign. For just as the bread is changed[27] into his true natural body[28] and the wine into his natural true blood, so truly are we also drawn and changed into the spiritual body, that is, into the fellowship of Christ and all saints and by this sacrament put into possession of all the virtues and mercies of Christ and his saints,

---

[27] *Vorwandelt.* While this term and the imagery involving change are associated with the doctrine of transubstantiation, it is clear that, through rejecting all scholastic speculation concerning substance (see p. 63), Luther is already beginning to call into question that very doctrine which within a year he was to condemn as "the second captivity of the sacrament" (*LW* 36, 28-35). Cf. Charles E. Hay (trans.) Reinhold Seeberg's *History of Doctrines* (Grand Rapids: Baker, 1952), II, 286, n. 1, "Literally, transubstantiation is here retained, but really Luther is only concerned to hold fast the idea that the body is 'in' the bread."

[28] *Leychnam;* cf. p. 49, n. 1.

as was said above[29] of a citizen who is taken and incorporated into the protection and freedom of the city and the entire community. For this reason he instituted not simply the one form, but two separate forms—his flesh under the bread, his blood under the wine—to indicate that not only his life and good works, which are indicated by his flesh and which he accomplished in his flesh, but also his passion and martyrdom, which are indicated by his blood and in which he poured out his blood, are all our own. And we, being drawn into them, may use and profit from them.

17. So it is clear from all this that this holy sacrament is nothing else than a divine sign, in which are pledged, granted, and imparted Christ and all saints together with all their works, sufferings, merits, mercies, and possessions, for the comfort and strengthening of all who are in anxiety and sorrow, persecuted by the devil, sins, the world, the flesh, and every evil. And to receive the sacrament is nothing else than to desire all this and firmly to believe that it is done.

Here, now, follows the third part of the sacrament,[30] that is, the *faith* on which everything depends. For it is not enough to know what the sacrament is and signifies. It is not enough that you know it is a fellov*ship and a gracious exchange or blending of our sin and suffering with the righteousness of Christ and his saints. You must also desire it and firmly believe that you have received it. Here the devil and our own nature wage their fiercest fight, so that faith may by no means stand firm. There are those who practice their arts and subtleties by trying [to fathom] what becomes of the bread when it is changed into Christ's flesh and of the wine when it is changed into his blood and how the whole Christ, his flesh and blood, can be encompassed in so small a portion of bread and wine. It does not matter if you do not see[31] it. It is enough to know that

---

[29]See pp. 243-248.

[30]The three parts are listed on p. 242.

[31] *Suchist*, literally "seek." WA 2, 750, n. 1 and *MA³* 1, 390, 17 both suggest that *siehest* may have been intended. There need not have been a typographical error here, however. The Indogermanic antecedent of *suchen* in meaning was close to the Latin *sagio*, to perceive. Luther may have been using the term with its early connotations, in the sense of tracing a thing down or ferreting it out until you fathom or grasp it. Cf. Jacob Grimm and Wilhelm Grimm (eds.), *Deutsches Wörterbuch* (16 vols.; Leipzig: Hirzel, 1854-1954), X, 835.

it is a divine sign in which Christ's flesh and blood are truly present. The how and the where, we leave to him.[32]

18. See to it that here you exercise and strengthen your faith, so that when you are sorrowful or when your sins press you and you go to the sacrament or hear mass, you do so with a hearty desire for this sacrament and for what it signifies. Then do not doubt that you have what the sacrament signifies, that is, be certain that Christ and all his saints are coming to you with all their virtues, sufferings, and mercies, to live, work, suffer, and die with you, and that they desire to be wholly yours, having all things in common with you. If you will exercise and strengthen this faith, then you will experience what a rich, joyous, and bountiful wedding feast your God has prepared for you upon the altar. Then you will understand what the great feast of King Ahasuerus signifies [Esther 1:5]; and you will see what that wedding feast is for which God slew his oxen and fat calves, as it is written in the gospel [Matt. 22:2-4]. Then your heart will become truly free and confident, strong and courageous against all enemies [Ps. 23:5]. For who will fear any calamity if he is sure that Christ and all his saints are with him and have all things, evil or good, in common with him? So we read in Acts 2[:46] that the disciples of Christ broke this bread and ate with great gladness of heart. Since, then, this work is so great that the smallness of our souls would not dare to desire it, to say nothing of hoping for it or expecting it, therefore it is necessary and profitable to go often to the sacrament, or at least in the daily mass to exercise and strengthen this faith on which the whole thing depends and for the sake of which it was instituted. For if you doubt, you do God the greatest dishonor and make him out to be a faithless liar; if you cannot believe, then pray for faith, as was said earlier in the other treatise.[38]

19. See to it also that you give yourself to everyone in fellowship and by no means exclude anyone in hatred or anger. For this sacrament of fellowship, love, and unity cannot tolerate discord and disunity. You must take to heart the infirmities and needs of others, as if they were your own. Then offer to others your strength, as if

---

[32] See *The Babylonian Captivity of the Church. LW* 36, 32-35.
[33]Cf. *The Sacrament of Penance,* 1519. *LW* 35, 3-22.

it were their own, just as Christ does for you in the sacrament. This is what it means to be changed into one another through love, out of many particles to become one bread and drink, to lose one's own form and take on that which is common to all.[34]

For this reason slanderers and those who wickedly judge and despise others cannot but receive death in the sacrament, as St. Paul writes in I Corinthians 11[:29]. For they do not do unto their neighbor what they seek from Christ, and what the sacrament indicates. They begrudge others anything good; they have no sympathy for them; they do not care for others as they themselves desire to be cared for by Christ. And then they fall into such blindness that they do not know what else to do in this sacrament except to fear and honor Christ there present[35] with their own prayers and devotion. When they have done this, they think they have done their whole duty. But Christ has given his holy body for this purpose, that the thing signified by the sacrament—the fellowship, the change wrought by love—may be put into practice. And Christ values his spiritual body, which is the fellowship of his saints, more than his own natural body. To him it is more important, especially in this sacrament, that faith in the fellowship with him and with his saints may be properly exercised and become strong in us; and that we, in keeping with it, may properly exercise our fellowship with one another. This purpose of Christ the blind worshipers do not perceive. In their devoutness they go on daily saying and hearing mass, but they remain every day the same; indeed every day they become worse but do not perceive it.

Therefore take heed. It is more needful that you discern the spiritual than the natural body of Christ; and faith in the spiritual body is more necessary than faith in the natural body. For the natural without the spiritual profits us nothing in this sacrament; a change must occur [in the communicant] and be exercised through love.

20. There are many who regardless of this change of love and faith rely upon the fact that the mass or the sacrament is, as they

---

[34] See pp. 252-253.

[35] *Kegenwertig*, i.e., present in the consecrated host.

say, *opus gratum opere operato*,[36] that is, a work which of itself pleases God, even though they who perform it do not please him. From this they conclude that however unworthily masses are said, it is nonetheless a good thing to have many masses, since harm comes [only] to those who say or use them unworthily. I grant everyone [the right to] his opinion, but such fables do not please me. For, [if you desire] to speak in these terms, there is no creature or work that does not of itself please God, as is written in Genesis 1[:31], "God saw all his works and they pleased him." What is the result if bread, wine, gold, and all good things are misused, even though of themselves they are pleasing to God? Why, the consequence of that is condemnation. So also here: the more precious the sacrament, the greater the harm which comes upon the whole community [of saints] from its misuse. For it was not instituted for its own sake, that it might please God, but for our sake, that we might use it right, exercise our faith by it, and through it become pleasing to God. If it is merely an *opus operatum*,[37] it works only harm everywhere; it must become an *opus operantis*.[38] Just as bread and wine, no matter how much they may please God in and of themselves, work only harm if they are not used, so it is not enough that the sacrament be merely completed (that is, *opus operatum*); it must also be used in faith (that is, *opus operantis*). And we must take care lest with such dangerous interpretations the sacrament's power and virtue be lost on us, and faith perish utterly through the false security of the [outwardly] completed sacrament.

All this comes from the fact that they pay more attention in this sacrament to Christ's natural body than to the fellowship, the spiritual body. Christ on the cross was also a completed work which was well pleasing to God. But to this day the Jews have found it a stumbling block because they did not construe it as a work that is made use of in faith. See to it, then, that for you the sacrament is an *opus*

---

[36] Literally, a work (that is) acceptable by (virtue of) the work (having been) performed.

[37] *Opus operatum* is an action that is done, completed, finished, considered as such without reference to the doer of it.

[38] *Opus operantis* is an action considered with reference to the doer of it, the action of the one acting.

operantis, that is, a work that is made use of, that is well pleasing to God not because of what it is in itself but because of your faith and your good use of it. The Word of God too is of itself pleasing to God, but it is harmful to me unless in me it also pleases God. In short, such expressions as *opus operatum* and *opus operantis* are vain words of men,[39] more of a hindrance than a help. And who could

---

[39] *Opus operatum* and *opus operantis* were terms used generally in discussion of the difference between the sacraments of the old law and those of the new. The latter, according to Alexander of Hales (d. 1245), are in their own right signs *and causes* of invisible grace, and hence superior to the former which were merely signs but *not causes.* "Otherwise," added Thomas Aquinas (d. 1274), "they would have obviated the necessity of Christ's passion (Gal. 2:21)." Thus the sacraments of the Old Testament *signified* the passion of Christ and its effects; but they had no *power* to justify—their effect depended rather on the faith they were able to stimulate in the believer. The sacraments of the New Testament, on the other hand, in and of themselves effectively impart grace *ex opere operato,* i.e., simply through the use of them, apart from any act of the soul. Thomas, however, still presupposed faith; not as the *cause* of the sacrament's effect to be sure, but as the *receptivity* for the sacrament's effect. Bonaventura (d. 1274) also included faith as a factor in the justification of the New Testament sacraments, only he regarded it as something supplementary to the *opus operatum,* the external action in and of itself, to which the justifying grace and its effect were inseparably attached.

From this reduction of faith to something *supplementary,* it was only a step to the elimination of it as something altogether *expendable.* The step was taken by Duns Scotus (d. 1308) and Gabriel Biel (d. 1495) when they defined the subjective condition for the sacrament's effecting a blessing no longer in terms of a positive disposition, but in terms of the negative absence of any impediment. Reception of the sacrament in and of itself invariably imparts grace so long as man does not "interpose an obstacle," such as positive disbelief or mortal sin. Thus the scholastics all agreed that the sacraments impart grace *ex opere operato.* They differed as to whether faith was necessary for the *reception* of that grace. According to Duns Scotus and Gabriel Biel the necessity of faith is expressly denied and a purely passive receptivity is held to be sufficient. Intended originally to affirm that the power and effect of the sacrament are caused not by any disposition on man's part but solely by God and the sufferings of Christ, the concept *ex opere operato* thus came ultimately to mean that the proper disposition on the part of the recipient need not be one of positive faith but of merely negative passivity. It was this latest, fullest, and perhaps logical development of the scholastic view that Luther is attacking. F. Kattenbusch in Hauck (ed.), *Realencyklopädie,* XVII, 363-365.

The concept of the *opus operatum* also proved useful for guaranteeing the validity of the sacrament irrespective of the personal worthiness of the celebrating priest (see *LW* 35, 102 and *LW* 36, 47, 55). Ultimately Luther's solution lay not in the preference for *operantis* over *operatum* but in the rejection of the *opus* altogether. The sacrament is not a good work or sacrifice on the part of man, but a testament or promise on the part of God, to be received by man in faith—not an *officium* but a *beneficium* (see *LW* 35, 93 and *LW* 36, 35-37).

tell of all the abominable abuses and misbeliefs which daily multiply about this blessed sacrament, some of which are so spiritual and holy that they might almost lead an angel astray?

Briefly, whoever would understand the abuses need only keep before him the aforesaid use and faith of this sacrament; namely, that there must be a sorrowing, hungry soul, who desires heartily the love, help, and support of the entire community—of Christ and of all Christendom—and who does not doubt that in faith [all these desires] are obtained, and who thereupon makes himself one with everyone. Whoever does not take this as his point of departure for arranging and ordering his hearing or reading of masses and his receiving of the sacrament is in error and does not use this sacrament to his salvation. It is for this reason also that the world is overrun with pestilences, wars, and other horrible plagues,[40] because with our many masses we only bring down upon us greater disfavor.

21. We see now how necessary this sacrament is for those who must face death, or other dangers of body and soul, that they not be left in them alone but be strengthened in the fellowship of Christ and all saints. This is why Christ instituted it and gave it to his disciples in the hour of their extreme need and peril. Since we then are all daily surrounded by all kinds of danger, and must at last die, we should humbly and heartily give thanks with all our powers to the God of all mercy for giving us such a gracious sign, by which—if we hold fast to it in faith—he leads and draws us through death and every danger unto himself, unto Christ and all saints.

Therefore it is also profitable and necessary that the love and fellowship of Christ and all saints be hidden, invisible, and spiritual, and that only a bodily, visible, and outward sign of it be given to us. For if this love, fellowship, and support were apparent to all, like the transient fellowship of men, we would not be strengthened or trained by it to desire or put our trust in the things that are unseen and eternal [II Cor. 4:18]. Instead we would be trained to put our trust only in things that are transient and seen, and would become so accustomed to them as to be unwilling to let them go; we would not

---

[40] Cf. I Cor. 11:30.

follow God, except so far as visible and tangible things led us. We would thereby be prevented from ever coming to God. For everything that is bound to time and sense must fall away, and we must learn to do without them, if we are to come to God.

For this reason the mass and this sacrament are a sign by which we train and accustom ourselves to let go of all visible love, help, and comfort, and to trust in the invisible love, help, and support of Christ and his saints. For death takes away all the things that are seen and separates us from men and transient things. To meet it, we must, therefore, have the help of the things that are unseen and eternal. And these are indicated to us in the sacrament and sign, to which we cling by faith until we finally attain to them also with sight and senses.

Thus the sacrament is for us a ford, a bridge, a door, a ship, and a stretcher, by which and in which we pass from this world into eternal life. Therefore everything depends on faith. He who does not believe is like the man who is supposed to cross the sea, but who is so timid that he does not trust the ship; and so he must remain and never be saved, because he will not embark and cross over. This is the fruit of our dependence on the senses and of our untrained faith, which shrinks from the passage across the Jordan of death; and the devil too has a gruesome hand in it.

22. This was signified long ago in Joshua 3[:14-17]. After the children of Israel had gone dry-shod through the Red Sea [Exod. 14:21-22]—in which [event] baptism was typified—they went through the Jordan also in like manner. But the priests stood with the ark in the Jordan, and the water below them was cut off, while the water above them rose up like a mountain—in which [event] this sacrament is typified. The priests hold and carry the ark in the Jordan when, in the hour of our death or peril, they preach and administer to us this sacrament, the fellowship of Christ and all saints. If we then believe, the waters below us depart; that is, the things that are seen and transient do nothing but flee from us. The waters above us, however, well up high; that is, the horrible torments of the other world, which we envision at the hour of death, terrify us as if they would overwhelm us. If, however, we pay no attention to them,

and walk over with a firm faith, then we shall enter dry-shod and unharmed into eternal life.

We have, therefore, two principal sacraments in the church, baptism and the bread. Baptism leads us into a new life on earth; the bread guides us through death into eternal life. And the two are signified by the Red Sea and the Jordan, and by the two lands, one beyond and one on this side of the Jordan. This is why our Lord said at the Last Supper, "I shall not drink again of this wine until I drink it new with you in my Father's kingdom" [Matt. 26:29]. So entirely is this sacrament intended and instituted for a strengthening against death and an entrance into eternal life.

In conclusion, the blessing of this sacrament is fellowship and love, by which we are strengthened against death and all evil. This fellowship is twofold: on the one hand we partake of Christ and all saints; on the other hand we permit all Christians to be partakers of us, in whatever way they and we are able. Thus by means of this sacrament, all self-seeking love is rooted out and gives place to that which seeks the common good of all; and through the change wrought by love there is one bread, one drink, one body, one community. This is the true unity of Christian brethren. Let us see, therefore, how the neat-looking brotherhoods, of which there are now so many, compare and square with this.

The Brotherhoods[41]

1. First let us consider the evil practices of the brotherhoods.

---

[41] Originally made up of monks and monasteries, later primarily of laymen, these sodalities ("fraternities," "confraternities") were associations for devotional purposes. Members were obligated to the recitation of certain prayers and the attendance upon certain masses at stipulated times. Each member was believed to participate—and, most important of all, even after death—in the benefits accruing from these "good works" of all the other members. In the case of most of the sodalities, membership (for which the fees ranged from one to twenty gulden) entitled the member to the enjoyment of certain indulgences. In 1520 little Wittenberg boasted of twenty such fraternities; Hamburg had more than one hundred. In 1519 Degenhard Peffinger, of Wittenberg, was a member of eight such fraternities in his home city and through their cartel relationships derived benefits from twenty-seven more in other places. The brotherhood of St. Peter in Salzburg was united in fellowship with eighty other fraternities. Hauck (ed.), *Realencyklopädie*, III, 434-437; Karl Benrath (ed.), *An den christlichen Adel deutscher Nation, von D. Martin Luther* (Halle: Verein für Reformationsgeschichte, 1884), pp. 106-107.

One of these is their gluttony and drunkenness. After one or more masses are held,[42] the rest of the day and night, and other days besides, are given over to the devil; they do only what displeases God. Such mad reveling has been introduced by the evil spirit, and he calls it a brotherhood, whereas, it is more a debauch and an altogether pagan, yes, a swinish way of life. It would be far better to have no brotherhoods in the world at all than to countenance such misconduct. Temporal lords and cities should unite with the clergy in abolishing it. For by it God, the saints, and all Christians are greatly dishonored; and the divine services and feast days are made into a laughingstock for the devil. Saints' days are supposed to be kept and hallowed by good works. And the brotherhood is also supposed to be a special convocation of good works; instead it has become a collecting of money for beer. What have the names of Our Lady,[43] St. Anne,[44] St. Sebastian,[45] or other saints to do with your brotherhoods, in which you have nothing but gluttony, drunkenness, useless squandering of money, howling, yelling, chattering, dancing, and wasting of time? If a sow were made the patron saint of such a brotherhood she would not consent. Why then do they afflict the dear saints so miserably by taking their names in vain in such shameful practices and sins, and by dishonoring and blaspheming with such evil practices the brotherhoods named after these saints? Woe unto them who do this, and [unto them who] permit it!

2. If men desire to maintain a brotherhood, they should gather provisions and feed and serve a tableful or two of poor people, for

---

[42] A brotherhood usually came together monthly—often weekly—as well as on the day of its particular saint and on festival days of its related monastic order, ostensibly for pious exercises but in reality for feasting and debauchery which had long been a source of concern to the civil and ecclesiastical authorities as well as to the Reformers. Henry C. Lea, *A History of Auricular Confession and Indulgences* (Philadelphia: Lea, 1896), III, 474-476.

[43] The Carmelites were possibly the first to form sodalities with the specific purpose of devotion to the Virgin Mary, having organized in the fourteenth century the "Confraternity of Our Lady of Mount Carmel." Jackson (ed.), *The New Schaff-Herzog Encyclopedia of Religious Knowledge*, III, 226.

[44] According to tradition, St. Anne was the mother of the Holy Virgin; sodalities to her honor and bearing her name spread, as Kolde says, "like an epidemic" after the fourteenth century. Hauck (ed.), *Realencyklopädie*, III, 437.

[45] St. Sebastian was martyred on January 20 (year unknown) in Rome under Diocletian, who was emperor in 284-305. *Schaff-Herzog*, X, 320.

the sake of God. The day before they should fast,[46] and on the feast day remain sober, passing the time in prayer and other good works. Then God and his saints would be truly honored; there would be improvement too, and a good example would be given to others. Or they should gather the money which they intend to squander for drink, and collect it into a common treasury, each craft for itself. Then in cases of hardship, needy fellow workmen might be helped to get started, and be lent money, or a young couple of the same craft might be fitted out respectably from this common treasury. These would be works of true brotherhood; they would make God and his saints look with favor upon the brotherhoods, of which they would then gladly be the patrons. But where men are unwilling to do this, where they insist on following the old ways of simulated brotherhood, I admonish that they not do it on the saints' days, nor in the name of the saints or of the brotherhood. Let them take some other weekday and leave the names of the saints and of their brotherhoods alone, lest the saints one day punish it. Although there is no day which is not dishonored by such doings, at least the festivals and the names of the saints should be spared. For such brotherhoods call themselves brotherhoods of the saints while they do the work of the devil.

3. There is another evil feature of the brotherhoods, and it is of a spiritual nature. That is the false opinion they have that their brotherhood is to be a benefit to no one but themselves, those who are members on the roll or who contribute. This damnably wicked opinion is an even worse evil than the first, and it is one of the reasons why God has brought it about that with their gluttony, drunkenness, and the like the brotherhoods are becoming such a mockery and blasphemy of God. For in them men learn to seek their own good, to love themselves, to be faithful only to one another, to despise others, to think themselves better than others, and to presume to stand higher before God than others. And so perishes the communion of saints, Christian love, and the true brotherhood which is established in the holy sacrament, while selfish love grows in them. That is, by means of these many external brotherhoods devoted to

---

[46]Cf. *LW* 35, 39-40.

works they oppose and destroy the one, inner, spiritual, essential brotherhood common to all saints.

When God sees this perverted state of affairs, he perverts it still more, as is written in Psalm 18[:26], "With the perverse thou wilt be perverted."[47] So God brings it to pass that they make themselves and their brotherhoods a mockery and a disgrace. And he casts them out of the common brotherhood of saints—which they have opposed and with which they do not make common cause—and into their own brotherhood of gluttony, drunkenness, and unchastity; so that they, who have neither sought nor thought of anything more than their own, may find their own. Then, too, God blinds them so that they do not recognize it as an abomination and disgrace, but adorn their misconduct with the names of saints, as though they were doing the right thing. Beyond this, God lets some fall into so deep an abyss that they boast publicly and say that whoever is in their brotherhood cannot be condemned; just as if baptism and the sacrament, instituted by God himself, were of less value and more uncertain than that which they have concocted out of their blinded heads. Thus will God dishonor and blind those who, with their crazed conduct and the swinish practices of their brotherhoods, mock and blaspheme his feasts, his name, and his saints, to the detriment of that common Christian brotherhood which flowed from the wounds of Christ.

4. Therefore for the correct understanding and use of the brotherhoods, one must learn to distinguish correctly between brotherhoods. The first is the divine, the heavenly, the noblest, which surpasses all others as gold surpasses copper or lead—this being the fellowship of all saints, of which we spoke above.[48] In this we are all brothers and sisters, so closely united that a closer relationship cannot be conceived. For here we have one baptism, one Christ, one sacrament, one food, one gospel, one faith, one Spirit, one spiritual body [Eph. 4:4-5], and each person is a member of the other [Rom. 12:5]. No other brotherhood is so close and strong.

---

[47] This rendering is according to the Douay Version, which is based on the Vulgate from which Luther is quoting.
[48] See pp. 243-260.

For natural brothers are, to be sure, of one flesh and blood, one heritage and home; yet they must separate and join themselves to the blood and heritage of others [in marriage]. The organized brotherhoods have one roll, one mass, one kind of good works, one festival day, one fee; and, as things are now, their common beer, common gluttony, and common drunkenness. But none of these penetrates so deeply as to produce one spirit, for that is done by Christ's brotherhood alone. For this reason, too, the greater, broader, and more comprehensive it is, the better it is.

Now all other brotherhoods should be so conducted as to keep this first and noblest brotherhood constantly before their eyes and regard it alone as great. With all their works they should be seeking nothing for themselves; they should rather do them for God's sake, entreating God that he keep and prosper this Christian fellowship and brotherhood from day to day. Thus when a brotherhood is formed, they should let it be seen that the members are a jump ahead of others in rendering Christendom some special service with their prayers, fastings, alms, and good works, and [that they do this] not in order to seek selfish profit or reward, or to exclude others, but to serve as the free servants of the whole community of Christians.

If men had such a correct conception, God would in return also restore good order, so that the brotherhoods might not be brought to shame by debauchery. Then blessing would follow: a general fund could be gathered, whereby material aid too could be given to other persons. Then the spiritual and material works[49] of the brotherhoods would be done in their proper order. And whoever does not want to follow this [proper] order in his brotherhood, I advise him to let the brotherhood go, and get out of it; it will [only] do him harm in body and soul.

But suppose you say, "If I do not get something special out of the brotherhood, of what use is it to me?" I answer: True, if you are seeking something special [for yourself], of what use indeed is the brotherhood, or the sisterhood either? But if by it you serve the community and other men, as is customarily the nature of love [to

---

[49] *Merck* (in WA 2, 757, l. 7) in all likelihood was intended to be *werck;* cf. WA 21, 161, l. 8.

do], you will have your reward for this love without any desire or search on your part. If, however, you consider the service and reward of love too small, this is evidence that yours is a perverted brotherhood. Love serves freely and without charge, which is why God in return also gives to it every blessing, freely and without charge. Since, then, everything must be done in love, if it is to please God at all, the brotherhood too must be a brotherhood in love. It is the nature of that which is done in love, however, not to seek its own,[50] or its own profit, but to seek that of others, and above all that of the community [of saints].

5. To return once more to the sacrament, since the Christian fellowship is at present in a bad way, such as it has never been before, and is daily growing worse, especially among those in high places, and since all places are full of sin and shame, you should be concerned not about how many masses are said, or how often the sacrament is celebrated—for this will make things worse rather than better—but about how much you and others increase in that which the sacrament signifies[51] and in the faith[52] which it demands. For therein alone lies improvement. And the more you find yourself being incorporated into the fellowship of Christ and his saints, the better it is with you. [It is good] if you find that you are becoming strong in the confidence of Christ and his dear saints, so that you are certain that they love you and stand by you in all the trials of life and of death; and that you, in turn, take to heart the shortcomings and lapses of all Christians and of the entire community [of saints] [as these occur] in any individual Christian, so that your love goes out to each one and you desire to help everyone, hate no one, suffer with all, and pray for all. See, as the work of the sacrament proceeds aright, you will come many times to weep, lament, and mourn over the wretched condition of Christendom today. If, however, you find no such confidence in Christ and his saints, and the needs of Christendom and of every single neighbor do not trouble or move you, then beware of all other good works, by which you

---

[50] I Cor. 13:5 (KJV); cf. I Cor. 10:24.
[51] Cf. p. 242 and pp. 243-255.
[52] Cf. p. 242 and pp. 255-260.

think you are godly and will be saved. They are surely nothing but hypocrisy, sham, and deceit, for they are without love and fellowship; and without these nothing is good. To sum it all up: *Plenitudo legis est dilectio,* "Love is the fulfilling of the law" [Rom. 13:10]. Amen.

[*Postscript*][53]

There are some who have unnecessarily rejected this treatise because I said in the third paragraph:[54] I should consider it a good thing if a Christian council were to decree that both kinds be given to everyone. They have opened their mouth so wide that they are saying, "This is an error and it is offensive." God in heaven have mercy! That we should live to see the day when Christ—the noble Lord and God—is publicly insulted and blasphemed by his own people, who rebuke his order as an error! It would have been enough had they allowed it to remain a permissive order and not turned it into a command. Then, at least, it would not be forbidden or regarded as an error. Yet I beg them to look carefully at the second and third paragraphs,[55] in which I have stated clearly that one kind is sufficient. I have experienced too that my writings are being rejected only by those who have not read them and who do not intend to do so. To such men I send my greetings and inform them that I am paying no attention to their blind and frivolous criticism; as long as God grants me life, I do not intend to tolerate it, that they so brazenly condemn and blaspheme my Lord Christ as an erring, offensive, and revolutionary teacher—they can act accordingly.

---

[53] This paragraph is found only in two of the Wittenberg printings, the so-called Editions C (*WA* 2, 739) and N (*WA* 9, 791), the only two which profess to having been corrected by Luther himself.

[54] See p. 243.

[55] See pp. 242-243.

16.

THE BABYLONIAN CAPTIVITY
OF THE CHURCH

A Prelude of Martin Luther
On the Babylonian Captivity of the Church

Jesus

Martin Luther, Augustinian, to his friend, Hermann Tulich,[1] greeting.

Whether I wish it or not, I am compelled to become more learned every day, with so many and such able masters eagerly driving me on and making me work. Some two years ago I wrote on indulgences, but in such a way that I now deeply regret having published that little book.[2] At that time I still clung with a mighty superstition to the tyranny of Rome, and so I held that indulgences should not be altogether rejected, seeing that they were approved by the common consent of so many. No wonder, for at the time I was still engaged singlehanded in this Sisyphean task. Afterwards, thanks to Sylvester,[3] and aided by those friars who so strenuously defended indulgences, I saw that they were nothing but impostures of the Roman flatterers, by which they rob men of their money and their faith in God. Would that I could prevail upon the booksellers and

---

[1] Tulich was born at Steinheim, near Paderborn, in Westphalia; graduated from Wittenberg (A.B., 1511); was a proofreader in Melchior Lotter's printing-house at Leipzig. He returned to Wittenberg in 1519 and received the doctorate in 1520; became professor of poetry at the university; rector of the same, 1525. He was a staunch supporter of Luther; rector of the school at Lüneberg from 1532 until his death in 1540.

[2] Probably the *Explanations of the Ninety-five Theses* (1518). LW 31, 83-252.

[3] Sylvester Prierias (more properly called Mazzolini), from Prierio in Piedmont (1456-1523), was a prior of the Dominicans. He became Grand Inquisitor and Censor of Books in 1515. He and others of the order (e.g., Tetzel and Hochstraten) had written against Luther.

persuade all who have read them to burn the whole of my booklets on indulgences, and instead of all that I have written on this subject adopt this proposition: INDULGENCES ARE WICKED DEVICES OF THE FLATTERERS OF ROME.

Next, Eck and Emser[4] and their fellow-conspirators undertook to instruct me concerning the primacy of the pope. Here too, not to prove ungrateful to such learned men, I acknowledge that I have profited much from their labors. For while I denied the divine authority of the papacy, I still admitted its human authority.[5] But after hearing and reading the super-subtle subtleties of these coxcombs,[6] with which they so adroitly prop up their idol (for my mind is not altogether unteachable in these matters), I now know for certain that the papacy is the kingdom of Babylon and the power of Nimrod, the mighty hunter [Gen. 10:8-9]. Once more, therefore, that all may turn out to my friends' advantage, I beg both the booksellers and my readers that after burning what I have published on this subject they hold to this proposition: THE PAPACY IS THE GRAND HUNTING OF THE BISHOP OF ROME. This is proved by the arguments of Eck, Emser, and the Leipzig lecturer on the Scriptures.[7]

Now they are making a game of schooling me concerning communion in both kinds and other weighty subjects: here I must take pains lest I listen in vain to these "eminent teachers" [8] of mine. A certain Italian friar of Cremona has written a "Recantation of

---

[4] Johann Eck (properly Maier) from Eck in the Allgäu (1486-1543), had become professor at Ingolstadt in 1510. His criticism of the Ninety-five Theses in his *Obelisci*, to which Luther replied with the *Asterisci* (*WA* 1, 281-314; *St.L.* 18, 536-589), culminated in their Leipzig disputation in 1519. Jerome Emser (1477-1527) had been a humanist professor at Erfurt during Luther's student days, and was later secretary to Duke George of Saxony in Dresden. Luther is referring to the treatises both men published against him as a consequence of the disputation.

[5] *Resolutio Lutheriana super propositione sua decima tertia de potestate papae (per autorem locupletata)* (1519). WA 2, 180-240.

[6] *Trossulorum*, originally a designation for Roman knights who had conquered the city Trossulum, later came to have the derogatory sense of a fop, someone who pretends to rank and authority. *St.L.* 19, 6 n. 1.

[7] Augustinus Alveld, a Franciscan. This reference by Luther is his chief claim to fame.

[8] *Cratippos.* Cratippus, a peripatetic philosopher of Mytilene, had taught Cicero's son at Athens and received the rights of Roman citizenship through the orator's efforts. In addition to instructing the youth of Athens, he wrote on divination and the interpretation of dreams.

Martin Luther before the Holy See,"[9] which is not that I revoke anything, as the words declare, but that he revokes me. This is the kind of Latin the Italians are beginning to write nowadays. Another friar, a German of Leipzig, that same lecturer, as you know, on the whole canon of Scripture [Alveld] has written against me concerning the sacrament in both kinds and is about to perform, as I understand, still greater and more marvelous things. The Italian [Isolani] was canny enough to conceal his name, fearing perhaps the fate of Cajetan[10] and Sylvester. The man of Leipzig, on the other hand, as becomes a fierce and vigorous German, boasts on his ample title page of his name, his life, his sanctity, his learning, his office, his fame, his honor, almost his very clogs.[11] From him I shall doubtless learn a great deal, since he writes his dedicatory epistle to the Son of God himself: so familiar are these saints with Christ who reigns in heaven! Here it seems three magpies are addressing me, the first in good Latin, the second in better Greek, the third in purest Hebrew. What do you think, my dear Hermann, I should do, but prick up my ears? The matter is being dealt with at Leipzig by the "Observance" of the Holy Cross.[12]

Fool that I was, I had hitherto thought that it would be well if a general council were to decide that the sacrament should be administered to the laity in both kinds.[13] This view our more than learned friar would correct, declaring that neither Christ nor the apostles had either commanded or advised that both kinds be administered to the laity; it was therefore left to the judgment of the church what to do or not to do in this matter, and the church must be obeyed. These are his words.

---

[9] *Revocatio Martini Lutheri Augustiniani ad sanctam sedem* by Isidoro Isolani. Cf. the Introduction. Cf. WA 6, 486-487.

[10] Thomas Cajetan (1469-1534), Italian cardinal, general of the Dominican order and foremost authority on Thomistic theology, found himself unequal to the task of testing and refuting Luther at Augsburg. Cf. *Proceedings at Augsburg* (1518). LW 31, 253-292.

[11] The title page of Alveld's treatise contained twenty-six lines. Luther's *Calopodia* (perhaps originally intended as *calcipodium*) may have been a reference to the wooden-soled sandals worn by Alveld's order.

[12] Concerning Alveld's lengthy title and his peculiar spelling, IHSVH, for Jesus, which he tried to justify by arguments involving an admixture of the three languages, cf. WA 6, 485. He was a member of the stricter Observantine Franciscans, at that time separate from the Conventuals.

[13] A *Treatise Concerning the Blessed Sacrament* (1519). PE 2, 9-10.

You will perhaps ask, what madness has entered into the man, or against whom is he writing? For I have not condemned the use of one kind, but have left the decision about the use of both kinds to the judgment of the church. This is the very thing he attempts to assert, in order to attack me with this same argument. My answer is that this sort of argument is common to all who write against Luther: either they assert the very things they assail, or they set up a man of straw whom they may attack. This is the way of Sylvester and Eck and Emser, and of the men of Cologne and Louvain,[14] and if this friar had not been one of their kind, he would never have written against Luther.

This man turned out to be more fortunate than his fellows, however, for in his effort to prove that the use of both kinds was neither commanded nor advised, but left to the judgment of the church, he brings forward the Scriptures to prove that the use of one kind for the laity was ordained by the command of Christ. So it is true, according to this new interpreter of the Scriptures, that the use of one kind was not commanded and at the same time was commanded by Christ! This novel kind of argument is, as you know, the one which these dialecticians of Leipzig are especially fond of using. Does not Emser profess to speak fairly of me in his earlier book,[15] and then, after I had convicted him of the foulest envy and shameful lies, confess, when about to confute me in his later book,[16] that both were true, and that he has written in both a friendly and an unfriendly spirit? A fine fellow, indeed, as you know!

But listen to our distinguished distinguisher of "kinds,"[17] to whom the decision of the church and the command of Christ are the same thing, and again the command of Christ and no command of Christ are the same thing. With such dexterity he proves that only one kind should be given to the laity, by the command of

---

[14] The universities of Cologne and Louvain had ratified Eck's "victory" over Luther at Leipzig.

[15] *De disputatione Lipsicensi* (1519).

[16] *A venatione Luteriana Aegocerotis Assertio* (1519).

[17] *speciosum speciatorem.* In this play on words, Luther coined the second word to hint at the *species* or elements in the sacrament, while at the same time connoting ironically someone who tries to make his case appear plausible and favorable. *St.L.* 19, 9 n. 1.

Christ, that is, by the decision of the church. He puts it in capital letters, thus: THE INFALLIBLE FOUNDATION. Then he treats John 6 [:35, 41] with incredible wisdom, where Christ speaks of the bread of heaven and the bread of life, which is He Himself. The most learned fellow not only refers these words to the Sacrament of the Altar, but because Christ says: "I am the living bread" [John 6:51] and not "I am the living cup," he actually concludes that we have in this passage the institution of the sacrament in only one kind for the laity. But here follow the words: "For my flesh is food indeed, and my blood is drink indeed" [John 6:55] and, "Unless you eat the flesh of the Son of man and drink his blood" [John 6:53]. When it dawned upon the good friar that these words speak undeniably for both kinds and against one kind—presto! how happily and learnedly he slips out of the quandary by asserting that in these words Christ means to say only that whoever receives the sacrament in one kind receives therein both flesh and blood. This he lays down as his "infallible foundation" of a structure so worthy of the holy and heavenly "Observance."

I pray you now to learn along with me from this that in John 6 Christ commands the administration of the sacrament in one kind, yet in such a way that his commanding means leaving it to the decision of the church; and further that Christ is speaking in this same chapter only of the laity and not of the priests. For to the latter the living bread of heaven, that is the sacrament in one kind, does not belong, but perhaps the bread of death from hell! But what is to be done with the deacons and subdeacons,[18] who are neither laymen nor priests? According to this distinguished writer they ought to use neither the one kind nor both kinds! You see, my dear Tulich, what a novel and "Observant" method of treating Scripture this is.

But learn this too: In John 6 Christ is speaking of the Sacrament of the Altar, although he himself teaches us that he is speaking of faith in the incarnate Word, for he says: "This is the work of God, that you believe in him whom he has sent" [John 6:29]. But we'll

---

[18] These are the sixth and fifth of the seven grades through which clergy advanced to the priesthood. Some then-contemporary Catholic theologians (e.g., Cajetan and Durandus) doubted whether the Sacrament of Order was actually received by deacons. They were later overruled by the Council of Trent which decided that it was. *The Catholic Encyclopedia* (15 vols.), IV, 650.

have to give him credit: this Leipzig professor of the Bible can prove anything he pleases from any passage of Scripture he pleases. For he is an Anaxagorian,[19] or rather an Aristotelian,[20] theologian for whom nouns and verbs when interchanged mean the same thing and any thing. Throughout the whole of his book he so fits together the testimony of the Scriptures that if he set out to prove that Christ is in the sacrament he would not hesitate to begin thus: "The lesson is from the book of the Revelation of St. John the Apostle." All his quotations are as apt as this one would be, and the wiseacre imagines he is adorning his drivel with the multitude of his quotations. The rest I will pass over, lest I smother you with the filth of this vile-smelling cloaca.

In conclusion, he brings forward I Cor. 11 [:23], where Paul says that he received from the Lord and delivered to the Corinthians the use of both the bread and the cup. Here again our distinguisher of kinds, treating the Scriptures with his usual brilliance, teaches that Paul permitted, but did not deliver, the use of both kinds. Do you ask where he gets his proof? Out of his own head, as he did in the case of John 6. For it does not behoove this lecturer to give a reason for his assertions; he belongs to that order whose members prove and teach everything by their visions.[21] Accordingly we are here taught that in this passage the apostle did not write to the whole Corinthian congregation, but to the laity alone—and therefore gave no "permission" at all to the clergy, but deprived them of the sacrament altogether! Further, according to a new kind of grammar, "I have received from the Lord" means the same as "it is permitted by the Lord," and "I have delivered to you" is the same as "I have permitted to you." I pray you, mark this well. For by this method not only the church, but any worthless fellow, will be at liberty, according to this master, to turn all the universal commands, institutions, and ordinances of Christ and the apostles into mere "permission."

I perceive therefore that this man is driven by a messenger of

---

[19] Anaxagoras (*circa* 500-428 B.C.), a Greek philosopher, was accused of atheism by his contemporaries because of his new interpretation of the myths of the gods.

[20] For Luther's opinion of Aristotle, cf. *An Open Letter to the Christian Nobility. PE* 2, 146-147.

[21] The Franciscans. Perhaps an allusion to the seraphic vision of St. Francis.

Pg 13 ≠ *Leipzig was trying to say that the Sacraments can only be partaken one by laity, one by PRRST.* Luther angers

The Babylonian Captivity of the Church

Satan [II Cor. 12:7] and that he and his partners are seeking to make a name for themselves in the world through me, as men who are worthy to cross swords with Luther. But their hopes shall be dashed. In my contempt for them I shall never even mention their names, but content myself with this one reply to all their books. If they are worthy of it, I pray that Christ in his mercy may bring them back to a sound mind. If they are not worthy, I pray that they may never leave off writing such books, and that the enemies of truth may never deserve to read any others. There is a true and popular saying:

"This I know for certain—whenever I fight with filth,

Victor or vanquished, I am sure to be defiled."[22]

And since I see that they have an abundance of leisure and writing paper, I shall furnish them with ample matter to write about. For I shall keep ahead of them, so that while they are triumphantly celebrating a glorious victory over one of my heresies (as it seems to them), I shall meanwhile be devising a new one. I too am desirous of seeing these illustrious leaders in battle decorated with many honors. Therefore, while they murmur that I approve of communion in both kinds, and are most happily engrossed with this important and worthy subject, I shall go one step further and undertake to show that all who deny communion in both kinds to the laity are wicked men. To do this more conveniently I shall compose *a prelude on the captivity of the Roman church*.[23] In due time, when the most learned papists have disposed of this book, I shall offer more.

I take this course, lest any pious reader who may chance upon this book, should be offended by the filthy matter with which I deal and should justly complain that he finds nothing in it which cultivates or instructs his mind or which furnishes any food for learned reflection. For you know how impatient my friends are that I waste my time on the sordid fictions of these men. They say that

---

[22] The saying was also used later (1530) in the explanation to the fable about the ass and the lion in Luther's little book on Aesop's Fables, which included his translation of 14 of the fables. *Luthers Werke*, ed. Arnold E. Berger, III, 113. Cf. *MA*[2] 2, 405-406.

[23] We have retained the italics of the original for the most part where they serve the purpose of emphasis, or of pointing up the organizational structure of the treatise, or both.

the mere reading of them is ample confutation; they look for better things from me, which Satan seeks to hinder through these men. I have finally resolved to follow the advice of my friends and to leave to those hornets the business of wrangling and hurling invectives.

Of that Italian friar of Cremona [Isolani] I shall say nothing. He is an unlearned man and a simpleton, who attempts with a few rhetorical passages to recall me to the Holy See, from which I am not as yet aware of having departed, nor has anyone proved that I have. His chief argument in those silly passages[24] is that I ought to be moved by my monastic vows and by the fact that the empire has been transferred to the Germans.[25] Thus he does not seem to have wanted to write my "recantation" so much as the praise of the French people and the Roman pontiff. Let him attest his allegiance in this little book, such as it is. He does not deserve to be harshly treated, for he seems to have been prompted by no malice; nor does he deserve to be learnedly refuted, since all his chatter is sheer ignorance and inexperience.

To begin with, I must deny that there are seven sacraments, and for the present[26] maintain that there are but three: baptism, penance, and the bread.[27] All three have been subjected to a miserable captivity by the Roman curia, and the church has been robbed of all her liberty. Yet, if I were to speak according to the usage of the Scriptures, I should have only one single sacrament,[28] but with three sacramental signs, of which I shall treat more fully at the proper time.

---

[24]Cf. p. 269 n. 9.

[25] Cf. *An Open Letter to the Christian Nobility*, PE 2, 153 n. 2, and 153-158. Luther is probably referring to the fact that German kings, since Charles the Great in 800 A.D., had been called Roman Emperors after receiving papal coronation. Perhaps, though, he is referring to the election of the half-German Charles V on May 28, 1519, despite the papal agitation in favor of a French king. *Luther's Werke für das christliche Haus*, ed. Buchwald, *et al.* (Braunschweig, 1890) [hereinafter cited as Buchwald], II, 386 n. 1. Cf. *LW* 35, 406, n. 88.

[26] The "present" did not last very long as far as penance was concerned. Cf. p. 124.

[27] Luther uses the commonly accepted designation for the Lord's Supper, a name derived from the fact that the wine was being withheld from the laity.

[28]In I Tim. 3:16 Christ himself is called the *sacramentum* (Vulgate). Cf. PE 2, 177 n. 5; Julius Köstlin, *The Theology of Luther*, trans. Charles E. Hay (Philadelphia, 1897), I, 403; and *LW* 36, 93-94.

Now concerning the sacrament of the bread first of all.[29]

I shall tell you now what progress I have made as a result of my studies on the administration of this sacrament. For at the time when I was publishing my treatise on the Eucharist,[30] I adhered to the common custom and did not concern myself at all with the question of whether the pope was right or wrong. But now that I have been challenged and attacked, nay, forcibly thrust into this arena, I shall freely speak my mind, whether all the papists laugh or weep together.

In the first place the sixth chapter of John must be entirely excluded from this discussion, since it does not refer to the sacrament in a single syllable. Not only because the sacrament was not yet instituted, but even more because the passage itself and the sentences following plainly show, as I have already stated,[31] that Christ is speaking of faith in the incarnate Word. For he says: "My words are spirit and life" [John 6:63], which shows that he was speaking of a spiritual eating, by which he who eats has life; whereas the Jews understood him to mean a bodily eating and therefore disputed with him. But no eating can give life except that which is by faith, for that is truly a spiritual and living eating. As Augustine[32] also says: "Why do you make ready your teeth and your stomach? Believe, and you have eaten." [33] For the sacramental eating does not give life, since many eat unworthily. Hence Christ cannot be understood in this passage to be speaking about the sacrament.

Some persons, to be sure, have misapplied these words in their teaching concerning the sacrament, as in the decretal *Dudum*[34] and many others. But it is one thing to misapply the Scriptures and another to understand them in their proper sense. Otherwise, if in this passage Christ were enjoining a sacramental eating, when he

---

[29]Luther inserted this sentence instead of a subtitle as in the case of the other sacraments to follow.

[30]A *Treatise Concerning the Blessed Sacrament* (1519). PE 2, 9-31.

[31]Cf. p. 271.

[32] St. Augustine (354-430), bishop of Hippo in North Africa.

[33] *Sermo* 112, cap. 5. Migne 38, 645.

[34] Luther's reference to the Decretals is correct. His citation of *Dudum* is wrong. It should have been *Quum Marthae, Decretalium Gregorii IX*, lib. iii, tit. XLI: *de celebratione missarum, et sacramento eucharistiae et divinis officiis*, cap. 6. Cf. the text in *Corpus Iuris Canonici*, ed. Aemilius Friedberg (Graz, 1955), II, col. 638.

says: "Unless you eat my flesh and drink my blood, you have no life in you" [John 6:53], he would be condemning all infants, all the sick, and all those absent or in any way hindered from the sacramental eating, however strong their faith might be. Thus Augustine, in his *Contra Julianum*,[35] Book II, proves from Innocent[36] that even infants eat the flesh and drink the blood of Christ without the sacrament; that is, they partake of them through the faith of the church. Let this then be accepted as proved: John 6 does not belong here. For this reason I have written elsewhere[37] that the Bohemians[38] cannot properly rely on this passage in support of the sacrament in both kinds.

Now there are two passages that do bear very clearly upon this matter: the Gospel narratives of the Lord's Supper and Paul in I Cor. 11. Let us examine these. Matthew [26], Mark [14], and Luke [22] agree that Christ gave the whole sacrament to all his disciples. That Paul delivered both kinds is so certain that no one has ever had the temerity to say otherwise. Add to this that Matt. [26:27] reports that Christ did not say of the bread, "eat of it, all of you," but of the cup, "drink of it, all of you." Mark [14:23] likewise does not say, "they all ate of it," but "they all drank of it." Both attach the note of universality to the cup, not to the bread, as though the Spirit foresaw this schism, by which some would be forbidden to partake of the cup, which Christ desired should be common to all. How furiously, do you suppose, would they rave against us, if they had found the word "all" attached to the bread instead of to the cup? They would certainly leave us no loophole to escape. They would cry out and brand us as heretics and damn us as schismatics. But now, when the Scripture is on our side and against them, they will not allow themselves to be bound by any force of logic. Men of the most free will[39] they are,

---

[35] *Contra Julianum* ii, cap. 36. Migne 44, 699-700.
[36] Innocent I, bishop of Rome 402-417, energetic opponent of Pelagius and other heretics.
[37] *Verklärung etlicher Artikel in einem Sermon vom heiligen Sakrament* (1520). WA 6, 80.
[38] Followers of the martyred John Huss (1369-1415); permitted by compromise agreements with Rome to administer Communion in both kinds.
[39] For Luther's denial of his opponents' doctrine of the complete freedom of the will, cf. his *De servo arbitrio* (1525), WA 18, 600-787, *St.L.* 18, 1668-1969; *The Bondage of the Will*, trans. J. I. Packer and O. R. Johnston (Westwood, New Jersey, 1957).

even in the things that are God's; they change and change again, and throw everything into confusion.

But imagine me standing over against them and interrogating my lords, the papists. In the Lord's Supper, the whole sacrament, or communion in both kinds, is given either to the priests alone or else it is at the same time given to the laity. If it is given only to the priests (as they would have it), then it is not right to give it to the laity in either kind. For it must not be given rashly to any to whom Christ did not give it when he instituted the sacrament. Otherwise, if we permit one institution of Christ to be changed, we make all of his laws invalid, and any man may make bold to say that he is not bound by any other law or institution of Christ. For a single exception, especially in the Scriptures, invalidates the whole. But if it is given also to the laity, it inevitably follows that it ought not to be withheld from them in either form. And if any do withhold it from them when they ask for it they are acting impiously and contrary to the act, example, and institution of Christ.

I acknowledge that I am conquered by this argument, which to me is irrefutable. I have neither read nor heard nor found anything to say against it. For here the word and example of Christ stand unshaken when he says, not by way of permission, but of command: "Drink of it, all of you" [Matt. 26:27]. For if all are to drink of it, and the words cannot be understood as addressed to the priests alone, then it is certainly an impious act to withhold the cup from the laymen when they desire it, even though an angel from heaven [Gal. 1:8] were to do it. For when they say that the distribution of both kinds is left to the decision of the church, they make this assertion without reason and put it forth without authority. It can be ignored just as readily as it can be proved. It is of no avail against an opponent who confronts us with the word and work of Christ; he must be refuted with the word of Christ, but this we[40] do not possess.

If, however, either kind may be withheld from the laity, then with equal right and reason a part of baptism or penance might also be taken away from them by this same authority of the church. Therefore, just as baptism and absolution must be administered in

---

[40] Here Luther identifies himself with the erring priesthood.

Bread only given to laity

their entirety, so the sacrament of the bread must be given in its entirety to all laymen, if they desire it. I am much amazed, however, by their assertion that the priests may never receive only one kind in the mass under pain of mortal sin; and that for no other reason except (as they unanimously say) that the two kinds constitute one complete sacrament, which may not be divided. I ask them, therefore, to tell me why it is lawful to divide it in the case of the laity, and why they are the only ones to whom the entire sacrament is not given? Do they not acknowledge, by their own testimony, either that both kinds are to be given to the laity or that the sacrament is not valid when only one kind is given to them? How can it be that the sacrament in one kind is not complete in the case of the priests, yet in the case of the laity it is complete? Why do they flaunt the authority of the church and the power of the pope in my face? These do not annul the words of God and the testimony of the truth.

It follows, further, that if the church can withhold from the laity one kind, the wine, it can also withhold from them the other, the bread. It could therefore withhold the entire Sacrament of the Altar from the laity and completely annul Christ's institution as far as they are concerned. By what authority, I ask. If the church cannot withhold the bread, or both kinds, neither can it withhold the wine. This cannot possibly be gainsaid; for the church's power must be the same over either kind as it is over both kinds, and if it has no power over both kinds, it has none over either kind. I am curious to hear what the flatterers of Rome will have to say to this.

But what carries most weight with me, however, and is quite decisive for me is that Christ says: "This is my blood, which is poured out for you and for many for the forgiveness of sins."[41] Here you see very clearly that the blood is given to all those for whose sins it was poured out. But who will dare to say that it was not poured out for the laity? And do you not see whom he addresses when he gives the cup? Does he not give it to all? Does he not say that it is poured out for all? "For you" [Luke 22:20], he says—let this refer to the priests. "And for many" [Matt. 26:28],

---

[41] A harmony of Matt. 26:28 and Luke 22:20 in the Vulgate, whereby "for you" and "for many" are conjoined in the traditional manner of the canon of the mass.

however, cannot possibly refer to the priests. Yet he says: "Drink of it, all of you" [Matt. 26:27]. I too could easily trifle here and with my words make a mockery of Christ's words, as my dear trifler[42] does. But those who rely on the Scriptures in opposing us must be refuted by the Scriptures.

This is what has prevented me from condemning the Bohemians,[43] who, whether they are wicked men or good, certainly have the word and act of Christ on their side, while we[44] have neither, but only that inane remark of men: "The church has so ordained." It was not the church which ordained these things, but the tyrants of the churches, without the consent of the church, which is the people of God.

But now I ask, where is the necessity, where is the religious duty, where is the practical use of denying both kinds, that is, the visible sign, to the laity, when everyone concedes to them the grace of the sacrament[45] without the sign? If they concede the grace, which is the greater, why not the sign, which is the lesser? For in every sacrament the sign as such is incomparably less than the thing signified. What then, I ask, is to prevent them from conceding the lesser, when they concede the greater? Unless indeed, as it seems to me, it has come about by the permission of an angry God in order to give occasion for a schism in the church, to bring home to us how, having long ago lost the grace of the sacrament, we contend for the sign, which is the lesser, against that which is the most important and the chief thing; just as some men for the sake of ceremonies contend against love. This monstrous perversion seems to date from the time when we began to rage against Christian love for the sake of the riches of this world. Thus God would show us, by this terrible sign, how we esteem signs more than the things they signify. How preposterous it would be to admit that the faith of baptism is granted to the candidate for baptism, and yet to deny him the sign of this very faith, namely, the water!

---

[42]Alveld, cf. above, p. 268 n. 7.

[43]Cf. p. 276 n. 38.

[44]Cf. p. 277 n. 41.

[45] The *res sacramenti*. The sacrament consisted of two parts—the *sacramentum*, or external sign, and the *res sacramenti*, or the thing signified, the sacramental grace.

Finally, Paul stands invincible and stops the mouth of everyone when he says in I Cor. 11 [:23]: "For I received from the Lord what I also delivered to you." He does not say: "I permitted to you," as this friar of ours lyingly asserts out of his own head.[46] Nor is it true that Paul delivered both kinds on account of the contention among the Corinthians. In the first place, the text shows that their contention was not about the reception of both kinds, but about the contempt and envy between rich and poor. The text clearly states: "One is hungry and another is drunk, and you humiliate those who have nothing" [I Cor. 11:21-22]. Moreover, Paul is not speaking of the time when he first delivered the sacrament to them, for he does not say "I receive from the Lord" and "I give to you," but "I received" and "I delivered"—namely, when he first began to preach among them, a long while before this contention. This shows that he delivered both kinds to them, for "delivered" means the same as "commanded," for elsewhere he uses the word in this sense. Consequently there is nothing in the friar's fuming about permission; he has raked it together without Scripture, without reason, without sense. His opponents do not ask what he has dreamed, but what the Scriptures decree in the matter, and out of the Scriptures he cannot adduce one jot or tittle in support of his dreams, while they can produce mighty thunderbolts in support of their faith.

Rise up then, you popish flatterers, one and all! Get busy and defend yourselves against the charges of impiety, tyranny, and lèse-majesté against the gospel, and of the crime of slandering your brethren. You decry as heretics those who refuse to contravene such plain and powerful words of Scripture in order to acknowledge the mere dreams of your brains! If any are to be called heretics and schismatics, it is not the Bohemians or the Greeks,[47] for they take their stand upon the Gospels. It is you Romans who are the heretics and godless schismatics, for you presume upon your figments alone against the clear Scriptures of God. Wash yourself of that, men!

But what could be more ridiculous and more worthy of this

---

[46] The passage from Alveld is quoted in WA 6, 505 n. 1.

[47] Greek Church is a common designation for that entire branch of Christendom known as Eastern Orthodoxy, which was split from Western or Latin Christianity in the year 1054. Its theologies and liturgies are written mostly in the Greek language.

friar's brains than his saying that the Apostle wrote these words and gave this permission, not to the church universal, but to a particular church, that is, the Corinthian? Where does he get his proof? Out of one storehouse, his own impious head. If the church universal receives, reads, and follows this epistle as written for itself in all other respects, why should it not do the same with this portion also? If we admit that any epistle, or any part of any epistle, of Paul does not apply to the church universal, then the whole authority of Paul falls to the ground. Then the Corinthians will say that what he teaches about faith in the Epistle to the Romans does not apply to them. What greater blasphemy and madness can be imagined than this! God forbid that there should be one jot or tittle in all of Paul which the whole church universal is not bound to follow and keep! The Fathers never held an opinion like this, not even down to these perilous times of which Paul was speaking [II Tim. 3:1-9] when he foretold that there would be blasphemers and blind, insensate men. This friar is one of them, perhaps even the chief.

However, suppose we grant the truth of this intolerable madness. If Paul gave his permission to a particular church, then, even from your own point of view, the Greeks and Bohemians are in the right, for they are particular churches. Hence it is sufficient that they do not act contrary to Paul, who at least gave permission. Moreover, Paul could not permit anything contrary to Christ's institution. Therefore, O Rome, I cast in your teeth, and in the teeth of all your flatterers, these sayings of Christ and Paul, on behalf of the Greeks and the Bohemians. I defy you to prove that you have been given any authority to change these things by as much as one hair, much less to accuse others of heresy because they disregard your arrogance. It is rather you who deserve to be charged with the crime of godlessness and despotism.

Concerning this point we may read Cyprian,[48] who alone is strong enough to refute all the Romanists. In the fifth book of his treatise, *On the Lapsed,* he testifies that it was the widespread custom in that church [at Carthage] to administer both kinds to the laity, even to children, indeed, to give the body of the Lord

---

[48] Bishop of Carthage, (249-258), who was beheaded as a martyr for the faith. The treatise was written about 251-252.

into their hands. And of this he gives many examples. Among other things, he reproves some of the people as follows: "The sacrilegious man is angered at the priests because he does not immediately receive the body of the Lord with unclean hands, or drink the blood of the Lord with unclean lips." [49] He is speaking here, you see, of irreverent laymen who desired to receive the body and the blood from the priests. Do you find anything to snarl at here, wretched flatterer? Will you say that this holy martyr, a doctor of the church endowed with the apostolic spirit, was a heretic, and that he used this permission in a particular church?

In the same place Cyprian narrates an incident that came under his own observation. He describes at length how a deacon was administering the cup to a little[50] girl, and when she drew away from him he poured the blood of the Lord into her mouth.[51] We read the same of St. Donatus, and how trivially does this wretched flatterer dispose of his broken chalice![52] "I read of a broken chalice," he says, "but I do not read that the blood was administered." [53] No wonder! He that finds what he pleases in the Holy Scriptures will also read what he pleases in the histories. But can the authority of the church be established, or the heretics be refuted, in this way?

But enough on this subject! I did not undertake this work for the purpose of answering one who is not worthy of a reply, but to bring the truth of the matter to light.

---

[49] St. Cyprian, "The Lapsed," trans. Maurice Bévenot, S. J. (Westminster, Maryland, 1957), p. 31. (Vol. 25 of *Ancient Christian Writers*.)

[50] *infanti*, a child under the age of seven years. *St.L.* 19, 21 n. 2.

[51] St. Cyprian, *op. cit.*, pp. 32-33.

[52] Donatus, bishop of Arezzo, whither he had fled during the persecution of Diocletian (303-305); martyred under Julian the Apostate, August 7, 362. In a collection of legendary lives of the saints, compiled by Jacobus de Voragine (*circa* 1230-1298), it is related: "And one day, as Gregory relates in his *Dialogue*, the people were receiving the holy Communion in the Mass, and the deacon was distributing the Blood of Christ, when the pagans pushed him so rudely that he fell, and the holy chalice was shattered. As he and the people were sorely grieved thereat, Donatus gathered the fragments of the chalice, and having prayed, restored it to its former shape." *The Golden Legend of Jacobus de Voragine*, trans. Granger Ryan and Helmut Ripperger (New York, 1941), Part Two, 433-434.

[53] Alveld quotes the story of the broken cup in order to refute the practice in administration of the sacrament which it implies. He says: "I read of the repairing of the chalice in Gregory, but do not find there the administration of the blood." Cf. *WA* 6, 506 n. 2.

I conclude, then, that it is wicked and despotic to deny both kinds to the laity, and that this is not within the power of any angel, much less of any pope or council. Nor does the Council of Constance[54] give me pause, for if its authority is valid, why not that of the Council of Basel as well, which decreed to the contrary that the Bohemians should be permitted to receive the sacrament in both kinds? That decision was reached only after considerable discussion, as the extant records and documents of the Council show. And to this Council the ignorant flatterer refers[55] in support of his dream; with such wisdom does he handle the whole matter.

The first captivity of this sacrament, therefore, concerns its substance or completeness, which the tyranny of Rome has wrested from us. Not that those who use only one kind sin against Christ, for Christ did not command the use of either kind, but left it to the choice of each individual, when he said: "As often as you do this, do it in remembrance of me" [I Cor. 11:25]. But they are the sinners, who forbid the giving of both kinds to those who wish to exercise this choice. The fault lies not with the laity, but with the priests. The sacrament does not belong to the priests, but to all men. The priests are not lords, but servants in duty bound to administer both kinds to those who desire them, as often as they desire them. If they wrest this right from the laity and deny it to them by force, they are tyrants; but the laity are without fault, whether they lack one kind or both kinds. In the meantime they must be preserved by their faith and by their desire for the complete sacrament. These same servants are likewise bound to administer baptism and absolution to everyone who seeks them, because he has a right to them; but if they do not administer them, the seeker has the full merit of his faith, while they will be accused before Christ as wicked servants. Thus the holy fathers of old in the desert did

[54] Alveld had cited the *Decretum Constantiense*, which approved the withholding of the cup from the laity. Cf. WA 6, 507 n. 1.
[55] The Council of Constance did sanction withholding of the cup from the laity, and burned John Huss at the stake for disputing it (July 6, 1415). Alveld, however, was wrong, as Luther says, in citing also the Council of Basel. That Council concluded the *Compactata* of Prague (November 30, 1433), granting to the followers of Huss (the "Bohemians") the privilege of administering the sacrament in both kinds.

not receive the sacrament in any form for many years at a time.[56]

Therefore I do not urge that both kinds be seized upon by force, as if we were bound to this form by a rigorous command, but I instruct men's consciences so that they may endure the Roman tyranny, knowing well that they have been forcibly deprived of their rightful share in the sacrament because of their own sin. This only do I desire—that no one should justify the tyranny of Rome, as if it were doing right in forbidding one kind to the laity. We ought rather to abhor it, withhold our consent, and endure it just as we should do if we were held captive by the Turk and not permitted to use either kind. This is what I meant by saying that it would be a good thing, in my opinion, if this captivity were ended by the decree of a general council,[57] our Christian liberty restored to us out of the hands of the Roman tyrant, and every one left free to seek and receive this sacrament, just as he is free to receive baptism and penance. But now we are compelled by the same tyranny to receive the one kind year after year, so utterly lost is the liberty which Christ has given us. This is the due reward of our godless ingratitude.

The second captivity of this sacrament is less grievous as far as the conscience is concerned, yet the gravest of dangers threatens the man who would attack it, to say nothing of condemning it. Here I shall be called a Wycliffite[58] and a heretic by six hundred names. But what of it? Since the Roman bishop has ceased to be a bishop and has become a tyrant, I fear none of his decrees; for I know that it is not within his power, nor that of any general council, to make new articles of faith.

Some time ago, when I was drinking in scholastic theology, the learned Cardinal of Cambrai[59] gave me food for thought in his

---

[56] Cf. *A Treatise Concerning the Ban*, PE 2, 40.

[57] Cf. above, p. 269 n. 13.

[58] John Wycliffe (d. 1384), the most prominent English reformer before the Reformation and keenest of medieval critics of the doctrine of transubstantiation, was posthumously condemned as a heretic by the Council of Constance on May 4, 1415.

[59] Pierre d'Ailly (1350-1420), a pupil of Ockham, influenced Luther greatly. He was chairman of that session of the Council of Constance which examined and condemned John Huss in 1415. Luther is referring to d' Ailly's *Questiones quarti libri sententiarum*, quest. 6, E; folio cclxiv a.

comments on the fourth book of the *Sentences*.[60] He argues with great acumen that to hold that real bread and real wine, and not merely their accidents,[61] are present on the altar, would be much more probable and require fewer superfluous miracles—if only the church had not decreed otherwise. When I learned later what church it was that had decreed this, namely the Thomistic[62]—that is, the Aristotelian church—I grew bolder, and after floating in a sea of doubt,[63] I at last found rest for my conscience in the above view, namely, that it is real bread and real wine, in which Christ's real flesh and real blood are present in no other way and to no less a degree than the others assert them to be under their accidents. I reached this conclusion because I saw that the opinions of the Thomists, whether approved by pope or by council, remain only opinions, and would not become articles of faith even if an angel from heaven were to decree otherwise [Gal. 1:8]. For what is asserted without the Scriptures or proven revelation may be held as an opinion, but need not be believed. But this opinion of Thomas hangs so completely in the air without support of Scripture or reason that it seems to me he knows neither his philosophy nor his logic. For Aristotle speaks of subject and accidents so very differently[64] from St. Thomas that it seems to me this great man is to be pitied not only for attempting to draw his opinions in matters of faith from Aristotle, but also for attempting to base them upon a man whom he did not understand, thus building an unfortunate superstructure upon an unfortunate foundation.

---

[60] Famous medieval textbook of theology, compiled *circa* 1150 by Peter Lombard (d. 1160), and containing brief statements or "sentences" of the main arguments pro and con with respect to the principal themes in Christian doctrine. The fourth book treats of the sacraments in general.

[61] The qualities which, in medieval thought, were held to adhere to the invisible "substance," and together with it, form the object. In transubstantiation the "substance" of the bread and wine was changed into the "substance" of Christ's body and blood, while only the "accidents" or "form" of the bread and wine (such as shape, color, and taste) remained.

[62] The name refers to Thomas Aquinas (1225-1274), a Dominican, greatest of the scholastic theologians, still regarded as the foremost doctrinal authority in the Roman Catholic church.

[63] *inter sacrum et saxum.* In his *Adagia*, Erasmus says the phrase is used of those who in their perplexity are carried to the point of grave danger. *CL* 1, 438 n. 29.

[64] Aristotle held that a subject and its accidents are inseparable; neither can exist apart from the other. Cf. *MA* 2, 406.

Therefore I permit every man to hold either of these opinions, as he chooses. My one concern at present is to remove all scruples of conscience, so that no one may fear being called a heretic if he believes that real bread and real wine are present on the altar, and that every one may feel at liberty to ponder, hold, and believe either one view or the other without endangering his salvation. However, I shall now set forth my own view.

In the first place, I do not intend to listen or attach the least importance to those who will cry out that this teaching of mine is Wycliffite, Hussite, heretical, and contrary to the decree of the church. No one will do this except those very persons whom I have convicted of manifold heresies in the matter of indulgences, freedom of the will and the grace of God, good works and sins, etc. If Wycliffe was once a heretic, they are heretics ten times over; and it is a pleasure to be blamed and accused by heretics and perverse sophists, since to please them would be the height of impiety. Besides, the only way in which they can prove their opinions and disprove contrary ones is by saying: "That is Wycliffite, Hussite, heretical!" They carry this feeble argument always on the tip of their tongues, and they have nothing else. If you ask for scriptural proof, they say: "This is our opinion, and the church (that is, we ourselves) has decided thus." To such an extent these men, who are reprobate concerning the faith [II Tim. 3:8] and untrustworthy, have the effrontery to set their own fancies before us in the name of the church as articles of faith.

But there are good grounds for my view, and this above all—no violence is to be done to the words of God, whether by man or angel. They are to be retained in their simplest meaning as far as possible. Unless the context manifestly compels it, they are not to be understood apart from their grammatical and proper sense, lest we give our adversaries occasion to make a mockery of all the Scriptures. Thus Origen[65] was rightly repudiated long ago because, ignoring the grammatical sense, he turned the trees and everything else written concerning Paradise into allegories, from which one could have inferred that trees were not created by God. Even so

---

[65] Origen of Alexandria (*circa* 184-253) whose principles of allegorical exegesis were the source of many lengthy controversies, beginning as early as the fourth century.

here, when the Evangelists plainly write that Christ took bread [Matt. 26:26; Mark 14:22; Luke 22:19] and blessed it, and when the Book of Acts and the Apostle Paul in turn call it bread [Acts 2:46; I Cor. 10:16; 11:23, 26-28], we have to think of real bread and real wine, just as we do of a real cup (for even they do not say that the cup was transubstantiated). Since it is not necessary, therefore, to assume a transubstantiation effected by divine power, it must be regarded as a figment of the human mind, for it rests neither on the Scriptures nor on reason, as we shall see.

Therefore it is an absurd and unheard-of juggling with words to understand "bread" to mean "the form or accidents[66] of bread," and "wine" to mean "the form or accidents of wine." Why do they not also understand all other things to mean their "forms or accidents"? And even if this might be done with all other things, it would still not be right to enfeeble the words of God in this way, and by depriving them of their meaning to cause so much harm.

Moreover, the church kept the true faith for more than twelve hundred years, during which time the holy fathers never, at any time or place, mentioned this transubstantiation (a monstrous word and a monstrous idea), until the pseudo philosophy of Aristotle began to make its inroads into the church in these last three hundred years.[67] During this time many things have been wrongly defined, as for example, that the divine essence is neither begotten nor begets; that the soul is the substantial form of the human body. These and like assertions are made without any reason or cause, as the Cardinal of Cambrai[68] himself admits.

Perhaps they will say that the danger of idolatry demands that the bread and wine should not be really present. How ridiculous! The laymen have never become familiar with their fine-spun philosophy of substance and accidents, and could not grasp it if it were taught to them. Besides, there is the same danger in the

---

[66]Cf. p. 285 n. 61.

[67] Luther is referring to the official establishment of transubstantiation as a fixed dogma by the Fourth Lateran Council of 1215 under Innocent III. The concept was perhaps several centuries in developing prior to that time, though the earliest documentable use of the term in its technical sense was probably in a treatise by Stephen of Autun (d. 1139). *The New Schaff-Herzog Encyclopedia of Religious Knowledge* (12 volumes) [hereinafter cited as Schaff-Herzog], XI, 494.

[68]Cf. p. 284 n. 59.

accidents which remain and which they see, as in the case of the substance which they do not see. If they do not worship the accidents, but the Christ hidden under them, why should they worship the [substance of the] bread, which they do not see?

And why could not Christ include his body in the substance of the bread just as well as in the accidents? In red-hot iron, for instance, the two substances, fire and iron, are so mingled that every part is both iron and fire. Why is it not even more possible that the body of Christ be contained in every part of the substance of the bread?

What will they reply? Christ is believed to have been born from the inviolate womb of his mother. Let them say here too that the flesh of the Virgin was meanwhile annihilated, or as they would more aptly say, transubstantiated, so that Christ, after being enfolded in its accidents, finally came forth through the accidents! The same thing will have to be said of the shut door [John 20:19, 26] and of the closed mouth of the sepulchre,[69] through which he went in and out without disturbing them.

Out of this has arisen that Babel of a philosophy of a constant quantity distinct from the substance,[70] until it has come to such a pass that they themselves no longer know what are accidents and what is substance. For who has ever proved beyond the shadow of a doubt that heat, color, cold, light, weight, or shape are mere accidents? Finally, they have been driven to pretend that a new substance is created by God for those accidents on the altar, all on account of Aristotle, who says: "It is the nature of an accident to be in something," and endless other monstrosities. They would be rid of all these if they simply permitted real bread to be present. I rejoice greatly that the simple faith of this sacrament is still to be found, at least among the common people. For as they do not understand, neither do they dispute whether accidents are present without substance, but believe with a simple faith that Christ's body and blood are truly contained there, and leave to those who have nothing else to do the argument about what contains them.

---

[69] Matt. 28:2; Mark 16:4; Luke 24:2; John 20:1.
[70] According to scholastic teaching the substance of the bread ceases to exist. Its quantity, however, together with the other accidents, remains the same.

But perhaps they will say: "Aristotle teaches that in an affirmative proposition subject and predicate must be identical," or (to quote the monster's own words in the sixth book of his *Metaphysics*)[71]: "An affirmative proposition requires the agreement of the subject and the predicate." They interpret argreement to mean identity. Hence, when I say: "This is my body," the subject cannot be identical with the bread, but must be identical with the body of Christ.

What shall we say when Aristotle and the doctrines of men are made to be the arbiters of such lofty and divine matters? Why do we not put aside such curiosity and cling simply to the words of Christ, willing to remain in ignorance of what takes place here and content that the real body of Christ is present by virtue of the words?[72] Or is it necessary to comprehend the manner of the divine working in every detail?

But what do they say when Aristotle admits that all of the categories[73] of accidents are themselves a subject—although he grants that substance is the chief subject? Hence for him "this white," "this large," "this something," are all subjects, of which something is predicated. If that is correct, I ask: If a "transubstantiation" must be assumed in order that Christ's body may not be identified with the bread, why not also a "transaccidentation," in order that the body of Christ may not be identified with the accidents? For the same danger remains if one understands the subject to be "this white or this round[74] is my body." And for the same reason that a "transubstantiation" must be assumed, a "transaccidentation" must also be assumed, because of this identity of subject and predicate.

If however, merely by an act of the intellect, you can do away with the accident, so that it will not be regarded as the subject

---

[71] Luther should be referred not to the *Metaphysics* but to the *Organon*, where in chapter 6 on *De Interpretatione,* Aristotle indicates that for affirmative and negative propositions having the same subject and predicate to be truly contradictory, subject and predicate must be unequivocally (univocally) identical. In chapter 10 he holds that "the subject and predicate in an affirmation must each denote a single thing." Richard McKeon (ed.), *The Basic Works of Aristotle* (New York, 1941), pp. 43, 49.

[72] Cf. A *Treatise Concerning the Blessed Sacrament* (1519). *PE* 2, 20.

[73] Namely: substance, quantity, quality, relation, place, time, position, state, action, and affection. McKeon, p. 8.

[74] i.e., the host, or wafer.

when you say, "this is my body," why not with equal ease transcend the substance of the bread, if you do not want it to be regarded either as the subject, so that "this my body" is no less in the substance than in the accident? After all, this is a divine work performed by God's almighty power, which can operate just as much and just as well in the accident as it can in the substance.

Let us not dabble too much in philosophy, however. Does not Christ appear to have anticipated this curiosity admirably by saying of the wine, not *Hoc est sanguis meus,* but *Hic est sanguis meus?* [Mark 14:24]. He speaks even more clearly when he brings in the word "cup" and says: "This cup [*Hic calix*] is the new testament in my blood" [Luke 22:20; I Cor. 11:25]. Does it not seem as though he desired to keep us in a simple faith, sufficient for us to believe that his blood was in the cup? For my part, if I cannot fathom how the bread is the body of Christ, yet I will take my reason captive to the obedience of Christ [II Cor. 10:5], and clinging simply to his words, firmly believe not only that the body of Christ is in the bread, but that the bread is the body of Christ. My warrant for this is the words which say: "He took bread, and when he had given thanks, he broke it and said, 'Take, eat, this (that is, this bread, which he had taken and broken) is my body'" [I Cor. 11:23-24]. And Paul says: "The bread which we break, is it not a participation in the body of Christ?" [I Cor. 10:16]. He does not say "in the bread there is," but "the bread itself is[75] the participation in the body of Christ." What does it matter if philosophy cannot fathom this? The Holy Spirit is greater than Aristotle. Does philosophy fathom their transubstantiation? Why, they themselves admit that here all philosophy breaks down. That the pronoun "this," in both Greek and Latin, is referred to "body," is due to the fact that in both of these languages the two words are of the same gender. In Hebrew, however, which has no neuter gender, "this" is referred to "bread," so that it would be proper to say *Hic* [bread] *est corpus meum.* Actually, the idiom of the language[76] and common sense both prove that the subject ["this"] obviously points to the bread and not to the body, when he says:

---

[75] Not *in pane est* but *ipse panis est.*

[76] Luther assumes that the language Jesus spoke on that occasion was certainly not Greek, but probably Hebrew.

Hoc est corpus meum, das ist meyn leyp, that is, "This very bread here [*iste panis*] is my body."

Thus, what is true in regard to Christ is also true in regard to the sacrament. In order for the divine nature to dwell in him bodily [Col. 2:9], it is not necessary for the human nature to be transubstantiated and the divine nature contained under the accidents of the human nature. Both natures are simply there in their entirety, and it is truly said: "This man is God; this God is man." Even though philosophy cannot grasp this, faith grasps it nonetheless. And the authority of God's Word is greater than the capacity of our intellect to grasp it. In like manner, it is not necessary in the sacrament that the bread and wine be transubstantiated and that Christ be contained under their accidents in order that the real body and real blood may be present. But both remain there at the same time, and it is truly said: "This bread is my body; this wine is my blood," and vice versa. Thus I will understand it for the time being to the honor of the holy words of God, to which I will allow no violence to be done by petty human arguments, nor will I allow them to be twisted into meanings which are foreign to them. At the same time, I permit other men to follow the other opinion, which is laid down in the decree, *Firmiter*,[77] only let them not press us to accept their opinions as articles of faith (as I have said above).[78]

The third captivity of this sacrament is by far the most wicked abuse of all, in consequence of which there is no opinion more generally held or more firmly believed in the church today than this, that the mass is a good work and a sacrifice. And this abuse has brought an endless host of other abuses in its train, so that the faith of this sacrament has become utterly extinct and the holy sacrament has been turned into mere merchandise, a market, and a profit-making business. Hence participations,[79] brotherhoods,[80]

---

[77]*Firmiter, Decretalium Gregorii IX*, lib. i, tit I: *de summa trinitate et fide catholica*, cap. 1, sec. 3. *Corpus Iuris Canonici, op. cit.*, II col. 5.
[78]Cf. p. 284.

[79] Though not actually present, one could obtain spiritual "participation" in masses which, for example, were read in a monastery.
[80] These confraternities and sodalities paid to have masses said for them, and engaged in devotional exercises for gaining merit. Membership in such an association provided each person the benefits accruing from the "good works" (prayers and attendance at masses) of all the other members.

intercessions, merits, anniversaries,[81] memorial days[82] and the like wares are bought and sold, traded and bartered, in the church. On these the priests and monks depend for their entire livelihood.

I am attacking a difficult matter, an abuse perhaps impossible to uproot, since through century-long custom and the common consent of men it has become so firmly entrenched that it would be necessary to abolish most of the books now in vogue, and to alter almost the entire external form of the churches and introduce, or rather re-introduce, a totally different kind of ceremonies. But my Christ lives, and we must be careful to give more heed to the Word of God than to all the thoughts of men and of angels. I will perform the duties of my office and bring to light the facts in the case. As I have received the truth freely [Matt. 10:8], I will impart it without malice. For the rest let every man look to his own salvation; I will do my part faithfully so that no one may be able to cast on me the blame for his lack of faith and his ignorance of the truth when we appear before the judgment seat of Christ [2 Cor. 5:10].

In the first place, in order that we might safely and happily attain to a true and free knowledge of this sacrament, we must be particularly careful to put aside whatever has been added to its original simple institution by the zeal and devotion of men: such things as vestments, ornaments, chants, prayers, organs, candles, and the whole pageantry of outward things.[83] We must turn our eyes and hearts simply to the institution of Christ and this alone, and set nothing before us but the very word of Christ by which he instituted the sacrament, made it perfect, and committed it to us. For in that word, and in that word alone, reside the power, the nature, and the whole substance of the mass. All the rest is the work of man, added to the word of Christ, and the mass can be held and remain a mass just as well without them. Now the words of Christ, in which he instituted this sacrament, are these:

"Now as they were eating, Jesus took bread, and blessed, and broke it, and gave it to his disciples and said, 'Take, eat; this is my body, which is given for you.' And he took a cup, and when he had

---

[81] Masses said on behalf of the soul of a deceased person daily for a year or annually on the anniversary of his death.

[82] Masses for the dead were read on memorial days.

[83] Cf. *A Treatise on the New Testament that is the Holy Mass.* PE 1, 296-297.

given thanks he gave it to them, saying, 'Drink of it, all of you; for this cup is the new testament in my blood, which is poured out for you and for many for the forgiveness of sins. Do this in remembrance of me.' [84]

These words the Apostle also delivers and more fully expounds in I Cor. 11 [:23-26]. On them we must rest; on them we must build as on a firm rock, if we would not be carried about with every wind of doctrine [Eph. 4:14], as we have till now been carried about by the wicked doctrines of men who reject the truth [Titus 1:14]. For in these words nothing is omitted that pertains to the completeness, the use, and the blessing of this sacrament; and nothing is included that is superfluous and not necessary for us to know. Whoever sets aside these words and meditates or teaches concerning the mass will teach monstrous and wicked doctrines, as they have done who have made of the sacrament an *opus operatum* [85] and a sacrifice.

Let this stand, therefore, as our first and infallible proposition—the mass or Sacrament of the Altar is Christ's testament, which he left behind him at his death to be distributed among his believers. For that is the meaning of his words, "This cup is the new testament in my blood" [Luke 22:20; I Cor. 11:25]. Let this truth stand, I say, as the immovable foundation on which we shall base all that we have to say. For, as you will see, we are going to overthrow all the godless opinions of men which have been imported into this most precious sacrament. Christ, who is the truth, truly says that this is the new testament in his blood, poured out for us [Luke 22:20]. Not without reason do I dwell on this sentence; the matter is of no small moment, and must be most deeply impressed on our minds.

Thus, if we enquire what a testament is, we shall learn at the

---

[84] Luther's rendering of the Words of Institution is similar to that of the canon of the mass in that it represents a harmony of the several scriptural accounts, incorporating features from all of them—Matt. 26:26-28; Mark 14:22-24; Luke 22:19-20; I Cor. 11:23-25. It differs from the canon of the mass in that it excludes all phrases not explicitly found in the scriptural accounts themselves, Vulgate version. Cf. the canon of the mass text on p. 319. Cf. also *PE* 6, 74, 107-108, 126, 160.

[85] A work accomplished or finished, which is supposed to impart grace simply by virtue of its having been properly performed, without reference to any faith or lack of faith on the part of the person for whom it is performed. Cf. *A Treatise Concerning the Blessed Sacrament* (1519), *PE* 2, 22-23, where Luther discusses this term.

same time what the mass is, what its right use and blessing, and what its wrong use.

A testament, as everyone knows, is a promise made by one about to die, in which he designates his bequest and appoints his heirs. A testament, therefore, involves first, the death of the testator, and second, the promise of an inheritance and the naming of the heir. Thus Paul discusses at length the nature of a testament in Rom. 4, Gal. 3 and 4, and Heb. 9. We see the same thing clearly also in these words of Christ. Christ testifies concerning his death when he says: "This is my body, which is given, this is my blood, which is poured out" [Luke 22:19-20]. He names and designates the bequest when he says "for the forgiveness of sins" [Matt. 26:28]. But he appoints the heirs when he says "For you [Luke 22:19-20; I Cor. 11:24] and for many" [Matt. 26:28; Mark 14:24], that is, for those who accept and believe the promise of the testator. For here it is faith that makes men heirs, as we shall see.

You see, therefore, that what we call the mass is a promise of the forgiveness of sins made to us by God, and such a promise as has been confirmed by the death of the Son of God. For the only difference between a promise and a testament is that the testament involves the death of the one who makes it. A testator is a promiser who is about to die, while a promiser (if I may put it thus) is a testator who is not about to die. This testament of Christ is foreshadowed in all the promises of God from the beginning of the world; indeed, whatever value those ancient promises possessed was altogether derived from this new promise that was to come in Christ. Hence the words "compact," "covenant," and "testament of the Lord" occur so frequently in the Scriptures. These words signified that God would one day die. "For where there is a testament, the death of the testator must of necessity occur" (Heb. 9 [:16]). Now God made a testament; therefore, it was necessary that he should die. But God could not die unless he became man. Thus the incarnation and the death of Christ are both comprehended most concisely in this one word, "testament."

From the above it will at once be seen what is the right and what is the wrong use of the mass, and what is the worthy and what the unworthy preparation for it. If the mass is a promise, as has been said, then access to it is to be gained, not with any works, or

powers, or merits of one's own, but by faith alone. For where there
is the Word of the promising God, there must necessarily be the
faith of the accepting man. It is plain therefore, that the beginning
of our salvation is a faith which clings to the Word of the promising
God, who, without any effort on our part, in free and unmerited
mercy takes the initiative and offers us the word of his promise.
"He sent forth his word, and thus [*sic*] healed them," [86] not: "He
accepted our work, and thus healed us." First of all there is God's
Word. After it follows faith; after faith, love; then love does every
good work, for it does no wrong, indeed, it is the fulfilling of the law
[Rom. 13:10]. In no other way can man come to God or deal with
him than through faith. That is to say, that the author of salvation
is not man, by any works of his own, but God, through his promise;
and that all things depend on, and are upheld and preserved by,
the word of his power [Heb. 1:3], through which he brought us
forth, to be a kind of first fruits of his creatures [Jas. 1:18].

Thus, in order to raise up Adam after the fall, God gave him
this promise when he said to the serpent: "I will put enmity between
you and the woman, and between your seed and her seed; he shall
bruise your head, and you shall bruise his heel" [Gen. 3:15]. In this
word of promise Adam, together with his descendants, was carried
as it were in God's bosom, and by faith in it he was preserved,
waiting patiently for the woman who should bruise the serpent's
head, as God had promised. And in that faith and expectation he
died, not knowing when or who she would be, yet never doubting
that she would come. For such a promise, being the truth of God,
preserves even in hell those who believe it and wait for it. After this
came another promise, made to Noah—to last until the time of
Abraham—when a bow was set in the clouds as a sign of the
covenant [Gen. 9:12-17], by faith in which Noah and his descendants
found God gracious. After that, he promised Abraham that all the
nations should be blessed in his seed [Gen. 22:18]. And this is
Abraham's bosom [Luke 16:22], into which his descendants have
been received. Then to Moses and the children of Israel [Deut.
18:18], especially to David [II Sam. 7:12-16], he gave the plainest
promise of Christ, and thereby at last made clear what the promise
to the men of old really was.

---

[86] Ps. 107:20. *Sic* is Luther's own interpolation into the Vulgate text.

And so it finally came to the most perfect promise of all, that of the new testament, in which, with plain words, life and salvation are freely promised, and actually granted to those who believe the promise. And he distinguishes this testament from the old one by a particular mark when he calls it the "new testament" [Luke 22:20; I Cor. 11:25]. For the old testament given through Moses was not a promise of forgiveness of sins or of eternal things, but of temporal things, namely, of the land of Canaan, by which no man was renewed in spirit to lay hold on the heavenly inheritance. Wherefore also it was necessary that, as a figure of Christ, a dumb beast should be slain, in whose blood the same testament might be confirmed, as the blood corresponded to the testament and the sacrifice corresponded to the promise. But here Christ says "the new testament in my blood" [Luke 22:20; I Cor. 11:25], not somebody else's, but his own, by which grace is promised through the Spirit for the forgiveness of sins, that we may obtain the inheritance.

According to its substance, therefore, the mass is nothing but the aforesaid words of Christ: "Take and eat, etc." [Matt. 26:26], as if he were saying: "Behold, O sinful and condemned man, out of the pure and unmerited love with which I love you, and by the will of the Father of mercies [II Cor. 1:3], apart from any merit or desire of yours, I promise you in these words the forgiveness of all your sins and life everlasting. And that you may be absolutely certain of this irrevocable promise of mine, I shall give my body and pour out my blood, confirming this promise by my very death, and leaving you my body and blood as a sign and memorial of this same promise. As often as you partake of them, remember me, proclaim and praise my love and bounty toward you, and give thanks."

From this you will see that nothing else is needed for a worthy holding of mass than a faith that relies confidently on this promise, believes Christ to be true in these words of his, and does not doubt that these infinite blessings have been bestowed upon it. Hard on this faith there follows, of itself, a most sweet stirring of the heart, whereby the spirit of man is enlarged and enriched (that is love, given by the Holy Spirit through faith in Christ), so that he is drawn to Christ, that gracious and bounteous testator, and made a thoroughly new and different man. Who would not shed tears of gladness, indeed, almost faint for joy in Christ, if he believed with unshaken faith that this inestimable promise of Christ belonged to him? How could he help loving so great a benefactor, who of his own accord offers, promises, and grants such great riches and this eternal inheritance to one who is unworthy and deserving of something far different?

Therefore it is our one and only misfortune that we have many masses in the world, and yet none, or very few of us, recognize, consider, and receive these promises and riches that are offered to us. Actually, during the mass, we should do nothing with greater zeal (indeed, it demands all our zeal) than to set before our eyes, meditate upon, and ponder these words, these promises of Christ—for they truly constitute the mass itself—in order to exercise, nourish, increase, and strengthen our faith in them by this daily remembrance. For this is what he commands, when he says: "Do this in remembrance of me" [Luke 22:19; I Cor. 11:24]. This should be done by the preachers of the gospel in order to impress this promise faithfully upon the people, to commend it to them, and to awaken their faith in it.

But how many are there today who know that the mass is the promise of Christ? I will say nothing of those godless preachers of fables, who teach human ordinances instead of this great promise. And even if they teach these words of Christ, they do not teach them as a promise or testament, neither therefore as a means of obtaining faith.

What we deplore in this captivity is that nowadays they take every precaution that no layman should hear these words of Christ, as if they were too sacred to be delivered to the common people. So mad are we priests[87] that we arrogate to ourselves alone the so-called words of consecration, to be said secretly,[88] yet in such a way that they do not profit even us, for we too fail to regard them as promises or as a testament for the strengthening of the faith. Instead of believing them, we reverence them with I know not what superstitious and godless fancies. What else is Satan trying to do to us through this misfortune of ours but to remove every trace of the

---

[87]Cf. p. 277 n. 40.
[88]The words of consecration, indeed of the whole canon of the mass, were spoken very softly. Cf. *The Abomination of the Secret Mass* (1525), LW 36, 310 and 314.

[true] mass out of the church, though he is meanwhile at work filling every corner of the globe with [false] masses, that is, with abuses and mockeries of God's testament—burdening the world more and more heavily with most grievous sins of idolatry, to its deeper condemnation? For what more sinful idolatry can there be than to abuse God's promises with perverse opinions and to neglect or extinguish faith in them?

For God does not deal, nor has he ever dealt, with man otherwise than through a word of promise, as I have said. We in turn cannot deal with God otherwise than through faith in the Word of his promise. He does not desire works, nor has he need of them; rather we deal with men and with ourselves on the basis of works. But God has need of this: that we consider him faithful in his promises [Heb. 10:23], and patiently persist in this belief, and thus worship him with faith, hope, and love. It is in this way that he obtains his glory among us, since it is not of ourselves who run, but of him who shows mercy [Rom. 9:16], promises, and gives, that we have and hold all good things. Behold, this is that true worship and service of God which we ought to perform in the mass. But if the words of promise are not delivered, what exercise of faith can there be? And without faith, who can have hope or love? Without faith, hope, and love, what service of God can there be? There is no doubt, therefore, that in our day all priests and monks, together with their bishops and all their superiors, are idolators, living in a most perilous state by reason of this ignorance, abuse, and mockery of the mass, or sacrament, or promise of God.

For anyone can easily see that these two, promise and faith, must necessarily go together. For without the promise there is nothing to be believed; while without faith the promise is useless, since it is established and fulfilled through faith. From this everyone will readily gather that the mass, since it is nothing but promise, can be approached and observed only in faith. Without this faith, whatever else is brought to it by way of prayers, preparations, works, signs, or gestures are incitements to impiety rather than exercises of piety. It usually happens that those who are thus prepared imagine themselves legitimately entitled to approach the altar, when in reality they are less prepared than at any other time or by any other work, by reason of the unbelief which they bring

Excellent pb

Where is our worship.

with them. How many celebrants you can see everywhere, every day, who imagine they—wretched men—have committed criminal offenses when they make some petty mistake, such as wearing the wrong vestment, or forgetting to wash their hands, or stumbling over their prayers! But the fact that they have no regard for or faith in the mass itself, namely, the divine promise, causes them not the slightest qualms of conscience. O worthless religion of this age of ours, the most godless and thankless of all ages!

Hence the only worthy preparation and proper observance is faith, the faith by which we believe in the mass, that is, in the divine promise. Whoever, therefore, desires to approach the altar or receive the sacrament, let him beware lest he appear empty-handed [Exod. 23:15; 34:20; Deut. 16:16] before the face of the Lord God. But he will be empty-handed unless he has faith in the mass, or this new testament. By what godless work could he sin more grievously against the truth of God, than by this unbelief of his? By it, as much as in him lies, he convicts God of being a liar and a maker of empty promises. The safest course, therefore, will be to go to the mass in the same spirit in which you would go to hear any other promise of God, that is, prepared not to do or contribute much yourself, but to believe and accept all that is promised you there, or proclaimed as promises through the ministry of the priest. If you do not come in this spirit, beware of attending at all, for you will surely be going to your condemnation [I Cor. 11:29].

I was right then in saying that the whole power of the mass consists in the words of Christ, in which he testifies that forgiveness of sins is bestowed on all those who believe that his body is given and his blood poured out for them. This is why nothing is more important for those who go to hear mass than to ponder these words diligently and in full faith. Unless they do this, all else that they do is in vain. This is surely true, that to every promise of his, God usually adds some sign as a memorial or remembrance of the promise, so that thereby we may serve him the more diligently and he may admonish us the more effectually. Thus, when he promised Noah that he would not again destroy the world by a flood, he added his bow in the clouds, to show that he would be mindful of his covenant [Gen. 9:8-17]. And after promising Abraham the inheritance in his seed, he gave him circumcision as a mark of his justification by faith [Gen. 17:3-11]. Thus he granted to Gideon the dry and the wet fleece to confirm his promise of victory over the Midianites [Judg. 6:36-40]. And through Isaiah he offered to Ahaz a sign that he would conquer the king of Syria and Samaria, to confirm in him his faith in the promise [Isa. 7:10-17]. And we read of many such signs of the promises of God in the Scriptures.

So in the mass also, the foremost promise of all, he adds as a memorial sign of such a great promise his own body and his own blood in the bread and wine, when he says: "Do this in remembrance of me" [Luke 22:19; I Cor. 11:24-25]. And so in baptism, to the words of promise he adds the sign of immersion in water. We may learn from this that in every promise of God two things are presented to us, the word and the sign, so that we are to understand the word to be the testament, but the sign to be the sacrament. Thus, in the mass, the word of Christ is the testament, and the bread and wine are the sacrament. And as there is greater power in the word than in the sign, so there is greater power in the testament than in the sacrament; for a man can have and use the word or testament apart from the sign or sacrament. "Believe," says Augustine, "and you have eaten." [89] But what does one believe, other than the word of the one who promises? Therefore I can hold mass every day, indeed, every hour, for I can set the words of Christ before me and with them feed and strengthen my faith as often as I choose. This is a truly spiritual eating and drinking.

Here you may see what great things our theologians of the *Sentences*[90] have produced in this matter. In the first place, not one of them treats of that which is first and foremost, namely, the testament and the word of promise. And thus they make us forget faith and the whole power of the mass. In addition, they discuss exclusively the second part of the mass, namely, the sign or sacrament; yet in such a way that here too they do not teach faith, but their preparations and *opera operata*,[91] participations[92] and fruits of the mass. They come then to the profundities, babble of transsub-

---

[89] Cf. p. 275 n. 33.
[90] Commentators on Peter Lombard's textbook. Cf. p. 285 n. 60.
[91] Cf. p. 293 n. 85.
[92] Cf. p. 291 n. 79.

stantiation and endless other metaphysical trivialities, destroy the proper understanding and use of both sacrament and testament together with faith as such, and cause Christ's people to forget their God—as the prophet says, days without number [Jer. 2:32]. Let the others tabulate the various benefits of hearing mass; you just apply your mind to this, that you may say and believe with the prophet that God has here prepared a table before you in the presence of your enemies [Ps. 23:5], at which your faith may feed and grow fat. But your faith is fed only with the word of divine promise, for "Man shall not live by bread alone, but by every word that proceeds from the mouth of God" [Deut. 8:3; Matt. 4:4]. Hence, in the mass you must pay closest heed above all to the word of promise, as to a most lavish banquet—your utterly green pastures and sacred still waters [Ps. 23:2], in order that you might esteem this word above everything else, trust in it supremely, and cling to it most firmly, even through death and all sins. If you do this, you will obtain not merely those tiny drops and crumbs of "fruits of the mass" which some have superstitiously invented, but the very fountainhead of life, namely, that faith in the Word out of which every good thing flows, as is said in John 4:[93] "He who believes in me, 'Out of his heart shall flow rivers of living water.'" And again, "Whoever drinks of the water that I shall give him, it will become in him a spring of water welling up to eternal life" [John 4:14].

Now there are two things that are constantly assailing us, so that we fail to gather the fruits of the mass. The first is that we are sinners, and unworthy of such great things because of our utter worthlessness. The second is that, even if we were worthy, these things are so high that our fainthearted nature does not dare to aspire to them or hope for them. For who would not simply stand awe-struck before the forgiveness of sins and life everlasting rather than seeking after them, once he had weighed properly the magnitude of the blessings which come through them, namely, to have God as father, to be his son and heir of all his goods! Against this twofold faintness of ours we must lay hold on the word of Christ, and fix our gaze much more steadfastly on it than on these thoughts of our own weakness. For "great are the works of the Lord, studied

---

[93] John 7:38. Luther apparently had his next quotation in mind when he cited John 4.

by all who have pleasure in them" [Ps. 111:2], who is able to give "more abundantly than all that we ask or think" [Eph. 3:20]. If they did not surpass our worthiness, our grasp, and all our thoughts, they would not be divine. Thus Christ also encourages us when he says: "Fear not, little flock, for it is your Father's good pleasure to give you the kingdom" [Luke 12:32]. For it is just this incomprehensible overflowing of God's goodness, showered upon us through Christ, that moves us above all to love him most ardently in return, to be drawn to him with fullest confidence, and, despising all else, be ready to suffer all things for him. Wherefore this sacrament is rightly called "a fountain of love."

Let us take an illustration of this from human experience.[94] If a very rich lord were to bequeath a thousand gulden to a beggar or to an unworthy and wicked servant, it is certain that he would boldly claim and accept them without regard to his unworthiness and the greatness of the bequest. And if anyone should seek to oppose him on the grounds of his unworthiness and the large amount of the legacy, what do you suppose the man would say? He would likely say: "What is that to you? What I accept, I accept not on my merits or by any right that I may personally have to it. I know that I am receiving more than a worthless one like me deserves; indeed, I have deserved the very opposite. But I claim what I claim by the right of a bequest and of another's goodness. If to him it was not an unworthy thing to bequeath so great a sum to an unworthy person, why should I refuse to accept it because of my unworthiness? Indeed, it is for this very reason that I cherish all the more his unmerited gift—because I am unworthy!" With that same thought every man ought to fortify his conscience against all qualms and scruples, so that he may lay hold on the promise of Christ with unwavering faith, and take the greatest care to approach the sacrament not trusting in confession, prayer, and preparation, but rather, despairing of all these, with firm confidence in Christ who gives the promise. For, as we have said often enough, the word of promise must reign alone here in pure faith; such faith is the one and only sufficient preparation.

Hence we see how great is God's wrath with us, in that he has

---

[94] Repeated in a similar context in *A Treatise on the New Testament that is the Holy Mass* (1520). PE 1, 304-305.

permitted godless teachers to conceal the words of this testament from us, and thereby to extinguish this same faith, as far as they could. It is already easy to see what is the inevitable result of this extinguishing of the faith, namely, the most godless superstition of works. For where faith dies and the word of faith is silent, there works and the prescribing of works immediately crowd into their place. By them we have been carried away out of our own land, as into a Babylonian captivity, and despoiled of all our precious possessions. This has been the fate of the mass; it has been con-verted by the teaching of godless men into a good work. They them-selves call it an *opus operatum*,[95] and by it they presume themselves to be all-powerful with God. Next they proceed to the very height of madness, and after inventing the lie that the mass is effective simply by virtue of the act having been performed, they add another one to the effect that the mass is none the less profitable to others even if it is harmful to some wicked priest who may be celebrating it. On such a foundation of sand they base their applications, participations,[96] brotherhoods,[97] anniversaries,[98] and numberless other lucrative and profitable schemes of that kind.

These fraudulent disguises are so powerful, so numerous, and so firmly entrenched that you can scarcely prevail against them unless you exercise unremitting care and bear well in mind what the mass is and what has been said above. You have seen that the mass is nothing else than the divine promise or testament of Christ, sealed with the sacrament of his body and blood. If that is true, you will understand that it cannot possibly be in any way a work; nobody can possibly do any thing in it, neither can it be dealt with in any other way than by faith alone. However, faith is not a work, but the lord and life of all works.[99] Who in the world is so foolish as to regard a promise received by him, or a testament given to him, as a good work, which he renders to the testator by his acceptance of it? What heir will imagine that he is doing his departed father

---

[95] Cf. p. 293 n. 85.
[96] Cf. p. 291 n. 79.
[97] Cf. p. 291 n. 80.
[98] Cf. p. 292 n. 81.

[99] On the relation between faith and works compare *A Treatise on Good Works* (1520), where Luther says faith is the first and highest of all good works. *PE* 1, 187.

a kindness by accepting the terms of the will and the inheritance it bequeaths to him? What godless audacity is it, therefore, when we who are to receive the testament of God come as those who would perform a good work for him! This ignorance of the testament, this captivity of so great a sacrament—are they not too sad for tears? When we ought to be grateful for benefits received, we come arrogantly to give that which we ought to take. With unheard-of perversity we mock the mercy of the giver by giving as a work the thing we receive as a gift, so that the testator, instead of being a dispenser of his own goods, becomes the recipient of ours. Woe to such sacrilege!

Who has ever been so mad as to regard baptism as a good work, or what candidate for baptism has believed that he was performing a work which he might offer to God on behalf of himself and communicate to others? If, then, there is no good work that can be communicated to others in this one sacrament and testament, neither will there be any in the mass, since it too is nothing else than a testament and sacrament. Hence it is a manifest and wicked error to offer or apply the mass for sins, for satisfactions, for the dead, or for any needs whatsoever of one's own or of others. You will readily see the obvious truth of this if you firmly hold that the mass is a divine promise, which can benefit no one, be applied to no one, intercede for no one, and be communicated to no one, except only to him who believes with a faith of his own. Who can receive or apply, in behalf of another, the promise of God, which demands the personal faith of each one individually? Can I give to another the promise of God, even if he does not believe? Can I believe for another, or cause another to believe? But this is what must happen if I am able to apply and communicate the mass to others; for there are but two things in the mass, the divine promise and the human faith, the latter accepting what the former promises. But if it is true that I can do this, then I can also hear and believe the gospel for another, I can be baptized for another, I can be absolved from sins for another, I can also partake of the Sacrament of the Altar for another, and—to go through the list of their sacraments also—I can marry a wife for another, get ordained for another, be confirmed for another, and receive extreme unction for another!

In short, why did not Abraham believe for all the Jews? Why

was faith in the promise made to Abraham demanded of every individual Jew?

Therefore, let this irrefutable truth stand fast: Where there is a divine promise, there every one must stand on his own feet; his own personal faith is demanded, he will give an account for himself and bear his own load [Gal. 6:5]; as it is said in the last chapter of Mark [16:16]: "He who believes and is baptized will be saved; but he who does not believe will be condemned." Even so each one can derive personal benefit from the mass only by his own personal faith. It is absolutely impossible to commune on behalf of anyone else. Just as the priest is unable to administer the sacrament to anyone on behalf of another, but administers the same sacrament to each one individually by himself. For in consecrating and administering, the priests are our servants. Through them we are not offering a good work or communicating something in an active sense. Rather, we are receiving through them the promises and the sign; we are being communicated unto in the passive sense. This is the view that has persisted with respect to the laity right up to the present day, for of them it is said not that they do something good but that they receive it. But the priests have strayed into godless ways; out of the sacrament and testament of God, which ought to be a good gift received, they have made for themselves a good deed performed, which they then give to others and offer up to God.

But you will say: What is this? Will you not overturn the practice and teaching of all the churches and monasteries, by virtue of which they have flourished all these centuries? For the mass is the foundation of their anniversaries, intercessions, applications, communications, etc., that is to say, of their fat income. I answer: This is the very thing that has constrained me to write of the captivity of the church. For it is in this manner that the sacred testament of God has been forced into the service of a most impious traffic. It has come through the opinions and ordinances of wicked men, who, passing over the Word of God, have dished up to us the thoughts of their own hearts and led the whole world astray. What do I care about the number and influence of those who are in this error? The truth is mightier than all of them. If you are able to refute Christ, who teaches that the mass is a testament and a sacrament, then I will admit that they are in the right. Or, if you can bring yourself to say that that man is doing a good work who receives the benefit of the testament, or to that end uses this sacrament of promise, then I will gladly condemn my teachings. But since you can do neither, why do you hesitate to turn your back on the multitude who go after evil? Why do you hesitate to give God the glory and to confess his truth—that all priests today are perversely mistaken who regard the mass as a work by which they may relieve their own needs and those of others, whether dead or alive? I am uttering unheard of and startling things, but if you will consider what the mass is, you will realize that I have spoken the truth. The fault lies with our false sense of security, which blinds us to the wrath of God that is raging against us.

I am ready to admit, however, that the prayers which we pour out before God when we are gathered together to partake of the mass are good works or benefits, which we impart, apply and communicate to one another, and which we offer for one another. Thus James [5:16] teaches us to pray for one another that we may be healed, and Paul in I Tim. 2 [:1-2] commands "that supplications, prayers, and intercessions be made for all men, for kings and all who are in high positions." Now these are not the mass, but works of the mass—if the prayers of heart and lips may be called works— for they flow from the faith that is kindled or increased in the sacrament. For the mass, or the promise of God, is not fulfilled by praying, but only by believing. However, as believers we pray and perform every good work. But what priest offers up the sacrifice in this sense, that he believes he is offering up only the prayers? They all imagine that they are offering up Christ himself to God the Father as an all-sufficient sacrifice, and performing a good work for all those whom they intend to benefit, for they put their trust in the work which the mass accomplishes, and they do not ascribe this work to prayer. In this way the error has gradually grown, until they have come to ascribe to the sacrament what belongs to the prayers, and to offer to God what should be received as a benefit.

We must therefore sharply distinguish the testament and sacrament itself from the prayers which we offer at the same time. Not only this, but we must also bear in mind that the prayers avail utterly nothing, either to him who offers them or to those for whom they are offered, unless the testament is first received in faith, so that it will be faith that offers the prayers; for faith alone is heard, as James teaches in his first chapter [Jas. 1:6]. There is therefore a great difference between prayer and the mass. Prayer may be extended to as many persons as one desires, while the mass is received only by the person who believes for himself, and only to the extent that he believes. It cannot be given either to God or to men. Rather it is God alone who through the ministration of the priest gives it to men, and men receive it by faith alone without any works or merits. Nor would anyone dare to be so foolish as to assert that a ragged beggar does a good work when he comes to receive a gift from a rich man. But the mass (as I have said)[100] is the gift of the divine promise, proffered to all men by the hand of the priest.

It is certain, therefore, that the mass is not a work which may be communicated to others, but the object of faith (as has been said),[101] for the strengthening and nourishing of each one's own faith.

Now there is yet a second stumbling block that must be removed, and this is much greater and the most dangerous of all. It is the common belief that the mass is a sacrifice, which is offered to God. Even the words of the canon[102] seem to imply this, when they speak of "these gifts, these presents, these holy sacrifices," and further on "this offering." Prayer is also made, in so many words, "that the sacrifice may be accepted even as the sacrifice of Abel," etc. Hence Christ is termed "the sacrifice of the altar." Added to these are the sayings of the holy fathers, the great number of examples, and the widespread practice uniformly observed throughout the world.

Over against all these things, firmly entrenched as they are, we must resolutely set the words and example of Christ. For unless we firmly hold that the mass is the promise or testament of Christ, as the words clearly say, we shall lose the whole gospel and all its comfort. Let us permit nothing to prevail against these words—

---

[100]Cf. pp. 294-299.
[101]*Ibid.*
[102]The canon of the mass is the invariable part of the liturgy of the mass in which the consecration of the bread and wine is effected. Its text was translated by Luther from the Latin in his treatises on *The Abomination of the Secret Mass* (1525), *LW 36*, 314-327.

even though an angel from heaven should teach otherwise [Gal. 1:8]—for they contain nothing about a work or a sacrifice. Moreover, we also have the example of Christ on our side. When he instituted this sacrament and established this testament at the Last Supper, Christ did not offer himself to God the Father, nor did he perform a good work on behalf of others, but, sitting at the table, he set this same testament before each one and proffered to him the sign. Now, the more closely our mass resembles that first mass of all, which Christ performed at the Last Supper, the more Christian it will be. But Christ's mass was most simple, without any display of vestments, gestures, chants, or other ceremonies, so that if it had been necessary to offer the mass as a sacrifice, then Christ's institution of it was not complete.

Not that any one should revile the church universal for embellishing and amplifying the mass with many additional rites and ceremonies. But what we contend for is this: No one should be deceived by the glamor of the ceremonies and entangled in the multitude of pompous forms, and thus lose the simplicity of the mass itself, and indeed practice a sort of transubstantiation by losing sight of the simple "substance" of the mass and clinging to the manifold "accidents" of outward pomp. For whatever has been added to the word and example of Christ is an "accident" of the mass, and ought to be regarded just as we regard the so-called monstrances and corporal cloths in which the host itself is contained. Therefore, just as distributing a testament or accepting a promise differs diametrically from offering a sacrifice, so it is a contradiction in terms to call the mass a sacrifice, for the former is something that we receive and the latter is something that we give. The same thing cannot be received and offered at the same time, nor can it be both given and accepted by the same person, any more than our prayer can be the same thing as that which our prayer obtains, or the act of praying be the same thing as the act of receiving that for which we pray.

What shall we say then of the canon of the mass and the patristic authorities? First of all, I would answer: If there were nothing at all to be said against them, it would be safer to reject them all than admit that the mass is a work or a sacrifice, lest we deny the word of Christ and destroy faith together with the mass.

Nevertheless, in order to retain them, we shall say that we are instructed by the Apostle in I Cor. 11 [:21, 33] that it was customary for Christ's believers, when they came together for mass, to bring with them food and drink. These they called "collections," and they distributed them among all who were in want, after the example of the apostles in Acts 4 [:34-35]. From this store was taken the portion of the bread and wine that was consecrated in the sacrament. And since all this store was consecrated by the word and prayer [I Tim. 4:5], by being "lifted up" according to the Hebrew rite of which we read in Moses [Num. 18:30-32],[103] the words and rite of this lifting up or offering have come down to us, although the custom of bringing along and collecting that which was offered or lifted up has long since fallen into disuse. Thus, in Isa. 37 [:4] Hezekiah commanded Isaiah to lift up his prayer in the sight of God for the remnant. In the Psalms we read: "Lift up your hands to the holy place" [Ps. 134:2]. And again: "To thee I will lift up my hands" [Ps. 63:4]. And in I Tim. 2 [:8]: "In every place lifting holy hands." For this reason the words "sacrifice" and "offering" must be taken to refer not to the sacrament and testament, but to the collections themselves. From this source also the word "collect" has come down to us for the prayers said in the mass.

The same thing happens when the priest elevates the bread and the cup immediately after consecrating them. By this he does not show that he is offering anything to God, for he does not say a single word here about a victim or an offering. But this elevation is either a survival of that Hebrew rite of lifting up what was received with thanksgiving and returned to God, or else it is an admonition to us to provoke us to faith in this testament which the priest has set forth and exhibited in the words of Christ, so that now he also shows us the sign of the testament. Thus the oblation of the bread properly accompanies the demonstrative "this" in the words, "this is my body," and by the sign the priest addresses us gathered about him; and in a like manner the oblation of the cup properly accompanies the demonstrative "this" in the words, "this cup is the new testament, etc." For it is faith that the priest ought to awaken in us by this act of elevation. And would to God that as he elevates the sign, or sacrament, openly before our eyes, he might

---

[103] Cf. *LW* 35, 95, n. 24

also sound in our ears the word, or testament, in a loud, clear voice, and in the language of the people, whatever it may be, in order that faith may be the more effectively awakened. For why may mass be said in Greek and Latin and Hebrew, but not in German or any other language?

Therefore, let the priests who offer the sacrifice of the mass in these corrupt and most perilous times take heed, first, that they do not refer to the sacrament the words of the greater and lesser canon,[104] together with the collects, because they smack too strongly of sacrifice. They should refer them instead to the bread and the wine to be consecrated, or to their own prayers. For the bread and wine are offered beforehand for blessing in order that they may be sanctified by the word and by prayer [I Tim. 4:5], but after they have been blessed and consecrated they are no longer offered, but received as a gift from God. And in this rite let the priest bear in mind that the gospel is to be set above all canons and collects devised by men, and that the gospel does not sanction the idea that the mass is a sacrifice, as has been shown.

Further, when a priest celebrates public mass, he should determine to do nothing else than to commune himself and others by means of the mass. At the same time, however, he may offer prayers for himself and others, but he must beware lest he presume to offer the mass. But let him that holds private masses[105] determine to commune himself. The private mass does not differ in the least from the ordinary communion which any layman receives at the hand of the priest, and has no greater effect. The difference is in the prayers, and in the fact that the priest consecrates the elements for himself and administers them to himself. As far as the blessing[106] of the mass and sacrament is concerned we are all equals, whether we are priests or laymen.

---

[104] In printed missals prior to the Council of Trent, *canon minor* was the term used to designate collectively those offertory prayers within the canon itself which immediately preceded the consecration of the elements. These collects were of comparatively late origin, coming only gradually into use during the late middle ages. Valentin Thalhofer, *Handbuch der katholischen Liturgik* (Freiburg im Breisgau, 1890), II, 159.

[105] The private mass does not require the presence of a congregation. Besides the celebrant there need be present only a ministrant. There is no music; the mass is only read.

[106] The *res sacramenti.*

If a priest is requested by others to celebrate so-called "votive" masses,[107] let him beware of accepting a fee for the mass, or of presuming to offer any votive sacrifice. Rather, he should take pains to refer all this to the prayers which he offers for the dead or the living, saying to himself: "Lo, I will go and receive the sacrament for myself alone, and while doing so I will pray for this one and that one." Thus he will receive his fee for the prayers, not for the mass, and can buy food and clothing with it. Let him not be disturbed because all the world holds and practices the contrary. You have the utmost certainty of the gospel, and by relying on it, you may well disregard the belief and opinions of men. But if you disregard me and insist upon offering the mass and not the prayers alone, remember that I have faithfully warned you, and that I will be without blame on the day of judgment; you will have to bear your sin alone. I have said what I was bound to say to you as brother to brother for your salvation; yours will be the gain if you observe it, yours the loss if you neglect it. And if some should even condemn what I have said, I will reply in the words of Paul: "But evil men and impostors will go on from bad to worse, deceiving and being deceived" [II Tim 3:13].

From the above every one will readily understand the often quoted saying of Gregory[108]: "A mass celebrated by a wicked priest is not to be considered of less effect than one celebrated by a good priest. Neither would a mass of St. Peter have been better than that of Judas the traitor, if they had offered the sacrifice of the mass." This saying has served many as a cloak to cover their godless doings, and because of it they have invented the distinction between the *opus operatum* and the *opus operantis*,[109] so as to be free to lead wicked lives themselves and yet benefit other men. Gregory speaks the truth, only they misunderstand his words. For it is true beyond a question that the testament or sacrament is given and received through the ministration of wicked priests no less completely

---

[107] Masses celebrated on the request of congregations or individuals in connection with specific purposes or occasions, or in honor of certain mysteries (e.g., of the Holy Trinity, of the Holy Spirit, or of angels).

[108] Pope Gregory I (590-604).

[109] The former is the properly executed performance of the ritual of the mass—"the work wrought" (cf. p. 293 n. 85). The latter is the inner disposition, the faith, either of the recipient or of the celebrant—"the work of the doer."

than through the ministration of the most saintly. For who has any doubt that the gospel is preached by the ungodly? Now the mass is part of the gospel; indeed, it is the sum and substance of it. For what is the whole gospel but the good tidings of the forgiveness of sins? Whatever can be said about forgiveness of sins and the mercy of God in the broadest and richest sense is all briefly comprehended in the word of this testament. For this reason popular sermons ought to be nothing else than expositions of the mass, or explanations of the divine promise of this testament; this would be to teach the faith and truly to edify the church. But in our day the expounders of the mass make mockery and jest with allegorical explanations of human ceremonies.

Therefore, just as a wicked priest may baptize, that is, apply the word of promise and the sign of water to the candidate for baptism, so he may also set forth the promise of this sacrament and administer it to those who partake, and even partake himself, as did Judas the traitor at the supper of the Lord [Matt. 26:23-25]. It still remains the same sacrament and testament, which works its own work in the believer but an "alien work" [110] in the unbeliever. But when it comes to offering a sacrifice the case is quite different. For not the mass but the prayers are offered to God, and therefore it is as plain as day that the offerings of a wicked priest avail nothing, but, as Gregory says again: When an unworthy person is sent as the intercessor, the heart of the judge is only turned to greater disfavor. Therefore these two things—mass and prayer, sacrament and work, testament and sacrifice—must not be confused; for the one comes from God to us through the ministration of the priest and demands our faith, the other proceeds from our faith to God through the priest and demands his hearing. The former descends, the latter ascends. The former, therefore, does not necessarily require a worthy and godly minister, but the latter does indeed require such a one, for "God does not listen to sinners" [John 9:31]. He knows how to do good through evil men, but he does not accept the work of any evil man; as he showed in the case of Cain [Gen. 4:5], and as is said in Prov. 15 [:8]: "The sacrifice of the wicked is

---

[110] Its own work is salvation. The "alien work" is condemnation. The expression derives from Isa. 28:21.

an abomination to the Lord," and in Rom. 14 [:23]: "Whatever does not proceed from faith is sin."

But let us bring this first part to an end, though I am ready to go on with the argument if an opponent should arise. From all that has been said we conclude that the mass was provided only for those who have a sad, afflicted, disturbed, perplexed and erring conscience, and that they alone commune worthily. For, since the word of divine promise in this sacrament sets forth the forgiveness of sins, let every one draw near fearlessly, whoever he may be, who is troubled by his sins, whether by remorse or by temptation. For this testament of Christ is the one remedy against sins, past, present and future, if you but cling to it with unwavering faith and believe that what the words of the testament declare is freely granted to you. But if you do not believe this, you will never, anywhere, by any works or efforts of your own, be able to find peace of conscience. For faith alone means peace of conscience. while unbelief means only distress of conscience.

---

[111] Letters of indulgence.

17.

THE SACRAMENT OF THE BODY AND BLOOD OF CHRIST— AGAINST THE FANATICS

In this sacrament there are two things that should be known and proclaimed. First, what one should believe. In Latin this is called the *objectum fidei*, that is, the work or thing in which one believes, or to which one is to adhere. Second, the faith itself, or the use which one should properly make of that in which he believes. The first lies outside the heart and is presented to our eyes externally, namely, the sacrament itself, concerning which we believe that Christ's body and blood are truly present in the bread and wine. The second is internal, within the heart, and cannot be externalized. It consists in the attitude which the heart should have toward the external sacrament. Up to now I have not preached very much about the first part, but have treated only the second, which is also the best part But because the first part is now being assailed by many, and the preachers, even those who are considered the best, are splitting up into factions over the matter, so that in foreign lands a large number are already pouncing upon it and maintaining that Christ's body and blood are not present in the bread and wine, the times demand that I say something on this subject also.

At the outset I will say this, however: if anyone is thought to be engulfed in such an error, I would earnestly advise him to abstain from the sacrament until he emerges from his error and becomes strong in the faith. For we have before us the clear text and the plain words of Christ: "Take, eat; this is my body, which is given for you. Drink of it, all of you, this is my blood, which is poured out for you. Do this in remembrance of me" [Matt. 26:26-28; Luke 22:19-20]. These are the words on which we take our stand.[1] They are so simply and clearly stated that even they, our adversaries, must confess that it is difficult to interpret them otherwise. Yet they pass these clear words by and follow their own thoughts, making darkness for themselves in the midst of the bright light.

If anyone wishes to pursue a true course and not come to grief, let him beware of the clever idea, inspired by the devil in this matter everywhere, that he may suck the egg dry and leave us the shell, that is, remove the body and blood of Christ from the bread and wine, so that it remains no more than mere bread, such as the baker bakes. In accordance with this clever idea our opponents mock us at their pleasure, charging that we are eaters of flesh and drinkers of blood and that we worship a baked God.[2] In former times that desperate renegade, Averroes,[3] who had himself been a Christian, similarly mocked and slandered the faithful, maintaining that there is no people on earth more despicable than the Christians, because they devour their own God, which no other people had ever done. Was this not an exquisitely clever saying? Such are the tricks which the devil is playing against us nowadays everywhere.

Now God is the sort of person who likes to do what is foolish and useless in the eyes of the world, as Paul says in I Cor. 1 [:23]: "We preach Christ crucified, a stumbling block to the Jews and folly to the Gentiles." And again: "For since, in the wisdom of God, the world did not know God through wisdom, it pleased God through the folly of what we preach to save those who believe in him" [I Cor. 1:21]. Well then, if anyone does not believe this, let him believe accordingly that it is mere bread, or a batch of bread.[4] Anyone who has failed to grasp the faith may thenceforth believe whatever he likes, it makes no difference. Just as when someone is

---

[1] Cf. p. 293 n. 84.

[2] In his *Billiche Antwort* of July 18, 1526, a reply to the Swabian Syngramma and Luther's preface to it, Oecolampadius defended his use of the terms *gotsfleischesser* and *gotsblutsauffer* to describe his opponents, and *brötenen* and *gebachnen* to describe their God. *WA* 19, 457 n. 2.

[3] Averroes (1126-98) was an Arab physician and philosopher whose commentary on Aristotle had a wide vogue in the Middle Ages and did much to revive the study of Aristotle.

[4] *Schusselbrod,* as much bread as is put into the oven at one time. *WA* 19, 484 n. 4.

on the point of drowning, whether he drowns in a brook or in the middle of a stream, he is drowned just the same. So I say of these fanatics: if they let go of the word, let them believe whatever they like and squabble as long as they like. It has already happened that six or seven sects have arisen over the sacrament, but all of them under the delusion that Christ's flesh and blood are not present.

This comes about, I maintain, because in the first place they have not adhered to the words, and then because they have followed their own thoughts and have seen that if Christ were present in the bread and wine and were distributed so widely everywhere and if each person were to eat this Christ, that would be an awkward situation. This has been their first thought. Hence they have a colored glass before their eyes, and therefore the words must mean what they think. This is what all factious spirits do: they first concoct an opinion. If it pleases them, they then attempt to force the Scriptures to agree with it. But whoever derives the right faith from the words will believe like this: Whether Christ enters into the bread or the cup or into whatever he will, God grant that as long as I have the words, I will not seek or speculate any further; what he says, I will keep. Thus the believer envelops himself in the Word, will not let himself be turned aside from it, and is also thereby sustained.

For we are not so simple-minded that we do not understand the words. If these words are not clear, I do not know how to speak German. Would I not understand, if someone were to place a roll before me and say: "Take, eat, this is white bread"? Or again, "Take and drink, this is a glass of wine"?[5] Therefore, when Christ says: "Take, eat, this is my body," even a child will understand perfectly well that he is speaking of that which he is offering. It is a natural way of speaking that when someone points to a thing, we know what he is saying. If I should now make this word obscure and invent some subtlety concerning it, I would only be confusing myself. These words are quite clear and explicit: take bread, give thanks, break, give, bid them eat and drink, this is my body, this

---

[5] The shorter of the two sermon copies, which is almost entirely in Latin, at this point has the German phrase: *"das ist wittenbergisch bier."* Cf. WA 19, 475, 481, and 485.

is my blood. The fanatics really knock themselves out struggling with these words. First they come up with a notion of their own; then they have to interpret the words according to what each one has dreamed up. For this reason we stick closely to the words and close our eyes and senses, because everyone knows what "this is my body" means, especially when he adds "given for you." We know what Christ's body is, namely, that which was born of Mary, suffered, died, and rose again.[6]

Now they have two points in particular which they bring up against us. First, they say it is not fitting that Christ's body and blood should be in the bread and wine. Second, it is not necessary. These are about the best foundations that they have to build on. Let us look at them.

To the first point I might say equally well that it is not reasonable that God should descend from heaven and enter into the womb; that he who nourishes, sustains, and encompasses all the world should allow himself to be nourished and encompassed by the Virgin. Likewise, that Christ, a king of glory [Ps. 24:10], at whose feet all angels must fall and before whom all creatures must tremble, should thus humble himself below all men and allow himself to be suspended upon the cross as a most notorious evil-doer and that by the most wicked and desperate of men. And I might conclude from this that God did not become man, or that the crucified Christ was not God. Thus they say it is not fitting that God should perform in the sacrament so many wondrous deeds that he does not perform anywhere else. For what we believe, they consider to be incongruous; they regard it as tremendous miracles, that the single body of Christ is in a hundred thousand places, wherever bread is broken, and that the massive limbs should there be so concealed that no one sees or feels them. But they do not see that these are vain and useless thoughts. If one wished to apply this kind of measurement, one would be forced to allow no creature to exist.

If it were possible and I should measure all creatures and describe them in words, you would see wonders just as great, nay, even greater, than in this sacrament. Behold the soul, which is a single creature, and yet at the same time is present throughout the

---

[6] The longer of the two sermon copies, the one by Rörer, adds: "he does not say 'is my stone, or table' but 'my body.'" *WA* 19, 500.

whole body, even in the smallest toe, so that when I prick the smallest member of the body with a needle, I affect the entire soul, and the whole man quivers. Now, if one soul can be present at one time in all the members—though I am unable to explain how that happens—should Christ not be capable of being present at one time in all places in the sacrament?

Again, my soul can think and speak simultaneously, and while speaking see, hear, feel, etc., and at the same time digest food into blood, flesh, bone, urine and feces. No one considers this a miracle, because we see it daily and are accustomed to it. The only thing that those people lack is that they have never observed any creature rightly, as we shall hear further.

Look at a grain of wheat in the field, and tell me how it comes about that the stalk grows out of the earth from a single seed and bears so many kernels on the ear, and gives each one its own form. Moreover, in a single kernel there are many, many miraculous works, which they neither perceive nor pay any heed to. Again, how does it happen, that I have only two eyes, and yet I am able to take in the heads of all men at one time with the sight of my eyes? Indeed, I can do it just as well with one eye as with two. Thus one eye can focus upon a thousand kernels, and on the other hand, a thousand eyes can focus on one kernel.

Take the word which I am speaking as a further example. The voice is a poor, miserable thing, to be reckoned as the least of creatures, not more than a breath of wind. As soon as the mouth ceases speaking, the voice is gone and is no more, so that there can be nothing weaker or more perishable. Yet it is so mighty, that I could rule a whole country with my voice. How does it come about, then, that I may capture so many hearts with words? I have a small voice, and there are several hundreds or thousands of ears, yet every single ear perceives the complete and entire voice. I do not distribute it, so that each ear has only a part of it, but each one has all of it. The fanatics see this, and do not consider it a miracle. Indeed, if we had never seen it, it would be the greatest of miracles. Now, if my voice can accomplish this so that it fills all ears, with each one receiving as much of it as the other, and my word is distributed so widely, should not Christ be able to do so all the more with his body? How much easier it is with a glorified body than with a bodily voice! You will find many more such miracles among the creatures, so that anyone who examines a creature rightly will not permit himself to be led astray by this article.

Again, I preach the gospel of Christ, and with my bodily voice I bring Christ into your heart, so that you may form him within yourself. If now you truly believe, so that your heart lays hold of the word and holds fast within it that voice, tell me, what have you in your heart? You must answer that you have the true Christ, not that he sits in there, as one sits on a chair, but as he is at the right hand of the Father. How that comes about you cannot know, but your heart truly feels his presence, and through the experience of faith you know for a certainty that he is there. Now I can accomplish this again, that the one Christ enters into so many hearts through the voice, and that each person who hears the sermon and accepts it takes the whole Christ into his heart. For Christ does not permit himself to be divided into parts; yet he is distributed whole among all the faithful, so that one heart receives no less, and a thousand hearts no more, than the one Christ. This we must ever confess, and it is a daily miracle. Indeed, it is as great a miracle as here in the sacrament. Why then should it not be reasonable that he also distributes himself in the bread?

But what happens when I bring Christ into the heart? Does it come about, as the fanatics imagine, that Christ descends on a ladder and climbs back up again? Christ still sits on the right hand of the Father, and also in your heart, the one Christ who fills heaven and earth. I preach that he sits on the right hand of God and rules over all creatures, sin, death, life, world, devils and angels; if you believe this, you already have him in your heart. Therefore your heart is in heaven, not in an apparition or dream, but truly. For where he is, there you are also. So he dwells and sits in your heart, yet he does not fall from the right hand of God. Christians experience and feel this clearly. But those people see none of these things, great as it is that Christ dwells thus in the heart and imparts himself completely in every heart and is distributed through the Word. Therefore, whoever can believe this does not find it difficult to believe also that his body and blood are in the sacrament. For if you try in this way to measure that wondrous sign with the measuring-rod of thought and reason, you will at last reach the point where you must also say that Christ does not dwell in the hearts of the faithful.

Now see, as I have said, how much the poor bodily voice is able to do. First of all it brings the whole Christ to the ears; then it brings him into the hearts of all who listen and believe. Should it then be so amazing that he enters into the bread and wine? Is not the heart much more tenuous and elusive than bread? You will probably not attempt to fathom how this comes about. Just as little as you are able to say how it comes about that Christ is in so many thousands of hearts and dwells in them—Christ as he died and rose again—and yet no man knows how he gets in, so also here in the sacrament, it is incomprehensible how this comes about. But this I do know, that the word is there: "Take, eat, this is my body, given for you, this do in remembrance of me." When we say these words over the bread, then he is truly present, and yet it is a mere word and voice that one hears. Just as he enters the heart without breaking a hole in it, but is comprehended only through the Word and hearing, so also he enters into the bread without needing to make any hole in it.

Take yet another example. How did his mother Mary become pregnant? Although it is a great miracle when a woman is made pregnant by a man, yet God reserved for him the privilege of being born of the Virgin. Now how does the Mother come to this? She has no husband [Luke 1:34] and her womb is entirely enclosed. Yet she conceives in her womb a real, natural child with flesh and blood. Is there not more of a miracle here than in the bread and wine? Where does it come from? The angel Gabriel brings the word: "Behold, you will conceive in your womb and bear a son, etc." [Luke 1:31]. With these words Christ comes not only into her heart, but also into her womb, as she hears, grasps, and believes it. No one can say otherwise, than that the power comes through the Word. As one cannot deny the fact that she thus becomes pregnant through the Word, and no one knows how it comes about, so it is in the sacrament also. For as soon as Christ says: "This is my body," his body is present through the Word and the power of the Holy Spirit. If the Word is not there, it is mere bread; but as soon as the words are added they bring with them that of which they speak.

Moreover, we believe that Christ, according to his human nature, is put over all creatures [Eph. 1:22] and fills all things, as Paul says in Eph. 4 [:10]. Not only according to his divine nature, but also according to his human nature, he is a lord of all things, has all things in his hand, and is present everywhere. If I am to follow the fanatics who say that this is not fitting, then I must deny Christ. We read of Stephen in Acts 7 [:56] that he said: "I see the heavens opened, and Jesus standing at the right hand of the Father." How does he see Christ? He need not raise his eyes on high. Christ is around us and in us in all places. Those people understand nothing of this. They also say that he sits at the right hand of God, but what it means that Christ ascends to heaven and sits there, they do not know. It is not the same as when you climb up a ladder into the house. It means rather that he is above all creatures and in all and beyond all creatures. That he was taken up bodily, however, occurred as a sign of this. Therefore he now has all things before his eyes, more than I have you before my eyes, and he is closer to us than any creature is to another. They speculate thus, that he must ascend and descend from the heavens through the air, and that he lets himself be drawn down into the bread when we eat his body. Such thoughts come from no other source than from foolish reason and the flesh. We must understand that it is not the words which we speak that draw him down. They have been given to us rather to assure us, that we may know we shall certainly find him.

Although he is present in all creatures, and I might find him in stone, in fire, in water, or even in a rope, for he certainly is there, yet he does not wish that I seek him there apart from the Word, and cast myself into the fire or the water, or hang myself on the rope. He is present everywhere, but he does not wish that you grope for him everywhere. Grope rather where the Word is, and there you will lay hold of him in the right way. Otherwise you are tempting God and committing idolatry. For this reason he has set down for us a definite way to show us how and where to find him, namely the Word. Those people, who say that it is unreasonable for Christ to be present in the bread and wine, do not know or see this at all, because they also do not understand what Christ's kingdom is, and the sitting at the right hand of God. If Christ were not with me in dungeon, torture, and death, where would I be? He is present there through the Word, although not in the same way as here in the sacrament, where through the Word he binds his body and blood so that they are also received corporeally in the bread and wine. If we believe the one, it is easy also to grasp and believe the other. Heaven and earth are his sack; as wheat fills the sack, so he fills all things. And as a seed bears a stalk, an ear, and many kernels; or again, as a single cherrystone cast into the ground brings forth a tree which bears many blossoms, leaves, inner and outer bark, and cherries; or again, as my voice reaches so many ears; much more is Christ able to distribute himself whole and undivided into so many particles.

Now because the fanatics do not see this, they come up with their man-made opinion to the effect that God is thereby performing some kind of hocus-pocus. Well, let them just go on making fools of themselves; but you cling to the thought that Christ, as I have said, does all these things through the Word, just as the wonders which he daily thereby performs are countless. Should he not through the same power know how to do these things also here in the sacrament? He has put himself into the Word, and through the Word he puts himself into the bread also. If he can break into the heart and spirit and dwell in the soul, he must have much easier access to the material object because the heart is much more tenuous and elusive. But he retains the lesser miracles in order that through them he may remind us of the greater ones. For that he enters the heart through faith is a much greater miracle than that he is present in the bread. Indeed, it is for the sake of faith that he uses that very bread or sacrament. If we would bear this in mind, we would not talk so much of miracles in the sacrament. But if we wanted to follow after and think of God with our reason we should have to say of faith too that no man is able to believe. For God is too far beyond all reason. Hence, to sum it all up, what those people keep saying—that because it is not in accord with reason it is not true—we shall simply turn about and say the opposite: God's Word is true, therefore your notions must be false. Is it necessarily unreasonable, just because it seems unreasonable to you and you think that the Word must be wrong and your ideas valid?

The other argument which they bring up is that it is not

necessary. So Christ has to let himself be taken to school and taught by them. The Holy Spirit hasn't hit it right. For this is what they say: If I believe in Jesus Christ, who died for me, what need is there for me to believe in a baked God? Wait and see, he will bake them when the time comes, so that their hides will sizzle. Who says this? God or a human being? A man says it. Why? Because Satan has taken possession of them; they have learned no more than to speak and preach the words: "Christ died for us, etc.," but in their hearts they do not feel it in the least. Do you wish to instruct God as to what is necessary and unnecessary, and have him decide according to your notions? It is better for us to reverse this and say: God wishes it thus, therefore your notions are false. Who are you, that you dare to speak against that which God regards as necessary? You are a liar, and therefore God is true [Rom. 3:4].

You might as well tell me also that because faith alone justifies, Christ is not necessary. So let us say to God: You had sin, death, devil, and everything in your power; what need was there to send down your Son, and permit him to be treated so cruelly and to die? You could indeed have allowed him to remain on high; it would have cost you only a word, and sin and death would have been destroyed, along with the devil. For you are certainly almighty. Again, let us conclude that Christ was not born of the Virgin, and say: Of what use was it? Could not God have caused him to be born of a man just as well, and still be fashioned so that he would have been conceived without sin and have remained innocent? Indeed, let us even go further and say that it is not necessary that Christ be God. For through God's power he could just as well have risen from the dead and saved us, even if he had been purely human. Thus the devil blinds people, and the result is, first, that they are incapable of seeing any work of God in the right light, and second, that they also fail to regard the Word, and accordingly want to find out everything with their own minds. If you were to search out everything about a kernel of wheat in the field, you would be so amazed that you would die. God's works are not like our works.

Therefore you should reply to these opponents: What is it to me, whether it is necessary or not? God knows well how it shall be and why it must be thus. If he says that it is necessary, then all creatures must be silent. But because in the sacrament Christ says in clear words: "Take, eat, this is my body, etc." it is my duty to believe these words, as firmly as I must believe all the words of Christ. If he handed me a mere straw and spoke these words, I should believe it. Therefore one must close mouth, eyes, and all the senses and say: "Lord, you know better than I." The same is true of baptism. The water is baptism, and in baptism is the Holy Spirit. So you might also say: "Why is it necessary to baptize with water?" But the Spirit says so, do you hear? Here is God's will and Word; adhere to it, and let your opinions go.

See, these are the two reasons they give for saying one should not believe that Christ's body and blood are in the sacrament. They are also the best reasons they can find, and the second one in particular they delineate at length. These are reasons, nevertheless, of the sort that sway devout hearts today, and have done so in the past. I myself have pondered much, what necessity there was in it, and how so great a body could be in so small a piece of bread, and how it could yet be undivided and whole in every particle. But if they examine a kernel of wheat or a cherrystone, it can well teach them manners. For why does God feed us through the bread, or under the bread, when he could do so just as well by the mere Word alone, without the bread? Why does he not create men as he created Adam and Eve, in a moment; he takes so long a time in doing it, in that man and woman must come together and the child must be trained so long with labor and effort. But he says: "What is that to you? [John 21:22]. I made Adam and Eve in this way at the beginning, but now I do not will to do it in this way any longer. I once caused a son to be born of the Virgin, and that also I do not will to do again." Thus those people would bind God by their laws, which is just as if I were to say: "Why have you given him a large body and me a small one? Why do you give this one black hair and that one blond, or this one brown eyes and that one gray?" Let this then be the sum of it: See only that you pay heed to God's Word and remain in it, like a child in the cradle. If you let go of it for a moment, then you fall out of it. This is the devil's sole aim, to tear people out of it and to cause them to measure God's will and work by human reason.

Those, I say, are still reasonable souls who concern themselves with the two points which I have touched on above; they can still be helped. The rest, however, are vain fanatics who proceed to force the words of Christ open and shut like pincers. Indeed, they are arch-fanatics, and do not have a leg to stand on. Those two points at least have some standing in the eyes of reason. But from the way in which the latter tear and twist the words, reason can well see that they are fools. There are only three words: "This is my body." So the one [Karlstadt] turns up his nose at the word "this" and severs it from the bread, claiming that one should interpret it thus: "Take, eat,—this is my body"; as if I were to say: "Take and eat; here sits Hans with the red jacket." [7] The second [Zwingli] seizes upon the little word "is"; to him it is the equivalent of "signifies." The third [Oecolampadius] says, "this is my body" means the same as, "this is a figure of my body." They set up these dreams of theirs without any scriptural basis. These fanatics do not disturb me, and are not worthy that one should fight with them. Some of them are crude, grammatical fanatics; the others are subtle, philosophical fanatics. Let them go, therefore, and let us adhere to the words as they read: that the body of Christ is present in the bread and that his blood is truly present in the wine. This does not mean that he is not present in other places also with his body and blood, for in believing hearts he is completely present with his body and blood. But it means that he wishes to make us certain as to where and how we are to lay hold of him. There is the Word, which says that when you eat the bread you eat his body, given for you. If the Word were not there, I would not pay any heed to the bread. Let this suffice for the first part.

Part II

Now that we have preserved the treasure, and not allowed the kernel to be taken out of the shell [8] so that we have only chaff left instead of grain,[9] we must now preach on the second part, namely, how one should make use of the sacrament and derive benefit from

---

[7] The shorter sermon copy at this point adds in Latin: "and behold the bread, I have money in my purse." WA 19, 498.
[8] Cf. *Sprichwörter-Lexikon, op. cit.,* IV, col. 78, *Schale,* No. 2.
[9] Cf. *Ibid.,* II, col. 1542, *Korn,* No. 53.

it. For it is not sufficient that we know what the sacrament is, namely, that Christ's body and blood are truly present, but it is also necessary to know why they are present and for what reason they are given to us to be received.

But here is where our opponents cause anguish. The devil cannot leave it alone; he must besmirch God's works and words. If he cannot tear it away completely, he makes an empty nut[10] of it. The pope took away from us one element of the sacrament. These people, however, leave us both elements; but they make a hole in the nut,[11] in order that we may lose the body and blood of Christ. In addition, both sides permit the right use to be lost from sight.

Thus we say now: Formerly we tortured ourselves with anxiety as to how we might approach this sacrament worthily. This worthy approach we now call the use of the sacrament. Then one advocated self-torment with many arduous works, with fasting and confession, and prepared one's self for it in such a way that it was used merely as a good work. The papists went that far with it, but still it remained intact. It is by grace that with respect to the gospel, the Scriptures, baptism, and the sacrament the thing has remained, as it is in itself. But the proper use of it they have destroyed and taken away from us. This use we must revive and preserve, as we have done heretofore. For when I was preaching against the misuse I did not foresee the heresy which is now gaining the upper hand; I merely contested with them concerning the proper use.

This is what I have taught: that one should not use the sacrament as a good work. They believed that whoever had confessed properly and knew of no mortal sin upon his conscience and so went to the sacrament was doing a precious, holy work, through which he merited heaven. If you wish to make the right use of it, you must not receive it in such a way that you say: "This I have done," just as if you had fasted or kept watch. But you ought to believe, not only that Christ is present with his body and blood, but also that he is given to you. You should always stand upon the words: "Take, eat, this is my body, which is given for you. Drink, this is my blood, which is poured out for you. Do this in remembrance of me." In these words his body and blood

[10] Cf. *Ibid.*, III, col. 1076, *Nuss*, No. 112.
[11] Cf. *Ibid.*, III, col. 1074, No. 78; and col. 1077, No. 129.

are given to us. So there are two things to be believed: that it is truly present, which the papists also believe; and that it is given to us, which they do not believe, and that we should use it as a gift.

There you hear it, expressed in clear German: he commands you to take his body and blood. Why? For what reason? Because the body is given for you and the blood is poured out for you. Here they have great anguish to inflict upon us, these new preachers of ours, in that they deprive us of this also, and in so cruel a manner that I believe the devil is trying his utmost and that the day of judgment is not far off. I should rather be dead than hear Christ so scorned and abused by them. They say that it is only a sign, by which one may recognize Christians and judge them, so that we have nothing more of it than the mere shell. So they come together, and eat and drink, in order that they may commemorate his death. All the power is said to be in this commemoration, the bread and wine are no more than a sign and a color by which one may recognize that we are Christians. Why do they do this? Because they cast to the winds the words: "Eat, this is my body, which is given for you." The words mean nothing to them; they rumble by over their heads. They are supposed to mean nothing more than the proclaiming and preaching of his death. To be sure, one should proclaim his death, and we have also preached it in grander fashion than they ever did. And if they did not have it from us, they would know nothing of it, because the papists have never spoken of it at all. Therefore, the fanatics have no right to teach this to us and make great boasts about it, as if they had invented something new.

Therefore we too are preaching the death of Christ according to the words: "Do this in remembrance of me." However, a distinction has to be made here. When I preach his death, it is in a public sermon in the congregation, in which I am addressing myself to no one individually; whoever grasps it, grasps it. But when I distribute the sacrament, I designate it for the individual who is receiving it; I give him Christ's body and blood that he may have forgiveness of sins, obtained through his death and preached in the congregation. This is something more than the congregational sermon; for although the same thing is present in the sermon as in the sacrament, here there is the advantage that it is directed at definite individuals. In the sermon one does not point out or portray any particular person, but in the sacrament it is given to you and to me in particular, so that the sermon comes to be our own. For when I say: "This is the body, which is given for you, this is the blood, which is poured out for you for the forgiveness of sins," I am there commemorating him; I proclaim and announce his death. Only it is not done publicly in the congregation but is directed at you alone.

Thus Christ has ordained that when we come together each one shall take of the bread and the cup, and afterwards preach of him. Why? For we are to give this to no one except those who are Christians and who have heard Christ preached beforehand. But the preaching or proclamation is intended for everyone in general, even for those who are not yet Christians. The Christians alone are to partake of the sacrament, but at the same time they are to take thought that their number may increase.

Therefore one should shout it out publicly and hold such public commemoration, that even those who do not yet know of it will attend. That they hold such commemoration privately is worthless. It should take place publicly before the congregation, and there should be preaching at the mass at all times. Therefore the words: "Do this in remembrance of me" are as much as to say: "As often as you do this, preach of me," as Paul interprets it in I Cor. 11 [:26], when he calls it "proclaiming the death of Christ." He uses the word, "proclaim," in order to show that it is not to be done privately, only among Christians who know of it beforehand and who stand in need, not of proclamation, but only of admonition. Rather it is to be done publicly before the multitude, for those who do not know of it. Thus both "remembrance" and "proclamation" mean nothing else than the preaching of him publicly, as is done in all sermons.

This, I say, we should always do when we receive the sacrament. Those who go to the sacrament, however, should believe and be assured, not only that they are receiving the true body and blood of Christ in it, but also that it is there given to them and is their own. Why? Not as a work for the sake of money or merit, as the monks and priests hold mass, but for the forgiveness of our sins. Now we surely know what forgiveness of sins means. When he forgives, he forgives everything completely and leaves nothing unforgiven. When I am free of sin, I am also free of death, devil, and hell; I am a son of God, a lord of heaven and earth.

Thus everyone, especially when he is attacked or subjected to persecution, should know how to answer and be able to say: "This is how I understand the words, that in the sacrament his body and blood are given to me for the forgiveness of sins." For this reason every Christian must know these words, letter for letter: "Here my Lord has given me his body and blood in the bread and wine, in order that I should eat and drink. And they are to be my very own, so that I may be certain that my sins are forgiven, that I am to be free of death and hell, have eternal life, and be a child of God and an heir of heaven. Therefore I go to the sacrament to seek these things. I am a poor sinner with death before me, I must go through it; and the devil threatens me with all kinds of trouble and danger. Because I am in sin, a captive of death and the devil, because I feel that I am weak in faith, cold in love, wayward, impatient, envious, with sin clinging to me before and behind; therefore I come hither where I find and hear Christ's word that I shall receive the gift of forgiveness of sins." Once we have the gift, we are then to proclaim it, so that we may bring other persons to it also. See, this is how one should instruct children and simple hearts concerning the sacrament, so that they may know what to seek in it.

This then is what we call the correct use of the sacrament. It is not a matter of mere performance and of rendering obedience to the church, for even a pig might go to the sacrament in this way. It is not to be done for the sake of a good work, but in order that your heart should be strengthened, as the words say: "Which is given for you, which is poured out for you." And even if the words were not there, as when Paul omits them [I Cor. 11:25], you still have the body which died for your sins and the blood which was poured out for them. But when Christ is given to you, forgiveness of sins is also given to you, and all that is procured through the treasure. If you have grasped it with your heart (and it cannot be grasped in any other way) and if you believe, you must say: "No work, no deed, will help me out of my sins, but I have another treasure, the body and blood of my Lord, given to me for the forgiveness of sins. This is the only treasure, the only forgiveness, and there is no other in heaven or on earth."

For this reason Christ has given himself to us completely, and wishes to be and remain with us until the day of judgment [Matt. 28:20]; not merely that he may be present, as the papists have him and carry him about to no avail, nor as the others say, *ut signum*, that is, as a mere sign, which would bring us neither improvement nor benefits. Should Christ institute so great a thing in vain, without any use or profit? No, this is the benefit that you ought to derive: that you strengthen your faith and make your conscience secure, so that afterwards you may also be able to preach. So they say that it is merely a useless commemoration, which can be of no advantage to you or to anyone else. Be on guard! May God continue to preserve us as he has done until now. The devil has nothing to do anywhere except to come and besmirch the place where the gospel has taken root. Therefore we must build firmly on these words and stand fast in them, and thus we will be able to give a proper answer to the heretics. For these words are expressed in clear enough German. In substance they say this: first, that here we obtain forgiveness of sins as a gift, and second, that we afterwards preach and proclaim the same.

Here then you have the distinction as to what the commemoration is, and how one should use the sacrament and derive benefit from it, namely, by simply correcting our shortcomings and failings. We share the common frailties of other people, and each has his own peculiar frailties; because of these we come here to seek strength. This is why this sacrament is called a food for hungry and thirsty souls, who feel their misery and would gladly be rescued from death and all misfortune. The papists have taught: "Beware, do not go thither unless you are pure and have no evil conscience," so that Christ may be certain to have a pure abode. They have so stupified and frightened the poor souls by this that they have fled from the sacrament, and yet have had to receive it under constraint—with such trembling that they would as gladly have entered a fiery furnace.

We are to be pure in the sense that we are sorry for our sins and would gladly be rid of them, and are vexed that we are such miserable people—insofar as we are serious about it and not just pretending. Complete sinlessness, however, no one will ever attain. Even if you should do so, you would not dare to go to the sacrament, for it was instituted specifically for the sake of the weak. So much for the use of the sacrament: it is to strengthen the conscience against all distress and temptation.

Now there remains the part concerning the fruit of the sacrament. Of this I have had much to say at other places. It is nothing other than love. The early fathers too have emphasized this most of all, and for this reason they called the sacrament *communio,* that is, a communion. This is also presented to us here in two ways—first, by way of an example, and second, by way of a symbol or sign which is the bread and wine—so every Christian, no matter how crude he may be, may be able to comprehend here in the sacrament the whole Christian doctrine, what he is to believe and what he is to do through faith. For it is necessary for each one to know that Christ has given his body, flesh, and blood on the cross to be our treasure and to help us to receive forgiveness of sins, that is, that we may be saved, redeemed from death and hell.

That is the first principle of Christian doctrine. It is presented to us in the words, and his body and blood are given to us to be received corporeally as a token and confirmation of this fact. To be sure, he did this only once, carrying it out and achieving it on the cross; but he causes it each day anew to be set before us, distributed and poured out through preaching, and he orders us to remember him always and never forget him.

The second principle is love. It is demonstrated in the first place by the fact that he has left us an example. As he gives himself for us with his body and blood in order to redeem us from all misery, so we too are to give ourselves with might and main for our neighbor. Whoever knows this and lives accordingly is holy, and has not much more to learn, nor will he find anything more in the whole Bible. For these two principles are here inscribed together as on a tablet which is always before our eyes and which we use daily.

Besides the example, there is also in the second place the figure or symbol. The teachers of old have diligently pointed out that he wished to give us his body and blood under the form of things which are of such a nature that they are themselves constituted by the fusing together of many individual things into one; just as a loaf is constituted by many kernels out of which one makes a single lump of dough, so that a loaf is nothing else than many kernels baked into one another. "We who are many" (says Paul in I Cor. 10 [:17]), "are nevertheless all one loaf and one body." Just as each grain loses its form and takes on a common form with the others, so that you cannot see or distinguish one from the other, and all of them are identical, yet separately present; so too should Christendom be one, without sects, that all may be one, of one heart, mind, and will, just as faith, the gospel, and baptism are one [Eph. 4:5]. That is how a Christian acts. He is conscious of nothing else than that the goods which are his are also given to his neighbor. He makes no distinction, but helps everyone with body and life, goods and honor, as much as he can. A similar picture is portrayed in the wine. Here many grapes are pressed together, and thereby each grape loses its form and a juice emerges. All the grapes are present in the wine, but there is nothing by which we could distinguish one from another; they have all flowed together and become one juice and one drink.

Thus Christ has beautifully portrayed and smoothly carved, as it were, the whole Christian way, so that, unless it is to be delineated at greater length, one needs no further books to perceive and grasp it clearly. Here we have a lesson, the study of which is sufficient to occupy us all our lives. You need not concern yourself with anything that others do not know, as our new sects are doing when they constantly invent new things. Here you have the whole thing. You can study it as long as you wish, but your flesh and blood will always be with you so that you will never be perfect in faith, love, and patience. Thus this sacrament is a taskmaster by which we order our lives and learn as long as we live. What good is it to try to know some special thing better than anybody else, if you do not know that which matters most of all? Whoever knows this, knows all that he ought to know. Without this, everything else that one might be able to know is nothing. I Cor. 13 [:2]: "And if I have prophetic powers and understand all mysteries and all knowledge, etc., but have not love, I am nothing."

The devil leads people by the nose, so that they pay no heed to the most important thing, but want to go beyond it and bring forth something special. Thus they lose the highest and only treasure. See—this is presented in the simplest of words, so that the simple souls can easily understand how to use the sacrament. They can know also the fruits by which they may see whether they have used it rightly. Let everyone follow this, and he will see wherein he is lacking; and let the others make up fables and prattle as they wish.

PART III

Concerning Confession

In addition we must also preach concerning confession [*beicht*], again in order to instruct the plain people. For it is a well-known fact that up to the present we have allowed ourselves to be tortured and humiliated with confession [*beichten*]. We have been troubled so much with it that there has been no more burdensome command since the world began. First, I hold that the word *beichten* comes from the little word *jahen*, from which is formed *bejychtet, bejehet*, that is, *bekennet* [confess]. From there we have reduced it to one syllable and call it *beichte*, that is, a confession.[12] Just as certain saints were called in Latin *Confessores*, in German *Beichtiger*, for *Bejychter*, that is, *bekenner* [confessors].

There are, however, as I have said before, three kinds of confession. One, before God: for it is necessary above all that I acknowledge before God that I am a sinner, as the gospel concludes in Rom. 3 [:23], and John 3 [:3]: "Unless one is born anew, he cannot see the kingdom of God." Whoever owns that he is born of woman must do God the honor of saying: I am nothing but a sinner, as David sings in Ps. 51 [:5]: "Behold, I was brought forth, or originated, in iniquity, and in sin did my mother conceive me." As if he were to say: I must indeed be a sinner, it was born in me;

---

[12] Luther's etymology is essentially correct. *Beichte* is derived from the Middle High German *biht*, a contraction of the Old High German *bijiht, bigiht* (meaning "declaration before the court"), which is the verbal noun for the Middle High German *bejëhen*, Old High German *bi-jëhan* (meaning "confess"). Though *jëhan* alone usually meant "say" or "declare" it also occasionally meant "admit" or "confess." Friedrich Kluge, *Etymologisches Wörterbuch der deutschen Sprache* (Berlin, 1957), *Beichte*.

as soon as I was formed in the womb, I was a sinner. For the flesh and blood of which I was made, were sin. As the saying has it: "Where hair and hide are bad, no good pelt will come of it." [13] Thus the clay, out of which we are made,[14] is not good. That which father and mother contribute is itself already sin.

Whoever refuses to confess this or will not admit that he is a sinner, but still claims to have a free will so that there may yet be some good in him, blasphemes God and gives him the lie, and must be eternally damned, as is proper. For he wants to be in the right and not suffer God's judgment. Therefore the prophet says again [Ps. 51:4]: "Against thee, thee only, have I sinned, and done that which is evil in thy sight, so that thou art justified in thy sentence and blameless in thy judgment." As if he would say again to God: I will not wrangle with you, but will let your Word be right and will confess that I am wrong and that you are right. But those who accuse you want to have the light of reason and something through which they will receive grace; surely you will remain blameless rather than they.

Now we must continue to make this confession as long as we live, always saying: "Lord, before thee I am a knave in the skin." [15] A distinction must be made, however; for even a knave and un-Christian person can say this, but he is certainly lying. No one but a true Christian says it from his heart, as Ps. 32 [:5-6] says: "I said, 'I will confess my transgressions to the Lord'; then thou didst forgive the guilt of my sin. Therefore let every one who is godly offer prayer to thee at an opportune time." All the godly, as many as there are of them, have this virtue in them, that they confess their sins to God and therefore pray. Hence none but those who are Christians and godly make such a confession. Now it is a marvelous thing that he who is righteous before God and has the Holy Spirit says that he is a sinner. It is right, however; he confesses what he has been and still is. He has the Holy Spirit, but he is still a sinner because of the flesh. For this reason all the godly cry out against the flesh. The devil, too, is not far off; he keeps stirring up the

---

[13] Cf. *Sprichwörter-Lexikon, op. cit.,* II, col. 441, *Haut,* Nos. 99 and 100.

[14] Cf. *Ibid.,* IV, col. 1155, *Thon,* No. 9: "He is made of the same clay."

[15] Rörer's sermon copy says instead: "As long as I am in this flesh, I am a sinner before thee."

flesh to cause it to sin. For this reason this is a great and lofty confession.

The others also say that they are sinners, but when other people say it of them they will not hear of it. But if one says this to the godly, or if God punishes them for their sins, they say: "Yes, it is right." Those hypocrites can indeed humble themselves, but they cease doing so whenever they wish. They do not want to be accused, but honored, by other people. It is the same with the priests and monks. They too say that they are sinners, but they will not hear it said by us. This is why God does not care about such confession. Genuine confession, now, is commanded and necessary and obligatory upon everybody. But no one makes it except the Christians.

The second kind of confession is that which one makes not to God but to one's neighbor. Of this Christ speaks in Matt. 5 [:23-25] and 6 [:14-15]. James also writes of it in his Epistle [Jas. 5:16]: "Confess your sins to one another," that is, conduct yourselves in such a way that each humbles himself before the other and confesses his guilt, if he has offended someone.

But there are many kinds of offense, both general and particular. In the general kind, I fear, we are all included; the Lord's Prayer puts us all there together [Matt. 6:12]. This kind consists in the fact that we do not help our neighbor as we are obligated to help him, namely, with words, preaching, advice, consolation, and with money, goods, honor, body, and life. This requirement is so rigorous that no one is so holy but that he is involved in guilt. Therefore we must all say to one another: "I am obligated to you; you are obligated to me." But especially the man to whom God has given much owes much in return [Luke 12:48]. I too owe him more than perhaps twenty or a hundred people. God will demand this from me, too. There is no other way, and he will reckon it down to the last farthing, how I have invested it and what profit I have gained from it. This obligation affects all in common and applies to no one in a particular way. I am under obligation to everyone; in return everyone owes consolation and assistance to me when I am in need and require help. We are not zealous enough, however, in seeking out the people who need us and offering them our service. It seems too much for us.

Now when we look at the account to see how much we owe we must quiver and quake and have no other recourse than to say: "I am in debt to others, but there are those who are in debt to me; I shall remit to them, one and all, whatever they owe me, and then O Lord, I pray thee, forgive me also." With that I draw a line through the reckoning and cancel it out. If we did not have this expedient we should be badly off. Therefore the Lord's Prayer remains valid, and it is necessary that we forgive our debtors, if our own debts are to be forgiven [Matt. 6:12-15], as Christ teaches in the Gospel (Matt. 18 [:21-35]).[16] This is one kind of confession, the kind which one must make openly before men, acknowledging one's guilt. I am not righteous before God; neither am I righteous before the world, when measured by the common kind of guilt. Each one has a claim on every other one, and no one satisfies that claim; therefore each must pray the other to forgive him.

Now no one but a Christian makes this confession. For un-Christian people do not permit this to be reckoned as sin. They cite the canon law which says: "To each man belongs his own";[17] and they believe that the goods which they possess they have for their own sakes. Therefore they use all sorts of goods only for their own honor and pleasure, as Solomon says in Proverbs: "The gain of the wicked leads to sin" [Prov. 10:16], "but the righteous is generous" [Ps. 37:21]. The wicked man uses his goods, his shrewdness, his skill, and honor in order to gain pleasure and profit from them. All this is sin, and sin of such a kind that he still believes that it is not sin, but right. God has created us in order that we should be our neighbor's steward, but in this we all fall short. We do have this advantage, however, that we recognize the fact and are sorry for it, and strive to do more and more every day, fearing God and doing as much as we can and as much as the Adam in us

---

[16] Both sermon copies follow the language of Matthew more closely, mentioning debts of 100, and of 1000 or 10,000 talents. WA 19, 517.

[17] The shorter sermon copy here quotes in Latin the Roman civil law: *unicuique tribuendum suum ius. Institutionum Justiniani*, lib. i, tit. I: *de Iustitia et Iure:* "Justice is the constant and perpetual wish to render every one his due." "The maxims of law are these: to . . . give every one his due." *The Institutes of Justinian*, trans. Thomas Collett Sandars (London, 1922), pp. 5-6. Cf. *A New Pandect of the Roman Civil Law* by John Ayliffe; folio (London, 1734), lib. i, tit. I, 2. Cf. also *Cicero's Three Books of Offices* (*De officiis*, I, 5), trans. Cyrus R. Edmonds (London, 1856), p. 11.

permits. What we fail to do above and beyond this, God cancels by drawing a line through it, as we have said before; we cannot hope to pay it, for it is too much. Therefore we say: "Forgive me, I will forgive in return."

Besides this general kind of guilt there is also a special kind. Of this Christ speaks in Matt. 5 [:22-24]. If a particular person is offended, deceived, injured, reviled or slandered, one should confess this too and admit that he has done wrong and ask forgiveness of his neighbor. O how it hurts, to break the Adam thus and to humble one's self toward a poor human being whom one despises, and to admit that he is right and grant to him the highest honor and to one's self the greatest shame. This was formerly a custom in monasteries, which the monks were forced to observe, but it was absurd.[18]

A godless person will not humiliate himself so deeply as to shame himself. He does not see that to humble himself would be a great honor to him before God and before devout people. Christians can guard against this kind of guilt to some extent, both for themselves and for others, by covering it up and punishing it where one hears of it or sees it in others. But from the general kind of guilt no one can escape.

However, we are not speaking here of those two kinds of confession, for they go on constantly throughout the year, and not merely when one wishes to go to the sacrament. We are speaking here of the private confession; and this, I maintain, has developed from the public confession. This took place in this way, that Christians put together into one the two kinds of confession we have described above. Thus everyone confessed publicly, before God and men, before he went to the sacrament. Where Christians were few in number, each individual said the confession separately to the other. From this they reached a point where they tried to classify and enumerate the sins. It would be better if they remained unenumerated, for you will never reckon up how much you have left undone of that which you ought to have done.

---

[18] Both sermon copies specify that this applied to the younger monks. The shorter calls it "a good custom," and adds: "they went to all the rest and begged forgiveness if they had offended them; but at least they would go to those whom they had never offended."

Concerning this last confession let me say this: if those other two kinds of confession take place in public, one is not obliged to make this last kind. God is well aware of your sins. If you only confess them before him, and then before your neighbor, your sins are forgiven. Yet for the sake of those who would like to make use of it, private confession is by no means to be rejected. The reason is this: there is much that is beneficial and precious in it. First of all, the absolution, in which your neighbor[19] absolves you in God's stead, is just as if God himself were speaking, and that should indeed be comforting to us. If I knew that God were in a certain place and would absolve me I would not go to some other place, but would receive absolution in that place as often as I could. Such absolution he has put into the mouth of man,[20] hence it is most comforting, especially to burdened consciences, to receive it there.

Second, private confession serves a good purpose for the simple, childlike people. For since the common herd is indolent, continually hearing sermons and learning nothing, there is no one in the homes either to urge anyone to do it. So, even if private confession did not serve any other purpose, it is at least useful because it gives opportunity to instruct the people and hear what they believe, teach them to pray, etc., otherwise they go along like cattle. For this reason I have said[21] that one ought to give the sacrament to no one unless he is able to explain what he is receiving and why he goes to the sacrament. This can be done most conveniently in confession.

Third, there is comfort in the fact that if anyone has an evil conscience, or some other desire or need, and would like advice, he may ask for advice here. Therefore we cannot despise private confession. For God's Word is present, which comforts us and strengthens us in faith, and in addition instructs us and teaches us what we lack, and also gives us advice in time of need. For this reason no one makes this confession properly either except devout Christians, because they must be the sort of people who feel that they really want advice and consolation. The difficulty with the matter, however, is that the people have not paid attention to the

---

[19] The shorter sermon copy has the word "priest."

[20] The Rörer sermon copy has "in the mouth of the priest."

[21] Cf. *Receiving Both Kinds of the Sacrament* (1522), *LW* 36, 231-267.

absolution, but to their own works, to how well and correctly they have made their confession. Moreover, they have attempted to enumerate their sins, and this cannot be done, because the number of them would be too great and it would be too great a task to hear them. Therefore the best way would be to make short work of it: "Dear brother, I come and want to lament my sins, that I am a sinner before God and man; I am especially concerned with this or that," etc. (whether you wish to say this or not, is up to you). Afterwards, conclude: "Therefore I pray, give me good comfort and strengthen my soul," etc. Thus it would require no effort and no toil. Moreover, it is a precious work, which none but a devout Christian does.

From all this you see that it is the devil's own doing when the pope commands private confession for everyone on pain of disobedience and mortal sin, and when he consigns to the devil those who do not practice it. For indeed this is not a matter which is in our power to take or give, but it is a gift which has come down from heaven. Because God has not commanded it, no man can command it. Even if I were to drive all men to it, how many of them would there be who would confess willingly and not merely out of compulsion? Not one in twenty thousand. With the rest one accomplishes no more than a mockery of God and dreadful blasphemy. For the priest there pronounces a judgment in God's stead that is wrong and will not be carried out. The man confesses unwillingly and hears the absolution unwillingly, and does not believe in it either. The fault does not lie with the priest, but with the one who confesses when he is insincere and does not truly wish the absolution from his heart. God has no desire that one should take his Word in vain [Exod. 20:7]. If you do not want to confess, then let it be, even all three kinds of confession. Confession is only for the devout people, and if you are not devout it is better to let it be, for then it is not righteous but damnable. So we have until now gone to confession only to serve the pope, not to serve our souls. This is rightly called obedience to the pope or to the church. He has had profit and honor from it. The rest, however, have had damnation of their souls.

Thus you have a brief and clear course of teaching concerning the two things, the sacrament and the confession. It should all be done willingly and freely. If you come of your own accord and recount your sins, if you seek consolation and strength, then it is beneficial and salutary. Children and simple people ought to be urged to do this. It should be taught, but with kind words and not with coercion. For, as has been said, it is especially useful also for that purpose, and should therefore be done. Amen.

18.

CONCERNING REBAPTISM

A *Letter of Martin Luther to Two Pastors*

Martin Luther, to the worthy and beloved pastors N. and N., my dear friends in Christ.

Grace and peace in Christ our Lord. Unfortunately, I know full well, dear sirs, that Balthasar Hubmaier[1] has included my name among others in his blasphemous booklet on rebaptism, as if I shared his perverted views. But I have comforted myself with the thought that no one, either friend or foe, would believe such a transparent lie as his. Not only is my conscience at rest in this, but my reputation is sufficiently safeguarded by the number of my sermons and especially by the latest Postil [containing sermons for the Sundays] from Epiphany to Easter, wherein I have made known abundantly my faith concerning infant baptism.[2] Therefore I have deemed it unnecessary to answer his kind of book. For who can stop the mouths of all people, even of all devils? I have long ago found that if I stop one mouth of the devil, he opens ten others, and the lie grows constantly greater. So, whether I wish it or not, I commit my cause to God, and if I have told the truth I depend on him as a true judge, who knows how to bring things to a right end. This he does daily as we may well discern.

---

[1] Balthasar Hubmaier studied theology at the University at Freiburg and became a professor in the theological faculty at Ingolstadt in 1512. In 1519, while serving as cathedral preacher at Regensburg, he declared himself in favor of the Reformation. Subsequently, he associated with rebellious peasants at Waldshut and embraced the cause of the Anabaptists. In thus denying the validity of infant baptism, Hubmaier became a heretic in Catholic and Protestant territories. After fleeing from Waldshut in Austria to Zurich in Switzerland and thence to Moravia, he was burned at the stake in Vienna in 1528.

[2] Cf. *EA'* 11, 52ff. The name, Postil, is derived from the Latin words, *Post illa verba textus* (after those words of the text), which were spoken after the reading of the text and prior to its interpretation in the sermon. In medieval times a collection of sermons was called a Postil (*postilla*). In his preface to the *Large Catechism*, Luther cites the titles of some of these volumes of sermons. Cf. *WA* 30I, 125.

So far we have escaped such rabble preachers in the territory of our prince, God be thanked and praised in eternity. We also have none of the foes of the sacrament, but are at peace and in harmony in doctrine, faith, and life. May it be God's will graciously to keep us thus. Amen. Since there has not been much occasion here for it, I have not, for my part, given much thought to these baptizers. But it serves you right as papists (I must call you such, as long as you are under your tyrants). You will not suffer the gospel, so you will have to endure these devil's rebels, as Christ says in John 5 [:43]: "I have come in my Father's name, and you do not receive me; if another comes in his own name, him you (i.e., the ones who are among you) will receive." Still, it is not right, and I truly grieve, that these miserable folk should be so lamentably murdered, burned, and tormented to death. We should allow everyone to believe what he wills. If his faith be false, he will be sufficiently punished in eternal hell-fire. Why then should we martyr these people also in this world, if their error be in faith alone and they are not guilty of rebellion or opposition to the government? Dear God, how quickly a person can become confused and fall into the trap of the devil! By the Scriptures and the Word of God, we ought to guard against and withstand him. By fire we accomplish little.

I am not sure as to the ground and reason of their faith, since you do not tell me, and yet ask advice as to what to do in such cases. My answer cannot be very definite. In a sense you are yourselves Anabaptists. For many among you rebaptize in Latin when someone has been baptized in German, though your pope neither does nor teaches thus. For we know well enough that the pope recognizes it as a baptism when midwives administer emergency baptism, even though it be in German. Still you rebaptize persons whom we have baptized in German, as if our German baptism by pastors were not as valid as German baptism by midwives. So the bonehead of Leipzig[3] recently did at Mühlhausen.

---

[3] A professor at Leipzig, Hieronymous Dungersheim, denied this accusation of Luther and wrote both a letter and a booklet to defend himself. The letter is in Enders, *Briefwechsel* 6:251ff., the treatise in *EA* (2d ed.; 28 vols.; 1862-1885), 26:322ff. Luther had carried on correspondence with Dungersheim in 1519 regarding the power of the papacy. *St. L* 18, 426ff.

But the pope has never commanded that baptism should be only in Latin and not in another language. So you have your reward. You favor rebaptism, so you get plenty of Anabaptists, though you will not tolerate them, and yet you want to be rebaptizers in opposition to your own teacher and master, the pope.

But I pass by now what wrong your people do in their rebaptizing. Your shame is the greater since by your rebaptizing you at the same time contradict your idol, the pope. Teacher and pupil do not agree with each other. I will not speak further of this, but rather help you by appearing to be a papist again and flattering the pope. For my dear enthusiasts will put no other interpretation on it (as they already have done) than that I hereby flatter the pope and seek his favor. Who does not follow their folly must bear the name of a new papist.

In the first place I hear and see that such rebaptism is undertaken by some in order to spite the pope and to be free of any taint of the Antichrist. In the same way the foes of the sacrament want to believe only in bread and wine, in opposition to the pope, thinking thereby really to overthrow the papacy. It is indeed a shaky foundation on which they can build nothing good. On that basis we would have to disown the whole of Scripture and the office of the ministry, which of course we have received from the papacy. We would also have to make a new Bible. Then, also, we would have to disavow the Old Testament, so that we would be under no obligation to the unbelieving Jews. And why the daily use of gold and goods which have been used by bad people, papists, Turks, and heretics? This, too, should be surrendered, if they are not to have anything good from evil persons.

The whole thing is nonsense. Christ himself came upon the errors of scribes and Pharisees among the Jewish people, but he did not on that account reject everything they had and thought (Matt. 23 [:3]). We on our part confess that there is much that is Christian and good under the papacy; indeed everything that is Christian and good is to be found there and has come to us from this source. For instance we confess that in the papal church there are the true holy Scriptures, true baptism, the true sacrament of the altar, the true keys to the forgiveness of sins, the true office of the ministry, the true catechism in the form of the Lord's Prayer, the Ten Commandments, and the articles of the creed. Similarly, the pope admits that we too, though condemned by him as heretics, and likewise all heretics, have the holy Scriptures, baptism, the keys, the catechism, etc. O how do you dissemble? How then do I dissemble? I speak of what the pope and we have in common. He on his part dissembles toward us and heretics and plainly admits what we and he have in common. I will continue to so dissemble, though it does me no good. I contend that in the papacy there is true Christianity, even the right kind of Christianity and many great and devoted saints. Shall I cease to make this pretense?

Listen to what St. Paul says to the Thessalonians [II Thess. 2:4]: "The Antichrist takes his seat in the temple of God." If now the pope is (and I cannot believe otherwise) the veritable Antichrist, he will not sit or reign in the devil's stall, but in the temple of God. No, he will not sit where there are only devils and unbelievers, or where no Christ or Christendom exist. For he is an Antichrist and must thus be among Christians. And since he is to sit and reign there it is necessary that there be Christians under him. God's temple is not the description for a pile of stones, but for the holy Christendom (I Cor. 3 [:17]), in which he is to reign. The Christendom that now is under the papacy is truly the body of Christ and a member of it. If it is his body, then it has the true spirit, gospel, faith, baptism, sacrament, keys, the office of the ministry, prayer, holy Scripture, and everything that pertains to Christendom. So we are all still under the papacy and therefrom have received our Christian treasures.

As a veritable Antichrist must conduct himself against Christendom, so the pope acts toward us: he persecutes us, curses us, bans us, pursues us, burns us, puts us to death. Christians need indeed to be truly baptized and right members of Christ if they are to win the victory in death over against the Antichrist. We do not rave as do the rebellious spirits, so as to reject everything that is found in the papal church. For then we would cast out even Christendom from the temple of God, and all that it contained of Christ. But when we oppose and reject the pope it is because he does not keep to these treasures of Christendom which he has inherited from the apostles. Instead he makes additions of the devil and does not use these treasures for the improvement of the temple. Rather he works toward its destruction, in setting his commandments and ordinances above the ordinance of Christ. But Christ preserves his Christendom even in the midst of such destruction, just as he rescued Lot at Sodom, as St. Peter recounts (I Pet. 2 [II Pet. 2:6]). In fact both remain, the Antichrist sits in the temple of God through the action of the devil, while the temple still is and remains the temple of God through the power of Christ. If the pope will suffer and accept this dissembling of mine, then I am and will be, to be sure, an obedient son and devoted papist, with a truly joyful heart, and take back everything that I have done to harm him.

So it is of no consequence when these Anabaptists and enthusiasts say, "Whatever is of the pope is wrong," or, "Whatever is in the papacy we must have and do differently," thinking thereby to prove themselves the foremost enemy of Antichrist. Not realizing that they thus give him most help, they hurt Christendom most and deceive themselves. For they should help us to reject abuse and accretion, but they would not get much credit for this because they realize they were not first to do this. So they attack what no one yet has attacked in the hope that here perchance they might have the honor of being first. But the honor turns to disgrace, for they attack the temple of God and miss the Antichrist who sits therein, just as the blind, who grope after water, take hold of fire.

In fact they remind us of what one brother in the forest of Thuringia did to the other. They were going through the woods with each other when they were set upon by a bear who threw one of them beneath him. The other brother sought to help and struck at the bear, but missed him and grievously wounded the brother under the bear. So these enthusiasts. They ought to come to the aid of Christendom which Antichrist has in his grip and tortures. They take a severe stand against the pope, but they miss their mark and murder the more terribly the Christendom under the pope. For if they would permit baptism and the sacrament of the altar to stand as they are, Christians under the pope might yet escape with their souls and be saved, as has been the case hitherto. But now when the sacraments are taken from them, they will most likely be lost, since even Christ himself is thereby taken away. Dear friend, this is not the way to blast the papacy while Christian saints are in his keeping. One needs a more cautious, discreet spirit, which attacks the accretion which threatens the temple without destroying the temple of God itself.

Again, those who depend on such arguments say that they know nothing of their baptism, and exclaim, "How do you know you have been baptized? You believe people who say you have been baptized. But you should believe God himself and not people, and you must be sure of your baptism." Surely this seems to me to be pretty shaky argument. For were I to reject everything which I have not seen or heard, I would indeed not have much left, either of faith or of love, either of spiritual or of temporal things. I might reply, "My friend, how do you know that this man is your father, this woman is your mother? You cannot trust people, you must be sure of your own birth." In this manner all children would forthwith be free from obedience to the commandment of God, "Thou shalt honor thy father and thy mother." For I could retort, "How do I know who is my father and mother? I can't believe people. So I will have to be born again by them in order to see for myself, else I will not obey them." By acting in this way God's command would indeed be made altogether null and void.

Likewise I might refuse to recognize anyone as brother, sister, cousin, or relative, constantly repeating, "I did not know we were related, because I am uncertain who my parents were," etc. But (if I were ruler of the land) I would repay such a spirit by forbidding him to retain, expect, or receive any inheritance, either house, land, or a single penny from his parents, and so play with him at his own game until his spirit takes on flesh for him again. For since he neither recognizes nor trusts his parents, he cannot know or hope for their possessions. O, how well society would be ordered when no one would want to be related to another as child, brother, sister, cousin, relative, heir, or neighbor! To be among such Christians would be no better than being among wild wolves.

Then too I might refuse to be subject to any lord or master, explaining that I am not sure he was born a prince, because I did not see it, but had to accept popular opinion. So I will be a free man, pay no attention to the command of God, have no authority above me, but run away from people to wolves, among whom there is no such commandment of God to honor parents and government. That the devil really desires this in these baptizers is apparent from the fact that these disciples of his are prepared (as it is said) to forsake wife and children, house and land, and go to heaven altogether alone. More of this later.

Indeed I might then claim that holy Scripture meant nothing, Christ meant nothing. The apostles, too, never preached. For I have not seen nor felt these things. I've only heard them from people. So I won't believe them unless they are re-enacted anew and happen and are done again before my eyes. So I am above all a wholly free fellow, free also from the commands of God. That's the way I would have it, if I could, the devil declares. That would be a foundation for the Anabaptists on which nothing in heaven and earth could stand.

You reply: Have you not yourself taught that we should obey God and not man? You think thereby to slay me with mine own sword, don't you? But since you are in such a fighting mood, I would ask you if we are to obey God when he commands us to honor parents and superiors? If you say, "Yes," I would ask, How then do you know who they are, since you don't want to believe men? Where are you then? I see full well that your mistake is in not knowing what it means to believe men, and so stumble into error as hopelessly as the Anabaptists do. Therefore listen to me.

When we teach that we are not to obey men, we mean of course that they are speaking entirely for themselves and God is not in their minds, that is, they speak only as men in what they think up, without reference to the Word and work of God, and cannot therefore prove anything either by the words or works of God. For who would call that a human teaching which is presented by God through man? And who would say that faith in such teaching meant faith in man and not in God? In Col. 2 [:23], Paul chides the human teaching which has never proven what it proclaims, that is, it is imagined only and cannot be proved by a single word or work of God. So when you hear that men are not tᵣ be believed you are to understand that this applies only to what is purely human speculation and not to statements wherein a word or work of God is declared or affirmed. You are to distinguish simply (as the words indicate) between faith in God and faith in what is only of man.

When you were born, for example, it was no secret event, nor was it a human invention. Your birth was a work of God which became publicly known and could not be denied. And if anyone wants to contradict it as the Jews presumed to contradict the miracles and signs of Christ, it is of no avail. For those who see and witness to the divine public deed will nonetheless prevail and stop the mouths of the others in deed and truth. For the law of God holds here rigorously, that by the mouths of two or three witnesses all things are to be confirmed [Deut. 19:15]. You must truly believe people like that. For they bear witness to the work of God, namely, your birth. They prove that these were your parents. Besides, no one but they took care of you, and no one but they alone strove and labored for you. God's work progresses in public so that neither devil nor man can controvert it, but every man can so know and declare it as he declares that you are living.

When anyone bears witness to the work of God it does not mean believing men, but God. In sum, when any one declares and bears witness to the work of God and which is not the figment of man's imagination, and this can be controverted neither by the devil nor man, then you believe God and not man, for it is the work of God which He so publicly discloses that even the devil cannot deny it.

This truth is in no way affected by the occasions when children are put or sent away and never know their true parents throughout their lifetime, for we are speaking here of ordinary divine public order. Such children are dishonestly and secretly dealt with, against the will of God, so it is not surprising that theirs is a different lot. They are reared in secret, so that who their parents are remains a secret to them. Whatever the devil does is darkness: let it remain in darkness. But God's order functions in the light.

If now you ask why I believe this man and this woman to be my parents I reply: First, I am sure that I am a work of God and am a human being, wherefore I have to have a mother and father and am not sprung from a rock.[4] God says in Gen. 1 [:28] to the man and woman, "Be fruitful and multiply," from which it is clear that all persons are born of man and woman, and have a father and mother. This is confirmed by the commandment to all men,

---

[4] The metaphor is derived from Homer's *Iliad* 22, 126.

"Thou shalt honor father and mother." (In both instances Christ as the Son of God is of course an exception.) Since I am sure that I came from parents and am not grown on a tree, I am compelled, secondly, to believe, that it is from this man and this woman, who are represented to me by other people as being my parents, according to the word, "On the evidence of two or three witnesses all things shall be established." So I am compelled by God to rely on such people. Thirdly, it is a work of God that no one other than these two in all the world in his own name has taken me as a natural child, or in case of their death, those relatives or pious people who took me in their name. Such an indisputable fact is like any other of God's evident works before devil and man. For neither world nor devil can doubt the evident works of God. They may try, but it will be to no avail. The devil can of course skilfully attack the Word of God, while the work is still hidden.

The reason that God speaks in Rom. 13 [:1], "Let every person be subject to the governing authorities," is that I might believe in him who is my prince or lord. I conclude from this word that I must have a superior and I must be a subject. Secondly, since all the world testifies and says this is he and everyone recognizes him as such and no one denies that this is an evident work of God, I must believe such testimony. If any one contradicts, he does so in vain, for finally every one admits that he lies. Thirdly, it is an evident work of God, that no one else considers me as his subject. I live under his protection, justice, law, and peace, as I should under government, and all other authorities leave me alone; nor do they call my status into question or oppose it, provided I keep my place in the light of law and God's order. Robbers and murderers may well find their place under foreign rulers in secrecy and darkness, but these are rightly judged as not being their subjects.

Wait, you say, I will test you. Why do you not now believe in the pope as your lord? Instead, you make him the Antichrist, though all the world testifies that he is the head of Christendom, and they will prove it indeed that he has the rule. I answer, there you almost caught me! But let me tell you, that if you can convince me that the papacy meets the three requirements I have shown to hold in regard to parents and government, then I will consider the papacy as a work of God, submitting to it, and deeming it a work of God. But, dear fellow, if you cannot do this, allow me to judge it as a human fancy, without the word and work of God, which is under no circumstances to be believed. I can forcefully prove that the papacy is a human fancy.

In the first place, the Word of God clearly tells me that parents and government exist, and that I should and must have parents and government as I have said. But there is no Word of God that says there is a pope, and that I must have a pope and be subject to him. Since the Scriptures command nothing concerning the pope and his rule, there is no papacy which can be considered the work of God. For the Scriptures give testimony concerning what are the works of God. Therefore I said above, that we should believe in men when they show and prove, not their own fancies or works, but the Word or work of God. For, before considering the question as to what a thing is, make sure that it exists.[5] Before you tell me what the pope is, you must convince me that there is a divinely appointed pope. If he cannot exist one does not ask who he is. Secondly, though many bear witness to him, their testimony is not only in vain, since it cannot make a work of God out of the papacy, or prove it to be such, but is not unanimous and complete. For not only has the Eastern church borne testimony against the papacy and opposed it, but also many subjects of the pope himself, who have been burned at the stake for their opposition and still are strangled daily. His rule thus has never been accepted or unopposed, or been peacefully established as has the rule of parents or government, as we have related already.

Thirdly, it is not a work of God. For he exercises no office to the welfare of his subjects. Indeed, he persecutes the gospel and Christians, let alone that he ought to be a teacher and guardian. He only teaches his filth and poison as human notions, discards the gospel, even persecutes it, though without avail. He makes a sacrifice out of the sacrament, faith out of works, work out of faith. He forbids marriage, [and issues prohibitions concerning] food, seasons, clothes, and places. He perverts and abuses all Christian treasures to the injury of souls, as we have sufficiently proved elsewhere. Since on all three counts the papacy is deficient, we

---

[5] Luther quotes a rule in medieval logic.

must judge it as a pure human invention, which is not worthy of belief and is in no way comparable to the institutions of parenthood and government.

Baptism, too, is a work of God, not invented by man but commanded by God and witnessed to by the gospel. Secondly, there are people who can witness to the fact that you have been baptized, and no one can contradict or prove the opposite. In the third place, there is the work, i.e., you are reckoned among Christians, admitted to the sacrament, and to the use of all Christian privileges. This would not be the case if you had not been baptized and all were not sure of it. So all of this is clear proof of your baptism. For all the world knows and sees that everyone is baptized as a child. Whoever refuses to believe all this refuses to believe God himself, since God says, Two witnesses are to be believed [Deut. 19:15; Matt. 18:16]. Such witnesses he does not punish, though he never leaves false witness unpunished or inviolate.

Herewith I have sufficiently proved that no one ought to have doubts as to his baptism, as if he did not know that he is baptized. He sins against God who will not believe it. For he is much more certain of his baptism through the witness of Christians, than if he himself had witnessed it. For the devil could easily have made him uncertain so that he imagined he had been dreaming or had an hallucination instead of being properly baptized. So he would have to fall back finally on the testimony of Christians to be at peace. This kind of testimony the devil cannot confuse or make dubious.

In the third place, it is said, as I also have read, that they base their faith on this verse, "He who believes and is baptized will be saved" [Mark 16:16]. This they interpret to mean that no man should be baptized before he believes. I must say that they are guilty of a great presumption. For if they follow this principle they cannot venture to baptize before they are certain that the one to be baptized believes. How and when can they ever know that for certain? Have they now become gods so that they can discern the hearts of men and know whether or not they believe? If they are not certain if they believe, why then do they baptize, since they contend so strenuously that faith must precede baptism? Are they not contradicting themselves when they baptize without being certain if faith is there or not? For whoever bases baptism on faith and baptizes on chance and not on certainty that faith is present does nothing better than he who baptizes him who has no faith. For unbelief and uncertain belief are one and the same thing, and both are contrary to the verse, "Whoever believes," which speaks of a sure faith which they who are to be baptized should have.

You say, I know, that he confesses that he believes, etc. Dear sir, confession is neither here nor there. The text does not say, "He who confesses," but "He who believes." To have his confession is not to know his faith. With all your reasoning you cannot do justice to this verse unless you also know he has faith, since all men are liars and God alone knows the heart. So whoever bases baptism on the faith of the one to be baptized can never baptize anyone. Even if you baptized a person a hundred times a day you would not at all know if he believes. Why then do you carry on with your rebaptizing, since you contradict yourself and baptize when you are not sure that faith is present, and yet you teach that faith must most certainly be present. This verse, "Whoever believes," altogether opposes their rebaptizing, since the verse speaks of a certain faith. They base their rebaptizing on an uncertain faith, and in not a syllable do they follow the meaning of the verse.

I say the same thing about the baptized one who receives or grounds his baptism on his faith. For he is not sure of his own faith. I would compare the man who lets himself be rebaptized with the man who broods and has scruples because perhaps he did not believe as a child. So when next day the devil comes, his heart is filled with scruples and he says, Ah, now for the first time I feel I have the right faith, yesterday I don't think I truly believed. So I need to be baptized a third time, the second baptism not being of any avail. You think the devil can't do such things? You had better get to know him better. He can do worse than that, dear friend. He can go on and cast doubt on the third, and the fourth and so on incessantly (as he indeed has in mind to do), just as he has done with me and many in the matter of confession. We never seemed able to confess sufficiently certain sins, and incessantly and restlessly sought one absolution after the other, one father confessor after the other. Just because we sought to rely on our confession, as those to be baptized now want to rely on their faith. What is the end result? Baptizing without end would result. All this is nonsense. Neither the baptizer nor the baptized can base baptism on a certain faith. This verse of Scripture is far more a judgment on them than on us. And these are the people who don't want to trust the men who are witnesses of their baptism, but now as men are ready to trust themselves that they are baptized as if they were not men, or as if they were more certain of their faith than the witness of Christendom allows.

So I contend that if they want to do justice to this passage, "Whoever believes," according to their understanding, they must condemn rebaptism much more earnestly than the first baptism. Neither the baptizer nor the baptized can maintain his position, for both are uncertain of their faith, or at least are in constant peril and anxiety. For it happens, indeed it is so in this matter of faith, that often he who claims to believe does not at all believe; and on the other hand, he who doesn't think he believes, but is in despair, has the greatest faith. So this verse, "Whoever believes," does not compel us to determine who has faith or not. Rather, it makes it a matter of every man's conscience to realize that if he is to be saved he must believe and not pretend that it is sufficient for a Christian to be baptized. For the verse does not say, "Whoever knows that he believes, or, if you know that anyone believes," but it says, "Whoever believes." Who has it, has it. One must believe, but we neither should nor can know it for certain.

Since our baptizing has been thus from the beginning of Christianity and the custom has been to baptize children, and since no one can prove with good reasons that they do not have faith, we should not make changes and build on such weak arguments. For if we are going to change or do away with customs that are traditional, it is necessary to prove convincingly that these are contrary to the Word of God. Otherwise (as Christ says), "For he that is not against us is for us" [Mark 9:40]. We have indeed overthrown monasteries, mass-priests, and clerical celibacy, but only by showing the clear and certain scriptural arguments against them. Had we not done this, we should truly have let them stand as they previously existed.

When they say, "Children cannot believe," how can they be sure of that? Where is the Scripture by which they would prove it and on which they would build? They imagine this, I suppose, because children do not speak or have understanding. But such a fancy is deceptive, yea, altogether false, and we cannot build on what we imagine.

There are Scripture passages that tell us that children may and can believe, though they do not speak or understand. So, Ps. 72 [106:37f.], describes how the Jews offered their sons and daughters to idols, shedding innocent blood. If, as the text says, it was innocent blood, then the children have to be considered pure and holy—this they could not be without spirit and faith. Likewise the innocent children whom Herod had murdered were not over two years of age [Matt. 2:16]. Admittedly they could not speak or understand. Yet they were holy and blessed. Christ himself says in Matt. 18 [19:14], "The kingdom of heaven belongs to children." And St. John was a child in his mother's womb [Luke 1:41] but, as I believe, could have faith.

Yes, you say, but John was an exception. This is not proof that all baptized children have faith. I answer, wait a minute. I am not yet at the point of proving that children believe. I am giving proof that your foundation for rebaptism is uncertain and false inasmuch as you cannot prove that there may not be faith in children. Inasmuch as John had faith, though he could not speak or understand, your argument fails, that children are not able to believe. To hold that a child believes, as St. John is an example, is not contrary to Scripture. If it is not contrary to the Scripture to hold that children believe, but rather in accord with Scripture, then your argument, that children cannot believe, must be unscriptural. That is my first point.

Who has made you so sure that baptized children do not believe in the face of what I here prove that they can believe? But if you are not sure, why then are you so bold as to discard the first baptism, since you do not and cannot know that it is meaningless? What if all children in baptism not only were able to believe but believed as well as John in his mother's womb? We can hardly deny that the same Christ is present at baptism and in baptism, in fact is himself the baptizer, who in those days came in his mother's womb to John. In baptism he can speak as well through the mouth of the priest, as when he spoke through his mother. Since then he is present,

speaks, and baptizes, why should not his Word and baptism call
forth spirit and faith in the child as then it produced faith in John?
He is the same one who speaks and acts then and now. Even before,
he had said through Isaiah [Isa. 55:11], "His word shall not return
empty." Now it is up to you to bring forth a single Scripture verse
which proves that children cannot believe in baptism. I have cited
these many verses showing that they can believe, and that it is
reasonable to hold that they do believe. I grant that we do not
understand how they do believe, or how faith is created. But that
is not the point here.

Furthermore, he commands us to bring the children to him.
In Matt. 19 [:14] he embraces them, kisses them, and says that
theirs is the kingdom of heaven. The misled spirits like to fend this
off by saying, Christ is not speaking of children, but of the humble.
But this is a false note, for the text clearly says that they brought
to him children, not the humble. And Christ does not say to let the
humble come to him, but the children, and reprimanded the
disciples, not because they kept the humble, but the children away.
He embraced and blessed the children, not the humble, when he
said, "Of such is the kingdom of heaven." So also Matt. 18 [:10],
"Their angels behold the face of my Father," is to be understood as
referring to such children, for he teaches us that we should also be
like these children. Were not these children holy, he would indeed
have given us a poor ideal with which to compare ourselves. He
would not have said, you must be like children, but rather, you must
be otherwise than children. In sum, the misled spiritualist cannot
make children here to mean the humble, except through his own
imagining, for the words are too clear and forceful.

Some want to take the force out of this text by saying that the
Jewish children were circumcised. Therefore they were holy and
could be brought to Christ, whereas our children are heathen, etc.
I answer: But suppose there were also girls among these children
who were brought to Jesus, and who were not circumcised? For
surely all kinds of children were among those brought to him, and
since it does not expressly say that they were boys only we cannot
exclude girls, but must let it mean children of both sexes. They
are not brought to him because of their circumcision, but that they
might be blessed, coming to Christ out of the Old into the New

Testament, according to his word, "Let the children come to me for of such is the kingdom of God." He says that those who come to him are of the kingdom of God. By their coming and being brought to Christ they are so holy that he embraces, blesses, and gives them the kingdom. Let him who wills follow his fancy. I maintain as I have written in the Postil[6] that the most certain form of baptism is child baptism. For an adult might deceive and come to Christ as a Judas and have himself baptized. But a child cannot deceive. He comes to Christ in baptism, as John came to him, and as the children were brought to him, that his word and work might be effective in them, move them, and make them holy, because his Word and work cannot be without fruit. Yet it has this effect alone in the child. Were it to fail here it would fail everywhere and be in vain, which is impossible.

It cannot be denied that Ps. 77 [106:37] speaks of girls and uncircumcised when it says that they were offered to the idols of Canaan. Yet they were described as innocent blood. And surely Moses in Lev. 12 [:5] included girls in the regulation of offerings for purification and atonement. Everybody knows that boys alone were subjected to circumcision, but that girls participated in its benefits also by virtue of the saying spoken by God to Abraham (Gen. 17 [:7]): "I will be the God of thy descendants, and circumcision shall be a covenant between me and you and your descendants after you." Surely girls are the descendants of Abraham, and through this promise God is indeed their God, though they are not circumcised as are the boys.

If they now believe that through the covenant of circumcision God accepts both boys and girls and is their God, why should he not also accept our children through the covenant of baptism? He has in fact promised us that he wants to be God not alone of the Jews but also of the Gentiles (Rom. 3 [:29]), and especially of the Christians and those who believe. If the circumcision of boys avails both boys and girls, so that they become the people of God because of the faith of Abraham from whom they are descended, how much more then should not baptism help each one to become a member of the people of God because of the merit of Christ to whom he is

---

[6] Cf. p. 341.

brought and by whom he is blessed. Let everyone know how uncertain is the foundation of the Anabaptists and how vainly they build thereon.

But, you say, he has not commanded the baptism of children, there is no reference to it in the writings or epistles of the apostles. I answer, neither has he specifically commanded the baptism of adults, nor of men or of women, so we had better not baptize anybody. But he has commanded us to baptize all Gentiles, none excepted, when he said, "Go and baptize all heathen in my name," etc. (Matt. 28 [:19]). Now children constitute a great part of the heathen. We read in Acts and the Epistles of St. Paul how whole households were baptized, and children are surely a good part of the household. So it seems that just as Christ commanded us to teach and baptize all heathen, without exception, so the apostles did, and baptized all who were in the household. Had they not overlooked that the troubling spirits would seek to differentiate between young and old, they would have considered this more expressly, since otherwise in all the Epistles they write so much about there being no respect or difference of persons among Christians. For St. John in I John 2 [:14] writes to the little children, that they know the Father. And, as St. Augustine writes, child baptism has come from the apostles.[7] So the Anabaptists proceed dangerously in everything. Not only are they not sure of themselves but also they act contrary to accepted tradition and out of their own imaginings create differences between persons which God has not made. For even if they contended that they had not been sufficiently subdued, they ought, however quarrelsome they are, to be concerned and frightened at their wrongdoing in rebaptizing on such uncertain grounds. For they are already convicted of doing wrong in their being so uncertain. For in divine matters one should act on certain, not on dubious, grounds.

For if an Anabaptist hears (that is, if he does not want to be obstinate but teachable) that just as John believed and was made holy when Christ came and spoke through the mouth of his mother, so a child becomes a believer if Christ in baptism speaks to him through the mouth of the one who baptizes, since it is his Word,

---

[7] *De Genesi ad literam* X. Cap 23. *Migne* 34, 426.

his commandment, and his word cannot be without fruit, then the Anabaptist must admit that it may be so, that he cannot altogether and firmly deny it, nor cite any Scripture to the contrary. But if he cannot clearly and convincingly deny it, then he cannot firmly defend his rebaptism. For he must first firmly prove that children are without faith when they are baptized, if he is to justify rebaptism. I hold that it has been sufficiently proved that his reasoning is uncertain and supercilious throughout.

Yet even if they could establish that children are without faith when they are baptized, it would make no difference to me. I would want to know their reason for rebaptizing when later on faith or the confession of faith is supposed to be present. For it is not enough to claim they were baptized without faith, therefore they should be rebaptized. Some reason is needed. You say it is not proper baptism. What does it matter, if it is still a baptism? It was a correct baptism in itself, regardless of whether it was received rightly. For the words were spoken and everything that pertains to baptism was done as fully as when faith is present. If a thing is in itself correct you do not have to repeat it even though it was not correctly received. You correct what was wrong and do not have to do the entire thing over. Abuse does not change the nature of a substance, indeed it proves the substance.[8] There can be no abuse unless the substance exists.

When ten years after baptism faith appears, what then is the need of a second baptism, if baptism was correctly administered in all respects? For now he believes, as baptism requires. For faith doesn't exist for the sake of baptism, but baptism for the sake of faith. When faith comes, baptism is complete. A second baptism is not necessary.

It is as if a girl married a man reluctantly and altogether without a wife's affection for the man. She is before God hardly to be considered his true wife. But after two years she gains affection for him. Would then a second engagement be required, a second wedding be celebrated, as if she had not previously been a wife, so that the earlier betrothal and wedding were in vain? Of course you would be considered a fool, if you believed that,

---

[8] A proverb in jurisprudence. Cf. WA 26, 159.

especially since everything is in order now because she has come into her right and properly keeps to the man she had not properly accepted. So also if an adult falsely allows himself to be baptized but after a year comes to faith, do you mean, dear sir, that he should be rebaptized? He received the correct baptism incorrectly, I hear you say. His impropriety makes baptism improper. Should then human error and wickedness be stronger than God's good and invincible order? God made a covenant with the people of Israel on Mt. Sinai. Some did not receive that covenant rightly and in faith. If now these later came to faith, should the covenant, dear sir, therefore be considered invalid, and must God come again to each one on Mt. Sinai in order to renew the covenant?

Likewise God provides for the preaching of the Ten Commandments. But since some people only grasp them with their ears, albeit improperly, they are not Ten Commandments, are no good, and God ought hence to issue ten new commandments in place of the former. It can't be enough that people let themselves be rightly converted and give heed to the original Ten Commandments. It would be a curious situation when the Word of God, which abides forever [Isa. 40:6-9; I Pet. 1:24], has to be changed and be renewed as often as men change and want something new. Yet it does remain firm and unique, so that they who do not now cleave to it or have fallen from it, may still have an immovable rock to which to return and to hold. If subjects paid homage to their liege with the intention of putting him to death, but after three days repented and gave sincere allegiance to him, dear fellow, would it be necessary here to set up anew the conditions of allegiance? Of course not, inasmuch as now their allegiance is sincere which formerly was treacherous.

Were we to follow their reasoning we would have to be baptizing all of the time. For I would take the verse, "Whoever believes," with me and whenever I find a Christian who has fallen or is without faith, I would say that this man is without faith, so his baptism is fruitless; he must be baptized again. If he falls a second time, I would again say, see, he has not faith, there must be something wrong about his first baptism. He will have to be baptized a third time, and so on and on. As often as he falls or there is doubt about his faith, I will say, he doesn't believe, his baptism is defective. In short, he will have to be baptized over again so often that he never again falls or is without faith, if he is to do justice to the verse, "Whoever believes." Tell me, what Christian will then ever be sufficiently baptized or consider that his baptism is completed? But verily baptism can be correct and sufficient even if the Christian falls from faith or sins a thousand times a year. It is enough that he rights himself and becomes faithful, without having to be rebaptized each time. Then why should not the first baptism be sufficient and proper if a person truly becomes a believing Christian? Since there is no difference in baptism whether lack of faith precedes or follows, baptism doesn't depend on faith. But if faith is lacking, the Anabaptists would have us believe we must alter the nature of baptism to accord with the verse, "Whoever believes."

I claim therefore that even if the Anabaptists could prove their thesis, that children are without faith (which they cannot do), they would not have proved more than that the correct baptism, instituted by God, has been wrongly and not properly received. But whoever proves only an abuse, only proves that the abuse should be corrected and not that the thing should be changed. For abuse does not alter the nature of a thing.[9] Gold does not become straw because a thief steals and misuses it. Silver doesn't turn into paper if it is dishonestly obtained by a usurer. Since then the Anabaptists demonstrate only the abuse of baptism, they fly in the face of God, nature, and reason, when they want to alter and make anew baptism itself in treating the abuse. All heretics do the same with regard to the gopsel. They perceive it wrongly and so hear it wrongly in connection with an abuse, and then hasten to change and make a new gopsel out of it. So no matter which way you look at it the Anabaptists are in error. They blaspheme and dishonor the order of God, calling baptism wrong on account of the wrongs and abuses of man, though even their claim of man's wrongs and abuses is unconvincing.

There is, however, a devil who promotes confidence in works [*Werkteufel*] among them. He feigns faith, whereas he really has a work in mind. He uses the name and guise of faith to lead the poor people to rely on a work. Just as it happened under the papacy,

---

[9]Cf. p. 358 n. 8.

when we were driven to the sacrament as a work of obedience. For no one went in order to nourish his faith, but everything was finished and the work accomplished when we had received the sacrament. So here again the Anabaptists are urging on to a work, so that when the people are baptized they may have confidence that everything is right and complete. In reality they pay little attention to faith, but only seem to praise it. For, as we have already said, were they to be sure beforehand of faith, they would never again baptize anyone. If they did not rely on works but earnestly sought for faith, they would not dare to rebaptize. The unchanging Word of God, once spoken in the first baptism, ever remains standing, so that afterwards they can come to faith in it, if they will, and the water with which they were baptized they can afterwards receive in faith, if they will. Even if they contradict the Word a hundred times, it still remains the Word spoken in the first baptism. Its power does not derive from the fact that it is repeated many times or is spoken anew, but from the fact that it was commanded once to be spoken.

It is the devil's masterpiece when he can get someone to compel the Christian to leave the righteousness of faith for a righteousness of works, as he forced the Galatians and Corinthians on to works though, as St. Paul writes, they were doing well in their faith and running rightly in Christ [Gal. 5:7]. So now, as he sees the Germans through the gospel acknowledging Christ in a fine way and believing as they should, so that they thereby were righteous before God, he interferes and tears them away from this righteousness, as if it were vain, and leads them into rebaptizing as if this were a better righteousness. He causes them thus to reject their former righteousness as ineffectual and to fall prey to a false righteousness. What shall I say? We Germans are and remain true Galatians.[10] For whoever permits himself be rebaptized rejects his former faith and righteousness, and is guilty of sin and condemnation. Of all things such behavior is most horrible. As St. Paul, says, the Galatians have severed themselves from Christ [Gal. 5:4], even making Christ a servant of sin, when they circumcise themselves.

Satan does these things against us, in order to make our teach-

---

[10] Cf. WA 18, 121.

ing seem contemptible, as if we could not have the right spirit or teaching because we had not been rightly baptized. But we know the tree by its fruits [Matt. 7:16f.]. For neither among the papists nor among these rebellious spirits do we find men who can handle and interpret Scripture as skilfully as do those on our side by the grace of God. This is not the least of the Spirit's gifts (I Cor. 12 [:10]). We see among them the natural fruit of the devil, namely, that some of them on account of rebaptism desert wife and child, house and land, and will recognize no authority. Yet St. Paul teaches that whoever does not provide for his own has disowned his faith and is worse than an unbeliever (I Tim. 6 [5:8]). And in I Cor. 7 [:13] he expresses as his desire that a wife who believes should not divorce an unbelieving husband. Nor does Christ want a marriage broken, except where adultery becomes a reason for it. Our spirit not only allows but commands that every estate should remain and be held in honor, and that faith should exercise itself peacefully in love [Cf. Gal. 5:6] so that no uprising or complaint could fairly be charged to our teaching. The papists of course by their lies blame us for all manner of ills, but even their own consciences are here in many instances their own judges.

This refutes too their position that baptism does not avail in case the priest or he who baptizes did not have faith. For even if St. Peter baptized, no one would know for certain if in that moment he stood in faith or in doubt. For no one can discern his heart. In brief, such arguments once led the Donatists[11] to separate themselves and to rebaptize, when they saw how unholy some were who preached and baptized. They began to base baptism on the holiness of men, though Christ had based it on his Word and commandment. That is also the attempt of our rebellious spirits, the foes of the sacrament. They maintain, of course, that the truth and Scripture compel them, but they lie nevertheless. They are offended (as they sometimes experience) that any rogue may bring Christ into the bread of the sacrament,[12] as if all the world were sure that they themselves have faith and are completely holy. They act as

---

[11] The Donatists were the group against whom Augustine defended the validity of the church's sacraments even if wicked priests administered them or wicked people received them. Cf. LW 13, 89.

[12] Cf. WA 18, 165ff.

though they were not great rogues in the eyes of God, just as much as they who sharply condemn wickedness and call others rascals, forgetting the beam in their own eye.

We recall that St. John was not averse to hearing the Word of God from Caiaphas and pays attention to his prophecy [John 11:49f.]. Moses and the people of Israel received the prophecy of the godless Balaam as a word from God [Num. 24:17]. So also St. Paul recognized the heathen poets Aratus and Epimenides and honored their saying (as a word of God).[13] And Christ bids us hear the godless Pharisees in the seat of Moses, though they are godless teachers. We need to be much less self-complacent. Let God judge their evil lies. We can still listen to their godly words. For if they are evil, it is to their own harm. If they teach correctly, we can be correctly instructed. Consider the pious Magi in Matt. 2 [:4ff.]. They heard the Word of God from the book of Micah through the mouth of Herod, the cruel king, who in turn had heard it from the godless high priests and scribes. Still on that Word they set out for Bethlehem and found Christ. It was no great hindrance that they heard the Word of God only through Herod the murderer of Christ.

Still we must admit that the enthusiasts have the Scriptures and the Word of God in other doctrines. Whoever hears it from them and believes will be saved, even though they are unholy heretics and blasphemers of Christ. It is not a minor grace that God gives his Word even through evil rogues and the godless. In fact it is in some respects more perilous when he proclaims it through holy than through unholy folk. For the thoughtless are tempted to attach themselves to the holiness of the people rather than to the Word of God. Greater honor is then given to man than to God and his Word. This danger does not exist when Judas, Caiaphas, and Herod preach, though no one can make this an excuse for an evil life if God can make some use of such. Now if a godless man can have and teach the Word of God correctly, much more can he baptize and give the sacrament properly. For it is a greater thing to teach the Word of God than to baptize, as St. Paul boasts

---

[13] "For we are indeed his offspring" [Acts 17:28], is a quotation from *Phainomena* 5, by Aratus of Sicily. "Cretans are always liars," etc. [Titus 1:12] is a quotation from the work of Epimenides of Gnossus (600 B.C.). WA 26, 163.

in I Cor. 1 [:17]. As we have said, whoever makes baptism dependent on the faith of him who baptizes will never receive baptism from anyone. For if I ask you if you have been rebaptized, and you say, yes, I again ask, how do you know that you now are rightly baptized? Were you to reply, because he who baptized me has faith, I would ask, how do you know that? Have you looked into his heart? So there you are, like butter in sunshine.

Our baptism, thus, is a strong and sure foundation, affirming that God has made a covenant with all the world to be a God of the heathen in all the world, as the gospel says. Also, that Christ has commanded the gospel to be preached in all the world, as also the prophets have declared in many ways. As a sign of this covenant he has instituted baptism, commanded and enjoined upon all heathen, as Matt. [28:19] declares: "Go therefore and make disciples of all nations, baptizing them in the name of the Father," etc. In the same manner he had made a covenant with Abraham and his descendants to be their God, and made circumcision a sign of this covenant. Here, namely, that we are baptized; not because we are certain of our faith but because it is the command and will of God. For even if I were never certain any more of faith, I still am certain of the command of God, that God has bidden to baptize, for this he has made known throughout the world. In this I cannot err, for God's command cannot deceive. But of my faith he has never said anything to anyone, nor issued an order or command concerning it.

True, one should add faith to baptism. But we are not to base baptism on faith. There is quite a difference between having faith, on the one hand, and depending on one's faith and making baptism depend on faith, on the other. Whoever allows himself to be baptized on the strength of his faith, is not only uncertain, but also an idolator who denies Christ. For he trusts in and builds on something of his own, namely, on a gift which he has from God, and not on God's Word alone. So another may build on and trust in his strength, wealth, power, wisdom, holiness, which also are gifts given him by God. But a baptism on the Word and command of God even when faith is not present is still a correct and certain baptism if it takes place as God commanded. Granted, it is not of benefit to the baptized one who is without faith, because of his lack of faith, but the baptism is not thereby incorrect, uncertain, or of no meaning. If we were to consider everything wrong or ineffectual which is of no value to the unbeliever, then nothing would be right or remain good. It has been commanded that the gospel should be preached to all the world. The unbeliever hears it but it has no meaning for him. Are we therefore to look on the gospel as not being a gospel or as being a false gospel? The godless see no value in God himself. Does that mean he is not God?

If an adult wants to be baptized and says, "Sir, I want to be baptized," you ask, "Do you believe?" Just as Philip asked the chamberlain in Acts 4 [8:37] and as we daily ask those to be baptized. Then he will not blurt out and say, "Yes, I intend to move mountains by my faith." Instead he will say, "Yes, Sir, I do believe, but I do not build on this my faith. It might be too weak or uncertain. I want to be baptized because it is God's command that I should be, and on the strength of this command I dare to be baptized. In time my faith may become what it may. If I am baptized on his bidding I know for certain that I am baptized. Were I to be baptized on my own faith, I might tomorrow find myself unbaptized, if faith failed me, or I became worried that I might not yesterday have had the faith rightly. But now that doesn't affect me. God and his command may be attacked, but I am certain enough that I have been baptized on his Word. My faith and I make this venture. If I believe, this baptism is of value to me. If I do not believe, it is not of value. But baptism in itself is not therefore wrong or uncertain, is not a matter of venture, but is as sure as are the Word and command of God."

Of his baptism as a child he would say, I thank God and am happy that I was baptized as a child, for thus I have done what God commanded. Whether I have believed or not, I have followed the command of God and been baptized and my baptism was correct and certain. God grant that whether my faith today be certain or uncertain, or I think that I believe and am certain, nothing is lacking in baptism. Always something is lacking in faith. However long our life, always there is enough to learn in regard to faith. It can happen that faith fails, so that it is said, "See, he had faith but has it no more." But one cannot say about baptism, "See, baptism was there but is no longer present." No, it remains, for the command of God remains, and what is done according to his command stands and will ever remain.

Up to this point we have clearly and sufficiently proved, in my opinion, that the Anabaptists do wrong in denying the first baptism, as if they were sure that children were baptized without faith, though of this they cannot be certain. On the other hand we cannot prove that children do believe with any Scripture verse that clearly and expressly declares in so many words, or the like, "You are to baptize children because they also believe." Whoever compels us to produce such a statement has the upper hand and wins, for we cannot find such words. But sincere and sensible Christians do not require such proof. The quarrelsome, obstinate rebellious spirits do in order to seem to be clever. But on their side they can produce no statement which says, "You are to baptize adults but no children." We are however persuaded by many good reasons to hold that child baptism is right and that children do believe.

First, because child baptism derives from the apostles and has been practiced since the days of the apostles. We cannot oppose it, but must let it continue, since no one has yet been able to prove that in baptism children do not believe or that such baptism is wrong. For even if I were not sure that they believed, yet for my conscience's sake I would have to let them be baptized. I would much rather allow them baptism than to keep them from it. For if, as we believe, baptism is right and useful and brings the children to salvation, and I then did away with it, then I would be responsible for all the children who were lost because they were unbaptized—a cruel and terrible thing. If baptism is not right, that is, without value or help to the children, then I would be guilty of no greater sin than the Word of God had been spoken and his sign given in vain. I would not be responsible for the loss of any soul, but only of an ineffectual use of the Word and sign of God.

But this God would easily forgive me, since it was done in ignorance and more than that out of fear. I did not invent it. It came to me by tradition and I was persuaded by no word of Scripture that it was wrong. I would have been unwilling to do it, had I been convinced otherwise. It would be very much as when I preach the Word, also according to his command, among the unbelieving and without fruit, or as it is said, cast pearls before swine, or holy things to the dogs [Matt. 7:6]. What could I do? Here, too, I would rather sin in preaching fruitlessly than in refusing to preach at all. For in fruitless preaching I would not be guilty of a soul [being lost] while in refusing to preach I might be held accountable for many souls. That would be too much for any individual. This I say even if there were uncertainty about the faith of children in baptism, for we cannot set aside baptism which is certain, on account of faith which is uncertain. Baptism did not originate with us, but with the apostles and we should not discard or alter what cannot be discarded or altered on clear scriptural authority. God is wonderful in his works. What he does not will, he clearly witnesses to in Scripture. What is not so witnessed to there, we can accept as his work. We are guiltless and he will not mislead us. If we knew or believed that child baptism was useless, it would be a wicked thing to still baptize. So the Waldenses do, but that is to despise God and his Word.

In the second place, this is an important consideration: No heresy endures to the end, but always, as St. Peter says, soon comes to light and is revealed as disgraceful. So St. Paul mentions Jannes and Jambres and their like [II Tim. 3:8f.], whose folly is finally plain to all. Were child baptism now wrong God would certainly not have permitted it to continue so long, nor let it become so universally and thoroughly established in all Christendom, but it would sometime have gone down in disgrace. The fact that the Anabaptists now dishonor it does not mean anything final or injurious to it. Just as God has established that Christians in all the world have accepted the Bible as Bible, the Lord's Prayer as Lord's Prayer, and faith of a child as faith, so also he has established child baptism and kept it from being rejected while all kinds of heresies have disappeared which are much more recent and later than child baptism. This miracle of God is an indication that child baptism must be right. He has not so upheld the papacy, which also is an innovation and has never been accepted by all Christians of the world as has child baptism, the Bible, faith, or the Lord's Prayer, etc.

You say, this does not prove that child baptism is certain. For there is no passage in Scripture for it. My answer: that is true. From Scripture we cannot clearly conclude that you could establish child baptism as a practice among the first Christians after the apostles. But you can well conclude that in our day no one may reject or neglect the practice of child baptism which has so long a tradition, since God actually not only has permitted it, but from the beginning so ordered, that it has not yet disappeared.

For where we see the work of God we should yield and believe in the same way as when we hear his Word, unless the plain Scripture tells us otherwise. I indeed am ready to let the papacy be considered as a work of God. But since Scripture is against it, I consider it as a work of God but not as a work of grace. It is a work of wrath from which to flee, as other plagues also are works of God, but works of wrath and displeasure.

In the third place, it is likewise the work of God that during all the time children were being baptized, he has given great and holy gifts to many of them, enlightened and strengthened them with the Holy Spirit and understanding of the Scripture, and accomplished great things in Christendom through them. John Huss[14] and his colleagues are examples from that time, and many other holy men before him. He does the same to very many of his people in our day. He has not hitherto driven them to the Anabaptists, which undoubtedly he would have done if he had judged his commandment concerning baptism improperly observed. He does not contradict himself, nor would he favor with his gifts those who disobey his commands. Since he thus gives such gifts as we must admit to be holy gifts of God, he confirms, of course, thereby the first baptism and considers us rightly baptized. By these works we thus prove the first baptism to be proper and rebaptism to be wrong, just as St. Peter and St. Paul (Acts 15 [:8f]) from the miracle of the gift of the Holy Spirit to the heathen proved that it was the will of God that heathen need not heed the law of Moses.

In the fourth place, if the first, or child, baptism were not right, it would follow that for more than a thousand years there was no baptism or any Christendom, which is impossible. For in that case the article of the creed, I believe in one holy Christian church, would be false. For over a thousand years there were hardly any

---

[14] John Huss, reformer of Bohemia, was burned at the stake at Constance on June 6, 1415, as a heretic. Luther found himself in agreement with many views held by Huss, notably concerning the papacy. Cf. *LW* 31, 321.

other but child baptisms. If this baptism is wrong then for that long period Christendom would have been without baptism, and if it were without baptism it would not be Christendom. For the Christian church is the bride of Christ, subject and obedient to him. It has his Spirit, his Word, his baptism, his sacrament, and all that Christ has. If, indeed, child baptism were not common throughout the world, but (like the papacy) were accepted only by some, then the Anabaptists might seem to have a case and might attack those who receive it, just as we oppose the clergy who have made a sacrifice out of the sacrament though among the laity it still remains a sacrament. But the fact that child baptism has spread throughout all the Christian world to this day gives rise to no probability that it is wrong, but rather to a strong indication that it is right.

In the fifth place, the words of St. Paul in II Thess. 2 [:4] concerning the Antichrist, that he shall sit in the temple of God, of which we have already spoken, accord with our position. If it is the temple of God it is not a haunt of heretics, but true Christendom, which must truly have a baptism which is right beyond any doubt. We see and hear of no other than child baptism, whether under the pope, among the Turks, or in all the world. Christ commands the children to come and to be brought to him, and, in Matt. 19 [:14] says that theirs is the kingdom of God. The apostles baptized entire households [Acts 16:15]. John writes to little children [I John 2:12]. St. John had faith even in his mother's womb, as we have heard [Luke 1:41]. If all of these passages do not suffice for the enthusiasts, I shall not be concerned. They are enough for me, to stop the mouth of anyone from saying that child baptism does not mean anything. If they are still uncertain, I am satisfied if they do not henceforth do away with it but let it be in doubt among themselves. We, however, are certain enough, because it is nowhere contrary to Scripture, but is rather in accord with Scripture.

In the sixth place, since God has made a covenant with all heathen through the gospel and ordained baptism as a sign thereof, who can exclude the children? If the old covenant and the sign of circumcision made the children of Abraham believe that they were, and were called the people of God, according to the promise, I will be the God of thy descendants [Gen. 17:7], then this new covenant and sign must be much more effectual and make those a people of God who receive it. Now he commands that all the world shall receive it. On the strength of that command (since none is excluded) we confidently and freely baptize everyone, excluding no one except those who oppose it and refuse to receive this covenant. If we follow his command and baptize everyone, we leave it to him to be concerned about the faith of those baptized. We have done our best when we have preached and baptized. If now we have no particular passage of Scripture on the baptism of children, they on their side have just as little of Scripture which bids us baptize adults. But we have the command to offer the common gospel and the common baptism to everyone, and herein the children must be included. We plant and water and leave the growth to God [Cf. I Cor. 3:6].

In sum, the Anabaptists are too frivolous and insolent. For they consider baptism, not as a God-given ordinance or command, but as a human trifle, like many other customs under the papacy relating to the consecration of salt, water, or herbs. For if they looked on it as a God-given ordinance and command they would not speak so disgracefully and shamefully about it even if it were not rightly used. But now they have the insane idea that baptism is something like the consecration of water and salt or the wearing of cowl and tonsure. So they carry on and call it a dog's bath, or a handful of water, and other such vile things. Those who hold the gospel to be the right Word of God do not speak lightly of it even though there are many who do not believe or accept it, or who falsely use it. He who does not hold it as the Word of God is the one who treats it lightly, blasphemes and says it is fable, fairy story, or a counsel of fools, and the like. It ought to be easy for such a one to acquire disciples who believe such blasphemy.

Observe this well, that if the Anabaptists at first had presented their idea with good arguments, they would not have misled or won many persons. For they have no substantial or certain arguments. But they attract a great many people by using great, high-sounding words of slander against baptism. For the devil well knows that if the mad mob hears high-sounding words of slander, it falls for and readily believes them, asking for neither reason nor proof. So they hear it said, baptism is a dog's bath and those who baptize are false and foolish servants of bathkeepers. So they conclude, aha, so the devil baptizes, and God shame the false servants of bathkeepers. That is the position they take and have nothing else with which to attack baptism. For all those to whom I have ever listened when discussing these things with me delivered themselves of these high-sounding words of slander (dog's bath, servant of a bathkeeper, handful of water, etc.) and then stood there as shorn monks, having nothing more with which to defend their errors.

Very much in the same manner the devil also deceives those who blaspheme the sacrament. When he realizes that his lies do not produce much effect, he fares forth and fills the ears of the mad mob with high-sounding sacrilege, such as, our sacrament is an eating of flesh and guzzling of blood and the like. When they have exhausted those same high-sounding words their art is soon exhausted, and they begin to talk about the ascension of Christ.[15] The Jews do the same to this day. In order to keep their children in their faith they blaspheme Christ shamelessly, refer to him as "the hanged one" and confidently lie about him. This frightens an innocent, simple heart and misleads it, as St. Paul observes in Rom. 16 [:18]. For this reason they always have an easy time of it, for their high-sounding sacrilege has enabled them to lead the people whither they wanted, nor have they dared to establish firm ground for their error. Had they first formulated a good and solid foundation for their case then it would be sufficient to give the lie a good blow and set it forth in its true light.

We who know that baptism is a God-given thing, instituted and commanded by God himself, look not at its abuse by godless persons, but simply at God's ordinance. We find baptism in itself to be a holy, blessed, glorious, and heavenly thing, to be held in honor with fear and trembling, just as it is reasonable and right to hold any other ordinance and command of God. It is not the fault of baptism that many people abuse it. It would be as wrong to call the gospel a vain babbling because there are many who abuse it. Since then, as far as I have been able to see and hear, the Anabaptists have no argument but high-sounding words of sacrilege, everyone ought properly to shun and avoid them as messengers of none

---

[15] An allusion to Zwingli's doctrine of the bodily presence of Christ at the right hand of God.

other than the devil, sent out into the world to blaspheme the Word and ordinance of God so that people might not believe therein and be saved. For they are the birds who eat the seed sown by the wayside (Matt. 13 [:4]).

Finally I claim that if some one had not been baptized, but did not know it and firmly believed that he had been rightly baptized, that faith would be sufficient for him. For before God he has what he believes. All things (Christ says) are possible to him who believes [Mark 9:23]. To rebaptize such a one would be to imperil his faith. How much less, then, should we rebaptize those who are sure they have been baptized! God grant they then believed, but it makes no difference if they did not. The Anabaptists cannot be sure their baptism is a right one, since they base their rebaptizing on a faith of which they cannot be sure. Hence they play a gambling game with those they rebaptize. To be uncertain and dubious in godly things is to sin and tempt God. Whoever teaches deceit for uncertainty in place of sure truth lies in the same way as he who speaks openly against the truth. For he speaks that of which he is himself not sure and yet wants it to be taken as truth. But whoever would base baptism on the commandment and ordinance of God would soon realize that rebaptism is neither necessary nor useful. The first baptism sufficiently meets the requirement of God.

They are guilty also of blaspheming and denying the commandment and work of God. For while the first baptism is in accord with the commandment of God and justice is done to it by its very performance, they still insist it is wrong and only a dog's bath. What else are they saying but that God's command and work are wrong and amount to a dog's bath? This they say for no other reason than that they demand a certainty of faith in baptism though it is impossible to have this certainty. This is to deny and blaspheme a sure command and work of God for an uncertain delusion.

Assume that the first baptism is without faith. Tell me which is the greater and the more important in the second baptism, the Word of God or faith? Is it not true that the Word of God is greater and more important than faith, since faith builds and is founded on the Word of God rather than God's Word on faith? Furthermore faith may waver and change, but God's Word remains forever [Isa. 40:6-9; I Pet. 1:24]. Then too, tell me, if one of these two should be otherwise, which should it rather be: the immutable Word or the changeable faith? Would it not more reasonably be the faith that should be subject to change rather than the Word of God? It is fairer to assume that the Word of God would change faith, if a right one were lacking, than that faith would change the Word of God. So they must confess that in the first baptism it was not the Word of God that was defective, but faith, and that what is needed is another faith and not another Word. Why then do they not concern themselves rather with a change of faith and let the Word remain unaltered? Shall we call God's Word and ordinance false because we do not truly believe it? In that case a true word would be rare and far between. If they were to act rightly according to their own peculiar logic they should be urging a rebelieving, not a rebaptizing. For baptism is by the Word and ordinance of God and dare not be opposed to it or other than it is, while faith may be otherwise than it is (if it is not present). So really they should be "Anabelievers" and not Anabaptists, if they were right, which, of course, they are not.

Since then these baptizers are altogether unsure of themselves, and reveal that they are lying, and thereby deny and blaspheme the ordinance of God through their deceitful uncertainty, making the last first, basing the Word and ordinance of God on human work and faith, urging baptism when they should be urging faith, every devout Christian, convinced that they are misleading, uncertain, and perverted spirits, should avoid them at the peril of his soul's salvation. May Christ, our Lord, grant this and help us. Amen.

This is as much as I can undertake now, briefly and hastily. For at this time I am not able to go into this matter more thoroughly. As mentioned I am not sure what they do believe. For the devil is mad and talks so wildly and stirs up so much confusion that absolutely no one knows what he believes. The Anabaptists agree with the foes of the sacrament that only bread and wine are in the Lord's Supper. Yet the sacramentarians disagree with the Anabaptists on baptism. Also, the sacramentarians are not agreed among themselves nor the Anabaptists among themselves. They are at one only in regard to and in opposition to us. Likewise the papacy is divided into innumerable factions of priests and monks who once devoured each other among themselves, until now, in their opposition to us, they are united. It is the same among temporal princes and lords. Pilate and Herod become one over against Christ, though previously they were mortal enemies. But in this particular case, the error of the Anabaptists is more tolerable than that of the sacramentarians. For the sacramentarians altogether destroy baptism, while the Anabaptists give it another character. Still there is reason to hope that they will right themselves. It is enough to have demonstrated that the Anabaptists' faith is uncertain and deceptive and that they cannot prove their case.

For Satan needs do no more through the enthusiasts than always to produce doubt. He thinks it is enough where he can speak haughtily and contemptuously about us, as the rebel sacramentarians do. None of them take pains to make clear and to prove their arrogance, but their concern is to make our interpretation contemptible and uncertain. They teach doubt, not faith, calling this Scripture and the Word of God. The devil knows he can accomplish nothing in the bright light of truth, so he stirs up the dust, hoping to raise a cloud before our eyes so that we cannot see the light. In the cloud he dazzles us with will o' the wisps to mislead us. Having made up their minds concerning their peculiar notions, they attempt to make the Scriptures agree with them by dragging passages in by the hair. But Christ has faithfully stood by our side up to this point and will continue to trod Satan under our foot. He will protect you all against the seductions of your tyrant and Antichrist and mercifully help us to gain his freedom. Amen.

19.

CONFESSION CONCERNING CHRIST'S SUPPER

* * *

Let this suffice to show that our interpretation is not contrary to Scripture or the Creed, as this mad spirit deludes himself into believing. Next he comes to the two principal points at which I have attacked most strongly, viz. that Christ is at the right hand of God, and that the flesh is of no avail,[61] where he was to prove that these two propositions make it impossible for Christ's body to be present in the Supper. I had called attention to these passages with capital letters,[62] so they might not skip over them. Now this dear spirit comes along with his figure, alloeosis,[63] to make everything plain, and teaches us that in the Scriptures one nature in Christ is taken for the other, until he falls into the abyss and concludes that the passage, "The Word became flesh," John 1 [:14], must not be understood as it reads, but thus: "The flesh became Word," or, "Man became God." This is to give the lie to Scripture.

I cannot at this time attack all this spirit's errors. But this I say: Whoever will take a warning, let him beware of Zwingli and shun his books as the prince of hell's poison. For the man is completely perverted and has entirely lost Christ. Other sacramen-

---

[61]*Christian Answer.* C. R. 92, 914ff.; *St. L.* 20, 1189 ff.

[62]See *That These Works of Christ, "This Is My Body,"* . . . (1527), *LW* 37, 144f.

[63] A section in *Friendly Exposition* is entitled, "On the Interchange (*De alloeosibus*) of the two natures in Christ." C. R. 92, 679 ff. (see footnotes there). A similar section is found in *Christian Answer.* C. R. 92, 922 ff.; *St. L.* 20, 1192 ff., and another in *Concerning Luther's Book Entitled "Confession,"* 1528, as printed in *St. L.* 20, 1309 ff. *Alloiōsis,* a word which in Plato and Aristotle and the Septuagint meant change, alteration, difference, became a technical rhetorical term in Plutarch's *Moralia,* ch. 41. Zwingli defines it as "an exchange [*abtuschen*] or interchange [*gegenwechsslen*] of the two natures which are in one person, by which in naming one nature we mean the other, or name them both but mean only the one." C. R. 92, 925 f., *St. L.* 20, 1194 f. Zwingli asserts that the patristic "communication of properties" concept involved just such a rhetorical *alloeosis.* Cf. *Clear Instruction.* LCC 24, 212 ff.

tarians settle on one error, but this man never publishes a book without spewing out new errors, more and more all the time. But anyone who rejects this warning may go his way, just so he knows that I warned him, and my conscience is clear.

You must not believe or admit that this figure, alloeosis, is to be found in these passages, or that you can put one nature of Christ in place of the other. The insane spirit dreamed this up in order to rob us of Christ, for he does not prove it to you nor can he do so. And even if this error of his were true and right, it still would not prove that Christ's body cannot be present in the Supper. I have pressed them to show conclusive grounds why these words, "This is my body," just as they read, are false, though Christ is in heaven. For the power of God is not known to us, and he can find a way to make both true, viz. Christ in heaven and his body present in the Supper. That was the principal question. What I demanded, writing in capital letters, was that they should show how the two were contradictory. But he is silent on this point, passes over it without one letter as if it did not concern him, and spouts meanwhile about his alloeosis.

When I proved that Christ's body is everywhere because the right hand of God is everywhere,[64] I did so—as I quite openly explained at the time—in order to show at least in one way how God could bring it about that Christ is in heaven and his body in the Supper at the same time, and that he reserved to his divine wisdom and power many more ways to accomplish the same result, because we do not know the limit or measure of his power.

Now if they had any intention or ability to answer, they should have proved incontrovertibly that there was no way within God's wisdom and power for Christ to be in heaven and at the same time for his body to be present in the Supper. Here is the difficulty over which these good fellows leap. For they did not need to teach us about the visible mode of existence, that according to our eyesight heaven is high above us and the Supper down here on earth. We know perfectly well that, to judge by our sight, what is here below cannot be above, and vice versa; for this is a human, visible mode of existence. But God's Word and works do

---

[64]See *LW* 37, 47ff., 55ff.

not proceed according to our eyesight, but in a way incomprehensible to all reason and even to the angels. So Christ is neither in heaven nor in the Supper in a visible manner, nor as fleshly eyes judge a thing to be at this place or that.

It certainly is a pitiful spirit who judges God's Word and works according to the eyes. For in this way God himself is not to be found wherever he may be, whether everywhere or somewhere. My friend, why then does this spirit cling to the one specific mode of existence which I pointed out? In the first place, because he is worried that his stomach may burst with all his cleverness. In the second place, because in this way he can fool the common people so that they will not see how he skips over questions which he ought to answer and starts a different game in order to sidetrack us and make us forget the matters which torment him. If I were to argue with them only over this one mode to which I referred, they would win the game. Why? Because then they would have an excuse to avoid answering the real problem which presses them, and still they would write one book after another to spew their useless chatter into the world. For they regard much spewing and writing of useless books as fitting rebuttal. So they betray the poor people.

This, then, is what you should do to protect yourself against them. If they prove conclusively that God's power and wisdom extend no farther than the range of our sight, and that he is able to do no more than we can physically see and judge with our eyes or touch with our fingers, then you should join their side. Then I too will believe that God knows of no other way whereby Christ can be at the same time in heaven and his body in the Supper. Demand and insist on this. They are bound to do it. Their teaching cannot be established until they have made this clear and certain, for on this their teaching rests.

The devil is well aware that he cannot furnish this proof; therefore he blusters loudly with his useless twaddle so that we may not press him for it. Meanwhile he spreads his cleverness which no one is asking for. Even if he could overthrow the mode to which I have referred—which he cannot—he still would have accomplished nothing by it, because it still would by no means have been proved a contradiction for Christ to be in heaven and his body in the bread. As I demanded in my previous book, he must prove not only that this mode of existence is impossible, but also that God himself cannot know or devise any other.[65] Since he does not do this, we now say: God is omnipotent; he can do more than we see; therefore I believe his words as they stand. See how these matters stand with this spirit and how he makes a fool of himself with all his learning!

To all his worthless spouting against the mode that I have mentioned, I answer with one little word: No! He brings in his alloeosis, which no one concedes him the right to do in this discussion; it is just as much in need of proof as the rest of his system of lies. But if he proved it, one could make further reply. So the mode of existence to which I have referred still stands absolutely firm, in spite of his alloeosis. Though he says it is an example of alloeosis, no one gives a rip about that; he might just as well say it was irony or some other trope. It simply won't do to play around with tropes[66] in the Scriptures. One must first prove that particular passages are tropes before one uses them in controversies. Oh, it is just as I have said: The devil has been hit so that he cannot answer, therefore he lashes about with vain words. God be praised and thanked that he knows how to arm us so well against the devil.

Dear brother, instead of alloeosis you should teach: Because Jesus Christ is true God and man in one person, in no passage of Scripture is one nature taken for the other. For he calls it alloeosis when something is said about the divinity of Christ which after all belongs to his humanity, or vice versa—for example, in Luke 24 [:26], "Was it not necessary that the Christ should suffer and so enter into his glory?" Here he performs a sleight-of-hand trick and substitutes the human nature for Christ. Beware, beware, I say, of this alloeosis, for it is the devil's mask since it will finally construct a kind of Christ after whom I would not want to be a Christian, that is, a Christ who is and does no more in his

---

[65]See *LW* 37, 47ff., 60ff.

[66] *Troppens odder troppelns.* The four chief kinds of trope were said to be metaphor, metonymy, synecdoche, and irony.

passion and his life than any other ordinary saint. For if I believe that only the human nature suffered for me, then Christ would be a poor Savior for me, in fact, he himself would need a Savior. In short, it is indescribable what the devil attempts with this alloeosis![67]

Indeed, this subject is an article of great importance and calls for a book itself, and should not come up in this matter at all. Briefly, however, a plain Christian should be satisfied with this: that the Holy Spirit knows quite well how to teach us the manner in which we should speak, and we need no trope-makers or crap-shooters.[68] The Holy Spirit speaks as follows, John 3 [:16], "God so loved the world that he gave his only Son"; Romans 8 [:32], "He did not spare his own Son but gave him up for us all." In the same way all his works, words, sufferings, and whatever Christ does, he does, accomplishes, speaks, and suffers as the true Son of God, so that it may properly be said, "The Son of God has died for us," "The Son of God preaches upon earth," "The Son of God washes his disciples' feet"; as the Epistle to the Hebrews says, chapter 6 [:6], "They crucify the Son of God on their own account," or I Corinthians 2: [:8], "If they had known, they would not have crucified the Lord of glory."

Now if the old witch, Lady Reason,[69] alloeosis' grandmother, should say that the Deity surely cannot suffer and die, then you must answer and say: That is true, but since the divinity and humanity are one person in Christ, the Scriptures ascribe to the divinity, because of this personal union, all that happens to humanity, and vice versa. And in reality it is so. Indeed, you must say that the person (pointing to Christ) suffers, and dies. But this person is truly God, and therefore it is correct to say: the Son of God suffers. Although, so to speak, the one part (namely, the divinity) does not suffer, nevertheless the person, who is God, suffers in the other part (namely, in the humanity).[70]

---

[67] Beginning with the second sentence of this paragraph, this passage is quoted in the *Formula of Concord,* Solid Declaration, VIII, 39 f.

[68] *Keiner troppeler noch toppeler.*

[69] Luther often referred to reason as the devil's bride or mother or grandmother, cf. *LW* 40, 174 f.

[70] This paragraph is quoted in the *Formula of Concord,* Solid Declaration, VIII, 41 f.

Just as we say: the king's son is wounded—when actually only his leg is wounded; Solomon is wise—though only his soul is wise; Absalom is handsome—though only his body is handsome; Peter is gray—though only his head is gray. For since body and soul are one person, everything that pertains to the body or the soul, yes, to the least member of the body, is correctly and properly ascribed to the entire person. This is the way people speak throughout the world, not only in Scripture, and it is the truth. For the Son of God truly is crucified for us, i.e. this person who is God. For that is what he is—this person, I say, is crucified according to his humanity.[71]

Thus we should ascribe to the whole person whatever pertains to one part of the person, because both parts constitute one person. This is the way all the ancient teachers speak; so do all modern theologians, all languages, and the whole Scripture. But this damned alloeosis exactly inverts the matter and changes it so that it ascribes to the parts what Scripture assigns to the whole person. He fashions his own tropes to pervert Scripture and divide the person of Christ, as he has also done with the word "is," just so he may bring to light his new teaching and his foolish ideas.

Well, if he is so fond of tropes, why isn't he satisfied with the old trope which Scripture and all teachers up to now have used? viz. *synecdoche*,[72] for example, "Christ died according to his humanity." But that would have been nothing new; no fame could have been won from it, and no new errors could have been produced. Therefore he had to bring forth alloeosis, and teach us that one nature is taken for the other. As if the apostles were so senseless and foolish that they could not speak of the divinity without calling it humanity, and vice versa. If John had wanted to use alloeosis, he could have said, "The flesh became Word," instead of saying, "The Word became flesh" [John 1:14].

Is this not a mischievous spirit, who blurts out his alloeosis in these passages? Who commanded him to do this? How does he prove there is an alloeosis here? No, this proof is not necessary;

---

[71] These last two sentences are quoted in the *Formula of Concord,* Solid Declaration, VIII, 42.

[72] Zwingli had actually cited the figure synecdoche in *On Baptism. LCC* 24, 147, *Friendly Rejoinder. C. R.* 92, 779; *St. L.* 20, 1111, and *Reply to Billican and Rhegius. C. R.* 91, 920.

it is enough if he says, "I, Zwingli, say there is an alloeosis here, therefore it is so. I was in the bosom of the Godhead yesterday and I have just come from heaven, therefore I must be believed!" He should prove first that there is an alloeosis here. This he fails to do, but assumes it as if he had established it a thousand years ago and no one may doubt it. But that there is an alloeosis here is much more in need of proof than that which he would like to establish with it. This is the principle of Zwinglian logic called "proving an uncertain proposition by something more uncertain, and an unknown by one more unknown." Oh, beautiful learning! The children should pelt it with dung and drive it away!

If it is proper for him to invent tropes and play around with figures as he pleases, and still be right in all he says, is it surprising that he ultimately makes a Belial out of Christ?[73] If anyone dares to assert whatever he pleases without being obliged to show his reasons, my friend, what conclusions may he not draw? It is no different from what I have complained of: this spirit appeals to Scripture to flatter people with fair words, and yet he produces nothing but his own dreams and his foolish imagination in opposition to Scripture. In this passage, however, we condemn and damn alloeosis right down to hell as the devil's own inspiration. We would like to see how he proposes to establish it. For what we want is Scripture and sound reasons, not his snot and slobber.

They raise a hue and cry against us, saying that we mingle the two natures into one essence.[74] This is not true. We do not say that divinity is humanity, or that the divine nature is the human nature, which would be confusing the natures into one essence. Rather, we merge the two distinct natures into one single person, and say: God is man and man is God. We in turn raise a hue and cry against them for separating the person of Christ as though there were two persons.[75] If Zwingli's alloeosis stands, then Christ

---

[73] Cf. II Cor. 6:15.

[74] *Christian Answer.* C. R. 92, 933 f.; *St. L.* 20, 1200. This is to accuse Luther of Monophysitism, which was condemned by the Fourth Ecumenical Council, at Chalcedon, in 451, and subsequently in the Athanasian Creed. For a discussion of the point at issue in another frame of reference see also Luther's *The Three Symbols or Creeds of the Christian Faith,* 1538. *LW* 34, 197 ff.

[75] Luther thus accuses the Zwinglians of Nestorianism, which was condemned by the Third Ecumenical Council, at Ephesus, 431, at Chalcedon as well,

will have to be two persons, one a divine and the other a human person, since Zwingli applies all the texts concerning the passion only to the human nature and completely excludes them from the divine nature. But if the works are divided and separated, the person will also have to be separated, since all the doing and suffering are not ascribed to natures but to persons. It is the person who does and suffers everything, the one thing according to this nature and the other thing according to the other nature, all of which scholars know perfectly well. Therefore we regard our Lord Christ as God and man in one person, "neither confusing the natures nor dividing the person." [76]

Let this suffice as a treatment of an incidental matter which would serve no useful purpose here, except that this spirit is so full of errors that he seeks occasion everywhere to dupe the simple, and meanwhile sidetrack the real issue. We stand firm, because this chatterbox will not and cannot prove that the two propositions, "Christ is in heaven, and his body is in the Supper," are contradictory. So the words, "This is my body," remain to us just as they read, for one letter of them is better and surer to us than the books of all the fanatics, even if they should fill the world with the books they write.

Again, since they do not prove that the right hand of God is a particular place in heaven,[77] the mode of existence of which I

---

and subsequently in the Athanasian Creed. The Chalcedonian Formula carefully steered between Monophysitism, which fused or *confused* the two natures of Christ and *converted* the human nature into the divine, and Nestorianism, which *divided* and *separated* the natures virtually into two persons. Zwingli defended himself at length against the charge of Nestorianizing in the section on Alloeosis in *Christian Answer. C. R.* 92, 922 ff.; *St. L.* 20, 1192 ff.

[76] Beginning with "If Zwingli's alloeosis . . .," this passage is quoted in the *Formula of Concord,* Solid Declaration, VIII, 43, which retouches it at two points: (a) in the second from the last sentence the Formula reads ". . . ascribed . . . to the person"; (b) in the last sentence the grammatical form of the Latin expression is emended from *confundens* to *confundendo* (as Luther's manuscript also had read), in better parallelism with *dividendo.*

[77] Zwingli had not argued that "the right hand of God" is a particular place in heaven; he acknowledged that God's right hand is everywhere, but asserted that Christ is not at God's right hand according to his humanity as he is according to his divinity. Zwingli distinguished between "Christ is everywhere" and "Christ's body is everywhere." *Christian Answer. C. R.* 92, 929 f.; *St. L.* 20, 1198 f.

have spoken also stands firm, that Christ's body is everywhere because it is at the right hand of God which is everywhere, although we do not know how that occurs. For we also do not know how it occurs that the right hand of God is everywhere. It is certainly not the mode by which we see with our eyes that an object is somewhere, as the fanatics regard the sacrament. But God no doubt has a mode by which it can be somewhere and that's the way it is until the fanatics prove the contrary.

Even if the alloeosis concept were valid, so that one nature could be taken for the other, still it would pertain only to the works or functions of the natures, and not the essence of the natures. For although in reference to his works—as when we say, "Christ preaches, drinks, prays, dies"—Christ might be taken as a designation for the human nature, the same could not be true in reference to his essence—as when we say, "God is man or man is God." Here there can be no alloeosis, indeed no synecdoche or other trope either, for here God must be taken as a designation for God, and man as a designation for man. Now when I write, "Christ's body is everywhere," I am treating not of the works of the natures, of course, but of the essence of the natures. Therefore neither alloeosis nor synecdoche can refute my argument, for essence is essence, each for itself and none for the other. Whoever wishes to refute my argument must not bring forth alloeoses or synecdoches or other tropes—these are good for nothing here—but he must refute my reasons on which my argument is based.

My grounds, on which I rest in this matter, are as follows: The first is this article of our faith, that Jesus Christ is essential, natural, true, complete God and man in one person, undivided and inseparable. The second, that the right hand of God is everywhere. The third, that the Word of God is not false or deceitful. The fourth, that God has and knows various ways to be present at a certain place, not only the single one of which the fanatics prattle, which the philosophers call "local." [78] Of this the sophists [79]

---

[78] This much of the paragraph is quoted in the *Formula of Concord*, Solid Declaration, VII, 93 ff., and (with an interpolation) Epitome, VII, 11 ff.

[79] Meaning in this case the Occamist Scholastics, from whom Luther adapted this analysis of the modes of existence or presence. Aquinas had recognized the first two modes. See Sasse, *This Is My Body*, pp. 155 ff.

properly say: There are three modes of being present in a given place: locally or circumscriptively, definitively, repletively.

Let me translate this for the sake of clearer understanding. In the first place, an object is circumscriptively or locally in a place, i.e. in a circumscribed manner,[80] if the space and the object occupying it exactly correspond and fit into the same measurements, such as wine or water in a cask, where the wine occupies no more space and the cask yields no more space than the volume of the wine. Or, a piece of wood or a tree in the water takes up no more space and the water yields no more than the size of the tree in it. Again, a man walking in the open air takes up no more space from the air around him, nor does the air yield more, than the size of the man. In this mode, space and object correspond exactly, item by item, just as a pewterer measures, pours off, and molds the tankard in its form.

In the second place, an object is in a place definitively,[81] i.e. in an uncircumscribed manner, if the object or body is not palpably in one place and is not measurable according to the dimensions of the place where it is, but can occupy either more room or less. Thus it is said that angels and spirits are in certain places. For an angel or devil can be present in an entire house or city; again, he can be in a room, a chest or a box, indeed, in a nutshell. The space is really material and circumscribed, and has its own dimensions of length, breadth, and depth; but that which occupies it has not the same length, breadth, or depth as the space which it occupies, indeed, it has no length or breadth at all. Thus we read in the gospel that the devil possesses men and enters them, and they also enter into swine. Indeed, in Matthew 8[82] we read that a whole legion were in one man. That would be about six thousand devils. This I call an uncircumscribed presence in a given place, since we cannot circumscribe or measure it as we measure a body, and yet it is obviously present in the place.

---

[80] *Begreifflich* could also be translated "comprehensible" or "determinate" in the sense of measurable.

[81] This is the more familiar spelling, cf. Aquinas. With the late medieval Occamists, Luther spelled the word *diffinitive.*

[82] Matt. 8:28 ff. relates the incident of the Gadarene (or Gerasene) demoniacs, but Luther's reference is to the parallel in Mark 5:9 ff. The Roman military legion numbered up to six thousand men.

This was the mode in which the body of Christ was present when he came out of the closed grave, and came to the disciples through a closed door, as the gospels show.[83] There was no measuring or defining of the space his head or foot occupied when he passed through the stone, yet he certainly had to pass through it. He took up no space, and the stone yielded him no space, but the stone remained stone, as entire and firm as before, and his body remained as large and thick as it was before. But he also was able, when he wished, to let himself be seen circumscribed in given places where he occupied space and his size could be measured. Just so, Christ can be and is in the bread, even though he can also show himself in circumscribed and visible form wherever he wills. For as the sealed stone and the closed door remained unaltered and unchanged, though his body at the same time was in the space entirely occupied by stone and wood, so he is also at the same time in the sacrament and where the bread and wine are, though the bread and wine in themselves remain unaltered and unchanged.

In the third place, an object occupies places repletively, i.e. supernaturally, if it is simultaneously present in all places whole and entire, and fills all places, yet without being measured or circumscribed by any place, in terms of the space which it occupies. This mode of existence belongs to God alone, as he says in the prophet Jeremiah [23:23 f.], "I am a God at hand and not afar off. I fill heaven and earth." This mode is altogether incomprehensible, beyond our reason, and can be maintained only with faith, in the Word.

All this I have related in order to show that there are more modes whereby an object may exist in a place than the one circumscribed, physical mode on which the fanatics insist. Moreover, Scripture irresistibly forces us to believe that Christ's body does not have to be present in a given place circumscriptively or corporeally, occupying and filling space in proportion to its size. For it was in the stone at the grave, but not in that circumscribed mode; similarly in the closed door, as they cannot deny. If it could be present there without space and place proportionate to

---

[83]Cf. Matt. 28:2 and John 20:19, 26.

its size, my friend, why can't it also be in the bread without space and room proportionate to its size? But if it can be present in this uncircumscribed manner, it is beyond the realm of material creatures and is not grasped or measured in their terms. Who can know how this takes place? Who will prove it false if someone declares that, since Christ's body is outside the realm of creation, it can assuredly be wherever he wishes, and that all creatures are as permeable and present to him as another body's material place or location is to it?

Consider our physical eyes and our power of vision. When we open our eyes, in one moment our sight is five or six miles[84] away, and simultaneously present everywhere within the range of those six miles. Yet this is only a matter of sight, the power of the eye. If physical sight can do this, do you not think that God's power can also find a way by which all creatures can be present and permeable to Christ's body? "Yes," you say, "but by this you do not prove that it is so." Thank you, I prove this much by it, that the fanatics also cannot refute me and prove that this is impossible to the divine power, which they should and must do. They should prove, I say, that God knows no other way by which the body of Christ can exist in a given place than corporeally and circumscriptively. If they cannot do this, their system stands disgraced. Of course, they cannot do it.

Because we prove from Scripture, however, that Christ's body can exist in a given place in other modes than this corporeal one, we have by the same token sufficiently argued that the words, "This is my body," ought to be believed as they read. For it is contrary to no article of faith, and moreover it is scriptural, in that Christ's body is held to have passed through the sealed stone and the closed door. Since we can point out a mode of existence other than the corporeal, circumscribed one, who will be so bold as to measure and span the power of God, as if He knows of no other modes? Yet the position of the fanatics cannot be maintained unless they can prove that the power of God can be thus measured and spanned, for their whole argument rests on the

---

[84] In terms of today's measurements this would be a distance of approximately twenty to twenty five miles.

assertion that the body of Christ can exist in a given place only in a corporeal and circumscribed manner. But here they are not answering but leaping over the question while they chatter about Lady Alloeosis.

And now to come to my own position: Our faith maintains that Christ is God and man, and the two natures are one person, so that this person may not be divided in two; therefore, he can surely show himself in a corporeal, circumscribed manner at whatever place he will, as he did after the resurrection and will do on the Last Day. But above and beyond this mode he can also use the second, uncircumscribed mode, as we have proved from the gospel[85] that he did at the grave and the closed door.

But now, since he is a man who is supernaturally one person with God, and apart from this man there is no God, it must follow that according to the third supernatural mode, he is and can be wherever God is and that everything is full of Christ through and through, even according to his humanity—not according to the first, corporeal, circumscribed mode, but according to the supernatural, divine mode. Here you must take your stand and say that wherever Christ is according to his divinity, he is there as a natural, divine person and he is also naturally and personally there, as his conception in his mother's womb proves conclusively. For if he was the Son of God, he had to be in his mother's womb naturally and personally and become man. But if he is present naturally and personally wherever he is, then he must be man there, too, since he is not two separate persons but a single person. Wherever this person is, it is the single, indivisible person, and if you can say, "Here is God," then you must also say, "Christ the man is present too."

And if you could show me one place where God is and not the man, then the person is already divided and I could at once say truthfully, "Here is God who is not man and has never become man." But no God like that for me! For it would follow from this that space and place had separated the two natures from one another and thus had divided the person, even though death and all the devils had been unable to separate and tear them apart.

---

[85]Cf. *LW* 37, 66.

This would leave me a poor sort of Christ, if he were present only at one single place, as a divine and human person, and if at all other places he had to be nothing more than a mere isolated God and a divine person without the humanity. No, comrade, wherever you place God for me, you must also place the humanity for me. They simply will not let themselves be separated and divided from each other. He has become one person and does not separate the humanity from himself[86] as Master Jack takes off his coat and lays it aside when he goes to bed.

Let me give a simple illustration for the common man. The humanity is more closely united with God than our skin with our flesh—yes, more closely than body and soul. Now as long as a man lives and remains in health, his skin and flesh, body and soul are so completely one being, one person, that they cannot be separated; on the contrary, wherever the soul is, there must the body be also, and wherever the flesh is, there must the skin be also. You cannot indicate a special place or space where the soul is present alone without the body, like a kernel without the shell, or where the flesh is without the skin, like a pea without a pod. On the contrary, wherever the one is, there must the other be also. Thus you cannot shell the divinity from the humanity and lay it aside at some place away from the humanity. For thereby you would be dividing the person and making the humanity merely a pod, indeed, a coat which the divinity put on and off according to the availability of place and space. Thus the physical space would have the power to divide the divine person, although neither angels nor all creation can do so.

Here you will say with Nicodemus, "How can this be?" [John 3:9]. Must all places and space now become one space and place? Or, as this dolt dreams according to his crude, fleshly sense, must the humanity of Christ stretch and extend itself like a skin as wide as all creation? I answer: Here you must with Moses take off your old shoes, and with Nicodemus be born anew.[87] According to your old notion, which perceives no more than the first, corporeal, circumscribed mode, you will understand this as little

---

[86] The entire two paragraphs down to this point are quoted in the *Formula of Concord*, Solid Declaration, VIII, 81 ff.
[87] Cf. Exod. 3:5, John 3:3.

as the fanatics, who cannot think of the Godhead in any other way than existing everywhere in a corporeal, circumscribed mode, as if God were some vast, extended entity that pervades and embraces all creation. This you may gather from their charge that we stretch and extend the humanity and thereby enclose the divinity.[88] Such words obviously apply to the corporeal, circumscribed mode of being, as a peasant stuffs himself into his jacket and trousers, when the jacket and trousers are expanded so that they will go around his body and his legs.

Get out of here, you stupid fanatic, with your worthless ideas! If you cannot think in higher and other terms than this, then sit behind the stove and stew pears and apples, and leave such subjects alone. If Christ passed through the closed door with his body, and the door was not on that account expanded nor his body compressed, why should the humanity here be expanded or the divinity enclosed, where there is a far different and more exalted mode of presence?

"This is a lofty subject," you say, "and I do not understand it." Yes, this is my complaint too, that these fleshly spirits who scarcely know how to crawl on the earth, untested in faith, inexperienced in spiritual matters, wish to fly aloft above the clouds and measure and judge these profound, mysterious, incomprehensible matters not according to God's words but according to their crawling and walking on the earth. They will fare as Icarus did in the poet's story.[89] For they too have stolen others' feathers —i.e. texts of Scripture—and fastened them on with wax—i.e. adjusted them to their own interpretation with reason—and now they fly aloft. But the wax melts, and they fall into the sea and drown in all kinds of errors.

Christ says, "If I have told you earthly things and you do not believe me, how can you believe it if I tell you heavenly things?" [John 3:12]. Behold, this is entirely an earthly and bodily thing, when Christ's body passes through the stone and the door. For his body is an object which can be laid hold of, as much so as the

---

[88]*Christian Answer.* C. R. 92, 935, 918; *St. L.* 20, 1201, 1190.
[89]The myth of Daedalus and Icarus is told in Ovid's *Metamorphoses*, II, 1 ff.

stone and the door. Still, no reason can grasp how his body and the stone are in one place at the same time when he passes through it, and yet neither does the stone become larger or expand more, nor Christ's body smaller or more compressed. Here faith must blind reason and lift it out of the physical, circumscribed mode into the second, uncircumscribed mode which it does not understand but cannot deny.

Now if this second mode must be understood by faith, and reason with its first, circumscribed mode must vanish, how much more must faith alone remain here and reason vanish in the case of the heavenly, supernatural mode, where Christ's body is one person with God in the Godhead? For everyone will grant me this, that it is a far different and higher mode when Christ's body is in the sealed stone and the closed door, than when according to the first mode it sits or stands in his clothes or walks in the open air about him. For here the air and the clothes extend and stretch themselves according to the size of his body which the eyes can see and the hands can touch. But in the stone and the door there is no expansion.

Further, everyone will grant me that it is a far more exalted existence and mode when Christ's body is one person with God, than when it is in the stone or the door. For God is no corporeal thing but a Spirit above all things. And Christ is not one person with the stone or the door, as he is with God. Therefore he must be in the Godhead in a greater and more profound manner than he is in the stone or the door, just as he is in the stone and the door more intimately and profoundly than in his clothes or in the open air. And if the stone and the door did not have to extend or expand themselves, nor enclose the body of Christ, much less in this most exalted mode does the humanity extend and expand itself or enclose and compress the divinity, as this fleshly spirit dreams.

The spirit must answer me and acknowledge that Christ's body has a far higher, supernatural existence, since he is one person with God, than he had when he was in the sealed stone and the door, since this is the highest mode and existence there is, and there cannot be anything higher than for a man to be one person with God. For the second mode, in which Christ's body existed in the stone, will also be common to all the saints in heaven; they will pass with their bodies through all the objects of creation, a property which is common even now to angels and devils. For the angel came to Peter in the prison, Acts 12 [:7]. And goblins come daily into closed chambers and storerooms. So he must also grant me that the stone does not extend itself or enclose Christ's body.

Why then does he babble about the highest existence and mode of all, where Christ is one person with God, saying that here the humanity had to expand and enclose God if it were to be omnipresent with God? Simply to flaunt his crude, fat, puffy ideas! He has never thought about God and Christ in any way but the first, corporeal, circumscribed mode. My friend, whether the humanity is in one place or in all places, it does not enclose the divinity; much less did the stone, which was in one place, enclose his body. Rather, it is one person with God, so that wherever God is, there also is the man; what God does, the man also is said to do; what the man suffers, God also is said to suffer.

Thus the one body of Christ has a threefold existence, or all three modes of being at a given place. First, the circumscribed corporeal mode of presence, as when he walked bodily on earth, when he occupied and yielded space according to his size. He can still employ this mode of presence when he wills to do so, as he did after his resurrection and as he will do on the Last Day, as Paul says in I Timothy [6:15], "Whom the blessed God will reveal," and Colossians 3 [:4], "When Christ your life reveals himself." He is not in God or with the Father or in heaven according to this mode, as this mad spirit dreams, for God is not a corporeal space or place. The passages which the spiritualists adduce concerning Christ's leaving the world and going to the Father[90] speak of this mode of presence.

Secondly, the uncircumscribed, spiritual mode of presence according to which he neither occupies nor yields space but passes through everything created as he wills. To use some crude illustrations, my vision passes through and exists in air, light, or water

---

[90] Especially John 16:28.

and does not occupy or yield any space; a sound or tone passes through and exists in air or water or a board and a wall and neither occupies nor yields space; likewise light and heat go through and exist in air, water, glass, or crystals and the like, but without occupying or yielding space, and many more like these. He employed this mode of presence when he left the closed grave and came through closed doors, in the bread and wine in the Supper, and, as people believe, when he was born in his mother.

Thirdly, since he is one person with God, the divine, heavenly mode, according to which all created things are indeed much more permeable and present to him than they are according to the second mode. For if according to the second mode he can be present in and with created things in such a way that they do not feel, touch, measure, or circumscribe him, how much more marvelously will he be present in all created things according to this exalted third mode, where they cannot measure or circumscribe him but where they are present to him so that he measures and circumscribes them. You must place this existence of Christ, which constitutes him one person with God, far, far beyond things created, as far as God transcends them; and on the other hand, place it as deep in and as near to all created things as God is in them. For he is one indivisible person with God, and wherever God is, he must be also, otherwise our faith is false.

But who can explain or even conceive how this occurs? We know indeed that it is so, that he is in God beyond all created things, and is one person with God. But how this happens, we do not know; it transcends nature and reason, even the comprehension of all the angels in heaven, and is known only to God. Since this is true, even though unknown to us, we should not give the lie to his words until we know how to prove certainly that the body of Christ cannot in any circumstances be where God is and that this mode of being is a fiction. Let the fanatics prove it! They will give it up.

I do not wish to have denied by the foregoing that God may have and know still other modes whereby Christ's body can be in a given place. My only purpose was to show what crass fools our fanatics are when they concede only the first, circumscribed mode of presence to the body of Christ although they are unable to prove that even this mode is contrary to our view. For I do not want to deny in any way that God's power is able to make a body be simultaneously in many places, even in a corporeal and circumscribed manner. For who wants to try to prove that God is unable to do that? Who has seen the limits of his power? The fanatics may indeed think that God is unable to do it, but who will believe their speculations? How will they establish the truth of that kind of speculation?[91]

If speculation is enough, then I too will speculate, better than they, and say: Even if Christ's body were just at one place, in heaven, as they prattle, yet all creatures may be present to him and around him even there, like the clear, transparent air. For, as has been said, a spirit can see, move, and hear through an iron wall as clearly and easily as I can see or hear through the air or through glass. And that which to our sight is solid and opaque, such as wood, stone, and brass, is to a spirit like glass, yes, like the clear air, as is well proved by goblins and angels, and as Christ also proved in the sealed stone and the closed door.

I have seen crystals or jewels within which was a kind of spark or flame, as in an opal, or a little cloud or bubble; and yet this little bubble or cloud shines as if it were at every side of the stone, for whichever way the stone is turned, the bubble can be seen as if it were at the very front of the stone, though it is really in the center of it. I am not speaking now from Scripture. But we must use our reason or else give way to the fanatics. If Christ also sat at one place in the center of the universe, like the bubble or spark in a crystal, and if a certain point in the universe were indicated to me, as the bread and wine are set forth to me by the Word, should I not be able to say, "See, there is the body of Christ actually in the bread," just as I say, when a certain side of the crystal is placed before my eyes, "See, there is the spark in the very front of the crystal"? Do you not suppose that God in a much truer and more miraculous way can set forth Christ's body in the bread, even if he were at a certain place in heaven, than show me the spark in a crystal?

---

[91] These five paragraphs, beginning with, "Thus the one body . . ." on p. 222, are quoted in the *Formula of Concord*, Solid Declaration, VII, 98 ff., which emends *dreyerley wesen*, "a threefold existence," in the first sentence of the passage, to *dreier* [*lei*] *Weisen*, "three different modes."

Not that I think this is certainly so, but it is not impossible with God. I only wish to give the fanatics something to mock and misinterpret, as they usually do. Yet I also wish to indicate thereby that they cannot maintain their position, or condemn our interpretation, even if it were true, as they say, that Christ is in heaven at a particular place. Of this, however, they too have no certain knowledge or proof. So far are they from demonstrated truth that even if their notions were correct—which they are not— still they cannot thereby prove their view of the Supper (that nothing but bread is there) nor refute ours.

Moreover, in order to show them that it takes no skill at all to speculate without Scripture, I give you the illustration of Lorenzo Valla.[92] A preacher stands and preaches. His voice is a single voice. It proceeds from his mouth, it is formed in his mouth, and it is in his mouth. But the same single voice, which is at one particular place, viz. in his mouth, passes in an instant into four, five, or ten thousand ears. And yet there is no other voice in those many thousand ears than the voice in the preacher's mouth, and it is at the same time, at the same instant, a single voice in the preacher's mouth and in all the people's ears, just as if his mouth and their ears were one point where his voice was located without any intervening space.

My friend, if God can do this with a physical voice, why should he not be able to do it far more easily with the body of Christ, even if it were at a particular place, as they say, and yet at the same time be truly in the bread and wine at many places, as it were in two ears? For his body is much quicker and lighter than any voice, and all creation is more permeable to him than the air is to the voice, as he proved in the ease of the grave-stone, inasmuch as no voice can pass through a stone as easily as Christ's body does.

These thoughts, however, I pursue no further than the point of truth in the fanatics' notions, that Christ is bodily and circum-

---

[92] In Valla's treatise, *On the Mystery of the Eucharist,* published in a Venetian edition of the works of Lactantius, 1521, as cited in *Nachträge* in WA 26, 656. Lorenzo Valla, 1405-1457, Italian humanist, Epicurean, and papal secretary, is best known for his demonstration that the "Donation of Constantine," for centuries a bulwark of papal claims to temporal authority, was a forgery.

scriptively at a particular place. Thus you may see, even to superfluity, that even though they contended for this, his body nonetheless can be in the Supper through God's power, because with created things even less significant, such as a voice, a tone, or a sound, it is not only possible but even natural and common, besides being palpable and tangible. Therefore their fancies are untenable that there must be nothing but bread in the Supper since Christ's body is in heaven.

One thing more. It was taught, even under the papacy, that if a mirror were broken into a thousand pieces, nevertheless the same complete image which had appeared previously in the whole mirror would remain in each piece. Here is the face of a man; he stands before the mirror and looks into it, and now in an instant the very same face is present, whole and entire, in every piece of the mirror. What if Christ also were in the bread and wine, and everywhere? For if God can do this with a man's face and a mirror, causing one face instantly to be in a thousand pieces or little mirrors, why should he not also make Christ's body so, that not only his image but he himself may be at many places at the same time, even if he were in heaven at a particular place, because it is much easier for his body to enter into the bread and wine than a face to enter into the mirror, since he passed through stone and iron, through which no image or face can pass?

"O you double papist!" they will shout. Well, let them shout if they please. With shouts they will be far from answering us, and nothing will be refuted; otherwise geese or asses or soused peasants might also become theologians. Nor have I seen any other point which the fanatics, these mighty Rolands[93] and giants, have won from the pope, that they should boast against the papists so loudly or justifiably. They have bared their teeth a little at the images—poor wood and stone!—but they have not bitten them yet. Now they attack baptism and the Supper, but so far they have not successfully carried out their aim.[94]

---

[93] Roland, in legend the nephew of Charlemagne, was the hero of many romantic tales, most famous being "The Song of Roland." Roland and the giants of mythology were favorite epithets of Luther against his ambitious opponents.

[94] Prominent in the overt break from Roman Catholicism in Zurich had been the removal of images from the churches, 1524. Luther implies that Zwingli's

I know very well that they may retort: The images in the mirror are not the face itself but its likeness, as bread and wine are signs of the Lord's body; hence the illustration is more for them than against them. But I also know, on the other hand, that bread and wine are not like the Lord's body, as the image in the mirror is like the face. Therefore the point of my illustration is this: If God can instantaneously make so many images of a face in a mirror, and if so marvelous a thing occurs naturally and visibly, it should be much more credible that he can cause Christ's body to be actually in many places in the bread and wine, even though he were in one physical place, as they dream. I have given this illustration to show how vacuous their notion is, which cannot imagine more than the single, circumscribed mode of existence in reference to Christ. And even if that were true, still what they would like to deduce from it would not follow. Far less will it follow since Christ's body does not exist in heaven in this physical, circumscribed mode, nor can they prove that he exists in heaven so.

Now this spirit rages against me that if Christ's body were everywhere that God is, I would become a Marcionite[95] and make a phantom Christ, because his body could not become so huge or so extended as to encompass the divinity, which is omnipresent. I reply, first: Perhaps this spirit is simply giving vent to his great petulance and rashness, for he does not prove that this follows from my argument, therefore I utterly disregard his prattle.

Secondly, he is well enough aware of the principle that to point out an inconsistency is not to refute arguments. If one inconsistent expression were sufficient, then no article of the Creed, indeed, no system of justice in the world could stand. But this proud, pompous spirit allows himself to imagine that if he simply declares a certain point inconsistent, such and such a consequence will necessarily follow, then it is inevitably so and needs no proof.

Thirdly, he reveals how crude and clumsy his ideas are by his inability to conceive of God's omnipresence except by imagining

doctrine would also destroy baptism and the Lord's Supper, cf. p. 16, n. 7, above.
[95] *Christian Answer. C. R.* 92, 937 ff., 918; *St. L.* 20, 1203 ff., 1190.

God as a vast, immense being that fills the world, pervades it and towers over it, just like a sack full of straw, bulging above and below, precisely according to the first, bodily, circumscribed mode. Then, of course, Christ's body would be a mere phantom and apparition, like an immense straw-sack with God and the heaven and the earth inside. Wouldn't that really be a crude way to think and speak of God?

But this is not the way we speak. We say that God is no such extended, long, broad, thick, high, deep being. He is a supernatural, inscrutable being who exists at the same time in every little seed, whole and entire, and yet also in all and above all and outside all created things. There is no need to enclose him here, as this spirit dreams, for a body is much, much too wide for the Godhead; it could contain many thousand Godheads. On the other hand, it is also far, far too narrow to contain one Godhead. Nothing is so small but God is still smaller, nothing so large but God is still larger, nothing is so short but God is still shorter, nothing so long but God is still longer, nothing is so broad but God is still broader, nothing so narrow but God is still narrower, and so on. He is an inexpressible being, above and beyond all that can be described or imagined.

But this is what this spirit should tell us: First, where there is Scripture or reason to prove that Christ's body has no other way of existing in a given place than the physical, circumscribed mode, like straw in a sack, or like bread in a basket or meat in a pot, especially since I have proved that he does have other modes, such as being in the gravestone. Again, that the right hand of God is a particular place in heaven. How does it happen that this spirit is so silent on this point, where there is the utmost necessity to speak out? Since he is so silent here, he has lost the argument, inasmuch as his belief rests upon this point, that Christ's body can have no other way to exist in heaven than the "local" mode, like straw in a sack, which however I have demonstrated to be obviously false. Here he should show his cleverness and prove his point. But how can he? He has got too deep in the mud and can't get out!

Secondly, the spirit should answer this: Christ is God and man, and his humanity has become one person with God, and is thus wholly and completely drawn into God above all creatures, so that he remains perfectly united with him. How is it possible, then, for God to be somewhere where Christ as man is not? How can it happen, without dividing the person, that God may be here without the humanity and there with the humanity?—especially since we have not two Gods but only one God, and yet this God is wholly and perfectly man according to one person, viz. the Son. What does it mean that he prattles so much at other places, but here where he needs to speaks, he skips over it and remains silent?

If God and man are one person and the two natures are so united that they belong together more intimately than body and soul, then Christ must also be man wherever he is God. If he is both God and man at one place, why should he not also be both man and God at a second place? If he is both man and God at a second place, why not at a third, fourth, or fifth, and so forth, at all places? But if the third, fourth, or fifth places do not permit him to be both man and God at the same time, neither would the first, original place permit him to be both man and God at the same time. For if place or space can divide the person, the first place can do it as well as all the others. Here an answer should have been forthcoming. It was on this point that I insisted when I showed that God and man were one person, and that Christ thereby had acquired a supernatural existence or mode of being whereby he can be everywhere.

If we wish to be Christians and think and speak rightly about Christ, we must regard his divinity as extending beyond and above all creatures. Secondly, we must assert that though his humanity is a created thing, yet since it is the only creature so united with God as to constitute it one person with the divinity, it must be higher than all other creatures and above and beyond them, under God alone. Well, this is our faith. Here we come with a Christ beyond all creatures, both according to his humanity and his divinity; with his humanity we enter a different land from that in which it moved here on earth, viz. beyond and above all creatures and purely in the Godhead. Now let faith be the judge and arbiter here. Beyond the creatures there is only God; accordingly, since this humanity also is beyond the creatures, it must be wherever God is, without fail. In essence, however, it cannot be God, but because it reaches up above all creation to the essential God and is united with him and is wherever God is, it must be at least in person God and thus exist everywhere that God is.

Of course, our reason takes a foolish attitude, since it is accustomed to understanding the word "in" only in a physical, circumscribed sense like straw in a sack and bread in a basket. Consequently, when it hears that God is in this or that object, it always thinks of the straw-sack and the breadbasket. But faith understands that in these matters "in" is equivalent to "above," "beyond," "beneath," "through and through," and "everywhere." Oh, why do I speak of such exalted matters? They are ineffable, and unnecessary for the common man; for the fanatics, though, they are utterly useless and even harmful. They understand the matter as little as an ass does the Psalter, except that they may wrench a little piece from it and abuse and mutilate it, as an excuse for ignoring and skipping over the main subjects. Thus Zwingli plays the fool and deduces from my argument that if Christ is everywhere, he cannot be received by the mouth, unless the mouth is everywhere too. This is plain, malicious perversion in which the devil shows his hand.

Therefore I will stop speaking about this subject here too. If anyone is open to advice, he has had enough; if anyone does not want it, let him go his way. For the common man, the simple words suffice which Christ spoke at the Supper, "This is my body," for the fanatics can produce nothing certain or irrefutable against it, nor do they answer correctly on any point. He who in these important matters is found standing on shaky ground, in even one point, should rightly be held in suspicion and shunned, especially since they boast with such arrogant self-confidence that they have Scripture on their side and everything is settled. How much more should they be regarded as erring, puffed up sectarians, since they are found standing not just upon one but upon a whole host of bad arguments, so frequently do they openly lie and fail to answer any point correctly.

Zwingli particularly is not worth answering further, unless he retracts his blasphemous alloeosis. As the saying goes, a manifest lie does not deserve an answer. Hence, also, one who denies a common article of faith is to be shunned as a manifest heretic. Now Zwingli not only denies this most exalted and necessary article, that the Son of God died for us; he actually blasphemes it, saying it is the most outrageous heresy that ever existed. His imagination and damned alloeosis lead him to divide the person of Christ, and he leaves us no other Christ than a mere man who died for us and redeemed us. But what Christian heart can hear or endure this? This teaching altogether rejects and condemns the entire Christian faith and the whole world's salvation. For whoever is redeemed by the humanity only, is certainly not yet redeemed, nor will he ever be redeemed.

There is neither time nor space to treat this matter further. I testify on my part that I regard Zwingli as un-Christian, with all his teaching, for he holds and teaches no part of the Christian faith rightly. He is seven times worse than when he was a papist, according to the declaration in Matthew 9 [12:45], "The last state of that man becomes worse than the first." I make this testimony in order that I may stand blameless before God and the world as one who never partook of Zwingli's teaching, nor will I ever do so.

The sum of the whole matter is this: we recognize here no alloeosis, no heterosis,[96] no ethopoeia,[97] nor any other trick that Zwingli produces out of his magician's kit. Reasons we demand out of Scripture, and not cleverness out of his imagination. We are not interested in his fearful fuming and foaming as if he were seized with a towering rage. Wrath and rage will not overthrow our interpretation. This wrathful spirit will not produce anything to convince us that Christ's body cannot be at the same time in heaven and in the Supper in accordance with the words, "This is my body." Perhaps in his great wrath, or out of lofty moderation, he is letting this subject rest, meanwhile roaring by and teaching us new tropes needlessly. He recklessly deduces and concludes that were my teaching to prevail, if Christ's body is present

---

[96] *Christian Answer. C. R.* 92, 935; *St. L.* 20, 1201. The word is used as a synonym for alloeosis.

[97] Zwingli defined *ēthopoiia* (which Luther transliterated *ithipeia*) as "the ascription of a common custom, used when one imputes to a person a character which the person does not by nature possess," e.g. describing God with anthropomorphisms, or Jesus in John 3:13 and Phil. 2:7 as Son of *man*. *Christian Answer. C. R.* 92, 938; *St. L.* 20, 1203.

wherever God is, then Christ's body would be a second infinite category, like God himself.[98] But he could easily see, if his wrath did not blind him, that this does not follow at all. If the world is not infinite in itself, how should it follow that Christ's body is infinite if he is everywhere? Besides this blind spirit draws his conclusion according to the crude, circumscribed mode; and yet we know that God has more than one way of causing a thing to be in a given place, as has been proved above. An angel can be at the same time in heaven and on earth, as Christ shows, Matthew 18 [:10]: "Their angels always behold the face of my Father in heaven." If they serve us, they are with us on earth; still, they always behold the Father's face in heaven. Yet they are not infinite beings.

This clumsy spirit does not yet know what it means to be in heaven, yet he wants to jump to conclusions on the subject. When I said that Christ was in heaven even while he was still walking on earth, as John 3 [:13] says, "The Son of man who is in heaven," God help us, how he jumped to weird conclusions! "How," he declared, "could Christ be in heaven at that time? Is there eating and drinking in heaven? Is there suffering and dying in heaven? Is there sleep and repose in heaven? See what you have got yourself into, you mad Luther? Phooey on you!" [99] What do you think of this spirit's victory? He has conquered Constantinople and devoured the Turks,[100] and his magician's kit full of alloeoses and ethopoeias begins to dance for joy.

Get out of here, you handsome devil! Let any faithful Christian tell me if it is not a higher and greater thing for the humanity to be in God, yes, to be one person with God, than for it merely to be in heaven. Isn't God higher and more glorious than heaven? Now, the humanity of Christ from his mother's womb was more profoundly and deeply in God and in God's presence than any angel, and certainly it was more profoundly in heaven than any angel. For whatever is in God and in God's presence is in heaven,

---

[98] *Christian Answer.* C. R. 92, 929 ff.; St. L. 20, 1197 ff.

[99] Here, as frequently, Luther is freely paraphrasing Zwingli. *Christian Answer.* C. R. 92, 940; St. L. 20, 1204.

[100] The fall of Constantinople in 1453 had been a fearful shock to Christendom. The Turks continued their conquests through the Balkans, and even besieged Vienna in 1529.

just as the angels are, even when they are on earth, as it is said in Matthew 18 [:10]. Unless God himself is no longer in heaven! So I might draw a Zwinglian conclusion and babble, "Is there eating and drinking in the Godhead? Is there suffering and dying in the Godhead? See what you have got yourself into, you mad John the Evangelist, who try to teach us that Christ is God and in the Godhead? For if there is no suffering or dying, or eating or drinking with God, the humanity of Christ cannot be with God, much less can it be one person with God." "This is what I was trying to do with my trickery," says the devil, "but, you spiteful Luther, you have ripped the bottom out of my magician's bag!"

Now if Christ can suffer and die on earth, even though he is at the same time in the Godhead and is one person with God, why should he not much more be able to suffer on earth, though he is at the same time in heaven? If heaven prevented it, much more would the Godhead prevent it. Indeed, what if I said that not only Christ was in heaven when he walked on earth, but also the apostles and all the rest of us mortals on earth, insofar as we believe in Christ? That would kick up a rumpus in Zwingli's magician's kit! He would start drawing conclusions and ask, "Is there also sin in heaven? Is there error in heaven? Does the devil assail us in heaven? Does the world persecute us in heaven? Do flesh and blood tempt us in heaven? And so forth. For we sin and err constantly, as we learn from the Lord's Prayer, 'Forgive us our trespasses' [Matt. 6:12], and we are continually being assailed by the devil, the world, and the flesh. In this way you would place the devil and the world and flesh and blood in heaven. See what you have got yourself into, you mad Luther! Phooey! Won't you ever learn that our spirit is no buffoon? Now, there you have it!"

What shall I do with him? St. Paul has misled me when he said, Ephesians 1 [:3], "God has blessed us with every spiritual blessing in the heavenly places," and again, chapter 2 [:5 f.], "He has made us alive together with Christ and raised us up with him, and made us sit with him in the heavenly places," and in Colossians 3 [:3] he says, "Our life is hid with Christ in God," which certainly means in heaven.

But here this spirit can call on his magician's kit to produce an alloeosis or an ethopoeia, which teach us to make an exchange and take one thing for another; so heaven must mean earth, just as he interprets John 6 [:51 ff.] to mean that Christ's flesh must mean his divinity. For alloeosis is the mistress in the Scriptures. And if we don't want to believe it, he will overpower us by logic and say, "But we are not on the Mount of Olives and from thence ascending to heaven, we are here in German countries;[101] therefore by heaven St. Paul must mean the earth." The only way this spirit can conceive of heaven is to point his finger and cast his eyes upward, where sun and moon are. I hold that since these bodies never stand still, they ascribe to Christ such a place in heaven that he can never sit still. For I cannot imagine or elicit from them what sort of place they ascribe to Christ in heaven. But let that go for what it is worth.

Thus, in regard to the text I quoted from Colossians 3 [2:9], "In Christ the whole fulness of deity dwells bodily," he thinks it unnecessary to say more than that "bodily" means "essentially," just as if Christ had not also been essentially God before God came to dwell bodily in Christ.[102] It is marvelous the way this spirit can explain whatever he wishes, with no need of proving it! The same with the passage in Ephesians 4 [:10], "Christ descended and ascended far above all the heavens, that he might fill all things." Here he explains "filling" as fulfilling the holy Scriptures,[103] and exults once more over the mad Luther as if he had stormed hell. But to prove this interpretation is quite unnecessary for him. It is enough that he says so; then the point is sufficiently answered and our interpretation is false.

He does hit Luther squarely for the first time, however, when he proves his powers of deduction on the word of Christ, "Where I am, there shall you be also" [John 14:3]. "You see," he says, "if Christ is everywhere, we must be everywhere also." [104] To my surprise he does not deduce also that because we are where Christ

---

[101] Cf. Acts 1:12. "German" in the sixteenth century had a linguistic and cultural, rather than a national connotation; Zwingli often referred to himself as a German. Luther here puts words into Zwingli's mouth, however.
[102] *Christian Answer. C. R.* 92, 956; *St. L.* 20, 1216.
[103] *Friendly Exposition. C. R.* 92, 676, 653, quoting Luther's *The Sacrament—Against the Fanatics*, 1526. *LW* 36, 342 f. Also *Friendly Rejoinder. C. R.* 92, 788; *St. L.* 20, 1118 f.
[104] *Christian Answer. C. R.* 92, 956; *St. L.* 20, 1216.

is, we must all be God and man also. For where Christ is, he is God and man. Again, Christ passed through the sealed stone and the closed door, therefore we must also pass through them. Again, Christ exists spiritually in us, therefore we also must exist spiritually in ourselves, etc.

Yes, on the other hand he might reasonably conclude that where Christ is, there we cannot be. For it is just as unreasonable for many bodies to be in one place as for one body to be in many places. But since Christ occupies a particular place in heaven, as they say, it must follow that each of us will have his particular place. Now, since this passage, "Where I am, there shall you be also," is contrary to Scripture and the Creed if it is understood literally, Lady Alloeosis, or heterosis, or perhaps the common figure *narrosis*[105] will stand godmother and help us on to a correct interpretation. Am I not clever too at their art of jumping to conclusions?

Now a sow cannot be a dove, nor a cuckoo a nightingale. This proud devil treats Scripture any way he pleases, and shows with his jugglery that since he cannot answer he will resort to ridiculing us. But we know that Scripture sets this man and no other at the right hand of God. Now although we shall be where he is, according to the first or second mode as described above, we shall not be where he is according to the third mode, viz. at the right hand of God as one person with God, according to which mode Christ exists wherever God is.[106] Indeed, since he is everywhere, of course we are wherever he is, for he must be with us if he is everywhere. This our master logician should have confuted, instead of which he confuses it all together, and refuses to recognize any but the one circumscribed mode. Beyond this he can understand nothing at all, and does not even comprehend what he is raving about.

---

[105] A coined word of sarcasm, based on the German word *narr*, "fool."
[106] Cf. pp. 385 ff.

PART V

THE REFORM OF THE CHURCH

In the first four parts of this anthology we have seen the various aspects of Luther's theology: his determination to re-center theology in the cross, his exposition of the Word as law and gospel, his confidence that the righteousness of God revealed in Christ stood over against all human goodness and wisdom, and his reinterpretation of the sacraments in light of the centrality of the gospel.

But how was this gospel-centered theology to be embodied in the actual life of the church? Luther was not only a professor, but also a pastor in Wittenberg, and one to whom the various supporters of the Reformation looked for leadership in the concrete task of structuring the church's life. The six documents in Part V show Luther at his task of practical reformer, struggling to structure the life of the church around this powerful new theology.

The course of reform was a stormy one, as readers of the first parts of this book will already have noticed. At an early point Luther thought that he so spoke for the hopes of Christendom that the reforms he proposed might sweep through the Roman Church, especially if assisted by a general council. The rapid spread of the Reformation as a popular movement in those first years gave credibility to this notion.

Luther eventually learned that there would be strong opposition to most of his reforming agenda from key leaders of the Roman Church. He also came to see that many devout Catholics did not agree with him, and either did not want the changes that he proposed or were not willing to struggle against the papacy and bishops to obtain them.

Trouble came from another direction as well. Luther's own agenda was a limited one, involving certain concrete changes that seemed to him absolutely necessary to correct current practices that obscured the gospel. But on other issues Luther was content to maintain the catholic tradition. He soon found himself outflanked by those, even among his supporters, who wanted more changes or more rapid transformation than seemed right to him.

20   Eight Sermons at Wittenberg

The first document in this part reflects those struggles about the nature of reform within the Wittenberg congregation itself. After his appearance before the Diet of Worms in 1521, Luther had been kidnapped by friends on the way home and taken into hiding at the Wartburg castle for his own protection. But while he was away from Wittenberg, those who wanted to move rapidly to eliminate Roman practices, under the leadership of Karlstadt, began to take dramatic action.

At Christmas in 1521, Karlstadt distributed both bread and the cup at communion. He also declared confession before communion unnecessary and held that images were not to be permitted in the church. This led to outbreaks of actual violence and destruction of images and altars. The disturbances became so strong that city schools had to be closed and the university itself was on the verge of collapse.

Luther had made a secret visit to Wittenberg in December of 1521, but now he decided that he needed to return, at whatever risk to his own personal safety, to lead a more orderly process of change. He arrived on Thursday, March 6, 1522, consulted with his friends, and then began on the following Sunday a series of daily sermons for the people about the current crisis. This series of "Eight Sermons at Wittenberg" (1522) is often called the "Invocabit Sermons," after the name of the Sunday in Lent when Luther began to preach.

In this series Luther acknowledges that many changes are needed, but he rebukes the Wittenbergers for their disorder. At the conclusion of the first sermon, Luther pleads that any changes be undertaken with patience and with education so that no persons fail to consent who might be able to agree, even if they do not yet understand:

> For there are many who are otherwise in accord with us and who would also gladly accept this thing, but they do not yet fully understand it—these we drive away. Therefore, let us show love to our neighbors; if we do not do this, our work will not endure. We must have patience with them for a time, and not cast out

him who is weak in faith; and do and omit to do many other things, so long as love requires it and it does no harm to faith. If we do not earnestly pray to God and act rightly in this matter, it looks to me as if all the misery which we have begun to heap upon the papists will fall upon us (p. 418).

Having restored order and having spoken to some of the most pressing issues in the "Eight Sermons," Luther turned his attention to how worship should in fact be restructured. The next two documents in this section, "Concerning the Order of Public Worship" and "An Order of Mass and Communion for the Church at Wittenberg" were both written in 1523 to deal with this question.

21   Concerning the Order of Public Worship

This short treatise appeared sometime in the spring of 1523. It offered general principles for the reform of worship. At the beginning Luther states three goals: (1) the recovery of the Word; (2) the elimination of "un-Christian fables and lies, in legends, hymns and sermons"; (3) and elimination of the sense of the "divine service . . . performed as a work whereby God's grace and salvation might be won."

Luther then outlines a program of worship for the entire week. Daily masses are to be replaced with morning and evening services of the Word, and all of them are to include preaching. If, however, any person wants the sacrament during the week, this is not forbidden. "Let mass be held as inclination and time dictate."

Sunday mass and vespers should continue "as has been customary," but both of these occasions should include preaching. Sung chants may be retained, but there is room for adjustment here. Festivals of the saints are to be discontinued, although those of Mary and the apostles may be retained (so long as the content of what they celebrate is "pure").

22   An Order of Mass and Communion for the Church at Wittenberg

In his brief principles of the reform of worship, Luther had said that his chief goal was "that the Word may have free course instead of the prattling and rattling that has been the rule until now." But he was soon pressed to provide more specific guidance for the Sunday service of the sacrament itself. So late in 1523 Luther published a detailed account of how he thought the Mass itself ought to be reformed. Its publication made it an influential standard not only in Saxony but wherever the Reformation was being introduced.

Several matters stand out clearly. First, Luther was concerned that lessons and preaching be in the language of the people. Second, he insisted on a thorough reform of the Eucharistic liturgy itself to take away every suggestion of sacrifice or human work. Third, there is his surprising flexibility—a reluctance to have every decision fixed. Local conditions, whether the scruples of the people or preference of the bishop, may rightly dictate that something be included in one place or time and eliminated in another.

23   The Small Catechism

The reader is next asked to consider two documents that are to be found in *The Book of Concord*, the official collection of teachings of the Lutheran churches. "The Small Catechism" and "The Smalcald Articles" show Luther's skill as a pastor and theological negotiator for the church.

A visitation to the churches of Saxony in 1528 sent Luther into real shock about the spiritual conditions that were found there. "Good God, what wretchedness I beheld! The common people . . . have no knowledge whatever of Christian teaching. . . ." Luther set out to remedy this situation by preparing a "Large Catechism" for pastors and teachers and a "Small Catechism" for use by the common people.

Luther presents the traditional catechetical material—Ten Commandments, Creed, sacraments—but offers his own explanations of each part. This has perhaps been Luther's most widely known writing in the centuries since its first publication in 1529, as it formed the basis for instruction in preparation for confirmation in the Lutheran churches.

Readers may be surprised at Luther's clear capacity to be a teacher of ordinary persons, presenting the Christian faith in a simple, positive, non-polemical way. Yet readers also should not fail to see several characteristic Luther themes—in the centering of all Ten Commandments on the first command to "fear and love God," in the description of faith itself as a gift in the third article of the creed, or in the teaching of a need for a daily return to baptism and of the "true body and blood of our Lord Jesus Christ" in the Supper.

In later editions Luther also included material on the daily life of a Christian—morning and evening prayer, grace at table, and tables of household duties. The time-conditioned character of much of this may seem curious (and not all subsequently published catechisms have included all of these parts). Yet here Luther was attempting to offer a pattern of spirituality for the Christian who lives in the world rather than the monastery.

24   The Smalcald Articles

In these decades of theological debate and political struggle, each party had to develop new norms or summaries of faith to speak to current controversy. Luther's personal statement of faith (see selection 4) played a significant part in the development of the "Augsburg Confession" of 1530 (although this confession was actually written by Melanchthon). But in 1537, when the long hoped for (and now feared) General Council had finally been called by the Pope, it was Luther who drew up a summary of Reformation faith in "The Smalcald Articles."

After a brief preface discussing the current situation, Luther presents these articles in three parts: First, there is a summary of trinitarian faith from the historic creeds. He admits, "these articles are not matters of dispute or contention for both parties confess them."

Second, Luther takes up four central Reformation concerns that the coming council must consider: Christ and justification by faith; the Mass; Chapters and Monasteries; and the Papacy. Christ, faith, and justification are not three separate topics, but a single reality, and "nothing in this article can be given up or compromised, even if heaven and earth and things temporal should be destroyed."

The Mass—not Holy Communion itself, but the way that it had been presented under the papacy—"must be regarded as the greatest and most horrible abomination because it runs into direct and violent conflict" with the fundamental article of Christ, faith, and justification. It is the misunderstanding of the Mass as a human work that has given rise to so many of the abuses against which Luther's writings had been focused: purgatory; masses for the dead; pilgrimages; the brotherhoods; relics; and indulgences.

The conclusion of this second part contains a good example of Luther's developed thinking about the papacy itself—an article that had been avoided in the "Augsburg Confession," but that now had to be faced. Luther denies that the papacy exists "by divine right or according to God's Word." He considers the possibility that some have suggested that the pope might be simply the bishop of Rome and as such the head of Christendom, preserving its unity. But Luther is skeptical by 1537 that such a development of the papal power could ever take place. (The reader will note in the signatures at the end of this document that the ever more irenic Melanchthon disagrees with Luther and makes a reservation about this confession at this very point.)

In the third and final part of the articles, Luther takes up fifteen matters that need discussion between the sides, although he is doubtful that the Roman party at the coming council "care much about these things; they are not concerned about matters of conscience but only about money, honor, and power." The articles throughout reflect Luther's fear that nothing good can emerge from the coming council. But those polemical notes aside, they provide an excellent summary of Luther's fully developed negotiating stance with Rome from a time twenty years after the beginnings of the conflict.

25 On the Councils and the Church—Part III

The final document in Part V is the concluding section of Luther's treatise "On the Councils and the Church" from 1539. In this section Luther provides a description of the marks of the church. Having reviewed the history of the council of Jerusalem and the first four ecumenical councils, Luther reaches a cautious conclusion about the positive role that such councils can play (in contrast to his earlier hopes that a true council might bring reform throughout Christendom). But he then goes on to present how the doctrine of the church is rightly to be understood.

For Luther the heart of the matter is the concept of church as *ecclesia*—neither building nor institution nor structure, but the gathered congregation, the people of God. But among the many communities claiming to bear the name of Christ, how can the true church be recognized? Luther proposes seven marks:

- □ possession of the holy Word of God
- □ the holy sacrament of baptism
- □ the holy sacrament of the altar
- □ the office of the keys (absolution for sin)
- □ the office of ministry (including bishops and pastors)
- □ prayer, public praise, and thanksgiving to God
- □ possession of the sacred cross—that is, experience of suffering

The treatise is written to continue the work of the "Smalcald Articles" in rallying the people to understand the treasure that they have received in a church re-formed around the gospel. Yet Luther knows that many in the reformation churches do not treasure sufficiently these seven great gifts of God. So the treatise contains this appeal and warning:

> If God were to bid you to pick up a straw or to pluck out a feather with the command, order, and promise that thereby you have forgiveness of all sin, grace, and eternal life, should you not accept this joyfully and gratefully, and cherish, praise, prize, and esteem that straw and that feather as a higher and holier possession than heaven and earth? No matter how insignificant the straw and feather may be, you would nonetheless acquire through them something more valuable than heaven and earth, indeed, than all the angels, are able to bestow on you. Why then are we such disgraceful people that we do not regard the water of baptism, the bread and wine, that is, Christ's body and blood, the spoken word, and that laying on of man's hands for the forgiveness of sin as such holy possessions, as we would the straw and the feather . . . ? (p. 569).

It could be fairly said that Luther's task as a reformer was to rally the church around the gospel in such a way that none of these precious gifts was lost, but so that the grace of God might be known clearly in these questions of structure and order.

EIGHT SERMONS AT WITTENBERG
1522

The First Sermon, March 9, 1522, Invocavit Sunday[1]

The summons of death comes to us all, and no one can die for another. Every one must fight his own battle with death by himself, alone. We can shout into another's ears, but every one must himself be prepared for the time of death, for I will not be with you then, nor you with me. Therefore every one must himself know and be armed with the chief things which concern a Christian. And these are what you, my beloved, have heard from me many days ago.

In the first place, we must know that we are the children of wrath, and all our works, intentions, and thoughts are nothing at all. Here we need a clear, strong text to bear out this point. Such is the saying of St. Paul in Eph. 2 [:3]. Note this well; and though there are many such in the Bible, I do not wish to overwhelm you with many texts. "We are all the children of wrath." And please do not undertake to say: I have built an altar, given a foundation for masses, etc.

---

[1] In the original there follow the words "Sermon, "D.M.L."

Secondly, that God has sent us his only-begotten Son that we may believe in him and that whoever trusts in him shall be free from sin and a child of God, as John declares in his first chapter, "To all who believed in his name, he gave power to become children of God" [John 1:12]. Here we should all be well versed in the Bible and ready to confront the devil with many passages. With respect to these two points I do not feel that there has been anything wrong or lacking. They have been rightly preached to you, and I should be sorry if it were otherwise. Indeed, I am well aware and I dare say that you are more learned than I, and that there are not only one, two, three, or four, but perhaps ten or more, who have this knowledge and enlightenment.

Thirdly, we must also have love and through love we must do to one another as God has done to us through faith. For without love faith is nothing, as St. Paul says (I Cor. 2 [13:1]): If I had the tongues of angels and could speak of the highest things in faith, and have not love, I am nothing. And here, dear friends, have you not grievously failed? I see no signs of love among you, and I observe very well that you have not been grateful to God for his rich gifts and treasures.

Here let us beware lest Wittenberg become Capernaum [cf. Matt. 11:23]. I notice that you have a great deal to say of the doctrine of faith and love which is preached to you, and this is no wonder; an ass can almost intone the lessons, and why should you not be able to repeat the doctrines and formulas? Dear friends, the kingdom of God,—and we are that kingdom—does not consist in talk or words [I Cor. 4:20], but in activity, in deeds, in works and exercises. God does not want hearers and repeaters of words [Jas. 1:22], but followers and doers, and this occurs in faith through love. For a faith without love is not enough—rather it is not faith at all, but a counterfeit of faith, just as a face seen in a mirror is not a real face, but merely the reflection of a face [I Cor. 13:12].

Fourthly, we also need patience. For whoever has faith, trusts in God, and shows love to his neighbor, practicing it day by day, must needs suffer persecution. For the devil never sleeps, but constantly gives him plenty of trouble. But patience works and produces hope [Rom. 5:4], which freely yields itself to God and vanishes away in him. Thus faith, by much affliction and persecution, ever increases, and is strengthened day by day. A heart thus blessed with virtues can never rest or restrain itself, but rather pours itself out again for the benefit and service of the brethren, just as God has done to it.

And here, dear friends, one must not insist upon his rights, but must see what may be useful and helpful to his brother, as Paul says, *Omnia mihi licent, sed non omnia expediunt*, " 'All things are lawful for me,' but not all things are helpful" [I Cor. 6:12]. For we are not all equally strong in faith, some of you have a stronger faith than I. Therefore we must not look upon ourselves, or our strength, or our prestige, but upon our neighbor, for God has said through Moses: I have borne and reared you, as a mother does her child [Deut. 1:31]. What does a mother do to her child? First she gives it milk, then gruel, then eggs and soft food, whereas if she turned about and gave it solid food, the child would never thrive [cf. I Cor. 3:2; Heb. 5:12-13]. So we should also deal with our brother, have patience with him for a time, have patience with his weakness and help him bear it; we should also give him milk-food, too [I Pet. 2:2; cf. Rom. 14:1-3], as was done with us, until he, too, grows strong, and thus we do not travel heavenward alone, but bring our brethren, who are not now our friends, with us. If all mothers were to abandon their children, where would we have been? Dear brother, if you have suckled long enough, do not at once cut off the breast, but let your brother be suckled as you were suckled. I would not have gone so far as you have done, if I had been here. The cause is good, but there has been too much haste. For there are still brothers and sisters on the other side who belong to us and must still be won.

Let me illustrate. The sun has two properties, light and heat. No king has power enough to bend or guide the light of the sun; it remains fixed in its place. But the heat may be turned and guided, and yet is ever about the sun. Thus faith must always remain pure and immovable in our hearts, never wavering; but love bends and turns so that our neighbor may grasp and follow it. There are some who can run, others must walk, still others can hardly creep [cf. I Cor. 8:7-13]. Therefore we must not look upon our own, but upon our brother's powers, so that he who is weak in faith, and attempts to follow the strong, may not be destroyed of the devil. Therefore, dear brethren, follow me; I have never been a destroyer. And I was also the very first whom God called to this work. I cannot run away, but will remain as long as God allows. I was also the one to whom God first revealed that his Word should be preached to you. I am also sure that you have the pure Word of God.

Let us, therefore, let us act with fear and humility, cast ourselves at one another's feet, join hands with each other, and help one another. I will do my part, which is no more than my duty, for I love you even as I love my own soul. For here we battle not against pope or bishop, but against the devil [cf. Eph. 6:12], and do you imagine he is asleep? He sleeps not, but sees the true light rising, and to keep it from shining into his eyes he would like to make a flank attack—and he will succeed, if we are not on our guard. I know him well, and I hope, too, that with the help of God, I am his master. But if we yield him but an inch, we must soon look to it how we may be rid of him. Therefore all those have erred who have helped and consented to abolish the mass; not that it was not a good thing, but that it was not done in an orderly way. You say it was right according to the Scriptures. I agree, but what becomes of order? For it was done in wantonness, with no regard for proper order and with offense to your neighbor. If, beforehand, you had called upon God in earnest prayer, and had obtained the aid of the authorities, one could be certain that it had come from God. I, too, would have taken steps toward the same end if it had been a good thing to do; and if the mass were not so evil a thing, I would introduce it again. For I cannot defend your action, as I have just said. To the papists and blockheads I could defend it, for I could say: How do you know whether it was done with good or bad intention, since the work in itself was really a good work? But I would not know what to assert before the devil. For if on their deathbeds the devil reminds those who began this affair of texts like these, "Every plant which my Father has not planted will be rooted up" [Matt. 15:13], or "I have not sent them, yet they ran" [Jer. 23:21],[2] how will they be able to withstand? He will cast them into hell. But I shall poke the one spear into his face, so that even the world will become too small for him, for I know that in spite of my reluctance I was called by the council to preach. Therefore I was willing to

---

[2] Scripture passages in Latin, though Luther undoubtedly spoke them in German.

accept you as you were willing to accept me, and, besides, you could have consulted me about the matter.

I was not so far away that you could not reach me with a letter, whereas not the slightest communication was sent to me. If you were going to begin something and make me responsible for it, that would have been too hard. I will not do it [i.e., assume the responsibility]. Here one can see that you do not have the Spirit, even though you do have a deep knowledge of the Scriptures. Take note of these two things, "must" and "free." The "must" is that which necessity requires, and which must ever be unyielding; as, for instance, the faith, which I shall never permit any one to take away from me, but must always keep in my heart and freely confess before every one. But "free" is that in which I have choice, and may use or not, yet in such a way that it profit my brother and not me. Now do not make a "must" out of what is "free," as you have done, so that you may not be called to account for those who were led astray by your loveless exercise of liberty. For if you entice any one to eat meat on Friday, and he is troubled about it on his deathbed, and thinks, Woe is me, for I have eaten meat and I am lost! God will call you to account for that soul. I, too, would like to begin many things, in which but few would follow me, but what is the use? For I know that, when it comes to the showdown, those who have begun this thing cannot maintain themselves, and will be the first to retreat. How would it be, if I brought the people to the point of attack, and though I had been the first to exhort others, I would then flee, and not face death with courage? How the poor people would be deceived!

Let us, therefore, feed others also with the milk which we received, until they, too, become strong in faith. For there are many who are otherwise in accord with us and who would also gladly accept this thing, but they do not yet fully understand it—these we drive away. Therefore, let us show love to our neighbors; if we do not do this, our work will not endure. We must have patience with them for a time, and not cast out him who is weak in faith; and do and omit to do many other things, so long as love requires it and it does no harm to our faith. If we do not earnestly pray to God and act rightly in this matter, it looks to me as if all the misery which we have begun to heap upon the papists will fall upon us. Therefore I could no longer remain away, but was compelled to come and say these things to you.

This is enough about the mass; tomorrow we shall speak about images.

The Second Sermon, March 10, 1522, Monday

after Invocavit[3]

Dear friends, you heard yesterday the chief characteristics of a Christian man, that his whole life and being is faith and love. Faith is directed toward God, love toward man and one's neighbor, and consists in such love and service for him as we have received from God without our work and merit. Thus, there are two things: the one, which is the most needful, and which must be done in one way and no other; the other, which is a matter of choice and not of necessity, which may be kept or not, without endangering faith or incurring hell. In both, love must deal with our neighbor in the same manner as God has dealt with us; it must walk the straight road, straying neither to the left nor to the right. In the things which are "musts" and are matters of necessity, such as believing in Christ, love nevertheless never uses force or undue constraint. Thus the mass is an evil thing, and God is displeased with it, because it is performed as if it were a sacrifice and work of merit. Therefore it must be abolished. Here there can be no question or doubt, any more than you should ask whether you should worship God. Here we are entirely agreed: the private masses must be abolished. As I have said in my writings,[4] I wish they would be abolished everywhere and only the ordinary evangelical mass be retained. Yet Christian love should not employ harshness here nor force the matter. However, it should be preached and taught with tongue and pen that

---

[3] The title reads: "Another sermon of D. M. Luther's on Monday after Invocavit."
[4] In the *Open Letter to the Christian Nobility* (1520), PE 2, 61-164, and *The Babylonian Captivity of the Church* (1520), PE 2, 170-293.

to hold mass in such a manner is sinful, and yet no one should be dragged away from it by the hair; for it should be left to God, and his Word should be allowed to work alone, without our work or interference. Why? Because it is not in my power or hand to fashion the hearts of men as the potter molds the clay and fashion them at my pleasure [Ecclus. 33:13]. I can get no farther than their ears; their hearts I cannot reach. And since I cannot pour faith into their hearts, I cannot, nor should I, force any one to have faith. That is God's work alone, who causes faith to live in the heart. Therefore we should give free course to the Word and not add our works to it. We have the *jus verbi* [right to speak] but not the *executio* [power to accomplish]. We should preach the Word, but the results must be left solely to God's good pleasure.

Now if I should rush in and abolish it by force, there are many who would be compelled to consent to it and yet not know where they stand, whether it is right or wrong, and they would say: I do not know if it is right or wrong, I do not know where I stand, I was compelled by force to submit to the majority. And this forcing and commanding results in a mere mockery, an external show, a fool's play, man-made ordinances, sham-saints, and hypocrites. For where the heart is not good, I care nothing at all for the work. We must first win the hearts of the people. But that is done when I teach only the Word of God, preach the gospel, and say: Dear lords or pastors, abandon the mass, it is not right, you are sinning when you do it; I cannot refrain from telling you this. But I would not make it an ordinance for them, nor urge a general law. He who would follow me could do so, and he who refused would remain outside. In the latter case the Word would sink into the heart and do its work. Thus he would become convinced and acknowledge his error, and fall away from the mass; tomorrow another would do the same, and thus God would accomplish more with his Word than if you and I were to merge all our power into one heap. So when you have won the heart, you have won the man—and thus the thing must finally fall of its own weight and come to an end. And if the hearts and minds of all are agreed and united, abolish it. But if all are not heart and soul for its abolishment—leave it in God's hands, I beseech you, otherwise the result will not be good. Not that I would again set up the mass; I let it lie in God's name. Faith must not be chained and imprisoned, nor bound by an ordinance to any work. This is the principle by which you must be governed. For I am sure you will not be able to carry out your plans. And if you should carry them out with such general laws, then I will recant everything that I have written and preached and I will not support you. This I am telling you now. What harm can it do you? You still have your faith in God, pure and strong so that this thing cannot hurt you.

Love, therefore, demands that you have compassion on the weak, as all the apostles had. Once, when Paul came to Athens (Acts 17 [:16-32]), a mighty city, he found in the temple many ancient altars, and he went from one to the other and looked at them all, but he did not kick down a single one of them with his foot. Rather he stood up in the middle of the market place and said they were nothing but idolatrous things and begged the people to forsake them; yet he did not destroy one of them by force. When the Word took hold of their hearts, they forsook them of their own accord, and in consequence the thing fell of itself. Likewise, if I had seen them holding mass, I would have preached to them and admonished them. Had they heeded my admonition, I would have won them; if not, I would nevertheless not have torn them from it by the hair or employed any force, but simply allowed the Word to act and prayed for them. For the Word created heaven and earth and all things [Ps. 33:6]; the Word must do this thing, and not we poor sinners.

In short, I will preach it, teach it, write it, but I will constrain no man by force, for faith must come freely without compulsion. Take myself as an example. I opposed indulgences and all the papists, but never with force. I simply taught, preached, and wrote God's Word; otherwise I did nothing. And while I slept [cf. Mark 4:26-29], or drank Wittenberg beer with my friends Philip[5] and Amsdorf,[6] the Word so greatly weakened the papacy that no prince or emperor ever inflicted such losses upon it. I did nothing; the Word did everything. Had I desired to foment trouble, I could have brought great bloodshed upon Germany; indeed, I could have started such a game that even the emperor would not have been safe. But what would it have been? Mere fool's play. I did

---

[5] Melanchthon.
[6] Nicholas von Amsdorf (1483-1565).

nothing; I let the Word do its work. What do you suppose is Satan's thought when one tries to do the thing by kicking up a row? He sits back in hell and thinks: Oh, what a fine game the poor fools are up to now! But when we spread the Word alone and let it alone do the work, that distresses him. For it is almighty and takes captive the hearts, and when the hearts are captured the work will fall of itself. Let me cite a simple instance. In former times there were sects, too, Jewish and Gentile Christians, differing on the law of Moses with respect to circumcision. The former wanted to keep it, the latter not. Then came Paul and preached that it might be kept or not, for it was of no consequence, and also that they should not make a "must" of it, but leave it to the choice of the individual; to keep it or not was immaterial [I Cor. 7:18-24; Gal. 5:1]. So it was up to the time of Jerome, who came and wanted to make a "must" out of it, desiring to make it an ordinance and a law that it be prohibited.[7] Then came St. Augustine and he was of the same opinion as St. Paul: it might be kept or not, as one wished. St. Jerome was a hundred miles away from St. Paul's opinion. The two doctors bumped heads rather hard, but when St. Augustine died, St. Jerome was successful in having it prohibited. After that came the popes, who also wanted to add something and they, too, made laws. Thus out of the making of one law grew a thousand laws, until they have completely buried us under laws. And this is what will happen here, too; one law will soon make two, two will increase to three, and so forth.

Let this be enough at this time concerning the things that are necessary, and let us beware lest we lead astray those of weak conscience [I Cor. 8:12].

---

[7] A note in *MA*[3], 4, 334 reads: "Luther correctly discerns that about the time of Jerome (*ca.* 345-420), the creator of the Latin translation of the Bible (the Vulgate), the peculiarly Roman character of the Christian church began to develop."

The Third Sermon, March 11, 1522, Tuesday

after Invocavit[8]

We have heard the things which are "musts," which are necessary and must be done, things which must be so and not otherwise: the private masses[9] must be abolished. For all works and things, which are either commanded or forbidden by God and thus have been instituted by the supreme Majesty, are "musts." Nevertheless, no one should be dragged to them or away from them by the hair, for I can drive no man to heaven or beat him into it with a club. I said this plainly enough; I believe you have understood what I said.

Now follow the things which are not necessary, but are left to our free choice by God and which we may keep or not, such as whether a person should marry or not, or whether monks and nuns should leave the cloisters. These things are matters of choice and must not be forbidden by any one, and if they are forbidden, the forbidding is wrong, since it is contrary to God's ordinance. In the things that are free, such as being married or remaining single, you should take this attitude: if you can keep to it without burdensomeness, then keep it; but it must not be made a general law; everyone must rather be free. So if there is a priest, monk, or nun, who cannot abstain, let him take a wife and be a husband, in order that your conscience may be relieved;[10] and see to it that you can stand before God and the world when you are assailed, especially when the devil attacks you in the hour of death. It is not enough to say: this man or that man did it, I followed the crowd, according to the preaching

---

[8] The title reads: "Another sermon of D. M. Luther's on Tuesday after Invocavit."

[9] *Winkelmessen oder sonderlichen Messen.*

[10] The contradiction of genders and the switch from impersonal to personal address reflects Luther's spoken style and is here retained.

of the dean,[11] Dr. Karlstadt,[12] or Gabriel,[13] or Michael.[14] Not so; every one must stand on his own feet and be prepared to give battle to the devil. You must rest upon a strong and clear text of Scripture if you would stand the test. If you cannot do that, you will never withstand—the devil will pluck you like a parched leaf. Therefore the priests who have taken wives and the nuns who have taken husbands in order to save their consciences must stand squarely upon a clear text of Scripture, such as this one by St. Paul, although there are many more: "In later times some will depart from the faith by giving heed to deceitful spirits and doctrines of the devil (I think St. Paul is outspoken enough here!) and will forbid marriage and the foods which God created" [I Tim. 4:1-3]. This text the devil will not overthrow nor devour, it will rather overthrow and devour him. Therefore any monk or nun who finds that he is too weak to maintain chastity should conscientiously examine himself; if his heart and conscience are thus strengthened, let him take a wife and be a husband. Would to God all monks and nuns could hear this sermon and properly understand this matter and would all forsake the cloisters, and thus all the cloisters in the world would cease to exist; this is what I would wish. But now they have no understanding of the matter (for no one preaches it to them); they hear about others who are leaving the cloisters in other places, who, however, are well prepared for such a step, and then they want to follow their example, but have not yet fortified their consciences and do not know that it is a matter of liberty. This is bad, and yet it is better that the evil should be outside than inside.[15] Therefore I say, what God has made free shall remain free. If anybody forbids it, as the pope, the Antichrist, has done, you should not obey. He who can do so without harm and for love of his neighbor may wear a cowl

---

[11] Justus Jonas (1493-1555), dean (*Probst*) of the Castle Church and professor in the Wittenberg faculty, at this time a radical advocate of liturgical reform. However, the omission of the comma in the original text may indicate that Luther did not refer to Jonas at all, since Karlstadt was dean of the faculty. Cf. WA 10^{III}, 438.

[12] Andreas Bodenstein Karlstadt (1480-1541).

[13] Gabriel Zwilling (Didymus) (*ca.* 1487-1558), Augustinian monk and champion of immediate reform of the mass.

[14] Zwilling's first name, Gabriel, probably suggested to Luther the addition of the name of the archangel Michael. Cf. Gal. 1:8.

[15] Namely, of the monasteries.

or a tonsure, since it will not injure your faith. The cowl will not strangle you, if you are already wearing one.

Thus, dear friends, I have said it clearly enough, and I believe you ought to understand it and not make liberty a law, saying: This priest has taken a wife, therefore all priests must take wives. Not at all. Or this monk or that nun has left the cloister, therefore they must all come out. Not at all. Or this man has broken the images and burnt them, therefore all images must be burned—not at all, dear brother! And again, this priest has no wife, therefore no priest dare marry. Not at all! For they who cannot retain their chastity should take wives, and for others who can be chaste, it is good that they restrain themselves, as those who live in the Spirit and not in the flesh [Rom. 8:4; I Cor. 7:40]. Neither should they be troubled about the vows they have made, such as the monks' vows of obedience, chastity, and poverty (though they are rich enough withal). For we cannot vow anything that is contrary to God's commands. God has made it a matter of liberty to marry or not to marry, and you, you fool, undertake to turn this liberty into a vow contrary to the ordinance of God! Therefore you must let it remain a liberty and not make a compulsion out of it; for your vow is contrary to God's liberty. For example, if I vowed to strike my father on the mouth, or to steal someone's property, do you believe God would be pleased with such a vow? Therefore, little as I ought to keep a vow to strike my father on the mouth, so little ought I to abstain from marriage because I am bound by a vow of chastity, for in both cases God has ordered it otherwise. God has ordained that I should be free to eat fish or flesh, and there should be no commandment concerning them. Therefore all the Carthusians[16] and all monks and nuns are departing from God's ordinance and liberty when they believe that if they eat meat they are defiled.

Concerning Images

But now we must come to the images, and concerning them also it is true that they are unnecessary, and we are free to have them or not, although it would be much better if we did not have them at all. I am not partial to them. A great controversy arose on the subject of images between the Roman emperor and the pope; the

---

[16] As he does frequently, Luther here names the strictest of the orders.

emperor held that he had the authority to banish the images, but the pope insisted that they should remain, and both were wrong. Much blood was shed, but the pope emerged as victor and the emperor lost.[17] What was it all about? They wished to make a "must" out of that which is free. This God cannot tolerate. Do you presume to do things differently from the way the supreme Majesty has decreed? Surely not; let it alone. You read in the Law (Exod. 20 [:4]), "You shall not make yourself a graven image, or any likeness of anything that is in heaven above, or that is in the earth beneath, or that is in the water under the earth." There you take your stand; that is your ground. Now let us see! When our adversaries say: The meaning of the first commandment is that we should worship only one God and not any image, even as it is said immediately following, "You shall not bow down to them or serve them" [Exod. 20:5], and when they say that it is the worship of images which is forbidden and not the making of them, they are shaking our foundation and making it uncertain. And if you reply: The text says, "You shall not make any images," then they say: It also says, "You shall not worship them." In the face of such uncertainty who would be so bold as to destroy the images? Not I. But let us go further. They say: Did not Noah, Abraham, Jacob build altars? [Gen. 8:20; 12:7; 13:4; 13:18; 33:20]. And who will deny that? We must admit it. Again, did not Moses erect a bronze serpent, as we read in his fourth book (Num. 22 [21:9])? How then can you say that Moses forbade the making of images when he himself made one? It seems to me that such a serpent is an image, too. How shall we answer that? Again, do we not read also that two birds were erected on the mercy seat [Exod. 37:7], the very place where God willed that he should be worshipped? Here we must admit that we may have images and make images, but we must not worship them, and if they are worshipped, they should be put away and destroyed, just as King Hezekiah broke in pieces the bronze serpent erected by Moses [II Kings 18:4]. And who will be so bold as to say, when he is challenged to give an answer: They worship the images. They will say:

---

[17] Luther has reference to the Iconoclastic Controversy, initiated by Emperor Leo III, who prohibited the veneration of images in 718, contested by Pope Gregory II, and finally settled in 843. Invocavit Sunday is the "Feast of Orthodoxy" in commemoration of the Seventh Ecumenical Council of 783, which dealt with this question.

Are you the man who dares to accuse us of worshipping them? Do not believe that they will acknowledge it. To be sure, it is true, but we cannot make them admit it. Just look how they acted when I condemned works without faith. They said: Do you believe that we have no faith, or that our works are performed without faith? Then I cannot press them any further, but must put my flute back in my pocket; for if they gain a hair's breadth, they make a hundred miles out of it.

Therefore it should have been preached that images were nothing and that no service is done to God by erecting them; then they would have fallen of themselves. That is what I did; that is what Paul did in Athens, when he went into their churches and saw all their idols. He did not strike at any of them, but stood in the market place and said, "You men of Athens, you are all idolatrous" [Acts 17:16, 22]. He preached against their idols, but he overthrew none by force. And you rush, create an uproar, break down altars, and overthrow images! Do you really believe you can abolish the altars in this way? No, you will only set them up more firmly. Even if you overthrew the images in this place, do you think you have overthrown those in Nürnberg and the rest of the world? Not at all. St. Paul, as we read in the Book of Acts [28:11], sat in a ship on whose prow were painted or carved the Twin Brothers [i.e., Castor and Pollux]. He went on board and did not bother about them at all, neither did he break them off. Why must Luke describe the Twins at this point? Without doubt he wanted to show that outward things could do no harm to faith, if only the heart does not cleave to them or put its trust in them. This is what we must preach and teach, and let the Word alone do the work, as I said before. The Word must first capture the hearts of men and enlighten them; we will not be the ones who will do it. Therefore the apostles magnified their ministry, *ministerium* [Rom. 11:13], and not its effect, *executio*.

Let this be enough for today.

The Fourth Sermon, March 12, 1522, Wednesday

after Invocavit[18]

Dear friends, we have now heard about the things which are "musts," such as that the mass is not to be observed as a sacrifice. Then we considered the things which are not necessary but free, such as marriage, the monastic life, and the abolishing of images. We have treated these four subjects, and have said that in all these matters love is the captain. On the subject of images, in particular, we saw that they ought to be abolished when they are worshipped; otherwise not,—although because of the abuses they give rise to, I wish they were everywhere abolished. This cannot be denied. For whoever places an image in a church imagines he has performed a service to God and done a good work, which is downright idolatry. But this, the greatest, foremost, and highest reason for abolishing images, you have passed by, and fastened on the least important reason of all. For I suppose there is nobody, or certainly very few, who do not understand that yonder crucifix is not my God, for my God is in heaven, but that this is simply a sign. But the world is full of that other abuse; for who would place a silver or wooden image in a church unless he thought that by so doing he was rendering God a service? Do you think that Duke Frederick, the bishop of Halle,[19] and the others would have dragged so many silver images into the churches, if they thought it counted for nothing before God? No, they would not bother to do it. But this is not sufficient reason to abolish, destroy, and burn all images. Why? Because we must admit that there are still some people who hold no such wrong opinion of them, but to whom they may well be useful, although they are few. Nevertheless, we cannot and ought not to condemn a thing which may be any way useful to a person. You should rather have taught that images are nothing, that God cares nothing for

---

[18] The title reads: "A Sermon preached by M. L. on Wednesday after Invocavit."
[19] Duke Frederick is Elector Frederick the Wise of Ernestine Saxony (1463-1525). The "bishop of Halle" is probably Albrecht of Hohenzollern, archbishop of Mainz and of Magdeburg; the cathedral was located in Halle.

them, and that he is not served nor pleased when we make an image for him, but that we would do better to give a poor man a gold-piece than God a golden image; for God has forbidden the latter, but not the former. If they had heard this teaching that images count for nothing, they would have ceased of their own accord, and the images would have fallen without any uproar or tumult, as they are already beginning to do.

We must, therefore, be on our guard, for the devil, through his apostles, is after us with all his craft and cunning. Now, although it is true and no one can deny that the images are evil because they are abused, nevertheless we must not on that account reject them, nor condemn anything because it is abused. This would result in utter confusion. God has commanded us in Deut. 4 [:19] not to lift up our eyes to the sun [and the moon and the stars], etc., that we may not worship them, for they are created to serve all nations. But there are many people who worship the sun and the stars. Therefore we propose to rush in and pull the sun and stars from the skies. No, we had better let it be. Again, wine and women bring many a man to misery and make a fool of him [Ecclus. 19:2; 31:30]; so we kill all the women and pour out all the wine. Again, gold and silver cause much evil, so we condemn them. Indeed, if we want to drive away our worst enemy, the one who does us the most harm, we shall have to kill ourselves, for we have no greater enemy than our own heart, as the prophet, Jer. 17 [:9], says, "The heart of man is crooked," or, as I take the meaning, "always twisting to one side." And so on—what would we not do?

He who would blacken the devil must have good charcoal, for he, too, wears fine clothes and is invited to the kermis.[20] But I can catch him by asking him: Do you not place the images in the churches because you think it a special service to God? And when he says Yes, as he must, you may conclude that what was meant as a service of God he has turned into idolatry by abusing the images and practicing what God has not commanded. But he has neglected God's command, which is that he should be helpful to his neighbor. But I have not yet caught him, though actually he is caught and will not admit it; he escapes me by saying: Yes, I help the poor,

---

[20] *Kirchmess:* service for the consecration or commemoration of the consecration of a church, an occasion for placing images or embellishments in the church.

too; cannot I give to my neighbor and at the same time donate images? This is not so, however, for who would not rather give his neighbor a gold-piece than God a golden image? No, he would not trouble himself about placing images in churches if he did not believe, as he actually does, that he was doing God a service. Therefore I must admit that images are neither here nor there, neither evil nor good, we may have them or not, as we please. This trouble has been caused by you; the devil would not have accomplished it with me, for I cannot deny that it is possible to find someone to whom images are useful. And if I were asked about it, I would confess that none of these things give offense to one, and if just one man were found on earth who used the images aright, the devil would soon draw the conclusion against me: Why, then, do you condemn what may be used properly? Then he has gained the offensive and I would have to admit it. He would not have got nearly so far if I had been here. Proudly he scattered us, though it has done no harm to the Word of God. You wanted to blacken the devil, but you forgot the charcoal and used chalk. If you want to fight the devil you must know the Scriptures well and, besides, use them at the right time.

Concerning Meats

Let us proceed and speak of the eating of meats and what our attitude should be in this matter. It is true that we are free to eat any kind of food, meats, fish, eggs, or butter. This no one can deny. God has given us this liberty; this is true. Nevertheless, we must know how to use our liberty, and in this matter treat the weak brother quite differently from the stubborn. Observe, then, how you ought to use this liberty.

First, if you cannot abstain from meat without harm to yourself, or if you are sick, you may eat whatever you like,[21] and if anyone takes offense, let him be offended. Even if the whole world took offense, you are not committing a sin, for God can approve it in view of the liberty he has so graciously bestowed upon you and of the necessities of your health, which would be endangered by your abstinence.

---

[21] For a discussion of this and related questions cf. also Luther's *Explanations of the Ninety-five Theses* (1518), LW 31, 86-87; 109-110.

Secondly, if you should be pressed to eat fish instead of meat on Friday, and to eat fish and abstain from eggs and butter during Lent, etc., as the pope has done with his fool's laws, then you must in no wise allow yourself to be drawn away from the liberty in which God has placed you, but do just the contrary to spite him, and say: Because you forbid me to eat meat and presume to turn my liberty into law, I will eat meat in spite of you. And thus you must do in all other things which are matters of liberty. To give you an example: if the pope, or anyone else were to force me to wear a cowl, just as he prescribes it, I would take off the cowl just to spite him. But since it is left to my own free choice, I wear it or take it off, according to my pleasure.

Thirdly, there are some who are still weak in faith, who ought to be instructed, and who would gladly believe as we do. But their ignorance prevents them, and if this were preached to them, as it was to us, they would be one with us. Toward such well-meaning people we must assume an entirely different attitude from that which we assume toward the stubborn. We must bear patiently with these people and not use our liberty; since it brings no peril or harm to body or soul; in fact, it is rather salutary, and we are doing our brothers and sisters a great service besides. But if we use our liberty unnecessarily, and deliberately cause offense to our neighbor, we drive away the very one who in time would come to our faith. Thus St. Paul circumcised Timothy [Acts 16:3] because simple-minded Jews had taken offense; he thought: What harm can it do, since they are offended because of their ignorance? But when, in Antioch, they insisted that he ought and must circumcise Titus [Gal. 2:3], Paul withstood them all and to spite them refused to have Titus circumcised [Gal. 2:11]. And he stood his ground. He did the same when St. Peter by the exercise of his liberty caused a wrong conception in the minds of the unlearned. It happened in this way: when Peter was with the Gentiles, he ate pork and sausages with them, but when the Jews came in, he abstained from this food and did not eat as he did before. Then the Gentiles who had become Christians thought: Alas! we, too, must be like the Jews, eat no pork, and live according to the law of Moses. But when Paul learned that they were acting to the injury of evangelical freedom, he reproved Peter publicly and read him an apostolic lecture, saying: "If you, though a Jew, live like a Gentile, how can you compel the Gentiles to live like Jews?" [Gal. 2:14]. Thus we, too, should order our lives and use our liberty at the proper time, so that Christian liberty may suffer no injury, and no offense be given to our weak brothers and sisters who are still without the knowledge of this liberty.

The Fifth Sermon, March 13, 1522, Thursday

after Invocavit

We have heard of the things that are necessary, such as that the mass is not to be performed as a sacrifice, and of the unnecessary things, such as monks' leaving the monasteries, the marriage of priests, and images. We have seen how we must treat these matters, that no compulsion or ordinance must be made of them, and that no one shall be dragged from them or to them by the hair, but that we must let the Word of God alone do the work. Let us now consider how we must observe the blessed sacrament.

You have heard how I preached against the foolish law of the pope and opposed his precept,[22] that no woman shall wash the altar linen on which the body of Christ has lain, even if it be a pure nun, except it first be washed by a pure priest.[23] Likewise, when any one has touched the body of Christ, the priests come running and scrape his fingers, and much more of the same sort. But when a maid has slept with a naked priest, the pope winks at it and lets it go. If she becomes pregnant and bears a child, he lets that pass, too. But to touch the altar linen and the sacrament [i.e., the host], this he will not allow. But when a priest grabs it, both top and bottom, this is all right.

Against such fool laws we have preached and exposed them, in order that it might be made known that no sin is involved in these

---

[22] Reference to *On the Abuse of the Mass* (1521). WA 8, 477-563, especially pp. 508, 540.
[23] *Decretum Gratiani*, dist. 23, cap. 25.

foolish laws and commandments of the pope, and that a layman does not commit sin if he touches the cup or the body of Christ with his hands. You should give thanks to God that you have come to such clear knowledge, which many great men have lacked. But now you go ahead and become as foolish as the pope, in that you think that a person must touch the sacrament with his hands. You want to prove that you are good Christians by touching the sacrament with your hands, and thus you have dealt with the sacrament, which is our highest treasure, in such a way that it is a wonder you were not struck to the ground by thunder and lightning. All the other things God might have suffered, but this he cannot allow, because you have made a compulsion of it. And if you do not stop this, neither the emperor nor anyone else need drive me from you, I will go without urging; and I dare say that none of my enemies, though they have caused me much sorrow, have wounded me as you have.

If you want to show that you are good Christians by handling the sacrament and boast of it before the world, then Herod and Pilate are the chief and best Christians, since it seems to me that they really handled the body of Christ when they had him nailed to the cross and put to death. No, my dear friends, the kingdom of God does not consist in outward things, which can be touched or perceived, but in faith [Luke 17:20; Rom. 14:17; I Cor. 4:20].

But you may say: We live and we ought to live according to the Scriptures, and God has so instituted the sacrament that we must take it with our hands, for he said, "Take, eat, this is my body" [Matt. 26:26]. The answer is this: though I am convinced beyond a doubt that the disciples of the Lord took it with their hands, and though I admit that you may do the same without committing sin, nevertheless I can neither make it compulsory nor defend it. And my reason is that the devil, when he really pushes us to the wall, will argue: Where have you read in the Scriptures that "take" means "grasping with the hands"? How, then, am I going to prove or defend it? Indeed, how will I answer him when he cites from the Scriptures the very opposite, and proves that "take" does not mean to receive with the hands only, but also to convey to ourselves in other ways? "Listen to this, my good fellow," he will say, "is not the word 'take' used by three evangelists when they described the Lord's taking of gall and vinegar? [Matt. 27:34; Mark 15:23; Luke 23:36].

You must admit that the Lord did not touch or handle it with his hands, for his hands were nailed to the cross." This verse is a strong argument against me. Again, he cites the passage: *Et accepit omnes timor*, "Fear seized them all" [Luke 7:16], where again we must admit that fear has no hands. Thus I am driven into a corner and must concede, even against my will, that "take" means not only to receive with the hands, but to convey to myself in any other way in which it can be done. Therefore, dear friends, we must be on firm ground, if we are to withstand the devil's attack [Eph. 6:11]. Although I must acknowledge that you committed no sin when you touched the sacrament with your hands, nevertheless I must tell you that it was not a good work, because it caused offense everywhere. For the universal custom is to receive the blessed sacrament from the hands of the priest. Why will you not in this respect also serve those who are weak in faith and abstain from your liberty, particularly since it does not help you if you do it, nor harm you if you do not do it.

Therefore no new practices should be introduced, unless the gospel has first been thoroughly preached and understood, as it has been among you. On this account, dear friends, let us deal soberly and wisely in the things that pertain to God, for God will not be mocked [Gal. 6:7]. The saints may endure mockery, but with God it is vastly different. Therefore, I beseech you, give up this practice.

Concerning Both Kinds in the Sacrament

Now let us speak of the two kinds. Although I hold that it is necessary that the sacrament should be received in both kinds, according to the institution of the Lord, nevertheless it must not be made compulsory nor a general law. We must rather promote and practice and preach the Word, and then afterwards leave the result and execution of it entirely to the Word, giving everyone his freedom in this matter. Where this is not done, the sacrament becomes for me an outward work and a hypocrisy, which is just what the devil wants. But when the Word is given free course and is not bound to any external observance, it takes hold of one today and sinks into his heart, tomorrow it touches another, and so on. Thus quietly and soberly it does its work, and no one will know how it all came about.

I was glad to know when some one wrote me, that some people here had begun to receive the sacrament in both kinds. You should have allowed it to remain thus and not forced it into a law. But now you go at it pell mell, and headlong force every one to it. Dear friends, you will not succeed in that way. For if you desire to be regarded as better Christians than others just because you take the sacrament into your hands and also receive it in both kinds, you are bad Christians as far as I am concerned. In this way even a sow could be a Christian, for she has a big enough snout to receive the sacrament outwardly. We must deal soberly with such high things. Dear friends, this dare be no mockery, and if you are going to follow me, stop it. If you are not going to follow me, however, then no one need drive me away from you—I will leave you unasked, and I shall regret that I ever preached so much as one sermon in this place. The other things could be passed by, but this cannot be overlooked; for you have gone so far that people are saying: At Wittenberg there are very good Christians, for they take the sacrament in their hands and grasp the cup, and then they go to their brandy and swill themselves full. So the weak and well-meaning people, who would come to us if they had received as much instruction as we have, are driven away.

But if there is any one who is so smart that he must touch the sacrament with his hands, let him have it brought home to his house and there let him handle it to his heart's content. But in public let him abstain, since that will bring him no harm and the offense will be avoided which is caused to our brothers, sisters, and neighbors, who are now so angry with us that they are ready to kill us. I may say that of all my enemies who have opposed me up to this time none have brought me so much grief as you.

This is enough for today; tomorrow we shall say more.

The Sixth Sermon, March 14, 1522, Friday

after Invocavit[24]

In our discussion of the chief thing we have come to the reception of the sacrament, which we have not yet finished. Today we shall see how me must conduct ourselves here, and also who is worthy to receive the sacrament and who belongs there.

It is very necessary here that your hearts and consciences be well instructed and that you make a big distinction between outward reception and inner and spiritual reception. Bodily and outward reception is that in which a man receives with his mouth the body of Christ and his blood, and doubtless any man can receive the sacrament in this way, without faith and love. But this does not make a man a Christian, for if it did, even a mouse would be a Christian, for it, too, can eat the bread and perchance even drink out of the cup. It is such a simple thing to do. But the true, inner, spiritual reception is a very different thing, for it consists in the right use of the sacrament and its fruits.

I would say in the first place that this reception occurs in faith and is inward and will have Christ. There is no external sign by which we Christians may be distinguished from others except this sacrament and baptism, but without faith outward reception is nothing. There must be faith to make the reception worthy and acceptable before God, otherwise it is nothing but sham and a mere external show, which is not Christianity at all. Christianity consists solely in faith, and no outward work must be attached to it.

But faith (which we all must have, if we wish to go to the sacrament worthily) is a firm trust that Christ, the Son of God, stands in our place and has taken all our sins upon his shoulders and that he is the eternal satisfaction for our sin and reconciles us with God the Father. He who has this faith is the very one who takes his rightful place at this sacrament, and neither devil nor hell nor sin can harm him. Why? Because God is his protector and

---

[24] The title reads: "Sermon of M. Luther preached on Friday after Invocavit."

defender. And when I have this faith, then I am certain God is fighting for me; I can defy the devil, death, hell, and sin, and all the harm with which they threaten me. This is the great, inestimable treasure given us in Christ, which no man can describe or grasp in words. Only faith can take hold of the heart, and not every one has such faith [II Thess. 3:2]. Therefore this sacrament must not be made a law, as the most holy father, the pope, has done with his fool's commandment: All Christians must go to the sacrament at the holy Eastertide, and he who does not go shall not be buried in consecrated ground.[25] Is not this a foolish law which the pope has set up? Why? Because we are not all alike; we do not all have equal faith; the faith of one is stronger than that of another. It is therefore impossible that the sacrament can be made a law, and the greatest sins are committed at Easter solely on account of this un-Christian command, whose purpose is to drive and force the people to the sacrament. And if robbery, usury, unchastity, and all sins were cast upon one big heap, this sin would overtop all others, at the very time when they [who come to the sacrament] want to be most holy. Why? Because the pope can look into no one's heart to see whether he has faith or not.

But if you believe that God steps in for you and stakes all he has and his blood for you, as if he were saying: Fall in behind me without fear or delay, and then let us see what can harm you; come devil, death, sin, and hell, and all creation, I shall go before you, for I will be your rear guard and your vanguard [Isa. 52:12]; trust me and boldly rely upon me. He who believes that can not be harmed by devil, hell, sin, or death; if God fights for him, what can you do to him?

He who has such faith has his rightful place here and receives the sacrament as an assurance, or seal, or sign to assure him of God's promise and grace. But, of course, we do not all have such faith; would God one-tenth of the Christians had it! See, such rich, immeasurable treasures [Eph. 2:7], which God in his grace showers upon us, cannot be the possession of everyone, but only of those who suffer tribulation, physical or spiritual, physically through the persecution of men, spiritually through despair of conscience, outwardly

---

[25] This law goes back to the Fourth Ecumenical Lateran Synod, 1215, under Innocent III. In the canon law: *C. 12, X, de poenitentiis.*

or inwardly, when the devil causes your heart to be weak, timid, and discouraged, so that you do not know how you stand with God, and when he casts your sins into your face. And in such terrified and trembling hearts alone God desires to dwell, as the prophet Isaiah says in the sixth chapter [Isa. 66:2]. For who desires a protector, defender, and shield to stand before him if he feels no conflict within himself, so that he is distressed because of his sins and daily tormented by them? That man is not yet ready for this food. This food demands a hungering and longing man,[26] for it delights to enter a hungry soul, which is constantly battling with its sins and eager to be rid of them.

He who is not thus prepared should abstain for a while from this sacrament, for this food will not enter a sated and full heart, and if it comes to such a heart, it is harmful.[27] Therefore, if we think upon and feel within us such distress of conscience and the fear of a timid heart, we shall come with all humbleness and reverence and not run to it brashly and hastily, without all fear and humility. So we do not always find that we are fit; today I have the grace and am fit for it, but not tomorrow. Indeed, it may be that for six months I may have no desire or fitness for it.

Therefore those who are most worthy, who are constantly being assailed by death and the devil, and they are the ones to whom it is most opportunely given, in order that they may remember and firmly believe that nothing can harm them, since they now have with them him from whom none can pluck them away; let come death, devil, or sin, they cannot harm them.

This is what Christ did when he was about to institute the blessed sacrament. First he terrified his disciples and shook their hearts by saying that he was going to leave them [Matt. 26:2], which was exceedingly painful to them; and then he went on to say, "One of you will betray me" [Matt. 26:21]. Do you think that that did not cut them to the heart? Of course they accepted that saying with all

---

[26] A quotation from Augustine, cf. *Enarratio in psalmos* XXI. Migne, 36, 178. Also quoted by Luther in *Treatise Concerning the Blessed Sacrament, etc.* WA 2, 746; PE 2, 15.

[27] This is a first indication of a doctrine which Luther later developed more emphatically, the doctrine of *manducatio impiorum*, i.e., to receive the sacrament unworthily, without faith, is to receive it to one's damnation. Cf. I Cor. 11:27-29.

fear and they sat there as though they had all been traitors to God. And after he had made them all tremble with fear and sorrow, only then did he institute the blessed sacrament as a comfort and consoled them again. For this bread is a comfort for the sorrowing, a healing for the sick, a life for the dying, a food for all the hungry, and a rich treasure for all the poor and needy.

Let this be enough for this time concerning the use of this sacrament. I commend you to God.

The Seventh Sermon, March 15, 1522, Saturday before Reminiscere[28]

Yesterday we heard about the use of this holy and blessed sacrament and saw who are worthy to receive it, namely, those in whom there is the fear of death, who have timid and despairing consciences and live in fear of hell. All such come prepared to partake of this food for the strengthening of their weak faith and the comforting of their conscience. This is the true use and practice of this sacrament, and whoever does not find himself in this state, let him refrain from coming until God also takes hold of him and draws him through his Word.

We shall now speak of the fruit of this sacrament, which is love; that is, that we should treat our neighbor as God has treated us. Now we have received from God nothing but love and favor, for Christ has pledged and given us his righteousness and everything he has; he has poured out upon us all his treasures, which no man can measure and no angel can understand or fathom, for God is a glowing furnace of love, reaching even from the earth to the heavens.

Love, I say, is a fruit of this sacrament. But this I do not yet

---

[28] The title reads: "A Sermon on the Eve of the Sunday or Saturday before Reminiscere. D. M. L."

perceive among you here in Wittenberg, even though you have had much preaching and, after all, you ought to have carried this out in practice. This is the chief thing, which is the only business of a Christian man. But nobody wants to be in this, though you want to practice all sorts of unnecessary things, which are of no account. If you do not want to show yourselves Christians by your love, then leave the other things undone, too, for St. Paul says in I Cor. 11 [I Cor. 13:1], "If I speak in the tongues of men and of angels, but have not love, I am a noisy gong or a clanging cymbal." This is a terrible saying of Paul. "And if I have prophetic powers, and understand all mysteries and all knowledge, and if I have all faith, so as to remove mountains, but have not love, I am nothing. If I give away all I have, and if I deliver my body to be burned, but have not love, I gain nothing" [I Cor. 13:2-3]. Not yet have you come so far as this, though you have received great and rich gifts from God, the highest of which is a knowledge of the Scriptures. It is true, you have the true gospel and the pure Word of God, but no one as yet has given his goods to the poor, no one has yet been burned, and even these things would be nothing without love. You are willing to take all of God's goods in the sacrament, but you are not willing to pour them out again in love. Nobody extends a helping hand to another, nobody seriously considers the other person, but everyone looks out for himself and his own gain, insists on his own way, and lets everything else go hang. If anybody is helped, well and good; but nobody looks after the poor to see how you might be able to help them. This is a pity. You have heard many sermons about it and all my books are full of it and have this one purpose, to urge you to faith and love.

And if you will not love one another, God will send a great plague upon you; let this be a warning to you, for God will not have his Word revealed and preached in vain. You are tempting God too far, my friends; for if in times past someone had preached the Word to our forefathers, they would perhaps have acted differently. Or if it were preached even now to many poor children in the cloisters, they would receive it more joyfully than you. You are not heeding it at all and you are playing around with all kinds of tomfoolery which does not amount to anything.

I commend you to God.

The Eighth Sermon, March 16, 1522,

Reminiscere Sunday

A Short Summary of the Sermon of D[r.] M[artin] L[uther]
Preached on Reminiscere Sunday on Private Confession

Now we have heard all the things which ought to be considered
here, except confession. Of this we shall speak now.

In the first place, there is a confession which is founded on the
Scriptures, and it is this: when anybody committed a sin publicly or
with other men's knowledge, he was accused before the congregation. If he abandoned his sin, they interceded for him with God.
But if he would not listen to the congregation [*häuffen*], he was cast
out and excluded from the assembly, so that no one would have anything to do with him. And this confession is commanded by God in
Matt. 18 [:15], "If your brother sins against you (so that you and
others are offended), go and tell him his fault, between you and
him alone." We no longer have any trace of this kind of confession
any more; at this point the gospel is in abeyance. Anybody who was
able to re-establish it would be doing a good work. Here is where
you should have exerted yourselves and re-established this kind of
confession, and let the other things go; for no one would have been
offended by this and everything would have gone smoothly and
quietly. It should be done in this way: When you see a usurer,
adulterer, thief, or drunkard, you should go to him in secret, and
admonish him to give up his sin. If he will not listen, you should
take two others with you and admonish him once more, in a brotherly way, to give up his sin. But if he scorns that, you should tell
the pastor before the whole congregation, have your witnesses with
you, and accuse him before the pastor in the presence of the people,
saying: Dear pastor, this man has done this and that and would not
take our brotherly admonition to give up his sin. Therefore I accuse
him, together with my witnesses, who have heard this. Then, if he
will not give up and willingly acknowledge his guilt, the pastor
should exclude him and put him under the ban before the whole

assembly, for the sake of the congregation, until he comes to himself and is received back again. This would be Christian. But I cannot undertake to carry it out single-handed.

Secondly, we need a kind of confession when we go into a corner by ourselves and confess to God himself and pour out before him all our faults. This kind of confession is also commanded. From this comes the familiar word of Scripture: *Facite judicium et justitiam.*[29] *Judicium facere est nos ipsos accusare et damnare; justitiam autem facere est fidere misericordiae Dei.*[30] As it is written, "Blessed are they who observe justice, who do righteousness at all times" [Ps. 106:3]. Judgment is nothing else than a man's knowing and judging and condemning himself, and this is true humility and self-abasement. Righteousness is nothing else than a man's knowing himself and praying to God for the mercy and help through which God raises him up again. This is what David means when he says, "I have sinned; I will confess my transgressions to the Lord and thou didst forgive the guilt of my sin; for this all thy saints shall pray to thee" [Ps. 32:5-6].

Thirdly, there is also the kind of confession in which one takes another aside and tells him what troubles one, so that one may hear from him a word of comfort; and this confession is commanded by the pope. It is this urging and forcing which I condemned when I wrote concerning confession,[31] and I refuse to go to confession simply because the pope has commanded it and insists upon it. For I wish him to keep his hands off the confession and not make of it a compulsion or command, which he has not the power to do. Nevertheless I will allow no man to take private confession away from me, and I would not give it up for all the treasures in the world, since I know what comfort and strength it has given me. No one knows what it can do for him except one who has struggled often and long with the devil. Yea, the devil would have slain me long ago, if the confession had not sustained me. For there are many doubtful matters which a man cannot resolve or find the answer to by himself, and so he takes his brother aside and tells him his trouble.

---

[29] Do judgment and righteousness. Cf. Gen. 18:19.
[30] To do judgment is to accuse and condemn ourselves; but to do righteousness is to trust in the mercy of God.
[31] *Von der Beichte, ob die der Papst Macht habe zu gebieten* (1521). WA 8, 138-204.

What harm is there if he humbles himself a little before his neighbor, puts himself to shame, looks for a word of comfort from him, accepts it, and believes it, as if he were hearing it from God himself, as we read in Matt. 18 [:19], "If two of you agree about anything they ask, it will be done for them."

Moreover, we must have many absolutions, so that we may strengthen our timid consciences and despairing hearts against the devil and against God. Therefore, no man shall forbid the confession nor keep or draw any one away from it. And if any one is wrestling with his sins and wants to be rid of them and desires a sure word on the matter, let him go and confess to another in secret, and accept what he says to him as if God himself had spoken it through the mouth of this person. However, one who has a strong, firm faith that his sins are forgiven may let this confession go and confess to God alone. But how many have such a strong faith? Therefore, as I have said, I will not let this private confession be taken from me. But I will not have anybody forced to it, but left to each one's free will.

For our God, the God we have, is not so niggardly that he has left us with only one comfort or strengthening for our conscience, or only one absolution, but we have many absolutions in the gospel and we are richly showered with many absolutions. For instance, we have this in the gospel: "If you forgive men their trespasses, your heavenly Father will also forgive you" [Matt. 6:14]. Another comfort we have in the Lord's Prayer: "Forgive us our trespasses," etc. [Matt. 6:12]. A third is our baptism, when I reason thus: See, my Lord, I have been baptized in thy name so that I may be assured of thy grace and mercy. Then we have private confession, when I go and receive a sure absolution as if God himself spoke it, so that I may be assured that my sins are forgiven. Finally, I take to myself the blessed sacrament, when I eat his body and drink his blood as a sign that I am rid of my sins and God has freed me from all my frailties; and in order to make me sure of this, he gives me his body to eat and his blood to drink, so that I shall not and cannot doubt that I have a gracious God.

Thus you see that confession must not be despised, but that it is a comforting thing. And since we need many absolutions and assurances, because we must fight against the devil, death, hell, and sin, we must not allow any of our weapons to be taken away, but keep intact the whole armor and equipment which God has given us to use against our enemies. For you do not yet know what labor it costs to fight with the devil and overcome him. But I know it well, for I have eaten a bit of salt or two with him. I know him well, and he knows me well, too. If you had known him, you would not have rejected confession in this way.

I commend you to God. Amen.

21.

CONCERNING THE
ORDER OF PUBLIC WORSHIP

The service now in common use everywhere goes back to genuine Christian beginnings, as does the office of preaching. But as the latter has been perverted by the spiritual tyrants, so the former has been corrupted by the hypocrites. As we do not on that account abolish the office of preaching, but aim to restore it again to its right and proper place, so it is not our intention to do away with the service, but to restore it again to its rightful use.

Three serious abuses have crept into the service. First, God's Word has been silenced, and only reading and singing remain in the churches. This is the worst abuse. Second, when God's Word had been silenced such a host of un-Christian fables and lies, in legends, hymns, and sermons were introduced that it is horrible to see. Third, such divine service was performed as a work whereby God's grace and salvation might be won. As a result, faith disappeared and everyone pressed to enter the priesthood, convents, and monasteries, and to build churches and endow them.

Now in order to correct these abuses, know first of all that a Christian congregation should never gather together without the preaching of God's Word and prayer, no matter how briefly, as Psalm 102[1] says, "When the kings and the people assemble to serve the Lord, they shall declare the name and the praise of God." And Paul in I Corinthians 14 [:26-31] says that when they come together, there should be prophesying, teaching, and admonition.[2] Therefore, when God's Word is not preached, one had better neither sing nor read, or even come together.

---

[1] A conflation and free rendering of Ps. 102:21-22.
[2] When Luther refers to I Corinthians 14, he assumes that the Scriptures are read in Latin, a practice he associates with speaking in tongues. Hence teaching and admonition, i.e., explanation of the lesson, should follow for the benefit of those who do not understand the Latin. WA 18, 124-125; WA 12, 31.

This was the custom among Christians at the time of the apostles and should also be the custom now. We should assemble daily at four or five in the morning and have [God's Word] read, either by pupils or priests, or whoever it may be, in the same manner as the lesson is still read at Matins; this should be done by one or two, or by one individual or choir after responding to the other,[3] as may seem most suitable.

Thereupon the preacher, or whoever has been appointed, shall come forward and interpret a part of the same lesson, so that all others may understand and learn it, and be admonished. The former[4] is called by Paul in I Corinthians 14 [:27] "speaking in tongues." The other he calls "interpreting" or "prophesying," or "speaking with sense or understanding." If this is not done, the congregation is not benefited by the lesson, as has been the case in cloisters and in convents, where they only bawled against the walls.

The lesson should be taken from the Old Testament; one of the books should be selected and one or two chapters, or half a chapter, be read, until the book is finished. After that another book should be selected, and so on, until the entire Bible has been read through; and where one does not understand it, pass on, and give glory to God. Thus Christian people will by daily training become proficient, skilful, and well versed in the Bible. For this is how genuine Christians were made in former times—both virgins and martyrs—and could also be made today.

Now when the lesson and its interpretation have lasted half an hour or so, the congregation shall unite in giving thanks to God, in praising him, and in praying for the fruits of the Word, etc. For this, the Psalms should be used and some good responsories and antiphons. In brief, let everything be completed in one hour or whatever time seems desirable; for one must not overload souls or weary them, as was the case until now in monasteries and convents, where they burdened themselves like mules.

---

[3] This is a reference to the two parts of a chancel choir which face each other in the stalls.
[4] I.e., the reading of the lesson just mentioned.

In like manner, come together at five or six in the evening. At this time one should really read again the Old Testament, book by book, namely the Prophets, even as Moses and the historical books are taken up in the morning. But since the New Testament is also a book, I read the Old Testament in the morning and the New Testament in the evening, or vice versa, and have reading, interpreting, praising, singing, and praying just as in the morning, also for an hour. For all that matters is that the Word of God be given free reign to uplift and quicken souls so that they do not become weary.

Should one desire to hold another such service during the day after lunch, that is a matter of choice.

And although these daily services might not be attended by the whole congregation, the priests and pupils, and especially those who, one hopes, will become good preachers and pastors,[5] should be present. And one should admonish them to do this willingly, not reluctantly or by constraint, or for the sake of reward, temporal or eternal, but alone to the glory of God and the neighbor's good.

Besides these daily services for a smaller group, the whole congregation should come together on Sundays, and mass and Vespers be sung, as has been customary. In both services there should be preaching for the whole congregation, in the morning on the Gospel for the day, in the evening on the Epistle; or the preacher may use his own judgment whether he would want to preach on a certain book or two.

If anyone desires to receive the sacrament at this time, let it be administered at a time convenient to all concerned.

The daily masses should be completely discontinued; for the Word is important and not the mass. But if any should desire the sacrament during the week, let mass be held as inclination and time dictate; for in this matter one cannot make hard and fast rules.

Let the chants in the Sunday masses and Vespers be retained; they are quite good and are taken from Scripture. However, one may lessen or increase their number. But to select the chants and

---

[5] *Seelsorger.*

Psalms for the daily morning and evening service shall be the duty of the pastor[6] and preacher. For every morning he shall appoint a fitting responsory or antiphon with a collect, likewise for the evening; this is to be read and chanted publicly after the lesson and exposition. But for the time being we can shelve the antiphons, responsories, and collects, as well as the legends of the saints and the cross, until they have been purged, for there is a horrible lot of filth in them.

All the festivals of saints are to be discontinued. Where there is a good Christian legend, it may be inserted as an example after the Gospel on Sunday. The festivals of the Purification and Annunciation of Mary may be continued, and for the time being also her Assumption and Nativity, although the songs in them are not pure. The festival of John the Baptist is also pure. Not one of the legends of the apostles is pure, except St. Paul's. They may either be transferred to the [closest] Sunday or be celebrated separately, if one so desires.

Other matters will adjust themselves as the need arises. And this is the sum of the matter: Let everything be done so that the Word may have free course instead of the prattling and rattling that has been the rule up to now. We can spare everything except the Word. Again, we profit by nothing as much as by the Word. For the whole Scripture shows that the Word should have free course among Christians. And in Luke 10 [:42], Christ himself says, "One thing is needful," i.e., that Mary sit at the feet of Christ and hear his word daily. This is the best part to choose and it shall not be taken away forever. It is an eternal Word. Everything else must pass away, no matter how much care and trouble it may give Martha. God help us achieve this. Amen.

---

6 *Pfarrer.*

22.

AN ORDER OF MASS AND COMMUNION FOR THE CHURCH AT WITTENBERG

Grace and peace in Christ to the venerable Doctor Nicholas Haus-mann, bishop of the church in Zwickau, saint in Christ, from Martin Luther.

Until now I have only used books and sermons to wean the hearts of people from their godless regard for ceremonial; for I believed it would be a Christian and helpful thing if I could prompt a peaceful removal of the abomination which Satan set up in the holy place through the man of sin [Matt. 24:15; II Thess. 2:3-4]. Therefore, I have used neither authority nor pressure. Nor did I make any innovations. For I have been hesitant and fearful, partly because of the weak in faith, who cannot suddenly exchange an old and accustomed order of worship for a new and unusual one, and more so because of the fickle and fastidious spirits who rush in like unclean swine without faith or reason, and who delight only in novelty and tire of it as quickly, when it has worn off. Such people are a nuisance even in other affairs, but in spiritual matters, they are absolutely unbearable. Nonetheless, at the risk of bursting with anger, I must bear with them, unless I want to let the gospel itself be denied to the people.

But since there is hope now that the hearts of many have been enlightened and strengthened by the grace of God, and since the cause of the kingdom of Christ demands that at long last offenses should be removed from it, we must dare something in the name of Christ. For it is right that we should provide at least for a few, lest by our desire to detach ourselves from the frivolous faddism of some people,[1] we provide for nobody, or by our fear

---

[1] I.e., the enthusiasts.

of ultimately offending others,[2] we endorse their universally held abominations.

Therefore, most excellent Nicholas, since you have requested it so often, we will deal with an evangelical[3] form of saying mass (as it is called) and of administering communion. And we will so deal with it that we shall no longer rule hearts by teaching alone, but we will put our hand to it and put the revision into practice in the public administration of communion, not wishing, however, to prejudice others against adopting and following a different order. Indeed, we heartily beg in the name of Christ that if in time something better should be revealed to them, they would tell us to be silent, so that by a common effort we may aid the common cause.

We therefore first assert: It is not now nor ever has been our intention to abolish the liturgical service of God[4] completely, but rather to purify the one that is now in use from the wretched accretions which corrupt it and to point out an evangelical use. We cannot deny that the mass, i.e., the communion of bread and wine, is a rite divinely instituted by Christ himself and that it was observed first by Christ and then by the apostles, quite simply and evangelically without any additions. But in the course of time so many human inventions were added to it that nothing except the names of the mass and communion has come down to us.

Now the additions of the early fathers who, it is reported, softly prayed one or two Psalms before blessing the bread and wine are commendable. Athanasius[5] and Cyprian[6] are supposed to be some of these. Those who added the Kyrie eleison also did

---

[2] I.e., the Romanists.

[3] Latin: *pia*. In Luther's usage in this context, the word *pius* means "in accord with the gospel." Speratus translates: "Christian." Similarly, *impius* denotes everything connected with work righteousness, in spite of the "piety" seemingly attached to it.

[4] *Cultus dei*.

[5] Cf. Athanasius, *De Fuga*. MPG 25, 676: "When I sat on the throne, I told the deacon to read the Psalm and the people to respond with 'for his mercy endureth forever' " [Ps. 136:1]; see also the reference to Athanasius' practice of Psalmody in Augustine, *Confessions*, X, 33, 50. MPL 32, 800.

[6] Cyprian (d. 258), bishop of Carthage. Perhaps Luther was thinking of Cyprian's advice to Donatus (*Epistle* I. ANF 5, 280), "Let the temperate meal resound with Psalms."

well. We read that under Basil the Great,[7] the Kyrie eleison was in common use by all the people. The reading of the Epistles and Gospels is necessary, too. Only it is wrong to read them in a language the common people do not understand. Later, when chanting began, the Psalms were changed into the introit; the Angelic Hymn *Gloria in Excelsis: et in terra pax*,[8] the graduals, the alleluias, the Nicene Creed, the Sanctus, the Agnus Dei, and the *communio*[9] were added. All of these are unobjectionable, especially the ones that are sung *de tempore*[10] or on Sundays. For these days by themselves testify to ancient purity, the canon excepted.

But when everyone felt free to add or change at will and when the tyranny of priestly greed and pride entered in, then our wicked kings, i.e., the bishops and pastors, began to erect those altars to the images of Baal and all gods in the Lord's temple. Then it was that wicked King Ahaz removed the brazen altar and erected another copied from one in Damascus.[11] What I am speaking of is the canon, that abominable concoction drawn from everyone's sewer and cesspool. The mass became a sacrifice. Offertories[12] and mercenary[13] collects were added. Sequences and proses[14] were inserted in the Sanctus and the Gloria in Excelsis. Whereupon the mass began to be a priestly monopoly devouring

Problem

---

[7] Luther seems to refer to the note in Guillaume Durand, *Rationale divinorum officiorum* (Argentine, 1484), lib. iv, fol. 12, 4, that before Pope Gregory the Great (*ca.* 540-604) and among the Greeks, the Kyrie was sung by both clergy and people. This note is contained in the paragraph which begins with a reference to the intonation of the Kyrie by Basil the Great, bishop of Caesarea (*ca.* 330-379).

[8] The Gloria in Excelsis was commonly called the Angelic Hymn because of its derivation from Luke 2:14.

[9] The chant sung during the distribution of the Lord's Supper.

[10] Cf. p. xiv, n. 4.

[11] Cf. II Kings 16:10-14.

[12] Of the propers of the mass, the offertory was the most offensive to Luther, because it stressed the sacrificial concept of the Lord's Supper.

[13] Luther calls the prayers (for the departed, for special favors, etc.) in the canon "mercenary" because they were based on the assumption that the sacrifice of the mass would evoke a readier response from God.

[14] As commonly understood, a sequence or prose is a kind of Latin hymn that was sung after the Alleluia. Luther thought highly of some of these (cf. p. 455). Here he seems to refer to tropes, which in a manner similar to the sequences and proses added new words to an existing melody in the Gloria or Sanctus.

the wealth of the whole world and engulfing it—as with an apoca‑ lyptic plague—with a host of rich, lazy, powerful, lascivious, and corrupt celibates. Thus came the masses for the departed, for journeys, for prosperity—but who can even name the causes for which the mass was made a sacrifice?

Nor do they cease to enlarge the canon even today: now it is for these feasts, then for others; now these *actiones* then other *communicantes*[15] are adopted—not to mention the commemoration of the living and the dead.[16] And there is no end of it yet. And what shall I say of the external additions of vestments, vessels, candles, and palls, of organs and all the music, and of images? There was scarcely a craft in all the world that did not depend on the mass for a large part of its business.

All these have been tolerated and—with the gospel revealing so many abominations—they can be tolerated until they can be completely removed. In the meanwhile we shall prove all things and hold fast what is good [I Thess. 5:21]. But in this book we are not going to prove again that the mass is neither a sacrifice nor a good work—we have amply demonstrated that elsewhere.[17] We do accept it as a sacrament, a testament, the blessing (as in Latin), the eucharist (as in Greek), the Table of the Lord, the Lord's Supper, the Lord's Memorial, communion, or by whatever evangelical name you please, so long as it is not polluted by the name of sacrifice or work. And we will set forth the rite accord‑ ing to which we think that it should be used.

First, we approve and retain the introits for the Lord's days and the festivals of Christ, such as Easter, Pentecost, and the Na‑ tivity, although we prefer the Psalms from which they were taken as of old.[18] But for the time being we permit the accepted use.

---

[15] The passage of canon called *intra actionem* and beginning with the word *communicantes* is altered on certain days.

[16] The canon contains prayers for the living (*Memento, Domine*) and for the dead (*Memento etiam*) that provide for the insertion of the names of certain beneficiaries.

[17] *A Treatise on the New Testament, that is, the Holy Mass*, 1520. LW 35, 79-111; *The Babylonian Captivity of the Church*, 1520. LW 36, 47-56, *passim; The Misuse of the Mass*, 1521. LW 36, 162-198.

[18] Cf. pp. 468-469.

And if any desire to approve the introits (inasmuch as they have been taken from Psalms or other passages of Scripture) for apostles' days, for feasts of the Virgin and of other saints, we do not condemn them. But we in Wittenberg intend to observe[19] only the Lord's days and the festivals of the Lord. We think that all the feasts of the saints should be abrogated, or if anything in them deserves it, it should be brought into the Sunday sermon. We regard the feasts of Purification[20] and Annunciation[21] as feasts of Christ, even as Epiphany[22] and Circumcision.[23] Instead of the feasts of St. Stephen[24] and of St. John the Evangelist,[25] we are pleased to use the office of the Nativity. The feasts of the Holy Cross[26] shall be anathema. Let others act according to their own conscience or in consideration of the weakness of some—whatever the Spirit may suggest.

Second, we accept the Kyrie eleison in the form in which it has been used until now, with the various melodies for different seasons, together with the Angelic Hymn, Gloria in Excelsis, which follows it. However, the bishop[27] may decide to omit the latter as often as he wishes.

Third, the prayer or collect which follows, if it is evangelical (and those for Sunday usually are), should be retained in its accepted form; but there should be only one. After this the Epistle is read. Certainly the time has not yet come to attempt revision here, as nothing unevangelical is read, except that those parts from the Epistles of Paul in which faith is taught are read only rarely, while the exhortations to morality are most frequently read. The Epistles seem to have been chosen by a singularly unlearned and

---

[19] Literally, to keep the Sabbath.
[20] February 2.
[21] March 25.
[22] January 6.
[23] January 1.
[24] December 26.
[25] December 27.
[26] The Invention of the Holy Cross, May 3; the Exaltation of the Cross, September 14. On Luther's marked opposition to these festivals, cf. WA 10ᴵᴵᴵ, 113-119; 332-341; 361-371.
[27] *Episcopus*, "bishop." Luther sometimes refers to the parish pastor as "bishop." Speratus translates *Pfarrherr*.

superstitious advocate of works. But for the service those sections in which faith in Christ is taught should have been given preference. The latter were certainly considered more often in the Gospels by whoever it was who chose these lessons. In the meantime, the sermon in the vernacular will have to supply what is lacking. If in the future the vernacular be used in the mass (which Christ may grant), one must see to it that Epistles and Gospels chosen from the best and most weighty parts of these writings be read in the mass.

Fourth, the gradual of two verses[28] shall be sung, either together with the Alleluia, or one of the two, as the bishop may decide. But the Quadragesima graduals and others like them that exceed two verses[29] may be sung at home by whoever wants them. In church we do not want to quench the spirit of the faithful with tedium. Nor is it proper to distinguish Lent, Holy Week, or Good Friday from other days, lest we seem to mock and ridicule Christ with half of a mass and the one part of the sacrament.[30] For the Alleluia is the perpetual voice of the church, just as the memorial of His passion and victory is perpetual.

Fifth, we allow no sequences or proses unless the bishop wishes to use the short one for the Nativity of Christ: *"Grates nunc*

---

[28] Most of the graduals consist of two verses, of which the first is repeated after the second. The Alleluias are usually short and consist of only one verse with its Alleluias.

[29] Quadragesima, the first Sunday in Lent, here refers to the whole Lenten season. In Lent the "tracts," consisting of up to thirteen verses, took the place of the gradual.

[30] The Mass of the Presanctified. This is a celebration without the consecration of the host or wine. Two hosts are consecrated on Maundy Thursday and one is reserved in a specially prepared place for use on Good Friday. On Good Friday the wine is not consecrated by the usual prayers, but rather by placing a third part of the preconsecrated host into it. The prayers in connection with the wine are omitted in this Good Friday use, but the unconsecrated wine together with the portion of the host placed in it is consumed by the priest. Though not forbidden to commune, the people at that time were directed to commune in silence (*sub silentio*). WA 12, 210, n. 2; PE 6, 104, n. 54. In his *Defense and Explanation of All the Articles*, 1521, Luther speaks of a "half-sacrament" (*halb sacrament*), though in a different context. LW 32, 56; WA 7, 389. Cf. also WA 7, 123, when he speaks of "the one part of the sacrament," *altera pars sacramenti.*

omnes."[31] There are hardly any which smack of the Spirit, save those of the Holy Spirit: *"Sancti Spiritus"*[32] and *"Veni sancte spiritus,"*[33] which may be sung after breakfast,[34] at Vespers, or at mass (if the bishop pleases).

Sixth, the Gospel lesson follows, for which we neither prohibit nor prescribe candles or incense. Let these things be free.

Seventh, the custom of singing the Nicene Creed does not displease us; yet this matter should also be left in the hands of the bishop. Likewise, we do not think that it matters whether the sermon in the vernacular comes after the Creed or before the introit of the mass; although it might be argued that since the Gospel is the voice crying in the wilderness[35] and calling unbelievers to faith, it seems particularly fitting to preach before mass. For properly speaking, the mass consists in using[36] the Gospel and communing at the table of the Lord. Inasmuch as it belongs to believers, it should be observed apart [from unbelievers].[37] Yet since we are free, this argument does not bind us, especially since everything in the mass up to the Creed is ours, free and not prescribed by God; therefore it does not necessarily have anything to do with the mass.

Eighth, that utter abomination follows which forces all that

---

[31] *"Grates nunc omnes reddamus Domino Deo, qui sua nativitate nos liberavit de diabolica potestate"*; attributed to Notker Balbulus of St. Gall (d. 912). *MPL* 131, 1005. Translated into German as *"Danksagen wir alle,"* it is found in many early Lutheran hymnals. Cf. Johannes Zahn, *Die Melodien der deutschen evangelischen Kirchenlieder* (Gütersloh: Bertelsmann), V (1892), No. 8619. Following John Julian's *Dictionary of Hymnology* (London, 1892), Strodach erroneously states that Luther's *"Gelobet seist du, Jesu Christ,"* was based on this sequence. *PE* 6, 105, n. 58.

[32] Attributed to Notker, *"Sancti Spiritus adsit nobis gratia, quaecorda nostra sibi faciat habitaculum"* was an eleventh-century sequence appointed for use following the reading of the Epistle for Pentecost. *MPL* 131, 1012.

[33] *"Veni sancte spiritus et emitte coelitus,"* a thirteenth-century sequence formerly used on Whitmonday (cf. Julian, *Dictionary of Hymnology,* pp. 1212-1215), which Luther prized highly; cf. *WA, TR* 4, No. 4627, p. 409. Strodach in *PE* 6, 105, confuses this sentence with the antiphon *"Veni sancte spiritus, reple tuorum corda fidelium,"* on which Luther's hymn "Come, Holy Spirit Lord and God" is based.

[34] Does Luther mean during Matins?

[35] Cf. Matt. 3:3.

[36] Luther distinguishes the "use" from the "preaching" of the gospel. It is heard by all, but "used" only by the believers.

[37] Cf. *LW* 53, 64.

precedes in the mass into its service and is, therefore, called the offertory. From here on almost everything smacks and savors of sacrifice. And the words of life and salvation [the Words of Institution] are imbedded in the midst of it all, just as the ark of the Lord once stood in the idol's temple next to Dagon.[38] And there was no Israelite who could approach or bring back the ark until it "smote his enemies in the hinder parts, putting them to a perpetual reproach,"[39] and forced them to return it—which is a parable of the present time. Let us, therefore, repudiate everything that smacks of sacrifice, together with the entire canon and retain only that which is pure and holy, and so order our mass.[40]

I. After the Creed or after the sermon[41] let bread and wine be made ready for blessing[42] in the customary manner. I have not yet decided whether or not water should be mixed with the wine. I rather incline, however, to favor pure wine without water; for the passage, "Thy wine is mixed with water," in Isaiah 1 [:22] gives the mixture a bad connotation.

Pure wine beautifully portrays the purity of gospel teaching. Further, the blood of Christ, whom we here commemorate, has been poured out unmixed with ours. Nor can the fancies of those be upheld who say that this is a sign of our union with Christ; for that is not what we commemorate. In fact, we are not united with Christ until he sheds his blood; or else we would be celebrating the shedding of our own blood together with the blood of Christ shed for us. Nonetheless, I have no intention of cramping anyone's freedom or of introducing a law that might again lead to superstition. Christ will not care very much about these matters, nor are they worth arguing about. Enough foolish controversies have been fought on these and many other matters by the Roman and Greek

---

[38] I Sam. 5:2.

[39] Ps. 78:66; cf. I Sam. 5:12.

[40] I.e., the mass in the narrower sense of the word, namely, the celebration of the Lord's Supper.

[41] Original: *post canonem*, an obvious misprint for *post concionem*.

[42] *Benedictio* is regularly translated as "blessing" or "benediction," except for *verba benedictionis*, which is translated "Words of Institution."

churches.[43] And though some[44] direct attention to the water and blood which flowed from the side of Jesus,[45] they prove nothing. For that water signified something entirely different from what they wish that mixed water to signify. Nor was it mixed with blood. The symbolism does not fit, and the reference is inapplicable. As a human invention, this mixing [of water and wine] cannot, therefore, be considered binding.

II. The bread and wine having been prepared, one may proceed as follows:

The Lord be with you.

Response: And with thy spirit.

Lift up your hearts.

Response: Let us lift them to the Lord.

Let us give thanks unto the Lord our God.

Response: It is meet and right.

It is truly meet and right, just and salutary for us to give thanks to Thee always and everywhere, Holy Lord, Father Almighty, Eternal God, through Christ our Lord . . .

III. Then:

. . . Who the day before he suffered, took bread, and when he had given thanks, brake it, and gave it to his disciples, saying, Take, eat; this is my body, which is given for you.

After the same manner also the cup, when he had

---

[43] Jerome Emser attacked Luther's restructuring of the mass on many points. On this point, he asserts: "Not only in Rome, but in Egypt, Asia, Africa, Europe, and throughout the whole Christian world, the rite of mixing water with wine is observed; and the Greek author, Theophilus, also approves." *Missa Christianorum contra Lutheranam missandi formulam assertio,* 1524. *Corpus Catholicorum,* 28, 30-31; cf. WA 12, 212, note.

In his argument Luther followed Guillaume Durand, a thirteenth-century French canonist and liturgical writer. Durand states: "It is said that the Greek church did not add water to the sacrament." *Rationale divinorum officiorum,* lib. iv, fol. 70. Similar statements were made by Peter Lombard, *Sententiarum* (Venice, 1563), lib. iv, dist. XI, ques. 8 (cf. *MPL* 192, 864), and by others (cf. *MPL* 58, 1044).

[44] Pseudo-Ambrose in *De sacramentis,* lib. v, cap. 1. *MPL* 16, 447; Gennadii, *De ecclesiasticis dogmatibus,* cap. 75. *MPL* 58, 998.

[45] John 19:34.

supped, saying, This cup is the New Testament in my blood, which is shed for you and for many, for the remission of sins; this do, as often as ye do it, in remembrance of me.

I wish these words of Christ—with a brief pause after the preface—to be recited in the same tone in which the Lord's Prayer is chanted elsewhere in the canon so that those who are present may be able to hear them, although the evangelically minded should be free about all these things and may recite these words either silently or audibly.

IV. The blessing ended, let the choir sing the Sanctus. And while the Benedictus is being sung, let the bread and cup be elevated according to the customary rite for the benefit of the weak in faith who might be offended if such an obvious change in this rite of the mass were suddenly made. This concession can be made especially where through sermons in the vernacular they have been taught what the elevation means.

V. After this, the Lord's Prayer shall be read. Thus, let us pray: "Taught by thy saving precepts. . . ."[46] The prayer which follows, "Deliver us, we beseech thee . . . ,"[47] is to be omitted together with all the signs[48] they were accustomed to make over the host and with the host over the chalice. Nor shall the host be broken or mixed into the chalice. But immediately after the Lord's Prayer shall be said, "The peace of the Lord," etc., which is, so to speak, a public absolution of the sins of the communicants, the true voice of the gospel announcing remission of sins, and there-

---

[46] The introduction to the Lord's Prayer in the Roman canon: "Taught by thy saving precepts and guided by the divine institution, we make bold to say: Our Father," etc.

[47] In the translation by Luther D. Reed (*The Lutheran Liturgy* [2nd ed.; Philadelphia: Muhlenberg Press, 1960], pp. 727-728), this prayer reads: "Deliver us, we beseech thee, O Lord, from all evils, past, present and to come, and by the intercession of the blessed and glorious ever Virgin Mary, Mother of God, together with thy blessed apostles Peter and Paul, and Andrew, and all the saints, mercifully grant peace in our days: that through the bounteous help of thy mercy we may be always free from sin and secure from all disturbance. Through the same Jesus Christ, thy Son our Lord, who liveth and reigneth with thee and the Holy Ghost, one God, world without end."

[48] The signs of the cross.

fore the one and most worthy preparation for the Lord's Table, if faith holds to these words as coming from the mouth of Christ himself. On this account I would like to have it pronounced facing the people, as the bishops are accustomed to do, which is the only custom of the ancient bishops that is left among our bishops.

VI. Then, while the Agnus Dei is sung, let him [the liturgist] communicate, first himself and then the people. But if he should wish to pray the prayer, "O Lord Jesus Christ, Son of the living God, who according to the will of the Father," etc.,[49] before communing, he does not pray wrongly, provided he changes the singular "mine" and "me" to the plural "ours" and "us." The same thing holds for the prayer, "The body of our Lord Jesus Christ preserve my (or thy) soul unto life eternal," and, "The blood of our Lord preserve thy soul unto life eternal."

VII. If he desires to have the communion sung,[50] let it be sung. But instead of the *complenda* or final collect,[51] because it sounds almost like a sacrifice, let the following prayer be read in the same tone: "What we have taken with our lips, O Lord . . . ."[52] The following one may also be read: "May thy body which we have received . . . (changing to the plural number) . . . who livest and reignest world without end."[53] "The Lord be with you," etc.

---

[49] In the Roman canon the prayer continues as follows: ". . . and the co-operation of the Holy Ghost, didst through thy death give life to the world: deliver me by this thy most sacred body and blood from all mine iniquities, and from all evils: and make me ever to cleave to thy commandments; nor ever suffer me to be separated from thee: who with the Father and the Holy Ghost livest and reignest with God, world without end. Amen."

[50] Literally, "If he desires to sing the communion." But the communion was one of the propers to be sung by the choir, not by the priest. Speratus also translates, "If one desires to have," etc.

[51] This is evidently a reference to the final collect in the canon of the Roman mass: "May the homage of my bounden duty be pleasing to thee, O holy Trinity; and grant that the sacrifice which I, though unworthy, have offered in the sight of thy majesty may be acceptable to thee, and through thy mercy be a propitiation for me and for all those for whom I have offered it. Through Christ our Lord. Amen." Reed, *op. cit.*, p. 734.

[52] In the Roman canon this prayer continues: ". . . may we with pure minds receive; and from a temporal gift, may it become to us an everlasting remedy."

[53] In the Roman canon, this prayer continues: ". . . cleave to mine [our] inmost parts: and grant that no stain of sin may remain in me [us] whom this pure and holy sacrament hath refreshed, O thou. . . ."

In place of the *Ite missa*[54] let the *Benedicamus domino*[55] be said, adding Alleluia according to its own melodies where and when it is desired. Or the *Benedicamus* may be borrowed from Vespers.

VIII. The customary benediction may be given;[56] or else the one from Numbers 6 [:24-27], which the Lord himself appointed:

"The Lord bless us and keep us. The Lord make his face shine upon us and be gracious unto us. The Lord lift up his countenance upon us, and give us peace."

Or the one from Psalm 67 [:6-7]:

"God, even our own God shall bless us. God shall bless us; and all the ends of the earth shall fear him."

I believe Christ used something like this when, ascending into heaven, he blessed his disciples [Luke 24:50-51].

The bishop should also be free to decide on the order in which he will receive and administer both species. He may choose to bless both bread and wine before he takes the bread. Or else he may, between the blessing of the bread and of the wine, give the bread both to himself and to as many as desire it, then bless the wine and administer it to all. This is the order Christ seems to have observed, as the words of the Gospel show, where he told them to eat the bread before he had blessed the cup [Mark 14:22-23]. Then is said expressly, "Likewise also the cup after he supped" [Luke 22:20; I Cor. 11:25]. Thus you see that the cup was not blessed until after the bread had been eaten. But this order is [now] quite new and allows no room for those prayers which heretofore were said after the blessing,[57] unless they would also be changed.

Thus we think about the mass. But in all these matters we will want to beware lest we make binding what should be free, or make sinners of those who may do some things differently or omit

---

[54] "Go, mass is ended," the closing versicle of the Roman canon.

[55] "Bless we the Lord," the closing versicle of the Roman canon for Advent and Lent. Vespers also closed with this versicle.

[56] In the Roman mass: "May Almighty God bless you: the Father, and the Son, and the Holy Ghost."

[57] The prayers listed under sections IV and V.

others. All that matters is that the Words of Institution[58] should be kept intact and that everything should be done by faith. For these rites are supposed to be for Christians, i.e., children of the "free woman" [Gal. 4:31], who observe them voluntarily and from the heart, but are free to change them how and when ever they may wish. Therefore, it is not in these matters that anyone should either seek or establish as law some indispensable form by which he might ensnare or harass consciences. Nor do we find any evidence for such an established rite, either in the early fathers or in the primitive church, but only in the Roman church. But even if they had decreed anything in this matter as a law, we would not have to observe it, because these things neither can nor should be bound by laws. Further, even if different people make use of different rites, let no one judge or despise the other, but every man be fully persuaded in his own mind [Rom. 14:5]. Let us feel and think the same, even though we may act differently. And let us approve each other's rites lest schisms and sects should result from this diversity in rites—as has happened in the Roman church. For external rites, even though we cannot do without them—just as we cannot do without food or drink—do not commend us to God, even as food does not commend us to him [I Cor. 8:8]. Faith and love commend us to God. Wherefore here let the word of Paul hold sway, "For the kingdom of God is not meat and drink; but righteousness and peace and joy in the Holy Ghost" [Rom. 14:17]. So the kingdom of God is not any rite, but faith within you, etc.

We have passed over the matter of vestments. But we think about these as we do about other forms. We permit them to be used in freedom, as long as people refrain from ostentation and pomp. For you are not more acceptable for consecrating in vestments. Nor are you less acceptable for consecrating without vestments. But I do not wish them to be consecrated or blessed—as if they were to become something sacred as compared with other garments—except that by general benediction of word and prayer by which every good creature of God is sanctified.[59] Otherwise,

---

[58] *Benedicationis verba.*
[59] Cf. I Tim. 4:4-5.

it is nothing but the superstition and mockery which the priests of Baal[60] introduced together with so many other abuses.

The Communion of the People

So far we have dealt with the mass and the function of the minister or bishop. Now we shall speak of the proper manner of communicating the people, for whom the Lord's Supper was primarily instituted and given this name. For just as it is absurd for a minister to make a fool of himself and publicly preach the Word where no one hears or to harangue himself in an empty room[61] or under the open sky, so it is equally nonsensical if the ministers prepare and embellish the Lord's Supper, which belongs to all, without having guests to eat and drink it, so that they who ought to minister to others, eat and drink by themselves alone at an empty table and in a vacant room. Therefore, if we really want to cherish Christ's command, no private mass should be allowed in the church, except as a temporary concession for the sake of necessity or for the weak in faith.

Here one should follow the same usage as with baptism, namely, that the bishop be informed of those who want to commune. They should request in person to receive the Lord's Supper so that he may be able to know both their names and manner of life. And let him not admit the applicants unless they can give a reason for their faith and can answer questions about what the Lord's Supper is, what its benefits are, and what they expect to derive from it. In other words, they should be able to repeat the Words of Institution from memory and to explain that they are coming because they are troubled by the consciousness of their sin, the fear of death, or some other evil, such as temptation of the flesh, the world, or the devil, and now hunger and thirst to receive the word and sign of grace and salvation from the Lord himself through the ministry of the bishop, so that they may be consoled and comforted; this was Christ's purpose, when he in priceless love gave and instituted this Supper, and said, "Take and eat," etc.

---

[60] *Abominationis pontifices,* "the pontiffs of abomination."
[61] Literally, *inter saxa et ligna,* "between stones and wood."

But I think it enough for the applicants for communion to be examined or explored once a year. Indeed, a man may be so understanding that he needs to be questioned only once in his lifetime or not at all. For, by this practice, we want to guard lest the worthy and unworthy alike rush to the Lord's Supper, as we have hitherto seen done in the Roman church. There they seek only to communicate; but the faith, the comfort, the use and benefit of the Supper are not even mentioned or considered. Nay, they have taken pains to hide the Words of Institution, which are the bread of life itself, and have furiously tried to make the communicants perform a work, supposedly good in itself, instead of letting their faith be nourished and strengthened by the goodness of Christ. Those, therefore, who are not able to answer in the manner described above should be completely excluded and banished from the communion of the Supper, since they are without the wedding garment [Matt. 22:11-12].

When the bishop has convinced himself that they understand all these things, he should also observe whether they prove their faith and understanding in their life and conduct. For Satan, too, understands and can talk about all these things. Thus if the pastor should see a fornicator, adulterer, drunkard, gambler, usurer, slanderer, or anyone else disgraced by a manifest vice, he should absolutely exclude such person from the Supper—unless he can give good evidence that his life has been changed. For the Supper need not be denied to those who sometimes fall and rise again, but grieve over their lapse. Indeed, we must realize that it was instituted just for such people so that they may be refreshed and strengthened. "For in many things we offend all" [Jas. 3:2]. And we "bear one another's burdens" [Gal. 6:2], since we are burdening one another. But I was speaking of those arrogant people who sin brazenly and without fear while they boast glorious things about the gospel.

When mass is being celebrated, those to receive communion should gather together by themselves in one place and in one group. The altar and the chancel were invented for this purpose. God does not care where we stand and it adds nothing to our faith. The communicants, however, ought to be seen and known openly, both by those who do and by those who do not commune, in order that their lives may be better observed, proved, and tested. For participation in the Supper is part of the confession by which they confess before God, angels, and men that they are Christians. Care must therefore be taken lest any, as it were, take the Supper on the sly and disappear in the crowd so that one cannot tell whether they live good or evil lives. On the other hand, even in this matter I do not want to make a law, but simply want to demonstrate a decent and fitting order to be used in freedom by free Christian men.

Now concerning private confession before communion, I still think as I have held heretofore, namely, that it neither is necessary nor should be demanded. Nevertheless, it is useful and should not be despised; for the Lord did not even require the Supper itself as necessary or establish it by law, but left it free to everyone when he said, "As often as you do this," etc. [I Cor. 11:25-26]. So concerning the preparation for the Supper, we think that preparing oneself by fasting and prayer is a matter of liberty. Certainly one ought to come sober and with a serious and attentive mind, even though one might not fast at all and pray ever so little. But the sobriety I speak of is not that superstitious practice of the papists. I demand it lest people should come belching their drink and bloated with overeating. For the best preparation is—as I have said—a soul troubled by sins, death, and temptation and hungering and thirsting for healing and strength. Teaching these matters to the people is up to the bishop.

It remains to be considered whether both forms,[62] as they call them, should be administered to the people. Here I say this: Now that the gospel has been instilled among us these two whole years, we have humored the weak in faith long enough. Hereafter we shall act according to the words of St. Paul, "If any man be ignorant, let him be ignorant" [I Cor. 14:38]. For if after all this time they have not understood the gospel, it matters little whether they receive either form. If we continue to make allowance for their weakness, we only run the risk of confirming their obstinacy and

---

[62] Both elements, i.e., bread and wine.

of making rules contrary to the gospel. Wherefore, both forms may be requested and shall be offered in simple compliance with the institution of Christ. Those who refuse them will be left alone and receive nothing. For we are devising this order of the mass for those to whom the gospel has been proclaimed and by whom it has been at least partly understood. Those who have not yet heard or understood it are also not ready to receive advice concerning this matter [of liturgical forms].

Nor is it necessary to wait for a council—as they prate—in order to have this practice sanctioned. We have the law of Christ on our side and are not minded to be delayed by or to listen to a council in matters which manifestly are part of the gospel. Nay, we say more: If by chance a council should establish and permit this practice, then we would be the last to partake of both forms. Nay, in contempt both of the council and of its statute, we should then wish to partake either of one or of neither, but never of both; and we would hold those to be wholly anathema who on the authority of such a council and statute would partake of both.

You wonder why and ask for a reason? Listen! If you know that the bread and wine were instituted by Christ and that both are to be received by all—as the Gospels and Paul testify so clearly that even our adversaries themselves are forced to admit it—and if you still dare not believe and trust in Him enough to receive both forms, but dare to do so after men decide this in a council, are you not preferring men to Christ? Do you not extol sinful men over Him who is named God and worshiped as such [II Thess. 2:3-4]? Do you not trust in the words of men more than in the words of God? Nay rather, do you not utterly distrust the words of God and believe only the words of men? And how great a rejection and denial of God the most high is that? What idolatry can be compared to the superstitious regard in which you hold the council of men? Should you not rather die a thousand deaths? Should you not rather receive one or no form at all, than [both] in the name of an obedience which is a sacrilege and of a faith that amounts to apostasy?

Therefore, let them stop prating of their councils. First, let them do this: Let them restore to God the glory which they have denied him. Let them confess that with Satan their master they have held back one form, that they have lifted themselves up above God, that they have condemned his word, and have led to perdition so many people for so long a time. And let them repent of this unspeakably cruel and godless tyranny. Then, let them solemnly declare that we have done right when on our part and even against their dogma we have taught and received both forms and have not waited for their council. And let them give thanks, because we have refused to follow their perditious abomination. When they have done this, we shall gladly and willingly honor and obey their council and [its] statute. In the meantime, while they fail to do so and instead continue to demand that we should await their authorization, we shall listen to nothing. Rather, we shall continue to teach and act against them, particularly where we know it displeases them most. For what do they require with their diabolical demand except that we should exalt them above God and their words above his, and that we should receive the phantoms of their fancy as idols in the place of God? It is our concern, however, that the whole world be completely subjected and obedient to God.

I also wish that we had as many songs as possible in the vernacular which the people could sing during mass, immediately after the gradual and also after the Sanctus and Agnus Dei. For who doubts that originally all the people sang these which now only the choir sings or responds to while the bishop is consecrating? The bishops may have these [congregational] hymns sung either after the Latin chants, or use the Latin on one [Sun]day and the vernacular on the next, until the time comes that the whole mass is sung in the vernacular. But poets are wanting among us, or not yet known, who could compose evangelical and spiritual songs, as Paul calls them [Col. 3:16], worthy to be used in the church of God. In the meantime, one may sing after communion, "Let God be blest, be praised, and thanked, Who to us himself hath granted,"[63] omitting the line, "And the holy sacrament, At our last end, From the consecrated priest's hand," which

---

[63]See *LW* 53, 252-254.

was added by some devotee of St. Barbara[64] who, having neglected
the sacrament all his life, hoped that he would on his deathbed be
able to obtain eternal life through this work rather than through
faith. For both the musical meter and structure prove this line to
be an interpolation.[65] Another good [hymn] is "Now Let Us Pray
to the Holy Ghost"[66] and also *"Ein Kindelein so löbelich."*[67] For
few are found that are written in a proper devotional style. I mention
this to encourage any German poets to compose evangelical
hymns for us.

This is enough for now about the mass and communion. What
is left can be decided by actual practice, as long as the Word of
God is diligently and faithfully preached in the church. And if
any should ask that all these [forms] be proved from Scriptures
and the example of the fathers, they do not disturb us; for as we
have said above, liberty must prevail in these matters and Christian consciences must not be bound by laws and ordinances. That
is why the Scriptures prescribe nothing in these matters, but allow
freedom for the Spirit to act according to his own understanding
as the respective place, time, and persons may require it. And as
for the example of the fathers, [their liturgical orders] are partly
unknown, partly so much at variance with each other that nothing
definite can be established about them, evidently because they
themselves used their liberty. And even if they would be perfectly
definite and clear, yet they could not impose on us a law or the
obligation to follow them.

As for the other days which are called weekdays,[68] I see nothing that we cannot put up with, provided the [weekday] masses be

---

[64] St. Barbara was called upon as intercessor to assure people that they would
be able to receive the sacraments of penance and the eucharist in the hour of
death.

[65] It was sung to the same melody which had already served the two previous
lines: "Let God be blessed," etc., and "That his own flesh and blood," etc.
The line censured by Luther is lacking in one of the two pre-Reformation
sources for this hymn.

[66]See *LW* 53, 263-264.

[67]A pre-Reformation Christmas hymn to the melody *"Dies est laetitiae."* See
Julian, *Dictionary of Hymnology,* p. 325. For text and melody of this hymn,
see Wilhelm Bäumker, *Das katholische deutsche Kirchenlied* (Freiburg: Herder, 1886), I, 286-289.

[68]*Feriae.*

discontinued. For Matins with its three lessons, the [minor] hours, Vespers, and Compline *de tempore* consist—with the exception of the propers for the Saints' days—of nothing but divine words of Scripture. And it is seemly, nay necessary, that the boys should get accustomed to reading and hearing the Psalms and lessons from the Holy Scripture. If anything should be changed, the bishop may reduce the great length [of the services] according to his own judgment so that three Psalms may be sung for Matins and three for Vespers with one or two responsories.[69] These matters are best left to the discretion of the bishop. He should choose the best of the responsories and antiphons and appoint them from Sunday to Sunday throughout the week, taking care lest the people should either be bored by too much repetition of the same or confused by too many changes in the chants and lessons. The whole Psalter, Psalm by Psalm, should remain in use, and the entire Scripture, lesson by lesson, should continue to be read to the people. But we must take care—as I have elsewhere explained—[70] lest the people sing only with their lips, like sounding pipes or harps [I Cor. 14:7], and without understanding. Daily lessons must therefore be appointed, one in the morning from the New or Old Testament, another for Vespers from the other Testament with an exposition in the vernacular. That this rite is an ancient one is proven by both the custom itself and by the words *homilia* in Matins and *capitulum*[71] in Vespers and in the other [canonical] hours, namely, that the Christians as often as they gathered together read something and then had it interpreted in the vernacular in the manner Paul describes in I Corinthians 14 [:26-27].[72] But when evil times came and there was a lack of prophets and interpreters, all that was left after the lessons and *capitula* was the

---

[69]Ordinarily, Matins had nine Psalms and eight responsories, Vespers and Compline eight Psalms and one responsory.

[70]See pp. 445-448.

[71] *Homilia*, i.e., "sermon," was the name of the lessons in Matins, which were taken both from Scripture and the writings of the church fathers. *Capitulum*, i.e., "chapter," is the name for the diminutive one-verse lesson read in Vespers. On this basis, Luther argues that Scripture readings had originally been longer—"chapter" rather than "verse"—and were followed by interpretative sermons.

[72]Cf. p. 445, n. 2.

response, "Thanks be to God."[73] And then, in place of the interpretation, lessons, Psalms, hymns, and other things were added in ~~boring repetition.~~ Although the hymns and the *Te Deum laudamus* at least confirm the same thing as the *Deo gratias*, namely, that after the exposition and homilies they used to praise God and give thanks for the revealed truth of his words. That is the kind of vernacular songs I should like us to have.

This much, excellent Nicholas, I have for you in writing about the rites and ceremonies which we either already have instituted in our Wittenberg church or expect to introduce, Christ willing, at an early date. If this example pleases you and others, you may imitate it. If not, we will gladly yield to your inspiration[74] and are prepared to accept corrections from you or from others. Nor should you or anyone else be deterred by the fact that here in Wittenberg the idolatrous "Topheth" [Jer. 7:31-32; 19:6] still continues as a shameless, ungodly source of revenue for the princes of Saxony. I am speaking of the Church of All Saints.[75] For by the mercy of God, we have so great an antidote among us in the riches of his Word that this plague languishes in its own little corner and can only contaminate itself. There are scarcely three or four swinish gluttons left to serve mammon in that house of perdition. To all others and to the whole populace, it is a loathsome and abominable thing. But we dare not proceed against them by force or by law, for Christians—as you know—should not fight except with the power of the sword of the Spirit. This is how I restrain the people every day. Otherwise, that house of all the saints—or rather of all the devils—would long be known by another name in all the earth. I have not used the power of the Spirit which the Lord has given me [II Cor. 13:10] against it, but patiently have borne this reproach if perchance God may give them repentance. Meanwhile,

---

[73] *Deo gratias.*

[74] Literally, "unction."

[75] This was the same church on the doors of which Luther had nailed the *Ninety-five Theses* six years earlier. It contained a famous collection of more than seventeen thousand relics which the Elector had amassed and which by attracting the seekers of indulgences were a lucrative revenue for the church. In 1522 they had once again been on exhibition, but on All Saints' Day, 1523, the custom was discontinued.

I am content that our house, which is more truly the house of all saints, reigns and stands here as a tower of Lebanon against the house of the devils [Song of Sol. 7:4]. Thus we torment Satan with the Word, even though he pretends to laugh. But Christ will grant that his hope will fail him and that he will be overthrown in the sight of all. Pray for me, you saint of God. Grace be with you and with us all. Amen.

The Reformation of
The church is centered in
the mass. —
The mass should:
1) Reflect promise of faith
2) God's word be certain
3) No mindless repetition
4) Be spoken/taught in the
people's language
5) Have music written in
devotional style.

23.

Enchiridion[1]

THE SMALL CATECHISM

Grace, mercy, and peace in Jesus Christ, our Lord, from Martin Luther to all faithful, godly pastors and preachers.

The deplorable conditions which I recently encountered 1 when I was a visitor[2] constrained me to prepare this brief and simple catechism or statement of Christian teaching. Good God, what 2 wretchedness I beheld! The common people, especially those who live in the country, have no knowledge whatever of Christian teaching, and unfortunately many pastors are quite incompetent and unfitted for teaching. Although the people are supposed to be 3 Christian, are baptized, and receive the holy sacrament, they do not know the Lord's Prayer, the Creed, or the Ten Commandments,[3] they live as if they were pigs and irrational beasts, and now that the Gospel has been restored they have mastered the fine art of abusing liberty.

How will you bishops answer for it before Christ that you 4 have so shamefully neglected the people and paid no attention at all to the duties of your office? May you escape punishment for this! 5 You withhold the cup in the Lord's Supper and insist on the observance of human laws, yet you do not take the slightest interest in teaching the people the Lord's Prayer, the Creed, the Ten Commandments, or a single part of the Word of God. Woe to you forever!

I therefore beg of you for God's sake, my beloved brethren 6 who are pastors and preachers, that you take the duties of your

---

[1]Greek: manual or handbook.

[2]Luther made visitations of congregations in Electoral Saxony and Meissen between Oct. 22, 1528, and Jan. 9, 1529.

[3]This is the order in which these materials appeared in late medieval manuals.

office seriously, that you have pity on the people who are entrusted to your care, and that you help me to teach the catechism to the people, especially those who are young. Let those who lack the qualifications to do better at least take this booklet and these forms and read them to the people word for word in this manner:

In the first place, the preacher should take the utmost care to 7 avoid changes or variations in the text and wording of the Ten Commandments, the Creed, the Lord's Prayer, the sacraments, etc. On the contrary, he should adopt one form, adhere to it, and use it repeatedly year after year. Young and inexperienced people must be instructed on the basis of a uniform, fixed text and form. They are easily confused if a teacher employs one form now and another form—perhaps with the intention of making improvements—later on. In this way all the time and labor will be lost.

This was well understood by our good fathers, who were 8 accustomed to use the same form in teaching the Lord's Prayer, the Creed, and the Ten Commandments. We, too, should teach these things to the young and unlearned in such a way that we do not alter a single syllable or recite the catechism differently from year to year. Choose the form that pleases you, therefore, and adhere to it henceforth. When you preach to intelligent and educated people, 9 you are at liberty to exhibit your learning and to discuss these topics from different angles and in such a variety of ways as you may be capable of. But when you are teaching the young, adhere to a fixed and unchanging form and method. Begin by teaching them the 10 Ten Commandments, the Creed, the Lord's Prayer, etc., following the text word for word so that the young may repeat these things after you and retain them in their memory.

If any refuse to receive your instruction, tell them that they 11 deny Christ and are no Christians. They should not be admitted to the sacrament, be accepted as sponsors in Baptism, or be allowed to participate in any Christian privileges.[4] On the contrary, they should

---

[4]Cf. Large Catechism, Short Preface, 1-5.

be turned over to the pope and his officials,[5] and even to the devil himself. In addition, parents and employers should refuse to 12 furnish them with food and drink and should notify them that the prince is disposed to banish such rude people from his land.

Although we cannot and should not compel anyone to be- 13 lieve, we should nevertheless insist that the people learn to know how to distinguish between right and wrong according to the standards of those among whom they live and make their living.[6] For anyone who desires to reside in a city is bound to know and observe the laws under whose protection he lives, no matter whether he is a believer or, at heart, a scoundrel or knave.

In the second place, after the people have become familiar 14 with the text, teach them what it means. For this purpose, take the explanations in this booklet, or choose any other brief and fixed explanations which you may prefer, and adhere to them with- 15 out changing a single syllable, as stated above with reference to the text. Moreover, allow yourself ample time, for it is not necessary 16 to take up all the parts at once. They can be presented one at a time. When the learners have a proper understanding of the First Commandment, proceed to the Second Commandment, and so on. Otherwise they will be so overwhelmed that they will hardly remember anything at all.

In the third place, after you have thus taught this brief 17 catechism, take up a large catechism[7] so that the people may have a richer and fuller understanding. Expound every commandment, petition, and part, pointing out their respective obligations, benefits, dangers, advantages, and disadvantages, as you will find all of this treated at length in the many books written for this purpose. 18 Lay the greatest weight on those commandments or other parts

---

[5]Diocesan judges who decided disciplinary and other cases; now often called vicar-generals.

[6]Cf. Large Catechism, Short Preface, 2.

[7]Luther here refers not only to his own Large Catechism but also to other treatments of the traditional parts of the catechism. See the reference to "many books" in the next sentence.

which seem to require special attention among the people where you are. For example, the Seventh Commandment, which treats of stealing, must be emphasized when instructing laborers and shopkeepers, and even farmers and servants, for many of these are guilty of dishonesty and thievery.[8] So, too, the Fourth Commandment must be stressed when instructing children and the common people in order that they may be encouraged to be orderly, faithful, obedient, and peaceful. Always adduce many examples from the Scriptures to show how God punished and blessed.

You should also take pains to urge governing authorities and   19
parents to rule wisely and educate their children. They must be shown that they are obliged to do so, and that they are guilty of damnable sin if they do not do so, for by such neglect they undermine and lay waste both the kingdom of God and the kingdom of the world and are the worst enemies of God and man. Make   20 very plain to them the shocking evils they introduce when they refuse their aid in the training of children to become pastors, preachers, notaries, etc., and tell them that God will inflict awful punishments on them for these sins. It is necessary to preach about such things. The extent to which parents and governing authorities sin in this respect is beyond telling. The devil also has a horrible purpose in mind.

Finally, now that the people are freed from the tyranny of   21
the pope, they are unwilling to receive the sacrament and they treat it with contempt. Here, too, there is need of exhortation, but with this understanding: No one is to be compelled to believe or to receive the sacrament, no law is to be made concerning it, and no time or place should be appointed for it. We should so preach that,   22
of their own accord and without any law, the people will desire the sacrament and, as it were, compel us pastors to administer it to them. This can be done by telling them: It is to be feared that anyone who does not desire to receive the sacrament at least three or four times a year despises the sacrament and is no Christian, just as he is no

---

[8]Cf. Large Catechism, Ten Commandments, 225, 226.

Christian who does not hear and believe the Gospel. Christ did not say, "Omit this," or "Despise this," but he said, "Do this, as often as you drink it," etc.[9] Surely he wishes that this be done and not that it be omitted and despised. "*Do* this," he said.

He who does not highly esteem the sacrament suggests   23 thereby that he has no sin, no flesh, no devil, no world, no death, no hell. That is to say, he believes in none of these, although he is deeply immersed in them and is held captive by the devil. On the other hand, he suggests that he needs no grace, no life, no paradise, no heaven, no Christ, no God, nothing good at all. For if he believed that he was involved in so much that is evil and was in need of so much that is good, he would not neglect the sacrament in which aid is afforded against such evil and in which such good is bestowed. It is not necessary to compel him by any law to receive the sacrament, for he will hasten to it of his own accord, he will feel constrained to receive it, he will insist that you administer it to him.

Accordingly you are not to make a law of this, as the pope   24 has done. All you need to do is clearly to set forth the advantage and disadvantage, the benefit and loss, the blessing and danger connected with this sacrament. Then the people will come of their own accord without compulsion on your part. But if they refuse to come, let them be, and tell them that those who do not feel and acknowledge their great need and God's gracious help belong to the   25 devil. If you do not give such admonitions, or if you adopt odious laws on the subject, it is your own fault if the people treat the sacrament with contempt. How can they be other than negligent if you fail to do your duty and remain silent. So it is up to you, dear pastor and preacher! Our office has become something different from   26 what it was under the pope. It is now a ministry of grace and salvation. It subjects us to greater burdens and labors, dangers and   27 temptations, with little reward or gratitude from the world. But Christ himself will be our reward if we labor faithfully. The Father

---

[9] I Cor. 11:25.

of all grace grant it! To him be praise and thanks forever, through Christ, our Lord. Amen.

[I]

THE TEN COMMANDMENTS

*in the plain form in which the head of the family
shall teach them to his household*[1]

The First

"You shall have no other gods."[2]   1

What does this mean?   2

Answer: We should fear,[3] love, and trust in God above all things.

The Second

"You shall not take the name of the Lord your God in vain."[4]   3

What does this mean?   4

Answer: We should fear and love God, and so[5] we should not use his name to curse, swear,[6] practice magic, lie, or deceive, but in every time of need call upon him, pray to him, praise him, and give him thanks.

---

[1]Latin title: Small Catechism for the Use of Children in School. How, in a very Plain Form, Schoolmasters Should Teach the Ten Commandments to their Pupils.

[2]The Nuremberg editions of 1531 and 1558 read: "I am the Lord your God. You shall have no other gods before me." In some editions since the sixteenth century "I am the Lord your God" was printed separately as an introduction to the entire Decalogue. The Ten Commandments are from Exod. 20:2-17 and Deut. 5:6-21.

[3]On filial and servile fear see Apology, XII, 38.

[4]The Nuremberg editions of 1531 and 1558 add: "for the Lord will not hold him guiltless who takes his name in vain."

[5]On the translation of *dass* see M. Reu in *Kirchliche Zeitschrift*, L (1926), pp. 626-689.

[6]For the meaning of "swear" see Large Catechism, Ten Commandments, 66.

The   Third

"Remember the Sabbath day,[7] *to keep it holy."*   5

What does this mean?   6

Answer: We should fear and love God, and so we should not despise his Word and the preaching of the same, but deem it holy and gladly hear and learn it.

The   Fourth

"Honor your father and your mother."   7

What does this mean?   8

Answer: We should fear and love God, and so we should not despise our parents and superiors, nor provoke them to anger, but honor, serve, obey, love, and esteem them.

The   Fifth

"You shall not kill."   9

What does this mean?   10

Answer: We should fear and love God, and we should not endanger our neighbor's life, nor cause him any harm, but help and befriend him in every necessity of life.

The   Sixth

"You shall not commit adultery."   11

What does this mean?   12

Answer: We should fear and love God, and so we should lead a chaste and pure life in word and deed, each one loving and honoring his wife or her husband.

---

[7]Luther's German word *Feiertag* means day of rest, and this is the original Hebrew meaning of Sabbath, the term employed in the Latin text. The Jewish observance of Saturday is not enjoined here, nor a Sabbatarian observance of Sunday; cf. Augsburg Confession, XXVIII, 57-60; Large Catechism, Ten Commandments, 79-82.

The Seventh

"You shall not steal."   13

What does this mean?   14

Answer: We should fear and love God, and so we should not rob our neighbor of his money or property, nor bring them into our possession by dishonest trade or by dealing in shoddy wares, but help him to improve and protect his income and property.

The Eighth

"You shall not bear false witness against your neighbor."   15

What does this mean?   16

Answer: We should fear and love God, and so we should not tell lies about our neighbor, nor betray, slander, or defame him, but should apologize for him, speak well of him, and interpret charitably all that he does.

The Ninth

"You shall not covet your neighbor's house."   17

What does this mean?   18

Answer: We should fear and love God, and so we should not seek by craftiness to gain possession of our neighbor's inheritance or home, nor to obtain them under pretext of legal right, but be of service and help to him so that he may keep what is his.

The Tenth

"You shall not covet your neighbor's wife, or his manservant,   19
*or his maidservant, or his ox, or his ass,[8] or anything that is your
neighbor's."*

What does this mean?   20

Answer: We should fear and love God, and so we should not abduct, estrange, or entice away our neighbor's wife, servants, or

---

[8]For "or his ox, or his ass" Luther's German text reads "or his cattle." The Latin text employs the fuller expression.

cattle, but encourage them to remain and discharge their duty to him.

[Conclusion]

What does God declare concerning all these command- 21 ments?

Answer: He says, "I the Lord your God am a jealous God, visiting the iniquity of the fathers upon the children to the third and the fourth generation of those who hate me, but showing steadfast love to thousands of those who love me and keep my commandments."

What does this mean? 22

Answer: God threatens to punish all who transgress these commandments. We should therefore fear his wrath and not disobey these commandments. On the other hand, he promises grace and every blessing to all who keep them. We should therefore love him, trust in him, and cheerfully do what he has commanded.

[II]

THE CREED

*in the plain form in which the head of the family
shall teach it to his household*[9]

The First Article: Creation 1

"*I believe in God, the Father almighty, maker of heaven and earth.*"

What does this mean? 2

Answer: I believe that God has created me and all that exists; that he has given me and still sustains my body and soul, all my limbs and senses, my reason and all the faculties of my mind, together with food and clothing, house and home, family and property; that he provides me daily and abundantly with all the necessities of life, protects me from all danger, and preserves me from all

---

[9]Latin text: How, in a very Plain Form, Schoolmasters Should Teach the Apostles' Creed to their Pupils.

evil. All this he does out of his pure, fatherly, and divine goodness and mercy, without any merit or worthiness on my part. For all of this I am bound to thank, praise, serve, and obey him. This is most certainly true.

The Second Article: Redemption   3

And in Jesus Christ, his only son, our Lord: who was conceived by the Holy Spirit, born of the virgin Mary, suffered under Pontius Pilate, was crucified, dead, and buried: he descended into hell, the third day he rose from the dead, he ascended into heaven, and is seated on the right hand of God, the Father almighty, whence he shall come to judge the living and the dead."

What does this mean?   4

Answer: I believe that Jesus Christ, true God, begotten of the Father from eternity, and also true man, born of the virgin Mary, is my Lord, who has redeemed me, a lost and condemned creature, delivered me and freed me from all sins, from death, and from the power of the devil, not with silver and gold but with his holy and precious blood and with his innocent sufferings and death, in order that I may be his, live under him in his kingdom, and serve him in everlasting righteousness, innocence, and blessedness, even as he is risen from the dead and lives and reigns to all eternity. This is most certainly true.

The Third Article: Sanctification   5

"I believe in the Holy Spirit, the holy Christian church, the communion of saints, the forgiveness of sins, the resurrection of the body, and the life everlasting. Amen."

What does this mean?   6

Answer: I believe that by my own reason or strength I cannot believe in Jesus Christ, my Lord, or come to him. But the Holy Spirit has called me through the Gospel, enlightened me with his gifts, and sanctified and preserved me in true faith, just as he calls, gathers, enlightens, and sanctifies the whole Christian church on earth and preserves it in union with Jesus Christ in the one true faith. In this Christian church he daily and abundantly forgives all my sins, and the sins of all believers, and on the last day he will raise me and all the dead and will grant eternal life to me and to all who believe in Christ. This is most certainly true.

[III]

THE LORD'S PRAYER

in the plain form in which the head of the family
shall teach it to his household[1]

[Introduction]

"Our Father who art in heaven."[2]   1

What does this mean?   2

Answer: Here God would encourage us to believe that he is truly our Father and we are truly his children in order that we may approach him boldly and confidently in prayer, even as beloved children approach their dear father.

The First Petition   3

"Hallowed be thy name."

What does this mean?   4

Answer: To be sure, God's name is holy in itself, but we pray in this petition that it may also be holy for us.

How is this done?

Answer: When the Word of God is taught clearly and purely and we, as children of God, lead holy lives in accordance with it. Help us to do this, dear Father in heaven! But whoever teaches and

---

[1] Latin title: How, in a very Plain Form, Schoolmasters Should Teach the Lord's Prayer to their Pupils.

[2] The "introduction" to the Lord's Prayer was not prepared by Luther until 1531. It does not appear in the Latin text, which begins with the First Petition. The text of the Prayer is from Matt. 6:9-13.

lives otherwise than as the Word of God teaches, profanes the name of God among us. From this preserve us, heavenly Father!

The Second Petition 6
"Thy kingdom come."

What does this mean? 7

Answer: To be sure, the kingdom of God comes of itself, without our prayer, but we pray in this petition that it may also come to us.

How is this done? 8

Answer: When the heavenly Father gives us his Holy Spirit so that by his grace we may believe in his holy Word and live a godly life, both here in time and hereafter forever.

The Third Petition 9
"Thy will be done, on earth as it is in heaven."

What does this mean? 10

Answer: To be sure, the good and gracious will of God is done without our prayer, but we pray in this petition that it may also be done by us.

How is this done? 11

Answer: When God curbs and destroys every evil counsel and purpose of the devil, of this world, and of our flesh which would hinder us from hallowing his name and prevent the coming of his kingdom, and when he strengthens us and keeps us steadfast in his Word and in faith even to the end. This is his good and gracious will.

The Fourth Petition 12
"Give us this day our daily bread."

What does this mean? 13

Answer: To be sure, God provides daily bread, even to the wicked, without our prayer, but we pray in this petition that God may make us aware of his gifts and enable us to receive our daily bread with thanksgiving.

What is meant by daily bread? 14

Answer: Everything required to satisfy our bodily needs, such as food and clothing, house and home, fields and flocks, money and property; a pious spouse and good children, trustworthy servants, godly and faithful rulers, good government; seasonal weather, peace and health, order and honor; true friends, faithful neighbors, and the like.

The Fifth Petition 15

"And forgive us our debts, as we have also forgiven our debtors."
What does this mean? 16

Answer: We pray in this petition that our heavenly Father may not look upon our sins, and on their account deny our prayers, for we neither merit nor deserve those things for which we pray. Although we sin daily and deserve nothing but punishment, we nevertheless pray that God may grant us all things by his grace. And assuredly we on our part will heartily forgive and cheerfully do good to those who may sin against us.

The Sixth Petition 17

"And lead us not into temptation."
What does this mean? 18

Answer: God tempts no one to sin, but we pray in this petition that God may so guard and preserve us that the devil, the world, and our flesh may not deceive us or mislead us into unbelief, despair, and other great and shameful sins, but that, although we may be so tempted, we may finally prevail and gain the victory.

The Seventh Petition 19

"But deliver us from evil."
What does this mean? 20

Answer: We pray in this petition, as in a summary, that our Father in heaven may deliver us from all manner of evil, whether it affect body or soul, property or reputation, and that at last, when the hour of death comes, he may grant us a blessed end and graciously take us from this world of sorrow to himself in heaven.

[Conclusion]

"Amen."[3]

What does this mean? 21

Answer: It means that I should be assured that such petitions are acceptable to our heavenly Father and are heard by him, for he himself commanded us to pray like this and promised to hear us. "Amen, amen" means "Yes, yes, it shall be so."

[IV]

THE SACRAMENT OF HOLY BAPTISM

in the plain form in which the head of the family shall teach it to his household[4]

First

What is Baptism? 1

Answer: Baptism is not merely water, but it is water used 2 according to God's command and connected with God's Word.

What is this Word of God? 3

Answer: As recorded in Matthew 28:19, our Lord Christ said, 4 "Go therefore and make disciples of all nations, baptizing them in the name of the Father and of the Son and of the Holy Spirit."

Second

What gifts or benefits does Baptism bestow? 5

Answer: It effects forgiveness of sins, delivers from death and 6

---

[3]The Nuremberg edition of 1558, and many later editions, inserted "For thine is the kingdom, and the power, and the glory, for ever and ever" before "Amen."

[4]Latin title: How, in a very Plain Form, Schoolmasters Should Teach the Sacrament of Baptism to their Pupils.

the devil, and grants eternal salvation to all who believe, as the Word and promise of God declare.

What is this Word and promise of God? 7

Answer: As recorded in Mark 16:16, our Lord Christ said, 8 "He who believes and is baptized will be saved; but he who does not believe will be condemned."

Third

How can water produce such great effects? 9

Answer: It is not the water that produces these effects, but 10 the Word of God connected with the water, and our faith which relies on the Word of God connected with the water. For without the Word of God that water is merely water and no Baptism. But when connected with the Word of God it is a Baptism, that is, a gracious water of life and a washing of regeneration in the Holy Spirit, as St. Paul wrote to Titus (3:5-8), "He saved us by the washing of regeneration and renewal in the Holy Spirit, which he poured out upon us richly through Jesus Christ our Saviour, so that we might be justified by his grace and become heirs in hope of eternal life. The saying is sure."

Fourth 11

What does such baptizing with water signify?

Answer: It signifies that the old Adam in us, together with 12 all sins and evil lusts, should be drowned by daily sorrow and repentance and be put to death, and that the new man should come forth daily and rise up, cleansed and righteous, to live forever in God's presence.

Where is this written? 13

Answer: In Romans 6:4, St. Paul wrote, "We were buried 14 therefore with him by baptism into death, so that as Christ was raised from the dead by the glory of the Father, we too might walk in newness of life."

[V]

[CONFESSION AND ABSOLUTION] 15

How Plain People Are to Be Taught to Confess[5]

What is confession? 16

Answer: Confession consists of two parts. One is that we confess
our sins. The other is that we receive absolution or forgiveness from
the confessor as from God himself, by no means doubting but firmly
believing that our sins are thereby forgiven before God in heaven.

What sins should we confess? 17

Answer: Before God we should acknowledge that we are 18
guilty of all manner of sins, even those of which we are not aware, as
we do in the Lord's Prayer. Before the confessor, however, we
should confess only those sins of which we have knowledge and
which trouble us.

What are such sins? 19

Answer: Reflect on your condition in the light of the Ten 20
Commandments: whether you are a father or mother, a son or
daughter, a master or servant; whether you have been disobedient,
unfaithful, lazy, ill-tempered, or quarrelsome; whether you have
harmed anyone by word or deed; and whether you have stolen,
neglected, or wasted anything, or done other evil.

Please give me a brief form of confession. 21

Answer: You should say to the confessor: "Dear Pastor, please
hear my confession and declare that my sins are forgiven for God's
sake."

"Proceed."

"I, a poor sinner, confess before God that I am guilty of all 22
sins. In particular I confess in your presence that, as a manservant or
maidservant, etc., I am unfaithful to my master, for here and there I

---

[5]In 1531 this section replaced the earlier "A Short Method of Confessing" (1529), *WA*, 30^I: 343-45. Luther intended confession especially
for those who were about to receive Communion.

have not done what I was told. I have made my master angry, caused him to curse, neglected to do my duty, and caused him to suffer loss. I have also been immodest in word and deed. I have quarreled with my equals. I have grumbled and sworn at my mistress, etc. For all this I am sorry and pray for grace. I mean to do better."

A master or mistress may say: "In particular I confess in   23 your presence that I have not been faithful in training my children, servants, and wife to the glory of God. I have cursed. I have set a bad example by my immodest language and actions. I have injured my neighbor by speaking evil of him, overcharging him, giving him inferior goods and short measure." Masters and mistresses should add whatever else they have done contrary to God's commandments and to their action in life, etc.

If, however, anyone does not feel that his conscience is bur-   24 dened by such or by greater sins, he should not worry, nor should he search for and invent other sins, for this would turn confession into torture;[6] he should simply mention one or two sins of which he is aware. For example, "In particular I confess that I once cursed. On one occasion I also spoke indecently. And I neglected this or that," etc. Let this suffice.

If you have knowledge of no sin at all (which is quite un-   25 likely), you should mention none in particular, but receive forgiveness upon the general confession[7] which you make to God in the presence of the confessor.

Then the confessor shall say: "God be merciful to you and   26 strengthen your faith. Amen."

Again he shall say: "Do you believe that this forgiveness is   27 the forgiveness of God?"

---

[6]Luther was here alluding to the medieval practice of confession; see also Smalcald Articles, Pt. II, Art. III, 19.

[7]See article "General Confession" in *New Schaff-Herzog Encyclopedia of Religious Knowledge*, IV, 449. Cf. Smalcald Articles, Pt. III, Art. III, 13.

Answer: "Yes, I do."

Then he shall say: "Be it done for you as you have believed.[8]   28 According to the command of our Lord Jesus Christ, I forgive you your sins in the name of the Father and of the Son and of the Holy Spirit. Amen. Go in peace."[9]

A confessor will know additional passages of the Scriptures   29 with which to comfort and to strengthen the faith of those whose consciences are heavily burdened or who are distressed and sorely tried. This is intended simply as an ordinary form of confession for plain people.

[VI]

THE SACRAMENT OF THE ALTAR

in the plain form in which the head of the family shall teach it to his household[1]

What is the Sacrament of the Altar?   1

Answer: Instituted by Christ himself, it is the true body and   2 blood of our Lord Jesus Christ, under the bread and wine, given to us Christians to eat and drink.

Where is this written?   3

Answer: The holy evangelists Matthew, Mark, and Luke, and   4 also St. Paul, write thus: "Our Lord Jesus Christ, on the night when he was betrayed, took bread, and when he had given thanks, he broke it, and gave it to the disciples and said, 'Take, eat; this is my body which is given for you. Do this in remembrance of me.' In the same way also he took the cup, after supper, and when he had given

---

[8]Matt. 8:13.

[9]Mark 5:34; Luke 7:50; 8:48.

[1]Latin title: How, in very Plain Form, Schoolmasters Should Teach the Sacrament of the Altar to their Pupils.

thanks he gave it to them, saying, 'Drink of it, all of you. This cup is the new covenant in my blood, which is poured out for many for the forgiveness of sins. Do this, as often as you drink it, in remembrance of me.' "[2]

What is the benefit of such eating and drinking?   5

Answer: We are told in the words "for you" and "for the   6 forgiveness of sins." By these words the forgiveness of sins, life, and salvation are given to us in the sacrament, for where there is forgiveness of sins, there are also life and salvation.

How can bodily eating and drinking produce such great   7 effects?

Answer: The eating and drinking do not in themselves pro-   8 duce them, but the words "for you" and "for the forgiveness of sins." These words, when accompanied by the bodily eating and drinking, are the chief thing in the sacrament, and he who believes these words has what they say and declare: the forgiveness of sins.

Who, then, receives this sacrament worthily?   9

Answer: Fasting and bodily preparation are a good external   10 discipline, but he is truly worthy and well prepared who believes these words: "for you" and "for the forgiveness of sins." On the other hand, he who does not believe these words, or doubts them, is unworthy and unprepared, for the words "for you" require truly believing hearts.

---

[2] A conflation of texts from I Cor. 11:23-25; Matt. 26:26-28; Mark 14:22-24; Luke 22:19, 20. Cf. Large Catechism, Sacrament of the Altar, 3.

[VII]

[MORNING AND EVENING PRAYERS]

How the head of the family shall teach his household
to say morning and evening prayers[3]

In the morning, when you rise, make the sign of the cross and   1
say, "In the name of God, the Father, the Son, and the Holy Spirit.
Amen."

Then, kneeling or standing, say the Apostles' Creed and the   2
Lord's Prayer. Then you may say this prayer:

"I give Thee thanks, heavenly Father, through thy dear Son Jesus
Christ, that Thou hast protected me through the night from all harm
and danger. I beseech Thee to keep me this day, too, from all sin
and evil, that in all my thoughts, words, and deeds I may please
Thee. Into thy hands I commend my body and soul and all that is
mine. Let the holy angel have charge of me, that the wicked one
may have no power over me. Amen."

After singing a hymn (possibly a hymn on the Ten Command-   3
ments)[4] or whatever your devotion may suggest, you should go to
your work joyfully.

In the evening, when you retire, make the sign of the cross   4
and say, "In the name of God, the Father, the Son, and the Holy
Spirit. Amen."

Then, kneeling or standing, say the Apostles' Creed and the   5
Lord's Prayer. Then you may say this prayer:

"I give Thee thanks, heavenly Father, through thy dear Son Jesus
Christ, that Thou hast this day graciously protected me. I beseech
Thee to forgive all my sin and the wrong which I have done. Gra-
ciously protect me during the coming night. Into thy hands I com-

---

[3]Latin title: How, in very Plain Form, Schoolmasters Should Teach
their Pupils to Say their Prayers in the Morning and in the Evening. (The
material in this section was adapted from the Roman Breviary.)

[4]See Large Catechism, Short Preface, 25.

mend my body and soul and all that is mine. Let thy holy angels have charge of me, that the wicked one may have no power over me. Amen."

Then quickly lie down and sleep in peace.

[VIII]

[GRACE AT TABLE]

How the head of the family shall teach his household   6
to offer blessing and thanksgiving at table[5]

[Blessing before Eating]

When children and the whole household gather at the table,   7
they should reverently fold their hands and say:

"The eyes of all look to Thee, O Lord, and Thou givest them their food in due season. Thou openest thy hand; Thou satisfiest the desire of every living thing."[6]

(It is to be observed that "satisfying the desire of every living   8
thing" means that all creatures receive enough to eat to make them joyful and of good cheer. Greed and anxiety about food prevent such satisfaction.)

Then the Lord's Prayer should be said, and afterwards this   9
prayer:

"Lord God, heavenly Father, bless us, and these thy gifts which of thy bountiful goodness Thou hast bestowed on us, through Jesus Christ our Lord. Amen."

---

[5]Latin title: How, in Plain Form, Schoolmasters Should Teach their Pupils to Offer Blessing and Thanksgiving at Table. (The material in this section was adapted from the Roman Breviary.)

[6]Ps. 145:15, 16. The gloss which follows, here given in parentheses, was intended to explain the meaning of *Wohlgefallen* or *benedictio* in the German and Latin translations of the Psalm.

[Thanksgiving after Eating]   10

After eating, likewise, they should fold their hands reverently and say:

"O give thanks to the Lord, for he is good; for his steadfast love endures forever. He gives to the beasts their food, and to the young ravens which cry. His delight is not in the strength of the horse, nor his pleasure in the legs of a man; but the Lord takes pleasure in those who fear him, in those who hope in his steadfast love."[7]

Then the Lord's Prayer should be said, and afterwards this   11 prayer:

"We give Thee thanks, Lord God, our Father, for all thy benefits, through Jesus Christ our Lord, who lives and reigns forever. Amen."

[IX]

TABLE OF DUTIES   1

*consisting of certain passages of the Scriptures, selected
for various estates and conditions of men, by
which they may be admonished to do
their respective duties*[8]

Bishops, Pastors, and Preachers   2

"A bishop must be above reproach, married only once, temperate, sensible, dignified, hospitable, an apt teacher, no drunkard, not violent but gentle, not quarrelsome, and no lover of money. He must manage his own household well, keeping his children submissive and respectful in every way. He must not be a recent convert," etc. (I Tim. 3:2-6).

---

[7] Ps. 106:1; 136:26; 147:9-11.

[8] This table of duties was probably suggested to Luther by John Gerson's *Tractatus de modo vivendi omnium fidelium.*

Duties Christians Owe Their Teachers and Pastors[9]   3

"Remain in the same house, eating and drinking what they provide, for the laborer deserves his wages" (Luke 10:7). "The Lord commanded that those who proclaim the gospel should get their living by the gospel" (I Cor. 9:14). "Let him who is taught the word share all good things with him who teaches. Do not be deceived; God is not mocked" (Gal. 6:6, 7). "Let the elders who rule well be considered worthy of double honor, especially those who labor in preaching and teaching; for the scripture says, 'You shall not muzzle an ox when it is treading out the grain,' and 'The laborer deserves his wages,'" (I Tim. 5:17, 18). "We beseech you, brethren, to respect those who labor among you and are over you in the Lord and admonish you, and to esteem them very highly in love because of their work. Be at peace among yourselves" (I Thess. 5:12, 13). "Obey your leaders and submit to them; for they are keeping watch over your souls, as men who will have to give account. Let them do this joyfully, and not sadly, for that would be of no advantage to you" (Heb. 13:17).

Governing Authorities[1]   4

"Let every person be subject to the governing authorities. For there is no authority except from God, and those that exist have been instituted by God. Therefore he who resists the authorities resists what God has appointed, and those who resist will incur judgment. He who is in authority does not bear the sword in vain; he is the servant of God to execute his wrath on the wrongdoer" (Rom. 13:1-4).

---

[9]This section was not prepared by Luther, but was later taken up into the Small Catechism, probably with Luther's consent. The passages from Luke 10 and I Thess. 5 are not included in the Latin text.

[1]This section was not prepared by Luther, but was later taken up into the Small Catechism, probably with Luther's consent.

Duties Subjects Owe Governing Authorities   5

"Render therefore to Caesar the things that are Caesar's, and to God the things that are God's" (Matt. 22:21). "Let every person be subject to the governing authorities. Therefore one must be subject, not only to avoid God's wrath but also for the sake of conscience. For the same reason you also pay taxes, for the authorities are ministers of God, attending to this very thing. Pay all of them their dues, taxes to whom taxes are due, revenue to whom revenue is due, respect to whom respect is due, honor to whom honor is due" (Rom. 13:1, 5-7). "I urge that supplications, prayers, intercessions, and thanksgivings be made for all men, for kings and all who are in high positions, that we may lead a quiet and peaceable life, godly and respectful in every way" (I Tim. 2:1, 2). "Remind them to be submissive to rulers and authorities, to be obedient, to be ready for any honest work" (Tit. 3:1). "Be subject for the Lord's sake to every human institution, whether it be to the emperor as supreme, or to governors as sent by him to punish those who do wrong and to praise those who do right" (I Pet. 2:13, 14).

Husbands   6

"You husbands, live considerately with your wives, bestowing honor on the woman as the weaker sex, since you are joint heirs of the grace of life, in order that your prayers not be hindered" (I Pet. 3:7). "Husbands, love your wives, and do not be harsh with them" (Col. 3:19).

Wives   7

"You wives, be submissive to your husbands, as Sarah obeyed Abraham, calling him lord. And you are now her children if you do right and let nothing terrify you" (I Pet. 3:1, 6).

Parents 8

"Fathers, do not provoke your children to anger, lest they become discouraged, but bring them up in the discipline and instruction of the Lord" (Eph. 6:4; Col. 3:21).

Children 9

"Children, obey your parents in the Lord, for this is right. 'Honor your father and mother' (this is the first commandment with a promise) 'that it may be well with you and that you may live long on the earth' " (Eph. 6:1-3).

Laborers and Servants, Male and Female 10

"Be obedient to those who are your earthly masters, with fear and trembling, with singleness of heart, as to Christ; not in the way of eye-service, as men-pleasers, but as servants of Christ, doing the will of God from the heart, rendering service with a good will as to the Lord and not to men, knowing that whatever good anyone does, he will receive the same again from the Lord, whether he is a slave or free" (Eph. 6:5-8).

Masters and Mistresses 11

"Masters, do the same to them, and forbear threatening, knowing that he who is both their Master and yours is in heaven, and that there is no partiality with him" (Eph. 6:9).

Young Persons in General 12

"You that are younger, be subject to the elders. Clothe yourselves, all of you, with humility toward one another, for 'God opposes the proud, but gives grace to the humble.' Humble yourselves therefore under the mighty hand of God, that in due time he may exalt you" (I Pet. 5:5, 6).

Widows 13

"She who is a real widow, and is left all alone, has set her hope on God and continues in supplication and prayers night and day; whereas she who is self-indulgent is dead even while she lives" (I Tim. 5:5, 6).

Christians in General 14

"The commandments are summed up in this sentence, 'You shall love your neighbor as yourself'" (Rom. 13:9). "I urge that supplications, prayers, intercessions, and thanksgivings be made for all men" (I Tim. 2:1).

Let each his lesson learn with care 15
And all the household well will fare.[2]

---

[2]On this rhyme by Luther see *WA*, 35:580.

24.

IV

THE SMALCALD ARTICLES

Pope Paul III called a council to meet in Mantua last year, in ⎸1
Whitsuntide. Afterwards he transferred the council from Mantua,
and it is not yet known where it will or can be held. In any case, we
had reason to expect that we might be summoned to appear before
the council or be condemned without being summoned. I was therefore instructed[2] to draft and assemble articles of our faith to serve
as a basis for possible deliberations and to indicate, on the one
hand, what and in how far we were willing and able to yield to the
papists and, on the other hand, what we intended to hold fast to
and persevere in.

Accordingly I assembled these articles and submitted them to ⎸2
our representatives.[3] The latter accepted them, unanimously adopted them as their confession, and resolved[4] that these articles should
be presented publicly as the confession of our faith if the pope and
his adherents ever became so bold as seriously, in good faith, and

---

[1]This preface was written by Luther in 1538, when he prepared the
Articles for publication.

[2]By Elector John Frederick of Saxony, early in December, 1536.

[3]The Articles were reviewed and somewhat modified in a conference of
theologians held in Wittenberg in December, 1536, and they were considered and signed by theologians at the meeting of the Smalcald League
held in Smalcald in February, 1537. However, the princes and free cities
of the Smalcald League ("our representatives") did not, as Luther mistakenly supposed, adopt the Articles.

[4]Luther was still laboring in 1538 under the misapprehension that
these things had happened in Smalcald.

without deception or treachery to hold a truly free council, as indeed the pope is in duty bound to do.

But the Roman court is dreadfully afraid of a free council   3 and flees from the light in a shameful fashion. Even adherents of that party have lost hope that the Roman court will ever permit a free council, to say nothing of calling one. They are deeply offended, as well they might be, and are not a little troubled on this account, for they perceive that the pope prefers to see all Christendom lost and all souls damned rather than suffer himself and his adherents to be reformed a little and allow limitations to be placed on his tyranny.

Nevertheless, I have decided to publish these articles so that, if I should die before a council meets (which I fully expect, for those knaves who shun the light and flee from the day take such wretched pains to postpone and prevent the council), those who live after me may have my testimony and confession (in addition to the confession[5] which I have previously given) to show where I have stood until now and where, by God's grace, I will continue to stand.

Why do I say this? Why should I complain? I am still alive. I   4 am still writing, preaching, and lecturing every day. Yet there are some who are so spiteful—not only among our adversaries, but also false brethren among those who profess to be adherents of our party—that they dare to cite my writings and teachings against me. They let me look on and listen, although they know very well that I teach otherwise. They try to clothe their venomous spirits in the garments of my labor and thus mislead the poor people in my name. Imagine what will happen after I am dead!

I suppose I should reply to everything while I am still living.   5 But how can I stop all the mouths of the devil? What, above all, can I do with those (for they are all poisoned) who do not pay attention to what I write and who keep themselves busy by shamefully twisting and corrupting my every word and letter? I shall let the devil—

---

[5]Luther's "Confession Concerning the Holy Supper" (1528).

or ultimately the wrath of God—answer them as they deserve. I 6
often think of the good Gerson,[6] who doubted whether one ought to
make good writings public. If one does not, many souls that might
have been saved are neglected. On the other hand, if one does, the
devil appears at once to poison and pervert everything by wagging
countless venomous and malicious tongues and thus destroying the
fruit. However, what such persons accomplish is manifest. For 7
although they slander us so shamefully and try by their lies to keep
the people on their side, God has constantly promoted his work, has
made their following smaller and smaller and ours ever larger, and
has caused, and still causes, them and their lies to be put to shame.

Let me illustrate this. There was a doctor[7] here in Wittenberg, 8
sent from France, who reported in our presence that his king had
been persuaded beyond a doubt that among us there is no church,
no government, and no state of matrimony, but that all live promis-
cuously like cattle and everybody does what he pleases. Imagine 9
how those will face us on the last day, before the judgment seat of
Christ, who in their writings have urged such big lies upon the king
and foreign peoples as if they were the unadulterated truth! Christ,
the lord and judge of us all, knows very well that they lie and have
lied. I am sure that he will pronounce sentence upon them. God convert those who are capable of conversion and turn them to repentance! As for the rest, wretchedness and woe will be their lot forever.

But let us return to the subject. I should be very happy to 10
see a true council assemble in order that many things and many
people might derive benefit from it. Not that we ourselves need such
a council, for by God's grace our churches have now been so enlightened and supplied with the pure Word and the right use of the
sacraments, with an understanding of the various callings of life,
and with true works, that we do not ask for a council for our own

---

[6]John Gerson (1363-1429) in his *De laude scriptorum,* XI.

[7]Dr. Gervasius Waim, or Wain, legate of King Francis I of France, was
in Saxony in 1531.

sake, and we have no reason to hope or expect that a council would improve our conditions. But in the dioceses of the papists we see so many vacant and desolate parishes everywhere that our hearts would break with grief.[8] Yet neither the bishops nor the canons care how the poor people live or die, although Christ died for them too. Those people cannot hear Christ speak to them as the true shepherd speaking to his sheep. This horrifies me and makes me fear that 11 he may cause a council of angels to descend on Germany and destroy us utterly, like Sodom and Gomorrah, because we mock him so shamefully with the council.[9]

Besides such necessary concerns of the church, there are 12 countless temporal matters that need reform. There is discord among princes and political estates. Usury and avarice have burst in like a deluge and have taken on the color of legality. Wantoness, lewdness, extravagance in dress, gluttony, gambling, vain display, all manner of vice and wickedness, disobedience of subjects, domestics, and laborers, extortion in every trade and on the part of peasants—who can enumerate everything?—these have gained the ascendancy to such an extent that ten councils and twenty diets would not be able to set things right again. If members of a council were to con- 13 sider such fundamental matters of the ecclesiastical and secular estates as are contrary to God, their hands would be so full that their trifling and tomfoolery with albs, great tonsures, broad cinctures, bishops' and cardinals' hats and crosiers, and similar nonsense would soon be forgotten. If we would first carry out God's commands and precepts in the spiritual and temporal estates, we would find enough time to reform the regulations concerning fasts, vestments, tonsures, and chasubles. But if we are willing to swallow camels and strain out gnats,[1] if we let logs stand and dispute about specks,[2] we might

---

[8] In Luther's table talk of Sept. 10, 1538 (*WA, TR*, 4: No. 4002), it was reported that 600 rich parishes in the diocese of Würzburg were vacant.

[9] Latin: pretext of a council.

[1] Cf. Matt. 23:24.

[2] Cf. Matt. 7:3-5.

just as well be satisfied with such a council.

I have drafted only a few articles, for, apart from these, God   14
has laid so many tasks upon us in church, state, and family that we
can never carry them out. What is the use of adopting a multitude of
decrees and canons in a council, especially when the primary things,
which are commanded by God, are neither regarded nor observed?
It is as if we were to expect God to acquiesce in our mummeries
while we trample his solemn commandments underfoot. But our sins
oppress us and keep God from being gracious to us, for we do not
repent and we even try to justify all our abominations.

Dear Lord Jesus Christ, assemble a council of thine own,   15
and by thy glorious advent deliver thy servants. The pope and his
adherents are lost. They will have nothing to do with Thee. But help
us, poor and wretched souls who cry unto Thee and earnestly seek
Thee according to the grace which Thou hast given us by the Holy
Spirit, who with Thee and the Father liveth and reigneth, blessed
forever. Amen.

[PART I]

The first part of the Articles treats the sublime articles of the
divine majesty, namely:

1. That Father, Son, and Holy Spirit, three distinct persons in one
divine essence and nature, are one God, who created heaven and
earth, etc.

2. That the Father was begotten by no one, the Son was begotten
by the Father, and the Holy Spirit proceeded from the Father and
the Son.

3. That only the Son became man, and neither the Father nor
the Holy Spirit.

4. That the Son became man in this manner: he was conceived
by the Holy Spirit, without the cooperation of man, and was born of

the pure, holy, and virgin Mary.[3] Afterwards he suffered, died, was buried, descended to hell, rose from the dead, and ascended to heaven; and he is seated at the right hand of God, will come to judge the living and the dead, etc., as the Apostles' Creed, the Athanasian Creed, and the Catechism in common use for children[4] teach.

These articles are not matters of dispute or contention, for both parties confess them.[5] Therefore, it is not necessary to treat them at greater length.

[PART II]

The second part treats the articles which pertain to the office and work of Jesus Christ, or to our redemption.

[Article I. Christ and Faith]

The first and chief article is this, that Jesus Christ, our God 1 and Lord, "was put to death for our trespasses and raised again for our justification" (Rom. 4:25). He alone is "the Lamb of God, 2 who takes away the sin of the world" (John 1:29). "God has laid upon him the iniquities of us all" (Isa. 53:6). Moreover, "all have 3 sinned," and "they are justified by his grace as a gift, through the redemption which is in Christ Jesus, by his blood" (Rom. 3:23-25).

Inasmuch as this must be believed and cannot be obtained or 4 apprehended by any work, law, or merit, it is clear and certain that such faith alone justifies us, as St. Paul says in Romans 3, "For we hold that a man is justified by faith apart from works of law" (Rom. 3:28), and again, "that he [God] himself is righteous and that he justifies him who has faith in Jesus" (Rom. 3:26).

---

[3]Latin: ever virgin Mary.

[4]The second article of the Creed in Luther's Small Catechism.

[5]I.e., Roman and Lutheran parties alike acknowledge the creeds of the ancient church. What follows in Part II makes it clear that, despite this, the two parties disagreed in their interpretation and application of these creeds.

Nothing in this article can be given up or compromised,[6] even   5
if heaven and earth and things temporal should be destroyed. For as
St. Peter says, "There is no other name under heaven given among
men by which we must be saved" (Acts 4:12). "And with his stripes
we are healed" (Isa. 53:5).

On this article rests all that we teach and practice against the
pope, the devil, and the world. Therefore we must be quite certain
and have no doubts about it. Otherwise all is lost, and the pope, the
devil, and all our adversaries will gain the victory.

Article II. [The Mass]

The mass in the papacy must be regarded as the greatest and   1
most horrible abomination because it runs into direct and violent
conflict with this fundamental article. Yet, above and beyond all
others, it has been the supreme and most precious of the papal idolatries, for it is held that this sacrifice or work of the Mass (even when
offered by an evil scoundrel) delivers men from their sins, both here
in this life and yonder in purgatory, although in reality this can and
must be done by the Lamb of God alone, as has been stated above.[7]
There is to be no concession or compromise in this article either, for
the first article does not permit it.

If there were reasonable papists, one would speak to them in   2
the following friendly fashion:

"Why do you cling so tenaciously to your Masses?

"1. After all, they are a purely human invention. They are not
commanded by God. And we can discard all human inventions, for
Christ says, 'In vain do they worship me, teaching as doctrines the
precepts of men' (Matt. 15:9).

"2. The Mass is unnecessary, and so it can be omitted without   3
sin and danger.

---

[6]Latin adds: nor can any believer concede or permit anything contrary
to it.

[7]Pt. II, Art I, above.

"3. The sacrament can be had in a far better and more blessed   4 manner—indeed, the only blessed manner—according to the institution of Christ. Why, then, do you drive the world into wretchedness and woe on account of an unnecessary and fictitious matter when the sacrament can be had in another and more blessed way?

"Let the people be told openly that the Mass, as trumpery,   5 can be omitted without sin, that no one will be damned for not observing it, and that one can be saved in a better way without the Mass. Will the Mass not then collapse of itself—not only for the rude rabble, but also for all godly, Christian, sensible, God-fearing people—especially if they hear that it is a dangerous thing which was fabricated and invented without God's Word and will?

"4. Since such countless and unspeakable abuses have arisen   6 everywhere through the buying and selling of Masses, it would be prudent to do without the Mass for no other reason than to curb such abuses, even if it actually possessed some value in and of itself. How much the more should it be discontinued in order to guard forever against such abuses when it is so unnecessary, useless, and dangerous and when we can obtain what is more necessary, more useful, and more certain without the Mass.

"5. The Mass is and can be nothing else than a human work,   7 even a work of evil scoundrels (as the canon[8] and all books on the subject declare), for by means of the Mass men try to reconcile themselves and others to God and obtain and merit grace and the forgiveness of sins. It is observed for this purpose when it is best observed. What other purpose could it have? Therefore, it should be condemned and must be abolished because it is a direct contradiction to the fundamental article, which asserts that it is not the celebrant of a Mass and what he does but the Lamb of God and the Son of God who takes away our sin."[9]

Somebody may seek to justify himself by saying that he wishes   8

---

[8] Roman canon of the Mass.
[9] Cf. John 1:29.

to communicate himself for the sake of his own devotion.[1] This is not honest, for if he really desires to commune, he can do so most fittingly and properly in the sacrament administered according to Christ's institution. To commune by himself is uncertain and unnecessary, and he does not know what he is doing because he follows a false human opinion and imagination without the sanction of God's Word. Nor is it right (even if everything else is in order) 9 for anyone to use the sacrament, which is the common possession of the church, to meet his own private need and thus trifle with it according to his own pleasure apart from the fellowship of the church.

This article concerning the Mass will be the decisive issue 10 in the council. Even if it were possible for the papists to make concessions to us in all other articles, it would not be possible for them to yield on this article. It is as Campegio[2] said in Augsburg: he would suffer himself to be torn to pieces before he would give up the Mass. So by God's help I would suffer myself to be burned to ashes before I would allow a celebrant of the Mass and what he does to be considered equal or superior to my Saviour, Jesus Christ. Accordingly we are and remain eternally divided and opposed the one to the other. The papists are well aware that if the Mass falls, the papacy will fall with it. Before they would permit this to happen, they would put us all to death.

Besides, this dragon's tail — that is, the Mass — has brought 11 forth a brood of vermin and the poison of manifold idolatries.

The first is purgatory. They were so occupied with requiem 12 Masses, with vigils, with the weekly, monthly, and yearly celebrations of requiems,[3] with the common week,[4] with All Souls' Day, and

---

[1]Cf. *WA, Br,* 5:504, 505; *WA,* 8:438, 514.

[2]Lorenzo Campegio (1474-1539), the papal legate. The same anecdote also appears elsewhere.

[3]The celebration of Mass on the anniversary of the deceased is referred to as early as Tertullian (*De corona,* III), and celebrations on the week and month following death are mentioned by Ambrose (*De obitu Theodosii oratio,* III).

with soul-baths[5] that the Mass was used almost exclusively for the dead although Christ instituted the sacrament for the living alone. Consequently purgatory and all the pomp, services, and business transactions associated with it are to be regarded as nothing else than illusions of the devil, for purgatory, too, is contrary to the fundamental article that Christ alone, and not the work of man, can help souls. Besides, nothing has been commanded or enjoined upon us with reference to the dead. All this may consequently be discarded, apart entirely from the fact that it is error and idolatry.

The papists here adduce passages from Augustine and some 13 of the Fathers[6] who are said to have written about purgatory. They suppose that we do not understand for what purpose and to what end the authors wrote these passages. St. Augustine[7] does not write that there is a purgatory, nor does he cite any passage of the Scriptures that would constrain him to adopt such an opinion. He leaves it undecided whether or not there is a purgatory and merely mentions that his mother asked that she be remembered at the altar or sacrament. Now, this is nothing but a human opinion of certain individuals and cannot establish an article of faith. That is the prerogative of God alone. But our papists make use of such human 14 opinions to make men believe their shameful, blasphemous, accursed traffic in Masses which are offered for souls in purgatory, etc. They can never demonstrate these things from Augustine. Only when they have abolished their traffic in purgatorial Masses (which St. Augustine never dreamed of) shall we be ready to discuss with them whether statements of St. Augustine are to be accepted when they are without the support of the Scriptures and whether the dead are to be commemorated in the sacrament. It will not do to 15

---

[4]The week following St. Michael's Day (Sept. 29), when many Masses were offered for the dead.

[5]Free baths endowed for the poor with the intention that the latter should pray for the donor's salvation.

[6]E.g., Gregory the Great, *Dialogs*, IV, 39.

[7]*Confessions*, IX, 11, 13.

make articles of faith out of the holy Fathers' words or works. Otherwise what they ate, how they dressed, and what kind of houses they lived in would have to become articles of faith—as has happened in the case of relics. This means that[8] the Word of God shall establish articles of faith and no one else, not even an angel.[9]

The second is a consequence of this: evil spirits have intro- 16 duced the knavery of appearing as spirits of the departed[1] and, with unspeakable lies and cunning, of demanding Masses, vigils, pilgrimages, and other alms. We had to accept all these things as arti- 17 cles of faith and had to live according to them. Moreover, the pope gave his approval to these things as well as to the Mass and all the other abominations. Here, too, there can be no concession or compromise.

The third are pilgrimages. Masses, forgiveness of sins, and 18 God's grace were sought here, too, for Masses dominated everything. It is certain that we have not been commanded to make pilgrimages, nor are they necessary, because we may obtain forgiveness and grace in a better way and may omit pilgrimages without sin and danger. Why do they neglect their own parishes, the Word of God, their wives and children, etc. and pursue these unnecessary, uncertain, harmful will-o'-the-wisps of the devil? They do so 19 simply because the devil has possessed the pope to praise and approve of these practices in order that great multitudes of people may turn aside from Christ to their own merits and (what is worst of all) become idolaters. Besides, it is an unnecessary, uncommanded, abortive, uncertain, and even harmful thing. Therefore there may be 20 no concession or compromise here either.

---

[8]Latin: We have another rule, namely, that.

[9]Cf. Gal. 1:8.

[1]The reference is to spirit manifestations reported by Gregory the Great (*Dialogs*, IV, 40) and Peter Damiani (*Opusculum*, XXXIV, 5).

The fourth are fraternities.[2] Here monasteries, chapters, and 21 vicars have obligated themselves to transfer (by legal and open sale) all Masses, good works, etc. for the benefit of the living and the dead. Not only is this mere human trumpery, utterly unnecessary and without command, but it is contrary to the first article, concerning redemption.[3] Therefore, it is under no circumstances to be tolerated.

The fifth are relics. In this connection so many manifest lies 22 and so much nonsense has been invented about the bones of dogs and horses that even the devil has laughed at such knavery. Even if there were some good in them, relics should long since have been condemned. They are neither commanded nor commended. They are utterly unnecessary and useless. Worst of all, however, is the 23 claim that relics effect indulgences and the forgiveness of sin and that, like the Mass, etc., their use is a good work and a service of God.

The sixth place belongs to the precious indulgences, which 24 are granted to the living and the dead (for money) and by which the pope sells the merits of Christ together with the superabundant merits of all the saints and the entire church. These are not to be tolerated. Not only are they unnecessary and without commandment, but they are also contrary to the first article, for the merits of Christ are obtained by grace, through faith, without our work or pennies. They are offered to us without our money or merit, not by the power of the pope but by the preaching of God's Word.

The Invocation of Saints

The invocation of saints is also one of the abuses of the 25 Antichrist. It is in conflict with the first, chief article and undermines

---

[2]Since the eighth century members of certain monasteries obligated themselves to offer prayers and engage in works of piety in behalf of deceased monks. In the Middle Ages similar obligations were assumed by groups of clergymen, clergymen and laymen, or only laymen.

[3]Pt. II, Art. I, above.

knowledge of Christ. It is neither commanded nor recommended, nor does it have any precedent in the Scriptures. Even if the invocation of saints were a precious practice (which it is not), we have everything a thousandfold better in Christ.

Although angels in heaven pray for us (as Christ himself 26 also does), and although saints on earth, and perhaps also in heaven, do likewise, it does not follow that we should invoke angels and saints, pray to them, keep fasts and festivals for them, say Masses and offer sacrifices to them, establish churches, altars, and services for them, serve them in still other ways, regard them as helpers in time of need, and attribute all sorts of help to them, assigning to each of them a special function,[4] as the papists teach and practice. This is idolatry. Such honor belongs to God alone. As a Chris- 27 tian and a saint on earth, you can pray for me, not in one particular necessity only, but in every kind of need. However, I should not on this account pray to you, invoke you, keep fasts and festivals and say Masses and offer sacrifices in your honor, or trust in you for my salvation. There are other ways in which I can honor, love, 28 and thank you in Christ. If such idolatrous honor is withdrawn from angels and dead saints, the honor that remains will do no harm and will quickly be forgotten. When spiritual and physical benefit and help are no longer expected, the saints will cease to be molested in their graves and in heaven, for no one will long remember, esteem, or honor them out of love when there is no expectation of return.

In short we cannot allow but must condemn the Mass, its 29 implications, and its consequences in order that we may retain the holy sacrament in its purity and certainty according to the institution of Christ and may use and receive it in faith.

---

[4]The notion that certain saints were specialists in intercession for specific afflictions is discussed, for example, in Luther's "The Fourteen of Consolation" (1520).

V. The Reform of the Church

Article III. [Chapters and Monasteries]

The chapters[5] and monasteries which in former times had ⏐ been founded with good intentions for the education of learned men and decent women should be restored to such purposes in order that we may have pastors, preachers, and other ministers in the church, others who are necessary for secular government in cities and states, and also well trained girls to become mothers, housekeepers, etc.

If they are unwilling to serve this purpose, it would be better ⏐ 2 to abandon them or tear them down rather than preserve them with their blasphemous services, invented by men, which claim to be superior to the ordinary Christian life and to the offices and callings established by God. All this, too, is in conflict with the first, fundamental article concerning redemption in Jesus Christ. Besides, like other human inventions, all this is without commandment, unnecessary, and useless. Moreover, it causes dangerous and needless effort, and accordingly the prophets call such service of God *aven,*[6] that is, vanity.

Article IV. [The Papacy]

The pope is not the head of all Christendom by divine right ⏐ or according to God's Word, for this position belongs only to one, namely, to Jesus Christ. The pope is only the bishop and pastor of the churches in Rome and of such other churches as have attached themselves to him voluntarily or through a human institution (that is, a secular government).[7] These churches did not choose to be under him as under an overlord but chose to stand beside him as

---

[5]Associations of secular priests, called canons. There were also canonesses, women who lived under a rule without taking the perpetual vows of nuns. Chapter schools were conducted for boys by canons and for girls by canonesses.

[6]Cf. Zech. 10:2, Hab. 1:3, Isa. 1:13, etc.

[7]The secular power of the pope, the patrimony of Peter.

Christian brethren and companions, as the ancient councils[8] and the time of Cyprian[9] prove. But now no bishop dares to call the pope   2 "brother," as was then customary,[1] but must address him as "most gracious lord," as if he were a king or emperor. This we neither will nor should nor can take upon our consciences. Those who wish to do so had better not count on us!

Hence it follows that all the things that the pope has under-   3 taken and done on the strength of such false, mischievous, blasphemous, usurped authority have been and still are purely diabolical transactions and deeds (except what pertains to secular government,[2] where God sometimes permits much good to come to a people through a tyrant or scoundrel) which contribute to the destruction of the entire holy Christian church (in so far as this lies in his power) and come into conflict with the first, fundamental article which is concerned with redemption in Jesus Christ.

All the pope's bulls and books, in which he roars like a lion   4 (as the angel in Rev. 10:3[3] suggests), are available. Here it is asserted that no Christian can be saved unless he is obedient to the pope and submits to him in all that he desires, says, and does.[4] This is nothing less than to say, "Although you believe in Christ, and in him have everything that is needful for salvation, this is nothing and all in vain unless you consider me your god and are obedient and subject to me." Yet it is manifest that the holy church was without a

---

[8]Luther here refers to the Councils of Nicea, Constantinople, Ephesus, and Chalcedon.

[9]See note 4, below, and also Melanchthon's "Treatise on the Power and Primacy of the Pope," below, 13-17.

[1]Luther often referred to the letters of Bishop Cyprian of Carthage (d. 258) to Pope Cornelius in which the pope is addressed as "very dear brother."

[2]See above, IV, 1, and note 1 at that place.

[3]The reference in Luther's text, probably set down from memory, is mistakenly given as Rev. 12.

[4]The classic statement of extreme papal claims was Boniface VIII's bull *Unam Sanctam* (1302): "It is altogether necessary to salvation for every human creature to be subject to the Roman pontiff."

pope for more than five hundred years at the least[5] and that the churches of the Greeks and many other nationalities have never been under the pope and are not at the present time. Manifestly 5 (to repeat what has already been said often) the papacy is a human invention, and it is not commanded, it is unnecessary, and it is useless. The holy Christian church can exist very well without such a head, and it would have remained much better if such a head had not been raised up by the devil. The papacy is of no use to the 6 church because it exercises no Christian office. Consequently the church must continue to exist without the pope.

Suppose that the pope would renounce the claim that he is 7 the head of the church by divine right or by God's command; suppose that it were necessary to have a head, to whom all others should adhere, in order that the unity of Christendom might better be preserved against the attacks of sects and heresies; and suppose that such a head would then be elected by men and it remained in their power and choice to change or depose this head. This is just the way in which the Council of Constance acted with reference to the popes when it deposed three and elected a fourth.[6] If, I say, the pope and the see of Rome were to concede and accept this (which is impossible), he would have to suffer the overthrow and destruction of his whole rule and estate, together with all his rights and pretensions. In short, he cannot do it. Even if he could, Christendom would not be helped in any way. There would be even more sects than 8

---

[5]Luther often thought of Gregory I (590-604) as the last Roman bishop before the succession of popes began. See also Melanchthon's Treatise on the Power and Primacy of the Pope, *The Book of Concord,* 319-335.

[6]John XXIII, Benedict XIV, and Gregory XII, rival claimants to the papacy, were removed from office (with the cooperation of the last-named) and Martin V was elected in their place by the Council of Constance (1414-1418).

before because, inasmuch as subjection to such a head would depend on the good pleasure of men rather than on a divine command, he would very easily and quickly be despised and would ultimately be without any adherents at all. He would not always have to have his residence in Rome or some other fixed place,[7] but it could be anywhere and in whatever church God would raise up a man fitted for such an office. What a complicated and confused state of affairs that would be!

Consequently the church cannot be better governed and maintained than by having all of us live under one head, Christ,[8] and by having all the bishops equal in office (however they may differ in gifts)[9] and diligently joined together in unity of doctrine, faith, sacraments, prayer, works of love, etc. So St. Jerome writes[1] that the priests of Alexandria governed the churches together and in common. The apostles did the same, and after them all the bishops throughout Christendom, until the pope raised his head over them all. 9

This[2] is a powerful demonstration that the pope is the real Antichrist[3] who has raised himself over and set himself against Christ, for the pope will not permit Christians to be saved except by his own power, which amounts to nothing since it is neither established nor commanded by God. This is actually what St. Paul calls exalting oneself over and against God.[4] Neither the Turks nor the Tartars, great as is their enmity against Christians, do this; those who desire to do so they allow to believe in Christ, and they receive bodily tribute and obedience from Christians. 10 11

---

[7]For example, the papal court was in Avignon from 1309 to 1377.

[8]Cf. Eph. 1:22; 4:15; 5:25; Col. 1:18.

[9]Cf. I Cor. 12:4, 8-10; Rom. 12:6-8.

[1]Quoting from memory, Luther here combines two citations from Jerome which he was fond of quoting: *Commentary on the Epistle to Titus*, 1:5, 6, and *Epistle to Euangelus the Presbyter*, No. 146.

[2]Latin: This doctrine.

[3]*Endechrist oder Widerchrist.*

[4]Cf. II Thess. 2:4.

However, the pope will not permit such faith but asserts that 12
one must be obedient to him in order to be saved.[5] This we are
unwilling to do even if we have to die for it in God's name. All 13
this is a consequence of his wishing to be the head of the Christian
church by divine right. He had to set himself up as equal to and
above Christ and to proclaim himself the head, and then the lord of
the church, and finally of the whole world. He went so far as to
claim to be an earthly god[6] and even presumed to issue orders to the
angels in heaven.[7]

When the teaching of the pope is distinguished from that of 14
the Holy Scriptures, or is compared with them, it becomes apparent
that, at its best, the teaching of the pope has been taken from the
imperial, pagan law[8] and is a teaching concerning secular transactions and judgments, as the papal decretals[9] show. In keeping with
such teaching, instructions are given concerning the ceremonies of
churches, vestments, food, personnel, and countless other puerilities,
fantasies, and follies without so much as a mention of Christ, faith,
and God's commandments.

Finally, it is most diabolical for the pope to promote his lies
about Masses, purgatory, monastic life, and human works and services (which are the essence of the papacy) in contradiction to God,
and to damn, slay, and plague all Christians who do not exalt and
honor these abominations of his above all things. Accordingly, just
as we cannot adore the devil himself as our lord or God, so we cannot suffer his apostle, the pope or Antichrist, to govern us as our
head or lord, for deception, murder, and the eternal destruction of

---

[5]See IV, 4, above, and note 2 at that place.

[6]So Augustinus de Ancona (d. 1328), Zenzelinus de Cassanis (d. ca.
1350), Francisus de Zabarellis (d. 1417).

[7]The reference is to the allegedly spurious bull of Pope Clement VI, *Ad
memoriam reducendo*, of June 27, 1346, in which the pope is said to have
commanded the angels "to lead to heaven the souls of the pilgrims who
might die on their way to Rome" during the "holy year" of 1350.

[8]That is, Roman law.

[9]Decisions of the popes in the form of letters.

body and soul are characteristic of his papal government,[1] as I have demonstrated in many books.[2]

In these four articles they will have enough to condemn in 15 the council, for they neither can nor will concede to us even the smallest fraction of these articles. Of this we may be certain, and we must rely on the hope that Christ, our Lord, has attacked his adversaries and will accomplish his purpose by his Spirit and his 16 coming.[3] Amen. In the council we shall not be standing before the emperor or the secular authority, as at Augsburg,[4] where we responded to a gracious summons and were given a kindly hearing, but we shall stand before the pope and the devil himself, who does not intend to give us a hearing but only to damn, murder, and drive us to idolatry. Consequently we ought not here kiss his feet[5] or say, "You are my gracious lord," but we ought rather speak as the angel spoke to the devil in Zechariah, "The Lord rebuke you, O Satan" (Zech. 3:2).[6]

[PART III]

The following articles treat matters which we may discuss with learned and sensible men, or even among ourselves. The pope and his court do not care much about these things; they are not concerned about matters of conscience but only about money, honor, and power.

---

[1]This passage is quoted below in the Formula of Concord, Solid Declaration, X, 20.

[2]E.g., *Resolutio super propositione de potestate papae* (1519).

[3]Cf. II Thess. 2:8.

[4]The diet of Augsburg in 1530, when the Augsburg Confession was presented. Here, as elsewhere, Luther spoke well of Emperor Charles V.

[5]All the faithful were required to kneel before the pope and kiss his foot in an act of homage (*adoratio*). This is still observed today at the election of a new pope. In 1520 Luther had written: "It is an unchristian, even anti-Christian, thing for a poor sinful man to allow his foot to be kissed by one who is a hundred times better than he is" (*WA*, 6:435).

[6]Originally Luther added here, *Pfui dein mal an,* "Shame on you!"

I. Sin

Here we must confess what St. Paul says in Rom. 5:12, name- 1
ly, that sin had its origin in one man, Adam, through whose disobedience all men were made sinners and became subject to death and
the devil. This is called original sin, or the root sin.

The fruits of this sin are all the subsequent evil deeds which 2
are forbidden in the Ten Commandments, such as unbelief, false
belief, idolatry, being without the fear of God, presumption, despair,
blindness—in short, ignorance or disregard of God—and then also
lying, swearing by God's name, failure to pray and call upon God,
neglect of God's Word, disobedience to parents, murder, unchastity,
theft, deceit, etc.

This hereditary sin[7] is so deep a corruption of nature that 3
reason cannot understand it. It must be believed because of the
revelation in the Scriptures (Ps. 51:5, Rom. 5:12ff., Exod. 33:20, Gen.
3:6ff.). What the scholastic theologians taught concerning this article is therefore nothing but error and stupidity, namely,

1. That after the fall of Adam the natural powers of man have 4
remained whole and uncorrupted, and that man by nature possesses
a right understanding and a good will, as the philosophers teach.[8]

2. Again, that man has a free will, either to do good and re- 5
frain from evil or refrain from good and do evil.

3. Again, that man is able by his natural powers to observe 6
and keep all the commandments of God.

4. Again, that man is able by his natural powers to love God 7
above all things and his neighbor as himself.

5. Again, if man does what he can, God is certain to grant 8
him his grace.

6. Again, when a man goes to the sacrament there is no need 9
of a good intention to do what he ought, but it is enough that he

---

[7]*Erbsunde; peccatum haereditarium.*
[8]E.g., Plato and Aristotle.

does not have an evil intention to commit sin, for such is the goodness of man's nature and such is the power of the sacrament.

7. That it cannot be proved from the Scriptures that the 10 Holy Spirit and his gifts are necessary for the performance of a good work.

Such and many similar notions have resulted from misun- 11 derstanding and ignorance concerning sin and concerning Christ, our Saviour. They are thoroughly pagan doctrines, and we cannot tolerate them. If such teachings were true, Christ would have died in vain, for there would be no defect or sin in man for which he would have had to die, or else he would have died only for the body and not for the soul inasmuch as the soul would be sound and only the body would be subject to death.

II. The Law

Here we maintain that the law was given by God first of all to 1 restrain sins by threats and fear of punishment and by the promise and offer of grace and favor. But this purpose failed because of the wickedness which sin has worked in man. Some, who hate the 2 law because it forbids what they desire to do and commands what they are unwilling to do, are made worse thereby. Accordingly, in so far as they are not restrained by punishment, they act against the law even more than before. These are the rude and wicked people who do evil whenever they have opportunity. Others become 3 blind and presumptuous, imagining that they can and do keep the law by their own powers, as was just said above[9] concerning the scholastic theologians. Hypocrites and false saints are produced in this way.

However, the chief function or power of the law is to make 4 original sin manifest and show man to what utter depths his nature has fallen and how corrupt it has become. So the law must tell him

---

[9]See Pt. III, Art. I, 3-10.

that he neither has nor cares for God or that he worships strange gods—something that he would not have believed before without a knowledge of the law. Thus he is terror-stricken and humbled, becomes despondent and despairing, anxiously desires help but does not know where to find it, and begins to be alienated from God, to murmur, etc. This is what is meant by Rom. 4:15,[1] "The law 5 brings wrath," and Rom. 5:20, "Law came in to increase the trespass."

III. Repentance

This function of the law is retained and taught by the New 1 Testament. So Paul says in Rom. 1:18, "The wrath of God is revealed from heaven against all ungodliness and wickedness of men," and in Rom. 3:19, 20, "The whole world may be held accountable to God, for no human being will be justified in his sight." Christ also says in John 16:8, "The Holy Spirit will convince the world of sin."

This, then, is the thunderbolt by means of which God with one 2 blow destroys both open sinners and false saints. He allows no one to justify himself. He drives all together into terror and despair. This is the hammer of which Jeremiah speaks, "Is not my word like a hammer which breaks the rock in pieces?" (Jer. 23:29). This is not *activa contritio* (artificial remorse), but *passiva contritio* (true sorrow of the heart, suffering, and pain of death).

This is what the beginning of true repentance is like. Here 3 man must hear such a judgment as this: "You are all of no account. Whether you are manifest sinners or saints,[2] you must all become other than you now are and do otherwise than you now do, no matter who you are and no matter how great, wise, mighty, and holy you may think yourselves. Here no one is godly," etc.

To this office of the law the New Testament immediately 4

---

[1]Luther mistakenly wrote Rom. 3.
[2]Latin adds: in your opinion.

adds the consoling promise of grace in the Gospel. This is to be believed, as Christ says in Mark 1:15. "Repent and believe in the Gospel," which is to say, "Become different, do otherwise, and believe my promise." John, who preceded Christ, is called a 5 preacher of repentance—but for the remission of sins. That is, John was to accuse them all and convince them that they were sinners in order that they might know how they stood before God and recognize themselves as lost men. In this way they were to be prepared to receive grace from the Lord and to expect and accept from him 6 the forgiveness of sins. Christ himself says this in Luke 24:47, "Repentance and the forgiveness of sins should be preached in his name to all nations."

But where the law exercises its office alone, without the addi- 7 tion of the Gospel, there is only death and hell, and man must despair like Saul and Judas.[3] As St. Paul says,[4] the law slays 8 through sin. Moreover, the Gospel offers consolation and forgiveness in more ways than one, for with God there is plenteous redemption (as Ps. 130:7 puts it) from the dreadful captivity to sin, and this comes to us through the Word, the sacraments, and the like, as we shall hear.[5]

Now we must compare the false repentance of the sophists[6] 9 with true repentance so that both may be better understood.

The False Repentance of the Papists

It was impossible for them to teach correctly about repen- 10 tance because they did not know what sin really is. For, as stated above,[7] they did not have the right teaching concerning original sin but asserted that the natural powers of man have remained whole

---

[3]Cf. I Sam. 28:20 and 31:4; Matt. 27:3-5.
[4]Cf. Rom. 7:10.
[5]See Pt. III, Art. IV.
[6]Scholastic theologians.
[7]Pt. III, Art. I, 4, 8.

and uncorrupted, that reason is capable of right understanding and the will is capable of acting accordingly, and that God will assuredly grant his grace to the man who does as much as he can according to his free will.

From this it follows that people did penance only for actual 11 sins, such as wicked thoughts to which they consented (for evil impulses, lust, and inclinations they did not consider sin), wicked words, and wicked works which man with his free will might well have avoided. Such repentance the sophists divided into three 12 parts—contrition, confession, and satisfaction—with the added consolation that a man who properly repents, confesses, and makes satisfaction has merited forgiveness and has paid for his sins before God. In their teaching of penance the sophists thus instructed the people to place their confidence in their own works. Hence the expression in the pulpit when the general confession was recited 13 to the people: "Prolong my life, Lord God, until I make satisfaction for my sins and amend my life."[8]

There was no mention here of Christ or of faith. Rather, men 14 hoped by their own works to overcome and blot out their sins before God. With this intention we, too, became priests and monks, that we might set ourselves against sin.

As for contrition, this was the situation: Since nobody could 15 recall all his sins (especially those committed during the course of a whole year),[9] the following loophole was resorted to, namely, that when a hidden sin was afterwards remembered, it had also to be repented of, confessed, etc., but meanwhile the sinner was commended to the grace of God. Moreover, since nobody knew how 16 much contrition he had to muster in order to avail before God, this

---

[8]Words from the general confession of sins, spoken by the priest in behalf of the congregation. See "General Confession" in *New Schaff-Herzog Encyclopedia,* IV, 449.

[9]The obligation of confession at least once a year was imposed at the Fourth Lateran Council (1215) on all who had reached years of discretion.

consolation was offered: If anybody could not be contrite (that is, really repentant), he should at least be attrite (which I might call half-way or partially repentant). They understood neither of these terms, and to this day they are as far from comprehending their meaning as I am. Nevertheless, such attrition was reckoned as a substitute for contrition when people went to confession. And when 17 somebody said that he was unable to repent or be sorry for his sin (which might have been committed, let us say, in whoredom, revenge, or the like), such a person was asked if he did not wish or desire to be repentant. If he said Yes (for who but the devil himself would want to say No?) it was accounted as contrition and, on the basis of this good work of his, his sin was forgiven. Here the example of St. Bernard, etc. was cited.[1]

Here we see how blind reason gropes about in matters 18 which pertain to God, seeking consolation in its own works, according to its own inventions, without being able to consider Christ and faith. If we examine this in the light, we see that such contrition is an artificial and imaginary idea evolved by man's own powers without faith and without knowledge of Christ. A poor sinner who reflected on his lust or revenge in this fashion would sooner have laughed than wept, unless perchance he was really smitten by the law or vainly vexed with a sorrowful spirit by the devil. Apart from cases like this, such repentance surely was pure hypocrisy. It did not extinguish the lust for sin. The person involved was obliged to grieve, but he would rather have sinned if he had been free to do so.

As for confession, the situation was like this: Everybody had 19 to give an account of all his sins—an impossibility and the source of great torture. The sins which had been forgotten were pardoned only when a man remembered them and thereupon confessed them. Accordingly he could never know when he had made a sufficiently complete or a sufficiently pure confession. At the same time his attention was directed to his own works, and he was told that the

---

[1]Cf. Bernard of Clairvaux, *Treatise on Grace and Free Will*, VI, 10.

more completely he confessed, the more he was ashamed, and the more he abased himself before the priest, the sooner and the better he would make satisfaction for his sins, for such humiliation would surely earn grace before God. Here, again, there was neither 20 faith nor Christ. A man did not become aware of the power of absolution, for his consolation was made to rest on his enumeration of sins and on his self-abasement. But this is not the place to recount the torture, rascality, and idolatry which such confession has produced.

Satisfaction was even more complicated,[2] for nobody could 21 know how much he was to do for one single sin, to say nothing of all his sins. Here the expedient was resorted to of imposing small satisfactions which were easy to render, like saying five Our Fathers, fasting for a day, etc. For the penance that was still lacking man was referred to purgatory.

Here, too, there was nothing but anguish and misery. Some 22 thought that they would never get out of purgatory because, according to the ancient canons, seven years of penance were required for a single mortal sin.[3] Nevertheless, confidence was placed in 23 man's own works of satisfaction. If the satisfaction could have been perfect, full confidence would have been placed in it, and neither faith nor Christ would have been of any value. But such confidence was impossible. Even if one had done penance in this way for a hundred years, one would still not have known whether this was enough. This is a case of always doing penance but never coming to repentance.

Here the holy see in Rome came to the aid of the poor church 24 and invented indulgences. By these satisfaction was remitted and canceled, first for seven years in a single case, then for a hundred, etc. The indulgences were distributed among the cardinals and bishops so that one could grant them for a hundred years, another

---

[2]Latin: perplexing.

[3]Such statements were to be found in the so-called *47 canones poenitentiales* which were well known at the close of the Middle Ages.

for a hundred days, but the pope reserved for himself alone the right to remit the entire satisfaction.[4]

When this began to yield money and the bull market be- 25 came profitable, the pope invented the jubilee year and attached it to Rome.[5] This was called remission of all penalty and guilt,[6] and the people came running, for everyone was eager to be delivered from the heavy, unbearable burden. Here we have the discovery and digging up of the treasures of the earth.[7] The popes went further and quickly multiplied the jubilee years.[8] The more money they swallowed, the wider became their maws. So they sent their legates out into all lands until every church and house was reached by 26 jubilee indulgences. Finally the popes forced their way into purgatory, first by instituting Masses and vigils for the dead and afterwards by offering indulgences for the dead through bulls and jubilee years.[9] In time souls got to be so cheap that they were released at six pence a head.

Even this did not help, however, for although the pope 27 taught the people to rely on and trust in such indulgences, he again introduced uncertainty when he declared in his bulls, "Whoever wishes to benefit from the indulgence or jubilee year must be contrite, make confession, and pay money."[1] But the contrition and confession practiced by these people, as we have heard above,[2] are

---

[4]Plenary indulgences were first granted in 1095 in connection with the crusades.

[5]The jubilee or holy year was instituted by Pope Boniface VIII in 1300 for the benefit of pilgrims to Rome.

[6]The expression *remissio poenae et culpae* was frequently used.

[7]There was a saying in the Middle Ages, based on Dan. 11:43, that the devil would show the Antichrist the hidden treasures of the earth in order that men might be seduced by them.

[8]From once every hundred years to once every twenty-five years.

[9]The first papal indulgence for the dead seems to have been offered in 1476. After 1500 such indulgences were connected with holy years.

[1]Contrition and confession were often mentioned as conditions for receiving indulgences.

[2]See sec. 16, 19.

uncertain and hypocritical. Moreover, nobody knew which soul was in purgatory, and nobody knew which of those in purgatory had truly repented and properly confessed. So the pope took the money, consoled the people with his power and indulgences, and once again directed attention to uncertain human works.

There were some who did not think they were guilty of ac-   28 tual sins—that is, of sinful thoughts, words, and deeds. I and others like myself who wished to be monks and priests in monasteries and chapters fought against evil thoughts by fasting, vigils, prayers, Masses, coarse clothing, and hard beds and tried earnestly and mightily to be holy, and yet the hereditary evil which is born in us did what is its nature to do, sometimes while we slept (as St. Augustine, St. Jerome, and others confess).[3] Each one, however, held that some of the others were, as we taught, without sin and full of good works, and so we shared our good works with others and sold them to others in the belief that they were more than we ourselves needed for heaven. This is certainly true, and there are seals, letters, and examples to show it. Such persons did not need to   29 repent, for what were they to repent of when they did not consent to evil thoughts? What should they confess when they refrained from evil words? What satisfaction should they render when they were innocent of evil deeds and could even sell their superfluous righteousness to other poor sinners? The scribes and Pharisees in Christ's time were just such saints.[4]

Here the fiery angel[5] St. John, the preacher of true repen-   30 tance, intervenes. With a single thunderbolt he strikes and destroys both. "Repent," he says.[6] On the one hand there are some who think, "We have already done penance," and on the other hand there   31 are others who suppose, "We need no repentance." But John   32

---

[3]Augustine, *Confessions*, II, 2; X, 30; Jerome, *Epistle to Eustochius,* 22:7.

[4]Latin adds: and hypocrites.

[5]Cf. Rev. 10:1.

[6]Matt. 3:2.

says: "Repent, both of you. Those of you in the former group are false penitents, and those of you in the latter are false saints. Both of you need the forgiveness of sins, for neither of you knows what sin really is, to say nothing of repenting and shunning sin. None of you is good. All of you are full of unbelief, blindness, and ignorance of God and God's will. For he is here present, and from his fullness have we all received, grace upon grace.[7] No man can be just before God without him. Accordingly, if you would repent, repent rightly. Your repentance accomplishes nothing. And you hypocrites who think you do not need to repent, you brood of vipers,[8] who has given you any assurance that you will escape the wrath to come?"

St. Paul teaches the same thing in Rom. 3:10-12: "None is 33 righteous, no, not one; no one understands, no one seeks for God. All have turned aside, together they have gone wrong." And in Acts 34 17:30, "Now he commands all men everywhere to repent." He says "all men," that is, excepting no one who is a man. Such repen- 35 tance teaches us to acknowledge sin—that is, to acknowledge that we are all utterly lost, that from head to foot there is no good in us, that we must become altogether new and different men.

This repentance is not partial and fragmentary like repen- 36 tance for actual sins, nor is it uncertain like that. It does not debate what is sin and what is not, but lumps everything together and says, "We are wholly and altogether sinful." We need not spend our time weighing, distinguishing, differentiating. On this account there is no uncertainty in such repentance, for nothing is left that we might imagine to be good enough to pay for our sin. One thing is sure: We cannot pin our hope on anything that we are, think, say, or do. And so our repentance cannot be false, uncertain, or partial, for a 37 person who confesses that he is altogether sinful embraces all sins in his confession without omitting or forgetting a single one. Nor 38 can our satisfaction be uncertain, for it consists not of the dubious, sinful works which we do but of the sufferings and blood of the

---

[7]John 1:16.
[8]Cf. Matt. 3:7.

innocent Lamb of God who takes away the sin of the world.[9]

This is the repentance which John preaches, which Christs 39 subsequently preaches in the Gospel, and which we also preach. With this repentance we overthrow the pope and everything that is built on our good works, for all of this is constructed on an unreal and rotten foundation which is called good works or the law, although no good work but only wicked works are there and although no one keeps the law (as Christ says in John 7:19) but all transgress it. Accordingly the entire building, even when it is most holy and beautiful, is nothing but deceitful falsehood and hypocrisy.

In the case of a Christian such repentance continues until 40 death, for all through life it contends with the sins that remain in the flesh. As St. Paul testifies in Rom. 7:23, he wars with the law in his members, and he does this not with his own powers but with the gift of the Holy Spirit which follows the forgiveness of sins. This gift daily cleanses and expels the sins that remain and enables man to become truly pure and holy.

This is something about which the pope, the theologians, the 41 jurists, and all men understand nothing. It is a teaching from heaven, revealed in the Gospel, and yet it is called a heresy by godless saints.

Some fanatics may appear (and perhaps they are already 42 present, such as I saw with my own eyes at the time of the uprising)[1] who hold that once they have received the Spirit or the forgiveness of sins, or once they have become believers, they will persevere in faith even if they sin afterwards, and such sin will not harm them. They cry out, "Do what you will, it matters not as long as you believe, for faith blots out all sins," etc. They add that if anyone sins after he has received faith and the Spirit, he never really had the Spirit and faith. I have encountered many foolish people like this and I fear that such a devil still dwells in some of them.

It is therefore necessary to know and to teach that when 43

---

[9]Cf. John 1:29.
[1]The Peasants' War in 1525.

holy people, aside from the fact that they still possess and feel original sin and daily repent and strive against it, fall into open sin (as David fell into adultery, murder, and blasphemy),[2] faith and the Spirit have departed from them. This is so because the Holy 44 Spirit does not permit sin to rule and gain the upper hand in such a way that sin is committed, but the Holy Spirit represses and restrains it so that it does not do what it wishes. If sin does what it wishes, the Holy Spirit and faith are not present, for St. John 45 says, "No one born of God commits sin; he cannot sin."[3] Yet it is also true, as the same St. John writes, "If we say we have no sin, we deceive ourselves, and the truth is not in us."[4]

IV. *The Gospel*

We shall now return to the Gospel, which offers counsel and help against sin in more than one way, for God is surpassingly rich in his grace: First, through the spoken word, by which the forgiveness of sin (the peculiar function of the Gospel) is preached to the whole world; second,[5] through Baptism; third, through the holy Sacrament of the Altar; fourth, through the power of keys; and finally, through the mutual conversation and consolation of brethren. Matt. 18:20, "Where two or three are gathered," etc.[6]

V. *Baptism*

Baptism is nothing else than the Word of God in water, com- 1 manded by the institution of Christ; or as Paul says, "the washing of water with the word";[7] or, again, as Augustine puts it, "The Word is

---

[2]Cf. II Sam. 11.
[3]I John 3:9; 5:18.
[4]I John 1:8.
[5]The order of succeeding topics is here indicated.
[6]Luther wrote: "Where two are gathered."
[7]Eph. 5:26.

added to the element and it becomes a sacrament."[8] Therefore 2
we do not agree with Thomas[9] and the Dominicans who forget the
Word (God's institution) and say that God has joined to the water a
spiritual power which, through the water, washes away sin. Nor 3
do we agree with Scotus[1] and the Franciscans who teach that Baptism washes away sin through the assistance of the divine will, as if
the washing takes place only through God's will and not at all
through the Word and the water.

As for infant Baptism, we hold that children should be bap- 4
tized, for they, too, are included in the promise of redemption which
Christ made,[2] and the church should administer Baptism to them.

VI. *The Sacrament of the Altar*

We hold that the bread and the wine in the Supper are the 1
true body and blood of Christ and that these are given and received
not only by godly but also by wicked Christians.

We also hold that it is not to be administered in one form 2
only.[3] We need not resort to the specious learning of the sophists[4]
and the Council of Constance[5] that as much is included under one
form as under both. Even if it were true that as much is included 3
under one form as under both, yet administration in one form is not
the whole order and institution as it was established and commanded by Christ. Especially do we condemn and curse in God's 4
name those who not only omit both forms but even go so far as auto-
cratically to prohibit, condemn, and slander the use of both as

---

[8]*Tractate 80,* on John 3.
[9]Cf. Thomas Aquinas, *Summa theologica,* III, q.62, a.4.
[1]Cf. Duns Scotus, *Sentences,* IV, dist. 1, q.2 ff.
[2]Cf. Matt. 19:14.
[3]That is, the bread alone, without the wine.
[4]Scholastic theologians.
[5]Decree of June 15, 1415, which defined the doctrine of sacramental
concomitance, namely, that the whole body and the whole blood of Christ
are under the form of the bread alone.

heresy and thus set themselves against and over Christ, our Lord and God, etc.

As for transubstantiation, we have no regard for the subtle 5 sophistry of those who teach that bread and wine surrender or lose their natural substance and retain only the appearance and shape of bread without any longer being real bread, for that bread is and remains there agrees better with the Scriptures, as St. Paul himself states, "The bread which we break" (I Cor. 10:16), and again, "Let a man so eat of the bread" (I Cor. 11:28).

VII. *The Keys*

The keys are a function and power given to the church by 1 Christ[6] to bind and loose sins, not only the gross and manifest sins but also those which are subtle and secret and which God alone perceives. So it is written, "Who can discern his errors?" (Ps. 19:12). And Paul himself complains (Rom. 7:23) that in his flesh he was a captive to "the law of sin." It is not in our power but in God's 2 alone to judge which, how great, and how many our sins are. As it is written, "Enter not into judgment with thy servant, for no man living is righteous before thee" (Ps. 143:2), and Paul also says in I Cor. 3 4:4, "I am not aware of anything against myself, but I am not thereby acquitted."

VIII. *Confession*

Since absolution or the power of the keys, which was insti- 1 tuted by Christ in the Gospel, is a consolation and help against sin and a bad conscience, confession and absolution should by no means be allowed to fall into disuse in the church, especially for the sake of timid consciences and for the sake of untrained young people who need to be examined and instructed in Christian doctrine.

---

[6]Cf. Matt. 16:19; 18:18.

However, the enumeration of sins should be left free to every- 2
body to do or not as he will. As long as we are in the flesh we shall
not be untruthful if we say, "I am a poor man, full of sin. I see in my
members another law," etc. (Rom. 7:23). Although private absolution is derived from the office of the keys, it should not be neglected;
on the contrary, it should be highly esteemed and valued, like all
other functions of the Christian church.

In these matters, which concern the external, spoken Word, 3
we must hold firmly to the conviction that God gives no one his
Spirit or grace except through or with the external Word which
comes before. Thus we shall be protected from the enthusiasts—that
is, from the spiritualists who boast that they possess the Spirit without and before the Word and who therefore judge, interpret, and
twist the Scriptures or spoken Word according to their pleasure.
Münzer[7] did this, and many still do it in our day who wish to distinguish sharply between the letter and the spirit without knowing 4
what they say or teach. The papacy, too, is nothing but enthusiasm,
for the pope boasts that "all laws are in the shrine of his heart,"[8] and
he claims that whatever he decides and commands in his churches
is spirit and law, even when it is above and contrary to the 5
Scriptures or spoken Word. All this is the old devil and the old serpent who made enthusiasts of Adam and Eve. He led them from the
external Word of God to spiritualizing and to their own imagina-
tions, and he did this through other external words. Even so, the
enthusiasts of our day condemn the external Word, yet they do 6
not remain silent but fill the world with their chattering and scrib-
bling, as if the Spirit could not come through the Scriptures or the
spoken word of the apostles but must come through their own
writings and words. Why do they not stop preaching and writing
until the Spirit himself comes to the people without and before their
writings since they boast that the Spirit came upon them without the

---

[7]Thomas Münzer.
[8]*Corpus juris canonici,* Book VI, I, 2, c.1.

testimony of the Scriptures?[9] There is no time to dispute further about these matters. After all, we have treated them sufficiently elsewhere.[1]

Even those who have come to faith before they were baptized 7 and those who came to faith in Baptism came to their faith through the external Word which preceded. Adults who have attained the age of reason must first have heard, "He who believes and is baptized will be saved" (Mark 16:16), even if they did not at once believe and did not receive the Spirit and Baptism until ten years 8 later. Cornelius (Acts 10:1ff.) had long since heard from the Jews about the coming Messiah through whom he was justified before God, and his prayers and alms were acceptable to God in this faith (Luke calls him "devout" and "God-fearing"),[2] but he could not have believed and been justified if the Word and his hearing of it had not preceded. However, St. Peter had to reveal to him that the Messiah, in whose coming he had previously believed, had already come, and his faith concerning the coming Messiah did not hold him captive with the hardened, unbelieving Jews, but he knew that he now had to be saved by the present Messiah and not deny or persecute him as the Jews did.

In short, enthusiasm clings to Adam and his descendants from 9 the beginning to the end of the world. It is a poison implanted and inoculated in man by the old dragon, and it is the source, strength, and power of all heresy, including that of the papacy and Mohammedanism. Accordingly, we should and must constantly main- 10 tain that God will not deal with us except through his external Word and sacrament. Whatever is attributed to the Spirit apart from such Word and sacrament is of the devil. For even to Moses God 11 wished to appear first through the burning bush and the spoken word,[3] and no prophet, whether Elijah or Elisha, received the Spirit

---

[9]Literally: without the preaching of the Scriptures.
[1]E.g., Luther's "Against the Heavenly Prophets" (1525).
[2]Cf. Acts 10:2, 22.
[3]Cf. Ex. 3:2, 4.

without the Ten Commandments. John the Baptist was not con- 12
ceived without the preceding word of Gabriel, nor did he leap 13
in his mother's womb until Mary spoke.[4] St. Peter says that when the
prophets spoke, they did not prophesy by the impulse of man but
were moved by the Holy Spirit, yet as holy men of God.[5] But without the external Word they were not holy, and the Holy Spirit would
not have moved them to speak while they were still unholy. They
were holy, St. Peter says, because the Holy Spirit spoke through
them.

IX. Excommunication

We consider the greater excommunication,[6] as the pope calls it,
to be merely a civil penalty which does not concern us ministers of
the church. However, the lesser (that is, the truly Christian) excommunication excludes those who are manifest and impenitent sinners
from the sacrament and other fellowship of the church until they
mend their ways and avoid sin. Preachers should not mingle civil
punishment with this spiritual penalty or excommunication.

X. Ordination and Vocation

If the bishops were true bishops and were concerned about 1
the church and the Gospel, they might be permitted (for the sake of
love and unity, but not of necessity) to ordain and confirm us and
our preachers,[7] provided this could be done without pretense, hum-
bug, and unchristian ostentation. However, they neither are nor
wish to be true bishops. They are temporal lords and princes 2

---

[4]Cf. Luke 1:13-42.

[5]II Peter 1:21.

[6]The Roman Church distinguished between a lesser ban, which excluded only from the sacraments, and a greater ban, which imposed civil
disabilities in addition to spiritual penalties.

[7]See also above, Apology, Art. XIV.

who are unwilling to preach or teach or baptize or administer Communion or discharge any office or work in the church. More than that, they expel, persecute, and condemn those who have been called to do these things. Yet the church must not be deprived of ministers on their account.

Accordingly, as we are taught by the examples of the ancient 3 churches and Fathers, we shall and ought ourselves ordain suitable persons to this office. The papists have no right to forbid or prevent us, not even according to their own laws, for their laws state that those who are ordained by heretics shall also be regarded as ordained and remain so.[8] St. Jerome, too, wrote concerning the church in Alexandria that it was originally governed without bishops by priests and preachers in common.[9]

XI. The Marriage of Priests

The papists had neither authority nor right to prohibit mar- 1 riage and burden the divine estate of priests with perpetual celibacy. On the contrary, they acted like antichristian, tyrannical, and wicked scoundrels, and thereby they gave occasion for all sorts of horrible, abominable, and countless sins, in which they are still involved. 2 As little as the power has been given to us or to them to make a woman out of a man or a man out of a woman or abolish distinctions of sex altogether, so little have they had the power to separate such creatures of God or forbid them to live together honestly in mar- 3 riage. We are therefore unwilling to consent to their abominable celibacy, nor shall we suffer it. On the contrary, we desire marriage to be free, as God ordained and instituted it, and we shall not disrupt or hinder God's work, for St. Paul says that to do so is a doctrine of demons.[1]

---

[8]Gratian, *Decretum*, Pt. I, dist. 68, chap. 1; Pt. III, dist. 4, chap. 107.
[9]See above. Pt. II, Art. IV, 9.
[1]Cf. I Tim. 4:1-3.

XII. The Church

We do not concede to the papists that they are the church,   1
for they are not. Nor shall we pay any attention to what they   2
command or forbid in the name of the church, for, thank God, a
seven-year-old child[2] knows what the church is, namely, holy believers and sheep who hear the voice of their Shepherd.[3] So children   3
pray, "I believe in one holy Christian church." Its holiness does not
consist of surplices, tonsures, albs, or other ceremonies of theirs
which they have invented over and above the Holy Scriptures, but
it consists of the Word of God and true faith.

XIII. How Man Is Justified Before God, and His Good Works

I do not know how I can change what I have heretofore con-   1
stantly taught on this subject, namely, that by faith (as St. Peter
says)[4] we get a new and clean heart and that God will and does
account us altogether righteous and holy for the sake of Christ, our
mediator. Although the sin in our flesh has not been completely removed or eradicated, he will not count or consider it.

Good works follow such faith, renewal, and forgiveness.   2
Whatever is still sinful or imperfect in these works will not be
reckoned as sin or defect for the sake of the same Christ. The whole
man, in respect both of his person and of his works, shall be accounted and shall be righteous and holy through the pure grace and
mercy which have been poured out upon us so abundantly in   3
Christ. Accordingly we cannot boast of the great merit in our works
if they are considered apart from God's grace and mercy, but, as it is
written, "Let him who boasts, boast of the Lord" (I Cor. 1:31). That
is to say, all is well if we boast that we have a gracious God. To this

---

2Seven years was the minimum age of discretion.
3John 10:3.
4Act 15:9.

we must add that if good works do not follow, our faith is false and not true.

XIV. *Monastic Vows*

Since monastic vows are in direct conflict with the first chief   1
article, they must be absolutely set aside. It is of these that Christ says in Matt. 24:5, "I am the Christ," etc. Whoever takes the vows of monastic life believes that he is entering upon a mode of life that is better than that of the ordinary Christian and proposes by means of his work to help not only himself but also others to get to heaven. This is to deny Christ, etc. And on the authority of their St. Thomas, such people boast that a monastic vow is equal to Baptism.[5] This is blasphemy.

XV. *Human Traditions*

The assertion of the papists that human traditions effect for-   1
giveness of sins or merit salvation is unchristian and to be condemned. As Christ says, "In vain do they worship me, teaching as doctrines the precepts of men" (Matt. 15:9), and it is written in Titus 1:14, "They are men who reject the truth." When the   2
papists say this it is a mortal sin to break such precepts of men, this, too, is false.

These are the articles on which I must stand and on which I   3
will stand, God willing, until my death. I do not know how I can change or concede anything in them. If anybody wishes to make some concessions, let him do so at the peril of his own conscience.

Finally, there remains the pope's bag of magic tricks which   4
contains silly and childish articles, such as the consecration of churches, the baptism of bells, the baptism of altar stones, the invitation to such ceremonies of sponsors who might make gifts, etc.

---

[5]Thomas Aquinas, *Summa theologica*, Pt. II, 2, q.189, a.3 ad 3.

Such baptizing is a ridicule and mockery of holy Baptism which should not be tolerated.[6] In addition, there are blessings of can- 5 dles, palms, spices, oats, cakes, etc.[7] These cannot be called blessings, and they are not, but are mere mockery and fraud. Such frauds, which are without number, we commend for adoration to their god and to themselves until they tire of them. We do not wish to have anything to do with them.

Dr. MARTIN LUTHER subscribed

Dr. JUSTUS JONAS, rector, subscribed with his own hand

Dr. JOHN BUGENHAGEN, of Pomerania, subscribed

Dr. CASPAR CREUTZIGER subscribed

NICHOLAS AMSDORF, of Madeburg, subscribed

GEORGE SPALATIN, of Altenburg, subscribed

I, PHILIP MELANCHTHON, regard the above articles as right and Christian. However, concerning the pope I hold that, if he would allow the Gospel, we, too, may concede to him that superiority over the bishops which he possesses by human right, making this concession for the sake of peace and general unity among the Christians who are now under him and who may be in the future.

JOHN AGRICOLA, of Eisleben, subscribed

GABRIEL DIDYMUS subscribed

I, Dr. URBAN RHEGIUS, superintendent of the churches in the Duchy of Lüneburg, subscribe in my own name and in the name of my brethren and of the church of Hanover

I, STEPHEN AGRICOLA, minister in Hof, subscribe

Also I, JOHN DRACH, professor and minister in Marburg, subscribe

---

[6]Bells were commonly named for saints, and when they were "blessed" with an order which closely resembled the order for the baptism of children, the "sponsors" who were present were obligated to pay fees.

[7]Priests "blessed" candles on Candlemas; palm branches on Palm Sunday; herbs, flowers, ears of corn, honey, and vines on the Feast of Assumption; oats on St. Stephen's Day; unleavened Easter cakes on Easter Eve.

I, CONRAD FIGENBOTZ, for the glory of God subscribe that I have thus believed and am still preaching and firmly believing as above.

I, ANDREW OSIANDER, minister in Nuremberg, subscribe

I, MASTER VEIT DIETRICH, minister in Nuremberg, subscribe

I, ERHARD SCHNEPF, preacher in Stuttgart, subscribe

CONRAD OETTINGER, preacher of Duke Ulric of Pforzheim

SIMON SCHNEEWEISS, pastor of the church in Crailsheim

I, JOHN SCHLAGENHAUFEN, pastor of the church in Köthen, subscribe

MASTER GEORGE HELT, of Forchheim

Master ADAM OF FULDA, preacher in Hesse

Master ANTHONY CORVINUS

I, Dr. John Bugenhagen of Pomerania, again subscribe in the name of Master JOHN BRENZ, who on his departure from Smalcald directed me orally and by a letter which I have shown to these brethren who have subscribed[8]

I, DIONYSIUS MELANDER, subscribe the Confession, the Apology, and the Concord[9] in the matter of the Eucharist

PAUL RHODE, superintendent of Stettin

GERARD OEMCKEN, superintendent of the church in Minden.

I, BRIXIUS NORTHANUS, minister of the church of Christ which is in Soest, subscribe the articles of the reverend father, Martin Luther, confess that I have hitherto thus believed and taught, and by the Spirit of Christ I will thus continue to believe and teach

MICHAEL CAELIUS, preacher in Mansfeld, subscribed

Master PETER GELTNER, preacher in Frankfurt, subscribed

WENDAL FABER, pastor of Seeburg in Mansfeld

I, JOHN AEPINUS, subscribe

Likewise I, JOHN AMSTERDAM, of Bremen

I, FREDERICK MYCONIUS, pastor of the church in Gotha, Thuringia, subscribe in my own name and in that of JUSTUS MENIUS, of Eisenach

---

[8]The letter was dated Feb. 23, 1537.

[9]The Wittenberg Concord of 1536, an attempt to bring about an understanding with the Swiss on the Lord's Supper.

I, Dr. John Lang, preacher of the church in Erfurt, in my own name and in the names of my other co-workers in the Gospel, namely:

the Rev. Licentiate Louis Platz, of Melsungen

the Rev. Master Sigismund Kirchner

the Rev. Wolfgang Kiswetter

the Rev. Melchior Weitmann

the Rev. John Thall

the Rev. John Kilian

the Rev. Nicholas Faber

the Rev. Andrew Menser (I subscribe with my hand)

And, I, Egidius Melcher, have subscribed with my hand

25.

ON THE COUNCILS AND THE CHURCH

* * *

Part III

Just as they scream about the fathers and the councils, without knowing what fathers and councils are, only to drown out our voices with mere letters, so they also scream about the church. But as for saying what, who, and where the church is, they do not render either the church or God even the service of asking the question or thinking about it. They like very much to be regarded as the church, as pope, cardinals, bishops, and yet to be allowed, under this glorious name, to be nothing but pupils of the devil, desiring nothing more than to practice sheer knavery and villainy.

Well then, setting aside various writings and analyses of the word "church," we shall this time confine ourselves simply to the Children's Creed, which says, "I believe in one holy Christian church, the communion of saints." Here the creed clearly indicates what the church is, namely, a communion of saints, that is, a crowd[378] or assembly of people who are Christians and holy, which is called a Christian holy assembly, or church. Yet this word "church" [379] is not German and does not convey the sense or meaning that should be taken from this article.

In Acts 19 [:39] the town clerk uses the word *ecclesia* for the congregation or the people who had gathered at the market place, saying, "It shall be settled in the regular assembly." Further, "When he said this, he dismissed the assembly" [vs. 41]. In these and other passages the *ecclesia* or church is nothing but an assembly of people, though they probably were heathens and not Christians. It is the same term used by town councilmen for their assembly which they summon to the city hall. Now there are many peoples in the world; the Christians, however, are a people with a special call and are therefore called not just *ecclesia*, "church," or "people," but *sancta catholica Christiana*, that is, "a Christian holy people" who believe in Christ. That is why they are called a Christian people and have the Holy Spirit, who sanctifies them daily, not only through the forgiveness of sin acquired for them by Christ (as the Antinomians foolishly believe), but also through the abolition,

---

378 *Hauffe.*
379 *Kirche.*

the purging, and the mortification of sins, on the basis of which they are called a holy people. Thus the "holy Christian church" is synonymous with a Christian and holy people or, as one is also wont to express it, with "holy Christendom," or "whole Christendom." The Old Testament uses the term "God's people."

If the words, "I believe that there is a holy Christian people," had been used in the Children's Creed, all the misery connected with this meaningless and obscure word ("church") might easily have been avoided. For the words "Christian holy people" would have brought with them, clearly and powerfully, the proper understanding and judgment of what is, and what is not, church. Whoever would have heard the words "Christian holy people" could have promptly concluded that the pope is no people, much less a holy Christian people. So too the bishops, priests, and monks are not holy, Christian people, for they do not believe in Christ, nor do they lead a holy life, but are rather the wicked and shameful people of the devil. He who does not truly believe in Christ is not Christian or a Christian. He who does not have the Holy Spirit against sin is not holy. Consequently, they cannot be "a Christian holy people," that is, *sancta et catholica ecclesia.*

But since we use this meaningless word "church" in the Children's Creed, the common man thinks of the stone house called a church, as painted by the artists; or, at best, they paint the apostles, disciples, and the mother of God, as on Pentecost, with the Holy Spirit hovering over them. This is still bearable; but they are the holy Christian people of a specific time, in this case, the beginning. *Ecclesia,* however, should mean the holy Christian people, not only of the days of the apostles, who are long since dead, but to the end of the world, so that there is always a holy Christian people on earth, in whom Christ lives, works, and rules, *per redemptionem,* "through grace and the remission of sin," and the Holy Spirit, *per vivificationem et sanctificationem,* "through daily purging of sin and renewal of life," so that we do not remain in sin but are enabled and obliged to lead a new life, abounding in all kinds of good works, as the Ten Commandments or the two tables of Moses' law command, and not in old, evil works. That is St. Paul's teaching. But the pope, with his followers, has applied both the name and the image of the church to himself and to his vile, accursed mob, under the meaningless word *ecclesia*, "church," etc.

Nevertheless, they give themselves the right name when they call themselves *ecclesia* (that is, if we interpret this term to agree with their way of life), either *Romana* or *sancta*, but do not add (as, indeed, they cannot) *catholica*. For *ecclesia* means "a people"; that they are, just as the Turks too, are *ecclesia*, "a people." *Ecclesia Romana* means "a Roman people"; that they are too, and indeed much more Roman than the heathen of ancient times were. *Ecclesia Romana sancta* means "a holy Roman people"; that they are too, for they have invented a holiness far greater than the holiness of Christians, or than the holy Christian people possess. Their holiness is a Roman holiness, *Romanae ecclesiae*, a holiness "of the Roman people," and they are now even called *sanctissimi*, *sacrosancti*, "the most holy," as Virgil speaks of a "holy thirst for gold,"[380] and Plautus of "the most holy one of all";[381] for they cannot stand Christian holiness. Therefore they are not entitled to the name "Christian church" or "Christian people," if for no other reason than that "Christian church" is a name and "Christian holiness" an entity common to all churches and all Christians in the world; therefore it is called "catholic." But they have little, if any, regard for this common name and holiness; instead, they invented a special, higher, different, better holiness than that of others. This is to be known as *sanctitas Romana et ecclesiae Romanae sanctitas*, that is, "Roman holiness and the holiness of the Roman people."

For Christian holiness, or the holiness common to Christendom, is found where the Holy Spirit gives people faith in Christ and thus sanctifies them, Acts 15 [:9], that is, he renews heart, soul, body, work, and conduct, inscribing the commandments of God not on tables of stone, but in hearts of flesh, II Corinthians 3 [:3]. Or, if I may speak plainly, he imparts true knowledge of God, accord-

---

[380] *Sacra fames, sacra hostia.* Virgil (70-19 B.C.), a Roman poet, in *Aeneid*, III, 57. See H. Rushton Fairclough (trans.), *Virgil: Eclogues, Georgics, Aeneid I-III* ("The Loeb Classical Library" [2nd ed., rev.; Cambridge: Harvard University Press, 1956]), p. 352. Luther, quoting from memory, leaves out the term "gold" (*auri*).

[381] *Omnium sacerrumus.* Plautus (d. 184 B.C.), another Roman poet, in *Mostellaria*, IV, 2, 67. Henry T. Riley (trans.), *The Comedies of Plautus* (2 vols.; London, 1884), II, 500.

ing to the first table, so that those whom he enlightens with true faith can resist all heresies, overcome all false ideas and errors, and thus remain pure in faith in opposition to the devil. He also bestows strength, and comforts timid, despondent, weak consciences against the accusation and turmoil of sin, so that the souls do not succumb or despair, and also do not become terrified of torment, pain, death, and the wrath and judgment of God, but rather, comforted and strengthened in hope, they cheerfully, boldly, and joyfully overcome the devil. He also imparts true fear and love of God, so that we do not despise God and become irritated and angry with his wondrous judgments, but love, praise, thank, and honor him for all that occurs, good or evil. That is called new holy life in the soul, in accordance with the first table of Moses. It is also called *tres virtutes theologicas,* "the three principal virtues of Christians,"[882] namely, faith, hope, and love; and the Holy Spirit, who imparts, does, and effects this (gained for us by Christ) is therefore called "sanctifier" or "life-giver."[883] For the old Adam is dead and cannot do it, and in addition has to learn from the law that he is unable to do it and that he is dead; he would not know this of himself.

In accordance with the second table, He also sanctifies the Christians in the body and induces them willingly to obey parents and rulers, to conduct themselves peacefully and humbly, to be not wrathful, vindictive, or malicious, but patient, friendly, obliging, brotherly, and loving, not unchaste, not adulterous or lewd, but chaste and pure with wife, child, and servants, or without wife and child. And on and on: they do not steal, are not usurious, avaricious, do not defraud, etc., but work honorably, support themselves honestly, lend willingly, and give and help wherever they can. Thus they do not lie, deceive, and backbite, but are kind, truthful, faithful, and trustworthy, and do whatever else the commandments of God prescribe. That is the work of the Holy Spirit, who sanctifies and also awakens the body to such a new life until it is perfected in the life beyond. That is what is called "Christian

---

[882] They became principal topics in scholastic theology after Augustine. Cf. I Cor. 13:13.

[883] *Sanctificator* or *vivificator.*

holiness." And there must always be such people on earth, even though it may be but two or three, or only children. Unfortunately, only a few of them are old folks. And those who are not, should not count themselves as Christians; nor should they be comforted with much babbling about the forgiveness of sins and the grace of Christ, as though they were Christians—like the Antinomians do.

For they, having rejected and being unable to understand the Ten Commandments, preach much about the grace of Christ, yet they strengthen and comfort only those who remain in their sins, telling them not to fear and be terrified by sins, since they are all removed by Christ. They see and yet they let the people go on in their public sins, without any renewal or reformation of their lives. Thus it becomes quite evident that they truly fail to understand the faith and Christ, and thereby abrogate both when they preach about it. How can he speak lightly about the works of the Holy Spirit in the first table—about comfort, grace, forgiveness of sins— who does not heed or practice the works of the Holy Spirit in the second table, which he can understand and experience, while he has never attempted or experienced those of the first table? Therefore it is certain that they neither have nor understand Christ or the Holy Spirit, and their talk is nothing but froth on the tongue, and they are as already said, true Nestoriuses and Eutycheses, who confess or teach Christ in the premise, in the substance, and yet deny him in the conclusion or *idiomata*; that is, they teach Christ and yet destroy him through their teaching.

All this then has been said about Christian holiness, which the pope does not want. He has to have one that is much holier, namely, that found in the prescription of chasubles, tonsures, cowls, garb, food, festivals, days, monkery, nunning, masses, saint-worship, and countless other items of an external, bodily, transitory nature. Whether one lives under it without faith, fear of God, hope, love, and whatever the Holy Spirit, according to the first table, effects, or in misbelief, uncertainty of heart, doubts, contempt of God, impatience with God, and false trust in works (that is, idolatry), not in the grace of Christ and his merit, but in the atonement by works, even selling the surplus ones to others and taking in exchange all the goods and wealth of the world as well earned—all that is of no consequence because a man may be holier than Christian holiness itself.

Thus, in the second table it matters not that they teach disobedience toward parents and rulers, that they even murder, make war, set people against each other, envy, hate, avenge, are unchaste, lie, steal, are usurious, defraud, and indulge in every villainy to the utmost. Just throw a surplice over your head and you are holy in accordance with the Roman church's holiness, and you can indeed be saved without the Christian holiness. But we will pay no attention to these filthy people, for any effort expended on them will be futile. "God's wrath has come upon them at last," as St. Paul says [I Thess. 2:16]. Instead, we shall discuss the church among ourselves.

Well then, the Children's Creed teaches us (as was said) that a Christian holy people is to be and to remain on earth until the end of the world. This is an article of faith that cannot be terminated until that which it believes comes, as Christ promises, "I am with you always, to the close of the age" [Matt. 28:20]. But how will or how can a poor confused person tell where such Christian holy people are to be found in this world? Indeed, they are supposed to be in this life and on earth, for they of course believe that a heavenly nature and an eternal life are to come, but as yet they do not possess them. Therefore they must still be in this life and remain in this life and in this world until the end of the world. For they profess, "I believe in another life"; thereby they confess that they have not yet arrived in the other life, but believe in it, hope for it, and love it as their true fatherland and life, while they must yet remain and tarry here in exile—as we sing in the hymn about the Holy Spirit, "As homeward we journey from this exile. Lord, have mercy."[384] We shall now speak of this.

First, the holy Christian people are recognized by their possession of the holy word of God. To be sure, not all have it in equal measure, as St. Paul says [I Cor. 3:12-14]. Some possess the word in its complete purity, others do not. Those who have the pure word are called those who "build on the foundation with

---

[384] The fourth line of a pre-Reformation hymn adapted by Luther in 1524, "Now Let Us Pray to the Holy Ghost." LW 53, 263-264.

gold, silver, and precious stones"; those who do not have it in its purity are the ones who "build on the foundation with wood, hay, and straw," and yet will be saved through fire. More than enough was said about this above. This is the principal item, and the holiest of holy possessions,[385] by reason of which the Christian people are called holy; for God's word is holy and sanctifies everything it touches; it is indeed the very holiness of God, Romans 1 [:16], "It is the power of God for salvation to every one who has faith," and I Timothy 4 [:5], "Everything is consecrated by the word of God and prayer." For the Holy Spirit himself administers it and anoints or sanctifies the Christian church with it rather than with the pope's chrism, with which he anoints or consecrates fingers, garb, cloaks, chalices, and stones. These objects will never teach one to love God, to believe, to praise, to be pious. They may adorn the bag of maggots,[386] but afterward they fall apart and decay with the chrism and whatever holiness it contains, and with the bag of maggots itself.

Yet this holy possession is the true holy possession, the true ointment that anoints unto life eternal, even though you cannot have a papal crown or a bishop's hat, but must die bare and naked, just like children (in fact, all of us), who are baptized naked and without any adornment. But we are speaking of the external word, preached orally by men like you and me, for this is what Christ left behind as an external sign, by which his church, or his Christian people in the world, should be recognized. We also speak of this external word as it is sincerely believed and openly professed before the world, as Christ says, "Every one who acknowledges me before men, I also will acknowledge before my Father and his angels" [Matt. 10:32]. There are many who know it in their hearts, but will not profess it openly. Many possess it, but do not believe in it or act by it, for the number of those who believe in and act by it is small—as the parable of the seed in Matthew

---

[385] *Heiligthum* or *Heilthum.* These words recur continually in the following section. The term "holy possession" (used in *PE* 5, 270) conveys both the meaning of "sanctuary" and "relic." Luther plays constantly on the idea of wonder-working objects of reverence when he speaks of the marks of the church.

[386] *Madensack,* i.e., the body that goes to decay.

13 [:4-8] says that three sections of the field receive and contain the seed, but only the fourth section, the fine and good soil, bears fruit with patience.

Now, wherever you hear or see this word preached, believed, professed, and lived, do not doubt that the true *ecclesia sancta catholica,* "a Christian holy people" must be there, even though their number is very small. For God's word "shall not return empty," Isaiah 55 [:11], but must have at least a fourth or a fraction of the field. And even if there were no other sign than this alone, it would still suffice to prove that a Christian, holy people must exist there, for God's word cannot be without God's people, and conversely, God's people cannot be without God's word. Otherwise, who would preach or hear it preached, if there were no people of God? And what could or would God's people believe, if there were no word of God?

This is the thing that performs all miracles, effects, sustains, carries out, and does everything, exorcises all devils, like pilgrimage-devils, indulgence-devils, bull-devils, brotherhood-devils, saint-devils, mass-devils, purgatory-devils, monastery-devils, priest-devils, mob-devils, insurrection-devils, heresy-devils, all pope-devils, also Antinomian-devils, but not without raving and rampaging, as is seen in the poor men mentioned in Mark 1 [:23-26] and 9 [:17-29]. No, he must depart with raving and rampaging as is evidenced by Emser,[387] Eck,[388] Snot-nose,[389] Schmid,[390] Wetzel,[391]

---

[387] Jerome Emser (1478-1527), a humanist who became an adviser to Duke George of Saxony, Catholic ruler of Saxony and an enemy of Luther. Cf. Luther's polemic tract *To the Leipzig Goat* (1521). *PE* 3, 275-286.

[388] John Eck (1486-1543), known for his debate with Luther at Leipzig in 1518. Cf. *LW* 31, 309-325.

[389] *Rotzleffel,* a German term for "impudent young rascal" and Luther's name for John Cochlaeus (1479-1552), a Catholic theologian who was a fanatic opponent of the Reformation and the author of *Memoirs on the Actions and Writings of Martin Luther* (*Commentaria de Actis et Scriptis M. Lutheri*) (1549), a polemic biography of Luther. See Adolf Herte, *Die Lutherkommentare des Johannes Cochlaeus* ("Religionsgeschichtliche Studien und Texte," Vol. XXXIII [Münster, 1935]).

[390] John Faber (1478-1541), the son of a smith (*faber* in Latin) and bishop in Vienna. He had been writing polemic tracts against Luther since 1521.

[391] Used as a name for dogs and as a pun on George Wetzel (1501-1573), who was originally a follower of Luther, but since 1533 had been an opponent of the Reformation and a protege of Duke George of Saxony.

Bumpkin, Boor, Churl, Brute, Sow, Ass,[392] and the rest of his screamers and scribes. They all are the devil's mouths and members, through whom he raves and rampages. But it does them no good. He must take his leave; he is unable to endure the power of the word. They themselves confess that it is God's word and Holy Scripture, claiming, however, that one fares better with the fathers and the councils. Let them go their way. It is enough for us to know how this chief holy possession purges, sustains, nourishes, strengthens, and protects the church, as St. Augustine also says, "The church is begotten, cared for, nourished, and strengthened by the word of God."[393] But those who persecute and condemn it identify themselves by their own fruits.

Second, God's people or the Christian holy people are recognized by the holy sacrament of baptism, wherever it is taught, believed, and administered correctly according to Christ's ordinance. That too is a public sign and a precious, holy possession by which God's people are sanctified. It is the holy bath of regeneration through the Holy Spirit [Titus 3:5], in which we bathe and with which we are washed of sin and death by the Holy Spirit, as in the innocent holy blood of the Lamb of God. Wherever you see this sign you may know that the church, or the holy Christian people, must surely be present, even if the pope does not baptize you or even if you know nothing of his holiness and power—just as the little children know nothing of it, although when they are grown, they are, sad to say, estranged from their baptism, as St. Peter laments in II Peter 2 [:18], "They entice with licentious passions of the flesh men who have barely escaped from those who live in error," etc. Indeed, you should not even pay attention to who baptizes, for baptism does not belong to the baptizer, nor is it given to him, but it belongs to the baptized. It was ordained for him by God, and given to him by God, just as the word of God is not the preacher's (except in so far as he too hears and believes it) but belongs to the disciple who hears and believes it; to him is it given.

---

[392] Probably names suggested by the sound of "Wetzel," which lose their force in translation.

[393] *Ecclesia verbo dei generatur, alitur nutritur, roboratur.* The saying could not be located in Augustine's writings.

Third, God's people, or Christian holy people, are recognized by the holy sacrament of the altar, wherever it is rightly administered, believed, and received, according to Christ's institution. This too is a public sign and a precious, holy possession left behind by Christ by which his people are sanctified so that they also exercise themselves in faith and openly confess that they are Christian, just as they do with the word and with baptism. And here too you need not be disturbed if the pope does not say mass for you, does not consecrate, anoint, or vest you with a chasuble. Indeed, you may, like a patient in bed, receive this sacrament without wearing any garb, except that outward decency obliges you to be properly covered. Moreover, you need not ask whether you have a tonsure or are anointed. In addition, the question of whether you are male or female, young or old, need not be argued—just as little as it matters in baptism and the preached word. It is enough that you are consecrated and anointed with the sublime and holy chrism of God, with the word of God, with baptism, and also this sacrament; then you are anointed highly and gloriously enough and sufficiently vested with priestly garments.

Moreover, don't be led astray by the question of whether the man who administers the sacrament is holy, or whether or not he has two wives.[394] The sacrament belongs to him who receives it, not to him who administers it, unless he also receives it. In that case he is one of those who receives it, and thus it is also given to him. Wherever you see this sacrament properly administered, there you may be assured of the presence of God's people. For, as was said above of the word, wherever God's word is, there the church must be; likewise, wherever baptism and the sacrament are, God's people must be, and vice versa. No others have, give, practice, use, and confess these holy possessions save God's people alone, even though some false and unbelieving Christians are secretly among them. They, however, do not profane the people of God because they are not known; the church, or God's people, does not tolerate known sinners in its midst, but reproves them and also makes them holy. Or, if they refuse, it casts them out from

---

[394]See pp. 551-561.

the sanctuary by means of the ban and regards them as heathen, Matthew 18 [:17].

Fourth, God's people or holy Christians are recognized by the office of the keys exercised publicly.[395] That is, as Christ decrees in Matthew 18 [:15-20], if a Christian sins, he should be reproved; and if he does not mend his ways, he should be bound in his sin and cast out. If he does mend his ways, he should be absolved. That is the office of the keys. Now the use of the keys is twofold, public and private. There are some people with consciences so tender and despairing that even if they have not been publicly condemned, they cannot find comfort until they have been individually absolved by the pastor. On the other hand, there are also some who are so obdurate that they neither recant in their heart and want their sins forgiven individually by the pastor, nor desist from their sins. Therefore the keys must be used differently, publicly and privately. Now where you see sins forgiven or reproved in some persons, be it publicly or privately, you may know that God's people are there. If God's people are not there, the keys are not there either; and if the keys are not present for Christ, God's people are not present. Christ bequeathed them as a public sign and a holy possession, whereby the Holy Spirit again sanctifies the fallen sinners redeemed by Christ's death, and whereby the Christians confess that they are a holy people in this world under Christ. And those who refuse to be converted or sanctified again shall be cast out from this holy people, that is, bound and excluded by means of the keys, as happened to the unrepentant Antinomians.

You must pay no heed here to the two keys of the pope, which he converted into two skeleton keys to the treasure chests and crowns of all kings. If he does not want to bind or reprove sin, whether it be publicly or privately (as he really does not), let it be reproved and bound in your parish. If he will not loose, or forgive it, let it be loosed and forgiven in your parish, for his retaining or binding, his remitting or releasing, makes you neither holy nor unholy, since he can only have skeleton keys, not the true

---

[395] Luther had previously discussed this subject at length in his treatise *The Keys* (1530). *LW* 40, 325-377.

keys. The keys belong not to the pope (as he lies) but to the church, that is, to God's people, or to the holy Christian people throughout the entire world, or wherever there are Christians. They cannot all be in Rome, unless it be that the whole world is there first—which will not happen in a long time. The keys are the pope's as little as baptism, the sacrament, and the word of God are, for they belong to the people of Christ and are called "the church's keys"[396] not "the pope's keys."[397]

Fifth, the church is recognized externally by the fact that it consecrates or calls ministers, or has offices that it is to administer. There must be bishops, pastors, or preachers, who publicly and privately give, administer, and use the aforementioned four things or holy possessions in behalf of and in the name of the church, or rather by reason of their institution by Christ, as St. Paul states in Ephesians 4 [:8], "He received gifts among men . . ."[398]—his gifts were that some should be apostles, some prophets, some evangelists, some teachers and governors, etc. The people as a whole cannot do these things, but must entrust or have them entrusted to one person. Otherwise, what would happen if everyone wanted to speak or administer, and no one wanted to give way to the other? It must be entrusted to one person, and he alone should be allowed to preach, to baptize, to absolve, and to administer the sacraments. The others should be content with this arrangement and agree to it. Wherever you see this done, be assured that God's people, the holy Christian people, are present.

It is, however, true that the Holy Spirit has excepted women, children, and incompetent people from this function, but chooses (except in emergencies) only competent males to fill this office, as one reads here and there in the epistles of St. Paul that a bishop must be pious, able to teach, and the husband of one wife[399]—and in I Corinthians 14 [:34] he says, "The women should keep silence in the churches." In summary, it must be a competent and chosen man. Children, women, and other persons are not qualified for this

---

[396] *Claves Ecclesiae.*
[397] *Claves Papae.*
[398] Luther is as usual quoting from memory, and confuses Eph. 4:8 with Ps. 68:18, from which the Ephesian passage quotes.
[399] For example, I Tim. 3:2; Titus 1:6.

office, even though they are able to hear God's word, to receive baptism, the sacrament, absolution, and are also true, holy Christians, as St. Peter says [I Pet. 3:7]. Even nature and God's creation makes this distinction, implying that women (much less children or fools) cannot and shall not occupy positions of sovereignty, as experience also suggests and as Moses says in Genesis 3 [:16], "You shall be subject to man." The gospel, however, does not abrogate this natural law, but confirms it as the ordinance and creation of God.

Here the pope will object through his loudmouths and brawlers of the devil, saying, "St. Paul does not speak only of pastors and preachers, but also of apostles, evangelists, prophets, and other high spiritual vocations; that is why there must be higher vocations in the church than those of pastors and preachers. What, Sir Luther, do you have to say now?" What do I have to say now? This is what I have to say: if they themselves would become apostles, evangelists, prophets, or would show me at least one among them—oh, what nonsense I am talking!—who is worth as much as a schoolboy or who is as well versed in Holy Scripture and in Christian doctrine as a seven-year-old girl, I shall declare myself caught. Now I know for certain that an apostle, an evangelist, a prophet knows more, or indeed as much, as a seven-year-old girl. (I am speaking about Holy Scripture and about faith.) For I thoroughly believe, more firmly than I believe in God, that they are acquainted with more human doctrine, and also with more villainy, because they are proving it before my very eyes by the things they are doing, and so they are apostles, evangelists, and prophets just as little as they are the church; that is to say, they are the devil's apostles, evangelists, and prophets. The true apostles, evangelists, and prophets preach God's word, not against God's word.

Now, if the apostles, evangelists, and prophets are no longer living, others must have replaced them and will replace them until the end of the world, for the church shall last until the end of the world [Matt. 28:20]. Apostles, evangelists, and prophets must therefore remain, no matter what their name, to promote God's word and work. The pope and his followers, who persecute God's word while admitting that it is true, must be very poor apostles, evangelists, and prophets, just like the devil and his angels. But why do I keep coming back to these shameful, filthy folk of the pope? Let them go again, and bid them not to return, or etc.

Just as was said earlier about the other four parts of the great, divine, holy possession by which the holy church is sanctified, that you need not care who or how those from whom you receive it are, so again you should not ask who and how he is who gives it to you or has the office. For all of it is given, not to him who has the office, but to him who is to receive it through this office, except that he can receive it together with you if he so desires. Let him be what he will. Because he is in office and is tolerated by the assembly, you put up with him too. His person will make God's word and sacraments neither worse nor better for you. What he says or does is not his, but Christ, your Lord, and the Holy Spirit say and do everything, in so far as he adheres to correct doctrine and practice. The church, of course, cannot and should not tolerate open vices; but you yourself be content and tolerant, since you, an individual, cannot be the whole assembly or the Christian holy people.

But you must pay no attention to the pope,[400] who bars any married man from being called to such an office. With Nestorian logic he declares that all must be chaste virgins; that is to say, all the clergy must be chaste, while they themselves may, of course, be unchaste. But look here! You bring up the pope again, and yet I did not want you any more. Well then, unwelcome guest that you are, I will receive you in Luther-like fashion.

The pope condemns the marriage of bishops or priests; that is now plain enough. Not content with that, he condemns bigamy[401] even more severely. Indeed, to express myself clearly, he distinguishes four, if not five, kinds of bigamy.[402] I will now call one who marries twice or who takes another's widow to wife a biga-

---

[400] This whole section repeats the ideas of a sermon preached by Luther on March 2, 1539. Cf. *WA* 47, 671-678.

[401] Luther calls it *digamia* (from the Greek *digamos*).

[402] See *Decreti Prima Pars*, dist. XXVI, C. I-III (*CIC* 1, 95-96); dist. XXXIII, C. II (*CIC* 1, 123); dist. XXXIV, C. IX-XVIII (*CIC* 1, 128-130); *Decretalium D. Gregorii Papae IX*, lib. i, tit. XXI (*CIC* 2, 146-148).

mist. The first kind of bigamist is one who marries two virgins successively; the second, one who marries a widow; the third, one who marries the betrothed whose deceased groom left her a virgin. The fourth acquires the name shamefully because he is the one who marries a "virgin," unknowingly or unwillingly, and later discovers that she is not at all pure or a virgin. And yet, in the pope's judgment this person must be more of a bigamist than the third type who married the virgin bride. All of these men stink and have an evil smell in canon law. They are not allowed to preach, baptize, administer the sacrament, or hold any office in the church, even if they were holier than St. John and their wives holier than the mother of God. So marvelously holy is the pope in his decretals!

However, if someone had ravished a hundred virgins, violated a hundred honorable widows, and lain with a hundred whores before that, he may become not only pastor or preacher but also bishop or pope. And even if he were to continue this kind of life, he would nonetheless be tolerated in those offices. But if he marries a bride who is a virgin, or a make-believe virgin, he cannot be a servant of God. It makes no difference that he is a true Christian, learned, pious, competent. He is a bigamist; thus, he must leave his office and never return to it. What do you think of that? Is that not a higher holiness than that of Christ himself, together with that of the Holy Spirit and his church? Christ spurns neither men with one wife or two successive wives, nor women with one husband or two successive husbands, if they believe in him. He lets them remain members of his holy, Christian people. He also make use of them for whatever work they are adapted. Scripture uses the term "bigamist" for one who, like Lamech, has two wives living at the same time [Gen. 4:19]. The pope, however, is more learned and calls one who marries two women successively a bigamist. He applies the same rule to women, for he is far more learned than God himself.

Better still, the pope himself admits that a bigamous marriage is a true marriage and does not constitute a sin against God, nor against the world or the church,[403] and that such a marriage is a

---

[403] *Decreti Prima Pars,* dist. XXVI, C. II. *CIC* 1, 95; *MPL* 187, 149c.

sacrament of the church; and yet such a man must be barred from holding an ecclesiastical office—as must the third or fourth type of bigamists, who really should be called husbands of one wife or husbands of virgins. Why? Well, here is the rub: such a marriage cannot be a sacrament or an image of Christ and his church, for Christ had but one bride, the church, and this bride has but one husband, Christ, and both remain virgins. So much sheer nonsense has been talked about this subject that it is impossible to relate it at all. The canonists should rightly be called lawyers for asses. First, if marriage is to be a sacrament of Christ and his church, then no marriage can be a sacrament unless both bridegroom and bride remain virgin, for Christ and the church remain virgins. But how will we get children and heirs under those conditions? What will become of the estate of marriage, instituted by God? In summary, there will be no marriage, other than that of Mary and Joseph and others like it. All the remaining marriages cannot be a sacrament, and may perhaps even be harlotry.

Second, who taught or decreed this, that we must keep it? St. Paul says (they say) in Ephesians 4 [5:31-32] that husband and wife are a great sacrament. I say, "Yes, in Christ and the church." My dear man, can you gather from these words of St. Paul that marriage is the kind of a sacrament of which they speak? He says that husband and wife are one body, which is a great sacrament. Then he interprets himself, saying, "I speak of Christ and the church, not of husband and wife." But they say that he is speaking of husband and wife. Paul envisages Christ and the church as a great sacrament or "mystery";[404] so they say that husband and wife are a great sacrament. Why then do they regard it as virtually the least of the sacraments, indeed, as sheer impurity and sin, in which one cannot serve God? Moreover, can you also deduce from St. Paul's words that men and women in bigamous marriages are not husband and wife or one body? If they are one body, why then are they not a sacrament of Christ and the church? After all, St. Paul is speaking generally about husbands and wives who become one body, whether they were single or widowed be-

---

[404] *Mysterium* (from the Greek *mysterion* used in Eph. 5:32).

fore, and calls them a sacrament (as you understand "sacrament"). Whence then are you so clever as to differentiate in marriage, taking only the single marriage as a sacrament of Christ and the church—that is, the marriage of a man with a virgin—and excluding all others? Who ordered you to martyr and force St. Paul's words in this manner?

Furthermore, you do not even call such a marriage a sacrament. For bridegrooms do not let their brides remain virgins, nor do the latter marry men in order that they may stay virgins; this they could do far better without husbands. No, they want and should bear children, for which God created them. What now becomes of the sacrament of Christ and the church, both of whom remained virgins? Is this the best argument "from image to historical fact or, conversely, from historical fact to image?"[405] Where did you learn such logic? Christ and the church are married, but remain virgins in the body; therefore husband and wife shall also remain virgins in the body. Furthermore, Christ is married to only one virgin; therefore a Christian or a priest shall also be married to only one virgin; otherwise, you say, there is no sacrament. Why, then, do you admit and say that the marriage of a widow is also a sacrament because it is a marriage, and again it is not a sacrament because the wife was not a virgin? Are you not mad, and crazy, and crass Nestorians, not knowing when you say yes and when you say no, stating one thing in the premise and another in the conclusion? Away with you stupid asses and fools!

Another crass error stemmed from the fact (unless, indeed, the former grew out of this) that they called and regarded bishops and popes as the bridegrooms of the church.[406] In verification of this view they cite the saying of St. Paul, "A bishop must be the husband of one wife" [I Tim. 3:2], that is to say, he must be the bishop of one church, as Christ is the bridegroom of one church; therefore they should not be bigamists. Popes and bishops, indeed,

---

[405] *A figura ad historiam, vel econtra, ab historia ad figuram.* A reference to the "dialectical" method of exegesis. Cf. Philip Melanchthon, *Dialectical Questions* (*Erotemata Dialectices*) (1527), VII, 653, 705. *C.R.* 13, 734. See also Clyde L. Manschreck, *Melanchthon* (New York and Nashville: Abingdon Press, 1958), p. 151.

[406] *Decreti Prima Pars,* dist. XXVI, C. II. *CIC* 1, 95; *MPL* 187, 149c.

are fine fellows to be bridegrooms of the church—yes, if she were a brothel-keeper or the devil's daughter in hell. True bishops are servants of this bride, and she is lady and mistress over them. St. Paul calls himself *diaconus*, a "servant of the church" [I Cor. 3:5]. He does not claim to be the bridegroom or the lord of this bride, rather, the true and only bridegroom of this bride is called Jesus Christ, God's Son. St. John does not say, "I am the bridegroom," but, "I am the friend of the bridegroom, who stands and hears him, and who rejoices greatly at the bridegroom's voice," for "he who has the bride" (he says) "is the bridegroom" [John 3:29]. One should gladly give ear to such speech and then conduct oneself as a servant.

But how nicely they themselves keep even this crass asininity and folly. A bishop may have three bishoprics, and yet he must be called husband of one wife. And even if he has but one bishopric, he still has one hundred, two hundred, five hundred, or more parishes or churches; yet he is the bridegroom of one church. The pope claims to be the bridegroom of all churches, both large and small, yet he is called the husband of one church. They are not bigamists or men with two wives, though they have all these brides at the same time. But he who marries a virgin who was betrothed to another is a bigamist. God will inflict gross, monstrous folly like this on us if we despise his word and want to do everything better than he commanded.

Indeed, they have an *acutius*[407] in their *Decretum*, in which St. Augustine holds, against St. Jerome, that he who had a wife before baptism and also one after baptism had two wives. Dear asses, does it therefore follow that St. Augustine, even though he views such a man as the husband of two wives (something Scripture does not do), wishes to have him condemned and barred from serving God, as you do? And even though this should follow, do you not have a strong *noli meis*[408] in dist. IX against it? How is it that you hold so fast to the *acutius* (though it is against Scripture) and pass so lightly over the *noli meis* and other chapters?

---

[407] A quotation from Augustine in *Decreti Prima Pars*, dist. XXVI, C. II: *Acutius intelligunt* . . . . *CIC* 1, 95; *MPL* 187, 149c.
[408] Augustine, *On the Trinity*, III, 2. *MPL* 42, 869; *PNF*[1] 3, 57.

This is, of course, your idea: you want to be lords of the church; whatever you say should be accepted as right. Marriage shall be right and a sacrament, if you will it so; on the other hand, marriage shall be an impurity, that is, a defiled sacrament that cannot serve God, if you will it so. Marriage shall bear children, and yet the wife shall remain a virgin or it is not a sacrament of Christ and the church, if you will it so. The bigamists are blameless and have a true marriage and sacrament, if you will it so; on the other hand, they are condemned and barred from serving God and have no sacrament of Christ and the church, if you will it so. Behold how the devil, who teaches you this nonsense, makes you reel and sway back and forth.

Why should I regard St. Augustine's statement as an article of faith if he himself does not wish to do so and if he himself does not even want to accept the sayings of his predecessors as articles of faith? Suppose that the dear fathers' opinion and teaching about a bigamist was such (as described)—what does it matter to us? It does not obligate us to hold and to teach that view. We must found our salvation on the words and works of man as little as we build our houses of hay and straw. But the canonists are such stupid asses and fools, with their idol in Rome, that they convert the words and deeds of the dear fathers into articles of faith against their will and without their consent. It should be proved by Scripture that such men may be called bigamists or trigamists; then their exclusion from the ministry of the church would be right and stand approved by St. Paul's instruction in I Timothy 3 [:2], "A bishop shall be the husband of one wife." But this frequently happened to the fathers—they sewed old patches on new cloth.[409] This is the case here: no bigamist shall be a servant of the church; that is right and that is the new cloth. But that this or that man is really a bigamist, that is the old patch of their own opinion because Scripture does not say it. Scripture regards the man who has two wives living at the same time as a bigamist; and it is assumed that St. Paul had had a wife, Philippians 4 [:3],[410] and that she died. So he too must have been a

---

[409]See LW 41, 63.

[410] Luther interprets the term "yokefellow" as an indication of Paul's marriage

man with two wives, obliged to give up his apostolic office; for in I Corinthians 7 [:8] he counts himself among the widowed, and yet in I Corinthians 9 [:5] he, along with Barnabas, claims the right to be accompanied by a wife. Who will assure us that the poor fishermen, Peter, Andrew, and James, were married to virgins and not to widows, or that they did not have two wives in succession?

These blockheads do not have the same idea of chastity that the fathers had, but would like to confuse the poor souls and jeopardize them, if only their stinking and filthy book[411] is regarded as right and their "science" is not found to err or to have erred. Otherwise, they would indeed see what chastity is—since, with regard to other "opinions"[412] (and what is their best and foremost but a matter of mere opinion?), they can say nicely, "It is not held; but hold this."[413] Why can they not do it here, especially since they do not hesitate to repudiate not only one father, but all of them, in "the cases to be decided,"[414] as their idol sputters and bellows? But they would like to rule the church, not with trustworthy wisdom, but with arbitrary opinions, and again confuse and perplex all the souls in the world, as they have done before. But just as they reject all the fathers and theologians in their petty canons, so do we, in turn, reject them in the church and in Scripture. They shall neither teach us Scripture nor rule in the church; they are not entitled to it, nor do they have the competence for it. But they shall attend to their trifling canons and squabbles over prebends—that is their holiness. They have cast us poor theologians, together with the fathers, from their books; for this we thank them most kindly. Now they propose to throw us out of the church and out of Scripture; and they themselves are not worthy to be in them. That is too much, and rips the bag

---

and assumes (on the basis of I Cor. 7:8) that he became a widower. Modern biblical scholarship does not agree. Cf., for example, George A. Buttrick *et al.* (eds.), *The Interpreter's Bible* (12 vols.; New York and Nashville: Abingdon, 1952-1957), IX, 107-108; X, 78-79.

[411] Canon law.

[412] *Opiniones.*

[413] *Non tenetur; hoc tene.*

[414] *Causis decidendis.* Here Luther mocks the slogans of medieval canonists who were frequently involved in court cases concerning ecclesiastical property.

wide open.[415] And furthermore, we shall not put up with it.

I truly believe that in accordance with their wisdom no man could marry a virgin and, after her death, become a priest among them, for who can guarantee or vouch that he is actually getting a virgin? "The road runs past the door"[416] (as they say). Now if he would find her not a virgin—and that is a chance he must take—he would, through no fault of his own, be a stinking bigamist. And if he wants to be certain that he can become a priest, he dare not marry a virgin either, for what assurance does he have that she is one? However, he may ravish virgins, widows, and wives, have many whores, commit all sorts of secret sins—he is still worthy of the priestly office. The sum and substance of it all is that the pope, the devil, and his church are averse to the estate of matrimony, as Daniel [11:37] says; therefore he wants it viewed as such a defilement that a married man cannot fill a priest's office. That is as much as to say that marriage is harlotry, sin, impure, and rejected by God. And even though they say, at the same time, that marriage is holy and a sacrament, that is hypocrisy and a lie, for if they would sincerely regard it as holy and a sacrament they would not forbid a priest to marry. But since they do prohibit it, it follows that they consider it impure and a sin—as they plainly say, "You must be clean, who bearest [the vessels of the lord]"[417] or (if some really are that pious) they must be stupid Nestorians and Eutychians, affirming a premise and denying the conclusion. May this be the reception that we, for the time being, accord the papal ass and the asinine papists, as we return to our own people.

Therefore do not worry (as was said) about the papists' talk concerning the personal qualifications for an ecclesiastical office, for these asses do not understand St. Paul's words, nor do they know what St. Paul's language calls a sacrament. He says [Eph. 5:31-32] that Christ and the church are a sacrament, that is, Christ and the church are one body, as husband and wife are, and that

---

[415] A German proverb, *"Das zurreisset den sack."* Cf. Thiele, *Luthers Sprichwörtersammlung,* No. 39.

[416] Another proverb, *"Der weg gehet fur der thür ruber."* Cf. *ibid.,* No. 10.

[417] *Mundamini, qui fertis [vasa Domini].* A reference to the formula used at the ordination of priests.

this is a great mystery, to be apprehended by faith. It is not visible or tangible; therefore it is a sacrament, that is, something secret, a mystery, invisible, hidden. But since not only virginal but also widowed people entering matrimony are one body, every marriage is a figure or symbol of this great sacrament or mystery in Christ and the church. St. Paul speaks of neither virgins nor widows; he speaks of marriage, in which husband and wife are one body. Now wherever you find these offices or officers, you may be assured that the holy Christian people are there; for the church cannot be without these bishops, pastors, preachers, priests; and conversely, they cannot be without the church. Both must be together.

Sixth, the holy Christian people are externally recognized by prayer, public praise, and thanksgiving to God. Where you see and hear the Lord's Prayer prayed and taught; or psalms or other spiritual songs sung, in accordance with the word of God and the true faith; also the creed, the Ten Commandments, and the catechism used in public, you may rest assured that a holy Christian people of God are present. For prayer, too, is one of the precious holy possessions whereby everything is sanctified, as St. Paul says [I Tim. 4:5]. The psalms too are nothing but prayers in which we praise, thank, and glorify God. The creed and the Ten Commandments are also God's word and belong to the holy possession, whereby the Holy Spirit sanctifies the holy people of Christ. However, we are now speaking of prayers and songs which are intelligible and from which we can learn and by means of which we can mend our ways. The clamor of monks and nuns and priests is not prayer, nor is it praise to God; for they do not understand it, nor do they learn anything from it; they do it like a donkey, only for the sake of the belly and not at all in quest of any reform or sanctification or of the will of God.

Seventh, the holy Christian people are externally recognized by the holy possession of the sacred cross. They must endure every misfortune and persecution, all kinds of trials and evil from the devil, the world, and the flesh (as the Lord's Prayer indicates) by inward sadness, timidity, fear, outward poverty, contempt, illness, and weakness, in order to become like their head, Christ.

And the only reason they must suffer is that they steadfastly adhere to Christ and God's word, enduring this for the sake of Christ, Matthew 5 [:11], "Blessed are you when men persecute you on my account." They must be pious, quiet, obedient, and prepared to serve the government and everybody with life and goods, doing no one any harm. No people on earth have to endure such bitter hate; they must be accounted worse than Jews, heathen, and Turks. In summary, they must be called heretics, knaves, and devils, the most pernicious people on earth, to the point where those who hang, drown, murder, torture, banish, and plague them to death are rendering God a service. No one has compassion on them; they are given myrrh and gall to drink when they thirst. And all of this is done not because they are adulterers, murderers, thieves, or rogues, but because they want to have none but Christ, and no other God. Wherever you see or hear this, you may know that the holy Christian church is there, as Christ says in Matthew 5 [:11-12], "Blessed are you when men revile you and utter all kinds of evil against you on my account. Rejoice and be glad, for your reward is great in heaven." This too is a holy possession whereby the Holy Spirit not only sanctifies his people, but also blesses them.

Meanwhile, pay no heed to the papists' holy possessions from dead saints, from the wood of the holy cross. For these are just as often bones taken from a carrion pit as bones of saints, and just as often wood taken from gallows as wood from the holy cross. There is nothing but fraud in this. The pope thus tricks people out of their money and alienates them from Christ. Even if it were a genuine holy possession, it would nonetheless not sanctify anyone. But when you are condemned, cursed, reviled, slandered, and plagued because of Christ, you are sanctified. It mortifies the old Adam and teaches him patience, humility, gentleness, praise and thanks, and good cheer in suffering. That is what it means to be sanctified by the Holy Spirit and to be renewed to a new life in Christ; in that way we learn to believe in God, to trust him, to love him, and to place our hope in him, as Romans 5 [:1-5] says, "Suffering produces hope," etc.

These are the true seven principal parts of the great holy possession whereby the Holy Spirit effects in us a daily sanctification and vivification in Christ, according to the first table of Moses. By this we obey it, albeit never as perfectly as Christ. But we constantly strive to attain the goal, under his redemption or remission of sin, until we too shall one day become perfectly holy and no longer stand in need of forgiveness. Everything is directed toward that goal. I would even call these seven parts the seven sacraments, but since that term has been misused by the papists and is used in a different sense in Scripture, I shall let them stand as the seven principal parts of Christian sanctification or the seven holy possessions of the church.

In addition to these seven principal parts there are other outward signs that identify the Christian church, namely, those signs whereby the Holy Spirit sanctifies us according to the second table of Moses; when he assists us in sincerely honoring our father and mother, and conversely, when he helps them to raise their children in a Christian way and to lead honorable lives; when we faithfully serve our princes and lords and are obedient and subject to them, and conversely, when they love their subjects and protect and guard them; also when we bear no one a grudge, entertain no anger, hatred, envy, or vengefulness toward our neighbors, but gladly forgive them, lend to them, help them, and counsel them; when we are not lewd, not drunkards, not proud, arrogant, overbearing, but chaste, self-controlled, sober, friendly, kind, gentle, and humble; when we do not steal, rob, are not usurious, greedy, do not overcharge, but are mild, kind, content, charitable; when we are not false, mendacious, perjurers, but truthful, trustworthy, and do whatever else is taught in these commandments—all of which St. Paul teaches abundantly in more than one place. We need the Decalogue not only to apprise us of our lawful obligations, but we also need it to discern how far the Holy Spirit has advanced us in his work of sanctification and by how much we still fall short of the goal, lest we become secure and imagine that we have now done all that is required. Thus we must constantly grow in sanctification and always become new creatures in Christ. This means "grow" and "do so more and more" [II Pet. 3:18].

However, these signs cannot be regarded as being as reliable as those noted before since some heathen too practice these works and indeed at times appear holier than Christians; yet their actions do not issue from the heart purely and simply, for the sake of God, but they search for some other end because they lack a real faith in and a true knowledge of God. But here is the Holy Spirit, who sanctifies the heart and produces these fruits from "an honest and good heart," as Christ says in the parable recorded in Matthew 13 [Luke 8:15]. Since the first table is greater and must be a holier possession, I have summarized everything in the second table. Otherwise, I could have divided it too into seven holy possessions or seven principal parts, according to the seven commandments.

Now we know for certain what, where, and who the holy Christian church is, that is, the holy Christian people of God; and we are quite certain that it cannot fail us. Everything else may fail and surely does, as we shall hear in part. Men should be selected from this people to form a council; that might be a council ruled by the Holy Spirit. Thus Lyra, too, writes that the church is not to be assessed by the high or spiritual vocations in it, but by the people who truly believe.[418] I am surprised that he was not burned at the stake for these words, for denying that popes, cardinals, bishops, and prelates compose the church; this amounts to abominable heresy, intolerable and offensive to the holy Roman church. More about this elsewhere.[419]

Now when the devil saw that God built such a holy church, he was not idle, and erected his chapel beside it, larger than God's temple. This is how he did it: he noticed that God utilized outward things, like baptism, word, sacrament, keys, etc., whereby he sanctified his church. And since the devil is always God's ape,

---

[418] Nicholas of Lyra (1270-1340), a Franciscan theologian and famous interpreter of the Bible. Luther frequently quotes him, as does Melanchthon, who quoted this statement of Lyra's in the *Apology of the Augsburg Confession*, Arts. VII, VIII. Tappert (ed.), *Book of Concord*, p. 172. The quotation Luther cites is found in *Comments on Matthew XVI* (*Annotationes in Matth. XVI*). See *WA* 50, 644, n. *a*. Five volumes of Lyra's works were published in 1471-1472 in Rome. *O.D.C.C.*, p. 957.

[419] Cf. *The Smalcald Articles*, Art. IV. Tappert (ed.), *Book of Concord*, pp. 298-301.

trying to imitate all God's things and to improve on them, he also tried his luck with external things purported to make man holy— just as he tries with rain-makers, sorcerers, exorcists of devils, etc. He even has the Lord's Prayer recited and the gospel read over them to make it appear a great holy possession. Thus he had popes and papists consecrate or sanctify water, salt, candles, herbs, bells, images, *Agnus Dei*,[420] pallia,[421] chasubles, tonsures, fingers, hands—who can tell it all?—finally the monks' cowls to a degree that many people died and were buried in them, believing that thereby they would be saved. Now it would have been fine indeed if God's word or a blessing or a prayer were spoken over these created things, as children do over their food or over themselves when they go to bed and when they arise. St. Paul says of this, "Everything created by God is good, and is consecrated by the word of God and prayer" [I Tim. 4:4-5]. The creature derives no new power from such a practice, but is strengthened in its former power.

But the devil has a different purpose in mind. He wants the creature to derive new strength and power from his aping tomfoolery. Just as water becomes baptism by the power of God, a bath unto eternal life, washing away sin and bringing salvation, a power which is not inherent in water; just as bread and wine become the body and blood of Christ; just as sins are remitted by the laying on of hands in accordance with God's institution—so the devil too wants his mummery and aping tomfoolery to be strong and imbued with supernatural power. Holy water is to blot out sin, exorcise devils, fend off evil spirits, protect women in childbed, as the pope teaches us in the *Aquam sale, de pe*;[422] consecrated salt is to have the same effect. An *Agnus Dei* consecrated by the pope is to do more than God himself can do, as this is described in verses that I should some day publish with marginal

---

[420] Luther refers to amulets usually made of wax and stamped with the image of a lamb.

[421] A woolen shoulder cape with the insignia of the archbishop's office on it.

[422] *Aquam sale*, a section in canon law dealing with consecration, according to which holy salt is used in rites of purification. *De pe* is either a slip of the pen for *de co* (*de consecratione*) or Luther's abbreviation for *de poenitentia*, the title of the chapter on penitence. Cf. *Decreti Tertia Pars: De Consecratione*, dist. III, C. XX. *CIC* 1, 1358; *MPL* 187, 1787c.

notes.[423] Bells are to drive away devils in thunderstorms. St. Anthony's knives stab the devil; consecrated herbs expel venomous worms; some blessings heal cows, keep off milk thieves,[424] and quench fire; certain letters give security in war and at other times against iron, fire, water, wild beasts, etc.;[425] monasticism, masses, and the like are said to confer more than ordinary salvation. Who can tell it all? There was no need so small that the devil did not institute a sacrament or holy possession for it, whereby one could receive advice and help. In addition, he had prophetesses, soothsayers, and sages able to reveal hidden things and to retrieve stolen goods.

Oh, he is far better equipped with sacraments, prophets, apostles, and evangelists than God, and his chapels are much larger than God's church; and he has far more people in his holiness than God. One is also more inclined to believe his promises, his sacraments, and his prophets than Christ. He is the great god of the world. Christ calls him "ruler of the world" [John 12:31; 14:30; 16:11] and Paul "the god of this world" [II Cor. 4:4]. With this aping tomfoolery he estranges men from faith in Christ and causes the word and the sacraments of Christ to be despised and almost unrecognizable because it is easier to perceive such things than to blot out sin, help in time of need, receive salvation through the devil's sacraments rather than through Christ's. For it is Christ's will to make people holy and pious in body and soul through the Holy Spirit and not let them remain in unbelief and sin. This is too hard for those who do not wish to be pious or to desist from sin. They can readily dispense with this work of the Holy Spirit after they learn how they can be saved more easily without him—for example, by holy water, *Agnus Dei*, bulls and breves, masses and cowls—thus making it unnecessary to seek or heed anything else.

But not only that! The devil has armed himself with these

---

[423] Cf. Luther's notes *On the Blessed Water and the Agnus Dei of the Pope* (*Von dem Geweihtem Wasser und des Papstes Agnus Dei*) (1539). WA 50, 668-673.

[424] I.e., witches who make cows go dry.

[425] In 1518 Luther dealt with these ecclesiastical customs more favorably. Cf. for example, *The Decalog, Preached to the People of Wittenberg* (*Decem Praecepta, Wittenbergensi Praedicata Populo*) (1518). WA 1, 401.

things in order to abolish God's word and sacraments with them. This is his line of thought: if someone arises to attack my church, sacraments, and bishops, saying that external things do not save, then God's word and sacraments shall perish with them, for these too are external signs and his church and bishops are also human beings. If mine do not stand approved, his will stand approved even less, especially because my church, bishops, and sacraments work promptly and help now and in this life, visibly and tangibly, for I am present in them and help quickly, as soon as it is desired. Christ's sacraments, however, work spiritually and invisibly and for the future so that his church and bishops can only be smelled, as it were, faintly and from afar, and the Holy Spirit behaves as though he were absent, permitting people to endure every misfortune and making them appear as heretics in the eyes of my church. Meanwhile, my church is not only so close that one can actually grasp it, but also my works follow very quickly; so everyone assumes that it is the true church of God. This is the advantage I have.

And that is what happened. When we began to teach, on the basis of the gospel, that these external things do not save, since they are merely physical and creatural and are often used by the devil for the purpose of sorcery, people, even great and learned people, concluded that baptism, being external water, that the word, being outward human speech, that Scripture, being physical letters made with ink, that the bread, being baked by the baker, and the wine were nothing more than outward, perishable things. So they devised the slogan, "Spirit! Spirit! The Spirit must do it! The letter kills!" So Münzer[426] called us Wittenberg theologians scribes of Scripture and himself the scribe of the Holy Spirit, and many others followed his example. There you see how the devil had armed himself and built up his barricades. If anyone were to attack his outward doctrine and sacraments (which afford quick, visible, and mighty aid), then the outward words and sacraments

---

[426] Thomas Münzer (1489-1525), labeled the "restless spirit of Allstedt" by Luther, became a leader of the rebellious peasants in the Peasants' War of 1525. The passage is found in Hans J. Hillerbrand, "Thomas Münzer's Last Tract Against Martin Luther," *The Mennonite Quarterly Review,* XXXVIII (1964), 26.

of Christ (attended by tardy or, at least, by invisible and feeble help) must go down to far worse destruction along with them.

Therefore the *ecclesia*, "the holy Christian people," does not have mere external words, sacraments, or offices, like God's ape Satan has, and in far greater numbers, but it has these as commanded, instituted, and ordained by God, so that he himself and not any angel will work through them with the Holy Spirit. They are called word, baptism, sacrament, and office of forgiveness, not of angels, men, or any other creature, but of God; only he does not choose to do it through his unveiled, brilliant, and glorious majesty, out of consideration for us poor, weak, and timid mortals and for our comfort, for who could bear such majesty for an instant in this poor and sinful flesh? As Moses says, "Man shall not see me and live" [Exod. 33:20]. If the Jews could not endure even the shoes of his feet on Mount Sinai, that is, the thunder and the clouds, how could they, with their feeble eyes, have endured the sight of the sun of his divine majesty and the clear light of his countenance? No, he wants to work through tolerable, kind, and pleasant means, which we ourselves could not have chosen better. He has, for instance, a godly and kind man speak to us, preach, lay his hands on us, remit sin, baptize, give us bread and wine to eat and to drink. Who can be terrified by these pleasing methods, and wouldn't rather delight in them with all his heart?

Well then, that is just what is done for us feeble human beings, and in it we see how God deals with us as with beloved children and not, as he surely would have a right to, in his majesty. And yet, in this guise he performs his majestic, divine works and exercises his might and power, such as forgiving sin, cleansing from sin, removing death, bestowing grace and eternal life. Indeed, these things are missing in the devil's sacraments and churches. No one can say there, "God commanded it, ordered it, instituted it, and ordained it; he himself is present and will do everything himself"; but one must say, "God did not command, but forbade it, that man, or rather that ape of God, invented it and misled the people with it." For he effects nothing except that which is temporal, or, if it purports to be spiritual, it is sheer fraud. He cannot forgive sin eternally and save, as he lyingly claims, by means of holy water, masses, and monkery, even though he may restore a cow's milk which he had first stolen from her by his prophetesses and priestesses. Among Christians these are called the devil's harlots and, when apprehended, are rightfully burned at the stake, not because of the theft of milk, but because of the blasphemy with which they fortify the devil, his sacraments, and his churches against Christ.

In summary, if God were to bid you to pick up a straw or to pluck out a feather with the command, order, and promise that thereby you would have forgiveness of all sin, grace, and eternal life, should you not accept this joyfully and gratefully, and cherish, praise, prize, and esteem that straw and that feather as a higher and holier possession than heaven and earth? No matter how insignificant the straw and the feather may be, you would nonetheless acquire through them something more valuable than heaven and earth, indeed, than all the angels, are able to bestow on you. Why then are we such disgraceful people that we do not regard the water of baptism, the bread and wine, that is, Christ's body and blood, the spoken word, and the laying on of man's hands for the forgiveness of sin as such holy possessions, as we would the straw and feather, though in the former, as we hear and know, God himself wishes to be effective and wants them to be his water, word, hand, bread, and wine, by means of which he wishes to sanctify and save you in Christ, who acquired this for us and who gave us the Holy Spirit from the Father for this work?

On the other hand, what good would it do you even if you went to St. James,[427] clad in armor, or let yourself be killed by the severe life of the Carthusians, Franciscans, or Dominicans in order to be saved, and God had neither commanded nor instituted it? He still knows nothing about all this, but you and the devil invented them, as special sacraments or classes of priests. And even if you were able to bear heaven and earth in order to be saved, it would still all be lost; and he who would pick up the straw (if this were commanded) would do more than you, even if you

---

[427] I.e., to the shrine of St. James of Compostella in Spain, where according to Spanish tradition the apostle was martyred in 44. See Acts 12:2.

could carry ten worlds. Why is that? It is God's will that we obey his word, use his sacraments, and honor his church. Then he will act graciously and gently enough, even more graciously and gently than we could desire; for it is written, "I am the Lord your God; you shall have no other gods before me" [Exod. 20:2-3]. And, "Listen to him and to no other" [Matt. 17:5]. May that suffice on the church. More cannot be said unless each point is elaborated further. The rest must deal with different ideas, about which we want to speak too.

Besides these external signs and holy possessions the church has other externals that do not sanctify it either in body or soul, nor were they instituted or commanded by God; but, as we said at length above, they are outwardly necessary or useful, proper and good—for instance, certain holidays and certain hours, forenoon or afternoon, set aside for preaching or praying, or the use of a church building or house, altar, pulpit, baptismal font, candlesticks, candles, bells, priestly vestments, and the like. These things have no more than their natural effects, just as food and drink accomplish no more by virtue of the grace the children say at the table,[428] for the ungodly or rude folk who don't say it, that is, who neither pray to God nor thank him, grow just as fat and strong from food and drink as Christians do. To be sure, Christians could be and remain sanctified even without these items, even if they were to preach on the street, outside a building, without a pulpit, if absolution were pronounced and the sacrament administered without an altar, and if baptism were performed without a font—as happens daily that for special reasons sermons are preached and baptisms and sacraments administered in the home. But for the sake of children and simple folk, it is a fine thing and conducive to good order to have a definite time, place, and hour to which people can adapt themselves and where they may assemble, as St. Paul says in I Corinthians 14 [:40], "All things should be done decently and in order." And no one should (as no Christian does) ignore such order without cause, out of mere pride or just to create disorder, but one should join in observing such order for the sake of the multitude, or at least should not disrupt or hinder

---

[428] These prayers are called *Benedicite* and *Gratias*.

it, for that would be acting contrary to love and friendliness.

Nevertheless, there should be freedom here: for instance, if we are unable, because of an emergency or another significant reason, to preach at six or seven, at twelve or one o'clock, on Sunday or Monday, in the choir or at St. Peter's, one may preach at a different hour, day, or place, just as long as one does not confuse the people, but properly apprises them of such a change. These matters are purely external (as far as time, place, and persons are concerned) and may be regulated entirely by reason, to which they are altogether subject. God, Christ, and the Holy Spirit are not interested in them—just as little as they are interested in what we wish to eat, drink, wear, and whom we marry, or where we want to dwell, walk, or stand; except that (as was said) no one should, without reason, adopt his own way and confuse or hinder the people. Just as at a wedding or other social event no one should offend the bride or the company by doing something special or something that interferes, but one should join the rest, and sit, walk, stand, dance, eat, and drink with them. For it is impossible to order a special table for each individual, and also a special kitchen, cellar, and servant. If he wants anything, let him leave the table without disturbing the others. Thus here too everything must be conducted peacefully and in order, and yet there must be freedom if time, person, or other reasons demand a change; then the masses will also follow harmoniously, since (as was said) no Christian is thereby made any more or less holy.

The pope, to be sure, has scribbled the whole world full of books about these things and fashioned them into bonds, laws, rights, articles of faith, sin, and holiness so that his decretal really deserves, once again, to be consigned to the fire.[429] For we could do well without this book[430] that has caused so much great harm. It has pushed Holy Scripture aside and practically suppressed Christian doctrine; it has also subjected the jurists, with their imperial law, to it. Thus it has trodden both church and emperor underfoot; in their stead it presented us with these stupid asses, the canonists, these will-o'-the-wisps who rule the church with it

---

[429] On December 10, 1520, in Wittenberg, Luther burned copies of the canon law along with the bull, *Exsurge, Domine,* excommunicating him.
[430] I.e., canon law.

and, still more deplorable, left the best parts in it and took the worst out, foisting them on the church. Whatever good there is in it, one can find much better and more richly in Holy Scripture, indeed, also in St. Augustine alone, as far as teaching Christendom is concerned; and then, as far as temporal government is concerned, also in the books of the jurists. For the jurists themselves once contemplated throwing this book out of jurisprudence and leaving it to the theologians. However, it would have been far better to throw it into the fire and reduce it to ashes, although there is something good in it, for how could sheer evil exist unless there was some good with it? But there is too much evil, so much that it crowds out the good, and (as was said) a greater measure of good is to be found in Scripture and also in the fathers and among the jurists. Of course, it might be kept in the libraries as evidence of the folly and the mistakes of the popes, some of the councils, and other teachers. That is why I am keeping it.

We will regard these externals as we do a christening robe[431] or swaddling clothes in which a child is clad for baptism. The child is not baptized or sanctified either by the christening robe or by the swaddling clothes, but only by the baptism. And yet reason dictates that a child be thus clothed. If this garment is soiled or torn, it is replaced by another, and the child grows up without any help from swaddling clothes or christening robe. Here too one must exercise moderation and not use too many of these garments, lest the child be smothered. Similarly, moderation should also be observed in the use of ceremonies, lest they become a burden and a chore. They must remain so light that they are not felt, just as at a wedding no one thinks it a chore or a burden to conform his actions to those of the other people present. I shall write on the special fasts when I write about the plague of the Germans, gluttony and drunkenness, for that properly belongs in the sphere of temporal government.[432]

---

[431] *Westerhemd* (from the Latin *vestis,* meaning "garment"). The robe was usually white (in accordance with Rev. 6:11) and was used in the early church to dress those to be baptized. Cf. WA 50, 651, n. *a.*

[432] Luther wrote about this in 1518 in his *Explanations of the Ninety-five Theses. LW* 31, 86-88.

Above and elsewhere[433] I have written much about the schools, urging firmness and diligence in caring for them. Although they may be viewed as something external and pagan, in as much as they instruct boys in languages and the arts, they are nevertheless extremely necessary. For if we fail to train pupils we will not have pastors and preachers very long—as we are finding out. The school must supply the church with persons who can be made apostles, evangelists, and prophets, that is, preachers, pastors, and rulers, in addition to other people needed throughout the world, such as chancellors, councilors, secretaries, and the like, men who can also lend a hand with the temporal government. In addition, if the schoolteacher is a godly man and teaches the boys to understand, to sing, and to practice God's word and the true faith and holds them to Christian discipline, then, as we said earlier, the schools are truly young and eternal councils, which perhaps do more good than many other great councils. Therefore the former emperors, kings, and princes did well when they showed such diligence in building many schools, high and low, monastic schools and convents, to provide the church with a rich and ample supply of people; but their successors shamefully perverted their use. Thus today princes and lords should do the same, and use the possessions of the cloisters for the maintenance of schools and provide many persons with the means for study.[434] If our descendants misuse these, we at least have done our duty in our day.

In summary, the schools must be second in importance only to the church, for in them young preachers and pastors are trained, and from them emerge those who replace the ones who die. Next, then, to the school comes the burgher's house, for it supplies the pupils; then the city hall and the castle, which must protect the schools so that they may train children to become pastors, and so that these, in turn, may create churches and children of God (whether they be burghers, princes, or emperors). But God must be over all and nearest to all, to preserve this ring or circle against

---

[433] See Luther's *To the Councilmen of All Cities in Germany that They Establish and Maintain Christian Schools* (*PE* 4, 101-130) and *A Sermon on Keeping Children in School* (*PE* 4, 133-178).

[434] Cf. *The Smalcald Articles*, Art. III. Tappert (ed.), *Book of Concord*, pp. 297-298.

the devil, and to do everything in all of life's vocations, indeed, in all creatures. Thus Psalm 127 [:1] says that there are only two temporal governments on earth, that of the city and that of the home, "Unless the Lord builds the house; unless the Lord watches over the city." The first government is that of the home, from which the people come; the second is that of the city, meaning the country, the people, princes and lords, which we call the secular government. These embrace everything—children, property, money, animals, etc. The home must produce, whereas the city must guard, protect, and defend. Then follows the third, God's own home and city, that is, the church, which must obtain people from the home and protection and defense from the city.

These are the three hierarchies ordained by God, and we need no more; indeed, we have enough and more than enough to do in living aright and resisting the devil in these three. Just look only at the home and at the duties it alone imposes: parents and landlords must be obeyed; children and servants must be nourished, trained, ruled, and provided for in a godly spirit. The rule of the home alone would give us enough to do, even if there were nothing else. Then the city, that is, the secular government, also gives us enough to do if we show ourselves really obedient, and conversely, if we are to judge, protect, and promote land and people. The devil keeps us busy enough, and with him God gave us the sweat of our brow, thorns and thistles in abundance [Gen. 3:18-19], so that we have more than enough to learn, to live, to do, and to suffer in these two governments. Then there is the third rule and government. If the Holy Spirit reigns there, Christ calls it a comforting, sweet, and light burden [Matt. 11:30]; if not, it is not only a heavy, severe, and terrible task, but also an impossible one, as St. Paul says in Romans 8 [:3], "What the law could not do," and elsewhere, "The letter kills" [II Cor. 3:6].

Now why should we have the blasphemous, bogus law or government of the pope over and above these three high divine governments, these three divine, natural, and temporal laws of God? It presumes to be everything, yet is in reality nothing. It leads us astray and tears us from these blessed, divine estates and laws. Instead, it dresses us in a mask or cowl, thereby making us the devil's fools and playthings, who are slothful and no longer know these three divine hierarchies or realms. That is why we no longer want to put up with it, but acting in conformity with St. Peter's, St. Paul's, and St. Augustine's teaching, want to be rid of it and turn the words of Psalm 2 [:3] against them, "Let us burst their bonds asunder, and cast their cords from us." Indeed, we shall sing with St. Paul, "Even if an angel from heaven should preach a gospel contrary to that, let him be accursed" [Gal. 1:8]; and we shall say with St. Peter, "Why do you make trial of God by putting such a yoke upon the neck?" [Acts 15:10]. Thus we shall again be the pope's masters and tread him underfoot, as Psalm 91 [:13] says, "You will tread on the lion and the adder, the young lion and the serpent you will trample under foot." And that we shall do by the power and with the help of the woman's seed, who has crushed and still crushes the serpent's head, although we must run the risk that he, in turn, will bite us in the heel [Gen. 3:15]. To this blessed seed of the woman be praise and honor, together with the Father and the Holy Spirit, to the one true God and Lord in eternity. Amen.

PART VI

LIVING AND DYING AS A CHRISTIAN

In some respects Luther is a one-issue theologian. The question of how humans are related to God runs through all his thought from the earliest documents in this anthology to the last ones. For Luther the gospel of the grace of God in Jesus Christ is such a surprising reality that it stands out above all other concerns. There is something right about the Reformation slogans of grace alone, faith alone, Christ alone, even Scripture alone in capturing Luther's passion for this God question.

But if the God-human question issue is the overriding concern in Luther's theology, then ethics, which for Luther includes the whole wide range of matters concerning how to live in this world, is the necessary second question. While ethics can never be equally important with the good news of forgiveness and reconciliation with God, it deserves careful attention. The six documents in Part VI show the rich range of Luther's reflections concerning how one is to live rightly in this world, never forgetting the centrality of what one has learned about God from the law and the gospel.

26   The Freedom of a Christian

In this section the first document is Luther's famous programmatic statement about Christian ethics, "The Freedom of a Christian." Published in November of his most productive year, 1520, it is written in a more conciliatory spirit than "Address to the German Nobility" and "The Babylonian Captivity of the Church" (see *Three Treatises* [Philadelphia: Fortress Press, 1970]). In fact, it includes an open letter to Pope Leo XIII, written in one of those moments in 1520 when Luther had been persuaded that a peaceful settlement of differences might still be possible.

In this classic definition of Christian freedom, Luther presents the central theological vision of how he sees the Christian's life. Building on the writings of St. Paul, and especially on his own earlier Galatians lectures, Luther presents the situation of the Christian who lives both in freedom and for service in a well-known paradox:

> A Christian is a perfectly free lord of all, subject to none.
> A Christian is a perfectly dutiful servant of all, subject to all
> (p. 596).

The first question of ethics for Luther is not V. I. Lenin's "What is to be done?", but rather "Why do we do what we do?" The woman or man who knows the grace of God in Jesus Christ is set free to act on the basis of responding love and the real needs of the neighbor. This action need not be contaminated by the continual pressure of the self wanting justification, praise, or credit for whatever is done.

At the end of the treatise, Luther identifies a danger: there are persons "for whom nothing can be said so well that they will not spoil it by misunderstanding it." They need to be warned that true Christian freedom is never "an occasion for the flesh" in which "now all things are allowed them." This worry about persons taking advantage of Christian liberty or freedom was a constant complaint of Luther's critics in both the catholic and reformed camps. He was never willing to back down from describing the Christian's life under the heading of freedom, but on several occasions after 1520 he addressed this danger again. (See, especially, "Against the Antinomians" from 1539 in *LW*, 47: 107-19).

27   A Sermon on the Estate of Marriage

With "The Freedom of a Christian" providing the theological framework for ethics, subsequent documents take up Luther's views on some concrete issues. Luther's ethic has often been summarized or even dismissed as conservative. It is conservative in many senses of the word, especially in Luther's lack of optimism about political change. But that term alone does not capture the dynamic quality of much of Luther's thinking about ethics and daily life.

The reader may remember that in Luther's personal theological testament (Part I. 4, excerpt from "Concerning Christ's Supper") he described the task of living in the world as summarized in the participation of Christians in God's created orders—family, civil society, and the church. It was his special achievement to help many ordinary Christians see the opportunities for service to the neighbor not only in churchly forms of ministry but also in their own settings.

This is well reflected in "A Sermon on the Estate of Marriage," from 1519. This sermon had been preached on the second Sunday after Epiphany of that year, taken down by a listener, and published without Luther's knowledge. Luther was dissatisfied enough to undertake a revision of the material, which he published that May.

In contrast to the ascetic traditions of medieval theology, Luther is enthusiastic about marriage as a gift from God. (His later claim that marriage was not a sacrament did not come from a low view of the institution, but rather from a sense that it was a universal order of creation and therefore not a distinctively Christian means of grace). His pastoral realism about all of the dimensions of marriage makes this an especially attractive presentation of one key aspect of ethics. (It is important to remember that this sermon was published six years before Luther's own marriage.)

28   A Sermon on Preparing to Die

Very different concerns were addressed that same year of 1519 in "A Sermon on Preparing to Die." This sermon was written under some duress, at a time when Luther was extraordinarily busy. But an importunate man, Mark Schart, kept making his request for help with dealing with fear of death, and by November 1, 1519, Luther was finally able to oblige him with this treatise.

In many respects it points back to the documents in Part III, celebrating the reasons for Christian confidence in the face of death. But it also belongs in this section because it represents Luther's commitment to offering a combination of spiritual and practical advice to troubled people.

The reader should note the concrete suggestion that Luther makes at the beginning of the treatise about the importance that the dying person "regulate his temporal goods properly or as he wishes to have them ordered, lest after death there be occasion for squabbles, quarrels, or other misunderstandings among his surviving friends" (p. 638).

Luther's tendency to stress the grace of God as the central truth did not destroy his ability to speak quite practically about how to live in this world. Rather, it gave him immense resources to continue speaking when one came to the limit of ethics—the boundary that death sets for all human projects.

29   Temporal Authority: To What Extent It Should Be Obeyed

Luther had high confidence not only in marriage and family life but also in the legitimate power of secular governments.

Over against many traditional Roman attempts to subordinate the power of government to that of the church (and especially the papacy), Luther saw the civil order as one of God's gifts, a way that minimal order was maintained in a violent, sinful world.

Luther's own reforming activities were possible only because of the support of princes and those free cities that embraced the Reformation. This surely added to his sense of support for secular authority, as did much traditional Christian teaching, especially St. Paul in Romans 13.

Yet Luther knew that the state could also be tyrannical, and even that it could persecute the faith and frustrate the preaching of the gospel. So he struggled throughout his authorship with the need to affirm the legitimate role of independent political power (independent of the church but never independent of the judgment of God) while at the same time acknowledging that limits to secular political power might be necessary.

One key document in Luther's developing understanding of politics is "Temporal Authority: To What Extent It Should Be Obeyed." Based on a sermon from 1522 that had made a favorable impression on Duke John of Saxony himself, this treatise is an early attempt by Luther to develop his own ethical concept of the legitimacy and limits of civil power.

Against radical ideas that were beginning to be spoken that the world could be governed in a directly Christian way, Luther insists that this will never be possible in this world:

> If anyone attempted to rule the world by the gospel and to abolish all temporal law and sword on the plea that all are baptized and Christian, and that, according to the gospel, there shall be among them no law or sword—or need for either—pray tell me, friend, what would he be doing? He would be loosing the ropes and chains of the savage wild beasts and letting them bite and mangle everyone. . . . But take heed and first fill the world with real Christians before you attempt to rule in a Christian and evangelical manner (p. 665).

But lest the reader jump to the conclusion that Luther's realism leads him to an unqualified apology for the rights of the state, it is important to go on to read Part II on the limits of authority, which Luther calls "the main part of this treatise." Luther insists that the state can have no ultimate jurisdiction over matters of faith. And he warns the princes against their own temptations toward tyranny:

> Men refuse to endure your tyranny and wantonness much longer. Dear princes and lords, be wise and guide yourselves accordingly. God will no longer tolerate it. . . . Abandon therefore your wicked use of force, give thought to dealing justly, and let God's word have its way, as it will anyway and must and shall; you cannot prevent it. If there is heresy somewhere, let it be overcome, as is proper, with God's word. But if you continue to brandish the sword, take heed lest someone come and compel you to sheathe it—and not in God's name (p. 690f.).

30   To the Councilmen of All Cities in Germany
That They Establish and Maintain Christian Schools

Luther's political views cannot be summarized at all adequately with the simple descriptor "conservative." This is especially evident in the fifth treatise in this part, "To the Councilmen of All Cities in Germany That They Establish and Maintain Christian Schools." This writing, from early in the year 1524, shows Luther deeply concerned with political issues and willing to argue quite vehemently with the authorities in advocating what he thought was needed.

It was a sad and unexpected consequence of the Reformation attack on monasticism that the immediate effects on education were negative. As persons left religious orders, and as their property was seized by nobles with evident greed, the traditional role that these institutions played in educating the young disappeared. It was clear that places which embraced the Reformation would either have to submit to a lowering of educational standards or find a new way.

In this treatise Luther urges the councilmen of all German cities to make new provision for public education. It shows us the continuing sense in which Luther was himself a humanist, and in which, for questions of living in the world, he placed much trust in learning and in reason.

The treatise contains a fine defense of non-practical liberal learning and a spirited attack by Luther on German miserliness. He also strongly defends educating both boys and girls, and chides parents for their selfishness in keeping children out of school for the short term gain of what they can earn. It is hardly an example of telling those in authority just what they wanted to hear.

31 Whether One May Flee from a Deadly Plague

The final selection in this section shows Luther's combination of theological and practical insight in addressing a typical and terrifying issue from his own day—how Christians should behave in the time of epidemic. Bubonic plague (or black death) swept through Europe many times after its initial terrible outbreak in 1350.

On August 2, 1527 a case of the plague was discovered in Wittenberg. The university was closed and the students sent home, but Luther remained in the city and was busy with the pastoral and practical care of the sick. He was urged by correspondents from various places to give advice on what a Christian's responsibility is at such a time. In November Luther finally got around to responding to a pastor in Breslau in what was published as an open letter to all.

Luther fought against the notion that faith would protect one against the plague, and he urged those who could rightly do so to leave. But some must stay, including doctors, pastors, public officials, and any person on whom an afflicted person is dependent.

Luther also shows a great deal of interest in practical reforms that could help the situation, from locating cemeteries outside the town, to the provision of hospitals for the care of the sick, to cautious behavior on the part of those who have been exposed to the plague.

But the note that sounds most clearly is his appeal for Christians to care for the sick despite any aversion to them and fear of disease. In his typical blunt way Luther says:

> This I well know, that if it were Christ or his mother who were laid low by illness, everybody would be so solicitous and would gladly become a servant or helper. Everyone would want to be bold and fearless; nobody would flee but everyone would come running. . . . If you wish to serve Christ and to wait on him, very well, you have your sick neighbor close at hand. Go to him and serve him, and you will surely find Christ in him . . . (p. 747).

The overall impression from these selections challenges the way in which Luther has popularly been taught as the theologian who fostered quiet submission to the powers that control this world. We see his reforming energies at work on a range of questions—political, sexual, educational, pastoral. He is a man feeling his way from the one thing he knows securely—the gospel of Jesus Christ—to a whole range of secondary but pressing questions that Christians must face in every generation.

26.

THE FREEDOM
OF A CHRISTIAN

LETTER OF DEDICATION TO MAYOR MÜHLPHORDT

To the learned and wise gentleman, Hieronymus Mühlphordt,[1] mayor of Zwickau, my exceptionally gracious friend and patron, I, Martin Luther, Augustinian, present my compliments and good wishes.

My learned and wise sir and gracious friend, the venerable Master Johann Egran, your praiseworthy preacher, spoke to me in terms of praise concerning your love for and pleasure in the Holy Scripture, which you also diligently confess and unceasingly praise before all men. For this reason he desired to make me acquainted with you. I yielded willingly and gladly to his persuasion, for it is a special pleasure to hear of someone who loves divine truth. Unfortunately there are many people, especially those who are proud of their titles, who oppose the truth with all their power and cunning. Admittedly it must be that Christ, set as a stumbling block and a sign that is spoken against, will be an offense and a cause for the fall and rising of many [I Cor. 1:23; Luke 2:34].

In order to make a good beginning of our acquaintance and friendship, I have wished to dedicate to you this treatise or discourse in German, which I have already dedicated to the people in Latin, in the hope that my teachings and writings concerning the papacy will not be considered objectionable by anybody. I commend myself to you and to the grace of God. Amen. Wittenberg, 1520.[2]

---

[1] The given name of Mühlphordt was Hermann, not Hieronymus, as Luther has it.

[2] In place of the German version of the treatise which Luther sent to Mühlphordt, the Latin version dedicated to the pope is used as the basis of the English translation in this volume.

AN OPEN LETTER TO POPE LEO X

To Leo X, Pope at Rome, Martin Luther wishes salvation in Christ Jesus our Lord. Amen.

Living among the monsters of this age with whom I am now for the third year waging war, I am compelled occasionally to look up to you, Leo, most blessed father, and to think of you. Indeed, since you are occasionally regarded as the sole cause of my warfare, I cannot help thinking of you. To be sure, the undeserved raging of your godless flatterers against me has compelled me to appeal from your see to a future council, despite the decrees of your predecessors Pius and Julius, who with a foolish tyranny forbade such an appeal. Nevertheless, I have never alienated myself from Your Blessedness to such an extent that I should not with all my heart wish you and your see every blessing, for which I have besought God with earnest prayers to the best of my ability. It is true that I have been so bold as to despise and look down upon those who have tried to frighten me with the majesty of your name and authority. There is one thing, however, which I cannot ignore and which is the cause of my writing once more to Your Blessedness. It has come to my attention that I am accused of great indiscretion, said to be my great fault, in which, it is said, I have not spared even your person.

I freely vow that I have, to my knowledge, spoken only good and honorable words concerning you whenever I have thought of you. If I had ever done otherwise, I myself could by no means condone it, but should agree entirely with the judgment which others have formed of me; and I should do nothing more gladly than recant such indiscretion and impiety. I have called you a Daniel in Babylon; and everyone who reads what I have written knows how zealously I defended your innocence against your defamer Sylvester.[3] Indeed, your reputation and the fame of your blameless life, celebrated as they are throughout the world by the

---

[3] Sylvester Mazzolini (1456-1523), usually called Prierias after Prierio, the city of his birth, had published three books against Luther. In these he had exaggerated the authority of the papacy.

writings of many great men, are too well known and too honorable to be assailed by anyone, no matter how great he is. I am not so foolish as to attack one whom all people praise. As a matter of fact, I have always tried, and will always continue, not to attack even those whom the public dishonors, for I take no pleasure in the faults of any man, since I am conscious of the beam in my own eye. I could not, indeed, be the first one to cast a stone at the adulteress [John 8:1-11].

I have, to be sure, sharply attacked ungodly doctrines in general, and I have snapped at my opponents, not because of their bad morals, but because of their ungodliness. Rather than repent this in the least, I have determined to persist in that fervent zeal and to despise the judgment of men, following the example of Christ who in his zeal called his opponents "a brood of vipers," "blind fools," "hypocrites," "children of the devil" [Matt. 23:13, 17, 33; John 8:44]. Paul branded Magus [Elymas, the magician] as the "son of the devil, . . . full of all deceit and villainy" [Acts 13:10], and he calls others "dogs," "deceivers," and "adulterers" [Phil 3:2; II Cor. 11:13; 2:17]. If you will allow people with sensitive feelings to judge, they would consider no person more stinging and unrestrained in his denunciations than Paul. Who is more stinging than the prophets? Nowadays, it is true, we are made so sensitive by the raving crowd of flatterers that we cry out that we are stung as soon as we meet with disapproval. When we cannot ward off the truth with any other pretext, we flee from it by ascribing it to a fierce temper, impatience, and immodesty. What is the good of salt if it does not bite? Of what use is the edge of a sword if it does not cut? "Cursed is he who does the work of the Lord deceitfully . . ." [Jer. 48:10].

Therefore, most excellent Leo, I beg you to give me a hearing after I have vindicated myself by this letter, and believe me when I say that I have never thought ill of you personally, that I am the kind of a person who would wish you all good things eternally, and that I have no quarrel with any man concerning his morals but only concerning the word of truth. In all other matters I will yield to any man whatsoever; but I have neither the power nor the will to deny the Word of God. If any man has a different opinion concerning me, he does not think straight or understand what I have actually said.

I have truly despised your see, the Roman Curia, which, however, neither you nor anyone else can deny is more corrupt than any Babylon or Sodom ever was, and which, as far as I can see, is characterized by a completely depraved, hopeless, and notorious godlessness. I have been thoroughly incensed over the fact that good Christians are mocked in your name and under the cloak of the Roman church I have resisted and will continue to resist your see as long as the spirit of faith lives in me. Not that I shall strive for the impossible or hope that by my efforts alone anything will be accomplished in that most disordered Babylon, where the fury of so many flatterers is turned against me; but I acknowledge my indebtedness to my Christian brethren, whom I am duty-bound to warn so that fewer of them may be destroyed by the plagues of Rome, at least so that their destruction may be less cruel.

As you well know, there has been flowing from Rome these many years—like a flood covering the world—nothing but a devastation of men's bodies and souls and possessions, the worst examples of the worst of all things. All this is clearer than day to all, and the Roman church, once the holiest of all, has become the most licentious den of thieves [Matt. 21:13], the most shameless of all brothels, the kingdom of sin, death, and hell. It is so bad that even Antichrist himself, if he should come, could think of nothing to add to its wickedness.

Meanwhile you, Leo, sit as a lamb in the midst of wolves [Matt. 10:16] and like Daniel in the midst of lions [Dan. 6:16]. With Ezekiel you live among scorpions [Ezek. 2:6]. How can you alone oppose these monsters? Even if you would call to your aid three or four well learned and thoroughly reliable cardinals, what are these among so many? You would all be poisoned[4] before you could begin to issue a decree for the purpose of remedying the situation. The Roman Curia is already lost, for God's wrath has relentlessly fallen upon it. It detests church councils, it fears a reformation, it cannot allay its own corruption; and what was

---

[4] An attempt to poison Leo X had been made in the summer of 1517.

said of its mother Babylon also applies to it: "We would have cured Babylon, but she was not healed. Let us forsake her" [Jer. 51:9].

It was your duty and that of your cardinals to remedy these evils, but the gout of these evils makes a mockery of the healing hand, and neither chariot nor horse responds to the rein [Virgil, *Georgics* i. 514]. Moved by this affection for you, I have always been sorry, most excellent Leo, that you were made pope in these times, for you are worthy of being pope in better days. The Roman Curia does not deserve to have you or men like you, but it should have Satan himself as pope, for he now actually rules in that Babylon more than you do.

Would that you might discard that which your most profligate enemies boastfully claim to be your glory and might live on a small priestly income of your own or on your family inheritance! No persons are worthy of glorying in that honor except the Iscariots, the sons of perdition. What do you accomplish in the Roman Curia, my Leo? The more criminal and detestable a man is, the more gladly will he use your name to destroy men's possessions and souls, to increase crime, to suppress faith and truth and God's whole church. O most unhappy Leo, you are sitting on a most dangerous throne. I am telling you the truth because I wish you well.

If Bernard felt sorry for Eugenius[5] at a time when the Roman See, which, although even then very corrupt, was ruled with better prospects for improvement, why should not we complain who for three hundred years have had such a great increase of corruption and wickedness? Is it not true that under the vast expanse of heaven there is nothing more corrupt, more pestilential, more offensive than the Roman Curia? It surpasses beyond all comparison the godlessness of the Turks so that, indeed, although it was once a gate of heaven, it is now an open mouth of hell, such a mouth that it cannot be shut because of the wrath of God. Only one thing can

---

[5] Bernard of Clairvaux wrote a devotional book, *On Consideration*, to Pope Eugenius III (1145-53), in which he discussed the duties of the pope and the dangers connected with his office. Migne 182, 727-808.

we try to do, as I have said:[6] we may be able to call back a few from that yawning chasm of Rome and save them.

Now you see, my Father Leo, how and why I have so violently attacked that pestilential see. So far have I been from raving against your person that I even hoped I might gain your favor and save you if I should make a strong and stinging assault upon that prison, that veritable hell of yours. For you and your salvation and the salvation of many others with you will be served by everything that men of ability can do against the confusion of this wicked Curia. They serve your office who do every harm to the Curia; they glorify Christ who in every way curse it. In short, they are Christians who are not Romans.

To enlarge upon this, I never intended to attack the Roman Curia or to raise any controversy concerning it. But when I saw all efforts to save it were hopeless, I despised it, gave it a bill of divorce [Deut. 24:1], and said, "Let the evildoer still do evil, and the filthy still be filthy" [Rev. 22:11]. Then I turned to the quiet and peaceful study of the Holy Scriptures so that I might be helpful to my brothers around me. When I had made some progress in these studies, Satan opened his eyes and then filled his servant Johann Eck, a notable enemy of Christ, with an insatiable lust for glory and thus aroused him to drag me unawares to a debate, seizing me by means of one little word which I had let slip concerning the primacy of the Roman church. Then that boastful braggart,[7] frothing and gnashing his teeth, declared that he would risk everything for the glory of God and the honor of the Apostolic See. Puffed up with the prospect of abusing your authority, he looked forward with great confidence to a victory over me. He was concerned not so much with establishing the primacy of Peter as he was with demonstrating his own leadership among the theologians of our time. To that end he considered it no small advantage to triumph over Luther. When the debate ended badly for the sophist, an unbelievable madness overcame the man, for he believed that it was his fault alone which was responsible for my disclosing all the infamy of Rome.

---

[6] Cf. p. 588, par. 1.

[7] Thrasó, in the original, is the name of a braggart soldier in Terence's *Eunuch.*

Allow me, I pray, most excellent Leo, this once to plead my cause and to indict your real enemies. You know, I believe, what dealings your legate, cardinal of St. Sisto,[8] an unwise and unfortunate, or rather, an unreliable man, had with me. When out of reverence for your name I had placed myself and my cause in his hands, he did not try to establish peace. He could easily have done so with a single word, for at that time I promised to keep silent and to end the controversy, provided my opponents were ordered to do likewise. As he was a man who sought glory, however, and was not content with such an agreement, he began to defend my opponents, to give them full freedom, and to order me to recant, even though this was not included in his instructions. When matters went fairly well, he with his churlish arbitrariness made them far worse. Therefore Luther is not to blame for what followed. All the blame is Cajetan's, who did not permit me to keep silent, as I at that time most earnestly requested him to do. What more should I have done?

There followed Karl Miltitz,[9] also a nuncio of Your Holiness, who exerted much effort and traveled back and forth, omitting nothing that might help restore the order which Cajetan had rashly and arrogantly disturbed. He finally, with the help of the most illustrious prince, the Elector Frederick, managed to arrange several private conferences with me.[10] Again I yielded out of respect for your name, was prepared to keep silent, and even accepted as arbiter either the archbishop of Trier or the bishop of Naumburg. So matters were arranged. But while this arrangement was being followed with good prospects of success, behold, that other and greater enemy of yours, Eck, broke in with the Leipzig Debate which he had undertaken against Dr. Karlstadt. When the new question of the primacy of the pope was raised, he suddenly turned his weapons against me and completely upset our arrangement for maintaining peace. Meanwhile Karl Miltitz waited. The debate was held and judges were selected. But again no decision was

---

[8]Cardinal Cajetan, cf. *LW* 31, 264 n. 10.
[9]Karl von Miltitz had induced Luther to be silent with respect to the indulgence controversy, provided his opponents did likewise.
[10] At Altenburg on January 5 or 6, 1519.

reached, which is not surprising, for through Eck's lies, tricks, and wiles everything was stirred up, aggravated, and confused worse than ever. Regardless of the decision which might have been reached, a greater conflagration would have resulted, for he sought glory, not the truth. Again I left undone nothing that I ought to have done.

I admit that on this occasion no small amount of corrupt Roman practices came to light, but whatever wrong was done was Eck's fault, who undertook a task beyond his capacities. Striving insanely for his own glory, he revealed the shame of Rome to all the world. This man is your enemy, my dear Leo, or rather the enemy of your Curia. From his example alone we can learn that no enemy is more pernicious than a flatterer. What did he accomplish with his flattery but an evil which not even a king could have accomplished? The name of the Roman Curia is today a stench throughout the world, papal authority languishes, and Roman ignorance, once honored, is in ill repute. We should have heard nothing of all this if Eck had not upset the peace arrangements made by Karl [von Miltitz] and myself. Eck himself now clearly sees this and, although it is too late and to no avail, he is furious that my books were published. He should have thought of this when, like a whinnying horse, he was madly seeking his own glory and preferred his own advantage through you and at the greatest peril to you. The vain man thought that I would stop and keep silent out of fear for your name, for I do not believe that he entirely trusted his cleverness and learning. Now that he sees that I have more courage than that and have not been silenced, he repents of his rashness, but too late, and perceives—if indeed he does finally understand—that there is One in heaven who opposes the proud and humbles the haughty [I Pet. 5:5; Jth. 6:15].

Since we gained nothing from this debate except greater confusion to the Roman cause, Karl Miltitz, in a third attempt to bring about peace, came to the fathers of the Augustinian Order assembled in their chapter and sought their advice in settling the controversy which had now grown most disturbing and dangerous. Because, by God's favor, they had no hope of proceeding against me by violent means, some of their most famous men were sent to me. These men asked me at least to show honor to the person of Your Blessedness and in a humble letter to plead as my excuse your innocence and mine in the matter. They said that the affair was not yet in a hopeless state, provided Leo X out of his innate goodness would take a hand in it. As I have always both offered and desired peace so that I might devote myself to quieter and more useful studies, and have stormed with such great fury merely for the purpose of overwhelming my unequal opponents by the volume and violence of words no less than of intellect, I not only gladly ceased but also joyfully and thankfully considered this suggestion a very welcome kindness to me, provided our hope could be realized.

So I come, most blessed father, and, prostrate before you, pray that if possible you intervene and stop those flatterers, who are the enemies of peace while they pretend to keep peace. But let no person imagine that I will recant unless he prefer to involve the whole question in even greater turmoil. Furthermore, I acknowledge no fixed rules for the interpretation of the Word of God, since the Word of God, which teaches freedom in all other matters, must not be bound [II Tim. 2:9]. If these two points are granted, there is nothing that I could not or would not most willingly do or endure. I detest contentions. I will challenge no one. On the other hand, I do not want others to challenge me. If they do, as Christ is my teacher, I will not be speechless. When once this controversy has been cited before you and settled, Your Blessedness will be able with a brief and ready word to silence both parties and command them to keep the peace. That is what I have always wished to hear.

Therefore, my Father Leo, do not listen to those sirens who pretend that you are no mere man but a demigod so that you may command and require whatever you wish. It will not be done in that manner and you will not have such remarkable power. You are a servant of servants,[11] and more than all other men you are in a most miserable and dangerous position. Be not deceived by those who pretend that you are lord of the world, allow no one

---

[11] *Servus servorum* was the usual title of the pope.

to be considered a Christian unless he accepts your authority, and prate that you have power over heaven, hell, and purgatory. These men are your enemies who seek to destroy your soul [I Kings 19:10], as Isaiah says: "O my people, they that call thee blessed, the same deceive thee" [Isa. 3:12]. They err who exalt you above a council and the church universal. They err who ascribe to you alone the right of interpreting Scripture. Under the protection of your name they seek to gain support for all their wicked deeds in the church. Alas! Through them Satan has already made much progress under your predecessors. In short, believe none who exalt you, believe those who humble you. This is the judgment of God, that ". . . he has put down the mighty from their thrones and exalted those of low degree" [Luke 1:52]. See how different Christ is from his successors, although they all would wish to be his vicars. I fear that most of them have been too literally his vicars. A man is a vicar only when his superior is absent. If the pope rules, while Christ is absent and does not dwell in his heart, what else is he but a vicar of Christ? What is the church under such a vicar but a mass of people without Christ? Indeed, what is such a vicar but an antichrist and an idol? How much more properly did the apostles call themselves servants of the present Christ and not vicars of an absent Christ?

Perhaps I am presumptuous in trying to instruct so exalted a personage from whom we all should learn and from whom the thrones of judges receive their decisions, as those pestilential fellows of yours boast. But I am following the example of St. Bernard in his book, *On Consideration*,[12] to Pope Eugenius, a book every pope should know from memory. I follow him, not because I am eager to instruct you, but out of pure and loyal concern which compels us to be interested in all the affairs of our neighbors, even when they are protected, and which does not permit us to take into consideration either their dignity or lack of dignity since it is only concerned with the dangers they face or the advantages they may gain. I know that Your Blessedness is driven and buffeted about in Rome, that is, that far out at sea you are threatened on all sides

---

[12]Cf. p. 589, n. 5.

by dangers and are working very hard in the miserable situation so that you are in need of even the slightest help of the least of your brothers. Therefore I do not consider it absurd if I now forget your exalted office and do what brotherly love demands. I have no desire to flatter you in so serious and dangerous a matter. If men do not perceive that I am your friend and your most humble subject in this matter, there is One who understands and judges [John 8:50].

Finally, that I may not approach you empty-handed, blessed father, I am sending you this little treatise[18] dedicated to you as a token of peace and good hope. From this book you may judge with what studies I should prefer to be more profitably occupied, as I could be, provided your godless flatterers would permit me and had permitted me in the past. It is a small book if you regard its size. Unless I am mistaken, however, it contains the whole of Christian life in a brief form, provided you grasp its meaning. I am a poor man and have no other gift to offer, and you do not need to be enriched by any but a spiritual gift. May the Lord Jesus preserve you forever. Amen.

Wittenberg, September 6, 1520.

MARTIN LUTHER'S TREATISE ON CHRISTIAN LIBERTY
[THE FREEDOM OF A CHRISTIAN]

Many people have considered Christian faith an easy thing, and not a few have given it a place among the virtues. They do this because they have not experienced it and have never tasted the great strength there is in faith. It is impossible to write well about it or to understand what has been written about it unless one has at one time or another experienced the courage which faith gives a man when trials oppress him. But he who has had even a faint taste of it can never write, speak, meditate, or hear enough concerning it. It is a living "spring of water welling up to eternal life," as Christ calls it in John 4 [:14].

As for me, although I have no wealth of faith to boast of and

---

[18] *The Freedom of a Christian.*

know how scant my supply is, I nevertheless hope that I have attained to a little faith, even though I have been assailed by great and various temptations; and I hope that I can discuss it, if not more elegantly, certainly more to the point, than those literalists and subtile disputants have previously done, who have not even understood what they have written.

To make the way smoother for the unlearned—for only them do I serve—I shall set down the following two propositions concerning the freedom and the bondage of the spirit:

A Christian is a perfectly free lord of all, subject to none.

A Christian is a perfectly dutiful servant of all, subject to all.

These two theses seem to contradict each other. If, however, they should be found to fit together they would serve our purpose beautifully. Both are Paul's own statements, who says in I Cor. 9 [:19], "For though I am free from all men, I have made myself a slave to all," and in Rom. 13 [:8], "Owe no one anything, except to love one another." Love by its very nature is ready to serve and be subject to him who is loved. So Christ, although he was Lord of all, was "born of woman, born under the law" [Gal. 4:4], and therefore was at the same time a free man and a servant, "in the form of God" and "of a servant" [Phil. 2:6-7].

Let us start, however, with something more remote from our subject, but more obvious. Man has a twofold nature, a spiritual and a bodily one. According to the spiritual nature, which men refer to as the soul, he is called a spiritual, inner, or new man. According to the bodily nature, which men refer to as flesh, he is called a carnal, outward, or old man, of whom the Apostle writes in II Cor. 4 [:16], "Though our outer nature is wasting away, our inner nature is being renewed every day." Because of this diversity of nature the Scriptures assert contradictory things concerning the same man, since these two men in the same man contradict each other, "for the desires of the flesh are against the Spirit, and the desires of the Spirit are against the flesh," according to Gal. 5 [:17].

First, let us consider the inner man to see how a righteous, free, and pious Christian, that is, a spiritual, new, and inner man, becomes what he is. It is evident that no external thing has any influence in producing Christian righteousness or freedom, or in producing unrighteousness or servitude. A simple argument will furnish the proof of this statement. What can it profit the soul if the body is well, free, and active, and eats, drinks, and does as it pleases? For in these respects even the most godless slaves of vice may prosper. On the other hand, how will poor health or imprisonment or hunger or thirst or any other external misfortune harm the soul? Even the most godly men, and those who are free because of clear consciences, are afflicted with these things. None of these things touch either the freedom or the servitude of the soul. It does not help the soul if the body is adorned with the sacred robes of priests or dwells in sacred places or is occupied with sacred duties or prays, fasts, abstains from certain kinds of food, or does any work that can be done by the body and in the body. The righteousness and the freedom of the soul require something far different since the things which have been mentioned could be done by any wicked person. Such works produce nothing but hypocrites. On the other hand, it will not harm the soul if the body is clothed in secular dress, dwells in unconsecrated places, eats and drinks as others do, does not pray aloud, and neglects to do all the above-mentioned things which hypocrites can do.

Furthermore, to put aside all kinds of works, even contemplation, meditation, and all that the soul can do, does not help. One thing, and only one thing, is necessary for Christian life, righteousness, and freedom. That one thing is the most holy Word of God, the gospel of Christ, as Christ says, John 11 [:25], "I am the resurrection and the life; he who believes in me, though he die, yet shall he live"; and John 8 [:36], "So if the Son makes you free, you will be free indeed"; and Matt. 4 [:4], "Man shall not live by bread alone, but by every word that proceeds from the mouth of God." Let us then consider it certain and firmly established that the soul can do without anything except the Word of God and that where the Word of God is missing there is no help at all for the soul. If it has the Word of God it is rich and lacks nothing since it is the Word of life, truth, light, peace, righteousness, salvation, joy, liberty, wisdom, power, grace, glory, and of every incalculable blessing. This is why the prophet in the entire Psalm [119] and in many other places yearns and sighs for the Word of God and uses so many names to describe it.

On the other hand, there is no more terrible disaster with which the wrath of God can afflict men than a famine of the hearing of his Word, as he says in Amos [8:11]. Likewise there is no greater mercy than when he sends forth his Word, as we read in Psalm 107 [:20]: "He sent forth his word, and healed them, and delivered them from destruction." Nor was Christ sent into the world for any other ministry except that of the Word. Moreover, the entire spiritual estate—all the apostles, bishops, and priests—has been called and instituted only for the ministry of the Word.

You may ask, "What then is the Word of God, and how shall it be used, since there are so many words of God?" I answer: The Apostle explains this in Romans 1. The Word is the gospel of God concerning his Son, who was made flesh, suffered, rose from the dead, and was glorified through the Spirit who sanctifies. To preach Christ means to feed the soul, make it righteous, set it free, and save it, provided it believes the preaching. Faith alone is the saving and efficacious use of the Word of God, according to Rom. 10 [:9]: "If you confess with your lips that Jesus is Lord and believe in your heart that God raised him from the dead, you will be saved." Furthermore, "Christ is the end of the law, that every one who has faith may be justified" [Rom. 10:4]. Again, in Rom. 1 [:17], "He who through faith is righteous shall live." The Word of God cannot be received and cherished by any works whatever but only by faith. Therefore it is clear that, as the soul needs only the Word of God for its life and righteousness, so it is justified by faith alone and not any works; for if it could be justified by anything else, it would not need the Word, and consequently it would not need faith.

This faith cannot exist in connection with works—that is to say, if you at the same time claim to be justified by works, whatever their character—for that would be the same as "limping with two different opinions" [I Kings 18:21], as worshiping Baal and kissing one's own hand [Job 31:27-28], which, as Job says, is a very great iniquity. Therefore the moment you begin to have faith you learn that all things in you are altogether blameworthy, sinful, and damnable, as the Apostle says in Rom. 3 [:23], "Since all have sinned and fall short of the glory of God," and, "None is righteous, no, not one; . . . all have turned aside, together they have gone wrong" (Rom. 3:10-12). When you have learned this you will know that you need Christ, who suffered and rose again for you so that, if you believe in him, you may through this faith become a new man in so far as your sins are forgiven and you are justified by the merits of another, namely, of Christ alone.

Since, therefore, this faith can rule only in the inner man, as Rom. 10 [:10] says, "For man believes with his heart and so is justified," and since faith alone justifies, it is clear that the inner man cannot be justified, freed, or saved by any outer work or action at all, and that these works, whatever their character, have nothing to do with this inner man. On the other hand, only ungodliness and unbelief of heart, and no outer work, make him guilty and a damnable servant of sin. Wherefore it ought to be the first concern of every Christian to lay aside all confidence in works and increasingly to strengthen faith alone and through faith to grow in the knowledge, not of works, but of Christ Jesus, who suffered and rose for him, as Peter teaches in the last chapter of his first Epistle (I Pet. 5:10). No other work makes a Christian. Thus when the Jews asked Christ, as related in John 6 [:28], what they must do "to be doing the work of God," he brushed aside the multitude of works which he saw they did in great profusion and suggested one work, saying, "This is the work of God, that you believe in him whom he has sent" [John 6:29]; "for on him has God the Father set his seal" [John 6:27].

Therefore true faith in Christ is a treasure beyond comparison which brings with it complete salvation and saves man from every evil, as Christ says in the last chapter of Mark [16:16]: "He who believes and is baptized will be saved; but he who does not believe will be condemned." Isaiah contemplated this treasure and foretold it in chapter 10: "The Lord will make a small and consuming word upon the land, and it will overflow with righteousness" [Cf. Isa. 10:22]. This is as though he said, "Faith, which is a small and perfect fulfilment of the law, will fill believers with so great a righteousness that they will need nothing more to become righteous." So Paul says, Rom. 10 [:10], "For man believes with his heart and so is justified."

Should you ask how it happens that faith alone justifies and offers us such a treasure of great benefits without works in view of the fact that so many works, ceremonies, and laws are prescribed in the Scriptures, I answer: First of all, remember what has been said, namely, that faith alone, without works, justifies, frees, and saves; we shall make this clearer later on. Here we must point out that the entire Scripture of God is divided into two parts: commandments and promises. Although the commandments teach things that are good, the things taught are not done as soon as they are taught, for the commandments show us what we ought to do but do not give us the power to do it. They are intended to teach man to know himself, that through them he may recognize his inability to do good and may despair of his own ability. That is why they are called the Old Testament and constitute the Old Testament. For example, the commandment, "You shall not covet" [Exod. 20:17], is a command which proves us all to be sinners, for no one can avoid coveting no matter how much he may struggle against it. Therefore, in order not to covet and to fulfil the commandment, a man is compelled to despair of himself, to seek the help which he does not find in himself elsewhere and from someone else, as stated in Hosea [13:9]: "Destruction is your own, O Israel: your help is only in me." As we fare with respect to one commandment, so we fare with all, for it is equally impossible for us to keep any one of them.

Now when a man has learned through the commandments to recognize his helplessness and is distressed about how he might satisfy the law—since the law must be fulfilled so that not a jot or tittle shall be lost, otherwise man will be condemned without hope—then, being truly humbled and reduced to nothing in his own eyes, he finds in himself nothing whereby he may be justified and saved. Here the second part of Scripture comes to our aid, namely, the promises of God which declare the glory of God, saying, "If you wish to fulfil the law and not covet, as the law demands, come, believe in Christ in whom grace, righteousness, peace, liberty, and all things are promised you. If you believe, you shall have all things; if you do not believe, you shall lack all things." That which is impossible for you to accomplish by trying to fulfil all the works of the law—many and useless as they all are—you will accomplish quickly and easily through faith. God our Father has made all things depend on faith so that whoever has faith will have everything, and whoever does not have faith will have nothing. "For God has consigned all men to disobedience, that he may have mercy upon all," as it is stated in Rom. 11 [:32]. Thus the promises of God give what the commandments of God demand and fulfil what the law prescribes so that all things may be God's alone, both the commandments and the fulfilling of the commandments. He alone commands, he alone fulfils. Therefore the promises of God belong to the New Testament. Indeed, they are the New Testament.

Since these promises of God are holy, true, righteous, free, and peaceful words, full of goodness, the soul which clings to them with a firm faith will be so closely united with them and altogether absorbed by them that it not only will share in all their power but will be saturated and intoxicated by them. If a touch of Christ healed, how much more will this most tender spiritual touch, this absorbing of the Word, communicate to the soul all things that belong to the Word. This, then, is how through faith alone without works the soul is justified by the Word of God, sanctified, made true, peaceful, and free, filled with every blessing and truly made a child of God, as John 1 [:12] says: "But to all who . . . believed in his name, he gave power to become children of God."

From what has been said it is easy to see from what source faith derives such great power and why a good work or all good works together cannot equal it. No good work can rely upon the Word of God or live in the soul, for faith alone and the Word of God rule in the soul. Just as the heated iron glows like fire because of the union of fire with it, so the Word imparts its qualities to the soul. It is clear, then, that a Christian has all that he needs in faith and needs no works to justify him; and if he has no need of works, he has no need of the law; and if he has no need of the law, surely he is free from the law. It is true that "the law is not laid down for the just" [I Tim. 1:9]. This is that Christian liberty, our faith, which does not induce us to live in idleness or wickedness but makes the law and works unnecessary for any man's righteousness and salvation.

This is the first power of faith. Let us now examine also the second. It is a further function of faith that it honors him whom it trusts with the most reverent and highest regard since it considers him truthful and trustworthy. There is no other honor equal to the estimate of truthfulness and righteousness with which we honor him whom we trust. Could we ascribe to a man anything greater than truthfulness and righteousness and perfect goodness? On the other hand, there is no way in which we can show greater contempt for a man than to regard him as false and wicked and to be suspicious of him, as we do when we do not trust him. So when the soul firmly trusts God's promises, it regards him as truthful and righteous. Nothing more excellent than this can be ascribed to God. The very highest worship of God is this that we ascribe to him truthfulness, righteousness, and whatever else should be ascribed to one who is trusted. When this is done, the soul consents to his will. Then it hallows his name and allows itself to be treated according to God's good pleasure for, clinging to God's promises, it does not doubt that he who is true, just, and wise will do, dispose, and provide all things well.

Is not such a soul most obedient to God in all things by this faith? What commandment is there that such obedience has not completely fulfilled? What more complete fulfilment is there than obedience in all things? This obedience, however, is not rendered by works, but by faith alone. On the other hand, what greater rebellion against God, what greater wickedness, what greater contempt of God is there than not believing his promise? For what is this but to make God a liar or to doubt that he is truthful?—that is, to ascribe truthfulness to one's self but lying and vanity to God? Does not a man who does this deny God and set himself up as an idol in his heart? Then of what good are works done in such wickedness, even if they were the works of angels and apostles? Therefore God has rightly included all things, not under anger or lust, but under unbelief, so that they who imagine that they are fulfilling the law by doing the works of chastity and mercy required by the law (the civil and human virtues) might not be saved. They are included under the sin of unbelief and must either seek mercy or be justly condemned.

When, however, God sees that we consider him truthful and by the faith of our heart pay him the great honor which is due him, he does us that great honor of considering us truthful and righteous for the sake of our faith. Faith works truth and righteousness by giving God what belongs to him. Therefore God in turn glorifies our righteousness. It is true and just that God is truthful and just, and to consider and confess him to be so is the same as being truthful and just. Accordingly he says in I Sam. 2 [:30], "Those who honor me I will honor, and those who despise me shall be lightly esteemed." So Paul says in Rom. 4 [:3] that Abraham's faith "was reckoned to him as righteousness" because by it he gave glory most perfectly to God, and that for the same reason our faith shall be reckoned to us as righteousness if we believe.

The third incomparable benefit of faith is that it unites the soul with Christ as a bride is united with her bridegroom. By this mystery, as the Apostle teaches, Christ and the soul become one flesh [Eph. 5:31-32]. And if they are one flesh and there is between them a true marriage—indeed the most perfect of all marriages, since human marriages are but poor examples of this one true marriage—it follows that everything they have they hold in common, the good as well as the evil. Accordingly the believing soul can boast of and glory in whatever Christ has as though it were its own, and whatever the soul has Christ claims as his own. Let us compare these and we shall see inestimable benefits. Christ is full of grace, life, and salvation. The soul is full of sins, death, and damnation. Now let faith come between them and sins, death, and damnation will be Christ's, while grace, life, and salvation will be the soul's; for if Christ is a bridegroom, he must take upon himself the things which are his bride's and bestow upon her the things that are his. If he gives her his body and very self, how shall he not give her all that is his? And if he takes the body of the bride, how shall he not take all that is hers?

Here we have a most pleasing vision not only of communion but of a blessed struggle and victory and salvation and redemption. Christ is God and man in one person. He has neither sinned nor died, and is not condemned, and he cannot sin, die, or be condemned; his righteousness, life, and salvation are unconquerable, eternal, omnipotent. By the wedding ring of faith he shares in the sins, death, and pains of hell which are his bride's. As a matter of fact, he makes them his own and acts as if they were his own and as if he himself had sinned; he suffered, died, and descended into hell that he might overcome them all. Now since it was such a one who did all this, and death and hell could not swallow him up, these were necessarily swallowed up by him in a mighty duel; for his righteousness is greater than the sins of all men, his life stronger than death, his salvation more invincible than hell. Thus the believing soul by means of the pledge of its faith is free in Christ, its bridegroom, free from all sins, secure against death and hell, and is endowed with the eternal righteousness, life, and salvation of Christ its bridegroom. So he takes to himself a glorious bride, "without spot or wrinkle, cleansing her by the washing of water with the word" [Cf. Eph. 5:26-27] of life, that is, by faith in the Word of life, righteousness, and salvation. In this way he marries her in faith, steadfast love, and in mercies, righteousness, and justice, as Hos. 2 [:19-20] says.

Who then can fully appreciate what this royal marriage means? Who can understand the riches of the glory of this grace? Here this rich and divine bridegroom Christ marries this poor, wicked harlot, redeems her from all her evil, and adorns her with all his goodness. Her sins cannot now destroy her, since they are laid upon Christ and swallowed up by him. And she has that righteousness in Christ, her husband, of which she may boast as of her own and which she can confidently display alongside her sins in the face of death and hell and say, "If I have sinned, yet my Christ, in whom I believe, has not sinned, and all his is mine and all mine is his," as the bride in the Song of Solomon [2:16] says, "My beloved is mine and I am his." This is what Paul means when he says in I Cor. 15 [:57], "Thanks be to God, who gives us the victory through our Lord Jesus Christ," that is, the victory over sin and death, as he also says there, "The sting of death is sin, and the power of sin is the law" [I Cor. 15:56].

From this you once more see that much is ascribed to faith,

namely, that it alone can fulfil the law and justify without works. You see that the First Commandment, which says, "You shall worship one God," is fulfilled by faith alone. Though you were nothing but good works from the soles of your feet to the crown of your head, you would still not be righteous or worship God or fulfil the First Commandment, since God cannot be worshiped unless you ascribe to him the glory of truthfulness and all goodness which is due him. This cannot be done by works but only by the faith of the heart. Not by the doing of works but by believing do we glorify God and acknowledge that he is truthful. Therefore faith alone is the righteousness of a Christian and the fulfilling of all the commandments, for he who fulfils the First Commandment has no difficulty in fulfilling all the rest.

But works, being inanimate things, cannot glorify God, although they can, if faith is present, be done to the glory of God. Here, however, we are not inquiring what works and what kind of works are done, but who it is that does them, who glorifies God and brings forth the works. This is done by faith which dwells in the heart and is the source and substance of all our righteousness. Therefore it is a blind and dangerous doctrine which teaches that the commandments must be fulfilled by works. The commandments must be fulfilled before any works can be done, and the works proceed from the fulfilment of the commandments [Rom. 13:10], as we shall hear.

That we may examine more profoundly that grace which our inner man has in Christ, we must realize that in the Old Testament God consecrated to himself all the first-born males. The birthright was highly prized for it involved a twofold honor, that of priesthood and that of kingship. The first-born brother was priest and lord over all the others and a type of Christ, the true and only first-born of God the Father and the Virgin Mary and true king and priest, but not after the fashion of the flesh and the world, for his kingdom is not of this world [John 18:36]. He reigns in heavenly and spiritual things and consecrates them—things such as righteousness, truth, wisdom, peace, salvation, etc. This does not mean that all things on earth and in hell are not also subject to him—otherwise how could he protect and save us from them?

—but that his kingdom consists neither in them nor of them. Nor does his priesthood consist in the outer splendor of robes and postures like those of the human priesthood of Aaron and our present-day church; but it consists of spiritual things through which he by an invisible service intercedes for us in heaven before God, there offers himself as a sacrifice, and does all things a priest should do, as Paul describes him under the type of Melchizedek in the Epistle to the Hebrews [Heb. 6-7]. Nor does he only pray and intercede for us but he teaches us inwardly through the living instruction of his Spirit, thus performing the two real functions of a priest, of which the prayers and the preaching of human priests are visible types.

Now just as Christ by his birthright obtained these two prerogatives, so he imparts them to and shares them with everyone who believes in him according to the law of the above-mentioned marriage, according to which the wife owns whatever belongs to the husband. Hence all of us who believe in Christ are priests and kings in Christ, as I Pet. 2 [:9] says: "You are a chosen race, God's own people, a royal priesthood, a priestly kingdom, that you may declare the wonderful deeds of him who called you out of darkness into his marvelous light."

The nature of this priesthood and kingship is something like this: First, with respect to the kingship, every Christian is by faith so exalted above all things that, by virtue of a spiritual power, he is lord of all things without exception, so that nothing can do him any harm. As a matter of fact, all things are made subject to him and are compelled to serve him in obtaining salvation. Accordingly Paul says in Rom. 8 [:28], "All things work together for good for the elect," and in I Cor. 3 [:21-23], "All things are yours whether . . . life or death or the present or the future, all are yours; and you are Christ's. . . ." This is not to say that every Christian is placed over all things to have and control them by physical power—a madness with which some churchmen are afflicted—for such power belongs to kings, princes, and other men on earth. Our ordinary experience in life shows us that we are subjected to all, suffer many things, and even die. As a matter of fact, the more Christian a man is, the more evils, sufferings, and deaths he must endure, as we see in

Christ the first-born prince himself, and in all his brethren, the saints. The power of which we speak is spirtual. It rules in the midst of enemies and is powerful in the midst of oppression. This means nothing else than that "power is made perfect in weakness" [II Cor. 12:9] and that in all things I can find profit toward salvation [Rom. 8:28], so that the cross and death itself are compelled to serve me and to work together with me for my salvation. This is a splendid privilege and hard to attain, a truly omnipotent power, a spiritual dominion in which there is nothing so good and nothing so evil but that it shall work together for good to me, if only I believe. Yes, since faith alone suffices for salvation, I need nothing except faith exercising the power and dominion of its own liberty. Lo, this is the inestimable power and liberty of Christians.

Not only are we the freest of kings, we are also priests forever, which is far more excellent than being kings, for as priests we are worthy to appear before God to pray for others and to teach one another divine things. These are the functions of priests, and they cannot be granted to any unbeliever. Thus Christ has made it possible for us, provided we believe in him, to be not only his brethren, co-heirs, and fellow-kings, but also his fellow-priests. Therefore we may boldly come into the presence of God in the spirit of faith [Heb. 10:19, 22] and cry "Abba, Father!" pray for one another, and do all things which we see done and foreshadowed in the outer and visible works of priests.

He, however, who does not believe is not served by anything. On the contrary, nothing works for his good, but he himself is a servant of all, and all things turn out badly for him because he wickedly uses them to his own advantage and not to the glory of God. So he is no priest but a wicked man whose prayer becomes sin and who never comes into the presence of God because God does not hear sinners [John 9:31]. Who then can comprehend the lofty dignity of the Christian? By virtue of his royal power he rules over all things, death, life, and sin, and through his priestly glory is omnipotent with God because he does the things which God asks and desires, as it is written, "He will fulfil the desire of those who fear him; he also will hear their cry and save them" [Cf.

Phil. 4:13]. To this glory a man attains, certainly not by any works of his, but by faith alone.

From this anyone can clearly see how a Christian is free from all things and over all things so that he needs no works to make him righteous and save him, since faith alone abundantly confers all these things. Should he grow so foolish, however, as to presume to become righteous, free, saved, and a Christian by means of some good work, he would instantly lose faith and all its benefits, a foolishness aptly illustrated in the fable of the dog who runs along a stream with a piece of meat in his mouth and, deceived by the reflection of the meat in the water, opens his mouth to snap at it and so loses both the meat and the reflection.[14]

You will ask, "If all who are in the church are priests, how do these whom we now call priests differ from laymen?" I answer: Injustice is done those words "priest," "cleric," "spiritual," "ecclesiastic," when they are transferred from all Christians to those few who are now by a mischievous usage called "ecclesiastics." Holy Scripture makes no distinction between them, although it gives the name "ministers," "servants," "stewards" to those who are now proudly called popes, bishops, and lords and who should according to the ministry of the Word serve others and teach them the faith of Christ and the freedom of believers. Although we are all equally priests, we cannot all publicly minister and teach. We ought not do so even if we could. Paul writes accordingly in I Cor. 4 [1], "This is how one should regard us, as servants of Christ and stewards of the mysteries of God."

That stewardship, however, has now been developed into so great a display of power and so terrible a tyranny that no heathen empire or other earthly power can be compared with it, just as if laymen were not also Christians. Through this perversion the knowledge of Christian grace, faith, liberty, and of Christ himself has altogether perished, and its place has been taken by an unbearable bondage of human works and laws until we have become, as the Lamentations of Jeremiah [1] say, servants of the vilest men on earth who abuse our misfortune to serve only their base and shameless will.

---

[14] Luther was fond of Aesop's Fables, of which this is one.

To return to our purpose, I believe that it has now become clear that it is not enough or in any sense Christian to preach the works, life, and words of Christ as historical facts, as if the knowledge of these would suffice for the conduct of life; yet this is the fashion among those who must today be regarded as our best preachers. Far less is it sufficient or Christian to say nothing at all about Christ and to teach instead the laws of men and the decrees of the fathers. Now there are not a few who preach Christ and read about him that they may move men's affections to sympathy with Christ, to anger against the Jews, and such childish and effeminate nonsense. Rather ought Christ to be preached to the end that faith in him may be established that he may not only be Christ, but be Christ for you and me, and that what is said of him and is denoted in his name may be effectual in us. Such faith is produced and preserved in us by preaching why Christ came, what he brought and bestowed, what benefit it is to us to accept him. This is done when that Christian liberty which he bestows is rightly taught and we are told in what way we Christians are all kings and priests and therefore lords of all and may firmly believe that whatever we have done is pleasing and acceptable in the sight of God, as I have already said.

What man is there whose heart, upon hearing these things, will not rejoice to its depth, and when receiving such comfort will not grow tender so that he will love Christ as he never could by means of any laws or works? Who would have the power to harm or frighten such a heart? If the knowledge of sin or the fear of death should break in upon it, it is ready to hope in the Lord. It does not grow afraid when it hears tidings of evil. It is not disturbed when it sees its enemies. This is so because it believes that the righteousness of Christ is its own and that its sin is not its own, but Christ's, and that all sin is swallowed up[15] by the righteousness of Christ. This, as has been said above,[15] is a necessary consequence on account of faith in Christ. So the heart learns to scoff at death and sin and to say with the Apostle, "O death, where is thy victory? O death, where is thy sting? The sting of death is sin, and the power of sin is the law. But thanks be to God, who gives us the

---

[15]Cf. p. 604.

victory through our Lord Jesus Christ" [I Cor. 15:55-57]. Death is swallowed up not only in the victory of Christ but also by our victory, because through faith his victory has become ours and in that faith we also are conquerors.

Let this suffice concerning the inner man, his liberty, and the source of his liberty, the righteousness of faith. He needs neither laws nor good works but, on the contrary, is injured by them if he believes that he is justified by them.

Now let us turn to the second part, the outer man. Here we shall answer all those who, offended by the word "faith" and by all that has been said, now ask, "If faith does all things and is alone sufficient unto righteousness, why then are good works commanded? We will take our ease and do no works and be content with faith." I answer: not so, you wicked men, not so. That would indeed be proper if we were wholly inner and perfectly spiritual men. But such we shall be only at the last day, the day of the resurrection of the dead. As long as we live in the flesh we only begin to make some progress in that which shall be perfected in the future life. For this reason the Apostle in Rom. 8 [:23] calls all that we attain in this life "the first fruits of the Spirit" because we shall indeed receive the greater portion, even the fulness of the Spirit, in the future. This is the place to assert that which was said above, namely, that a Christian is the servant of all and made subject to all. Insofar as he is free he does no works, but insofar as he is a servant he does all kinds of works. How this is possible we shall see.

Although, as I have said, a man is abundantly and sufficiently justified by faith inwardly, in his spirit, and so has all that he needs, except insofar as this faith and these riches must grow from day to day even to the future life; yet he remains in this mortal life on earth. In this life he must control his own body and have dealings with men. Here the works begin; here a man cannot enjoy leisure; here he must indeed take care to discipline his body by fastings, watchings, labors, and other reasonable discipline and to subject it to the Spirit so that it will obey and conform to the inner man and faith and not revolt against faith and hinder the inner man, as it is the nature of the body to do if it is not held in check. The inner man, who by faith is created in the image of God, is both joyful and happy because of Christ in whom so many benefits are conferred upon him; and therefore it is his one occupation to serve God joyfully and without thought of gain, in love that is not constrained.

While he is doing this, behold, he meets a contrary will in his own flesh which strives to serve the world and seeks its own advantage. This the spirit of faith cannot tolerate, but with joyful zeal it attempts to put the body under control and hold it in check, as Paul says in Rom. 7 [:22-23], "For I delight in the law of God, in my inmost self, but I see in my members another law at war with the law of my mind and making me captive to the law of sin," and in another place, "But I pommel my body and subdue it, lest after preaching to others I myself should be disqualified" [I Cor. 9:27], and in Galatians [5:24], "And those who belong to Christ Jesus have crucified the flesh with its passions and desires."

In doing these works, however, we must not think that a man is justified before God by them, for faith, which alone is righteousness before God, cannot endure that erroneous opinion. We must, however, realize that these works reduce the body to subjection and purify it of its evil lusts, and our whole purpose is to be directed only toward the driving out of lusts. Since by faith the soul is cleansed and made to love God, it desires that all things, and especially its own body, shall be purified so that all things may join with it in loving and praising God. Hence a man cannot be idle, for the need of his body drives him and he is compelled to do many good works to reduce it to subjection. Nevertheless the works themselves do not justify him before God, but he does the works out of spontaneous love in obedience to God and considers nothing except the approval of God, whom he would most scrupulously obey in all things.

In this way everyone will easily be able to learn for himself the limit and discretion, as they say, of his bodily castigations, for he will fast, watch, and labor as much as he finds sufficient to repress the lasciviousness and lust of his body. But those who presume to be justified by works do not regard the mortifying of the lusts, but only the works themselves, and think that if only they have done as many and as great works as are possible, they have done well and have become righteous. At times they even addle their brains and destroy, or at least render useless, their natural strength with their works. This is the height of folly and utter ignorance of Christian life and faith, that a man should seek to be justified and saved by works and without faith.

In order to make that which we have said more easily understood, we shall explain by analogies. We should think of the works of a Christian who is justified and saved by faith because of the pure and free mercy of God, just as we would think of the works which Adam and Eve did in Paradise, and all their children would have done if they had not sinned. We read in Gen. 2 [:15] that "The Lord God took the man and put him in the garden of Eden to till it and keep it." Now Adam was created righteous and upright and without sin by God so that he had no need of being justified and made upright through his tilling and keeping the garden; but, that he might not be idle, the Lord gave him a task to do, to cultivate and protect the garden. This task would truly have been the freest of works, done only to please God and not to obtain righteousness, which Adam already had in full measure and which would have been the birthright of us all.

The works of a believer are like this. Through his faith he has been restored to Paradise and created anew, has no need of works that he may become or be righteous; but that he may not be idle and may provide for and keep his body, he must do such works freely only to please God. Since, however, we are not wholly recreated, and our faith and love are not yet perfect, these are to be increased, not by external works, however, but of themselves.

A second example: A bishop, when he consecrates a church, confirms children, or performs some other duty belonging to his office, is not made a bishop by these works. Indeed, if he had not first been made a bishop, none of these works would be valid. They would be foolish, childish, and farcical. So the Christian who is consecrated by his faith does good works, but the works do not make him holier or more Christian, for that is the work of faith alone. And if a man were not first a believer and a Christian, all his works would amount to nothing and would be truly wicked and damnable sins.

The following statements are therefore true: "Good works do not make a good man, but a good man does good works; evil works do not make a wicked man, but a wicked man does evil works." Consequently it is always necessary that the substance or person himself be good before there can be any good works, and that good works follow and proceed from the good person, as Christ also says, "A good tree cannot bear evil fruit, nor can a bad tree bear good fruit" [Matt. 7:18]. It is clear that the fruits do not bear the tree and that the tree does not grow on the fruits, also that, on the contrary, the trees bear the fruits and the fruits grow on the trees. As it is necessary, therefore, that the trees exist before their fruits and the fruits do not make trees either good or bad, but rather as the trees are, so are the fruits they bear; so a man must first be good or wicked before he does a good or wicked work, and his works do not make him good or wicked, but he himself makes his works either good or wicked.

Illustrations of the same truth can be seen in all trades. A good or a bad house does not make a good or a bad builder; but a good or a bad builder makes a good or a bad house. And in general, the work never makes the workman like itself, but the workman makes the work like himself. So it is with the works of man. As the man is, whether believer or unbeliever, so also is his work —good if it was done in faith, wicked if it was done in unbelief. But the converse is not true, that the work makes the man either a believer or an unbeliever. As works do not make a man a believer, so also they do not make him righteous. But as faith makes a man a believer and righteous, so faith does good works. Since, then, works justify no one, and a man must be righteous before he does a good work, it is very evident that it is faith alone which, because of the pure mercy of God through Christ and in his Word, worthily and sufficiently justifies and saves the person. A Christian has no need of any work or law in order to be saved since through faith he is free from every law and does everything out of pure liberty and freely. He seeks neither benefit nor salvation since he already abounds in all things and is saved through the grace of God because in his faith he now seeks only to please God.

Furthermore, no good work helps justify or save an unbeliever. On the other hand, no evil work makes him wicked or damns him; but the unbelief which makes the person and the tree evil does the evil and damnable works. Hence when a man is good or evil, this is effected not by the works, but by faith or unbelief, as the Wise Man says, "This is the beginning of sin, that a man falls away from God" [Cf. Sirach 10:14-15], which happens when he does not believe. And Paul says in Heb. 11 [:6], "For whoever would draw near to God must believe. . . ." And Christ says the same: "Either make the tree good, and its fruit good; or make the tree bad, and its fruit bad" [Matt. 12:33], as if he would say, "Let him who wishes to have good fruit begin by planting a good tree." So let him who wishes to do good works begin not with the doing of works, but with believing, which makes the person good, for nothing makes a man good except faith, or evil except unbelief.

It is indeed true that in the sight of men a man is made good or evil by his works; but this being made good or evil only means that the man who is good or evil is pointed out and known as such, as Christ says in Matt. 7 [:20], "Thus you will know them by their fruits." All this remains on the surface, however, and very many have been deceived by this outward appearance and have presumed to write and teach concerning good works by which we may be justified without even mentioning faith. They go their way, always being deceived and deceiving [II Tim. 3:13], progressing, indeed, but into a worse state, blind leaders of the blind, wearying themselves with many works and still never attaining to true righteousness [Matt. 15:14]. Of such people Paul says in II Tim. 3 [5, 7], "Holding the form of religion but denying the power of it . . . who will listen to anybody and can never arrive at a knowledge of the truth."

Whoever, therefore, does not wish to go astray with those blind men must look beyond works, and beyond laws and doctrines about works. Turning his eyes from works, he must look upon the person and ask how he is justified. For the person is justified and saved, not by works or laws, but by the Word of God, that is, by the promise of his grace, and by faith, that the glory may remain God's, who saved us not by works of righteousness which we have done [Titus 3:5], but by virtue of his mercy by the word of his grace when we believed [I Cor. 1:21].

From this it is easy to know how far good works are to be rejected or not, and by what standard all the teachings of men concerning works are to be interpreted. If works are sought after as a means to righteousness, are burdened with this perverse leviathan,[16] and are done under the false impression that through them one is justified, they are made necessary and freedom and faith are destroyed; and this addition to them makes them no longer good but truly damnable works. They are not free, and they blaspheme the grace of God since to justify and to save by faith belongs to the grace of God alone. What the works have no power to do they nevertheless—by a godless presumption through this folly of ours—pretend to do and thus violently force themselves into the office and glory of grace. We do not, therefore, reject good works; on the contrary, we cherish and teach them as much as possible. We do not condemn them for their own sake but on account of this godless addition to them and the perverse idea that righteousness is to be sought through them; for that makes them appear good outwardly, when in truth they are not good. They deceive men and lead them to deceive one another like ravening wolves in sheep's clothing [Matt. 7:15].

But this leviathan, or perverse notion concerning works, is unconquerable where sincere faith is wanting. Those work-saints cannot get rid of it unless faith, its destroyer, comes and rules in their hearts. Nature of itself cannot drive it out or even recognize it, but rather regards it as a mark of the most holy will. If the influence of custom is added and confirms this perverseness of nature, as wicked teachers have caused it to do, it becomes an incurable evil and leads astray and destroys countless men beyond all hope of restoration. Therefore, although it is good to preach and write about penitence, confession, and satisfaction, our teaching is unquestionably deceitful and diabolical if we stop with that and do not go on to teach about faith.

---

[16] Probably a reminiscence of Leviathan, the twisting serpent, in Isa. 27:1.

Christ, like his forerunner John, not only said, "Repent" [Matt. 3:2; 4:17], but added the word of faith, saying, "The kingdom of heaven is at hand." We are not to preach only one of these words of God, but both; we are to bring forth out of our treasure things new and old, the voice of the law as well as the word of grace [Matt. 13:52]. We must bring forth the voice of the law that men may be made to fear and come to a knowledge of their sins and so be converted to repentance and a better life. But we must not stop with that, for that would only amount to wounding and not binding up, smiting and not healing, killing and not making alive, leading down into hell and not bringing back again, humbling and not exalting. Therefore we must also preach the word of grace and the promise of forgiveness by which faith is taught and aroused. Without this word of grace the works of the law, contrition, penitence, and all the rest are done and taught in vain.

Preachers of repentance and grace remain even to our day, but they do not explain God's law and promise that a man might learn from them the source of repentance and grace. Repentance proceeds from the law of God, but faith or grace from the promise of God, as Rom. 10 [:17] says: "So faith comes from what is heard, and what is heard comes by the preaching of Christ." Accordingly man is consoled and exalted by faith in the divine promise after he has been humbled and led to a knowledge of himself by the threats and the fear of the divine law. So we read in Psalm 30 [:5]: "Weeping may tarry for the night, but joy comes with the morning."

Let this suffice concerning works in general and at the same time concerning the works which a Christian does for himself. Lastly, we shall also speak of the things which he does toward his neighbor. A man does not live for himself alone in this mortal body to work for it alone, but he lives also for all men on earth; rather, he lives only for others and not for himself. To this end he brings his body into subjection that he may the more sincerely and freely serve others, as Paul says in Rom. 14 [:7-8], "None of us lives to himself, and none of us dies to himself. If we live, we live to the Lord, and if we die, we die to the Lord." He cannot ever in this life be idle and without works toward his neighbors, for he will necessarily speak, deal with, and exchange views with men, as Christ also, being made in the likeness of men [Phil. 2:7], was found in form as a man and conversed with men, as Baruch 3 [:38] says.

Man, however, needs none of these things for his righteousness and salvation. Therefore he should be guided in all his works by this thought and contemplate this one thing alone, that he may serve and benefit others in all that he does, considering nothing except the need and the advantage of his neighbor. Accordingly the Apostle commands us to work with our hands so that we may give to the needy, although he might have said that we should work to support ourselves. He says, however, "that he may be able to give to those in need" [Eph. 4:28]. This is what makes caring for the body a Christian work, that through its health and comfort we may be able to work, to acquire, and lay by funds with which to aid those who are in need, that in this way the strong member may serve the weaker, and we may be sons of God, each caring for and working for the other, bearing one another's burdens and so fulfilling the law of Christ [Gal. 6:2]. This is a truly Christian life. Here faith is truly active through love [Gal. 5:6], that is, it finds expression in works of the freest service, cheerfully and lovingly done, with which a man willingly serves another without hope of reward; and for himself he is satisfied with the fullness and wealth of his faith.

Accordingly Paul, after teaching the Philippians how rich they were made through faith in Christ, in which they obtained all things, thereafter teaches them, saying, "So if there is any encouragement in Christ, any incentive of love, any participation in the Spirit, any affection and sympathy, complete my joy by being of the same mind, having the same love, being in full accord and of one mind. Do nothing from selfishness or conceit, but in humility count others better than yourselves. Let each of you look not only to his own interests, but also to the interests of others" [Phil. 2:1-4]. Here we see clearly that the Apostle has prescribed this rule for the life of Christians, namely, that we should devote all our works to the welfare of others, since each has such abundant riches in his faith that all his other works and his whole life are a surplus with which he can by voluntary benevolence serve and do good to his neighbor.

As an example of such life the Apostle cites Christ, saying, "Have this mind among yourselves, which you have in Christ Jesus, who, though he was in the form of God, did not count equality with God a thing to be grasped, but emptied himself, taking the form of a servant, being born in the likeness of men. And being found in human form he humbled himself and became obedient unto death" [Phil. 2:5-8]. This salutary word of the Apostle has been obscured for us by those who have not at all understood his words, "form of God," "form of a servant," "human form," "likeness of men," and have applied them to the divine and the human nature. Paul means this: Although Christ was filled with the form of God and rich in all good things, so that he needed no work and no suffering to make him righteous and saved (for he had all this eternally), yet he was not puffed up by them and did not exalt himself above us and assume power over us, although he could rightly have done so; but, on the contrary, he so lived, labored, worked, suffered, and died that he might be like other men and in fashion and in actions be nothing else than a man, just as if he had need of all these things and had nothing of the form of God. But he did all this for our sake, that he might serve us and that all things which he accomplished in this form of a servant might become ours.

So a Christian, like Christ his head, is filled and made rich by faith and should be content with this form of God which he has obtained by faith; only, as I have said, he should increase this faith until it is made perfect. For this faith is his life, his righteousness, and his salvation: it saves him and makes him acceptable, and bestows upon him all things that are Christ's, as has been said above, and as Paul asserts in Gal. 2 [:20] when he says, "And the life I now live in the flesh I live by faith in the Son of God." Although the Christian is thus free from all works, he ought in this liberty to empty himself, take upon himself the form of a servant, be made in the likeness of men, be found in human form, and to serve, help, and in every way deal with his neighbor as he sees that God through Christ has dealt and still deals with him. This he should do freely, having regard for nothing but divine approval.

He ought to think: "Although I am an unworthy and condemned man, my God has given me in Christ all the riches of righteousness and salvation without any merit on my part, out of pure, free mercy, so that from now on I need nothing except faith which believes that this is true. Why should I not therefore freely, joyfully, with all my heart, and with an eager will do all things which I know are pleasing and acceptable to such a Father who has overwhelmed me with his inestimable riches? I will therefore give myself as a Christ to my neighbor, just as Christ offered himself to me; I will do nothing in this life except what I see is necessary, profitable, and salutary to my neighbor, since through faith I have an abundance of all good things in Christ."

Behold, from faith thus flow forth love and joy in the Lord, and from love a joyful, willing, and free mind that serves one's neighbor willingly and takes no account of gratitude or ingratitude, of praise or blame, of gain or loss. For a man does not serve that he may put men under obligations. He does not distinguish between friends and enemies or anticipate their thankfulness or unthankfulness, but he most freely and most willingly spends himself and all that he has, whether he wastes all on the thankless or whether he gains a reward. As his Father does, distributing all things to all men richly and freely, making "his sun rise on the evil and on the good" [Matt. 5:45], so also the son does all things and suffers all things with that freely bestowing joy which is his delight when through Christ he sees it in God, the dispenser of such great benefits.

Therefore, if we recognize the great and precious things which are given us, as Paul says [Rom. 5:5], our hearts will be filled by the Holy Spirit with the love which makes us free, joyful, almighty workers and conquerors over all tribulations, servants of our neighbors, and yet lords of all. For those who do not recognize the gifts bestowed upon them through Christ, however, Christ has been born in vain; they go their way with their works and shall never come to taste or feel those things. Just as our neighbor is in need and lacks that in which we abound, so we were in need before God and lacked his mercy. Hence, as our heavenly Father has in Christ freely come to our aid, we also ought freely to help our neighbor through our body and its works, and each one should become as it were a

Christ to the other that we may be Christs to one another and Christ may be the same in all, that is, that we may be truly Christians.

Who then can comprehend the riches and the glory of the Christian life? It can do all things and has all things and lacks nothing. It is lord over sin, death, and hell, and yet at the same time it serves, ministers to, and benefits all men. But alas in our day this life is unknown throughout the world; it is neither preached about nor sought after; we are altogether ignorant of our own name and do not know why we are Christians or bear the name of Christians. Surely we are named after Christ, not because he is absent from us, but because he dwells in us, that is, because we believe in him and are Christs one to another and do to our neighbors as Christ does to us. But in our day we are taught by the doctrine of men to seek nothing but merits, rewards, and the things that are ours; of Christ we have made only a taskmaster far harsher than Moses.

We have a pre-eminent example of such a faith in the blessed Virgin. As is written in Luke 2 [:22], she was purified according to the law of Moses according to the custom of all women, although she was not bound by that law and did not need to be purified. Out of free and willing love, however, she submitted to the law like other women that she might not offend or despise them. She was not justified by this work, but being righteous she did it freely and willingly. So also our works should be done, not that we may be justified by them, since, being justified beforehand by faith, we ought to do all things freely and joyfully for the sake of others.

St. Paul also circumcised his disciple Timothy, not because circumcision was necessary for his righteousness, but that he might not offend or despise the Jews who were weak in the faith and could not yet grasp the liberty of faith. But, on the other hand, when they despised the liberty of faith and insisted that circumcision was necessary for righteousness, he resisted them and did not allow Titus to be circumcised Gal. 2 [:3]. Just as he was unwilling to offend or despise any man's weak faith and yielded to their will for a time, so he was also unwilling that the liberty of faith should be offended against or despised by stubborn, work-righteous men. He chose a middle way, sparing the weak for a time, but always withstanding the stubborn, that he might convert all to the liberty of faith. What we do should be done with the same zeal to sustain the weak in faith, as in Rom. 14 [:1]; but we should firmly resist the stubborn teachers of works. Of this we shall say more later.

Christ also, in Matt. 17 [:24-27], when the tax money was demanded of his disciples, discussed with St. Peter whether the sons of the king were not free from the payment of tribute, and Peter affirmed that they were. Nonetheless, Christ commanded Peter to go to the sea and said, "Not to give offense to them, go to the sea and cast a hook, and take the first fish that comes up, and when you open its mouth you will find a shekel; take that and give it to them for me and for yourself." This incident fits our subject beautifully for Christ here calls himself and those who are his children sons of the king, who need nothing; and yet he freely submits and pays the tribute. Just as necessary and helpful as this work was to Christ's righteousness or salvation, just so much do all other works of his or his followers avail for righteousness, since they all follow after righteousness and are free and are done only to serve others and to give them an example of good works.

Of the same nature are the precepts which Paul gives in Rom. 13 [:1-7], namely, that Christians should be subject to the governing authorities and be ready to do every good work, not that they shall in this way be justified, since they already are righteous through faith, but that in the liberty of the Spirit they shall by so doing serve others and the authorities themselves and obey their will freely and out of love. The works of all colleges,[17] monasteries, and priests should be of this nature. Each one should do the works of his profession and station, not that by them he may strive after righteousness, but that through them he may keep his body under control, be an example to others who also need to keep their bodies under control, and finally that by such works he may submit his will to that of others in the freedom of love. But very great care must always be exercised so that no man in a false confidence imagines that by such works he will be justified or acquire merit

---

[17] The word "college" here denotes a corporation of clergy supported by a foundation and performing certain religious services.

or be saved; for this is the work of faith alone, as I have repeatedly said.

Anyone knowing this could easily and without danger find his way through those numberless mandates and precepts of pope, bishops, monasteries, churches, princes, and magistrates upon which some ignorant pastors insist as if they were necessary to righteousness and salvation, calling them "precepts of the church," although they are nothing of the kind. For a Christian, as a free man, will say, "I will fast, pray, do this and that as men command, not because it is necessary to my righteousness or salvation; but that I may show due respect to the pope, the bishop, the community, a magistrate, or my neighbor, and give them an example. I will do and suffer all things, just as Christ did and suffered far more for me, although he needed nothing of it all for himself, and was made under the law for my sake, although he was not under the law." Although tyrants do violence or injustice in making their demands, yet it will do no harm as long as they demand nothing contrary to God.

From what has been said, everyone can pass a safe judgment on all works and laws and make a trustworthy distinction between them and know who are the blind and ignorant pastors and who are the good and true. Any work that is not done solely for the purpose of keeping the body under control or of serving one's neighbor, as long as he asks nothing contrary to God, is not good or Christian. For this reason I greatly fear that few or no colleges, monasteries, altars, and offices of the church are really Christian in our day—nor the special fasts and prayers on certain saints' days. I fear, I say, that in all these we seek only our profit, thinking that through them our sins are purged away and that we find salvation in them. In this way Christian liberty perishes altogether. This is a consequence of our ignorance of Christian faith and liberty.

This ignorance and suppression of liberty very many blind pastors take pains to encourage. They stir up and urge on their people in these practices by praising such works, puffing them up with their indulgences, and never teaching faith. If, however, you wish to pray, fast, or establish a foundation in the church, I advise you to be careful not to do it in order to obtain some benefit, whether temporal or eternal, for you would do injury to your faith which alone offers you all things. Your one care should be that faith may grow, whether it is trained by works or sufferings. Make your gifts freely and for no consideration, so that others may profit by them and fare well because of you and your goodness. In this way you shall be truly good and Christian. Of what benefit to you are the good works which you do not need for keeping your body under control? Your faith is sufficient for you, through which God has given you all things.

See, according to this rule the good things we have from God should flow from one to the other and be common to all, so that everyone should "put on" his neighbor and so conduct himself toward him as if he himself were in the other's place. From Christ the good things have flowed and are flowing into us. He has so "put on" us and acted for us as if he had been what we are. From us they flow on to those who have need of them so that I should lay before God my faith and my righteousness that they may cover and intercede for the sins of my neighbor which I take upon myself and so labor and serve in them as if they were my very own. That is what Christ did for us. This is true love and the genuine rule of a Christian life. Love is true and genuine where there is true and genuine faith. Hence the Apostle says of love in I Cor. 13 [:5] that "it does not seek its own."

We conclude, therefore, that a Christian lives not in himself, but in Christ and in his neighbor. Otherwise he is not a Christian. He lives in Christ through faith, in his neighbor through love. By faith he is caught up beyond himself into God. By love he descends beneath himself into his neighbor. Yet he always remains in God and in his love, as Christ says in John 1 [:51], "Truly, truly, I say to you, you will see heaven opened, and the angels of God ascending and descending upon the Son of man."

Enough now of freedom. As you see, it is a spiritual and true freedom and makes our hearts free from all sins, laws and commands, as Paul says, I Tim. 1 [:9], "The law is not laid down for the just." It is more excellent than all other liberty, which is external, as heaven is more excellent than earth. May Christ give us this liberty both to understand and to preserve. Amen.

Finally, something must be added for the sake of those for

whom nothing can be said so well that they will not spoil it by misunderstanding it. It is questionable whether they will understand even what will be said here. There are very many who, when they hear of this freedom of faith, immediately turn it into an occasion for the flesh and think that now all things are allowed them. They want to show that they are free men and Christians only by despising and finding fault with ceremonies, traditions, and human laws; as if they were Christians because on stated days they do not fast or eat meat when others fast, or because they do not use the accustomed prayers, and with upturned nose scoff at the precepts of men, although they utterly disregard all else that pertains to the Christian religion. The extreme opposite of these are those who rely for their salvation solely on their reverent observance of ceremonies, as if they would be saved because on certain days they fast or abstain from meats, or pray certain prayers; these make a boast of the precepts of the church and of the fathers, and do not care a fig for the things which are of the essence of our faith. Plainly, both are in error because they neglect the weightier things which are necessary to salvation, and quarrel so noisily about trifling and unnecessary matters.

How much better is the teaching of the Apostle Paul who bids us take a middle course and condemns both sides when he says, "Let not him who eats despise him who abstains, and let not him who abstains pass judgment on him who eats" [Rom. 14:3]. Here you see that they who neglect and disparage ceremonies, not out of piety, but out of mere contempt, are reproved, since the Apostle teaches us not to despise them. Such men are puffed up by knowledge. On the other hand, he teaches those who insist on the ceremonies not to judge the others, for neither party acts toward the other according to the love that edifies. Wherefore we ought to listen to Scripture which teaches that we should not go aside to the right or to the left [Deut. 28:14] but follow the statutes of the Lord which are right, "rejoicing the heart" [Ps. 19:8]. As a man is not righteous because he keeps and clings to the works and forms of the ceremonies, so also will a man not be counted righteous merely because he neglects and despises them.

Our faith in Christ does not free us from works but from false opinions concerning works, that is, from the foolish presumption that justification is acquired by works. Faith redeems, corrects, and preserves our consciences so that we know that righteousness does not consist in works, although works neither can nor ought to be wanting; just as we cannot be without food and drink and all the works of this mortal body, yet our righteousness is not in them, but in faith; and yet those works of the body are not to be despised or neglected on that account. In this world we are bound by the needs of our bodily life, but we are not righteous because of them. "My kingship is not of this world" [John 18:36], says Christ. He does not, however, say, "My kingship is not here, that is, in this world." And Paul says, "Though we live in the world we are not carrying on a worldly war" [II Cor. 10:3], and in Gal. 2 [:20], "The life I now live in the flesh I live by faith in the Son of God." Thus what we do, live, and are in works and ceremonies, we do because of the necessities of this life and of the effort to rule our body. Nevertheless we are righteous, not in these, but in the faith of the Son of God.

Hence the Christian must take a middle course and face those two classes of men. He will meet first the unyielding, stubborn ceremonialists who like deaf adders are not willing to hear the truth of liberty [Ps. 58:4] but, having no faith, boast of, prescribe, and insist upon their ceremonies as means of justification. Such were the Jews of old, who were unwilling to learn how to do good. These he must resist, do the very opposite, and offend them boldly lest by their impious views they drag many with them into error. In the presence of such men it is good to eat meat, break the fasts, and for the sake of the liberty of faith do other things which they regard as the greatest of sins. Of them we must say, "Let them alone; they are blind guides." According to this principle Paul would not circumcise Titus when the Jews insisted that he should [Gal. 2:3], and Christ excused the apostles when they plucked ears of grain on the sabbath [Matt. 12: 1-8]. There are many similar instances. The other class of men whom a Christian will meet are the simple-minded, ignorant men, weak in the faith, as the Apostle calls them, who cannot yet grasp the liberty of faith, even if they were willing to do so [Rom. 14:1]. These he must take care not to offend. He must yield to their weakness until they are more fully instructed. Since they do and think as they do, not because they are stubbornly wicked, but only because their faith is weak, the fasts and other things which they consider necessary must be observed to avoid giving them offense. This is the command of love which would harm no one but would serve all men. It is not by their fault that they are weak, but by that of their pastors who have taken them captive with the snares of their traditions and have wickedly used these traditions as rods with which to beat them. They should have been delivered from these pastors by the teachings of faith and freedom. So the Apostle teaches us in Romans 14: "If food is a cause of my brother's falling, I will never eat meat" [Cf. Rom. 14:21 and I Cor. 8:13]; and again, "I know and am persuaded in the Lord Jesus that nothing is unclean in itself; but it is unclean for any one who thinks it unclean" [Rom. 14:14].

For this reason, although we should boldly resist those teachers of traditions and sharply censure the laws of the popes by means of which they plunder the people of God, yet we must spare the timid multitude whom those impious tyrants hold captive by means of these laws until they are set free. Therefore fight strenuously against the wolves, but for the sheep and not also against the sheep. This you will do if you inveigh against the laws and the lawgivers and at the same time observe the laws with the weak so that they will not be offended, until they also recognize tyranny and understand their freedom. If you wish to use your freedom, do so in secret, as Paul says, Rom. 14 [:22], "The faith that you have, keep between yourself and God"; but take care not to use your freedom in the sight of the weak. On the other hand, use your freedom constantly and consistently in the sight of and despite the tyrants and the stubborn so that they also may learn that they are impious, that their laws are of no avail for righteousness, and that they had no right to set them up.

Since we cannot live our lives without ceremonies and works, and the perverse and untrained youth need to be restrained and saved from harm by such bonds; and since each one should keep his body under control by means of such works, there is need that the minister of Christ be far-seeing and faithful. He ought so to govern and teach Christians in all these matters that their conscience and faith will not be offended and that there will not spring up in them a suspicion and a root of bitterness and many will thereby be defiled, as Paul admonishes the Hebrews [Heb. 12:15]; that is, that they may not lose faith and become defiled by the false estimate of the value of works and think that they must be justified by works. Unless faith is at the same time constantly taught, this happens easily and defiles a great many, as has been done until now through the pestilent, impious, soul-destroying traditions of our popes and the opinions of our theologians. By these snares numberless souls have been dragged down to hell, so that you might see in this the work of Antichrist.

In brief, as wealth is the test of poverty, business the test of faithfulness, honors the test of humility, feasts the test of temperance, pleasures the test of chastity, so ceremonies are the test of the righteousness of faith. "Can a man," asks Solomon, "carry fire in his bosom and his clothes and not be burned?" [Prov. 6:27]. Yet as a man must live in the midst of wealth, business, honors, pleasures, and feasts, so also must he live in the midst of ceremonies, that is, in the midst of dangers. Indeed, as infant boys need beyond all else to be cherished in the bosoms and by the hands of maidens to keep them from perishing, yet when they are grown up their salvation is endangered if they associate with maidens, so the inexperienced and perverse youth need to be restrained and trained by the iron bars of ceremonies lest their unchecked ardor rush headlong into vice after vice. On the other hand, it would be death for them always to be held in bondage to ceremonies, thinking that these justify them. They are rather to be taught that they have been so imprisoned in ceremonies, not that they should be made righteous or gain great merit by them, but that they might thus be kept from doing evil and might more easily be instructed to the righteousness of faith. Such instruction they would not endure if the impulsiveness of their youth were not restrained.

Hence ceremonies are to be given the same place in the life of a Christian as models and plans have among builders and artisans. They are prepared, not as a permanent structure, but because without them nothing could be built or made. When the structure is complete the models and plans are laid aside. You see, they are not despised, rather they are greatly sought after; but what we despise is the false estimate of them since no one holds them to be the real and permanent structure.

If any man were so flagrantly foolish as to care for nothing all his life long except the most costly, careful, and persistent preparation of plans and models and never to think of the structure itself, and were satisfied with his work in producing such plans and mere aids to work, and boasted of it, would not all men pity his insanity and think that something great might have been built with what he has wasted? Thus we do not despise ceremonies and works, but we set great store by them; but we despise the false estimate placed upon works in order that no one may think that they are true righteousness, as those hypocrites believe who spend and lose their whole lives in zeal for works and never reach that goal for the sake of which the works are to be done, who, as the Apostle says, "will listen to anybody and can never arrive at a knowledge of the truth" [II Tim. 3:7]. They seem to wish to build, they make their preparations, and yet they never build. Thus they remain caught in the form of religion and do not attain unto its power [II Tim. 3:5]. Meanwhile they are pleased with their efforts and even dare to judge all others whom they do not see shining with a like show of works. Yet with the gifts of God which they have spent and abused in vain they might, if they had been filled with faith, have accomplished great things to their own salvation and that of others.

Since human nature and natural reason, as it is called, are by nature superstitious and ready to imagine, when laws and works are prescribed, that righteousness must be obtained through laws and works; and further, since they are trained and confirmed in this opinion by the practice of all earthly lawgivers, it is impossible that they should of themselves escape from the slavery of works and come to a knowledge of the freedom of faith. Therefore there is need of the prayer that the Lord may give us and make us *theodidacti*, that is, those taught by God [John 6:45], and himself, as he has promised, write his law in our hearts; otherwise there is no hope for us. If he himself does not teach our hearts this wisdom hidden in mystery [I Cor. 2:7], nature can only condemn it and judge it to be heretical because nature is offended by it and regards it as foolishness. So we see that it happened in the old days in the case of the apostles and prophets, and so godless and blind popes and their flatterers do to me and to those who are like me. May God at last be merciful to them and to us and cause his face to shine upon us that we may know his way upon earth [Ps. 67:1-2], his salvation among all nations, God, who is blessed forever [II Cor. 11:31]. Amen.

A SERMON ON THE ESTATE OF MARRIAGE

Preface

A sermon on the estate of marriage has already been published in my name, but I would much rather it had not. I know perfectly well that I have preached on the subject, but it has never been put into writing yet, as I am about to do at this moment. For this reason I determined to revise this same sermon, and improve it as much as possible. I ask every good soul to disregard the first sermon published and discard it. Further, if anybody wants to start writing my sermons for me, let him restrain himself, and let me have a say in the publication of my words as well. There is a vast difference between using the spoken word to make something clear and having to use the written word.

A Sermon on the Estate of Marriage Revised and Corrected by Dr. Martin Luther Augustinian at Wittenberg

1. God created Adam and brought all the animals before him. Adam did not find a proper companion among them suitable for marriage, so God then said, "It is not good that Adam should be alone. I will create a helpmeet for him to be with him always." And he sent a deep sleep upon Adam, and took a rib from him, and closed his side up again. And out of this very rib taken from Adam, God created a woman and brought her to him. Then Adam said, "This is bone of my bone, and flesh of my flesh. She shall be called a woman, because she was taken from her man. This is why a man shall leave his father and mother and cleave to his wife, and the two shall be one flesh" [Gen. 2:18-24].

All of this is from God's word. These words teach us where man and woman come from, how they were given to one another, for what purpose a wife was created, and what kind of love there should be in the estate of marriage.

2. If God himself does not give the wife or the husband, anything can happen. For the truth indicated here is that Adam found no marriageable partner for himself, but as soon as God had created Eve and brought her to him, he felt a real married love toward her, and recognized that she was his wife. Those who want to enter into the estate of marriage should learn from this that they should earnestly pray to God for a spouse. For the sage says that parents provide goods and houses for their children, but a wife is given by God alone [Prov. 19:14], everyone according to his need, just as Eve was given to Adam by God alone. And true though it is that because of excessive lust of the flesh lighthearted youth pays scant attention to these matters, marriage is nevertheless a weighty matter in the sight of God. For it was not by accident that Almighty God instituted the estate of matrimony only for man and above all animals, and gave such forethought and consideration to marriage. To the other animals God says quite simply, "Be fruitful and multiply" [Gen. 1:22]. It is not written that he brings the female to the male. Therefore, there is no such thing as marriage among animals. But in the case of Adam, God creates for him a unique, special kind of wife out of his own flesh. He brings her to him, he gives her to him, and Adam agrees to accept her. Therefore, that is what marriage is.

3. A woman is created to be a companionable helpmeet to the man in everything, particularly to bear children. And that still holds good, except that since the fall marriage has been adulterated with wicked lust. And now [i.e., after the fall] the desire of the man for the woman, and vice versa, is sought after not only for companionship and children, for which purposes alone marriage was instituted, but also for the pursuance of wicked lust, which is almost as strong a motive.

4. God makes distinctions between the different kinds of love, and shows that the love of a man and woman is (or should be) the greatest and purest of all loves. For he says, "A man shall leave his

father and mother and cleave to his wife" [Gen. 2:24], and the wife does the same, as we see happening around us every day. Now there are three kinds of love: false love, natural love, and married love. False love is that which seeks its own, as a man loves money, possessions, honor, and women taken outside of marriage and against God's command. Natural love is that between father and child, brother and sister, friend and relative, and similar relationships. But over and above all these is married love, that is, a bride's love, which glows like a fire and desires nothing but the husband. She says, "It is you I want, not what is yours: I want neither your silver nor your gold; I want neither. I want only you. I want you in your entirety, or not at all." All other kinds of love seek something other than the loved one: this kind wants only to have the beloved's own self completely. If Adam had not fallen, the love of bride and groom would have been the loveliest thing. Now this love is not pure either, for admittedly a married partner desires to have the other, yet each seeks to satisfy his desire with the other, and it is this desire which corrupts this kind of love. Therefore, the married state is now no longer pure and free from sin. The temptation of the flesh has become so strong and consuming that marriage may be likened to a hospital for incurables which prevents inmates from falling into graver sin.[1] Before Adam fell it was a simple matter to remain virgin and chaste, but now it is hardly possible, and without special grace from God, quite impossible. For this very reason neither Christ nor the apostles sought to make chastity a matter of obligation. It is true that Christ counseled chastity,[2] and he left it up to each one to test himself, so that if he could not be continent he was free to marry, but if by the grace of God he could be continent, then chastity is better.[3]

Thus the doctors[4] have found three good and useful things about the married estate, by means of which the sin of lust, which flows beneath the surface, is counteracted and ceases to be a cause of damnation.

---

[1] It was not until 1523 that Luther complemented his view of marriage as a "remedy against sin" with that of marriage as an "estate of faith." Cf. Lazareth, *Luther on the Christian Home,* pp. 233-234.
[2] Cf. Matt. 19:10-12.
[3] Cf. I Cor. 7:8-10.
[4] Luther means the church's theologians.

First, [the doctors say] that it is a sacrament. A sacrament is a sacred sign of something spiritual, holy, heavenly, and eternal, just as the water of baptism, when the priest pours it over the child, means that the holy, divine, eternal grace is poured into the soul and body of that child at the same time, and cleanses him from his 'original sin. This also means that the kingdom of God, which is an inestimable benefit, in fact immeasurably greater than the water which conveys this meaning, is within him. In the same way the estate of marriage is a sacrament. It is an outward and spiritual sign of the greatest, holiest, worthiest, and noblest thing that has ever existed or ever will exist: the union of the divine and human natures in Christ. The holy apostle Paul says that as man and wife united in the estate of matrimony are two in one flesh, so God and man are united in the one person Christ, and so Christ and Christendom are one body. It is indeed a wonderful sacrament, as Paul says [Eph. 5:32], that the estate of marriage truly signifies such a great reality. Is it not a wonderful thing that God is man and that he gives himself to man and will be his, just as the husband gives himself to his wife and is hers? But if God is ours, then everything is ours.[5]

Consider this matter with the respect it deserves. Because the union of man and woman signifies such a great mystery, the estate of marriage has to have this special significance. This means that the wicked lust of the flesh, which nobody is without, is a conjugal obligation and is not reprehensible when expressed within marriage, but in all other cases outside the bond of marriage, it is mortal sin. In a parallel way the holy manhood of God covers[6] the shame of the wicked lust of the flesh. Therefore, a married man should have regard for such a sacrament, honor it as sacred, and behave properly in marital obligations, so that those things which originate in the lust of the flesh do not occur [among us] as they do in the world of brute beasts.

Second, [the doctors say] that marriage is a covenant of fidelity. The whole basis and essence of marriage is that each gives himself or herself to the other, and they promise to remain faithful to each

---

[5] Cf. I Cor. 3:21-23.
[6] Cf. Ps. 32:1; Rom. 4:7.

other and not give themselves to any other. By binding themselves to each other, and surrendering themselves to each other, the way is barred to the body of anyone else, and they content themselves in the marriage bed with their one companion. In this way God sees to it that the flesh is subdued so as not to rage wherever and however it pleases, and, within this plighted troth, permits even more occasion than is necessary for the begetting of children. But, of course, a man has to control himself and not make a filthy sow's sty of his marriage.

At this point I want to say what kind of words[7] should be used when two people are betrothed[8] to each other. The matter has been dealt with at such length, in such depth, and in such concise fashion that I myself am much too inadequate to understand it all, but I am afraid that there are many who are as married people, whom before now we thought unmarried. But because the estate of marriage consists essentially in consent having been freely and previously given one to another, and also because God is wonderfully merciful in all his judgments, I will leave it all to his care. The generally accepted formula is "I am thine, thou art mine," and though some intended it most strictly, it is not enough when they say, "I will take thee" or "I am willing to take thee" or when they use some other form of words. Nevertheless I would still prefer to consider the words in the sense in which they have been understood up to the present.

Similarly, when someone has made a clandestine betrothal, and subsequently takes another, either clandestinely or publicly, I am still not sure whether what we write about it or the judgment we make on it is altogether right. My advice is that parents persuade their children not to be ashamed to ask their parents to find a marriage partner for them. Parents should make it clear from the start that they want to advise their children so that they in their turn may remain chaste and persevere in expectation of marriage.

---

[7] In the earlier sermon Luther mentioned briefly the significance of the words used in betrothal. Cf. *WA* 9, 216-217.

[8] Luther generally regarded betrothal (engagement) as equivalent to marriage. Opposed to long engagements, he expressed the opinion that it would be best if engagement, marriage, and consummation took place on the same night. *WA*, TR 3, No. 3179. Cf. Olavi Lähteenmaki, *Sexus und Ehe bei Luther* ("Schriften der Luther-Agricola Gesellschaft," No. 10 [Turku, 1955]), pp. 99-128.

In return, children should not become engaged without the knowledge of their parents. You are not ashamed, are you, to ask your parents for a coat or a house? Why be foolish then, and not ask for what is far greater, a partner in marriage? Samson did it. He entered a city and saw a young maiden who pleased him. Thereupon he immediately goes back home and says to his father and mother, "I have seen a young maiden whom I love. Dear parents, get me this girl for a wife" [Judg. 14:1-2].

Third, [the doctors say] that marriage produces offspring, for that is the end and chief purpose of marriage. It is not enough, however, merely for children to be born, and so what they say about marriage excusing sin does not apply in this case. Heathen, too, bear offspring. But unfortunately it seldom happens that we bring up children to serve God, to praise and honor him, and want nothing else of them. People seek only heirs in their children, or pleasure in them; the serving of God finds what place it can. You also see people rush into marriage and become mothers and fathers before they know what the commandments are or can pray.

But this at least all married people should know. They can do no better work and do nothing more valuable either for God, for Christendom, for all the world, for themselves, and for their children than to bring up their children well. In comparison with this one work, that married people should bring up their children properly, there is nothing at all in pilgrimages to Rome, Jerusalem, or Compostella,[9] nothing at all in building churches, endowing masses, or whatever good works could be named. For bringing up their children properly is their shortest road to heaven. In fact, heaven itself could not be made nearer or achieved more easily than by doing this work. It is also their appointed work. Where parents are not conscientious about this, it is as if everything were the wrong way around, like fire that will not burn or water that is not wet.

By the same token, hell is no more easily earned than with

---

[9] Compostella, a Spanish town, was a famous and popular shrine. According to Spanish tradition, James the son of Zebedee was martyred there (see Acts 12:2). The name Compostella is a corruption of Giacomo Postolo, i.e., James the Apostle. Luther mentions this shrine frequently.

respect to one's own children. You could do no more disastrous work than to spoil the children, let them curse and swear, let them learn profane words and vulgar songs, and just let them do as they please. What is more, some parents use enticements to be more alluring to meet the dictates of the world of fashion, so that they may please only the world, get ahead, and become rich, all the time giving more attention to the care of the body than to the due care of the soul. There is no greater tragedy in Christendom than spoiling children. If we want to help Christendom, we most certainly have to start with the children, as happened in earlier times.

This third point seems to me to be the most important of all, as well as being the most useful. For without a shadow of doubt it is not only a matter of marital obligation, but can completely eclipse all other sins. False natural love blinds parents so that they have more regard for the bodies of their children than they have for their souls. It was because of this that the sage said, "He who spares the rod hates his son, but he who loves him is diligent to discipline him" [Prov. 13:24]. Again, "Folly is bound up in the heart of a child, but the rod of discipline drives it far from him" [Prov. 22:15]. Or again, "If you beat him with the rod you will save his life from hell" [Prov. 23:14]. Therefore, it is of the greatest importance for every married man to pay closer, more thorough, and continuous attention to the health of his child's soul than to the body which he has begotten, and to regard his child as nothing else but an eternal treasure God has commanded him to protect, and so prevent the world, the flesh, and the devil from stealing the child away and bringing him to destruction. For at his death and on the day of judgment he will be asked about his child and will have to give a most solemn account. For what do you think is the cause of the horrible wailing and howling of those who will cry, "O blessed are the wombs which have not bore children, and the breasts which have never suckled" [Luke 23:29]? There is not the slightest doubt that it is because they have failed to restore their children to God, from whom they received them to take care of them.

O what a truly noble, important, and blessed condition the estate of marriage is if it is properly regarded! O what a truly pitiable, horrible, and dangerous condition it is if it is not properly regarded! And to him who bears these things in mind the desire of the flesh may well pass away, and perhaps he could just as well take on chastity as the married state. The young people take a poor view of this and follow only their desires, but God will consider it important and wait on him who is in the right.

Finally, if you really want to atone for all your sins, if you want to obtain the fullest remission[10] of them on earth as well as in heaven, if you want to see many generations of your children, then look but at this third point with all the seriousness you can muster and bring up your children properly. If you cannot do so, seek out other people who can and ask them to do it. Spare yourself neither money nor expense, neither trouble nor effort, for your children are the churches, the altar, the testament, the vigils and masses for the dead for which you make provision in your will.[11] It is they who will lighten you in your hour of death, and to your journey's end.

---

10 Luther uses the word *ablasz*, which also means "indulgence."
11 Testamentary bequests endowing masses to be said in one's behalf after death were not uncommon in Luther's day. He treats this practice at some length in *To the Christian Nobility*, pp. 180-181.

28.

A SERMON ON
PREPARING TO DIE

Martin Luther, Augustinian Monk

First, since death marks a farewell from this world and all its activities, it is necessary that a man regulate his temporal goods properly or as he wishes to have them ordered, lest after his death there be occasion for squabbles, quarrels, or other misunderstanding among his surviving friends. This pertains to the physical or external departure from this world and to the surrender of our possessions.

Second, we must also take leave spiritually. That is, we must cheerfully and sincerely forgive, for God's sake, all men who have offended us. At the same time we must also, for God's sake, earnestly seek the forgiveness of all the people whom we undoubtedly have greatly offended by setting them a bad example or by bestowing too few of the kindnesses demanded by the law of Christian brotherly love. This is necessary lest the soul remain burdened by its actions here on earth.

Third, since everyone must depart, we must turn our eyes to God, to whom the path of death leads and directs us. Here we find the beginning of the narrow gate and of the straight path to life [Matt. 7:14]. All must joyfully venture forth on this path, for though the gate is quite narrow, the path is not long. Just as an infant is born with peril and pain from the small abode of its mother's womb into this immense heaven and earth, that is, into this world, so man departs this life through the narrow gate of death. And although the heavens and the earth in which we dwell at present seem large and wide to us, they are nevertheless much narrower and smaller than the mother's womb in comparison with the future heaven. Therefore, the death of the dear saints is called a new birth, and their feast day is known in Latin as *natale,* that is, the day of their birth.[1] However, the narrow passage of death makes us think of this life as expansive and the life beyond as confined. Therefore, we must believe this and learn a lesson from the physical birth of a child, as Christ declares, "When a woman is in travail she has sorrow; but when she has recovered, she no longer remembers the anguish, since a child is born by her into the world" [John 16:21]. So it is that in dying we must bear this anguish and know that a large mansion and joy will follow [John 14:2].

Fourth, such preparation and readiness for this journey are accomplished first of all by providing ourselves with a sincere confession (of at least the greatest sins and those which by diligent search can be recalled by our memory), with the holy Christian sacrament of the holy and true body of Christ, and with the unction.[2] If these can be had, one should devoutly desire them and receive them with great confidence. If they cannot be had, our longing and yearning for them should nevertheless be a comfort and we should not be too dismayed by this circumstance.[3] Christ says, "All things are possible to him who believes" [Mark 9:23]. The sacraments are nothing else than signs which help and incite us to faith, as we shall see. Without this faith they serve no purpose.

Fifth, we must earnestly, diligently, and highly esteem the holy sacraments, hold them in honor, freely and cheerfully rely on them, and so balance them against sin, death, and hell that they will outweigh these by far. We must occupy ourselves much more with the sacraments and their virtues than with our sins. However, we must know how to give them due honor and we must know what

---

[1] *Natale* (usually spelled *natalis*) dates back to the second century and was observed originally with a religious service commemorating a relative on the anniversary of his death. In the course of time the observance commemorated especially saints and martyrs.

[2] Extreme Unction, one of the seven sacraments of the Roman Catholic Church, is administered to the gravely ill, the dying, or the just deceased. At this point Luther did not openly reject the nonscriptural sacraments. By December, 1519, however, he rejected all the sacraments but penance, baptism, and the Lord's Supper. See his December 18, 1519, letter to Spalatin in WA, Br 1, 594-595. On his views of the sacraments in general, see particularly *The Babylonian Captivity of the Church* (1520). LW 36, 3-126.

[3] Luther expresses a similar view in the case of those who for humanly ordained reasons (i.e., church regulations) are denied the sacrament. See *An Instruction to Penitents* (1521). LW 44, 219-229.

their virtues are. I show them due honor when I believe that I truly receive what the sacraments signify and all that God declares and indicates in them, so that I can say with Mary in firm faith, "Let it be to me according to your words and signs" [Luke 1:38]. Since God himself here speaks and acts through the priest, we would do him in his Word and work no greater dishonor than to doubt whether it is true. And we can do him no greater honor than to believe that his Word and work are true and to firmly rely on them.

Sixth, to recognize the virtues[4] of the sacraments, we must know the evils which they contend with and which we face. There are three such evils: first, the terrifying image of death; second, the awesomely manifold image of sin; third, the unbearable and unavoidable image of hell and eternal damnation.[5] Every other evil issues from these three and grows large and strong as a result of such mingling.

Death looms so large and is terrifying because our foolish and fainthearted nature has etched its image too vividly within itself and constantly fixes its gaze on it. Moreover, the devil presses man to look closely at the gruesome mien and image of death to add to his worry, timidity, and despair. Indeed, he conjures up before man's eyes all the kinds of sudden and terrible death ever seen, heard, or read by man. And then he also slyly suggests the wrath of God with which he [the devil] in days past now and then tormented and destroyed sinners. In that way he fills our foolish human nature with the dread of death while cultivating a love and concern for life, so that burdened with such thoughts man forgets God, flees and abhors death, and thus, in the end, is and remains disobedient to God.

We should familiarize ourselves with death during our lifetime, inviting death into our presence when it is still at a distance

---

[4] In speaking here of virtues and evils, Luther uses the contrasting German words *Tugend* and *Untugend*, today meaning "virtue" and "evil" or "vice." However, just as the English word "virtue" originally meant "strength," so the word *Tugend* (derived from *taugen*, meaning "to be useful" or "to be capable of") in Luther's day implied strength, power, ability, and good characteristics.

[5] The images of which Luther speaks are probably not just theological or symbolic, but allusions to contemporary art exemplified in the works of Dürer and others who depicted dreadful scenes of life in purgatory and hell.

and not on the move. At the time of dying, however, this is hazardous and useless, for then death looms large of its own accord. In that hour we must put the thought of death out of mind and refuse to see it, as we shall hear. The power and might of death are rooted in the fearfulness of our nature and in our untimely and undue viewing and contemplating of it.

Seventh, sin also grows large and important when we dwell on it and brood over it too much. This is increased by the fearfulness of our conscience, which is ashamed before God and accuses itself terribly. That is the water that the devil has been seeking for his mill. He makes our sins seem large and numerous. He reminds us of all who have sinned and of the many who were damned for lesser sins than ours so as to make us despair or die reluctantly, thus forgetting God and being found disobedient in the hour of death. This is true especially since man feels that he should think of his sins at that time and that it is right and useful for him to engage in such contemplation. But he finds himself so unprepared and unfit that now even all his good works are turned into sins. As a result, this must lead to an unwillingness to die, disobedience to the will of God, and eternal damnation. That is not the fitting time to meditate on sin. That must be done during one's lifetime. Thus the evil spirit turns everything upside down for us. During our lifetime, when we should constantly have our eyes fixed on the image of death, sin, and hell—as we read in Psalm 51 [:3], "My sin is ever before me"—the devil closes our eyes and hides these images. But in the hour of death when our eyes should see only life, grace, and salvation, he at once opens our eyes and frightens us with these untimely images so that we shall not see the true ones.

Eighth, hell also looms large because of undue scrutiny and stern thought devoted to it out of season. This is increased immeasurably by our ignorance of God's counsel. The evil spirit prods the soul so that it burdens itself with all kinds of useless presumptions, especially with the most dangerous undertaking of delving into the mystery of God's will to ascertain whether one is "chosen" or not.

Here the devil practices his ultimate, greatest, and most cunning art and power. By this he sets man above God, insofar as man seeks signs of God's will and becomes impatient because he is not supposed to know whether he is among the elect. Man looks with suspicion upon God, so that he soon desires a different God. In brief, the devil is determined to blast God's love from a man's mind and to arouse thoughts of God's wrath. The more docilely man follows the devil and accepts these thoughts, the more imperiled his position is. In the end he cannot save himself, and he falls prey to hatred and blasphemy of God. What is my desire to know whether I am chosen other than a presumption to know all that God knows and to be equal with him so that he will know no more than I do? Thus God is no longer God with a knowledge surpassing mine. Then the devil reminds us of the many heathen, Jews, and Christians who are lost, agitating such dangerous and pernicious thoughts so violently that man, who would otherwise gladly die, now becomes loath to depart this life. When man is assailed by thoughts regarding his election, he is being assailed by hell, as the psalms lament so much.[6] He who surmounts this temptation has vanquished sin, hell, and death all in one.

Ninth, in this affair we must exercise all diligence not to open our homes to any of these images and not to paint the devil over the door.[7] These foes will of themselves boldly rush in and seek to occupy the heart completely with their image, their arguments, and their signs. And when that happens man is doomed and God is entirely forgotten. The only thing to do with these pictures at that time is to combat and expel them. Indeed, where they are found alone and not in conjunction with other pictures, they belong nowhere else than in hell among the devils.

But he who wants to fight against them and drive them out will find that it is not enough just to wrestle and tussle and scuffle with them. They will prove too strong for him, and matters will go from bad to worse. The one and only approach is to drop them entirely and have nothing to do with them. But how is that done? It is done in this way: You must look at death while you are alive and see sin in the light of grace and hell in the light of heaven, permitting nothing to divert you from that view. Adhere to that even

---

[6] Cf. Psalm 65:4; 78:67-68; 106:4-5.
[7] I.e., don't invite the devil's presence.

if all angels, all creatures, yes, even your own thoughts, depict God in a different light—something these will not do. It is only the evil spirit who lends that impression. What shall we do about that?

Tenth, you must not view or ponder death as such, not in yourself or in your nature, nor in those who were killed by God's wrath and were overcome by death. If you do that you will be lost and defeated with them. But you must resolutely turn your gaze, the thoughts of your heart, and all your senses away from this picture and look at death closely and untiringly only as seen in those who died in God's grace and who have overcome death, particularly in Christ and then also in all his saints.

In such pictures death will not appear terrible and gruesome. No, it will seem contemptible and dead, slain and overcome in life. For Christ is nothing other than sheer life, as his saints are likewise. The more profoundly you impress that image upon your heart and gaze upon it, the more the image of death will pale and vanish of itself without struggle or battle. Thus your heart will be at peace and you will be able to die calmly in Christ and with Christ, as we read in Revelation [14:13], "Blessed are they who die in the Lord Christ." This was foreshown in Exodus 21 [Num. 21:6-9], where we hear that when the children of Israel were bitten by fiery serpents they did not struggle with these serpents, but merely had to raise their eyes to the dead bronze serpent and the living ones dropped from them by themselves and perished. Thus you must concern yourself solely with the death of Christ and then you will find life. But if you look at death in any other way, it will kill you with great anxiety and anguish. This is why Christ says, "In the world—that is, in yourselves—you have unrest, but in me you will find peace" [John 16:33].

Eleventh, you must not look at sin in sinners, or in your conscience, or in those who abide in sin to the end and are damned. If you do, you will surely follow them and also be overcome. You must turn your thoughts away from that and look at sin only within the picture of grace. Engrave that picture in yourself with all your power and keep it before your eyes. The picture of grace is nothing else but that of Christ on the cross and of all his dear saints.

How is that to be understood? Grace and mercy are there where Christ on the cross takes your sin from you, bears it for you, and destroys it. To believe this firmly, to keep it before your eyes and not to doubt it, means to view the picture of Christ and to engrave it in yourself. Likewise, all the saints who suffer and die in Christ also bear your sins and suffer and labor for you, as we find it written, "Bear one another's burdens and thus fulfil the command of Christ" [Gal. 6:2]. Christ himself exclaims in Matthew 11 [:28], "Come to me, all who labor and are heavy-laden, and I will help you." In this way you may view your sins in safety without tormenting your conscience. Here sins are never sins, for here they are overcome and swallowed up in Christ. He takes your death upon himself and strangles it so that it may not harm you, if you believe that he does it for you and see your death in him and not in yourself. Likewise, he also takes your sins upon himself and overcomes them with his righteousness out of sheer mercy, and if you believe that, your sins will never work you harm. In that way Christ, the picture of life and of grace over against the picture of death and sin, is our consolation. Paul states that in I Corinthians 15 [:57], "Thanks and praise be to God, who through Christ gives us the victory over sin and death."

Twelfth, you must not regard hell and eternal pain in relation to predestination, not in yourself, or in itself, or in those who are damned, nor must you be worried by the many people in the world who are not chosen. If you are not careful, that picture will quickly upset you and be your downfall. You must force yourself to keep your eyes closed tightly to such a view, for it can never help you, even though you were to occupy yourself with it for a thousand years and fret yourself to death. After all, you will have to let God be God and grant that he knows more about you than you do yourself.

So then, gaze at the heavenly picture of Christ, who descended into hell [I Pet. 3:19] for your sake and was forsaken by God as one eternally damned when he spoke the words on the cross, "Eli, Eli, lama sabachthani!"—"My God, my God, why hast thou forsaken me?" [Matt. 27:46]. In that picture your hell is defeated and your uncertain election is made sure. If you concern yourself solely with that and believe that it was done for you, you will surely be preserved in this same faith. Never, therefore, let this be erased from your vision. Seek yourself only in Christ and not in yourself and you will find yourself in him eternally.

Thus when you look at Christ and all his saints and delight in the grace of God, who elected them, and continue steadfastly in this joy, then you too are already elected. He says in Genesis 12 [:3], "All who bless you shall be blessed." However, if you do not adhere solely to this but have recourse to yourself, you will become adverse to God and all saints, and thus you will find nothing good in yourself. Beware of this, for the evil spirit will strive with much cunning to bring you to such a pass.

Thirteenth, these three pictures or conflicts are foreshadowed in Judges 7 [:16-22], where we read that Gideon attacked the Midianites at night with three hundred men in three different places, but did no more than have trumpets blown and glass fragments smashed. The foe fled and destroyed himself. Similarly, death, sin, and hell will flee with all their might if in the night we but keep our eyes on the glowing picture of Christ and his saints and abide in the faith, which does not see and does not want to see the false pictures. Furthermore, we must encourage and strengthen ourselves with the Word of God as with the sound of trumpets.

Isaiah [9:4] introduces this same figure very aptly against these three images, saying of Christ, "For the yoke of his burden, and the staff for his shoulder, the rod of his oppressor, thou hast broken as in the days of the Midianites," who were overcome by Gideon. He says as it were: The sins of your people (which are a heavy "yoke of his burden" for his conscience), and death (which is a "staff" or punishment laid upon his shoulder), and hell (which is a powerful "rod of the oppressor" with which eternal punishment for sin is exacted)—all these you have broken and defeated. This came to pass in the days of Gideon, that is, when Gideon, by faith and without wielding his sword, put his enemies to flight.

And when did Christ do this? On the cross! There he prepared himself as a threefold picture for us, to be held before the eyes of our faith against the three evil pictures with which the evil spirit and our nature would assail us to rob us of this faith. He is the living and immortal image against death, which he suffered, yet by his resurrection from the dead he vanquished death in his life. He is the image of the grace of God against sin, which he assumed, and yet overcame by his perfect obedience. He is the heavenly image, the one who was forsaken by God as damned, yet he conquered hell through his omnipotent love, thereby proving that he is the dearest Son, who gives this to us all if we but believe.

Fourteenth, beyond all this he not only defeated sin, death, and hell in himself and offered his victory to our faith, but for our further comfort he himself suffered and overcame the temptation which these pictures entail for us. He was assailed by the images of death, sin, and hell just as we are. The Jews confronted Christ with death's image when they said, "Let him come down from the cross; he has healed others, let him now help himself" [Matt. 27: 40-42]. They said as it were, "Here you are facing death; now you must die; nothing can save you from that." Likewise, the devil holds the image of death before the eyes of a dying person and frightens his fearful nature with this horrible picture.

The Jews held the image of sin before Christ's eyes when they said to him, "He healed others. If he is the Son of God, let him come down from the cross, etc."—as though they were to say, "His works were all fraud and deception. He is not the Son of God but the son of the devil, whose own he is with body and soul. He never worked any good, only iniquity." And just as the Jews cast these three pictures at Christ in wild confusion, so man too is assailed by all three at the same time in disarray to bewilder him and ultimately to drive him to despair. The Lord describes the destruction of Jerusalem in Luke 19 [:43-44], saying that the city's enemies will surround it with such devastation as to cut off escape—that is death. Furthermore, he says that its enemies will terrify the inhabitants and drive them hither and yon so that they will not know where to turn—that is sin. In the third place, he says that the foe will dash them to the ground and not leave one stone upon another —that is hell and despair.

The Jews pressed the picture of hell before Christ's eyes when they said, "He trusts in God; let us see whether God will deliver him now, for he said he is the Son of God" [Matt. 27:43]—as though they were to say, "His place is in hell; God did not elect him; he is rejected forever. All his confidence and hope will not help him. All is in vain."

And now we mark that Christ remained silent in the face of all these words[8] and horrible pictures. He does not argue with his foes; he acts as though he does not hear or see them and makes no reply. Even if he had replied, he would only have given them cause to rave and rant even more horribly. He is so completely devoted to the dearest will of his Father that he forgets about his own death, his sin, and his hell imposed on him, and he intercedes for his enemies, for their sin, death, and hell [Luke 23:34]. We must, similarly, let these images slip away from us to wherever they wish or care to go, and remember only that we cling to God's will, which is that we hold to Christ and firmly believe our sin, death, and hell are overcome in him and no longer able to harm us. Only Christ's image must abide in us. With him alone we must confer and deal.

Fifteenth, we now turn to the holy sacraments and their blessings to learn to know their benefits and how to use them. Anyone who is granted the time and the grace to confess, to be absolved, and to receive the sacrament and Extreme Unction before his death has great cause indeed to love, praise, and thank God and to die cheerfully, if he relies firmly on and believes in the sacraments, as we said earlier. In the sacraments your God, Christ himself, deals, speaks, and works with you through the priest. His are not the works and words of man. In the sacraments God himself grants you all the blessings we just mentioned in connection with Christ. God wants the sacraments to be a sign and testimony that Christ's life has taken your death, his obedience your sin, his love your hell, upon themselves and overcome them. Moreover, through the same sacraments you are included and made one with all the saints. You thereby enter into the true communion of saints so that they die with you in Christ, bear sin, and vanquish hell.

It follows from this that the sacraments, that is, the external words of God as spoken by a priest, are a truly great comfort and at the same time a visible sign of divine intent. We must cling to

---

[8] According to Matthew, Jesus spoke only once during his agony on the cross. See Matt. 27:46.

them with a staunch faith as to the good staff which the patriarch Jacob used when crossing the Jordan [Gen. 32:10], or as to a lantern by which we must be guided, and carefully walk with open eyes the dark path of death, sin, and hell, as the prophet says, "Thy word is a light to my feet" [Ps. 119:105]. St. Peter also declares, "And we have a sure word from God. You will do well to pay attention to it" [II Pet. 1:19]. There is no other help in death's agonies, for everyone who is saved is saved only by that sign. It points to Christ and his image, enabling you to say when faced by the image of death, sin, and hell, "God promised and in his sacraments he gave me a sure sign of his grace that Christ's life overcame my death in his death, that his obedience blotted out my sin in his suffering, that his love destroyed my hell in his forsakenness. This sign and promise of my salvation will not lie to me or deceive me. It is God who has promised it, and he cannot lie either in words or in deeds." He who thus insists and relies on the sacraments will find that his election and predestination will turn out well without his worry and effort.[9]

Sixteenth, it is of utmost importance that we highly esteem, honor, and rely upon the holy sacraments, which contain nothing but God's words, promises, and signs. This means that we have no doubts about the sacraments or the things of which they are certain signs, for if we doubt these we lose everything. Christ says that it will happen to us as we believe.[10] What will it profit you to assume and to believe that sin, death, and hell are overcome in Christ for others, but not to believe that your sin, your death, and your hell are also vanquished and wiped out and that you are thus redeemed? Under those circumstances the sacraments will be completely fruitless, since you do not believe the things which are indicated, given, and promised there to you. That is the vilest sin that can be committed, for God himself is looked upon as a liar in his Word, signs, and works, as one who speaks, shows, and promises something which he neither means nor intends to keep. Therefore we dare not

---

[9] In contrast to the Roman church, which emphasized what Luther called the "monster of uncertainty," Luther stressed the certainty of salvation for him who believes and trusts in the truth of the sacraments. Cf. WA 40^{I}, 588; WA 48, 227.

[10] Matt. 15:28; 21.

trifle with the sacraments. Faith must be present for a firm reliance and cheerful venturing on such signs and promises of God. What sort of a God or Savior would he be who could not or would not save us from sin, death, and hell? Whatever the true God promises and effects must be something big.

But then the devil comes along and whispers into your ear, "But suppose you received the sacraments unworthily and through your unworthiness robbed yourself of such grace?" [11] In that event cross yourself[12] and do not let the question of your worthiness or unworthiness assail you. Just see to it that you believe that these are sure signs, true words of God, and then you will indeed be and remain worthy. Belief makes you worthy; unbelief makes you unworthy. The evil spirit brings up the question of worthiness and unworthiness to stir up doubts within you, thus nullifying the sacraments with their benefits and making God a liar in what he says.

God gives you nothing because of your worthiness, nor does he build his Word and sacraments on your worthiness, but out of sheer grace he establishes you, unworthy one, on the foundation of his Word and signs. Hold fast to that and say, "He who gives and has given me his signs and his Word, which assure me that Christ's life, grace, and heaven have kept my sin, death, and hell from harming me, is truly God, who will surely preserve these things for me. When the priest absolves me, I trust in this as in God's Word itself. Since it is God's Word, it must come true. That is my stand, and on that stand I will die." You must trust in the priest's absolution as firmly as though God had sent a special angel or apostle to you, yes, as though Christ himself were absolving you.

Seventeenth, we must note that he who receives the sacraments has a great advantage, for he has received a sign and a promise from God with which he can exercise and strengthen his belief that he has been called into Christ's image and to his benefits. The others who must do without these signs labor solely in faith and must obtain these benefits with the desires of their hearts. They will, of course, also receive these benefits if they persevere in that

---

[11] Cf. Luther's discussion of this point, *LW* 42, 174-175.

[12] Signing or blessing oneself with the sign of the cross was, among other things, an affirmation of the power of Christ against evil spirits and demons.

same faith. Thus you must also say with regard to the Sacrament of the Altar, "If the priest gave me the holy body of Christ, which is a sign and promise of the communion of all angels and saints that they love me, provide and pray for me, suffer and die with me, bear my sin and overcome hell, it will and must therefore be true that the divine sign does not deceive me. I will not let anyone rob me of it. I would rather deny all the world and myself than doubt my God's trustworthiness and truthfulness in his signs and promises. Whether worthy or unworthy of him, I am, according to the text and the declaration of this sacrament, a member of Christendom. It is better that I be unworthy than that God's truthfulness be questioned. Devil, away with you if you advise me differently."

Just see how many people there are who would like to be certain or to have a sign from heaven to tell them how they stand with God and whether they are elected. But what help would it be to them to receive such a sign if they would still not believe? What good are all the signs without faith? How did Christ's signs and the apostles' signs help the Jews? What help are the venerable signs of the sacraments and the words of God even today? Why do people not hold to the sacraments, which are sure and appointed signs, tested and tried by all saints and found reliable by all who believed and who received all that they indicate?

We should, then, learn what the sacraments are, what purpose they serve, and how they are to be used. We will find that there is no better way on earth to comfort downcast hearts and bad consciences. In the sacraments we find God's Word—which reveals and promises Christ to us with all his blessing and which he himself is—against sin, death, and hell. Nothing is more pleasing and desirable to the ear than to hear that sin, death, and hell are wiped out. That very thing is effected in us through Christ if we see the sacraments properly.

The right use of the sacraments involves nothing more than believing that all will be as the sacraments promise and pledge through God's Word. Therefore, it is necessary not only to look at the three pictures in Christ and with these to drive out the counterpictures, but also to have a definite sign which assures us that this has surely been given to us. That is the function of the sacraments.

Eighteenth, in the hour of his death no Christian should doubt that he is not alone. He can be certain, as the sacraments point out, that a great many eyes are upon him: first, the eyes of God and of Christ himself, for the Christian believes his words and clings to his sacraments; then also, the eyes of the dear angels, of the saints, and of all Christians. There is no doubt, as the Sacrament of the Altar indicates, that all of these in a body run to him as one of their own, help him overcome sin, death, and hell, and bear all things with him. In that hour the work of love and the communion of saints are seriously and mightily active. A Christian must see this for himself and have no doubt regarding it, for then he will be bold in death. He who doubts this does not believe in the most venerable Sacrament of the Body of Christ, in which are pointed out, promised, and pledged the communion, help, love, comfort, and support of all the saints in all times of need. If you believe in the signs and words of God, his eyes rest upon you, as he says in Psalm 32 [:8], "*Firmabo*, etc., my eyes will constantly be upon you lest you perish." If God looks upon you, all the angels, saints, and all creatures will fix their eyes upon you. And if you remain in that faith, all of them will uphold you with their hands. And when your soul leaves your body, they will be on hand to receive it, and you cannot perish.

This is borne out in the person of Elisha, who according to II Kings 6 [:16-17] said to his servant, "Fear not, for those who are with us are more than those who are with them." This he said although enemies had surrounded them and they could see nothing but these. The Lord opened the eyes of the young man, and they were surrounded by a huge mass of horses and chariots of fire.

The same is true of everyone who trusts God. Then the words found in Psalm 34 [:7] apply, "The angel of the Lord will encamp around those who fear him, and deliver them." And in Psalm 125 [:1-2], "Those who trust in the Lord are like Mount Zion, which cannot be moved, but abides forever. As the mountains (that is, the angels) are round about Jerusalem, so the Lord is round about his people, from this time forth and forevermore." And in Psalm 91 [:11-16], "For he has charged his angels to bear you on their hands and to guard you wherever you go lest you dash your foot against a stone. You will tread on the lion and the adder, the young lion and the serpent you will trample under foot (this means that all the power and the cunning of the devil will be unable to harm you), because he has trusted in me and I will deliver him; I will protect him because he knows my name. When he calls to me, I will answer him; I will be with him in all his trials, I will rescue him and honor him. With eternal life will I satisfy him, and show him my eternal grace."

Thus the Apostle also declares that the angels, whose number is legion, are all ministering spirits and are sent out for the sake of those who are to be saved [Heb. 1:14]. These are all such great matters that who can believe them? Therefore, we must know that even though the works of God surpass human understanding, God yet effects all of this through such insignificant signs as the sacraments to teach us what a great thing a true faith in God really is.

Nineteenth, let no one presume to perform such things by his own power, but humbly ask God to create and preserve such faith in and such understanding of his holy sacraments in him. He must practice awe and humility in all this, lest he ascribe these works to himself instead of allowing God the glory. To this end he must call upon the holy angels, particularly his own angel,[13] the Mother of God, and all the apostles and saints,[14] especially since God has granted him exceptional zeal for this. However, he dare not doubt, but must believe that his prayer will be heard. He has two reasons for this. The first one is that he has just heard from the Scriptures how God commanded the angels to give love and help to all who believe and how the sacrament conveys this. We must hold this before them and remind them of it, not that the angels do not know this, or would otherwise not do it, but to make our faith and trust in them, and through them in God, stronger and bolder as we face death. The other reason is that God has enjoined us firmly to believe in the fulfilment of our prayer [Mark 11:24] and that it is truly an Amen.[15] We must also bring this command of God to his

---

[13] On guardian angels, see Gal. 1:8; I Tim. 3:16; 1 Pet. 1:12.
[14] On Luther's later opposition to the invocation of Mary and the saints, see *On Translating: An Open Letter* (1530). LW 35, 198-200.
[15] See Luther's treatment of "Amen" on pp. 76-77.

attention and say, "My God, you have commanded me to pray and to believe that my prayer will be heard. For this reason I come to you in prayer and am assured that you will not forsake me but will grant me a genuine faith."

Moreover, we should implore God and his dear saints our whole life long for true faith in the last hour, as we sing so very fittingly on the day of Pentecost, "Now let us pray to the Holy Spirit for the true faith of all things the most, that in our last moments he may befriend us, and as home we go, he may tend us." [16] When the hour of death is at hand we must offer this prayer to God and, in addition, remind him of his command and of his promise and not doubt that our prayer will be fulfilled. After all, if God commanded us to pray and to trust in prayer, and, furthermore, has granted us the grace to pray, why should we doubt that his purpose in this was also to hear and to fulfil it?

Twentieth, what more should God do to persuade you to accept death willingly and not to dread but to overcome it? In Christ he offers you the image of life, of grace, and of salvation so that you may not be horrified by the images of sin, death, and hell. Furthermore, he lays your sin, your death, and your hell on his dearest Son, vanquishes them, and renders them harmless for you. In addition, he lets the trials of sin, death, and hell that come to you also assail his Son and teaches you how to preserve yourself in the midst of these and how to make them harmless and bearable. And to relieve you of all doubt, he grants you a sure sign, namely, the holy sacraments. He commands his angels, all saints, all creatures to join him in watching over you, to be concerned about your soul, and to receive it. He commands you to ask him for this and to be assured of fulfilment. What more can or should he do?

From this you can see that he is a true God and that he performs great, right, and divine works for you. Why, then, should he not impose something big upon you (such as dying), as long as he adds to it great benefits, help, and strength, and thereby wants to test the power of his grace. Thus we read in Psalm 111 [:2],

---

[16] Luther quotes a well-known hymn of which he thought very highly. He later translated it into German and added three verses of his own composition. See *LW* 53, 263-264 for the full text.

"Great are the works of the Lord, selected according to his pleasure." Therefore, we ought to thank him with a joyful heart for showing us such wonderful, rich, and immeasurable grace and mercy against death, hell, and sin, and to laud and love his grace rather than fearing death so greatly. Love and praise make dying very much easier, as God tells us through Isaiah, "For the sake of my praise I restrain it [wrath] for you, that I may not cut you off." [17] To that end may God help us. Amen.

[17] Isa. 48:9 (RSV). Luther actually uses a more literal translation of the original and says of God, who is willing to forgo being honored by his people, "I shall curb your mouth in its praise of me, so that you will not perish." Cf. WA 2, 697.

29.

TEMPORAL AUTHORITY: TO WHAT EXTENT IT SHOULD BE OBEYED

To the illustrious, highborn prince and lord, Lord John,[1] Duke of Saxony, Landgrave of Thuringia, Margrave of Meissen, my gracious lord.

Grace and peace in Christ. Again,[2] illustrious, highborn prince, gracious lord, necessity is laid upon me, and the entreaties of many, and above all your Princely Grace's wishes,[3] impel me to write about temporal authority and the sword it bears, how to use it in a Christian manner, and to what extent men are obligated to obey it. You are perturbed over Christ's injunction in Matthew 5 [:39, 25, 40], "Do not resist evil, but make friends with your accuser; and if any one would take your coat, let him have your cloak as well"; and Romans 12 [:19], "Vengeance is mine, I will repay, says the Lord." These very texts were used long ago against St. Augustine by the prince Volusian, who charged that Christian teaching permits the wicked to do evil, and is incompatible with the temporal sword.[4]

---

[1] John the Steadfast (1468-1532) was the brother of Frederick the Wise, whom he succeeded in the Electorate in 1525. Politically less sagacious than his brother, John nevertheless was a man of fearless courage and deep evangelical conviction. It was he who in the elector's absence refused to publish the bull directed against Luther. It was he who advised his brother to adopt the Reformer's cause more openly. It was he to whom Luther sent single sheets of the Wartburg New Testament as they became available, that John might be able daily to read the Scriptures.

[2] Luther had treated this same matter before in *A Sincere Admonition* (1522) (*LW* 45, 51-74) and in *An Open Letter to the Christian Nobility* (1520). PE 2, 61-164. Cf. p. 657.

[3] Duke John himself was among those who requested Luther to write this treatise.

[4] Volusian was the brother of Albina to whom, with her daughter Melania and son-in-law Pirian, Augustine had dedicated his treatise *Contra Pelagium et Coelestium.* Volusian carried on some correspondence in the year A.D. 412 with Augustine, then Bishop of Hippo, on theological matters which troubled him (*Letters* 132, 135, 137). His doubts concerning the compatibility of

The sophists[5] in the universities have also been perplexed by these texts, because they could not reconcile the two things. In order not to make heathen of the princes, they taught that Christ did not command these things but merely offered them as advice or counsel to those who would be perfect.[6] So Christ had to become a liar and be in error in order that the princes might come off with honor, for they could not exalt the princes without degrading Christ—wretched, blind sophists that they are. And their poisonous error has spread thus through the whole world until everyone regards these teachings of Christ not as precepts binding on all Christians alike but as mere counsels for the perfect. It has gone so far that they have granted the imperfect estate of the sword and of temporal authority not only to the perfect estate of the bishops, but even to the pope, that most perfect estate of all; in fact, they have ascribed it to no one on earth so completely as to him! So thoroughly has the devil taken possession of the sophists and the universities that they themselves do not know what and how they speak or teach.

Christ's doctrine of nonresistance with the laws and customs of the state, however, was discussed in an exchange of letters between Augustine and Marcellinus that same year (*Letters* 136 and 138). Marcellinus, proconsul of Africa, was the tribune appointed by Emperor Honorius to preside over the June, 411, conference which put an end to the Donatist schism; to him Augustine dedicated the first two books of his *City of God*. The texts of these letters are in Sister Wilfrid Parsons (trans.), Roy J. Deferrari's (ed.), *Saint Augustine: Letters*, Vol. III. FC 20; see especially pp. 17, 41-48. MPL 33, 514-515 and 525-535.

[5] Luther often referred to the scholastic theologians as "Sophisten."

[6] Cf. Luther's detailed treatment of the second table of the law, in which his dispute with the Paris theologians on this issue of command vs. counsel looms large, in his *Misuse of the Mass* (1521). LW 36, 204-210, especially p. 205, n. 66. The distinction between commands (*praecepta*) and counsels (*consilia*) was already discussed by Tertullian (*ca.* 160-*ca.* 220) in connection with Paul's own treatment of the subject in I Corinthians 7 (see Tertullian's *Second Book to His Wife*, par. 1). Thomas Aquinas (*ca.* 1225-1274) too distinguished between commandment and counsel in terms of obligation and option. It was held that the New Law—of liberty—fittingly added counsels to the commandments, as the Old Law—of bondage—did not. These "evangelical counsels" were to enable man more speedily to attain to eternal happiness through the renunciation of the things of the world, through poverty, chastity, and obedience in keeping with 1 John 2:16. They were not proposed for all, but for those who are fit to observe them, as in Matt. 19:12, 21. The same injunction of Christ, e.g., to love the enemy, is said to be a command, necessary to salvation, in the sense that we should be mentally prepared to do good; "but that anybody should actually and promptly behave thus toward an enemy when there is no

I hope, however, that I may instruct the princes and the temporal authorities in such a way that they will remain Christians —and Christ will remain Lord—and yet Christ's commands will not for their sake have to become mere counsels.

I do this as a humble service to your Princely Grace, for the benefit of everyone who may need it, and to the praise and glory of Christ our Lord. I commend your Princely Grace with all your kin to the grace of God. May he mercifully have you in his keeping.

At Wittenberg, New Year's Day,[7] 1523.

Your Princely Grace's obedient servant,
Martin Luther

Some time ago I addressed a little book to the German nobility,[8] setting forth their Christian office and functions. How far they acted on my suggestions is only too evident.[9] Hence, I must change my tactics and write them, this time, what they should omit and not do. I fear this new effort will have as little effect on them as the other, and that they will continue to be princes and never become Christians. For God the Almighty has made our rulers mad; they actually think they can do—and order their subjects to do—whatever they please. And the subjects make the mistake of believing that they, in turn, are bound to obey their rulers in everything. It has gone so far that the rulers have begun ordering the people to get rid of certain books,[10] and to

---

special need, is to be referred to the particular counsels." *Summa Theologica,* I, II, ques. 108, art. 4. FC 3, 319. Cf. *Summa Theologica,* 2, II, ques. 184, arts. 3 and 7, where the state of perfection is said to be most nearly realized in the monastic kind of life, and more so in the "episcopal" than in the "religious" state. Further bibliography on this question is given in MA³ 5, 395, n. 9, 21; see also MA³ 5, 421, n. 146, 32. See Luther's discussion of the question in this volume, pp. 661-662 and LW 45, 255-256, 275-276, 283, and 289-290.

[7] Thinking of the new year as beginning with the day of Christ's birth, Luther undoubtedly meant here Christmas Day, December 25, 1522. Cf. the reference to New Year in the concluding line of his Christmas hymn, *"Vom himmel hoch"*: *"und singen uns solch neues Jahr,"* translated by Catherine Winkworth as "a glad new year to all the earth." *Service Book and Hymnal* (published by eight co-operating Lutheran churches), No. 22.

[8] *An Open Letter to the Christian Nobility* (1520). PE 2, 61-164; WA 6 (381), 404-469. See p. 81, n. 2.

[9] This is a reference to the Edict of Worms and its implementation.

[10] Luther's books.

believe and conform to what the rulers prescribe. They are thereby presumptuously setting themselves in God's place, lording it over men's consciences and faith, and schooling the Holy Spirit according to their own crackbrained ideas. Nevertheless, they let it be known that they are not to be contradicted, and are to be called gracious lords all the same.

They issue public proclamations, and say that this is the emperor's command[11] and that they want to be obedient Christian princes, just as if they really meant it and no one noticed the scoundrel behind the mask. If the emperor were to take a castle or a city from them or command some other injustice, we should then see how quickly they would find themselves obliged to resist the emperor and disobey him. But when it comes to fleecing the poor or venting their spite on the word of God, it becomes a matter of "obedience to the imperial command." Such people were formerly called scoundrels; now they have to be called obedient Christians princes. Still they will not permit anyone to appear before them for a hearing or to defend himself, no matter how humbly he may petition. If the emperor or anyone else were to treat them this way, they would regard it as quite intolerable. Such are the princes who today rule the empire in the German lands.[12] This is also why things are necessarily going so well in all the lands, as we see!

Because the raging of such fools tends toward the suppression of the Christian faith, the denying of the divine word, and the blaspheming of the Divine Majesty, I can and will no longer just look at my ungracious lords and angry nobles; I shall have to

---

[11] A proclamation dated November 7, 1522, issued by Duke George of ducal Saxony and printed and posted at various places in his realm, reminds his subjects of previous prohibitions of buying or reading Luther's books, mentions that Luther has recently published the New Testament in a German translation adorned with disgraceful drawings of the pope, and commands all subjects to deliver up their copies to the duke's nearest representative and receive the purchase price in return. A time limit is set for this surrender; after that, failure to comply will be punished. See the text in Gess, *op. cit.*, I, 386-387. Cf. also Duke George's proclamation of February 10, 1522 (see p. 77, n. 2), in which he bases his "Christian duty" upon the imperial edict of Charles V which placed Luther under the ban and proscribed the reading and printing of his books.

[12] Luther is apparently thinking particularly of the Imperial Council of Regency set up by Charles V to act as a central government during his absence from the German nation.

resist them, at least with words. And since I have not been in
terror of their idol, the pope,[13] who threatens to deprive me of
soul and of heaven, I must show that I am not in terror of his
lackeys[14] and bullies[15] who threaten to deprive me of body and
of earth. God grant that they may have to rage until the gray
coats[16] perish, and help us that we may not die of their threatenings. Amen.

First, we must provide a sound basis for the civil law and
sword so no one will doubt that it is in the world by God's will
and ordinance. The passages which do this are the following:
Romans 12, "Let every soul [*seele*] be subject to the governing
authority, for there is no authority except from God; the authority

---

[13] Luther's criticism is thus directed against the Catholic princes.

[14] *Schupen*, literally, "scales," is a favorite term of Luther for designating
the adherents of the pope. He takes it from the figure in Job 41:15-17,
where the devil is pictured as a dragon thickly covered with scales which
stick close together. Grimm, *Deutsches Wörterbuch*, IX, 2014.

[15] *Wasserblassen* (literally, "water bubble") was a derogatory German
rendering of the Latin term *bulla*, which was the common designation for
an official papal mandate or "bull." The *bulla* (literally, "bubble") actually
took its name from the leaden plate with which the document was authen-
ticated in the middle ages, namely, a circular plate in form resembling an air
bubble floating upon the water (*LW* 36, 77, n. 137). Luther delighted
in recalling the etymology of the term as a way of deflating the ego of
the bull's author (see his sarcastic *Bulla Coenae Domini* of 1522 in *WA*
8, 712-713). He used the term *Wasserblassen* also in a derived sense for
such "blusterers" or "windbags" as were devotees and adherents of the
pope and his bulls. This is the epithet which was applied to Duke George
of Saxony in a letter from Luther to Hartmuth von Cronberg of March 26 or
27, 1522. It is possible that Luther did not actually mention Duke George
by name and that in a printing not authorized by Luther the duke's name
was inserted, though Otto Clemen believes the conjunction of name and
epithet was original with Luther (*WA*, Br 2, 484-485). At any rate, when
the letter was brought to his attention, Duke George wrote Luther on
December 30, 1522, a dignified letter of protest inquiring as to Luther's part
and purpose in the matter. Luther replied on January 3, 1523, in impolite
terms, neither denying nor accepting responsibility but repeating the offensive
term in a context where the reference to Duke George had to be unmistakable. See the text of the three letters in *S-J* 2, 104-110, 153-154, 158-159;
WA 10ᴵᴵ, (42) 53-60; *WA*, Br 2, 642, and 3, 4.

[16] *Grawen röck* could have reference here to the plain and humble garb
of the peasant, utterly unpretentious and, presumably, forever plentiful. *WA*
30ᴵᴵ, 711, n. 42, 19. Usually it has reference to the world-renunciation of
monasticism, which people could hardly imagine ever passing away, as in
LW 21, 254-255; *LW* 14, 24, n. 24. In view of Luther's own anticipation
of monasticism's imminent decline (see, e.g., p. 143 in this volume), he
may here be simply borrowing—imprecisely—a current expression for indicating
a period without end. Grimm, *Deutsches Wörterbuch*, VIII, 1097.

which everywhere [*allenthalben*] exists has been ordained by God. He then who resists the governing authority resists the ordinance of God, and he who resists God's ordinance will incur judgment."[17] Again, in I Peter 2 [:13-14], "Be subject to every kind of human ordinance, whether it be to the king as supreme, or to governors,[18] as those who have been sent by him to punish the wicked and to praise the righteous."

The law of this temporal sword has existed from the beginning of the world. For when Cain slew his brother Abel, he was in such great terror of being killed in turn that God even placed a special prohibition on it and suspended the sword for his sake, so that no one was to slay him [Gen. 4:14-15]. He would not have had this fear if he had not seen and heard from Adam that murderers are to be slain. Moreover, after the Flood, God reestablished and confirmed this in unmistakable terms when he said in Genesis 9 [:6], "Whoever sheds the blood of man, by man shall his blood be shed." This cannot be understood as a plague or punishment of God upon murderers, for many murderers who are punished in other ways or pardoned altogether[19] continue to live, and eventually die by means other than the sword. Rather, it is said of the law of the sword, that a murderer is guilty of death and in justice is to be slain by the sword. Now if justice should be hindered or the sword have become negligent so that the murderer dies a natural death, Scripture is not on that account false when it says, "Whoever sheds the blood of man, by man shall his blood be shed." The credit or blame belongs to men if this law instituted by God is not carried out; just as other commandments of God, too, are broken.

Afterward it was also confirmed by the law of Moses, Exodus 21 [:14], "If a man wilfully kills another, you shall take him from

---

[17] Luther's citation here of Rom. 13:1-2 differs slightly from his rendering of the same passage in his New Testament; cf *WA*, DB 7, 68-69. Emser approved heartily of the word *"seele,"* which Luther dropped from his 1522 Testament, and of the word *"allenthalben,"* which Luther dropped from his 1546 Testament. *WA*, DB 7, 569-570. Luther's chapter reference for the same passage is given correctly on other occasions in this same treatise.

[18] *Pflegern* could have reference to any kind of administrators, supervisors, trustees, guardians, or stewards; not simply to politically appointed executive officers. Grimm, *Deutsches Wörterbuch*, VII, 1748. Luther substituted the term *Heubtleuten* in his 1546 New Testament. *WA*, DB 7, 305.

[19] *Durch pusss oder gunst;* see MA³ 5, 396, n. 11, 32.

my altar, that he may die." And again, in the same chapter,[20] "A life for a life, an eye for an eye, a tooth for a tooth, a foot for a foot, a hand for a hand, a wound for a wound, a stripe for a stripe." In addition, Christ also confirms it when he says to Peter in the garden, "He that takes the sword will perish by the sword" [Matt. 26:52], which is to be interpreted exactly like the Genesis 9 [:6] passage, "Whoever sheds the blood of man," etc. Christ is undoubtedly referring in these words to that very passage which he thereby wishes to cite and to confirm. John the Baptist also teaches the same thing. When the soldiers asked him what they should do, he answered, "Do neither violence nor injustice to any one, and be content with your wages" [Luke 3:14]. If the sword were not a godly estate, he should have directed them to get out of it, since he was supposed to make the people perfect and instruct them in a proper Christian way.[21] Hence, it is certain and clear enough that it is God's will that the temporal sword and law be used for the punishment of the wicked and the protection of the upright.

Second. There appear to be powerful arguments to the contrary. Christ says in Matthew 5 [:38-41], "You have heard that it was said to them of old: An eye for an eye, a tooth for a tooth. But I say to you, Do not resist evil; but if anyone strikes you on the right cheek, turn to him the other also. And if anyone would sue you and take your coat, let him have your cloak as well. And if anyone forces you to go one mile, go with him two miles," etc. Likewise Paul in Romans 12 [:19], "Beloved, defend[22] not yourselves, but leave it to the wrath of God; for it is written, 'Vengeance is mine; I will repay, says the Lord.'" And in Matthew 5 [:44], "Love your enemies, do good to them that hate you." And again, in I Peter 2 [3:9], "Do not return evil for evil, or reviling for reviling," etc. These and similar passages would certainly make it appear as though in the New Testament Christians were to have no temporal sword.

Hence, the sophists also say that Christ has thereby abolished the law of Moses. Of such commandments they make "counsels"

---

[20] In the sequence of Exod. 21:23-25 Luther omits "a burn for a burn."
[21] Cf. Matt. 11:9-11.
[22] *Schützet* is closer to the Vulgate's *defendentes* than to the *Rechnet* (literally, "avenge") of Luther's 1522 New Testament. WA, DB 7, 68.

for the perfect. They divide Christian teaching and Christians into two classes. One part they call the perfect, and assign to it such counsels. The other they call the imperfect, and assign to it the commandments. This they do out of sheer wantonness and caprice, without any scriptural basis. They fail to see that in the same passage Christ lays such stress on his teaching that he is unwilling to have the least word of it set aside, and condemns to hell those who do not love their enemies.[23] Therefore, we must interpret these passages differently, so that Christ's words may apply to everyone alike, be he perfect or imperfect. For perfection and imperfection do not consist in works, and do not establish any distinct external order among Christians. They exist in the heart, in faith and love, so that those who believe and love the most are the perfect ones, whether they be outwardly male or female, prince or peasant, monk or layman. For love and faith produce no sects[24] or outward differences.

Third. Here we must divide the children of Adam and all mankind into two classes, the first belonging to the kingdom of God, the second to the kingdom of the world. Those who belong to the kingdom of God are all the true believers who are in Christ and under Christ, for Christ is King and Lord in the kingdom of God, as Psalm 2 [:6] and all of Scripture says. For this reason he came into the world, that he might begin God's kingdom and establish it in the world. Therefore, he says before Pilate, "My kingdom is not of the world, but every one who is of the truth hears my voice" [John 18:36-37]. In the gospel he continually refers to the kingdom of God, and says, "Amend your ways, the kingdom of God is at hand" [Matt. 4:17, 10:7]; again, "Seek first the kingdom of God and his righteousness" [Matt. 6:33]. He also calls the gospel a gospel of the kingdom of God;[25] because it teaches, governs, and upholds[26] God's kingdom.

---

23 Cf. Matt. 5:17-22.
24 Cf. Gal. 3:28; 5:6. By "sect" Luther means the divergences, rivalries, and jealousies between the various monastic orders and theological factions. Cf. *LW* 35, 80, and *LW* 36, 78, n. 138.
25 In Mark 1:14 the KJV phrase is more accurate than that of the RSV, which omits the term "kingdom." George Arthur Buttrick (commentary ed.), *The Interpreter's Bible* (New York: Abingdon-Cokesbury, 1951-1957), VII, 655.
26 *Enthellt* is here taken to mean *erhält*, following *CL* 2, 365, n. 6.

Now observe, these people need no temporal law or sword. If all the world were composed of real Christians, that is, true believers, there would be no need for or benefits from prince, king, lord, sword, or law. They would serve no purpose, since Christians have in their heart the Holy Spirit, who both teaches and makes them to do injustice to no one, to love everyone, and to suffer injustice and even death willingly and cheerfully at the hands of anyone. Where there is nothing but the unadulterated doing of right and bearing of wrong, there is no need for any suit, litigation, court, judge, penalty, law, or sword. For this reason it is impossible that the temporal sword and law should find any work to do among Christians, since they do of their own accord much more than all laws and teachings can demand, just as Paul says in I Timothy 1 [:9], "The law is not laid down for the just but for the lawless."

Why is this? It is because the righteous man of his own accord does all and more than the law demands. But the unrighteous do nothing that the law demands; therefore, they need the law to instruct, constrain, and compel them to do good. A good tree needs no instruction or law to bear good fruit;[27] its nature causes it to bear according to its kind without any law or instruction. I would take to be quite a fool any man who would make a book full of laws and statutes for an apple tree telling it how to bear apples and not thorns, when the tree is able by its own nature to do this better than the man with all his books can describe and demand. Just so, by the Spirit and by faith all Christians are so thoroughly disposed and conditioned in their very nature[28] that they do right and keep the law better than one can teach them with all manner of statutes; so far as they themselves are concerned, no statutes or laws are needed.

You ask: Why, then, did God give so many commandments to all mankind, and why does Christ prescribe in the gospel so many things for us to do? Of this I have written at length in the

---

[27] Cf. Matt. 7:17-18.
[28] *Aller ding genaturt;* cf. MA³ 5, 396, n. 14, 3, *"durchaus von Natur geartet,"* and Grimm, *Deutsches Wörterbuch,* IV, 3347, *"die damalige form des sog. determinismus."*

Postils[29] and elsewhere. To put it here as briefly as possible, Paul says that the law has been laid down for the sake of the lawless [I Tim. 1:9], that is, so that those who are not Christians may through the law be restrained outwardly from evil deeds, as we shall hear later. Now since no one is by nature Christian or righteous, but altogether sinful and wicked, God through the law puts them all under restraint so they dare not wilfully implement their wickedness in actual deeds. In addition, Paul ascribes to the law another function in Romans 7 and Galatians 2,[30] that of teaching men to recognize sin in order that it may make them humble unto grace and unto faith in Christ. Christ does the same thing here in Matthew 5 [:39], where he teaches that we should not resist evil; by this he is interpreting the law and teaching what ought to be and must be the state and temper of a true Christian, as we shall hear further later on.[31]

Fourth. All who are not Christians belong to the kingdom of the world and are under the law. There are few true believers, and still fewer who live a Christian life, who do not resist evil and indeed themselves do no evil. For this reason God has provided for them a different government beyond the Christian estate and kingdom of God. He has subjected them to the sword so that, even though they would like to, they are unable to practice their wickedness, and if they do practice it they cannot do so without fear or with success and impunity. In the same way a savage wild beast is bound with chains and ropes so that it cannot bite and tear as it would normally do, even though it would like to; whereas a tame and gentle animal needs no restraint, but is harmless despite the lack of chains and ropes.

---

[29] The Postils were a collection of sermons expounding the Epistles and Gospels for the Sundays and festivals of the church year. Luther had published the Advent Postil in Latin in March of 1521 (see the text in WA 7 [458] 463-537). His German Postil, the so-called Wartburg Postil, began to appear in March, 1522, with the Christmas-Epiphany cycle, which preceded the German Advent sermons by more than a month (see the respective texts in WA 10I, 1, [vii] 1-728 and WA 10I, 2, [ix] 1-208). On the function of the law see especially WA 7, 476-477, and 504-505; see also in Luther's 1521 *A Brief Instruction on What to Look for and Expect in the Gospels*, originally intended as an introduction to the entire Wartburg Postil, "The fact that Christ and the apostles . . . explain the law is to be counted a benefit just like any other work of Christ." LW 35, 120.

[30] Rom. 7:7-13; Gal. 3:19, 24; cf. Rom. 3:20.

[31] See pp. 676-677.

If this were not so, men would devour one another, seeing that the whole world is evil and that among thousands there is scarcely a single true Christian. No one could support wife and child, feed himself, and serve God. The world would be reduced to chaos. For this reason God has ordained two governments: the spiritual, by which the Holy Spirit produces Christians and righteous people under Christ; and the temporal, which restrains the un-Christian and wicked so that—no thanks to them—they are obliged to keep still and to maintain an outward peace. Thus does St. Paul interpret the temporal sword in Romans 13 [:3], when he says it is not a terror to good conduct but to bad. And Peter says it is for the punishment of the wicked [I Pet. 2:14].

If anyone attempted to rule the world by the gospel and to abolish all temporal law and sword on the plea that all are baptized and Christian, and that, according to the gospel, there shall be among them no law or sword—or need for either—pray tell me, friend, what would he be doing? He would be loosing the ropes and chains of the savage wild beasts and letting them bite and mangle everyone, meanwhile insisting that they were harmless, tame, and gentle creatures; but I would have the proof in my wounds. Just so would the wicked under the name of Christian abuse evangelical freedom, carry on their rascality, and insist that they were Christians subject neither to law nor sword, as some are already raving and ranting.[32]

To such a one we must say: Certainly it is true that Christians, so far as they themselves are concerned, are subject neither to law nor sword, and have need of neither. But take heed and first fill the world with real Christians before you attempt to rule it in a Christian and evangelical manner. This you will never accomplish; for the world and the masses are and always will be un-Christian, even if they are all baptized and Christian in name. Christians are few and far between (as the saying is). Therefore, it is out of the question that there should be a common Christian government over the whole world, or indeed over a single country or any considerable body of people, for the wicked always outnumber the good. Hence, a man who would venture to govern

---

32 The allusion is to the Anabaptists.

an entire country or the world with the gospel would be like a shepherd who should put together in one fold wolves, lions, eagles, and sheep, and let them mingle freely with one another, saying, "Help yourselves, and be good and peaceful toward one another. The fold is open, there is plenty of food. You need have no fear of dogs and clubs." The sheep would doubtless keep the peace and allow themselves to be fed and governed peacefully, but they would not live long, nor would one beast survive another.

For this reason one must carefully distinguish between these two governments. Both must be permitted to remain; the one to produce righteousness, the other to bring about external peace and prevent evil deeds. Neither one is sufficient in the world without the other. No one can become righteous in the sight of God by means of the temporal government, without Christ's spiritual government. Christ's government does not extend over all men; rather, Christians are always a minority in the midst of non-Christians. Now where temporal government or law alone prevails, there sheer hypocrisy is inevitable, even though the commandments be God's very own. For without the Holy Spirit in the heart no one becomes truly righteous, no matter how fine the works he does. On the other hand, where the spiritual government alone prevails over land and people, there wickedness is given free rein and the door is open for all manner of rascality, for the world as a whole cannot receive or comprehend it.

Now you see the intent of Christ's words which we quoted above from Matthew 5,[33] that Christians should not go to law or use the temporal sword among themselves. Actually, he says this only to his beloved Christians, those who alone accept it and act accordingly, who do not make "counsels"[34] out of it as the sophists do, but in their heart are so disposed and conditioned [*genaturt*] by the Spirit that they do evil to no one and willingly endure evil at the hands of others. If now the whole world were Christian in this sense, then these words would apply to all, and all would act accordingly. Since the world is un-Christian, however, these words do not apply to all; and all do not act accordingly, but are under another government in which those who are

---

[33]See the quotation of Matt. 5:38-41 on p. 661.
[34]See p. 656, n. 6.

not Christian are kept under external constraint and compelled to keep the peace and do what is good.

This is also why Christ did not wield the sword, or give it a place in his kingdom.[35] For he is a king over Christians and rules by his Holy Spirit alone, without law. Although he sanctions the sword, he did not make use of it, for it serves no purpose in his kingdom, in which there are none but the upright. Hence, David of old was not permitted to build the temple [II Sam. 7:4-13], because he had wielded the sword and had shed much blood. Not that he had done wrong thereby, but because he could not be a type of Christ, who without the sword was to have a kingdom of peace. It had to be built instead by Solomon, whose name in German means "Friedrich" or "peaceful";[36] he had a peaceful kingdom, by which the truly peaceful kingdom of Christ, the real Friedrich and Solomon, could be represented. Again, "during the entire building of the temple no tool of iron was heard," as the text says [I Kings 6:7]; all for this reason, that Christ, without constraint and force, without law and sword, was to have a people who would serve him willingly.

That is what the prophets mean in Psalm 110 [:3], "Your people will act of their free volition"; and in Isaiah 11 [:9], "They shall not hurt or destroy in all my holy mountain"; and again in Isaiah 2 [:4], "They shall beat their swords into plowshares and their spears into pruning hooks, and no one shall lift up the sword against another, neither shall they put their efforts into war any more," etc. Whoever would extend the application of these and similar passages to wherever Christ's name is mentioned, would entirely pervert the Scripture; rather, they are spoken only of true Christians, who really do this among themselves.

Fifth. But you say: if Christians then do not need the temporal sword or law, why does Paul say to all Christians in Romans 13 [:1], "Let all souls be subject to the governing authority," and St. Peter, "Be subject to every human ordinance"

---

[35] Cf. Matt. 26:52-53; John 18:36.
[36] "Solomon" is derived from the Hebrew word for "peace," *shalom.* The equivalent German "Friedrich" means literally "one who is rich in peace." Cf. Jerome's *Liber de Nominibus Hebraicis: "Salomon, pacificus, sive pacatus erit." MPL* 23, 843.

[I Pet. 2:13], etc., as quoted above?[37] Answer: I have just said that Christians, among themselves and by and for themselves, need no law or sword, since it is neither necessary nor useful for them. Since a true Christian lives and labors on earth not for himself alone but for his neighbor, he does by the very nature of his spirit even what he himself has no need of, but is needful and useful to his neighbor. Because the sword is most beneficial and necessary for the whole world in order to preserve peace, punish sin, and restrain the wicked, the Christian submits most willingly to the rule of the sword, pays his taxes, honors those in authority,[38] serves, helps, and does all he can to assist the governing authority, that it may continue to function and be held in honor and fear. Although he has no need of these things for himself—to him they are not essential—nevertheless, he concerns himself about what is serviceable and of benefit to others, as Paul teaches in Ephesians 5 [:21—6:9].

Just as he performs all other works of love which he himself does not need—he does not visit the sick in order that he himself may be made well, or feed others because he himself needs food—so he serves the governing authority not because he needs it but for the sake of others, that they may be protected and that the wicked may not become worse. He loses nothing by this; such service in no way harms him, yet it is of great benefit to the world. If he did not so serve he would be acting not as a Christian but even contrary to love; he would also be setting a bad example to others who in like manner would not submit to authority, even though they were not Christians. In this way the gospel would be brought into disrepute, as though it taught insurrection and produced self-willed people unwilling to benefit or serve others, when in fact it makes a Christian the servant of all.[39] Thus in Matthew 17 [:27] Christ paid the half-shekel tax that he might not offend them, although he had no need to do so.

Thus you observe in the words of Christ quoted above from

---

[37] See p. 660.

[38] Cf. Rom. 13:6-7.

[39] See Luther's 1520 *The Freedom of a Christian* where Romans 13 and Matthew 17 are also cited in illustration of the Christian's willing service to others. *LW* 31, 343-377, especially p. 369.

Matthew 5⁴⁰ that he clearly teaches that Christians among themselves should have no temporal sword or law. He does not, however, forbid one to serve and be subject to those who do have the secular sword and law. Rather, since you do not need it and should not have it, you are to serve all the more those who have not attained to such heights as you and who therefore do still need it. Although you do not need to have your enemy punished, your afflicted neighbor does. You should help him that he may have peace and that his enemy may be curbed, but this is not possible unless the governing authority is honored and feared. Christ does not say, "You shall not serve the governing authority or be subject to it," but rather, "Do not resist evil" [Matt. 5:39], as much as to say, "Behave in such a way that you bear everything, so that you may not need the governing authority to help you and serve you or be beneficial or essential for you, but that you in turn may help and serve it, being beneficial and essential to it. I would have you be too exalted and far too noble to have any need of it; it should rather have need of you."

Sixth. You ask whether a Christian too may bear the temporal sword and punish the wicked, since Christ's words, "Do not resist evil," are so clear and definite that the sophists have had to make of them a "counsel." Answer: You have now heard two propositions. One is that the sword can have no place among Christians; therefore, you cannot bear it among Christians or hold it over them, for they do not need it. The question, therefore, must be referred to the other group, the non-Christians, whether you may bear it there in a Christian manner. Here the other proposition applies, that you are under obligation to serve and assist the sword by whatever means you can, with body, goods, honor, and soul. For it is something which you do not need, but which is very beneficial and essential for the whole world and for your neighbor. Therefore, if you see that there is a lack of hangmen, constables, judges, lords, or princes, and you find that you are qualified, you should offer your services and seek the position, that the essential governmental authority may not be despised and become enfeebled or perish. The world cannot and dare not dispense with it.

Here is the reason why you should do this: In such a case

---

⁴⁰Matt. 5:38-41 was quoted on p. 661.

you would be entering entirely into the service and work of others, which would be of advantage neither to yourself nor your property or honor, but only to your neighbor and to others. You would be doing it not with the purpose of avenging yourself or returning evil for evil, but for the good of your neighbor and for the maintenance of the safety and peace of others. For yourself, you would abide by the gospel and govern yourself according to Christ's word [Matt. 5:39-40], gladly turning the other cheek and letting the cloak go with the coat when the matter concerned you and your cause.

In this way the two propositions are brought into harmony with one another: at one and the same time you satisfy God's kingdom inwardly and the kingdom of the world outwardly. You suffer evil and injustice, and yet at the same time you punish evil and injustice; you do not resist evil, and yet at the same time, you do resist it. In the one case, you consider yourself and what is yours; in the other, you consider your neighbor and what is his. In what concerns you and yours, you govern yourself by the gospel and suffer injustice toward yourself as a true Christian; in what concerns the person or property of others, you govern yourself according to love and tolerate no injustice toward your neighbor. The gospel does not forbid this; in fact, in other places it actually commands it.

From the beginning of the world all the saints have wielded the sword in this way: Adam and his descendants; Abraham when he rescued Lot, his brother's son, and routed the four kings as related in Genesis 14 [:8-16], although he was a thoroughly evangelical man. Thus did Samuel, the holy prophet, slay King Agag, as we read in I Samuel 15 [:33]; and Elijah slew the prophets of Baal, I Kings 18 [:40]. So too did Moses, Joshua, the children of Israel, Samson, David, and all the kings and princes in the Old Testament wield the sword; also Daniel and his associates, Hananiah, Azariah, and Mishael, in Babylon; and Joseph in Egypt, and so on.

Should anyone contend that the Old Testament is abrogated and no longer in effect, and that therefore such examples cannot be set before Christians, I answer: That is not so. St. Paul says in I Corinthians 10 [:3-4], "They ate the same spiritual food as we, and drank the same spiritual drink from the Rock, which is Christ." That is, they had the same Spirit and faith in Christ as we have, and were just as much Christians as we are. Therefore, wherein they did right, all Christians do right, from the beginning of the world unto the end. For time and external circumstances make no difference among Christians. Neither is it true that the Old Testament was abrogated in such a way that it must not be kept, or that whoever kept it fully would be doing wrong, as St. Jerome and many others[41] mistakenly held. Rather, it is abrogated in the sense that we are free to keep it or not to keep it, and it is no longer necessary to keep it on penalty of losing one's soul, as was the case at that time.

Paul says in I Corinthians 7 [:19] and Galatians 6 [:15] that neither uncircumcision nor circumcision counts for anything, but only a new creature in Christ. That is, it is not sin to be uncircumcised, as the Jews thought, nor is it sin to be circumcised, as the Gentiles thought. Either is right and permissible for him who does not think he will thereby become righteous or be saved. The same is true of all other parts of the Old Testament; it is not wrong to ignore them and it is not wrong to abide by them, but it is permissible and proper either to follow them or to omit them. Indeed, if it were necessary or profitable for the salvation of one's neighbor, it would be necessary to keep all of them. For everyone is under obligation to do what is for his neighbor's good, be it Old Testament or New, Jewish or Gentile, as Paul teaches

---

[41] Jerome (*ca.* 342-420), translator of the Vulgate and distinguished biblical commentator, had been attacked by Augustine (354-430) in 394 or 395 for his interpretation of Gal. 2:11-14. In the ensuing lively and sometimes bitter literary exchange between the Roman scholar and the North African bishop, Jerome had at one point crystallized the debate in these terms, admittedly derived from the philosophers, "To carry out the ceremonies of the Law cannot be an indifferent act; it is either bad or good. You say it is good; I insist that it is wrong." See Jerome's letter 112, 16, dated *ca.* A.D. 404 in *MPL* 22, 926; *FC* 20, 360.

Jerome enumerated among those who were his guides in the matter particularly Origen, and also Didymus the Blind, Apollinaris of Laodicea, Alexander ("the former heretic" who had ordained Origen), Eusebius of Emesa, Theodore of Heraclea, and John Chrysostom. *FC* 20, 345-348; cf. pp. 410-411.

Luther apparently sided with Augustine, whose rebuttal was that "these observances [circumcision, *et al*] were neither to be required as necessary, nor condemned as sacrilegious." *FC* 20, 399. On the whole issue, see Luther's *How Christians Should Regard Moses* (1525). *LW* 35, (155) 161-174.

in I Corinthians 12.[42] For love pervades all and transcends all; it considers only what is necessary and beneficial to others, and does not ask whether it is old or new. Hence, the precedents for the use of the sword also are matters of freedom, and you may follow them or not. But where you see that your neighbor needs it, there love constrains you to do as a matter of necessity that which would otherwise be optional and not necessary for you either to do or to leave undone. Only do not suppose that you will thereby become righteous or be saved—as the Jews presumed to be saved by their works—but leave this to faith, which without works makes you a new creature.

To prove our position also by the New Testament, the testimony of John the Baptist in Luke 3 [:14] stands unshaken on this point. There can be no doubt that it was his task to point to Christ, witness for him, and teach about him; that is to say, the teaching of the man who was to lead a truly perfected people to Christ had of necessity to be purely New Testament and evangelical. John confirms the soldiers' calling, saying they should be content with their wages. Now if it had been un-Christian to bear the sword, he ought to have censured them for it and told them to abandon both wages and sword, else he would not have been teaching them Christianity aright. So likewise, when St. Peter in Acts 10 [:34-43] preached Christ to Cornelius, he did not tell him to abandon his profession, which he would have had to do if it had prevented Cornelius from being a Christian. Moreover, before he was baptized the Holy Spirit came upon him [Acts 10:44-48]. St. Luke[43] also praises him as an upright man prior to St. Peter's sermon, and does not criticize him for being a soldier, the centurion of a pagan emperor [Acts 10:1-2]. It is only right that what the Holy Spirit permitted to remain and did not censure in the case of Cornelius, we too should permit and not censure.

A similar case is that of the Ethiopian captain, the eunuch in Acts 8 [:27-39], whom Philip the evangelist converted and baptized and permitted to return home and remain in office, although without the sword he could not possibly have been so high an official under the queen of Ethiopia. It was the same too

---

[42] I Cor. 12:13; cf. 9:19-22.
[43] Luther accepted the Lucan authorship of the book of Acts. *LW* 35, 363-364.

with the proconsul of Cyprus, Sergius Paulus, in Acts 13 [:7-12];
St. Paul converted him, and yet permitted him to remain proconsul
over and among heathen. The same policy was followed by many
holy martyrs who continued obedient to pagan Roman emperors,
went into battle under them, and undoubtedly slew people for
the sake of preserving peace, as is written of St. Maurice, St.
Acacius, St. Gereon, and many others under the emperor Julian.[44]

Moreover, we have the clear and compelling text of St. Paul
in Romans 13 [:1], where he says, "The governing authority has
been ordained by God"; and further, "The governing authority
does not bear the sword in vain. It is God's servant for your good,
an avenger upon him who does evil" [Rom. 13:4]. Be not so
wicked, my friend, as to say, "A Christian may not do that which
is God's own peculiar work, ordinance, and creation." Else you
must also say, "A Christian must not eat, drink, or be married,"
for these are also God's work and ordinance. If it is God's work
and creation, then it is good, so good that everyone can use it
in a Christian and salutary way, as Paul says in II Timothy 4 [I
Tim. 4:4, 3], "Everything created by God is good, and nothing
is to be rejected by those who believe and know the truth." Under
"everything created by God" you must include not simply food
and drink, clothing and shoes, but also authority and subjection,
protection and punishment.

In short, since Paul says here that the governing authority
is God's servant, we must allow it to be exercised not only by

----

44 Maurice, the patron saint of Magdeburg, was commander of the Theban
legion which, according to legend, was composed entirely of Christians, sixty-
six thousand men from Thebes in North Africa. They were willing to
"render unto Caesar" military service in a just war, but were massacred (*ca.*
287) on order of the emperor Maximian Herculius (285-310) when they
refused to make the usual sacrifice to the pagan gods and aid in the extermi-
nation of the Christians in Gaul. See Ryan and Ripperger, *The Golden
Legend of Jacobus de Voragine*, II, 566-569.

Acacius, a Cappadocian centurian in the Roman army stationed at Thrace,
was tortured and beheaded at Byzantium (*ca.* 303) under Diocletian (284-
305). The Benedictine Monks of St. Augustine's Abbey, Ramsgate, *The Book
of the Saints* (New York: Macmillan, 1947), p. 4.

Gereon, according to unreliable tradition, was a member of the Theban
legion, 319 of whom were martyred as a group near Cologne. *Ibid.*, p. 262.

Julian the Apostate was Roman emperor in 361-363. Luther probably confused him here with Diocletian and Maximian, under whom the specifically
named saints were martyred. Julian's policy was to degrade Christianity
and promote paganism, but without resort to force or persecution.

the heathen but by all men. What can be the meaning of the phrase, "It is God's servant," except that governing authority is by its very nature such that through it one may serve God? Now it would be quite un-Christian to say that there is any service of God in which a Christian should not or must not take part, when service of God is actually more characteristic[45] of Christians than of anyone else. It would even be fine and fitting if all princes were good, true Christians. For the sword and authority, as a particular service of God, belong more appropriately[46] to Christians than to any other men on earth. Therefore, you should esteem the sword or governmental authority as highly as the estate of marriage, or husbandry, or any other calling which God has instituted. Just as one can serve God in the estate of marriage, or in farming or a trade, for the benefit of others—and must so serve if his neighbor needs it—so one can serve God in government, and should there serve if the needs of his neighbor demand it. For those who punish evil and protect the good are God's servants and workmen. Only, one should also be free not to do it if there is no need for it, just as we are free not to marry or farm where there is no need for them.

You ask: Why did not Christ and the apostles bear the sword? Answer: You tell me, why did Christ not take a wife, or become a cobbler or a tailor. If an office or vocation were to be regarded as disreputable on the ground that Christ did not pursue it himself, what would become of all the offices and vocations other than the ministry, the one occupation he did follow? Christ pursued his own office and vocation, but he did not thereby reject any other. It was not incumbent upon him to bear the sword, for he was to exercise only that function by which his kingdom is governed and which properly serves his kingdom. Now, it is not essential to his kingdom that he be a married man, a cobbler, tailor, farmer, prince, hangman, or constable; neither is the temporal sword or law essential to it, but only God's Word and Spirit. It is by these that his people are ruled inwardly. This is the office which he also exercised then and still exercises now,

---

[45] *So eben eygent.* Cf. MA³ 5, 397, n. 21, 13, "*So ganz zu seinem Wesen Gehört.*"
[46] *Gepürt . . . zu eygen.* Cf. Grimm, *Deutsches Wörterbuch*, IV¹, 1893-1895.

always bestowing God's Word and Spirit. And in this office the apostles and all spiritual rulers had to follow him. For in order to do their job right they are so busily occupied with the spiritual sword, the Word of God, that they must perforce neglect the temporal sword and leave it to others who do not have to preach, although it is not contrary to their calling to use it, as I have said. For each one must attend to the duties of his own calling.

Therefore, although Christ did not bear or prescribe the sword, it is sufficient that he did not forbid or abolish it but actually confirmed it; just as it is sufficient that he did not abolish the estate of marriage but confirmed it, though without himself taking a wife or setting forth a teaching concerning it. He had to manifest himself wholly in connection with that estate and calling which alone expressly served his kingdom, lest from his example there should be deduced the justification or necessity of teaching and believing that the kingdom of God could not exist without matrimony and the sword and similar externals (since Christ's example is necessarily binding), when in fact it exists solely by God's Word and Spirit. This was and had to be Christ's peculiar function as the Supreme King in this kingdom. Since not all Christians, however, have this same function (although they are entitled to it), it is fitting that they should have some other external office by which God may also be served.

From all this we gain the true meaning of Christ's words in Matthew 5 [:39], "Do not resist evil," etc. It is this: A Christian should be so disposed that he will suffer every evil and injustice without avenging himself; neither will he seek legal redress in the courts but have utterly no need of temporal authority and law for his own sake. On behalf of others, however, he may and should seek vengeance, justice, protection, and help, and do as much as he can to achieve it. Likewise, the governing authority should, on its own initiative or through the instigation of others, help and protect him too, without any complaint, application, or instigation on his own part. If it fails to do this, he should permit himself to be despoiled and slandered; he should not resist evil, as Christ's words say.

Be certain too that this teaching of Christ is not a counsel for those who would be perfect, as our sophists blasphemously and falsely say,[47] but a universally obligatory command for all Christians. Then you will realize that all those who avenge themselves or go to law and wrangle in the courts over their property and honor are nothing but heathen masquerading under the name of Christians. It cannot be otherwise, I tell you. Do not be dissuaded by the multitude and common practice; for there are few Christians on earth—have no doubt about it—and God's word is something very different from the common practice.[48]

Here you see that Christ is not abrogating the law when he says, "You have heard that it was said to them of old, 'An eye for an eye'; but I say to you: Do not resist evil," etc. [Matt. 5:38-39]. On the contrary, he is expounding the meaning of the law as it is to be understood, as if he were to say, "You Jews think that it is right and proper in the sight of God to recover by law what is yours. You rely on what Moses said, 'An eye for an eye,' etc. But I say to you that Moses set this law over the wicked, who do not belong to God's kingdom, in order that they might not avenge themselves or do worse but be compelled by such outward law to desist from evil, in order that by outward law and rule they might be kept subordinate to the governing authority. You, however, should so conduct yourselves that you neither need nor resort to such law. Although the temporal authority must have such a law by which to judge unbelievers, and although you yourselves may also use it for judging others, still you should not invoke or use it for yourselves and in your own affairs. You have the kingdom of heaven; therefore, you should leave the kingdom of earth to anyone who wants to take it."

There you see that Christ does not interpret his words to mean that he is abrogating the law of Moses or prohibiting temporal authority. He is rather making an exception of his own people. They are not to use the secular authority for themselves but leave it to unbelievers. Yet they may also serve these unbelievers, even with their own law, since they are not Christians and no one can be forced into Christianity. That Christ's words apply only to his own is evident from the fact that later on he says they should love their enemies and be perfect like their

---

[47] See p. 82, n. 6.

[48] Cf. Tertullian, *De virginibus velandis*, chap. i, "Christ did not say, 'I am the common practice,' but, 'I am the truth.'" *MPL* 2, 889.

heavenly Father [Matt. 5:44, 48]. But he who loves his enemies and is perfect leaves the law alone and does not use it to demand an eye for an eye. Neither does he restrain the non-Christians, however, who do not love their enemies and who do wish to make use of the law; indeed, he lends his help that these laws may hinder the wicked from doing worse.

Thus the word of Christ is now reconciled, I believe, with the passages which establish the sword, and the meaning is this: No Christian shall wield or invoke the sword for himself and his cause. In behalf of another, however, he may and should wield it and invoke it to restrain wickedness and to defend godliness. Even as the Lord says in the same chapter [Matt. 5:34-37], "A Christian should not swear, but his word should be Yes, yes; No, no." That is, for himself and of his own volition and desire, he should not swear. When it is needful or necessary, however, and salvation or the honor of God demands it, he should swear. Thus, he uses the forbidden oath to serve another, just as he uses the forbidden sword to serve another. Christ and Paul often swore in order to make their teaching and testimony valuable and credible to others,[49] as men do and have the right to do in covenants and compacts, etc., of which Psalm 63 [:11] says, "They shall be praised who swear by his name."

Here you inquire further, whether constables, hangmen, jurists, lawyers, and others of similar function can also be Christians and in a state of salvation. Answer: If the governing authority and its sword are a divine service, as was proved above, then everything that is essential for the authority's bearing of the sword must also be divine service. There must be those who arrest, prosecute, execute, and destroy the wicked, and who protect, acquit, defend, and save the good. Therefore, when they perform their duties, not with the intention of seeking their own ends but only of helping the law and the governing authority function to coerce the wicked, there is no peril in that; they may use their office like anybody else would use his trade, as a means of livelihood. For, as has been said, love of neighbor is not concerned about its own; it considers not how great or humble, but how

---

[49] Cf., e.g., Christ's frequent use of the expression, "Truly, I say to you," and Paul's mentioning of God as his witness in II Cor. 11:31 and Gal. 1:20.

profitable and needful the works are for neighbor or community.

You may ask, "Why may I not use the sword for myself and for my own cause, so long as it is my intention not to seek my own advantage but to punish evil?" Answer: Such a miracle is not impossible, but very rare and hazardous. Where the Spirit is so richly present it may well happen. For we read thus of Samson in Judges 15 [:11], that he said, "As they did to me, so have I done to them," [50] even though Proverbs 24 [:29] says to the contrary, "Do not say, I will do to him as he has done to me," and Proverbs 20 [:22] adds, "Do not say, I will repay him his evil." Samson was called of God to harass the Philistines and deliver the children of Israel. Although he used them as an occasion to further his own cause, still he did not do so in order to avenge himself or to seek his own interests, but to serve others and to punish the Philistines [Judg. 14:4]. No one but a true Christian, filled with the Spirit, will follow this example. Where reason too tries to do likewise, it will probably contend that it is not trying to seek its own, but this will be basically untrue, for it cannot be done without grace. Therefore first become like Samson, and then you can also do as Samson did.

Part Two [51]

How Far Temporal Authority Extends

We come now to the main part of this treatise.[52] Having learned that there must be temporal authority on earth, and how it is to be exercised in a Christian and salutary manner, we must now learn how far its arm extends and how widely its hand stretches, lest it extend too far and encroach upon God's kingdom and government. It is essential for us to know this, for where it is given too wide a scope, intolerable and terrible injury follows; on the other hand, injury is also inevitable where it is restricted too narrowly. In the former case, the temporal authority punishes too much; in the latter case, it punishes too little. To err in this

[50] Luther had used this same verse to close his important 1520 statement on *Why the Books of the Pope and His Disciples Were Burned by Doctor Martin Luther.* LW 31, (379) 383-395.

[51] The main divisions of the treatise are suggested in Luther's dedication to Duke John; see p. 655.

[52] *Sermon.*

direction, however, and punish too little is more tolerable, for it is always better to let a scoundrel live than to put a godly man to death. The world has plenty of scoundrels anyway and must continue to have them, but godly men are scarce.

It is to be noted first that the two classes of Adam's children—the one in God's kingdom under Christ and the other in the kingdom of the world under the governing authority, as was said above—have two kinds of law. For every kingdom must have its own laws and statutes; without law no kingdom or government can survive, as everyday experience amply shows. The temporal government has laws which extend no further than to life and property and external affairs on earth, for God cannot and will not permit anyone but himself to rule over the soul. Therefore, where the temporal authority presumes to prescribe laws for the soul, it encroaches upon God's government and only misleads souls and destroys them. We want to make this so clear that everyone will grasp it, and that our fine gentlemen, the princes and bishops, will see what fools they are when they seek to coerce the people with their laws and commandments into believing this or that.

When a man-made law is imposed upon the soul to make it believe this or that as its human author may prescribe, there is certainly no word of God for it. If there is no word of God for it, then we cannot be sure whether God wishes to have it so, for we cannot be certain that something which he does not command is pleasing to him. Indeed, we are sure that it does not please him, for he desires that our faith be based simply and entirely on his divine word alone. He says in Matthew 18 [16:18], "On this rock I will build my church"; and in John 10 [:27, 14, 5], "My sheep hear my voice and know me; however, they will not hear the voice of a stranger, but flee from him." From this it follows that with such a wicked command the temporal power is driving souls to eternal death. For it compels them to believe as right and certainly pleasing to God that which is in fact uncertain, indeed, certain to be displeasing to him since there is no clear word of God for it. Whoever believes something to be right which is wrong or uncertain is denying the truth, which is God himself. He is believing in lies and errors, and counting as right that which is wrong.

Hence, it is the height of folly when they command that one shall believe the Church,[53] the fathers, and the councils, though there be no word of God for it. It is not the church but the devil's apostles who command such things, for the church commands nothing unless it knows for certain that it is God's word. As St. Peter puts it, "Whoever speaks, let him speak as the word of God" [I Pet. 4:11]. It will be a long time, however, before they can ever prove that the decrees of the councils are God's word.[54] Still more foolish is it when they assert that kings, princes, and the mass of mankind believe thus and so. My dear man, we are not baptized into kings, or princes, or even into the mass of mankind, but into Christ and God himself. Neither are we called kings, princes, or common folk, but Christians. No one shall or can command the soul unless he is able to show it the way to heaven; but this no man can do, only God alone. Therefore, in matters which concern the salvation of souls nothing but God's word shall be taught and accepted.

Again, consummate fools though they are, they must confess that they have no power over souls. For no human being can kill a soul or give it life, or conduct it to heaven or hell. If they will not take our word for it, Christ himself will attend to it strongly enough where he says in the tenth chapter of Matthew, "Do not fear those who kill the body, and after that have nothing that they can do; rather fear him who after he has killed the body, has power to condemn to hell." [55] I think it is clear enough here that the soul is taken out of all human hands and is placed under the authority of God alone.

Now tell me: How much wit must there be in the head of a person who imposes commands in an area where he has no authority whatsoever? Would you not judge the person insane

---

[53] In this paragraph Luther uses the term *Kirche* in two different senses. Here, spelled with a capital "K" it signifies the external organization, which to his contemporaries meant the pope, cardinals, *et al.* In the next sentence, spelled with a lower case "k," it signifies the totality of true believers.

[54] This was a conviction which the Leipzig debate of 1519 with Johann Eck helped to bring into sharp focus for Luther. See Schwiebert, *Luther and His Times*, pp. 410-411, 416-417.

[55] Luther might even have strengthened his case had he actually quoted Matt. 10:28 ("who kill the body but cannot kill the soul," etc.) rather than its less specific parallel in Luke 12:4-5.

who commanded the moon to shine whenever he wanted it to? How well would it go if the Leipzigers were to impose laws on us Wittenbergers, or if, conversely, we in Wittenberg were to legislate for the people of Leipzig![56] They would certainly send the lawmakers a thank-offering of hellebore[57] to purge their brains and cure their sniffles. Yet our emperor and clever princes are doing just that today. They are allowing pope, bishop, and sophists to lead them on—one blind man leading the other—[58] to command their subjects to believe, without God's word, whatever they please. And still they would be known as Christian princes,[59] God forbid!

Besides, we cannot conceive how an authority could or should act in a situation except where it can see, know, judge, condemn, change, and modify. What would I think of a judge who should blindly decide cases which he neither hears nor sees? Tell me then: How can a mere man see, know, judge, condemn, and change hearts? That is reserved for God alone, as Psalm 7 [:9] says, "God tries the hearts and reins"; and [v. 8], "The Lord judges the peoples." And Acts 10[60] says, "God knows the hearts"; and Jeremiah 1 [17:9-10], "Wicked and unsearchable is the human heart; who can understand it? I the Lord, who search the heart and reins." A court should and must be quite certain and clear about everything if it is to render judgment. But the thoughts and inclinations of the soul can be known to no one but God. Therefore, it is futile and impossible to command or compel anyone by force to believe this or that. The matter must be approached in a different way. Force will not accomplish it. And I am surprised at the big fools, for they themselves all say: *De*

---

[56] Leipzig was the capital of Albertine Saxony, ruled by the hostile Duke George the Bearded from 1500-1539 (see p. 77, n. 2), while Wittenberg was the capital of Ernestine Saxony, ruled by the friendly Elector Frederick the Wise from 1486-1525.

[57] *Nysse wortz* was a plant whose pulverized roots were used to induce sneezing, which since ancient times was thought to be a cure for various mental disorders including insanity and epilepsy. Grimm, *Deutsches Wörterbuch*, VII, 837.

[58] Cf. Matt. 15:14; Luke 6:39.

[59] See *LW* 45, 77.

[60] Cf. Acts 1:24; 15:8.

occultis non iudicat Ecclesia,[61] the church does not judge secret matters. If the spiritual rule of the church governs only public matters, how dare the mad temporal authority judge and control such a secret, spiritual, hidden matter as faith?

Furthermore, every man runs his own risk in believing as he does, and he must see to it himself that he believes rightly. As nobody else can go to heaven or hell for me, so nobody else can believe or disbelieve for me; as nobody else can open or close heaven or hell to me, so nobody else can drive me to belief or unbelief. How he believes or disbelieves is a matter for the conscience of each individual, and since this takes nothing away from the temporal authority the latter should be content to attend to its own affairs and let men believe this or that as they are able and willing, and constrain no one by force. For faith is a free act, to which no one can be forced. Indeed, it is a work of God in the spirit, not something which outward authority should compel or create. Hence arises the common saying,[62] found also in Augustine,[63] "No one can or ought to be forced to believe."

Moreover, the blind, wretched fellows fail to see how utterly hopeless and impossible a thing they are attempting. For no matter how harshly they lay down the law, or how violently they rage, they can do no more than force an outward compliance of the mouth and the hand; the heart they cannot compel, though they work themselves to a frazzle. For the proverb is true: "Thoughts are tax-free." [64] Why do they persist in trying to force people to believe from the heart when they see that it is impossible? In so doing they only compel weak consciences to lie, to disavow, and to utter what is not in their hearts. They thereby load themselves down with dreadful alien sins,[65] for all the lies and false

---

[61] This is a gloss to the canon *Erubescant impii,* dist. XXXII, C. XI, in the *Decreti Magistri Gratiani Prima Pars,* where the glossed phrase reads, *De manifestis quidem loquimur, secretorum autem cognitor et iudex est Deus* ("We indeed speak of open things, but God is the witness and judge of secret things"). *Corpus Iuris Canonici,* I, col. 120. This marginal gloss is found in *Decretum Gratiani emendatum et notationibus illustratum una cum glossis* (Paris, 1612), col. 175.
[62] Cf. Wander (ed.), *Sprichwörter-Lexikon,* I, 1697, "*Glaube,*" No. 36, and *ibid.,* V, 1352, No. 176.
[63] See Augustine's *Contra litteras Petiliani,* II, 184. *MPL* 43, 315.
[64] See Wander (ed.), *Sprichwörter-Lexikon,* I, 1395, "*Gedanke,*" No. 44.
[65] Scholastic theology had distinguished, among its many other classifications

confessions which such weak consciences utter fall back upon him who compels them. Even if their subjects were in error, it would be much easier simply to let them err than to compel them to lie and to utter what is not in their hearts. In addition, it is not right to prevent evil by something even worse.

Would you like to know why God ordains that the temporal princes must offend so frightfully? I will tell you. God has given them up to a base mind [Rom. 1:28] and will make an end of them just as he does of the spiritual nobility. For my ungracious lords, the pope and the bishops, are supposed to be bishops[66] and preach God's word. This they leave undone, and have become temporal princes who govern with laws which concern only life and property. How completely they have turned things topsy-turvy! They are supposed to be ruling souls inwardly by God's word; so they rule castles, cities, lands, and people outwardly, torturing souls with unspeakable outrages.

Similarly, the temporal lords are supposed to govern lands and people outwardly. This they leave undone. They can do no more than strip and fleece, heap tax upon tax and tribute upon tribute, letting loose here a bear and there a wolf.[67] Besides this, there is no justice, integrity, or truth to be found among them. They behave worse than any thief or scoundrel, and their temporal rule has sunk quite as low as that of the spiritual tyrants. For this reason God so perverts their minds also, that they rush on into the absurdity of trying to exercise a spiritual rule over souls, just as their counterparts try to establish a temporal rule. They blithely heap alien sins upon themselves and incur the hatred of God and man, until they come to ruin together with bishops, popes, and monks, one scoundrel with the other. Then they lay all the blame

---

of sin, nine so-called *peccata aliena* (see PE 1, 91; and 2, 364)—the term derives from the Vulgate rendering of I Tim. 5:22—such as commanding, counseling, consenting, approving, participating, co-operating, or simply failing to speak, hinder, punish, or expose where the sin of another party is involved. *Lexikon für Theologie und Kirche* (2nd ed.; 10 vols.; Freiburg im Breisgau: Herder, 1930-1938), IX, 900.

66 In the sense of the New Testament, bishops were to be overseers of Christ's flock.

67 Not only were the beasts which were set free for purposes of hunting a threat to the lives of the peasants, but the hunts themselves were destructive of their lands and property. MA³ 5, 398, n. 28, 22.

on the gospel, and instead of confessing their sin they blaspheme God and say that our preaching has brought about that which their perverse wickedness has deserved—and still unceasingly deserves—just as the Romans did when they were destroyed.[68] Here then you have God's decree concerning the high and mighty.[69] They are not to believe it, however, lest this stern decree of God be hindered by their repentance.

But, you say: Paul said in Romans 13 [:1] that every soul [*seele*] [70] should be subject to the governing authority; and Peter says that we should be subject to every human ordinance [I Pet. 2:13]. Answer: Now you are on the right track, for these passages are in my favor. St. Paul is speaking of the governing authority. Now you have just heard that no one but God can have authority over souls. Hence, St. Paul cannot possibly be speaking of any obedience except where there can be corresponding authority. From this it follows that he is not speaking of faith, to the effect that temporal authority should have the right to command faith. He is speaking rather of external things, that they should be ordered and governed on earth. His words too make this perfectly clear, where he prescribes limits for both authority and obedience, saying, "Pay all of them their dues, taxes to whom taxes are due, revenue to whom revenue is due, honor to whom honor is due, respect to whom respect is due" [Rom. 13:7]. Temporal obedience and authority, you see, apply only externally to taxes, revenue, honor, and respect. Again, where he says, "The governing authority is not a terror to good conduct, but to bad" [Rom. 13:3], he again so limits the governing authority that it is not to have the mastery over faith or the word of God, but over evil works.

This is also what St. Peter means by the phrase, "Human

---

[68] When Rome was captured and sacked by the Goths in A.D. 410, the pagans blamed the disaster on the Christian desertion of the Roman gods. Augustine wrote *The City of God* to refute this charge. In dedicating his *Seven Books Against the Pagans* to Augustine, the early fifth century historian Paulus Orosius wrote, "You bade me reply to the empty chatter and perversity of those . . . pagans . . . [who] charge that the present times [*ca.* 417] are unusually beset with calamities for the sole reason that men believe in Christ and worship God while idols are increasingly neglected." Irving W. Raymond (trans.), *Seven Books of History Against the Pagans* (New York: Columbia University Press, 1936), p. 30.
[69] *Grossen hanssen;* cf. WA 10II, 507, n. 21, 22, and WA, DB 3, 78, ll. 10-11.
[70] See p. 660, n. 17.

ordinance" [I Pet. 2:13]. A human ordinance cannot possibly extend its authority into heaven and over souls; it is limited to the earth, to external dealings men have with one another, where they can see, know, judge, evaluate, punish, and acquit.

Christ himself made this distinction, and summed it all up very nicely when he said in Matthew 22 [:21], "Render to Caesar the things that are Caesar's and to God the things that are God's." Now, if the imperial power extended into God's kingdom and authority, and were not something separate, Christ would not have made this distinction. For, as has been said, the soul is not under the authority of Caesar; he can neither teach it nor guide it, neither kill it nor give it life, neither bind it nor loose it,[71] neither judge it nor condemn it, neither hold it fast nor release it. All this he would have to do, had he the authority to command it and to impose laws upon it. But with respect to body, property, and honor he has indeed to do these things, for such matters are under his authority.

David too summarized all this long ago in an excellent brief passage, when he said in Psalm 113 [115:16], "He has given heaven to the Lord of heaven, but the earth he has given to the sons of men." That is, over what is on earth and belongs to the temporal, earthly kingdom, man has authority from God; but whatever belongs to heaven and to the eternal kingdom is exclusively under the Lord of heaven. Neither did Moses forget this when he said in Genesis 1 [:26], "God said, 'Let us make man to have dominion over the beasts of the earth, the fish of the sea, and the birds of the air.'" There only external dominion is ascribed to man. In short, this is the meaning as St. Peter says in Acts 4 [5:29], "We must obey God rather than men." Thereby, he clearly sets a limit to the temporal authority, for if we had to do everything that the temporal authority wanted there would have been no point in saying, "We must obey God rather than men."

If your prince or temporal ruler commands you to side with the pope, to believe thus and so, or to get rid of certain books,[72]

---

[71] *Binden* and *lössen* have reference to the power of the keys derived from Matt. 16:19. See *LW* 35, 9-22.
[72] See *LW* 45, 77, n. 2.

you should say, "It is not fitting that Lucifer[73] should sit at the side of God. Gracious sir, I owe you obedience in body and property; command me within the limits of your authority on earth, and I will obey. But if you command me to believe or to get rid of certain books, I will not obey; for then you are a tyrant and overreach yourself, commanding where you have neither the right nor the authority," etc. Should he seize your property on account of this and punish such disobedience, then blessed are you; thank God that you are worthy to suffer for the sake of the divine word. Let him rage, fool that he is; he will meet his judge. For I tell you, if you fail to withstand him, if you give in to him and let him take away your faith and your books, you have truly denied God.

Let me illustrate. In Meissen,[74] Bavaria,[75] the Mark,[76] and other places, the tyrants have issued an order that all copies of the New Testament are everywhere to be turned in to the officials.[77] This should be the response of their subjects: They should not turn in a single page, not even a letter, on pain of losing their salvation. Whoever does so is delivering Christ up into the hands of Herod, for these tyrants act as murderers of Christ just like Herod.[78] If their homes are ordered searched and books or property taken by force, they should suffer it to be done. Outrage is not to be resisted but endured; yet we should not sanction it, or lift a little finger to conform, or obey. For such tyrants are

---

[73] Since the third century, especially among the poets, the name Lucifer had been applied to Satan, the rebel angel hurled from heaven, on the grounds of an allegorical interpretation of Isa. 14:12 in terms of Luke 10:18.

[74] Duke George of Saxony was also the margrave of Meissen; see p. 84, n. 11.

[75] Bavaria was ruled at the time by Duke Wilhelm IV (1493-1550), a vigorous opponent of the Reformation.

[76] Brandenburg was ruled at the time by Duke Joachim I (1484-1535), who remained an enemy of the Reformation despite his wife's espousal of it.

[77] Luther's German New Testament had appeared in September, 1522. On its prohibition in Meissen, see J. K. Seidemann, *Beiträge zur Reformationsgeschichte* (Dresden, 1846), I, 51; in Bavaria: Winter, *Schicksale der evangelischen Lehre*, II, 189; in the Mark: Paul Steinmüller, *Einführung der Reformation in die Kurmark Brandenburg* (Halle: Verein für Reformationsgeschichte, 1903), p. 22; and in Austria (the prohibition of November 6 and 17, 1522, by Ferdinand I): Johann Loserth, *Die Reformation und Gegenreformation in den innerösterreichischen Ländern im XVI Jahrhundert* (Stuttgart: Cotta, 1898), p. 23, n. 1.

[78] The reference is doubtless to Matt. 2:16 rather than Luke 23:7.

acting as worldly[79] princes are supposed to act, and worldly princes they surely are. But the world is God's enemy; hence, they too have to do what is antagonistic to God and agreeable to the world, that they may not be bereft of honor, but remain worldly princes. Do not wonder, therefore, that they rage and mock at the gospel; they have to live up to their name and title.

You must know that since the beginning of the world a wise prince is a mighty rare bird,[80] and an upright prince even rarer.[81] They are generally the biggest fools or the worst scoundrels on earth; therefore, one must constantly expect the worst from them and look for little good, especially in divine matters which concern the salvation of souls. They are God's executioners[82] and hangmen; his divine wrath uses them to punish the wicked and to maintain outward peace. Our God is a great lord and ruler; this is why he must also have such noble, highborn, and rich hangmen and constables. He desires that everyone shall copiously accord them riches, honor, and fear in abundance. It pleases his divine will that we call his hangmen gracious lords, fall at their feet, and be subject to them in all humility, so long as they do not ply their trade too far and try to become shepherds instead of hangmen. If a prince should happen to be wise, upright, or a Christian, that is one of the great miracles, the most precious token of divine grace upon that land. Ordinarily the course of events is in accordance with the passage from Isaiah 3 [:4], "I

---

[79] *Welltlich*, usually translated as "temporal," here is given its cognate rendering because of the play on words intended.

[80] *Seltzam vogel*; see Wander (ed.), *Sprichwörter-Lexikon*, I, 1285, *"Fürst,"* No. 61.

[81] Cf. *ibid.*, I, 1283, *"Fürst,"* No. 31.

[82]The term *stockmeyster*, meaning "jailer," is also used by Luther synonomously with *Zuchtmeister* for Paul's "custodian" of Gal. 3:24-25. See his exegesis of the Nunc Dimittis in a sermon preached on the Day of the Purification of Mary, February 2, 1526, where the term must mean more than merely a guard or warden; it refers actually to one who flogs or otherwise inflicts legal punishment in execution of a sentence. WA 20, 247. See also in the fourth of his Weimar sermons (on which this treatise is based) Luther's statement that "princes are the hangmen and *Stockblöcher* of Christ" (WA 10^{III},381, l. 31), the latter term being a tautological construction of the two words for "stock" and "block" and signifying an instrument of torture or punishment. Grimm, *Deutsches Wörterbuch*, X^3, 54.

will make boys their princes, and gaping fools[83] shall rule over them"; and in Hosea 13 [:11], "I will give you a king in my anger, and take him away in my wrath." The world is too wicked, and does not deserve to have many wise and upright princes. Frogs must have their storks.[84]

Again you say, "The temporal power is not forcing men to believe; it is simply seeing to it externally that no one deceives the people by false doctrine;[85] how could heretics otherwise be restrained?" Answer: This the bishops should do; it is a function entrusted to them[86] and not to the princes. Heresy can never be restrained by force. One will have to tackle the problem in some other way, for heresy must be opposed and dealt with otherwise than with the sword. Here God's word must do the fighting. If it does not succeed, certainly the temporal power will not succeed either, even if it were to drench the world in blood. Heresy is a spiritual matter which you cannot hack to pieces with iron, consume with fire, or drown in water. God's word alone avails here, as Paul says in II Corinthians 10 [:4-5], "Our weapons are not carnal, but mighty in God to destroy every argument and proud obstacle that exalts itself against the knowledge of God, and to take every thought captive in the service of Christ."

Moreover, faith and heresy are never so strong as when men oppose them by sheer force, without God's word. For men count it certain that such force is for a wrong cause and is directed against the right, since it proceeds without God's word and knows not how to further its cause except by naked force, as brute beasts do. Even in temporal affairs force can be used only after the wrong has been legally condemned. How much less possible it is

---

[83] *Maulaffen* is literally an ape with a wide or open mouth. Grimm, *Deutsches Wörterbuch*, VI, 1796. In his 1522 *Wider den falsch genannten geistlichen stand* Luther defined the word in these terms, "They open their mouths up wide and preach of great things but there is nothing back of it." WA 10II, 125. The various meanings of the term in Luther are discussed in WA 10II, 510, n. 121, 22.

[84] The proverb means in effect: "like people, like prince" according to Wander (ed.), *Sprichwörter-Lexikon*, I, 1230, "Frosch," No. 34. It derives from the Aesop fable about the frogs who insisted on having a king, and were finally granted a stork who devoured them all.

[85] On Luther's approval in another connection of the position here rejected, see Kawerau (ed.), Köstlin's *Martin Luther*, I, 584.

[86] Cf. Titus 1:9ff.

to act with force, without justice and God's word, in these lofty spiritual matters! See, therefore, what fine, clever nobles they are! They would drive out heresy, but set about it in such a way that they only strengthen the opposition, rousing suspicion against themselves and justifying the heretics. My friend, if you wish to drive out heresy, you must find some way to tear it first of all from the heart and completely turn men's wills away from it. With force you will not stop it, but only strengthen it. What do you gain by strengthening heresy in the heart, while weakening only its outward expression and forcing the tongue to lie? God's word, however, enlightens the heart, and so all heresies and errors vanish from the heart of their own accord.

This way of destroying heresy was proclaimed by Isaiah in his eleventh chapter where he says, "He shall smite the earth with the rod of his mouth, and with the breath of his lips he shall slay the wicked."[87] There you see that if the wicked are to be slain and converted, it will be accomplished with the mouth. In short, these princes and tyrants do not realize that to fight against heresy is to fight against the devil, who fills men's hearts with error, as Paul says in Ephesians 6 [:12], "We are not contending against flesh and blood, but against spiritual wickedness, against the principalities which rule this present darkness," etc. Therefore, so long as the devil is not repelled and driven from the heart, it is agreeable to him that I destroy his vessels[88] with fire or sword; it's as if I were to fight lightning with a straw. Job bore abundant witness to this when in his forty-first chapter he said that the devil counts iron as straw, and fears no power on earth.[89] We learn it also from experience, for even if all Jews and heretics were forcibly burned no one ever has been or will be convinced or converted thereby.

Nevertheless, such a world as this deserves such princes, none of whom attends to his duties. The bishops are to leave God's word alone and not use it to rule souls; instead they are to turn over to the worldly princes the job of ruling souls with the sword. The worldly princes, in turn, are to permit usury, robbery, adultery,

---

[87] See Luther's application of Isa. 11:4 in *LW* 45, 59-60.
[88] *Gefesss;* cf. Rom. 9:22.
[89] Job 41:25-34, especially v. 27.

murder, and other evil deeds, and even commit these offenses themselves, and then allow the bishops to punish with letters of excommunication. Thus, they neatly put the shoe on the wrong foot: they rule the souls with iron and the bodies with letters, so that worldly princes rule in a spiritual way, and spiritual princes rule in a worldly way. What else does the devil have to do on earth than to masquerade[90] and play the fool with his people? These are our Christian princes, who defend the faith and devour the Turk![91] Fine fellows, indeed, whom we may well trust to accomplish something by such refined wisdom, namely, to break their necks and plunge land and people into misery and want.

I would in all good faith advise these blind fellows to take heed to a little phrase that occurs in Psalm 107: *"Effundit contemptum super principes."*[92] I swear to you by God that if you fail to see that this little text is applicable to you, then you are lost, even though each one of you be as mighty as the Turk; and your fuming and raging will avail you nothing. A goodly part of it has already come true. For there are very few princes who are not regarded as fools or scoundrels; that is because they show themselves to be so. The common man is learning to think, and the scourge of princes (that which God calls *contemptum*) is gathering force among the mob and with the common man.[93] I fear there will be no way to avert it, unless the princes conduct themselves in a princely manner and begin again to rule decently and reasonably. Men will not, men cannot, men refuse to endure your tyranny and wantonness much longer. Dear princes and lords be wise and guide yourselves accordingly. God will no longer tolerate it. The world is no longer what it once was, when you hunted and drove the people like game. Abandon therefore your

---

[90] *Fassnacht spiel treybe. Fastnacht,* literally "eve of the fast," was that period just prior to Lent which was observed with feasting, revelry, parades, masquerades, and mummery, and also simple dramatic episodes in which the people could anonymously mimic and ridicule their superiors.

[91] The Mohammedans were at that time a threat to all of Western Christendom; see *LW* 35, 300, n. 152. The very princes who were displaying their "Christianity" abroad by forcibly stemming the encroachment of the Turks were denying it at home, according to Luther, by presuming to rule souls with the sword.

[92] Ps. 107:40, "He pours contempt upon princes."

[93] The smoldering dissatisfaction of the oppressed serfs was to erupt a couple years later in the Peasants' Revolt of 1524-1526.

wicked use of force, give thought to dealing justly, and let God's word have its way, as it will anyway and must and shall; you cannot prevent it. If there is heresy somewhere, let it be overcome, as is proper, with God's word. But if you continue to brandish the sword, take heed lest someone come and compel you to sheathe it—and not in God's name!

But you might say, "Since there is to be no temporal sword among Christians, how then are they to be ruled outwardly? There certainly must be authority even among Christians." Answer: Among Christians there shall and can be no authority; rather all are alike subject to one another, as Paul says in Romans 12: "Each shall consider the other his superior";[94] and Peter says in I Peter 5 [:5], "All of you be subject to one another." This is also what Christ means in Luke 14 [:10], "When you are invited to a wedding, go and sit in the lowest place." Among Christians there is no superior but Christ himself, and him alone. What kind of authority can there be where all are equal and have the same right, power, possession, and honor, and where no one desires to be the other's superior, but each the other's subordinate? Where there are such people, one could not establish authority even if he wanted to, since in the nature of things it is impossible to have superiors where no one is able or willing to be a superior. Where there are no such people, however, there are no real Christians either.

What, then, are the priests and bishops? Answer: Their government is not a matter of authority or power, but a service and an office, for they are neither higher nor better than other Christians.[95] Therefore, they should impose no law or decree on others without their will and consent. Their ruling is rather nothing more than the inculcating of God's word, by which they guide Christians and overcome heresy. As we have said, Christians can be ruled by nothing except God's word, for Christians must be ruled in faith, not with outward works. Faith, however, can come through no word of man, but only through the word of God, as Paul says in Romans 10 [:17], "Faith comes through hearing, and hear-

---

[94] Cf. Rom. 12:10.
[95] See Luther's comments on the sacrament of ordination in *The Babylonian Captivity of the Church* (1520). LW 36, 106-117.

ing through the word of God." Those who do not believe are not Christians; they do not belong to Christ's kingdom, but to the worldly kingdom where they are constrained and governed by the sword and by outward rule. Christians do every good thing of their own accord and without constraint, and find God's word alone sufficient for them. Of this I have written frequently and at length elsewhere.[96]

Part Three

Now that we know the limits of temporal authority, it is time to inquire also how a prince should use it. We do this for the sake of those very few who would also like very much to be Christian princes and lords, and who desire to enter into the life in heaven. Christ himself describes the nature of worldly princes in Luke 22 [:25], where he says, "The princes of this world exercise lordship, and those that are in authority proceed with force." For if they are lords by birth or by election they think it only right that they should be served and should rule by force. He who would be a Christian prince must certainly lay aside any intent to exercise lordship or to proceed with force. For cursed and condemned is every sort of life lived and sought for the benefit and good of self; cursed are all works not done in love. They are done in love, however, when they are directed wholeheartedly toward the benefit, honor, and salvation of others, and not toward the pleasure, benefit, honor, comfort, and salvation of self.

I will say nothing here of the temporal dealings and laws of the governing authority. That is a large subject, and there are too many lawbooks already, although if a prince is himself no wiser than his jurists and knows no more than what is in the lawbooks, he will surely rule according to the saying in Proverbs 28: "A prince who lacks understanding will oppress many with injustice."[97] For no matter how good and equitable[98] the laws

---

[96] See, for example, *A Treatise on Good Works* (1520). PE 1, 184-285; and *The Freedom of a Christian* (1520). LW 31, 343-377.
[97] Prov. 28:16 (Vulgate).
[98] *Billich* in this connection for Luther has reference to equity. See his 1526 treatise, *Whether Soldiers, Too, Can Be Saved,*" where he identifies *Billigkeit* with the latin *aequitas* and the Greek *epieikeia*. PE 5, 42.

are, they all make an exception in the case of necessity,[99] in the face of which they cannot insist upon being strictly enforced. Therefore, a prince must have the law as firmly in hand as the sword, and determine in his own mind when and where the law is to be applied strictly or with moderation, so that law may prevail at all times and in all cases, and reason may be the highest law and the master of all administration of law. To take an analogy, the head of a family fixes both the time and the amount when it comes to matters of work and of food for his servants and children; still, he must reserve the right to modify or suspend these regulations if his servants happen to be ill, imprisoned, detained, deceived, or otherwise hindered; he must not deal as severely with the sick as with the well. I say this in order that men may not think it sufficiently praiseworthy merely to follow the written law or the opinions of jurists. There is more to it than that.

What, then, is a prince to do if he lacks the requisite wisdom and has to be guided by the jurists and the lawbooks? Answer: This is why I said that the princely estate is a perilous one. If he be not wise enough himself to master both his laws and his advisers, then the maxim of Solomon applies, "Woe to the land whose prince is a child" [Eccles 10:16]. Solomon recognized this too. This is why he despaired of all law—even of that which Moses through God had prescribed for him—and of all his princes and counselors. He turned to God himself and besought him for an understanding heart to govern the people [I Kings 3:9]. A prince must follow this example and proceed in fear; he must depend neither upon dead books nor living heads, but cling solely to God, and be at him constantly, praying for a right understanding, beyond that of all books and teachers, to rule his subjects wisely. For this reason I know of no law to prescribe for a prince; instead, I will simply instruct his heart and mind on what his attitude should be toward all laws, counsels, judgments, and actions. If he governs himself accordingly, God will surely grant

---

[99] Cf. the proverb quoted frequently by Luther (see, e.g., LW 36, 255) and also by Thomas Aquinas (*Summa theologica*, 2, I, ques. 96, art. 6), "Necessity knows no law." Wander (ed.), *Sprichwörter-Lexikon*, III, 1051, "*Noth*," No. 146.

him the ability to carry out all laws, counsels, and actions in a proper and godly way.

First. He must give consideration and attention to his subjects, and really devote himself to it. This he does when he directs his every thought to making himself useful and beneficial to them; when instead of thinking, "The land and people belong to me, I will do what best pleases me," he thinks rather, "I belong to the land and the people, I shall do what is useful and good for them. My concern will be not how to lord it over them and dominate them, but how to protect and maintain them in peace and plenty." He should picture Christ to himself, and say, "Behold, Christ, the supreme ruler, came to serve me; he did not seek to gain power, estate, and honor from me, but considered only my need, and directed all things to the end that I should gain power, estate, and honor from him and through him. I will do likewise, seeking from my subjects not my own advantage but theirs. I will use my office to serve and protect them, listen to their problems and defend them, and govern to the sole end that they, not I, may benefit and profit from my rule." In such manner should a prince in his heart empty himself of his power and authority, and take unto himself the needs of his subjects, dealing with them as though they were his own needs. For this is what Christ did to us [Phil. 2:7]; and these are the proper works of Christian love.

Now you will say, "Who would then want to be a prince? That would make the princely estate the worst on earth, full of trouble, labor, and sorrow. What would become of the princely amusements—dancing, hunting, racing, gaming, and similar worldly pleasures?"[100] I answer: We are not here teaching how a temporal prince is to live, but how a temporal prince is to be a Christian, such that he may also reach heaven. Who is not aware that a prince is a rare prize in heaven?[101] I do not speak with any hope that temporal princes will give heed, but on the chance that there

---

[100]See Luther's criticism of the ruler's preoccupation with amusements to the neglect of their office, LW 45, 249-250, 367-368.

[101]*Eyn furst wiltprett ym hymel ist.* Cf. p. 687, n. 80. This proverbial expression (cf. Wander [ed.]), *Sprichwörter-Lexikon*, I, 1288, "*Fürst*," No. 119) was a favorite of Luther (cf. *PE* 2, 163; *LW* 21, 345). A *Wildbret* was a bird or beast hunted as game; the term came also to mean anything rare, precious, and desirable. Grimm, *Deutsches Wörterbuch*, XIV², 53.

might be one who would also like to be a Christian, and to know how he should act. Of this I am certain, that God's word will neither turn nor bend for princes, but princes must bend themselves to God's word.

I am satisfied simply to point out that it is not impossible for a prince to be a Christian, although it is a rare thing and beset with difficulties. If they would so manage that their dancing, hunting, and racing were done without injury to their subjects, and if they would otherwise conduct their office in love toward them, God would not be so harsh as to begrudge them their dancing and hunting and racing. But they would soon find out for themselves that if they gave their subjects the care and attention required by their office, many a fine dance, hunt, race, and game would have to be missed.

Second. He must beware of the high and mighty[102] and of his counselors, and so conduct himself toward them that he despises none, but also trusts none enough to leave everything to him.[103] God cannot tolerate either course. He once spoke through the mouth of an ass [Num. 22:28]; therefore, no man is to be despised, however humble he may be. On the other hand, he permitted the highest angel to fall from heaven;[104] therefore, no man is to be trusted, no matter how wise, holy, or great he may be. One should rather give a hearing to all, and wait to see through which one of them God will speak and act. The greatest harm is done at court when the prince gives his mind into the captivity of the high and mighty and of the flatterers, and does not look into things himself. When a prince fails and plays the fool, not just one person is affected, but land and people must bear the result of such foolishness.

Therefore, a prince should trust his officials and allow them to act, but only in such a way that he will still keep the reins of government in his own hands. He must not be overconfident but keep his eyes open and attend to things, and (like Jehoshaphat did [II Chron. 19:4-7]) ride through the land and observe everywhere how the government and the law are being administered.

---

[102]See p. 684, n. 69.
[103]Cf. Luther's earlier exposition of the *Magnificat*. LW 21, 357.
[104]See p. 686, n. 73, on this reference to Isa. 14:12 and Luke 10:18.

In this way he will learn for himself that one cannot place complete trust in any man. You have no right to assume that somebody else will take as deep an interest in you and your land as you do yourself, unless he be a good Christian filled with the Spirit. The natural man will not. And since you cannot know whether he is a Christian or how long he will remain one, you cannot safely depend upon him.

Beware especially of those who say, "Oh, gracious lord, does your grace not have greater confidence in me? Who is so willing to serve your grace?" etc. Such a person is certainly not guileless; he wants to be lord in the land and make a monkey[105] of you. If he were a true and devout Christian he would be glad that you entrust nothing to him, and would praise and approve you for keeping so close a watch on him. Since he acts in accord with God's will, he is willing and content to have his actions brought to light by you or anyone else. As Christ says in John 8 [3:21], "He who does what is good comes to the light, that it may be clearly seen that his deeds have been wrought in God." The former, however, would blind your eyes, and act under cover of darkness; as Christ also says in the same place, "He who does evil shuns the light, lest his deeds should be exposed" [John 3:20]. Therefore, beware of him. And if he complains about it, say to him, "Friend, I do you no wrong; God is unwilling that I trust myself or any other man. Find fault with Him because He will have it so, or because He has not made you something more than a man. But even if you were an angel, I still would not fully trust you—Lucifer[106] was not to be trusted—for we should trust God alone."

Let no prince think that he will fare better than David, who is an example to all princes. He had so wise a counselor, Ahithophel by name, that the text says: The counsel which Ahithophel gave was as if one had consulted God himself [II Sam. 16:23]. Yet Ahithophel fell, and sank so low that he tried to betray, slay, and destroy David, his own lord [II Sam. 17:1-23]. Thus did David at that time have to learn that no man is to be trusted. Why do you suppose God permitted such a horrible incident to occur

[105]*Maulaffen;* see p. 688, n. 83.
[106]See p. 686, n. 73.

and be recorded? It could only be in order to warn princes and lords against putting their trust in any man, which is the most perilous misfortune that could befall them. For it is most deplorable when flatterers reign at court, or when the prince relies upon others and puts himself in their hands, and lets everyone do as he will.

Now you will say, "If no one is to be trusted, how can land and people be governed?" Answer: You are to take the risk of entrusting matters to others, but you are yourself to trust and rely upon God alone. You will certainly have to entrust duties to somebody else and take a chance on him, but you should trust him only as one who might fail you, whom you must continue to watch with unceasing vigilance. A coachman has confidence in the horses and wagon he drives; yet he does not let them proceed on their own, but holds rein and lash in his hands and keeps his eyes open. Remember the old proverbs—which are the sure fruit of experience—"The master's eye makes the horse fat"; and, "The master's footprints fertilize the soil best."[107] That is, if the master does not look after things himself but depends on advisers and servants, things never go right. God also wills it that way and causes it to be so in order that the lords may be driven of necessity to care for their office themselves, just as everyone has to fulfil his own calling and every creature do its own work. Otherwise, the lords will become fatted pigs and worthless fellows, of benefit to no one but themselves.

Third. He must take care to deal justly with evildoers. Here he must be very wise and prudent, so he can inflict punishment without injury to others. Again, I know of no better example of this than David. He had a commander, Joab by name, who committed two underhanded crimes when he treacherously murdered two upright commanders [II Sam. 3:27; 20:10], whereby

---

107 The first proverb may derive from the Greek Xenophon who wrote of a king's inquiry as to the best fodder for improving his horse, and of the wise man's answer, "Experience has taught me that the master's eye best feeds the horse." Both proverbs in various versions, and even in conjunction, are listed in Wander (ed.), *Sprichwörter-Lexikon*, II, 541-542, "Herr," Nos. 147-155, 158-161. The meaning is clear: the master must attend to things himself if they are to go well. *Ibid.*, I, 171, "Auge," No. 45. See WA 10III, 384, ll. 4-7.

he justly merited death twice over. Yet David, during his own lifetime, did not have him put to death but commanded his son Solomon to do so without fail [I Kings 2:5-6], doubtless because he himself could not do it without causing even greater damage and tumult. A prince must punish the wicked in such a way that he does not step on the dish while picking up the spoon,[108] and for the sake of one man's head plunge country and people into want and fill the land with widows and orphans. Therefore, he must not follow the advice of those counselors and fire-eaters who would stir and incite him to start a war, saying, "What, must we suffer such insult and injustice?" He is a mighty poor Christian who for the sake of a single castle would put the whole land in jeopardy.

In short, here one must go by the proverb, "He cannot govern who cannot wink at faults."[109] Let this be his rule: Where wrong cannot be punished without greater wrong, there let him waive his rights, however just they may be. He should not have regard to his own injury, but to the wrong others must suffer in consequence of the penalty he imposes. What have the many women and children done to deserve being made widows and orphans in order that you may avenge yourself on a worthless tongue or an evil hand which has injured you?

Here you will ask: "Is a prince then not to go to war, and are his subjects not to follow him into battle?" Answer: This is a far-reaching question, but let me answer it very briefly. To act here as a Christian, I say, a prince should not go to war against his overlord—king, emperor, or other liege lord[110]—but let him who takes, take. For the governing authority must not be resisted by force, but only by confession of the truth. If it is influenced by this, well and good; if not, you are excused, you suffer wrong

---

[108] See *ibid.*, III, 224-226, "*Löffel*," Nos. 55, 56, 73, 106. The proverb actually has reference to one who misses or neglects the big thing because he is too intent on that which is insignificant; cf. LW 21, 337, n. 35.

[109] See Wander (ed.), *Sprichwörter-Lexikon*, I, 1019, "*Finger*," No. 77. Luther used the same figure in his fourth Weimar sermon (WA 10 II, 383-384) and in his exposition of *The Magnificat* (LW 21, 337). In his 1526 lectures on Ecclesiastes he ascribed the saying to Emperor Frederick III (1415-1493); WA 20, 97-98.

[110] The *Lehen herrnn* was the feudal sovereign who actually owned a vassal's property. Grimm, *Deutsches Wörterbuch*, VI, 540.

for God's sake. If, however, the antagonist is your equal, your inferior, or of a foreign government, you should first offer him justice and peace, as Moses taught the children of Israel. If he refuses, then—mindful of what is best for you[111]—defend yourself against force by force, as Moses so well describes it in Deuteronomy 20 [:10-12]. But in doing this you must not consider your personal interests and how you may remain lord, but those of your subjects to whom you owe help and protection, that such action may proceed in love. Since your entire land is in peril you must make the venture, so that with God's help all may not be lost. If you cannot prevent some from becoming widows and orphans as a consequence, you must at least see that not everything goes to ruin until there is nothing left except widows and orphans.

In this matter subjects are in duty bound to follow, and to devote their life and property, for in such a case one must risk his goods and himself for the sake of others. In a war of this sort it is both Christian and an act of love to kill the enemy without hesitation, to plunder and burn and injure him by every method of warfare[112] until he is conquered (except that one must beware of sin, and not violate wives and virgins). And when victory has been achieved, one should offer mercy and peace to those who surrender and humble themselves. In such a case let the proverb apply, "God helps the strongest."[113] This is what Abraham did when he smote the four kings, Genesis 14; he certainly slaughtered many, and showed little mercy until he conquered them. Such a case must be regarded as sent by God as a means to cleanse the land for once and drive out the rascals.

What if a prince is in the wrong? Are his people bound to follow him then too? Answer: No, for it is no one's duty to do wrong; we must obey God (who desires the right) rather than men [Acts 5:29]. What if the subjects do not know whether their

---

111 *Gedenck deyn bestes;* see Berger, *Die Sturmtruppen der Reformation,* p. 109, n. 3; and MA³ 5, 399, n. 39, 14.

112 *Kriegs leufften* means simply "the wars," that is, war and everything that goes with it, including, as the context here demands though the syntax is somewhat ambiguous, the notion of usages, conventions, and rules of war. See Grimm, *Deutsches Wörterbuch,* V, 2280, and MA³ 5, 399, n. 39, 28.

113 See Wander (ed.), *Sprichwörter-Lexikon,* II, 30, "Gott," No. 656.

prince is in the right or not? Answer: So long as they do not know, and cannot with all possible diligence find out, they may obey him without peril to their souls. For in such a case one must apply the law of Moses in Exodus 21,[114] where he writes that a murderer who has unknowingly and unintentionally killed a man shall through flight to a city of refuge and by judgment of a court be declared acquitted. Whichever side then suffers defeat, whether it be in the right or in the wrong, must accept it as a punishment from God. Whichever side fights and wins in such ignorance, however, must regard its battle as though someone fell from a roof and killed another, and leave the matter to God. It is all the same to God whether he deprives you of life and property by a just or by an unjust lord. You are His creature and He can do with you as He wills, just so your conscience is clear. Thus in Genesis 20 [:2-7] God himself excuses Abimelech for taking Abraham's wife; not because he had done right, but because he had not known that she was Abraham's wife.

Fourth. Here we come to what should really have been placed first, and of which we spoke above.[115] A prince must act in a Christian way toward his God also; that is, he must subject himself to him in entire confidence and pray for wisdom to rule well, as Solomon did [I Kings 3:9]. But of faith and trust in God I have written so much that it is not necessary to say more here. Therefore, we will close with this brief summation, that a prince's duty is fourfold: First, toward God there must be true confidence and earnest prayer; second, toward his subjects there must be love and Christian service; third, with respect to his counselors and officials he must maintain an untrammeled reason and unfettered judgment; fourth, with respect to evildoers he must manifest a restrained severity and firmness. Then the prince's job will be done right, both outwardly and inwardly; it will be pleasing to God and to the people. But he will have to expect much envy and sorrow on account of it; the cross will soon rest on the shoulders of such a prince.

Finally, I must add an appendix in answer to those who raise

---

[114] Exod. 21:13; Num. 35:10-25.
[115] See p. 692.

questions about restitution,[116] that is, about the return of goods wrongfully acquired. This is a matter about which the temporal sword is commonly concerned; much has been written about it, and many fantastically severe judgments have been sought in cases of this sort. I will put it all in a few words, however, and at one fell swoop dispose of all such laws and of the harsh judgments based upon them, thus: No surer law can be found in this matter than the law of love. In the first place, when a case of this sort is brought before you in which one is to make restitution to another, if they are both Christians the matter is soon settled; neither will withhold what belongs to the other, and neither will demand that it be returned. If only one of them is a Christian, namely, the one to whom restitution is due, it is again easy to settle, for he does not care whether restitution is ever made to him. The same is true if the one who is supposed to make restitution is a Christian, for he will do so.

But whether one be a Christian or not a Christian, you should decide the question of restitution as follows. If the debtor is poor and unable to make restitution, and the other party is not poor, then you should let the law of love prevail and acquit the debtor; for according to the law of love the other party is in any event obliged to relinquish the debt and, if necessary, to give him something besides. But if the debtor is not poor, then have him restore as much as he can, whether it be all, a half, a third, or a fourth of it, provided that you leave him enough to assure a house, food, and clothing for himself, his wife, and his children. This much you would owe him in any case, if you could afford it; so much the less ought you to take it away now, since you do not need it and he cannot get along without it.

If neither party is a Christian, or if one of them is unwilling to be judged by the law of love, then you may have them call in some other judge, and tell the obstinate one that they are acting contrary to God and natural law,[117] even if they obtain a

---

[116] The background of this specific question is not known. It may have been raised by Duke John of Saxony, to whom the treatise is dedicated. MA³ 5, 400, n. 40, 31.
[117] See the 1521 definition of "natural law" deduced by Melanchthon from Rom. 2:15, "A natural law is a common judgment to which all men alike assent, and therefore one which God has inscribed upon the soul of each

strict judgment in terms of human law. For nature teaches—as does love—that I should do as I would be done by [Luke 6:31]. Therefore, I cannot strip another of his possessions, no matter how clear a right I have, so long as I am unwilling myself to be stripped of my goods. Rather, just as I would that another, in such circumstances, should relinquish his right in my favor, even so should I relinquish my rights.

Thus should one deal with all property unlawfully held, whether in public or in private, that love and natural law may always prevail. For when you judge according to love you will easily decide and adjust matters without any lawbooks. But when you ignore love and natural law you will never hit upon the solution that pleases God, though you may have devoured all the lawbooks and jurists. Instead, the more you depend on them, the further they will lead you astray. A good and just decision must not and cannot be pronounced out of books, but must come from a free mind, as though there were no books. Such a free decision is given, however, by love and by natural law, with which all reason is filled; out of the books come extravagant and untenable judgments. Let me give you an example of this.

This story is told of Duke Charles of Burgundy.[118] A certain nobleman took an enemy prisoner. The prisoner's wife came to ransom her husband. The nobleman promised to give back the husband on condition that she would lie with him. The woman was virtuous, yet wished to set her husband free; so she goes and asks her husband whether she should do this thing in order

---

man." Charles Leander Hill (trans.), *The "Loci Communes" of Philip Melanchthon* (Boston: Meador, 1944), p. 112. Cf. *LW* 40, 97-98. Luther frequently cited Matt. 7:12 and Luke 6:31 when speaking of the natural law of love. See, e.g., *LW* 45, 287, 292, 296. Cf. Karl Holl, *Gesammelte Aufsätze zur Kirchengeschichte*, Vol. I, Luther (6th ed.; Tübingen: Mohr, 1932), p. 265, n. 1.

[118] Charles the Bold, Duke of Burgundy in 1467-1477, had actually been involved in such a unique case at Vlissingen in 1469 according to the Dutch historian Pontus Heuter (1535-1602), *Rerum Burgundicarum libri sex* (Hagae-Comitis, 1639), pp. 393ff. In Luther's fourth sermon at Weimar, October 25, 1522, on which this treatise is based, he had referred to the wise ruler simply as a "king." *WA* 10III, 384. Melanchthon relates the same incident in *C. R.* 20, 531, No. XLII. Both accounts may derive from a contemporary lyrical poem. *CL* 2, 393, n. 32.

to set him free. The husband wished to be set free and to save his life, so he gives his wife permission. After the nobleman had lain with the wife, he had the husband beheaded the next day and gave him to her as a corpse. She laid the whole case before Duke Charles. He summoned the nobleman and commanded him to marry the woman. When the wedding day was over he had the nobleman beheaded, gave the woman possession of his property, and restored her to honor. Thus he punished the crime in a princely way.

Observe: No pope, no jurist, no lawbook could have given him such a decision. It sprang from untrammeled reason, above the law in all the books, and is so excellent that everyone must approve of it and find the justice of it written in his own heart. St. Augustine relates a similar story in *The Lord's Sermon on the Mount*.[119] Therefore, we should keep written laws subject to reason, from which they originally welled forth as from the spring of justice. We should not make the spring dependent on its rivulets, or make reason a captive of letters.

---

[119] *Sermon on the Mount* I, xvi, 50. An abridged version of Augustine's story, dealing with a similar deception involving a woman's fornication by consent of her husband who was imprisoned for defaulting on a debt to the public treasury, was appended to a German edition of the treatise already in 1523 (WA 11, 280-281). The full text of the original story is in Denis J. Kavanagh (trans.), *Saint Augustine: Commentary on the Lord's Sermon on the Mount*. FC, p. 71-73, MPL 34, 1254.

30.

TO THE COUNCILMEN
OF ALL CITIES IN GERMANY
THAT THEY ESTABLISH AND
MAINTAIN CHRISTIAN SCHOOLS

Grace and peace from God our Father and the Lord Jesus Christ. Honorable, wise, and dear sirs: Had I feared the command of men more than God[1] I should have remained silent on this subject, for it is now some three years since I was put under the ban and declared an outlaw,[2] and there are in Germany many of both high and low degree who on that account attack whatever I say and write, and shed much blood over it.[3] But God has opened my mouth and bidden me speak, and he supports me mightily. The more they rage against me, the more he strengthens and extends my cause—without any help or advice from me—as if he were laughing and holding their rage in derision, as it says in Psalm 2 [:4]. By this fact alone anyone whose mind is not hardened can see that this cause must be God's own, for it plainly bears the mark of a divine word and work; they always thrive best when men are most determined to persecute and suppress them.

Therefore, I will speak and (as Isaiah says) not keep silent as long as I live,[4] until Christ's righteousness goes forth as brightness, and his saving grace is lighted as a lamp [Isa. 62:1]. I beg of you now, all my dear sirs and friends, to receive this letter

---

[1] Cf. Acts 5:29.

[2] Pope Leo X's formal bull of excommunication against Luther, the *Decet Romanum pontificem,* was published January 3, 1521. On May 26 Emperor Charles V signed the Edict of Worms putting Luther under the ban of the empire. Schwiebert, *Luther and His Times,* pp. 492, 511-512.

[3] The earliest martyrs to the cause of Lutheranism were Henry Vos and Johann van den Esschen, who were burned at Brussels July 1, 1523. *LW* 32, 263.

[4] In a letter to Spalatin November 30, 1524, Luther remarked, "I daily expect the death decreed to the heretic." *S-J* 2, 264; *WA,* Br 3, 394.

kindly and take to heart my admonition. For no matter what I may be personally, still I can boast before God with a good conscience that in this matter I am not seeking my own advantage— which I could more readily attain by keeping silent—but am dealing sincerely and faithfully with you, and with the whole German nation into which God has placed me, whether men believe it or not. And I wish to assure you and declare to you frankly and openly that he who heeds me in this matter is most certainly heeding not me, but Christ; and he who gives me no heed is despising not me, but Christ [Luke 10:16]. For I know very well and am quite certain of the content and thrust of what I say and teach; and anyone who will rightly consider my teaching will also discover it for himself.

First of all, we are today experiencing in all the German lands how schools are everywhere being left to go to wrack and ruin. The universities are growing weak, and monasteries are declining. The grass withers and the flower fades, as Isaiah [40:7-8] says, because the breath of the Lord blows upon it through his word and shines upon it so hot through the gospel. For now it is becoming known through God's word how un-Christian these institutions are, and how they are devoted only to men's bellies. The carnal-minded masses are beginning to realize that they no longer have either the obligation or the opportunity to thrust their sons, daughters, and relatives into cloisters and foundations, and to turn them out of their own homes and property and establish them in others' property. For this reason no one is any longer willing to have his children get an education. "Why," they say, "should we bother to have them go to school if they are not to become priests, monks, or nuns? 'Twere better they should learn a livelihood to earn." [5]

---

[5] *Man las sie so mehr leren, da mit sie sich erneren.* The precise connection and meaning of this last sentence—a rhyming couplet—is obscure. We have been guided in our rendering by the arguments of Albrecht who construes the sentence as the concluding part of the protest of the opponents of education (hence included within the quotation marks) rather than as a quick rejoinder by Luther to their protest ("all the more then do they need a practical education"). "Studien zu Luther's Schrift 'An die Ratsherren aller Städte deutschen Lands, dass sie christliche Schulen aufrichten und halten sollen, 1524,'" *Theologische Studien und Kritiken,* Jahrgang 70, I[1] (Gotha: Perthes, 1897) pp. 696-698, 725-726.

The thoughts and purposes of such people are plainly evident from this confession of theirs. If in the cloisters and foundations, or the spiritual estate, they had been seeking not only the belly and the temporal welfare of their children but were earnestly concerned for their children's salvation and eternal bliss, they would not thus fold their hands and relapse into indifference, saying, "If the spiritual estate is no longer to be of any account, we can just as well let education go and not bother our heads about it." Instead, they would say, "If it be true, as the gospel teaches, that this estate is a perilous one for our children, then, dear sirs, show us some other way which will be pleasing to God and of benefit to them. For we certainly want to provide not only for our children's bellies, but for their souls as well." At least that is what truly Christian parents would say about it.

It is not surprising that the wicked devil takes a position in this matter and induces carnal and worldly hearts thus to neglect the children and young people. Who can blame him for it? He is the ruler and god of this world [John 14:30]; how can he possibly be pleased to see the gospel destroy his nests, the monasteries and the clerical gangs, in which he corrupts above all the young folks who mean so much, in fact everything, to him? How can we expect him to permit or promote the proper training of the young? He would indeed be a fool to allow and promote the establishment in his kingdom of the very thing by which that kingdom must be most speedily overthrown, which would happen if he were to lose that choice morsel—our dear young people—and have to suffer them to be supported at his own expense and by means of his own resources for the service of God.

Therefore, he acted most adroitly at the time when Christians were having their children trained and taught in a Christian manner. The young crowd bade fair to escape him entirely and to establish within his kingdom something that was quite intolerable. So he went to work, spread his nets, and set up such monasteries, schools, and estates that it was impossible for any lad to escape him, apart from a special miracle of God. But now that he sees his snares exposed through the word of God, he goes to the other extreme and will permit no learning at all.

Again he does the right and smart thing to preserve his kingdom and by all means retain his hold on the young crowd. If he can hold them, and they grow up under him and remain his, who can take anything from him? He then maintains undisputed possession of the world. For if he is to be dealt a blow that really hurts, it must be done through young people who have come to maturity in the knowledge of God, and who spread His word and teach it to others.

No one, positively no one, realizes that this is a despicable trick of the devil. It proceeds so unobtrusively that no one notices it, and the damage is done before one can take steps to prevent and remedy it. We are on the alert against Turks,[6] wars, and floods, because in such matters we can see what is harmful and what is beneficial. But no one is aware of the devil's wily purpose. No one is on the alert, but just goes quietly along. Even though only a single boy could thereby be trained to become a real Christian, we ought properly to give a hundred gulden to this cause for every gulden we would give to fight the Turk, even if he were breathing down our necks. For one real Christian is better and can do more good than all the men on earth.

Therefore, I beg all of you, my dear sirs and friends, for the sake of God and our poor young people, not to treat this matter as lightly as many do, who fail to realize what the ruler of this world [John 14:30] is up to. For it is a grave and important matter, and one which is of vital concern both to Christ and the world at large, that we take steps to help the youth. By so doing we will be taking steps to help also ourselves and everybody else. Bear in mind that such insidious, subtle, and crafty attacks of the devil must be met with great Christian determination. My dear sirs, if we have to spend such large sums every year on guns, roads, bridges, dams, and countless similar items to insure the temporal peace and prosperity of a city, why should not much more be devoted to the poor neglected youth—at least enough to engage one or two competent men to teach school?

Moreover, every citizen should be influenced by the following consideration. Formerly he was obliged to waste a great deal of

---

[6]See *LW* 45, 44, n. 44; 116, n. 91; 352, n. 12.

money and property on indulgences, masses, vigils,[7] endowments, bequests, anniversaries,[8] mendicant friars, brotherhoods,[9] pilgrimages, and similar nonsense. Now that he is, by the grace of God, rid of such pillage and compulsory giving, he ought henceforth, out of gratitude to God and for his glory, to contribute a part of that amount toward schools for the training of the poor children. That would be an excellent investment. If the light of the gospel had not dawned and set him free, he would have had to continue indefinitely giving up to the above-mentioned robbers ten times that sum and more, without hope of return. Know also that where there arise hindrances, objections, impediments, and opposition to this proposal, there the devil is surely at work, the devil who voiced no such objection when men gave their money for monasteries and masses, pouring it out in a veritable stream; for he senses that this kind of giving is not to his advantage. Let this, then, my dear sirs and friends, be the first consideration to influence you, namely, that herein we are fighting against the devil as the most dangerous and subtle enemy of all.

A second consideration is, as St. Paul says in II Corinthians 6 [:1-2], that we should not accept the grace of God in vain and neglect the time of salvation. Almighty God has indeed graciously visited us Germans and proclaimed a true year of jubilee.[10] We have today the finest and most learned group of men, adorned with languages and all the arts, who could also render real service if only we would make use of them as instructors of the young people. Is it not evident that we are now able to prepare a boy in three years, so that at the age of fifteen or eighteen he will know more than all the universities and monasteries have known before? Indeed, what have men been learning till now in the universities and monasteries except to become asses, blockheads,

---

[7]*Vigilien* were services held in the cloisters at night. *LW* 36, 198, n. 59.
[8]On the *jartagen*, see *LW* 45, 180, n. 37.
[9]On the *bruderschafften*, see *LW* 45, 181, n. 39.
[10] *Ein recht gülden jar* means literally, "a truly golden year." Luther is alluding to the papal practice of proclaiming from time to time a jubilee year, which in Germany was popularly called a *"Güldenjahr."* During such a year throngs of pilgrims would visit Rome to earn the promised papal indulgence; their substantial gifts made it literally a "golden" year indeed for the church. *PE* 4, 107, n. 1. The reference, of course, is to the recent advances in humanistic education.

and numbskulls? For twenty, even forty, years they pored over their books, and still failed to master either Latin or German, to say nothing of the scandalous and immoral life there in which many a fine young fellow was shamefully corrupted.

It is perfectly true that if universities and monasteries were to continue as they have been in the past, and there were no other place available where youth could study and live, then I could wish that no boy would ever study at all, but just remain dumb. For it is my earnest purpose, prayer, and desire that these asses' stalls and devil's training centers should either sink into the abyss or be converted into Christian schools. Now that God has so richly blessed us, however, and provided us with so many men able to instruct and train our youth aright, it is surely imperative that we not throw his blessing to the winds and let him knock in vain. He is standing at the door;[11] happy are we who open to him! He is calling us; blessed is he who answers him! If we turn a deaf ear and he should pass us by, who will bring him back again?

Let us remember our former misery, and the darkness in which we dwelt. Germany, I am sure, has never before heard so much of God's word as it is hearing today; certainly we read nothing of it in history. If we let it just slip by without thanks and honor, I fear we shall suffer a still more dreadful darkness and plague. O my beloved Germans, buy while the market is at your door; gather in the harvest while there is sunshine and fair weather; make use of God's grace and word while it is there! For you should know that God's word and grace is like a passing shower of rain which does not return where it has once been. It has been with the Jews, but when it's gone it's gone, and now they have nothing. Paul brought it to the Greeks; but again when it's gone it's gone, and now they have the Turk.[12] Rome and the Latins also had it; but when it's gone it's gone, and now they have the pope. And you Germans need not think that you will have it forever, for ingratitude and contempt will not make

---

11 Cf. Rev. 3:20.

12 From the conquest of Syria beginning in 635 until the fall of Constantinople in 1453 the Byzantines were constantly pressed by Islam, and the Greek church gradually lost its best territories to the Turks.

it stay. Therefore, seize it and hold it fast, whoever can; for lazy hands are bound to have a lean year.[13]

The third consideration is by far the most important of all, namely, the command of God, who through Moses urges and enjoins parents so often to instruct their children that Psalm 78 says: How earnestly he commanded our fathers to teach their children and to instruct their children's children [Ps. 78:5-6]. This is also evident in God's fourth commandment, in which the injunction that children shall obey their parents is so stern that he would even have rebellious children sentenced to death [Deut. 21:18-21]. Indeed, for what purpose do we older folks exist, other than to care for, instruct, and bring up the young? It is utterly impossible for these foolish young people to instruct and protect themselves. This is why God has entrusted them to us who are older and know from experience what is best for them. And God will hold us strictly accountable for them. This is also why Moses commands in Deuteronomy 32 [:7], "Ask your father and he will tell you; your elders, and they will show you."

It is a sin and a shame that matters have come to such a pass that we have to urge and be urged to educate our children and young people and to seek their best interests, when nature itself should drive us to do this and even the heathen afford us abundant examples of it. There is not a dumb animal which fails to care for its young and teach them what they need to know; the only exception is the ostrich, of which God says in Job 31 [39:16, 14] that she deals cruelly with her young as if they were not hers, and leaves her eggs upon the ground. What would it profit us to possess and perform everything else and be like pure saints, if we meanwhile neglected our chief purpose in life, namely, the care of the young? I also think that in the sight of God none among the outward sins so heavily burdens the world and merits such severe punishment as this very sin which we commit against the children by not educating them.

When I was a lad they had this maxim in school: *"Non minus est negligere scholarem quam corrumpere virginem"*; "It is just as bad to neglect a pupil as to despoil a virgin." The purpose

---

[13] *Faule haende müssen eyn bösses jar haben.* Wander (ed.), *Sprichwörter-Lexikon,* II, 300, "Hand," No. 153.

of this maxim was to keep the schoolmasters on their toes, for in those days no greater sin was known that that of despoiling a virgin. But, dear Lord God, how light a sin it is to despoil virgins or wives (which, being a bodily and recognized sin, may be atoned for) in comparison with this sin of neglecting and despoiling precious souls, for the latter sin is not even recognized or acknowledged and is never atoned for.[14] O woe unto the world for ever and ever! Children are born every day and grow up in our midst, but, alas! there is no one to take charge of the youngsters and direct them. We just let matters take their own course. The monasteries and foundations should have seen to it; therefore, they are the very ones of whom Christ says, "Woe unto the world because of offenses! Whoever causes one of these little ones who believe in me to sin, it would be better for him to have a millstone fastened round his neck, and to be drowned in the depth of the sea" (Matt. 18:7, 6). They are nothing but devourers and destroyers of children.

Ah, you say, but all that is spoken to the parents; what business is it of councilmen and the authorities? Yes, that is true; but what if the parents fail to do their duty? Who then is to do it? Is it for this reason to be left undone, and the children neglected? How will the authorities and council then justify their position, that such matters are not their responsibility?

There are various reasons why parents neglect this duty. In

---

14 Our rendering of the several ambiguous words in this sentence is based on considerations advanced by Albrecht, *op. cit.*, pp. 698-702. Luther does not mean to say that a light sin—one against the body—because it is acknowledged can be atoned for, while a grave sin—one against the soul—even if acknowledged cannot be atoned for. His purpose is not to diminish the gravity of sexual sin, which was universally recognized, but by way of comparison to assert the generally unrecognized gravity of the sin of omission in matters of education. His assessment of the seriousness of a sin in terms of its detriment to body or to soul must be seen in the light of the fact that it derives from a proverb not of his own coinage which he is exploiting by way of hyperbole for his own purpose. It certainly runs in the direction of such biblical estimates of sin as those found in Matt. 21:31-32, Rom. 14:23, and Luke 18:9-13, where the chief sins are defined in terms of unbelief, a view utterly remote from the current Roman teaching and practice regarding confession. Cf. Luther's distinction between open sins and unbelief of the heart in his 1522 sermon on the Pharisee and the publican (WA 10III, 301) and in his later expositions of Galatians (WA 40I, 221) and Isaiah (WA 25. 121).

the first place, there are some who lack the goodness and decency to do it, even if they had the ability. Instead, like the ostrich [Job 39:14-16], they deal cruelly with their young. They are content to have laid the eggs and brought children into the world; beyond this they will do nothing more. But these children are supposed to live among us and with us in the community. How then can reason, and especially Christian charity, allow that they grow up uneducated, to poison and pollute the other children until at last the whole city is ruined, as happened in Sodom and Gomorrah [Gen. 19:1-25], and Gibeah [Judges 19–20], and a number of other cities?

In the second place, the great majority of parents unfortunately are wholly unfitted for this task. They do not know how children should be brought up and taught, for they themselves have learned nothing but how to care for their bellies. It takes extraordinary people to bring children up right and teach them well.

In the third place, even if parents had the ability and desire to do it themselves, they have neither the time nor the opportunity for it, what with their other duties and the care of the household. Necessity compels us, therefore, to engage public school-teachers for the children—unless each one were willing to engage his own private tutor. But that would be too heavy a burden for the common man, and many a promising boy would again be neglected on account of poverty. Besides, many parents die, leaving orphans, and if we do not know from experience how they are cared for by their guardians it should be quite clear from the fact that God calls himself Father of the fatherless [Ps 68:5], of those who are neglected by everyone else. Then too there are others who have no children of their own, and therefore take no interest in the training of children.

It therefore behooves the council and the authorities to devote the greatest care and attention to the young. Since the property, honor, and life of the whole city have been committed to their faithful keeping, they would be remiss in their duty before God and man if they did not seek its welfare and improvement day and night with all the means at their command. Now the welfare of a city does not consist solely in accumulating vast treasures, building mighty walls and magnificent buildings, and producing a goodly supply of guns and armor. Indeed, where such things are plentiful, and reckless fools get control of them, it is so much the worse and the city suffers even greater loss. A city's best and greatest welfare, safety, and strength consist rather in its having many able, learned, wise, honorable, and well-educated citizens. They can then readily gather, protect, and properly use treasure and all manner of property.

So it was done in ancient Rome. There boys were so taught that by the time they reached their fifteenth, eighteenth, or twentieth year they were well versed in Latin, Greek, and all the liberal arts[15] (as they are called), and then immediately entered upon a political or military career. Their system produced intelligent, wise, and competent men, so skilled in every art and rich in experience that if all the bishops, priests, and monks in the whole of Germany today were rolled into one, you would not have the equal of a single Roman soldier. As a result their country prospered; they had capable and trained men for every position. So at all times throughout the world simple necessity has forced men, even among the heathen, to maintain pedagogues and schoolmasters if their nation was to be brought to a high standard. Hence, the word "schoolmaster" is used by Paul in Galatians 4[16] as a word taken from the common usage and practice of mankind, where he says, "The law was our schoolmaster."

Since a city should and must have [educated] people, and since there is a universal dearth of them and complaint that they are nowhere to be found, we dare not wait until they grow up of themselves; neither can we carve them out of stone nor hew them out of wood. Nor will God perform miracles as long as men can solve their problems by means of the other gifts he has

---

[15] The liberal arts were traditionally seven in number. Grammar, rhetoric, and dialectic comprised the trivium of the medieval elementary schools; music, arithmetic, geometry, and astronomy comprised the quadrivium of the secondary schools. BG 3, 32, n. 6. Luther's description has reference to Roman education in the shape it took after the end of the republic, as he had come to know it through his own reading of Cicero, Quintilian, and others. Albrecht, *Studien zu . . . "die Ratsherren,"* p. 710.

[16] Luther consistently rendered the *paidagōgos* of Gal. 3:24 (literally, "attendant" or "custodian"; cf. RSV) as *Zuchtmeyster* (literally, one who educates, trains, or disciplines in home, court, or school; cf. KJV). WA, DB 7, 182-183; Grimm, *Deutsches Wörterbuch,* VII, 275.

already granted them. Therefore, we must do our part and spare no labor or expense to produce and train such people ourselves. For whose fault is it that today our cities have so few capable people? Whose fault, if not that of authorities, who have left the young people to grow up like saplings in the forest, and have given no thought to their instruction and training? This is also why they have grown to maturity so misshapen that they cannot be used for building purposes, but are mere brushwood, fit only for kindling fires.[17]

After all, temporal government has to continue.[18] Are we then to permit none but louts and boors to rule, when we can do better than that? That would certainly be a crude and senseless policy. We might as well make lords out of swine and wolves, and set them to rule over those who refuse to give any thought to how they are ruled by men. Moreover, it is barbarous wickedness to think no further than this: We will rule now; what concern is it of ours how they will fare who come after us? Not over human beings, but over swine and dogs should such persons rule who in ruling seek only their own profit or glory. Even if we took the utmost pains to develop a group of able, learned, and skilled people for positions in government, there would still be plenty of labor and anxious care involved in seeing that things went well. What then is to happen if we take no pains at all?

"All right," you say again,[19] "suppose we do have to have schools; what is the use of teaching Latin, Greek, and Hebrew, and the other liberal arts? We could just as well use German for teaching the Bible and God's word, which is enough for our salvation."[20] I reply: Alas! I am only too well aware that we Germans must always be and remain brutes and stupid beasts, as the neighboring nations call us, epithets which we richly de-

---

[17]Cf. Matt. 13:30.

[18]On Luther's view of temporal government as an abiding divine institution, see his 1523 treatise on *Temporal Authority*, pp. 659-661.

[19]*Aber mal* refers back to the last four lines of p. 707. Having discussed the need for education, Luther now considers its content.

[20]This was the position of the ex-monks at Erfurt, who disparaged higher education in the name of their new evangelical religion.

serve.[21] But I wonder why we never ask, "What is the use of silks, wine, spices, and other strange foreign wares[22] when we ourselves have in Germany wine, grain, wool, flax, wood, and stone not only in quantities sufficient for our needs, but also of the best and choicest quality for our glory and ornament?" Languages and the arts, which can do us no harm, but are actually a greater ornament, profit, glory, and benefit, both for the understanding of Holy Scripture and the conduct of temporal government—these we despise. But foreign wares, which are neither necessary nor useful, and in addition strip us down to a mere skeleton—these we cannot do without. Are not we Germans justly dubbed fools and beasts?

Truly, if there were no other benefit connected with the languages, this should be enough to delight and inspire us, namely, that they are so fine and noble a gift of God, with which he is now so richly visiting and blessing us Germans above all other lands. We do not see many instances where the devil has allowed them to flourish by means of the universities and monasteries; indeed, these have always raged against languages and are even now raging. For the devil smelled a rat, and perceived that if the languages were revived a hole would be knocked in his kingdom which he could not easily stop up again. Since he found he could not prevent their revival, he now aims to keep them on such slender rations that they will of themselves decline and pass away. They are not a welcome guest in his house, so he plans to offer them such meager entertainment that they will not prolong their stay. Very few of us, my dear sirs, see through this evil design of the devil.

Therefore, my beloved Germans, let us get our eyes open, thank God for this precious treasure, and guard it well, lest the devil vent his spite and it be taken away from us again. Although the gospel came and still comes to us through the Holy Spirit alone, we cannot deny that it came through the medium of languages, was spread abroad by that means, and must be preserved

---

21 Luther is alluding to the common sneers of the Italian humanists at German crudities. *WA* 15, 36, n. 3.
22 On Luther's opposition to foreign wares, see his 1524 treatise on *Trade, LW* 45, 246-247.

by the same means. For just when God wanted to spread the gospel throughout the world by means of the apostles he gave the tongues for that purpose [Acts 2:1-11]. Even before that, by means of the Roman Empire he had spread the Latin and Greek languages widely in every land in order that his gospel might the more speedily bear fruit far and wide. He has done the same thing now as well. Formerly no one knew why God had the languages revived, but now for the first time we see that it was done for the sake of the gospel, which he intended to bring to light and use in exposing and destroying the kingdom of Antichrist.[23] To this end he gave over Greece to the Turk in order that the Greeks, driven out and scattered, might disseminate their language and provide an incentive to the study of other languages as well.

In proportion then as we value the gospel, let us zealously hold to the languages. For it was not without purpose that God caused his Scriptures to be set down in these two languages alone—the Old Testament in Hebrew, the New in Greek. Now if God did not despise them but chose them above all others for his word, then we too ought to honor them above all others. St. Paul declared it to be the peculiar glory and distinction of Hebrew that God's word was given in that language, when he said in Romans 3 [:1-2], "What advantage or profit have those who are circumcised? Much indeed. To begin with, God's speech[24] is entrusted to them." King David too boasts in Psalm 147 [:19-20], "He declares his word to Jacob, his statutes and ordinances to Israel. He has not dealt thus with any other nation or revealed to them his ordinances." Hence, too, the Hebrew language is called sacred. And St. Paul, in Romans 1 [:2], calls it "the holy scriptures," doubtless on account of the holy word of God which is comprehended [*verfasset*] therein. Similarly, the Greek language too may be called sacred, because it was chosen above all others as the language in which the New Testament was to be written, and because by it other languages too have been sanctified as it

---

[23] On Luther's identification of the pope with Antichrist, see p. 60, n. 8.
[24] *Gottes rede* was rendered as *was Gott gered hat* (literally, "what God has spoken") in Luther's 1522 New Testament and in subsequent editions until the complete Bible of 1546 where it was rendered as *Gotteswort* (literally, "God's Word"). WA, DB 7, 36-37.

spilled over into them like a fountain through the medium of translation.[25]

And let us be sure of this: we will not long preserve the gospel without the languages. The languages are the sheath in which this sword of the Spirit [Eph. 6:17] is contained; they are the casket in which this jewel is enshrined; they are the vessel in which this wine is held; they are the larder in which this food is stored; and, as the gospel itself points out [Matt. 14:20], they are the baskets in which are kept these loaves and fishes and fragments. If through our neglect we let the languages go (which God forbid!), we shall not only lose the gospel, but the time will come when we shall be unable either to speak or write a correct Latin or German. As proof and warning of this, let us take the deplorable and dreadful example of the universities and monasteries, in which men have not only unlearned the gospel, but have in addition so corrupted the Latin and German languages that the miserable folk have been fairly turned into beasts, unable to speak or write a correct German or Latin, and have wellnigh lost their natural reason to boot.

For this reason even the apostles themselves considered it necessary to set down the New Testament and hold it fast in the Greek language, doubtless in order to preserve it for us there safe and sound as in a sacred ark. For they foresaw all that was to come, and now has come to pass; they knew that if it was left exclusively to men's memory, wild and fearful disorder and confusion and a host of varied interpretations, fancies, and doctrines would arise in the Christian church, and that this could not be prevented and the simple folk protected unless the New Testament were set down with certainty in written language. Hence, it is inevitable that unless the languages remain, the gospel must finally perish.

Experience too has proved this and still gives evidence of it. For as soon as the languages declined to the vanishing point, after the apostolic age, the gospel and faith and Christianity itself declined more and more until under the pope they disappeared entirely. After the decline of the languages Christianity witnessed

---

25 Our rendering of the difficult sentence is based on the suggestions of Albrecht, *Studien zu . . . "die Ratsherren,"* pp. 702-703.

little that was worth anything; instead, a great many dreadful abominations arose because of ignorance of the languages. On the other hand, now that the languages have been revived, they are bringing with them so bright a light and accomplishing such great things that the whole world stands amazed and has to acknowledge that we have the gospel just as pure and undefiled as the apostles had it, that it has been wholly restored to its original purity, far beyond what it was in the days of St. Jerome and St. Augustine. In short, the Holy Spirit is no fool. He does not busy himself with inconsequential or useless matters. He regarded the languages as so useful and necessary to Christianity that he ofttimes brought them down with him from heaven.[26] This alone should be a sufficient motive for us to pursue them with diligence and reverence and not to despise them, for he himself has now revived them again upon the earth.

Yes, you say, but many of the fathers were saved and even became teachers without the languages. That is true. But how do you account for the fact that they so often erred in the Scriptures? How often does not St. Augustine err in the Psalms and in his other expositions, and Hilary[27] too—in fact, all those who have undertaken to expound Scripture without a knowledge of the languages? Even though what they said about a subject at times was perfectly true, they were never quite sure whether it really was present there in the passage where by their interpretation they thought to find it. Let me give you an example: It is rightly said that Christ is the Son of God; but how ridiculous it must have sounded to the ears of their adversaries when they attempted to prove this by citing from Psalm 110: "*Tecum principium in die virtutis tuae*,"[28] though in the Hebrew there is not a word about the

---

[26] Acts 2:4; 10:46; I Cor. 12:10; 14:2-19.

[27] Hilary (*ca.* 315-367), the Bishop of Poitiers, was important to Luther primarily because of his commentaries on the psalms. See, e.g., *LW* 14, 285.

[28] This Vulgate version of Ps. 110:3 (translated literally, "With thee is sovereignty in the day of thy strength") is derived in part from the Septuagint text (*meta sou . . .*), which itself rests upon a misunderstanding of the Hebrew text whereby "your people" (cf. RSV) was read as "with you" through the simple change of one vowel point. The error of course could never be discovered without renewed examination of the Hebrew original. Luther was critical of the Vulgate rendering already in his earliest (1513-1516) commentary on the Psalms (see *WA* 4, 227, 233, 516-517). Au-

Deity in this passage! When men attempt to defend the faith with such uncertain arguments and mistaken proof texts, are not Christians put to shame and made a laughingstock in the eyes of adversaries who know the language? The adversaries only become more stiff-necked in their error and have an excellent pretext for regarding our faith as a mere human delusion.

When our faith is thus held up to ridicule, where does the fault lie? It lies in our ignorance of the languages; and there is no other way out than to learn the languages. Was not St. Jerome compelled to translate the Psalter anew from the Hebrew[29] because, when we quoted our [Latin] Psalter in disputes with the Jews, they sneered at us, pointing out that our texts did not read that way in the original Hebrew? Now the expositions of all the early fathers who dealt with Scripture apart from a knowledge of the languages (even when their teaching is not in error) are such that they often employ uncertain, indefensible, and inappropriate expressions. They grope their way like a blind man along the wall, frequently missing the sense of the text and twisting it to suit their fancy, as in the case of the verse mentioned above, *"Tecum principium,"* etc. Even St. Augustine himself is obliged to confess, as he does in his *Christian Instruction,*[30]

---

gustine had interpreted *principium* not in terms of spontaneity or voluntariness as did Luther (WA 4, 233; see also his constant rendering of the Psalter from 1524 on—*williglich*—in WA, DB 10ᴵ, 476-477), but in terms of God the Father. See Albrecht, *Studien zu . . . "die Ratsherren,"* pp. 713-714.

[29] Jerome's first revision of the Old Latin Psalter, done in 383 at Rome and known as the *Psalterium Romanum,* was based on the Septuagint. His second revision, done in Palestine about four years later and known as the Gallican Psalter was also based on the Septuagint; it became the current version in the Latin Church and is still printed in most Vulgate Bibles. Finally, at the suggestion of Sophronius about 392, Jerome translated the Psalms from the Hebrew. Luther is probably thinking of the exchange of letters between Augustine and Jerome in which the former placed great confidence in the accuracy of the Septuagint—over against the great diversity of Latin Scriptures—while the latter's purpose was "not so much . . . to do away with the old texts, which, with their emendations, I translated from Greek into Latin for men of my own tongue, but rather to bring out that evidence which was passed over or corrupted by the Jews, so that our people might know what the Hebrew text really contained." See Sister Wilfrid Parsons (trans.), *Saint Augustine: Letters, I. FC* 9, 95, 325-328, 363-367, especially p. 365.

[30] "Men who know the Latin language . . . have need of two others in order to understand the sacred Scriptures. These are Hebrew and Greek, by which they may turn back to the originals if the infinite variance of Latin translators cause any uncertainty." John J. Gavigan (trans.), "Christian Instruc-

that a Christian teacher who is to expound the Scriptures must know Greek and Hebrew in addition to Latin. Otherwise, it is impossible to avoid constant stumbling; indeed, there are plenty of problems to work out even when one is well versed in the languages.

There is a vast difference therefore between a simple preacher of the faith and a person who expounds Scripture, or, as St. Paul puts it [I Cor. 12:28-30; 14:26-32], a prophet. A simple preacher (it is true) has so many clear passages and texts available through translations that he can know and teach Christ, lead a holy life, and preach to others. But when it comes to interpreting Scripture, and working with it on your own, and disputing with those who cite it incorrectly, he is unequal to the task; that cannot be done without languages. Now there must always be such prophets in the Christian church who can dig into Scripture, expound it, and carry on disputations. A saintly life and right doctrine are not enough. Hence, languages are absolutely and altogether necessary in the Christian church, as are the prophets or interpreters; although it is not necessary that every Christian or every preacher be such a prophet, as St. Paul points out in I Corinthians 12 [:4-30] and Ephesians 4 [:11].

Thus, it has come about that since the days of the apostles Scripture has remained so obscure, and no sure and trustworthy expositions of it have ever been written. For even the holy fathers (as we have said) frequently erred. And because of their ignorance of the languages they seldom agree; one says this, another that. St. Bernard[31] was a man so lofty in spirit that I almost venture to set him above all other celebrated teachers both ancient and modern. But note how often he plays (spiritually to be sure) with the Scriptures and twists them out of their true sense. This is also why the sophists[32] have contended that Scripture is obscure; they have held that God's word by its very nature is obscure and

---

tion" (*De doctrina Christiana* II, 11), *Writings of Saint Augustine*. FC 4, 73. *MPL* 34, 42.

[31] Bernard (1090-1153), abbot of Clairvaux, foremost leader of the rigorist Cistercian order and founder of one hundred sixty-three Cistercian monasteries, was a prominent mystic renowned for his preaching. For an example of Luther's critique of Bernard's exegesis, see LW 35, 217, n. 25.

[32] See p. 656, n. 5.

employs a peculiar style of speech. But they fail to realize that the whole trouble lies in the languages. If we understood the languages nothing clearer would ever have been spoken than God's word. A Turk's speech must needs be obscure to me—because I do not know the language—while a Turkish child of seven would understand him easily.

Hence, it is also a stupid undertaking to attempt to gain an understanding of Scripture by laboring through the commentaries of the fathers and a multitude of books and glosses.[33] Instead of this, men should have devoted themselves to the languages. Because they were ignorant of languages, the dear fathers at times expended many words in dealing with a text. Yet when they were all done they had scarcely taken its measure; they were half right and half wrong. Still, you continue to pore over them with immense labor even though, if you knew the languages, you could get further with the passage than they whom you are following. As sunshine is to shadow, so is the language itself compared to all the glosses of the fathers.

Since it becomes Christians then to make good use of the Holy Scriptures as their one and only book and it is a sin and a shame not to know our own book or to understand the speech and words of our God, it is a still greater sin and loss that we do not study languages, especially in these days when God is offering and giving us men and books and every facility and inducement to this study, and desires his Bible to be an open book. O how happy the dear fathers would have been if they had had our opportunity to study the languages and come thus prepared to the Holy Scriptures! What great toil and effort it cost them to gather up a few crumbs, while we with half the labor—yes, almost without any labor at all—can acquire the whole loaf! O how their effort puts our indolence to shame! Yes, how sternly God will judge our lethargy and ingratitude!

---

[33] Having finally read the Bible along with the *glossa ordinaria* as a monk at Erfurt and carefully taken into account the exegesis of the fathers in his own early lectures, Luther did not sharply distinguish between the authority of Scripture and that of the fathers, traditionally set alongside or above Scripture in the common scholastic method of studying theology, until his 1520 *Assertio omnium articulorum* (cf. *LW* 32, 11-12, which is based on the German version) and his 1521 controversy with Emser (see *PE* 3, 332-353). Albrecht, *Studien zu . . . "die Ratsherren,"* pp. 743-745.

Here belongs also what St. Paul calls for in I Corinthians 14 [:27, 29], namely, that in the Christian church all teachings must be judged. For this a knowledge of the language is needful above all else. The preacher or teacher can expound the Bible from beginning to end as he pleases, accurately or inaccurately, if there is no one there to judge whether he is doing it right or wrong. But in order to judge, one must have a knowledge of the languages; it cannot be done in any other way. Therefore, although faith and the gospel may indeed be proclaimed by simple preachers without a knowledge of languages, such preaching is flat and tame; people finally become weary and bored with it, and it falls to the ground. But where the preacher is versed in the languages, there is a freshness and vigor in his preaching, Scripture is treated in its entirety, and faith finds itself constantly renewed by a continual variety of words and illustrations. Hence, Psalm 129[34] likens such scriptural studies to a hunt, saying: to the deer God opens the dense forests; and Psalm 1 [:3] likens them to a tree with a plentiful supply of water, whose leaves are always green.

We should not be led astray because some boast of the Spirit and consider Scripture of little worth,[35] and others, such as the Waldensian Brethren,[36] think the languages are unnecessary. Dear friend, say what you will about the Spirit, I too have been in

---

[34] Ps. 29:9; Luther, or his printer, by mistake slipped in another digit. His understanding of the verse is based on the Vulgate, whose obscurity is compounded by Luther's reading of *cervas* ("deer") for *cervos* ("forked stakes"; Douay: "oaks"). This understanding, including the interpretation of "forests" in terms of "the obscure books of the Old Testament," goes back to Luther's earliest commentary of 1513-1516 on the psalms. *WA* 3, 157. Actually, both psalm passages are here interpreted allegorically.

[35] This is an allusion to zealots and fanatics such as Karlstadt, Münzer, and the Zwickau prophets. Luther had begun to warn against Münzer already in 1523 and was soon to publish further writings culminating in his *Against the Heavenly Prophets* of 1525. See *LW* 40, 47-223.

[36] Luther commonly referred to the Bohemian Brethren as "Waldensians," as in his treatise of less than a year earlier, *The Adoration of the Sacrament* (1523), the treatise in which he also urged them not to "neglect the languages." See *LW* 36, 271-276 and 304. Paul Speratus, who had originally established the relationship between Luther and the Brethren was at the time of this writing a guest in Luther's house, having been driven out of Moravia. Luther's incidental reference to the Bohemians may be significant for an understanding of the various other groups inimical to education; Albrecht suggests the possibility of their being influenced directly by the radical Taborites. *Studien zu . . . "die Ratsherren,"* pp. 727-728.

the Spirit and have seen the Spirit, perhaps even more of it (if it comes to boasting of one's own flesh[37]) than those fellows with all their boasting will see in a year. Moreover, my spirit has given some account of itself, while theirs sits quietly in its corner and does little more than brag about itself. I know full well that while it is the Spirit alone who accomplishes everything, I would surely have never flushed a covey[38] if the languages had not helped me and given me a sure and certain knowledge of Scripture. I too could have lived uprightly and preached the truth in seclusion; but then I should have left undisturbed the pope, the sophists, and the whole anti-Christian regime. The devil does not respect my spirit as highly as he does my speech and pen when they deal with Scripture. For my spirit takes from him nothing but myself alone; but Holy Scripture and the languages leave him little room on earth, and wreak havoc in his kingdom.

So I can by no means commend the Waldensian Brethren for their neglect of the languages. For even though they may teach the truth, they inevitably often miss the true meaning of the text, and thus are neither equipped nor fit for defending the faith against error. Moreover, their teaching is so obscure and couched in such peculiar terms, differing from the language of Scripture, that I fear it is not or will not remain pure. For there is great danger in speaking of things of God in a different manner and in different terms than God himself employs. In short, they may lead saintly lives and teach sacred things among themselves, but so long as they remain without the languages they cannot but lack what all the rest lack, namely, the ability to treat Scripture with certainty and thoroughness and to be useful to other nations. Because they could do this, but will not, they have to figure out for themselves how they will answer for it to God.

To this point we have been speaking about the necessity and

---

[37] Cf. II Cor. 12:1-6 and Phil. 3:4.
[38] *Were ich doch allen püsschen zu ferne gewest.* We have been guided in the rendering of this difficult clause, and in the construing of its obscure syntactical relationship to the clauses preceding it, by the suggestions of Albrecht, *Studien zu . . . "die Ratsherren,"* pp. 703-705. It seems clearly to have reference to the matter of success, and to be derived in all likelihood from some proverbial expression, perhaps one connected with the hunt to which Luther had just alluded in connection with Ps. 29:9.

value of languages and Christian schools for the spiritual realm and the salvation of souls. Now let us consider also the body. Let us suppose that there were no soul, no heaven or hell, and that we were to consider solely the temporal government from the standpoint of its worldly functions. Does it not need good schools and educated persons even more than the spiritual realm? Hitherto, the sophists have shown no concern whatever for the temporal government, and have designed their schools so exclusively for the spiritual estate that it has become almost a disgrace for an educated man to marry. He has had to hear such remarks as, "Well! so he is turning worldly and does not want to become spiritual," just as if their spiritual estate alone were pleasing to God, and the worldly estate (as they call it) were altogether of the devil and un-Christian. But in the sight of God it is they themselves who are meanwhile becoming the devil's own (as happened to the nation of Israel during the Babylonian Captivity [II Kings 24:14]); only the despised rabble has remained in the land and in the right estate, while the better class of people and the leaders are carried off with tonsure and cowl to the devil in Babylon.[39]

It is not necessary to repeat here that the temporal government is a divinely ordained estate (I have elsewhere[40] treated this subject so fully that I trust no one has any doubt about it). The question is rather: How are we to get good and capable men into it? Here we are excelled and put to shame by the pagans of old, especially the Romans and the Greeks. Although they had no idea of whether this estate were pleasing to God or not, they were so earnest and diligent in educating and training their young boys and girls to fit them for the task, that when I call it to mind I am forced to blush for us Christians, and especially for us Germans. We are such utter blockheads and beasts that we dare to say, "Pray, why have schools for people who are not going to become spiritual?" Yet we know, or at least we ought to know, how essential and beneficial it is—and pleasing to God—that a

---

[39] Luther had used this same illustration in his 1520 *The Babylonian Captivity of the Church.* LW 36, 78.
[40] See Luther's *Temporal Authority: To What Extent it Should be Obeyed* (1523), pp. 659-678.

prince, lord, councilman, or other person in a position of authority be educated and qualified to perform the functions of his office as a Christian should.

Now if (as we have assumed) there were no souls, and there were no need at all of schools and languages for the sake of the Scriptures and of God, this one consideration alone would be sufficient to justify the establishment everywhere of the very best schools for both boys and girls, namely, that in order to maintain its temporal estate outwardly the world must have good and capable men and women, men able to rule well over land and people, women able to manage the household and train children and servants aright. Now such men must come from our boys, and such women from our girls. Therefore, it is a matter of properly educating and training our boys and girls to that end. I have pointed out above that the common man is doing nothing about it; he is incapable of it, unwilling, and ignorant of what to do. Princes and lords ought to be doing it, but they must needs be sleigh riding, drinking, and parading about in masquerades.[41] They are burdened with high and important functions in cellar, kitchen, and bedroom. And the few who might want to do it must stand in fear of the rest lest they be taken for fools or heretics. Therefore, dear councilmen, it rests with you alone; you have a better authority and occasion to do it than princes and lords.

But, you say, everyone may teach his sons and daughters himself, or at least train them in proper discipline. Answer: Yes, we can readily see what such teaching and training amount to. Even when the training is done to perfection and succeeds, the net result is little more than a certain enforced outward respectability; underneath, they are nothing but the same old blockheads, unable to converse intelligently on any subject, or to assist or counsel anyone. But if children were instructed and trained in schools, or wherever learned and well-trained schoolmasters and schoolmistresses were available to teach the languages, the other arts, and history, they would then hear of the doings and sayings of the entire world, and how things went with various cities, kingdoms, princes, men, and women. Thus, they could in a short time set

---

[41] See Luther's criticism of the ruler's preoccupation with amusements to the neglect of their office, e.g. pp. 694-695 and *LW* 45, 249-250.

before themselves as in a mirror the character, life, counsels, and purposes—successful and unsuccessful—of the whole world from the beginning; on the basis of which they could then draw the proper inferences and in the fear of God take their own place in the stream of human events. In addition, they could gain from history the knowledge and understanding of what to seek and what to avoid in this outward life, and be able to advise and direct others accordingly. The training we undertake at home, apart from such schools, is intended to make us wise through our own experience. Before that can be accomplished we will be dead a hundred times over, and will have acted rashly throughout our mortal life, for it takes a long time to acquire personal experience.

Now since the young must always be hopping and skipping, or at least doing something that they enjoy, and since one cannot very well forbid this—nor would it be wise to forbid them everything—why then should we not set up such schools for them and introduce them to such studies? By the grace of God it is now possible for children to study with pleasure and in play languages, or other arts, or history. Today, schools are not what they once were, a hell and purgatory in which we were tormented with *casualibus* and *temporalibus*,[42] and yet learned less than nothing despite all the flogging, trembling, anguish, and misery. If we take so much time and trouble to teach children card-playing, singing, and dancing, why do we not take as much time to teach them reading and other disciplines while they are young and have the time, and are apt and eager to learn? For my part, if I had children[43] and could manage it, I would have them study not only languages and history, but also singing and music together with the whole of mathematics.[44] For what is all this but

---

[42] Luther did not object to "cases" and "tenses" as such but to the perverted methods whereby declining and conjugating were made disciplinary exercises in the classroom. Albrecht, *Studien zu . . . "die Ratsherren,"* p. 709.

[43] Luther, still a bachelor, married Katherine von Bora some sixteen months later on June 13, 1525, and eventually became the father of three sons and three daughters.

[44] Luther here distinguishes between the practical art of singing and the theoretical discipline of music, the latter being, with arithmetic, geometry, and astronomy, a part of the quadrivium, generally termed the mathematical disciplines in the Middle Ages.

mere child's play? The ancient Greeks trained their children in these disciplines; yet they grew up to be people of wondrous ability, subsequently fit for everything. How I regret now that I did not read more poets and historians, and that no one taught me them! Instead, I was obliged to read at great cost, toil, and detriment to myself, that devil's dung, the philosophers and sophists, from which I have all I can do to purge myself.

So you say, "But who can thus spare his children and train them all to be young gentlemen? There is work for them to do at home," etc. Answer: It is not my intention either to have such schools established as we have had heretofore, where a boy slaved away at his Donatus[45] and Alexander[46] for twenty or thirty years and still learned nothing. Today we are living in a different world, and things are being done differently. My idea is to have the boys attend such a school for one or two hours during the day, and spend the remainder of the time working at home, learning a trade, or doing whatever is expected of them. In this way, study and work will go hand-in-hand while the boys are young and able to do both. Otherwise, they spend at least ten times as much time anyway with their pea shooters, ballplaying, racing, and tussling.

In like manner, a girl can surely find time enough to attend school for an hour a day, and still take care of her duties at home. She spends much more time than that anyway in sleeping, dancing, and playing. Only one thing is lacking, the earnest desire to train the young and to benefit and serve the world with

---

[45] Aelius Donatus, teacher of St. Jerome at Rome about the year 355, wrote the elementary Latin grammar which bears his name. It was originally in two parts, the *Ars minor* and *Ars grammatica.* The latter soon fell into disuse, but the former remained for more than a thousand years the chief textbook for teaching the rudiments of Latin grammar. It was among the earliest products of Gutenberg's press. See the English translation by Wayland Johnson Chase, *The Ars minor of Donatus* ("Wisconsin Studies in the Social Sciences and History," No. 11 [Madison, Wis., 1926]).

[46] Alexander de Villa-Dei, a Franciscan in Normandy, in 1199 composed the *Doctrinale puerorum,* a grammatical treatise in hexameters designed to help pupils memorize the necessary rules; it became immensely popular for over three hundred years. Alexander drew his illustrations from the later Christian poets rather than from the ancient classics, and is largely responsible for the decadence of Latin style in the later Middle Ages. See the text in Dietrich Reichling (ed.), *Doctrinale* ("Monumenta Germaniae Paedagogica," Vol. XII [Berlin: Hofmann, 1893]). See Henry Osborn Taylor, *The Medieval Mind* (3rd American ed., 2 vols.; New York: Macmillan, 1919), II, 152-154.

able men and women. The devil very much prefers coarse block-heads and ne'er-do-wells, lest men get along too well on earth. The exceptional pupils, who give promise of becoming skilled teachers, preachers, or holders of other ecclesiastical positions, should be allowed to continue in school longer, or even be dedicated to a life of study, as we read of [those who trained][47] the holy martyrs SS. Agnes, Agatha, Lucy,[48] and others. That is how the monasteries and foundations originated; they have since been wholly perverted to a different and damnable use. There is great need of such advanced study, for the tonsured crowd is fast dwindling. Besides, most of them are unfit to teach or to rule, for all they know is to care for their bellies, which is indeed all they have been taught. We must certainly have men to administer God's word and sacraments and to be shepherds of souls. But where shall we get them if we let our schools go by the board, and fail to replace them with others that are Christian? The schools that have been maintained hitherto, even though they do not die out entirely, can produce nothing but lost and pernicious deceivers.

It is highly necessary, therefore, that we take some positive action in this matter before it is too late; not only on account of the young people, but also in order to preserve both our spiritual and temporal estates. If we miss this opportunity, we

---

[47] The text itself actually speaks of the training imparted by, rather than given to, the martyrs. Albrecht (*op. cit.*, pp. 693-694), however, suggests that our present rendering may have been intended. Parallels for this line of thought are to be found elsewhere in Luther, particularly in his 1520 *Open Letter to the Christian Nobility* (PE 2, 118 and 152), his 1521 *Against Latomus* (LW 32, 258), and his 1523 *Ordering of Divine Worship* (PE 6, 61). Several early manuscripts as well as the Latin translation of Obsopoeus so construe the meaning. *The Golden Legend of Jacobus de Voragine* affords no evidence of the teaching activity of these women. Paul Pietsch, on the other hand, thinks that Luther may perhaps have used a different source, or been himself in error, but that it is distinctly possible that Luther actually intended to speak of instruction imparted by, rather than received by, the martyrs; he cites the ambiguity of PE 2, 152, in this regard, and might have cited the 1521 *De votis monasticis* (WA 8, 615) as well.

[48]The Roman maiden Agnes, traditionally esteemed for her youthful chastity and innocence, was martyred under Dioclethian, ca. A.D. 304. Both born in Sicily, Agatha was martyred under Decius, *c.a.* A.D. 250, and Lucy was martyred under Diocletioan, ca. A.D. 304. All three names occur in the litany of the saints in the canon of the mass (see the text in LW 36, 322).

may perhaps find our hands tied later on when we would gladly attend to it, and ever after have to suffer in vain the pangs of remorse. God is offering us ample help; he stretches forth his hand and gives us all things needful for this task. If we disdain his offer we are already judged with the people of Israel, of whom Isaiah says [65:2], "I spread out my hand all the day to an unbelieving and rebellious people"; and in Proverbs 1 [:24-26] we read, "I have stretched out my hand, and no one has heeded; you have ignored all my counsel. Very well, then I will also laugh at your calamity, and will mock when your misfortune overtakes you," etc. Of this let us beware! Consider, for example, what a great effort King Solomon made in this matter; so deeply was he concerned for the young that in the midst of his royal duties he wrote for them a book called Proverbs. Consider Christ himself, how he draws little children to him, how urgently in Matthew 18 [:5, 10] he commends them to us and praises the angels who wait upon them, in order to show us how great a service it is when we train the young properly. On the other hand, how terrible is his wrath when we offend them and suffer them to perish! [Matt. 18:6].

Therefore, dear sirs, take this task to heart which God so earnestly requires of you, which your office imposes upon you, which is so necessary for our youth, and with which neither church [*geyst*] nor world can dispense. Alas! we have lain idle and rotting in the darkness long enough; we have been German beasts all too long. Let us for once make use of our reason, that God may perceive our thankfulness for his benefits, and other nations see that we too are human beings, able either to learn something useful from others or to teach them in order that even through us the world may be made better. I have done my part. It has truly been my purpose to counsel and assist the German nation. If there be some who despise me for this and refuse to listen to my sincere advice because they think they know better, I cannot help it. I know full well that others could have done this better; since they keep silent, I am doing it as well as I can. It is surely better to have spoken out on the subject, however inadequately, than to have remained altogether silent about it. It is my hope that God will awaken some of you, so that my well-meant advice may not be offered in vain, and instead of having regard for the one who utters it you will rather be stirred by the cause itself to do something about it.

Finally, one thing more merits serious consideration by all those who earnestly desire to have such schools and languages established and maintained in Germany. It is this: no effort or expense should be spared to provide good libraries or book repositories, especially in the larger cities which can well afford it. For if the gospel and all the arts are to be preserved, they must be set down and held fast in books and writings (as was done by the prophets and apostles themselves, as I have said above).[49] This is essential, not only that those who are to be our spiritual and temporal leaders may have books to read and study, but also that the good books may be preserved and not lost, together with the arts and languages which we now have by the grace of God. St. Paul too was concerned about this when he charged Timothy to give attention to reading [I Tim. 4:13], and bade him bring with him the parchments from Troas [II Tim. 4:13].

Indeed, all the kingdoms which ever amounted to anything gave careful attention to this matter. This is especially true of the people of Israel, among whom Moses was the first to begin the practice when he had the book of the law kept in the ark of God [Deut. 31:25-26]. He put it in charge of the Levites so that whoever needed a copy might obtain one from them. He even commanded the king to procure from them a copy of this book [Deut. 17:18]. Thus, we see how God directed the Levitical priesthood, among its other duties, to watch over and care for the books. Later this library was added to and improved by Joshua, then by Samuel, David, Solomon, Isaiah, and by many other kings and prophets. Thence have come the Holy Scriptures of the Old Testament, which would never have been collected or preserved had God not required such care to be bestowed upon them.

Following this example, the monasteries and foundations of old also established libraries, although there were few good books among them. What a loss it was that they neglected to

---

[49]See pp. 715-729.

acquire books and good libraries at that time, when the books and men for it were available, became painfully evident later when, as time went on, unfortunately all the arts and languages declined. Instead of worthwhile books, the stupid, useless, and harmful books of the monks, such as *Catholicon, Florista, Grecista, Labyrinthus, Dormi secure*,[50] and the like asses' dung were introduced by the devil. Because of such books the Latin language was ruined, and there remained nowhere a decent school, course of instruction, or method of study. This situation lasted until, as we have experienced and observed, the languages and arts were laboriously recovered—although imperfectly—from bits and fragments of old books hidden among dust and worms. Men are still painfully searching for them every day, just as people poke through the ashes of a ruined city seeking the treasures and jewels.

This served us right; God has properly repaid us for our ingratitude in not considering his kindness toward us and failing to provide for a constant supply of good books and learned men while we had the time and opportunity. When we neglected this, as though it were no concern of ours, he in turn did the same; instead of Holy Scripture and good books, he suffered Aristotle[51]

---

[50] The Latin lexicon *Summa grammaticalis,* commonly known as *Catholicon,* was compiled about 1286 by the Dominican John of Genoa, sometimes called Balbi or de Balbis (d. *ca.* 1298) comprising treatises on orthography, etymology, grammar, prosody, rhetoric, and an etymological dictionary of the Latin language, it appeared in a number of printed editions before 1500.

A rhymed Latin syntax, composed in 1317 by Ludolf von Luchow of Hildesheim, the *Flores grammaticae* gave its author the nickname "Florista," and the book itself subsequently came to be called by that name. The *Graecismus,* a grammatical treatise in hexameters, interposed with elegiacs, ascribed to Eberhard of Bethune (*fl.* 1212), got its name from the tenth chapter, which takes up Greek etymologies; this book too came to be called by the nickname it had won for its author.

The *Labyrinthus* was an early thirteenth-century poem, *De miseriis rectorum scholarum,* also by Eberhard of Bethune.

The *Dormi secure* was a collection of seventy-one sermons for the church year and holy days, compiled ostensibly by the Franciscan, Johann von Werden (*ca.* 1450); the title implies that it was for the benefit of preachers too ignorant or too lazy to compose their own sermons. Luther attributes to the bad Latin of these books the medieval decline of the language. See Albrecht, *Studien zu . . . "die Ratsherren,"* pp. 705-707.

[51] On Luther's view of Aristotle, the ancient Greek philosopher whose ideas became basic for scholastic theology, and for a bibliography on the subject see Peter Petersen, *Geschichte der aristotelischen Philosophie im protestantischen*

to come in, together with countless harmful books which drew us farther from the Bible. In addition to these he let in those devil's masks, the monks, and those phantoms which are the universities, which we endowed with vast properties. We have taken upon ourselves the support of a host of doctors, preaching friars, masters, priests, and monks; that is to say, great, coarse, fat asses decked out in red and brown birettas, looking like a sow bedecked with a gold chain and jewels. They taught us nothing good, but only made us all the more blind and stupid. In return, they devoured all our goods and filled every monastery, indeed every nook and cranny, with the filth and dung of their foul and poisonous books, until it is appalling to think of it.

Isn't it a crying shame that heretofore a boy was obliged to study for twenty years or even longer merely to learn enough bad Latin to become a priest and mumble through the mass? Whoever got that far was accounted blessed, and blessed was the mother who bore such a child! And yet he remained all his life a poor ignoramus, unable either to cackle or to lay an egg.[52] Everywhere we were obliged to put up with teachers and masters who knew nothing themselves, and were incapable of teaching anything good or worthwhile. In fact, they did not even know how to study or teach. Where does the fault lie? There were no other books available than the stupid books of the monks and the sophists. What else could come out of them but pupils and teachers as stupid as the books they used? A jackdaw hatches no doves,[53] and a fool cannot produce a sage. That is the reward of our ingratitude, that men failed to found libraries but let the good books perish and kept the poor ones.

My advice is not to heap together all manner of books indiscriminately and think only of the number and size of the collection. I would make a judicious selection, for it is not necessary

---

Deutschland (Leipzig: Meiner, 1921), pp. 31-38. Cf. also Luther's own judgment of Aristotle's several works in his 1520 *Open Letter to the Christian Nobility. PE* 2, 146-147.

[52] Cackling (*Glucken*) was said to be easier than laying an egg; Wander (ed.), *Sprichwörter-Lexikon*, I, 1774. Whoever could do neither the harder nor the easier was presumably pretty worthless. *WA* 15, 51, n. 1
[53] See Wander (ed.), *Sprichwörter-Lexikon*, I, 671, "*Dohle,*" No. 4.

to have all the commentaries of the jurists, all the sentences[54] of the theologians, all the *quaestiones*[55] of the philosophers, and all the sermons of the monks. Indeed, I would discard all such dung, and furnish my library with the right sort of books, consulting with scholars as to my choice.

First of all, there would be the Holy Scriptures, in Latin, Greek, Hebrew, and German, and any other language in which they might be found. Next, the best commentaries, and, if I could find them, the most ancient, in Greek, Hebrew, and Latin. Then, books that would be helpful in learning the languages, such as the poets and orators, regardless of whether they were pagan or Christian, Greek or Latin, for it is from such books that one must learn grammar.[56] After that would come books on the liberal arts,[57] and all the other arts. Finally, there would be books of law and medicine; here too there should be careful choice among commentaries.

Among the foremost would be the chronicles and histories, in whatever languages they are to be had. For they are a wonderful help in understanding and guiding the course of events, and especially for observing the marvelous works of God.[58] How many fine tales and sayings we should have today of things that took place and were current in German lands, not one of which is known to us, simply because there was no one to write them down, and no one to preserve the books had they been written. That is why nothing is known in other lands about us

---

[54] The term should properly be "books of sentences." "Sentences" was a common title for dogmatic-theological treatises of the Middle Ages. Luther probably had in mind the countless commentaries on the *Sentences* compiled ca. 1150 by Peter Lombard (d. 1160), for centuries the most influential textbook of theology.

[55] Scholastic philosophers, in dealing with almost any subject, customarily split it up into *quaestiones,* i.e., specific topics to be discussed in the form of question and answer.

[56] *Grammatica,* the most basic of the liberal arts, included much more than we understand by the term "grammar" today. Perhaps "English" would be the closest modern equivalent, for it included besides the rules of a language such things as vocabulary, reading, interpretation, and creative expression. Albrecht, *Studien zu . . . "die Ratsherren,"* p. 711.

[57] See p. 713, n. 15.

[58] Luther set forth his ideas on the value of history at greater length in his 1538 preface to Wenceslaus Link's translation of Capella's history of Francesco Sforza, WA 50, 383-385.

Germans, and we must be content to have the rest of the world refer to us as German beasts who know only how to fight, gorge, and guzzle.[59] The Greeks and Latins, however, and even the Hebrews, wrote their things down so accurately and diligently that if even a woman or a child said or did something out of the ordinary the whole world must read of it and know it. Meanwhile, we Germans are nothing but Germans, and will remain Germans.

Now that God has today so graciously bestowed upon us an abundance of arts, scholars, and books, it is time to reap and gather in the best as well as we can, and lay up treasure in order to preserve for the future something from these years of jubilee,[60] and not lose this bountiful harvest. For it is to be feared—and the beginning of it is already apparent—that men will go on writing new and different books until finally, because of the devil's activity, we will come to the point where the good books which are now being produced and printed will again be suppressed, and the worthless and harmful books with their useless and sense-less rubbish will swarm back and litter every nook and corner. The devil certainly intends that we shall again be burdened and plagued as before with nothing but *Catholicons, Floristae, Modernists,*[61] and the accursed dung of monks and sophists, for-ever studying but never learning anything.

Therefore, I beseech you, my dear sirs, to let this sincere effort of mine bear fruit among you. Should there be any who think me too insignificant to profit by my advice, or who despise me as one condemned by the tyrants,[62] I pray them to consider that I am not seeking my own advantage, but the welfare and

---

[59]On the bitter comments especially of the Italians, who frequently character-ized the Germans as uncultured barbarians, see Albrecht, *Studien zu . . . "die Ratsherren,"* p. 712.

[60]See p. 708, n. 10.

[61] The *Moderni* were the followers of Occam and opponents of the *Antiqui* who adhered strictly to the interpretation of Aristotle as delivered by Al-bertus Magnus, Thomas Aquinas, and Duns Scotus. Their quarrel over the best methods of introducing young students to logic and dialectics became bitter enough to split faculties and require intervention by authorities. While the former called themselves nominalists and the latter realists, the controversy was essentially not that which divided the two great systems of scholastic thought going by the same names. Albrecht, *Studien zu . . . "die Ratsherren,"* p. 708.

[62]See p. 704, n. 2.

salvation of all Germany. Even if I were a fool and had hit upon a good idea, surely no wise man would think it a disgrace to follow me. And if I were a very Turk or a heathen, and my plan were nevertheless seen to benefit not myself but the Christians, they ought not in fairness to spurn my offer. It has happened before that a fool gave better advice than a whole council of wise men.[63] Moses was obliged to take advice from Jethro [Exod. 18:17-24].

Herewith I commend all of you to the grace of God. May he soften and kindle your hearts that they may be deeply concerned for the poor, miserable, and neglected youth, and with the help of God aid and assist them, to the end that there may be a blessed and Christian government in the German lands with respect to both body and soul, with all plenty and abundance, to the glory and honor of God the Father, through our Savior Jesus Christ. Amen.

---

[63] See Luther's similar statement in the address to Amsdorf with which he began his 1520 *Open Letter to the Christian Nobility.* PE 2, 62.

31.

WHETHER ONE MAY FLEE
FROM A DEADLY PLAGUE

To the Reverend Doctor Johann Hess,
pastor at Breslau, and to his fellow-
servants of the gospel of Jesus Christ

Martinus Luther

Grace and peace from God our Father and our Lord Jesus Christ.
Your letter, sent to me at Wittenberg, was received some time ago.
You wish to know whether it is proper for a Christian to run away
from a deadly plague. I should have answered long ago, but God
has for some time disciplined and scourged me so severely that I
have been unable to do much reading or writing.[1] Furthermore, it
occurred to me that God, the merciful Father, has endowed you so
richly with wisdom and truth in Christ that you yourself should be
well qualified to decide this matter or even weightier problems in
his Spirit and grace without our assistance.

But now that you keep on writing to me and have, so to speak,
humbled yourself in requesting our view on this matter so that, as
St. Paul repeatedly teaches, we may always agree with one another
and be of one mind [I Cor. 1:10; II Cor. 13:11; Phil. 2:2]. Therefore we here give you our opinion as far as God grants us to understand and perceive. This we would humbly submit to your judgment
and to that of all devout Christians for them, as is proper, to come
to their own decision and conclusion. Since the rumor of death is to

---

[1] On July 6, 1527, Luther suffered a severe attack of cerebral anemia, an
illness from which he suffered repeatedly. The deep depression which followed may be one reason for the mild tone of the first portion of this pamphlet.

be heard in these and many other parts also, we have permitted these instructions of ours to be printed because others might also want to make use of them.

To begin with, some people are of the firm opinion that one need not and should not run away from a deadly plague. Rather, since death is God's punishment, which he sends upon us for our sins, we must submit to God and with a true and firm faith patiently await our punishment. They look upon running away as an outright wrong and as lack of belief in God. Others take the position that one may properly flee, particularly if one holds no public office.

I cannot censure the former for their excellent decision. They uphold a good cause, namely, a strong faith in God, and deserve commendation because they desire every Christian to hold to a strong, firm faith. It takes more than a milk[2] faith to await a death before which most of the saints themselves have been and still are in dread. Who would not acclaim these earnest people to whom death is a little thing? They willingly accept God's chastisement, doing so without tempting God, as we shall hear later on.

Since it is generally true of Christians that few are strong and many are weak, one simply cannot place the same burden upon everyone. A person who has a strong faith can drink poison and suffer no harm, Mark 16 [:18], while one who has a weak faith would thereby drink to his death. Peter could walk upon the water because he was strong in faith. When he began to doubt and his faith weakened, he sank and almost drowned.[3] When a strong man travels with a weak man, he must restrain himself so as not to walk at a speed proportionate to his strength lest he set a killing pace for his weak companion. Christ does not want his weak ones to be abandoned, as St. Paul teaches in Romans 15 [:1] and I Corinthians 12 [:22 ff.]. To put it briefly and concisely, running away from death may happen in one of two ways. First, it may happen in disobedience to God's word and command. For instance, in the case of a man who is imprisoned for the sake of God's word and who, to escape death, denies and repudiates God's word. In such a situation everyone has Christ's plain mandate and command not to flee but

---

[2] See I Cor. 3:2.
[3] Cf. Matt. 14:30.

rather to suffer death, as he says, "Whoever denies me before men, I will also deny before my Father who is in heaven" and "Do not fear those who kill the body but cannot kill the soul," Matthew 10 [:28, 33].

Those who are engaged in a spiritual ministry such as preachers and pastors must likewise remain steadfast before the peril of death.[4] We have a plain command from Christ, "A good shepherd lays down his life for the sheep but the hireling sees the wolf coming and flees" [John 10:11]. For when people are dying, they most need a spiritual ministry which strengthens and comforts their consciences by word and sacrament and in faith overcomes death. However, where enough preachers are available in one locality and they agree to encourage the other clergy to leave in order not to expose themselves needlessly to danger, I do not consider such conduct sinful because spiritual services are provided for and because they would have been ready and willing to stay if it had been necessary. We read that St. Athanasius[5] fled from his church that his life might be spared because many others were there to administer his office. Similarly, the brethren in Damascus lowered Paul in a basket over the wall to make it possible for him to escape, Acts 9 [:25]. And also in Acts 19 [:30] Paul allowed himself to be kept from risking danger in the marketplace because it was not essential for him to do so.

Accordingly, all those in public office such as mayors, judges, and the like are under obligation to remain. This, too, is God's word, which institutes secular authority and commands that town and country be ruled, protected, and preserved, as St. Paul teaches in Romans 13 [:4], "The governing authorities are God's ministers for your own good." To abandon an entire community which one has been called to govern and to leave it without official or government, exposed to all kinds of danger such as fires, murder, riots, and every imaginable disaster is a great sin. It is the kind of disaster the devil would like to instigate wherever there is no law and order. St. Paul says, "Anyone who does not provide for his own

---

[4] Elector John wrote Luther and urged him and the professors at the university to leave on account of the plague and go to Jena. Luther, Bugenhagen, and two chaplains, however, stayed on at Wittenberg.
[5] Augustine in *MPL* 30, 1017.

family denies the faith and is worse than an unbeliever" [I Tim. 5:8]. On the other hand, if in great weakness they flee but provide capable substitutes to make sure that the community is well governed and protected, as we previously indicated, and if they continually and carefully supervise them [i.e., the substitutes], all that would be proper.

What applies to these two offices [church and state] should also apply to persons who stand in a relationship of service or duty toward one another. A servant should not leave his master nor a maid her mistress except with the knowledge and permission of master or mistress. Again, a master should not desert his servant or a lady her maid unless suitable provision for their care has been made somewhere. In all these matters it is a divine command that servants and maids should render obedience and by the same token masters and ladies should take care of their servants.[6] Likewise, fathers and mothers are bound by God's law to serve and help their children, and children their fathers and mothers. Likewise, paid public servants such as city physicians, city clerks and constables, or whatever their titles, should not flee unless they furnish capable substitutes who are acceptable to their employer.

In the case of children who are orphaned, guardians or close friends are under obligation either to stay with them or to arrange diligently for other nursing care for their sick friends. Yes, no one should dare leave his neighbor unless there are others who will take care of the sick in their stead and nurse them. In such cases we must respect the word of Christ, "I was sick and you did not visit me . . ." [Matt. 25:41-46]. According to this passage we are bound to each other in such a way that no one may forsake the other in his distress but is obliged to assist and help him as he himself would like to be helped.[7]

Where no such emergency exists and where enough people are available for nursing and taking care of the sick, and where, voluntarily or by orders, those who are weak in faith make provision so that there is no need for additional helpers, or where the sick do not want them and have refused their services, I judge that they

---

[6] Cf. Eph. 6:5-9.
[7] Cf. Matt. 7:12.

have an equal choice either to flee or to remain. If someone is sufficiently bold and strong in his faith, let him stay in God's name; that is certainly no sin. If someone is weak and fearful, let him flee in God's name as long as he does not neglect his duty toward his neighbor but has made adequate provision for others to provide nursing care. To flee from death and to save one's life is a natural tendency, implanted by God and not forbidden unless it be against God and neighbor, as St. Paul says in Ephesians 4 [5:29], "No man ever hates his own flesh, but nourishes and cherishes it." It is even commanded that every man should as much as possible preserve body and life and not neglect them, as St. Paul says in I Corinthians 12 [:21-26] that God has so ordered the members of the body that each one cares and works for the other.

It is not forbidden but rather commanded that by the sweat of our brow we should seek our daily food, clothing, and all we need and avoid destruction and disaster whenever we can, as long as we do so without detracting from our love and duty toward our neighbor. How much more appropriate it is therefore to seek to preserve life and avoid death if this can be done without harm to our neighbor, inasmuch as life is more than food and clothing, as Christ himself says in Matthew 5 [6:25]. If someone is so strong in faith, however, that he can willingly suffer nakedness, hunger, and want without tempting God and not trying to escape, although he could do so, let him continue that way, but let him not condemn those who will not or cannot do the same.

Examples in Holy Scripture abundantly prove that to flee from death is not wrong in itself. Abraham was a great saint but he feared death and escaped it by pretending that his wife, Sarah, was his sister.[8] Because he did so without neglecting or adversely affecting his neighbor, it was not counted as a sin against him. His son, Isaac, did likewise.[9] Jacob also fled from his brother Esau to avoid death at his hands.[10] Likewise, David fled from Saul, and from Absalom.[11] The prophet Uriah escaped from King Jehoiakim and fled into Egypt.[12] The valiant prophet, Elijah, I Kings 19 [:3],

[8] Gen. 12:13.
[9] Gen. 26:7.
[10] Cf. Gen. 27:43-45.
[11] Cf. I Sam. 19:10-17; II Sam. 15:14.
[12] Jer. 26:21.

had destroyed all the prophets of Baal by his great faith, but afterward, when Queen Jezebel threatened him, he became afraid and fled into the desert. Before that, Moses fled into the land of Midian when the king searched for him in Egypt.[13] Many others have done likewise. All of them fled from death when it was possible and saved their lives, yet without depriving their neighbors of anything but first meeting their obligations toward them.

Yes, you may reply, but these examples do not refer to dying by pestilence but to death under persecution. Answer: Death is death, no matter how it occurs. According to Holy Scripture God sent his four scourges: pestilence, famine, sword, and wild beasts.[14] If it is permissible to flee from one or the other in clear conscience, why not from all four? Our examples demonstrate how the holy fathers escaped from the sword; it is quite evident that Abraham, Isaac, and Jacob fled from the other scourge, namely, hunger and death, when they went to Egypt to escape famine, as we are told in Genesis [40–47]. Likewise, why should one not run away from wild beasts? I hear people say, "If war or the Turks come, one should not flee from his village or town but stay and await God's punishment by the sword." That is quite true; let him who has a strong faith wait for his death, but he should not condemn those who take flight.

By such reasoning, when a house is on fire, no one should run outside or rush to help because such a fire is also a punishment from God. Anyone who falls into deep water dare not save himself by swimming but must surrender to the water as to a divine punishment. Very well, do so if you can but do not tempt God, and allow others to do as much as they are capable of doing. Likewise, if someone breaks a leg, is wounded or bitten, he should not seek medical aid but say, "It is God's punishment. I shall bear it until it heals by itself." Freezing weather and winter are also God's punishment and can cause death. Why run to get inside or near a fire? Be strong and stay outside until it becomes warm again. We should then need no apothecaries or drugs or physicians because all illnesses are punishment from God. Hunger and thirst are also great

---

[13] Cf. Exod. 2:15.
[14] Cf. Ezek. 14:21.

punishments and torture. Why do you eat and drink instead of letting yourself be punished until hunger and thirst stop of themselves? Ultimately such talk will lead to the point where we abbreviate the Lord's Prayer and no longer pray, "deliver us from evil, Amen," since we would have to stop praying to be saved from hell and stop seeking to escape it. It, too, is God's punishment as is every kind of evil. Where would all this end?

From what has been said we derive this guidance: We must pray against every form of evil and guard against it to the best of our ability in order not to act contrary to God, as was previously explained. If it be God's will that evil come upon us and destroy us, none of our precautions will help us. Everybody must take this to heart: first of all, if he feels bound to remain where death rages in order to serve his neighbor, let him commend himself to God and say, "Lord, I am in thy hands; thou hast kept me here; thy will be done. I am thy lowly creature. Thou canst kill me or preserve me in this pestilence in the same way as if I were in fire, water, drought, or any other danger." If a man is free, however, and can escape, let him commend himself and say, "Lord God, I am weak and fearful. Therefore I am running away from evil and am doing what I can to protect myself against it. I am nevertheless in thy hands in this danger as in any other which might overtake me. Thy will be done. My flight alone will not succeed of itself because calamity and harm are everywhere. Moreover, the devil never sleeps. He is a murderer from the beginning [John 8:44] and tries everywhere to instigate murder and misfortune."[15]

In the same way we must and we owe it to our neighbor to accord him the same treatment in other troubles and perils, also. If his house is on fire, love compels me to run to help him extinguish the flames. If there are enough other people around to put the fire out, I may either go home or remain to help. If he falls into the water or into a pit I dare not turn away but must hurry to help him as best I can. If there are others to do it, I am released. If I see that he is hungry or thirsty, I cannot ignore him but must offer food and drink, not considering whether I would risk impoverishing

---

[15] At this point Luther interrupted his writing. He resumed it no later than early September, as a reference in a sermon on September 15 or 21 indicates. The second part of the pamphlet reflects the plague's arrival in Wittenberg.

myself by doing so. A man who will not help or support others unless he can do so without affecting his safety or his property will never help his neighbor. He will always reckon with the possibility that doing so will bring some disadvantage and damage, danger and loss. No neighbor can live alongside another without risk to his safety, property, wife, or child. He must run the risk that fire or some other accident will start in the neighbor's house and destroy him bodily or deprive him of his goods, wife, children, and all he has.

Anyone who does not do that for his neighbor, but forsakes him and leaves him to his misfortune, becomes a murderer in the sight of God, as St. John states in his epistles, "Whoever does not love his brother is a murderer," and again, "If anyone has the world's goods, and sees his brother in need [yet closes his heart against him], how does God's love abide in him?" [I John 3:15, 17]. That is also one of the sins which God attributed to the city of Sodom when he speaks through the prophet Ezekiel [16:49], "Behold, this was the guilt of your sister Sodom: she and her daughters had pride, surfeit of food, and prosperous ease, but did not aid the poor and needy." Christ, therefore, will condemn them as murderers on the Last Day when he will say, "I was sick and you did not visit me" [Matt. 25:43]. If that shall be the judgment upon those who have failed to visit the sick and needy or to offer them relief, what will become of those who abandoned them and let them lie there like dogs and pigs? Yes, how will they fare who rob the poor of the little they have and plague them in all kinds of ways? That is what the tyrants do to the poor who accept the gospel. But let that be; they have their condemnation.

It would be well, where there is such an efficient government in cities and states, to maintain municipal homes and hospitals staffed with people to take care of the sick so that patients from private homes can be sent there—as was the intent and purpose of our forefathers with so many pious bequests, hospices, hospitals, and infirmaries so that it should not be necessary for every citizen to maintain a hospital in his own home. That would indeed be a fine, commendable, and Christian arrangement to which everyone should offer generous help and contributions, particularly the government. Where there are no such institutions—and they exist in only a few places—we must give hospital care and be nurses for one another in any extremity or risk the loss of salvation and the grace of God. Thus it is written in God's word and command, "Love your neighbor as yourself," and in Matthew 7 [:12], "So whatever you wish that men would do to you, do so to them."

Now if a deadly epidemic strikes, we should stay where we are, make our preparations, and take courage in the fact that we are mutually bound together (as previously indicated) so that we cannot desert one another or flee from one another. First, we can be sure that God's punishment has come upon us, not only to chastise us for our sins but also to test our faith and love—our faith in that we may see and experience how we should act toward God; our love in that we may recognize how we should act toward our neighbor. I am of the opinion that all the epidemics, like any plague, are spread among the people by evil spirits who poison the air or exhale a pestilential breath which puts a deadly poison into the flesh. Nevertheless, this is God's decree and punishment to which we must patiently submit and serve our neighbor, risking our lives in this manner as St. John teaches, "If Christ laid down his life for us, we ought to lay down our lives for the brethren" [I John 3:16].

When anyone is overcome by horror and repugnance in the presence of a sick person he should take courage and strength in the firm assurance that it is the devil who stirs up such abhorrence, fear, and loathing in his heart. He is such a bitter, knavish devil that he not only unceasingly tries to slay and kill, but also takes delight in making us deathly afraid, worried, and apprehensive so that we should regard dying as horrible and have no rest or peace all through our life. And so the devil would excrete us out of this life as he tries to make us despair of God, become unwilling and unprepared to die, and, under the stormy and dark sky of fear and anxiety, make us forget and lose Christ, our light and life, and desert our neighbor in his troubles. We would sin thereby against God and man; that would be the devil's glory and delight. Because we know that it is the devil's game to induce such fear and dread, we should in turn minimize it, take such courage as to spite and annoy him, and send those terrors right back to him. And we should arm ourselves with this answer to the devil:

"Get away, you devil, with your terrors! Just because you hate it, I'll spite you by going the more quickly to help my sick neighbor. I'll pay no attention to you: I've got two heavy blows to use against you: the first one is that I know that helping my neighbor is a deed well-pleasing to God and all the angels; by this deed I do God's will and render true service and obedience to him. All the more so because if you hate it so and are so strongly opposed to it, it must be particularly acceptable to God. I'd do this readily and gladly if I could please only one angel who might look with delight on it. But now that it pleases my Lord Jesus Christ and the whole heavenly host because it is the will and command of God, my Father, then how could any fear of you cause me to spoil such joy in heaven or such delight for my Lord? Or how could I, by flattering you, give you and your devils in hell reason to mock and laugh at me? No, you'll not have the last word! If Christ shed his blood for me and died for me, why should I not expose myself to some small dangers for his sake and disregard this feeble plague? If you can terrorize, Christ can strengthen me. If you can kill, Christ can give life. If you have poison in your fangs, Christ has far greater medicine. Should not my dear Christ, with his precepts, his kindness, and all his encouragement, be more important in my spirit than you, roguish devil, with your false terrors in my weak flesh? God forbid! Get away, devil. Here is Christ and here am I, his servant in this work. Let Christ prevail! Amen."

The second blow against the devil is God's mighty promise by which he encourages those who minister to the needy. He says in Psalm 41 [:1-3], "Blessed is he who considers the poor. The Lord will deliver him in the day of trouble. The Lord will protect him and keep him alive; the Lord will bless him on earth and not give him up to the will of his enemies. The Lord will sustain him on his sickbed. In his illness he will heal all his infirmities." Are not these glorious and mighty promises of God heaped up upon those who minister to the needy? What should terrorize us or frighten us away from such great and divine comfort? The service we can render to the needy is indeed such a small thing in comparison with God's promises and rewards that St. Paul says to Timothy, "Godliness is of value in every way, and it holds promise both for the present life and for the life to come" [I Tim. 4:8]. Godliness is nothing else but service to God. Service to God is indeed service to our neighbor. It is proved by experience that those who nurse the sick with love, devotion, and sincerity are generally protected. Though they are poisoned, they are not harmed. As the psalm says, "in his illness you heal all his infirmities" [Ps. 41:3], that is, you change his bed of sickness into a bed of health. A person who attends a patient because of greed, or with the expectation of an inheritance or some personal advantage in such services, should not be surprised if eventually he is infected, disfigured, or even dies before he comes into possession of that estate or inheritance.

But whoever serves the sick for the sake of God's gracious promise, though he may accept a suitable reward to which he is entitled, inasmuch as every laborer is worthy of his hire—whoever does so has the great assurance that he shall in turn be cared for. God himself shall be his attendant and his physician, too. What an attendant he is! What a physician! Friend, what are all the physicians, apothecaries, and attendants in comparison to God? Should that not encourage one to go and serve a sick person, even though he might have as many contagious boils on him as hairs on his body, and though he might be bent double carrying a hundred plague-ridden bodies! What do all kinds of pestilence or devils mean over against God, who binds and obliges himself to be our attendant and physician? Shame and more shame on you, you out-and-out unbeliever, for despising such great comfort and letting yourself become more frightened by some small boil or some uncertain danger than emboldened by such sure and faithful promises of God! What would it avail you if all physicians and the entire world were at your service, but God were not present? Again, what harm could overtake you if the whole world were to desert you and no physician would remain with you, but God would abide with you with his assurance? Do you not know that you are surrounded as by thousands of angels who watch over you in such a way that you can indeed trample upon the plague, as it is written in Psalm 91 [:11-13], "He has given his angels charge of you to guard you in all your ways. On their hands they will bear you up lest you dash your foot against a stone. You will tread upon the lion and the adder, and trample the young lion and the serpent under foot."

Therefore, dear friends, let us not become so desperate as to desert our own whom we are duty-bound to help and flee in such a cowardly way from the terror of the devil, or allow him the joy of mocking us and vexing and distressing God and all his angels. For it is certainly true that he who despises such great promises and commands of God and leaves his own people destitute, violates all of God's laws and is guilty of the murder of his neighbor whom he abandons. I fear that in such a case God's promise will be reversed and changed into horrible threats and the psalm [41] will then read this way against them: "Accursed is he who does not provide for the needy but escapes and forsakes them. The Lord in turn will not spare him in evil days but will flee from him and desert him. The Lord will not preserve him and keep him alive and will not prosper him on earth but will deliver him into the hands of his enemies. The Lord will not refresh him on his sickbed nor take him from the couch of his illness." For "the measure you give will be the measure you get" [Matt. 7:2]. Nothing else can come of it. It is terrible to hear this, more terrible to be waiting for this to happen, most terrible to experience it. What else can happen if God withdraws his hand and forsakes us except sheer devilment and every kind of evil? It cannot be otherwise if, against God's command, one abandons his neighbor. This fate will surely overtake anyone of this sort, unless he sincerely repents.

This I well know, that if it were Christ or his mother who were laid low by illness, everybody would be so solicitous and would gladly become a servant or helper. Everyone would want to be bold and fearless; nobody would flee but everyone would come running. And yet they don't hear what Christ himself says, "As you did to one of the least, you did it to me" [Matt. 25:40]. When he speaks of the greatest commandment he says, "The other commandment is like unto it, you shall love your neighbor as yourself" [Matt. 22:39]. There you hear that the command to love your neighbor is equal to the greatest commandment to love God, and that what you do or fail to do for your neighbor means doing the same to God. If you wish to serve Christ and to wait on him, very well, you have your sick neighbor close at hand. Go to him and serve him, and you will surely find Christ in him, not outwardly but in his word. If you do not wish or care to serve your neighbor you can be sure that if Christ lay there instead you would not do so either and would let him lie there. Those are nothing but illusions on your part which puff you up with vain pride, namely, that you would really serve Christ if he were there in person. Those are nothing but lies; whoever wants to serve Christ in person would surely serve his neighbor as well. This is said as an admonition and encouragement against fear and a disgraceful flight to which the devil would tempt us so that we would disregard God's command in our dealings with our neighbor and so we would fall into sin on the left hand.

Others sin on the right hand. They are much too rash and reckless, tempting God and disregarding everything which might counteract death and the plague. They disdain the use of medicines; they do not avoid places and persons infected by the plague, but lightheartedly make sport of it and wish to prove how independent they are. They say that it is God's punishment; if he wants to protect them he can do so without medicines or our carefulness. This is not trusting God but tempting him. God has created medicines and provided us with intelligence to guard and take good care of the body so that we can live in good health.

If one makes no use of intelligence or medicine when he could do so without detriment to his neighbor, such a person injures his body and must beware lest he become a suicide in God's eyes. By the same reasoning a person might forego eating and drinking, clothing and shelter, and boldly proclaim his faith that if God wanted to preserve him from starvation and cold, he could do so without food and clothing. Actually that would be suicide. It is even more shameful for a person to pay no heed to his own body and to fail to protect it against the plague the best he is able, and then to infect and poison others who might have remained alive if he had taken care of his body as he should have. He is thus responsible before God for his neighbor's death and is a murderer many times over. Indeed, such people behave as though a house were burning in the city and nobody were trying to put the fire out. Instead they give leeway to the flames so that the whole city is consumed, saying that if God so willed, he could save the city without water to quench the fire.

No, my dear friends, that is no good. Use medicine; take potions which can help you; fumigate house, yard, and street; shun persons and places wherever your neighbor does not need your presence or has recovered, and act like a man who wants to help put out the burning city. What else is the epidemic but a fire which instead of consuming wood and straw devours life and body? You ought to think this way: "Very well, by God's decree the enemy has sent us poison and deadly offal. Therefore I shall ask God mercifully to protect us. Then I shall fumigate, help purify the air, administer medicine, and take it. I shall avoid places and persons where my presence is not needed in order not to become contaminated and thus perchance infect and pollute others, and so cause their death as a result of my negligence. If God should wish to take me, he will surely find me and I have done what he has expected of me and so I am not responsible for either my own death or the death of others. If my neighbor needs me, however, I shall not avoid place or person but will go freely, as stated above. See, this is such a God-fearing faith because it is neither brash nor foolhardy and does not tempt God.

Moreover, he who has contracted the disease and recovered should keep away from others and not admit them into his presence unless it be necessary. Though one should aid him in his time of need, as previously pointed out, he in turn should, after his recovery, so act toward others that no one becomes unnecessarily endangered on his account and so cause another's death. "Whoever loves danger," says the wise man, "will perish by it" [Ecclus. 3:26]. If the people in a city were to show themselves bold in their faith when a neighbor's need so demands, and cautious when no emergency exists, and if everyone would help ward off contagion as best he can, then the death toll would indeed be moderate. But if some are too panicky and desert their neighbors in their plight, and if some are so foolish as not to take precautions but aggravate the contagion, then the devil has a heyday and many will die. On both counts this is a grievous offense to God and to man—here it is tempting God; there it is bringing man into despair. Then the one who flees, the devil will pursue; the one who stays behind, the devil will hold captive so that no one escapes him.

Some are even worse than that. They keep it secret that they have the disease and go among others in the belief that by contaminating and poisoning others they can rid themselves of the plague and so recover. With this idea they enter streets and homes, trying to saddle children or servants with the disease and thus save themselves. I certainly believe that this is the devil's doing, who helps turn the wheel of fate to make this happen. I have been told that some are so incredibly vicious that they circulate among people and enter homes because they are sorry that the plague has not reached that far and wish to carry it in, as though it were a prank like putting lice into fur garments or flies into someone's living room. I do not know whether I should believe this; if it is true, I do not know whether we Germans are not really devils instead of human beings. It must be admitted that there are some extremely coarse and wicked people. The devil is never idle. My advice is that if any such persons are discovered, the judge should take them by the ear and turn them over to Master Jack, the hangman, as outright and deliberate murderers. What else are such people but assassins in our town? Here and there an assassin will jab a knife through someone and no one can find the culprit. So these folk infect a child here, a woman there, and can never be caught. They go on laughing as though they had accomplished something. Where this is the case, it would be better to live among wild beasts than with such murderers. I do not know how to preach to such killers. They pay no heed. I appeal to the authorities to take charge and turn them over to the help and advice not of physicians, but of Master Jack, the hangman.

If in the Old Testament God himself ordered lepers to be banished from the community and compelled to live outside the city to prevent contamination [Leviticus 13–14], we must do the same with this dangerous pestilence so that anyone who becomes infected will stay away from other persons, or allow himself to be taken away and given speedy help with medicine. Under such circumstances it is our duty to assist such a person and not forsake him in his plight, as I have repeatedly pointed out before. Then the poison is stopped in time, which benefits not only the individual but also the whole community, which might be contaminated if one person is permitted to infect others. Our plague here in Wittenberg has been caused by nothing but filth. The air, thank God, is still clean and pure, but some few have been contaminated because of the laziness or recklessness of some. So the devil enjoys himself at the terror and flight which he causes among us. May God thwart him! Amen.

This is what we think and conclude on this subject of fleeing from death by the plague. If you are of a different opinion, may God enlighten you. Amen.[16]

Because this letter will go out in print for people to read, I regard it useful to add some brief instructions on how one should care and provide for the soul in time of death. We have done this orally from the pulpit, and still do so every day in fulfilment of the ministry to which we have been called as pastors.

First, one must admonish the people to attend church and listen to the sermon so that they learn through God's word how to live and how to die. It must be noted that those who are so uncouth and wicked as to despise God's word while they are in good health should be left unattended when they are sick unless they demonstrate their remorse and repentance with great earnestness, tears, and lamentation. A person who wants to live like a heathen or a dog and does not publicly repent should not expect us to administer the sacrament to him or have us count him a Christian. Let him die as he has lived because we shall not throw pearls before swine nor give to dogs what is holy [Matt. 7:6]. Sad to say, there are many churlish, hardened ruffians who do not care for their souls when they live or when they die. They simply lie down and die like unthinking hulks.

Second, everyone should prepare in time and get ready for death by going to confession and taking the sacrament once every week or fortnight. He should become reconciled with his neighbor and make his will so that if the Lord knocks and he departs before a pastor or chaplain can arrive, he has provided for his soul, has left nothing undone, and has committed himself to God. When there are many fatalities and only two or three pastors on duty, it is impossible to visit everyone, to give instruction, and to teach each one what a Christian ought to know in the anguish of death. Those who have been careless and negligent in these matters must account for themselves. That is their own fault. After all, we cannot set up a private pulpit and altar daily at their bedside simply because they

---

[16] The following section was added later by Luther.

have despised the public pulpit and altar to which God has summoned and called them.

Third, if someone wants the chaplain or pastor to come, let the sick person send word in time to call him and let him do so early enough while he is still in his right mind before the illness overwhelms the patient. The reason I say this is that some are so negligent that they make no request and send no message until the soul is perched for flight on the tip of their tongues[17] and they are no longer rational or able to speak. Then we are told, "Dear Sir, say the very best you can to him," etc. But earlier, when the illness first began, they wanted no visit from the pastor, but would say, "Oh, there's no need. I hope he'll get better." What should a diligent pastor do with such people who neglect both body and soul? They live and die like beasts in the field. They want us to teach them the gospel at the last minute and administer the sacrament to them as they were accustomed to it under the papacy when nobody asked whether they believed or understood the gospel but just stuffed the sacrament down their throats as if into a bread bag.

This won't do. If someone cannot talk or indicate by a sign that he believes, understands, and desires the sacrament—particularly if he has wilfully neglected it—we will not give it to him just anytime he asks for it. We have been commanded not to offer the holy sacrament to unbelievers but rather to believers who can state and confess their faith. Let the others alone in their unbelief; we are guiltless because we have not been slothful in preaching, teaching, exhortation, consolation, visitation, or in anything else that pertains to our ministry and office. This, in brief, is our instruction and what we practice here. We do not write this for you in Breslau, because Christ is with you and without our aid he will amply instruct you and supply your needs with his own ointment. To him be praise and honor together with God the Father and the Holy Spirit, world without end. Amen.[18]

Because we have come upon the subject of death, I cannot refrain from saying something about burials. First of all, I leave it to the

---

[17] According to popular belief the soul left the body at death through the mouth.
[18] What follows up to the concluding paragraph is a further insert written on a separate page which Luther evidently added before the pamphlet was published.

doctors of medicine and others with greater experience than mine in such matters to decide whether it is dangerous to maintain cemeteries within the city limits. I do not know and do not claim to understand whether vapors and mists arise out of graves to pollute the air. If this were so my previously stated warnings constitute ample reason to locate cemeteries outside the city. As we have learned, all of us have the responsibility of warding off this poison to the best of our ability because God has commanded us to care for the body, to protect and nurse it so that we are not exposed needlessly. In an emergency, however, we must be bold enough to risk our health if that is necessary. Thus we should be ready for both—to live and to die according to God's will. For "none of us lives to himself and none of us dies to himself," as St. Paul says, Romans 15 [14:7].

It is very well known that the custom in antiquity, both among Jews and pagans, among saints and sinners, was to bury the dead outside the city. Those people were just as prudent as we claim to be ourselves. This is also evident in St. Luke's Gospel, when Christ raised from the dead the widow's son at the gates of Nain (for the text [Luke 7:12] states, "He was being carried out of the city to the grave and a large crowd from the city was with her"). In that country it was the practice to bury the dead outside the town.

Christ's tomb, also, was prepared outside the city. Abraham, too, bought a burial plot in the field of Ephron near the double cave[19] where all the patriarchs wished to be buried. The Latin therefore employs the term *efferi*, that is, "to carry out," by which we mean "carry to the grave." They not only carried the dead out but also burned them to powder to keep the air as pure as possible.

My advice, therefore, is to follow these examples and to bury the dead outside the town. Not only necessity but piety and decency should induce us to provide a public burial ground outside the town, that is, our town of Wittenberg.

A cemetery rightfully ought to be a fine quiet place, removed from all other localities, to which one can go and reverently meditate

---

[19] Gen. 23:9 (Luther's German translation). Ancient Hebrew burial caves usually had a second chamber into which the bones of previous burials were placed to make room for new interments.

upon death, the Last Judgment, the resurrection, and say one's prayers. Such a place should properly be a decent, hallowed place, to be entered with trepidation and reverence because doubtlessly some saints rest there. It might even be arranged to have religious pictures and portraits painted on the walls.

But our cemetery, what is it like? Four or five alleys, two or three marketplaces, with the result that no place in the whole town is busier or noisier than the cemetery. People and cattle roam over it at any time, night and day. Everyone has a door or pathway to it from his house and all sorts of things take place there, probably even some that are not fit to be mentioned. This totally destroys respect and reverence for the graves, and people think no more about walking across it than if it were a burial ground for executed criminals. Not even the Turk would dishonor the place the way we do. And yet a cemetery should inspire us to devout thoughts, to the contemplation of death and the resurrection, and to respect for the saints who rest there. How can that be done at such a common place through which everyone must walk and into which every man's door opens? If a cemetery is to have some dignity, I would rather be put to rest in the Elbe or in the forest. If a graveyard were located at a quiet, remote spot where no one could make a path through it, it would be a spiritual, proper, and holy sight and could be so arranged that it would inspire devotion in those who go there. That would be my advice. Follow it, who so wishes. If anyone knows better, let him go ahead. I am no man's master.

In closing, we admonish and plead with you in Christ's name to help us with your prayers to God so that we may do battle with word and precept against the real and spiritual pestilence of Satan in his wickedness with which he now poisons and defiles the world. That is, particularly against those who blaspheme the sacrament, though there are other sectarians also. Satan is infuriated and perhaps he feels that the day of Christ is at hand. That is why he raves so fiercely and tries through the enthusiasts[20] to rob us of the Savior, Jesus Christ. Under the papacy Satan was simply "flesh" so

---

[20] I.e., the *Schwärmer*, who stressed a "spiritual" use of the sacrament. Cf. *That These Words of Christ, "This Is My Body," etc., Still Stand Firm Against the Fanatics* (1527). LW 37, 3-150, especially p. 18, n. 14.

that even a monk's cap had to be regarded as sacred. Now he is nothing more than sheer "spirit" and Christ's flesh and word are no longer supposed to mean anything. They made an answer to my treatise[21] long ago, but I am surprised that it has not yet reached me at Wittenberg.[22] [When it does] I shall, God willing, answer them once again and let the matter drop. I can see that they will only become worse. They are like a bedbug which itself has a foul smell, but the harder you rub to crush it, the more it stinks. I hope that I've written enough in this pamphlet for those who can be saved so that—God be praised—many may thereby be snatched from their jaws and many more may be strengthened and confirmed in the truth. May Christ our Lord and Savior preserve us all in pure faith and fervent love, unspotted and pure until his day. Amen. Pray for me, a poor sinner.

---

[21] The treatise mentioned in note 20.
[22] This statement helps in dating the end of this letter. The communication, a diatribe by Zwingli, arrived November 11, 1527.

Praise for *WAR DANCES:*

"Sherman Alexie is not a finicky writer. He is often messy and in-your-face in a way that can make you laugh (or shudder) when you least expect to. . . . *War Dances* is Alexie's fiercely freewheeling collection of stories and poems about the tragicomedies of ordinary lives." —*O, the Oprah Magazine*

"Alexie has a wry, subversive sensibility. . . . The structure [in *War Dances*] is sophisticated yet playful, a subtle way to bring lightness to heavy topics such as senility, bigotry, cancer, and loneliness. . . . A mix tape of a book, with many voices, pieces of different length, shifting rhythms, an evolving story." —Carolyn Kellogg, *Los Angeles Times*

"Smart modern stories interspersed with witty and deep-feeling verse." —Alan Cheuse, *San Francisco Chronicle*

"Sherman Alexie mixes up comedy and tragedy, shoots it through with tenderness, then delivers with a provocateur's don't-give-a-damn flourish. He's unique, and his new book, *War Dances*, is another case in point." —Mary Ann Gwinn, *Seattle Times*

"[With *War Dances*], Sherman Alexie enhances his stature as a multitalented writer and an astute observer of life among Native Americans in the Pacific Northwest. . . . [An] edgy and frequently surprising collection." —Harvey Freedenberg, *Bookpage*

"Few other contemporary writers seem willing to deal with issues of race, class, and sexuality as explicitly as Alexie . . . ["War Dances" is] a virtuoso performance of wit and pathos, a cultural and familial critique and a son's quiet, worthless scream against the night as his father expires . . . [that] reminds me of the early twentieth-century master of the short form Akutagawa Riyunosuke. . . . Yet again Sherman Alexie has given us a hell of a ride." —Anthony Swofford, Barnes & Noble Reviews

"Complex . . . Unpredictable . . . Thought-provoking." —Michelle Peters, *Winnipeg Free Press*

"Alexie's works are piercing yet rueful. He writes odes to anguished pay-phone calls, to boys who would drive through blizzards to see a girl, to couples who need to sit together on airplane flights even though the computer thinks otherwise. . . . [A] marvelous collection."   —Connie Ogle, *The Miami Herald*

"Sherman Alexie is a rare creature in contemporary literature, a writer who can make you laugh as easily as he can make you cry. He's also frighteningly versatile, as a poet, screenwriter, short-story author, and novelist."   —Ben Fulton, *Salt Lake Tribune*

" *War Dances* is maybe the most personal book Alexie has ever published, and it's certainly one of his most readable. The closest thing to a historical precedent for this book is *Palm Sunday*, Kurt Vonnegut's wildly entertaining self-described 'autobiographical collage' of anecdotes, fiction, reminiscences, and other work. . . . Each piece firmly builds on some part of the other, like the songs on a good mix tape. . . . The asymmetrical collection on display in *War Dances* works as a supremely gratifying reading experience."
—Paul Constant, *The Stranger*

"Alexie is a master storyteller whose prose is laced with metaphoric realities of life, mixed with triumph and tragedy. . . . *War Dances* is vintage Alexie . . . [and] should be savored. . . . Fans will not be disappointed."
—Levi Rickert, *The Grand Rapids Press*

"Remarkable . . . Wonderful . . . [Alexie's] work reveals both the light and dark within Native American life. A paradox in his writing is that you can be in the middle of delighted laughter when he will hit you with a sentence so true to the core of a character's pain that you suck your breath or are startled to realize you are crying."
—Gale Zoe Garnett, *The Globe and Mail*

"May be his best work yet . . . An odd grab bag of images, insights, and loose ends . . . yet each piece asks a similar set of questions: What's the point of all this? If there is a point, what's the point of that? And isn't life really goddamn funny? . . . A book about searching."   —Mike Dumke, *Chicago Reader*

WAR DANCES

Also by Sherman Alexie

FICTION

The Absolutely True Diary of a Part-Time Indian

Flight

Ten Little Indians

The Toughest Indian in the World

The Lone Ranger and Tonto Fistfight in Heaven

Indian Killer

Reservation Blues

SCREENPLAYS

The Business of Fancy Dancing

Smoke Signals

POETRY

Face

Dangerous Astronomy

Il powwow della fine del mondo

One Stick Song

The Man Who Loves Salmon

The Summer of Black Widows

Water Flowing Home

Seven Mourning Songs for the Cedar Flute
I Have Yet to Learn to Play

First Indian on the Moon

Old Shirts & New Skins

I Would Steal Horses

The Business of Fancy Dancing

WAR DANCES

by

Sherman Alexie

Grove Press
New York

ISBN 978-0-8021-4489-8

Grove Press
an imprint of Grove/Atlantic, Inc.
154 West 14th Street
New York, NY 10011

Distributed by Publishers Group West
www.groveatlantic.com

15 16 17 18   6 5 4 3

For
Elisabeth, Morgan, Eric, and Deb

CONTENTS

Contents

WAR DANCES

THE LIMITED

I saw a man swerve his car
And try to hit a stray dog,
But the quick mutt dodged
Between two parked cars

And made his escape.
God, I thought, did I just see
What I think I saw?
At the next red light,

I pulled up beside the man
And stared hard at him.
He knew that'd I seen
His murder attempt,

But he didn't care.
He smiled and yelled loud
Enough for me to hear him
Through our closed windows:

"Don't give me that face
Unless you're going to do
Something about it.
Come on, tough guy,

What are you going to do?"
I didn't do anything.
I turned right on the green.
He turned left against traffic.

I don't know what happened
To that man or the dog,
But I drove home
And wrote this poem.

Why do poets think
They can change the world?
The only life I can save
Is my own.

BREAKING AND ENTERING

Back in college, when I was first learning how to edit film—how to construct a scene—my professor, Mr. Baron, said to me, "You don't have to show people using a door to walk into a room. If people are already in the room, the audience will understand that they didn't crawl through a window or drop from the ceiling or just materialize. The audience understands that a door has been used—the eyes and mind will make the connection—so you can just skip the door."

Mr. Baron, a full-time visual aid, skipped as he said, "Skip the door." And I laughed, not knowing that I would always remember his bit of teaching, though of course, when I tell the story now, I turn my emotive professor into the scene-eating lead of a Broadway musical.

"Skip the door, young man!" Mr. Baron sings in my stories—my lies and exaggerations—skipping across the stage with a top hat in one hand and a cane in the other. "Skip the door, old friend! And you will be set free!"

"Skip the door" is a good piece of advice—a maxim, if you will—that I've applied to my entire editorial career, if not my entire life. To state it in less poetic terms, one would say, "An editor must omit all unnecessary information." So in telling you this story—with words, not film or video stock—in constructing its scenes, I will attempt to omit all unnecessary information. But oddly enough, in order to skip the door in telling this story, I am forced to begin with a door: the front door of my home on Twenty-seventh Avenue in the Central District neighborhood of Seattle, Washington.

One year ago, there was a knock on that door. I heard it, but I did not rise from my chair to answer. As a freelance editor, I work at home, and I had been struggling with a scene from a locally made film, an independent. Written, directed, and shot by amateurs, the footage was both incomplete and voluminous. Simply stated, there was far too much of nothing. Moreover, it was a love scene—a graphic sex scene, in fact—and the director and the producer had somehow convinced a naive and ambitious local actress to shoot the scene full frontal, graphically so. This was not supposed to be a pornographic movie; this was to be a tender coming-of-age work of art. But it wasn't artistic, or not the kind of art it pretended to be. This young woman had been exploited—with her permission, of course—but I was still going to do my best to protect her.

Don't get me wrong. I'm not a prude—I've edited and enjoyed sexual and violent films that were far more graphic—but I'd spotted honest transformative vulnerability in that young actress's performance. Though the director and the producer thought she'd just been acting—had created her fear and shame through technical skill—I knew better. And so, by editing out the more gratuitous nudity and focusing on faces and small pieces of dialogue—and by paying more attention to fingertips than to what those fingertips were touching—I was hoping to turn a sleazy gymnastic sex scene into an exchange that resembled how two people in new love might actually touch each other.

Was I being paternalistic, condescending, and hypocritical? Sure. After all, I was being paid to work with exploiters, so didn't that mean I was also being exploited as I helped exploit the woman? And what about the young man, the actor, in the scene? Was he dumb and vulnerable as well? Though he was allowed—was legally bound—to keep his penis hidden, wasn't he more exploited than exploiter? These things are hard to define. Still, even in the most compromised of situations, one must find a moral center.

But how could I find any center with that knocking on the door? It had become an evangelical pounding: *Bang, bang, bang, bang!* It had to be the four/four beat of a Jehovah's Witness or a Mormon. *Bang, cha, bang, cha!* It had to be the iambic pentameter of a Sierra Club shill or a magazine sales kid.

Trust me, nobody interesting or vital has ever knocked on a front door at three in the afternoon, so I ignored the knocking and kept at my good work. And, sure enough, my potential guest stopped the noise and went away. I could hear feet pounding down the stairs and there was only silence—or, rather, the relative silence of my urban neighborhood.

But then, a few moments later, I heard a window shatter in my basement. Is shatter too strong a verb? I heard my window break. But break seems too weak a verb. As I visualize the moment—as I edit in my mind—I add the sound track, or rather I completely silence the sound track. I cut the sounds of the city—the planes overhead, the cars on the streets, the boats on the lake, the televisions and the voices and the music and the wind through the trees—until one can hear only shards of glass dropping onto a hardwood floor.

And then one hears—feels—the epic thump of two feet landing on that same floor.

Somebody—the same person who had knocked on my front door to ascertain if anybody was home, had just broken and entered my life.

Now please forgive me if my tenses—my past, present, and future—blend, but one must understand that I happen to be one editor who is not afraid of jump cuts—of rapid flashbacks and flash-forwards. In order to be terrified, one must lose all sense of time and place. When I heard those feet hit the floor, I traveled back in time—I de-evolved, I suppose—and became a primitive version of myself. I had been a complex organism—but I'd turned into a two-hundred-and-two pound one-celled amoeba. And that amoeba knew only fear.

Looking back, I suppose I should have just run away. I could have run out the front door into the street, or the back door onto the patio, or the side door off the kitchen into the alley, or even through the door into the garage—where I could have dived through the dog door cut into the garage and made my caninelike escape.

But here's the salt of the thing: though I cannot be certain, I believe that I was making my way toward the front door—after all, the front door was the only place in my house where I could be positive that my intruder was *not* waiting. But in order to get from my office to the front door, I had to walk past the basement door. And as I walked past the basement door, I spotted the baseball bat.

It wasn't my baseball bat. Now, when one thinks of baseball bats, one conjures images of huge slabs of ash wielded by steroid-fueled freaks. But that particular bat belonged to my ten-year-old son. It was a Little League bat, so it was comically small. I could easily swing it with one hand and had, in fact, often swung it one-handed as I hit practice grounders to the little second baseman of my heart, my son, my Maximilian, my Max. Yes, I am a father. And a husband. That is information you need to know. My wife, Wendy, and my son were not in the house. To give me the space and time I needed to finish editing the film, my wife had taken our son to visit her mother and father in Chicago; they'd been gone for one week and would be gone for another. So, to be truthful, I was in no sense being forced to defend my family, and I'd never been the kind of man to defend his home, his property, his shit. In fact, I'd often laughed at the news footage of silly men armed with garden hoses as they tried to defend their homes from wildfires. I always figured those men would die, go to hell, and spend the rest of eternity having squirt-gun fights with demons.

So with all that information in mind, why did I grab my son's baseball bat and open the basement door? Why did I creep down the stairs? Trust me, I've spent many long nights awake, asking myself those questions. There are no easy answers. Of course, there are many men—and more than a few women—who believe I was fully within my rights to head down those stairs and confront my intruder. There are laws that define—that frankly encourage—the art of self-defense. But since I wasn't interested in defending my property, and since my family and I were not being directly threatened, what part of my self could I have possibly been defending?

In the end, I think I wasn't defending anything at all. I'm an editor—an artist—and I like to make connections; I am paid to make connections. And so I wonder. Did I walk down those stairs because I was curious? Because a question had been asked (Who owned the feet that landed on my basement floor?) and I, the editor, wanted to discover the answer?

So, yes, slowly I made my way down the stairs and through the dark hallway and turned the corner into our downstairs family room—the man cave, really, with the big television and the pool table—and saw a teenaged burglar. I stood still and silent. Standing with his back to me, obsessed with the task—the crime—at hand, he hadn't yet realized that I was in the room with him.

Let me get something straight. Up until that point I hadn't made any guesses as to the identity of my intruder. I mean, yes, I live in a black neighborhood—and I'm not black—and there had been news of a series of local burglaries perpetrated by black teenagers, but I swear none of that entered my mind. And when I saw him, the burglar, rifling through my DVD collection and shoving selected titles into his backpack—he was a felon with cinematic taste, I guess, and that was a strangely pleasing observation—I didn't think, There's a black teenager stealing from me. I only remembering being afraid and wanting to make my fear go away.

"Get the fuck out of here!" I screamed. "You fucking fucker!"

The black kid was so startled that he staggered into my television—cracking the screen—and nearly fell before he caught his balance and ran for the broken window. I could have—would have—let him make his escape, but he stopped and turned back toward me. Why did he do that? I don't know. He was young and scared and made an irrational decision. Or maybe it wasn't irrational at all. He'd slashed his right hand when he crawled through the broken window, so he must have decided the opening with its jagged glass edges was not a valid or safe exit—who'd ever think a broken window was a proper entry or exit—so he searched for a door. But the door was behind me. He paused, weighed his options, and sprinted toward me. He was going to bulldoze me. Once again, I could have made the decision to avoid conflict and step aside. But I didn't. As that kid ran toward me I swung the baseball bat with one hand.

I often wonder what would have happened if that bat had been made of wood. When Max and I had gone shopping for bats, I'd tried to convince him to let me buy him a wooden one, an old-fashioned slugger, the type I'd used when I was a Little Leaguer. I've always been a nostalgic guy. But my son recognized that a ten-dollar wooden bat purchased at Target was not a good investment.

"That wood one will break easy," Max had said. "I want the lum-a-lum one."

Of course, he'd meant to say *aluminum;* we'd both laughed at his mispronunciation. And I'd purchased the lum-a-lum bat.

So it was a metal bat that I swung one-handed at the black teenager's head. If it had been cheap and wooden, perhaps the bat would have snapped upon contact and dissipated the force. Perhaps. But this bat did not snap. It was strong and sure, so when it made full contact with the kid's temple, he dropped to the floor and did not move.

He was dead. I had killed him.

I fell to my knees next to the kid, dropped my head onto his chest, and wept.

I don't remember much else about the next few hours, but I called 911, opened the door for the police, and led them to the body. And I answered and asked questions.

"Did he have a gun or knife?"

"I don't know. No. Well, I didn't see one."

"He attacked you first?"

"He ran at me. He was going to run me over."

"And that's when you hit him with the bat?"

"Yes. It's my son's bat. It's so small. I can't believe it's strong enough to—is he really dead?"

"Yes."

"Who is he?"

"We don't know yet."

His name was Elder Briggs. Elder: such an unusual name for anybody, especially a sixteen-year-old kid. He was a junior at Garfield High School, a B student and backup point guard for the basketball team, an average kid. A good kid, by all accounts. He had no criminal record—had never committed even a minor infraction in school, at home, or in the community—so why had this good kid broken into my house? Why had he decided to steal from me? Why had he made all the bad decisions that had led to his death?

The investigation was quick but thorough, and I was not charged with any crime. It was self-defense. But then nothing is ever clear, is it? I was legally innocent, that much is true, but was I morally innocent? I wasn't sure, and neither were a significant percentage of my fellow citizens. Shortly after the police held the press conference that exonerated me, Elder's family—his mother, father, older brother, aunts, uncles, cousins, friends, and priest—organized a protest. It was small, only forty or fifty people, but how truly small can a protest feel when you are the subject—the object—of that protest?

I watched the live coverage of the event. My wife and son, after briefly returning from Chicago, had only spent a few days with me before they fled back to her parents. We wanted to protect our child from the media. An ironic wish, considering that the media were only interested in me because I'd killed somebody else's child.

"The police don't care about my son because he's black," Elder's mother, Althea, said to a dozen different microphones and as many cameras. "He's just another black boy killed by a white man. And none of these white men care."

As Althea continued to rant about my whiteness, some clever producer—and his editor—cut into footage of me, the white man who owned a baseball bat, walking out of the police station as a free man. It was a powerful piece of editing. It made me look pale and guilty. But all of them—Althea, the other protesters, the reporters, producers, and editors—were unaware of one crucial piece of information: I am not a white man.

I am an enrolled member of the Spokane Tribe of Indians. Oh, I don't look Indian, or at least not typically Indian. Some folks assume I'm a little bit Italian or Spanish or perhaps Middle Eastern. Most folks think I'm just another white guy who tans well. And since I'd just spent months in a dark editing room, I was at my palest. But I grew up on the Spokane Indian Reservation, the only son of a mother and father who were also Spokane Indians who grew up on our reservation. Yes, both of my grandfathers had been half-white, but they'd both died before I was born.

I'm not trying to be holy here. I wasn't a traditional Indian. I didn't dance or sing powwow or speak my language or spend my free time marching for Indian sovereignty. And I'd married a white woman. One could easily mock my lack of cultural connection, but one could not question my race. That's not true, of course. People, especially other Indians, always doubted my race. And I'd always tried to pretend it didn't matter—I was confident about my identity—but it did hurt my feelings. So when I heard Althea Riggs misidentify my race—and watched the media covertly use editing techniques to confirm her misdiagnosis—I picked up my cell phone and dialed the news station.

"Hello," I said to the receptionist. "This is George Wilson. I'm watching your coverage of the protests and I must issue a correction."

"Wait, what?" the receptionist asked. "Are you really George Wilson?"

"Yes, I am."

"Hold on," she said. "Let me put you straight through to the producer."

So the producer took the call and, after asking a few questions to further confirm my identity, he put me on live. So my voice played over images of Althea Riggs weeping and wailing, of her screaming at the sky, at God. How could I have allowed myself to be placed into such a compromising position? How could I have been such an idiot? How could I have been so goddamn callous and self-centered?

"Hello, Mr. Wilson," the evening news anchor said. "I understand you have something you'd like to say."

"Yes." My voice carried into tens of thousands of Seattle homes. "I am watching the coverage of the protest, and I insist on a correction. I am not a white man. I am an enrolled member of the Spokane Tribe of Indians."

Yes, that was my first official public statement about the death of Elder Briggs. It didn't take clever editing to make me look evil; I had accomplished this in one take, live and uncut.

I was suddenly the most hated man in Seattle. And the most beloved. My fellow liberals spoke of my lateral violence and the destructive influence of colonialism on the indigenous, while conservatives lauded my defensive stand and lonely struggle against urban crime. Local bloggers posted hijacked footage of the most graphically violent films I'd edited.

And finally, a local news program obtained rough footage of the film I'd been working on when Elder Briggs broke into my house. Though I had, through judicious editing, been trying to protect the young actress, a black actress, the news only played the uncut footage of the obviously frightened and confused woman. And when the reporters ambushed her—her name was Tracy—she, of course, could only respond that, yes, she felt as if she'd been violated. I didn't blame her for that; I agreed with her. But none of that mattered. I could in no way dispute the story—the cleverly edited series of short films—

that had been made about me. Yes, I was a victim, but I didn't for one second forget that Elder Briggs was dead. I was ashamed and vilified, but I was alive.

I spent most of that time alone in my basement, in the room where I had killed Elder Briggs. When one spends that much time alone, one ponders. And when one ponders, one creates theories—hypotheses, to explain the world. Oh, hell, forget rationalization; I was pissed, mostly at myself for failing to walk away from a dangerous situation. And I was certainly pissed at the local media, who had become as exploitative as any pornographic moviemaker. But I was also pissed at Althea and Elder Briggs.

Yes, the kid was a decent athlete; yes, the kid was a decent student; yes, the kid was a decent person. But he had broken into my house. He had smashed my window and was stealing my DVDs and, if I had not been home, would have stolen my computer and television and stereo and every other valuable thing in my house. And his mother, Althea, instead of explaining why her good and decent son had broken and entered a stranger's house, committing a felony, had instead decided to blame me and accuse me of being yet another white man who was always looking to maim another black kid—had already maimed generations of black kids—when in fact I was a reservation Indian who had been plenty fucked myself by generations of white men. So, Althea, do you want to get into a pain contest? Do you want to participate in the Genocidal Olympics? Whose tragic history has more breadth and depth and length?

Oh, Althea, why the hell was your son in my house? And oh, my God, it was a *Little League* baseball bat! It was only twenty inches long and weighed less than three pounds. I could have hit one hundred men in the head—maybe one thousand or one million—and not done anything more than given them a headache. But on that one day, on that one bitter afternoon, I took a swing—a stupid, one-handed, unlucky cut—and killed a kid, a son, a young man who was making a bad decision but who maybe had brains and heart and soul enough to stop making bad decisions.

Oh, Jesus, I murdered somebody's potential.

Oh, Mary, it was self-defense, but it was still murder. I confess: I am a killer.

How does one survive these revelations? One just lives. Or, rather, one just finally walks out of his basement and realizes that the story is over. It's old news. There are new villains and heroes, criminals and victims, to be defined and examined and tossed aside.

Elder Briggs and I were suddenly and equally unimportant.

My life became quiet again. I took a job teaching private-school white teenagers how to edit video. They used their newly developed skills to make documentaries about poor brown people in other countries. It's not oil that runs the world, it's shame. My Max was always going to love me, even when he began to understand my limitations, I didn't know what my wife thought of my weaknesses.

Weeks later, in bed, after lovemaking, she interrogated me.

"Honey," she said.

"Yes," I said.

"Can I ask you something?"

"Anything."

"With that kid, did you lose your temper?"

"What do you mean?" I asked.

"Well, you have lost your temper before."

"Just one time."

"Yes, but you broke your hand when you punched the wall."

"Do you think I lost my temper with Elder Briggs?" I asked.

My wife paused before answering, and in that pause I heard all her doubt and fear. So I got out of bed, dressed, and left the house. I decided to drive to see a hot new independent film—a gory war flick that pretended to be antiwar—but first stepped into a mini-mart to buy candy I could smuggle into the theater.

I was standing in the candy aisle, trying to decide between a PayDay and a Snickers, when a group of young black men walked into the store. They were drunk or high and they were cursing the world, but in a strangely friendly way. How is it that black men can make a word like *motherfucker* sound jovial?

There are people—white folks, mostly—who are extremely uncomfortable in the presence of black people. And I know plenty of Indians—my parents, for example—who are also uncomfortable around black folks. As for me? I suppose I'd always been the kind of nonblack person who celebrated himself for not being uncomfortable around blacks. But now, as I watched those black men jostle one another up and down the aisles, I was afraid—no, I was nervous. What if they recognized me? What if they were friends of Elder Briggs? What if they attacked me?

Nothing happened, of course. Nothing ever really happens, you know. Life is infinitesimal and incremental and inconsequential. Those young black men paid for their energy drinks and left the store. I paid for my candy bar, walked out to my car, and drove toward the movie theater.

One block later, I had to hit my brakes when those same black guys jaywalked across the street in front of me. All of them stared me down and walked as slowly as possible through the crosswalk. I'd lived in this neighborhood for years and I'd often had this same encounter with young black men. It was some remnant of the warrior culture, I suppose.

When it had happened before, I had always made it a point to smile goofily and wave to the black men who were challenging me. Since they thought I was a dorky white guy, I'd behave like one. I'd be what they wanted me to be.

But this time, when those black men walked in slow motion in front of me, I did not smile or laugh. I just stared back at them. I knew I could hit the gas and slam into them and hurt them, maybe even kill them. I knew I had that power. And I knew that I would not use that power. But what about these black guys? What power did they have? They could only make me wait at an intersection. And so I waited. I waited until they walked around the corner and out of my vision. I waited until another driver pulled up behind me and honked his horn. I was supposed to move, and so I went.

Go, Ghost, Go

At this university upon a hill,
      I meet a tenured professor
            Who's strangely thrilled
      To list all of the oppressors—
Past, present, and future—who have killed,
Are killing, and will kill the indigenous.
      O, he names the standard suspects—
            Rich, white, and unjust—
      And I, a red man, think he's correct,
But why does he have to be so humorless?

And how can he, a white man, fondly speak
      Of the Ghost Dance, the strange and cruel
            Ceremony
      That, if performed well, would have doomed
All white men to hell, destroyed their colonies,
And brought every dead Indian back to life?
      The professor says, "Brown people
            From all brown tribes
      Will burn skyscrapers and steeples.
They'll speak Spanish and carry guns and knives.

Sherman, can't you see that immigration
              Is the new and improved Ghost Dance?"
              All I can do is laugh and laugh
And say, "Damn, you've got some imagination.
You should write a screenplay about this shit—
              About some fictional city,
              Grown fat and pale and pretty,
That's destroyed by a Chicano apocalypse."
The professor doesn't speak. He shakes his head
              And assaults me with his pity.
              I wonder how he can believe
In a ceremony that requires his death.
I think that he thinks he's the new Jesus.
              He's eager to get on that cross
              And pay the ultimate cost
Because he's addicted to the indigenous.

Bird-watching at Night

What kind of bird is that?

An owl.

What kind of bird was that?

Another owl.

Oh, that one was too quick and small to be an owl. What was it?

A quick and small owl.

One night, when I was sixteen, I was driving with my girlfriend up on Little Falls Flat and this barn owl swooped down over the road, maybe fifty feet or so in front of us, and came flying straight toward our windshield. It was huge, pterodactyl-size, and my girlfriend screamed. And—well, I screamed, too, because that thing was heading straight for us, but you know what I did? I slammed on the gas and sped toward that owl. Do you know why I did that?

Because you wanted to play chicken with the owl?

Exactly.

So what happened?

When we were maybe a second from smashing into each other, that owl just flapped its wings, but barely. What's a better word than *flap*? What's a word that still means *flap*, but a smaller *flap*?

How about slant?

Oh, yes, that's pretty good. So, like I was saying, as that owl was just about to smash into our windshield, it slanted its wings, and slanted up into the dark. And it was so friggin' amazing, you know? I just slammed on the brakes and nearly slid into the ditch. And my girlfriend and I were sitting there in the dark with the engine *tick, tick, tick*ing like some kind of bomb, but an existential bomb, like it was just measuring out the endless nothingness of our lives because that owl had nearly touched us but was gone forever. And I said something like, "That was magnificent," and my girlfriend—you want to know what she said?

She said something like, "I'm breaking up with you."

Damn, that's exactly what she said. And I asked her, "Why are you breaking up with me?" And do you know what she said?

She said, "I'm breaking up with you because you are not an owl."

Yes, yes, yes, and you know what? I have never stopped thinking about her. It's been twenty-seven years, and I still miss her. Why is that?

Brother, you don't miss her. You miss the owl.

AFTER BUILDING THE LEGO *STAR WARS* ULTIMATE DEATH STAR

How many planets do you want to destroy?
Don't worry, Daddy, this is just a big toy,
And there is nothing more fun than making noise.

My sons, when I was a boy, I threw dirt clods
And snow grenades stuffed with hidden rocks, and fought
Enemies—other Indian boys—who thought,

Like me, that joyful war turned us into gods.

WAR DANCES

1. My Kafka Baggage

A few years ago, after I returned from a trip to Los Angeles, I unpacked my bag and found a dead cockroach, shrouded by a dirty sock, in a bottom corner. "Shit," I thought. "We're being invaded." And so I threw the unpacked clothes, books, shoes, and toiletries back into the suitcase, carried it out onto the driveway, and dumped the contents onto the pavement, ready to stomp on any other cockroach stowaways. But there was only the one cockroach, stiff and dead. As he lay on the pavement, I leaned closer to him. His legs were curled under his body. His head was tilted at a sad angle. Sad? Yes, sad. For who is lonelier than the cockroach without his tribe? I laughed at myself. I was feeling empathy for a dead cockroach. I wondered about its story. How had it got into my bag? And where? At the hotel in Los Angeles? In an airport baggage system? It didn't originate in our house. We've kept those tiny bastards away from our place for fifteen years. So what had happened to this little vermin? Did he smell something delicious in my bag—my musky deodorant or some crumb of chocolate Power Bar—and climb inside, only to be crushed by the shifts of fate and garment bags? As he died, did he feel fear? Isolation? Existential dread?

2. SYMPTOMS

Last summer, in reaction to various allergies I was suffering from, defensive mucous flooded my inner right ear and confused, frightened, untied, and unmoored me. Simply stated, I could not fucking hear a thing from that side, so I had to turn my head to understand what my two sons, ages eight and ten, were saying.

"We're hungry," they said. "We keep telling you."

They wanted to be fed. And I had not heard them.

"Mom would have fed us by now," they said.

Their mother had left for Italy with her mother two days ago. My sons and I were going to enjoy a boys' week, filled with unwashed socks, REI rock wall climbing, and ridiculous heaps of pasta.

"What are you going to cook?" my sons asked. "Why haven't you cooked yet?"

I'd been lying on the couch reading a book while they played and I had not realized that I'd gone partially deaf. So I, for just a moment, could only weakly blame the silence—no, the contradictory roar that only I could hear.

Then I recalled the man who went to the emergency room because he'd woken having lost most, if not all, of his hearing. The doctor peered into one ear, saw an obstruction, reached in with small tweezers, and pulled out a cockroach, then reached into the other ear, and extracted a much larger cockroach. Did you know that ear wax is a delicacy for roaches?

I cooked dinner for my sons—overfed them out of guilt—and cleaned the hell out of our home. Then I walked into the bathroom and stood close to my mirror. I turned my head and body at weird angles, and tried to see deeply into my congested ear. I sang hymns and prayed that I'd see a small angel trapped in the canal. I would free the poor thing, and she'd unfurl and pat dry her tiny wings, then fly to my lips and give me a sweet kiss for sheltering her metamorphosis.

3. The Symptoms Worsen

When I woke at three a.m., completely unable to hear out of my clogged right ear, and positive that a damn swarm of locusts was wedged inside, I left a message for my doctor, and told him that I would be sitting outside his office when he reported to work.

This would be the first time I had been inside a health-care facility since my father's last surgery.

4. Blankets

After the surgeon cut off my father's right foot—no, half of my father's right foot—and three toes from the left, I sat with him in the recovery room. It was more like a recovery hallway. There was no privacy, not even a thin curtain. I guessed it made it easier for the nurses to monitor the postsurgical patients, but still, my father was exposed—his decades of poor health and worse decisions were illuminated—on white sheets in a white hallway under white lights.

"Are you okay?" I asked. It was a stupid question. Who could be okay after such a thing? Yesterday, my father had *walked* into the hospital. Okay, he'd shuffled while balanced on two canes, but that was still called walking. A few hours ago, my father still had both of his feet. Yes, his feet and toes had been black with rot and disease but they'd still been, technically speaking, feet and toes. And, most important, those feet and toes had belonged to my father. But now they were gone, sliced off. Where were they? What did they do with the right foot and the toes from the left foot? Did they throw them in the incinerator? Were their ashes floating over the city?

"Doctor, I'm cold," my father said.

"Dad, it's me," I said.

"I know who are you. You're my son." But considering the blankness in my father's eyes, I assumed he was just guessing at my identity.

"Dad, you're in the hospital. You just had surgery."

"I know where I am. I'm cold."

"Do you want another blanket?" Another stupid question. Of course, he wanted another blanket. He probably wanted me to build a fucking campfire or drag in one of those giant propane heaters that NFL football teams used on the sidelines.

I walked down the hallway—the recovery hallway—to the nurses' station. There were three women nurses, two white and one black. Being Native American-Spokane and Coeur d'Alene Indian, I hoped my darker pigment would give me an edge with the black nurse, so I addressed her directly.

"My father is cold," I said. "Can I get another blanket?"

The black nurse glanced up from her paperwork and regarded me. Her expression was neither compassionate nor callous.

"How can I help you, sir?" she asked.

"I'd like another blanket for my father. He's cold."

"I'll be with you in a moment, sir."

She looked back down at her paperwork. She made a few notes. Not knowing what else to do, I stood there and waited.

"Sir," the black nurse said. "I'll be with you in a moment."

She was irritated. I understood. After all, how many thousands of times had she been asked for an extra blanket? She was a nurse, an educated woman, not a damn housekeeper. And it was never really about an extra blanket, was it? No, when people asked for an extra blanket, they were asking for a time machine. And, yes, she knew she was a health care provider, and she knew she was supposed to be compassionate, but my father, an alcoholic, diabetic Indian with terminally damaged kidneys, had just endured an incredibly expensive surgery for what? So he could ride his motorized wheelchair to the bar and win bets by showing off his disfigured foot? I know she didn't want to be cruel, but she believed there was a point when doctors should stop rescuing people from their own self-destructive impulses. And I couldn't disagree with her but I could ask for the most basic of comforts, couldn't I?

"My father," I said. "An extra blanket, please."

"Fine," she said, then stood and walked back to a linen closet, grabbed a white blanket, and handed it to me. "If you need anything else—"

I didn't wait around for the end of her sentence. With the blanket in hand, I walked back to my father. It was a thin blanket, laundered and sterilized a hundred times. In fact, it was too thin. It wasn't really a blanket. It was more like a large beach towel. Hell, it wasn't even good enough for that. It was more like the world's largest coffee filter. Jesus, had health care finally come to this? Everybody was uninsured and unblanketed.

"Dad, I'm back."

He looked so small and pale lying in that hospital bed. How had that change happened? For the first sixty-seven years of his life, my father had been a large and dark man. And now, he was just another pale and sick drone in a hallway of pale and sick drones. A hive, I thought, this place looks like a beehive with colony collapse disorder.

"Dad, it's me."

"I'm cold."

"I have a blanket."

As I draped it over my father and tucked it around his body, I felt the first sting of grief. I'd read the hospital literature about this moment. There would come a time when roles would reverse and the adult child would become the caretaker of the ill parent. The circle of life. Such poetic bullshit.

"I can't get warm," my father said. "I'm freezing."

"I brought you a blanket, Dad, I put it on you."

"Get me another one. Please. I'm so cold. I need another blanket."

I knew that ten more of these cheap blankets wouldn't be enough. My father needed a real blanket, a good blanket.

I walked out of the recovery hallway and made my way through various doorways and other hallways, peering into the rooms, looking at the patients and their families, looking for a particular kind of patient and family.

I walked through the ER, cancer, heart and vascular, neuro-science, orthopedic, women's health, pediatrics, and surgical services. Nobody stopped me. My expression and posture were that of a man with a sick father and so I belonged.

And then I saw him, another Native man, leaning against a wall near the gift shop. Well, maybe he was Asian; lots of those in Seattle. He was a small man, pale brown, with muscular arms and a soft belly. Maybe he was Mexican, which is really a kind of Indian, too, but not the kind that I needed. It was hard to tell sometimes what people were. Even brown people guessed at the identity of other brown people.

"Hey," I said.

"Hey," the other man said.

"You Indian?" I asked.

"Yeah."

"What tribe?"

"Lummi."

"I'm Spokane."

"My first wife was Spokane. I hated her."

"My first wife was Lummi. She hated me."

We laughed at the new jokes that instantly sounded old.

"Why are you in here?" I asked.

"My sister is having a baby," he said. "But don't worry, it's not mine."

"Ayyyyyy," I said—another Indian idiom—and laughed.

"I don't even want to be here," the other Indian said. "But my dad started, like, this new Indian tradition. He says it's a thousand years old. But that's bullshit. He just made it up to impress himself. And the whole family just goes along, even when we know it's bullshit. He's in the delivery room waving eagle feathers around. Jesus."

"What's the tradition?"

"Oh, he does a naming ceremony right in the hospital. Like, it's supposed to protect the baby from all the technology and shit. Like hospitals are the big problem. You know how many babies died before we had good hospitals?"

"I don't know."

"Most of them. Well, shit, a lot of them, at least."

This guy was talking out of his ass. I liked him immediately.

"I mean," the guy said. "You should see my dad right now. He's pretending to go into this, like, fucking trance and is dancing around my sister's bed, and he says he's trying to, you know, see into her womb, to see who the baby is, to see its true nature, so he can give it a name—a protective name—before it's born."

The guy laughed and threw his head back and banged it on the wall.

"I mean, come on, I'm a loser," he said and rubbed his sore skull. "My whole family is filled with losers."

The Indian world is filled with charlatans, men and women who pretended—hell, who might have come to believe—that they were holy. Last year, I had gone to a lecture at the University of Washington. An elderly Indian woman, a Sioux writer and scholar and charlatan, had come to orate on Indian sovereignty and literature. She kept arguing for some kind of separate indigenous literary identity, which was ironic considering that she was speaking English to a room full of white professors. But I wasn't angry with the woman, or even bored. No, I felt sorry for her. I realized that she was dying of nostalgia. She had taken nostalgia as her false idol—her thin blanket—and it was murdering her.

"Nostalgia," I said to the other Indian man in the hospital.

"What?"

"Your dad, he sounds like he's got a bad case of nostalgia."

"Yeah, I hear you catch that from fucking old high school girlfriends," the man said. "What the hell you doing here anyway?"

"My dad just got his feet cut off," I said.

"Diabetes?"

"And vodka."

"Vodka straight up or with a nostalgia chaser?"

"Both."

"Natural causes for an Indian."

"Yep."

There wasn't much to say after that.

"Well, I better get back," the man said. "Otherwise, my dad might wave an eagle feather and change my name."

"Hey, wait," I said.

"Yeah?"

"Can I ask you a favor?"

"What?"

"My dad, he's in the recovery room," I said. "Well, it's more like a hallway, and he's freezing, and they've only got these shitty little blankets, and I came looking for Indians in the hospital because I figured—well, I guessed if I found any Indians, they might have some good blankets."

"So you want to borrow a blanket from us?" the man asked.

"Yeah."

"Because you thought some Indians would just happen to have some extra blankets lying around?"

"Yeah."

"That's fucking ridiculous."

"I know."

"And it's racist."

"I know."

"You're stereotyping your own damn people."

"I know."

"But damn if we don't have a room full of Pendleton blankets. New ones. Jesus, you'd think my sister was having, like, a dozen babies."

Five minutes later, carrying a Pendleton Star Blanket, the Indian man walked out of his sister's hospital room, accompanied by his father, who wore Levi's, a black T-shirt, and eagle feathers in his gray braids.

"We want to give your father this blanket," the old man said. "It was meant for my grandson, but I think it will be good for your father, too."

"Thank you."

"Let me bless it. I will sing a healing song for the blanket. And for your father."

I flinched. This guy wanted to sing a song? That was dangerous. This song could take two minutes or two hours. It was impossible to know. Hell, considering how desperate this old man was to be seen as holy, he might sing for a week. I couldn't let this guy begin his song without issuing a caveat.

"My dad," I said. "I really need to get back to him. He's really sick."

"Don't worry," the old man said and winked. "I'll sing one of my short ones."

Jesus, who'd ever heard of a self-aware fundamentalist? The son, perhaps not the unbeliever he'd pretended to be, sang backup as his father launched into his radio-friendly honor song, just three-and-a-half minutes, like the length of any Top 40 rock song of the last fifty years. But here's the funny thing: the old man couldn't sing very well. If you were going to have the balls to sing healing songs in hospital hallways, then you should logically have a great voice, right? But, no, this guy couldn't keep the tune. And his voice cracked and wavered. Does a holy song lose its power if its singer is untalented?

"That is your father's song," the old man said when he was finished. "I give it to him. I will never sing it again. It belongs to your father now."

Behind his back, the old man's son rolled his eyes and walked back into his sister's room.

"Okay, thank you," I said. I felt like an ass, accepting the blanket and the old man's good wishes, but silently mocking them at the same time. But maybe the old man did have some power, some real medicine, because he peeked into my brain.

"It doesn't matter if you believe in the healing song," the old man said. "It only matters that the blanket heard."

"Where have you been?" my father asked when I returned. "I'm cold."

"I know, I know," I said. "I found you a blanket. A good one. It will keep you warm."

I draped the Star Blanket over my father. He pulled the thick wool up to his chin. And then he began to sing. It was a healing song, not the same song that I had just heard, but a healing song nonetheless. My father could sing beautifully. I wondered if it was proper for a man to sing a healing song for himself. I wondered if my father needed help with the song. I hadn't sung for many years, not like that, but I joined him. I knew this song would not bring back my father's feet. This song would not repair my father's bladder, kidneys, lungs, and heart. This song would not prevent my father from drinking a bottle of vodka as soon as he could sit up in bed. This song would not defeat death. No, I thought, this song is temporary, but right now, temporary is good enough. And it was a good song. Our voices filled the recovery hallway. The sick and healthy stopped to listen. The nurses, even the remote black one, unconsciously took a few steps toward us. The black nurse sighed and smiled. I smiled back. I knew what she was thinking. Sometimes, even after all of these years, she could still be surprised by her work. She still marveled at the infinite and ridiculous faith of other people.

5. DOCTOR'S OFFICE

I took my kids with me to my doctor, a handsome man—a reservist—who'd served in both Iraq wars. I told him I could not hear. He said his nurse would likely have to clear wax and fluid, but when he scoped inside, he discovered nothing.

"Nope, it's all dry in there," he said.

He led my sons and me to the audiologist in the other half of the building. I was scared, but I wanted my children to remain calm, so I tried to stay measured. More than anything, I wanted my wife to materialize.

During the hearing test, I heard only 30 percent of the clicks, bells, and words—I apparently had nerve and bone conductive deafness. My inner ear thumped and thumped.

How many cockroaches were in my head?

My doctor said, "We need an MRI of your ear and brain, and maybe we'll find out what's going on."

Maybe? That word terrified me.

What the fuck was wrong with my fucking head? Had my hydrocephalus come back for blood? Had my levees burst? Was I going to flood?

6. HYDROCEPHALUS

Merriam-Webster's dictionary defines hydrocephalus as "an abnormal increase in the amount of cerebrospinal fluid within the cranial cavity that is accompanied by expansion of the cerebral ventricles, enlargement of the skull and especially the forehead, and atrophy of the brain." I define hydrocephalus as "the obese, imperialistic water demon that nearly killed me when I was six months old."

In order to save my life, and stop the water demon, I had brain surgery in 1967 when I was six months old. I was supposed to die. Obviously, I didn't. I was supposed to be severely mentally disabled. I have only minor to moderate brain damage. I was supposed to have epileptic seizures. Those I did have, until I was seven years old. I was on phenobarbital, a major league antiseizure medication, for six years.

Some of the side effects of phenobarbital—all of which I suffered to some degree or another as a child—include sleepwalking, agitation, confusion, depression, nightmares, hallucinations, insomnia, apnea, vomiting, constipation, dermatitis, fever, liver and bladder dysfunction, and psychiatric disturbance.

How do you like them cockroaches?

And now, as an adult, thirty-three years removed from phenobarbital, I still suffer—to one degree or another—from sleepwalking, agitation, confusion, depression, nightmares, hallucinations, insomnia, bladder dysfunction, apnea, and dermatitis.

Is there such a disease as post-phenobarbital traumatic stress syndrome?

Most hydrocephalics are shunted. A shunt is essentially brain plumbing that drains away excess cerebrospinal fluid. Those shunts often fuck up and stop working. I know hydrocephalics who've had a hundred or more shunt revisions and repairs. That's over a hundred brain surgeries. There are ten fingers on any surgeon's hand. There are two or three surgeons working on any particular brain. That means certain hydrocephalics have had their brains fondled by three thousand fingers.

I'm lucky. I was only temporarily shunted. And I hadn't suffered any hydrocephalic symptoms since I was seven years old.

And then, in July 2008, at the age of forty-one, I went deaf in my right ear.

7. CONVERSATION

Sitting in my car in the hospital parking garage, I called my brother-in-law, who was babysitting my sons.

"Hey, it's me. I just got done with the MRI on my head."

My brother-in-law said something unintelligible. I realized I was holding my cell to my bad ear. And switched it to the good ear.

"The MRI dude didn't look happy," I said.

"That's not good," my brother-in-law said.

"No, it's not. But he's just a tech guy, right? He's not an expert on brains or anything. He's just the photographer, really. And he doesn't know anything about ears or deafness or anything, I don't think. Ah, hell, I don't know what he knows. I just didn't like the look on his face when I was done."

"Maybe he just didn't like you."

"Well, I got worried when I told him I had hydrocephalus when I was a baby and he didn't seem to know what that was."

"Nobody knows what that is."

"That's the truth. Have you fed the boys dinner?"

"Yeah, but I was scrounging. There's not much here."

"I better go shopping."

"Are you sure? I can do it if you need me to. I can shop the shit out of Trader Joe's."

"No, it'll be good for me. I feel good. I fell asleep during the MRI. And I kept twitching. So we had to do it twice. Otherwise, I would've been done earlier."

"That's okay; I'm okay; the boys are okay"

"You know, before you go in that MRI tube, they ask you what kind of music you want to listen to—jazz, classical, rock, or country—and I remembered how my dad spent a lot of time in MRI tubes near the end of his life. So I was wondering what kind of music he always chose. I mean, he couldn't hear shit anyway by that time, but he still must have chosen something. And I wanted to choose the same thing he chose. So I picked country."

"Was it good country?"

"It was fucking Shania Twain and Faith Hill shit. I was hoping for George Jones or Loretta Lynn, or even some George Strait. Hell, I would've cried if they'd played Charley Pride or Freddy Fender."

"You wanted to hear the alcoholic Indian father jukebox."

"Hey, that's my line. You can't quote me to me."

"Why not? You're always quoting you to you."

"Kiss my ass. So, hey, I'm okay, I think. And I'm going to the store. But I think I already said that. Anyway, I'll see you in a bit. You want anything?"

"Ah, man, I love Trader Joe's. But you know what's bad about them? You fall in love with something they have—they stock it for a year—and then it just disappears. They had those wontons I loved and now they don't. I was willing to shop for you and the boys, but I don't want anything for me. I'm on a one-man hunger strike against them."

8. World Phone Conversation, 3 a.m.

After I got home with yogurt and turkey dogs and Cinnamon Toast Crunch and my brother-in-law had left, I watched George Romero's *Diary of the Dead,* and laughed at myself for choosing a movie that featured dozens of zombies getting shot in the head.

When the movie was over, I called my wife, nine hours ahead in Italy.

"I should come home," she said.

"No, I'm okay," I said. "Come on, you're in Rome. What are you seeing today?"

"The Vatican."

"You can't leave now. You have to go and steal something. It will be revenge for every Indian. Or maybe you can plant an eagle feather and claim that you just discovered Catholicism."

"I'm worried."

"Yeah, Catholicism has always worried me."

"Stop being funny. I should see if I can get Mom and me on a flight tonight."

"No, no, listen, your mom is old. This might be her last adventure. It might be your last adventure with her. Stay there. Say Hi to the Pope for me. Tell him I like his shoes."

That night, my sons climbed into bed with me. We all slept curled around one another like sled dogs in a snowstorm. I woke, hour by hour, and touched my head and neck to check if they had changed shape—to feel if antennae were growing. Some insects "hear" with their antennae. Maybe that's what was happening to me.

9. VALEDICTION

My father, a part-time blue collar construction worker, died in March 2003, from full-time alcoholism. On his deathbed, he asked me to "Turn down that light, please."

"Which light?" I asked.

"The light on the ceiling."

"Dad, there's no light."

"It burns my skin, son. It's too bright. It hurts my eyes."

"Dad, I promise you there's no light."

"Don't lie to me, son, it's God passing judgment on Earth."

"Dad, you've been an atheist since '79. Come on, you're just remembering your birth. On your last day, you're going back to your first."

"No, son, it's God telling me I'm doomed. He's using the brightest lights in the universe to show me the way to my flame-filled tomb."

"No, Dad, those lights were in your delivery room."

"If that's true, son, then turn down my mother's womb."

We buried my father in the tiny Catholic cemetery on our reservation. Since I am named after him, I had to stare at a tombstone with my name on it.

10. BATTLE FATIGUE

Two months after my father's death, I began research on a book about our family's history with war. I had a cousin who had served as a cook in the first Iraq war in 1991; I had another cousin who served in the Vietnam War in 1964–65, also as a cook; and my father's father, Adolph, served in WWII and was killed in action on Okinawa Island, on April 5, 1946.

During my research, I interviewed thirteen men who'd served with my cousin in Vietnam but could find only one surviving man who'd served with my grandfather. This is a partial transcript of that taped interview, recorded with a microphone and an iPod on January 14, 2008:

Me: Ah, yes, hello, I'm here in Livonia, Michigan, to interview—well, perhaps you should introduce yourself, please?

Leonard Elmore: What?

Me: Um, oh, I'm sorry, I was asking if you could perhaps introduce yourself.

LE: You're going to have to speak up. I think my hearing aid is going low on power or something.

Me: That is a fancy thing in your ear.

LE: Yeah, let me mess with it a bit. I got a remote control for it. I can listen to the TV, the stereo, and the telephone with this thing. It's fancy. It's one of them blue tooth hearing aids. My grandson bought it for me. Wait, okay, there we go. I can hear now. So what were you asking?

Me: I was hoping you could introduce yourself into my recorder here.

LE: Sure, my name is Leonard Elmore.

Me: How old are you?

LE: I'm eighty-five-and-a-half years old (laughter). My great-grandkids are always saying they're seven-and-a-half or nine-and-a-half or whatever. It just cracks me up to say the same thing at my age.

Me: So, that's funny, um, but I'm here to ask you some questions about my grandfather—

LE: Adolph. It's hard to forget a name like that. An Indian named Adolph and there was that Nazi bastard named Adolph. Your grandfather caught plenty of grief over that. But we mostly called him "Chief," did you know that?

Me: I could have guessed.

LE: Yeah, nowadays, I suppose it isn't a good thing to call an Indian "Chief," but back then, it was what we did. I served with a few Indians. They didn't segregate them Indians, you know, not like the black boys. I know you aren't supposed to call them boys anymore, but they were boys. All of us were boys, I guess. But the thing is, those Indian boys lived and slept and ate with us white boys. They were right there with us. But, anyway, we called all them Indians "Chief." I bet you've been called "Chief" a few times yourself.

Me: Just once.

LE: Were you all right with it?

Me: I threw a basketball in the guy's face.

LE: (laughter)

Me: We live in different times.

LE: Yes, we do. Yes, we do.

Me: So, perhaps you could, uh, tell me something about my grandfather.

LE: I can tell you how he died.

Me: Really?

LE: Yeah, it was on Okinawa, and we hit the beach, and, well, it's hard to talk about it—it was the worst thing—it was Hell—no, that's not even a good way to describe it. I'm not a writer like you—I'm not a poet—so I don't have the words—but just think of it this way—that beach, that island—was filled with sons and fathers—men who loved and were loved—American and Japanese and Okinawan—and all of us were dying—were being killed by other sons and fathers who also loved and were loved.

Me: That sounds like poetry—tragic poetry—to me.

LE: Well, anyway, it was like that. Fire everywhere. And two of our boys—Jonesy and O'Neal—went down—were wounded in the open on the sand. And your grandfather—who was just this little man—barely five feet tall and maybe one hundred and thirty pounds—he just ran out there and picked up those two guys—one on each shoulder—and carried them to cover. Hey, are you okay, son?

Me: Yes, I'm sorry. But, well, the thing is, I knew my grandfather was a war hero—he won twelve medals—but I could never find out what he did to win the medals.

LE: I didn't know about any medals. I just know what I saw. Your grandfather saved those two boys, but he got shot in the back doing it. And he laid there in the sand—I was lying right beside him—and he died.

Me: Did he say anything before he died?

LE: Hold on. I need to—

49

Me: Are you okay?

LE: It's just—I can't—

Me: I'm sorry. Is there something wrong?

LE: No, it's just—with your book and everything—I know you want something big here. I know you want something big from your grandfather. I knew you hoped he'd said something huge and poetic, like maybe something you could have written, and, honestly, I was thinking about lying to you. I was thinking about making up something as beautiful as I could. Something about love and forgiveness and courage and all that. But I couldn't think of anything good enough. And I didn't want to lie to you. So I have to be honest and say that your grandfather didn't say anything. He just died there in the sand. In silence.

11. ORPHANS

I was worried that I had a brain tumor. Or that my hydrocephalus had returned. I was scared that I was going to die and orphan my sons. But, no, their mother was coming home from Italy. No matter what happened to me, their mother would rescue them.

"I'll be home in sixteen hours," my wife said over the phone.

"I'll be here," I said. "I'm just waiting on news from my doctor."

12. COFFEE SHOP NEWS

While I waited, I asked my brother-in-law to watch the boys again because I didn't want to get bad news with them in the room.

Alone and haunted, I wandered the mall, tried on new clothes, and waited for my cell phone to ring.

Two hours later, I was uncomposed and wanted to murder everything, so I drove south to a coffee joint, a spotless place called Dirty Joe's.

Yes, I was silly enough to think that I'd be calmer with a caffeinated drink.

As I sat outside on a wooden chair and sipped my coffee, I cursed the vague, rumbling, ringing noise in my ear. And yet, when my cell phone rang, I held it to my deaf ear.

"Hello, hello," I said and wondered if it was a prank call, then remembered and switched the phone to my left ear.

"Hello," my doctor said. "Are you there?"

"Yes," I said. "So, what's going on?"

"There are irregularities in your head."

"My head's always been wrong,"

"It's good to have a sense of humor," my doctor said. "You have a small tumor that is called a meningioma. They grow in the meninges membranes that lie between your brain and your skull."

"Shit," I said. "I have cancer."

"Well," my doctor said. "These kinds of tumors are usually noncancerous. And they grow very slowly, so in six months or so, we'll do another MRI. Don't worry. You're going to be okay."

"What about my hearing?" I asked.

"We don't know what might be causing the hearing loss, but you should start a course of prednisone, the steroid, just to go with the odds. Your deafness might lessen if left alone, but we've had success with the steroids in bringing back hearing. There *are* side effects, like insomnia, weight gain, night sweats, and depression."

"Oh, boy," I said. "Those side effects might make up most of my personality already. Will the 'roids also make me quick to pass judgment? And I've always wished I had a dozen more skin tags and moles."

The doctor chuckled. "You're a funny man."

I wanted to throw my phone into a wall but I said good-bye instead and glared at the tumorless people and their pretty tumorless heads.

13. MENINGIOMA

Mayoclinic.com defines "meningioma" as "a tumor that arises from the meninges—the membranes that surround your brain and spinal cord. The majority of meningioma cases are noncancerous (benign), though rarely a meningioma can be cancerous (malignant)."

Okay, that was a scary and yet strangely positive definition. No one ever wants to read the word "malignant" unless one is reading a Charles Dickens novel about an evil landlord, but "benign" and "majority" are two things that go great together.

From the University of Washington Medical School Web site I learned that meningioma tumors "are usually benign, slow growing and do not spread into normal brain tissue. Typically, a meningioma grows inward, causing pressure on the brain or spinal cord. It may grow outward toward the skull, causing it to thicken."

So, wait, what the fuck? A meningioma can cause pressure on the brain and spinal fluid? Oh, you mean, just like fucking hydrocephalus? Just like the water demon that once tried to crush my brain and kill me? Armed with this new information—with these new questions—I called my doctor.

"Hey, you're okay," he said. "We're going to closely monitor you. And your meningioma is very small."

"Okay, but I just read—"

"Did you go on the Internet?"

"Yes."

"Which sites?"

"Mayo Clinic and the University of Washington."

"Okay, so those are pretty good sites. Let me look at them."

I listened to my doctor type.

"Okay, those are accurate," he said.

"What do you mean by accurate?" I asked. "I mean, the whole pressure on the brain thing, that sounds like hydrocephalus."

"Well, there were some irregularities in your MRI that were the burr holes from your surgery and there seems to be some scarring and perhaps you had an old concussion, but other than that, it all looks fine."

"But what about me going deaf? Can't these tumors make you lose hearing?"

"Yes, but only if they're located near an auditory nerve. And your tumor is not."

"Can this tumor cause pressure on my brain?"

"It could, but yours is too small for that."

"So, I'm supposed to trust you on the tumor thing when you can't figure out the hearing thing?"

"The MRI revealed the meningioma, but that's just an image. There is no physical correlation between your deafness and the tumor. Do the twenty-day treatment of Prednisone and the audiologist and I will examine your ear, and your hearing. Then, if there's no improvement, we'll figure out other ways of treating you."

"But you won't be treating the tumor?"

"Like I said, we'll scan you again in six to nine months—"

"You said six before."

"Okay, in six months we'll take another MRI, and if it has grown significantly—or has changed shape or location or anything dramatic—then we'll talk about treatment options. But if you look on the Internet, and I know you're going to spend a lot of time obsessing on this—as you should—I'll tell you what you'll find. About 5 percent of the population has these things and they live their whole lives with these undetected meningiomas. And they can become quite large—without any side effects—and are only found at autopsies conducted for other causes of death. And even when these kinds of tumors become invasive or dangerous they are still rarely fatal. And your tumor, even if it grows fairly quickly, will not likely become an issue for many years, decades. So that's what I can tell you right now. How are you feeling?"

"Freaked and fucked."

I wanted to feel reassured, but I had a brain tumor. How does one feel any optimism about being diagnosed with a brain tumor? Even if that brain tumor is neither cancerous nor interested in crushing one's brain?

14. DRUGSTORE INDIAN

In Bartell's Drugs, I gave the pharmacist my prescription for Prednisone.

"Is this your first fill with us?" she asked.

"No," I said. "And it won't be the last."

I felt like an ass, but she looked bored.

"It'll take thirty minutes," she said, "more or less. We'll page you over the speakers."

I don't think I'd ever felt weaker, or more vulnerable, or more absurd. I was the weak antelope in the herd—yeah, the mangy fucker with the big limp and a sign that read, "Eat me! I'm a gimp!"

So, for thirty minutes, I walked through the store and found myself shoving more and more useful shit into my shopping basket, as if I were filling my casket with the things I'd need in the afterlife. I grabbed toothpaste, a Swiss Army knife, moisturizer, mouthwash, non-stick Band-Aids, antacid, protein bars, and extra razor blades. I grabbed pen and paper. And I also grabbed an ice scraper and sunscreen. Who can predict what weather awaits us in Heaven?

This random shopping made me feel better for a few minutes but then I stopped and walked to the toy aisle. My boys needed gifts: Lego cars or something, for a lift, a shot of capitalistic joy. But the selection of proper toys is art and science. I have been wrong as often as right and heard the sad song of a disappointed son.

Shit, if I died, I knew my sons would survive, even thrive, because of their graceful mother.

I thought of my father's life: he was just six when his father was killed in World War II. Then his mother, ill with tuberculosis, died a few months later. Six years old, my father was cratered. In most ways, he never stopped being six. There was no religion, no magic tricks, and no song or dance that helped my father.

Jesus, I needed a drink of water, so I found the fountain and drank and drank until the pharmacist called my name.

"Have you taken these before?" she asked.

"No," I said, "but they're going to kick my ass, aren't they?"

That made the pharmacist smile, so I felt sadly and briefly worthwhile. But another customer, some nosy hag, said, "You've got a lot of sleepless nights ahead of you."

I was shocked. I stammered, glared at her, and said, "Miss, how is this any of your business? Please, just fuck all the way off, okay?"

She had no idea what to say, so she just turned and walked away and I pulled out my credit card and paid far too much for my goddamn steroids, and forgot to bring the toys home to my boys.

15. Exit Interview for My Father

- True or False?: when a reservation-raised Native American dies of alcoholism it should be considered death by natural causes.

- Do you understand the term *wanderlust,* and if you do, can you please tell us, in twenty-five words or less, what place made you wanderlust the most?
- Did you, when drunk, ever get behind the tattered wheel of a '76 Ford three-speed van and somehow drive your family one thousand miles on an empty tank of gas?
- Is it true that the only literary term that has any real meaning in the Native American world is *road movie?*
- During the last road movie you saw, how many times did the characters ask, "Are we there yet?"
- How many times, during any of your road trips, did your children ask, "Are we there yet?"
- In twenty-five words or less, please define *there.*
- Sir, in your thirty-nine years as a parent, you broke your children's hearts, collectively and individually, 612 times and you did this without ever striking any human being in anger. Does this absence of physical violence make you a better man than you might otherwise have been?
- Without using the words *man* or *good,* can you please define what it means to be a good man?
- Do you think you will see angels before you die? Do you think angels will come to escort you to Heaven? As the angels are carrying you to Heaven, how many times will you ask, "Are we there yet?"
- Your son distinctly remembers stopping once or twice a month at that grocery store in Freeman, Washington, where you would buy him a red-white-and-blue rocket popsicle and purchase for yourself a pickled pig foot. Your son

distinctly remembers the feet still had their toenails and little tufts of pig fur. Could this be true? Did you actually eat such horrendous food?

- Your son has often made the joke that you were the only Indian of your generation who went to Catholic school on purpose. This is, of course, a tasteless joke that makes light of the forced incarceration and subsequent physical, spiritual, cultural, and sexual abuse of tens of thousands of Native American children in Catholic and Protestant boarding schools. In consideration of your son's questionable judgment in telling jokes, do you think there should be any moral limits placed on comedy?
- Your oldest son and your two daughters, all over thirty-six years of age, still live in your house. Do you think this is a lovely expression of tribal culture? Or is it a symptom of extreme familial codependence? Or is it both things at the same time?
- F. Scott Fitzgerald wrote that the sign of a superior mind "is the ability to hold two opposing ideas at the same time." Do you believe this is true? And is it also true that you once said, "The only time white people tell the truth is when they keep their mouths shut"?
- A poet once wrote, "Pain is never added to pain. It multiplies." Can you tell us, in twenty-five words or less, exactly how much we all hate mathematical blackmail?
- Your son, in defining you, wrote this poem to explain one of the most significant nights in his life:

MUTUALLY ASSURED DESTRUCTION

When I was nine, my father sliced his knee
With a chain saw. But he let himself bleed
And finished cutting down one more tree
Before his boss drove him to EMERGENCY.

Late that night, stoned on morphine and beer,
My father needed my help to steer
His pickup into the woods. "Watch for deer,"
My father said. "Those things just appear

Like magic." It was an Indian summer
And we drove through warm rain and thunder,
Until we found that chain saw, lying under
The fallen pine. Then I watched, with wonder,

As my father, shotgun-rich and impulse-poor,
Blasted that chain saw dead. "What was that for?"
I asked. "Son," my father said, "here's the score.
Once a thing tastes blood, it will come for more."

- Well, first of all, as you know, you did cut your knee with a
  chain saw, but in direct contradiction to your son's poem:

  A) You immediately went to the emergency room after in-
      juring yourself.
  B) Your boss called your wife, who drove you to the emer-
      gency room.

C) You were given morphine but even you were not alco-holically stupid enough to drink alcohol while on seri-ous narcotics.

D) You and your son did not get into the pickup that night.

E) And even if you had driven the pickup, you were not in-jured seriously enough to need your son's help with the pedals and/or steering wheel.

F) You never in your life used the word, *appear*, and cer-tainly never used the phrase, like magic.

G) You also agree that Indian summer is a fairly question-able seasonal reference for an Indian poet to use.

H) What the fuck is "warm rain and thunder"? Well, every-body knows what warm rain is, but what the fuck is warm thunder?

I) You never went looking for that chain saw because it be-longed to the Spokane tribe of Indians and what kind of freak would want to reclaim the chain saw that had just cut the shit out of his knee?

J) You also agree that the entire third stanza of this poem sounds like a Bruce Springsteen song and not necessar-ily one of the great ones.

K) And yet, "shotgun-rich and impulse-poor" is one of the greatest descriptions your son has ever written and probably redeems the entire poem.

L) You never owned a shotgun. You did own a few rifles during your lifetime, but did not own even so much as a pellet gun during the last thirty years of your life.

M) You never said, in any context, "Once a thing tastes your blood, it will come for more."

N) But you, as you read it, know that it is absolutely true and does indeed sound suspiciously like your entire life philosophy.

O) Other summations of your life philosophy include: "I'll be there before the next teardrop falls."

P) And: "If God really loved Indians, he would have made us white people."

Q) And: "Oscar Robertson should be the man on the NBA logo. They only put Jerry West on there because he's a white guy."

R) And: "A peanut butter sandwich with onions. Damn, that's the way to go."

S) And: "Why eat a pomegranate when you can eat a plain old apple. Or peach. Or orange. When it comes to fruit and vegetables, only eat the stuff you know how to grow."

T) And: "If you really want a woman to love you, then you have to dance. And if you don't want to dance, then you're going to have to work extrahard to make a woman love you forever, and you will always run the risk that she will leave you at any second for a man who knows how to tango."

U) And: "I really miss those cafeterias they use to have in Kmart. I don't know why they stopped having those. If there is a Heaven then I firmly believe it's a Kmart cafeteria."

V) And: "A father always knows what his sons are doing. For instance, boys, I knew you were sneaking that *Hustler* magazine out of my bedroom. You remember that one? Where actors who looked like Captain Kirk and

Lieutenant Uhura were screwing on the bridge of the *Enterprise*. Yeah, that one. I know you kept borrowing it. I let you borrow it. Remember this: men and pornography are like plants and sunshine. To me, porn is photosynthesis."

W) And: "Your mother is a better man than me. Mothers are almost always better men than men are."

16. REUNION

After she returned from Italy, my wife climbed into bed with me. I felt like I had not slept comfortably in years.

I said, "There was a rumor that I'd grown a tumor but I killed it with humor."

"How long have you been waiting to tell me that one?" she asked.

"Oh, probably since the first time some doctor put his fingers in my brain."

We made love. We fell asleep. But I, agitated by the steroids, woke at two, three, four, and five a.m. The bed was killing my back so I lay flat on the floor. I wasn't going to die anytime soon, at least not because of my little friend, Mr. Tumor, but that didn't make me feel any more comfortable or comforted. I felt distant from the world—from my wife and sons, from my mother and siblings—from all of my friends. I felt closer to those who've always had fingers in their brains.

And I didn't feel any closer to the world six months later when another MRI revealed that my meningioma had not grown in size or changed its shape.

"You're looking good," my doctor said. "How's your hearing?"

"I think I've got about 90 percent of it back."

"Well, then, the steroids worked. Good."

And I didn't feel any more intimate with God nine months later when one more MRI made my doctor hypothesize that my meningioma might only be more scar tissue from the hydrocephalus.

"Frankly," my doctor said. "Your brain is beautiful."

"Thank you," I said, though it was the oddest compliment I'd ever received.

I wanted to call up my father and tell him that a white man thought my brain was beautiful. But I couldn't tell him anything. He was dead. I told my wife and sons that I was okay. I told my mother and siblings. I told my friends. But none of them laughed as hard about my beautiful brain as I knew my father would have. I miss him, the drunk bastard. I would always feel closest to the man who had most disappointed me.

THE THEOLOGY OF REPTILES

We found a snake, dead in midmolt.
"It's almost like two snakes," I said.
My brother grabbed it by the head
And said, "It just needs lightning bolts."

Laughing, he jumped the creek and draped
The snake over an electric fence.
Was my brother being cruel? Yes,
But we were shocked when that damn snake

Spiraled off the wire and splayed,
Alive, on the grass, made a fist
Of itself, then, gorgeous and pissed,
Uncurled, stood on end, and swayed

For my brother, who, bemused and odd,
Had somehow become one snake's god.

CATECHISM

Why did your big brother, during one hot summer, sleep in the hall-way closet?

My mother, a Spokane Indian, kept bags of fabric scraps in that hallway closet. My brother arranged these scrap bags into shapes that approximated a mattress and pillows. My mother used these scraps to make quilts.

As an Indian, were you taught to worship the sun or the moon?

My mother was (and is) a Protestant of random varieties. My late father, a Coeur d'Alene, was a Catholic until the day that he decided to become an atheist. But it wasn't until twelve years after he decided to become an atheist that he made this infor-mation public.
MY MOTHER: "Why did you wait so long to tell us?"
MY FATHER: "I didn't want to make a quick decision."

Do you think that religious ceremony is an effective treatment for grief?

My mother once made a quilt from dozens of pairs of second-and third- and fourth-hand blue jeans that she bought at Goodwill, the Salvation Army, Value Village, and garage sales.

My late sister studied my mother's denim quilt and said, "That's a lot of pants. There's been a lot of ass in those pants. This is a blanket of asses."

If your reservation is surrounded on all sides by two rivers and a creek, doesn't that make it an island?

A Coeur d'Alene Indian holy man—on my father's side—received this vision: Three crows, luminescent and black, except for collars of white feathers, perched in a pine tree above my ancestor's camp and told him that three strangers would soon be arriving and their advice must be heeded or the Coeur d'Alene would vanish from the earth. The next day, the first Jesuits—three men in black robes with white collars—walked into a Coeur d'Alene Indian fishing camp.

Do you believe that God, in the form of his son, Jesus Christ, once walked the Earth?

Thus the Coeur d'Alene soon became, and remain, among the most Catholicized Indians in the country.

Has any member of the clergy ever given you a clear and concise explanation of this Holy Ghost business?

Therefore, nuns taught my father, as a child, to play classical piano.

Do you think that Beethoven was not actually deaf and was just having a laugh at his family's expense?

By the time I was born, my father had long since stopped playing piano.

ME: "Dad, what did the nuns teach you to play?

HIM: "I don't want to talk about that shit."

After you catch a sliver from a wooden crucifix, how soon afterward will you gain superpowers?

When he was drunk, my father would sit at the kitchen table and hum an indecipherable tune while playing an imaginary keyboard.

Did your mother ever make a quilt that featured a real piano keyboard?

I have mounted my father's imaginary keyboard on my office wall.

ME: "And, here, on the wall, is my favorite work of art."

GUEST: "I don't see anything."

ME: "It's an installation piece created by my father."

GUEST: "I still can't see anything."

ME: "Exactly."

If you could only pick one word to describe your family, then what would that word be?

Honorificabilitudinitas.

Is that a real word?

Yes, Shakespeare used it. It means "The state of being able to achieve honors."

So you're stating your multisyllabic, overeducated, and pretentious belief that your family is and was in a state of being able to achieve honors?

Yep.

What kind of honors?

Whenever anybody in my family did something good, my mother would make an honor blanket. She used pieces of people's clothes and stitched in little photographs and images or important dates and names. Very ornate.

So if your mother were going to honor your family's religious history with an honor blanket, what shape would it take?

It wouldn't be an honor blanket. It would be a quilt of guilt.

Do you actually believe in God?

My mother kept scraps of God in our hallway closet. My big brother arranged these scraps of God into shapes that approximated a mattress and pillows, and slept in that closet. My mother once used these scraps of God to make an epic quilt. My late sister studied this quilt and said, "That's a lot of God. There's been a lot of God in this God. This is a blanket of God."

However, my late father, when drunk, would sit at the kitchen table and sing to an indecipherable God while playing an imaginary keyboard.

But what do you think about God?

I'm at my kitchen window, and I'm watching three crows perched on the telephone wire. I think they're talking trash about me.

ODE TO SMALL-TOWN SWEETHEARTS

O, when you are driving through a blizzard
   And your vision has been reduced—
     Has been scissored—
   Into two headlights and a noose,
How joyous to come upon the Wizard
Of Snowplows driving his glorious machine.
    Now you will survive if you ride
      In his slipstream.
   He pushes back the fear and ice.
This is not a time for prayer, so you scream

With joy (*Snowplow! Snowplow! Snowplow! Snowplow!*)
   As he leads you into the next
     Snowed-in town.
   You are not dead! You did not wreck!
And you know a family who live here—the Browns.
They run that little diner on Main Street.
    It must be shut at this dark hour—
      Quarter past three—
   But the son, Mark, plays power
Forward for the high school, the Wolverines—

And once broke your nose with a stray elbow
    While playing some tough-ass defense—
    And you know him and call him friend.
So you park your car and trudge through the snow—
Cursing and/or blessing this fierce winter—
    To find Mark and his dad awake
    And cooking chicken-fried steaks
For a dozen other survivors and sinners.
"Dang," Mark says. "Why are you out in this stuff?"
    "For a girl," you say. And Mark nods.
    Mortals have always fought the gods
And braved epic storms for love and/or lust.
So don't be afraid to speak honestly
    About how you obeyed beauty's call.
    And though your triumph was small,
You can still sing of your teenage odyssey.

THE SENATOR'S SON

I hadn't seen my best friend in sixteen years, half of our lives ago, so I didn't recognize him when I pulled him out of the car and hit him in the face. I'd taken a few self-defense classes, so I'd learned to strike with the heel of my open hand. It's too easy to break fingers if one slams a fist against the hard bones of the head. A good student, I also remembered to stand with my feet a shoulder's width apart, for maximum balance, and to twist my hips and shoulders back before I thrust forward, for maximum leverage and striking power. And so, maximally educated, I hit my best friend and snapped his nose.

It made an astonishing noise. I imagine it could have been heard a block away. And the blood! Oh, his red glow drenched my shirt. He screamed, slumped back against his car, and slid to the ground. After that, it would have been impossible to recognize him because his face was a bloody mask. Drunk and enraged, I tried to kick him and might have beaten him unconscious or worse, but Bernard, my old college friend and drinking buddy, wrapped me in a bear hug and dragged me away.

Meanwhile, on the other side of the car, a faggot was winning his fight with Spence and Eddie, my other friends. They'd picked the wrong guy to bash. He was a talented fighter and danced, ducked, and threw mean kicks and elbows that *snap-snap-snap*ped into my friends' faces. This guy had to be one of those ultimate fighters, a mixed-martial artist.

This was in Seattle, on a dark street on Capitol Hill, the Pacific Northwest center of all things shabby, leftist, and gay. What was I, a straight Republican boy, doing on Capitol Hill? Well, it's also the home of my favorite Thai joint. I love peanut sauce and Asian beer. So my friends and I had feasted in celebration of my new junior partnership in the law firm of Robber Baron, Tax Dodger & Guilt-ridden Pro Bono. I was cash-heavy, lived in a three-bedroom condo overlooking Elliott Bay, and drove a hybrid Lexus SUV.

My father was in his first term as U.S. senator from Washington State, and he was already being talked about as a candidate for U.S. president. "I'm something different," he said to me once. "This country wants Jimmy Stewart. And I am Jimmy Stewart."

It was true. My father was handsome without being beautiful, intelligent without being pretentious, and charming without being sexual. And he was a widower, a single father who'd raised an accomplished son. My mother had died of breast cancer when I was six years old, and my father, too much in love with her memory, had never remarried. He was now as devoted and loyal to curing breast cancer as he had been to my mother.

A University of Washington Law graduate, he had begun life as the only son of a wheat farmer and his schoolteacher wife. Eagle Scout, captain of the basketball team, and homecoming king, my father was the perfect candidate. He was a city commissioner, then a state representative, and then he ran for the U.S. Senate. After decades of voting for the sons and grandsons of privilege, the state's conservatives were excited, even proud, to vote for a public school veteran, a blue-collar prince, a farmer's son, a boy with dirt in his shoes.

His best moment during his senatorial campaign was during the final debate with his Democratic rival. "My opponent keeps talking about how hard he's worked for his country, for our state. And I'm sure he has. But my grandfather and my father taught me how to be a farmer. They taught me how to plant the seed and grow the wheat that feeds our country. I worked so hard that my hands bled; look, you can still see my scars. And I promise you, my fellow Washingtonians, that I will work hard for you. And I will work hard *with* you."

My father lost liberal King County by a surprisingly close margin but kicked ass in the rest of the state and was declared senator at 9:35 P.M. on the night of the election.

Yes, my father had become Jefferson Smith and had marched into the other Washington as the first real populist in decades.

I'm not ashamed to admit that I cried a little on the night my father was elected. You've seen the photograph. It was on the cover of the *Seattle Times* and was reprinted all over the country. Everybody assumed that I was happy for my father. Overjoyed, in fact. But I was also slapped hard by grief. I desperately missed my mother, but I desperately missed my father as well. You see, he was now a U.S. senator with presidential ambitions, and that meant he belonged to everybody. I knew I'd forever lost a huge part of his energy and time and, yes, his love; I'd have to share my father with the world. I also knew I'd lost my chance to ever be anything other than an all-star politician's son.

But who wants to hear the sob story of a senator's son? The real question is this: Why the hell would I risk my reputation and future and my father's political career—the entire meaning of his life—for a street fight—for a gay bashing? I don't know, but it was high comedy.

So I laughed while that tough faggot beat Spence and Eddie into the pavement. And I laughed as Bernard dragged me toward his car, shoved me into the backseat, and slammed the door shut. Then he popped open his trunk, grabbed his tire iron, and ran back toward the fight.

I powered down the window and watched Bernard race up to that black-belt fag and threaten him with the tire iron.

"Stop this shit," Bernard yelled. "Or I'll club you."

"Why the hell are you waving that thing at me?" he screamed back. "You started it."

It was true, playground true. Spence, Eddie, Bernie, and I had started it. We'd been drunkenly ambling down the street, cussing and singing, when Spence spotted the amorous boys in their car.

"Lookit," he said. "I hate them fucking fags."

That's all it took. With banshee war cries, Spence and Eddie flung open the driver's door and dragged out the tough guy. I dragged my best friend (whom I didn't recognize) from the passenger seat and broke his nose.

And now, I was drunk in Bernard's car and he was waving a tire iron at the guy we'd assaulted.

"Come on, Spence, Eddie," Bernard said.

Bloodied and embarrassed by their beating, Spence and Eddie staggered to their feet and made their way to the car. Still waving that tire iron, Bernard also came back to me. I laughed as Spence and Eddie slid into the backseat beside me. I laughed when Bernard climbed into the driver's seat and sped us away. And I was still laughing when I looked out the rear window and saw the tough guy tending to his broken and bloody lover boy. But even as I laughed, I knew that I had committed an awful and premeditated crime: I had threatened my father's career.

Sixteen years before I dragged him out of his car and punched him in the face, my best friend Jeremy and I were smart, handsome, and ambitious young Republicans at Madison Park School in Seattle. Private and wealthy, Madison Park was filled with leftist children, parents, and faculty. Jeremy and I were the founders and leaders of the Madison Park Carnivores, a conservative club whose mission was to challenge and ridicule all things leftist. Our self-published newspaper was called *Tooth & Claw*, borrowed from the poem by Alfred Tennyson, of course, and we filled its pages with lame satire, poorly drawn cartoons, impulsive editorials, and gushing profiles of local conservative heroes, including my father, a Republican city commissioner in a Democratic city.

Looking back, I suppose I became a Republican simply because my father was a Republican. It had never occurred to me to be something different. I loved and respected my father and wanted to be exactly like him. If he'd been a plumber or a housepainter, I suppose I would have followed him into those careers. But my father's politics and vocation were only the outward manifestations of his greatness. He was my hero because of his strict moral sense. Simply put, my father kept his promises.

Jeremy, a scholarship kid and the only child of a construction worker and a housewife, was far more right wing than I was. He worried that my father, who'd enjoyed bipartisan support as city commissioner, was a leftist in conservative disguise.

"He's going to Souter us," Jeremy said. "Just you watch, he's going to Souter us in the ass."

Jeremy and I always made fun of each other's fathers. Since black kids told momma jokes, we figured we should do the opposite.

"I bet your daddy sucks David Souter's dick," Jeremy said.

Jeremy hated Supreme Court Justice David Souter, who'd been named to the court by the first President Bush. Thought to be a typical constitutional conservative, Souter had turned into a moderate maverick, a supporter of abortion rights and opponent of sodomy laws, and was widely seen by the right as a political traitor. Jeremy thought Souter should be executed for treason. Was it hyperbole? Sure, but I think he almost meant it. He was a romantic when it came to political assassination.

"When I close one eye, you look just like Lee Harvey," I said.

"I'm not Oswald," he said. "Oswald was a communist. I'm more like John Wilkes Booth."

"Come on, man, read your history. Booth killed Lincoln over slavery."

"It wasn't about slavery. It was about states' rights."

Jeremy had always enjoyed a major-league hard-on for states' rights. If it had been up to him, the United States would be fifty separate countries with fifty separate interpretations of the Constitution.

Yes, compared to Jeremy, I was more Mao than Goldwater.

It was in January of our sophomore year at Madison Park that Jeremy stole me out of class and drove me to the McDonald's in North Bend, high up in the Cascade Mountains, more than thirty miles away from our hometown of Seattle.

"What are we doing way up here?" I asked.

"Getting lunch," he said.

So we ordered hamburgers and fries from the drive-thru and ate in the car.

"I love McDonald's fries," he said.

"Yeah, they're great," I said. "But you know the best thing about them?"

"What?"

"I love that McDonald's fries are exactly the same everywhere you go. The McDonald's fries in Washington, DC, are exactly like the fries in Seattle. Heck, the McDonald's fries in Paris, France, are exactly like the fries in Seattle."

"Yeah, so what's your point?" Jeremy asked.

"Well, I think the McDonald's fries in North Bend are also exactly like the fries in Washington, DC, Paris, and Seattle. Do you agree?"

"Yeah, that seems reasonable."

"Okay, then," I said. "If all the McDonald's fries in the world are the same, why did you drive me all the way up into the mountains to buy fries we could have gotten anywhere else in the world and, most especially, in Seattle?"

"To celebrate capitalism?"

"That's funny, but it's not true," I said. "What's really going on?"

"I have something I need to tell you," Jeremy said.

"And you couldn't have told me in Seattle?"

"I didn't want anybody to hear," he said.

"Oh, nobody is going to hear anything up here," I said.

Jeremy stared out the window at Mount Si, a four-thousand-foot-tall rock left behind by one glacier or another. I usually don't pay attention to such things, but I did that day. Along with my best friend, I stared at the mountain and wondered how old it was. That's the thing: the world is old. Ancient. And humans are so temporary. But who wants to think about such things? Who wants to feel small?

"I'm getting bored," I said.

"It's beautiful up here," he said. "So green and golden."

"Yeah, whatever, Robert Frost. Now tell me why we're here."

He looked me in the eye. Stared at me for a long time. *Regarded* me.

"What?" I said, and laughed, uncomfortable as hell.

"I'm a fag," he said.

"What?" I said, and laughed.

"I'm a fag," he repeated.

"That's not funny," I said, and laughed again.

"It's kind of funny."

"Okay, yeah, it's a little funny, but it's not true."

"Yes, it is. I am a fag."

I looked into his eyes. I stared at him for a long time. I *regarded* him.

"You're telling the truth," I said.

"Yeah."

"You're a fag."

"Yeah."

"Wow."

"That's all you have to say?"

"What else am I supposed to say?" I asked.

"I was hoping you would say more than 'Wow.'"

"Well, 'Wow' is all I got."

"Damn," he said. "And I had this all planned out."

He'd been thinking about coming out to me, his unveiling, for months. At first, he'd thought about telling me while we were engaged in some overtly masculine activity, like shouting out "I'm gay!" while we were butchering a hog. Or whispering, "I'm a really good shot—for a homosexual," while we were duck hunting. Or saying, "After I'm done with Sally's vagina, it's penis and scrotum from now on," as we were screwing twin sisters in their living room.

"I'm not gay," I said.

"I know."

"I'm just saying it, so it's out there, I'm not gay. Not at all."

"Jeez, come on, I'm not interested in you like that," he said. "I'm gay, but I'm not blind."

"That's funny," I said, but I didn't laugh. I was pissed. I felt betrayed. I'd been his best friend since we were five years old, and he'd never told me how he felt. He'd never told me who he was. He'd lied to me all those years. It made me wonder what else he had lied about. After all, don't liars tell lies about everything? And sure, maybe he'd lied to protect himself from hatred and judgment. And, yes, maybe he lied because he was scared of my reaction. But a lie is a lie, right? And lying is contagious.

"You're a liar," I said.

"I know," he said, and cried.

"Ah, man," I said, "don't cry."

And then I realized how many times I'd said that to girls, to *naked* girls. I mean, don't get me wrong. I'd seen him cry before—we'd wept together at baseball games and funerals—but not in that particular context.

"I'm getting sick to my stomach," I said, which made him cry all that much harder. It felt like I was breaking up with him or something.

Maybe I wasn't being fair. But all you ever hear about are gay people's feelings. What about the feelings of the gay people's friends and family? Nobody talks about our rights. Maybe people are born gay, okay? I can deal with that, but maybe some people, like me, are born afraid of gay people. Maybe that fear is encoded in my DNA.

"I'm not gay," I said.

"Stop saying that," he said.

But I couldn't help it. I had to keep saying it. I was scared. I wondered if I was gay and didn't know it. After all, I was best friends with a fag, and he'd seen me naked. I'd seen him naked so often I could have described him to a police sketch artist. It was crazy.

"I can't take this," I said, and got out of the car. I walked over to a picnic bench and sat.

Jeremy stayed in the car and stared through the windshield at me. He wanted my love, my sweet, predictable, platonic love, the same love I'd given to him for so many years. He'd chosen me as his confessor. I was supposed to be sacred for him. But I felt like God had put a shotgun against my head and pulled the trigger. I was suddenly Hamlet, and all the uses of the world were weary, stale, flat, and unprofitable.

Jeremy stared at me. He waited for me to take action. And yes, you can condemn me for my inaction and fear. But I was only sixteen years old. Nobody had taught me how to react in such a situation. I was young and terrified and I could not move. Jeremy waited for several long minutes. I sat still, so he gave me the finger and shouted, "Fuck off!" I gave him the finger and shouted, "Fuck off!" And then Jeremy drove away.

I sat there for a few hours, bewildered. Yes, I was bewildered. When was the last time a white American male was truly bewildered or would admit to such a thing? We had taken the world from covered wagons to space shuttles in seventy-five years. After such accomplishment, how could we ever get lost in the wilderness again? How could we not invent a device to guide our souls through the darkness?

I prayed to Our Father and I called my father. And one father remained silent and the other quickly came to get me.

In that North Bend parking lot, in his staid sedan, my father trembled with anger. "What the hell are you doing up here?" he asked. He'd left a meeting with the lame-duck mayor to rescue me.

"Jeremy drove me up."

"And where is Jeremy?"

"We got in a fight. He left."

"You got into a fight?" my father asked. "What are you, a couple of girls?"

"Jeremy is a fag," I said.

"What?"

"Jeremy told me he's a fag."

"Are you homosexual?" my father asked.

I laughed.

"This is not funny," he said.

"No, it's just that word, *homosexual;* it's a goofy word."

"You haven't answered the question."

"What question?"

"Are you homosexual?"

I knew that my father still loved me, that he was still my defender. But I wondered how strong he would defend me if I were indeed gay.

"Dad, I'm not a fag. I promise."

"Okay."

"Okay."

We sat there in silence. A masculine silence. Thick and strong. Oh, I'm full of shit. We were terrified and clueless.

"Okay, Dad, what happens next?"

"I was hoping to tell you this at a better time, but I'm going to run for the State House."

"Oh, wow," I said. "Congratulations."

"I'm happy you're happy. I hated to make the decision without your input, but it had to be that way."

"I understand."

"Yes, I knew you would. And I hope you understand a few other things."

And so my father, who'd never been comfortable with my private school privilege, transferred me from Madison Park to Garfield High, a racially mixed public school in a racially mixed neighborhood.

Let my father tell you why: "The Republican Party has, for decades, silently ignored the pernicious effects of racial segregation, while simultaneously resisting any public or private efforts at integration. That time has come to an end. I am a Republican, and I love my fellow Americans, regardless of race, color, or creed. But, of course, you've heard that before. Many Republicans have issued that same kind of lofty statement while living lives entirely separate from people of other races, other classes, and other religions. Many Republicans have lied to you. And many Democrats have told you those same lies. But I will not lie, in word or deed. I have just purchased a house in the historically black Central District neighborhood of Seattle, and my son will attend Garfield High School. I am moving because I believe in action. And I am issuing a challenge to my fellow Republicans and to all Democrats, as well: Put your money, and your house, where your mouth is."

And so my father, who won the state seat with 62 percent of the vote, moved me away from Jeremy, who also left Madison Park and was homeschooled by his mother. Over the next year or so, I must have called his house twenty times. But I always hung up when he or his parents answered. And he called my private line more than twenty times, but would stay on the line and silently wait for me to speak. And then it stopped. We became rumors to each other.

Five hours after I punched Jeremy in the face, I sat alone in the living room of my childhood home in Seattle. Bernard, Spence, and Eddie were gone. I felt terrible. I prayed that I would be forgiven. No, I didn't deserve forgiveness. I prayed that I would be fairly judged. So I called the fairest man I know—my father—and told him what I had done.

The sun was rising when my father strode alone into the room and slapped me: once, twice, three times.

"Shit," he said, and stepped away.

I wiped the blood from my mouth.

"Shit," my father said once more, stepped up close to me, and slapped me again.

I was five inches taller, thirty years younger, and forty pounds heavier than my father and could have easily stopped him from hitting me. I could have hurt him. But I knew that I deserved his anger. A good son, I might have let him kill me. And, of course, I know that you doubt me. But I believe in justice. And I was a criminal who deserved punishment.

"What did you do?" my father asked.

"I don't know," I said. "I was drunk and stupid and—I don't know what happened."

"This is going to ruin everything. You've ruined me with this, this *thing*, do you understand that?"

"No, it's okay. I'll confess to it. It's all my fault. Nobody will blame you."

"Of course they'll blame me. And they *should* blame me. I'm your father."

"You're a great father."

"No, I'm not. I can't be. What kind of father could raise a son who is capable of such a thing?"

I wanted to rise up and tell my father the truth, that his son was a bloody, bawdy villain. A remorseless, treacherous, lecherous, kindless villain. But such sad and selfish talk is reserved for one's own ears. So I insulted myself with a silence that insulted my father as well.

"Don't just sit there," he said. "You can't just sit there. You have to account for yourself."

My father had always believed in truth, and in the real and vast differences between good and evil. But he'd also taught me, as he had learned, that each man is as fragile and finite as any other.

On the morning of September 11, 2001, my father prayed aloud for the victims. All day, the media worried that the body count might reach twenty or thirty thousand, so my father's prayers were the most desperate of his life. But, surprisingly, my father also prayed for the nineteen men who'd attacked us. He didn't pray for their forgiveness or redemption. No, he believed they were going to burn in a real hell. After all, what's the point of a metaphorical hell? But my father was compassionate and Christian enough to know that those nineteen men, no matter how evil their actions and corrupt their souls, could have been saved.

This is what my father taught me on that terrible day: "We are tested, all of us. We are constantly and consistently given the choice. Good or evil. Light or darkness. Love or hate. Some of those decisions are huge and tragic. Think of those nineteen men and you must curse them. But you must also curse their mothers and fathers. Curse their brothers and sisters. Curse their teachers and priests. Curse everybody who failed them. I pray for those nineteen men because I believe that some part of them, the original sliver of God that still resided in them, was calling out for guidance, for goodness and beauty. I pray for them because they chose evil and thus became evil, and I pray for them because nobody taught them how to choose goodness and become good."

Of course, my father, being a politician, could never have uttered those words in public. His supporters would not have understood the difference between empathy for a lost soul and sympathy with a terrorist's politics. Make no mistake: My father was no moral relativist. He wanted each criminal to be judged by his crimes, not by his motivations or biography.

My father refused to believe that all cultures were equal. He believed that representative democracy was a God-given gift to humans.

"I think that our perfect God will protect us in a perfect afterlife," he was fond of saying in public. "But in this highly imperfect world, we highly imperfect humans need to be protected from one another, and only a progressive republican government can guarantee any sort of protection."

In private, my father said this: "Fuck the fucking leftists and their fucking love of secularism and communism. Those bastards haven't yet figured out that the secular Hitler and the communist Stalin slaughtered millions and millions of people."

Don't get me wrong. My father knew that the world was complicated and unpredictable—and that only God knew the ultimate truth—but he also knew that each citizen of that world was ultimately responsible for his actions. My father staked his political career, his entire life, on one basic principle: An unpredictable world demands a predictable moral code.

"Son," my father said to me many a time in the years after September 11, "a thief should be judged by the theft. A rapist should be judged by the rape. A murderer should be judged by the murder. A terrorist should be judged by the terror."

And so I sat, a man capable of inexplicable violence against an innocent, eager to be judged by my God and by my father. I wanted to account and be held accountable.

"I'm sorry," I said. "I shouldn't have attacked those men. I shouldn't have walked away from the scene. At least, I should have gone back to the scene. I should go back now and turn myself in to the police."

"But you're not telling me why you did it," my father said. "Can you tell me that? Why did you do it?"

I searched my soul for an answer and could not find one. I could not make sense of it. But if I'd known that it was Jeremy I'd assaulted, I could have spoken about Cain and Abel and let my father determine the moral of the story.

"Spence and Eddie—"

"No," my father interrupted. "This is not about them. This is about you."

"Okay," I said. "I'm really confused here, Dad. I'm trying to do the right thing. And I need you to help me. Tell me what the right thing is. Tell me what I'm supposed to do."

And so my father told me what he had learned from confidential sources. The gay men had reported the assault but, obviously shocked and confused, had provided conflicting descriptions of Spence, Eddie, and Bernard and no description of me other than "white male, twenties to thirties, five-eight to six feet, one-eighty to two hundred pounds." In other words, I could have been almost any Caucasian guy in Seattle. The victims didn't catch the license plate of the suspects' car and could only describe it as a "dark four-door." There were no other witnesses to the assault as of yet. Most curious, the victims disagreed on whether or not the perpetrators brandished guns.

"What do the police think?" I asked.

"They think the victims are hiding something," my father said.

"They're just scared and freaked out."

"No. I agree with the police. I think they're hiding something."

"No, they're not hiding anything, Dad. They're just confused. I'd be confused if somebody attacked me like that."

"No, they're hiding the fact that they started the fight and they don't want the police to know it."

I was shocked. Was this really my father or his lying twin? Was I talking to my father or his murderous brother?

"Listen," he said. "I don't think the police really have anything to go on. And I don't think they're going to pursue this much further. But we're going to monitor the investigation very closely. And we're going to be preemptive if we sense any real danger."

"What are you talking about? Are you going to hurt them?"

More enraged than ever before, my father grabbed me by the shirt. "Don't you say such things. Don't you dare! This is the United States of America, not some third world shit heap! I am not in the business of intimidation or violence. I am not in the business of murder."

It was true. My father believed in life, the sacred spark of humans, more strongly than any other man I'd ever known. As a Republican, he was predictably antiabortion, but he was also against capital punishment. His famous speech: "It is the business of man to judge and punish on this mortal Earth; but it is the business of God to give and take away life. I believe that abortion is a great evil, but it is just as evil to abandon any child to the vagaries of economics. I believe it is evil to murder another human being, but it is just as evil for a government to kill its citizens based on the vagaries of justice."

Yes, this was the man I had accused of conspiracy. I had insulted my father. I'd questioned his honor. I'd deemed him capable of murder. He was right to shake me.

"I'm sorry," I said. "I'm sorry. I'm just confused. Help me. Please, Daddy, help me. I love you. Please, please help me."

And so he held me while I wept.

"I love you, son," he said. "But you have to listen to me. You have to understand. I know that you were wrong to do what you did. It was a mortal sin. You sinned against God, against those men, and against me. And you should pay for those sins."

My good father wanted me to be a good man.

"But it's not that easy," my father said. "If you turn yourself in to the police, I will also pay for your sins. And I know I should pay for your sins because I am your father, and I have obviously failed to raise you well. But I will also pay for your sins as a U.S. senator, so our state and country will also pay for them. A scandal like this will ruin my career. It will ruin our party. And it will ruin our country. And though I know I will be judged harshly by God, I can't let you tell the truth."

My father wanted me to lie. No, he was forcing me to lie.

"William, Willy," he said. "If we begin to suspect that you might be implicated in this, we're going to go on the offensive. We're going to kill their reputations."

If it is true that children pay for the sins of their fathers, is it also true that fathers pay for the sins of their children?

Three days later, I returned to my condominium in downtown Seattle and found a message waiting on my voice mail.

"Hey, William, it's—um, me, Jeremy. You really need to call me."

And so I called Jeremy and agreed to meet him at his house in Magnolia, an upper-class neighborhood of Seattle. It was a small but lovely house, painted blue and chocolate.

I rang the doorbell. Jeremy answered. His face and nose were swollen purple, yellow, and black; his eyes were bloodshot and tear-filled.

"It was you," I said, suddenly caught in an inferno of shame.

"Of course it was me. Get your ass in here."

Inside, we sat in his study, a modernist room decorated with beautiful and useless furniture. What good is a filing cabinet that can only hold an inch of paperwork?

"I'm so sorry, Jeremy," I said. "I didn't know it was you."

"Oh, so I'm supposed to be happy about that? Things would be okay if you'd beaten the shit out of a fag you didn't know?"

"That's not what I meant."

"Okay, then, what did you mean?"

"I was wrong to do what I did. Completely wrong."

"Yes, you were," he said.

He was smiling. I recognized that smile. Jeremy was giving me shit. Was he going to torture me before he killed me?

"Why didn't you tell the police it was me?" I asked.

"Because the police don't give a shit about fags."

"But we assaulted you. We could have killed you."

"Doubtful. James had already kicked the crap out of your friends. And he would have kicked the crap out of you and the guy with the tire iron. Let's just call it a split decision."

"You didn't tell James it was me, did you?"

"No, of course not. I told the police a completely different story than James did. And I was the one with the broken face, so they believed me."

"But what about James? What's he going to do?"

"Oh, who cares? I barely knew him."

"But it was a hate crime."

"Aren't all crimes, by definition, hate crimes? I mean, people don't rob banks because they love tellers."

"I don't understand you. Why haven't you gone public with this? You could destroy my father. And me."

Jeremy sighed.

"Oh, William," he said. "You're still such an adolescent. And so romantic. I haven't turned you in because I'm a Republican, a good one, and I think your father is the finest senator we've ever had. I used to think he was a closet Democrat. But he's become something special. This kind of shit would completely fuck his chance at the presidency."

Jesus, was this guy more a son to my father than I was?

"And, okay, maybe I'm a romantic, too," Jeremy said. "I didn't turn you in because we were best friends and because I still consider you my best friend."

"But my father hates gay people."

"It's more complicated than that."

And so Jeremy explained to me that his sexual preference had nothing to do with his political beliefs.

"Hey," he said. "I don't expect to be judged negatively for my fuck buddies. But I don't want to be judged positively, either. It's just sex. It's not like it's some specialized skill or something. Hell, right now, in this house, one hundred thousand bugs are fucking away. In this city, millions of bugs are fucking at this very moment. And, hey, probably ten thousand humans—and registered voters—are fucking somewhere in this city. Four or five of them might even be married."

"So what's your point?"

"Anybody who thinks that sex somehow relates to the national debt or terrorism or poverty or crime or moral values or any kind of politics is just an idiot."

"Damn, Jeremy, you've gotten hard."

"That's what all the boys say."

"And what does James say? What if he goes to the press? What if he sees my face in the newspapers or on TV and recognizes me?"

"James is a little fag coffee barista from Bumfuck, Idaho. Nobody cares what he has to say. Little James could deliver a Martian directly to the White House and people would think it was a green poodle with funny ears."

I wondered if I'd completely scrambled Jeremy's brains when I punched him in the head.

"Will you listen to me?" I said. "My father will destroy your life if he feels threatened."

"Did you know your father called my father that day up in North Bend?" Jeremy asked.

"What day?" I asked. But I knew.

"Don't be obtuse. After I told you I was gay, you told your father, and your father told my father. And my father beat the shit out of me."

"You're lying," I said. But I knew he wasn't.

"You think my face looks bad now? Oh, man, my dad broke my cheekbone. Broke my arm. Broke my leg. A hairline fracture of the skull. A severe concussion. I saw double for two months."

"How come you didn't go to the police?"

"Oh, my dad took me to the police. Said a gang of kids did it to me. Hoodlums, he called them."

"How come you didn't tell the police the truth?"

"Because my dad said he'd kill my mom if I told the truth."

"I don't think I believe any of this."

"You can believe what you want. I know what happened. My father beat the shit out of me because he was ashamed of me. And I let him because I was ashamed of myself. And because I loved my mom."

I stared at him. Could he possibly be telling the truth? Are there truths as horrible as this one? In abandoning him when he was sixteen, did I doom him to a life with a violent father and a beaten mother?

"But you know the best thing about all of this?" he asked.

I couldn't believe there'd be any good in this story.

"When my father was lying in his hospital bed, he asked for me," Jeremy said. "Think about it. My father was dying of cancer. And he called for me. He needed me to forgive him. And you know what?"

"What?" I asked, though I didn't want to know.

"I went into his room, hugged him and told him I forgave him and I loved him, and we cried and then he died."

"I can't believe any of this."

"It's all true."

"You forgave your father?" I asked.

"Yeah," Jeremy said. "It really made me wish I was Roman or Greek, you know? A classical Greek god would have killed his lying, cheating father and *then* given him forgiveness. And a classical Greek god would have better abs, too. That's what Greek gods are all about, you know? Patricide and low body fat."

How could anybody be capable of that much forgiveness? I was reminded of the black man, the convicted rapist, who'd quietly proclaimed his innocence all during his thirty years in prison. After he was exonerated by DNA evidence and finally freed, that black man completely forgave the white woman who'd identified him as her rapist. He said he forgave her because it would do him no good to carry that much anger in his heart. I often wonder if that man was Jesus come back.

"The thing is, Willy," Jeremy said, "you've always been such a moral guy. Six years old, and you made sure that everybody got equal time on the swings, on the teeter-totter, on the baseball field. Even the losers. And you learned that from your father."

"My father is a great man," I said, but I wasn't sure I believed it. I had to believe it, though, or my foundations would collapse.

"No," Jeremy said. "Your father has great ideas, but he's an ordinary man, just like all of us. No, your father is more of an asshole than usual. He likes to hit people."

"He's only hit me a couple of times."

"That you can remember."

"What does that mean?"

"We wouldn't practice denial if it didn't work."

"Fuck you," I said.

"Oh, you're scary. What are you going to do, punch me in the face?"

We laughed.

"It comes down to this," Jeremy said. "You can't be a great father and a great politician at the same time. Impossible. Can't be a great father and a great writer, either. Just ask Hemingway's kids."

"I prefer Faulkner."

"Yeah, there's another candidate for Father of the Year."

"Okay, okay, writers are bad dads. What's your point?"

"Your father is great because of his ideas. And those great ideas will make him a great president."

"Why do you believe in him so much?"

"It's about sacrifice. Listen, I am a wealthy American male. I can't campaign for something as silly and fractured as gay marriage when there are millions of Muslim women who can't even show their ankles. Your daddy knows that. Everybody knows it."

"I don't know anything."

"I hate to sound like a campaign worker or something, but listen to me. I believe in him so much that I'll pay ten bucks for a gallon of gas. I believe in him so much that I'm going to let you go free."

I wondered if Jeremy had been beaten so often that it had destroyed his spirit. Had he lost the ability to defend himself? How many times could he forgive the men who had bloodied and broken him? Is there a finite amount of forgiveness in the world? Was there a point after which forgiveness, even the most divinely inspired, is simply the act of a coward? Or has forgiveness always been used as political capital?

"Jeremy," I asked, "what am I supposed to do with all this information?"

"That's up to you, sweetheart."

Oh, there are more things in heaven and earth than can be explained by *Meet the Press*.

Jeremy and I haven't talked since that day. We agreed that our friendship was best left abandoned in the past. My crime against him was also left in the past. As expected, the police did not pursue the case, and it was soon filed away. There was never any need to invent a story.

I cannot tell you what happened to James, or to Eddie and Spence, or to Bernard. We who shared the most important moment of our lives no longer have any part in the lives of the others. It happens that way. I imagine that someday one of them might try to tell the whole story. And I imagine nobody would believe them. Who would believe any of them? Or me? Has a liar ever told the truth?

As for my father, he lost his reelection bid and retired to the relatively sad life of an ex-senator. He plays golf three times a week. State leaders beg for his advice.

My father and I have never again discussed that horrible night. We have no need or right to judge each other for sins that might have already doomed us to a fiery afterlife. Instead, we both silently forgave each other, and separately and loudly pray to God for his forgiveness. I'll let you know how that works out.

ANOTHER PROCLAMATION

When
Lincoln
Delivered
The
Emancipation
Proclamation,
Who
Knew

that, one year earlier, in 1862, he'd signed and approved the
order for the largest public execution in United States history?
Who did they execute? "Mulatto, mixed-bloods, and Indians."
Why did they execute them? "For uprisings against the State
and her citizens." Where did they execute them? Mankato,
Minnesota. How did they execute them? Well, Abraham Lincoln thought it was good

And
Just
To
Hang
Thirty-eight
Sioux

simultaneously. Yes, in front of a large and cheering crowd, thirty-eight Indians dropped to their deaths. Yes, thirty-eight necks snapped. But before they died, thirty-eight Indians sang their death songs. Can you imagine the cacophony of thirty-eight different death songs? But wait, one Indian was pardoned at the last minute, so only thirty-seven Indians had to sing their death songs. But, O, O, O, O, can you imagine the cacophony of that one survivor's mourning song? If he taught you the words, do you think you would sing along?

———

Invisible Dog on a Leash

1.

In 1973, my father and I saw *Enter the Dragon*, the greatest martial arts movie of all time. I loved Bruce Lee. I wanted to be Bruce Lee. Afterward, as we walked to our car, I threw punches and kicks at the air.

"Hey, Dad," I asked, "is Bruce Lee the toughest guy in the world?"

My father said, "No way. There are five guys in Spokane who could probably kick Bruce Lee's ass."

"Really? You mean in a fair fistfight and everything?"

"Who said anything about fair? And who'd want to throw punches with Bruce Lee? I'm not talking about fists. I'm saying there are at least five guys in Spokane who, if they even saw Bruce Lee, they'd walk up to him and just sucker punch him with a baseball bat or a two-by-four or something."

"That's not right."

"You didn't ask me about right. You asked me about tough."

"Are you tougher than Bruce Lee?"

"Well, I'm tough in some ways, I guess. But I'm not the kind of guy who will knock somebody in the head with a baseball bat. I'm not going to do that to Bruce Lee. But let me tell you, there are more than five guys in Spokane who would do that. As I'm thinking more and more about it, I'm thinking there are probably fifty crazy guys who'd sneak up behind Bruce Lee at a restaurant and just knock him out with a big frying pan or something."

"Okay, Dad, that's enough."

"And I haven't even talked about prison dudes. Shoot, every other guy in prison would be happy to sucker punch Bruce Lee. They'd wait in a dark corner for a week, just waiting to ambush Bruce Lee with a chain saw or something. Man, those prison guys aren't going to mess around with a Jeet Kune Do guy like Bruce Lee. No way. Those prison dudes would build a catapult and fling giant boulders at Bruce Lee."

"Okay, Dad, I believe you. I've heard enough. Stop it, Dad, stop it!"

"Okay, Okay, I'm sorry. I'm just telling you the truth."

2.

On TV, Uri Geller was bending spoons
With just his mind. "Wow," I said. "That's so cool."

Then, three days later, as I browsed through Rick's
Pawn Shop, I picked up a book of magic tricks

And learned how to bend spoons almost as well.
I called my act URI GELLER IS GOING TO HELL.

3.

At Expo '74, in Spokane, I saw my first invisible dog on a leash. A hilarious and agile Chinese man was selling them.

"My dog is fast," he said. And his little pet, in its leash and harness, dragged him across the grass. I thought it was real magic. I didn't know it was just an illusion. I didn't know that thick and flexible wires had been threaded through the leash and harness and then shaped to look like a dog—an invisible dog. In fact, I didn't discover the truth until two years later at our tribe's powwow, when a felonious-looking white man tried to sell me an invisible dog with a broken leash. Without a taut leash, that invisible dog didn't move or dance in its harness. The magic was gone. I was an emotional kid, so I started to cry, and the felonious dude said, "Shit, kid, take it, I found it in the garbage anyway."

4.

In '76, I also saw the remake of *King Kong*. It was terrible. Even my father, who loved the worst drive-in exploitation crap, said, "It's Kong, man. What went so wrong?" But that does remind me of a drive-in flick whose name I can't recall. It's about a herd of Sasquatch who sneak into a biker gang's house and kidnap all of the biker women. Later, the biker gang puts spiked wheels on their rods, roars into the woods, somehow finds the Sasquatch, and battles for the women. As the Sasquatch fight and fall and pretend to die, two or three of them lose their costume heads. Their furry masks just go sailing but the actors playing Sasquatch, and the other actors, and the director, and the writer, and the producers, and God just keep on going as if it didn't matter. And I suppose, for the sake of budget, it *didn't* matter, but I stood on the top of our van and shouted, "It's not real. It's not real. It's not real. It's not real!" And some politically aware but unseen dude shouted from out of the dark, "Okay, Little Crazy Horse, we know it's not real, so get your ass back in your van."

5.

Speaking of Sasquatch, I met the love of my life in 1979, in Redding, California, the heart of Bigfoot Country. Okay, she wasn't the love of my life, she just happened to be the first world-class beauty I'd ever seen. Honestly. She could have been on the cover of *Glamour* magazine. But she was just a teenage girl from Redding, California, which, like I said, was the heart of Bigfoot Country. And I was obsessed with Bigfoot, with the real Sasquatch, not the fake biker-gang-fighting and biker-chick-kidnapping type. So, as this gorgeous girl asked me what I wanted (my family had stopped to eat at some fast-food joint on our way to Disneyland), I said, "Isn't it cool to live in Bigfoot Country? In the heart of Bigfoot Country. In the heart of the heart of Bigfoot Country."

"Oh," she said. "That stuff ain't real. It's my two uncles— Little Jim and Big Jim—who make all those footprints with these big wooden feet they carved out and tie up on their boots."

"What?"

"Yeah. If you've ever seen that movie *Planet of the Apes*, you've seen my uncles, because they played gorillas."

"Are you kidding?"

"No, my uncles used to work at the San Francisco Zoo when they were in college. They helped feed the gorillas and monkeys and chimps and stuff. So they really learned how to walk around like apes. But those Hollywood people didn't appreciate them, you know? Didn't pay them hardly anything for being in that first *Planet* movie. So my uncles didn't work on any of the sequels."

"I can't believe what I'm hearing."

"Well, it's all true. You can even go visit my uncles if you want. They've got a bunch of those fake Bigfoot feet you can buy. And if you tell them I sent you over, they'll even show you their Bigfoot costumes."

"They have costumes?"

"Yeah, and you will not believe how much those costumes look like a real Bigfoot. It was Big Jim who was playing Bigfoot in that famous movie. You've seen that one, right? The one where Bigfoot is walking across the riverbed? Yeah, whenever I see that video on TV, I scream, "Hey, Uncle Big Jim!" Anyway, I have to remember my job. What do you want to eat, little man?"

"A corn dog, I guess."

6.

O, the '70s broke my heart. No,
The '70s broke my heart's ass.

HOME OF THE BRAVES

When my female friends are left
By horrid spouses and lovers,
I commiserate. I send gifts—
Powwow songs and poems—and wonder

Why my gorgeous friends cannot find
Someone who knows them as I do.
Is the whole world deaf and blind?
I tell my friends, "I'd marry you

Tomorrow." I think I'm engaged
To thirty-six women, my harem:
Platonic, bookish, and enraged.
I love them! But it would scare them—

No, of course, they already know
That I can be just one more boy,
A toy warrior who explodes
Into silence and warpaths with joy.

THE BALLAD OF
PAUL NONETHELESS

In Chicago's O'Hare Airport, walking east on a moving sidewalk, Paul saw a beautiful woman walking west. She'd pulled her hair back into a messy ponytail, and her blue jeans were dark-rinsed boot-cut, and her white T-shirt was a size too small, and her pale arms were muscular. And—ah, she wore a pair of glorious red shoes. Pumas. Paul knew those shoes. He'd seen them in an ad in a fashion magazine, or maybe on an Internet site, and fallen in love with them. Allegedly an athletic shoe, the red Pumas were really a thing of beauty. On any woman, they'd be lovely; on this woman, they were glorious. Who knew that Paul would someday see those shoes on a woman's feet and feel compelled to pursue her?

Paul wanted to shout out, *I love your Pumas!* He wanted to orate it with all the profundity and passion of a Shakespearean couplet, but that seemed too eccentric and desperate and—well, literate. He wanted the woman to know he was instantly but ordinarily attracted to her, so he smiled and waved instead. But bored with her beauty, or more likely bored with the men who noticed her beauty, she ignored Paul and rolled her baggage on toward the taxi or parking shuttle or town car.

"'She's gone, she's gone.'" Paul sang the chorus of that Hall & Oates song. He sang without irony, for he was a twenty-first-century American who'd been taught to mourn his small and large losses by singing Top 40 hits.

There was a rule book: When a man is rebuffed by a beautiful stranger he must sing blue-eyed soul; when a man is drunk with the loneliness of being a frequent flyer he must sing Mississippi Delta blues; when a man wants revenge he must whistle the sound track of *The Good, the Bad, and the Ugly*. When a man's father and mother die within three months of each other, he must sing Rodgers and Hammerstein: "Oklahoma! Oklahoma Okay!"

Despite all the talk of diversity and division—of red and blue states, of black and white and brown people, of rich and poor, gay and straight—Paul believed that Americans were shockingly similar. How can we be so different, thought Paul, if we all know the lyrics to the same one thousand songs? Paul knew the same lyrics as any random guy from Mobile, Alabama, or woman from Orono, Maine. Hell, Paul had memorized, without effort or ever purchasing or downloading one of their CDs—or even one of their songs—the complete works of Garth Brooks, Neil Diamond, and AC/DC. And if words and music can wind their way into and around our DNA strands—and Paul believed they could—wouldn't American pop music be passed from generation to generation as easily as blue eyes or baldness? Hadn't pop music created a new and invisible organ, a pituitary gland of the soul, in the American body? Or were these lies and exaggerations? Could one honestly say that Elvis is a more important figure in American history than Einstein? Could one posit that Aretha Franklin's version of "Respect" was more kinetic and relevant to American life than Dwight D. Eisenhower's 1961 speech that warned us about the dangers of a military-industrial complex? Could a reasonable person think that Madonna's "Like a Prayer" was as integral and universal to everyday life as the fork or wheel? Paul believed all these heresies about pop music but would never say them aloud for fear of being viewed as a less-than-serious person.

Or wait, maybe Paul wasn't a serious person. Maybe he was an utterly contemporary and callow human being. Maybe he was an American ironic. Maybe he was obsessed with pop music because it so perfectly reflected his current desires. And yet, Paul sold secondhand clothes for a living. He owned five vintage clothing stores in the Pacific Northwest and was currently wearing a gray tweed three-piece suit once owned by Gene Kelly. So Paul was certainly not addicted to the present day. On the contrary, Paul believed that the present, past, and future were all happening simultaneously, and that any era's pop culture was *his* pop culture. And sure, pop culture could be crass and manipulative, and sometimes evil, but it could also be magical and redemptive.

Take Irving Berlin, for example. He was born Israel Baline in Russia in 1888, emigrated with his family in 1893 to the United States, and would eventually write dozens, if not hundreds, of classic tunes, including, most famously, "Alexander's Ragtime Band." Yes, it was a Russian Jew who wrote the American love song that suggested we better hurry and meander at the same time. Can a person simultaneously hurry and meander? Yes, in the United States a romantic is, by definition, a person filled with those contradictions. And, the romantic American is in love with his contradictions. And the most romantic Americans (see Walt Whitman) want to have contradictory sex. Walt Whitman would have wanted to have sex with Irving Berlin. Paul loved Irving Berlin and Walt Whitman. He loved the thought of their sexual union. And most of all, Paul loved the fact that Irving Berlin had lived a long and glorious life and died in 1989, only sixteen years earlier.

Yes, Irving Berlin was still alive in 1989. It's quite possible that Irving Berlin voted for Michael Dukakis for United States president. How can you not love a country and a culture where that kind of beautiful insanity can flourish? But wait—did any of this really matter anyway? Was it just the musical trivia of a trivial man in a trivial country? And beyond all that, why was Paul compelled to defend his obsessions? Why was he forced to define and self-define? After all, one doesn't choose his culture nearly as much as one trips and falls into it.

Splat! Paul was a forty-year-old man from Seattle, Washington, who lived only ten minutes from the house where Kurt Cobain shotgunned himself, and only fifteen minutes from the stretch of Jackson Street where Ray Charles and Quincy Jones began their careers in bygone jazz clubs. *Splat!* Paul's office, and the headquarters of his small used-clothes empire, was down the street from a life-size statue of Jimi Hendrix ripping an all-weather solo. *Splat!* Paul bought his morning coffee at the same independent joint where a dozen of Courtney Love's bounced checks decorated the walls.

Paul believed American greatness and the ghosts of that greatness surrounded him. But who could publicly express such a belief and not be ridiculed as a patriotic fool? Paul believed in his fellow Americans, in their extraordinary decency, in their awesome ability to transcend religion, race, and class, but what leftist could state such things and ever hope to get laid by any other lefty? And yet Paul was the perfect example of American possibility: He made a great living (nearly $325,000 the previous tax year) by selling secondhand clothes.

For God's sake, Paul was flying to Durham, North Carolina, for a denim auction. A Baptist minister had found one hundred pairs of vintage Levi's (including one pair dating back to the nineteenth century that was likely to fetch $25,000 or more!) in his father's attic, and was selling them to help raise money for the construction of a new church. Blue jeans for God! Blue jeans for Jesus! Blue Jeans for the Holy Ghost!

Used clothes for sale! Used clothes for sale! That was Paul's capitalistic war cry. That was his mating song.

Thus unhinged and aroused, Paul turned around and ran against the moving sidewalk. He chased after the beautiful woman—in her gorgeous red Pumas—who had rebuffed him. He wanted to tell her everything that he believed about his country. No, he just wanted to tell her that music—pop music—was the most important thing in the world. He would show her the top twenty-five songs played on his iPod, and she'd have sex with him in the taxi or parking shuttle or town car.

And there she was, on the escalator above him, with her perfect jeans and powerful yoga thighs. Paul could hear her denim singing friction ballads across her skin. Paul couldn't remember the last time he'd had sex with a woman who wore red shoes. Paul dreamed of taking them off and taking a deep whiff. Ha! He'd instantly developed a foot fetish. He wanted to smell this woman's feet. Yes, that was the crazy desire in his brain and his crotch when he ran off the escalator and caught the woman outside of the security exit.

"Excuse me, I'm sorry, hello," Paul said.

She stared at him. She studied his face, wondering if she knew him, or if he was a gypsy cab driver, or if he was a creep.

"I saw you back there on the moving sidewalk," Paul said.

Wow, that was a stupid thing to say. That meant nothing. No, that meant Paul had noticed the lovely shapes of her green eyes, breasts, and ass—their mystical geometry—and that made him as ordinary, if slightly more mathematical, as any other man in the airport. He needed to say something extraordinary, something poetic, in order to make her see that he was capable of creating, well, extraordinary poetry. Could he talk about her shoes? Was that a convincing way to begin this relationship? Or maybe he could tell her that Irving Berlin's real name was Israel.

"I mean," Paul said, "well, I wanted to—well, the thing is, I saw you—no, I mean—well, I did see you, but it wasn't sight that made me chase after you, you know? I mean—it wasn't really any of my five senses that did it. It was something beyond that. You exist beyond the senses; I just know that without really knowing it, you know?"

She smiled. The teeth were a little crowded. The lines around her eyes were new. She was short, a little over five feet tall, and, ah, she wore those spectacular red shoes. If this didn't work out, Paul was going to run home and buy the DVD version of that movie about the ballerina's red dance slippers. Or was he thinking of the movie about the kid who lost his red balloon? Somewhere there must be a movie about a ballerina who ties her dance shoes to a balloon and watches them float away. *Jesus*, Paul said to himself. *Focus, focus.*

"You have a beautiful smile," Paul said to the stranger. "And if your name is Sara, I'm going to lose my mind."

"My name isn't Sara," she said. "Why would you think my name is Sara?"

"You know, great smile, name is Sara. 'Sara Smile'? The song by Hall and Oates."

"Oh, yeah, that's a good one."

"You've made me think of two Hall and Oates songs in, like, five minutes. I think that's a sign. Of what, I don't know, but a sign nonetheless."

"I think that's the first time I've ever heard a man say *nonetheless* in normal conversation."

Was she mocking him? Yes, she was. Was that a positive step in their relationship? Did it imply a certain familiarity or the desire for a certain familiarity? And, by the way, when exactly had he become the kind of man who uses *nonetheless* in everyday conversation?

"Listen," Paul said to the beautiful stranger. "I don't know you. And you don't know me. But I want to talk to you—and listen to you; that's even more important—I want to talk and listen to you for a few hours. I want to share stories. That's it. That's it exactly. I think you have important stories to tell. Stories I need to hear."

She laughed and shook her head. Did he amuse her? Or bemuse her? There was an important difference: Women sometimes slept with bemusing men, but they usually *married* amusing men.

"So, listen," Paul said. "I am perfectly willing to miss my flight and have coffee with you right here in the airport—and if that makes you feel vulnerable, just remember there are dozens of heavily armed security guards all around us—so, please, if you're inclined to spend some time with a complete but devastatingly handsome stranger, I would love your company."

"Well," she said. "You *are* cute. And I like your suit."

"It used to belong to Gene Kelly. He wore it in one of his movies."

"*Singin' in the Rain?*"

"No, one of the bad ones. When people talk about the golden age of Hollywood musicals, they don't realize that almost all of them were bad."

"Are you a musician?"

"Uh, no, I sell used clothes. Vintage clothes. But only the beautiful stuff, you know?"

"Like your suit."

"Yes, like my suit."

"Sounds like a cool job."

"It *is* a cool job. I have, like, one of the coolest lives ever. You should know that."

"I'm sure you are a very cool individual. But I'm married, and my husband is waiting for me at baggage claim."

"I don't want this to be a comment on the institution of marriage itself, which I believe in, but I want you to know that your marriage, while great for your husband and you, is an absolute tragedy for me. I'm talking Greek tragedy. I'm talking mothers-killing-their-children level of tragedy. If you listened to my heart, you'd hear that it just keeps beating *Medea, Medea, Medea*. And yes, I know the rhythm is off on that. Makes me sound like I have a heart murmur."

She laughed. He'd made her laugh three or four times since they'd met. He'd turned the avenging and murderous Medea into a sexy punch line. How many men could do that?

"Hey," she said. "Thank you for the—uh—attention. You've made my day. Really. But I must go. I'll see you in the next life."

She turned to leave, but then she paused—O, *che sarà!*—leaned in close to Paul, and gave him a soft kiss on the cheek. Then she laughed again and walked away. No, it wasn't just a walk. It was a magical act of transportation. Delirious, Paul watched her leave. He marveled at the gifts of strangers, at the way in which a five-minute relationship can be as gratifying and complete (and sexless!) as a thirteen-year marriage. Then he made his way back through security and to his gate, caught his flight to North Carolina, and bought a pair of 1962 Levi's for $1,250.

Of course, Paul was a liar, a cheater, and a thief. He'd pursued the beautiful airport stranger without giving much thought to his own marriage. And sure, he was separated, and his wife and three teenage daughters were living in the family home while Paul lived in a one-bedroom on Capitol Hill, but he was still married and wanted to remain married. He loved his wife, didn't he? Well, of course he did. She was lovely (was more than that, really) and smart and funny and all those things an attractive human being is supposed to be, and she in turn thought Paul was a lovely, smart, funny, and attractive human being. They had built a marriage based on their shared love of sixties soul music on vinyl—and vintage clothes, of course. Or perhaps

Paul had built this life and his wife had followed along. In any case, they were happy, extraordinarily happy, right? Jesus, it was easy to stay happy in a first-world democracy. What kind of madman would stay that long in an unhappy marriage, especially in an age when people divorced so easily? Yes, Paul loved his wife; he was in love with her. He was sure he could pass a lie-detector test on that one. And he loved his three daughters. He was more sure about that.

But if he was so happy, if he was so in love with his wife and daughters, why was he separated from them? Sadly, it was all about sex—or, rather, the lack of sex. Simply and crudely stated, Paul had lost the desire to fuck his wife. How had that happened? Paul didn't know, exactly. And he couldn't talk to anybody about it. How could he tell his friends, his circle of men, that he had no interest in sleeping with the sexiest woman any of them had ever met? She was so beautiful that she intimidated many of his friends. His best friend, Jacob, had once drunkenly confessed that he still couldn't look her directly in the eyes.

"I've known her, what, almost twenty years?" Jacob had said. "And I still have to look at her out of the corner of my eye. I'm the godfather to your daughters, and I have to talk to their mother with my sideways vision. You remember the time we all got drunk and naked in my hot tub? She was so amazing, so perfect, that I had to run around the corner and throw up. Your wife was so beautiful she made me sick. I hope you know how lucky you are, you lucky bastard."

Yes, Paul knew he was lucky: He had a great job, great daughters, and a great wife that he didn't want to fuck. And so he, the lucky bastard, had sex with every other possible part-ner. During his marriage, Paul had had sex with eight other women: two employees, three ex-girlfriends, two of his friends' wives, and a woman with one of the largest used-clothing stores on eBay.

After that last affair, a clumsy and incomplete coupling in a San Francisco apartment crowded with vintage sundresses and UPS boxes, Paul had confessed to his wife. Oh, no, he didn't confess to all his infidelities. That would have been too much. It would have been cruel. Instead, he only admitted to the one but carefully inserted details of the other seven, so that his confession would be at least fractionally honest. His wife had listened silently, packed him a bag, and kicked him out of the house. What was the last thing she'd said? "I can't believe you fucked somebody from eBay."

And so, for a year now, Paul had lived apart from his family. And had been working hard to win back their love. He'd been chaste while recourting his wife. But he was quite sure that she doubted his newly found fidelity—he traveled too damn much ever to be thought of as a good candidate for stability—and he'd heard from his daughters that a couple of men, handsome strangers, had come calling on his wife. He couldn't sleep some nights when he thought about other men's hands and cocks and mouths touching his wife. How strange, Paul thought, to be jealous of other men's lust for the woman who had only wanted, and had lost, her husband's lust. And stranger and more con-tradictory, Paul vanquished his jealousy by furiously mas-turbating while fantasizing about his dream wife fucking dream men. Feeling like a fool, but hard anyway, Paul stroked as other men—nightmares—pushed into his wife. And when those vision men came hard, Paul also came hard. Everybody was arched and twisted. And oh, Paul was afraid—terrified—of how good it felt. What oath, what marital vow, did he break by imagining his wife's infidelity? None, he supposed, but he felt primitive, like the first ape that fell from the high trees and, upon landing, decided to live upright, use tools, and evolve. *Dear wife,* Paul wanted to say, *I'm quite sure that you will despise me for these thoughts, and I respect your need to keep our lives private, to relock the doors of our home, but I, primal and vain, still need to boast about my fears and sins. Inside my cave, I build fires to scare away the ghosts and keep the local predators at bay, or perhaps I build fires to attract hungry carnivores. Could I be that dumb? Dear wife, watch me celebrate what I lack. I am as opposable as my thumbs.* Ah, Paul thought, who cares about the color of a man's skin when his true identity is much deeper—subterranean—and far more diverse and disturbing than the ethnicity of his mother and father? And yet, nobody had ever argued for the civil rights of contradictory masturbators. "Chances are," Paul often sang to himself while thinking of his marriage. "Chances are." And he was singing that song in a Los Angeles International Airport bookstore—on his way home from the largest flea market in Southern California—when he saw the beautiful stranger who had rebuffed him three months earlier at O'Hare.

"Hey," he said. "It's Sara Smile."

She looked up from the book she was skimming—some best-selling and clever book about the one hundred greatest movies ever made—and stared at Paul. She was puzzled at first, but then she remembered him.

"Hey," she said. "It's Nonetheless."

Paul was quite sure this was the first time in the history of English that the word *nonetheless* had caused a massive erection. He fought mightily against the desire to kiss the stranger hard on the mouth.

"Wow," she said. "This is surprising, huh?"

"I can't believe you remember me," Paul said.

"I can't believe it either," she said. Then she quickly set down the book she'd been browsing. "These airport books, you know? They're entertaining crap."

Her embarrassment was lovely.

"I don't underestimate the power of popular entertainment," Paul said.

"Oh, okay, I guess," she said. "Wait, no. Let me amend that. I actually have no idea what you're talking about."

"I guess I don't either," Paul said. "I was trying to impress you with some faux philosophy."

She smiled. Paul wanted to lick her teeth. Once again, she was wearing blue jeans and a white T-shirt. Why is it that some women can turn that simple outfit into royal garb? God, he wanted her. *Want, want, want.* Can you buy and sell *want* on eBay?

"Are you still married?" he asked.

She laughed.

"Damn," she said. "You're as obvious as a thirteen-year-old. When are you going to start pawing at my breasts?"

"It's okay that you're married," he said. "I'm married, too."

"Oh, well, now, you didn't mention that the last time we met."

She was teasing him again. Mocking. Insulting. But she was not walking away. She had remembered him, had remembered a brief encounter from months earlier, and she was interested in him, in his possibilities. Wasn't she?

"No, I didn't mention my marriage," he said. "But I didn't mention it because I'm not sure how to define it. Technically speaking, I'm separated."

"Are you separated because you like to hit on strangers in airports?" she asked.

Wow. How exactly was he supposed to respond to that? He supposed his answer was going to forever change his life. Or at least decide if this woman was going to have sex with him. But he was not afraid of rejection, so why not tell the truth?

"Strictly speaking," he said, "I am not separated because I hit on strangers in airports. In fact, I can't recall another time when I hit on anybody in an airport. I am separated because I cheated on my wife."

Paul couldn't read her expression. Was she impressed or disgusted by his honesty?

"Do you have kids?" she asked.

"Three daughters. Eighteen, sixteen, and fifteen. I am surrounded by women."

"So you cheated on your daughters, not just your wife?"

Yes, it was true. Paul hated to think of it that way. But he knew his betrayal of his wife was, in some primal way, the lesser crime. What kind of message was he sending to the world when he betrayed the young women—his offspring—who would carry his name—his DNA—into the future?

"Yes," Paul said. "I cheated on my daughters. And that's pathetic. It's like I've put a letter in a bottle, and I've dropped it in the ocean, and it will someday wash up onshore, and somebody will find it, open it, and read it, and it will say, *Hello, People of the Future, my name is Paul Nonetheless, and I was a small and lonely man.*"

"You have a wife and three daughters and you still feel lonely?"

"Yes," he said. "It's true. Sad and true."

"Do you think you're as lonely, let's say, as a Russian orphan sleeping with thirty other orphans in a communal crib in the basement of a hospital in Tragikistan or somewhere?"

"No," Paul said. "I am not that lonely."

"Last week, outside of Spokane, a man and his kids got into a car wreck. He was critically injured, paralyzed from the neck down, and all five of his kids were killed. They were driving to pick up the mother at the train station. So tell me, do you think you are as lonely as that woman is right now?"

Wow, this woman had a gift for shaming!

"No," Paul said. "I am not that lonely. Not even close."

"Okay, good. You do realize that, grading on a curve, your loneliness is completely average."

"Yes, I realize that. Compared to all the lonely in the world, mine is pretty boring."

"Good," she said. "You might be an adulterous bastard, but at least you're a self-aware adulterous bastard."

She waited for his response, but he had nothing to say. He couldn't dispute the accuracy of her judgment of his questionable morals, nor could he offer her compelling evidence of his goodness. He was as she thought he was.

"My father cheated on us, too," she said. "We all knew it. My mother knew it. But he never admitted to it. He kept cheating and my mother kept ignoring it. They were married for fifty-two years and he cheated during all of them. Had to go on the damn Viagra so he could cheat well into his golden years. I think Viagra was invented so that extramarital assholes could have extra years to be assholes.

"But you know the worst thing?" she asked. "At the end, my father got cancer and he was dying and you'd think that would be the time to confess all, to get right with God, you know? But nope, on his deathbed, my father pledged his eternal and undying love to my mother. And you know what?"

"What?"

"She believed him."

Paul wanted to ask her why she doubted her father's love. Well, of course, Paul knew why she doubted it, but why couldn't her father have been telling the truth? Despite all the adultery and lies, all the shame and anger, perhaps her father had deeply and honestly loved her mother. If his last act on earth was a declaration of love, didn't that make him a loving man? Could an adulterous man also be a good man? But Paul couldn't say any of this, couldn't ask these questions. He knew it would only sound like the moral relativism of a liar, a cheater, and a thief.

"Listen to me," she said. "I can't believe I'm saying this stuff to you. I don't say this stuff to anybody, and here I am, talking to you like we're friends."

Paul figured silence was the best possible response to her candor.

"Okay, then," she said, "I guess that's it. I don't want to miss my flight. It was really nice to see you again. I'm not sure why. But it was."

She walked away. He watched her. He knew he should let her go. What attraction could he have for her now? He was the cheating husband of a cheated wife and the lying father of deceived daughters. But he couldn't let her go. Not yet. So he chased after her again.

"Hey," he said, and touched her shoulder.

"Just let me go," she said. A flash of anger. Her first flash of anger at him.

"Listen," he said. "I was going to let you go. But I couldn't. I mean, don't you think it's amazing that we've run into each other twice in two different airports?"

"It's just a coincidence."

"It's more than that. You know it's more than that. We've got some connection. I can feel it. And I think you can feel it, too."

"I have a nice ass. And a great smile. And you have pretty eyes and good hair. And you wear movie stars' clothes. That's why we noticed each other. But I have news for us, buddy, there's about two hundred women in this airport who are better-looking than me, and about two hundred and one men who are better-looking than you."

"But we've seen each other twice. And you remembered me."

"We saw each other twice because we are traveling salespeople in a capitalistic country. If we paid attention, I bet you we would notice the same twelve people over and over again."

Okay, so she was belittling him and their magical connection. And insulting his beloved country, too. But she was still talking to him. She'd tried to walk away, but he'd caught her, and she was engaged in a somewhat real conversation with him. He suddenly realized that he knew nothing of substance about this woman. He only knew her opinions of his character.

"Okay," he said. "We're making progress. I sell clothes. But you already knew that. What do you sell?"

"You don't want to know," she said.

"Yes, I do."

"No, you don't."

"Tell me."

"It will kill your dreams," she said.

That hyperbole made Paul laugh.

"Come on, it can't be that bad."

"I work for a bank," she said.

"So, wow, you're a banker," Paul said, and tried to hide his disappointment. She could have said that she did live-animal testing—smeared mascara directly into the eyes of chimpanzees—and Paul would have felt better about her career choice.

"But I'm not the kind of banker you're thinking about," she said.

"What kind of banker are you?" Paul asked, and studied her casual, if stylish, clothing. What kind of banker wore blue jeans? Perhaps a trustworthy banker? Perhaps the morality of any banker was inversely proportional to the quality of his or her clothing?

"Have you ever heard of microlending?" she asked.

"Yeah, that's where you get regular people to loan money to poor people in other countries. To start small businesses and stuff, right?"

"Basically, yes, but my company focuses on microlending to unique entrepreneurs in the United States."

"Ah, so what's your bank called?"

"We're in the start-up phase, so I don't want to get into that quite yet."

He was a little insulted, but then he realized that he was a stranger, after all, so her secrecy was understandable.

"You're just starting out then?" Paul asked. "That's why you're traveling so much?"

"Yes. We have initial funding from one source," she said, "and I'm meeting with other potential funders around the country."

"Sounds exciting," Paul said. He lied. Paul didn't trust the concept of using money to make more money. He believed it was all imaginary. He preferred his job—the selling of tangible goods. Paul trusted his merchandise. He knew a pair of blue jeans would never betray him.

"It's good work, but it's not exciting," she said. "Fund-raising is fucking humiliating. You know what I really do? You know what I'm good at? I'm good at making millionaires cry. And crying millionaires are generous with their money."

"I'm a millionaire," Paul said, "and you haven't made me cry yet."

"I haven't tried to," she said. She patted Paul on the cheek—let the hounds of condescension loose!—and walked out of the bookstore.

After she left, Paul bought the book she'd been browsing—the list of the greatest movies of all time—and read it on the flight back to Seattle. It was a book composed entirely of information taken from other sources. But Paul set it on his nightstand, then set his alarm clock on the book, and thought about the beautiful microbanker whenever he glanced at the time.

On a Tuesday, a year and a half into their separation, while sitting in their marriage counselor's office, Paul turned to his wife and tried to tell the truth.

"I love you," he said. "You're my best friend. I can't imagine a life without you as my wife. But, the thing is, I've lost my desire—my sexual desire—for you."

Could there be a more painful thing to say to her? To say to anyone? *You are not desirable.* That was a treasonous, even murderous, statement inside of a marriage. What kind of person could say that to his wife? To the person who'd most often allowed herself to be naked and vulnerable in front of him? Paul supposed he was being honest, but fuck honesty completely, fuck honesty all the way to the spine, and fuck the honest man who tells the truth on his way out the door.

"How can you say this shit to me?" she asked. "We've been separated for almost two years. You keep telling me you don't want a divorce. You keep begging me for another chance. For months, you have begged me. So here we are, Paul, this is your chance. And all you can say is that you don't desire me? What are you talking about?"

"I remember when we used to have sex all day and night," he said. "I remember we used to count your orgasms."

It was true. On a cool Saturday in early April, in the first year of their marriage, Paul had orgasmed six times while his wife had come eleven times. What had happened to those Olympian days?

"Is that the only way you can think about a marriage?" she asked. "Jesus, Paul, we were young. Our marriage was young. Everything is easier when you're young."

Paul didn't think that was true. His life had steadily improved over the years and, even in the middle of a marital blowup, Paul was still pleased with his progress and place in the world.

"I don't know why I feel the way I do," Paul said. "I just feel that way. I feel like we have gone cold to each other."

"I haven't gone cold," she said. "I'm burning, okay? You know how long it's been since I've had sex? It's been almost four years. Four years! And you know what? I'm ashamed to say that aloud. Listen to me. I'm ashamed that I'm still married to the man who has not fucked me in four years."

Paul looked to the marriage counselor for help. He felt lost in the ocean of his wife's rage and needed a friggin' lifeguard. But the counselor sat in silence. In *learned* silence, the bastard.

"Don't you have anything to say?" she asked Paul. "I'm your wife. I'm the mother of your children. I deserve some respect. No, I demand it. I demand your respect."

He wanted to tell her the truth. He wanted to tell himself the truth, really. But was he capable of such a thing? Could he tell her what he suspected? Could he share his theory about the loss of desire? If he sang to her, would that make it easier? Is honesty easier in four/four time?

"Are you just going to sit there?" she asked. "Is this what it comes down to, you sitting there?"

My love, he wanted to say to her, I began to lose my desire for you during the birth of our first child, and it was gone by the birth of our third. Something happened to me in those delivery rooms. I saw too much. I saw your body do things— I saw it change—and I have not been able to look at you, to see you naked, without remembering all the blood and pain and fear. *All the changes.* I was terrified. I thought you were dying. I felt like I was in the triage room of a wartime hospital, and there was nothing I could do. I felt so powerless. I felt like I was failing you. I know it's irrational. Jesus, I know it's immature and ignorant and completely irrational. *I know it's wrong.* I should have told you that I didn't want to be in the delivery room for the first birth. And I should have never been in the delivery room during the second and third. Maybe my desire would have survived, would have recovered, if I had not seen the second and third births. Maybe I wouldn't feel like such a failure. But how was I supposed to admit to these things? In the twenty-first-century United States, what kind of father and husband chooses not to be in the delivery room?

My love, Paul wanted to say, I am a small and lonely man made smaller and lonelier by my unspoken fears.

"Paul!" his wife screamed. "Talk to me!"

"I don't know," Paul said. "I don't know why I feel this way. I just do."

"Paul." The counselor finally spoke, finally had an opinion. "Have you considered that your lack of desire might be a physical issue? Have you consulted a doctor about this? There are—"

"He has no problem fucking other women," she said. "He's fucked plenty of other women. He just has a problem fucking me."

She was right. Even now, as they fought to save their marriage, Paul was thinking of the woman in the airport. He was thinking about all other women and not the woman in his life.

That night, on eBay, Paul bid on a suit once worn by Sean Connery during the publicity tour for *Thunderball*. It would be too big for Paul; Connery is a big man. But Paul still wanted it. Maybe he'd frame it and put it on the wall of his apartment. Maybe he'd drink martinis and stare at it. Maybe he'd imagine that a crisp white pocket square made all the difference in the world. But he lost track of the auction and lost the suit to somebody whose screen name was Shaken, Not Stirred.

Jesus, Paul thought, I'm wasting my life.

After the divorce, Paul's daughters spent every other weekend with him. It was not enough time. It would never be enough. And he rarely saw them during his weekends anyway because they were teenagers. Everywhere he looked, he saw happy men—good and present fathers—and he was not one of them. A wealthy man, an educated man, a privileged man, he had failed his family—his children—as easily and brutally as the poorest, most illiterate, and helpless man in the country. And didn't that prove the greatness of the United States? All of us wealthy and imperial Americans are the children of bad fathers! Ha! thought Paul. Each of us—rich and poor, gay and straight, black and white—we are fragile and finite. We all go through this glorious life without guarantees, without promise of rescue or redemption. We have freedom of speech and religion, and the absolute freedom to leave behind our loved ones, to force them to unhappily pursue us. How can I possibly protect my daughters from their nightmares, from their waking fears, Paul thought, if I am not sleeping in the room next door? Oh, God, he missed them! Pure and simple, he ached. But who has sympathy for the failed father? Who sings honor songs for the monster?

And what could he do for his daughters? He could outfit them in gorgeous vintage clothing. So he gave them dresses and shoes and pants that were worn by Doris Day, Marilyn Monroe, and Audrey Hepburn.

"Who is Audrey Hepburn?" his youngest daughter had asked.

"She was perfect," Paul said.

"But who is she?"

"An actress. A movie star."

"What movies has she been in?"

"I don't think you've seen any of them."

"If I don't know who she is, why did you buy me her dress?"

It was a good question. Paul didn't have an answer. He just looked at this young woman in front of him—his daughter—and felt powerless.

"I thought maybe if you wore different clothes at school," Paul said, "maybe you could start a trend. You'd be original."

"Oh, my God," she said. "It's high school, Dad. People get beat up for being original."

Jesus, Paul had thought he was giving her social capital. He thought he could be a microlender of art—the art of the pop song. So he gave music to his daughters. Yes, he'd once romanced their mother with mix tapes, dozens of mix tapes, so he'd romance his daughters—in an entirely different way—with iPods. So Paul bought three iPods and loaded them with a thousand songs each. Three iPods, three thousand songs. Instead of just a few songs on a CD or a cassette tape, Paul had made epic mixes. Paul had given each daughter a third of his musical history. And, oh, they were delighted—were ecstatic—when they opened their gifts and saw new iPods, but, oh, how disappointed—how disgusted—they were when they discovered that their new iPods were already filled with songs, songs chosen by their father. By their sad and desperate father.

"Daddy," his eldest daughter said. "Why did you put all *your* music on here?"

"I chose all those songs for you," he said. "They're specifically for you."

"But all these songs are *your* songs," she said. "They're not mine."

"But if you listen to them," he said, "if you learn them, then maybe they can become *our* songs."

"We don't have to love the same things," she said.

"But I want you to love what I love."

Did I say that? Paul asked himself. Did I just sound that love starved and socially inept? Am I intimidated by my own daughter? In place of romantic love for my wife, am I trying to feel romantic love for my daughters? No, no, no, no, Paul thought. But he wasn't sure. How could he be sure? He was surrounded by women he did not understand.

"It's okay, Daddy," she said. "I can just load my music over your music. Thank you for the iPod."

She shook her head—a dismissive gesture she'd learned from her mother—kissed her incompetent father on the cheek, and left the room.

Three years after his divorce had finalized, after two of his daughters had gone off to college, one to Brown and the other to Oberlin, and his third daughter had disowned him, Paul saw Sara Smile again in the Detroit Airport. They saw each other at the same time, both walking toward a coffee kiosk.

"Sara Smile," he said.

"Excuse me?" the woman said.

"It's me," he said. "Paul Nonetheless."

"I'm sorry," she said. "Do I know you?"

He realized this woman only looked like his Sara Smile. It would have been too much to ask for a third chance meeting. If he'd run into Sara Smile again, they would have had to make their way over to the airport hotel—the Hyatt or Hilton or whatever it was—and get a room. He could imagine them barely making it inside the door before their hands were down each other's pants. God, he'd drop to his knees, unbutton her pants, pull them down to her ankles, and kiss her thighs. He'd pull aside her panties and push his mouth against her crotch and she'd want it for a few moments—she'd moan her approvals—and then she'd remember her husband and her life—substantial—and she'd push Paul away. She'd pull up her pants and apologize and rush out of the room. And Paul would be there, alone again, on his knees again, in a room where thousands of people had slept, eaten, fucked, and made lonely phone calls home. And who would Paul call? Who was waiting for his voice on the line? But wait, none of this had happened. It wasn't real. Paul was still standing in the Detroit Airport next to a woman—a stranger—who only strongly resembled Sara Smile.

"Are you going to call this coincidental now?" he asked this stranger.

"You have me confused with somebody else," she said. She was smiling. She was enjoying this odd and humorous interaction with the eccentric man in his old-fashioned suit.

"Can I buy you a coffee?" he asked. He knew she was the wrong woman. But he wasn't going to let that become an impediment.

"Sir," she said. "I'm not who you think I am."

She wasn't smiling now. She realized that something was wrong with this man. Yes, she was in an airport, surrounded by people—by security—but she was still a little afraid.

"How's your marriage?" he asked.

"Sir, please," she said. "Stop bothering me."

She walked away, but Paul followed her. He couldn't stop himself. He needed her. He walked a few feet behind her.

"Me asking about your marriage is just a way of talking about my marriage," he said. "But you knew that, right? Anyway, I'm divorced now."

"Sir, if you don't leave me alone, I am going to find a cop." She stopped and put her hands up as if to ward off a punch.

"My wife left me," Paul said. "Or I left her. We left each other. It's hard to say who left first."

Paul shrugged his shoulders. And then he sang the first few bars of "She's Gone." But he couldn't quite hit Daryl Hall's falsetto notes.

"I can't hit those high notes," Paul said. "But it's not about the notes, is it? It's about the heat behind the notes."

"What's wrong with you?" the woman asked.

Two hours later, Paul sat in a simple room at a simple table while two men in suits leaned against the far wall and studied him.

"I'm not a terrorist," Paul said. "If that's what you're thinking."

The men didn't speak. Maybe they couldn't speak. Maybe there were rules against speaking. Maybe this was some advanced interrogation technique. Maybe they were silent because they knew Paul would want to fill the room with his voice.

"Come on, guys," he said. "I got a little carried away. I knew it wasn't her. I knew it wasn't Sara. I just needed to pretend for a while. Just a few moments. If she'd let me buy her some coffee or something. If she'd talked to me, everything would have been okay."

The men whispered to each other.

Paul decided it might be best if he stopped talking, if he stopped trying to explain himself.

Instead he would sing. Yes, he would find the perfect song for this situation and he would sing it. And these men—police officers, federal agents, mysterious suits—would recognize the song. They certainly wouldn't (or couldn't) sing along, but they'd smile and nod their heads in recognition. They'd share a moment with Paul. They'd have a common history, maybe even a common destiny. Rock music had that kind of power. But what song? What song would do?

And Paul knew—understood with a bracing clarity—that he must sing Marvin Gaye's "What's Going On." And so he began to hum at first, finding the tune, before he sang the first few lyrics—mumbled them, really, because he couldn't quite remember them—but when he came to the chorus, Paul belted it out. He sang loudly, and his imperfect, ragged vocals echoed in that small and simple room.

What's going on?
What's going on?
What's going on?

And, yes, Paul recognized that his singing—his spontaneous talent show—could easily be seen as troublesome. It could even be seen as crazy. Paul knew he wasn't crazy. He was just sad, very sad. And he was trying to sing his way out of the sadness.

What's going on?
What's going on?
What's going on?

The men kept staring at Paul. They wouldn't smile. They wouldn't even acknowledge the song. Why not? But then Paul remembered what had happened to Marvin Gaye. Broken, depressed, alcoholic, drug-addicted, Marvin had ended up living back home with his parents. Even as his last hit, "Sexual Healing," was selling millions of copies, Marvin was sleeping in his parents' house.

And, oh, how Marvin fought with his father. Day after day, Marvin Gaye Sr. and Marvin Gaye Jr. *screamed* at each other.

"What happened to you?"

"It's all your fault."

"You had it all and you lost it."

"You're wasting your life."

"Where's my money?"

"You have stolen from me."

"You owe me."

"I don't owe you shit."

Had any father and son ever disappointed each other so completely? But Paul couldn't stop singing. Even as he remembered that Marvin Gaye Sr. had shot and killed his son—killed his song.

What's going on?
What's going on?
What's going on?

And then it was over. Paul stopped singing. This was the wrong song. Yes, it was the worst possible song to be singing at this moment. There had to be a better one, but Paul couldn't think of it, couldn't even think of another inappropriate song. *What's wrong with me? Why can't I remember?* Paul laughed at himself as he sat in the airport interrogation room. How had he come to this? Wasn't Paul a great man who lived in a great country? Hadn't he succeeded? Jesus, he was good at everything he had ever attempted. Well, he had failed at marriage, but couldn't he be good at grief? Couldn't he be an all-star griever? Couldn't he, through his own fierce tears, tell his captors that he wasn't going to die? Couldn't he survive? Couldn't he pause now and rest his voice—rest his soul—and then start singing again when he felt strong enough? Could he do that? Was he ever going to be that strong?

"Officers," Paul said, "I'm very tired. Can I please have some time? The thing is, I'm sorry for everything. And I know this is no excuse, but I think—I realize now that I want to remember everything—every song, every article of clothing—because I'm afraid they will be forgotten."

One of the men shook his head; the other turned his back and spoke into a cell phone.

Paul bowed his head with shame.

And then he spoke so softly that he wasn't sure the men heard him. Paul thought of his wife and his daughters, of Sara Smile, and he said, "I don't want to be forgotten. I don't want to be forgotten. Don't forget me. Don't forget me. Don't forget me. Don't forget me."

On Airplanes

I am always amused
By those couples—

Lovers and spouses—
Who perform and ask

Others to perform
Musical chairs

Whenever they, by
Random seat selection,

Are separated
From each other.

"Can you switch
Seats with me?"

A woman asked me.
"So I can sit

With my husband?"
She wanted me,

A big man, who
Always books early,

And will gratefully
Pay extra for the exit row,

To trade my aisle seat
For her middle seat.

By asking me to change
My location for hers,

The woman is actually
Saying to me:

"Dear stranger, dear
Sir, my comfort is

More important than yours.
Dear solitary traveler,

My love and fear—
As contained

Within my marriage—
Are larger than yours."

O, the insult!
O, the condescension!

And this is not
An isolated incident.

I've been asked
To trade seats

Twenty or thirty times
Over the years.

How dare you!
How dare you

Ask me to change
My life for you!

How imperial!
How colonial!

But, ah, here is
The strange truth:

Whenever I'm asked
To trade seats

For somebody else's love,
I do, I always do.

Big Bang Theory

After our earliest ancestors crawled out of the oceans, how soon did they feel the desire to crawl back in?

At age nine, I stepped into the pool at the YWCA. I didn't know how to swim, but the other Indian boys had grown salmon and eagle wings and could fly in water and sky.

Wouldn't the crow, that ubiquitous trickster, make a more compelling and accurate national symbol for the United States than the bald eagle?

Okay, that Indian-boy salmon-and-eagle-wings transformation thing is bullshit, but I'm trying to tell a creation story here, and by definition all creation stories are bullshit. Scientifically speaking, we all descend from one man and woman who lived in what we now call Africa—yes, we are all African at our cores—but why should we all live with the same metaphorical creation story? The Kiowa think they were created when lightning struck the mud inside a log. I think the Hopis are crashlanded aliens who are still waiting for a rescue mission. Christians think God built everything in a week—well, in six days—and then rested. Yeah, like God created the universe in anticipation of the Sunday funny pages.

Q: In the singles bar, over nonalcoholic beer, what did the Palestinian say to the Israeli?
A: "Your holy war or mine?"

But wait, before I get too critical or metaphysical, let me return to that YWCA on Maple Street in Spokane, Washington. I stood alone in the shallow end while my big brother, cousins, best friend, and little warrior enemies swam in the deep end. I was so ashamed, but then our female swim instructors shouted my name and challenged me to dive off the five-foot board. Fuck that! I jumped out of the pool and ran into the locker room.

There is a myth that drowning is a peaceful death. I've heard people say, "I would just open my mouth and breathe death in." In truth, drowning is torture. The fear of drowning is used as torture.

At the YWCA, I quickly dressed and waited for the other Indian boys, who mocked me for my aquatic cowardice and locked me in a towel bin. But I escaped and made it onto the bus that took us to the Fox Theater for a matinee showing of *Jaws*, the blockbuster that changed the way our country looks at sharks and at films.

Did you know that when a shark stops swimming, it dies?

As we walked past the endless line of movie lovers, the other boys kept pitching me crap, but then our female swim instructors, one Japanese and one Korean, shouted my name again and insisted that I join them in the line. "But what about us?" my brother asked. "You go to the deep end," the Japanese girl said.

A wise man once said that revenge is not more important than love or compassion. Until it is.

I was nine. The Asian girls were sixteen. I sat between them and they each held one of my hands as we watched a great white shark devour people. At one point, when a little boy was in danger, I hid my face in the Korean girl's chest. Oh, it was the first time I had ever been that close to a woman's breast.

Do you think the universe is expanding or contracting?

I wish I knew what happened to those Asian girls. Are they still living in Spokane? Do you realize how much they mean to me? Did they love me? Or was I just a sad-ass kid who needed their help? If I could talk to them, I would tell them this creation story: "A bonnethead shark in Omaha, Nebraska, conceived and gave birth to a baby that soon died. But this mother shark had never shared water with a male. Scientists were puzzled. So they performed a DNA test and discovered the dead baby only had its mother's DNA. Yes, that bonnethead shark had given virgin birth. Do you think this is amazing? Well, it's not. Dozens of species of insects give virgin birth. Crayfish give virgin birth. Some honeybees give virgin birth. And Komodo dragons—yeah, those big lizards give virgin birth, too. Jeez, one human gives virgin birth and that jump-starts one of the world's great religions. But when a Komodo dragon gives virgin birth, do you know what it's thinking? It's thinking, *This is Tuesday, right? I think this is Tuesday. What am I going to do on Wednesday?*

ODE FOR PAY PHONES

All

That

Autumn,

I walked from

The apartment (shared

With my sisters) to that pay phone

On Third Avenue, next to a sleazy gas station

And down the block from the International House of Pan-
cakes. I was working the night

Shift at a pizza joint and you were away at college. You dated a
series of inconsequential boys. Well, each boy meant little on his

Own, but their cumulative effect devastated my brain and
balls. I wanted you to stop kissing relative strangers, so I called
you at midnight as often as I could afford. If I talked to you
that late, I knew

(Or hoped) you couldn't rush into anybody's bed. But, O, I still
recall the misery of hearing the *ring, ring, ring, ring*

Of your unanswered phone. These days, I'd text you to find
you, but where's the delicious pain

In that? God, I miss standing in the mosquito dark

At this or that pay phone. I wish

That I could find one

And call back

All that

I

Loved.

FEARFUL SYMMETRY

When he was eighteen and a senior in high school, Sherwin Polatkin and a group of his schoolmates jumped into two cars and drove into Spokane to see *The Breakfast Club*. Sherwin sat next to Karen, a smart and confident sophomore—a farm-town white girl with the sun-bleached hair and tanned skin of a harvest truck driver. She'd never been of romantic interest, so Sherwin slouched in his seat and munched on popcorn. It was just the random draw of a dozen friends choosing seats.

But near the end of the movie, as Molly Ringwald and Judd Nelson were making out in a supply closet, Sherwin was surprised to discover that Karen was holding his hand and even more surprised when she started playing with his fingers. Their friends had no idea this was happening. Karen lightly ran her fingertips along Sherwin's palm, the backs of his fingers, and his wrist. It was simple—and nearly innocent—but it still felt like sex.

Sherwin was not a virgin—he'd had sex with three girls—but this was the first time a girl had been so indirect with her desires. He'd touched naked women, but this hand-holding—this skin against skin—seemed far more intimate. He loved it. He was a Spokane Indian, the lead singer for his drum group, and had a sudden urge to sing an honor song for Karen—for her tenderness. He was nervous they'd be discovered. He knew their friends would be both titillated and slightly offended by this contact. It seemed like a betrayal of what was otherwise a platonic gathering. But Sherwin could not stop it. And Karen certainly didn't want to stop it. He would never touch her again, and they would never speak of the moment and would not see each other again after high school, but Sherwin always considered it one of the best moments of his life.

So, years later, when he became a professional writer, Sherwin would tell curious journalists that he loved movies and his favorite movie of all time was *The Breakfast Club*, but he would never tell them why. He knew that the best defense against fame was keeping certain secrets. He hoped that Karen, wherever she was, would someday read an interview with him and smile when she read about his cinematic preference.

On August 11, 1948, sixteen smoke jumpers, led by a taciturn man named Wayne Ford, parachuted into Sirois Canyon, a remote area near Wenatchee, Washington, to fight a small wildfire. However, the fire, unpredictable as such fires can be, exploded into a fifty-foot-tall wall of flame, jumped the canyon, and chased the smoke jumpers up a steep and grassy hillside. Fifteen smoke jumpers tried to outrun the fire, an impossible race to win, but Wayne Ford didn't run. Instead, he did something that was new and crazy: He built the first U.S. Forest Service escape fire.

Did you know that you can escape a fire by setting another fire at your feet? You might seem to be building a funeral pyre, but you're creating a circle of safety. In order to save your endangered ass, all you have to do is burn down the grass surrounding you, lie facedown in the ash, and pray that the bigger fire will pass over you like a flock of blind and burning angels.

I know you're thinking, *You're crazy. There's no way I'm going to set a fire when another fire is already chasing me.* And that's exactly what Wayne Ford's men thought. They had never seen any firefighter set one fire to escape another. It was unprecedented— for white folks. Indians had set many such escape fires before white men had arrived in the Americas, but Wayne Ford and his men had no way of knowing this.

Wise Wayne Ford—who before the fire had the same color and sinewy bite as one hundred and fifty pounds of deer jerky— could never fully explain why he set his escape fire. All he ever said is that it just made sense. Ford's men tried to outrun the murderous flames, but one by one they all succumbed to the fire and smoke. Ford calmly lay down in the ash, in his circle of safety, and lived.

Thirty years after the Sirois Canyon fire, Harris Tolkin, a former smoke jumper, began to write a nonfiction chronicle of the tragedy, *Fearful Symmetry: The True Story of the Sirois Canyon Fire*. Tolkin borrowed the title of his book from the first and last stanzas of William Blake's most famous poem:

> Tyger! Tyger! burning bright
> In the forests of the night,
> What immortal hand or eye
> Could frame thy fearful symmetry?

In exploring the meanings of the Sirois Canyon fire and its aftermath, Tolkin relied heavily on William Blake's notions of *innocence* and *experience* and on the dichotomies of joy and sorrow, childhood and adulthood, religious faith and doubt, and good and evil. Tolkin died before completing the book, but it was edited by his daughter, Diane Tolkin, and was posthumously published in 2002 and was a surprise *New York Times* best seller for twenty-six weeks. In 2003, Tesla Studios, fresh off a Best Picture Oscar for their Civil War epic, *Leaves of Grass*, approached a hot young short-story writer, poet and first-time screenwriter, Sherwin Polatkin, to adapt *Fearful Symmetry* for the big screen.

Sitting in the Tesla offices, Sherwin stared through a glass desk at the bare feet of the executive producer, a short thin man who was otherwise completely dressed in a gorgeous bespoke suit.

"So, Sherwin," the producer said, "why are you here?"

That was a strange question, considering that Sherwin had been invited. He decided that it must be an existential query. Or no, maybe it was just the first question of a job interview. This was Hollywood, yes, but Sherwin was really just a typist—a *creative* typist—trying to get a job.

"Well, number one," Sherwin said, "I know fire like no other screenwriter in this town. I was a hotshot, a forest firefighter, for ten summers. It's how I paid for college."

That was a lie. Sherwin had only fought one fire in his life—a burning hay bale—and he'd only had to pour ten buckets of water on it. But this executive had no way of knowing Sherwin was a liar. Wasn't everybody in Hollywood a liar? Maybe Sherwin could only distinguish himself by the quality of his lies and not their quantity.

"And number two, I'm a Native American," Sherwin said. "I'm indigenous to the West, to the idea of the West, and you're not going to find that sort of experience in film school."

That couldn't be true. Wasn't Hollywood filled with small-town folks from the West—hell, from everywhere? Wasn't Hollywood filled with nomads? Yes, Jewish folks, those original nomads, created the movie business, and it had not really changed in all the decades since, had it? Wasn't Sherwin really just one more nomad in a business filled with nomads? How could he really distinguish himself?

"Listen," Sherwin said to the executive, "I'm nervous and I'm exaggerating, and I'm sounding like an arrogant bastard, so let's just start over. Is that okay? Can we call *cut* and start this scene over? Can we do a reshoot?"

The executive smiled and tugged at his toes. Yes, they were well-manicured toes, but it was still disconcerting, in the context of a business meeting, to see something—ten things—so naked and—well, toelike.

"We've had about a dozen screenwriters work on this project," the executive said. "And had three different directors attached. And none of them could crack this thing. So tell me, how are you going to crack it?"

Sherwin didn't quite understand the terminology. He assumed it had something to do with secret codes and languages. So he went with that.

"Well, the book itself is a tragedy." Sherwin said.

"Tragedies are fucked at the box office," the executive said.

Sherwin didn't know if that was true. It didn't feel true. Or maybe it was truer than Sherwin wanted to believe. Weren't

Americans afraid of tragedy? As a Native American, Sherwin was, by definition, trapped in a difficult but lustful marriage with tragedy. But that cultural fact wouldn't get him this job.

"I think there's redemption in this story," Sherwin said. "I know I can find the redemption."

"Redemption," the executive said. "Yes, that's exactly what we need."

Thus hired on the basis of one word—one universal concept—Sherwin tried to transform a tragedy into a redemptive action-adventure movie. How did he go about his task? First he pulled the story out of the past and reset it in the present. Why? Because the studio thought the audience wouldn't watch another period piece, and because the director—an old studio pro who was rumored to have had sex with at least three of the actresses who'd starred in *Dallas,* the TV series—wanted his Chinese girlfriend to play the female lead. Ah, the things one does for diversity!

But in changing the time frame of the Sirois Canyon fire at the behest of the capitalistic studio and the love-struck director, Polatkin was confronted with a logical problem. If the fictional Wayne Ford were to set an escape fire in 2003 and still be ignored by his crew members for such a crazy idea, Polatkin would have to pretend that forest-fire fighters still didn't know about escape fires. This, of course, was a nasty insult to the intelligence of firefighters. So Polatkin only had one option. He had to change the narrative and eliminate Wayne Ford's escape fire—or, rather, the concept of a man setting the first escape fire in U.S. Forest Service history. But Harris Tolkin's book revolves around the revolutionary nature of this escape fire. Thus, by eliminating the escape fire and its aftermath, Polatkin created a screenplay that had little connection to the narrative and moral concerns of the sourcebook.

Such are the dangers of creating art based on other art. Such are the dangers of Hollywood, where it is contractually understood that screenwriters will write first drafts with verve, and then, with each revision, lose more nerve and individuality. It's fucked, but Polatkin got paid five hundred thousand bucks to write a first draft where the killing fire burned as brightly as William Blake's tygers. In fact, Wayne Ford, younger and renamed for the film, saw tygers inside the flames as they chased his team up the steep slope. The others lost all innocence and hope and died before they reached the summit. But Ford reached the top and made the mad plummet down the back slope with the fire tygers in pursuit. He didn't build an escape fire—no time for that old tactic—he just ran, and he survived because he was so damn fast.

There is real inspiration for this fictional flight from fiery death. On July 3, 1999, near Boulder, Colorado, another relatively small wildfire exploded into a conflagration and chased sixteen firefighters up a steep slope and killed fifteen of them. Only Richard McPhee, an experienced smoke jumper out of Bonners Ferry, Idaho, was able to outrun the flames. Later, when researchers did the math, they estimated that McPhee ran the equivalent of a hundred-yard dash in nine seconds. That would be a world-record speed on a *flat* surface, but McPhee ran it while carrying a forty-pound backpack up a heavily forested sixty-degree slope. The man *wanted* to live. It gives one pleasure to take the measure of a man's fight to survive. Ask

yourself: Could I have run that fast and won the right to live?
This might be glib, but certain men are born to be stars—to be
at their best when faced with death. Richard McPhee only believes he was lucky.

"Yeah, I've got speed," he said. "But hell, what if I had fallen
or tripped or just hit some bad luck? What if I had started in
back and had to run past everyone? I lived because nobody was
running slowly in front of me."

Richard McPhee refuses to be called a hero, which makes
him the perfect real-life model for a cinematic star. So, in
writing his first-draft screenplay, Polatkin blended aspects
of Wayne Ford and Richard McPhee's heroism and created
an entirely fictional smoke jumper, now named Joseph Adams,
who survived a murderous inferno but was emotionally and
spiritually crippled by survivor's guilt. Angry and drinking
alcoholically, Joseph Adams falls apart in the first act, stag-
gers his way through the second act, and finds redemption in
the third act when he again faces a monster fire but sacrifices
his own life to save his entire team, including the love of his
life, a Vietnamese-American smoke jumper named Grace.
Yes, Sherwin decided that the director's Chinese girlfriend
would cross over racial borders and play a Vietnamese-
American woman, a first-generation immigrant, who had
fled the Vietnam War and was adopted and raised by a white
American family. And yes, Polatkin, the possessor of a res-
ervation-inspired messiah complex ("I am the smartest Indian
in the universe and I will save all you other Indians!"), decided that the hero, Joseph Adams, should die so that others
might live.

Okay, Polatkin wasn't writing Shakespeare, but he did write an interesting screenplay, maybe even a good one. But as he'd feared, the studio had notes. They wanted to change a few things so Polatkin flew to Hollywood, met his town-car driver, and was driven to a meeting room in L.A. Sherwin kept thinking of Survivor's eighties hit, "Eye of the Tiger," as twenty studio executives shuttled into the room. The director, angry because his other project had been scuttled, rolled in late, stuffed his face with a muffin, and said, while spewing food, "This screenplay is seriously flawed, but it's nothing we can't fix."

The director was wearing cargo shorts. Sherwin was convinced that nobody over the age of thirty-three should ever wear cargo shorts.

For the rest of the day, the director and the executives made suggestions and demands: "The hero can't die. Get rid of the William Blake shit. And you need more action, more fistfights and fucking. Maybe you could write a scene where the hero fucks his girl in the ash after a fire. The hero could leave ashy handprints on his girl's back—on her whole body. That would be primal and hot. Jesus, it would be poetry."

Polatkin fought for his screenplay's survival, but it was a pathetic and lonely battle. He was a writer-for-hire and was contractually bound to follow studio orders or he would be fired and replaced. So, feeling hollow and violated, he took careful notes as a roomful of businessmen wrested art into commodity. He thought of how much he had always loved movies and how, for most his life, he'd had no idea how they were made. He thought of the boy he had been, sitting in that dark theater with Karen, the girl from high school, and how innocent it was.

Not perfect, not at all, but better—cleaner—than this meeting. How had the boy who loved movies become so different from this man who wrote them?

And then Sherwin saw the latest issue of *The New Yorker*, crisp and unread, on the table. He had just published his first short story in the magazine. It's every fiction writer's wish to be published in the same magazine that has published Cheever, Munro, Yates, and ten thousand other greats and near-greats and goods.

"Hey," Sherwin said. "I've got a short story in that *New Yorker*."

The director flipped through the magazine, coughed and sighed, and said, "You should let me be your editor because you would win the fucking Pulitzer if I were in charge of your career."

The room went cold and silent. The professionally cold studio executives couldn't believe that any human being, even a film director, had said something so deluded and imperial.

Polatkin was baffled. No, it was worse than that. At that moment, something broke inside him. He didn't know it at the time, but he'd fractured some part of his soul. He only realized the extent of his spiritual injuries a few months later. While writing nine drafts of the screenplay, Sherwin—who had already taken out the concept of the first escape fire set in U.S. Forest Service history—discovered that he could not take the William Blake out of a book whose title and themes were based on Blake's poetry.

"I can't do it," he said to the director. "The book is about Blake. How can you take Blake out if the book is about Blake?"

"Fuck Blake," the director said. "And fuck this book. Do you think this book is the fucking Bible? Do you think it's sacred? Jesus, we're making a movie, and that's more fucking important than this book. I'm going to make a movie that's ten times—a hundred times—greater than this fucking book. So are you going to take out the fucking Blake or what?"

"I can't do it," Sherwin said.

"Then fuck you. You're fired."

It was easy to fire screenwriters. But Sherwin was not just a screenwriter. He was also the author of a book of short stories and two volumes of poetry, and he still wanted to explore the notion of heroic self-sacrifice, so he decided to write a series of sonnets dedicated to smoke jumpers. At his home in San Francisco, he sat at his computer and stared at the blank screen. He sat, silent and unworking, for hours, for weeks, for months. Every time he tried to write a word, a metaphor, a line of poetry, he could only hear the critical voices of the studio executives and the director: *The hero can't die. Get rid of the William Blake shit*. Sherwin had fallen victim to his own imagination. He couldn't create anything on the page, but he was fully capable of creating fictional and aural ghosts who prevented him from writing.

Desperate, he decided the computer's advanced technology was creating the impediment. He decided to go back to the beginning—to the Adam and Eve of writing—the pen and paper. Yes, he tried to write by hand. He reasoned that if Herman Melville could write *Moby-fucking-Dick* with an inky feather, he could write one measly goddamn sonnet with a felt tip pen and

graph paper. But he could still hear the executives and director talking. *The hero can't die. Get rid of the William Blake shit.*
He was suffering from Hollywood-induced schizophrenia and
couldn't produce a word. Polatkin had always mocked those
folks who'd claimed to suffer from writer's block. But now, he
was a writer . . .

> Who could not produce one goddamn word.
> The poems had migrated like goddamn birds.
> And no matter what you may have heard,
> Writer's block causes physical hurt.
> The fool couldn't wear a goddamn shirt
> Because the cotton scratched, bruised, and burned
> His skin. His stomach ached; his vision blurred.
> What happens to a soul that's shaken *and* stirred?
>
> What happens to a writer who can't write?
> Who flees his office and drives through the night,
> In search of some solace, some goddamn streetlight
> That will illuminate and give back his life,
> His odes and lyrics? The desperate fool tried
> Every workshop trick. The agnostic fool cried
> To God for relief. God, can a man die
> Of writer's block? Well, the fool did survive

. . . the early and most painful stages of his creative disease.
Sherwin grew numb. He became strangely complacent with
the idea that he would never write again. Oh, Sherwin still
loved words, but he found other ways to play with them. He
discovered the magic and terror of crossword puzzles. He read

dictionaries and encyclopedias that promised to help him solve the most difficult ones. He soon became good at crossword puzzles. By testing himself using the same crosswords the best puzzlers solved in competition, Sherwin learned that he was probably one of the best five hundred crossword puzzle solvers in the English-speaking world.

He'd become that good after only six months of part-time work. How good could he become if he dedicated himself fully to the task? He figured that by living even more frugally than he had for the last decade, he had enough cash to survive for one more decade. So he decided to become, for lack of a better term, a crossword monk. But instead of praying, instead of keeping a diary, instead of transcribing by hand every page of some holy book, Sherwin made lists of words, the most common crossword-puzzle answers:

AREA	OLE
ERA	IRE
ERE	ESE
ELI	ENE
ALE	ARE
ALOE	ATE
EDEN	NEE
ALI	ALA
ETA	AGE
ESS	IRA
ERIE	ACE
ANTE	ELSE
ARIA	ODE

ERR	EVE
ADO	ETNA
IDEA	ASEA
EEL	ASH
END	ANTI
ANT	EAR
APE	ARI
ACRE	ETAL
EST	

That was just the short list. There were a thousand or more common answers. They were the building blocks of crossword puzzles. But the quality—the comedy and tragedy—of a puzzle often had less to do with the answers than with the clues. A great solver understood the poetry of the clues. The most difficult puzzles used puns, misdirection, verb-noun elision, and camouflage in their clueing.

Sherwin believed himself to be a great solver, so he traveled to the American Crossword Puzzle Championship in Stamford, Connecticut.

When he stepped into the conference room, crowded with solvers who all seemed to know one another, Sherwin was nervous and vaguely ashamed of himself. Was this what his life had come to? He'd been flying first class to Hollywood, and now he was paying too much for a king bed nonsmoking in a Hilton in Connecticut? Yes, it was a wealthy, lovely, and privileged part of the state, but it still felt like a descent.

But wait, Sherwin thought, stop judging people. These solvers were a group of people who had to be clever. These people were thinkers. Yes, there had to be plenty of eccentrics—compulsive hand-washers, functioning autistics, encyclopedia readers, and compulsive cat collectors—but didn't that actually make them a highly attractive group of people? When had Sherwin been anything other than a weird fucker? Didn't he get paid to be a weird fucker?

"Hello," he said to the woman at the registration desk. She wore a name tag with her name, *Sue*, spelled out on a crossword grid.

"Hello," Sue said. "Welcome to the tournament. Are you a contestant or a journalist?"

"A contestant."

"So this must be your first time here?" she asked.

"How do you know that?"

"Oh, this is a family, really, a highly dysfunctional family." She laughed. "I know everybody. But I don't know you. So that makes you new."

"You've got me."

"Okay, I'll sign you up for the C Group."

"C? What's that?"

"It's for new solvers."

"I'm new," Sherwin said, "but I'm good."

"Oh, first-timers are always C Group. If you do well enough on the first few puzzles, they'll consider moving you up right away, but that rarely happens."

"Why not?"

"Because the puzzles are always more difficult than you'd expect. And because the pressure—well, first-timers have no idea how much pressure there is. And—well, they tend to choke a bit."

Sue laughed again.

"Are you laughing at me?" Sherwin asked.

"Oh, no," she said. "I'm sorry. I'm laughing at myself. I've been coming to this tournament for seventeen years and I'm still a C Group. I keep choking year after year."

"I'm used to pressure."

"Oh, I'm not judging you. It's all supposed to be fun. It *is* fun. Just sign up with the C Group and have fun. This is your first time. You have years of fun ahead of you."

Years of fun? When had anybody ever said such a thing and meant it? Sue meant it. Sherwin shrugged and signed up for C Group.

Later that afternoon, he sat at a long table in a room filled with long tables. He had four pencils and a good eraser. He sat beside an elderly Korean woman who looked as if she'd been born in her sweater.

"Hello," she said. "You must be new?"

She had a slight accent, so she was probably a first-generation immigrant. She'd probably been in the United States for twenty-five years. She'd been here long enough to become a crossword solver. Sherwin realized that he had no idea if crossword puzzles were written in other languages. Were other languages flexible enough?

"Are you new?" the Korean woman asked again. She was missing a lower front tooth. This made her look somehow younger, even impish. Don't be condescending, Sherwin chastised himself.

"Yes, I'm new," he said. "C Group."

"Welcome, welcome," she said. "We're like a family here."

"So I've heard."

"Yes, just like a family. Like my family. My big sister is a legendary bitch. Just like that bitch over there."

She pointed a pencil at another elderly woman, a white woman wearing thick glasses. Didn't she know that one could purchase plastic lenses these days?

"Why is she a bitch?" Sherwin asked.

"Because she always beats me. And because she always apologizes for beating me. Young man, you must never apologize for being good. It makes the rest of us feel worse about ourselves."

"Okay, good advice," Sherwin said. "So I guess I should tell you that I really don't belong in Group C. I'm better than that."

"So you think you can beat me?"

"I've timed myself with puzzles. I'm fast."

"I'm sure you are."

A volunteer set the first puzzle—freshly printed on fine cotton paper—facedown on the table in front of Sherwin.

"So what happens now?" Sherwin asked.

"When they say *go,* you turn over the paper and do your puzzle. When you're finished, raise your hand, and somebody will mark your time, and then they'll collect your puzzle and check it for accuracy. And they'll measure your score against all the other C Group puzzlers."

"The woman said they'd move me up to B if I did well enough."

"Why don't you just do the first puzzle and see what happens? What's your name anyway?"

"Sherwin."

"I'm Mai. What do you do when you aren't solving puzzles?"

"I'm a writer."

"Oh. Have you written anything I might have heard of?"

"Doubtful. I wrote poems and short stories. I never sold much. And never won any awards. I wrote a couple of movies, too. But they never got made."

"What are you working on now?"

"Oh, I don't write anymore."

"Why not?"

"My talent dried up and blew away in the wind," Sherwin said. "I am the Dust Bowl."

"I'm sorry to hear that."

"I'm sorry to say it."

Sherwin had never before confessed aloud his fears that his talent was gone forever. And now that he had, he realized that he would never write again. Not like he had. Was that so bad? He'd written two decent books and two bad ones. How many people in the world had written and published anything? Because he'd stopped writing, Sherwin had been thinking of himself as a failure. But perhaps that wasn't it. Perhaps he had only been destined to be a writer for that brief period of time. After all, there must be at least one person in the world who had loved his books—who still loved his work— so perhaps that made it all worthwhile. Wasn't everything temporary anyway?

"Okay, wait, Sherwin, enough of the biography," the Korean woman said. "Here we go."

"Puzzlers," the emcee said, "start your puzzles."

Sherwin and the Korean woman, and a few hundred other puzzlers, flipped over their papers and started working. Sherwin quickly filled three Across answers and one Down, but then stalled. He read through the clues and found that he didn't know any of them offhand. He was stuck already. Thirty seconds into his first puzzle and he was frozen. Words were failing him. Again and again, they failed him. He stared blankly at his mostly empty grid for one minute and three seconds and was shocked when the Korean woman raised her hand.

"You're done?" he asked.

"You're not supposed to talk," she said.

"But you're really done that fast?"

"Yes, but that bitch up there beat me again."

Sherwin checked out of the hotel, caught a taxi to the airport, and the flight to Chicago that would connect him to the flight back home to San Francisco.

On the second leg, somewhere over Wyoming, Sherwin pulled out the *New York Times* and found the crossword. It was Saturday, so this puzzle would probably be difficult to solve. Sherwin vowed to solve it, quickly and accurately. He wanted redemption. Here, in the airplane, he was able to fill in a few boxes, but not many. The puzzle remained mostly unsolved.

He was ready to crumple the paper into a ball and stuff it into the seat pocket in front of him when he became aware that he was being watched. One row behind him, to the left and across the aisle, a man was simultaneously working the airline magazine crossword puzzle and watching Sherwin work his *New York Times* puzzle. The airline magazine puzzles were embarrassingly easy. But the man was obviously struggling and was embarrassed by his struggles.

"I'll figure this out," he said to Sherwin, "but you, man, you're working the *Times* puzzle. You must be a genius."

"Maybe," Sherwin said.

Wanting to confirm the man's opinion, Sherwin again studied the puzzle. He tentatively filled in one answer. It was wrong, surely it was wrong; ALPINE could not be the right answer. It made no sense. But it fit the squares. It put ink on the page. Sherwin felt good about that, so he filled in another answer with the wrong word. And then he filled in another. In a minute, he finished the puzzle. He'd filled nearly all the boxes with incorrect and random words like *music* and *screenwriter* and *fear* but the man behind him could not tell that Sherwin was faking it. He could only see Sherwin finishing the difficult puzzle in record time. Wow, the man thought, he's barely even reading the clues. He's a crossword machine. He's a crossword cyborg. He's a crossword killer. He's a crossword Terminator.

When Sherwin filled in the last blank, he sighed with satisfaction, folded the paper in half, and slid it into the seat pocket in front of him. Then he looked back at the man behind him and smiled. The man gave him a thumbs-up. It was such an eager and innocent gesture that Sherwin felt guilty for his deception. But then he laughed at himself, at his gift for lying.

I am a lying genius, Sherwin thought. And what is lying but a form of storytelling? Sherwin realized that he'd told a story, the first story he'd told in public for any kind of audience since he left Hollywood. But wait, did this really count as story-telling? Well, he'd entertained one man, right? And then Sherwin realized what he'd truly just done. And he roared with laughter and startled a few of his fellow passengers with the volume of his joy.

Sherwin realized that, for years, he'd been running away from a wildfire, an all-consuming inferno that had turned his words into cinder and ash, but he'd just now set an escape fire; he'd told a lie, a story, that convinced him he might be capable of putting a story on the page. Or was this all delusion? Sherwin knew there was a pen in his left inside coat pocket. He could feel it there. And there was paper everywhere on this airplane. He had ink; he could get paper. Oh, he wondered, oh, do I have the strength to begin again? Do I have the courage to step into a dark theater, hold hands with a beautiful woman, and fall back in love with my innocence?

ODE TO MIX TAPES

These days, it's too easy to make mix tapes.
CD burners, iPods, and iTunes
Have taken the place
Of vinyl and cassette. And, soon
Enough, clever introverts will create
Quicker point-and-click ways to declare
One's love, lust, friendship, and favor.
But I miss the labor
Of making old-school mix tapes—the midair

Acrobatics of recording one song
At a time. It sometimes took days
To play, choose, pause,
Ponder, record, replay, erase,
And replace. But there was no magic wand.
It was blue-collar work. A great mix tape
Was sculpture designed to seduce
And let the hounds loose.
A great mix tape was a three-chord parade

Led by the first song, something bold and brave,
　　　A heat-seeker like Prince with "Cream,"
　　　Or "Let's Get It On," by Marvin Gaye.
The next song was always Patsy Cline's "Sweet Dreams,"
or something by Hank. But O, the last track
　　　Was the vessel that contained
　　　The most devotion and pain
And made promises that you couldn't take back.

Roman Catholic Haiku

Humans

In 1985, while attending Gonzaga University—a Jesuit institution—students shared the dining hall with fifty or sixty nuns who lived in a dormitory-turned-convent. We students didn't think positively or negatively about this situation. We barely had any interaction with the holy women, though a few of us took to shouting, "Get thee to a nunnery!" at one another—but never at the nuns—after we took a Shakespeare class. I'm sure the nuns must have heard us shouting Hamlet's curse at one another, but being a rather scholarly bunch, they were probably more amused than insulted.

Nature

The brown recluse spider is not an aggressive spider and attacks only when hurt or threatened. Its bite, however, contains a very aggressive poison that can form a necrotizing ulcer that destroys soft tissue and sometimes bone. So this six-eyed spider is passive and dangerous. And it's strangely beautiful. It often has markings on its stomach and back that resemble violins. Yes, this spider could be thought of as a tattooed musician.

COLLISION

While waiting in the lunch line behind a nun, I noticed a brown recluse spider perched on her shoulder. I reflexively slapped the arachnid to the floor. The nun must have thought I'd slapped her in jest or cruelty because she turned and glared at me. But then I pointed at the brown recluse spider scuttling across the floor away from us. At first, the nun stepped back, but then she took two huge steps forward and crushed the spider underfoot. The nun gasped; I gasped. Mortified, she looked at me and said, "I'm sorry." And then she looked down at the mutilated spider and said, "You, too."

Looking Glass

On October 5, 1877, in Montana's Bear Paw Mountains, the
starved and exhausted Nez Perce ended their two-thousand-
mile flight and surrendered to General Oliver Howard and his
Ninth Cavalry. When the legendary Nez Perce leader, Chief
Joseph, stood and said, "My heart is sick

And
Sad.
From
Where
The
Sun
Now
Stands,

I
Will
Fight
No
More
Forever"

he thought they were his final words. He had no idea that he
would live for another twenty-seven years. First, he watched

hundreds of his people die of exile in Oklahoma. Then Joseph and his fellow survivors were allowed to move back to the Pacific Northwest but were forced to live on the Colville Indian Reservation, hundreds of miles away from their tribe's ancestral home in Oregon's Wallowa Valley. Exiled twice, Joseph still led his tribe into the twentieth century, though he eventually died of depression. But my grandmother, who was born on the Colville Indian Reservation, always said she remembered Joseph as a kind and peaceful man. She always said that Chief Joseph was her favorite babysitter.

Yes,
He
Would
Sit
In
His
Rocking
Chair

And
Braid
My
Grandmother's
Epic
Hair.

SALT

I wrote the obituary for the obituaries editor. Her name was Lois Andrews. Breast cancer. She was only forty-five. One in eight women get breast cancer, an epidemic. Lois's parents had died years earlier. Dad's cigarettes kept their promises. Mom's Parkinson's shook her into the ground. Lois had no siblings and had never been married. No kids. No significant other at present. No significant others in recent memory. Nobody remembered meeting one of her others. Some wondered if there had been any others. Perhaps Lois had been that rarest of holy people, the secular and chaste nun. So, yes, her sexuality was a mystery often discussed but never solved. She had many friends. All of them worked at the paper.

I wasn't her friend, not really. I was only eighteen, a summer intern at the newspaper, moving from department to department as need and boredom required, and had only spent a few days working with Lois. But she'd left a note, a handwritten will and testament, with the editor in chief, and she'd named me as the person she wanted to write her obituary.

"Why me?" I asked the chief. He was a bucket of pizza and beer tied to a broomstick.

"I don't know," he said. "It's what she wanted."

"I didn't even know her."

"She was a strange duck," he said.

I wanted to ask him how to tell the difference between strange and typical ducks. But he was a humorless white man with power, and I was a reservation Indian boy intern. I was to be admired for my ethnic tenacity but barely tolerated because of my callow youth.

"I've never written an obituary by myself," I said. During my hours at her desk, Lois had carefully supervised my work.

"It may seem bureaucratic and formal," she'd said. "But we have to be perfect. This is a sacred thing. We have to do this perfectly."

"Come on," the chief said. "What did you do when you were working with her? She taught you how to write one, didn't she?"

"Well, yeah, but—"

"Just do your best," he said and handed me her note. It was short, rather brutal, and witty. She didn't want any ceremony. She didn't want a moment of silence. Or a moment of indistinct noise, either. And she didn't want anybody to gather at a local bar and tell drunken stories about her because those stories would inevitably be romantic and false. And she'd rather be forgotten than inaccurately remembered. And she wanted me to write the obituary.

It was an honor, I guess. It would have been difficult, maybe impossible, to write a good obituary about a woman I didn't know. But she made it easy. She insisted in her letter that I use the standard fill-in-the-blanks form.

"If it was good enough for others," she'd written, "it is good enough for me."

A pragmatic and lonely woman, sure. And serious about her work. But, trust me, she was able to tell jokes without insulting the dead. At least, not directly.

That June, a few days before she went on the medical leave that she'd never return from, Lois had typed *surveyed* instead of *survived* in the obituary for a locally famous banker. That error made it past the copy editors and was printed: *Mr. X is surveyed by his family and friends.*

Mr. X's widow called Lois to ask about the odd word choice.

"I'm sorry," Lois said. She was mortified. It was the only serious typo of her career. "It was my error. It's entirely my fault. I apologize. I will correct it for tomorrow's issue."

"Oh, no, please don't," the widow said. "My husband would have loved it. He was a poet. Never published or anything like that. But he loved poems. And that word, *survey*—well, it might be accidental, but it's poetry, I think. I mean, my husband would have been delighted to know that his family and friends were surveying him at the funeral."

And so a surprised and delighted Lois spent the rest of the day thinking of verbs that more accurately reflected our interactions with the dead.

Mr. X is assailed by his family and friends.
Mr. X is superseded by his family and friends.
Mr. X is superimposed by his family and friends.
Mr. X is sensationalized by his family and friends.
Mr. X is shadowboxed by his family and friends.

Lois laughed as she composed her imaginary obituaries. I'd never seen her laugh that much, and I suspected that very few people had seen her react that strongly to anything. She wasn't remote or strained, she was just private. And so her laughter—her public joy—was frankly erotic. Though I'd always thought of her as a sexy librarian—with her wire-rimmed glasses and curly brown hair and serious panty hose and suits—I'd never really thought of going to bed with her. Not to any serious degree. I was eighteen, so I fantasized about having sex with nearly every woman I saw, but I hadn't obsessed about Lois. Not really. I'd certainly noticed that her calves were a miracle of muscle—her best feature—but I'd only occasionally thought of kissing my way up and down her legs. But at that moment, as she laughed about death, I had to shift my legs to hide my erection.

"Hey, kid," she said, "when you die, how do you want your friends and family to remember you?"

"Jeez," I said. "I don't want to think about that stuff. I'm eighteen."

"Oh, so young," she said. "So young and handsome. You're going to be very popular with the college girls."

I almost whimpered. But I froze, knowing that the slightest movement, the softest brush of my pants against my skin, would cause me to orgasm.

Forgive me, I was only a kid.

"Ah, look at you," Lois said. "You're blushing."

And so I grabbed a random file off her desk and ran. I made my escape. But, oh, I was in love with the obituaries editor. And she—well, she taught me how to write an obituary.

And so this is how I wrote hers:

Lois Andrews, age 45, of Spokane, died Friday, August 24, 1985, at Sacred Heart Hospital.

There will be no funeral service. She donated her body to Washington State University. An only child, Lois Anne Andrews was born January 16, 1940, at Sacred Heart Hospital, to Martin and Betsy (Harrison) Andrews. She never married. She was the obituaries editor at the *Spokesman-Review* for twenty-two years. She is survived by her friends and colleagues at the newspaper.

Yes, that was the story of her death. It was not enough. I felt morally compelled to write a few more sentences, as if those extra words would somehow compensate for what had been a brief and solitary life.

I was also bothered that Lois had donated her body to science. Of course, her skin and organs would become training tools for doctors and scientists, and that was absolutely vital, but the whole process still felt disrespectful to me. I thought of her, dead and naked, lying on a gurney while dozens of students stuck their hands inside of her. It seemed—well, pornographic. But I also knew that my distaste was cultural.

Indians respect dead bodies even more than the live ones.

Of course, I never said anything. I was young and frightened and craved respect and its ugly cousin, approval, so I did as I was told. And that's why, five days after Lois's death and a few minutes after the editor in chief had told me I would be writing the obituaries until they found "somebody official," I found myself sitting at her desk.

"What am I supposed to do first?" I asked the chief.

"Well, she must have unfiled files and unwritten obits and unmailed letters."

"Okay, but where?"

"I don't know. It was *her* desk."

This was in the paper days, and Lois kept five tall filing cabinets stuffed with her job.

"I don't know what to do," I said, panicked.

"Jesus, boy," the editor in chief said. "If you want to be a journalist, you'll have to work under pressure. Jesus. And this is hardly any pressure at all. All these people are dead. The dead will not pressure you."

I stared at him. I couldn't believe what he was saying. He seemed so cruel. He was a cruel duck, that's what he was.

"Jesus," he said yet again, and grabbed a folder off the top of the pile. "Start with this one."

He handed me the file and walked away. I wanted to shout at him that he'd said Jesus three times in less than fifteen seconds. I wasn't a Christian and didn't know much about the definition of blasphemy, but it seemed like he'd committed some kind of sin.

But I kept my peace, opened the file, and read the handwritten letter inside. A woman had lost her husband. Heart attack. And she wanted to write the obituary and run his picture. She included her phone number. I figured it was okay to call her. So I did.

"Hello?" she said. Her name was Mona.

"Oh, hi," I said. "I'm calling from the *Spokesman-Review*. About your—uh, late husband?"

"Oh. Oh, did you get my letter? I'm so happy you called. I wasn't sure if anybody down there would pay attention to me."

"This is sacred," I said, remembering Lois's lessons. "We take this very seriously."

"Oh, well, that's good—that's great—and, well, do you think it will be okay for me to write the obituary? I'm a good writer. And I'd love to run my husband's photo—his name was Dean—I'd love to run his photo with the—with his—with my remembrance of him."

I had no idea if it was okay for her to write the obituary. And I believed that the newspaper generally ran only the photographs of famous dead people. But then I looked at the desktop and noticed Lois's neatly written notes trapped beneath the glass. I gave praise for her organizational skills.

"Okay, okay," I said, scanning the notes. "Yes. Yes, it's okay if you want to write the obituary yourself."

I paused and then read aloud the official response to such a request.

"Because we understand, in your time of grieving, that you want your loved one to be honored with the perfect words—"

"Oh, that's lovely."

"—but, and we're truly sorry about this, it will cost you extra," I said.

"Oh," she said. "Oh, I didn't know that. How much extra?"

"Fifty dollars."

"Wow, that's a lot of money."

"Yes," I said. It was one-fifth of my monthly rent.

"And how about running the photograph?" Mona asked. "How much extra does that cost?"

"It depends on the size of the photo."

"How much is the smallest size?"

"Fifty dollars, as well."

"So it will be one hundred dollars to do this for my husband?"

"Yes."

"I don't know if I can afford it. I'm a retired schoolteacher on a fixed income."

"What did you teach?" I asked.

"I taught elementary school—mostly second grade—at Meadow Hills for forty-five years. I taught three generations." She was proud, even boastful. "I'll have you know that I taught the grandchildren of three of my original students."

"Well, listen," I said, making an immediate and inappropriate decision to fuck the duck in chief. "We have a special rate for—uh, retired public employees. So the rate for your own obituary and your husband's photograph is—uh, let's say twenty dollars. Does that sound okay?"

"Twenty dollars? Twenty dollars? I can do twenty dollars. Yes, that's lovely. Oh, thank you, thank you."

"You're welcome, ma'am. So—uh, tell me, when do you want this to run?"

"Well, I told my daughters and sons that it would run tomorrow."

"Tomorrow?"

"Yes, the funeral is tomorrow. I really want this to run on the same day. Is that okay? Will that be possible?"

I had no idea if it was possible. "Let me talk to the boys down in the print room," I said, as if I knew them. "And I'll call you back in a few minutes, okay?"

"Oh, yes, yes, I'll be waiting by the phone."

We said our good-byes and I slumped in my chair. In Lois's chair. What had I done? I'd made a promise I could not keep. I counted to one hundred, trying to find a cool center, and walked over to the chief's office.

"What do you want?" he asked.

"I think I screwed up."

"Well, isn't that a surprise," he said. I wanted to punch the sarcasm out of his throat.

"This woman—her husband died," I said. "And she wanted to write the obituary and run his photo—"

"That costs extra."

"I know. I read that on Lois's desk. But I read incorrectly, I think."

"How incorrectly?"

"Well, I think it's supposed to cost, like, one hundred dollars to run the obit and the size photo she wants—"

"How much did you tell her it would cost?"

"Twenty."

"So you gave her an eighty-percent discount?"

"I guess."

He stared at me. Judged me. He'd once been a Pulitzer finalist for a story about a rural drug syndicate.

"And there's more," I said.

"Yes?" His anger was shrinking his vocabulary.

"I told her we'd run it tomorrow."

"Jesus," he said. "Damn it, kid."

I think he wanted to fire me, to throw me out of his office, out of his building, out of his city and country. I suddenly realized that he was grieving for Lois, that he was angry about her death. Of course he was. They had worked together for two decades. They were friends. So I tried to forgive him for his short temper. And I did forgive him, a little.

"I'm sorry," I said.

"Well, shit on a rooster," he said, and leaned back in his chair. "Listen. I know this is a tough gig here. This is not your job. I know that. But this is a newspaper and we measure the world by column inches, okay? We have to make tough decisions about what can fit and what cannot fit. And by telling this woman—this poor woman—that she could have this space tomorrow, you have fucked with the shape of my world, okay?"

"Yes, sir," I said.

He ran his fingers through his hair (my father did the same thing when he was pissed), made a quick decision, picked up his phone, and made the call.

"Hey, Charlie, it's me," he said. "Do we have any room for another obituary? With a photo?"

I could hear the man screaming on the other end.

"I know, I know," the chief said. "But this is an important one. It's a family thing."

The chief listened to more screaming, then hung up on the other guy.

"All right," he said. "The woman gets one column inch for the obit."

"That's not much," I said.

"She's going to have to write a haiku, isn't she?"

I wanted to tell him that haikus were not supposed to be elegies, but then I realized that I wasn't too sure about that literary hypothesis.

"What do I do now?" I asked.

"We need the obit and the photo by three o'clock."

It was almost one.

"How do I get them?" I asked.

"Well, you could do something crazy like get in a car, drive to this woman's house, pick up the obit and the photo, and bring them back here."

"I don't have a car," I said.

"Do you have a driver's license?"

"Yes."

"Well, then, why don't you go sign a vehicle out of the car pool and do your fucking job?"

I fled. Obtained the car. And while cursing Lois and her early death, and then apologizing to Lois for cursing her, I drove up Maple to the widow's small house on Francis. A green house with a white fence that was maybe one foot tall. A useless fence. It couldn't keep out anything.

I rang the doorbell and waited a long time for the woman— Mona, her name was Mona—to answer. She was scrawny, thin-haired, dark for a white woman. At least eighty years old. Maybe ninety. Maybe older than that. I did the math. Geronimo was still alive when this woman was born. An old raven, I thought. No, too small to be a raven. She was a starling.

"Hello," she said.

"Hi, Mona," I said. "I'm from the *Spokesman;* we talked on the phone."

"Oh, yes, oh, yes, please come in."

I followed her inside into the living room. She slowly, painfully, sat on a wooden chair. She was too weak and frail to lower herself into a soft chair, I guess. I sat on her couch. I looked around the room and realized that every piece of furniture, every painting, every knickknack and candlestick, was older than me. Most of the stuff was probably older than my parents. I saw photographs of Mona, a man I assumed was her husband, and five or six children, and a few dozen grandchildren. Her children and grandchildren, I guess. Damn, her children were older than my parents. Her grandchildren were older than me.

"You have a nice house," I said.

"My husband and I lived here for sixty years. We raised five children here."

"Where are your children now?"

"Oh, they live all over the country. But they're all flying in tonight and tomorrow for the funeral. They loved their father. Do you love your father?"

My father was a drunken liar.

"Yes," I said. "I love him very much."

"That's good, you're a good son. A very good son."

She smiled at me. I realized she'd forgotten why I was there.

"Ma'am, about the obituary and the photograph?"

"Yes?" she said, still confused.

"We need them, the obituary you wrote for your husband, and his photograph?"

And then she remembered.

"Oh, yes, oh, yes, I have them right here in my pocket."

She handed me the photograph and the obit. And yes, it was clumsily written and mercifully short. The man in the photograph was quite handsome. A soldier in uniform. Black hair, blue eyes. I wondered if his portrait had been taken before or after he'd killed somebody.

"My husband was a looker, wasn't he?" she asked.

"Yes, very much so."

"I couldn't decide which photograph to give you. I mean, I thought I might give you a more recent one. To show you what he looks like now. He's still very handsome. But then I thought, No, let's find the most beautiful picture of them all. Let the world see my husband at his best. Don't you think that's romantic?"

"Yes, you must have loved him very much," I said.

"Oh, yes, he was ninety percent perfect. Nobody's all perfect, of course. But he was close, he was very close."

Her sentiment was brutal.

"Listen, ma'am," I said. "I'm sorry, but I have to get these photographs back to the newspaper if they're going to run on time."

"Oh, don't worry, young man, there's no rush."

Now I was confused. "But I thought the funeral was tomorrow?" I asked.

"Oh, no, silly, I buried my husband six months ago. In Veterans' Cemetery. He was at D-Day."

"And your children?"

"Oh, they were here for the funeral, but they went away."

But she looked around the room as if she could still see her kids. Or maybe she was remembering them as they had been, the children who'd indiscriminately filled the house and then, just as indiscriminately, had moved away and into their own houses. Or maybe everything was ghosts, ghosts, ghosts. She scared me. Maybe this house was lousy with ghosts. I was afraid that Lois's ghost was going to touch me on the shoulder and gently correct my errors.

"Mona, are you alone here?" I asked. I didn't want to know the answer.

"No, no—well, yes, I suppose. But my Henry, he's buried in the backyard."

"Henry?"

"My cat. Oh, my beloved cat."

And then she told me about Henry and his death. The poor cat, just as widowed as Mona, had fallen into a depression after her husband's death. Cat and wife mourned together.

"You know," she said. "I read once that grief can cause cancer. I think it's true. At least, it's true for cats. Because that's what my Henry had, cancer of the blood. Cats get it all the time. They see a lot of death, they do."

And so she, dependent on the veterinarian's kindness and charity, had arranged for her Henry to be put down.

"What's that big word for killing cats?" she asked me.

"Euthanasia," I said.

"Yes, that's it. That's the word. It's kind of a pretty word, isn't it? It sounds pretty, don't you think?"

"Yes."

"Such a pretty word for such a sad and lonely thing," she said.

"Yes, it is," I said.

"You can name your daughter Euthanasia and nobody would even notice if they didn't know what the word meant."

"I suppose," I said.

"My cat was too sick to live," Mona said.

And then she told me how she'd held Henry as the vet injected him with the death shot. And, oh, how she cried when Henry's heart and breath slowed and stopped. He was gone, gone, gone. And so she brought him home, carried him into the backyard, and laid him beside the hole she'd paid a neighbor boy to dig. That neighbor boy was probably fifty years old.

"I prayed for a long time," she said. "I wanted God to know that my cat deserved to be in Heaven. And I didn't want Henry to be in cat heaven. Not at all. I wanted Henry to go find my husband. I want them both to be waiting for me."

And so she prayed for hours. Who can tell the exact time at such moments? And then she kneeled beside her cat. And that was painful because her knees were so old, so used—like the ancient sedan in the garage—and she pushed her Henry into the grave and poured salt over him.

"I read once," she said, "that the Egyptians used to cover dead bodies with salt. It helps people get to Heaven quicker. That's what I read."

When she poured the salt on her cat, a few grains dropped and burned in his eyes.

"And let me tell you," she said. "I almost fell in that grave when my Henry meowed. Just a little one. I barely heard it. But it was there. I put my hand on his chest and his little heart was beating. Just barely. But it was beating. I couldn't believe it. The salt brought him back to life."

Shit, I thought, the damn vet hadn't injected enough death juice into the cat. Shit, shit, shit.

"Oh, that's awful," I said.

"No, I was happy. My cat was alive. Because of the salt. So I called my doctor—"

"You mean you called the vet?"

"No, I called my doctor, Ed Marashi, and I told him that it was a miracle, that the salt brought Henry back to life."

I wanted to scream at her senile hope. I wanted to run to Lois's grave and cover her with salt so she'd rise, replace me, and be forced to hear this story. This was her job; this was her responsibility.

"And let me tell you," the old woman said. "My doctor was amazed, too, so he said he'd call the vet and they'd both be over, and it wasn't too long before they were both in my home. Imagine! Two doctors on a house call. That doesn't happen anymore, does it?"

It happens when two graceful men want to help a fragile and finite woman.

And so she told me that the doctors went to work on the cat. And, oh, how they tried to bring him back all the way, but there just wasn't enough salt in the world to make it happen. So the doctors helped her sing and pray and bury her Henry. And, oh, yes—Dr. Marashi had sworn to her that he'd tried to help her husband with salt.

"Dr. Marashi said he poured salt on my husband," she said. "But it didn't work. There are some people too sick to be salted."

She looked around the room as if she expected her husband and cat to materialize. How well can you mourn if you continually forget that the dead are dead?

I needed to escape.

"I'm really sorry, ma'am," I said. "I really am. But I have to get back to the newspaper with these."

"Is that my husband's photograph?" she asked.

"Yes."

"And is that his obituary?"

"Yes," I said. "It's the one you wrote."

"I remember, I remember."

She studied the artifacts in my hands.

"Can I have them back?" she asked.

"Excuse me?"

"The photo, and my letter, that's all I have to remember my husband. He died, you know?"

"Yes, I know," I said.

"He was at D-Day."

"If I give you these back," I said. "I won't be able to run them in the newspaper."

"Oh, I don't want them in the newspaper," she said. "My husband was a very private man."

Ah, Lois, I thought, you never told me about this kind of death.

"I have to go now," I said. I wanted to crash through the door and run away from this house fire.

"Okay, okay. Thank you for visiting," she said. "Will you come back? I love visitors."

"Yes," I said. I lied. I knew I should call somebody about her dementia. She surely couldn't take care of herself anymore. I knew I should call the police or her doctor or find her children and tell them. I knew I had responsibilities to her—to this grieving and confused stranger—but I was young and terrified.

So I left her on her porch. She was still waving when I turned the corner. Ah, Lois, I thought, are you with me, are you with me? I drove the newspaper's car out of the city and onto the freeway. I drove for three hours to the shore of Soap Lake, an inland sea heavy with iron, calcium, and salt. For thousands of years, my indigenous ancestors had traveled here to be healed. They're all gone now, dead by disease and self-destruction. Why had they believed so strongly in this magic water when it never protected them for long? When it might not have protected them at all? But you, Lois, you were never afraid of death, were you? You laughed and played. And you honored the dead with your brief and serious prayers.

Standing on the shore, I prayed for my dead. I praised them. I stupidly hoped the lake would heal my small wounds. Then I stripped off my clothes and waded naked into the water.

Jesus, I don't want to die today or tomorrow, but I don't want to live forever.

Food Chain

This is my will:

Bury me
In an anthill.

After one week
Of this feast,

Set the ants on fire.
Make me a funeral pyre.

Let my smoke rise
Into the eyes

Of those crows
On the telephone wire.

Startle those birds
Into flight

With my last words:
I loved my life.

Good News
for
Married Lovers

Good News
for
Married Lovers

A Scriptural Path for
Marriage Renewal

CHARLES GALLAGHER, S.J., & MARY ANGELEE SEITZ

Liguori
LIGUORI, MISSOURI

Imprimi Potest:
Richard Thibodeau, C.Ss.R.
Provincial, Denver Province
The Redemptorists

Published by Liguori Publications
Liguori, Missouri
www.liguori.org
www.catholicbooksonline.com

Excerpts from *The New Jerusalem Bible*, copyright © 1985 by Doubleday,
a division of Bantam, Doubleday, Dell Publishing Group, Inc. and Darton,
Longman & Todd, Ltd. Used by permission of the publisher.

Library of Congress Cataloging-in-Publication Data

Gallagher Chuck, 1927–
        Good news for married lovers : a scriptural path to marriage renewal /
Chuck Gallagher, Mary Angelee Seitz.—Rev. ed.
            p.   cm.
        ISBN 0-7648-0998-9 (pbk.)
        1. Marriage—Religious aspects—Christianity. 2. Love—Religious as-
pects—Christianity. I. Seitz, Mary Angelee. II. Title.

BV835.G34 2003
248.8'44—dc21   2003044618

Contents

Introduction

Two thousand years ago, Jesus Christ came into the world with a promise. "Give," he said, "and there will be gifts for you: a full measure, pressed down, shaken together and overflowing, will be poured into your lap" (Lk 6:38).

In married couples today, there is a full measure of goodness, pressed down, shaken together and overflowing. There's confusion, too. We've been taught to grab what we can, to satisfy ourselves with things instead of people: with hobbies, careers, clothes, cars.

Thus there are legalistic prenuptial agreements and long-distance two-career families. That's why logic has taken the place of trust, and we seek to fill the emptiness with purchases from the store.

Lord, we're making ourselves so unhappy. And we don't even know why. We need to let go; to trust. To hope and to dream. We need to face the wrongs we've done and forget those done against us. We need to forgive and be forgiven.

There is no easy recipe for happiness, but a promise: of gifts, a full measure, pressed down, shaken together and overflowing. To seek those gifts, we have to reach outside ourselves. We have to have the courage to love, even when it isn't easy. We begin by cherishing those marvelous gifts God has already given us: our husbands and wives.

This book will challenge you to heal each other's hurts, to love each other more deeply than you could ever have imagined, to paint for each other a vivid portrait of God's unbounded love.

Unfortunately, a hurried glance through this book—or any other—won't renew your marriage. But if you read this book carefully, thoughtfully, applying it to your life, the rewards will astonish you. Summer romance, even honeymoon delirium, is nothing compared to the loving, warm, passionate relationship you can share when you invite God—and each other—into your lives.

Ideally, this book isn't for only one of you. It's written for couples. If possible, both of you should read each chapter, pray over it, and discuss it between you. As you read, don't think of yourself as having failed so far. See, instead, how beautiful you are and how much more the Lord is offering you. Growing in love is like learning a language. The more accomplished we become, the more we are able to speak. We are learning to speak the language of the Lord.

That language begins with Scripture. Through the Scriptures, the Lord tells us how we can receive his gifts of happiness and peace. In this book, the Scriptures are applied specifically to married couples to help you think about each other more tenderly, to be more open to each other, to talk with freedom and trust.

In each chapter, you'll find problems and explanations, examples and questions to help you be open: to yourself, to God, and to your spouse. Many of the questions will be for you to ponder in private. Others are to be shared with your love. During your discussions, each of you should express only your own feelings. Describe how each chapter relates to you. Never blame your spouse; always treat his or her sharing with gratitude and respect. Remember, your beloved will be entrusting you with his or her most intimate feelings. No gift is more fragile, or more precious.

At the end of each chapter, you will have the option to write to your love. Please take it. When writing, your words come forth just as you intend them: clear, uninterrupted, unchanged by body language. You will discover hidden feelings of pain and joy, fear and comfort, both in yourself and in your beloved. Chapter by chapter, you'll find yourselves growing closer. In a few months, read this book again. Its meaning will have grown, even as you have.

If you must read alone, by all means do so. Then put this book under your love's pillow, or on top of his or her coffee cup. Speak gently. And pray, really pray, for your love to pick it up.

CHAPTER 1

What Is Love?

"If I Am Without Love, I Am Nothing."
(1 COR 13:1–13)

If you were asked the question, "What is love?" what would you answer? Many of us would define love in terms of warmth, closeness, or sexual attraction. Others would define love in terms of feelings: maybe the glow we feel when someone is nice to us. Most of us see love as "what's going on inside me."

Philosophical types might define love in terms of action: love is doing the right thing. Married couples often use this definition. It brings to mind phrases like "Love is living up to your responsibilities. Love is fulfilling the commitments you've made."

There's a third definition of love, one that isn't passive and self-centered, contained within ourselves, or dependent on a personal mood. Instead, it is joyful: reaching out, celebrating the good around us, casting off the mundane weight of everyday troubles.

This definition of love was written by Saint Paul in his first letter to the Corinthians. He says love is more important than anything else.

Though I command languages both human and angelic—if I speak without love, I am no more than a gong booming or a cymbal clashing. And though I have the power of prophecy, to penetrate all mysteries and knowledge, and though I have all the faith necessary to move mountains—if I am without love, I am nothing. Though I should give away to the poor all that I possess, and even give up my body to be burned—if I am without love, it will do me no good whatever.

Love is always patient and kind; love is never jealous; love is not boastful or conceited, it is never rude and never seeks its own advantage, it does not take offense or store up grievances. Love does not rejoice at wrongdoing, but finds its joy in the truth. It is always ready to make allowances, to trust, to hope and to endure whatever comes.

Love never comes to an end. But if there are prophecies, they will be done away with; if tongues, they will fall silent; and if knowledge, it will be done away with. For we know only imperfectly, and we prophesy imperfectly; but once perfection comes, all imperfect things will be done away with. When I was a child, I used to talk like a child, and see things as a child does, and think like a child, but now that I have become an adult, I have finished with all childish ways. Now we see only reflections in a mirror, mere riddles, but then we shall be seeing face to face. Now, I can know only imperfectly; but then I shall know just as fully as I am myself known.

As it is, these remain: faith, hope and love, the three of them; and the greatest of them is love.

1 CORINTHIANS 13:1–13

Most of us don't believe that this Scripture passage is a practical definition of love. That's tragic. This kind of love is, indeed, real. But so many of us pass it by, searching all the while somewhere else.

To understand why Saint Paul wrote this passage, we need to understand the apostle himself. We think of him as a great apostle, a brilliant man who came out with magnificent theology. That's true, but Paul was, first of all, a lover. He was driven to bring Jesus to all those he could reach.

To see how loving he is, read the greetings that close his epistles. They're full of phrases like "Remember me to this person," or "Tell that person I was thinking about her." He closes his first letter to the Romans, for instance, with the hope that, "after longing for many years past to visit you, to see you when I am on the way to Spain" (1 Rom 15:23).

Although Saint Paul was always facing forward, he constantly left his heart behind, among the people to whom he had already announced the glad tidings of Jesus Christ. Saint Paul speaks of love and, in doing so, speaks of his ambition for his beloved people. He wants them to be happy, to live in harmony with Jesus Christ. He offers them a way to truly enjoy life.

Paul knew there were no easy follow-the-directions recipes for perfect love. Paul doesn't say, "If you follow these instructions, you'll be a successful woman, a great man." Instead, he says, "Love is...." He isn't talking about good deeds; he's talking about a quality of life.

Love, according to Paul, is in the very fiber of our being. If we're loving people, anyone who touches our lives will be better off. We simply couldn't resist someone who is living a life of love. In our hearts, we know Saint Paul is right, and even hearing that passage is a moving experience.

Love Is Always Patient

Let's look at the qualities Paul lists in his model for love. Which one does he choose first? Patience. If we were writing that first letter to the Corinthians, would patience have been the first loving virtue that popped into our minds? Probably not. That's why the Lord chose Saint Paul, not us, to write that letter.

Often, we're difficult to live with because we're in such a rush. We want that other person to love us immediately.

We are impatient and now-oriented: "I want you to talk to me *now*. I want supper *now*. I want to go out *now*. I want you off the phone *now*." How often does this simple lack of patience cause friction in our relationships with one another? Saint Paul was wise when he wrote that love is patient. If we could just get "now" out of our vocabularies, our marriages would be so much happier.

Our urgency isn't confined to small daily concerns. Sometimes we're terribly impatient about serious issues. We withdraw from our loves simply because they aren't changing fast enough. We give up on each other in sex, for instance, or in understanding.

"He'll never change," we say to ourselves, or perhaps, "That's the way she is." Translated, these phrases mean, "I've tried hard enough."

We've given a great deal of attention, energy, effort, persuasion, encouragement, or affection; whatever we thought was needed. We've reached out to the other person and we haven't received a proper response. Nothing seems to be happening, so we decide to leave the other person alone. We don't do that because it's good for that person, but because we're disheartened and weary of trying.

Women are practiced at being much more persistently loving. Take, for example, a day when a woman's husband is angry or moody. She tries to put a hand on his arm, but he shakes it off. She smiles, but he frowns. She backs off, then comes back again with a nice word. Perhaps she tries the hand on his arm again or brings him a drink. Saint Paul was writing about this type of patient love. We have to be willing to stay with each other, not to take no for an answer but to try again in gentleness and tenderness.

Perhaps the husband comes home and sees his wife has had a tough day. She's so down, she doesn't want to talk. He gives her a hug and squeeze. He says, "Honey, what's the matter?"

She says, "Nothing."

He tries again. "Ah, come on, really, what's the matter? I can tell there's something wrong."

"No, I'm fine," she says, with that special overtone to the word "fine."

He rolls his eyes. Maybe he pours himself a drink and tries again. He is a good man. He puts his hands on her shoulders and she shrugs them off.

At this point, he decides, "Well, I did as much as I could." He takes his drink, goes to another room, and reads the paper. "She'll come out of it," he thinks. "When she wants to talk, she'll talk."

But he's really not present to her anymore. He's back in his own world and she'll have to recover alone.

We limit our patience with our husbands, wives, and children to what we think is reasonable. How can something be wrong if it feels so—reasonable?

It is, nonetheless. The devil doesn't tempt good people into doing bad things. The devil always tempts us into doing something less good. Often, we're awfully proud of ourselves because we're avoiding the biggest sins. We haven't robbed any banks or had any orgies.

Reasonableness is one of the most common anti-love concepts in our lives. Why? Because it limits patience. We'll be patient only to a certain point. Once that point is reached, we think we don't have to try anymore.

How many times have we used, "It's against good reason" as an excuse for not being lovers? The lines we draw between reasonable and unreasonable may differ greatly from person to person, but they're always there.

Saint Paul didn't say, "Be patient when it makes sense." He didn't say that love is patient and reasonable either. In fact, reason isn't mentioned once in Paul's entire list. He did say love is patient; it is always ready to make allowances, it endures whatever comes.

We stop being patient because this level of self-sacrifice doesn't meet our needs. Perhaps we get fed up or we don't think we're getting enough consideration. Perhaps anger is starting to churn within us.

"I have really been loving," a wife might say. "What more can I do? He takes me for granted; the least he could do is appreciate my efforts." A man might think, "How much longer is she planning to sulk? I've done all I can."

Love Works Overtime

We're all good, generous people, but even good people tend to ration patience like a precious jewel. We allot a certain amount of time to coax our husbands out of their bad moods or to help our wives solve their problems of the moment. If they don't respond in the proper time frame, we give up. We've done our best, and now we're off the hook.

Remember, it's not whether your effort is reasonable but whether it's successful. If, like Saint Paul, we're lovers, we simply have to keep on until it works.

Patience is other-centered. When I'm a lover, you become my agenda. If, instead, there's something else on my agenda, I can't help but think, "How much more time can I spend with you before I have to leave?" I don't have to leave physically. Maybe my favorite television show is coming on in thirty minutes. Perhaps it's getting late and if we don't wind this up, I won't get my sleep. Maybe I have to make lunches for the kids, fix that faucet.

I simply can't have something else to do when my spouse needs me. If you, my lover, need me to be present to you, I simply have to make you my priority. No matter how long it takes, I'm yours. If later I get around to my other plans, fine, but I'm not counting on that right now because you need me.

That can be very hard to do sometimes. Especially if you're well organized, you might be tempted to think, "But I just can't live that way. There are things that have to be done around here. He understands it as well as I do," or "She knows I can't spend twenty-four hours a day with her."

Our lovers know about all our other obligations; they're very conscious of them, indeed. If they still feel they need us right now, their needs are obviously important. What if the dishes did go unwashed? What if the kids' lunches didn't get made and we had to take them to school later on? What if we did go to work a little sleepy because we stayed up late talking to our spouses? We'd be happier, that's all.

Still, we keep fitting our lovers into our schedules. Think about it. Are our husbands less important than a set of dishes? Are our wives less valuable than the scores of last night's game?

Of course not. Yet our priorities speak louder than our words.

That's why Saint Paul was wise when he chose patience as the first quality of love. If we could just discipline ourselves to give our lovers absolute priority in our lives, our marriages would be so much better.

A "Give" Proposition

We often think of patience as passivity, but Saint Paul's definition has nothing to do with an even temper. "If I don't say anything abrasive," we might think, "I'm patient." Not necessarily. We may be steaming inside, or perhaps we're people who never get angry. It may not be virtue; it may be indifference.

On the other hand, maybe our husbands do shout sometimes, or our wives snap at the children, but they never quit trying to reach out when we need them. Patience is sticking with each other, regardless of response.

That takes trust and sometimes even strength. We can't say, "I love you, but you have to respond to me pretty soon because I have to feel your love, too." That's like saying, "Hurry up and love me before it's too late, because my love won't last."

Paul says that real love loves regardless. Love doesn't say, "I'll give you my love as long as I feel good about it." It doesn't say, "As soon as I start getting frustrated because you're not listening, I'll stop talking to you. I won't say anything nasty, but I'll wait until you're ready." We make love a give-and-take proposition. It's not. It's a give proposition: I give love because I love you.

Love Is Kind

Kindness is a very special gift. Probably the closest we can come to canonizing someone in normal, human terms is to say, "She's really kind," or "He's a kind person." Kindness is something quite different. Saint Paul says love *is* kind. Paul is not talking about performing a number of kind actions. He is talking about living a kind lifestyle, creating that atmosphere in the home. When a husband and wife are living in kindness, there is joy, peace, and delight in that place.

This quality should be the one you most desire for yourselves, because it's the best gift you can give to another. Kindness is a gentle concern for the needs of others, a desire to make them happy and relieve their pain. Affection is a very strong ingredient in kindness.

Kindness can be present in small, everyday actions, but the same actions may not reflect kindness at all. Perhaps you're being kind when you put out the garbage. Maybe not; maybe you're just being obedient or trying to avoid trouble.

The same activity can be good or neutral. Fixing the faucet or dusting a table can be either a chore or an act of kindness. In the second instance, there is an obvious affection in the way you do it. But in the first, you're just doing the work.

This affection, this tenderness, this gentleness, come from a reverence for the other person. That's why kindness is not present merely in our actions, no matter how good they may be. For kindness to be truly present, there must be warmth in our hearts. We can't be thinking only of what we're doing; we have to be conscious of whom we're doing it for, and our feelings of love must be evident.

Do you see yourself as a kind person, not just one who does kind things? We all do kind things, and frequently, too, but that doesn't mean we're living a kind way of life.

Perhaps you are thinking, "I really wish I could look at myself in a mirror and say, 'Yes, you are a kind person.' I can't. I know how wonderful that would be for my spouse. But I just wasn't put together that way."

Maybe you are finding it difficult to even think of yourself as kind. Don't be discouraged and don't give up. Each of us has the potential to be as kind as Mother Teresa of Calcutta.

Kindness is a virtue, not a talent. Talent, I either have or don't have. I'm either six foot ten with a great deal of agility and a good shooting eye or I'm five foot six and I'm just not going to make it as a big-time basketball player. I either have an IQ of 190 and can earn a doctorate in geophysics at a school like Harvard, or I just can't do that.

Virtue, though, is there for the taking. If I go into the bank and take money, I'm a thief, but if I go to an undiscovered island and find diamonds on the beach, they're mine to keep. Like those diamonds, virtue is a free gift.

I can't say I'm not kind because kindness wasn't given to me. I can't think that some people are naturally kind, and I'm not one of them. Some people have better personalities than others, yes. Some people have less abrasive temperaments or are less driven. But nobody, by nature, is kinder than I am.

When someone is kinder than I am, it's because that person has chosen to be kind and I have not. I have to decide: will I be kind? Notice, it's "will I?" This "will" is not the future tense of the verb "to be." It's "will" in the sense of the Latin word *volo:* I will it, I choose; I decide to be a kind person.

I can't value kindness just because it makes me a better man or woman. I shouldn't make a checklist of my virtues, then study it to decide where I score high and where I need work.

I should take on kindness for the sake of my lover, not for my own sake. That's a very important lesson and a very hard one. We humans really are so self-centered, even in our virtues. I'll say, "Yes, this is the kind of person I should be." Then I go out to further my own integrity. Rather, I should be saying, "This is the kind of spouse my partner should have."

We can't excuse a lack of kindness by saying everyone has defects, that we'll make up for our lack in other ways. That's a self-centered response. It's like saying, "Well, I score pretty well when you consider everything."

We can't say, "Well, I'm kind enough to suit my taste. I don't think I'm bad at it." We have to concentrate, instead, on how others perceive us. Do they believe we're approachable? Do they think they have to warm us up—or thaw us out—before mentioning certain subjects? Are they nervous because they don't know how we're going to react? We might discover that we frighten them.

We should all ask ourselves, "Am I a fearsome person?" We're dodging the issue if we ask merely, "Do I sometimes get mad?" Anger is only a symptom of a larger ill. Must our lovers go through all sorts of contortions, building up the courage to risk talking to us about something important?

We can inspire fear in our spouses without shouting. Maybe we're soft-spoken on the outside. Maybe we don't get angry at all, but there is a tenseness about us; our lovers never know when the volcano is going to erupt. It never has because it never has to. Like a nuclear warhead, it's a deterrent.

When we're in the presence of a kind person, we always feel relaxed and at ease. We can be ourselves. We don't have to weigh our words or wonder how to bring up certain topics.

Those around us best experience our kindness when they believe we're pleased with them. When we're kind, they know we're always on their side. That doesn't mean we agree with everything they say, do, and think. It means that no matter what happens, we're always with them. That type of mentality, expressed both verbally and nonverbally, brings our lovers tremendous security and a sense of well-being.

Our natural reaction is to want to do something about acting kind. We say, "Okay, how do I do it?" Ask yourselves these questions: "When I'm sitting on the sofa, reading the paper, or stirring soup at the stove, how tender am I toward my spouse?"

If we find a hardness in ourselves or even just a shoulder shrug, we have to change. We have to stop, breathe deeply, and deliberately build up some kind thoughts about our husbands or wives. We have to reflect on those qualities that originally attracted us to them.

There are many practical ways to be kind. What about the kindness of a truly gentle kiss, or a look across the kitchen table that's misted over a bit with gratitude and affection, or a hug during the evening, for no reason at all? Often, kindness is translated into perfume, flowers, and restaurant meals. That's fine, but it's much kinder to be alert on the days we're not going out or buying gifts.

We have trouble achieving kindness because we aren't spontaneous. We tend to practice it only when it's needed: when something is wrong or when we've hurt someone. More important are the small kindnesses we can do every day, not for any reason but just to be kind. Of course, we do have to respond to our lovers' needs, but it's even better to have kindness flowing from our very being. Then we're going beyond healing hurts. We're creating an environment in which our lovers truly enjoy life.

Love Is Never Jealous

We imagine typical pictures of jealousy, for example, of a woman who tells her husband, "We're going home," because another woman talked to him for thirty seconds; of a man who won't let his wife out of the house unless he's with her. Most of us don't have that type of jealousy. We're jealous in subtler, more significant ways, and we're jealous more often than we think.

What makes us jealous? Usually, it's the small things. If our spouse is heavily praised, we think it's great—providing we get equal time. Sometimes we're jealous when the children bring their needs to our spouse. "Why do they always go to her?" we grumble. "Why don't they come to me?"

Sometimes the jealousy is more serious, an envy of lifestyles: "He has it so good," we think. "He spends money on his clothes and people respect him. I stay home all the time, just like the family dog."

Part of the reason for this jealousy is that we're expected to be that way. Ever since we were little, we've been trained to resent others' good fortune. Sometimes the other person doesn't even deserve our envy. Maybe a neighbor goes on trips and stays in interesting places, but once a person's comfortable with the idea of checking into a hotel, those "interesting" places all begin to look the same, whether in Paris or San Diego, Hawaii or Hartford.

Jealously is anti-love. Jealousy is thinking about me. It's concentrating on what I'm getting out of our marriage. It's not finding delight in the other person's delight. It's a mean, ugly little vice.

Too often we excuse ourselves by saying, "Well, that's the kind of person I am. He knew that when he married me," or "She knew I wouldn't want her spending all her time with the kids."

Jealousy, of course, is not necessarily an overall attitude. It can be restricted to one or a few areas of a couple's life together. Maybe I'm not generally jealous of you, but I am jealous of your relationship with your mother, your success at work, or the way the children obey you. That jealousy strongly interferes with the love and trust that should be between us.

Love Is Not Boastful or Conceited

We have a hard time believing this passage of Scripture was meant for us. Maybe the Corinthians were conceited, but we aren't. To the contrary, Paul knew what he was talking about. We can be conceited no matter what our circumstances.

When does our conceit cause us to obey the loveless rules of this world? When do we turn our backs on the love that could be ours? We could think, for instance, that we're superior in logic. "If he'd only listen to *me...*" we might think, or "If only she'd take *my* advice."

Maybe we're overly proud because of our professional credentials. We might be overly proud of our openness or even our reserve: "I'm in touch with my feelings. Now if he would only get in touch with his, we'd have a great marriage." Or "I don't say anything if I can't improve on silence."

We can even feel smug about our insecurities. We might think, "I'm so sensitive, I'm better at love than he is," or "Where would she be without my support?"

We can also feel superior about our jobs. We might say, "I have to earn a living. I don't have time for...." Fill in any number of things. We can use this as an excuse not to work on our personalities at home, or to dodge out of spiritual growth or church work.

We can put on airs in our faith too. I grew up in an Irish Catholic neighborhood in New York City. My mother went to daily Mass and Communion, had attended Catholic schools, and was very active in church affairs.

My father never set foot inside a Catholic school. He went to Confession on Thursday before First Friday, went to Communion on First Friday and the following Sunday, and that was that until the next month. He worked nights, so he wasn't able to involve himself in church activities. He was a good man, but when it came to "real faith" in the family, we looked to our mother. Only after I had left home, when my dad was dead, did I realize that he was every bit as good a Catholic as my mother was.

Sometimes we can fool ourselves by looking at the externals. We might feel virtuous if we belong to a prayer group, or go to daily Mass and Communion. We're not putting anyone else down, but isn't there a hint of smugness there?

A good personal appearance is a mark of healthy self-respect, but we can also use it as a tool for conceit. We might think, "I'm pretty attractive. It would be a shame for me not to look my best." We can be equally conceited and think just the opposite: "I don't need to look good to feel good about myself. If you think I'm a slob, that shows how shallow you are."

❧❧

We can also be overly proud of the way we handle money, whether that means spending it or saving it. We may even be proud of the unselfish priority we give our lovers' needs. That's not pure generosity; it can also mean control.

We may seek to prove our lack of materialism by spending little and letting the money pile up in a bank account. Because we don't accumulate visible possessions, we deceive ourselves into thinking we're not acquisitive.

Most of us think we're not attached to money. Paradoxically, most of us also think we don't have enough of it. Money is an addiction; it's even stronger than heroin. People can break away from heroin, but how many of us can break away from money? Most of us probably think the idea's ridiculous. That's an indication of how addicted we really are.

Money can be a real area of conflict even between good husbands and wives, especially if one of them is not particularly good with the budget. Family finances might bore them or they're afraid they don't have any skills for dealing with bills and mortgages. Then their spouses are strongly tempted to feel superior. They may not be especially good at it, either, but they judge they are.

We're also yielding to superiority when we see ourselves as the givers in a love relationship: "Oh, he's a great guy. I'm glad I married him, but I'm the one who holds this marriage together," or "She's a wonderful woman, but she couldn't make it without me."

This feeling of superiority can encompass an entire marriage or only one specific area. In either case, it's not a harmless little idiosyncrasy. If we're going to live lives of love, we must thoroughly explore this attitude of superiority toward each other. Conceit and boastfulness aren't pretty words, and it's hard to be honest with ourselves about them. None of us like to see ourselves as haughty braggarts. Nonetheless, all of us do have feelings of superiority, no matter how good we are.

We're not speaking now of whether I can drive the car better, or sew a better seam, or change a flat tire on the highway. Those are skills; they pale in significance beside our personal qualities: kindness, understanding, listening, thoughtfulness.

Where do I consider myself superior to you? Sometimes we excuse ourselves by saying, "Well, my superiority is my contribution to our marriage. I'm more thoughtful and my spouse is more understanding. We work as a team."

That's not teamwork; it's competition. Superiority, no matter how gracious, is never a plus in a love relationship. Each of us brings special qualities into our love relationships, and that's great, unless they come with a price tag.

Sometimes we don't realize the superiority that hides even behind our compliments. We may say, "Yes, you are much more sensitive than I am. But I'm much better at making money." Or "Why don't you do the entertaining when people come over? After all, you're much better at it than I am." Or "Why don't you discipline the kids? You don't lose your temper like I do."

Conflict grows even more intense when we believe we're superior in the same area. Most often, couples clash over their children, because both of them think they know more about child-raising. But when parents clash over strict or lenient philosophies, a child doesn't see a philosophical debate. He sees the trauma of discord in the home and the lack of guidance.

Love Is Never Rude

Until now, Saint Paul's Scripture passage was serious. What happened here? Love is never rude? That's hardly worth bothering about, is it?

Wait. Let's think for a moment what a gift it would be to have a spouse who was naturally full of small courtesies. When you put all those courtesies together, they're no longer small.

During your dating days, you were delighted by all the little favors you did for each other. You wanted to show your reverence for each other; to let him know he was important to you, that she counted in your life. If we could put our best foot forward when we were dating, why can't we keep it there after we're married?

Why don't you take some time to think of all the tender little courtesies you performed for each other in your dating days and in the early days of your marriage? They really make quite a list, and you did them spontaneously, without thinking too much about them. Write them down, and when you're through, ask yourself a question. How could it be wrong to perform these little courtesies once again?

Maybe by now, you're squirming in your chair or rolling your eyes toward the ceiling. People would wonder what was going on. Even your spouse might be puzzled. But why not do them anyway? People would probably decide you were in love.

Unfortunately, we tend to wonder, "Are these things necessary anymore?" Don't look at them that way; look from the opposite perspective: "How could it hurt my beloved wife, my beloved husband, if I did these nice little things?"

When we think like that, we can't come up with any good reasons. We dropped those courtesies because they cost too much: too much effort, too much trouble.

That's why Saint Paul says love is not rude. When we're courteous toward our spouses, we're never rude. These courtesies may look small, but they create an atmosphere of kindness and concern. How often do we permit ourselves the sharp tone of voice, the imperious manner, the orders given, the demands we make.

Another form of rudeness is name calling. Language doesn't have to earn an "R" rating to be hurtful. Maybe I've cleaned up my vocabulary, but still there's a cynical tone of voice or a biting harshness in the way I say my love's name. It's only a name, I argue. But in truth, I've turned a vital part of my spouse's identity into a curse.

Perhaps I use a term of affection in a bitter tone: "Why don't you do the dishes—*honey*," or "I hear you—*dear.*" If I do this, I rob the endearment of its power. It will never hold the same loving meaning for my spouse again.

Perhaps we also need to examine our habits of teasing. Teasing can be a gentle gift, but it can also deliver a fist to the face.

Maybe I embarrassed my wife in front of others by a "little joke." At home that night, she told me she didn't like that. Even before she spoke, I knew she was unhappy, but I pointedly told her no one else was bothered by the joke.

If no one had been bothered—my wife included—it would have been all right. But since she was hurt, I should stop that kind of teasing. It's rude to be indifferent to her feelings.

We insist that our children say "thank you" and "please," but when we're angry with our husbands or wives, our "pleases" and "thank yous" become absolutely chilled with ice.

Saint Paul knew what he was saying when he wrote that love isn't rude. We've come to tolerate rudeness on daily basis, and we pay by losing happiness and peace in our homes. We're especially careless of the little courtesies, those small gifts of respect we once gave to each other. Now we're too busy or too "married" to work on them.

Love Never Seeks Its Own Advantage

In other words, love is not selfish. It's easy to be self-centered, to seek our own advantage, no matter how good we may be in so many ways. We certainly want our spouses to be happy, and we'll even help them seek their own happiness. But there's a difference: if they're not happy, we feel sad. If we're not happy, we feel a desperate sense of urgency. Instead of unity, we create a sense of distance, with ourselves irresistibly coming first.

This can happen in sex. We might think, "You want to watch television? Well, *I* want to make love," or "I can't make love to you tonight. I'm angry with you right now, and you wouldn't want me if my heart wasn't in it."

We can be self-seeking in conversation, too. "If your subject turns me on," we imply, "I'll listen. But you can't expect me to listen to a subject that doesn't interest me." In other words, I'm seeking my own entertainment rather than your satisfaction.

An early bird married to a night owl can be (an example of lovers) trapped in the lonely cycle of seeking their own advantage. For example: "For some reason, he likes getting up early," the wife says. "He whistles around the house when it's pitch-dark outside. I can hardly find my coffee before eight A.M., but I have lots of energy at night. I like to watch the late show after he goes to bed."

"I doze off in front of the television after supper," her husband adds. "I can't seem to help it. She threatens to put a construction sign over me that says: 'Man Sleeping.'"

If she worked during the day and he worked the night shift, they would realize how much they were suffering. But they—and many of us—establish such patterns in our own homes. It's a self-seeking way of life. We're really saying, "I'm not going to change my way of life for him," or "She can't seriously expect me to change the habits I've had for years."

God didn't create day people and night people, though. He made all people in his own image; he made them to be lovers.

It's both ironic and sad: many husbands feel despair because married passion "naturally" fades, but they arrange their lives so love has little chance to bloom. Likewise, many women feel lonely for their husbands' company, but create schedules that force their husbands to go to bed alone. No wonder these people are unhappy. But how do they make themselves feel better? By retreating even further into their estranged schedules.

Of course, these schedules often begin as a reaction to hurt or loneliness. A wife may think, "He doesn't pay any attention to me anyway. I might as well read a book," while her husband decides, "I might as well begin that big painting project. She won't want to make love tonight. She'll be reading." These situations call for healing, not retreat.

Who determines the schedule at your house: when meals are served, which activities and social events take place? If you're the one, ask yourself, "Am I being self-serving?" Selfishness often masquerades as efficiency or rightness. Do any of these sound like you:

"Nothing is going to happen around this house until the supper dishes are done."

"I'm not going to have those things hanging over me. I don't want to think about them for the rest of the night."

"Monday night football is my one form of relaxation, so don't plan anything for that night, and keep the kids out of the way."

"I have a right to enjoy myself and I don't care if you're tired. We're going out tonight."

Love Does Not Take Offense

Anger is probably the greatest source of friction in our homes. Its damage isn't confined to the trauma of fighting or even the chill of indifference. Often, anger is held in reserve as a threat, creating an air of constant tension.

How angry are you? That doesn't always mean, "How often do you shout?" You may be a very angry person, even though you never express your anger. Your anger is a method of control.

Perhaps you have to explode only once a year, because when you do, it's earth-shattering. The rest of the time, you have only to threaten to get angry and your lover will surrender.

How many wives are afraid their husbands might lose their tempers? Such a husband may control himself, but the effort is so intense, she'll say, "Settle down. I give in. I don't want you having a heart attack." Either way, he wins, and when there are winners in a marriage, everyone loses.

The threat of anger is especially effective when it promises to undermine the need for peace in the home. When a woman wants peace, she usually means, "There's something between us; let's get it out, even if it means a fight." The man's definition of peace, though, is closer to "I don't want to fight about it. If we have to resolve it in anger, let it lie buried."

A husband and wife could avoid many hurts if they would both think through a problem before talking it through. Often, we calm down when we take time to think. We can see our lover's side and we don't blurt out the first angry words that come to mind. The hurt from those angry words lasts a long time and it causes both of us to be wary in the future.

Many of us have learned to talk through our problems, and that's a marvelous improvement over keeping our problems inside, where they can poison a relationship. It's not good, though, to voice every angry feeling, no matter how much it hurts.

Let's add thinking things through to our repertoire of marital skills. When we know we're losing control, one of us should just say, "Time out." Then both of us should sit quietly holding hands for ten to fifteen minutes, thinking of where we stand on this problem, what we want resolved, and how we can talk calmly and lovingly.

We've talked about coping with our own anger. Now, how about our spouses' anger? Can we do anything about that? Yes, indeed, and not with blame or accusations. Each of us can ask ourselves, "How much do I provoke my lover's anger?"

We look on anger as a small failing, but it's probably the biggest cause of marital unhappiness. Anger is destructive because we use it as an excuse to say things we've been storing inside. We'll let something fester within us until it gets so painful, it spurts out. Then we'll excuse ourselves: "I only said that because I was angry."

The insults we deliver in anger often take months and even years to heal. In the meantime, those grudges poison the happiness of the person who's holding them.

Love Does Not Store Up Grievances

Love is not supposed to be resentful, but all of us do hold resentments at one time or another. How many of us are like the Greek hero Achilles, who sulked in his tent during the Trojan War because the king had taken away his girl?

We may think we're nursing our own hurts. Really, we're punishing our partners. We're creating a miserable environment in our homes, even if we do excuse ourselves with a phrase like "Well, I don't do this very often, but sometimes I just can't help it."

We need to find some other way to air those frustrations. Maybe we should talk them out more frequently, long before they have a chance to build up. If we let resentments silently churn inside, they grow into big issues, which could have been resolved so much more easily.

I remember going home for supper with a man once, a lawyer; when he opened the door and saw his wife's face, he knew a storm was coming. "Honey," he said, "can we have a statute of limitations of five years?" Actually, that statute should be much shorter. Why store up our pain and anguish for years when we can get rid of it right away?

How long should we be able to cling to a slight or an injury? No more than two days. If you haven't resolved a grievance within two days, forget it, and once you've talked it out, don't bring it up again. We can't keep bludgeoning our spouses with the same complaints.

Why don't you make a list of your grievances: grievances against your spouse that are in your heart right now. Be honest with yourself. What grudge do you have against her? What gripes do you have against him?

Think about them, one by one, then decide how you'll get rid of them. You'll be tempted to say, "I'll go ahead and list them, then we'll talk them out. That'll get rid of them." That won't work in this case. You've probably already talked out a lot of them without success. But even if you haven't, if they're more than two days old, consider them dead. Forget them.

You can do it if you truly want to. You remember them because you think about them and bring them up and mull them over. Now stop the brooding and start to ponder the good things instead. Try to remember the positive aspects of your relationship with each other rather than the negative ones. It's hard sometimes, but it works wonders.

If you're feeling some reluctance, don't be surprised. We really don't want to give up all our gripes. We treasure them; they're precious possessions, like wedding pictures or old athletic trophies. We think about them; we take them out and polish them whenever they start to fade.

Often we proclaim our hurts and declare our innocence by airing our marital grievances with our friends. Don't some wives put on halos and say, "That's what men do"? And some men do exactly the same thing, a bit more subtly, when they say, "Aren't women touchy about little things? They're always complaining." But listeners know that the speaker is talking about his wife. Somehow the conversation stirs up trouble. It may make your companions aware of flaws in their own wives—flaws they hadn't noticed before.

How often do wives talk to one another about their husbands? The conversations take different forms, but they usually all mean,

"See what I have to put up with?" Often, we're telling our own version of events, slanted by our own feelings. This is actually detraction and, often, it's slander. We're not free to destroy our spouses' reputations.

Worse, talking about our gripes can establish them more firmly in our minds. When friends respond sympathetically, we begin to feel justified. These friends aren't really friends; if they were, they'd work toward harmony, not division.

We each have a choice: we can continue to brood over our slights or mull over our spouses' virtues. Don't think that you can't stop brooding. That's an attitude of hopelessness. Your negativity is a bad habit, not a personality trait given to you by the Lord. Let today be the day you change. You've probably changed your goals in life, your job, even your values and ideals. Why not change your attitude as well?

We're all afraid to let go of the hurts; we think our spouses will take advantage of us. Even if they did, though, we'd be happier than we are now. Brooding certainly doesn't add joy to our lives. Our rights are very cold bedmates.

We have to be absolutely practical: do we want to live loving and happy lives or not? If we choose, we can be sharp-tongued and on target; our lovers won't get away with a thing. Then what have we accomplished?

Love Does Not Rejoice at Wrongdoing, But Finds Its Joy in the Truth

Sometimes we really do rejoice in wrongdoing: when the kids stand up to Mom or Dad, for instance. Occasionally we rejoice in saying. "I told you so"; "Now maybe he'll listen to me"; "She'll hear me next time and things will get better around here." Sometimes we're glad when we've said something hurtful to our lovers. Rather than feeling their pain, we're smug, at least for a moment. "Well, he hurt me," we say defensively. "She hurt me first. Maybe she ought to know how it feels."

Of course, we don't usually behave this way, but these things do happen, and they happen entirely too often. We'll yield to the temptation to take our lovers down a peg, or we'll be angry with them, angry enough to be pleased when something bad happens. We don't like to admit that about ourselves; it's too petty and mean. That's exactly what it is, and that's what we should remind ourselves when we're doing it. After all, we are people of God; we're truly free to change.

Love Always Makes Allowances

This means no retaliation. That's a real gift in marriage, isn't it? Too often, our spouses will do one small thing and we'll want to send in the army.

Because we're human, there is a streak of vengeance in each of us. We're good people with the strength to conquer it, but first we have to look it in the eye. Most of us don't see ourselves as vengeful, however. We want to believe retaliation is justified. We hold back for a while, but if we don't get satisfaction one way or another, we attack.

Let's ask ourselves, "How do we fight?" Are we all-out fighters? Maybe we pride ourselves on that. We're not peace-at-any-price types; we really fight. Then God help us. There are times when a fight is good to clear the air, but too often we fight so we can hurt our lovers as much as they've hurt us.

How do we react to unfairness? Do we seek fair play? Maybe we shouldn't. Fairness in a relationship is not a good thing. Christ calls us all to be givers, not to establish compromises.

In my study of Scripture, I found that Jesus never used the word *fair,* not even once. Fairness is a pagan standard, rather a nicely dressed "eye for an eye" philosophy. When we love, we're not preoccupied with our fair share.

A little child will pout when his parents say he can't have a toy. "It's not fair," he wails. He really means, "I have to have that toy; I'll be miserable if you don't give it to me."

Unfortunately, our definition of "unfair" is the same. We're saying, "I'm not getting enough"; enough attention, sex, money, time out, or relief from the chores. It really has nothing to do with injustice.

Do we keep score of the hurts in our marriages? Do we keep score in housework and chores?

How about with money? Do we keep mental ledgers on the amounts our partners spend? Usually we don't care how much it is, but if we really want something, we often find we can remember those expenditures.

How often do we keep score on time to ourselves? "She spent the whole afternoon at the mall, so why can't I watch the game for a few minutes?" or "He spent the whole afternoon watching that darned game. I have a right to run out for a few minutes to buy *his* socks."

We keep score in sex: "We made love last night; that ought to be enough to satisfy him"; "Why should she complain?"

We keep score in time spent with the family: "We stayed with his family for Thanksgiving; now it's my family's turn," or "Don't the kids have two sets of grandparents?"

Love Is Trust

Do you trust your spouse to respect and like you, or do you keep parts of yourself secret, afraid they'll provoke scorn or disapproval?

Men, ask yourselves a few questions to determine how you feel about trusting your wives: Do I trust her to make the basic family decisions, or do I decide how much to save and whether to sell the house? Do I discipline the children because I think I'm better equipped or because I don't really trust her with them? Do I trust her with money; with all of it or just the amount I allocate? When we get into the car, do I automatically sit in the driver's seat or do I trust her to drive me?

Wives, ask yourselves: Do I trust him enough to give him his paternity, or do I take his fatherhood away, letting him know the children are my responsibility? Do I trust him to care for myself and our children, or have I limited our family size because I can't handle it all by myself? Do I trust him to care for me better than I care for myself, or do I fend for myself, establishing a home life of my own and expecting him to fit in? Do I trust him to understand me or do I believe only another woman can understand a woman's heart?

Many times, we don't trust because of past hurts or failures. We can't remain locked in our own pain; that's a slow, miserable death. Our Lord is anxious to renew us. We must be willing to open ourselves to his healing.

Love Is Hope

How do you know if you're hopeful? It's not hard. The sign of hope is a willingness to change. I can say I have all the hope in the world, but unless I'm willing to change, I don't have any. If we're hopeless, we decide to continue living in mediocrity and making do with what we have.

Why don't you look at each other and silently ask, "Am I willing to change my relationship with you?" Your answer will show whether you have hope. Be careful with this one. You'll be tempted to look at each other and say, instead, "Yes, we do need changes around here. Are you ready to make them, dear?"

We humans are constantly aware of the good things others are failing to do and the bad things they ought to stop doing. We fail to realize that if we became more understanding, they'd be under less pressure.

Love Endures

We're good people; we really want to love our wives and husbands. So often, though, we think, "He makes it too hard." "She's so difficult to deal with." "I do my best, but how can you expect me to love him when he's behaving this way?" "How can you expect me to love her all my life?"

Saint Paul never asked you to love for fifty years. You can't. It's not human to be able, after being hurt deeply, to love day after day. You don't have to do that. You just have to love for today.

It's not possible to keep talking for thirty, forty, or fifty years to a person who doesn't understand you, but that lack of understanding will only have to be endured for today. We think because we've endured for a long time, we're excused from continuing. Really, that long track record of love is proof we can do it.

Too much of our love is based on our own perceptions. We're saying, "This is the way I want to be loved. Therefore, it must be the way you want to be loved, too." Without knowing it, we impose our style of loving on our spouses.

For example, a man may think sex will make everything all right. His wife may not feel that way, but she needs to know that it will, indeed, make things all right for him. She must heal his hurt the way he needs to be healed. Meanwhile, her husband must understand that sex isn't enough to heal her hurt. He may become frustrated with her renewing desire to talk, but he must realize how important it is to her.

One way isn't better than the other, and we shouldn't trade off: "How do you expect me to desire you when you won't even pay me any attention?" or "Okay, I'll listen awhile—and then we'll make love." Love has the power to endure. We don't want to endure. We'd rather our lovers change instead. Saint Paul calls us to the grace of endurance, to accept our spouses and respond to them in love.

If we're going to be true lovers, we must concentrate on our spouses. We must see love as a means to bring delight to them, not as a gift meant only for ourselves. When we become other-centered, we become happier as well. Small annoyances no longer bother us, and we become more cheerful and full of peace, no longer consumed with worries and regrets.

We can, indeed, live such lives if we ask for God's help. Each of us is supremely capable of patience and kindness and generosity of spirit.

Resources for Reflection

It would be very beautiful to go back and reread that passage from Saint Paul at the beginning of this chapter. As you do, remember that love doesn't exist in the abstract. This beloved woman or man of yours is your love. Then read that passage a second time, saying the name of your spouse wherever you see the word *love*.

You might read, "Jane is always patient and kind. She is never jealous....Mike is not boastful or conceited; he is never rude and never seeks his own advantage.... My beloved husband, you do not take offense or store up grievances....My dear wife, you are always ready to make allowances, to trust and to hope. My darling, you can endure whatever comes...."

Just mull that over. Think of specific ways she lives out her kindness, her hope, her endurance; ways you've experienced his patience, his refusal to be rude, his trust.

Then write these down, specifically listing the ways your spouse lives out these qualities. Don't write generalities, but memories: examples of what you have personally experienced.

Make a full list. The more detailed you are, the more meaningful it will be. Don't remember only the spectacular occasions. The little ones count, too, and they definitely add up.

When you're through, take that list and exchange it with your spouse. This can be a moment of great tenderness between you.

Maybe your love won't write his or her list. That's all right. Write yours anyway, then give it to your spouse. See, we keep falling into that trap of fairness: "If he doesn't write his list, mine will be a waste. Why should I bother?" Your list alone will be a great gift for both of you, giving you an increased awareness of yourself and a greater opportunity to truly understand each other.

My Letter to You, Dear:

This is a love letter; it should be written in your own words, using the name of your beloved. Don't be afraid to use that name as often as you can. The more often you call your love by name, the more he or she will feel truly cherished. Perhaps you would like to write something like this:

My dearest one,

I can't help but remember the many times you have been patient and kind with me. I remember when [examples are added here]... You have a great heart and I see there's room in it for me. Thank you for your compliments and for watching with love when it was my turn to shine....You know I'm proud of you, and perhaps I'm most proud of the times when you stood back and smiled at my accomplishments when you had so many of your own....You are so concerned about me, you treat me with care. You have been unselfish so many times in our years together....

My dear, you are so loving. I haven't been aware enough of your eagerness to forgive me for my mistakes. There are so many times when you could have taken offense or stored up grievances, but you chose love instead....

You are such a treasure to me, beloved. You are always ready to understand....You give me a feeling of self-worth by trusting me, even when I don't deserve it. I have never thanked you for the time when [examples are added here]... You never give up working on our relationship. Your hope for the growth of our love never seems to end; in that hope, I can see my own value. Your love makes you strong; you have endured all the trials of our life together without bitterness. I remember...

I believe your love, dear, will never end. It is more lasting than my finest goals and ambitions, greater than the wisdom of those I admire, even stronger than death itself.

Your love is real to me and, through it, I can see the love that God our Father has for me. Without you, I would be lost and alone. I love you.

Prayer for Wives:

Dear God, I want to thank you for the wonderful treasure you have given me: my beloved husband. Help me to appreciate him and to never take his love for granted.

Please give me the grace to love him as generously as he loves me. Help me love him the way You intend: by making his life worthwhile rather than by selfishly focusing on my own life.

Help us both to grow together in love so we can heal each other and protect each other from the troubles of this world. Amen.

Prayer for Husbands:

Dear God, I want to thank you for the wonderful treasure you have given me: my beloved wife. Help me to appreciate her and to never take her love for granted.

Please give me the grace to love her as generously as she loves me. Help me love her the way You intend, by making her life worthwhile rather than by selfishly focusing on my own life.

Help us both to grow together in love, so we can heal each other and protect each other from the troubles of this world. Amen.

Search and Sharing

The end of each chapter in this book will include questions for self-search to share with your spouse. It will also include a prayer. It's good to respond to the self-search questions with pencil in hand, even though this section of the exercise is private. Most of us think far more seriously when we write down our thoughts. If your spouse does not participate in this, do these questions anyway. Your growth in love will inspire your spouse to a greater love, too.

When working through the sharing questions with your spouse, each of you should write. Write for ten minutes. If you feel you have nothing to say, the enforced timing will often help stimulate your mind. Begin writing immediately and, if you don't know what to say, say so, and try to explain why.

Your written sharing is really a love letter, so begin with "Dear" and end with "Love." Remember to focus on your own feelings and to never, under any circumstances, lay blame on your spouse. If you can insert the word "that" in your feeling, you are expressing a judgment instead.

This expression is all wrong and a love-killer: "I feel that your low-down, selfish way of life makes me miserable and lonely." This one is much better: "I feel miserable and lonely when you tinker with the car after work. I feel a yearning to spend more time together."

After you have both written, exchange your letters. Read them twice, then discuss them with love.

Consider These Questions Privately:

What type of husband, what type of wife, would my spouse like to have? (Make a list.) How can I become that person?

How do I feel about growing in patience, kindness, and generosity of heart? If I am resisting these virtues, why? Am I willing to work and pray for them?

Share This Question With Your Spouse:

How do I feel, knowing that my role as your husband, as your wife, is to make your life delightful and worthwhile?

CHAPTER 2

Do I Love You Enough?

"When the Son of Man Comes...
He Will Place the Sheep on His Right."
(MT 25:31–35)

It was two days until Passover, two days until Jesus would suffer his Passion and Resurrection. He was alone with his disciples on the Mount of Olives, readying them—and us—for that time when he would no longer walk the earth as a flesh-and-blood man.

His disciples still had lessons to learn; none of these would be easy. This last one would be the toughest of all. He said:

> When the Son of man comes in his glory, escorted by all the angels, then he will take his seat on his throne of glory. All nations will be assembled before him and he will separate people one from another as the shepherd separates sheep from goats. He will place the sheep on his right hand and the goats on his left. Then the King will say to those on his right hand, "Come, you whom my Father has blessed, take as your heritage the kingdom prepared for you since the foundation of the world. For I was hungry and you gave me food, I was thirsty and you gave me drink, I was a stranger and you made me welcome, lacking clothes and you clothed me, sick and you visited me, in prison and you came to see me." Then the upright will say to him in reply, "Lord, when did we see you hungry and feed you, or thirsty and give you drink? When did we see you a stranger and make you welcome, lacking clothes and clothe you? When did we find you sick or in prison and go to see you?" And the King will answer, "In truth I tell you,

in so far as you did this to one of the least of these brothers of mine, you did it to me." Then he will say to those on his left hand, "Go away from me, with your curse upon you, to the eternal fire prepared for the devil and his angels. For I was hungry and you never gave me food, I was thirsty and you never gave me anything to drink, I was a stranger and you never made me welcome, lacking clothes and you never clothed me, sick and in prison and you never visited me." Then it will be their turn to ask, "Lord, when did we see you hungry or thirsty, a stranger or lacking clothes, sick or in prison, and did not come to your help?" Then he will answer, "In truth I tell you, in so far as you neglected to do this to one of the least of these, you neglected to do it to me." And they will go away to eternal punishment, and the upright to eternal life.

MATTHEW 25:31–46

The Hidden Poor

This Scripture passage might cause us to do a bit of squirming. We feel a little guilty; we wish we were more like Mother Teresa. Then we're rather glad we're not. We think of all those we aren't helping: the poor sleeping in the gutters in Calcutta, the junkies in the slums of New York, the abused children on the pornography strips in Fort Lauderdale and Houston. We feel frustrated. We don't even know these people; what does Jesus expect us to do?

The Lord doesn't expect us all to abandon our houses, resign from our jobs, and give our bank accounts to the poor. He works more compassionately than we can imagine. Before we step outside to care for those on the street, he wants us to begin at home.

When we hear this Scripture passage, we never think about our own families. They're well provided for, we believe. Let's think for a moment. We're not cruel people who are deliberately ignoring our husbands and wives, living invisible and dejected right beneath our noses. We've simply slipped into blind thinking. When the Lord speaks of poverty and the desperate needs of others, we look at our lovers' dry, warm homes, their bounteous food and clothing, and say, "Well, they're well provided for—compared to the tough kids on the Minnesota Strip or the homeless in Newark."

It sounds sensible; fair, even, but you can't fill your lover's needs by saying other people are worse off. It would be like telling a heat-struck desert wanderer he doesn't have it so bad; the other guys who came this way are dead.

By taking care of those at home, we aren't sacrificing the needy. We're building spiritual muscle. The more compassion we display toward our spouses, the more our hearts will be moved by all people. If we can live with a husband or a wife and not notice his need, her hurts, how can we be sensitive to people who aren't even close?

When we think of the poor and the downtrodden, we see a vast wave of despairing people on the scale of a Hollywood movie. We feel sorry for them, but they're not real to us. We don't know their names; we don't see their hunger; we don't know when they die. This total anonymity makes them less than human to us.

We can't touch these faceless poor for the same reason we stay aloof from our lovers. We're trapped—as captive as the most wretched prisoner in solitary confinement in a third-world prison. We're imprisoned in a middle-class lifestyle that keeps us enslaved to a false god, money. Money is a jealous god; it demands more and more devotion. We find ourselves working overtime to make money— taking on second jobs just to own newer cars and have dinners out and DVD players. All our purchases would be fair and reasonable, if they weren't paid for with the loneliness of our families.

Another false god is independence. We think happiness is a solo quest, best achieved by becoming more successful, more creative, more fun-loving, but not more loving of others. If we live this way long enough, we find ourselves angry and frustrated, shouting "I am happy! I must be happy, because I finally have all the things I wanted."

What's Wrong?

We don't fully let Jesus into our hearts because we know it means trouble. If we really listen to him, we will have to change completely.

That's why Jesus said no person can serve two masters. We want to live according to the world's standards, but we also want Jesus in our lives. It simply doesn't work that way. We must make a choice.

It's rather like a man who's in love with two women. If he came home and said, "Honey, I can't decide whether I love you or my secretary. Can I have you both?" he'd get quite an answer. Yet we think it's unfair when we have to choose between Jesus and our self-centered ways of life.

We're not doing anything *wrong,* we think. But Jesus didn't say only the wrong things had to change. He came to earth to offer a complete change, a better way. We can take him or leave him, but we can't have him both ways.

When we're dealing with a moral issue, we tend to say, "But what's wrong with… ?" That's the worst question we can ask. It simply misses the whole point. It's an attempt to excuse ourselves; to wriggle by with the minimal amount of work. It's antilove.

"What's wrong with… ?" says our hearts are set on what we want or what we're already doing. To avoid this trap, we must look at what Jesus is offering rather than what we're losing if we follow his way.

The "what's wrong with… ?" trap caught the rich young man in the Bible, too. Remember him? He asked Jesus what he must do to inherit eternal life. Jesus told him to keep the ten commandments. When he replied that he had kept them since he was a child, Jesus said he could do one thing more to become perfect: give up all his money. The young man went away sad; he couldn't do it.

Jesus didn't tell the young man his riches were evil. He didn't say he had to give them up because he was misspending them. He simply offered that young man himself.

It upsets us to read this passage because we know the rich young man wasn't a terrible sinner. He was already a beautiful person, and that's why Jesus offered him more. He's offering us more, too, for Jesus is never outdone in generosity. Our bread cast upon the waters comes back one hundredfold.

Doing Good at Home

That's why when we speak of doing good for others, we must start in our own homes. One of the reasons we don't do better in the inner cities is that we don't do very well where we live.

We certainly can't excuse ourselves from the call to social justice, but it won't be successful unless we personally love the people in our ministries. At best, our work will be a dutiful responding to needs rather than to people.

We may be indefatigable in the way we spend ourselves and our talents, but something will be sadly lacking. We won't be spending our goodness on our families and friends: the people Jesus gave us especially to care for, to make the Gospel come alive in their hearts. If I have a greater concern for the hunger of a stranger than for my lover, something is missing. It doesn't mean I'm a hypocrite; it means I haven't learned to really love.

I Was Hungry; Did You Feed Me Food?

Where are we in our relationship with each other compared to where the Lord wants us to be? Husbands and wives are hungry for the gift of self. Have we given them the food of our company?

Most of us have, over the years, grown separate from our spouses. We relax over the newspaper or the program on television, or we pursue hobbies like golf or reading. We probably spend eight hours a day, at least, earning a paycheck that keeps the family afloat. Our paychecks, though, do not provide the love and companionship our partners so eagerly desire from us.

To be lovers, we must talk with our spouses. We can't tell the Lord we're not naturally loving. He said, "I was hungry. Did you give me food?" We can discuss business topics for hours. Perhaps when we encounter problems in conversation with our spouses, we're simply having trouble with the subject. We can learn to be just as interested in our partners' subjects as we are in our own.

"But it's not natural; I just don't talk that way," we might protest.

It's not natural for a visitor from Spain, Ireland, or Italy to talk about football, but he soon learns, even if he's never seen a football game. Marriage, after all, is a form of immigration; when we take on a new lifestyle, we're living in a new country. There's a naturalization process: we have to learn the language, and that language is sharing with our partners.

Learning to Talk

Marriage, after all, is belonging fully and totally to one person. We simply can't do this without a great deal of verbal communication. Real communication, by the way, is one part talking to two parts listening.

The number one question should be: "How much do I communicate with my spouse?" This question is answered not by looking at other people's habits but by looking at your spouse. Is he or she happy? Does he or she feel thoroughly listened to? That's all that matters.

Don't ask if you're satisfied with your level of listening or whether you're doing your best. Your best can mean "Considering all my responsibilities, I listen fairly well." Your partner may still be lonely.

Marriage partners must also learn to reveal themselves in conversation. We can't speak only when we feel like it; we must always be honest and open. Ask yourselves, "Does my partner feel shut out of my life, shut away and hungry for a fuller part of who I am?" You must look at this hunger, not at the amount you've already given.

Your greatest call as a spouse is to feed this hunger to be understood. So often, we humans want to give on our terms, and only as much as we wish. This turning in toward self is almost as natural as breathing, but it's unhealthy and imprisoning. When we're turned inward, we're not tuned in to our lovers.

How often do we fall into a lonely married holding pattern: we aren't fighting, but we simply stop growing closer? How often do our schedules prevent us from being really present to our partners?

So often, when you come home from work, your partner is less than thrilled with your presence and wrapped up in getting supper, taking care of the kids, or getting tomorrow's events arranged. That's wrong. Where is the eagerness for each other?

But answer this question: if your partner were eager for you, how much would you have to give? Think it over.

Frenzy vs. Freedom

A number of years ago, someone studied the behavior of an infant chimpanzee whose natural mother was replaced with a wire "mother" with a bottle attached. Although the little one's physical needs were met, he was obviously starved for living affection. Covering the wire "mother" with fur helped a bit, but no humane observer could believe it was a good substitute for the real thing. It's frighteningly easy to become a wire imitation of a real parent, to forget how important we are to one another.

This habit of consuming spiritually empty calories is symptomatic of a rush-rush lifestyle that puts priority on the family's itinerary, destinations, and achievements. It sees no value in enjoying one another's company. It says that breaking bread together isn't that important.

If we're in step with society, we don't have time for a sweet, old-fashioned idea like a leisurely meal. It would be great, certainly—but at the cost of piano lessons or soccer or parish council?
Blinded by our options, we find ourselves rushing through our meals so we can chauffeur ourselves or our children to the evening's activities. As Jesus said, we have to choose. Will we choose things or people?

How do we change? First, we must examine our unconscious beliefs. Our friends, relatives, and neighbors will probably think it's selfish, perhaps even abusive, to let a child walk or bike to an activity when he could have had a ride. But they don't realize the virtue of a lifestyle where children burn energy while developing muscle and self-reliance.

We must be in charge of our families. Too often, we allow friends, coaches, instructors, and committees to persuade us their activities are more important than our family love and unity.

Some of us must find the courage to slow down. Sometimes creative scheduling won't work and the only real answer is "No, we won't get involved in that," or even "I resign." This may be the hardest decision of all, especially when it baffles others.

Love's True Food

After Jesus rose from the dead, he visited his disciples near the Sea of Tiberias. They were fishing, and when they came ashore, they found him grilling fish for them. "Come and have breakfast," he said (Jn 21:1-12).

Cooking is a religious ministry. Too often, we neglect a great calling and choose lesser ones instead.

Cooking is a tangible way to tell all four senses that we are nurturers. There's nothing more comforting than the smell, sight, and taste of good food. The Lord knew that; that's why Jesus cooked.

Most likely, one of the partners in your marriage has been chief cook ever since you were married. You, and only you, will have the commitment to get a return to family meals project going and to keep it afloat.

A full dinner can be an intimidating request. It can make us feel we're giving up hard-earned ground. We might think we're being "returned to the kitchen."

I'm not asking you to do KP. I'm asking you to take shelter from the pressures of the world in your own private oasis. You and your spouse need a place of peace, fellowship, and harmony. That place should be the dinner table.

Please don't think of how much time and effort it will cost. That's the world's way, and it's loveless and lonely. Your time together is precious; you don't have much of it. Most of the day is spent at work. How do you prepare for that important time of togetherness? One of the best ways is to plan a beautiful meal. When you spend that time anticipating your partner's company at the table, you'll be much more sensitive to that person. The meal will be the high point of your day.

Please don't compare your family to others' families, and don't fall into the trap of saying, "But no one really cares," or "That kind of meal just doesn't fit our lifestyle." Instead, explore the alternatives.

Just how many chores can the kids truly do? You can teach them to shop or pare vegetables. You might also discover that some of your adult or family activities really sapped energy rather than adding to everyone's quality of life.

My Beloved or My Life?

It's a difficult choice: our activities or each other. Most of us attempt to compromise, although it doesn't make us happy. Both husbands and wives keep their freedom at the expense of their relationships. Too often, they schedule their lives the way they wish. They accommodate their spouses when it seems terribly important or when there's an emergency, but basically they live side by side rather than in unity. They try to avoid clashes. They're not fighters, but are they lovers?

Your life's success is determined not by your happiness but by your beloved's. How much is your spouse getting from your marriage? It isn't enough to ask, "How does our schedule improve the quality of my own life?" or "How does our conversation please me?" We must be lovers. We must ask, instead, "Am I filling my beloved's hunger?"

I Was Thirsty; Did You Give Me Drink?

Paternity and maternity are thirsts. How often do we control our lovers' childbearing and child rearing? Perhaps we're worried about finances, poor health, or the long burden children will lay on both of us.

So often, men and women assume that our only real value in the world is to bring home paychecks. We ask at parties, "What do you *do?*" If the spouse works outside the home, then a sophisticated speech that implies that work is more important than people is supposed to follow. If the spouse doesn't work outside the home, we conclude that person doesn't have anything to add to the conversation. So often, we're so very, very thirsty, and no one even knows how to give us a drink.

Is my wife, my husband, thirsty for love? There's no doubt about it: our spouses' throats are parched. Each of us should ask ourselves, "How do I rate today as a lover?" Just today, not generally. Rate yourself on a scale of one to ten. Don't explain why you chose a number: "I only rate a two today because my spouse was bad-tempered," or "I only rate a one because I had a terrible day."

Now then, how does today compare with my average Monday love? What's my number on Thursdays? How do I rate myself regularly as a lover? How do my spouse and I rate as a couple?

When we say, "How are we doing in our marriage?" it usually means, "Am I satisfied?" Sometimes it means, "Are you doing well enough for me?" When we truly rate ourselves as partners, we don't even face ourselves. We face our lovers instead.

Right now, forget how the other person rates. What's your score? Wives, ask yourselves this: if you were a man, would you like to have a wife like yourself? Husbands, ask yourselves: if your daughter brought home a man just like you, would you say, "Wow, is she going to have a great life!"

We really are good people, and we do make resolutions: "I need to talk to her more." "I ought to spend more time with him." "I need to pay more attention to her." "I ought to get home earlier." "I ought to be more positive." "I shouldn't shout so much." "I shouldn't nag."

Those are good resolutions, and they come from our sincere desire to please our lovers. But do we ever go all the way and resolve to be full-fledged, no-holds-barred, all-out lovers, with no ifs, ands, or buts?

We tend to compromise just a little. We admit we're wrong in a certain area, so we'll clean up there and do a little better. But we don't go for broke.

We should be lovers, not judges who look at the defendants' records and decide what's fair. When we're lovers, we don't ask, "Am I satisfied?" or "Am I doing all right?" Instead, we ask, "Is she totally loved?" "Does he experience every ounce of love I have?" Only this depth of commitment will slake our beloved's thirst.

Resources for Reflection

I hope you recognize that I don't want you to feel like a failure. I want you to see how beautiful you are and how much more the Lord is holding out to you. It's like learning a language. The more accomplished we become in a language, the more we are able to read and the more full of thought we become in that language. As we learn the language of love, the language of the Lord, we become more aware of our possibilities.

I don't want you to close this book, discouraged, or feel that you have such a long way to go. Instead, celebrate how far you have come and how good you truly are. If you weren't already blessed in your love and openness, you wouldn't still be with me here on this page. So thank God, because you are wonderful.

Consider These Questions Privately:

How do I worship materialism and independence? In what ways do I follow the world's standards instead of God's?

What will I do to feed my wife's hunger for my companionship? What will I do to feed my husband's hunger for affection?

How do I rate today as a lover? How do I rate through the week? How do we rate as a couple?

Share These Questions With Your Spouse:

How are my schedule, my priorities, and my conveniences excluding you from my life? How do I feel about my answer?

What will I do, dear, to make our love life a "10"? What are some of my best memories of time we spent together?

Express Your Love:

Husbands, when you come home from work tonight, take a good look at this woman the Lord chose for you. Feel how delighted you are to be with her this evening.... You are so happy with her, you don't want to be anywhere else. You want to spend time with her, to hug her and see her smile.

Wives, prepare tonight's meal as if it's the last one you'll ever make for him. Sprinkle it with love. Use the best tablecloth; use candles. Tonight is your night to celebrate because the Lord has given you this man to love and to love you.

When it's appropriate, you can suggest a commitment to a special family meal. Don't worry about doing this every day. You only have to do it tonight. When tomorrow comes, that will be tonight. You won't have to face a long and weary future. You'll merely get to celebrate tonight—again and again.

Finally, Let Us Invite God Into Our Marriages:

Dear Lord, thank you for this wonderful gift of my wife. Help me realize she is the most important part of my life. Let me delight in her; let me enjoy our time together above all other things. Help me tell her how much I love her, not only with those words, but with every word I speak. Help me give her the gift of myself: my enthusiasm and affection for her, my eagerness to be with her. Amen.

Dear Lord, thank you for this wonderful gift of my husband. Help me realize he is the most important part of my life. Let me delight in him; let me look forward to seeing him when we are apart. Help me enjoy our time together above all other things. Help me show him how much I love him, how worthy he is of my time and my attention. Help me show him that he is indeed the center of my life. Amen.

CHAPTER 3

Welcome Home, Beloved Stranger

"For I Was Hungry and You Gave Me Food."
(MT 25:35–46)

In Matthew 25:35, Jesus said, "I was a stranger and you made me welcome." Strangers are living in our own households. We know their faces intimately, but we don't understand their hearts.

We men and women come into marriage with a myriad of goals and values. That's normal, but fiercely clinging to those differences is a love-killer. We may think our ways are right, but rightness isn't the issue. Love and happiness are the issues.

So now let's read the list below, putting ourselves into each area and thinking, "Where do we stand? How much have we changed to become one couple? How much are we willing to change?"

Be wary of finger pointing here. It's easy to say, "Yes, if only he'd stay home a little more," or "If only she'd learn to save a little." Think, instead, "Do I really want to give up my own values?"

If you don't, beware. You're forcing your spouse to remain a stranger in your home. You'll each retreat to your own corners, clinging to your beliefs instead of to each other. You'll be separate but equal—but it won't make anyone happy.

So now read these over carefully, opening your hearts to change—and love:

Money. One of us might have a freewheeling "spend it now" philosophy while the other saves for a rainy day. One thinks we have enough; the other believes we need more. One is careless; the other is a precise household accountant.

Housing. To one, a house could be the center of life; to the other, it's only a place to sleep. To one, it's "mine"; to the other, it's "yours." For one, a house needs square footage; for the other, cozy comfort is best.

Faith. For one, it's an experience; for the other, it's a practice. In one of us, it's increasing; in the other, it's stagnating.

Friends. To one, they're pleasant but not that necessary; to the other, they're vital. To one, they're only social acquaintances; to the other, they're like family.

Families. For one spouse, they're people to enjoy on holidays; for the other, they're part of daily life. For one, they're a support network; for the other, a problem.

Children. To one, they're "yours"; to the other, they're "ours." To one, they're a pleasure; to the other, a burden. To one, they mean responsibility; to the other, love.

Lifestyles. For one spouse, livelier is best; the other seeks peace. One wants a busy social life; the other is a homebody. One likes single pursuits; the other wants to go out as a couple.

Charity. For one, it's terribly important; for the other, it's only an option for spending extra time and money.

The neighborhood. To one, it's just a place where we plant ourselves; to the other, it's part of our way of life.

No Surrender

Differences can cause doubt and pain, so we just surrender. "He's going to believe what he wants," we think, "so why bother?" "She's going to get her own way, so I'll get mine, too."

That's hopelessness at work. It's also stubbornness, camouflaged so well we don't recognize it. It's probably good to surrender at this point, because we haven't been trying to meld with our lovers. We've really been trying to change them. We'd really be thinking: "You need to be thinking my way." Of course that doesn't work, so we back off in frustration and disappointment. We had the right idea: becoming one in our goals and values. We simply had the wrong method.

It can be frightening to think of changing to your lover's point of view. You sincerely believe that you are right. So, first, work on the areas you can easily change.

Then when you get to the tough subjects, try to see his point, her view. Talk it through until you understand where your lover's coming from. There could be hidden hurts—or hidden wisdom. Suppose, for instance, that your husband embarrasses you by wearing torn-up jeans to a party. He may be happier than you are; he's looking forward to seeing his friends, and he knows they'll be glad to see him no matter what he's wearing. He'll have a great time, but you'll spend the evening worrying about the run in your hose. You don't have to dress like he does, but you do have to understand his heart. Why not let him teach you to be carefree?

I Lacked Clothes and You Clothed Me

In other words, my husband, my wife, was naked. Did I clothe my spouse?

There's more to clothing than driving off to the mall. So many of our wives say, "He never notices how I'm dressed. I could color my hair chartreuse and he wouldn't comment for weeks."

Men, it's important to notice, for instance, that she's dressed up tonight, or even that she's wearing her favorite pin. You must notice her vocally. You must compliment her until she believes the compliment.

How many spouses are so self-sacrificing, so concerned about watching the family budget that they won't buy anything for themselves? That's wonderful but if self-sacrificing spouses won't buy for themselves, the other partner must buy for them.

You may say, "How could I ever buy women's/men's clothes?" As with everything, you learn with practice. Buying clothing for your spouse is an art form. It can, indeed, be learned. First, when you can do so unnoticed, go through the closet. Find something that fits and look at the size on the label. If that doesn't work, look for a salesperson who's knowledgeable about sizes and styles.

You don't have to buy an entire outfit each time. You could bring home a tie, a piece of jewelry, a scarf. Something that doesn't fit can be exchanged, but if you never buy your spouse anything, there's nothing to exchange. And, don't just give money to sponsor a shopping trip. What is wanted is your praise, and money can't buy that.

In the beginning, there will be times when your gifts are opened and your spouse gasps, "You've got to be kidding." You'll learn not to buy *that* again.

Unfortunately, we learn not to *buy* again. That's wrong. Clothes, after all, are important. They announce us to one another, saying, "I'm this kind of guy"; "This is the type of woman I am." Our clothing tells everyone how we're feeling.

Stripped by Insults

We can use an attitude about money to strip our husbands and wives of clothes, hairdos, accessories, and the like. Perhaps we make pointed comments like "How much did that cost?" Our robbery could be subtle; it could voice itself in gestures or comments: "It's a good thing I don't spend like that"; "I'm glad both of us aren't clothes-horses."

We can also fail to clothe our spouses in ways that don't involve wearing apparel. Is your spouse criticized by friends and neighbors, perhaps because of the size of the family or because the in-laws live with you? Is your wife put down because of her faith, her tenderness toward her children, or her love for you? Most likely these put-downs are subtle barbs, which are much more devastating than frontal attacks.

Do you stand aloof while friends strip your spouse naked? Do you think they're just petty insults and you shouldn't get involved?

Do you believe that? Do you merely nod your approval when told about the hurt over these insults? When we do this, we're fooling no one. Our partners know we aren't serious about their pain.

Sometimes we're right there on center stage when someone attacks our lovers. What do we do then? If we say nothing, we're letting our spouse stand there, naked and hurt and vulnerable.

We can't just comfort our lovers later. We must stand up right away and tell that hurtful person, "This is my wife; you don't talk to her like that." "This is my husband; I love him and there is no way I'm going to let you get away with that." We certainly do not want to protect false friends at our lovers' expense. After a while, digs and insults become less motivated by malice than by habit. They become habits because we don't say, "Stop."

Not all criticism comes from outside, however. Sometimes we ourselves are the hurtful people who criticize our lovers in front of friends, relatives, or the children. Sometimes we merely criticize them in private; that's harmful enough by itself.

We must be strictly on guard against being critical. All too often we make excuses for this failing.

We may say, "Me? I'd never do that kind of thing. I never criticize my husband"; "I never say anything negative about my wife." By "never," we really mean "not at parties" or "not before strangers." We feel perfectly free to criticize in front of the children, with our mothers, buddies, or very close friends.

We're stripping our lovers when we do that. We're exposing them to embarrassment and shame. We're tempted to defend ourselves: Our children, relatives, and friends are close to the situation. After all, they understand.

Quiet criticism before friends and family does far more damage, though, than the angriest screaming match in public. After all, we'll walk away from those strangers and won't see them again. But our children are right there, and they'll remember that Mom isn't so special; that Dad is a grumpy man. Our friends and relatives will remember, too. Every time they see our lovers, they'll recall the defect that upset us so.

I Was Sick and You Visited Me

How do we treat each other when we're sick? Is our lover's sickness an inconvenience? How sensitive are we to each other's needs in sickness?

Have you ever seriously discussed what it's like to be sick and what your spouse could do to please you then? How does your husband want to be treated when he's sick? "Very, very carefully," you may say. "It's like tending a wounded bear." Why? Perhaps that last time he had the flu, he felt humiliated because you were fussing over him. He became annoyed, so you backed off, neither of you understanding each other's feelings.

How does your wife want to be treated when she's sick? "Not how. How much. She wants me there all the time, even when she doesn't need me." Perhaps she wants all those little attentions she tried to give you. She doesn't want you at her bedside holding her hand; she just wants more of you than you're giving. She feels lonely, thinking that her physical pain doesn't matter to you. Why not talk to her about it?

Since we're good people, we try to guess why our lovers act so oddly when they're sick. But often we can't, so we shrug our shoulders and give up. When we surrender like this, we're giving up any real effort to take each other into our lives. That would mean change, and sometimes we don't want to change. We prefer our own attitudes, values, priorities, and goals. We'll let our lovers work on their own goals; we won't interfere with them, but neither will we give up ours.

In doing so, we miss our overriding goal as a couple: to take our husbands and wives into our own lives; to become one. A marriage is not composed of two people who get along well with each other. It's composed of two people who become part of each other.

Sickness is a part of marriage; it will happen increasingly as the years go by. So we must concentrate on being "married" when we're sick as well as when we're healthy.

In marriage, tending the sick includes tolerance for each other's small flaws. How do we respond to baldness, thinness, fat, buck teeth, warts, an extremely heavy beard, a large nose, or excessive height? Do we ignore these little flaws? If so, we're really reinforcing the idea that they're disfiguring.

Maybe we tease our lovers about their flaws. It proves we're open about them. After all, it's just affectionate teasing. It's also a good way to avoid revealing our feelings. That may be all right for acquaintances, but couples are called to do more than evade an issue. Do we comfort each other about our flaws? It's extremely important to handle this well, because these little defects make a significant difference in our spouses' lives.

Our flaws may not be visible, either. Maybe we're afraid of flying, or snakes, or of driving a car. Maybe one of us is an easy crier. Maybe the other one can't cry at all. Either of us could get unnerved in a crisis.

We each seem to have married a person with a flaw. Sometimes, we're not very sympathetic. We think, "He believes he's so calm, but when trouble starts, I'm better off without him," or "She's had these cramps every month for twenty-five years, so why should I get upset?"

We humans have a very high threshold of others' pain. We need to be sensitive to our spouses' needs. First we must realize what those needs are. It's not hard; all we have to do is think awhile. The evidence is everywhere.

It's easy to say, "Yes, she's always that way," or "I know exactly how he's going to behave." How are we using that knowledge? We shouldn't be trying to change our lovers, but we should be responding to their needs. Jesus said, "I was sick and you visited me." I was hurting and you reached inside to heal the hurt.

If we choose, we can use our illnesses to manipulate our spouses. It's an effective way to get the attention we need, to inspire feelings of guilt, or change plans that seemed unchangeable.

This is one of our most typical and most devious ways of control-

ling each other. We might withhold affection or sex, or begin showing signs of an emotional crisis. We're saying, "Look how awful I
feel. How can you do this to me?"

I Was in Prison and You Came to See Me

This one can't possibly apply to matrimony—can it? After all, we
didn't marry criminals. No, we didn't marry criminals, but our
spouses are still in jail.

Men, how many of our wives are imprisoned by the children?
How often do they feel cut out of life? There is a slice of your wife's
life from age twenty-one until fifty that just disappears. Those kids
are always there. She can't think of anything else.

If she works in the home, she lives and breathes kids from dawn
until bedtime. If she works outside the home, she lives in a state of
exhaustion, worrying about everything from child care to when she's
going to find time to sleep.

The heart of the problem isn't mere physical "imprisonment,"
but the intellectual prison she's experiencing. Even if she works outside the home, whom does she spend time with at a family picnic?
The children, of course.

Part-Time Fathers

No wonder so many young women today are skeptical of motherhood. Today's mothers see themselves as having the whole burden
of child-rearing because many men are part-time fathers.

We men don't take full responsibility for our parenthood. We're
relief pitchers, waiting in the bull pen. We'll come in if she gets hit,
but until then, it's her ball game.

By now, you're tempted to say, "I pitch in when the going gets
rough. But I can't do it all the time. I have my responsibilities." You
do. They're called Johnny, Mary, Frances. "But I couldn't do more if
I wanted to. She likes things the way they are. If I tried what you're
suggesting, she'd tell me to go away."

If this is true, you need to find out why. Maybe she doesn't believe you'll do as well as she does. Maybe she's right; maybe not. Maybe she wants you to pretend to care, but she doesn't want real changes.

That's when you both need to talk. She is probably afraid to change because she doesn't believe you'll stick with your new role. She's afraid you'll start with a big fanfare, then let her down. Your change has to be a real commitment.

Maybe you're the one who doesn't want change. You think the present system is fine: "I do my share; now you want me to do my wife's work, too." If you put it that way, yes, I do.

You can't say "I love you" to your wife if you're not a father to her children. It's just not believable. I'm not speaking just of time spent with the children, either. I'm speaking of the whole mentality in the home. Many men are tempted to see the home as a place of rest where we gather the strength to be our best when we go out in the world. We should want to be our best when we're at home with the people who love us.

You might say, "That's not realistic. My boss won't understand that." Your boss is no sacrament. You and your wife are, though. You're supposed to belong to her. Let's hope you don't belong to your boss.

You're not filling your wife's needs when she does most of the work and you merely give her the money to do it. That's when the home becomes a prison. If you're really as much of a parent as she is, the children are not a burden. She realizes how much you're missing when work takes priority over the children. She won't feel that way, though, until *you* realize how much you're missing.

The Chain Gang

Spouses, are you both in prison? If you're both employed, you probably are. Your jobs take away almost all your spare time. You're on treadmills, wearily going nowhere, unless it's to newer or bigger treadmills. Spending day after day at jobs in which you can have no real fulfillment results in no real sense of purpose.

Materially, this generation's families are doing better. We have better homes than our parents did while we were growing up. Our children's educations are far superior to our own. We have more vacations, better meals, and more expensive clothes, but we aren't any better off. We need to see the poverty behind the wealth; we need to see those chains attached to our husbands' well-dressed ankles.

How often does one spouse chain the other to their jobs? They're imprisoned so the children can have what they need in order to have a better life. Ironic, isn't it?

The culprit is our expectations: the homes we think we need, the possessions our children are supposed to need, the expenses we've created. Now, I'm not speaking against basic living expenses or good things for our children. I'm speaking against a middle-class mentality that looks only at purchases and never at the peace and happiness of the buyers. Use this mentality to buy the best house you can "afford" and a couple of new cars, and the prison walls grow even thicker.

Earlier, I told husbands especially to save their best for home. Be careful, wives, that this remains his gift, not something you feel he owes you. You don't want to judge him. Besides, no matter how good his intentions are, maybe he doesn't have anything to give when he comes home. Maybe he has to be filled before he can even say anything to you. He needs human warmth: compliments, gratitude for both his job and work at home, knowledge that you enjoy his company, peace, and cheerfulness.

What about the peace and justice we need at home? You might say, "He does his job and I do mine. I do have sympathy for him, but I work as hard as he does. It's tough being a woman today."

We're not running a contest to see who has it tougher. What's important is this: do wives always see the call to treat their husbands specially? Do we see his needs and lack of freedom?

Often, men don't really know what they need. It's not because they're refusing to be open. It's because needs are a weakness in their eyes. The average man has been trained not to have any needs. At least if he does, he fills them himself.

Wives, not husbands, are supposed to want things. It's a man's job, they think, to respond to his wife's needs. Now, that sounds generous and loving. It isn't necessarily so. It can be a way of saying, "I won't let you in; I don't need you. I will take care of you, but I won't allow you to take care of me."

Husbands, don't be proud that you ask her for nothing. That's a way of putting her out of your life, of not responding to her fully.

When we're working on our marriages, we must be careful when it comes to "fairness." We're always tempted to say, "When do we get to change the other person?"

I'm asking marriage partners to reach out to heal each other without worrying about fairness. If you say, "I'll change if you will," we'll get nowhere.

Should you change or not? If the answer is yes, it doesn't matter whether your spouse changes or not. That's a hard saying, isn't it? But it's God's honest truth.

A Different Kind of Marriage

In Matthew 13:11, the Lord said to his disciples, "To you it is granted to understand the mysteries of the kingdom of Heaven, but to [others] it is not granted..." or, in other words, "I'm telling you some things I don't tell the world." Too often we live the world's way with holy water. We have the sign of the cross hovering over our heads, but the world is imprinted in our hearts.

The Lord is really saying, "I'm offering you a different kind of marriage." He's offering you a greater marriage than others have. His offer isn't a marriage in which you get along better, but a marriage in which the whole value system is different. It's not a marriage with improved communication, but a sacrament of unity which celebrates different decisions about the outside world.

He's offering you a happier marriage. All you have to do is begin. Begin with simple actions like defending your spouse if somebody criticizes him or her. It's your call not to tolerate such insults. Or begin by welcoming your spouse back into your life by learning to understand his or her thinking about family, children, religion, housing....

There are so many graces in this Scripture passage. Ponder it in your hearts, so you can freely let the sacrament of matrimony be present in your lives.

Resources for Reflection

Don't look at this marital soul-search as a weighty obligation. You shouldn't have to gather courage for it. Rather, look on it as an opportunity. Because you have been so good as a husband or wife, you've now discovered even more potential. You have even more ability to respond to the needs of your lover and to the Lord. What you have just read has meant something to you, and that's a gift from God. The fact that you thought, "Gee, I should do something about this" shows how tremendous you are. It's in no way, shape, or form an indication of any failure. It is a definite sign of your success.

It's best if the two of you can talk these ideas over. You can't become a good wife, for instance, by yourself. Why? Because you're not "a wife." You're *his* wife. He needs to be fully involved in your plans. Men, each of you belongs to a special woman. If you decide in private how to be a better husband, you're missing the whole point. Your change must be based on what she's seeking from you, what responses she desires, how she believes you can improve the quality of her life.

If your spouse doesn't want to read this book, don't be judgmental. Try to talk to him about what you've read, ask her how she thinks you should change. Don't hit your lover with a statement like, "I see you're dehumanized by your job, dear." He'll say, "What are you talking about?" or something even less polite.

Say, instead, "I read this book today, and it says... Do you feel like that? Does it hurt your feelings when I...? How would you feel if I changed in this area...?" And of course, never, ever say, "I think you should..."

See if you can get your spouse to write on the sharing questions that follow, or at least talk about them. And pray. Our Lord is a loving God who wants us to be happy in our marriages; he will certainly hear your prayer. Trust, too, in the goodness of your lover. Our spouses are good men and women who perhaps have been hurt in the past and are afraid to be open and trusting. Your sincerity and willingness to change create a greenhouse effect in your home: it becomes a place of light and warmth where souls can bloom.

This book is not a think book; it's a love book. It's written so you will feel more tender toward each other, be more open to each other, speak more freely. It's intended to help you think of subjects that need to be talked over. In order for it all to work, you have to go to each other, so turn to each other and enjoy.

Consider These Questions Privately:

Is my husband, my wife, a stranger in our home? Am I willing to change that?

How is my spouse naked?

How do I treat my lover when he or she is sick? How can I improve?

Do I comfort my lover for those little flaws?

How is my beloved spouse in prison, and what can I do about that?

Share These Questions With Your Spouse:

My love, when do I treat you as a stranger in our home? How does my answer make me feel?

When do I feel most vulnerable? When would I like your support?

How do I plan to make you feel clothed, dear? Am I on target?

How do I want to be treated when I'm sick?... How am I going to change to fill your needs when you're sick?

How am I in prison?...What will I do to free you from your prison, my love?

Finally, Let Us Invite God Into Our Marriages:
Dear Lord,

Thank you for giving me the grace to realize I've been hurting my beloved spouse. Please let me see this truthfully, and let me see with equal truth my goodness and generosity of heart. Help me understand how much you love me, just as I am.

Lord, please make me willing to change. Help me understand that you want me to be happy and that following your way will enrich the lives of both myself and my beloved.

Help me fill my beloved's life with love and warmth and acceptance. Help me treat my dear spouse as I would treat you. Amen.

CHAPTER 4

How Delighted Is Your Life?

"Love Your Enemies,
Do Good to Those Who Hate You."
(LK 6:27–29)

It would be an exciting day, not only for his disciples but for Jesus as well. He had passed the entire night on a mountain, praying to his Father. Now it was dawn and he would come down to the foot of the mountain and preach to the crowd. He already knew what he wanted to say:

> ... I say this to you who are listening: Love your enemies, do good to those who hate you, bless those who curse you, pray for those who treat you badly. To anyone who slaps you on one cheek, present the other cheek as well; to anyone who takes your cloak from you, do not refuse your tunic. Give to everyone who asks you, and do not ask for your property back from someone who takes it. Treat others as you would like people to treat you. If you love those who love you, what credit can you expect? Even sinners love those who love them. And if you do good to those who do good to you, what credit can you expect? For even sinners do that much. And if you lend to those from whom you hope to get money back, what credit can you expect? Even sinners lend to sinners to get back the same amount. Instead, love your enemies and do good to them, and lend without any hope of return. You will have a great reward, and you will be children of the Most High, for he himself is kind to the ungrateful and the wicked.
>
> Be compassionate just as your Father is compassionate. Do

not judge, and you will not be judged; do not condemn, and you will not be condemned; forgive, and you will be forgiven. Give, and there will be gifts for you: a full measure, pressed down, shaken together, and overflowing, will be poured into your lap; because the standard you use will be the standard used for you.

LUKE 6:27–38

This passage of Scripture is magnificent, isn't it? If everyone could live this one, no unhappiness would be left in the world. It would end the get-ahead mentality that leads to such aggressiveness and aggrandizement. We'd all stop looking over our shoulders to see who was gaining on us.

The Golden Rule is such a wonderful plan for living. Jesus makes a great deal of sense, but everything he says is not so easy to accept. If we're honest, most of us will admit that Jesus' "turn the other cheek" message is most comfortable when we keep a safe distance.

There's No Place Like Home

We can almost imagine Jesus' message being given in a major television address or United Nations forum. We see global implications. But implementation of his message really starts at home, in the context of our own lives. Further, Jesus spoke to each of us individually. It's not as if he finished his sermon, then muttered, "Whew. I'm glad that's over. I hope someone gives it a try." Instead, he's whispering in your ear right now, something to the effect of "I'm serious about this, and I want you to go first." And he's holding this message out as a gift, not delivering it like a jail sentence. He really wants us to live our daily lives this way.

For husbands and wives, Jesus wants us to pay strictest attention to his words when we're in communication with each other. It's unfortunate but true: sometimes your lover is your enemy, at least for an hour or two. That's when she's angry with you; he won't talk to you. When we think of enemies, though, we think of someone with a gun. It's sad, even frightening, to think our enemies share our beds.

Our enemies are people who hurt us emotionally, who take away things we believe are ours, like attention or free time, or who make our lives less rewarding than they ought to be. Who's in the best position to hurt us in these ways? Our spouses, of course.

Often enough, we make the tragic mistake of retaliation. We follow the world's way instead of letting go as the Lord suggests. The Lord said, more or less, "It's easy to be nice to a husband who's romancing you." When he's buried in the computer or glued to the Super Bowl, though, he becomes your enemy. Are you afraid to be nice to him then? How about a spouse who's on your back, who never seems satisfied. Are you hesitant to follow the Lord's message then, afraid you'll encourage even more antagonism? Luckily, it doesn't work that way. There's a difference between encouraging anger and encouraging love.

So often, spouses shout simply to let us know they're there. They wonder if they really come first. We say they do, but we seem to put our jobs first during the day, while the other responsibilities come first at night. Perhaps dinner is taken for granted. We're certainly glad to have it, but we don't often praise our spouses' efforts. Maybe we should but, after all, people don't *really* thank each other for daily chores or for going to work. Do they?

The Lord has told us in no uncertain terms that we must love, even when someone is making us angry and taking our peace away. In other words, when someone is an enemy, even if that enemy is a marriage partner.

Besides, why get into an argument? It merely upsets both parties, and makes everyone feel guilty and uncomfortable. The basic question is simpler: Will we really live the Lord's way, or will we follow society's footpath? Will we continue to take each other for granted?

Now I'm asking you to praise your spouses for coming home at night. Consider this: your spouse's presence is a gift to you, and deserving of praise for faithfulness.

We must begin by seeing our spouses as the Lord sees them: as wonderful, beautiful children created by the Father to be our beloveds.

Then we can't help but find delight in them, from the smallest shrug of their shoulders to their biggest accomplishments. Our partners deserve praise just for being themselves.

We pledged to praise each other when we were married, yet we're very grudging with our compliments. We reserve them for special occasions. When we withhold our praise, though, we signal that we are wary and distrustful, not wanting to commit ourselves. We're not acting in anger or malice; we're simply withholding the beautiful gifts we have to give.

Normal, Everyday Saints

Why don't we live the Gospel more fully? Partly because we think we're not supposed to. At least, not while we're doing the dishes or going through the bills. We're supposed to live the Gospel on Sundays. The rest of our lives are filled with normal, everyday events.

We draw a sharp line between the great bulk of the world and those few items that fit into a spiritual category. We may practice those spiritual pursuits fervently and faithfully, but the world takes up most of our time.

In the worldly category, though, we let Jesus in reluctantly and carefully. We don't want his idealism ruining our relationships with other people.

The rules we use to govern our worldly lives are gathered from our peers. We strive toward good common sense. Common sense is defined as whatever the average, normal person would do under the circumstances.

But Jesus didn't come to proclaim good common sense. He came to tell us salvation was at hand. If we'd let him, he would change our lives, but we often don't give him free reign. Jesus is calling us to himself as whole beings, not just when we're in church or doing volunteer work. The glad tidings apply to every facet of our existence and every relationship under all circumstances. If we accept him wholeheartedly, it will be a conversion experience.

It's the Good News

Today, Jesus' message is just as new—and as difficult to accept—as it was when he first preached it. Our world still doesn't believe the Good News. Husbands and wives are still treating each other with fairness and common sense. When everything's going smoothly, they're smooth; when things are rough, they're rough, too. They're not responding to each other, they're responding to themselves. They're unconsciously deciding, "I feel upset, so I'm going to behave that way."

Jesus is saying, "Let's do it differently. Let's not talk about how you're feeling or how she's treating you. Let's talk about loving her, not because she deserves it, but because I'm asking you to."

He's asking us to question ourselves: "Do I love her when everyone would say I ought to withdraw? Maybe I won't be nasty, but I won't hear a thing. I'll just let her voice roll off me like water off a duck. Then she'll learn."

When we behave this way, we're playing a power game with each other. We're saying, "I won't punish you if you act the way I want." We're forcing our lovers to meet our approval—or else. "My obligation toward you is absolved," we add, "if you don't live up to your obligation toward me." We're trying to "teach" our spouses to treat us better, but we're really teaching them anger, hopelessness, and resentment.

We're behaving like children then. We're not trusting our lovers' goodness. We're saying, "I really don't believe she'll respond; I don't think he cares enough to change. Furthermore, I really don't believe in Jesus' way. I have to use force; it's the only thing I trust."

Perhaps you're thinking Jesus' way is the right way, but it's a big change. It could leave you looking foolish and it might not work: "If I'm nice to her when she's in a rotten mood, she'll die of the shock." What a way to go.

You Are So Nice, Dear,
What Do You Want?

I'm not promising instant success. It might take some time for our new behavior to affect our lovers. At first, our lovers might not notice we're acting nicely. They might be suspicious, waiting for the other shoe to drop. So we must be patient, knowing it takes time to undo the previous training.

Sometimes we'd rather look for another way to happiness. Sometimes we even prefer hard work. We keep the house clean and painted, we cook or do repairs, take good care of the children and carefully watch the budget. Yes, we're very good to each other.

That's still a policy of loneliness. We need to add compassion to constant, relentless love. Both men and women crave that type of love. Let's be generous with it. Our lovers need our goodness the most when they're angry or unhappy, and having trouble being lovers themselves.

How could weak human beings ever succeed at such an idealistic program? Basically, because we're the Lord's own people. We have been chosen to reveal him through the way we love one another. Jesus has raised us to the dignity of children of God. That wasn't a reward for good conduct. It was a free gift, made possible by his passion and death on the cross.

We must see beyond our lovers' pouting, shouting, or anger. We must see that immortal being whom God calls his son or daughter. Above all, we must rise above our own feelings.

Feelings are neither right nor wrong, and we shouldn't deny our resentment or hurt. But we must decide whether to love, and that decision can't be based on our own feelings. It must be based on others' needs. We must ask ourselves, "What expression of love does my spouse need right now?" "Right now" should be in the middle of an argument or whenever it is hardest. It's a tough thing to do. If it came naturally, Jesus wouldn't have had to tell us about it.

The real test of a marriage is not when everything is sweetness and light. Then it's easy to do things for each other. The real test of a marriage comes when we're disillusioned with each other. How do we respond when our spouses aren't responding to us? How do we reach out when they're pushing us away? How do we speak to them when their language is harsh and rejecting?

Bless Those Who Curse You

It's tragic but sometimes we curse each other. Some of us are too proper to use so-called bad language. But bad language is not the use of certain nasty words. It's the intention behind the statement. We could cut someone to ribbons with perfectly respectable language.

When we curse people, we're taking away their blessedness. We're depriving them of our approval. Sometimes a curse is best accomplished through silence, or by politeness or pleasant chitchat.

We can also degrade our lovers through sarcasm. We can demean others by superiority or scorn. We can humiliate them by the simple, unspoken assumption that they're not worthy of our attention.

Do we pray for those who curse us, or do we handle them without any help from God? Do we wish God would help us, but doubt that he will? Do we feel that prayer is such a weak little tool when used toward a cold, selfish spouse? When we do pray, what do we pray? "Lord, make him straighten up. Make her see how she's hurting me."

Instead, let's ask the Lord to bless them. How about a prayer to celebrate their goodness, to make us see the log in our own eye rather than the splinter in theirs?

Next time, let's ask the Lord to help us respond rather than react. Let's seek the graces of tenderness and love rather than the knee-jerk defensiveness of coldness and rejection.

We must ask him to help us respond on his terms, not ours. We must listen and wait as he gentles our hearts and pares the calluses off our tenderness. This type of prayer breaks the vicious circle of negativity. Soon we will see our spouses responding to our love with love of their own.

If Anyone Slaps You on One Cheek,
Present the Other Cheek As Well

We slap each other, too, don't we? Not physically, but we find other ways to let our lovers know we're upset. For a while, we put up with these hidden negative messages. But sooner or later, we reach the end of our rope. "I've run out of patience," we think. "I've had enough."

We don't always put it into words. Sometimes we say it with angry looks or the way we slam the pots and pans. Our lovers know these signals.

Again, we're measuring out our generosity. It's as if marriage is a recipe, and too much love will ruin the batter. The Good News is this: the more love you add, the better it gets.

So often, though, we find ourselves searching for some minimum standard of behavior: "What is the least I can do and still have reasonable peace at home?"

We must get away from that miserable trap of being satisfied with the minimum. We aren't satisfied with the minimum in anything else. We don't say, "More clothes? No; I don't want 'em. I'll wear what I bought last year." We don't say (at least, without a twinge), "A vacation away? Why would I want one of those?"

Yet we're comfortable with our limited generosity. We believe we're virtuous because we don't lose patience right away. Actually, we're not concentrating on our lovers at all. We're simply being "good."

Jesus is telling us, "Stop concentrating on yourself. Don't see things in terms of how much is 'reasonable'; see your lover's needs instead." He really intends for our unbounded love to be an everyday occurrence.

We want to listen to the Lord, but we have learned this world's lessons all too well. We do the kindly thing: we tune him out. We decide he's not talking about us. If he is, he really can't be serious. He'll understand, we think, when we don't live up to his godlike ideals. Our problem, then, isn't failure. It's that we don't even try.

If Anyone Takes Your Cloak, Do Not Refuse Your Tunic

Do you really give your tunic to the spouse who takes your cloak? There's a good way to find out. What happens when you're both in the car and it's time to pay for gas or a toll? Do you look at each other, waiting for the other one to pay?

Free giving doesn't always involve money. It can involve our lives at home. Maybe I have my chair, and God help you if I catch you in it.

Do we really give the tunic when the cloak is taken, or do we just establish a nice way of life in which both of us can keep our cloaks? Maybe my cloak is smaller than my lover's, but I like smaller cloaks.

The Lord has great ambitions for us, and scorekeeping is not part of his plan. Yet we carefully measure the minimum amount of satisfaction we'll tolerate in a relationship, and we spend tremendous amounts of energy making sure we get it. We all recognize how sad it is when a divorcing couple divides their property, each of them trying to get an edge on the other one.

Too often that can be just as true in a marriage. It doesn't necessarily involve property. We may be perfectly willing to concede a greater amount of time, money, or energy, but we're going to get at least a minimum amount of what we want. Nobody had better take that away from us or we'll let them know about it.

Resources for Reflection

From time to time, we hear stories of the saints who loved their persecutors. We tend to wonder if these people were for real. They were; now go and do likewise.

I am asking you to be saints. The community of faith needs you; you embody our sacrament of matrimony and we need you. It may be difficult for you to realize that you are, indeed, a sacrament. But it's true. The Lord always calls us to greater things than we could imagine on our own.

Once we realize our importance in God's plan, we're called to action. Do we live God's plan with each other? Remember, the man you're angry with is half that sacrament; the woman you wish would go away is the other half.

Do we ever turn the other cheek with each other? Yes, we often do. It's not fair to ourselves, nor is it helpful, to call ourselves failures. There are many times when we are most understanding and compassionate toward each other.

I'm not suggesting that we're reprobates and it's time to shape up. I'm saying, let's expand our goodness. Let's make a real campaign of being our best. We sometimes think if we can't do our best, we might as well give up. That's hopelessness, though, not the Lord's way. Jesus didn't say either we're flawless or we flunk. He expected our goodness to be a journey of growth.

We should ask ourselves whether we're turning the other cheek more frequently than we did last week, last month, or last year. We should ask: "Am I limiting my growth in goodness by thinking I'm already generous enough, or am I willing to push myself a little beyond."

That's all. Don't tell yourselves, "I won't be impatient with him again, ever"; "I'll turn the other cheek with her from now on." The step beyond today's success, however small or large it may have been, is a big stride ahead.

Consider These Questions Privately:

Do I love my spouse when everyone would say it's all right not to?

When am I my spouse's enemy?

What specific steps can I take in order to do better than I did today?

Share These Questions With Your Spouse:

I remember a certain time when you reached out to me, even though my actions or words were pushing you away. Let me tell you about it....How does that memory make me feel?

Which parts of my life did I once think were worldly, and now realize are spiritual? (Make a list and explain why.)

My dear, you are God's immortal son or daughter. I can see this because of your goodness, which shines forth when you... I remember when you....

Finally, Let Us Invite God Into Our Marriages:

Dear Father, I ask you today for the grace of trust. Help me realize your plan is one of happiness and strength, not hopelessness. Help me see my lover's needs, not mine; lift me beyond the trap of my own hurts and resentments. Let me see the pain behind my spouse's anger; fill me with mercy and forgiveness.

Please give me the patience to wait while you gentle my heart, replacing the hardness with tenderness, and the rigidness with happiness and love.

Thank you for my wonderful spouse, who is so good to me. Bless my spouse and fill her (him) with peace. Amen.

CHAPTER 5

We Are Instruments of His Love

"Give, and There Will Be Gifts for You."
(LK 6:30–38)

This guy didn't look much like a psychologist, she thought. He was too young, his hair was too long, and he was entirely too cheerful. "Don't smile at me," she told him. "We're talking about misery here, you know."

"I understand," he said. "I understand it all."

For a strange moment, she believed he did. Behind the smile, his eyes were full of compassion. But wait a minute. He hadn't heard her story yet. "How can you—"

"You don't have to leave him, you know," he said. "I know how to repair your marriage."

"You do?" For a moment, she felt a surge of excitement. Then practicality took over. No; it was too late now. She wouldn't indulge fool's hopes.

"Don't think that way," he said. "Listen to me."

"You know what I'm thinking? But—you can't read minds."

"You're the one who said it. Now then, dear, I want you to turn the other cheek."

"Turn the other cheek? No one does that."

His gaze was steady; she could see he didn't agree. She began to feel a little guilty. "I mean—well, I know we're supposed to, but we can't really do it. It's not realistic."

The counselor went on as if he hadn't heard. "You need to be good to him, even when he hurts you. You need to say nice things to him; things that make him feel good about himself, especially when he's cold or sarcastic. I also want you to pray for him."

"Pray that God straightens him out?"

"No, pray that our Father blesses him, makes him happy, gives him peace. It wouldn't hurt if you prayed for yourself, too."

She shrugged.

"When he insults you or snubs you, don't fight with him. When he trespasses on your rights, don't hold back. Give him what he seems to need."

"Now you're insulting me," she said. "That's nonsense."

"No it's not. All I'm saying is to treat him the way you wish he'd treat you. It's not enough to love him when things are all moonlight and roses. Any woman could do that."

"Moonlight and roses?" she said. "We haven't had moonlight and roses since the garden show."

He didn't look happy. "I'm not excusing him. But if you're good to him when he's good to you, that isn't love. That's common sense. His wife should love him more than that. Now then, I want you to give him everything he needs without expecting him to return any favors."

"And what do I get out of it?"

"How about holiness?"

"I don't want holiness. I want love."

"Love is the same thing."

She didn't understand that at all. "You're saying it's all my fault."

"No, I'm not. Not at all. I'm complimenting you. You have the goodness and the strength to turn this marriage around—with the Father's help, of course. If I didn't have faith in you, I would have said, take a cruise. Pretend things are going well and be satisfied with mediocrity. But if you do what I'm telling you, you two will have the best marriage on the block. You'll have such a good marriage, everyone will think you're crazy."

"I almost believe you," she said.

"That's almost good. Why don't you pray about it?"

"Pray about it? Who, me?"

"Yes, you." He walked her to the door. "I think you'll do well."

"Am I supposed to make another appointment?" she asked.

"No. I'll see you in church."

She stood outside on the sidewalk. "Church? He doesn't even know if I go to church." She flung open the door to confront him with it. Of course, he wasn't there.

Give to Everyone Who Asks You

Jesus said, "Give to everyone who begs from you, and do not ask for your property back from someone who takes it." We may not like the idea that our husbands and wives have to beg from us, but all too frequently it happens. How often do our lovers have to beg us to pay attention? Are they afraid to initiate lovemaking because they know we might reject them?

There are so many things our spouses like us to do, yet they never seem important enough for us to remember. We're sporadic with our thoughtfulness, which makes our lovers suspicious, sometimes rightly so. When a husband brings home flowers, his wife is tempted to say, "You've quit your job, haven't you? Or have you done something else?"

If a wife does something special for her husband, he runs through a list of occasions to discover if he forgot one. When he realizes it's just an ordinary weekday, he thinks, "I wonder what she's up to."

Sometimes our thoughtfulness is a form of apology: "I'm sorry I fought with you." Why don't we expand our repertory? Let's add, "There's no particular reason for this; I'm just so glad I have you. Let's have a party." The Lord doesn't want his people to wear long faces or think only about "serious" spiritual things. He wants us to be happy.

We force our spouses to beg when they want something we don't approve of, when their needs are a burden on us, or when we think their requests can't really be important to them. Sometimes we make them beg because we're still concentrating on our own satisfaction. We might even withhold something deliberately because our spouses aren't responding to us, and turnabout is fair play. For whatever reason, we humans do a lot of withholding. When we do give, it may be grudging, partial, or seldom. Again, we're not bad people. We're good people who don't see our bad habits. Now that we do, we're free to change.

We're often quite generous with each other. I don't want to imply otherwise. But, often, our generosity is only for special occasions. Many men graciously pitch in with the dishes, the children, or the housework, but pitching in is exactly what we're doing. We're helping our wives do their own jobs; we're not taking responsibility.

Wives can also limit their generosity. Maybe they work outside the home, and when they come home, they feel they ought to be off duty. They may not go anywhere, but they're vividly aware that it's their time to themselves. If our husbands want time for themselves, too, how do we react?

Sometimes our "property" that is not "shared" is an attitude or belief. Clashes in child-raising philosophies are an all-too-frequent example. Often, we think our ideas are the right ones. If our lovers start to "interfere" by using their own methods, how do we respond? Do we feel they're taking the children away from us?

In a sense, we're like dogs clinging to a bone. Our attention is totally centered on what's being taken away from us. Maybe we growl self-righteously about it, and maybe we just clamp our jaws.

Such bones of contention can be sources of conflict and unhappiness. The Lord wants to free us from that. He's telling us to stop being possessive, not just about money or belongings, but about attitudes, preferences, and styles of living.

Let's stop and examine ourselves now: what hidden demands do we have of our spouses? Do we have mental lists of their responsibilities, which can only be postponed under special circumstances? What happens when those special circumstances are over? Do our spouses shoulder the same loads once again? Do they have to carry even more for a while to pay us for our help? "Remember how nice I was to you?" we imply. "Well, now you can let me off the hook."

Jesus reminds us, "If you love those who love you, what credit can you expect? Even sinners love those who love them." If you love your spouses when they're lovable, how different are you from any other couple? How are you a sacrament in anything but name?

Prickly Pair

We have been so carefully trained to be prickly, defensive, and, above all, in charge. When we can't control others' responses, we worry: are we getting our share? Yes, we're less defensive with our spouses than with others, but our training has been so thorough, we unconsciously bring it into our homes.

I'm not suggesting a debate about who's right and who's wrong. What I'm calling for is a surrender of defenses, a throwing down of arms, and a lasting, peaceful embrace. It's indeed not a fool's hope. It's God's plan.

The Lord is saying, "Let go; be free. Don't treat others as they treat you. That's the world's teaching."

"But I'm afraid. My spouse is hurting me. If I don't look out for myself, who will?"

The Lord isn't as heartless as we sometimes think he is. "Why, I will, of course," he answers. "I'm looking out for you right now."

The more we require, the less satisfied we become. We see how much we're not getting, and that certainly doesn't make us happy. The Lord is offering us happiness. He's offering us fullness in life. If we follow his way, there will be much more joy in our marriages. Our husbands and wives will certainly respond to our goodness if we'll only let it shine forth.

If the truth be known, we desperately want our spouses to love us freely. When we force "love" from them, no matter how subtle we are, we're fooling no one.

Besides, if we wait for our lovers to earn our trust, we'll have a long wait indeed. Our lovers simply cannot prove they're trustworthy. They, like all of us, have faults. Our trust must be our gift to them.

We All Have a Stake in Your Marriage

No matter how adeptly we extort good behavior from our spouses, we still can't make them into the people we want them to be. Many a fiancée, for instance, thinks, "Oh, I can make him stop drinking (attend the symphony/enjoy family life/change in other ways)." Of course not. Only he can change himself. Likewise, a husband can't force changes on a wife.

Our sacrament calls us to love our spouses, whether or not they earn it. Your relationship is not just a marriage; it's the sacrament of matrimony. Practically anyone can be married, but your relationship is more significant than a document in city hall. We, the church, have a stake in your marriage. Your good relationship nourishes us, and its rough moments drag us down. You are our community, and we need you to be your loving best.

Perhaps you're satisfied in your marriage. That doesn't necessarily mean you're answering your call to be sacramental. All too often, we compare our marriages with the failures around us:

"Thank God our marriage isn't like Joe and Mary's. They just endure each other. They never go out together, and when they're home, they're in opposite corners of the house. We're not perfect, but we still have some passion in our marriage. At least we still fight."

Maybe we're not judgmental, but just a little smug: "We have a date every Saturday night. We go to dinner, take in a movie. We don't know any other couple who does that." The idea's a great one, but the pride in that sentence can be blinding.

Put the Pedal to the Metal

Let's not ask ourselves, "Am I a good wife?" or "Am I a good husband?" if it means, "Am I living up to certain minimal standards?" or "Am I doing all right?"

Let's do ask, "Is this the best I can do? Am I really going all out, every moment of every day?"

Don't ask, "Does he gripe?" "Is she reasonably pleased?" It isn't enough to wonder, "Am I living up to my responsibilities?" Ask, instead, "How delighted is his life?" "How full is her life?" "How can I add to that enjoyment?"

If you compared many of today's marriages to schoolrooms, you'd find a lot of students content to earn Cs, sometimes a D, or even an F. But we didn't marry to get passing marks. We each have the capability to make our marriages an A+.

The Lord said, "Treat others as you would like people to treat you." We don't want others to do the minimum for us. We need so much more than that. We want to know that our husbands and wives are eager for us to be happy. We want to know that they'll treat us kindly, make sure our lives are filled with wonder because they love us so much.

If You Do Good to Those Who Do Good to You, What Credit Can You Expect?

When do we exercise our good qualities? If it's mainly when our spouses are appreciative or when they're good to us, we've changed loving into banking. We're lending to each other and expecting repayment.

The Lord says, "If you lend to those from whom you hope to get money back, what credit can you expect? Even sinners lend to sinners to get back the same amount."

So many couples practice a system of trade-offs. They may be very good people; it may be all they know. How are we different? Do we live Christian lives during the week and not just on Sunday? Are you living your sacrament right this minute?

If you live as a sacrament, you and your spouse will naturally benefit more than anyone else does. But you're living for more than your spouse's sake, though. The Church is only as credible as you are.

The words of the Bible are great and certainly necessary, but people aren't drawn to God because they're impressed with his book. They are drawn through a love relationship, beginning with his love as it is lived in you: your willingness to seek the happiness of others instead of yourself. That's best demonstrated by the way you love your spouse.

Love Your Enemies and Do Good to Them

In full, this passage says, "Love your enemies and do good to them, and lend without any hope of return. You will have a great reward, and you will be children of the Most High, for he himself is kind to the ungrateful and the wicked."

Our defensive instincts urge us to reject this teaching. We want to say, "Wait a minute. That's a nice thought, but we have to live in this world. My spouse is a good person; better than I am, most likely. But if you let people get away with rude behavior, they'll just get worse."

That's a little crude, but it gets to the point. How do we overcome the tendency to follow such love-killing advice? By telling ourselves, "I am not that kind of person. I am a loving person, and I will be a lover no matter what anyone else says or thinks."

We must teach ourselves that sulking, shouting back, the cold shoulder, forgetfulness of anniversaries—whatever—is unacceptable in the Lord's plan. We'll still make mistakes. We're human. But we must resolve not to lower our standards, even when we can't live up to them.

Prayer opens us to the Father's love. By understanding that love, we better understand how to love others. Prayer can be quiet thought in church. It can be meditation on the Scriptures. It can involve the rosary, spontaneous group prayer, or any number of expressions.

We Catholics, especially if we're older, are familiar with the concept of penance. Penance strengthens our prayer lives and the goodness within us. It is our widow's mite of suffering offered to the Father.

The strength to live his way is also found in trust. We humans are tempted to rely on force, making marriage into a power struggle.

Instead, we must truly trust our partners to want to love us. And the best way to encourage your spouse's desire to love you is to love your partner with everything you've got.

If we allow ourselves even a little laxity, we're being less than we can be. We're called to love each other as much as we can. That exuberant maximum will be different for each person. You might find yourself excelling in gentleness and forgiveness while your spouse grows in spontaneity and joy. Each of us is stronger in some graces, needing more prayer in others.

How to Grow a Lover

Some years ago, researchers placed two sets of plants in separate parts of a greenhouse, making sure the physical conditions were exactly the same. For one set of plants, they made life as miserable as possible. They constantly played harsh music, yelled, and insulted the poor things. To the other plants, they played soft, gentle music and offered constant praise.

The second set of plants blossomed incredibly, way beyond the capacity of the soil, fertilizer, sun, and water. The first set of plants withered and died.

The way to grow a lover is to talk gently and lovingly and in praise. The more criticism you dish out, the more your prophecies will be fulfilled. The harsher you are, the less love will be returned.

The following statements are, in a twisted way, the kind that usually turns into self-fulfilling prophecies:

"You don't care about me. All you care about is yourself."

"How could you *do* such a thing?"

"I don't know why I bother (…with you)."

"I forgot (…because you aren't important enough to make me remember)."

Our spouses are much more likely to become the kinds of people we "speak" them to be than the kinds of people we're trying to make them. Pressure, punishment, and force simply do not work in a husband-wife relationship.

To some degree, we're all guilty, even if we aren't extraordinary scoundrels or suffering in bad relationships. Less than perfect conduct is present even in the best marriages.

If we're clever and we apply enough pressure, we could probably force our spouses to perform as we wish, at least sometimes. But their hearts won't be in it and, after all, aren't hearts what marriage is all about?

It's our responsibility to bolster the good self-images of our spouses. The better their self-images are, the better they'll respond to us. They'll be more capable of loving; freer from defensiveness, narrowness, and rejection.

If our lovers see themselves as inadequate in our eyes, they simply won't have the confidence to love. But if we're frequently telling them how much they mean to us, how much more joyful our lives are because of their presence, the more they'll pour out their love on us. There will be a tremendous increase in their capacity to love because we have expanded them with our praise.

Resources for Reflection

"Words flow out of what fills the heart," Jesus told the Pharisees in Matthew 12:34. Out of those words a home is created. When you provide an environment of unconditional tenderness, your beloved becomes the kind of person who does fit your life. Spouses bloom when they believe they're so wonderful in your eyes that you just can't resist them.

If they receive love only when they perform correctly, they can never believe in that love. When that love is constant, relentless, when it is absolutely, totally poured out, the rewards are great.

There is no man who is loved by a tender woman who does not discover riches in himself that he never believed were there. There is no woman who is loved by a gentle man who does not live way beyond her outward potential. Every bit of love you ever expressed throughout your marriage has been more than returned.

The Lord's way really does work. We're losing so much if we

don't try it. But it won't work if we try a little of it for a little while. We really must make a commitment to love our spouses the way the Lord intends. Husbands, the Lord has specifically chosen each of you to love this particular woman the way he wants her to be loved. Wives, you are each called by Jesus to touch, to heal, to console, and to bring this man to life the way he wants to do it himself.

Do you see the wonder of it? This is an awesome commitment and a great honor. Jesus trusts you the way he trusted his disciples. He wants you to make his Kingdom come alive in the hearts of his people. Matrimony is a magnificent call to love totally and unreservedly.

Consider These Questions Privately:

When do I best increase my spouse's self-esteem? When do I wither my spouse by failing to love? What steps can I take to nourish my lover more?

What is holding me back from being a more perfect lover? Fear of hurt and rejection? Indignation? Fear of losing my "rights"?

Am I willing to incorporate prayer and/or penance into my life for the sake of my beloved? What, specifically, will I do?

Before we cover the next questions, let's review how to share. Remember to focus on your own feelings. These questions are meant to stimulate dialogue between you and to clear up misunderstandings. They are absolutely not a place to lay even the slightest blame. Don't, for instance, say, "I have trouble loving you when you're acting like a jerk, because that's when you make me the angriest." Do say something like "When we quarrel, I feel afraid that you'll stop loving me. I feel ashamed of myself, too. I'm afraid to share those feelings, so I cover them up with anger."

A warning: if you can add a "like" or "that" after "feel," it's a judgment, not a feeling.

Remember: use at least ten minutes to write and at least ten minutes to talk. Enjoy.

Share These Questions With Your Spouse:

My dear, I know that sometimes I love you less than I am able. I want to be closer to you; I want to love you more. These are the feelings that hold me back...

My dear, I want to increase my life of prayer and/or penance so I can love you more perfectly. I am thinking of doing the following... I would like you to support me by.... Will you please...?

What do I like best about you? What are your special goodnesses, the things that fill me with delight?

An Exercise in Happiness:

At least once a month in the next five months, find a way to tell your lover just how wonderful he or she is.

- Bring home flowers or a small gift.
- Plan a surprise dinner out or perhaps brunch on Sunday.
- Spend an evening or a Saturday being completely present to your partner. Do anything your spouse wants, providing you can share it together. A walk on the beach is great; reading books on the beach is not.
- Hide a love note in your spouse's lunch bag/box or briefcase.
- Fix a special food that you know your partner likes.

Finally, Let Us Invite God Into Our Marriages:

Eternal Father, my prayer today is for freedom: freedom from my cage of resentment and anxiety. Please grant me the grace to love as bountifully as you do. Please free me from the fear of rejection and hopelessness; give me the greatness of heart to trust my spouse's goodness.

Thank you, Lord, for choosing me to be the one to love my wonderful husband (wife). Thank you for trusting in me and believing in my goodness. Please help me love my spouse the way you want to do it yourself. Amen.

CHAPTER 6

Beloved, I Belong to You

The Prodigal Son.
(Lk 15:11–20)

One day, while sinners and tax collectors were crowding around Jesus, the scribes and Pharisees began to complain. "This man welcomes sinners and even eats with them"(Lk 15:2). Evidently they thought their virtue made them better company at dinner and probably in heaven as well. Jesus, who didn't agree, told them the story of the prodigal son.

Let's read this parable carefully to see where we fit in, particularly in relation to our spouses.

> There was a man who had two sons. The younger one said to his father, "Father, let me have the share of the estate that will come to me." So the father divided the property between them. A few days later, the younger son got together everything he had and left for a distant country where he squandered his money on a life of debauchery.
>
> When he had spent it all, that country experienced a severe famine, and now he began to feel the pinch; so he hired himself out to one of the local inhabitants who put him on his farm to feed the pigs. And he would willingly have filled himself with the husks the pigs were eating but no one would let him have them. Then he came to his senses and said, "How many of my father's hired men have all the food they want and more, and here am I dying of hunger! I will leave this place and go to my father and say: Father, I have sinned against heaven and against you; I no

longer deserve to be called your son; treat me as one of your hired men." So he left the place and went back to his father.

While he was still a long way off, his father saw him and was moved with pity. He ran to the boy, clasped him in his arms and kissed him. Then his son said, "Father, I have sinned against heaven and against you. I no longer deserve to be called your son. But the father said to his servants, "Quick! Bring out the best robe and put it on him; put a ring on his finger and sandals on his feet. Bring the calf we have been fattening, and kill it; we will celebrate by having a feast, because this son of mine was dead and has come back to life; he was lost and is found." And they began to celebrate.

Now the elder son was out in the fields, and on his way back, as he drew near the house, he could hear music and dancing. Calling one of the servants he asked what it was all about. The servant told him, "Your brother has come, and your father has killed the calf we had been fattening because he has got him back safe and sound." He was angry then and refused to go in, and his father came out and began to urge him to come in; but he retorted to his father, "All these years I have slaved for you and never once disobeyed any orders of yours, yet you never offered me so much as a kid for me to celebrate with my friends. But, for this son of yours, when he comes back after swallowing up your property—he and his loose women—you kill the calf we had been fattening."

The father said, "My son, you are with me always and all that I have is yours. But it was only right we should celebrate and rejoice, because your brother here was dead and has come to life; he was lost and is found."

LUKE 15:11–32

Let's try putting ourselves in the place of each character in the drama: the loving father, the indignant elder son, and the penitent younger one. You don't have to pretend you're an aging farmer or a swinging single. Jesus meant this parable to be generously interpreted. For the purposes of this chapter, then, let's think of ourselves as the loving spouse, the indignant spouse, and the penitent one.

The Wounds of Marriage

Remember the old saying "You only hurt the one you love"? That's because the one you love is the only one who lets you get close enough to cause that hurt.

Rejection isn't ever pleasant, but we can shrug it off more readily if it doesn't come from the ones we love. We all like to impress others, but we aren't seriously hurt when we don't succeed.

Most of the time, we don't expect everyone to have a burning desire for our companionship. But when a husband or wife doesn't desire our company, day after day, night after night, we hurt deeply.

When we love, our defenses are down. We don't want our words to be judged by someone who is supposed to love us. After all, we trust our loves, so we speak spontaneously.

Spontaneous speech is a rare gift, and we don't usually share it. We're always personal with our spouses, though, so when we're faced with indifference, cruelness, or even anger, we're wide open to the pain.

That's why forgiveness is the single most essential blessing a husband or wife can ask from God.

The Gift of Trust

There's a tremendous vulnerability in the love relationship, and often we forget how fragile a gift our spouses are giving us.

Sometimes we don't forget. We may even take advantage of it. A spouse who chooses the newspaper over his partner may say, "I'm not trying to hurt her. I'm just trying to unwind from work." A woman who gives her husband the cold shoulder may argue, "I'm not ignoring him. I'm just busy—doing *his* laundry."

We try to persuade ourselves that we're not deliberately hurting the other person, though we really know better. Once we know our actions will pain our loves, we can't pretend innocence. Even though some of us take advantage of this gift of trust, don't be discouraged. Our goodness is not determined by our flaws, but by our willingness to change those flaws.

Let's Call Ourselves Leaders

Anytime we're tempted to justify our actions by watching our friends' marriages, we're headed for trouble. There are unhappy marriages all around us, but that's because so many around us have already thrown in the towel.

In the parable of the prodigal son, Jesus calls us to be leaders. He calls us to be happy—and to be brave enough to face our mistakes. We're dodging the issue if we say, "There's misunderstanding and pain in every love relationship. We'd be naive to expect anything else."

Why settle for a wounded, hurting relationship when we have a much better choice?

Remember, in 1 Peter 2:9,10, the apostle says, "You are a chosen race, a royal priesthood, a holy nation, a people set apart to sing the praises of God who called you out of the darkness into his wonderful light. Once, you were no people and now you are the People of God...." Jesus Christ came to earth to free us all from the hopeless limitations of humanity. With God's grace, you can, indeed, have a truly loving relationship. It's your choice. Hurry! Your family's happiness is at stake.

The lack of happiness in today's marriages is a life-threatening illness. If a husband was vomiting and feverish, and had a sharp pain on the lower right side of his abdomen, his wife wouldn't shrug her shoulders and say, "Oh, well. Must be appendicitis; that's pretty common. Most people get it sooner or later." Instead, she'd rush her husband to the hospital. When our husbands or wives hurt from wounds we inflict, though, we're much more relaxed.

We humans are much more likely to excuse our own defects, and much less likely to excuse our lovers' flaws. There's a good rule of thumb we can all follow: when we find ourselves making excuses for our behavior, that's when our loves are feeling their greatest pain.

To Love or Be Loved?

We are only happy when we're focused on others, and we're miserably unhappy when we focus on ourselves. We think we would much rather be loved than love. That's not because we're bad people. It's because we've learned to look for happiness the wrong way.

This self focus is a recipe for trouble. Love is supposed to pull us outward until we're taking the other person even more seriously than we do ourselves. As our love grows, we start to find our own well-being in our loves' well-being.

Marriage is not supposed to be a business deal in which each partner receives separate rewards for a joint effort. It's a call for both husband and wife to be totally absorbed in each other. It's a call to spend all our talents, our energy, enthusiasm, and responsiveness for one precious purchase: bringing true joy to our loves.

If we think the purpose of marriage is to be loved, we are clinging to an illusion: that the more we are loved, the happier we are.

If we are experiencing hurt in our marriages, we need to find out why. We must go beyond the specific incident that triggered the pain: "He forgot our anniversary." "She doesn't care how hard I work." We may be choosing to experience the pain. If we have a whole series of hidden expectations for our partners and lists of our own rights, we're headed for heartache.

Sin Is a Four-Letter Word

Ask yourselves, "What causes the most pain in this world?" Terrorism? Cancer? Prejudice? No, sin does.

We don't realize that pain is intimately connected with sin. If we could wipe out sin in a husband/wife relationship, we would eliminate ninety percent of that couple's emotional pain.

"We're sinners." How does this expression make us feel?

Most likely we're probably not too offended, although this statement is worse than any obscene phrase we could imagine.

It's a far more horrible insult to say that we're sinners. Instead, it doesn't faze us in the least. This admission that we're all sinners doesn't make that sinful condition less lethal. When we say, "We're sinners," we're really saying we are people who inflict pain. We are infectious with unhappiness; we make those around us suffer.

We're passive about sin because we don't recognize what it means to be a sinner. An admission of sin is of the greatest and most important seriousness. It's an opening of our hearts to those around us and, for Catholics, a necessary preliminary to receiving the Body and Blood of Christ. Do we realize it's our opportunity for a true conversion experience, or is our admission of sin rather like brushing dust off our coats before we walk into church? For many of us, it's only a lighthearted "I'm a sinner, you're a sinner, all God's children are sinners."

We resist an awareness of our sinfulness because we don't want to go on any guilt trips. We're determined to avoid guilt, even to the point of ignoring our wrongs. It's easier to ignore those wrongs when we don't accept God's view of life. We may admit that, yes, in his eyes we've committed a sin, but we add that we're normal human beings, no worse than anyone else.

That excuse isn't worthy of you. Remember, we're called to be leaders, not sheep following the rest of society on a downhill road. Everyone else's sins don't excuse our own; they merely add to the world's problems.

Ask yourselves, "Do I really stand before God as a sinner and see the pain my sin is inflicting upon his people, especially my spouse? Or do I see it with this world's eyes and pass it off with a shoulder shrug?" Honesty will give you the answer, and your goodness will tell you what to do.

A Way of Life

We must recognize sin as a way of life. It is not merely doing something that is bad in itself, nor is it merely a neutral action that is motivated by a sinful purpose. Sin is a whole orientation toward life: "I am a sinner," not "I did sinful things."

When I say, "I am a sinner," I'm saying I'm committed to a way of life that is self-centered and unloving.

To many of us, that's a threatening truth. We want to deny it; to say, "Most of my actions are good, or at least neutral. They're not bad." Again, we have to stop deluding ourselves. Sin isn't merely action.

We're living a sinful way of life when we're living for our own satisfaction, our own advancement. In sin, others fit best into our lives when they give us these things. That's what it means to say, "I am a sinner." That's why some husbands and wives focus on being loved rather than on loving. We can perform all sorts of good actions sinfully if our attention is fundamentally on us.

In a marriage relationship, the basic choice is between you and me. We sin when we choose me over you. We do this in many subtle ways:

We don't say we're self-centered. We say we're independent. We stand on our own two feet.

We don't say we're indifferent to the needs of our spouses. We say there has to be give and take.

We don't say the other person is less important than we are; we say we have a lot of responsibilities and we can only do so much.

It's no wonder we say such things; it's the way we've been trained. We've all seen tests that measure marital happiness. These tests ask spouses whether they're satisfied in their marriages. A real test should ask, "Is my spouse satisfied? What am I contributing to his or her satisfaction?"

We also need to recognize that sin is never "out there." There is probably no such thing as sin in itself. There are only sinners. Sin is personal. We can't sin when we're asleep or out of our minds. The deed does not make the sin; the person does.

Right now, you're probably admitting that sometimes you don't always do as well as a spouse should. When we think that way, we're still isolating ourselves from our sin. We have to learn a new way of thinking that takes openness and courage. We have to let go of our defenses; we have to stop depersonalizing sin. We have to stop thinking it's outside us, like stained clothes or scaly skin.

The Prodigal Son

We are horrified by the prodigal son's gall. He went to his father and said, "Okay, I'm old enough, I want to be independent. Give me my share." Most of us wouldn't be as generous as his father; we'd put that brat in his place. We'd ask, "What do you mean your share?"

We're indignant that he could have been so greedy and cold-blooded. Our feelings are right. His heartless demand for money was much more sinful than the way he spent it.

We think the sleeping around, the drinking, and the reckless spending were the younger son's sins. They weren't. The sin had already been committed. Those activities were merely expressions of the life-style he had chosen to live; a life-style in which he had divorced himself from his father. Demanding his share of the estate was more than rude. It was a statement: "I no longer belong to you." In effect, he was saying, "I want to live my own way." That's when he decided to be a sinner.

The relationship between father and son is the most important part of this parable. The debauchery is a very small part of the story, like the famine and the degradation of starving while feeding the pigs.

The prodigal son probably could have said, "Look, I don't have anything against the old man. I'm not doing these things because I dislike him. I just want my due. I don't want to live on a farm all my life; I have other plans."

Have you ever really felt yourself to be a sinner with your wife, with your husband? We limit sin in a marriage to adultery, wife beating, and desertion. Most of us find it easy to refrain from those. Often, our virtue is lack of opportunity. Adultery isn't merely sleeping in someone else's bed. Adultery happens when you don't enjoy the bed you're in. Many good husbands and wives would never look at another man or touch another woman, but their sexual response to each other is dutiful or grudging. That's infidelity.

In other words, infidelity is not the actual act of intercourse with another person. It's the severing of relationship with your spouse. It's the putting him or her out of your life. That's because, like the prodigal son's debauchery, an act of adultery isn't the primary sin. It's the expression of a sin that's already been committed.

If you're really involved with your wife or husband, you won't have your mind on adultery; if the opportunity comes up, you won't be interested. Your heart's already taken.

It's much more difficult not to live adulterously, now that we know where adultery really begins. Many of us call ourselves married, but we're really "married singles." That means we don't fully belong to our loves. We just eliminate certain activities like dating others or staying out all night. We're living a single way of life with occasional limitations.

Let's Stamp Out Spouse Abuse

Like adultery, spouse abuse isn't always as obvious as it seems. A husband or wife may not be innocent, even if a spouse has never been touched. Emotional pain is a subtle, terrible thing.

Do you really listen to your spouses—all the time, not just when they talk about something interesting? When you stood at the altar, you didn't pledge to listen to specific topics. You promised to listen to *a person.*

The emotional pain of being ignored is as real as a migraine headache. The pain recurs again and again; it becomes a regular part of life. We can't say, "Well, that's the way I am. My partner will have to get used to it."

Wives can match their husbands blow for blow. More than a million husbands in the United States have been physically beaten by their wives. Many more have been tongue-lashed, and the tongue is a sharper weapon than any fist or pot.

When I say this to an audience, the women will tell me, "If you were married to my husband, you'd do it too!" But I didn't choose to marry those men. They did. Every wife has promised to love her husband without fail until death parts him from her.

Again, remember the prodigal son. Like adultery, tongue-lashing isn't the real sin. The real sin is that we haven't really decided to be married. We're living together with benefit of clergy, but that's not marriage.

Tongue-lashing happens because we store up hurts and grudges. Then we explode. We don't feel any particular obligation to hold ourselves back. It's a shame, but tongue-lashing is what works. What else can we do?

If you're thinking like that, you're asking the wrong question. Don't wonder if your anger is justified. Ask yourself—is your partner afraid of your tongue?

Cast off the right to vent your anger on your love. Don't say, "Well, I know it's not the nicest way to act. I wouldn't do it all the time, but I can only take so much." In those thoughts, the focus is on yourself, not on your love.

Whether you're examining your listening habits, your anger, or any other flaw, don't let yourself be deluded into saying, "Well, I don't do it that often. I'm not like you-know-who." Live for yourself and your own family. Living next door to the neighborhood ogre doesn't make your household any happier. We shouldn't compare ourselves to our spouses, either. Our spouses could be the greatest sinners in the world, but that doesn't reduce our sin in the slightest.

Your Love Is Your Life

Do you really belong to your spouses? We're not talking about whether you love them, whether you're nice or do all the right things. Those are good beginnings, but have you really put yourself in your partner's hands?

The issue is one of trust. Do you really believe your spouse loves you even more than you love yourself? That's what marriage is all about. As anniversaries go by, you should become two in one flesh.

Jesus gives us a great challenge, one in startling disagreement with the lessons of our me-first society. It's a challenge that asks you to give your all. It isn't enough for two independent souls to live side by side. When you're really married, you're no longer running your life. There are two of you inside, and you can no more ignore the needs and desires of your love than you can ignore yourself.

Of course, that perfect oneness is an ideal; most of us probably won't reach it in a lifetime. Instead, begin with a question: Do you really want your spouse to be your way of life?

Have you really decided to get married, or are you taking your portion of the marriage and just not living riotously? Remember, riotous living was not the prodigal son's sin. Refusing the relationship was his sin. Had he been married, he might have run to the store for his wife at midnight, but he would have wanted to live his own life.

How Much Love Is Enough?

No matter how good you are, it's a constant temptation to look toward your spouse instead: to test the waters, to see if he's up to this kind of relationship, if she's responding the way you think she should. Sometimes we all fear that our goodness will bounce off our loves like water off rocks. Then we'll be left alone, with nothing but stark reality.

Of course, behind all those fears is the unspoken judgment that we're better people than our spouses are. That isn't a good way to think. Ask yourselves: "Am I truly willing to be a full-fledged husband?" "Am I truly willing to be a full-fledged wife?" You mustn't decide what that means by watching your friends and neighbors. You must make your decision in accordance with your beloved's needs and your vocation from God himself.

Ask yourself, "Am I willing to accept a life of total love, not of being loved but loving?" If the answer is "yes," then look at yourself clearly. All of us are good people, yet we could all honestly say, "Why, I haven't been married at all. I've been doing married things, the right ones and very well, but I've been expecting rewards. I've been paying entirely too much attention to *me*."

That's when we truly become aware that we are sinners. When the prodigal son chose to be a sinner, to breach his relationship with his father, he was young and single. He used harlots as his sin of choice.

We might choose a job instead of a full love relationship. We might choose our children instead, or the television, a book, or friends. It isn't riotous living, but it's the product of sin just the same.

Now, there's nothing wrong with doing well at your job. There's nothing wrong with being a good parent, being well-read or talented. But don't be an "unwed" mother or father. Don't be married to the boss; be married to this lover you have chosen.

Hitting Rock Bottom

If we're to make the prodigal son's final choice of love over self-interest, we must first become disillusioned with ourselves. The prodigal son hit rock bottom. Then, the parable says, he "came to his senses." It didn't say he recognized debauchery was wrong, that he spent a lot of money on nothing, or that getting drunk wasn't that great, after all. The parable says, simply, that he came to his senses.

Then Scripture tells us what coming to his senses means. Immediately he said, "I will leave this place and go to my father." When he came to his senses, he realized who he was: his father's son.

You see, when we come to our senses, we do more than admit we ought to do better or we've been wrong. This coming to our senses concentrates on the other person, because our spouses are who we are. The prodigal was his father's son. You are your wife's husband; your husband's wife.

We all need to understand that there is no such thing as a full, independent life with relationships on the side. Because we are so intimately defined by our relationships, our coming to our senses makes us look outside ourselves. It makes you, a lover, look to your wife or husband.

We all have selfish impulses. I'm going to outline a few below. And we all need to look at them. Remember; admitting our sins gives us a true feeling of freedom.

Hopeless popular wisdom urges us to think these thoughts:

"I'm not getting enough from this marriage. Why should I stay with you?"

"You're not the person I thought you were. You aren't living up to my expectations. I have plans and dreams, and you're holding me back."

"Darling, I love you so much. But you have to love me, too."

"I'm not going to love you unless you love me. I'll measure out my love."

Or, in a nutshell, "This marriage is about my satisfaction. I married you for my own pleasure, and pleasure is what I expect."

The urge to excuse ourselves is almost irresistible. We want to say, "Oh, no, that's not really the way it is, because I give. I know I have to give, but he has to give too; she has to pull her load."

Again, comparisons only defeat our goal. The prodigal son didn't think about how much he owed his father. He simply faced the truth: he didn't belong to his father any more because he hadn't wanted to.

This parable wasn't a lesson in fairness. It was a lesson in recognition. When the prodigal left home, he stopped being a son, not because his father didn't want him, and not because his father deserved a better son. The breach was his own personal choice.

Resources for Reflection

We have to face that choice. How have we chosen? Are we married, really married, or are we single? Do we live as lovers, as husbands or wives? Or do we live as we wish, earnestly hoping our spouses can accept our decisions?

Consider These Questions Privately:

What thoughts and attitudes of mine keep me from living as a lover: a husband or a wife?

How does my marriage fit my life-style? What changes must I make so my life-style will fit my marriage?

Do I really believe I am a sinner? Why or why not?

Share These With Your Spouse:

What dream has this chapter inspired in me? (Be as idealistic as you choose.) How can you, my love, and I make this dream come true?

"Thank you, dear." Spend ten minutes writing a simple letter to your love, a letter of thanks for that delicate gift of trust. For instance, does she trust you to care about her problems? Does he let down his mask of masculine toughness to be tender during lovemaking? (Remember, focus on your own feelings. Be respectful; never judge your spouse.)

Finally, Let Us Invite God Into Our Marriages:

Dear Lord, let me stop dwelling within myself and live instead in relationship with my beloved spouse.

Let me be grateful for that fragile gift he (she) has given me: his (her) trust. Let me treat it with gentleness and return it in full measure.

Let me forgive my lover's wrongs and ask forgiveness for mine.

Like the prodigal son, let me be open to my sinfulness and yearn for your presence in my life. And like the prodigal, help me realize that we are born to be lovers, not lonely, loveless individuals.

Give me healing and the grace to grow in you. Amen.

CHAPTER 7

I Am Unworthy to Be Called Your Spouse

"This Son of Mine Was Dead and Has Come Back to Life."
(LK 15:20–32)

Jesus spoke in parables, but he expects us to apply his lessons to our own lives. For us, the parable of the prodigal son might become the parable of the prodigal spouse. But the prodigal spouse may not be the husband who runs off with a young blonde, or the wife who heads down the highway with a salesman from Las Vegas.

Prodigal spouses may spend every night at home. They may be proud of their beautiful home, which both may work overtime to finance, and which they work hard to keep clean. And neither of them seriously thinks of looking for another mate.

But are they married? They may have stopped living as spouses to each other, just as the prodigal son decided not to be a son to his father.

Now, suppose a prodigal couple wanted to reconcile. How would they do it? They might make a catalog of sins: "I worked on the car when you wanted to talk"; "I let you work overtime so I could have a nice house." It would be a noble effort, but it wouldn't even touch their real problem. Their sin was more than a grocery list of mistakes. Their sin was choosing self-centered ways of life.

Instead, they should look to the parable of the prodigal son to find an ideal example of reconciliation. When the prodigal wanted to reconcile, he said, "Father, I have sinned against heaven and against you; I no longer deserve to be called your son." He didn't say, "Let me tell you all the rotten things I've done." He said only, "I no longer deserve to be called your son." He knew that his breach of relationship was more serious than his sleeping around, his drunkenness, or his carelessness with money.

Fairness Doesn't Work

In sin, we deny who we are by denying the loves in our lives. It's the normal, everyday sinfulness that says, "You are a man who's supposed to make me happy," or "You're not flesh of my flesh. You're here because I like what you do for me."

This focus on reciprocal fairness is a pagan standard that has nothing to do with God. We try to structure our marriages in terms of fairness. We say marriage is a 50–50 proposition. That sounds like an ideal compromise, but it's not God-centered and it simply doesn't work. What happens if that perfect balance slips a little? If it's 51–49, our favor, that probably feels all right to us. But what if it's 60–40? Do we think it's about time we got our share, or do we begin to feel a little guilty? What if the scale tips to 70–30, and we're giving the seventy? Do we say, "It's all right; we're just having a rough time right now"?

If we want to become real husbands and wives, we must reconcile with each other. We can't merely say, "I'm sorry I nag you," or "I'm sorry I close up." These are the expressions of sin, not the sin itself.

They're also easy to confess. Instead, we must be honest and trusting, both with ourselves and our lovers. We must say, "I have been unworthy to be called your husband"; "I have been unworthy to be called your wife."

Those are strong statements, but we need strong statements when we're speaking of sin. Sin is serious, and we have to challenge it face-to-face. As long as we resist saying, "I am unworthy to be called your spouse," we're refusing to come to our senses as sinners.

Sin Is Comparing

Sometimes we judge the success of a marriage by the level of unhappiness. We lie to ourselves, saying we're not doing too badly. We have carefully rationed interludes of romance: birthdays, anniversaries, and the like. Forget all that; it's organized misery.

The only way we should be single is in recognition of our sins. Even then, we must be thinking of how our sins harm our lovers. We must come to our senses and say, "I am a sinner." We can't pretend our sins don't exist. The only way to erase sin is to seek forgiveness.

The prodigal son didn't say, "It's normal for young men to sow their wild oats." Instead, he came to his senses and said, "I no longer deserve to be called your son."

We shouldn't say, "I don't deserve to be called your wife because of what I've done." Instead, we should realize, "I don't deserve to be called your wife because I have not *been* your wife, and because I have not allowed you to be my husband."

Sin is the keeping of ourselves to ourselves, whether it's expressed in reprehensible actions or even in praiseworthy ones.

"I am unworthy to be called your husband" may be hard to say. We might disagree: "I always support her, I don't drink up the paycheck." But have we been part of her heart?

We must say, "I am unworthy to be called your husband because I haven't been living for you. I've been living with myself, and you're nearby. I have taken my share of the marriage and squandered it."

Sin Is Reasonable

On your wedding day, you said your body wasn't yours anymore; it belonged to your beloved. Later on, you can't change your mind.

Saint Paul states very clearly in his first letter to the Corinthians that a husband's body belongs to his wife and a wife's body belongs to her husband. In 1 Corinthians 7:3–4, he says: "The husband must give to his wife what she has a right to expect, and so too the wife to her husband. The wife does not have authority over her own body, but the husband does; and in the same way, the husband does not have authority over his own body, but the wife does."

Yet we tend to think it's normal to deny sex to our lovers. We don't realize it's a form of theft. We must stop thinking that marriage is like living with a roommate. Marriage is a real integration. It is truly becoming one in mind, heart, and body.

With today's emphasis on careers and materialism, both husbands and wives are finding themselves too exhausted and even too busy to physically love each other. Doesn't that sound bizarre?

Go make love. It'll keep you out of trouble. The goodness of a passionate relationship spills over onto your friends, your neighbors, and especially your family. A passionate love relationship, for instance, fosters patience. When you're passionate toward each other and your son misbehaves, you'll say, "Ah, isn't that cute? He's just like his father." When you're not passionate toward each other, you'll shout, "You little brat! You're just like your *father.*"

Marriage is more than a piece of paper you signed one, ten, or fifty years ago. It's a sacrament, and your love, including physical love, is sacramental.

Am I Sorry? Or Am I Married?

"I'm sorry" means "I know my action was inappropriate and unworthy of a good person like me." It's a very self-centered awareness. "I'm sorry" can mean other things as well. It might mean, "You're very angry about what I did. I can't understand why; I don't think it was that bad. But you're not going to get over it until I say I'm sorry, so I'll say I'm sorry and get it over with." In this case, I really do want to reconcile, but I'm not admitting I'm wrong.

Or maybe "I'm sorry" means, "Gee, you're hurt and I don't like to see you hurt. I'm not hung up about saying I'm sorry, so if it makes you feel better, I'll say it." It's a remedy, like bringing you chicken broth when you're sick.

"I'm sorry" is a request. We're really asking our loves to say, "Ah, that's all right; forget it. I do things like that too."

That's why when we say, "I'm sorry," we're selling ourselves short, we're not facing the truth that we denied our relationship. We're only facing the symptom: what we did. If the prodigal son had behaved this way, he would have said, "It's not worthy of me to be sleeping around, so I won't do it anymore." That doesn't touch his sin, does it? His sin is against his relationship with his father. The prodigal could have stopped sleeping around and drinking; he could have worked very hard, earned back all the money he squandered, and sent it home to his father, and still he would not have come to his senses.

When we say, "I'm sorry," we're avoiding both the Gospel story and our own identities: those of husband or wife, not just man or woman. When our loves tell us, "I'm sorry," and we answer, "Well, that's all right," we're really saying, "Okay, let's be friends—until this happens again."

We have memory rights when we excuse that way; we're allowed to revive the old hurts whenever appropriate. This way, we can protect ourselves. We don't have to trust as much because, after all, our loves let us down before.

Most husbands and wives excuse instead of forgiving. It's the normal thing to do. It's also impersonal; it isn't open.

Excusing is too shallow an option for two good lovers. Instead, we must forgive and seek forgiveness. The prodigal son said, "I will go to my father and say: Father, I have sinned against heaven and against you; I no longer deserve to be called your son; treat me as one of your hired men." He didn't invite his father to excuse him. He knew better. He knew that "I'm sorry" so often means "I'm hurting too much for any more of this fighting, so let's make up."

We appear to be the heroes when we say "I'm sorry," but we're really looking for something: for peace in the home or for our lovers to be nice to us again. The prodigal son saw through all of it. He simply said, "I'm not worthy to be called your son. Treat me like a hired hand."

That's what it's like to come to our senses. Ordinarily we wouldn't see the need for it unless we'd dealt with a great trauma like physical adultery or beating. That's where we're wrong. The trauma of sin surrounds us every day.

Sin: Not What It's Cracked Up to Be

Most evil isn't glamorous. It's trite and everyday. Adolf Eichmann, for instance, lived quietly in Argentina for more than a decade. His neighbors probably never dreamed that this almost kindly looking man would eventually be hung as a mass murderer, condemned for the deaths of millions of Jews.

Take that idea one step further: imagine yourself living next door to such a criminal, thinking, "I'm not sure I agree, but my neighbor seems happy enough. Well, it must be all right, because there's nothing wrong with him."

As a society, we're obsessed with the desire to be like those around us. Why? Because watching others absolves us of having to try harder than they do. If all our friends are getting divorced, we reason that it must somehow be all right. If they dive into the computer every night or throw dishes at each other, we can decide that's normal, too.

"But everyone does it." The answer comes automatically. Other people work overtime. Other people don't date after marriage; they stay home like old married couples are supposed to. Other people don't hold hands and they don't feel too rotten when they insult each other in a fight.

Now, why did Jesus come to earth? He came to change everyone. There's no Gospel passage that says, "Thou shalt do as everyone else does." Nor did he say that when we appear before him in heaven, he'd reward us because "I was hungry, and you behaved like everyone else."

We're called to a better goal. Everyone else doesn't recognize that we're called to be higher than a blind average. Everyone else doesn't recognize sin. They think sin is the normal human condition; sin is to be expected.

No, it isn't. Sin is why Jesus came to die on the cross. God thinks sin was serious enough to merit the suffering and death of his only Son. He didn't just shrug his shoulders and say, "So this person didn't listen to his spouse, so what's new?"

Rightness is another reason Jesus came to earth. Being right kills a love relationship. Rightness doesn't justify inflicting hurt. The prodigal son didn't say, "After all, Father, I only took what was coming to me. It's my business how I spent it." He said, "I will go to my father and say: Father, I have sinned against heaven and against you; I no longer deserve to be called your son."

Hurry to Forgive

The parable of the prodigal son continues, "So he left the place and went back to his father." His father was standing a long way off, looking, hoping, yearning. The father didn't say, "I hope my kid comes to his senses and knows what he's done to me."

A husband and wife must have that same yearning to embrace. We must also be looking from a long way off, watching and hoping for that first sign that our spouses are seeking forgiveness. When our loves try to reconcile, we too often make them go through their paces: "I want her to realize this is serious"; "I want to make sure he knows how much he hurt me."

The prodigal's father cast all that aside. The parable says, "While he was still a long way off, his father saw him and was moved with pity. He ran to the boy, clasped him in his arms and kissed him." At the first sign of his son, the father was overwhelmed with eagerness to reach his son. He didn't test the waters; the slightest sign that his son was responsive again was enough for him.

Do we do likewise, or do we cling to our hurts and our righteousness? We test our loves' sincerity, thinking, "He has to earn his way back. She has to prove she's reformed." That's not forgiveness.

The father didn't exact any fee from his son. The father was simply drawing him in with love, hoping against hope they could reconcile. Even though the boy saw his father's openness, he didn't feel extremely sure because he was so aware of his sinfulness. He insisted on saying what he'd come to say: "Father, I have sinned against heaven and against you. I no longer deserve to be called your son."

But his father ignored the past. He hugged that boy and leaped up and down for joy. He shouted, "Come on, everyone, get him a robe, get him a ring, put sandals on his feet, kill the best beef on the farm. Let's have a party!"

He wasn't rejoicing because his son was going to change or because he was penitent. The father rejoiced simply because he could touch him. When our loves seek our forgiveness, our response must be the same. It can in no way, shape, or form be judgmental or superior.

The Long Memory

When our loves seek forgiveness, we must pledge to wipe out the memory of their wrongs. As long as we remember those wrongs, we have not yet forgiven. We may be virtuous enough never to bring them up, but their memory can poison our love. When our loves ask for forgiveness, our response in joy is to reaffirm our relationship by saying, "My beloved wife…" or "My beloved husband…." What we remember from now on is his humility, her goodness.

This is a key point. Too often, we give ourselves great credit for being long-suffering. We're long-suffering, though, because we have such long memories.

If you want to know just how forgiving you are, ask yourselves, "What do I remember?" Do we remember our own goodness in forgiving so graciously, or do we recall with wonder our loves' humility? Do we recall the sin? If we recall the sin, our spouses can never be touched by the forgiveness. We could say, "Well, I'm not holding it against him"; "I'm not using it against her." If we're keeping it alive in memory, though, it's more important than our relationship.

We're called to give total forgiveness, not lukewarm excuses and apologies. We are called to remember the sinner's seeking of reconciliation, not the sin. The prodigal's father illustrates this beautifully. He didn't ask, "Are you going to be a good boy now? Are you going to settle down? Did you learn a lesson?"

The father did say, "This son of mine was dead and has come back to life." With that statement, he wiped out the boy's denial and reestablished their relationship. A truly forgiving wife or husband says the same: "Yes, dear, you are my spouse. I could never let you go. I'm so glad to have you back."

That celebration marks not your love's sin, but your renewed belonging. It rejoices: "How good you are in wanting to belong to me. I thought I had lost you. But you are my husband (wife). You're so wonderful, I'm so lucky to have you. Come, let us be merry, let everyone know: not that I who have been offended have finally been justified, but that you are so good, and my belonging to you is precious to me." When we forgive like this, we follow Jesus' teaching and become true lovers.

Sin Unseen

This parable of the prodigal son prompts us to think of a few prodigals we know and hope our spouses get the point. We don't really apply it to ourselves. We don't realize the Lord is seeking to teach us through this story.

Perhaps we mentally cast ourselves in the role of the son who stayed. The older boy wasn't all that gracious, but we might have real empathy for his position.

We shouldn't feel sorry for the second son. He had no more relationship with his father than his brother did. Both boys were sinners. Both boys were living their own ways of life, centered around themselves. One of them expressed it in a spectacular way by going to a far-off country and doing all sorts of extravagant things. The other boy looked good on the outside, but where was he in relationship with his father? Obviously, not very close, since he never shared his father's pain over the other boy's absence.

If the older son had been in relationship with his father, he would have known what the younger boy meant to his father and he would have rejoiced for his father's sake. But he was thinking only of himself for all those years when his brother was gone.

The second son had equal need to go to his father for forgiveness. He might have said, "I am no longer worthy to be called your son, not because I live riotously but because I don't understand you. Otherwise I could not be so cold and indifferent, so wrapped up in myself."

There are plenty of second sons in our marriages. Maybe our spouses do more "bad" things, but we are equally guilty of failing to love. If we've realized this, we can go to our spouses and say, "My beloved, I am unworthy to be called your spouse, not because I've done anything, but because I haven't belonged to you. I belong to myself. I haven't been responding to you, my dear. I've really been responding to my own sense of self."

Remember, in the parable of the prodigal son, the father never gave any grudging replies like "Oh, it's all right," or "I'm glad that's over." When his younger son came to him, he merely reaffirmed the relationship. That's true forgiveness.

Accepting Forgiveness

We should be eager to seek such forgiveness ourselves. First, of course, we must search inside for our sins. One area we all overlook is the memories of our spouses' failings. These memories become our own failing; that of cold-heartedness. If we are guilty of this, we must say, "My beloved, I have been remembering your failings. I am unworthy to be called your wife (husband)."

It isn't easy to accept our spouses' forgiveness. It's easier to keep concentrating on ourselves. Even after we've been forgiven, it's normal to wish we could make up for the hurt. Don't do that.

After your love forgives you, you must simply rejoice at being accepted back. You should concentrate on your love's acceptance, rather than on the sins you've committed. Focusing on your sins may be virtuously self-punishing, but it's also self-centered. Besides, you can never really make up for the pain you caused.

You can avoid this self-defeating trap by welcoming the goodness of your lover. The more you can concentrate on how good she is, how forgiving he is, the more you'll be able to accept that forgiveness. If you look to yourself and try to make up for the past, you'll prevent your own healing. Furthermore, scorekeeping is a subtle method of avoiding relationship. It's a way of canceling sin, not admitting it as a way of life and accepting your lover's goodness.

Often, we don't live in relationship with our loves because we think "husband" and "wife" are job descriptions, like "homemaker" or "diplomat." That's not true. Being a spouse is not an occupation, it's a relationship with another human being.

It doesn't matter how many children you have by each other or how long you've lived in the same house. Only your choice of each other on a daily basis makes you husband and wife. So does a constant seeking of forgiveness, because we are all sinners. We will continue to be sinners, even after we are reconciled. Marriage is a constant offering of forgiveness as well.

Forgive Me? What Did I Do?

You can't offer forgiveness to someone who doesn't ask for it. The father couldn't search out the youngest son and say, "You're forgiven." He didn't know he'd sinned. Likewise, you can't go to your spouses and say, "You are forgiven." They'll ask, "What for?" But when forgiveness is sought, it has to be given generously, as the Lord teaches us.

Jesus said, "Do not judge, and you will not be judged; do not condemn, and you will not be condemned; forgive, and you will be forgiven. Give, and there will be gifts for you: a full measure, pressed down, shaken together, and overflowing, will be poured into your lap; because the standard you use will be the standard used for you" (Lk 6:37, 38).

Ask yourselves: "Can I stand before my heavenly Father and say, "Father, I ask nothing more than the forgiveness I have given my spouse"? Don't worry about whether you forgive others. Concentrate on your spouse; that's where it all begins.

Jesus has placed himself in our hands. We really are the body of Jesus; that's not just a nice theological notion. We have been called to express him, his view of life, and his way of living. We do this by the way we live. Specifically, we do this by the way we live with our husbands and wives.

The Lord says forgiveness is part of the kingdom of heaven. When my beloved experiences that goodness within me, the kingdom of heaven becomes real to him or her. The believability of God and God's way of life is in your hands. Please, search within yourselves to discover how you are a sinner and then spend some real time with each other and seek forgiveness, regardless of whether your spouse seeks forgiveness, too.

Beloved, I Have Sinned

You may be thinking, "How can anyone just presume we're in sin and need to be forgiven?" That very question indicates that we're in the position of the older son. We think because we've been doing the right things, we don't have any sin. We're fooling ourselves. We know that someday we must stand before our Father and say, "I am a sinner."

It's not presumptuous or unreasonable to say that each of us as husband or wife really needs to seek forgiveness, not just in the sense of "Well, I have these little defects," but in the sense of "I am a sinner before God. I am unworthy to be called your spouse because of my whole attitude; because of my whole lack of belonging; because I have lived my own way instead of putting myself in your hands."

Maybe you're willing but you're tempted to tell your spouse, "Okay, I'll go first, you go second." Don't; you're not ready.

If you're really conscious that you're a sinner, you're completely unconscious of your spouse as a sinner. It works in reverse as well: the more conscious you are of your spouse's sin, the less conscious you are of your own. If you're still focusing on your spouse's sin, you are in no state to seek forgiveness, and maybe you should say that. You could say, "Help me, beloved. Let us go to the Lord together to soften the hardness of my heart. How could I be so indifferent to my own sins and so conscious of yours?"

Resources for Reflection

This is a wonderful opportunity to discover each other, to come to your senses. As soon as you finish this chapter, go to your beloved and say, "My beloved, I have sinned against heaven and against you." Then specify the ways. General confessions aren't much help.

You should describe the specific ways you've established your independent lifestyle; how you've shown your indifference; how you've chosen self over your beloved; how you really haven't been married.

If I'm a sinner, I need forgiveness. The more I recognize I am a sinner, the more unworthy I become in my own eyes and the less conscious I become of my spouse's growth—or lack of growth—toward God. I need forgiveness. I need to belong again. I need to come to my senses; I need that awakening to be truly recognized, not only by myself, but by that person I have pledged myself to.

All too often, we'll ask for forgiveness, then add, "Now it's your turn. What? You're not going to say anything? Well, I take mine back." We must seek a healing, not a trade-off. This is not an event where we come together to confess to each other. Here, each of us must come to his senses alone.

Go ask forgiveness of each other, not next week or next fight; do it right now. This reconciliation can be a real moment of grace. It can be a profound occasion for love. Read the questions below and search inside yourself to discover how you have sinned against God and against your spouse. Pray together for the grace to seek forgiveness and to freely forgive.

How Have I Sinned Against God and Against My Beloved Husband or Wife?

- Have I believed the purpose of my marriage is to make my lover happy? Or have I thought this marriage is for my happiness instead?
- Have I been living my own life-style, expecting my spouse to fit into my demands?
- Am I sensitive to my spouse's hurts and needs? Or do I react only to myself?
- Have I kept my lover out of my heart, not allowing my husband, my wife, to truly be part of me?
- Have I withheld my attention and approval?
- Have I withheld my body?
- Have I yielded to the temptation to hurt with words?
- Have I insisted I was right instead of working toward a solution in love?
- Have I insisted on fairness in our marriage instead of unbounded love?
- Am I more conscious of my love's sins than I am my own? Have I refused to forget my love's failings? Do I keep them alive in my heart to use as weapons?
- Have I been imitating the life-styles of "everyone else" instead of imitating Christ?
- Have I made our family meals a real time of sharing? Do I show my love for our children?

A Prayer for Grace:

Lord, let me truly come to an understanding of my own sinfulness. Help me see myself as I really am, not hidden behind a mask of pride, fear, and self-interest.

I want to ask my spouse to forgive me for denying our relationship, for not living as a lover. Give me courage; help me to be sincere.

Help me to not expect my spouse to ask for forgiveness in return. Give me the grace to understand that each person grows at different rates. Let me wait lovingly and patiently until my spouse is ready.

Should my spouse ask forgiveness of me, help me to give it whole-heartedly. Let my love's failings be wiped forever from my mind so we can live together in joy.

Thank you for the wonderful goodness of my spouse. Let us both rejoice in your gift of healing; let us always see each other through your generous and all-forgiving eyes.

Be with us as we celebrate Your love for us and our love for each other. Amen.

The Reconciliation:

Your own words might be similar to this:

"My beloved, I have sinned against God and against you. I can see how wrong, how selfish, I've been. I've been living with myself, not with you, dear…. (Add specifics.)

"My sin has isolated me from your love, and I can see how lonely I've made both of us. I want to truly live as your husband (wife). I love you so much. Please forgive me."

When your spouse seeks forgiveness, your response might be similar to this:

"I forgive you, my beloved. You are such a good, loving person. I thank God for giving you to me and for bringing us closer to each other right now.

"I want to belong to you, too. I love you so much; you are the most important treasure I have. I'm so glad I have you, because my life would be empty if you weren't here. I want to celebrate, to tell everyone how wonderful you are and how much you mean to me. I will always remember your goodness and love in coming to me to-day. I will never forget it."

CHAPTER 8

My Talent Is Loving You

*"A Man...Summoned His Servants and
Entrusted His Property to Them."*
(MT 25:14–30)

The scribes and Pharisees provoked Jesus to some marvelous retorts. These were more than snappy comebacks, though, they were lessons. After one fierce debate with the Pharisees, Jesus sat on the Mount of Olives and told his disciples about the Kingdom of Heaven:

> It is like a man about to go abroad who summoned his servants and entrusted his property to them. To one he gave five talents, to another two, to a third one, each in proportion to his ability. Then he set out on his journey. The man who had received the five talents promptly went and traded with them and made five more. The man who had received two made two more in the same way. But the man who had received one went off and dug a hole in the ground and hid his master's money. Now a long time afterwards, the master of those servants came back and went through his accounts with them. The man who had received the five talents came forward bringing five more. "Sir," he said, "you entrusted me with five talents; here are five more that I have made." His master said to him, "Well done, good and trustworthy servant; you have shown you are trustworthy in small things; I will trust you with greater; come and join in your master's happiness." Next the man with the two talents came forward. "Sir," he said, "you entrusted me with two talents; here are two more that I have made." His

master said to him, "Well done, good and trustworthy servant; you have shown you are trustworthy in small things; I will trust you with greater; come and join in your master's happiness." Last came forward the man who had the single talent. "Sir," said he, "I had heard you were a hard man, reaping where you had not sown and gathering where you had not scattered; so I was afraid, and I went off and hid your talent in the ground. Here it is; it was yours, you have it back." But his master answered him, "You wicked and lazy servant! So you knew that I reap where I have not sown and gather where I have not scattered? Well, then, you should have deposited my money with the bankers, and on my return I would have got my money back with interest. So now, take the talent from him and give it to the man who has the ten talents. For to everyone who has will be given more, and he will have more than enough; but anyone who has not, will be deprived even of what he has. As for this good-for-nothing servant, throw him into the darkness outside, where there will be weeping and grinding of teeth."

MATTHEW 25:14–30

What Are My Talents?

God himself has given us our talents. He generously asks us to use these investments for his people's sake; most specifically, for those people we have chosen to marry.

First, of course, we must realize what capabilities, skills, and graces almighty God has given each of us, specifically as husbands and wives.

Some of us may say, "My talent is in accounting, or finance, or...." But many of us don't believe we have a special talent to love, to be generous or tender or forgiving. Oh, we can summon up that behavior if we try hard enough, but it's work.

However, if we want to live as whole, healed people, we must recognize that God has given each of us a marvelous capability to love our spouses. In 1 Corinthians, Saint Paul tells us that we can do it. Paul wrote, "None of the trials which have come upon you is more than a human being can stand. You can trust that God will not let you be put to the test beyond your strength, but with any trial will also provide a way out by enabling you to put up with it" (1 Cor 10:13).

Now, let's look at our resources from our spouses' point of view. Sometimes we're not good judges when it comes to ourselves. Ask, "Why did my spouse choose me? What was it my partner saw in me that caused a lifetime commitment?"

Some of you will say, "Oh, I suppose I could name a few things." Now, stop insulting yourself. Your lover wasn't that naive. Your spouse saw good qualities in you and was so taken by that goodness that he or she promised to live with you until death. You don't make promises like that lightly.

What is inside you, as a person, that caused your spouse to say, "Will you be mine?" Start thinking of the words that have been said over the years, especially the compliments you don't believe.

One reason we disbelieve compliments is that we've never been taught to think kindly of ourselves. In this culture, criticism is often the only acceptable opinion of self.

Compliments are also challenges. If a compliment has been accepted, for example, for gentleness, then the partner will have to live up to it. Even though it destroys us inside, we find it easier to say, "No, I'm really not gentle (considerate/funny/ beautiful/sexy). I just was this time."

Always Inferior

We humans always find people who are better in one area or another.

"She's so patient. Compared to her, I'm a shrew." "He's such a wonderful person. He must be closer to God than I am." How destructive to think that way.

It simply doesn't matter how we rate compared to others. We're missing the Lord's lesson if we say, "Well, I'm not as good as my mother was with my father," or "I'm not as good as the guy down the block." The Lord has indeed invested in us. Earthshaking talents often look normal, even humdrum.

How about the gift of time? We have time; maybe not as much as we'd like, but we do have it. We each have a certain number of hours per day to spend as we will. There is lunchtime and coffee break time. There is unwind-from-the-day time and recreation time. We also have double time; that is, when we're doing things we don't have to think about. Housekeeping chores like taking out the trash keep our hands busy, but our minds are free to think, to rest, or to share with our mates.

We also have the time that we waste. How many of those moments you call "your own" are your lover's, and how many belong to you?

Too often, we'll measure our marriages against an ideal relationship. The result is wishful thinking, feelings of inferiority, and despair. The Lord didn't ask for such comparisons. In the parable of the talents, he didn't differentiate between the servant with five talents and the servant with two. All that mattered was the servant's stewardship.

So, examine an ordinary day. How much did you think about your lover today? With affection and eagerness, that is? "If I don't call, I'll have hell to pay" doesn't count. That's not thinking about your spouse. That's self-preservation.

Perhaps we call our mates to ask what's in the mail, what our friends had to say, and so on. Our mouths are moving, but we aren't really talking to each other. We're being safe and amiable. But let's be lovers. Let's use our time during the day to plan how we'll be more effective with each other that night.

Time Costs More Than Money

Do we value time together as our most precious commodity? How many hours do we spend worrying about our lack of time together? In contrast, how many hours do we spend worrying about the disposal of our income? We probably spend considerably less time saying, "Dear, when are we going to sit down and talk tonight?" and much more time saying, "What are we going to do about the orthodontist?" or "Dear, how much is in your wallet?"

We all know people who just can't handle money. Some of us are that way ourselves. These people get in terrible binds because the money just seeps away from them. Most of us are like that when it comes to time, not because we lack natural talent but because we lack attention, self-discipline, and even knowledge. Many of us don't realize how many wonderful things our time can buy.

It's much more important to budget your time than your dollars. Get out paper and pencil; write it all down. How much time do you have on an average day? How much of that time is used productively? How much of it is spent sitting on the sofa, dreading to do the chores? How much time is spent pursuing hobbies and outside commitments you "ought" to love, but in reality make you feel weary and burdened?

What are your weekends like? That's when we're together the most, but we don't do well with each other on weekends because we cram them full of activities that aren't family activities at all. They're merely entertainments the family attends, such as the amusement park, the beach, or a swimming party. No wonder our weekends aren't warm and peaceful and happy. We spend our precious hours rushing from one activity to the next and wondering if we're having fun yet.

We may rub shoulders all weekend, but we don't specifically plan how to be with each other as persons. Don't let that weekend slip by. It's a wonderful opportunity to really be present to each other.

My Time Is Your Time

How many of our evening chores could have been done earlier in the day? Do we spend our valuable time together reading the mail, paying the bills, or writing the grocery list?

We have to stop squandering the time the Lord gives us to spend with each other. There isn't that much of it. We're probably awake about sixteen hours a day, but we only have between four and six hours with our spouses.

How much of that time is poured into dry ground because we haven't thought ahead and put each other first? Time is critical if we're going to use our God-given talents for our lovers' well-being.

All too often, though, we think, "How am I going to spend *my* time?" Sometimes, even time with our lovers is really spent for our own sake.

Our gestures may be self-motivated. Many spouses will say, "Look, honey. I know you're upset. Let's go out tomorrow evening; we'll spend some time together…" The unspoken finishing line to that phrase is "…because you've been looking so unhappy and I want to see you smile," or is it more like "…because when you get a break, I get a break too"?

In the latter example, the spouse is only placating. It isn't time spent together on the agenda, but a peaceful relationship that's uppermost.

The Fifteen-Minute Lover

We need to reevaluate our time in minutes, not in hours. How many hours' worth of minutes do we throw away every day?

We treat our minutes with the same indifference as we do pennies. How about that extra free fifteen minutes just before supper? Do we use it to phone friends or take a nap? Or is it the husband's time to sneak off and read the paper?

But when you add fifteen minutes here, fifteen minutes there, and fifteen minutes somewhere else, you've counted almost an hour of the evening. We just fritter away the time we could spend together. The whole evening ends up lost, as far as loving each other is concerned.

We must decide to prioritize our time for each other. That doesn't mean adopting a rigid schedule: "Seven o'clock's our time together, son, so run along. We'll set that broken arm at seven-thirty."

We should value our time, though, the way we do our money.

Businesses succeed or fail because they follow the principle "Time is money." Time is also love. If a business used "Time is money" as earnestly as we use "Time is love," would that business be among the Fortune 500, or would it be bankrupt?

My Talent Is Tenderness

How do you spend your tenderness? Some men may have raised your eyebrows. "Tenderness? That's my wife's department."

Maybe you only have one share of tenderness and she has five. That's all right. We're not asking how you spend five; we're asking how you spend one.

Wives, be careful not to use the same argument: "I'm much more tender than he is, so I relax. I don't need to improve." Are you sure? You may be spending five shares of tenderness, but you have fifty. Don't ask whether you're giving more tenderness than he is. Ask whether you're giving the level of tenderness the Lord has invested in you.

How tender is your relationship with each other? Now, don't compare it with any other couple; compare it with your own capabilities. How tender are you right now? Maybe this isn't a time that calls for tenderness, but that's all right. The Lord didn't say, "Invest the money when the opportunity arises." He said, "Invest the money." Furthermore, when you do invest, you get the interest, and the Lord's return is a hundredfold.

❧❧❧

When we don't think much about each other, we react to one another instead of responding. Suppose you went home after work or greeted your spouse at the door with a different attitude: a determination to give every bit of tenderness you have tonight. You may not have all that much. That's all right; just give what you have.

Do we ever really resolve to be tender, not just for some special occasion but because I have this tenderness to spend? How thoroughly do we examine what we've given, and how frequently do we focus on what we're getting? Especially when pain's involved, it's easy to measure out the first by weighing the second.

A woman, for instance, might think, "He isn't very tender, so I don't have to be tender with him. Even if I was, he wouldn't understand it." But maybe he isn't tender because he hasn't experienced much tenderness.

If It Doesn't Earn Money, It Can't Be Talent

Do you ever smother your God-given talents with a cash-flow mentality? You could have natural talent for woodworking, ceramics, flower decoration, or any number of skills you don't pursue.

Every one of us has talents that go unused. "I'd love to do that," we tell ourselves. "Too bad I couldn't make a living at it." Evidently the Lord didn't think we needed regular income before he gave us a loan. Why can't we use it?

He also didn't say we should wait for others' approval. He said we should use the gifts he gave us.

Let's examine the talents we do have. What would we do well, if only we had the time? What do other people seem to like about us? What do we think is fun?

Maybe your talent is writing poetry.

"Yes, but I could never get it published."

Don't worry about that; write for your spouse, your beloved.

Ask yourself: why are our talents worth less if we spend them on our spouses and children? Let's' forget how much we're "not worth" and start spending ourselves.

In order to do so, we must take another look at our expenditures of time. By the way, don't be comforted because everyone else is wasting time, too. Let's just ask ourselves: how much of our time is spent doing things that are not only unnecessary but also harmful?

Children can give a sterling example of how our best efforts can be misguided. We spend a lot of time chauffeuring them from activity to activity. That's bad for them. Dance class, scouts, sports, and music lessons all round out our children's education—and encourage them to be independent, unloving people. By keeping our kids in constantly moving cars, going from "experience" to "experience," we're teaching them a strong lesson about values. We're telling them these experiences are more important than the people in their lives. We're making them value things over people.

When we fill our children's evenings with activities, we're institutionalizing them. We're turning the home into a taxi stand and building up a peer group mentality. Has anyone noticed? Today, kids are socializing with one another at age nine the way we did when we were fifteen. They don't have even an older child's knowledge of how to stay out of trouble.

This chauffeured culture isn't any healthier for Mom and Dad. We shouldn't have time to chauffeur our kids. We should be too busy creating a home and family to spend that much time in the car.

Sex Is a Talent, Too

Some of us don't realize our sexuality is a God-given talent. Others wish our spouses would wake up to that fact. I honestly believe most couples fail to invest their sexual talents far more than they fail to be tender, forgiving, or generous.

When most of us ask, "How well do I use my sexual talents?" we think of frequency. We reduce sex to intercourse, and that's a problem.

If we believe that a husband and wife must communicate intimately with each other on a daily basis—and I strongly support that statement—it must include physical intimacy as well as verbal. They must set aside time when they are free to experience each other physically. And I don't mean at eleven-thirty or twelve at night. Whether that is expressed ultimately in intercourse is not the point.

If a couple does take time to physically experience each other, intercourse will probably happen more frequently. One reason it doesn't happen is that it's unavailable. We're too busy.

God did, indeed, give us sex as a resource. Are we spending it or are we hiding it in the ground? Are we using our full capacity for sexual experience of each other?

Again, I'm not speaking of frequency but of passion. Physical communication is like verbal: it can be intimate or superficial. A couple may talk to each other every night, but perhaps they're just chattering. Are you making love, or are you engaging in sexual chatter?

Some of you will say, "What we have is quality rather than quantity." Quality is good, but this can be a means of avoiding each other. If you applied this phrase to conversation, it could create a pretty chilly relationship: "Find a significant topic, dear, and I'll talk to you."

When you were married, you gave your bodies to each other so you could be healed of your hurts and aloneness. If a husband has to say to himself, "I wonder if she's in the mood tonight," her body is not his. If a wife has to figure out ways to seduce him, his body is not hers.

Again, I want to emphasize that we're not just talking about the completed act. Why don't you set aside fifteen minutes to half an hour each day for physical intimacy? Perhaps just to go into your room and experience each other, skin to skin. Now, maybe "nothing will happen." Isn't that a terrible statement? All sorts of things can happen: in awareness, in sensitivity, and tenderness. Yet we seem to think if we merely grow in love, our lovemaking has failed.

Compliments Are Free

To fully invest in our marital relationship, we should use all the resources at our disposal, and compliments are a powerful resource.

Even if we think we don't notice details, we're probably better at it than we suppose. Do we turn our observations into compliments, or do we keep them hidden from our loves?

Do we note only the negative things? Some of us have been taught that it's "discerning" to see flaws, but it's a weakness to pay too much attention to goodnesses. That attitude smothers our hearts.

Do you give your partners a full measure of compliments? Mind you, I didn't say, "compliments that are deserved." It's arrogant to judge whether someone deserves a compliment. The question is, rather, "Right now, do I have a compliment in me?"

We may be afraid to offer compliments. But if we hold back our compliments, our spouses will think we don't care. We might also hold back our compliments for fear that praise will make our partner impossible to live with. A person can actually be overflowing with false pride because deep and sincere praise—backed by understanding and real affection—are lacking.

Because we've been trained to criticize, it's tremendously difficult for many of us to give compliments. It's even tougher to accept a compliment. Most of us will squirm every which way to dodge praise. "Well, thank you, but...," we begin, "...but I'm not really pretty." "But this is just an old shirt." "But I'm not a forgiving person."

We must understand what's happening behind the scenes when our lovers cast off our heartfelt praise. They may laugh or say, "You don't mean that," or even, "What do you want?" Have patience. Again, the Lord doesn't say, "Spend your resources when they'll be accepted." He says, "Spend your resources."

There is nothing like praise. Our highest call, in relationship with our Father in heaven, is to praise him. How can we praise God unless we praise our spouses? Further, God is really more pleased when we praise the daughter or son he gave us than when we praise him directly.

Now, let's ask ourselves specifically, "Do I give my spouse the praise I have inside? Do I give it all?" We humans tend to hold back; to give praise only when it's appropriate, when we're feeling warm and affectionate, when we've been complimented, or when someone has earned it.

That's wonderful. Now, is it all you have? Is there any more in you? If there is, spit it out. Don't keep it to yourself; it's just rusting in there. Keeping a compliment inside doesn't help anyone, unless you're praising yourself.

Our Talents Are for Eternity

One of our greatest talents is our desire to love each other. We do, indeed, wish to put each other first. The difficulties we face in doing so are just that: difficulties. They're not failures. We can overcome our difficulties with prayer, with soul-searching, and by keeping our eyes wide open to the love-killing lessons society has taught us.

The toughest part is facing the fact that, often, we have to give up something in order to have love instead. What makes it tough is that we don't realize how marvelous and fulfilling that love will be. Our present life seems pretty attractive, even if it is somewhat hollow.

Decide what kind of relationship you'd like to have, then go for it. Don't worry about looking back; there are better roads ahead.

That brings us back to the subject of time management. In order to love each other, we simply have to spend time with each other, and that may mean cutting something out of our schedules and changing our agendas.

Who, really, is more important? Your spouse, or your friends, coworkers, fellow volunteers, or children's sports coaches? You didn't marry those people. The Lord is not going to ask how passionate you were about them. Nor will he ask you if you did the laundry, the ironing, the lawn, or the house repairs after you came home from work. He might ask, though, why you didn't put your feet up for an hour after dinner so you'd be enthusiastic about your lover.

We all have beautiful excuses about time, but they aren't cast in stone. Our problem is that we don't want to find the time: not unless it fits into our current schedules.

That's when we have to cut loose from that love-smothering focus on self; to trust our spouses to make us happy, just as we did when we were first married. We must also trust God, who truly wants us to be happy. He's offering us a way; let's take it.

Resources for Reflection

Let's list the talents God gave us. Let's add all the skills, big and little, that we now realize are ours. Take every talent, one by one, and ask, "Am I using every bit of it for my beloved?" not "Am I doing well?" "Is she satisfied?" "Is he content?" and not "Would he understand if I suddenly did all those things?" "Would she be shocked if I became that full-fledged?"

"How much am I keeping to myself? Am I using my talent for the sake of my beloved, or am I just letting it rust, maybe to disappear in bitterness because I haven't been able to live up to my potential?"

Let's ask ourselves if we're ready to stand before the Lord and say, "You gave me this talent of listening. You gave me five shares of it and I have spent five shares. You gave me two shares of sexuality and I spent it all. You gave me five units of understanding and I poured it all out. Now I have ten because you returned it in abundance."

I have faith in you; you are truly good people. Even now, as you spend your talent of hope, remember the Master's promise: "Well done, my son; well done, my daughter. You have shown you are trustworthy in small things; I will trust you with greater; come and join in your master's happiness. To everyone who has will be given more, and he will have more than enough."

Consider These Questions Privately:

What qualities prompted my spouse to spend his/her life with me? What compliments has my spouse given me that I just pass off?

Make a time budget. How much time do I have with my spouse? What can I make more efficient, shuffle around, or omit entirely to give me more time with my lover?

What talents have I been given for my beloved's sake? There are at least three kinds:

Spiritual (like kindness or patience)...

Enriching (like creativity, intelligence, or humor)...

Uplifting (like lightheartedness, optimism, or sexuality)...

Do I use each of these talents for the benefit of my beloved? What can I do to use each one to the utmost?

Share These Questions With Your Spouse:

What compliments do I give you, dear, that you don't seem to believe?

I want to spend more time with you, dear. I'm willing to do these things... so we can spend more time together.

My beloved, I yearn to spend more time being intimate with you physically. Why don't we do the following...?

Finally, Let Us Invite God Into Our Marriages:

Loving Father, it is hard for me to truly believe that You have given me so much goodness. Please help me appreciate all the talents you have given me, especially the ones I don't yet see. Let me use these every day, to the utmost, for the sake of my beloved spouse. Let me fill his/her life with warmth and joy and trust. When I believe my talents are lacking, gently remind me that, when I have spent all the talents I have, you will fill me with so many more. Thank you for loving me so much. Amen.

CHAPTER 9

We Are One

*"Who Among You Delights in Life,
Longs for Time to Enjoy Prosperity?"*
(1 PET 3:8–12)

Peter's first letter really was written for you. You'll find it just as relevant today as it was to the early Christians, who were also bearing "all sorts of trials" (1 Pet 1:6).

> *Finally: you should all agree among yourselves and be
> sympathetic; love the brothers, have compassion and be
> self-effacing. Never repay one wrong with another, or one
> abusive word with another; instead, repay with a blessing.
> That is what you are called to do, so that you inherit a
> blessing. For who among you delights in life,
> longs for time to enjoy prosperity?
> Guard your tongue from evil,
> your lips from any breath of deceit.
> Turn away from evil and do good, seek peace and pursue it.
> For the eyes of the Lord are on the upright,
> his ear turned to their cry.
> But the Lord's face is set against those who do evil.*
>
> 1 PETER 3:8–12

Here, Peter is referring to the whole church. That's a lot to deal with, so let's take it down to the little church: the family. More specifically, we'll see how Peter's words apply to the husband-wife relationship.

Delights in Life, Longs for Time to Enjoy Prosperity?

We certainly don't hesitate to wish for happy lives. As for prosperity, we'd probably translate that somewhat differently from the way Peter would. The key to this prosperity of peace, happiness, and goodwill is found in the next two lines:

Guard your tongue from evil,
your lips from any breath of deceit.

These verses make sense. None of us would defend the virtues of malicious conversation and deceitful talk. Maliciousness and deceit are so repugnant to us, in fact, that we don't apply them to ourselves. It's far more comfortable to see malice "out there" in our coworkers and neighbors.

Maliciousness can crop up when we're hurt, especially if we've evolved a lifelong attitude of defensiveness. It's a way of protecting ourselves first—before someone else runs us down. It can arise when we're called to change but are afraid to let go of the safe and comfortable. It happens frequently when envy gets the best of us.

Personally, I find it difficult to admit I have malice. I don't fall into the trap of claiming I'm perfect, but I do tend to write off the bad things I say: "Well, sometimes I sound malicious, but most of the time it's provoked" or "Maybe I was malicious, but I wasn't nearly as bad as he was."

But Peter didn't tell me, "Guard your tongue from evil unless you're provoked." Nor did he say, "Make sure your deceit isn't as bad as the other guy's."

Silence Can Be Golden

In most marriages, there is usually a silent partner and a speaking partner. The roles can switch any time; one spouse might be the silent partner on politics, while the other is silent on religion. That silent partner may fail to talk, but keeping silent curbs the tendency toward a malicious tongue.

Yet we humans excuse ourselves for thoughtlessly blurting out our problems. After all, we say, we're not "holding it inside." Perhaps you've had a tough day at work, and you just can't wait to get home and vent your feelings. Wait a minute. Maybe it would be better to wait until tomorrow night, when you have a little more perspective.

Maybe you're the type of person who stores up the frustrations of the day until your spouse comes home. You're not on a personal attack. You're just venting what's wrong with your life.

We've all behaved that way at some time, haven't we? It's not that we're mean, it's that we can hardly resist. We know we'll be in pain if we don't vent it on someone, and secretly we decide, "Better them than me."

That takes us back to Saint Peter's use of the word "prosperity." Most of us tend to define prosperity in terms of cash, but also in terms of comfort. Now, some of that comfort is material, but some of it is emotional, too.

It's ironic, isn't it? Our very longing for prosperity is what keeps us from having it.

Talk It Up

We truly must examine our consciences when it comes to our conversations with each other. This especially applies to the talkers.

Free speech—and I mean speech free from fear or shyness—is a real grace in a marriage. But we do want to look at the content of that speech. Sometimes, because we so highly praise communication, we underemphasize the virtue of thinking a problem through first.

Our society tends to make a talker feel superior. Those of us who can lay it on the line feel skilled, and may even consider our quiet spouses handicapped.

Not necessarily. Study a normal day in your lives. How much does your lover enjoy your company? Not your conversation; communication is beyond conversation. Even when it concerns a tough subject, it's beyond merely venting your anger. To twist the old say-ing, where there's fire, there's probably so much smoke that nobody can see clearly anyway.

Let's take an imaginary scene again. Supposing, wives, that your husband forgot your birthday. He didn't say anything in the morn-ing and he didn't ask you out to lunch. That evening you waited for your surprise, but surprise! It didn't come. The next day you went off to work angry and, as the day progressed, you rehearsed the blistering comments you'd make when you both got home that night.

You weren't able to make them, though; you had to work late. You also had time to think—and to cool off; to remember how busy he'd been at work, with the kids, fixing the plumbing. Now you had an honest chance at communication.

If you'd said what you'd originally planned, there would have been no communication whatever. An angry "Did you intend to forget my birthday, or was that just the best you could do?" would provoke nothing but defensiveness and shame.

A comment based on compassion might have had a different effect:

"Yesterday was my birthday, Joe."

"Oh, no. Not the twenty-first?"

"That's right. Shall we do something anyway?"

Joe is a good man, even if he did forget, and this gives him a chance to exercise his goodness: to take you out, bring you belated flowers. It also gives him a chance to apologize, and for you to ex-press your hurt feelings in a nonthreatening way.

Blurting it out isn't always wrong, but it isn't always right, either. Blurting it out has nothing to do with openness, honesty, or commu-nication. It's a knee-jerk response to pain, an action that is supposed to make us feel better. It doesn't, really. It takes away the feeling that we're going to explode, but it causes anguish in the family, and that can't possibly make us feel good.

Sometimes blurting it out does help rid us of negative feelings. It's like writing a hate letter. By the time we've finished the letter, we've changed our minds and maybe feel a little silly.

So write, if you have to. It's much better to wield that poison pen than a malicious tongue. You can always trash the letter, but you can never erase your lover's memory of your harsh words. If you have to, shout at the mirror. Say those angry things into a tape recorder. Then play it back. Believe me, once you've heard yourself at your worst, you won't be tempted to speak that way again. Then sit down and think your problem through.

Sometimes malice is disguised as self-awareness. We each have years of experience in knowing which subjects, phrases, or tones of voice will pain our lovers. Still, we yield to the impulse to use them again and again.

How about changing that to this statement: "That's the kind of person I am, all right. And I want to do better."

Marriage Means Change

Change is marriage's whole purpose. In matrimony, you become one couple, not two good people being themselves.

The matrimonial union creates a whole new life, just as the sacrament of baptism does. We may not realize it until years after the ceremony, but baptism is a commitment not to be ourselves anymore. It's a commitment to become bodied with the Lord in his people, to become so much more than we could ever be ourselves. That commitment doesn't take away our identities or make us less than we are.

Marriage, in a very real way, is the same. We're called to become bodied with our beloveds; to become bone of his bone, flesh of her flesh.

Those are inspiring words. Many of us will read them with pride and gratitude, perhaps even saying, "Good. People are finally starting to recognize our dignity as a married couple." We have to watch, though, that we don't close this book and return to our old selves: two good people living side by side, except on special occasions.

It's difficult not to do that, especially when we try to force virtue on ourselves. We should do it the easy way: by praying for the grace to become one with our beloveds.

Are We Alike?

We must ask ourselves, "How similar have I become to my spouse in the last twelve months?" Again, we shouldn't ask, "Am I satisfied with our marriage?" or "Do I think I'm a good wife (husband)?" That last question is a fine one, but it's only a beginning. Let's ask, "How much of her has become part of me?" "Do I speak as he does?"

I'm not speaking of tone of voice or even vocabulary. I'm speaking of desiring to converse the way he converses; talking about her topics in her way. Ideally, it should happen spontaneously. The more we become like our spouses, the more sincerely we enjoy their conversation, the less malicious we'll become. This is not easy. That's why you're a sacrament.

If we're like the pagans—good pagans—we get along well with each other, provided there are some understandings: "He's used to my spouting off." "She has to take my ranting and raving in stride."

Instead, ask, "Am I used to talking to her in the tone of voice and in the way that touches her heart? Am I used to listening to myself with his ears rather than just shouting it out?"

We excuse ourselves for our flaws in conversation. We say, "I'm only human," or "Let's be reasonable." First, you're not "only human." The Lord came to make you greater than mere flesh. Second, you're not just a man, not just a woman. You're a husband; you're a wife.

Your marriage license isn't just a contract to support a family, put out the garbage, and cook the meals. Your marriage is a call to put him on like a beautiful garment, to make her an integral, intimate part of you. Too many of us really haven't changed much since we were single. Sure, we'd find it difficult to sleep alone, and we might not want to sit down to an empty table. Those changes are good; they're a beginning. But ask yourselves, "How different am I inside, compared with my single days or with any single person?"

"Well, I'm thinking about him all the time." "She's my whole life;

she's the reason why I do so many of the things I do." That's great. That's also an exaggeration, isn't it? But it's good; it shows ambition.

It's not enough, though, to be thinking about your lover all the time. You're called to bring her inside yourself, to draw him close. In a very real way she has to be doing some of the thinking for you. He has to be so much a part of you that it's difficult to imagine where you end and he begins. That does lead to prosperity and a happy life.

The Marriage Bomb

It certainly isn't easy to keep the tongue under control. If the tongue were a beast, it would be more of a Komodo dragon than a house pet. Saint James puts it bluntly: "Wild animals and birds, reptiles and fish of every kind can all be tamed, and have been tamed, by humans; but nobody can tame the tongue—it is a pest that will not keep still…." (Jas 3:7, 8).

That makes us stop and think, doesn't it? We'd probably agree that a thunderstorm is very powerful. But its aftereffects don't compare with the path of destruction wreaked by a truly nasty tongue. That becomes most clear when we look at the damage in our own lives.

That's certainly true in marriage. How many of us really work on our tongues? Most of us probably don't, except when it comes to extremes.

Now, remember, I'm not addressing the shrews and spouse beaters who make the headlines in the local paper, and I'm not talking about verbally abusive relationships. I'm talking to you: good people who are nevertheless capable of malice, especially when you're wounded by insult, envy, or what have you.

We all have shameful memories of a quickly slung insult that really made him crumble, a cheap word we know she never forgot. Those memories make us feel awful, and we know to work on that kind of behavior. Let's work, too, on the peace and prosperity of our everyday speech.

Let's examine the power speech has over men and women.

For many women, sex lasts longer than it does with their men. These wives are still basking in the afterglow while their husbands are saying, "Let's do it again."

Likewise, conversation usually lasts longer with a man that it does with a woman. When a wife talks out her problem, the talking itself is her cure. Her husband, though, tends to think out his problem. It may take days.

This trait has both positive and negative implications. If she insults him, he may feel the sting for a long time. If she compliments him, he will savor that goodness for a long time, too.

A really sincere compliment lasts longer with a man than with a woman. That's why our women think their husbands are so sparing with their praise. That accusation baffles their men, who protest, "I *said* I loved you. Didn't you believe me?"

Bite Your Tongue

If you're the talker in your marriage, why don't you ask your lover how to stop and think before you talk? After all, marriage is a relationship where we share and learn from each other.

At first, it may sound like asking the leopard to change his spots, but that's not the case. A long history of spouting off isn't virtuous. It's a powerful reason for change.

Choose a time when the two of you aren't in conflict, then ask: "When you want to blow up at me, how do you stop yourself? I'm sure you have feelings as strong as mine, and I know you'd like to blurt it out sometimes. Yet you don't. How do you succeed?"

Next, ask, "How do you stand it?"

Then listen to the answer. Much of it will probably be along these lines:

First, your spouse trusts you. He (or she) knows you make mistakes, but believes you are a good person who honestly loves him.

Second, calmness and confidence are involved. There will be a solution to your dispute.

Third, follow this two-part rule: One, "Don't sweat the small stuff." Two, "Everything is the small stuff." When you think about it, it really is.

Fourth, focus on learning to forgive. Sometimes it can be rough on our pride, but it always pays off. In a real crisis, forgiveness may be a pure act of will. The forgiving person may say silently, "Lord, even though I am furious with this person, I forgive her (him). At least, that's what I want to do, even though I don't feel it now. So help me to really forgive; to really have compassion."

Forgiveness also frees us from a myriad of unconscious reactions; it is a way of choosing life-giving thoughts and rejecting the negative thoughts induced by someone else's behavior. If your next-door neighbor drives you absolutely up a tree, forgive him or her; think of pleasant things instead and silently insist that you won't let him bother you.

If you don't do this, you'll remain a puppet on angry strings. If you relieve that tension by dumping it on your spouse, both of you will be trapped.

Discussion or Slander?

Evil or malicious speech isn't always kept within the four walls of our homes. Sometimes we defuse our anger at our spouses by dumping it off with friends. It's all right, we think, because we've purged ourselves of it and now we won't fight with our lovers.

Like nuclear waste, the poison of complaints doesn't just disappear. It can seep and spread and remain constantly virulent. Even the nicest, the noblest, of friends won't refrain from looking at your spouse and thinking, "Why does he leave her at home when he goes out on Saturdays? Just selfish, I guess," or "Boy, I'm glad I don't have that old spendthrift pulling the purse strings."

Do your girlfriends wish they had married your husband, or do they think he's a lot like their own men: partly good and partly bad? Is every man at work anxious to see the paragon you go home to, or is she just another woman?

It's ironic; we say things about our spouses that no one else would even dare hint. If a friend said, "Your wife couldn't balance the checkbook if she tried. What an airhead!" we'd bristle instantly. If a neighbor said, "Poor dear. Your husband must not love you very much. He's always going off to play poker," we'd let her have it. But we'll deliver similar insults ourselves. What in the world are we doing?

What kind of reputations are we crafting for our lovers? It doesn't matter if our complaints are true. That just makes us guilty of detraction instead of calumny.

Like nuclear waste, it's difficult to erase the poison once it's spilled. Once we gripe to our mothers, neighbors, bosses, or the people in our car pools, we find it difficult to retract that gripe. We rarely say, "You know, my back was really aching and that's why I was so mad at my wife," or "He said one wrong word and I made a whole paragraph of it."

At best, we just don't repeat it again. If our friends bring up the gripe at some later time, we'll probably support it again. Especially after ten or twenty years of marriage, we don't want people to think we're too much in love. Too much in love? What a terrible cage we've locked ourselves into.

Of course, when we criticize our spouses to others, we wind up feeling guilty. Whenever we think of our lovers or see those friends we complained to, we remember our hasty words. The result of it all is definitely not prosperity.

Turn Away From Evil and Do Good, Seek Peace and Pursue It

Do we seek peace in our homes or do we seek personal satisfaction? When someone asks you how your marriage is do you say, "Yes, I have a happy marriage," or "Well, it could be better, but in general, I'm happy"?

A man or woman of peace should answer, "I honestly believe my wife is happy"; "I truly think my husband has a happy marriage."

Now, if you believe your husband or wife truly isn't happy, don't feel like a failure. You are here, loving that person, ready to change. Praise the Lord for your goodness.

This focus on self begins in our dating years. When I went on a date, my mother, father, and aunt always waited up for me. "Did you have a good time?" they asked. They were sincerely interested, and that was beautiful.

Never once, though, did they ask if my date had a good time. Maybe it's good that I didn't get married. My whole preparation for marriage was to enjoy myself. That's an exaggeration, of course. But we are indeed trained to judge our romantic relationships by how well we're satisfied.

That's also true for our priests. If you asked me, "Are you satisfied with your priesthood?" I would not automatically look at you, my people, and ask in return if you're pleased with me. Instead, I'd say, "Well, gee, I couldn't imagine myself doing anything else. I feel very fulfilled."

My answer is a denial of our relationship. It becomes "my" priesthood, not "ours." Then it's reduced to a ministry instead of a network of love relationships.

Likewise, a marriage becomes "my" marriage instead of "our" marriage. It becomes a list of duties, balanced by the benefits of the spouse living up to their responsibilities, too. That's good business. True peace in the home comes, instead, when we find satisfaction and joy by experiencing our spouses' happiness.

We have to bow reverently to our husbands when it comes to love-making. Most good husbands simply don't enjoy sex unless their wives do. Without her delight, he has only the minimal physical satisfaction.

Conversation should be the same way. But, too often, we evaluate a conversation by asking, "Did she listen to me?" "Did he understand what I was saying?" Instead, we should be thinking, "I truly believe I understood her tonight"; "I really think I listened to him." That's when conversation brings joy.

Our homes aren't truly at peace when we're merely getting along or when we've succeeded in hashing out an issue. Peace doesn't come when we're doing all the right things by each other. Peace comes when we're more interested in our lovers' well-being than in our own.

It sounds great, but we find ourselves saying, "Yes, that's nice, but it's unreal. I'd like to be that way, but I'm human and I fail."

We keep concentrating on our humanity. Remember, Peter said, "You are a chosen race, a royal priesthood, a holy nation, a people set apart to sing the praises of God who called you out of the darkness into his wonderful light. Once you were no people and now you are the People of God..." (1 Pet 2:9, 10).

He didn't say we're people. He didn't even say we're good people. He said we're a holy people, a people set apart. Frankly, we don't accept that. We don't deny the theology of it, but it sounds too good to be true. Why not take Peter's word for it? We're so used to limiting ourselves. In material possessions or career goals, our society is insatiable, but when it comes to something like love, we throw up our hands and say, "Infatuation doesn't last forever, you know. Real love is—uh, comfortable."

Agree With Each Other

Peter's First Letter was directed to the whole Church, but it also applies to our fellow Christian (our spouse) with whom we sleep.

How much do we agree among ourselves? How much do we disagree? We may even say, "Ah, but opposites attract." That explains why we get married. It doesn't explain why we're still married and reading this book.

After one, ten, or thirty years together, are we still opposites? In marriage, we're not called to be rugged individualists. We're called to be one in the Lord, models of how Jesus loves his church.

Do we live in harmony, or do we ascribe to the "separate but equal" philosophy: "She takes care of this part of our life together and I take care of the other part." Do we agree among ourselves or do we just avoid fights? Giving in isn't enough. That's a good start, but we have to become part of the other person.

An obvious area to consider is the struggle between a silent partner and a talker. If a talker is overwhelming a thinker, they must both examine that situation and decide how to fix it. The thinker can't just say, "Well, he (she) always takes the stage. I'll just have to live that way." That's not agreement. That's toleration.

Another area of disagreement may be love-making. One partner may have more physical desire than the other. That's fine; that's the starting point. After ten years, the gap should have narrowed a great deal. Has it?

Sex with teeth gritted and a false smile would be a form of prostitution. You don't have to pretend, though; it can happen naturally. You can pray for passion. You can ask your spouse how to yearn more for him or her. If exhaustion or worry is sapping your energy, you can address those issues as well. You can also work at it. In this case, practice has a great deal to do with desire. But, too often, the person who doesn't have the desire says, "Well, when I get the desire, I'll practice."

There are a myriad of other possible disagreements. For example, how do you both feel about working overtime, hobbies, furniture buying, faith, friends? In Chapter 4, you found a list of possible disagreements. Go back and read them over with a new eye.

Now, ask yourselves where you need to agree more. Don't ask what conflicts you need to resolve. Many of your disagreements will be hidden within your lifestyles. They don't always surface as conflicts. After all, you are good couples, and whether or not you realize it, you've already begun your search for peace.

Over the years, there may have been a great deal of polarization of views between partners. Many, weary of it all, have taken refuge in indifference. Have you settled into indifference about in-laws, money, the number of your children, the raising of those children? That's not agreement.

Remember, I don't recommend artificial smiles pasted over angry faces. Start with "I want to agree with you." That may sound trivial, but it isn't. Once we say, "I don't agree with you," we've closed a door. We don't even want to agree.

So, first, build up the desire to agree, not because our lovers are right but because they're our lovers. Loving each other will help us agree.

Don't think, "I'll lose my integrity if I knuckle under all the time." As a married couple, your integrity is formed not by maintaining opinions but by becoming one with each other. Think instead, "I just can't understand why she feels this way, but I want us to work it out." "I love him so much, I don't want there to be anything between us."

Of course, we're not talking about violations of conscience. If your spouse wants to rob a bank, agreement is not an issue. Instead, we're talking about the kind of opinions that are a dime a dozen. What isn't a dime a dozen is your spouse. He or she is infinitely precious.

Sympathy for Spouses

Saint Peter is telling us not to take each other's sacrifices for granted. Perhaps your husband's most magnificent trait is his consistency. That's what attracted you to him. You knew he would never let you down. Do you still delight in that, or do you sometimes feel there's no excitement in your life?

Perhaps you married your wife because she was so practical and level-headed. You knew she'd take good care of a family. Do you still bless her for that, or do you feel weary because she keeps suggesting financial and home improvement projects?

Too often, we can take for granted the goodness that we deliberately brought into our lives. Instead, we focus on the miserable.

How sympathetic are we toward our lovers' trials and responsibilities? Sometimes we're too envious to be sympathetic. So often, we believe our lovers' ways of life are much easier than our own.

Our lovers' responsibilities are more than drudgery. They're gifts. Unfortunately, though, we rarely see them that way. Instead, we're always focusing on what we don't have. Deep down, we think we're supposed to be that way. If we're too grateful, someone might say, "Pollyanna, get your head out of the clouds."

We deliberately torture ourselves with hurtful fantasies; ones that aren't even true. How about the old classic "I wish I'd married...." So on we go, having our "fun," making ourselves feel terrible. That isn't what Christ called us to do.

Are you sympathetic toward your lover? I'm speaking of more now than doing the housework or watching the family budget. Let your lover know you appreciate his or her work. Find meaningful ways to say: "I'm so grateful that you do all these things for me, and for the children, too. You do them so well, and I know they're not easy." This must be more than an occasional pat on the back or a nice word that almost sounds dutiful.

Sympathy needs a little imagination. To convey it, speak your thoughts a little differently from the way you otherwise might; use, maybe, a change of intonation or facial expression. Your lover is used to hearing you say, "Yeah, thanks." You want to convey an added message: "How wonderful you are to do that."

Have Compassion

Compassion is deeper than sympathy. Husbands, do you really know your wives' pain? Wives, do you experience your husbands' suffering?

How compassionate are you because her father never hugged her; because she just doesn't feel comfortable with her body? How much tenderness is in your heart because his mother nagged him to pieces? It doesn't have to be that extreme. Maybe a husband just doesn't see himself as all that lovable, or a wife doesn't see herself as all that capable.

Maybe our lovers' wounds are long buried, but still alive and painful. Our lovers probably don't complain of them; they don't realize how much they hurt. Maybe he lost his father at twelve, or she always wanted a sister and was raised with six brothers. We can't rectify these lifelong hurts, but we can help the healing process by giving our lovers our compassionate hearts today.

Maybe our lovers' hurts are physical. We're usually more compassionate about physical pain, but how often do we stretch ourselves to be as compassionate as we can be?

It's especially hard when physical pain becomes a way of life. Maybe a wife has constant migraine headaches. After a while her husband gets used to them. He encourages her to lie down; he takes over around the house, then entertains himself with the paper until she's up and around again. He isn't fully suffering with her.

What happens when a husband has a touch of bursitis? Perhaps his wife thinks, "What can I do about it?" She notices the flash of pain across his face and says, "Pretty bad tonight, isn't it?" She's sympathetic, but she isn't fully suffering with him, either.

In both cases, these actions are good. They're probably better than someone else's actions, but they're not filled to the brim with compassion. We have much more compassion than we use, amd we are asked to use that compassion to the full.

Be Self-Effacing

This command of Saint Peter's is probably the hardest one in this Scripture passage. Can we honestly say we're self-effacing?

Now, I'm not speaking of a milquetoast. I'm speaking of a person like John the Baptist. If you'll recall, his thundering denunciations and unswerving proclamation of the Lord's message were anything but spineless. He was also self-effacing. In John 3:30, he said of Jesus, "He must grow greater, I must grow less."

I'm not speaking of becoming a slave to others. I'm speaking of selflessness, of seeing that our lovers get the attention, affection, and healing they need, while we cease being preoccupied with our own.

For instance, who gets the attention at home? Maybe we make sure it's us. On the other hand, maybe we're a bit shy, so our spouses really do get the lion's share. That may not mean we're self-effacing. We may merely lack assertiveness. Perhaps we don't need much attention, but when we do, everything screeches to a stop while the family gives us our due.

On the other hand, people who are not self-effacing—let's call them proud—may not demonstrate that pride by ranting and raving. The proud person can be a quiet type who controls the atmosphere in the home by his or her very quietness. The proud person can be dedicated to fairness or even generosity. "In fact," he or she seems to say, "I'll give you even more than you give me, but I have to have mine."

We also need to look at that notion of "You deserve it." We "deserve" all kinds of things that cost money; everything from hair color to exercise equipment. In order to get the things we "deserve," we work harder and harder at jobs we like less and less. We set our sights on objects like restaurant meals and cars and clothes; there's no time or energy left for the God-given people in our lives. We feel more and more out of control, so we wander the shopping malls in search of inner peace. "After all," we say, "I deserve that much." When we're exhausted and broke, have we gotten what we deserved?

"Deserve" crops up sometimes as an excuse. "After all, I pull a double shift. I deserve a break now and then." But when it comes to God's generosity, none of us is more deserving than the rest. If we struggle for what we "deserve" in a relationship, that struggle can deprive us of God's peace.

Let's not ask ourselves what we deserve. Let's ask, instead, "Is my life about him, is my life about her? Or is it about myself?" We have a natural tendency to think that happiness starts with ourselves. "If I'm happy," we think, "I'll make her happy. If I'm pleased, I can be so much more responsive to him." Unfortunately, it doesn't work that way.

Now, I'm in no way suggesting that you allow yourself to live in anger, unforgiveness, or self-loathing while trying to please others. Not only is that hurtful, it isn't necessary. If your focus is on the loves in your life, you will naturally be happy. You'll be like a physically healthy person who feels great without thinking about it. If you're constantly focused on your need to be happier, you'll be like a hypochondriac who's miserably absorbed in minor aches and pains.

Never Repay One Wrong With Another

Now Saint Peter's really hitting below the belt, isn't he? We don't like to think we do this. The truth is, we will graciously put up with a certain amount of trouble. Then our dignity becomes at stake. This happens especially when we're under attack. Suddenly our husband or wife is angry. He's furious; she's shouting—and not kind words, either. What do we do? Shout back. Tell them off. After all, they have no right to do this to us.

We're responding to a challenge to fight. What we're not doing is thinking. On a calmer day, we'd realize he or she is naturally a good, loving person who doesn't really hate us. So what's wrong? It must be something.

Saint Peter says in this passage, "Never repay one wrong with another, or one abusive word with another; instead, repay with a blessing."

What does he mean? That we should be mealy-mouthed? Not at all. Saint Peter is not recommending this type of exchange:

"You silly ninny. Can't you do anything right?"

"God bless you, dear."

That's not good-hearted; it's unnatural. Instead, Saint Peter wants us to respond with a kind word, a gentle word, a soft word. That will, indeed, turn away wrath. We're called to see behind the anger, to learn what our lovers are really trying to say.

If you do this, Peter says, you inherit a blessing, because the eyes of the Lord are on the upright, his ear turned to their cry. That means he won't abandon you to an eternally angry spouse.

Resources for Reflection

Are we really taking our values from the Lord, or are we taking our values from the world around us, saying: "Well, I'm not doing badly"?

You are a holy people. You are not called to be a "not bad" people. You are saints. I'm not just writing nice words, and I'm not just repeating them because they were good enough for Peter. They really come from the depths of my heart because I couldn't have written these words to any but a holy people.

Consider These Questions Privately:

When have my words at home caused unhappiness or hurt? What would have happened if, instead of blurting it out, I had taken time to think? Exactly how would I have done that?

When have I complained of my spouse to others? How could I have stopped myself?

What are my spouse's hurts and responsibilities? How can I show sympathy and compassion for my spouse?

What steps can I take to be more in unity and agreement with my spouse?

Share These Questions With Your Spouse:

Each of us takes turns being the speaking partner and the silent one. With that in mind, ask: Dear, how do you keep from blurting out harsh words?

Saint Peter said we are a holy people, meant to sing the praises of God who called us into his wonderful light. How would I think, speak, and act if I really believed that?

Finally, Let Us Invite God Into Our Marriages:

Glorious Father, we ask you to be present in our marriage this day and always. Thank you for your gift of grace, which allows us to see our flaws and gives us the courage to become more loving and selfless. Help keep us from hurting others with our anger. Let us see each other's goodness so we can speak gently and with love. Give us your peace and prosperity, and help us to truly become one. Amen.

CHAPTER 10

Scriptural Marriage

"I Am Here, Beloved, to Give You Life."
(EPH 5:21–33)

In this chapter, we're tackling that most misunderstood passage in the New Testament, the one where Saint Paul is supposed to tell husbands they have dominion over their wives, and that wives should be their submissive servants. Do I have your attention?

Honestly, Saint Paul doesn't say that at all. Saint Paul was inspired by God to make not a document of slavery, but a case for equality of the sexes. He's recommending peace, love, and great respect. Trust him as you read this passage of Saint Paul's letter to the Ephesians:

> Be subject to one another out of reverence for Christ. Wives should be subject to their husbands as to the Lord, since, as Christ is head of the Church and saves the whole body, so is a husband the head of his wife; and as the Church is subject to Christ, so should wives be to their husbands, in everything. Husbands should love their wives, just as Christ loved the Church and sacrificed himself for her to make her holy by washing her in cleansing water with a form of words, so that when he took the Church to himself she would be glorious, with no speck or wrinkle or anything like that, but holy and faultless. In the same way, husbands must love their wives as they love their own bodies; for a man to love his wife is for him to love himself. A man never hates his own body, but he feeds it and looks after it; and that is the way Christ treats the Church, because we are parts of his Body. This is why a man

leaves his father and mother and becomes attached to his wife, and the two become one flesh. This mystery has great significance, but I am applying it to Christ and the Church. To sum up: you also, each one of you, must love his wife as he loves himself; and let every wife respect her husband.

EPHESIANS 5:21–33

Saint Paul's message is this: husbands, be one with your wives; love them as fully and completely as Christ loves his Church. To wives he says, let them love you as Christ loves his Church.

Neither of these commands is easy. They both require dying to self. But as you well know, dying to self means opening your heart to others and especially to our good God. It's like Jesus' parable of the mustard seed. That smallest of seeds—our sin-bound, hurting self—when healed and allowed to bloom, becomes the biggest of trees.

Pass the Dynamite

Before we do some honest soul-searching, let's blast, once and for all, some centuries-old misconceptions about this passage of Ephesians. First, it doesn't mean that the husband is Lord. It doesn't say the husband's decisions, ideas, or attitudes represent the will of God.

Second, this passage is concerned only with relationships, not with gender issues. It certainly does not say, "Women, be subject to men." That would be completely out of character with the freedom and dignity Jesus offers all men and women. The idea of prostrating oneself before another in order to be dominated is alien to the message of the Gospel.

None of Scripture relegates women to the role of passive rag dolls. Women played an active role in Jesus' life and he always responded with reverence and respect. Submission, as expressed in Scripture, cannot mean a lessening of women as persons.

Paul's words, then, speak to a couple who have already chosen to love each other. He and she have already established a relationship of understanding, communication, and responsiveness. They're totally committed to each other. Only then could he consider treating her as he treats his own body; only then could she be called to be respond to his love as she is to that of Jesus.

Because of the uniqueness of sacramental marriage, a wife's role is shaped by her interaction with her husband. She can't be subject to him unless he draws forth that response. The two of them must be bonded together in making this happen.

This bonding happens in love. The husband loves his wife as his own body; he gives himself up for her. The wife becomes responsive to that love because its invitation at this depth is irresistible. Her joyous response inspires an even deeper love from him.

We should keep this in mind at all times. Paul's Letter to the Ephesians isn't a burden; it's a game plan for joy. We have to work to get rid of our own game plan and the world's game plan. We have to integrate the Lord's plan into our way of living.

Marriage Is a Prayer

Now let us reexamine our call to the sacrament of matrimony. Do we believe our marriages are spiritual? Are we sure? It's easy to say a quick yes.

Marriage is spiritual twenty-four hours a day. It's not spiritual just at Christmas, at Mass or church services, or after a wonderful sexual experience. Marriage is spiritual on Tuesday, even if it's spaghetti night and the food is all over the floor. It's spiritual on Friday when we come home shell-shocked from the week.

Too often, we see God's plan as a list of "shouldn'ts." We shouldn't fight, we shouldn't be angry with one another or hurt one another.

God's definition of love, though, isn't like calf roping. We're not supposed to subdue our anger and annoyance like a wild beast. We're supposed to transcend our humanity by, again, dying to self and believing in the wonderful goodness of our lovers. That is our spirituality.

We Catholics are invited to attend Mass and receive the Eucharist every day. We consider the Eucharist a sacrament. Matrimony is a sacrament, too. Do we see marriage as a grace that we receive daily?

Sometimes we think loving others is more in tune with the Gospel message than is loving our own spouses. If someone works in the inner city, Appalachia, or the local Sunday School program, we think they're being especially spiritual. If we, on the other hand, spend time with our families, we're only doing what comes naturally.

Do we realize our marriages are spiritualizing us, or do we merely see our spirituality helping our marriages? There's a difference.

Do we realize that our marriages are our fundamental prayer, or do we merely believe prayer helps our marriages? Of course, we should certainly use prayer to help our marriages, but our first prayer is our relationship with one another. The best way husbands and wives can acknowledge God is by loving one another in his name.

Our relationship is more than a series of actions that please God; it's more than doing the right thing, as he commanded us. It's an act of liturgy. All the normal little everyday acts of love in the living room, bedroom, dining room, and kitchen are religious acts because we are faithful couples.

Husbands loving their wives as they love their own bodies—or of wives trusting husbands to do that—seems so extreme that we tune this Gospel message out. It's like one of those oldtime prayers we Catholics used to say after Holy Communion. They sounded beautiful and they were appropriately spiritual for the occasion, but we had no serious intention of living the type of life they spoke of.

People who hear Saint Paul's message that "Husbands should love their wives, just as Christ loved the Church; wives should be subject to their husbands as to the Lord," shouldn't think it sounds bizarre. They should be able to say, "Oh, you mean Christ loves us in the Church as much as we love each other? You know, that's really something."

Vocation to Love

Sacred Scripture really does give couples a vocation to love each other with the same passionate faithfulness that exists between Christ and his Church. Imagine Saint Paul looking you right in the eye and saying, "Will you love her as you love yourself? Will you treat him as you'd treat Jesus?" Not just "Are you doing a good job?"

We, the people of the Church, are calling you to a totally different relationship. It's not a lofty ideal that an occasional saint or two might embrace. It's just as attainable as reconciliation with God, Holy Communion, or the sacrament of baptism.

When you're baptized, you seek admission into the community of God, the very body of Jesus. We, the Church, respond to you with trust and confidence. We baptize you into the death and resurrection of Jesus: we immerse you in the saving waters of baptism.

That's not fantasy; that's a fact. When we call you a matrimonial sacrament, that's a fact, too. When we say that we, God's chosen people, believe you are to love each other as Jesus loves his Church, that's not an exaggeration. We're serious.

We are called to be prophets. A prophet, despite the popular misconception, is not someone who predicts the future. A prophet is someone who announces God's presence in our midst by living an exemplary life. As married couples, we are specifically called to live out those words of Saint Paul. We are called to a scriptural marriage, not just a human marriage.

That means a total lifestyle change; it's more than being a little kinder to each other today. Instead, we're called to be moved toward God.

The Heart of Matrimony

Imagine yourself being interviewed by a newspaper reporter who says, "My editor thought your life would be worth a story. Why don't you tell me about it?"

What would you tell the reporter? Would your story center around your job, your avocation, or outside interests? Better, you might mention a cause you've lived for or some people you've served with responsibility and love.

Even better, you might describe your personal qualities: "I'm a very prayerful person," or "I'm really good with children." Now, that's an improvement but, still, is that all? Would you tell this reporter, "The most important thing I've ever done is become a husband or a wife"?

Too often, we think marriage is something each of us accomplishes separately: the wife does wifely things and her husband does husbandly things. The two halves somehow equal one whole.

It doesn't work that way. Marriage is purely a relationship, and that relationship is determined by how much we become each other.

The heart of matrimony is the community of life we establish in each other. The key to that community of life is not merely to live in the same house, sleep in the same bed, eat at the same table, or go together to the same party. The key is to have the same goals and values. It's not merely avoiding conflicts or disagreements; it's two hearts beating as one. It has to be a constant effort, not just something that's nice when it happens.

We may have very good and lofty dreams; probably the dreams we had even before we were married. We should take on our lovers' dreams, not because the dreams are so good, but because our lovers are.

This kind of unity is possible, but we must be open to God's grace. Saint Paul admits that this is not something we would think of ourselves. He says this is a mystery of great significance. He also explains why we are called to it. When we accomplish this or even strive to accomplish it, we are revealing Jesus' love relationship with his Church.

Husbands Should Love Their Wives
Just As Christ Loved the Church

We must take Saint Paul's teaching to heart. He says, "Husbands should love their wives, just as Christ loved the Church...." How did Christ love the Church? He "sacrificed himself for her." In other words, he submitted himself to her.

From the very beginning, Jesus submitted himself to his people. He came down to earth and became one of us. As a child, and even as an adult, he was subject to Mary and Joseph. He was also obedient to his Father's will. In John 8:28–29, he said, "...I do nothing of my own accord. What I say is what the Father has taught me; he who sent me is with me, and has not left me to myself, for I always do what pleases him."

He died in submission to us, too. He didn't have to be mocked, beaten, and crucified, but he let us do that to him. You'll recall that when Jesus was betrayed by Judas in the garden of Gethsemane, one of his followers cut off the high priest's servant's ear. In Matthew 26:53,54, Jesus asked that disciple, "...do you think that I cannot appeal to my Father, who would promptly send more than twelve legions of angels to my defense? But then, how would the scriptures be fulfilled that say this is the way it must be?"

If a husband is to answer the Lord's call to sacramental marriage, he must take the leadership in submitting himself to his wife, exactly as Jesus submitted himself to the Church. He must surrender himself profoundly, relentlessly, and totally to this woman who is flesh of his flesh.

A sacramental wife is called to subject herself to her husband *in response to his subjection to her.* If she seems to have difficulty doing this, it's because she has no model. The Lord says that model is you—her husband. He's calling you to take the lead.

Sacrament of Marriage

A sacramental marriage calls a man to become incarnate with his wife just as Jesus enfleshes himself with us. A sacramental husband makes no distinction between his wife and himself. Saint Paul says, "...husbands must love their wives as they love their own bodies; for a man to love his wife is for him to love himself." Ask yourselves, "Do I see her as my body, or as an important but very separate person?"

Husbands may acknowledge their responsibilities toward their wives and admit to opportunities to make their lives more pleasant. Beyond that, though, husbands may live their own lives because they don't want to take on the responsibility for the kind of overwhelming intimacy Jesus is calling us to.

Husbands are tempted to say this total intimacy isn't real; it's something no one really does. Before we actually voice those words, let's take a good look at our wives. Do we see their needs, their search for oneness?

A man has to ask himself, "How married am I?" Sure, we do a lot of married things and we've stopped a lot of single ones, but are we living a married way of life? Or are we merely two nice people who have affection for each other, some concern, a history together, and are living side by side in peace and harmony?

Married to the Job

Many husbands form their identities watching other men rather than by becoming one body with their wives. These men tend to judge success by their nonmarital accomplishments.

If a man lets others determine his identity, his wife is an outside interest. She has rights, and he respects these. She has needs and desires, and he knows his responsibility to respond. He does his best, but his wife is definitely a distinct entity. This undercuts Paul's whole message. If different and distinct, she's not part of a man's own body. She's a separate body, albeit an attractive one.

Many men are married to their jobs. We can't just say, "Well, that's the way things are." Saint Paul is saying very clearly that sacramental husbands are *not* supposed to be that way.

We can allow the job to keep us from relationship in other ways. For instance, we can bring the job home with us. Sometimes we do it literally: "I just have a few plans to make, honey," or "I have to go over these reports."

Even worse, we bring home the job's atmosphere. This happens more frequently, drowning the whole family in work-related anger or depression. Maybe the boss has been on our back, or maybe we're the boss and we've been on everyone else's back. When we come home, everybody has to deal with our job traumas.

Show a Little Tenderness

Physical, mental, and spiritual tenderness is such a beautiful gift from a man to his spouse. Sometimes we husbands are tender physically but not mentally. Tenderness means so much to a woman. Ask any woman what qualities she wants in her lover, and tenderness is always there. Some women will say they want certain qualities, but all look for tenderness in their partner.

Men are inclined to be tender only when we feel like it. If we're in a tender mood tonight, we show our tenderness. But that's a response to ourselves, not to our lovers.

Tenderness, whether mentally, physically, or psychologically, can be a decision. Its reward isn't the mere pleasure of feeling tender, but the fulfillment that tenderness gives and the unity it helps achieve.

We have to start thinking about how we can improve our tenderness quotient. We have to force ourselves to do this just as we force ourselves to jog, study for an exam, or drag into the office when we're sick. We can ask for the grace to create an environment of tenderness within our homes. It won't happen overnight, but each day we'll improve a little. In time, we will truly see the results.

First, we must remember when we've been tender, what helped create that feeling and helped express it meaningfully. We should recall what destroys a tender mood or an attitude that would lead to tenderness. Then we must take steps to eliminate those destructive influences, thoughts, or behaviors.

Men are called to take the lead in creating that tender environment in the home. To do so, they have to be as willing to work on tenderness in their marriages as they are to work on success in their jobs. We can't leave our marriages at the mercy of accidents, and we shouldn't leave the initiative to our wives.

Tenderness of heart and soul, mind and conversation, is an inestimable gift to our beloved wives. To give it, we should place three thoughts where we'll never forget them: a memory of how much she desires our tenderness, how significantly that tenderness impacts her, and how much more it would mean if she could look forward to tenderness as a normal, everyday occurrence.

Heavenly Treatment

Since we've been called to treat our wives as Jesus treats the Church, let's examine Jesus' life. Let's take some cases in point.

In John 15:15, he said, "...I have made known to you everything I have learned from my Father."

Do we men let our wives know what is inside us? Many husbands keep private places within themselves. Can we truthfully say to our beloved wives, "I have told you everything that's inside me. There isn't any of me today that you don't know"?

"But that isn't so easy to do," you might want to say. "I'm naturally not too reflective a guy. I don't look inside myself that much, much less talk about it."

That's all right. That's where you are right now. But you should start being different for your wife's sake. She needs to be part of you, and she can't be part of you unless you tell her what's in there.

In John 10:10, Jesus said, "I have come so that they may have life and have it to the full."

Why have you come into marriage? Many husbands don't understand that their life's purpose is to give their beloved wives abundant happiness. They believe they can add to her well-being. But her fulfillment is her own responsibility, they think.

Jesus doesn't think that way. He doesn't teach us a little more than we knew before; he doesn't improve things. He came to give us a totally new way of being, and he did this because we are his flesh.

Likewise, your wife's whole life should be totally different, fresh and new in hope and joy because she is one with you. You have let her into your life so she wouldn't be alone any longer. Now she is full of you and your love for her.

❧❧❧

Jesus said, "Come to me, all you who labor and are overburdened, and I will give you rest" (Mt 11:28).

Many husbands offer their wives every refreshment but themselves. They suggest a night out with the girls, a trip to the mall, freedom from the children for a Saturday.

When our wives are frazzled, lonely, disturbed, or not feeling up to par, do we say, "Come to me," or do we offer all sorts of suggestions to take them outside themselves? We do this largely because we don't believe in our power to heal. Saint Paul doesn't agree. Neither does the Lord. They not only believe we can do it, they are calling us to.

Without question, our wives' heaviest burdens are the children. That's partly because of the children's natural demands, but also because they don't have full-time fathers. Many husbands are well-intentioned, but they're not really there.

A wife is not fundamentally refreshed if her husband pitches in only when she's desperate, or if he gives her little rewards like praise and an occasional dinner out. The only true refreshment a loving husband can give is to become an actively involved father.

A woman can't believe her husband truly loves her unless he loves those children. No matter what else he may do, she's going to feel deserted and alone.

Women can receive a lot of negativity about having children, especially if there are more than two. These insults come from family, friends, neighbors, even strangers. It hurts our loves when others think they are foolish or lacking independence and creativity because they have families. If a woman's husband is as involved with the children as she is, those attacks don't bother her. If they do sting, it's because they are echoed at home.

In John 10:14, Jesus said, "I am the good shepherd; I know my own and my own know me."

Often, husbands don't really know their wives. Do you *really* know your wife, not just know about her?

"Sure, I know her; we've been married for twenty years. She likes to sleep with the window open and she likes anchovy pizzas. She gets mad when I'm five minutes late and even madder when she hears about cruelty to animals."

That's fine; it has to start there. But really knowing the other person is a much deeper matter. Often, a husband doesn't take enough time for that.

Jesus was referring to the Lord's knowledge: the knowledge of belonging. He said, "I know my own," not merely "I know this person because we've lived side by side for two decades." Do we know with intimacy, and do ours—our wives—know we belong to them, or are we very much our own men? We may do all the right things by them; we may live up to our responsibilities in marriage. That's good for a start, but Jesus went much further when forming a love relationship with his Church.

In John 15:11, Jesus said, "I have told you this so that my own joy may be in you and your joy be complete."

How often do we talk to our wives to bring them joy? In comparison, how often do we talk to provide information or a suitable response?

Do we even want our speech to make our beloved wives joyous? Then that's where we must concentrate. It isn't as difficult as it seems, nor does it call us to do all sorts of exotic tasks. We must simply tell her who we are. We must believe our wives have a need to know us. Nothing brings a wife more joy than for her husband to let her inside.

Resources for Reflection I

Near the end of Saint Paul's passage on married love, he wrote, "This is why a man leaves his father and mother and becomes attached to his wife, and the two become one flesh."

If I were to ask whether you were living in accordance with this passage, you'd sincerely say yes. You'd be puzzled, wondering why I even asked. After all, you left your father and mother's house years ago.

Why not put a new slant on the question? Ask yourself this: "Have I left myself and my habits, attitudes, and demands? Have I left my single way of life and become one with her?"

"This mystery has great significance," Paul added. A mystery is never understood completely; it's only gradually revealed. That's why the Lord gives you fifty years to love your wife.

Consider These Questions Privately:

Below is a list of Scripture passages. Each describes Christ's intimate love for his Church.

Read and interpret each of these. How do they apply to your relationship with your wife? What are you doing well? What can you do better?

Matthew 11:28: "Come to me, all you who labor and are over-burdened, and I will give you rest."

Matthew 19:13, Mark 10:13–16, Luke 18:15–17: Jesus and the children.

Matthew 26:6–11, Mark 14:3–6, John 12:1–7: The woman and the oil.

Luke 10:38–42: Martha and Mary.

John 8:2–11: The adulterous woman.

John 13:3–16: The washing of the feet.

John 13:34, 35: "Love one another as I have loved you."

Share With Your Spouse:

After you and your wife finish reading Chapter 10, write to each other on these themes:

Beloved, you are such a delightful spouse; I have such wonderful memories of your goodness. I can see you following God's plan for our relationship when you...." (Write on more than one if you wish.)

My dear, I realize I haven't always followed God's plan for our relationship. I am going to make the following change(s). This makes me feel....

Finally, Let Us Invite the Lord Into Our Marriages:

Almighty Father, I truly want to follow your plan for our marriage. I know that, without your help, I don't have the grace to do what you ask of me. Please send me your Spirit so I can fully live out your plan with my beloved wife.

I thank you for her beauty and goodness, and for the graces you have already given me: the grace of openness to your word, the grace of trust, the grace of generosity, the grace of hope. Thank you; praise you for your gifts to my beloved and myself. Amen.

I Am Here, Beloved, to Give You Life

Wives, Saint Paul's passage from Ephesians 5 calls us not to servitude, but to healing. Our Lord wants us to be free to live in the warmth of his love, and he shows us that love through our beloved husbands. He wants us to be free; free to share ourselves with others, free to believe we are wonderful and good, free to accept and give love, free to use our talents.

Let's review that Scripture passage again (on pp. 143–144). Some of it describes what the Lord is asking us to do. The rest describes his promise.

For years, many women have listened to Ephesians 5 in anger and despair. They thought it was just another demand that they continue to be passive.

It's not that at all. Allowing yourself to be healed and loved is anything but passive. It's tremendously hard work. It will take everything you've got, spiritually, intellectually, and emotionally. It's rather like a crisis, except that exhilarating things are happening instead of traumatic ones.

The sad truth is, many people will never be healed. Terrified of trust, they develop alternate ways of dealing with—and sometimes manipulating—others. Each victory through masquerade or manipulation is another nail in their spiritual coffins. Ultimately they can turn away from God and humanity, living half-lives of empty loneliness.

Allowing yourself to be healed and loved, though, takes more than courage. It takes self-confidence, love, and trust. All these are graces from God, and we should pray for them. God loves it when we ask for his graces. He'll give them to us every time. Pray for them every day; it may take hours, weeks, or even a few months, but you'll begin to notice changes. Grace, by the way, snowballs. It may start small and slow, but if you're willing, it picks up depth and speed until it's a magnificent avalanche.

Some of you must be wondering why the Lord places such emphasis on self-stroking. If our purpose on earth is to love others, why are we wasting time in these selfish pursuits?

Now, that's a put-down par excellence. Who are we to say we don't deserve healing and wholeness? The Lord made us, he wants to heal us, and that should be enough.

There's another reason why we should allow ourselves to be whole: we must be healed and loved before we can give love. Maybe it doesn't seem logical, but it's like this: Trying to love others while neglecting your inner self is like trying to draw water from an empty well. You can put mud in the bucket instead, but people who drink it will be able to tell the difference.

Healing Us

Now that we've talked about individual healing, let's apply that to you as a couple. The Lord is calling you as a couple to be healed, to be one whole body, just as Jesus is one with his Church. He wants you to give each other his life to the full. When that happens, you can show his love to all other people.

Before we tackle the world at large, though, we should be healing our husbands. Many of our husbands have hidden wounds, too, and are suffering from lack of love. As you both begin to grow, him loving you, you accepting that love and loving in return, your bond of oneness will grow stronger.

By the way, your husband needs love the way he defines it. That's not because his idea is right and yours is wrong. It's because love happens not with the giver, but with the receiver. For instance, imagine you and your spouse have been conversing, and he was doing most of the talking. Now, have you listened to him? Only he can say for sure. You can tell him, "I have tried to listen to you," but only he can say, "I feel listened to." Likewise, you can say, "But I did love you. Didn't you feel it?" He's the one who decides, "Yes, I feel loved by you," or "No, it's not getting through to me."

Know You Are Loved

Saint Paul's message calls us to accept our husbands' love, to let them consider us part of their own bodies and to make absolutely no distinction between us and themselves.

After all, we're celebrating the sacrament of matrimony. It's much more than marriage, which is a secular contract. In marriage, two people who love each other merely come together to their mutual advantage, Instead, we've taken on a whole new way of being; we're living in, with, and through the other person.

Matrimony is not two people doing nice things for each other. It is two people *being* each other. This is Saint Paul's meaning when he says the two become one flesh.

The Gospel calls your husband to live for you. It asks you to let him make you his world and his happiness. You are the woman for whom he pours out his life, just as Christ poured out his life for his Church. As his center, you are the place where he discovers his true identity. Your scriptural call is to accept his gift and support him in giving it.

Saint Paul calls each of you to complete, absolute, and relentless responsiveness to your chosen husband. You must draw from him a willingness to share totally in your life. Ask yourselves, "How can I belong more deeply to my husband?"

As you read this, you may be thinking, "I just can't respond that way forever. It's too much."

But you can respond today. We live only in the present; right now, today's love is all that matters. C. S. Lewis, in his book *The Screwtape Letters,* says, "… the Present is the point at which time touches eternity… in it alone, freedom and actuality are offered…." Tomorrow doesn't exist yet, and the past is over. Besides, God gives us graces on a daily basis. He even told us that the burden of our whole future is too much for us to bear.

What If the Leader Gets Lost?

By the way, what if your husband isn't impressed with God's plan and isn't interested in following it?

Then you are called to pray for him, and for yourself. Not a prayer like "Dear God, make him do what he's supposed to do," but a prayer to bless him, to surround him with God's infinite love, and to help him feel that love. He needs compassion, as much as you can give. He isn't making the first move for a number of reasons.

First, he may not know what he's supposed to do. If he does, he may believe it's too challenging or too wonderful to be real. He may be alienated from God by suffering or negative experiences with organized religion.

Perhaps you have been sending out signals that say, "Love me, but don't get too close." Maybe you unknowingly have sent him the message that his best—that is, what he considers his best—isn't enough for you. Perhaps he feels inadequate.

Perhaps he needs healing. This will come with time, prayer, and effort.

Perhaps he's afraid of the depth of involvement that would happen if he followed Saint Paul's message. Not only would it drain his resources, he wouldn't know how to handle it.

Each husband may have a different combination of reasons for reluctance. In all cases, your prayer is a good first step. Especially, pray for compassion. As Jesus said in Matthew 6:8, "...your Father knows what you need before you ask him." And as he said in Luke 11:9,10, "Ask, and it will be given to you; search, and you will find; knock, and the door will be opened to you. For everyone who asks receives; everyone who searches finds; everyone who knocks will have the door opened."

The Many Faces of Anger

Now let's examine the ways in which we fail to follow God's plan for our marriages.

First, we tend to finger-point. Be careful not to think that way because it will throw a whole lot of heat and not very much light. If you tried to keep score, you would have to list which of his actions caused the flaws he's accusing you of: "Sure, I yell sometimes. It's because he doesn't care; but he doesn't care because...." You'd need a full notebook to keep track of all the blame and misery, and when you finished, you'd have two wounded hearts and no resolution.

The second way we lose track of God's plan is in our expression of anger. When we speak of anger, we're usually speaking of fights.

Let's examine how each partner reacts to a fight, and how these natural, harmful reactions damage love relationships and clear no air anyway. In most fights, good men and women will behave in ways that only worsen the conflict.

Men dread their wives' anger; it makes them feel hopeless and leaves heavy lumps of anguish in the pits of their stomachs. Worse, it makes them feel unloved.

Anger is a feeling, and feelings are neither right nor wrong. But the by-products of anger are definitely worth giving up:

First is the desire for retaliation. Perhaps a man hurts his wife by being indifferent to her needs; by ignoring her, working overtime, whatever. She feels betrayed; she believes he doesn't care. There's no way she can *make* him care or repent his actions. He just walks all over her any time he feels like it. So, partly in despair, partly in indignation, she delivers verbal punishment for his crime.

Second is the urge to provoke guilt. If a wife yields to this impulse, her husband will feel like an absolute blockhead by the time the fight is finished. This is certainly easy for a woman to achieve, and a natural human impulse, but it doesn't come from God. She would never do it in cold blood; if a friend tried to make him feel equally worthless, she'd go in swinging to defend him. After the fight is over, the man may insist he still feels good about what he's done, but he nevertheless feels like garbage. This lowers his self-respect and his ability to love. It starts a downward spiral.

Third, this anger can be ongoing. We don't think, "Yes, he failed me, but that's okay. It's over. I'll forget it." Instead, we have a panic reaction: "Dear God, he really worked me over. Is this a trend? I have to deal with it or my life will fall apart." The hurtful emotions that accompany this don't rise to the conscious surface, but they do come out in the fight.

In a fight, a woman's emotions are in full swing. She's upset; she's hurt; she's afraid and downright furious. She gives vent to most of her impulses.

The man feels attacked. The person he loves most in the world suddenly hates him from the inside out. He knows that isn't really true, but if she doesn't hate, loathe, or blame him, she's certainly giving a good imitation of it. He decides to stay calm; his getting angry won't solve anything. He tries to apologize, calm her down, tell her the situation isn't that bad. In other words, he placates her which increases her anger.

The fight escalates from there until the man really is angry. As his adrenaline flows, he wants to fight or flee. He can't do either. If he leaves, the trouble will be waiting when he comes back. And he certainly can't hit her. All he can do is survive the situation and swallow that heavy pit in the center of his stomach.

Eventually, harsh words fly back and forth. Everyone is hurt; both parties wish it had never happened.

So often, though, it happens again. What can be done about it? There's no quick answer. Understanding and compassion for each other work; so does prayer. So does a calm, nonfrantic life-style. The biggest healer, though, is trust.

Fear of Trust

Trust is like quadruple bypass heart surgery. If you don't get it, you'll live a restricted life and you may even die. But the thought of climbing onto that operating table is equally terrifying.

Many women don't trust. They have a deeply ingrained fear that they don't have equilibrium in the relationship. The details may be different. Perhaps there's a fear of being mastered, of losing one's identity, of being taken for granted or becoming a servant. Certainly there's the fear of not being loved and cherished. Often, at the bottom of it is a feeling of worthlessness—that we're not important and deserve no more than second-rate love. We're constantly on the watch for skirmishes in the disputed territory of self-worth and lovableness. If we can defend ourselves vigorously enough, maybe that empty feeling inside us will go away.

It all boils down to lack of faith in our spouses. Because we cannot trust, we deny ourselves the life-giving, self-affirming knowledge that our husbands will always love us and will be there for us, no matter what.

"But he does let me down. I'm not imagining that." That's true. But you let him down, too. You're both good, imperfect people who love each other. Flaws don't stop healthy, whole people from trusting. None of us can earn trust; it's a free gift. In fact, it's an essential gift if we want to follow God's plan.

This trust is, in a nutshell, the subjection Saint Paul speaks of. Paul asks us to say to our beloved husbands, "I am yours; I belong to you. I find my true self in your love. I place myself in your hands and I give myself over to you. You will determine the quality of my life."

The reward for trusting him isn't betrayal; it's peace of mind. It's happiness. It's trading that heavy burden we all drag around for the lighthearted freedom of God's plan.

Lack of Enthusiasm

How often do our husbands go out with their own friends? For all the talk about nights out with the boys, it's probably pretty seldom. Often, when a man gets married, his whole social life becomes restricted to his wife and her choices of what to do.

Take one example: wilderness trips. They're a typical male recreation, but many men don't get to experience them because of their responsibilities at home. If he goes off with the boys to fish or hunt, he feels guilty because his wife is left at home with the children. But often, he can't take her with him because she doesn't enjoy the rugged outdoors. Now, she rarely says, "Don't you dare do that to me." She may not even mind if he goes, but after years of her unenthusiasm, he is so dispirited, he decides he doesn't want to do it anyway. It remains a wistful dream or a memory of his youth.

A lack of enthusiasm, by the way, is devastating. It's every bit as effective as disapproval; it just takes a little longer. If you hear yourself laughing about "men's stuff," take note of it. Stop, because once he's convinced that the things that turn him on are worthless, he'll be partly dead inside. You'll then have less of a husband. He'll love himself less, and he'll be less capable of loving you the way God wants.

A lack of enthusiasm is particularly devastating in sex. When a wife tells her man "No," or even "Oh, I suppose so," he feels alone, even abandoned. Especially if he's afraid to speak of his love and desire for unity, so he expresses it physically. When you imply "I'm not really interested in you right now," you've done more than deprive him of his evening's entertainment; you've told him you don't love him. He takes it personally, and he's right to do so.

The Hebrew word for *memory* means "make me present to you." In sex, you make yourselves totally present to each other through your bodies, which are no longer your own but are given up for the other. When you make love to your husband, you are saying, "I have given up my body for you. It is yours. Make me present to you, and become present to me, as we speak to each other physically."

It sounds like a paradox, but we humans are happiest when we forgo control and become truly one with our lovers. If the oneness is a coming together in sex, it suffuses our being for a long time afterward. We are not lonely because we are no longer alone.

"Time to Think"

"I just want some peace," says the husband. "So do I," responds the wife. "That's why I want to get this problem solved."

That, in a nutshell, is the difference between men's and women's views of peace. What's defined as "quiet" to a man is, to a woman, the final solution. To her, remaining quiet when there's an unresolved problem is as silly as sweeping dirt under the rug. Her husband, though, just wants time to think. How can he solve anything when he doesn't even have the silence he needs to ponder the problem?

Wives, let's have compassion. Let's understand they're not stonewalling us. They just work differently. They need that silence in order to love us as Christ loved his Church. Even if it feels sometimes as if we're living with the emotionless man from outer space, let's give them thinking space.

Both husbands and wives need an atmosphere of peace and harmony in order to let Christ's love flourish in our homes. Only when there's peace—peace for both parties, peace because we show compassionate understanding—can he work on loving you.

Peace is particularly difficult to find in our tense, driven society. We don't allow ourselves any time to think, and we make sure our lives are crammed full: so full, our tempers fray. "I shouldn't feel this upset," we tell ourselves. "Mary (Melissa/Joanne/whoever) works much harder than I do. *Plus* she has an exercise program and that wonderful hobby. She seems so happy and cheerful. Why can't I do it, too?"

Search for Happiness

Of course, that other woman isn't as happy and cheerful as we imagine. She's working like a field ox; how can she possibly be happy? She—and we—are like Richard Cory. Do you know the poem by E. A. Robinson? Richard Cory was the rich man who had everything: women, money, honor in the church, the respect of his fellow men. But, as the song says, Richard Cory went home one night and put a bullet through his head. He ought to have been happy, with all his achievements and luxuries, but in fact, he was in despair.

We simply can't be superheroes, yet we don't allow ourselves the dignity of our own limitations. We deny our feelings of frustration and, instead, dance to the piping of "You'd better do it or you'll be inadequate."

Let's ask ourselves a question: "What do I need to do in order to feel really good about myself?" Most likely, the answers will be in the form of exacting demands: lose twenty pounds, dress better, have thicker hair, wash out that gray, make more money, be able to do more work in a day, take up an exotic hobby like jewelry making, increase my IQ....The grind goes on and on. When we do get a color, lose twenty pounds, and buy some clothes, we'll find another reason to feel inadequate.

Of course, the problem goes much deeper. At the root of it are two facts: we don't value ourselves as ourselves, and we are lonely in our personal relationships. If we asked ourselves, "Would I rather lose twenty pounds and keep my relationship with my husband just as it is? Or would I rather my husband was wildly romantic and after me all the time just as I am?" what would we answer? We'd have to think about it, wouldn't we?

What are we doing to ourselves? We're saying, "No, I won't subject myself to freely given love. It can't be worth anything unless I earn it."

We don't seem to place a very high value on plain and simple happiness. Furthermore, we don't even know what it is. We think happiness comes when we have what we ought to have. The idea that we ought to take time to watch the sun go down sounds romantic and rather frivolous. We don't do it very often because it wouldn't get us anywhere.

Part of our pain exists because we think we're not worthwhile people unless we do worthwhile things. We have to have our own hobbies, do our own housekeeping and child-raising, make our own money. It's like a computerized formula for self-worth.

Imagine feeding this into the computer: "My greatest accomplishment is loving my husband with everything I've got." Where does that fit in? In our society, if we said it out loud, people would answer, "What are you talking about?" or "Oh, you can do that anytime." It's time to reprogram ourselves.

We're happiest when we're in love. Remember your courtship and your honeymoon? People are desperate to recapture that feeling. They'll rip their lives apart trying to do so. That's why there are so many divorces, so many affairs, so many lonely women lost in beautiful novels. We all wish like crazy to be in love, but we work like crazy at things that drive us apart. We love love, but it isn't "worthwhile" according to society's standards. We don't agree out loud, but our actions speak louder than words. Love is a waste of time, a waste of ambition.

Now, I'm not saying we should abandon our talents. God gave them to us to be used. I am saying that your transcendent calling in life is to love that man; your calling as a couple is to echo Christ's passionate love affair with his Church.

Are you ready? The world—and your lovers—are waiting.

Resources for Reflection II

Dear wives, dear husbands, it has been such a pleasure writing these words to you. So much of God's presence in this world is shown through loving couples like you who are willing and courageous enough to embrace his way. The world needs you so much; your spouses need you; your children need you. Our society desperately needs you as an example and a guiding light. We hope these words will take root and grow in you, so that Christ's joy may be in you and your own joy may be complete.

Love, Chuck and Mary Angelee.

Consider These Questions Privately:

Below is a list of Scripture passages. Each describes a response to Christ's love for His church.

Read and interpret each of these. How do they apply to your relationship with your husband? What are you doing well? What can you do better?

Trusting the goodness of our spouse:
> Matthew 11:28: "Come to me, all you who labor and are over-burdened, and I will give you rest."

Accepting unconditional love:
> John 13:3–16: The washing of the feet.

Relentless love:
> John 13:34, 35: "Love one another as I have loved you."

Oneness:
> Acts 4:32–35. The early Church.

God's will for our love:
Romans 8:28–39.

God's great love for us and our response:
1 John 4:7–19.

Share These Thoughts:

After you and your husband read this chapter, write to each other on these topics:

Beloved, you are such a delightful spouse; I have such wonderful memories of your goodness. I can see you following God's plan for our relationship when you...." (Write on more than one if you wish.)

My dear, I realize I haven't always followed God's plan for our relationship. I am going to make the following change(s). This makes me feel....

Finally, Let Us Invite the Lord Into Our Marriages:

Dear Father, I truly want to follow your plan for our marriage. Please help me to trust my husband's goodness; give me your peace, your patience, and enthusiasm for your will. Please send me your Spirit so I can fully live out your plan with my beloved husband.

Thank you for his wonderful goodness and for the graces you have already given me: the grace of openness to your word, the grace of compassion, the grace of generosity, the grace of hope. Thank you; praise you for your gifts to my beloved and myself. Amen.